California

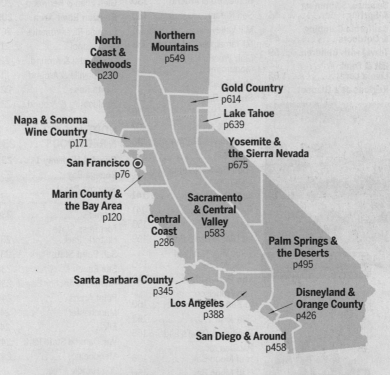

Andrea Schulte-Peevers,
Brett Atkinson, Andrew Bender, Sara Benson, Alison Bing,
Cristian Bonetto, Celeste Brash, Jade Bremner, Nate Cavalieri,
Michael Grosberg, Ashley Harrell, Josephine Quintero, Helena
Smith, John A Vlahides, Benedict Walker, Clifton Wilkinson

PLAN YOUR TRIP

YOSEMITE VALLEY P678

A CALIFORNIA BEACH

ON THE ROAD

PAUL ROJAS / GETTY IMAGES ©

ONEINCHPUNCH / SHUTTERSTOCK ©

California's
Top 25

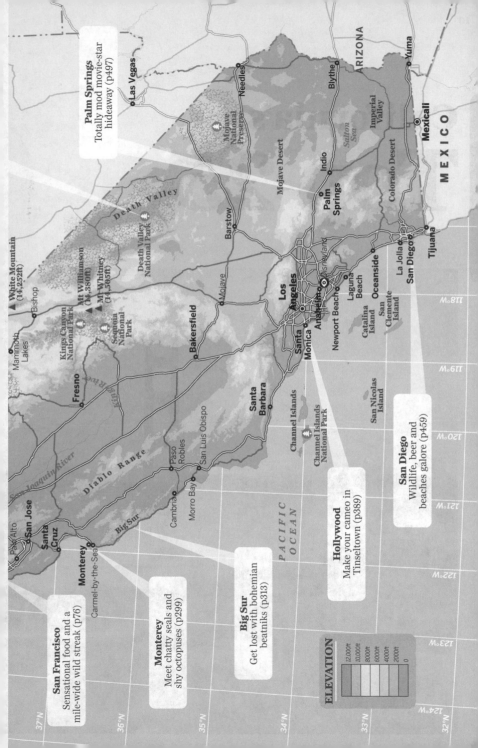

San Francisco
Sensational food and a mile-wide wild streak (p76)

Monterey
Meet chatty seals and shy octopuses (p299)

Big Sur
Get lost with bohemian beatniks (p313)

Hollywood
Make your cameo in Tinseltown (p389)

San Diego
Wildlife, beer and beaches galore (p459)

Palm Springs
Totally mod movie-star hideaway (p497)

ELEVATION
12,000ft
10,000ft
8000ft
6000ft
4000ft
2000ft
0

California

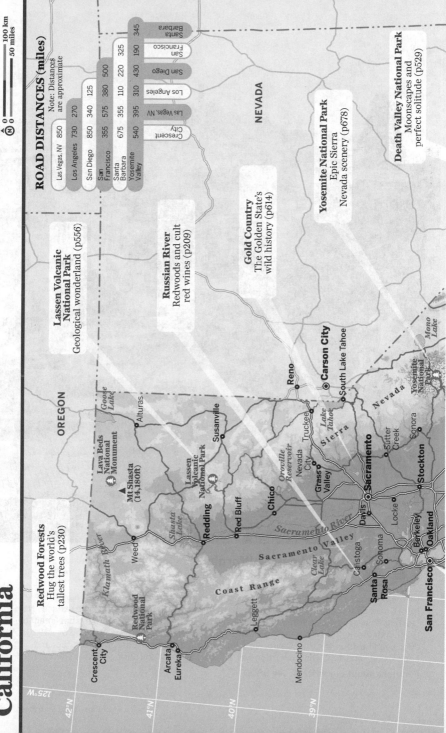

Redwood Forests
Hug the world's tallest trees (p230)

Lassen Volcanic National Park
Geological wonderland (p556)

Russian River
Redwoods and cult red wines (p209)

Gold Country
The Golden State's wild history (p614)

Yosemite National Park
Epic Sierra Nevada scenery (p678)

Death Valley National Park
Moonscapes and perfect solitude (p529)

ROAD DISTANCES (miles)

Note: Distances are approximate

	Crescent City	Las Vegas, NV	Los Angeles	San Diego	San Francisco	Santa Barbara
Las Vegas, NV	850					
Los Angeles	730	270				
San Diego	850	340	125			
San Francisco	355	575	380	500		
Santa Barbara	675	355	110	220	325	
Yosemite Valley	540	395	310	430	190	345

Why I Love California

By Alison Bing, Writer

On my way from Hong Kong to New York, I stopped through San Francisco for a day. I walked from Geary St art galleries through Chinatown to Waverly Place, just as temple services were starting. The fog was scented with incense and roast duck. I wandered into the basement of City Lights Bookstore, and near the Muckraking section, I noticed a sign painted by a 1920s cult: 'I am the door.' It's true: California is the threshold between East and West, fact and fiction, body and soul. That revelation was 20 years ago. I'm still here. You have been warned.

For more about our writers, see p800

Above: Lombard Street (p95), San Francisco

Welcome to California

From misty Northern California redwood forests to sun-kissed Southern California beaches, the enchanted Golden State makes Disneyland seem normal.

Natural Beauty

Don't be fooled by its perpetually fresh outlook and adventurous attitude: California is older than it seems. Coastal bluffs and snowy peaks were created over millennia of tectonic upheavals that threatened to shake California right off the continent. After 19th-century mining, logging and oil-drilling threatened the state's natural splendors, California's pioneering environmentalists rescued old-growth trees, reclaimed rivers and cleaned the beaches. Thanks to the leadership of Californian conservationist John Muir and his Sierra Club, California's national and state parks continue to astound visitors today.

Fabulous Food & Drink

Without California, America's menu would be drab: the Golden State produces most of the country's fresh produce and kicks off nationwide food trends. Every time they sit down to eat, Californians take a stand on food issues: would you like that salad certified organic or spray-free, your toast with farm-to-table jam or urban-beehive honey, and your burger vegan or with humanely raised grass-fed meat? No matter what you order, it's bound to be local and creative. For a chaser, California produces over 90% of the nation's wine-making grapes, and has twice as many breweries as any other state.

From Hollywood to Silicon Valley

Hollywood still makes most of the world's movies and TV shows, and launches new talents nightly on stages statewide. But California dreams don't begin with moguls in office towers – they're invented by California's artists, adventurers and resident weirdos in their own backyards. Wild schemes that started at psychedelic music festivals and in San Jose garages have gone mainstream – perhaps you've heard of smartphones, streaming video and Burning Man? – but there are plenty of outlandish ideas here still awaiting discovery.

City Lights

California's cities hit maximum dazzle as the sun sets over the Pacific. Lamps illuminate San Diego's Gaslamp Quarter, the Hollywood sign glows bright as the moon over LA, and Bay Bridge lights welcome San Francisco arrivals with a wink and a shimmy. Consider this your invitation to come out and play at LA's star-studded nightclubs and movie palaces, San Francisco's historic LGBT hot spots, Santa Barbara's swanky beach bars and San Diego's booming brewpubs. Tomorrow there will be neighborhoods, beaches, spas and boutiques to explore – but tonight is a night on the town like no other.

Contents

ON THE ROAD

DANCESTROKES / SHUTTERSTOCK ©

DOWNTOWN SAN DIEGO
P459

Contents

San Francisco

1 This is as far out as you can get without winding up in the Pacific – San Francisco (p76) keeps pushing boundaries with trendsetting food, social movements, art and technology. This town is defined by bold moves: the iconic Golden Gate Bridge is an engineering marvel in a color chosen over the Navy's objections; nature lovers elbowed aside speculators to establish Golden Gate Park; and Alcatraz was occupied by Native American protestors and turned into a museum. Discover the weirdest tech in the west at the Exploratorium, and find inspiration in new-media installations at supersized SFMOMA. Golden Gate Bridge (p83)

Redwood Forests

2 Hugging a tree never came so naturally as it does in California's sun-dappled groves of ancient redwoods (p230), the world's tallest trees. These gentle giants are quintessentially Californian: their roots may be shallow, but they hold each other up and reach dizzying heights. Even a short stroll on the soft forest floor beneath them puts the rest of the world into perspective. Redwoods thrive along the coast from Big Sur north to the Oregon, and you'll find old-growth groves at Muir Woods National Monument, Humboldt Redwoods State Park and Redwood National and State Parks.

MICHAEL LAWENKO DELA PAZ / GETTY IMAGES ©

JORDAN SIEMENS / GETTY IMAGES ©

LOIC LAGARDE / GETTY IMAGES ©

TRINETTE REED / GETTY IMAGES ©

Yosemite National Park

3 Everything is monumental at Yosemite National Park (p678): thunderous waterfalls tumble over sheer cliffs, granite domes tower overhead and the world's biggest trees cluster in mighty groves of giant sequoias. Conservationist John Muir considered Yosemite a great temple, and awe is the natural reaction to these vast wildflower-strewn meadows and steep valleys carved over millennia by glaciers, avalanches and earthquakes. To achieve maximum wonder, stop at Glacier Point under a full moon or drive the high country's Tioga Rd on a cloudless summer day. Yosemite Valley (p678)

Palm Springs

4 The desert gets hot, but Palm Springs has kept its cool since the '50s. This resort getaway is where stars like Sinatra, Elvis, and Leonardo DiCaprio have come out to play away from the paparazzi and lounge by the pool in mid-Century Modern digs. Hit brunch hot spots, vintage stores and the Palm Springs Art Museum (p497) until happy hour in tiki speakeasies and LGBT cabarets. Tomorrow you could explore desert canyons across Native American tribal lands, summit the San Jacinto Mountains the easy way on an aerial tramway...or you can just lounge the day away. A Palm Springs resort

DOUG MEEK / SHUTTERSTOCK ©

N.ITTO1.00 / GETTY IMAGES ©

Big Sur

5 Following your bliss inevitably leads to Big Sur (p313). Waterfalls splash down sandy bluffs in rainbow mists, and yurt retreats perch at the edge of redwood forests. Beyond purple-sand beaches and coves lined with California jade, pods of migrating whales dot the sparkling Pacific. But don't forget to turn around: hiding behind these coastal bluffs are hot springs and Beat literary retreats, with California condors circling over the cliffs. Time your visit for peak waterfall season in May, or after summer vacation for maximum meditation. McWay Falls (p316)

Santa Monica & Venice

6 How do you beat LA traffic? Hit the beach instead. Sunny Santa Monica (p397) delivers an endless summer with iconic surf spots, a solar-powered Ferris wheel, carnival games on the old-fashioned pier, tidal touch pools in the aquarium and beach sunsets that go on forever. Arrive at nearby Venice Beach (pictured, p420) to join the nonstop parade of New Agers, muscled bodybuilders, goth punks and hippie drummers – around here you'll never need an excuse to let your freak flag fly.

Hollywood

7 When you're ready for your close-up, there's only one place to go. The stars come out at night for red-carpet premieres at restored movie palaces, and you too can have your Hollywood moment on the pink-starred Walk of Fame (pictured, p392). This once-gritty LA neighborhood is making a glorious comeback, bringing old Hollywood glamour to glitzy velvet-roped bars, VIP nightclubs and hip hotels. Snap a selfie outside Grauman's Chinese Theatre (p389) or duck into Hollywood & Highland's Babylon Court for a photo op with the iconic Hollywood sign.

Disneyland Resort

8 Where orange groves and walnut trees once grew, Walt Disney built his dream world. Since his 'Magic Kingdom' opened in 1955, Disneyland (p428) has expanded to neighboring Disney California Adventure to become SoCal's most-visited tourist attraction. Main Street, U.S.A. with your favorite cartoon characters, ride movie-themed roller coasters and watch fireworks explode over Sleeping Beauty Castle on hot summer nights. For a day, leave your troubles behind, suspend disbelief and join throngs of gleeful kids.

OSCITY / SHUTTERSTOCK ©

© DISNEY

San Diego

9 San Diego (p459) is known for its beaches and craft beer – but there's another side to this seaside town. Beautiful Balboa Park (pictured, p460) is the pride of San Diego, with Spanish Colonial and Mission Revival–style architecture along El Prado promenade and more than a dozen art, cultural and science museums. Glimpse exotic wildlife and ride the 'Skyfari' aerial tram at San Diego's world-famous zoo, or nab tickets for a show at the Old Globe Theaters, modeled on the famous Shakespearean original.

Death Valley

10 The daunting name brings to mind Wild West ghost towns, broken-down pioneer wagon trains and tumbleweed blowing past skulls on desert sand dunes – but Death Valley (p529) is full of life. Spring wildflowers daub the dunes with a painter's palette of colors, adrenaline-seekers zoom across crackled salt flats, and shy desert wildlife lives by starlight. Twist your way up narrow canyons past geological oddities, and teeter over volcanic craters formed by violent prehistoric explosions.

Mendocino

11 Along the coast around the weathered Victorian port of Mendocino (p242), tides roll back to reveal driftwood, abalone, and boulders that'll make you think some sea monsters have lost their marbles. Mendocino is a legendary bohemian outpost, with bookstores, natural food shops and redwood water towers swirled in mists carrying fragrant bursts of lavender, jasmine and THC – but there's more to explore inland in Mendocino County. You've probably heard of Mendocino's now-legal cash crop, but you'll also find some of the state's best-value wines lining sunny Anderson Valley. Point Arena (p240), Mendocino County

FEIFEI CUI-PAOLUZZO / GETTY IMAGES ©

CLAY MCLACHLAN / GETTY IMAGES ©

Gold Country

12 'Go west, young man!' was the rallying cry of tens of thousands of pioneers who arrived here during California's gold rush, starting in 1848. Today, the Sierra Nevada foothills (p675) are a stronghold of Golden State history, with thrilling, mostly true tales of banditry, bordellos and bloodlust. Wind past sleepy townships and abandoned mines on Hwy 49 to discover swimming holes, white-water rafting, downhill mountain-biking bomber runs and saloon wine-tasting rooms supplied by the state's oldest grapevines. Eureka! You've found your California adventure. Bodie State Historic Park (p713)

Russian River

13 Sonoma's Russian River Valley (p209) is one of California's best-kept secrets. This wine country is Napa's rebel cousin, with cult biodynamic Pinot Noirs you won't find anywhere else. Hippies headed back to the land here in the '60s, and you can taste their organic farm-to-table cuisine and feel the groovy vibes in Occidental and Sebastopol. Riverside cabin retreats date from the 1900s, when San Franciscan socialites headed here for sunshine and privacy – Guerneville has been an LGBT getaway for a century, and Lazy Bear Weekend (July/August) is a major gay holiday.

Santa Barbara

14 Nicknamed the 'American Riviera' for its seaside elegance and culinary decadence, Santa Barbara (p347) might sound fancy, but it's all laidback California vibes. Palm trees, powdery beaches, fishing boats in the harbor – it'd be a cliché if it wasn't true. But Santa Barbara worked hard to stay so idyllic: downtown was rebuilt in signature Spanish Colonial Revival style after a 1925 earthquake and environmentalists lobbied to clean up the beaches in the '60s and '70s. California's 'Queen of the Missions' is a rare beauty, with its signature red-roofed, whitewashed adobe building.

ED-NI PHOTO / SHUTTERSTOCK ©

CHASE DEKKER / SHUTTERSTOCK ©

Monterey

15 Get up close and personal with California marine life in the fishing village of Monterey (p299), where John Steinbeck brought colorful local wharf characters to life – and the seals are pretty outrageous too. Hop aboard a whale-watching cruise, or walk right into the bay at the aquarium to spot golden sea dragons, shy pink Pacific octopuses and scene-stealing rescued otters at play. Explore Monterey's hidden gardens, villa art museums and historic adobe-walled buildings, then visit monarch butterflies and the West Coast's oldest light-house in neighboring Pacific Grove. Humpback whale

Lake Tahoe

16 High in the Sierra Nevada Mountains, this all-seasons adventure base camp centers on the USA's second-deepest lake (p639). In summer, startlingly clear blue waters invite splashing, kayaking and even scuba diving. Meanwhile, mountain bikers career down epic single-track runs and hikers follow trails through thick forests to staggering views. After dark, retreat to cozy lakefront cottages and toast s'mores in firepits. When the lake turns into a winter wonderland, gold-medal ski resorts amp up the adrenaline for downhill fanatics, snowboarders and Nordic traditionalists.

Lassen Volcanic National Park

17 Anchoring the Cascades' chain of volcanoes to the south, this alien landscape bubbles over with roiling mud pots, noxious sulfur vents and steamy fumaroles. But Lassen (pictured, p556) also delights the senses with colorful cinder cones and azure crater lakes. Ditch the crowds and head to this off-the-beaten-path destination to discover fresh peaks to be conquered, pristine waters for dipping, forested campgrounds for comfort, and boardwalks through Bumpass Hell that will leave you awestruck.

TOPSELLER / SHUTTERSTOCK ©

KOJIHIRANO / GETTY IMAGES ©

Laguna Beach

18 While surfers hang loose in Huntington Beach and yachties mingle dockside in Newport Beach, Orange County's Laguna Beach (p450) lures them all with culture and natural beauty. Startling seascapes led an early-20th century artists' colony to put down roots here, and Laguna's bohemian past lives on in downtown art galleries, adorable arts-and-crafts bungalows tucked beside multimillion-dollar mansions, and the annual Summer Festival of Arts and Pageant of the Masters.

Heisler Park (p451)

Mt Shasta

19 No other pile of rock in California stirs the imagination quite like Mt Shasta (p565). There's something mystical about this peak – Native Californians believed that it was home to a sky-spirit chief. Tales swirl around Mt Shasta: New Age pilgrims say it's an energy vortex, and one late-19th-century explorer reported that survivors of a lost continent were living in tunnels below its surface. Experience spine-tingling chills on its windblown peak, and see for yourself why conservationist John Muir said its beauty made his 'blood turn to wine.'

Surfing

20 Even if you never set foot on a board – but, like, you should totally check out this gnarly break, brah – surfing (p46) defines Californian pop culture, from street slang to movies and laid-back fashion. Pros ride world-class breaks off Malibu, Huntington Beach (aka 'Surf City USA'), La Jolla and Santa Barbara, while newbies get schooled at 'surfari' camps along the coast from San Diego north to Santa Cruz.

RABENA / SHUTTERSTOCK © USED WITH PERMISSION OF MISSION SAN JUAN CAPISTRANO

NICK FOX / SHUTTERSTOCK ©

DOUGLAS KLUG / GETTY IMAGES ©

California's Missions

21 Road-trip along the coast between San Diego and Sonoma, and follow in the footsteps of early Spanish conquistadors and Catholic priests. Franciscan friar Junípero Serra founded many of California's 21 missions in the late 18th century, and many are restored to their original stark beauty. Legend has it that ghosts still pace the cloisters of many missions, built by Native California conscripts – many of whom didn't survive to see their completion. Mission San Juan Capistrano (pictured, p454) is one of best restores, with flowering gardens, stone arcades, fountains, and chapels adorned by frescoes.

Point Reyes National Seashore

22 California may be sunnier down south, but Point Reyes (p139) is more poetic. Step across the San Andreas Fault to find windswept beaches, where the horizon stretches toward infinity. Way off at land's end, climb the lighthouse (pictured, p140) and scan the Pacific for migratory whales. In this wild place you'll find good company: there's a seasonal colony of raucous giant elephant seals at Chimney Rock and free-ranging herds of hulking tule elk, especially on the north end. Return to civilization the easy way at Point Reyes Station for lazy brunches and splendid local cheese.

Channel Islands

23 Tossed like lost pearls off the coast, the Channel Islands (p384) have been California's last outpost of civilization ever since seafaring Chumash people established villages on these remote rocks. Marine life thrives on these islands, from coral reefs to giant elephant seals. Get back to nature with fantastic sea kayaking and snorkeling in Channel Islands National Park, or plan a posh getaway at the harborfront hotels of Mediterranean-style Catalina Island. Seal

Coastin' on Amtrak

24 All aboard! Evocatively named routes like *Coast Starlight* and *Pacific Surfliner* will tempt you to leave your car behind and ride the rails (p784), from Oakland to SoCal. South of San Luis Obispo, glimpse remote beaches from Amtrak's panoramic-view observation cars. Blink and you're already in Santa Barbara, in time for wine. Hop off for a seaside swim at whistle-stop Carpinteria or Ventura, before rolling into LA's architecturally grand Union Station. Keep rolling south to historic Mission San Juan Capistrano and North County beach towns before landing in downtown San Diego.

Coronado

25 Who says you can't turn back time? Speed over the curved bay bridge or hop the ferry from San Diego to swanky, retro, seaside Coronado. You don't need a costume to enjoy the period drama of the palatial 19th-century Hotel del Coronado (pictured, p469), where royalty and presidents escaped from their duties and Marilyn Monroe cavorted in the 1950s screwball classic *Some Like It Hot*. Pedal past impossibly while beaches all the way down the peninsula's Silver Strand, stopping at old-fashioned ice-cream parlors and vintage photo ops – no sepia-tone filter necessary.

HAL BERGMAN PHOTOGRAPHY / GETTY IMAGES ©

GAGLIARDIIMAGES / SHUTTERSTOCK ©

Need to Know

For more information, see Survival Guide (p767)

Currency
US dollars ($)

Language
English

Visas
Generally not required for stays of 90 days or less for citizens of Visa Waiver Program (VWP) countries with Electronic System for Travel Authorization (ESTA) approval (https://esta.cbp.dhs.gov) – apply online at least 72 hours in advance.

Money
ATMs are widely available. Credit cards are usually required for reservations. Traveler's checks (US dollars) are rarely accepted. Tipping is customary, not optional.

Cell Phones
The only foreign phones that will work in the USA are GSM multiband models. Buy prepaid SIM cards locally. Coverage can be spotty in remote areas.

Time
Pacific Standard Time (GMT/UTC minus eight hours)

When to Go

Arcata
GO Apr–Oct

San Francisco
GO Apr–Oct

Yosemite Village
GO Apr–Oct

Los Angeles
GO Apr–Oct

Palm Springs
GO Dec–Apr

- Desert, dry climate
- Dry climate
- Warm to hot summers, mild winters
- Warm to hot summers, cold winters

High Season
(Jun–Aug)

➔ Accommodations prices up 50% to 100% on average.

➔ Major holidays are even busier and more expensive.

➔ Summer is low season in the desert, where temperatures exceed 100°F (38°C).

Shoulder
(Apr–May & Sep–Oct)

➔ Crowds and prices drop, especially on the coast and in the mountains.

➔ Mild temperatures and sunny, cloudless days.

➔ Typically wetter in spring, drier in autumn.

Low Season
(Nov–Mar)

➔ Accommodations rates lowest along the coast.

➔ Chilly temperatures, frequent rainstorms and heavy snow in the mountains.

➔ Winter is peak season in SoCal's desert regions.

Useful Websites

California Travel & Tourism Commission (www.visit california.com) Multilingual trip-planning guides.

Lonely Planet (www.lonely planet.com/usa/california) Destination information, hotel bookings, traveler forum and more.

LA Times Travel (www.latimes.com/travel) Travel news, deals and blogs.

Sunset (www.sunset.com/travel/california) Local and insider travel tips.

California State Parks (www.parks.ca.gov) Outdoor activities and camping.

CalTrans (www.dot.ca.gov) Current highway conditions.

Important Numbers

All phone numbers have a three-digit area code followed by a seven-digit local number. For long-distance and toll-free calls, dial ☑1 plus all 10 digits.

Country code	☑1
International dialing code	☑011
Operator	☑0
Emergency (ambulance, fire & police)	☑911
Directory assistance (local)	☑411

Exchange Rates

Australia	A$1	$0.74
Canada	C$1	$0.74
China	Y10	$1.45
Euro zone	€1	$1.11
Japan	¥100	$0.89
Mexico	MXN10	$0.53
New Zealand	NZ$1	$0.70
UK	£1	$1.29

For current exchange rates see www.xe.com.

Daily Costs

Budget: Less than $100

➡ Hostel dorm beds: $30–55

➡ Take-out meal: $7–12

Midrange: $100–200

➡ Motel or hotel double room: $100–150

➡ Rental car per day, excluding insurance and gas: $50–80

Top End: More than $200

➡ Upscale hotel or beach resort room: $150–300

➡ Three-course meal in top restaurant excluding drinks: $80–120

Opening Hours

Businesses, restaurants and shops may close earlier and on additional days during the winter off-season (November to March). Otherwise, standard opening hours are as follows:

Banks 9am–6pm Monday to Friday, some 9am–1pm or later Saturday

Bars 5pm–2am daily

Business hours (general) 9am–5pm Monday to Friday

Nightclubs 10pm–4am Thursday to Saturday

Post offices 8:30am–5pm Monday to Friday, some 8:30am–noon or later Saturday

Restaurants 7:30am–10am, 11:30am–2pm and 5pm–9pm daily, some open later Friday and Saturday

Shops 10am–6pm Monday to Saturday, noon–5pm Sunday (malls open later)

Supermarkets 8am–9pm or 10pm daily, some 24 hours

Arriving in California

Los Angeles International Airport (p779) Taxis to most destinations ($30 to $50) take 30 minutes to one hour. Door-to-door shuttles ($15 to $20) operate 24 hours. FlyAway bus ($9.75) runs to Downtown LA. Free shuttles connect with LAX City Bus Center and Metro Rail station.

San Francisco International Airport (p779) Taxis into the city ($45 to $65) take 25 to 50 minutes. Door-to-door shuttles (from $17) operate 24 hours. BART trains ($8.95, 30 minutes) serve the airport, running from 5:30am (later on weekends) to midnight daily.

Getting Around

Most people drive themselves around California. You can also fly (it's expensive) or take cheaper long-distance buses or scenic trains. In cities, when distances are too far to walk, hop aboard buses, trains, streetcars, cable cars or trolleys, or grab a taxi.

Car Metro-area traffic can be nightmarish, especially during weekday commuter rush hours (roughly 6am to 10am and 3pm to 7pm). City parking is often an expensive hassle.

Train The fastest way to get around the San Francisco Bay Area and LA, but lines don't go everywhere. Pricier regional and long-distance Amtrak trains connect some destinations.

Bus Usually the cheapest and slowest option, but with extensive metro-area networks. Inter-city, regional and long-distance Greyhound routes are limited and more expensive.

For much more on **getting around**, see p780

What's New

Recreational Marijuana

Two decades after legalizing medical cannabis, California followed Colorado's lead in legalizing marijuana for recreational use, with 56% of voters approving Proposition 64 in 2016. How will this change the local economy and tourism, especially in the North Coast's Mendocino and Humboldt Counties? Find out first hand – or through second hand smoke.

SFMOMA

San Francisco is undergoing an arts renaissance, against the long odds of rising rents and federal funding cuts. Reopened in 2016, an expanded San Francisco Museum of Modern Art has tripled its collections, while blockbuster museum and gallery shows elsewhere keep raising the city's artistic profile. (p78)

Expo Line extension

Los Angeles's public transportation system reached a new milestone with the opening of the Metro Rail's Expo Line, which now offers a direct rail connection between downtown LA and Santa Monica. (www.metro.net)

Big Sur

Heavy winter rains in 2016 and 2017 washed out several areas of California's coastal highways, but nowhere was damaged more severely than Big Sur, cut off from the rest of the coast for more than six months. Pfeiffer Canyon Bridge is scheduled to reopen in late 2017. (www.dot.ca.gov) (p313)

Broad

Big-name modern and contemporary art and eye-popping architecture are drawing crowds to LA's newest museum, the Broad. The $140-million wonder has free general admission. (p389)

CIA at Copia

The Culinary Institute of America's new Napa campus offers a different kind of restaurant – diners approach cooking stations where rotating chefs prepare food and answer questions – along with a lifestyle shop and countless food and wine-tasting classes and cooking demonstrations. (p179)

DTLA

Internationally renowned gallery Hauser & Wirth has moved into a sprawling industrial space in Downtown LA's vibrant Arts District, one of the city's hottest destinations for contemporary art, dining and nightlife. (p389)

Tin City

In Paso Robles on the Central Coast, this ever-expanding precinct features craft breweries, urban wineries and innovative distilleries. Weekend afternoons often add live music and food trucks. (p332)

Highland Park

In Los Angeles, indie-cool Echo Park and Silver Lake are sharing the spotlight with Highland Park, a booming neighborhood of creative galleries, vintage stores and brand-new bars and eateries.

Santa Barbara's Funk Zone

It's just what this sometimes stuffy seaside city needed: an edgy, creative neighborhood space with art, food, craft beer and regional wines, all just a short walk from the beach. (p355)

For more recommendations and reviews, see lonelyplanet.com/california

If You Like...

Fantastic Food

New cravings have been invented at California's cultural crossroads for over 200 years, so don't hold back – try something new and get adventurous with the latest food trends, from Peking duck empanadas to vegan soul food.

Chez Panisse Chef Alice Waters revolutionized California cuisine back in the '70s with seasonal, sustainable, locavore cooking. The tradition continues in this iconic Berkeley restaurant. (p156)

French Laundry The north star of contemporary cuisine. Thomas Keller continually takes home international awards to tiny Yountville. (p186)

LA's food trucks LA sparked the mobile foodie revolution, with chefs on wheels offering gourmet cuisine from downtown strips to Pacific beachfronts.

Ferry Building Duck inside San Francisco's landmark to good taste, featuring local, sustainable food producers and a legendary farmers market. (p79)

Fish tacos Join surfers on the quest for the ultimate Mexicali snack, starting in San Diego with Baja Betty's and all the way up to Malibu.

Craft Beer

California's vineyards may steal the scene, but big copper vats hidden in garages across the state are producing award-winning brews.

Lost Coast Brewery In Eureka, knock back a pint of Downtown Brown while admiring conceptual-art beer labels.

Anderson Valley Brewing Company Mendocino County's solar-powered brewhouse lets you play disc golf while drinking a bottle of oatmeal stout. (p255)

Stone Brewing Company This San Diego upstart brews big, bold character into Arrogant Bastard Ale and chipotle-spiked porter. (p476)

Anchor Brewing Company San Francisco lets off steam with the help of Gold Rush steam-brewing techniques innovated by this historic brewer. (p70)

Sierra Nevada Brewing Company Get tours and pours of this mega-popular pale ale in Chico. (p597)

Theme Parks

SoCal is theme-park heaven, bringing Hollywood movie magic, Disneyland and roller coasters galore.

Disneyland Topping almost every family's must-do list is Walt Disney's 'imagineered' theme park, with Disney California Adventure next door. (p428)

Universal Studios Hollywood The legendary movie studio offers a studio backlot tram tour, movie-themed rides, live-action shows and slick special effects. (p393)

Legoland California Resort Creative kids love this low-key theme park with a resort hotel and endless building possibilities. (p491)

San Diego Zoo Safari Park Take a safari-style tram tour through an 'open-range' zoo. (p489)

Hiking

Ever since Native Americans blazed the first trails through this wilderness, Californians have been hikers. Oceanside rambles, desert palm oases, skyscraping peaks and silent forests await.

Sierra Nevada Spend a lifetime trekking in national parks and alpine wilderness, or just a day summiting Mt Whitney. (p730)

North Coast Hardy backpackers tackle the Lost Coast Trail, while wanderers ramble misty old-growth redwood forests. (p265)

Marin County Tawny headlands tempt hikers across SF's Golden Gate Bridge north to wild, wind-blown Point Reyes. (p139)

PLAN YOUR TRIP IF YOU LIKE...

Palm Springs & the Deserts
Discover hidden oases, stroll across salt flats and visit Native Californian canyons. (p497)

Small Towns

When California's crowded metropolises wear you out, restore your spirits at friendly locales by the beach, up in the mountains and down the road from vineyards.

Calistoga Napa Valley's blue-jeans-and-boots crowd heads to this quaint downtown for mud baths and BBQ. (p192)

Bolinas This quirky end-of-the-road beach hamlet is Marin County's best-kept secret. (p136)

Ferndale A charming Victorian-era farm town tucked away on the North Coast. (p268)

Mammoth Lakes All-seasons outdoor adventures begin at eastern Sierra's jumping-off point. (p718)

Seal Beach Discover an old-fashioned Orange County surf town, complete with period-perfect main street and wooden pier. (p440)

National & State Parks

Jagged mountain peaks, high-country meadows and desert sand dunes lure you inland – and you'll be astonished by California's wild diversity, from the Nevada border ranges to wind-tossed offshore islands.

Yosemite National Park Ascend into the Sierra Nevada, where waterfalls tumble into glacier-carved valleys and wildflower meadows bloom. (p678)

Redwood National & State Parks Get lost ambling among

Top: Half Dome, Yosemite National Park (p678)

Bottom: Hollywood Boulevard, Los Angeles (p389)

ancient groves of the world's tallest trees on the foggy North Coast. (p279)

Death Valley National Park Uncover secret pockets of life in this austere desert landscape, peppered with geological oddities. (p529)

Lassen Volcanic National Park Camp by northern alpine lakes and traipse around the boiling mud pots of Bumpass Hell. (p556)

Channel Islands National Park Escape civilization on SoCal's isolated islands, nicknamed 'California's Galapagos.' (p384)

Nightlife

Go VIP all the way at California's chic city nightclubs – or skip the velvet ropes and dress codes, and hit California's come-as-you-are watering holes.

Los Angeles DJs spin at glam Hollywood clubs, and all of LGBT LA hits the 'WeHo' scene. (p415)

San Francisco Become a beatnik in North Beach, mingle with Mission hipsters or party with the Castro's rainbow-flag nation. (p111)

San Diego Put on your best flip-flops for surfer bars, or your walking shows for pub crawls through the Gaslamp Quarter, downtown's historic red-light district. (p477)

Las Vegas, Nevada The Strip's high-wattage nightclubs are the stuff of legend – but what happens in Vegas, stays in Vegas. (p546)

Film & TV Locations

For a century California has made audiences laugh,

cry, and come back for more. To witness the magic in action, join a live studio audience or tour a movie studio in LA.

Los Angeles You can't throw a director's megaphone without hitting a celluloid sight, from Mulholland Drive to Malibu. (p388)

San Francisco Bay Area Relive film-noir classics like *The Maltese Falcon* and Hitchcock's thrillers *Vertigo* and *The Birds*.

Lone Pine Get misty-eyed over old-fashioned Westerns filmed in the Alabama Hills over in the Eastern Sierra. (p729)

Orange County Where soap operas, 'dramedies' and reality TV series have struck pop-culture gold. (p426)

Mendocino This tiny North Coast town has starred in dozens of movies, from *East of Eden* to *The Majestic*. (p242)

Weird Stuff

SoCal's deserts and the North Coast are magnets for free spirits, but loopy LA and bohemian SF are just as jam-packed with memorable oddities.

Venice Boardwalk Gawk at the human zoo of bodybuilders, chainsaw-jugglers and Speedo-clad snake-charmers. (p398)

Kinetic Grand Championship Outrageously whimsical, artistic and human-powered sculptures race along the North Coast. (p274)

Integratron Allegedly built with aliens' help, this giant 'rejuvenation and time machine' awaits near Joshua Tree. (p513)

Madonna Inn Fantastically campy Central Coast hotel with 110 bizarrely themed rooms, from 'Caveman' to 'Hot Pink.' (p336)

Mystery Spot Santa Cruz's shamelessly kitschy 1940s tourist trap will turn your world upside down. (p289)

Solvang Danish-flavored village in Santa Barbara's wine country spirited out of a Hans Christian Andersen fairy tale. (p373)

Las Vegas, Nevada Exploding faux volcanoes, a mock Eiffel Tower and an Egyptian-esque pyramid. (p538)

Museums

Who says California only has pop culture? You could spend most of your trip viewing multimillion-dollar art galleries, high-tech science exhibits, out-of-this-world planetariums and more.

San Francisco Museum of Modern Art (SFMOMA) The supersized museum has more space than ever for photography, new media and walk-in installation art. (p78)

Getty Center & **Getty Villa** Art museums that are as beautiful as their elevated settings and ocean views in West LA and Malibu. (p395) (p397)

Los Angeles County Museum of Art More than 150,000 works of art span the ages and cross all borders. (p393)

Griffith Observatory There's no better place to see stars in Hollywood than at this hilltop planetarium. (p392)

de Young Museum A copper-skinned temple to art from around the globe in SF's Golden Gate Park. (p98)

Balboa Park Museums Spend all day in San Diego hopping between top-notch art, history and science museums, including those for kids. (p460)

DENTOK / GETTY IMAGES ©

Ferndale (p268), Humboldt County

Exploratorium Even adults love the zany interactive science-learning fun at this indoor/outdoor landmark on San Francisco Bay. (p87)

History

Native American nations, Spanish Colonial *presidios* (forts) and Catholic missions, Mexican *pueblos* (towns) and mining ghost towns have all left traces here for you to find.

Mission San Juan Capistrano Painstakingly restored jewel along California's mission trail, stretching from San Diego to Sonoma. (p455)

Gold Country Follow in the tracks of Western pioneers and hardscrabble miners, or pan for gold yourself. (p614)

Old Town San Diego Time travel on the site of California's first civilian Spanish Colonial *pueblo.* (p461)

Monterey State Historic Park Get a feel for California's Spanish, Mexican and early American days inside adobe buildings. (p300)

Bodie State Historic Park Haunting mining ghost town in the Eastern Sierra, above Mono Lake. (p713)

Manzanar National Historic Site WWII Japanese American internment camp interprets a painful chapter of the USA's past. (p729)

Shopping

It doesn't matter where you go in California, especially along the coast: there's a rack of haute couture, outlet-mall bargains or vintage finds begging to be stashed in your suitcase.

Los Angeles Forget Beverly Hills. Robertson Blvd has more star-worthy boutiques per block, and youthful Melrose Ave is more fashion-forward. (p418)

San Francisco Elevating thrift-store fashion to a high art, while indie boutiques spread from the Marina to the Mission. (p116)

Orange County Hit Costa Mesa's offbeat mini-malls, or browse boutiques with beautiful people in Laguna Beach. (p454)

Palm Springs Heaven for vintage and thrift-store shoppers seeking retro 20th-century gems, with outlet shopping too. (p507)

Month by Month

January

January is the wettest month in California, and a slow time for coastal travel – but this is when mountain ski resorts and Southern California deserts hit their stride.

☆ Rose Bowl & Parade

The famous New Year's parade held before the Tournament of Roses college football game draws over 700,000 spectators to the LA suburb of Pasadena with flower-festooned floats, marching bands and prancing equestrians.

🦁 Lunar New Year

Firecrackers, parades, lion dances and Chinatown night markets usher in the lunar new year, falling in late January or early February. California's biggest and most historic parade happens in San Francisco, where tiny-tot martial artists chase a 200ft dragon. (p101)

February

As California sunshine breaks through the drizzle, skiers hit the slopes in T-shirts, wildflowers burst into bloom, and romantics scramble for Valentine's Day reservations at restaurants and hotels.

☆ Academy Awards

Hollywood rolls out the red carpet for movie-star entrances on Oscar night at the Dolby Theatre in late February or early March. Fans wait patiently in bleachers and jostle paparazzi for a glimpse of the action when stretch limos arrive.

March

As ski season winds down the beaches warm up, just in time for spring break (exact dates vary with school schedules and the Easter holiday).

🏃 Mendocino Coast Whale Festivals

Mendocino, Fort Bragg and nearby towns toast the whale migration with wining and dining, art shows and naturalist-guided walks and talks over three weekends in March. (p244)

🎭 Festival of the Swallows

After wintering in South America, the swallows return to Mission San Juan Capistrano in Orange County around March 19 – and the historic mission town celebrates its Spanish and Mexican heritage all month long.

April

As wildflower season peaks in the high desert, the southern desert bursts into song and San Francisco twinkles with international film stars. Shoulder season in the mountains and along the coast brings lower hotel prices.

☆ Coachella Music & Arts Festival

Headliners, indie rockers, rappers and cult DJs converge outside Palm Springs for a three-day musical extravaganza held over two weekends in mid-April. Book well ahead – this festival is huge. (p501)

☆ San Francisco International Film Festival

The nation's oldest film festival lights up San Francisco nights with star-studded US premieres of 325 films from around the globe, held over two weeks from late April to early May. (p101)

May

Weather starts to heat up statewide, although some coastal areas are blanketed by 'May gray' fog. Memorial Day holiday weekend marks the official start of summer, and one of the year's busiest travel times.

🎎 Cinco de Mayo

¡Viva México! California celebrates its Mexican heritage and the victory of Mexican forces over the French army on May 5, 1862. LA and San Diego have the biggest celebrations, but you'll find margaritas, music and dancing across the state.

◉ Jumping Frog Jubilee & Calaveras County Fair

Taking inspiration from Mark Twain's famous short story, the Gold Rush pioneer town of Angels Camp fills a long weekend in mid-May with rodeo cowboys, live country-and-western music and old-fashioned family fun.

🏃 Bay to Breakers

On the third Sunday in May, costumed joggers, inebriated idlers and renegade streakers make the annual dash from San Francisco's Embarcadero to Ocean Beach. Watch out for participants dressed as salmon, who run upstream from the finish line. (p101)

🎎 Kinetic Grand Championship

Artists spend months preparing for this 'triathlon of the art world,' inventing outlandish human-powered and self-propelled sculptural contraptions to cover 42 miles from Arcata to Ferndale over three days. (p274)

June

Once school lets out for the summer, everyone heads to California beaches – only to shiver through San Francisco as 'June gloom' coastal fog descends. Mountain resorts offer cool escapes, but the deserts are just too darn hot.

🎎 Pride Month

California celebrates LGBT pride not just for a day but for the entire month of June, with costumed parades, film fests, marches and streets parties. SF Pride sets the global parade standard, with 1.2 million people, tons of glitter and ounces of bikinis. San Diego also celebrates in mid-July.

July

California's campgrounds, beaches and theme parks hit peak popularity, especially on the July 4 holiday – summer's biggest travel weekend.

◉ California State Fair

A million people come to this fair to ride the giant Ferris wheel, cheer on pie-eating contests and horseback jockeys, browse the blue-ribbon agricultural and arts-and-crafts exhibits, taste California wines and craft beers, and listen to live bands. It's held in Sacramento over two weeks in late July. (p588)

☆ Reggae on the River

Come party with Humboldt's finest haul of hippies, Rastafarians, tree huggers, jugglers, unicyclists and iconoclasts. Festivities last for (at least) two days in late July/early August, featuring live bands, arts and crafts, food vendors, camping and swimming.

🎎 Festival of Arts & Pageant of the Masters

Laguna Beach is so prolifically creative, the local Festival of Arts stretches over July and August, featuring art shows and demos by 140 artists in media ranging from scrimshaw to furniture. The festival culminates with a reenactment of famous paintings by costumed actors, accompanied by an orchestra. (p452)

☆ Comic-Con International

Affectionately known as 'Nerd Prom,' the nation's biggest annual convention of comic-book fans, hardcore pop-culture collectors, and sci-fi and anime devotees brings out-of-this-world costumed madness to San Diego in late July. (p468)

August

School summer vacations may technically be over, but you'd never guess in California – beaches and parks are still packed. Travel slows only slightly before the Labor Day holiday weekend.

☆ Outside Lands

Three days of debauchery in Golden Gate Park: Outside Lands is out to reinvent the Summer of Love every August with headliner music and comedy acts plus gourmet food, beer and wine.

☆ Old Spanish Days Fiesta

Santa Barbara shows off its early Spanish, Mexican and American *rancho* roots with parades, rodeo events, arts-and-crafts exhibits, and live music and dance shows in early August.

September

Summer's last hurrah is Labor Day holiday weekend, which is busy almost everywhere in California (except hot SoCal deserts). After Labor Day, prices drop and availability goes up statewide.

☉ Tall Ships Festival

In early September, the West Coast's biggest gathering of historical tall ships happens at Dana Point in Orange County, with knot-tying and scrimshaw-carving demonstrations and other kid-friendly maritime activities.

☆ Monterrey Jazz Festival

Old-school jazz cats, cross-cultural sensations and fusion rebels all line up to play the West Coast's legendary jazz festival, held on the Central Coast over a long weekend in mid-September. (p304)

October

Summer arrives at last in Northern California, and Southern Californians take a breather after a long summer of nonstop beach-going. The mellow fall shoulder season is a prime time for sweet travel deals along the coast and in cities.

☆ Hardly Strictly Bluegrass

Over half a million people converge for free outdoor concerts in Golden Gate Park during the first weekend in October. Headliners like Emmylou Harris, Elvis Costello and Gillian Welch share seven stages with 100-plus folk, blues and jazz musicians. (p102)

🍷 Vineyard Festivals

All month long under sunny skies, California's wine countries celebrate bringing in the vineyard harvest with food-and-wine events, harvest fairs, barrel tastings and grape-stomping 'crush' parties.

☆ Halloween

Hundreds of thousands of revelers come out to play in LA's West Hollywood LGBTQ neighborhood for all-day partying and live entertainment. Over-the-top scary and NSFW costumes must be seen to be believed.

November

Temperatures drop statewide, the first raindrops fall along the coast, and with any luck, ski season begins in the mountains. Consider this your opportunity to explore without crowds or traffic, except around the Thanksgiving holiday.

☉ Dia de los Muertos

Mexican communities honor deceased relatives on November 2 with costumed parades, sugar skulls, graveyard picnics, candlelight processions and fabulous altars, including in San Francisco, LA and San Diego.

☉ Death Valley '49ers

Take a trip back to California's 19th-century gold rush during this annual encampment at Furnace Creek, with campfire sing-alongs, cowboy poetry readings, horseshoe tournaments and a Western art show in early to mid-November. (p532)

December

As winter rains reach coastal areas, SoCal's sunny, dry deserts become magnets for travelers. Christmas and New Year's Eve are extremely crowded travel times, but worth it for California's palm-tree light displays and holiday cheer.

☉ Parades of Lights

Deck the decks with boughs of holly: boats bedecked with holiday cheer and twinkling lights float through coastal California harbors, including Orange County's Newport Beach and San Diego.

Itineraries

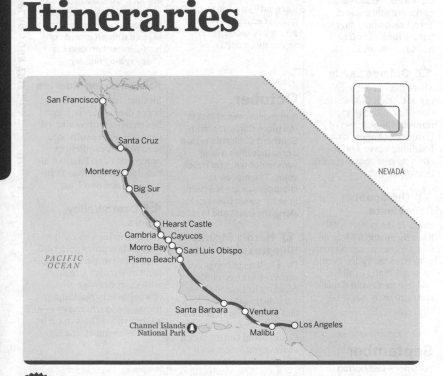

San Francisco

Santa Cruz

Monterey

Big Sur

Hearst Castle

Cambria   Cayucos

Morro Bay   San Luis Obispo

Pismo Beach

PACIFIC
OCEAN

NEVADA

Santa Barbara

Ventura

Channel Islands
National Park

Malibu

Los Angeles

1 WEEK Los Angeles to San Francisco

You've got one week to settle California's longest-running debate: which is California's better half, North or South? Start in **Los Angeles** for Hollywood star-spotting, movie premieres and live music. Cruise north to the idyllic beaches of **Malibu**, and hop a boat from **Ventura** to explore island wildlife at **Channel Islands National Park**. Arrive just in time for happy hour at sophisticated **Santa Barbara**, conveniently bordering SoCal wine country.

Follow the monarch butterfly trail to retro-1950s **Pismo Beach**, and plan to arrive in **San Luis Obispo** good and hungry for legendary local BBQ. Take coastal Hwy 1 past offbeat beach towns like **Morro Bay**, **Cayucos** and **Cambria** before you stop and stare at the sprawling landmark to eccentricity known as **Hearst Castle**.

Wind north along dizzying cliff edges through soul-stirring **Big Sur**, where redwood forests rise and waterfalls crash onto the beach in a rainbow shimmer. Dive into California's best aquarium in maritime **Monterey**, and take a bone-rattling antique roller-coaster ride over the beach boardwalk in **Santa Cruz**.

Hwy 1 leads you past lighthouses and strawberry farms, staggering bluffs and fishing harbors to the countercultural capital of **San Francisco**. Now that you've arrived, you may not have settled the great North/South debate – but you can definitely see both sides.

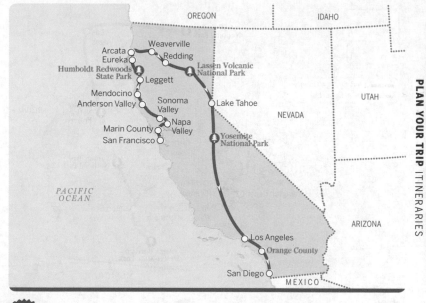

3 WEEKS California Classics

Cover the Golden State's greatest hits on this grand tour, starting in San Francisco and ending up over 1400 unforgettable miles later with your toes in the warm sands of San Diego.

Jump aboard a cable car in **San Francisco**, take a walk on the wild side in Golden Gate Park, and hop a ferry to infamous Alcatraz prison. Plan your jailbreak in time for dinner at the Ferry Building, San Francisco's local food landmark.

Cross the Golden Gate Bridge into the rolling hills of **Marin County**. California's most famous grapes grow just east in down-home **Sonoma Valley** and chichi **Napa Valley**. Detour west through more vineyards and apple orchards in rural **Anderson Valley**, and head through redwood forests to **Mendocino**, a postcard-perfect Victorian seaside town.

Swing onto Hwy 101 at **Leggett**, where your magical tour of the Redwood Empire really begins. In **Humboldt Redwoods State Park**, you'll stand in the shadows of the tallest trees on earth. Kick back in the candy-colored Victorian harbor town of **Eureka**, or head north to hang out with artists and environmentalists in the outlandish outpost of **Arcata**.

Turn east on Hwy 299 for a long, scenic trip to hidden **Weaverville**, skirting the lake-laced Trinity Alps. Keep trucking east, then south on I-5 to **Redding**, where families throng Turtle Bay Exploration Park. Climb east on Hwy 44 to the otherworldly moonscapes of **Lassen Volcanic National Park**, at the southern tip of the Cascades Range.

Go southeast on Hwy 89 to **Lake Tahoe**, the Sierra Nevada's scenic outdoor playground. Roll down the Eastern Sierra's Hwy 395, taking the back-door route via Tioga Rd (open seasonally) into **Yosemite National Park**. Feel your jaw drop as you watch waterfalls tumble over granite cliffs, and enjoy moments of profound silence in groves of giant sequoias.

Zoom south to **Los Angeles** to find as-seen-on-TV beaches, fleets of food trucks and colorful neighborhood characters. Walk in stars' footsteps through Hollywood, then sprawl on the sand in hip Santa Monica or quirky Venice Beach. Cruise south past the beautiful beaches of swanky **Orange County** to hang-loose **San Diego** for epic surf and serious fish tacos. Dude, you've totally got the hang of California.

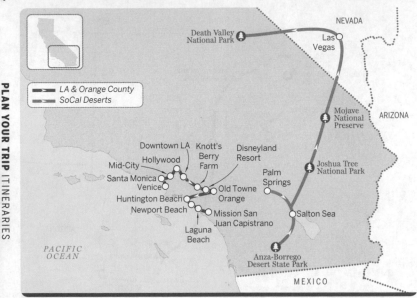

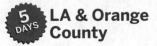

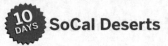

5 DAYS LA & Orange County

All-star attractions, bodacious beaches and fresh seafood are yours to discover on this 100-mile Southern California sojourn.

Kick things off in Los Angeles. Skate north from oddball **Venice** to oceanfront **Santa Monica** for sunset carnival rides on the pier. Cram your social feeds with selfies on the star-studded sidewalks of **Hollywood**, then go highbrow with art musuems in **Mid-City**, and the symphony hall and Grammy Museum in **downtown LA**.

Over in Anaheim, you've got a hot date with Mickey at Disneyland and wild rides at Disney California Adventure. If **Disneyland Resort** isn't enough adrenaline for you, hit the thrill rides over at **Knott's Berry Farm**, then recuperate in **Old Towne Orange**.

Cruise west to 'Surf City USA': **Huntington Beach**, where you can rent a board, join beach volleyball games and make s'mores over a beach bonfire. Swing by **Newport Beach** for sunset strolls and people-watching by the piers, then roll south to the upscale artists' colony of **Laguna Beach**. Slingshot back toward the I-5, and see what SoCal looked like before achieving international stardom at historic **Mission San Juan Capistrano**.

10 DAYS SoCal Deserts

You might think you've arrived on another planet, with giant sand dunes, palm-tree oases, volcanic craters, and rainbow cinder cones – but you're just a few hours from LA. Go get lost – and find yourself – on this 800-mile desert drive.

Start in glam **Palm Springs**, where you can sip mojitos poolside, hike to palm-studded canyons and ride a tram into cool pine-scented mountains.

Drive past the Coachella Valley's date farms and along the shores of the mirage-like **Salton Sea**, turning west into wild **Anza-Borrego Desert State Park** to see bighorn sheep and wind-sculpted caves.

Boomerang north to **Joshua Tree National Park**, with its precariously balanced boulders and iconic namesake trees. Keep motoring north into the **Mojave National Preserve**, where you can hear sand dunes sing with the wind and wander the world's largest Joshua-tree forest.

Ready for a change of pace? **Las Vegas**, baby. Quit while you're ahead at the Strip's casinos and run to **Death Valley National Park**. These crackled salt flats and marbled canyons make Mars seem overrated – California is totally out of this world.

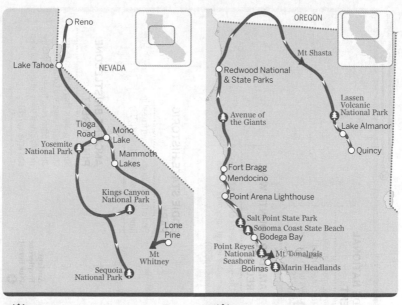

10 DAYS Sierra Nevada Ramble

Nothing can prepare our tiny human minds for the monumental mountain scenery of the Sierra Nevada, with acres of wildflower meadows, gleaming alpine lakes and sun-catching peaks John Muir called the 'Range of Light.' Take this 850-mile trip in summer, when all roads are open to exploration.

To gaze up at the world's biggest trees and down at a gorge deeper than the Grand Canyon, start in **Sequoia and Kings Canyon National Parks**. Go west, then north to **Yosemite National Park**, where thunderous waterfalls and eroded granite monoliths overhang a verdant valley.

Soar over the Sierra Nevada's snowy rooftop on Yosemite's high-elevation **Tioga Rd** (open seasonally). It's a quick trip south on Hwy 395 to **Mammoth Lakes**, an all-seasons adventure base camp, and 100 more miles to **Lone Pine**, in the shadow of mighty **Mt Whitney**.

Backtracking north, gaze out over **Mono Lake** and its odd-looking tufa formations, which you can paddle past in a kayak. Head to **Lake Tahoe**, a deep-blue jewel framed by jutting peaks with hiking trails and ski-resort slopes. Roll across the Nevada state line for casino nightlife in **Reno**, and return to Tahoe for restorative hot springs.

2 WEEKS North Coast & Mountains

Follow the ruggedly handsome coastline north of San Francisco past rocky shores, secluded coves and wind-sculpted beaches. Loop back via the majestic Northern Mountains for a memorable 800-mile journey.

Across the Golden Gate Bridge, hike over the **Marin Headlands** or around **Mt Tamalpais**. Locals keep hiding the road signs to **Bolinas**, but you'll find this eccentric cove north of Stinson Beach. Head up to blustery **Point Reyes National Seashore**, and, passing **Bodega Bay**, picnic at stunning **Sonoma Coast State Beach** or **Salt Point State Park**. Next, climb to the tip of **Point Arena Lighthouse**, step through pot-scented mists into enchanted **Mendocino** and ride the Skunk Train at **Fort Bragg**.

Hwy 1 curves inland to Hwy 101, running north into hippie Humboldt County. Hug ancient redwood trees on the **Avenue of the Giants** or head further north through misty **Redwood National and State Parks**.

Cutting east through Oregon to the I-5 southbound, arrive at majestic **Mt Shasta**. Treat yourself to a rest here before heading southeast to **Lassen Volcanic National Park**, a geological wonderland. Take a bracing dip in **Lake Almanor**, near the laid-back mountain town of **Quincy**, and emerge from your trip renewed, body and soul.

Off the Beaten Track

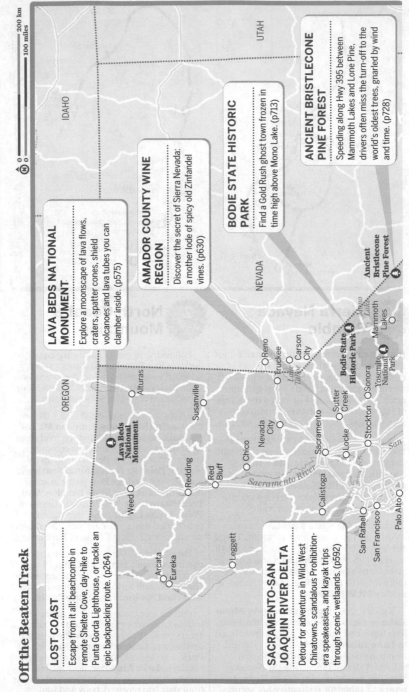

LOST COAST

Escape from it all: beachcomb in remote Shelter Cove, day-hike to Punta Gorda Lighthouse, or tackle an epic backpacking route. (p264)

LAVA BEDS NATIONAL MONUMENT

Explore a moonscape of lava flows, craters, spatter cones, shield volcanoes and lava tubes you can clamber inside. (p575)

AMADOR COUNTY WINE REGION

Discover the secret of Sierra Nevada: a mother lode of spicy old Zinfandel vines. (p630)

BODIE STATE HISTORIC PARK

Find a Gold Rush ghost town frozen in time high above Mono Lake. (p713)

ANCIENT BRISTLECONE PINE FOREST

Speeding along Hwy 395 between Mammoth Lakes and Lone Pine, drivers often miss the turn-off to the world's oldest trees, gnarled by wind and time. (p728)

SACRAMENTO-SAN JOAQUIN RIVER DELTA

Detour for adventure in Wild West Chinatowns, scandalous Prohibition-era speakeasies, and kayak trips through scenic wetlaands. (p592)

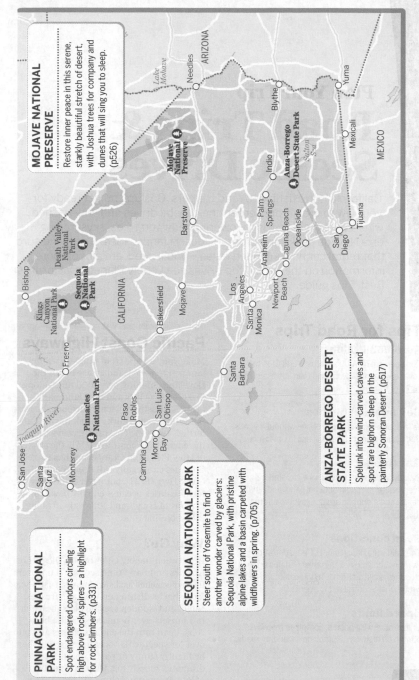

MOJAVE NATIONAL PRESERVE

Restore inner peace in this serene, starkly beautiful stretch of desert, with Joshua trees for company and dunes that will sing you to sleep. (p526)

PINNACLES NATIONAL PARK

Spot endangered condors circling high above rocky spires – a highlight for rock climbers. (p331)

SEQUOIA NATIONAL PARK

Steer south of Yosemite to find another wonder carved by glaciers: Sequoia National Park, with pristine alpine lakes and a basin carpeted with wildflowers in spring. (p705)

ANZA-BORREGO DESERT STATE PARK

Spelunk into wind-carved caves and spot rare bighorn sheep in the painterly Sonoran Desert. (p517)

Plan Your Trip

Road Trips & Scenic Drives

California is irresistible to road trippers. Gas up and get ready for your jaw to drop, from serpentine coastal drives and sun-washed wine-country vineyards to towering redwood trees, skyscraping Sierra Nevada peaks and dramatic desert landscapes. Just make sure that rental car has unlimited miles – you'll need 'em all. For more information on the state's top drives see Lonely Planet's California's Best Trips guide.

Tips for Road Trips

Automobile clubs

Consider joining AAA or Better World Club to cover emergency towing and roadside assistance service.

Cell (mobile) phones

Talking or texting on a cell phone without a hands-free device while driving is illegal in California.

Gas (fuel)

Readily available at self-service gas stations everywhere, except in national parks and remote desert and mountain areas. Expect to pay more than $4 per US gallon.

Road conditions

The California Department of Transportation (www.dot.ca.gov) has the latest updates on road closures, construction delays and detours, and winter chain-control requirements.

Speed limits

Unless otherwise posted, 65mph on freeways, 55mph on highways, 35mph on secondary roads.

Pacific Coast Highways

Make your escape from tangled, traffic-jammed freeways and cruise life in the slow lane. Snaking over 1000 miles along dizzying sea cliffs and over landmark bridges, passing ancient redwoods, historic lighthouses and quirky beach towns, California's two-lane coastal highways trace the edge of the continent. Only the stretch of Hwy 1 through Orange and Los Angeles Counties can legally call itself the Pacific Coast Hwy (PCH), but never mind those technicalities because equally bewitching ribbons of Hwy 1 and 101 await all along this shoreline route.

Why Go?

In between the big cities of San Diego, Los Angeles and San Francisco, you'll uncover hidden beaches and surf breaks, rustic seafood shacks dishing up the day's freshest catch, and wooden seaside piers for catching sunsets over boundless Pacific horizons. Lean into the endless curves and pull over for spectacular ocean views, whether brilliantly sunny or partly obscured by dramatic, moody fog. Once you get north of San Francisco, fishing villages are the gateways to wilder beaches and old-growth redwood forests.

When to Go

You can drive this route year-round, but July through September and sometimes into October brings the sunniest skies. Beware of 'May grey' and 'June gloom,' when clouds can blanket the coast almost everywhere south of San Francisco. Winter brings rain and chilly temperatures, especially on the North Coast.

The Route

If you drive the state's entire coastline, you'll get the best of both worlds – sunny SoCal beach life and foggy NorCal forests – with chances to stop and explore cities too. If you only have time to drive part of this coastal route, start with Orange County's beaches on PCH in SoCal; Hwy 1 from hippie Big Sur all the way north to Mendocino, crossing San Francisco's Golden Gate Bridge; or the verdant northern 'Redwood Coast' between Eureka and Crescent City.

Best Detour

Alongside Hwy 101, the incredible 32-mile Avenue of the Giants winds underneath a canopy of the world's tallest trees inside Humboldt Redwoods State Park (p266).

Time & Mileage

Seven to 10 days, 1000 miles

Eastern Sierra Scenic Byway

US Hwy 395 traces the rugged back side of the Sierra Nevada Mountains, passing the otherworldly tufa columns of Mono Lake, thick pine forests, crystal alpine lakes and hot springs galore. Endless outdoor activities – camping, hiking, rock climbing and more – beckon beyond the asphalt.

Why Go?

This road trip is riddled with amazing geological spectacles, like the bizarre volcanic formations at Mono Lake and Devils Postpile, as well as soaring Mt Whitney

(14,505ft), the highest peak in the lower 48 states. To unwind, spend an afternoon soaking in one of the area's hot springs. Also along the way are fascinating historical sites like Bodie, a gold-mining ghost town, and heartbreaking Manzanar, where 10,000 people of Japanese ancestry were unjustly interned during WWII.

When to Go

June to September is peak season, although the shoulder months of May and June may be snow-free at lower elevations. The golden fall foliage of aspen trees is beautiful during October. Driving in winter isn't recommended, because roads can be icy or even closed by snow.

The Route

If you're coming from SoCal's deserts, pick up Hwy 395 south of Lone Pine. Reno, Nevada, is the closest major access point from the north. Travelers coming from Yosemite National Park via Hwy 120 over Tioga Pass (usually open from May or June to October or November) intersect Hwy 395 at Lee Vining.

Best Detour

The Ancient Bristlecone Pine Forest has some of the oldest living trees on the planet (one named Methuselah has been around for over 4700 years). It's a 22-mile drive east of Big Pine via Hwy 168, then north on White Mountain Rd.

Time & Mileage

Three to five days, 350 miles

Hwy 49 Through Gold Country

That highway number is no coincidence: it commemorates the '49ers who came to get rich in California's gold rush. Today Hwy 49 (Golden Chain Hwy) connects the historic towns and rolling hills of Gold Country up in the Sierra Nevada foothills, a short drive from the state capitol of Sacramento.

Why Go?

Get a taste of California's early pioneer days, when hell-raising mine prospectors, railroad workers and ruffians rushed helter-skelter into the Wild West. Ride an antique steam train, try your own hand at panning for gold or be entertained at living-history museums and old-fashioned saloons. Hwy 49 also passes through little-known wine countries such as Amador County, where old-vine Zinfandel grapes grow. When the heat of the blistering summer sun gets to be too much, hop into a swimming hole, go underground and explore a cave or climb aboard a raft for a white-water river adventure.

When to Go

Sunshine is almost guaranteed from May to October, with daytime highs spiking over 100°F (38°C) during July and August. A few rain showers in April and November shouldn't deter you much.

The Route

Start following Hwy 49 from either its southern end in Jamestown, just down the road from Sonora, or at its northern finish line in Nevada City. Don't count on driving any faster than 35mph along much of this twisting route.

Best Detour

Hwy 49 crosses US Hwy 50 at Placerville and the I-5 Fwy at Auburn; from either place, it's under an hour's drive west to Sacramento. Spend the day at the state capital's museums and riverside historical sites. In July, join the crowds at the California State Fair.

Time & Mileage

Three to four days, 200 miles

Route 66

For a classic American road trip, nothing beats Route 66, connecting small-town streets and rural byways. What California novelist John Steinbeck nicknamed the 'Mother Road' triumphantly ends in SoCal, rolling through the Mojave Desert to the Pacific Ocean. You'll know you've finally found this legendary road when you're cruising by neon-lit diners, drive-in movie theaters, 20th-century motor courts and kitschy roadside attractions.

Why Go?

Speed west through eerie ghost towns beside railroad tracks in the Mojave Desert, starting from hot, hot Needles on the Arizona border. Stop into the Route 66 and train museum in whistle-stop railway town of Barstow. Atop Cajoin Pass, order an ostrich burger and a date shake at the Summit Inn, then sleep inside a faux wigwam outside San Bernardino before getting your final kicks in Pasadena and LA, ending with waving palm trees and a carnival pier in Santa Monica.

When to Go

Springtime in the desert brings wildflower blooms and milder temperatures before the scorching heat of summer hits. Route 66 from Los Angeles to San Bernardino or even Victorville can be driven year-round.

The Route

You need to be an amateur sleuth to follow Route 66 these days. Historical realignments of the highway, dead ends and stretches paved over by the interstate are all par for the course. Getting lost every now and then is inevitable, but you can get turn-by-turn driving directions from the website www.historic66.com. Be prepared for rough, rutted driving conditions in the desert – take it easy on that gas pedal.

Best Detour

From nearby the desert pit stop of Amboy, it's about a 40-mile drive northeast to Kelso in the heart of the vast Mojave National Preserve, strewn with volcanic cinder cones, Joshua trees, sand dunes and hiking trails.

Time & Mileage

Two to three days, 320 miles

WEST
SAN BERNARDINO
66
COUNTY

Top: Motorcycles on
Route 66 (p522)

Bottom: Bixby Bridge
(p313)

California's Best Road Trips & Scenic Drives

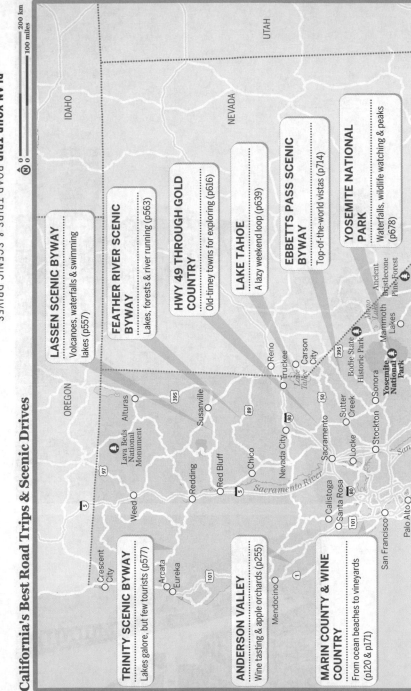

LASSEN SCENIC BYWAY
Volcanoes, waterfalls & swimming lakes (p557)

FEATHER RIVER SCENIC BYWAY
Lakes, forests & river running (p563)

HWY 49 THROUGH GOLD COUNTRY
Old-timey towns for exploring (p616)

LAKE TAHOE
A lazy weekend loop (p639)

EBBETTS PASS SCENIC BYWAY
Top-of-the-world vistas (p714)

YOSEMITE NATIONAL PARK
Waterfalls, wildlife watching & peaks (p678)

TRINITY SCENIC BYWAY
Lakes galore, but few tourists (p577)

ANDERSON VALLEY
Wine tasting & apple orchards (p255)

MARIN COUNTY & WINE COUNTRY
From ocean beaches to vineyards (p120 & p171)

0 100 miles
0 200 km

N

IDAHO
UTAH
NEVADA
OREGON

Crescent City
Arcata
Eureka
Weed
Lava Beds National Monument
Alturas
Redding
Red Bluff
Susanville
Chico
Nevada City
Reno
Truckee
Lake Tahoe
Carson City
Sacramento
Sutter Creek
Stockton
Locke
Sonora
Yosemite National Park
Bodie State Historic Park
Mono Lake
Mammoth Lakes
Ancient Bristlecone Pine Forest
Calistoga
Santa Rosa
San Francisco
Palo Alto
Mendocino
Sacramento River

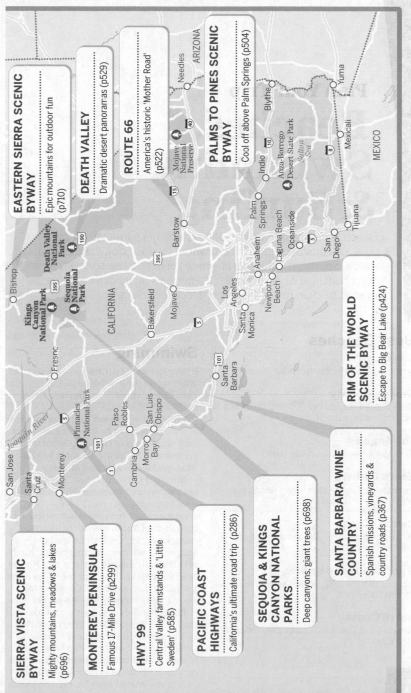

SIERRA VISTA SCENIC BYWAY

Mighty mountains, meadows & lakes (p696)

MONTEREY PENINSULA

Famous 17-Mile Drive (p299)

HWY 99

Central Valley farmstands & 'Little Sweden' (p585)

PACIFIC COAST HIGHWAYS

California's ultimate road trip (p286)

SEQUOIA & KINGS CANYON NATIONAL PARKS

Deep canyons, giant trees (p698)

SANTA BARBARA WINE COUNTRY

Spanish missions, vineyards & country roads (p367)

EASTERN SIERRA SCENIC BYWAY

Epic mountains for outdoor fun (p710)

DEATH VALLEY

Dramatic desert panoramas (p529)

ROUTE 66

America's historic 'Mother Road' (p522)

PALMS TO PINES SCENIC BYWAY

Cool off above Palm Springs (p504)

RIM OF THE WORLD SCENIC BYWAY

Escape to Big Bear Lake (p424)

Plan Your Trip
Beaches, Swimming & Surfing

Beach life and surf culture define California's freewheeling life-style, so consider permission granted to play hooky and hit the waves. Southern California is where you'll find the sunniest swimming beaches, while Northern California's misty cliffs and blustery strands beckon romantics and hardcore surfers.

Best Beaches

San Diego
Coronado, Mission Beach, Pacific Beach, La Jolla

Orange County
Newport Beach, Laguna Beach, Crystal Cove State Park, Doheny State Beach

Los Angeles
Santa Monica, Venice, South Bay, Malibu

Santa Barbara
East Beach, El Capitán State Beach, Refugio State Beach, Carpinteria State Beach

Central Coast
Main Beach (Santa Cruz), Moonstone Beach, Cayucos, Pismo State Beach

San Francisco Bay Area
Stinson Beach, Point Reyes National Seashore, Pacifica State Beach

North Coast
Sonoma Coast State Beach, Lost Coast, Trinidad State Beach

Swimming

If your California dream vacation means bronzing on the beach and paddling in the Pacific, head directly to Southern California (SoCal). With mile after mile of wide, sandy beaches between Santa Barbara and San Diego, you can be living the dream at least six months of the year. Ocean temperatures in SoCal are tolerable by May or June, peaking in July and August.

Northern California (NorCal) beaches are blustery and dramatic, with high swells crashing into rocky bluffs – not great for casual swimmers but perfect for the Titans of Mavericks (http://titansof mavericks.com), the world's most challenging big-wave pro surfing competition, held annually near Half Moon Bay. NorCal beaches remain chilly year-round, so bring a windbreaker – and if you're going to brave these waters, bring or rent a wetsuit.

Beach bonfires at sunset are a California tradition – Burning Man Festival started as a massive bonfire on San Francisco's Ocean Beach – but they're no longer permitted at most beaches for environmental reasons. Legally, you can build bonfires only in designated fire pits, even on Ocean Beach. Show up early in the day to snag

Top: La Jolla, San Diego (p483)

Bottom: Santa Monica beach (p398)

one (no reservations) and bring your own firewood. Unless otherwise posted, drinking alcohol is usually prohibited on beaches, except at campgrounds.

During the hottest dog days of summer, families skip the beach and head inland for a dip at Legoland (p491) in San Diego's North County, Knott's Soak City (p438) near Disneyland and Wet 'n' Wild Palm Springs (p500) in the SoCal desert.

Safety Tips

➡ Most California beaches have flags to distinguish between surfer-only sections and sections for swimmers. Flags also alert beachgoers to dangerous water conditions – and even seasoned California surfers know these warnings need to be taken seriously.

➡ Popular beaches in Southern California have lifeguards, but can still be dangerous places to swim. Obey all posted warning signs and ask about local conditions before venturing out.

➡ Stay out of the ocean for at least three days after a major rainstorm, when dangerously high levels of pollutants flush out through storm drains.

➡ Water quality varies from beach to beach and day to day. For current water-safety conditions and beach closures, check the Beach Report Card issued by the nonprofit organization Heal the Bay (http://brc.healthebay.org).

Best Family-Friendly Beaches

➡ **Silver Strand State Beach** (☎619-435-5184; www.parks.ca.gov; 5000 Hwy 75; per car/RV site $10/from $50; ⊗7am-sunset; P ⛱) Coronado

➡ **Santa Monica State Beach** (p398) Los Angeles

WARNING! RIPTIDES

If you find yourself being carried offshore by a dangerous ocean current called a riptide, the important thing is to just keep afloat. Don't panic or try to swim against the current, as this will quickly exhaust you. Instead, swim parallel to the shoreline and once the current stops pulling you out, swim back to shore.

➡ **Leo Carrillo State Park** (☎310-457-8143; www.parks.ca.gov; 35000 W Pacific Coast Hwy; per car $12; ⊗8am-10pm; P ⛱) Malibu

➡ **Balboa Peninsula** (p444) Newport Beach

➡ **Carpinteria State Beach** (p378) Santa Barbara County

➡ **Arroyo Burro Beach County Park** (p349) Santa Barbara

➡ **Avila Beach** (p339) San Luis Obispo County

➡ **Natural Bridges State Beach** (p289) Santa Cruz

➡ **Stinson Beach** (p136) Marin County

➡ **Trinidad State Beach** (p277) North Coast

Best Places for Beach Volleyball

➡ **Manhattan Beach** (www.citymb.info; ▣MTA 126, 439) LA's South Bay

➡ **Hermosa Beach** LA's South Bay

➡ **Huntington City Beach** (p441) Orange County

➡ **Mission Bay** (p465) San Diego

➡ **East Beach** (p349) Santa Barbara

Books & Maps

California Coastal Access Guide (University of California Press, 2014) has comprehensive maps of every public beach, reef, harbor, cover, overlook and coastal campground, with valuable information about parking, hiking trails, facilities and wheelchair access – and secluded beaches only locals know.

Surfing

Surf's up! Are you down? Even if you've never set foot on a board, there's no denying the influence of surfing on every aspect of California life, from street clothing to slang. Surfing is an obsession up and down the coast, particularly in Santa Cruz, San Diego and Orange County.

The most powerful ocean swells arrive along California's coast during late fall and winter. May and June are generally the flattest months, although they do bring warmer water. Speaking of temperature, don't believe the Hollywood hype about blondes surfing in skimpy bikinis; without

GABRIELE MALTINTI / SHUTTERSTOCK ©

Laguna Beach (p450)

a wetsuit, you'll likely freeze your butt off except at the height of summer – especially anywhere north of Santa Barbara.

Crowds can be a problem at many surf spots, as are overly territorial surfers. Befriend a local surfer for an introduction before hitting Cali's most famous waves, such as notoriously agro Windansea Beach and Malibu Surfrider Beach.

Sharks do inhabit California waters, but attacks are rare. Most take place in the so-called 'Red Triangle' between Monterey on the Central Coast, Tomales Bay north of San Francisco and the offshore Farallon Islands.

Rentals & Lessons

You'll find board rentals on just about every patch of beach where surfing is possible. Expect to pay about $25 per half day for a board, with wetsuit rental costing another $10 or so.

Two-hour group lessons for beginners start at around $100 per person, while private, two-hour instruction easily costs more than $125. If you've got bigger ambitions and deeper pockets, many surf schools offer weekend surf clinics and week-long 'surfari' camps.

Only a few Californians are hardcore surfers, but many enjoy boogie boarding, paddle boarding and kitesurfing. Stand-up paddleboarding (SUP) is easier than learning to surf, and it's skyrocketing in popularity. You'll find board-and-paddle rentals and lessons popping up all along the coast, from San Diego to north of San Francisco Bay. Kiteboarding is also big along NorCal's windy coast, and you can get started with rentals in Santa Cruz and San Francisco.

Best Surf Breaks for Beginners

The best spots to learn to surf are long, shallow bays where waves are small and rolling. Surf schools dot the California coast from San Diego to Santa Cruz, and popular places for beginners include:

San Diego

➡ **Mission Beach** (☎858-483-8837; www. missionsurf.com; 4320 Mission Blvd, Pacific

Beach; surfboard rentals from $10 (softtop) $20 (hardboard); ⊙10am-7pm)

➡ **Pacific Beach** (☎858-373-1138; www. pbsurfshop.com; 4150 Mission Blvd; group surfing lessons from $75; ⊙store 9am-6pm (winter), 9am-7pm (summer))

➡ **La Jolla** (☎858-454-8273; www.surfdiva. com; 2160 Avenida de la Playa; ⊙store 8:30am-5pm, lesson hours vary from season to season), Oceanside (p494)

Orange County

➡ **Seal Beach** (p440)

➡ **Huntington Beach** (p442)

➡ **Newport Beach** (p444)

➡ **Laguna Beach** (☎949-497-1423; www. casurfshop.com; 695 S Coast Hwy; lessons group/private $75/95; ⊙8am-9pm most days)

Los Angeles

➡ **Santa Monica** (☎310-663-2479; www. learntosurfla.com; group lesson per person from $85),

➡ **Malibu** (☎310-456-8508; www. malibusurfshack.com; 22935 Pacific Coast Hwy, Malibu; kayaks per day $35, surfboards per day $25-35, SUP per 2hr/overnight $45/75, wetsuits per day $10-15, surf/SUP lessons per person $125/100; ⊙10am-6pm)

Santa Barbara County

➡ **Leadbetter Beach** (p349)

➡ **Carpinteria** (p378)

Central Coast

➡ **Santa Cruz** (p292),

➡ **Cayucos** (p325)

Bodyboarding & Bodysurfing

If you don't have the time or inclination to conquer California's surf breaks on a long-board, there are other ways to catch your dream wave. Bodysurfing and bodyboard-ing (aka boogie boarding) let you ride rolling waves for 100ft or more. To increase your speed and control, use some flippers. If you're not sure how to get started, just watch how locals do it – or strike up a con-versation in the water and ask for pointers. It's pretty easy, and you'll be beaming with glee once you catch that first wave.

Online Resources

➡ Browse the comprehensive atlas, live webcams and surf reports at Surfline (www.surfline.com), and get the lowdown on the best swells from San Diego to Humboldt County on the North Coast.

➡ Orange County–based *Surfer* magazine's website (www.surfermag.com) has travel reports, gear reviews, blogs, forums and totally gnarly videos.

➡ Surfers have led California's coastal conservation efforts for 40 years, and you can join their ongoing efforts through the nonprofit Surfrider Foundation (www.surfrider.org).

➡ If you're a kook, bone up on surf-speak so brahs don't go agro and give you stinkeye. For translations, use Riptionary (www.riptionary.com).

Plan Your Trip
California Camping & Outdoors

California is an all-seasons outdoor playground. Hike among desert wildflowers in spring, dive into the Pacific in summer, mountain bike through fall foliage and ski down wintry mountain slopes. Once California gets your adrenaline pumping, you'll also be ready to hang glide off ocean bluffs, scuba past coastal shipwrecks, scale sheer granite cliffs or white-water raft the rapids.

Camping

In California, camping is much more than just a cheap way to spend the night. Pitch a tent beside alpine lakes and streams beneath snaggletoothed Sierra Nevada peaks, nestle into shimmering SoCal sand dunes beneath the full moon, and drift off on NorCal redwood forest floors beneath the tallest trees on earth. No five-star-hotel views can compare to this kind of scenery. If you didn't bring your own tent, you can buy (and occasionally rent) camping gear at outdoor outfitters and sporting-goods shops in most cities and some towns, especially near national parks.

Campground Types & Amenities

➡ **Primitive campsites** Usually have fire pits, picnic tables and access to drinking water and vault toilets; most common in United States Forest Service (USFS) forests and on Bureau of Land Management (BLM) land.

➡ **Developed campgrounds** Typically found in state and national parks, these offer more amenities, including flush toilets, barbecue grills and occasionally hot showers.

➡ **Private campgrounds** Often cater to RVs (recreational vehicles), with full electricity and

When & Where

Best Times to Go

Cycling & mountain biking Apr–Oct

Hiking Apr–Oct

Kayaking, snorkeling & scuba diving Jul–Oct

Rock climbing Apr–Oct

Skiing & snowboarding Dec–Mar

Whale-watching Jan–Mar

White-water rafting Apr–Oct

Windsurfing Apr–Oct

Top Experiences

Backpacking John Muir Trail

Cycling Pacific Coast Hwy

Hiking Redwood National & State Parks

Mountain biking Lake Tahoe

Rock climbing Yosemite National Park

Sea kayaking Channel Islands

Snorkeling & scuba diving La Jolla

White-water rafting Sierra Nevada

California's Best Places to Camp

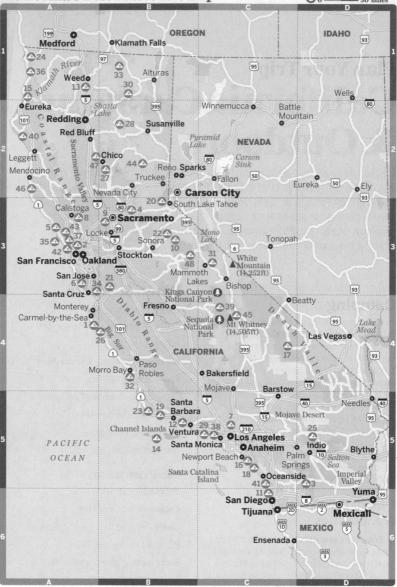

water hookups and dump stations; tent sites may be sparse and uninviting. Hot showers and a coin-operated laundry are usually available, plus possibly a swimming pool, wi-fi and camping cabins.

➡ **Walk-in (environmental) sites** Provide more peace and privacy, and may be significantly cheaper than drive-in sites. A few state-park campgrounds reserve walk-in sites for long-distance hikers and cyclists only.

California's Best Places to Camp

Seasons, Rates & Reservations

Many campgrounds are closed from late fall through to early spring or summer, especially in the mountains and Northern California. Opening and closing dates vary each year, depending on weather conditions and the previous winter's snowfall. Private campgrounds are often open year-round, especially those closest to cities, beaches and major highways.

Many public and private campgrounds accept reservations for all or some of their sites, while a few are strictly first-come, first-served. Overnight rates range from free for the most primitive campsites to $60 or more for pull-through RV sites with full hookups.

Booking services let you search for public and private campground locations and amenities, check availability and reserve campsites online. They may charge a reservation fee of up to $10.

Last-Minute Camping

If you can't get a campsite reservation, plan to show up at the campground between 10am and noon, when the previous night's campers may be leaving. Don't be too choosy, or you may end up with no site at all – especially on holidays, summer weekends and spring days when wildflowers are in bloom. Park rangers, visitor centers and campground hosts can often tell you where spaces may still be available, if there are any. Otherwise, ask about overflow and dispersed camping nearby.

Cycling & Mountain-Biking

Strap on that helmet! California is outstanding cycling terrain, whether you're looking for a leisurely spin along the beach, an adrenaline-fueled mountain ride or a multiday road-cycling tour down the coast. The cycling season runs year-round in most coastal areas, although coastal fog may rob you of views both in winter and during 'May gray' and 'June gloom.' Avoid the North Coast and the mountains during winter (too much rain and snow at higher elevations) and SoCal's deserts in summer (too dang hot).

BUT WAIT, THERE'S MORE

ACTIVITY	LOCATION	REGION
Bird-watching	Klamath Basin National Wildlife Refuges	Northern Mountains
	Mono Lake	Sierra Nevada
	Sonny Bono Salton Sea National Wildlife Refuge	The Deserts
Caving	Lava Beds National Monument)	Northern Mountains
	Crystal Cave	Sierra Nevada
	Pinnacles National Park	Central Coast
Fishing	Dana Point	Orange County
	San Diego	San Diego
	Bodega Bay	North Coast
	Trinity Alps	North Coast & Mountains
Golf	Palm Springs & Coachella Valley	The Deserts
	Pebble Beach	Central Coast
	Torrey Pines	San Diego
Hang gliding & paragliding	Torrey Pines	San Diego
	Santa Barbara	Santa Barbara County
Horseback riding	Yosemite National Park	Sierra Nevada
	Wild Horse Sanctuary	Northern Mountains
	South Lake Tahoe	Lake Tahoe
Hot-air ballooning	Del Mar	San Diego
	Temecula	San Diego
	Napa Valley	Napa & Sonoma Wine Country
Kayaking & canoeing	Channel Islands National Park	Santa Barbara County
	Elkhorn Slough	Central Coast
	Mendocino	North Coast
	Tomales Bay	Marin County
	Russian River	Napa & Sonoma Wine Country
	Morro Bay	Central Coast
	San Diego	San Diego
	Sacramento Delta	Sacramento County
Kiteboarding & windsurfing	Crissy Field	San Francisco
	Mission Bay	San Diego
	Donner Lake	Lake Tahoe
Rock climbing	Yosemite National Park	Sierra Nevada
	Joshua Tree National Park	The Deserts
	Pinnacles National Park	Central Coast
	Bishop	Eastern Sierra
	Truckee	Lake Tahoe

Road Rules

➡ In national parks, bicycles are usually limited to paved and dirt roads, and are not allowed on trails or in designated wilderness areas.

➡ Most national forests and BLM lands are open to mountain bikers. Stay on already established tracks and always yield to hikers and horseback riders.

➡ At California's state parks, trails are off-limits to bikes unless otherwise posted, while paved and dirt roads are usually open to cyclists and mountain bikers.

Best Places to Cycle

➡ Even heavily trafficked urban areas may have good cycling routes, especially in SoCal. Take the scenic route along LA's beachside South Bay Bicycle Trail (p398) and down shoreline bike paths in Santa Barbara, Newport Beach and other beach towns.

➡ In the Bay Area, cruise through San Francisco's Golden Gate Park (p98) and over the Golden Gate Bridge (p83), then hop on the ferry back across the bay from Sausalito. Angel Island is another great bike-and-ferry combo.

➡ On the Central Coast, ocean-view Monterey Peninsula Recreational Trail and scenic 17-Mile Drive (p311) attract cyclists of all skill levels.

➡ California's wine countries offer beautiful DIY and guided bike tours, especially in Napa (p174) and Sonoma's Dry Creek Valley (p211).

➡ For road cyclists, nothing surpasses winding, coastal Hwy 1, especially the dizzying stretch through Big Sur (p313).

➡ Up north in Humboldt Redwoods State Park (p266), take a gentle ride past the world's tallest trees on the Avenue of the Giants.

➡ In Sierra Nevada, Yosemite Valley (p675) has paved recreational paths that pass meadows, waterfalls and granite spires.

Best Mountain-Biking Areas

➡ Just north of San Francisco, the Marin Headlands offer a bonanza of trails for fat-tire fliers. Mt Tamalpais State Park (p133) is where the sport of mountain biking began, and the adrenaline-pumping trails here have inspired video games.

➡ Top-rated single-track rides near Lake Tahoe include Mr Toad's Wild Ride and the Flume Trail (p670). In the neighboring Gold Country,

Downieville offers an enormous downhill rush (p623).

➡ Speed freaks can't get enough of Eastern Sierra's Mammoth Mountain (p719), where the summer bike park offers more than 80 miles of single-track challenges. Other ski areas also open trails and chairlifts to mountain bikers in summer, including Big Bear Mountain Resort (p425) outside LA and Northstar (p662) at Lake Tahoe.

➡ Joshua Tree (p508) and Death Valley (p529) national parks offer miles of backcountry roads for desert mountain biking. For more desert terrain, hit Anza-Borrego Desert State Park (p517) outside San Diego and the Santa Monica Mountains (www.nps.gov/samo/index.htm) north of LA.

➡ State parks especially popular with mountain bikers include NorCal's **Prairie Creek Redwoods** (☑707-488-2039; www.parks. ca.gov; Newton B Drury Scenic Pkwy; ⊘9am-5pm May-Sep, to 4pm Wed-Sun Oct-Apr; ☑), Montaña de Oro (p328) on the Central Coast and Orange County's Crystal Cove (p449).

➡ A hidden gem inland from Monterey, Fort Ord National Monument (p303) has more than 80 miles of dirt single tracks and fire roads for mountain bikers.

Maps & Online Resources

Local bike shops and some tourist offices can supply you with more cycling route ideas, maps and advice. For online forums and reviews of mountain-biking trails in California, search www.mtbr.com and www.socaltrailriders.org.

➡ **California Bicycle Coalition** (http://calbike. org) Links to free online cycling maps, bike-sharing programs and community bike shops.

➡ **Adventure Cycling Association** (www. adventurecycling.org) Sells long-distance cycling route guides and touring maps covering the entire Pacific Coast.

➡ **League of American Bicyclists** (www. bikeleague.org) Can help you find bicycle specialty shops and local cycling clubs.

Hiking

With epic scenery, California is the perfect place to explore on foot. If you stay in the car, you'll miss the state's iconic highlights: strolling the beach at sunset, trekking past

TAKE A HIKE

An invitation to get lost may sound like an insult elsewhere, but in California, it's a fantastic dare. Legendary long-distance trails cut right through the state, including the 2650-mile **Pacific Crest National Scenic Trail** (PCT; www.pcta.org), which takes hikers from Mexico to Canada. Running mostly along the PCT, the 211-mile **John Muir Trail** (JMT; www.pcta.org) links Yosemite Valley and Mt Whitney via Sierra Nevada's high country. Trace the footsteps of pioneers and Native Americans along the 165-mile **Tahoe Rim Trail** (www.tahoerimtrail.org), and you'll swear you've never seen a bluer lake or brighter sky. But there are still more trails to blaze here: the **California Coastal Trail Association** (www.coastwalk.org) is already halfway through building a 1200-mile trail along California's shoreline.

Joshua trees in desert oases, summitting 14,000-ft craggy peaks and walking under the world's tallest, largest and oldest trees. In spring and early summer, the Golden State is touched with a painter's palette as wildflowers bloom down coastal hillsides, across mountain meadows and along desert sands.

Best Places to Hike

No matter where you find yourself in California, you're never far from a trail, even in metropolitan areas. National and state parks offer a wide variety of trails, from easy nature walks negotiable by wheelchairs and strollers to multiday backpacking routes through rugged wilderness.

➡ **Sierra Nevada** In Yosemite (p678), Sequoia & Kings Canyon National Parks (p698) and around Lake Tahoe (p639), clamber toward waterfalls, wildflower meadows and alpine lakes, tackle mighty granite domes and peaks, and wander through pine-scented forests.

➡ **SoCal's Deserts** Best hiked in spring and fall, Death Valley (p529) and Joshua Tree (p508) national parks, Mojave National Preserve (p526) and Anza-Borrego Desert State Park (p517) lead you to palm-canyon oases and mining ghost towns, up volcanic cinder cones and across sand dunes and salt flats.

➡ **San Francisco Bay Area** Marin Headlands (p122), Muir Woods National Monument (p135), Mt Tamalpais State Park (p133) and Point Reyes National Seashore (p139) are crisscrossed by dozens of superb hiking trails – and they're all within a 90-minute drive of San Francisco.

➡ **North Coast** Redwood National and State Parks (p279) and the Avenue of the Giants (p266) offer misty walks through groves of old-growth redwoods, or you can scout out wilder beaches along the challenging Lost Coast Trail (p265).

➡ **Northern Mountains** Summiting Mt Shasta (p565) is a spiritually uplifting experience, while Lassen Volcanic National Park (p556) is a bizarre landscape of smoking fumaroles, cinder cones and craters.

➡ **Los Angeles** Ditch your car in the Santa Monica Mountains National Recreation Area (p53), where many movies and TV shows are filmed – or get away from the LA scene in the cool mountain climate of Big Bear Lake (p424).

Fees & Wilderness Permits

➡ Most California state parks charge a daily parking fee of $4 to $15. There's often no charge for pedestrians or cyclists. Californians give serious side-eye to people who park their cars just outside the gate then walk in – California's state parks are chronically underfunded and need the support.

➡ National park entry averages $15 to $20 per vehicle for seven consecutive days. Some national parks offer free admission, including the Channel Islands and Redwood national parks.

➡ For unlimited admission to national parks, national forests and other federal recreation lands, buy an 'America the Beautiful' annual pass (12-month pass $80). It's sold at national park visitor centers and entry stations, online (https://store.usgs.gov/pass) and at most USFS ranger stations.

➡ If you don't have an 'American the Beautiful' annual pass, you'll need a National Forest Adventure Pass (per day $5; annual pass $30) to park in some recreational areas of SoCal's national forests. Buy passes from USFS ranger stations and local vendors, such as sporting-goods stores.

Top: Kings Canyon
National Park (p699)

Bottom: Cycling in
Marin County (p122)

➡ Often required for overnight backpacking trips and a few extended day hikes, wilderness permits are issued at ranger stations and park visitor centers. Costs vary from free to more than $20. Daily quotas may be in effect during peak periods, usually late spring through early fall. Some wilderness permits can be reserved, and the most popular trails (such as Mt Whitney) may sell out several months in advance.

Maps & Online Resources

➡ There are bulletin boards showing basic trail maps and safety information at most major trailheads, some of which also have trail-guide brochure dispensers.

➡ For short, established hikes in national and state parks, free maps handed out at visitor centers or ranger stations are usually sufficient. A more detailed topographical map may be necessary for longer backcountry hikes.

➡ Topo maps are sold at park bookstores, visitor centers, ranger stations and outdoor-gear shops. The USGS Store (https://store.usgs.gov) offers its (sometimes outdated) topographic maps as free downloadable PDFs, or you can order print copies online.

➡ Learn how to minimize your impact on the environment while traipsing through the wilderness at the Leave No Trace Center for Outdoor Ethics online (http://lnt.org).

Scuba Diving & Snorkeling

All along California's coast, rocky reefs, shipwrecks and kelp beds teem with sea creatures ready for their close-up. Ocean waters are warmest in SoCal, but wetsuits are recommended for divers year-round.

Local dive shops are your best resource for equipment, guides, instructors and boat trips. With PADI certification, you can book one-tank boat dives for $65 to $150; reserve at least a day in advance. For diving with no previous experience, local outfitters offer beginners' courses that include basic instruction followed by a shallow beach or boat dive for around $150.

Snorkelers can rent a mask, snorkel and fins from most dive shops or beach concessionaires for about $20 to $45 per day. If you're going to take the plunge more than once or twice, it's probably worth buying your own mask and fins. Remember not to touch anything while you're out snorkeling, and never snorkel alone.

Best Scuba Diving & Snorkeling Spots

➡ **San Diego–La Jolla Underwater Park Ecological Reserve** (p483) is a great place for beginning divers, while La Jolla Cove attracts snorkelers.

BEST WHITE-WATER RAFTING RIVERS

RIVER	CLASS	SEASON	DESCRIPTION
American	II-V	Apr-Oct	The South Fork is best for rafting newbies, while the more challenging Middle and North Forks carve through deep gorges.
Kaweah	II-V	Apr-Jul	Expect steep drops past Sequoia National Park, then mellow out past Three Rivers.
Kern	III-V	Apr-Sep	The Upper and Lower Forks offer some of the southern Sierra's best white water.
Kings	III	Apr-Jul	One of California's most powerful rivers, with put-ins (starting points) outside Kings Canyon National Park.
Merced	III-IV	Apr-Jul	Starting near Yosemite National Park, this canyon run is the Sierra Nevada's best one-day intermediate trip.
Stanislaus	II-IV	Apr-Oct	The North Fork provides rafting trips for all, from novices to the more adventure-minded.
Truckee	I-IV	Apr-Aug	Near Lake Tahoe, this gentle river is a great beginners' run, especially for families.
Tuolumne	IV-V	Apr-Sep	Experienced paddlers prefer ferocious runs on 'the T'; in summer, experts-only Cherry Creek is a legendary Sierra Nevada run.

Snowboarding at Lake Tahoe (p641)

➡ More experienced divers and snorkelers head for Orange County's Crystal Cove State Park (p449), Divers Cove (p452) in Laguna Beach or explore shipwrecks off San Diego's Mission Beach (p464).

➡ Offshore from LA and Ventura, Catalina Island (p423) and Channel Islands National Park (p384) are major diving and snorkeling destinations.

➡ With its national marine sanctuary, Monterey Bay (p299) offers world-renowned diving and snorkeling – although in these chilly waters, you'll need a thick wetsuit.

➡ Just south of Monterey, Point Lobos State Natural Reserve (p310) is another gem for scuba divers and snorkelers (permit reservations required).

White-Water Rafting

California has dozens of white-water rivers, and hurtling down their surging rapids beats any roller-coaster ride. Swelled by snowmelt and ripping through sheer canyons, these river rapids collapse your entire vocabulary into just two words: 'dude!' and 'go!' You'll find river challenges here to suit any skill level, from beginning paddlers to hardcore river rats. The premier river runs are in the Sierra Nevada and Gold Country, but the Northern Mountains also offer some rollicking rides.

You don't get thrills without some spills – in rough conditions, it's not unusual for participants to fall out of the raft. But serious injuries are rare, and most trips are without incident. No prior experience is needed for guided river trips up to Class III, but Class IV is recommended for excellent swimmers in good shape, with paddling experience under your life-jacket belt.

Seasons, Rates & Online Resources

The main river-running season is from April to October, although exact months depend on which river you're rafting and the spring snowmelt runoff from the mountains. You'll be hurtling along either in large rafts holding a dozen or more people, or in smaller ones seating half a dozen. Smaller rafts tend to be more exhilarating because everyone paddles and they can tackle rougher rapids.

California Whitewater Rafting (www.c-w-r.com) covers all of California's prime river-running spots, with links to outfitters and river conservation groups. Commercial rafting outfitters run a variety of trips, from morning or afternoon floats to overnight and multiday expeditions. Book ahead and expect to pay more than $100 for a one-day trip.

Whale-Watching

During their annual migration, gray whales can be spotted off the California coast from December to April, while blue, humpback and sperm whales pass by in summer and fall. You can try your luck whale-watching from lighthouses and other coastal perches along the shore – but you're less likely to see whales and you'll be removed from all the action.

Just about every port town along the coast worth its sea salt offers whale-watching boat excursions, especially during winter. Bring binoculars and dress in warm, waterproof layers. Fair warning: choppy seas can be nauseating. To avoid seasickness, sit outside on the boat's second level – but not too close to the diesel fumes in the back.

Half-day whale-watching cruises cost from $30 to $100 per adult (up to 50% less for children). Make reservations at least a day ahead. Better tour boats limit the number of passengers and have a trained naturalist on board. Some tour companies let you go again for free if you don't spot any whales on your first trip.

Snow Sports

California winter vacations have it all: alpine scenery, luxury mountain cabins, killer après-ski happy hours, high-speed modern ski lifts, slopes dusted with fresh powder, and trails ranging from easy-peasy 'Sesame Street' to black-diamond 'Death Wish.' All that, and you're still just a short drive from a beach. Now you get why people move here.

Ski season runs from late November or early December until late March or early April, although this depends on weather conditions and elevation. The Sierra Nevada Mountains offer the best slopes and trails for skiers and snowboarders, although snow conditions have been unreliable in recent years due to unusually low winter snowfall. All resorts have ski schools, rent equipment and offer a variety of lift tickets, including cheaper half-day and multiday versions. Prices vary tremendously, from $50 to $125 per day for adults; discounts for children, teens and seniors are typically available. 'Ski & stay' lodging packages may offer big savings.

Best Places for Snow Sports

➡ **Around Lake Tahoe** For sheer variety, the dozen-plus downhill skiing and snowboarding resorts ringing Lake Tahoe are unbeatable. Alongside world-famous ski resorts like Squaw Valley (p661), site of the 1960 Winter Olympic Games, you'll find scores of smaller operations, many of them with lower lift-ticket prices, smaller crowds and great runs for beginners and families. Royal Gorge (p663), near Truckee, is North America's largest cross-country ski resort. Family-friendly 'sno-parks' offer sledding hills and snow play.

➡ **Mammoth & June Mountains** Mammoth Mountain (p718) is a favorite of downhill devotees, because it usually has the longest ski and snowboarding season. Beginning and intermediate skiers and snowboarders hit the less-crowded slopes of nearby June Mountain (p717).

➡ **Yosemite National Park** In the glacier-carved winter wonderland of Yosemite National Park, Yosemite Ski & Snowboard Area – Badger Pass (p689) welcomes families and beginning skiers and snowboarders. This is California's oldest ski resort and a launchpad for cross-country skiing and snowshoe treks – and kids will love the snow-tubing hill. You can snowshoe or cross-country ski among giant sequoias elsewhere in Yosemite, as well as at Panoramic Point (p701) in Kings Canyon National Park.

➡ **Northern Mountains** Mt Shasta Ski Park (p567) is popular with families, offering a range of challenges for all skill levels.

➡ **Near Los Angeles** Sunny Southern California gets in on the snow action at Big Bear Mountain Resort (p425). In the San Jacinto Mountains, Palm Springs' aerial tramway whisks you to the Winter Adventure Center (p501), where you can rent snowshoes or cross-country skis.

Plan Your Trip

Travel with Children

California is a tailor-made destination for family travel. The kids will be begging to go to theme parks, and teens to celebrity hot spots. Then take 'em into the great outdoors – from sunny beaches shaded by palm trees to misty redwood forests to four-seasons mountain playgrounds.

California for Kids

There's not too much to worry about when traveling in California with your kids, as long as you keep them covered in sunblock.

Children's discounts are available for everything from museum admission and movie tickets to bus fares and motel stays. The definition of a 'child' varies – from 'under 18' to age six. At theme parks, some rides may have minimum-height requirements, so let younger kids know about this in advance to avoid disappointment and tears.

It's fine to bring kids along to most restaurants, except top-end places. Casual restaurants usually have high chairs and children's menus and break out paper place mats and crayons for drawing. At theme parks, pack a cooler in the car and have a picnic in the parking lot to save money. On the road many supermarkets have wholesome, ready-to-eat takeout dishes.

Baby food, infant formula, disposable diapers (nappies) and other necessities are widely sold at supermarkets and pharmacies. Many public toilets have a baby-changing table, while private gender-neutral 'family' bathrooms may be available at airports, museums, etc.

Best Regions for Kids

Los Angeles

See stars in Hollywood and get behind the movie magic at Universal Studios then hit the beaches and Griffith Park for fun in the sun. What, it's raining? Dive into the city's many kid-friendly museums instead.

San Diego, Disneyland & Orange County

SoCal theme parks galore: Disneyland, Knott's Berry Farm, the San Diego Zoo & Safari Park, Legoland and more. Oh, and those sandy beaches just couldn't be more beautiful.

San Francisco Bay Area

Explore hands-on, whimsical and 'Wow!' museums, hear the barking sea lions at Pier 39 or Point Reyes National Seashore, traipse through Golden Gate Park and ride San Francisco's famous cable cars.

Yosemite & the Sierra Nevada

Watch your kids gawk at Yosemite's waterfalls and granite domes, then go hiking among groves of giant sequoias, the world's biggest trees. In the Eastern Sierra, Mammoth Lakes is a year-round outdoor-adventure base camp.

Children's Highlights

It's easy to keep kids entertained no matter where you travel in California. At national and state parks, ask at visitor centers about family-friendly, ranger-led activities and self-guided 'Junior Ranger' programs, in which kids earn themselves a badge after completing an activity booklet.

Theme Parks

➡ **Disneyland Park** (p428) and Disney California Adventure (p432) Kids of all ages, even teens, and the young-at-heart adore the 'Magic Kingdom'.

➡ **Knott's Berry Farm** (p437) Near Disneyland, SoCal's original theme park offers thrills-a-minute, especially on spooky, haunted Halloween nights.

➡ **Universal Studios Hollywood** (☏800-864-8377; www.universalstudioshollywood.com; 100 Universal City Plaza, Universal City; admission from $99, child under 3yr free; ☉daily, hours vary; P 🚻; Ⓜ Red Line to Universal City) Movie-themed action rides, special-effects shows, the Wizarding World of Harry Potter and a working studio backlot tram tour entertain tweens and teens.

➡ **Legoland California Resort** (p491) This fantasyland of building blocks in San Diego's North County is made for tots and youngsters.

Aquariums & Zoos

➡ **Monterey Bay Aquarium** (p299) Meet denizens of the deep at a national marine sanctuary.

➡ **San Diego Zoo** (p460) and Safari Park (p489) Journey around the world with exotic wildlife at California's best and biggest zoo then go on safari.

➡ **Aquarium of the Pacific** (p398) Long Beach's aquarium houses critters from balmy Baja California to the chilly north Pacific, including a shark lagoon.

➡ **Los Angeles Zoo & Botanical Gardens** (☏323-644-4200; www.lazoo.org; 5333 Zoo Dr, Griffith Park; adult/senior/child $20/17/15; ☉10am-5pm, closed Christmas Day; P 🚻) What was once the home of retired circus animals is today a center for endangered-species conservation.

➡ **Living Desert Zoo & Gardens** (p500) Outside Palm Springs, this educational zoo features a walk-through animal hospital and family campouts under the stars.

➡ **Seymour Marine Discovery Center** (p288) Santa Cruz's university-run aquarium makes interactive science fun, with tide pools for exploring by the beach.

Beaches

➡ **Los Angeles** (p388) Carnival fun and an aquarium await on Santa Monica Pier, or hit perfect beaches just up Hwy 1 in Malibu.

➡ **Orange County** (p426) Pick from beautiful pier-side strands in Newport Beach and miles of million-dollar sands in Laguna Beach, Huntington Beach (aka 'Surf City, USA') or old-fashioned Seal Beach.

➡ **San Diego** (p458) Head over to Coronado's idyllic Silver Strand, play in Mission Bay by SeaWorld, lap up La Jolla or unwind in a half-dozen surf-style beach towns in North County.

➡ **Santa Barbara County** (p345) and Central Coast (p286) Laze on unmatched beaches in Santa Barbara then roll all the way north to the famous beach boardwalk in Santa Cruz.

➡ **Lake Tahoe** (p639) In summer it's California's favorite high-altitude escape: a sparkling diamond tucked in the craggy Sierra Nevada Mountains.

Parks

➡ **Yosemite National Park** Get an epic slice of Sierra Nevada scenery, with gushing waterfalls, alpine lakes, glacier-carved valleys and peaks.

➡ **Redwood National & State Parks** (p279) A string of nature preserves on the North Coast protect magnificent wildlife and the planet's tallest trees.

➡ **Lassen Volcanic National Park** (p556) A peaceful destination in Northern California for otherworldly volcanic scenery and lakeside camping and cabins.

➡ **Griffith Park** (p392) Bigger than NYC's Central Park, this LA greenspace has tons of fun for younger kids, from miniature train rides and a merry-go-round to planetarium shows.

➡ **Channel Islands National Park** (p384) Sail across to California's version of the Galapagos for wildlife-watching, sea kayaking, hiking and camping adventures – best for teens.

Museums

➡ **San Francisco** (p76) The city is a mind-bending classroom for kids, especially at the interactive Exploratorium, multimedia Children's Creativity Museum and eco friendly California Academy of Sciences in Golden Gate Park.

➡ **Los Angeles** (p388) See stars (the real ones) at the Griffith Observatory, dinosaur bones at the Natural History Museum of Los Angeles and the La Brea Tar Pits & Museum then have hands-on fun at the California Science Center, home of the retired space shuttle *Endeavour*.

➡ **San Diego** (p458) Balboa Park is jam-packed with museums and a world-famous zoo, or take younger kids to the engaging New Children's Museum downtown and let teens and tweens clamber aboard the USS Midway Museum.

➡ **Orange County** (p426) Bring budding lab geeks to the Discovery Cube and get a pint-sized dose of arts and culture in the Kidseum at the Bowers Museum, all near Disneyland Resort.

➡ **Northern Mountains** (p549) Redding's Turtle Bay Exploration Park combines an eco-museum, an arboretum and botanical and butterfly gardens beside the Sacramento River.

Planning

Don't pack your schedule too tightly. When navigating metro areas such as LA, San Diego and San Francisco, allow extra time for traffic jams, parking and getting lost.

Accommodations & Child Care

Rule one: if you're traveling with kids, always mention it when making reservations. At a few places, notably B&Bs, you may have a hard time if you show up with little ones. When booking, be sure to request the specific room type you want, although requests often aren't guaranteed.

Motels and hotels typically have rooms with two beds or an extra sofa bed. They also may have rollaway beds or cots, usually available for a surcharge (request these when making reservations). Some offer 'kids stay free' promotions, which may apply only if no extra bedding is required.

Resorts may offer daytime activity programs for kids and child-care services. At other hotels, front-desk staff or a concierge might be able to help you make babysitting arrangements. Ask whether babysitters are licensed and bonded, what they charge per hour per child, whether there's a minimum fee and if they charge extra for transportation and meals.

Transportation

Airlines usually allow infants (up to age two) to fly for free – bring proof of age – while older children require a seat of their own and don't usually qualify for reduced fares. Children receive substantial discounts on most trains and buses.

While driving in California, any child under age eight who is shorter than 4ft, 9in must be buckled up in the back seat of the car in a child or infant safety seat. Most car-rental agencies offer these for about $10 to $15 per day, but you must specifically book them in advance.

On the road, rest stops are few and far between, and gas stations and fast-food bathrooms tend to be icky. However, you're usually never far from a shopping mall, which generally have well-kept restrooms.

What to Pack

Sunscreen. And bringing sunscreen should remind you to bring hats, swimsuits, flip-flops and goggles. If you like beach umbrellas and sand chairs, pails and shovels, you'll probably want to bring your own, or buy them at local supermarkets and pharmacies. At many beaches you can rent bicycles and water-sports gear.

For outdoor vacations, bring broken-in hiking shoes and your own camping equipment. Outdoor gear can be purchased or sometimes rented from local outdoor outfitters and sporting-goods shops. But the best time to test out gear is before you take your trip. Murphy's Law dictates that wearing brand-new hiking shoes always results in blisters, and setting up a new tent in the dark ain't easy.

If you forget some critical piece of equipment, **Traveling Baby Company** (☎800-304-4866; www.travelingbaby.com) and **Baby's Away** (☎800-571-0077; https://babysaway.com) rent cribs, strollers, car seats, high chairs, backpacks, beach gear and more.

Helpful Resources

➡ Lonely Planet's *Travel with Children* is loaded with valuable tips and amusing anecdotes, especially for families who haven't traveled before.

➡ **Lonelyplanet.com** (www.lonelyplanet.com) Ask questions and get advice from other travelers in the Thorn Tree's 'Kids to Go' and 'USA' forums.

➡ **Visit California** (www.visitcalifornia.com) The state's official tourism website lists family-friendly attractions, activities and more – just search for 'Family Experiences' and 'Kids'.

➡ **Travel for Kids** (www.travelforkids.com) Listings of kid-friendly sights, activities, hotels and recommended children's books for every region of California.

Hog Island Oyster Bar, Ferry Building (p79)

Plan Your Trip
Eat & Drink
Like a Local

As you graze the Golden State, you'll often want to compliment
the chef – and that chef will pass it on to the local farmers, fishers,
ranchers, winemakers and artisan food producers that make their
menu possible. California cuisine is a team effort that changes
with every season – and it's changed the way the world eats.

The Year in Food

Most of America's fruit and specialty vegetables are grown in California and you get the pick of the crop year-round.

Fall

Experience your first crush at harvest in wine country, get lost in corn mazes and pumpkin patches, and give thanks for California's bounty of fresh-fruit pies.

Winter

Make the most of long winter nights with seafood feasts of Dungeness crab, oysters and sand dabs. Celebrate lunar new year with lucky mandarins, and let citrus-spiked craft cocktails with locally distilled spirits warm you from the inside out.

Spring

When the sun comes out, farmers markets fill city streets with salad makings, fish-taco trucks flock to California beaches, and lines bend around the block for organic artisanal ice-cream studded with just-picked berries.

Summer

Beach barbecues with wild coho salmon, Brentwood corn on the cob, fresh salsa made with heirloom tomatoes, and grilled peaches topped with edible lavender flowers.

California Cuisine: Then & Now

'Let the ingredients speak for themselves!' is the rallying cry of California cuisine. With fruit, vegetables, meats and seafood this fresh, heavy French sauces and fussy molecular-gastronomy foams aren't required to make meals memorable. So when New York chefs David Chang and Anthony Bourdain mocked California cuisine as merely putting an organic fig on a plate, Californian chefs retorted that New Yorkers shouldn't knock it until they tried real Mission figs. They are one of hundreds of rare California heirloom produce varietals cultivated here since the late 18th century for their unique flavor, not their refrigerator shelf life. In California, even fast food gets the California-fresh treatment: one grass-fed burger with heirloom-tomato ketchup, coming right up!

California's 20th-Century Food Revolution

Seasonal, locavore eating has become mainstream, but California started the movement more than 40 years ago. As the turbulent 1960s wound down, many disillusioned idealists concluded that the revolution was not about to be delivered on a platter – but California's pioneering organic farmers weren't about to give up.

In 1971 Alice Waters opened her now-legendary restaurant Chez Panisse (p156) in a converted house in Berkeley with the then-radical notion of making the most of California's organically farmed, sustainably sourced bounty. Waters combined rustic French finesse with California's seasonal flavors, and diners tasted the difference.

Waters' call for 'good, clean, fair food' was heard around the world, inspiring Italy's Carlo Petrini to cofound the worldwide Slow Food movement in the 1980s. Meanwhile in California, crowds flock year-round to 800 certified California farmers markets across the state, stocking up on farm-fresh ingredients direct from 2500 local producers.

Global Soul Food

Beyond its exceptionally fertile farmland, California has another culinary advantage: an experimental attitude toward food that dates from its Wild West days. Most gold-rush miners were men not accustomed to cooking for themselves, which resulted in such doomed mining-camp experiments as jelly omelets. But the era also introduced California to the Hangtown fry, a strike-it-rich scramble of eggs, bacon and deep-fried cornbread-battered oysters – a combination of ingredients that cost around $200 in today's terms. Miners were adventurous eaters, pairing whiskey and wine with tamales and Chinese noodles, and becoming regulars at America's first Italian restaurant, which opened in San Francisco in 1886.

Some 150 years later, fusion is not a fad but second nature in California, where chefs can hardly resist adding international twists to local flavors. Menus often infuse ingredients and kitchen craft borrowed from neighbors across the Pacific in Asia, from California's deep Latin American heritage, and from Europe's distant Mediterranean, where the climate and soil are similar to California's.

Keep in mind that California belonged to Mexico before it became a US state in 1850, and Latinos make up almost 40% of the state's population today. It's no surprise that Californian versions of Mexican classics remain go-to comfort foods, and upscale restaurants are adding new twists to staple tamales and tacos. Culinary cross-pollination has yielded the California burrito – a mega-meal bursting out of a giant flour tortilla – and the Korean taco, with grilled marinated beef and spicy pickled kimchi.

California's Regional Specialties

San Francisco Bay Area

For miners converging here for the gold rush, San Francisco offered an unrivaled variety of novelties and cuisines, from cheap Chinese street food to French fine dining for those who struck it rich. Today, San Francisco's adventurous eaters support the most restaurants per capita of any US city – five times more than NYC, ahem – and farmers markets every day of the week, year-round.

Some of San Francisco's novelty dishes have extraordinary staying power, including chocolate bars (invented by the Ghirardelli family as power bars for miners), ever-popular cioppino (seafood stew), and sourdough bread, with original gold-rush era mother dough still yielding local loaves with a distinctive tang. To sample SF classics and the latest local inventions, stop by San Francisco's monument to food: the Ferry Building (p79).

Today no Bay Area star chef's tasting menu would be complete without a few foraged ingredients – including wild chanterelles found beneath California oaks, miner's lettuce from Berkeley hillsides, and edible nasturtium flowers from SF backyards. But some pioneering San Francisco chefs are taking local a step further, growing herbs and hosting beehives right on their restaurant rooftops. Don't laugh:

Oysters on the half shell

urban farming may be coming soon to a green roof near you.

Napa & Sonoma Wine Country

With international acclaim for Napa and Sonoma wines in the 1970s came woozy Wine Country visitors in need of food, and local cheese-makers and restaurateurs graciously obliged. In 1994 chef Thomas Keller transformed a 1900s Yountville saloon into an international foodie landmark called French Laundry (p186), showcasing garden-grown organic produce and casual elegance in multicourse feasts. Other chefs eager to make their names and fortunes among free-spending wine tasters descended on this 30-mile valley – and now the night skies over Napa are crowded with 11 Michelin stars. To sample the artisanal food scene, stop by Napa's Oxbow Public Market (p181).

North Coast

San Francisco hippies headed back to the land here in the 1960s to find a more self-sufficient lifestyle, reviving traditions of

Cioppino (seafood stew)

making breads and cheeses from scratch and growing their own *everything*. Early adopters of pesticide-free farming, these hippie homesteaders innovated hearty, organic cuisine that was health-minded – yet still satisfied pot-smoking munchies.

On the North Coast today, you can taste the influence of Ohlone and Miwok traditions. Alongside traditional shellfish collection, sustainable oyster farms have sprung up. Nature has been kind to this landscape, yielding bonanzas of wildflower honey and berries. Fearless foragers have identified every edible plant from wood sorrel to Mendocino sea vegetables – though key spots for wild mushrooms remain closely guarded local secrets. To try wild Mendo morels at their peak, don't miss the Mendocino Wine & Mushroom Festival (p244).

Central Valley & Central Coast

Most of California's produce is grown in the hot, irrigated Central Valley, south of Sacramento – but road-tripping foodies tend to bolt through the sunny farmlands, if only to make it past stinky cattle feed-lots without losing their appetites. Much of the region remains dedicated to large-scale agribusiness, but valley farms that have converted to organic methods have helped make California the top US producer of organic foods.

Over on the Central Coast, some of California's freshest seafood is harvested from Monterey Bay. For help choosing the most sustainable catch on restaurant menus, check out the handy report card of the Monterey Bay Aquarium (p299) at www.seafoodwatch.org. Excellent wine tasting awaits in the fog-kissed Santa Cruz Mountains, the sun-drenched hills around Paso Robles and the lush valleys north of Santa Barbara. Look for farm-stand produce pit stops all along the coast, offering everything from Watsonville strawberries to Carpinteria avocados. In San Luis Obispo, the weekly farmers market celebrates local farms with Santa Maria–style barbecue.

Southern California

Follow authenticity-seeking Angelenos to Koreatown for flavor-bursting *kalbi* (marinated, grilled beef short ribs), East LA for tacos *al pastor* (marinated, fried pork), Torrance for ramen noodles made fresh daily, and the San Gabriel Valley for Chinese dim sum. Further south, San Diego and Orange County surfers cruise from Ocean Beach to Huntington Beach in search of epic waves, but also for the ultimate Cal-Mex fish taco.

Austrian-born chef Wolfgang Puck launched the celebrity-chef trend with his Sunset Strip restaurant Spago in 1982. Reservations at chefs' tables are now as sought-after as entry into nightclub VIP rooms. As with Hollywood blockbusters, trendy LA restaurants don't always live up to the hype though – for brutally honest opinions, read reviews by respected food critic Jonathan Gold in the *Los Angeles Times*, or follow him on Twitter (@thejgold).

True Californian foodies insist that immortality isn't achieved with a star in a Michelin guide or on the Hollywood Walk of Fame, but by having a dish named in your honor. Bob Cobb was the celebrity-owner of Hollywood's Brown Derby Restaurant, and his legend lives on with his namesake salad: lettuce, tomato, avocado, egg, chicken and blue cheese. First concocted in the 1930s, it's been ordered by countless starlets since.

When salads fail to satisfy, make late-night raids on local food trucks – fleets are standing by in LA and San Diego. In Hollywood, barflies hit diners that have survived since the '50s with only minor remodeling – more than you can say for some celebrities around here.

Wine, Beer & Beyond

Powerful drink explains a lot about California. Mission vineyards planted in the 18th century gave California a taste for wine, and the mid-19th-century gold rush brought a rush on the bar. By 1850 San Francisco had one woman per 100 men, but 500 saloons selling hooch for consolation. Today California's traditions of wine, beer and cocktails are being reinvented by cult winemakers, craft brewers and microdistillers – and, for the morning after, specialty coffee roasters come in mighty handy.

Wine

During the gold rush, when imported French wine was slow to arrive in California via Australia, three brothers from Bohemia named Korbel started making their own bubbly in 1882. Today, the Russian River winery they founded has become the biggest US maker of sparkling wines.

Many California vines survived federal scrutiny during Prohibition (1920–33) with a flimsy alibi: the grapes were needed for sacramental wines back east. The authorities bought this story, or at least the bribes that came with it. The ensuing bootlegging bonanza kept West Coast speakeasies well supplied, and saved old vinestock from being torn out by the authorities.

By 1976 California had an established reputation for mass-market plonk and bottled wine spritzers, when upstart Napa Valley and Santa Cruz Mountains wineries suddenly gained international status. At a landmark blind tasting by international critics, their Cabernet Sauvignon and Chardonnay beat venerable French wines to take top honors. This event became known as the Judgment of Paris, as amusingly retold in the movie *Bottle Shock* (2008).

During the internet bubble of the late 1990s, owning a vineyard became the ultimate Silicon Valley status symbol. It seemed like a comparatively solid investment – until a phylloxera blight made a catastrophic comeback, and acres of infected vines across the state had to be dug out from the roots. But disaster brought breakthroughs: winemakers rethought their approach, using organic and biodynamic methods to keep the soil healthy and pests at bay. So whether you order a red, white or pink small-production California vintage, chances are your wine is green.

Wine-Tasting Tips

➡ **Swirl** Before tasting a vintage red, swirl your glass to oxygenate the wine and release the flavors.

➡ **Sniff** Dip your nose (without getting it wet) into the glass for a good whiff.

➡ **Swish** Take a swig, and roll it over the front of your teeth and sides of your tongue to get the full effect of complex flavors and textures. After you swallow, breathe out through your nose to appreciate the finish.

Top: Wine tasting at
Iron Horse vineyard,
Sonoma County (p210)

Bottom: Grapes in
Napa Valley (p174)

JUANCAT / SHUTTERSTOCK ©

➡ **If you're driving or cycling, don't swallow** Sips are hard to keep track of at tastings, so perfect your graceful arc into the spit bucket.

➡ **You don't have to buy anything** No one expects you to buy, especially if you're paying to taste or take a tour – but it's customary to buy a bottle before winery picnics.

➡ **Take it slow and easy** There's no need for speed. Plan to visit three or four wineries a day maximum.

➡ **Don't smoke** Not in the gardens either. Wait until you're off-property so you don't kill that mellow buzz your fellow wine-tasters have worked so diligently to achieve.

Beer

Some 400 craft breweries are based in California – more than any other US state. Even the most laid-back surfer here geeks out over Belgian tripels, and will passionately debate optimum hoppiness levels. You won't get attitude for ordering beer with fancy food here, and many sommeliers are happy to suggest beer pairings with your five-star meal.

Any self-respecting California city has at least one brewery or brewpub of note, serving quality small-batch brews you won't find elsewhere. The well-established craft beer scenes in San Diego and on the North Coast will spoil you for choice – but you'll also find memorable microbrews around the San Francisco Bay Area and along the Central Coast, especially around Santa Cruz and Santa Barbara.

Some of the best beer you'll try in California might actually come in a can. California's craft breweries are increasingly canning craft beer to make it cheaper, more ecofriendly and easier to distribute across California. There's nothing as satisfying as popping the tab of a cold one after a hot California day on hiking trails or at the beach.

Cocktails

Cocktails have been shaken in Northern California since San Francisco's Barbary Coast days, when they were used to sedate men in order to deliver them onto outbound ships in need of crews. Now hip bartenders across the state are researching old recipes and inventing new cocktail traditions, aided and abetted by local distillers. Don't be surprised to see NorCal's own St George absinthe poured into cordial glasses of Sazerac, or holiday eggnog spiked with Sonoma County Distilling rye and organic orange peel.

Legend has it that the martini was invented when a boozehound walked into an

---

TOP 10 CALIFORNIA FOOD & DRINK FESTIVALS

Arcata Bay Oyster Festival (p274) Get yours raw or Rockefeller on the North Coast in mid-June.

California Avocado Festival (p378) Guacamole for days in Santa Barbara County in early October.

Castroville Artichoke Food & Wine Festival (p303) Master tricky pairings near Monterey in May or June.

Eat Real Fest (http://eatrealfest.com) Oakland celebrates sustainable, local food in late September.

Gilroy Garlic Festival (p329) Tons of garlic fries and zero vampires in late July.

Gravenstein Apple Fair (p213) Pies galore in Sonoma County in mid-August.

Mendocino Wine & Mushroom Festival (p244) Morels and pinot make perfect Mendo pairings in early November.

National Date Festival (www.datefest.org; Riverside County Fairgrounds, 82503 Hwy 111, Indio; adult $10, child 6-12 $8; ☉Feb; 🖲) The best dates ever await outside Palm Springs in February.

San Diego Beer Week (p468) Craft brews flow citywide in early November.

Strawberry Festival at Monterey Bay (www.celebratestrawberries.com; ☉early Aug) Juicy and ripe on the Central Coast in early August.

California's Best Wine Countries

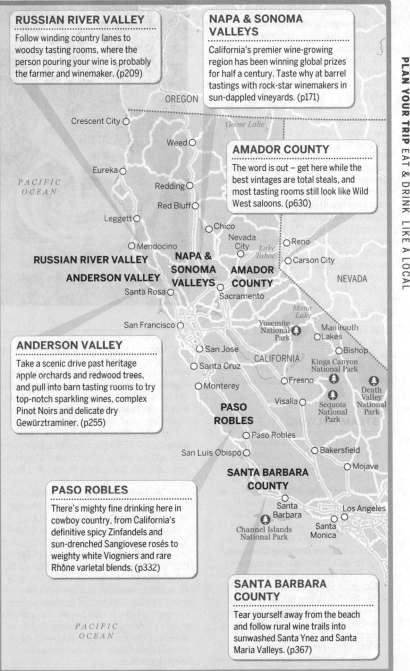

RUSSIAN RIVER VALLEY

Follow winding country lanes to woodsy tasting rooms, where the person pouring your wine is probably the farmer and winemaker. (p209)

NAPA & SONOMA VALLEYS

California's premier wine-growing region has been winning global prizes for half a century. Taste why at barrel tastings with rock-star winemakers in sun-dappled vineyards. (p171)

AMADOR COUNTY

The word is out – get here while the best vintages are total steals, and most tasting rooms still look like Wild West saloons. (p630)

ANDERSON VALLEY

Take a scenic drive past heritage apple orchards and redwood trees, and pull into barn tasting rooms to try top-notch sparkling wines, complex Pinot Noirs and delicate dry Gewürztraminer. (p255)

PASO ROBLES

There's mighty fine drinking here in cowboy country, from California's definitive spicy Zinfandels and sun-drenched Sangiovese rosés to weighty white Viogniers and rare Rhône varietal blends. (p332)

SANTA BARBARA COUNTY

Tear yourself away from the beach and follow rural wine trails into sunwashed Santa Ynez and Santa Maria Valleys. (p367)

SF bar and demanded something to tide him over until he reached Martinez across the bay – a likely story, but we'll drink to that. The original was made with vermouth, gin, bitters, lemon, maraschino cherry and ice, although by the days of Sinatra's Rat Pack, the recipe was reduced to gin with vermouth vapors and an olive or two.

Beach weather calls for tropical drinks, and California obliges at legendary tiki bars such as Bootlegger Tiki (p507) in Palm Springs, Trader Sam's Enchanted Tiki Lounge (p435) in Disneyland and San Francisco's Tonga Room (p113). The mai tai (with rum, orgeat, curaçao and lime juice) is another cocktail allegedly invented in the Bay Area, at Trader Vic's tiki bar in Oakland in the 1940s – and you can try another original version with Chinese *baijiu* (white lightning) in San Francisco Chinatown's historic Li Po (p112). For those who like their cocktails less sweet and sometimes downright mean, margaritas (made with tequila, lime, Cointreau, ice and salt) have been SoCal's poolside drink of choice since the 1940s.

Coffee

Coffee

California has become a hub for 'third-wave' coffee. Pulitzer Prize–winning critic Jonathan Gold defines this as coffee directly sourced from small farms instead of plantations, and roasted to maximize the

STEAM BREWING

Blowing off steam took on new meaning during the gold rush, when entrepreneurs trying to keep up with the demand for drink started brewing beer at higher temperatures. The result was an amber color, malted flavor and such powerful effervescence that when a keg was tapped a mist would rise like steam. San Francisco's **Anchor Brewing Company** (☑415-863-8350; www.anchorbrewing.com; 1705 Mariposa St; tours adult $20-25, child free; ☉tours 10am & 1pm Mon-Fri, 11am & 1pm Sat; ☐10, 19, 22) has made its signature Anchor Steam amber ale this way since 1896, using copper distilling equipment – and a tour of the facilities makes a fine excuse for daytime drinking.

bean's unique characteristics. The university towns of Berkeley and Santa Cruz were early adopters, and Santa Cruz still sets coffee standards at Verve Coffee Roasters (p296). LA's third-wave coffee shops tend not to roast their own, but cherry-pick the best beans from microroasters along the West Coast and Chicago.

Oakland's **Blue Bottle Coffee Company** (☑510-653-3394; http://bluebottlecoffee.com; 300 Webster St; ☉7am-5:30pm Mon-Fri, to 6pm Sat & Sun; ☐Broadway Shuttle) ✆ added a 'fourth-wave' element of showmanship to coffee geekery, introducing a $20,000 Japanese coffee siphon to filter its brews. SF's **Sightglass Coffee** (☑415-861-1313; www.sightglasscoffee.com; 270 7th St; ☉7am-7pm; ☐12, 14, 19, ⒷCivic Center, ⓂCivic Center) and **Ritual Coffee Roasters** (☑415-641-1011; www.ritualroasters.com; 1026 Valencia St; ☉6am-8pm Mon-Fri, from 7am Sat & Sun; ☐14, 49, Ⓑ24th St Mission) roast beans in-house in small batches and leaded guided tastings at cupping bars. It may sound precious, but there's no denying the laid-back California appeal of their popular 'pour-over': water poured slooooowly over custom-ground specialty coffees.

Food truck, Los Angeles

Food Trucks & Pop-Up Restaurants

Weekday lunches may last only 30 minutes for Californians, and every minute counts. California's legendary food trucks deliver gourmet options on the go, from Indian curry-and-naan wraps to Chinese buns packed with roast duck and fresh mango. One way to find trucks coming soon to a curb near you is by searching for 'food truck' and your location on Twitter. Come prepared with cash and sunblock: most trucks don't accept plastic cards, and lines can be long.

Dinner has recently also been popping up in unexpected urban spaces, including art galleries, warehouses and storefronts. Chefs at pop-up restaurants prepare wildly creative meals around a theme, such as all-chocolate meals or winemakers' dinners. Foodies seek out these overnight taste sensations via Twitter and websites such as www.eater.com. Bring cash and arrive early, as popular dishes run out fast.

Vegans & Vegetarians Welcome

To all you beleaguered vegetarians accustomed to making do with reheated vegetarian lasagna: relax, you're in California now. Your needs are not an afterthought in California cuisine, which revolves around seasonal produce instead of the usual American meat and potatoes. Decades before actress Alicia Silverstone (of *Clueless* fame) championed a vegan diet in her cookbook *The Kind Diet* and website (www.thekindlife.com), LA, SF and North Coast restaurants were already catering to vegans. You don't have to go out of your way to find vegetarian and vegan options: bakeries, bistros and even mom-and-pop joints in the remote Sierras are ready for meat-free, dairy-free, eggless requests. To locate vegetarian and vegan restaurants and health-food stores near you in California, consult the free online directory at Happy Cow (www.happycow.net).

Regions at a Glance

California's cities have more flavors than a jar of jellybeans. Start from San Francisco, where earth mother meets geek chic, and head toward Los Angeles, where even juice-cleansing starlets can't resist Koreatown BBQ. On sunny days when the coastal fog lifts, over 1100 miles of ocean beaches await. Drift down the coast past palm-lined avenues to surfer-dude-central San Diego – and when you're tanned enough and ready for a change of scenery, escape to the craggy Sierra Nevada mountains, soul-search in SoCal's desert moonscapes, and find your better nature in northern redwood forests. And no matter where you go, California's vineyards never seem far away.

San Francisco

Food
Culture
Arts

California's 'Left Coast' reputation is made in SF, where DIY self-expression, sustainability and spontaneity are the highest virtues. Freethinkers, techies, chefs and renegade artists all conspire to create the world's most out-there ideas, food and technology.

p76

Marin County & the Bay Area

Hiking & Cycling
Food
Cities

Outdoorsy people love Marin County for its beaches, wildlife and hiking and cycling trails – but indoorsy people will find something to love about the entire Bay Area, from the counterculture 'Bezerkely' and 'Oaktown' to Silicon Valley.

p120

Napa & Sonoma Wine Country

Wineries
Food
Cycling & Canoeing

Sun-washed valleys and cool coastal fog have turned Napa, Sonoma and the Russian River into California's most iconic wine-growing region. But this isn't a monoculture: local ranches and specialty produce thrive.

p171

North Coast & the Redwoods

Wildlife
Hiking
Scenic Drives

Lumber barons who had a change of heart helped conserve primeval redwood forests along the misty, rugged and wild North Coast. Let your hippie flag fly in Humboldt County, and swap seafaring stories at fishing villages from Bodega Bay to Eureka.

p230

Central Coast

Beaches
Wildlife
Scenic Drives

Surf south from hippy-dippy Santa Cruz to studious San Luis Obispo, stopping to whale-watch at Monterey Bay, hike past Big Sur's coastal waterfalls and gawk at Hearst Castle.

p286

Santa Barbara County

Beaches
Wineries
Outdoor Sports

Unlike certain neighbors, Santa Barbara keeps a low, Spanish Colonial profile behind white-sand beaches, and world-class vineyards are less than an hour's drive away. Sparkling waters invite you to snorkel, dive or sea kayak in the Channel Islands National Park.

p345

Los Angeles

Nightlife
Food
Beaches

There's more to life in La La Land than just sunny beaches and air-kissing celebrities. Get a dose of culture downtown, then dive into LA's iconic neighborhoods, from historic Little Tokyo to movie-palace Hollywood.

p386

Disneyland & Orange County

Theme Parks
Beaches
Surfing

The OC's beaches are packed bronze-shoulder-to-shoulder with rugged surfers, ripped beach-volleyball champions and retouched reality stars. If you think the scenery is surreal here, wait until you spend a day at Disney's Magic Kingdom.

p426

San Diego & Around

Beaches
Mexican Food
Museums

California's southernmost city is on permanent vacation, with a near-perfect year-round climate and booming craft-brewery scene. Explore Balboa Park's quirky museums and lush gardens, or wander laid-back beach towns on a quest for the ultimate fish taco.

p458

Palm Springs & the Deserts

Resorts & Spas
Wildflowers
Hiking & Climbing

The retro resort playground of Palm Springs is making a comeback with its Coachella festival, LGBT scene, tiki speakeasies and restored mid-Century Modern motels. Go hiking or climbing in Joshua Tree, then test your 4WD mettle in Death Valley, where spring wildflowers dazzle.

p495

Northern Mountains

Mountains
Lakes
Scenic Drives

Sacred Mt Shasta is a magnet for Native American shamans, new-age poets and ice-axe-wielding alpinists. There's more wilderness as you head north along backcountry byways, passing pristine lakes to Lassen's volcanic Bumpass Hell.

p549

Sacramento & Central Valley

History
Museums
Farms & Fairs

Start exploring California's roots in the state capital – show up in July for the state fair, then visit the Sacramento River Delta, where riverside towns look much as they did in their 1930s heyday. Explore the Wild West Chinatowns of Locke and Isleton or Walnut Grove's Japantown.

p583

Gold Country

History
Caving & Rafting
Wineries

Head for the Sierra Nevada foothills to find the Wild West alive and well in California's historic goldmining country. Get thrills on river-rafting trips, chills on underground cave tours and swills at rustic winery tasting rooms.

p614

Lake Tahoe

Winter Sports
Water Sports
Cabins & Camping

North America's largest alpine lake is a year-round outdoor playground. Come for Olympic-worthy skiing in winter, or cool off by the beaches in summer. Flashy casinos are a bonus nearby attraction.

p639

Yosemite & the Sierra Nevada

Wildlife
Hiking & Climbing
Scenic Drives

California's iconic mountain range is a world of wonder, with granite peaks, natural hot springs, deep canyons, groves of giant sequoias, and alpine meadows and lakes. Summer is prime time for outdoor adventures in America's wildest backyard.

p675

On the Road

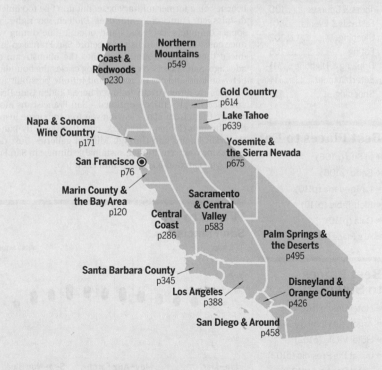

North Coast & Redwoods
p230

Northern Mountains
p549

Gold Country
p614

Lake Tahoe
p639

Napa & Sonoma Wine Country
p171

Yosemite & the Sierra Nevada
p675

San Francisco ◉
p76

Marin County & the Bay Area
p120

Sacramento & Central Valley
p583

Central Coast
p286

Palm Springs & the Deserts
p495

Santa Barbara County
p345

Disneyland & Orange County
p426

Los Angeles
p388

San Diego & Around
p458

San Francisco

POP 870,887

Best Places to Eat

➡ In Situ (p106)
➡ Benu (p106)
➡ La Taqueria (p110)
➡ Rich Table (p110)
➡ Cala (p110)
➡ Al's Place (p111)

Best Places to Sleep

➡ Hotel Drisco (p104)
➡ Argonaut Hotel (p104)
➡ Hotel Vitale (p102)
➡ Inn at the Presidio (p103)
➡ Hotel Bohème (p103)

Why Go?

Get to know the capital of weird from the inside out, from mural-lined alleyways named after poets to clothing-optional beaches on a former military base. But don't be too quick to dismiss San Francisco's wild ideas. Biotech, gay rights, personal computers, cable cars and organic fine dining were once considered outlandish too, before San Francisco introduced these underground ideas into the mainstream decades ago. San Francisco's morning fog erases the boundaries between land and ocean, reality and infinite possibility.

Rules are never strictly followed here. Golden Gate Bridge and Alcatraz are entirely optional – San Franciscans mostly admire them from afar – leaving you free to pursue inspiration through Golden Gate Park, past flamboyantly painted Victorian homes and through Mission galleries. Just don't be late for your sensational, sustainable dinner: in San Francisco, you can find happiness and eat it too.

When to Go
San Francisco

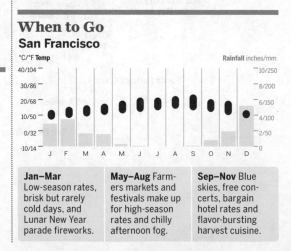

Jan–Mar	May–Aug	Sep–Nov
Low-season rates, brisk but rarely cold days, and Lunar New Year parade fireworks.	Farmers markets and festivals make up for high-season rates and chilly afternoon fog.	Blue skies, free concerts, bargain hotel rates and flavor-bursting harvest cuisine.

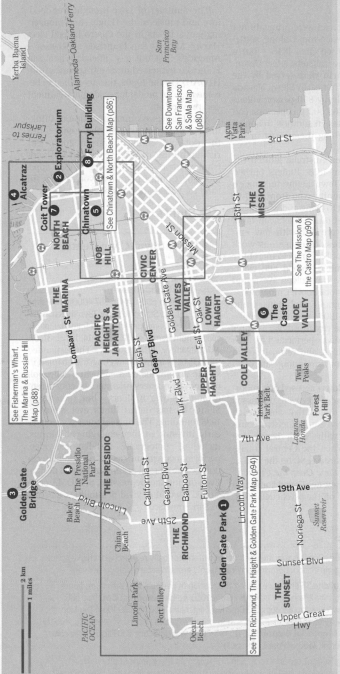

San Francisco Highlights

1 Following your bliss through SF's mile-wide wild streak: **Golden Gate Park** (p96).

2 Seeing how real life is cooler than science fiction at the **Exploratorium** (p87).

3 Watching fog dance atop the deco towers of the **Golden Gate Bridge** (p83).

4 Plotting your escape from **Alcatraz** (p83). SF's notorious island prison.

5 Wandering through 150 years of California history in **Chinatown** (p88).

6 Coming out and celebrating LGBTQ history in the **Castro** (p94).

7 Climbing **Coit Tower** (p83), taking in the murals as you go before gazing at the panoramic views.

8 Grazing at **Ferry Building** (p79), SF's local, sustainable-food destination.

The Castro (p94), the center of the gay universe.

History

Oysters and acorn bread were prime dinner options in the Mexico-run Ohlone settlement of San Francisco circa 1848 – but a year and some gold nuggets later, Champagne and chow mein were served by the bucket. Gold found in nearby Sierra Nevada foothills turned a sleepy 800-person village into a port city of 100,000 prospectors, con artists and prostitutes, in addition to honest folk – good luck telling them apart in the city's 200 saloons.

Panic struck when Australia glutted the market with gold in 1854. Rioters burned waterfront 'Sydney-Town' before turning on SF's Chinese community, who from 1877 to 1945 were restricted to living and working in Chinatown by anti-Chinese exclusion laws. Chinese laborers were left with few employment options besides dangerous work building railroads for San Francisco's robber barons, who dynamited, mined and clear-cut their way across the Golden West, and built Nob Hill mansions above Chinatown.

But the city's grand ambitions came crashing down in 1906, when earthquake and fire reduced the city to rubble. Theater troupes and opera divas performed for free amid smoldering ruins, and reconstruction hummed along at an astounding rate of 15 buildings per day.

During WWII, soldiers accused of insubordination and homosexuality were dismissed in San Francisco, as though that would teach them a lesson. Instead San Francisco's counterculture thrived, with North Beach jazz and Beat poetry. When the Central Intelligence Agency (CIA) tested LSD on the willing volunteer and *One Flew Over the Cuckoo's Nest* author Ken Kesey, he slipped some into Kool-Aid and kicked off the psychedelic '60s.

The Summer of Love brought free food, love and music to the Haight, and pioneering gay activists in the Castro helped elect Harvey Milk as San Francisco supervisor – America's first out gay official. When San Francisco witnessed devastating losses from HIV/AIDS in the 1980s, the city rallied to become a global model for epidemic treatment and prevention.

San Francisco's unconventional thinking spawned the web in the 1990s, until the dot-com bubble burst in 2000. But risk-taking SF continues to float outlandish new ideas – social media, mobile apps, biotech. Congratulations: you're just in time for San Francisco's next wild ride.

⊙ Sights

◉ Downtown, Civic Center & SoMa

⭐ **San Francisco Museum of Modern Art**   MUSEUM
(SFMOMA; Map p80; ☑415-357-4000; www.sfmoma.org; 151 3rd St; adult/under 18yr/student $25/free/$19; ⊙10am-5pm Fri-Tue, to 9pm Thu, public spaces from 9am; 📶; 🚌5, 6, 7, 14, 19, 21, 31, 38, Ⓜ Montgomery, Ⓑ Montgomery) The expanded SFMOMA is a mind-boggling feat, tripled in size to accommodate a sprawling collection of modern masterworks and 19 concurrent exhibitions over 10 floors – but, then again, SFMOMA has defied limits ever since its 1935 founding. The museum was a visionary early investor in then-emerging art forms, including photography, installations, video, performance art, and (as befits a global technology hub) digital art and industrial design. Even during the Depression, SFMOMA envisioned a world of vivid possibilities, starting in San Francisco.

DON'T MISS...

Saloons The Barbary Coast is roaring back to life with historically researched whiskey cocktails and staggering gin concoctions in San Francisco's great Western-saloon revival.

Rooftop-garden cuisine SF chefs are raising the roof on hyperlocal fare with ingredients raised right upstairs: city-bee honey at Jardinière (p109), edible pansies at **Coi** (Map p86; ☑415-393-9000; www.coirestaurant.com; 373 Broadway; set menu $250; ⊙5:30-10pm Thu-Mon; 🅿; 🚌8, 10, 12, 30, 41, 45, 🚋Powell-Mason) 🌿, herbs at farm:table (p105) and salad greens to feed the homeless at **Glide Memorial** (Map p80; ☑415-674-6090; www.glide.org; 330 Ellis St; ⊙celebrations 9am & 11am Sun; 📶; 🚌38, Ⓜ Powell, Ⓑ Powell).

Green everything Recent reports rank San Francisco as the greenest city in North America, with its pioneering parklets, citywide composting laws and the USA's biggest stretch of urban greenery: Golden Gate Park (p90).

★ **Asian Art Museum**   MUSEUM

(Map p80; ☑415-581-3500; www.asianart.org; 200 Larkin St; adult/student/child $15/10/free; 1st Sun of month free; ⊘10am-5pm Tue, Wed & Fri-Sun, to 9pm Thu; 🚹; Ⓜ Civic Center, Ⓑ Civic Center) Imaginations race from ancient Persian miniatures to cutting-edge Japanese minimalism across three floors spanning 6000 years of Asian art. Besides the largest collection outside Asia – 18,000 works – the museum offers excellent programs for all ages, from shadow-puppet shows and tea tastings with star chefs to mixers with cross-cultural DJ mash-ups.

★ **Contemporary Jewish Museum**   MUSEUM

(Map p80; ☑415-344-8800; www.thecjm.org; 736 Mission St; adult/student/child $14/12/free; after 5pm Thu $5; ⊘11am-5pm Mon, Tue & Fri-Sun, to 8pm Thu; 🚹; 🚌14, 30, 45, Ⓑ Montgomery, Ⓜ Montgomery) That upended blue-steel box miraculously balancing on one corner isn't sculpture but the Yerba Buena Lane entry to the Contemporary Jewish Museum – an institution that upends conventional ideas about art and religion. Exhibits here are compelling explorations of Jewish ideals and visionaries, including writer Gertrude Stein, rock promoter Bill Graham, cartoonist Roz Chast and filmmaker Stanley Kubrick.

★ **Luggage Store Gallery**   GALLERY

(Map p80; ☑415-255-5971; www.luggagestore gallery.org; 1007 Market St; ⊘noon-5pm Wed-Sat; 🚌5, 6, 7, 21, 31, Ⓜ Civic Center, Ⓑ Civic Center) Like a dandelion pushing through sidewalk cracks, this plucky nonprofit gallery has brought signs of life to one of the Tenderloin's toughest blocks for two decades. By giving SF street artists a gallery platform, the Luggage Store helped launch graffiti-art star Barry McGee, muralist Rigo and street photographer Cheryl Dunn. Find the graffitied door and climb to the 2nd-floor gallery, which rises above the street without losing sight of it.

★ **SF Camerawork**   GALLERY

(Map p80; ☑415-487-1011; www.sfcamerawork. org; 1011 Market St, 2nd fl; ⊘noon-6pm Tue-Sat; 🚌6, 7, 9, 21, Ⓑ Civic Center, Ⓜ Civic Center) **FREE** Since 1974, this nonprofit art organization has championed experimental photo-based imagery beyond classic B&W prints and casual digital snapshots. Since moving into this spacious new Market St gallery, Camerawork's far-reaching exhibitions have examined memories of love and war in Southeast

---

BEFORE YOU GO
....

➡ Make reservations at top San Francisco restaurants – some accept early/late walk-ins, but not all do.

➡ Reserve Alcatraz tickets two to four weeks ahead, especially for popular night tours.

➡ Download SF-invented apps for ride sharing (Lyft, Uber), home sharing (Airbnb), restaurant booking (Yelp) and audio walking tours (Detour) – all widely used here.

Asia, taken imaginary holidays with slide shows of vacation snapshots scavenged from the San Francisco Dump and showcased SF-based artist Sanaz Mazinani's mesmerizing Islamic-inspired photo montages made of tiny Trumps.

★ **Ferry Building**   LANDMARK

(Map p80; ☑415-983-8030; www.ferrybuilding marketplace.com; cnr Market St & the Embarcadero; ⊘10am-7pm Mon-Fri, 8am-6pm Sat, 11am-5pm Sun; 🚹; 🚌2, 6, 9, 14, 21, 31, Ⓜ Embarcadero, Ⓑ Embarcadero) Hedonism is alive and well at this transit hub turned gourmet emporium, where foodies happily miss their ferries over Sonoma oysters and bubbly, SF craft beer and Marin-raised beef burgers, or locally roasted coffee and just-baked cupcakes. Star chefs are frequently spotted at the farmers market (p107) that wraps around the building all year.

Diego Rivera's Allegory of California Fresco   PUBLIC ART

(Map p80; www.sfcityguides.org/desc.html? tour=96; 155 Sansome St; tours free; ⊘tours by reservation with SF City Guides 3pm 1st & 3rd Mon of month; Ⓑ Montgomery, Ⓜ Montgomery) **FREE** Hidden inside San Francisco's Stock Exchange tower is a priceless treasure: Diego Rivera's 1930–31 *Allegory of California* fresco. Spanning a two-story stairwell between the 10th and 11th floors, the fresco shows California as a giant golden goddess offering farm-fresh produce, while gold miners toil beneath her and oil refineries loom on the horizon. Rivera's *Allegory* is glorious, but cautionary – while Californian workers, inventors and dreamers go about their business, the pressure gauge in the left-hand corner is entering the red zone.

Downtown San Francisco & SoMa

SAN FRANCISCO

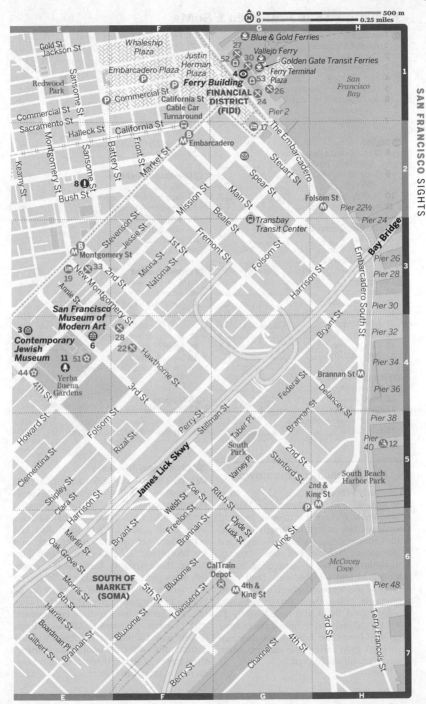

Downtown San Francisco & SoMa

⊙ North Beach & Chinatown

★**Waverly Place**   STREET

(Map p86; ⊟1, 30, ⊠California, Powell-Mason)
Grant Ave may be the economic heart of
Chinatown, but its soul is Waverly Pl, lined
with historic clinker-brick buildings and
flag-festooned temple balconies. Due to
19th-century race-based restrictions, family
associations and temples were built right
on top of the barber shops, laundries and
restaurants lining these two city blocks.
Through good times and bad, Waverly Pl
stood its ground, and temple services have
been held here since 1852 – even after San
Francisco's 1906 earthquake and fire, when
altars were still smoldering.

★**Chinatown Alleyways**   AREA

(Map p86; btwn Grant Ave, Stockton St, California
St & Broadway; ⊟1, 30, 45, ⊠Powell-Hyde, Powell-
Mason, California) The 41 historic alleyways
packed into Chinatown's 22 blocks have
seen it all since 1849: gold rushes and
revolution, incense and opium, fire and
icy receptions. In clinker-brick buildings
lining these narrow backstreets, temple
balconies jut out over bakeries, laundries
and barbers – there was nowhere to go
but up in Chinatown after 1870, when laws
limited Chinese immigration, employment
and housing. Chinatown Alleyway Tours
(p100) and Chinatown Heritage Walking
Tours (p100) offer community-supporting,
time-traveling strolls through defining moments in American history.

★**City Lights Books** CULTURAL CENTER
(Map p86; 415-362-8193; www.citylights.com; 261
Columbus Ave; 10am-midnight; ; 8, 10, 12, 30,
41, 45, Powell-Mason, Powell-Hyde) Free speech
and free spirits have flourished here since
1957, when City Lights founder and poet Lawrence Ferlinghetti and manager Shigeyoshi
Murao won a landmark ruling defending
their right to publish Allen Ginsberg's magnificent epic poem *Howl*. Celebrate your freedom to read freely in the designated Poet's
Chair upstairs overlooking Jack Kerouac Alley, load up on 'zines on the mezzanine and
entertain radical ideas downstairs in the new
Pedagogies of Resistance section.

★**Coit Tower** PUBLIC ART
(Map p86; 415-249-0995; www.sfrecpark.org; Telegraph Hill Blvd; nonresident elevator fee adult/child
$8/5; 10am-6pm Apr-Oct, to 5pm Nov-Mar; 39)
The exclamation mark on San Francisco's
skyline is Coit Tower, with 360-degree views
of downtown and wraparound 1930s Works
Progress Administration (WPA) murals glo-
rifying SF workers. Initially denounced as
communist, the murals are now a national
landmark. For a wild-parrot's panoramic view
of San Francisco 210ft above the city, take the
elevator to the tower's open-air platform. To
glimpse seven recently restored murals up
a hidden stairwell on the 2nd floor, join the
11am tour Wednesday or Saturday (free; donations welcome).

Beat Museum MUSEUM
(Map p86; 800-537-6822; www.kerouac.com;
540 Broadway; adult/student $8/5, walking tours
$25; museum 10am-7pm, walking tours 2-4pm
Sat; 8, 10, 12, 30, 41, 45, Powell-Mason) The
closest you can get to the complete Beat
experience without breaking a law. The
1000-plus artifacts in this museum's liter-
ary-ephemera collection include the sublime
(the banned edition of Ginsberg's *Howl*, with
the author's own annotations) and the ridiculous (those Kerouac bobblehead dolls are
definite head-shakers). Downstairs, watch
Beat-era films in ramshackle theater seats
redolent with the odors of literary giants,
pets and pot. Upstairs, pay your respects at
shrines to individual Beat writers.

**Chinese Historical Society
of America** MUSEUM
(CHSA; Map p86; 415-391-1188; www.chsa.
org; 965 Clay St; adult/student/child $15/10/free;
noon-5pm Tue-Fri, 10am-4pm Sat & Sun; ; 1,
8, 30, 45, California, Powell-Mason, Powell-Hyde)

FREE Picture what it was like to be Chinese
in America during the gold rush, transcontinental railroad construction or Beat heyday
in this 1932 landmark, built as Chinatown's
YWCA by Julia Morgan (chief architect of
Hearst Castle). CHSA historians unearth
fascinating artifacts, from 1920s silk *qipao*
dresses to Chinatown miniatures created
by set designer Frank Wong. Exhibits reveal
once-popular views of Chinatown, including
the sensationalist opium-den exhibit at San
Francisco's 1915 Panama-Pacific International Expo inviting fairgoers to 'Go Slumming'
in Chinatown.

The Marina, Fisherman's Wharf & the Piers

★**Alcatraz** HISTORIC SITE
(Alcatraz Cruises 415-981-7625; www.nps.gov/
alcatraz; tours adult/child 5-11yr day $37.25/23, night
$44.25/26.50; call center 8am-7pm, ferries de-
part Pier 33 half-hourly 8:45am-3:50pm, night tours
5:55pm & 6:30pm;) Alcatraz: for over 150
years, the name has given the innocent chills
and the guilty cold sweats. Over the decades,
it's been the nation's first military prison, a
forbidding maximum-security penitentiary
and disputed territory between Native American activists and the FBI. No wonder that
first step you take onto 'the Rock' seems to
cue ominous music: dunh-dunh-dunnnnh!

★**Maritime National
Historical Park** HISTORIC SITE
(Map p88; 415-447-5000; www.nps.gov/safr;
499 Jefferson St, Hyde St Pier; 7-day ticket adult/
child $10/free; 9:30am-5pm Oct-May, to 5:30pm
Jun-Sep; ; 19, 30, 47, Powell-Hyde, M F)
Four historic ships are floating museums

DON'T MISS

GOLDEN GATE BRIDGE

Hard to believe the Navy almost nixed
SF's signature art-deco **landmark** (www.
goldengatebridge.org/visitors; Hwy 1; northbound free, southbound $6.50-7.50; 28,
all Golden Gate Transit buses) by architects
Gertrude and Irving Murrow and engineer
Joseph B Strauss. Photographers, take
your cue from Hitchcock: seen from **Fort
Point** (p89), the 1937 bridge induces a
thrilling case of vertigo. Fog aficionados
prefer Marin's Vista Point, watching gusts
billow through bridge cables. For the full
effect, hike or bike the 2-mile span.

Alcatraz

A HALF-DAY TOUR

Book a ferry from Pier 33 and ride 1.5 miles across the bay to explore America's most notorious former prison. The trip itself is worth the money, providing stunning views of the city skyline. Once you've landed at the ❶ **Ferry Dock & Pier**, you begin the 580-yard walk to the top of the island and prison; if you need assistance to reach the top, there's a twice-hourly tram.

As you climb toward the ❷ **Guardhouse**, notice the island's steep slope; before it was a prison, Alcatraz was a fort. In the 1850s, the military quarried the rocky shores into near-vertical cliffs. Ships could then only dock at a single port, separated from the main buildings by a sally port (a drawbridge and moat in what became the guardhouse). Inside, peer through floor grates to see Alcatraz' original prison.

Volunteers tend the brilliant ❸ **Officer's Row Gardens** an orderly counterpoint to the overgrown rose bushes surrounding the burned-out shell of the ❹ **Warden's House**. At the top of the hill, by the front door of the ❺ **Main Cellhouse**, beautiful shots unfurl all around, including a view of the ❻ **Golden Gate Bridge**. Above the main door of the administration building, notice the ❼ **historic signs & graffiti**, before you step inside the dank, cold prison to find the ❽ **Frank Morris cell**, former home to Alcatraz' most notorious jail-breaker.

TOP TIPS

➡ Book at least one month prior for self-guided daytime visits, longer for ranger-led night tours. For info on garden tours, see www.alcatraz gardens.org.

➡ Be prepared to hike; a steep path ascends from the ferry landing to the cell block. Most people spend two to three hours on the island. You need only reserve for the outbound ferry; take any ferry back.

➡ There's no food (just water) but you can bring your own; picnicking is allowed at the ferry dock only. Dress in layers as weather changes fast and it's usually windy.

ADRIEN_G/SHUTTERSTOCK ©

Historic Signs & Graffiti
During their 1969–71 occupation, Native Americans graffitied the water tower: 'Home of the Free Indian Land.' Above the cellhouse door, examine the eagle-and-flag crest to see how the red-and-white stripes were changed to spell 'Free.'

DOPTIS/SHUTTERSTOCK ©

Warden's House
Fires destroyed the warden's house and other structures during the Indian Occupation. The government blamed the Native Americans; the Native Americans blamed agents provocateurs acting on behalf of the Nixon Administration to undermine public sympathy.

Parade Grounds

Officer's Row Gardens
In the 19th century soldiers imported topsoil to beautify the island with gardens. Well-trusted prisoners later gardened – Elliott Michener said it kept him sane. Historians, ornithologists and archaeologists choose today's plants.

Main Cellhouse
During the mid-20th century, the maximum-security prison housed the day's most notorious troublemakers, including Al Capone and Robert Stroud, the 'Birdman of Alcatraz' (who actually conducted his ornithology studies at Leavenworth).

View of Golden Gate Bridge
The Golden Gate Bridge stretches wide on the horizon. Best views are from atop the island at Eagle Plaza, near the cellhouse entrance, and at water level along the Agave Trail (September to January only).

Power House

Recreation Yard

Water Tower

Officers' Club

(6)

(5)

(8)

(7)

(3)

(4)

Lighthouse

(2)

Guard Tower

Guardhouse
Alcatraz' oldest building dates to 1857 and retains remnants of the original drawbridge and moat. During the Civil War the basement was transformed into a military dungeon – the genesis of Alcatraz as prison.

Frank Morris Cell
Peer into cell 138 on B-Block to see a recreation of the dummy's head that Frank Morris left in his bed as a decoy to aid his notorious – and successful – 1962 escape from Alcatraz.

(1)

Ferry Dock & Pier
A giant wall map helps you get your bearings. Inside nearby Bldg 64, short films and exhibits provide historical perspective on the prison and details about the Indian Occupation.

Chinatown & North Beach

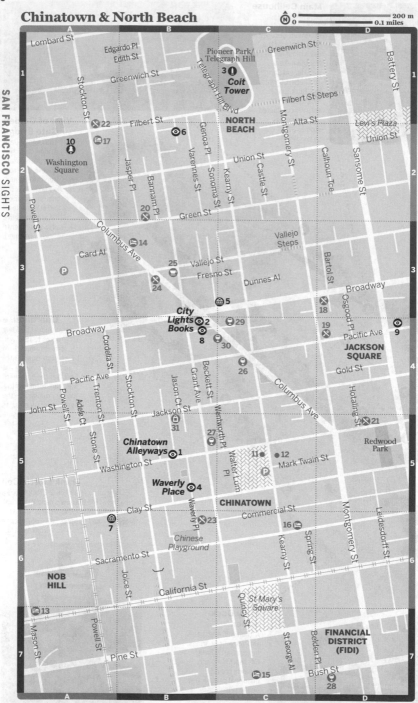

Chinatown & North Beach

at this maritime national park, Fisherman's Wharf's most authentic attraction. Moored along Hyde St Pier, standouts include the 1891 schooner *Alma*, which hosts guided sailing trips in summer; 1890 steamboat *Eureka*; paddlewheel tugboat *Eppleton Hall*; and iron-hulled *Balclutha*, which brought coal to San Francisco. It's free to walk the pier; pay only to board ships.

★ **Baker Beach** BEACH
(Map p94; ☑10am-5pm 415-561-4323; www.nps.
gov/prsf; ☉sunrise-sunset; Ⓟ; ☑29, PresidiGo Shuttle) Picnic amid wind-sculpted pines, fish from craggy rocks or frolic nude at mile-long Baker Beach, with spectacular views of the Golden Gate. Crowds come weekends, especially on fog-free days; arrive early. For nude sunbathing (mostly straight girls and gay boys), head to the north. Families in clothing stick to the south, nearer parking. Mind the currents and the c-c-cold water.

★ **Musée Mécanique** AMUSEMENT PARK
(Map p88; ☑415 346-2000; www.musee
mechanique.org; Pier 45, Shed A; ☉10am-8pm; ♿; ☑47, ☑Powell-Mason, Powell-Hyde, Ⓜ E, F) A flashback to penny arcades, the Musée Mécanique houses a mind-blowing collection of vintage mechanical amusements. Sinister, freckle-faced Laughing Sal has creeped out kids for over a century, but don't let this manic mannequin deter you from the best

arcade west of Coney Island. A quarter lets you start brawls in Wild West saloons, peep at belly dancers through a vintage Mutoscope and even learn a cautionary tale about smoking opium.

★ **Exploratorium** MUSEUM
(Map p88; ☑415-528-4444; www.exploratorium.
edu; Pier 15; adult/child $30/20, 6-10pm Thu $15; ☉10am-5pm Tue-Sun, over 18yr only 6-10pm Thu; Ⓟ♿; Ⓜ E, F) 🐾 Is there a science to skateboarding? Do toilets really flush counterclockwise in Australia? Find out things you'll wish you learned in school at San Francisco's hands-on science museum. Combining science with art and investigating human perception, the Exploratorium nudges you to question how you perceive the world around you. The setting is thrilling: a 9-acre, glass-walled pier jutting straight into San Francisco Bay, with large outdoor portions you can explore free of charge, 24 hours a day.

★ **Crissy Field** PARK
(Map p88; ☑415-561-4700; www.crissyfield.org; 1199 East Beach; Ⓟ; ☑30, PresidiGo Shuttle) War is for the birds at Crissy Field, a military airstrip turned waterfront nature preserve with knockout Golden Gate views. Where military aircraft once zoomed in for landings, bird-watchers now huddle in the silent rushes of a reclaimed tidal marsh. Joggers pound beachside trails and the only security

Fisherman's Wharf, The Marina & Russian Hill

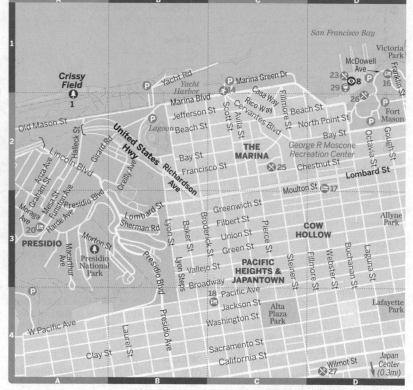

Fisherman's Wharf, The Marina & Russian Hill

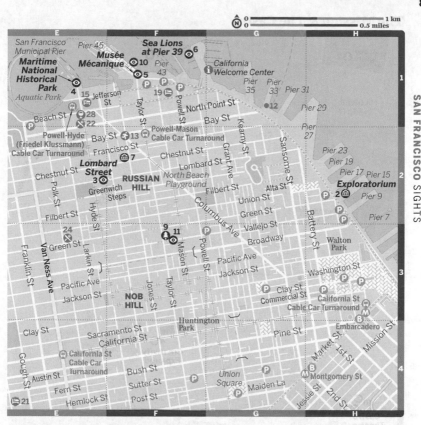

alerts are raised by puppies suspiciously sniffing surfers. On foggy days, stop by the certified-green **Warming Hut** (Map p126; ☑415-561-3042; www.parksconservancy.org/visit/eat/warming-hut.html; 983 Marine Dr; items $4-9; ⊙9am-5pm; P⬛; 🚌PresidiGo shuttle) 🍃 to browse regional-nature books and warm up with fair-trade coffee.

Fort Mason Center AREA

(Map p88; ☑415-345-7500; www.fortmason.org; cnr Marina Blvd & Laguna St; P; 🚌22, 28, 30, 43, 47, 49) San Francisco takes subversive glee in turning military installations into venues for nature, fine dining and out-there experimental art. Evidence: Fort Mason, once a shipyard and embarkation point for WWII troops, now a vast cultural center and gathering place for events, drinking and eating. Wander the waterfront, keeping your eyes peeled for fascinating outdoor art-and-science installations designed by the Exploratorium (p87).

Fort Point HISTORIC SITE

(Map p126; ☑415-556-1693; www.nps.gov/fopo; Marine Dr; ⊙10am-5pm Fri-Sun; P; 🚌28) **FREE** This triple-decker, brick-walled US military fortress was completed in 1861, with 126 cannons, to protect the bay against certain invasion during the Civil War...or not, as it turned out. Without a single shot having been fired, Fort Point was abandoned in 1900. Alfred Hitchcock made it famous in his 1956 film *Vertigo* – this is where Kim Novak jumped into the bay. Now the fort showcases Civil War displays and knockout panoramic viewing decks of the bridge's underside.

Pier 39 PIER

(Map p88; ☑415-705-5500; www.pier39.com; cnr Beach St & the Embarcadero; P⬛; 🚌47, 🚋Powell-Mason, Ⓜ E, F) The focal point of Fisherman's Wharf isn't the waning fishing fleet but the carousel, carnival-like attractions, shops and restaurants of Pier 39 – and, of course, the

The Mission & The Castro

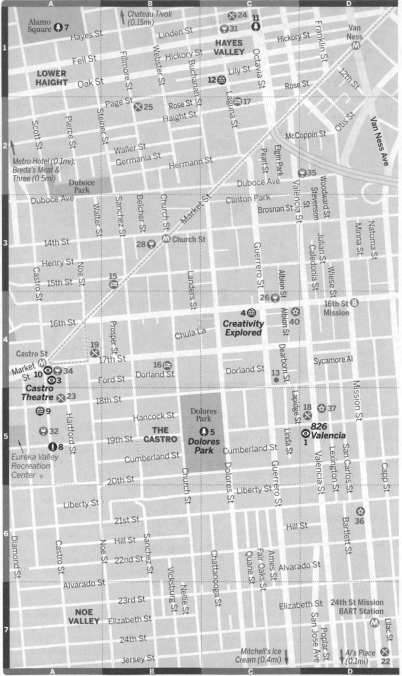

The Mission & The Castro

◉ Top Sights

◎ Sights

● Activities, Courses & Tours

● Sleeping

● Eating

● Drinking & Nightlife

● Entertainment

Top: Powell-Mason cable car
Bottom: Powell-Hyde cable car

San Francisco by Cable Car

Carnival rides can't compare to cable cars, San Francisco's vintage public transit. Novices slide into strangers' laps – cable cars were invented in 1873, long before seat belts – but regular commuters just grip the leather hand straps, lean back and enjoy the ride. On this trip, you'll master the San Francisco stance, and conquer SF hills without breaking a sweat.

At the ❶ **Powell St Cable Car Turnaround** operators turn the car atop a revolving wooden platform and there's a vintage kiosk where you can buy an all-day Muni Passport for $21, instead of paying $7 per ride. Board the red-signed Powell-Hyde cable car, and begin your 338ft ascent up Nob Hill.

Nineteenth-century city planners were skeptical of inventor Andrew Hallidie's 'wire-rope railway' – but after more than a century of near-continuous operation, his wire-and-hemp cables have seldom broken. On the ❷ **Powell-Hyde car**, you'll enjoy Bay views as you careen past flower-lined Lombard Street toward ❸ **Fisherman's Wharf**. At the wharf you can see SF as sailors did, as you emerge from the submarine ❹ **USS Pampanito** (p95). Witness Western saloon brawls in vintage arcade games at the ❺ **Musée Mécanique** (p87) before hitching the Powell-Mason cable car to North Beach. Hop off to see Diego Rivera's 1931 cityscape in the ❻ **Diego Rivera Gallery** (p95) at the San Francisco Art Institute, or follow your rumbling stomach directly to ❼ **Liguria Bakery** (p106). Stroll through North Beach and Chinatown alleyways, or take the Powell-Mason line to time-travel through the ❽ **Chinese Historical Society of America** (p83). Nearby, catch a ride on the city's oldest line: the California St cable car. The terminus is near the ❾ **Ferry Building** (p79), where champagne-and-oyster happy hour awaits.

The Richmond, The Haight & Golden Gate Park

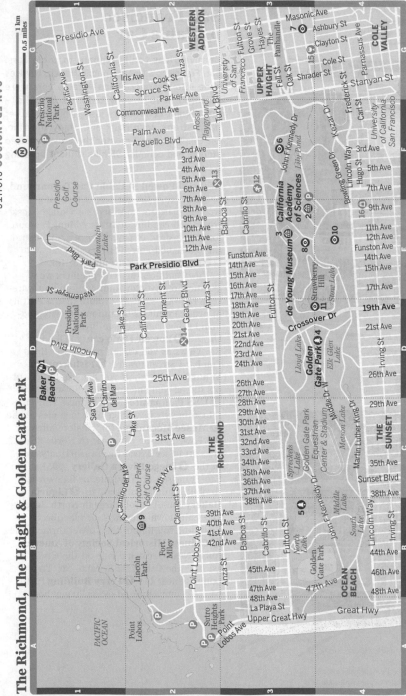

The Richmond, The Haight & Golden Gate Park

famous **sea lions** (Map p88; www.pier39.com; Pier 39, cnr Beach St & the Embarcadero; ⊙24hr; 🚺; 🚌15, 37, 49, Ⓜ E, F). Developed in the 1970s to revitalize tourism, the pier draws thousands of tourists daily, but it's really just a big outdoor shopping mall. On the plus side, its visitors center rents strollers, stores luggage and has free phone-charging stations.

USS Pampanito　　　　　　HISTORIC SITE
(Map p88; ☑415-775-1943, tickets 855-384-6410; www.maritime.org/pamphome.htm; Pier 45; adult/child/family $20/10/45; ⊙9am-8pm Thu-Tue, to 6pm Wed; 🚺; 🚌19, 30, 47, 🚋Powell-Hyde; Ⓜ E, F) Explore a restored WWII submarine that survived six tours of duty while you listen to submariners' tales of stealth mode and sudden attacks in a riveting audio tour that makes surfacing afterwards a relief (caution, claustrophobes).

◉ Nob Hill, Russian Hill & Fillmore

★Lombard Street　　　　　　STREET
(Map p88; 🚋Powell-Hyde) You've seen the eight switchbacks of Lombard St's 900 block in a thousand photographs. The tourist board has dubbed it 'the world's crookedest street,' which is factually incorrect: Vermont St in Potrero Hill deserves that award, but Lombard is much more scenic, with its redbrick pavement and lovingly tended flowerbeds. It wasn't always so bent; before the arrival of the car it lunged straight down the hill.

★Cable Car Museum　　　　　　HISTORIC SITE
(Map p80; ☑415-474-1887; www.cablecarmuseum.org; 1201 Mason St; donations appreciated; ⊙10am-6pm Apr-Sep, to 5pm Oct-Mar; 🚺; 🚋Powell-Mason, Powell-Hyde) FREE Hear that whirring beneath the cable-car tracks?

That's the sound of the cables that pull the cars, and they all connect inside the city's long-functioning cable-car barn. Grips, engines, braking mechanisms...if these warm your gearhead heart, you'll be besotted with the Cable Car Museum.

Huntington Park　　　　　　PARK
(Map p80; http://sfrecpark.org; California St, btwn Mason & Taylor Sts; 🚺; 🚌1, 🚋California) San Francisco's poshest park, Huntington's 1.3 acres mark the crest of Nob Hill. At the center rises the four-sided 'Fountain of the Tortoises,' a century-old recreation of a 400-year-old limestone fountain in Rome. If you're staying down the hill and don't have a lot of time to explore, the park makes a perfect picnic destination – especially with kids, who love the little playground, kitted out with spongy-soft ground cover.

Vallejo Street Steps　　　　　　ARCHITECTURE
(Map p88; Vallejo St, btwn Mason & Jones Sts; 🚋Powell-Mason, Powell-Hyde) This glorious high staircase connects North Beach with Russian Hill – ideal for working off a pasta dinner. Ascend Vallejo toward Mason St; stairs rise toward Jones St, passing **Ina Coolbrith Park** (Map p88; cnr Vallejo & Taylor Sts; 🚌10, 12, 🚋Powell-Mason). Sit at the top for brilliant views of the Bay Bridge lights, then continue west to Polk St for nightlife.

Diego Rivera Gallery　　　　　　GALLERY
(Map p88; ☑415-771-7020; www.sfai.edu; 800 Chestnut St; ⊙9am-7pm; 🚌30, 🚋Powell-Mason) FREE Diego Rivera's 1931 *The Making of a Fresco Showing the Building of a City* is a trompe l'oeil fresco within a fresco, showing the artist himself, pausing to admire his work, as well as the work in progress that is San Francisco. The fresco covers an entire

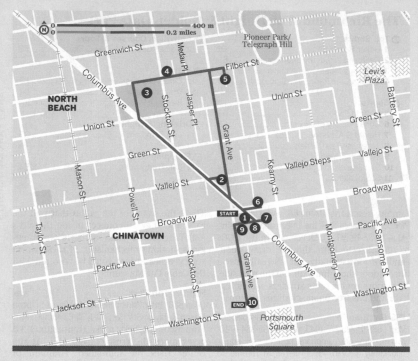

City Walk
North Beach Beat

START CITY LIGHTS BOOKS
END LI PO
LENGTH 1.5 MILES; TWO HOURS

At ❶ **City Lights Books** (p83), home of Beat poetry and free speech, pick up something to inspire your journey into literary North Beach – Ferlinghetti's *San Francisco Poems* and Ginsberg's *Howl* make excellent company.

Head to ❷ **Caffe Trieste** (p112) for opera on the jukebox and potent espresso in the back booth, where Francis Ford Coppola allegedly drafted *The Godfather* screenplay.

At ❸ **Washington Square**, you'll spot parrots in the treetops and octogenarians in tai chi tiger stances on the lawn – pure poetry in motion. At the corner, ❹ **Liguria Bakery** (p106) will give you something to write home about: focaccia hot from a 100-year-old oven.

Peaceful ❺ **Bob Kaufman Alley** was named for the legendary street-corner poet, who broke a 12-year vow of silence that lasted until the Vietnam War ended, whereupon he finally walked into a North Beach cafe and recited his poem 'All Those Ships That Never Sailed': 'Today I bring them back/Huge and transitory/And let them sail/Forever.'

Dylan jam sessions erupt in the bookshop, Allen Ginsberg spouts poetry nude in backroom documentary screenings, and onlookers grin beatifically at it all. Welcome to the ❻ **Beat Museum** (p83), where visitors are all (to quote Ginsberg's *Howl*) 'angelheaded hipsters burning for the ancient heavenly connection.'

The obligatory literary bar crawl begins at ❼ **Specs** (p112) amid merchant-marine memorabilia, tall tales and pitchers of Anchor Steam. *On the Road* author Jack Kerouac once blew off Henry Miller to go on a bender across the street at ❽ **Vesuvio** (p112), until bartenders ejected him into the street now named for him: ❾ **Jack Kerouac Alley**. Note the words of Chinese poet Li Po embedded in the alley: 'In the company of friends, there is never enough wine.'

Follow the lead of Kerouac and Ginsberg and end your night under the laughing Buddha at ❿ **Li Po** (p112) – there may not be enough wine, but there's plenty of beer.

wall in the Diego Rivera Gallery at the San Francisco Art Institute. For a memorable San Francisco aspect, head to the terrace cafe for espresso and panoramic bay views.

◉ The Haight & Hayes Valley

Haight & Ashbury   LANDMARK
(Map p94; 🖸 6, 7, 33, 37, 43) This legendary intersection was the epicenter of the psychedelic '60s, and 'Hashbury' remains a counterculture magnet. On average Saturdays here you can sign Green Party petitions, commission a poem and hear Hare Krishna on keyboards and Bob Dylan on banjo. The clock overhead always reads 4:20 – better known in herbal circles as International Bong-Hit Time. A local clockmaker recently fixed the clock; within a week it was stuck again at 4:20.

Zen Center   HISTORIC BUILDING
(Map p90; 🖉415-863-3136; http://sfzc.org; 300 Page St; ⊙9:30am-12:30pm & 1:30-4pm Mon-Fri, 8:30am-noon Sat; 🖸6, 7, 21, 22) With its sunny courtyard and generous cased windows, this uplifting 1922 building is an interfaith landmark. Since 1969 it's been home to the largest Buddhist community outside Asia. Before she built Hearst Castle, Julia Morgan (California's first licensed woman architect) designed this Italianate brick structure to house the Emanu-El Sisterhood, a residence for low-income Jewish working women – note the ironwork Stars of David on the 1st-floor loggia.

Today the Zen Center opens to the public for visits, meditation (see the website for a schedule), introductions to Zen practice (8:45am Saturdays) and other Zen workshops.

Alamo Square Park   PARK
(Map p90; www.sfparksalliance.org/our-parks/parks/alamo square; cnr Hayes & Steiner Sts; ⊙sunrise-sunset; 🖪🎠; 🖸5, 21, 22, 24) Hippie communes and Victorian bordellos, jazz greats and opera stars, earthquakes and Church of Satan services: these genteel **'Painted Lady' Victorian mansions** have hosted them all since 1857, and survived elegantly intact. Pastel Postcard Row mansions along Alamo Sq's eastern side pale in comparison with the colorful characters along the northwestern end of this hilltop park. The northern side features Barbary Coast baroque mansions at their most bombastic, bedecked with fish-scale shingles and gingerbread trim dripping from peaked roofs.

◉ The Castro & Noe Valley

★Castro Theatre   THEATER
(Map p90; 🖉415-621-6120; www.castrotheatre.com; 429 Castro St; ⊙Tue-Sun; Ⓜ Castro St) The city's grandest movie palace opened in 1922. The Spanish-Moorish exterior yields to mishmash styles inside, from Italianate to Oriental. Ask nicely and staff may let you take a peek, or come for the nightly cult or classic films (p116), or one of the many film festivals – check calendars online. At evening shows, arrive early to hear the organist play before the curtain rises.

Barbie-Doll Window   PUBLIC ART
(Map p90; 4099 19th St; 🖸24, Ⓜ Castro) No first-time loop through the Castro would be complete without a peek at the Barbie-Doll Window – better called the Billy-Doll Window, a gay spin-off of Barbie, notable for its shockingly huge penis. Dolls are dressed – well, some of them – in outrageous costumes and arranged in miniature protest lines, complete with signs. One of them says it best: 'It's Castro, Bitch.'

Harvey Milk & Jane Warner Plazas   SQUARE
(Map p90; cnr Market & Castro Sts; Ⓜ Castro St) A huge rainbow flag flaps above Castro and Market Sts, officially Harvey Milk Plaza. Look closer and spot a plaque honoring the man whose legacy is gay civic pride and political clout. Across Castro, by the F-train terminus, is Jane Warner Plaza, where ragtag oddballs and kids too young for the bars congregate at public tables and chairs.

◉ The Mission, Dogpatch & Potrero Hill

★Anglim Gilbert Gallery   GALLERY
(🖉415-528-7258; http://anglimgilbertgallery.com; 1275 Minnesota St, 2nd fl; ⊙11am-6pm Tue-Sat; 🖸48, 🖪T) 𝐅𝐑𝐄𝐄 The Bay Area hits the big time here, with gallerist Ed Gilbert continuing Anglim's 30-year legacy of launching art movements from Beat assemblage to Bay Area conceptualists. Major gallery artists range from political provocateur Enrique Chagoya to sublime sculptor Deborah Butterfield, yet shows here maintain a hair-raising edge, such as an upraised fist pushed through gallery walls in David Huffman's *Panther*. Check the website for concurrent Anglim Gilbert shows at the gallery's downtown location at 14 Geary St.

DON'T MISS

GOLDEN GATE PARK

When San Franciscans refer to 'the park,' there's only one that gets the definite article. Everything they hold dear is in **Golden Gate Park** (Map p94; www.golden-gate-park.com; btwn Stanyan St & Great Hwy; **P** 🚻 👶; 🚌5, 7, 18, 21, 28, 29, 33, 44, Ⓜ N) 🚲, including free spirits, free music, Frisbee and bison.

At the east end you can join year-round drum circles at **Hippie Hill**, sweater-clad athletes at the historic **Lawn Bowling Club**, toddlers clinging for dear life onto the 100-year-old carousel and meditators in the AIDS Memorial Grove. To the west, turtles paddle past model yachts at Spreckels Lake, offerings are made at pagan altars behind the baseball diamond and free concerts are held in the Polo Fields, site of 1967's hippie Human Be-In.

This scenery seems far-fetched now, but impossible when proposed in 1866. When New York's Central Park architect Frederick Law Olmsted balked at transforming 1017 acres of dunes into the world's largest developed park, San Francisco's green scheme fell to tenacious young civil engineer William Hammond Hall. He insisted that instead of casinos, race tracks and an igloo village, park features should include **botanical gardens** (Strybing Arboretum; Map p94; 🗹415-661-1316; www.strybing.org; 1199 9th Ave; adult/child $8/2, before 9am daily & 2nd Tue of month free; ☯7:30am-7pm Mar-Sep, to 6pm Oct–mid-Nov & Feb, to 5pm mid-Nov–Jan, last entry 1hr before closing, bookstore 10am-4pm; 🚻; 🚌6, 7, 44, Ⓜ N) 🚲, a dedicated **buffalo paddock** (Map p94; www.golden-gate-park.com/buffalo-paddock.html; ☯sunrise-sunset; 🚌5, 21) FREE and waterfalls at **Stow Lake** (Map p94; www.sfrecpark.org; ☯sunrise-sunset; 🚻; 🚌7, 44, Ⓜ N). Today the park offers 7.5 miles of bicycle trails, 12 miles of equestrian trails, an archery range, fly-casting pools, four soccer fields and 21 tennis courts. Sundays, when John F Kennedy Dr closes to traffic around 9th Ave, don't miss roller disco and lindy-hopping in the park. Other times, catch these park highlights:

de Young Museum (Map p94; 🗹415-750-3600; http://deyoung.famsf.org; 50 Hagiwara Tea Garden Dr; adult/child $15/free, 1st Tue of month free; ☯9:30am-5:15pm Tue-Sun, to 8:45pm Fri Apr-Nov; 🚻; 🚌5, 7, 44, Ⓜ N) Follow sculptor Andy Goldsworthy's artificial fault line in the sidewalk into Herzog & de Meuron's sleek, copper-clad building that's oxidizing green to blend into the park. Don't be fooled by the de Young's camouflaged exterior: shows here boldly broaden artistic horizons, from Oceanic ceremonial masks and trippy-hippie handmade fashion to James Turrell's domed *Skyspace* installation, built into a hill in the sculpture garden. Ticket includes free same-day entry to the **Legion of Honor** (Map p94; 🗹415-750-3600; http://legionofhonor.famsf.org; 100 34th Ave; adult/child $15/free, discount with Muni ticket $2, 1st Tue of month free; 🚻; 🚌1, 2, 18, 38); $2 discount with Muni ticket.

California Academy of Sciences (Map p94; 🗹415-379-8000; www.calacademy.org; 55 Music Concourse Dr; adult/student/child $35/30/25; ☯9:30am-5pm Mon-Sat, from 11am Sun; **P** 🚻; 🚌5, 6, 7, 21, 31, 33, 44, Ⓜ N) Architect Renzo Piano's 2008 landmark LEED-certified green building houses 40,000 weird and wonderful animals in a four-story rainforest, split-level aquarium and planetarium all under a 'living roof' of California wildflowers. After the penguins nod off to sleep, the wild rumpus starts at the kids-only Penguins+Pajamas Sleepovers ($109 including snack and breakfast; ages five to 17, plus adult chaperones; 6pm to 8am) and the over-21 NightLife Thursdays ($15; 6pm to 10pm), when rainforest-themed cocktails encourage strange mating rituals among shy internet daters.

Japanese Tea Garden (Map p94; 🗹415-752-1171; www.japaneseteagardensf.com; 75 Hagiwara Tea Garden Dr; adult/child $8/2, before 10am Mon, Wed & Fri free; ☯9am-6pm Mar-Oct, to 4:45pm Nov-Feb; **P** 🚻; 🚌5, 7, 44, Ⓜ N) Since 1894, this picturesque 5-acre garden has blushed with cherry blossoms in spring, flamed red with maple leaves in fall, and induced visitors to lose track of time in its meditative Zen Garden. The bonsai grove was cultivated by the Hagiwara family, who returned from WWII Japanese American internment camps to discover that many of their prized miniature evergreens had been sold – they spent decades recovering them. Visit the Tea House for tea and fortune cookies, introduced to the US right here.

Conservatory of Flowers (Map p94; 🗹info 415-831-2090; www.conservatoryofflowers.org; 100 John F Kennedy Dr; adult/student/child $8/6/2, 1st Tue of month free; ☯10am-4pm Tue-Sun; 🚻; 🚌5, 7, 21, 33, Ⓜ N) Flower power is alive and well at San Francisco's Conservatory of Flowers. This gloriously restored 1878 Victorian greenhouse is home to freaky outer-space orchids, contemplative floating lilies and creepy carnivorous plants gulping down insect lunches.

★**826 Valencia** CULTURAL CENTER
(Map p90; ☑415-642-5905; www.826valencia.org; 826 Valencia St; ⊙noon-6pm; ⓓ; ⊒14, 33, 49, Ⓑ16th St Mission, ⓂJ) Avast, ye scurvy scalawags! If ye be shipwrecked without yer eye patch or McSweeney's literary anthology, lay down ye doubloons and claim yer booty at this here nonprofit Pirate Store. Below decks, kids be writing tall tales for dark nights a'sea, and ye can study writing movies and science fiction and suchlike, if that be yer dastardly inclination. Arrrr!

★**Dolores Park** PARK
(Map p90; http://sfrecpark.org/destination/mission-dolores-park; Dolores St, btwn 18th & 20th Sts; ⊙6am-10pm; ⓓⓔ; ⊒14, 33, 49, Ⓑ16th St Mission, ⓂJ) Semiprofessional tanning and taco picnics: welcome to San Francisco's sunny side. Dolores Park has something for everyone, from street ball and tennis to the Mayan-pyramid playground (sorry, kids: no blood sacrifices allowed). Political protests and other favorite local sports happen year-round, and there are free movie nights and mime troupe performances in summer. Climb to the upper southwestern corner for superb views of downtown, framed by palm trees.

★**Balmy Alley** PUBLIC ART
(Map p90; ☑415-285-2287; www.precitaeyes.org; btwn 24th & 25th Sts; ⊒10, 12, 14, 27, 48, Ⓑ24th St Mission) Inspired by Diego Rivera's 1930s San Francisco murals and provoked by US foreign policy in Central America, 1970s Mission *muralistas* (muralists) led by Mia Gonzalez set out to transform the political landscape, one mural-covered garage door at a time. Today, Balmy Alley murals span three decades, from an early memorial for El Salvador activist Archbishop Óscar Romero to a homage to Frida Kahlo, Georgia O'Keeffe and other trailblazing female modern artists.

★**Creativity Explored** GALLERY
(Map p90; ☑415-863-2108; www.creativityex plored.org; 3245 16th St; donations welcome; ⊙10am-3pm Mon-Wed & Fri, to 7pm Thu, noon-5pm Sat & Sun; ⓓ; ⊒14, 22, 33, 49, Ⓑ16th St Mission, ⓂJ) Brave new worlds are captured in celebrated artworks destined for museum retrospectives, international shows, and even Marc Jacobs handbags and CB2 pillowcases – all by local artists with developmental disabilities, who create at this nonprofit center. Intriguing themes range from monsters to Morse code, and openings are joyous celebrations with the artists, their families and rock-star fan base.

★**Galería de la Raza** GALLERY
(Map p90; ☑415-826-8009; www.galeriadelaraza.org; 2857 24th St; donations welcome; ⊙during exhibitions noon-6pm Wed-Sat; ⓓ; ⊒10, 14, 33, 48, 49, Ⓑ24th St Mission) Art never forgets its roots at this nonprofit that has showcased Latino art since 1970. Culture and community are constantly being redefined here, from contemporary Mexican photography and group shows exploring Latin gay culture to performances capturing community responses to Mission gentrification. Outside is the Digital Mural Project, where, in place of the usual cigarette advertisements, a billboard features slogans like 'Abolish borders!' in English, Arabic and Spanish.

🏃 Activities

Cycling & Skating

Basically Free Bike Rentals CYCLING
(Map p88; ☑415-741-1196; www.sportsbasement.com/annex; 1196 Columbus Ave; half-/full-day bike rentals adult from $24/32, child $15/20; ⊙9am-7pm Mon-Fri, 8am-7pm Sat & Sun; ⓓ; ⊒F, 30, 47, ⓐPowell-Mason, Powell-Hyde) This quality bike-rental shop cleverly gives you the choice of paying for your rental or taking the cost as credit for purchases (valid for 72 hours) at sporting-goods store **Sports Basement** (☑415-437-0100; www.sportsbase ment.com; 610 Old Mason St; ⊙9am-9pm Mon-Fri, 8am-8pm Sat & Sun; ⊒30, 43, PresidiGo Shuttle), in the Presidio en route to the Golden Gate Bridge. (If you buy too much to carry, Sports Basement staff will mount panniers or mail your stuff home.)

Blazing Saddles CYCLING
(Map p88; ☑415-202-8888; www.blazingsaddles.com/san-francisco; 2715 Hyde St; bicycle rental per hour $8-15, per day $32-88, electric bikes per day $48-88; ⊙8am-8pm; ⓓ; ⓐPowell-Hyde) Blazing Saddles is tailored to visitors, with a main shop on Hyde St and six rental stands around Fisherman's Wharf, convenient for biking the Embarcadero or to the Golden Gate Bridge. It also rents electric bikes and offers a 24-hour return service – a big plus. Reserve online for a 20% discount; rental includes all extras (bungee cords, packs etc).

Golden Gate Park Bike & Skate CYCLING
(Map p94; ☑415-668-1117; www.goldengatepark bikeandskate.com; 3038 Fulton St; skates per hour $5-6, per day $20-24, bikes per hour $3-5, per day

$15-25, tandem bikes per hour/day $15/75, discs $6/25; ⏲10am-6pm Mon-Fri, to 7pm Sat & Sun; 👪; 🚌5, 21, 31, 44) Besides bikes (for kids and adults) and skates (four-wheeled and inline), this rental shop just outside Golden Gate Park rents disc putters and drivers for the park's free Frisbee golf course. Bargain rates; helmets included with rentals. Call ahead to confirm it's open if the weather looks iffy.

Kayaking & Whale-Watching

★Oceanic Society Expeditions CRUISE

(Map p88; ☎415-256-9604; www.oceanicsociety.org; 3950 Scott St; whale-watching trips per person $128; ⏲office 9am-5pm Mon-Fri, to 2pm Sat; 🚌30) The Oceanic Society runs top-notch, naturalist-led, ocean-going weekend boat trips – sometimes to the Farallon Islands – during both whale-migration seasons. Cruises depart from the yacht harbor and last all day. Kids must be 10 years or older. Reservations required.

City Kayak KAYAKING

(Map p80; ☎415-294-1050, 888-966-0953; www.citykayak.com; Pier 40, South Beach Harbor; kayak rentals per hour $35-125, 3hr lesson & rental $49, tours $59-75; ⏲rentals noon-3pm, return by 5pm Thu-Mon; 🚌30, 45, Ⓜ N, T) You haven't seen San Francisco until you've seen it from the water. Newbies to kayaking can take lessons and paddle calm waters near the Bay Bridge; experienced paddlers can rent kayaks to brave currents near the Golden Gate (conditions permitting; get advice first). Sporty romantics: twilight tours past the Bay Bridge lights are ideal for proposals. Check website for details.

Spas

★Kabuki Springs & Spa SPA

(☎415-922-6000; www.kabukisprings.com; 1750 Geary Blvd; adult $25; ⏲10am-9:45pm, co-ed Tue, women only Wed, Fri & Sun, men only Mon, Thu & Sat; 🚌22, 38) This favorite urban retreat recreates communal, clothing-optional Japanese baths. Salt-scrub in the steam room, soak in the hot pool, then cold-plunge and reheat in the sauna. Rinse and repeat. Silence is mandatory, fostering a meditative mood – if you hear the gong, it means Shhhh! Men and women alternate days, except on co-ed Tuesdays (bathing suits required Tuesdays).

The look befits the location – slightly dated Japanese modern, with vaulted lacquered-wood ceilings, tile mosaics and low lighting. Plan on two hours minimum, plus a 30- to 60-minute wait at peak times (add your name to the waiting list, then go next door to slurp noodles or shop; they'll text you when your key is ready). Communal bathing is discounted with massage appointments; book ahead and come on the gender-appropriate day.

Tours & Courses

★Chinatown Alleyway Tours WALKING

(Map p86; ☎415-984-1478; www.chinatownalleywaytours.org; Portsmouth Sq; adult/student $26/16; ⏲tours 11am Sat; 👪; 🚌1, 8, 10, 12, 30, 41, 45, 🚋California, Powell-Mason, Powell-Hyde) Teenage Chinatown residents guide you on two-hour tours through backstreets that have seen it all – Sun Yat-sen plotting China's revolution, forty-niners squandering fortunes on opium, services held in temple ruins after the 1906 earthquake. Your presence here helps the community remember its history and shape its future – Chinatown Alleyway Tours is a nonprofit youth-led program of the Chinatown Community Development Center.

Chinatown Heritage Walking Tours WALKING

(Map p86; ☎415-986-1822; www.cccsf.us; Chinese Culture Center, Hilton Hotel, 3rd fl, 750 Kearny St; group tour adult $25-30, student $15-20, private tour (1-4 people) $60; ⏲tours 10am, noon & 2pm Tue-Sat; 👪; 🚌1, 8, 10, 12, 30, 41, 45, 🚋California, Powell-Mason, Powell-Hyde) These local-led tours pack discoveries into a kid-friendly, school-accredited program. One-hour Public Art walks explore Chinatown's history through its murals – including new Wentworth Alley murals. Two-hour Democracy Walks reveal Chinatown's role in US civil rights and international human-rights movements. Proceeds support the nonprofit Chinese Culture Center; book online or by phone three days ahead.

★Precita Eyes Mission Mural Tours WALKING

(Map p90; ☎415-285-2287; www.precitaeyes.org; 2981 24th St; adult $15-20, child $3; 👪; 🚌12, 14, 48, 49, Ⓑ24th St Mission) Muralists lead weekend walking tours covering 60 to 70 Mission murals within a six- to 10-block radius of mural-bedecked Balmy Alley (p95). Tours last 90 minutes to two hours and 15 minutes (for the more in-depth Classic Mural Walk). Proceeds fund mural upkeep at this community arts nonprofit.

★Emperor Norton's Fantastic Time Machine WALKING

(Map p80; ☎415-644-8513; www.emperornortontour.com; $20; ⏲11am & 2:30pm Thu & Sat, 11am Sun; 🚌30, 38, Ⓑ Powell St, Ⓜ Powell St, 🚋Powell-Mason, Powell-Hyde) Huzzah, San Francisco invented time-travel contraptions! They're called shoes, and you wear them to follow the self-appointed Emperor Norton (aka historian Joseph Amster) across 2 miles of the most dastardly, scheming, uplifting and urban-legendary terrain on Earth...or at least west of Berkeley. Sunday waterfront tours depart from the Ferry Building; all others depart from Union Sq's Dewey Monument. Cash only.

★ **18 Reasons** COOKING
(Map p90; ☏415-568-2710; www.18reasons.org; 3674 18th St; classes & dining events $12-125; ♿; ▣22, 33, Ⓜ J) ✎ Go gourmet at this Bi-Rite–affiliated community food nonprofit offering deliciously educational events: wine tastings, knife-skills and cheese-making workshops, and chef-led classes. Mingle with fellow foodies at family-friendly, $12 community suppers and multicourse wine-maker dinners ($95 to $125). Check the website for bargain guest-chef pop-ups and low-cost classes with cookbook authors. Spots fill quickly for excellent hands-on cooking classes – book early.

✺ Festivals & Events

Lunar New Year CULTURAL
(www.chineseparade.com; ⊙ Feb) Chase the 200ft dragon, legions of lion dancers and frozen-smile runners-up for the Miss Chinatown title during Lunar New Year celebrations. Firecrackers and fierce troops of tiny-tot martial artists make this parade the highlight of San Francisco winters.

SF International Film Festival FILM
(www.sffs.org; ⊙ Apr) The nation's oldest film festival is still looking stellar, featuring hundreds of films and directors, and plenty of star-studded premieres. Plan ahead for two weeks of screenings citywide, including showcases at the Castro Theatre (p116), Alamo Drafthouse (p116) and Roxie Cinema (p116).

SF Pride Celebration LGBT
(⊙ Jun) A day isn't enough to do SF proud: June begins with the San Francisco LGBTQ Film Festival and goes out in style over the last weekend with Saturday's **Dyke March** (www.thedykemarch.org) to the Castro's Pink Party and the joyous, million-strong **Pride Parade** (www.sfpride.org; ⊙ last Sun Jun) on Sunday.

Bay to Breakers SPORTS
(www.baytobreakers.com; race registration from $65; ⊙ 3rd Sun May) Run costumed or in not much at all from the Embarcadero to Ocean Beach; joggers dressed as salmon run upstream.

San Francisco LGBTQ Film Festival FILM
(www.frameline.org; tickets $10-35; ⊙ Jun) Here, queer and ready for a premiere since 1976, the San Francisco LGBTQ Film Festival is the oldest, biggest lesbian/gay/bisexual/transgender/queer film fest anywhere. Binge-watch up to 300 films from 30 countries over two weeks. If you can afford a festival pass, get one: pass holders can show up at the last minute and avoid the ubiquitous lines.

AIDS Walk San Francisco SPORTS
(http://sf.aidswalk.net/; ⊙ 3rd Sun Jul) Until AIDS takes a hike, you can: this 10km fundraiser walk through Golden Gate Park benefits 43 AIDS organizations. Over three decades, $88 million has been raised to fight the pandemic and support those living with HIV.

BAY BRIDGE

San Francisco's other landmark bridge was inspired by a madman. Joshua Norton lost his shirt and his mind in the Gold Rush before proclaiming himself 'Emperor of these United States and Protector of Mexico,' and ordering construction of a trans-bay bridge in 1872. Taxpayers took some convincing: the Bay Bridge was completed in 1936. But the eastern span collapsed in the 1989 Loma Prieta earthquake, taking 12 years and $6.4 billion to repair.

Emperor Norton's idea seemed not quite so bright anymore – until artist Leo Villareal installed 25,000 LED lights along the western span, mesmerizing commuters with a 1.8-mile-long light show that shimmers and pulses in patterns that never repeat. The show ran from dusk until 2am nightly from March 2013 through to March 2015 – but a crowdfunding campaign in collaboration with the State of California brought the installation back in January 2016, and now the lights are now set to twinkle indefinitely. For more, see www.thebaylights.org.

RESOURCES

SFGate (www.sfgate.com) *San Francisco Chronicle* news and event listings.

7x7 (www.7x7.com) Trend-spotting SF restaurants, bars and style.

Craigslist (http://sfbay.craigslist.org) SF-based source for jobs, dates and free junk.

Lonely Planet (www.lonelyplanet.com/san-francisco) Destination information, hotel bookings, traveler forum and more.

Stern Grove Festival MUSIC
(www.sterngrove.org) Music for free among the redwood and eucalyptus trees every summer since 1938. Stern Grove's 2pm Sunday concerts include hip-hop, world music and jazz, but the biggest events are performances by the SF Ballet, SF Symphony and SF Opera.

Hardly Strictly Bluegrass MUSIC
(www.hardlystrictlybluegrass.com; ⊙Oct) The West goes wild for free bluegrass at Golden Gate Park, with three days of concerts by 100-plus bands and seven stages of headliners.

Litquake LITERATURE
(www.litquake.org; ⊙2nd week Oct) Stranger-than-fiction literary events take place during SF's outlandish literary festival, with authors leading lunchtime story sessions and spilling trade secrets over drinks at the legendary Lit Crawl.

Día de los Muertos FESTIVAL
(Day of the Dead; www.dayofthedeadsf.org; ⊙2 Nov) Zombie brides and Aztec dancers in feather regalia party to wake the dead on Día de los Muertos, paying their respects to the dead at altars along the Mission processional route.

🛏 Sleeping

🛏 Downtown, Civic Center & SoMa

★**Marker** BOUTIQUE HOTEL $$
(Map p80; ☎844-736-2753, 415-292-0100; http://themarkersanfrancisco.com; 501 Geary St; r from $209; ❋@🛜❄❄; 🚌38, 🚋Powell-Hyde, Powell-Mason) 🐾 Snazzy Marker gets details right, with guest-room decor in bold colors – lipstick-red lacquer, navy-blue velvet and shiny purple silk – and thoughtful amenities like high-thread-count sheets, ergonomic workspaces, digital-library access, multiple electrical outlets and ample space in drawers, closets and bathroom vanities. Extras include a spa with a Jacuzzi, a small gym, evening wine reception and bragging rights to stylish downtown digs.

★**Axiom** BOUTIQUE HOTEL $$
(Map p80; ☎415-392-9466; www.axiomhotel.com; 28 Cyril Magnin St; d $189-342; @🛜❄; 🚋Powell-Mason, Powell-Hyde, 🅱Powell, Ⓜ Powell) Of all the downtown SF hotels aiming for high-tech appeal, this one gets it right. The lobby is razzle-dazzle LED, marble and riveted steel, but the game room looks like a start-up HQ, with arcade games and foosball tables. Guest rooms have low-slung, gray-flannel couches, king platform beds, dedicated routers for high-speed wireless streaming to Apple/Google/Samsung devices, and Bluetooth-enabled everything.

Hotel Carlton DESIGN HOTEL $$
(Map p80; ☎800-922-7586, 415-673-0242; www.hotelcarltonsf.com; 1075 Sutter St; r $269-309; @🛜❄; 🚌2, 3, 19, 38, 47, 49) 🐾 World travelers feel right at home at the Carlton amid Moroccan tea tables, Indian bedspreads, West African wax-print throw pillows and carbon-offsetting, LEED-certified initiatives (note the rooftop solar panels). It's not the most convenient location – 10 minutes from Union Sq – but offers good value for colorful, spotlessly clean rooms. The quietest rooms are those with the suffix -08 to -19.

★**Hotel Vitale** BOUTIQUE HOTEL $$$
(Map p80; ☎415-278-3700, 888-890-8688; www.hotelvitale.com; 8 Mission St; r $385-675; ❋@🛜❄; Ⓜ Embarcadero, 🅱Embarcadero) When your love interest or executive recruiter books you into the waterfront Vitale, you know it's serious. The office-tower exterior disguises a snazzy hotel with sleek, up-to-the-minute luxuries. Beds are dressed with silky-soft, 450-thread-count sheets, and there's an excellent on-site spa with two rooftop hot tubs. Rooms facing the bay offer spectacular Bay Bridge views, and Ferry Building dining awaits across the street.

★**Palace Hotel** HOTEL $$$
(Map p80; ☎415-512-1111; www.sfpalace.com; 2 New Montgomery St; r from $300; ❋@🛜❄❄; Ⓜ Montgomery, 🅱Montgomery) The 1906 landmark Palace remains a monument to turn-of-the-century grandeur, with 100-year-old Austrian-crystal chandeliers and Maxfield Parrish paintings. Cushy (if staid) accommo-

dations cater to expense-account travelers, but prices drop at weekends. Even if you're not staying here, visit the opulent Garden Court to sip tea beneath a translucent glass ceiling. There's also a spa; kids love the big pool.

North Beach & Chinatown

Pacific Tradewinds Hostel HOSTEL $
(Map p86; ☑ 415-433-7970; www.san-francisco -hostel.com; 680 Sacramento St; dm $35-45; ☺ front desk 8am-midnight; ☻@☎; ☐1, ☐California, ⓑ Montgomery) San Francisco's smartest all-dorm hostel has a blue-and-white nautical theme, a fully equipped kitchen (free peanut butter and jelly sandwiches all day!), spotless glass-brick showers, a laundry (free sock wash!), luggage storage and no lockout time. Bunks are bolted to the wall, so there's no bed-shaking when bunkmates roll. No elevator means hauling bags up three flights – but it's worth it. Great service; fun staff.

★Hotel Bohème BOUTIQUE HOTEL $$
(Map p86; ☑ 415-433-9111; www.hotelboheme. com; 444 Columbus Ave; r $235–295; ☻@☎; ☐10, 12, 30, 41, 45) Eclectic, historic and unabashedly poetic, this quintessential North Beach boutique hotel has jazz-era color schemes, pagoda-print upholstery and photos from the Beat years on the walls. The vintage rooms are smallish, some face noisy Columbus Ave (quieter rooms are in back) and bathrooms are teensy, but novels beg to be written here – especially after bar crawls. No elevator or parking lot.

★Orchard Garden Hotel BOUTIQUE HOTEL $$
(Map p86; ☑ 415-399-9807, 888-717-2881; www. theorchardgardenhotel.com; 466 Bush St; r $207– 390; ℗☀@☎; ☐2, 3, 30, 45, ⓑ Montgomery) ◢ San Francisco's original LEED-certified, all-green-practices hotel uses sustainably grown wood, chemical-free cleaning products and recycled fabrics in its soothingly quiet rooms. Don't think you'll be trading comfort for conscience: rooms have unexpectedly luxe touches, like high-end down pillows, Egyptian-cotton sheets and organic bath products. Don't miss the sunny rooftop terrace – a sweet spot at day's end.

Washington Square Inn B&B $$
(Map p86; ☑ 415-981-4220, 800-388-0220; www.wsisf.com; 1660 Stockton St; r $209-359; @☎; ☐30, 41, 45, ☐Powell-Mason) On leafy, sun-dappled Washington Sq, this restored

1910 inn offers European style, complete with wine-and-cheese receptions and continental breakfasts in bed. The tasteful rooms are styled with a few choice antiques, including carved wooden armoires. The least-expensive rooms don't leave much room for North Beach shopping, but this is a stellar location for people-watching, dining and exploring. No elevator.

The Marina, Fisherman's Wharf & the Piers

★HI San Francisco Fisherman's Wharf HOSTEL $
(Map p88; ☑ 415-771-7277; www.sfhostels.com; Fort Mason, Bldg 240; dm $30-53, r $116-134; ℗@☎; ☐28, 30, 47, 49) Trading downtown convenience for a glorious park-like setting with million-dollar waterfront views, this hostel occupies a former army-hospital building, with bargain-priced private rooms and dorms (some co-ed) with four to 22 beds (avoid bunks one and two – they're by doorways). Huge kitchen. No curfew, but no heat during daytime: bring warm clothes. Limited free parking.

★Inn at the Presidio HOTEL $$
(Map p88; ☑ 415-800-7356; www.innatthe presidio.com; 42 Moraga Ave; r $295-380; ℗☻@☎☀; ☐43, PresidiGo Shuttle) ◢ Built in 1903 as bachelor quarters for army officers, this three-story, redbrick building in the Presidio was transformed in 2012 into a spiffy national-park lodge, styled with leather, linen and wood. Oversized rooms are plush, including feather beds with Egyptian-cotton sheets. Suites have gas fireplaces. Nature surrounds you, with hiking trailheads out back, but taxis downtown cost $25. Free parking.

Hotel Zephyr DESIGN HOTEL $$
(Map p88; ☑ 844-617-6555, 415-617-6565; www. hotelzephyrsf.com; 250 Beach St; r $250-400; ℗☀@☎; ☐8, 39, 47, ☐Powell-Mason, Ⓜ E, F) ◢ Completely revamped in 2015, this vintage-1960s hotel surrounds a vast courtyard with fire pits and lounge chairs, modern art from nautical junk, and games like table tennis in a tube – reminders you're here to play, not work. Rooms are fresh and spiffy, with up-to-date amenities, including smart TVs that link with your devices. Best rooms face the water. Parking costs $57.

Hotel del Sol
MOTEL $$

(Map p88; ☑877-433-5765, 415-921-5520; www.
jdvhotels.com; 3100 Webster St; d $259-359;
P❋@☎❄❄; ☐22, 28, 30, 43) ✈ The spiffy,
kid-friendly Marina District Hotel del Sol is
a riot of color, with tropical-themed decor.
This is a quiet, revamped 1950s motor lodge
with a palm-lined central courtyard, and is
one of the few San Francisco hotels with a
heated outdoor pool. Family suites have
trundle beds and board games. Free parking.

★ Hotel Drisco
BOUTIQUE HOTEL $$$

(Map p88; ☑800-634-7277, 415-346-2880; www.
hoteldrisco.com; 2901 Pacific Ave; r $338-475;
@☎; ☐3, 24) The only hotel in Pacific
Heights, a stately 1903 apartment-hotel
tucked between mansions, stands high on
the ridgeline. It's notable for its architecture,
attentive service and chic rooms, with their
elegantly austere decor, but the high-on-a-
hill location is convenient only to the Marina; anywhere else requires a bus or taxi.
Still, for a real boutique hotel, it's tops.

★ Argonaut Hotel
BOUTIQUE HOTEL $$$

(Map p88; ☑800-790-1415, 415-563-0800; www.
argonauthotel.com; 495 Jefferson St; r from $389;
P➡❋☎❄; ☐19, 47, 49, ☐Powell-Hyde) ✈
Fisherman's Wharf's top hotel was built as a
cannery in 1908 and has century-old wooden
beams and exposed-brick walls. Rooms sport
an over-the-top nautical theme, with port-
hole-shaped mirrors and plush, deep-blue
carpets. Though all rooms have the amenities
of an upper-end hotel – ultra-comfy beds,
iPod docks – some are tiny with limited sun-
light. Parking is $59.

🏨 Nob Hill, Russian Hill & Fillmore

Golden Gate Hotel
HOTEL $$

(Map p80; ☑800-835-1118, 415-392-3702; www.
goldengatehotel.com; 775 Bush St; r $215, with-
out bath $145; @☎; ☐2, 3, ☐Powell-Hyde,
Powell-Mason) Like an old-fashioned *pension*,
the Golden Gate has kindly owners and
simple rooms with mismatched furniture,
in a 1913 Edwardian hotel safely up the hill
from the Tenderloin. Rooms are small, clean
and comfortable, and most have private
bathrooms (some with antique claw-foot
bathtubs). Enormous croissants, homemade
cookies and a resident cat provide TLC after
long days of sightseeing.

Petite Auberge
BOUTIQUE HOTEL $$

(Map p80; ☑800-365-3004, 415-928-6000; www.
petiteaubergesf.com; 863 Bush St; r $270-410;
☎; ☐2, 3, 27) Petite Auberge feels like a
French country inn, with floral-print fabrics,
sunny-yellow colors and in-room gas fire-
places – it's among central SF's most charm-
ing midprice stays. Alas, several rooms are
dark (especially tiny 22) and face an alley
where rubbish collectors rattle cans ear-
ly (request a quiet room). Breakfast and
afternoon wine are served fireside in the
cozy salon.

Queen Anne Hotel
B&B $$

(Map p88; ☑415-441-2828, 800-227-3970; www.
queenanne.com; 1590 Sutter St; r $210-350; @☎;
☐2, 3) The Queen Anne occupies a lovely
1890 Victorian mansion, formerly a girls'
boarding school, long on character and architectural charm. Though the chintz decor borders on twee, it matches the stately
house. Rooms are comfy (some are tiny) and
have a mishmash of antiques; some have romantic wood-burning fireplaces.

★ Fairmont San Francisco
HOTEL $$$

(Map p86; ☑800-441-1414, 415-772-5000; www.
fairmont.com; 950 Mason St; r from $329;
P❋@☎❄; ☐California) Heads of state
choose the Fairmont, whose magnificent
lobby is decked out with crystal chan-
deliers, marble floors and towering yel-
low-marble columns. Notwithstanding the
opulent presidential suite, rooms have tra-
ditional business-class furnishings and lack
the finer details of top-end luxury hotels.
Still, few addresses compare. For old-fash-
ioned character, reserve in the original 1906
building; for jaw-dropping views, go for the
tower.

🏨 The Castro & Noe Valley

★ Parker Guest House
B&B $$

(Map p90; ☑888-520-7275, 415-621-3222; www.
parkerguesthouse.com; 520 Church St; r $219-
279, without bath $179-99; @☎; ☐33, ⓂJ) The
Castro's stateliest gay digs occupy two side-
by-side Edwardian mansions. Details are
elegant and formal, never froufrou. Rooms
feel like they belong more to a swanky hotel
than to a B&B, with super-comfortable beds
and down duvets. Bathroom fixtures gleam.
The garden is ideal for a lovers' tryst – as is
the steam room. No elevator.

Beck's Motor Lodge   MOTEL $$
(Map p90; ☑415-621-8212; www.becksmotor
lodge.com; 2222 Market St; r $189-279; P❋❋🅟;
Ⓜ Castro St) This three-story motor-lodge
motel got a makeover in 2016 and its
rooms look colorful, sharp and clean.
Though technically not gay oriented,
its placement at the center of the Castro
makes it a de facto gay favorite. Bringing
kids isn't recommended, especially dur-
ing big gay events, when rooms book out
months ahead.

🏠 The Haight & Hayes Valley

Metro Hotel   HOTEL $
(☑415-861-5364; www.metrohotelsf.com; 319
Divisadero St; r $107; @🅟; 🚌6, 24, 71) Trendy
Divisadero St offers boutiques and res-
taurants galore, and the Metro Hotel has
a prime position – some rooms overlook
the garden patio of top-notch Ragazza
Pizzeria. Rooms are cheap and clean, if
bland – if possible, get the one with the SF
mural. Some have two double beds; one
room sleeps six ($150). The hotel's handy
to the Haight and has 24-hour reception;
no elevator.

★ Chateau Tivoli   B&B $$
(☑415-776-5462, 800-228-1647; www.chateau
tivoli.com; 1057 Steiner St; r $195-300, without
bath $150-200; 🅟; 🚌5, 22) The source of
neighborhood gossip since 1892, this gilded
and turreted mansion once hosted Isadora
Duncan, Mark Twain and (rumor has it) the
ghost of a Victorian opera diva – and now
you can be the Chateau Tivoli's guest. Nine
antique-filled rooms and suites set the scene
for romance; most have claw-foot bathtubs,
though two share a bathroom. No elevator;
no TVs.

Parsonage   B&B $$
(Map p90; ☑415-863-3699; www.theparsonage.
com; 198 Haight St; r $220-280; @🅟; 🚌6, 71,
Ⓜ F) With rooms named for San Francisco's
grand dames, this 23-room 1883 Italianate
Victorian retains gorgeous original details,
including rose-brass chandeliers and Carr-
ara-marble fireplaces. Spacious, airy rooms
offer antique beds with cushy SF-made
McRoskey mattresses; some rooms have
wood-burning fireplaces. Take breakfast in
the formal dining room, and brandy and
chocolates before bed. Charming owners.
There's even an elevator.

✕ Eating

✕ Downtown, Civic Center & SoMa

★ farm:table   AMERICAN $
(Map p80; ☑415-292-7089; www.farmtablesf.
com; 754 Post St; dishes $6-9; ⏱7.30am-2pm
Tue-Fri, 8am-3pm Sat & Sun; 🖉; 🚌2, 3, 27, 38)
🖉 A ray of sunshine in the concrete heart
of the city, this plucky little storefront
showcases seasonal California organics in
just-baked breakfasts and farmstead-fresh
lunches. Check the menu on Twitter (@
farmtable) for today's homemade cereals,
savory tarts and game-changing toast –
mmmm, ginger peach and mascarpone on
whole-wheat sourdough. Tiny space, but
immaculate kitchen and great coffee. Cash
only.

Red Chilli   NEPALI $
(Map p80; ☑415-931-3529; www.redchillisf.com;
522 Jones St; mains $8-11; ⏱11:30am-10:30pm;
🚌2, 3, 27, 38) Mt Everest is for amateurs –
gourmet adventurers brave the Tenderloin's
mean streets for Red Chilli's bargain butter
chicken, Kathmandu rolls (naan wraps) and
pickle-spice lamb *achar*. Can't decide? Get
rice-plate combos, but don't skip the *mo-
mos* (Nepalese dumplings). This family-run
storefront diner is welcoming, charmingly
kitschy and convenient before/after Bour-
bon & Branch (p111) cocktails – otherwise,
get delivery.

El Porteño Empanadas   ARGENTINE $
(Map p80; ☑415-513-4529; www.elportenosf.com;
1 Ferry Bldg, cnr Market St & the Embarcadero; em-
panadas $4.50; ⏱9am-7pm Mon-Sat, 10am-5pm
Sun; 🖉🚼; Ⓑ Embarcadero, Ⓜ Embarcadero) 🖉
Pocket change left over from farmers-market
shopping scores Argentine pocket pastries
packed with local flavor at El Porteño. Veg-
etarian versions like *acelga* (organic Swiss
chard and Gruyère) and *humita* (Brentwood
sweet corn and caramelized onions) are just
as mouthwatering as classic *jamon y que-
so* (prosciutto and fontina). Save room for
dulce de leche alfajores (cookies with gooey
caramel centers).

Sentinel   SANDWICHES $
(Map p80; ☑415-284-9960; www.thesentinelsf.
com; 37 New Montgomery St; sandwiches $9-12;
⏱7:30am-2:30pm Mon-Fri; 🚌12, 14, Ⓜ Mont-
gomery, Ⓑ Montgomery) Rebel SF chef Dennis
Leary revolutionizes the humble sandwich

with top-notch seasonal ingredients: lamb gyros get radical with pesto and eggplant, and corned beef crosses borders with Swiss cheese and housemade Russian dressing. Check the website for daily menus and call in your order, or expect a 10-minute wait – sandwiches are made to order. Enjoy in nearby **Yerba Buena Gardens** (cnr 3rd & Mission Sts).

★**Cotogna** ITALIAN $$
(Map p86; ✆415-775-8508; www.cotognasf. com; 490 Pacific Ave; mains $19-35; ☻11:30am-10:30pm Mon-Thu, to 11pm Fri & Sat, 5-9:30pm Sun; ✐; ☐10, 12) Chef-owner Michael Tusk racks up James Beard Awards for a quintessentially Italian culinary balancing act: he strikes ideal proportions among a few pristine flavors in rustic pastas, wood-fired pizzas and salt-crusted branzino. Reserve, especially for bargain $55 four-course Sunday suppers with $35 wine pairings – or plan a walk-in late lunch/early dinner. Top-value Italian wine list (most bottles are $55).

★**In Situ** CALIFORNIAN, INTERNATIONAL $$
(Map p80; ✆415-941-6050; http://insitu. sfmoma.org; SFMOMA, 151 3rd St; mains $14-34; ☻11am-3:30pm Mon & Tue, 11am-3:30pm & 5-9pm Thu-Sun; ☐5, 6, 7, 14, 19, 21, 31, 38, ⬚Montgomery, Ⓜ︎Montgomery) The landmark gallery of modern cuisine attached to SFMOMA also showcases avant-garde masterpieces – but these ones you'll lick clean. Chef Corey Lee collaborates with star chefs worldwide, scrupulously recreating their signature dishes with California-grown ingredients so that you can enjoy Harald Wohlfahrt's impeccable anise-marinated salmon, Hiroshi Sasaki's decadent chicken thighs and Albert Adrià's gravity-defying cocoa-bubble cake in one unforgettable sitting.

★**Benu** CALIFORNIAN, FUSION $$$
(Map p80; ✆415-685-4860; www.benusf.com; 22 Hawthorne St; tasting menu $285; ☻6-9pm seatings Tue-Sat; ☐10, 12, 14, 30, 45) SF has pioneered Asian fusion cuisine for 150 years, but the pan-Pacific innovation chef-owner Corey Lee brings to the plate is gasp-inducing: foie-gras soup dumplings – what?! Dungeness crab and truffle custard pack such outsize flavor into Lee's faux–shark's fin soup, you'll swear Jaws is in there. Benu dinners are investments, but don't miss star sommelier Yoon Ha's ingenious pairings ($185).

★**Kusakabe** SUSHI, JAPANESE $$$
(Map p86; ✆415-757-0155; http://kusakabe-sf. com; 584 Washington St; prix fixe $95; ☻5-10pm, last seating 8:30pm; ☐8, 10, 12, 41) Trust chef Mitsunori Kusakabe's *omakase* (tasting menu). Sit at the counter while the chef adds a herbal hint to fatty tuna with the *inside* of a *shiso* leaf. After you devour the menu – mostly with your hands, 'to release flavors' – you can special-order Hokkaido sea urchin, which the chef perfumes with the *outside* of the *shiso* leaf. Soy sauce isn't provided – or missed.

North Beach & Chinatown

★**Golden Boy** PIZZA $
(Map p86; ✆415-982-9738; www.goldenboypizza. com; 542 Green St; slices $2.75-3.75; ☻11:30am-11:30pm Sun-Thu, to 2:30am Fri & Sat; ☐8, 30, 39, 41, 45, ☐Powell-Mason) Looking for the ultimate post-bar-crawl or morning-after slice? Here you're golden. Since 1978, second-generation Sodini family *pizzaioli* (pizza makers) have perfected Genovese-style focaccia-crust pizza, achieving that mystical balance between chewy and crunchy with the ideal amount of olive oil. Go for toppings like clam and garlic or pesto, and bliss out with hot slices and draft beer at the tin-shed counter.

★**Liguria Bakery** BAKERY $
(Map p86; ✆415-421-3786; 1700 Stockton St; focaccia $4-6; ☻8am-1pm Tue-Fri, from 7am Sat; ✐🖐; ☐8, 30, 39, 41, 45, ☐Powell-Mason) Bleary-eyed art students and Italian grandmothers are in line by 8am for cinnamon-raisin focaccia hot out of the 100-year-old oven, leaving 9am dawdlers a choice of tomato or classic rosemary and garlic, and 11am stragglers out of luck. Take yours in waxed paper or boxed for picnics – but don't kid yourself that you're going to save some for later. Cash only.

★**Molinari** DELI $
(Map p86; ✆415-421-2337; www.molinari salame.com; 373 Columbus Ave; sandwiches $10-13.50; ☻9am-6pm Mon-Fri, to 5:30pm Sat; ☐8, 10, 12, 30, 39, 41, 45, ☐Powell-Mason) Observe quasi-religious North Beach noontime rituals: enter Molinari, and grab a number and a crusty roll. When your num-

THE FERRY BUILDING

San Francisco's monument to food, the Ferry Building (p79) still doubles as a trans-bay transit hub – but with dining options like these, you may never leave.

Ferry Plaza Farmers Market (Map p80; ☎415-291-3276; www.cuesa.org; street food $3-12; ⏰10am-2pm Tue & Thu, from 8am Sat; ☒☒;) The pride and joy of SF foodies, the Ferry Building market showcases 50 to 100 prime purveyors of California-grown, organic produce, pasture-raised meats and gourmet prepared foods at accessible prices. On Saturdays, join top chefs early for prime browsing, and stay for eclectic bayside picnics of Namu Korean tacos, RoliRoti porchetta, Dirty Girl tomatoes, Nicasio cheese samples, and Frog Hollow fruit turnovers.

Slanted Door (Map p80; ☎415-861-8032; www.slanteddoor.com; mains $18-42; ⏰11am-4:30pm & 5:30-10pm Mon-Sat, 11:30am-10pm Sun) Live the dream at this bayfront bistro, where California-fresh, Vietnamese-inspired dishes are served with sparkling waterfront views. Chinatown-raised chef-owner Charles Phan is a James Beard Award winner and a local hero for championing California-grown ingredients in signature dishes like garlicky grass-fed 'shaking beef' and Dungeness crab heaped atop cellophane noodles. Book weeks ahead, or settle for Out the Door takeout.

Hog Island Oyster Company (Map p80; ☎415-391-7117; www.hogislandoysters.com; 4 oysters $14; ⏰11am-9pm) Slurp the bounty of the North Bay with East Bay views at this local, sustainable oyster bar. Get them raw, grilled with chipotle-bourbon butter, or Rockefeller (cooked with spinach, Pernod and cream). Not the cheapest oysters in town, but consistently the best – with excellent wines. Stop by Hog Island's farmers-market stall 8am to 2pm Saturday for $2 oysters.

Mijita (Map p80; ☎415-399-0814; www.mijitasf.com; dishes $4-10; ⏰10am-7pm Mon-Thu, to 8pm Fri, 9am-8pm Sat, 9am-3pm Sun; ☒☒) Jealous seagulls circle above your outdoor bayside table, eyeing your sustainable fish tacos and tangy jicama and grapefruit salad. James Beard Award–winning chef Traci Des Jardins honors her Mexican grandmother's cooking at this sunny taqueria – the Mexico City–style quesadilla is laced with *epazote* (Mayan herbs) and the *agua fresca* (fruit punch) is made from just-squeezed juice.

ber's called, wisecracking staff pile your roll with heavenly fixings: milky buffalo mozzarella, tangy sun-dried tomatoes, translucent sheets of prosciutto di Parma, slabs of legendary house-cured salami, drizzles of olive oil and balsamic. Enjoy hot from the panini press at sidewalk tables.

⭐ **Mister Jiu's** CHINESE $$
(Map p86; ☎415-857-9688; http://misterjius. com; 28 Waverly Pl; mains $14-45; ⏰5:30-10:30pm Tue-Sat; ☒30, ☒California) Ever since the gold rush, San Francisco has craved Chinese food, powerful cocktails and hyperlocal specialties – and Mister Jiu's satisfies on all counts. Build your own banquet of Chinese classics with California twists: chanterelle chow mein, Dungeness-crab rice noodles, quail and Mission-fig sticky rice. Cocktail pairings are equally inspired – try the jasmine-infused-gin Happiness ($13) with tea-smoked Sonoma-duck confit.

🍴 The Marina, Fisherman's Wharf & the Piers

⭐ **Off the Grid** FOOD TRUCK $
(Map p88; www.offthegridsf.com; Fort Mason Center, 2 Marina Blvd; items $6-14; ⏰5-10pm Fri Apr-Oct; ☒; ☒22, 28) Spring through fall, some 30 food trucks circle their wagons at SF's largest mobile-gourmet hootenannies on Friday night at Fort Mason Center, and 11am to 4pm Sunday for **Picnic at the Presidio** on the Main Post lawn. Arrive early for the best selection and to minimize waits. Cash only.

Lucca Delicatessen DELI $
(Map p88; ☎415-921-7873; www.luccadeli.com; 2120 Chestnut St; sandwiches $9-12; ⏰9am-6pm; ☒28, 30, 43) Open since 1929, this classic

Italian deli is an ideal spot to assemble picnics for Marina Green. Besides perfect prosciutto and salami, nutty cheeses and fruity Chiantis, expect made-to-order sandwiches on fresh-baked Acme bread, including yummy meatball subs. There's hot homemade soup from 11am to 3pm.

★**Greens** VEGETARIAN, CALIFORNIAN **$$**
(Map p126; ☑415-771-6222; www.greensrestaurant. com; Fort Mason Center, 2 Marina Blvd, Bldg A; mains lunch $16-19, dinner $20-28; ⊙11:45am-2:30pm & 5:30-9pm; ☑⑂; ☐22, 28, 30, 43, 47, 49) ⌖ Career carnivores won't realize there's zero meat in the hearty black-bean chili, or in Greens' other flavor-packed vegetarian dishes, made using ingredients from a Zen farm in Marin. And, oh, what views! The Golden Gate rises just outside the window-lined dining room. The on-site cafe serves to-go lunches, but for sit-down meals, including Sunday brunch, reservations are essential.

★**Gary Danko** CALIFORNIAN **$$$**
(Map p88; ☑415-749-2060; www.garydanko.com; 800 North Point St; 3-/5-course menu $86/124; ⊙5:30-10pm; ☐19, 30, 47, ☐Powell-Hyde) Gary Danko wins James Beard Awards for his

impeccable Californian *haute cuisine*. Smoked-glass windows prevent passersby from tripping over their tongues at the exquisite presentations – roasted lobster with blood oranges, blushing duck breast with port-roasted grapes, lavish cheeses and trios of crèmes brûlées. Reservations a must.

✖ Nob Hill, Russian Hill & Fillmore

★**Swan Oyster Depot** SEAFOOD **$$**
(Map p80; ☑415-673-1101; 1517 Polk St; dishes $10-25; ⊙10:30am-5:30pm Mon-Sat; ☐1, 19, 47, 49, ☐California) Superior flavor without the superior attitude of typical seafood restaurants – Swan's downside is an inevitable wait for the few stools at its vintage lunch counter, but the upside of high turnover is incredibly fresh seafood.

Out the Door VIETNAMESE **$$**
(Map p88; ☑415-923 9575; www.outthedoors. com; 2232 Bush St; mains lunch $14-22, dinner $20-36; ⊙11am-2:30pm & 5:30-9:30pm Mon-Fri, 9am-2:30pm & 5:30-9:30pm Sat & Sun; ☐2, 3, 22) Offshoot of the famous Slanted Door (p107), this casual outpost jump-starts after-

---

SAN FRANCISCO TREATS

Life is sweet in San Francisco, where chocolate bars were invented in the gold rush and velvet ropes keep ice-cream lines from getting ugly. Before you dismiss dessert, consider these temptations.

Tout Sweet (Map p80; ☑415-385-1679; www.toutsweetsf.com; Macy's, 3rd fl, cnr Geary & Stockton Sts; baked goods $2-8; ⊙11am-6pm Sun-Wed, to 8pm Thu-Sat; ☎⑂; ☐2, 38, ☐Powell-Mason, Powell-Hyde, ☐Powell) Mango with Thai chili or peanut butter and jelly? Choosing your favorite California-French macaron isn't easy at Tout Sweet, where *Top Chef Just Desserts* champion Yigit Pura keeps outdoing his own inventions – he's like the love child of Julia Child and Steve Jobs. Chef Pura's sweet retreat on Macy's 3rd floor offers unbeatable views overlooking Union Sq, excellent teas and free wi-fi.

Craftsman & Wolves (Map p90; ☑415-913-7713; http://craftsman-wolves.com; 746 Valencia St; pastries $3-8; ⊙7am-6pm Mon-Fri, from 8am Sat & Sun; ☐14, 22, 33, 49, ☐16th St Mission, ☐J) Breakfast routines are made to be broken by the infamous Rebel Within: a sausage-spiked Asiago-cheese muffin with a silken soft-boiled egg baked inside. SF's surest pick-me-up is a Highwire macchiato with *matcha* (green tea) cookies; a Thai coconut-curry scone enjoyed with pea soup and rosé is lunch perfected. Exquisite hazelnut cube-cakes and vanilla-violet cheesecakes are ideal for celebrating unbirthdays and imaginary holidays.

Humphry Slocombe (Map p90; ☑415-550-6971; www.humphryslocombe.com; 2790 Harrison St; ice creams $4-6; ⊙1-11pm Mon-Fri, from noon Sat & Sun; ⑂; ☐12, 14, 49, ☐24th St Mission) Indie-rock organic ice cream may permanently spoil you for Top 40 flavors. Once 'Elvis: The Fat Years' (banana and peanut butter) and 'Hibiscus Beet Sorbet' have rocked your taste buds, cookie dough seems so basic – and ordinary sundaes can't compare to 'Secret Breakfast' (bourbon and cornflakes) and 'Blue Bottle Vietnamese Coffee' drizzled with hot fudge, California olive oil and sea salt.

noon shopping with stellar Dungeness-crab noodles, five-spice chicken and rice plates and Vietnamese coffee. At dinner, rice plates and noodles are replaced with savory clay-pot meats and fish – an evening you won't soon forget. Make reservations.

★**La Folie**   FRENCH $$$
(Map p88; ☑ 415-776-5577; www.lafolie.com; 2316 Polk St; 3-/4-/5-course menu $100/120/140; ⊙ 5:30-10pm Tue-Sat; ☐ 19, 41, 45, 47) Casually sophisticated La Folie remains one of SF's top tables – even after 30 years. Its success lies in the French-born chef-owner's uncanny ability to balance formal and playful. He's a true artist, whose cooking references classical tradition but also nods to California sensibilities. The colorful flourishes on the plate are mirrored in the *très professionnel* staff. Book a week ahead.

★**Acquerello**   CALIFORNIAN, ITALIAN $$$
(Map p80; ☑ 415-567-5432; www.acquerello.com; 1722 Sacramento St; 3-/4-/5-course menu $95/120/140; ⊙ 5:30-9:30pm Tue-Sat; ☐ 1, 19, 47, 49, ☐ California) A converted chapel is a fitting location for a meal that'll turn Italian culinary purists into true believers in Cal-Italian cuisine. Chef Suzette Gresham's generous pastas and ingenious seasonal meat dishes include heavenly quail salad, devilish lobster *panzerotti* and venison loin chops. Suave *maître d'hôtel* Giancarlo Paterlini indulges every whim, even providing black-linen napkins if you're worried about lint.

★**Seven Hills**   ITALIAN $$$
(Map p80; ☑ 415-775-1550; www.sevenhillssf.com; 1550 Hyde St; mains $19-31; ⊙ 5:30-9:30pm Sun-Thu, to 10pm Fri & Sat; ☐ 10, 12, ☐ Powell-Hyde) Anthony Florian has studied with some of the great chefs of California and Italy, and he's an expert at taking several seasonal ingredients and making them shine. His short, market-driven menu features housemade pastas with elements such as rabbit and house-cured pancetta. The four mains showcase quality California meats. Tables are close in the elegant little storefront, but brilliant sound-canceling technology eliminates noise. Stellar service, too.

★**State Bird Provisions**   CALIFORNIAN $$$
(☑ 415-795-1272; http://statebirdsf.com; 1529 Fillmore St; dishes $9-30; ⊙ 5:30-10pm Sun-Thu, to 11pm Fri & Sat; ☐ 22, 38) Even before winning back-to-back James Beard Awards, State Bird attracted lines for 5:30pm seatings

not seen since the Dead played neighboring Fillmore Auditorium. The draw is a thrilling play on dim sum, wildly inventive with seasonal-regional ingredients and esoteric flavors, like fennel pollen and garum. Plan to order multiple dishes. Book exactly 60 days ahead. The staff couldn't be lovelier.

✕ The Haight & Hayes Valley

★**Souvla**   GREEK $
(Map p90; ☑ 415-400-5458; www.souvlasf.com; 517 Hayes St; sandwiches & salads $11-14; ⊙ 11am-10pm; ☐ 5, 21, 47, 49, Ⓜ Van Ness) Ancient Greek philosophers didn't think too hard about lunch, and neither should you at Souvla. Get in line and make no-fail choices: pita or salad, wine or not. Instead of go-to gyros, try roast lamb atop kale with yogurt dressing, or tangy chicken salad with pickled onion and *mizithra* cheese. Go early/late for skylit communal seating, or head to **Patricia's Green** (Map p90; http://proxysf.net; cnr Octavia Blvd & Fell St; ☐ 5, 21) with takeout.

★**Brenda's Meat & Three**   SOUTHERN US $
(☑ 415-926-8657; http://brendasmeatandthree.com; 919 Divisadero St; mains $8-15; ⊙ 8am-10pm Wed-Mon; ☐ 5, 21, 24, 38) The name means one meaty main course plus three sides – though only superheroes finish ham steak with Creole red-eye gravy and exemplary grits, let alone cream biscuits and eggs. Chef Brenda Buenviaje's portions are defiantly Southern, which explains brunch lines of marathoners and partiers who forgot to eat last night. Arrive early, share sweet-potato pancakes, and pray for crawfish specials.

Three Twins Ice Cream   ICE CREAM $
(Map p90; ☑ 415-487-8946; www.threetwinsicecream.com; 254 Fillmore St; cones $3-5.75; ⊙ 3-10pm Mon, 2-10pm Tue-Thu, 2-11pm Fri, 1-11pm Sat, 1-10pm Sun; ⊞; ☐ 6, 7, 22, Ⓜ N) 🍃 For local flavor, join the motley crowd of Lower Haighters lining up for extra-creamy organic ice cream in seasonal flavors. To guess who gets what, here's a cheat sheet: Wiggle bikers brake for dad's cardamom, foodie babies coo over lemon cookie, and stoned skaters feast on California clichés (two scoops, pistachios, olive oil, sea salt, caramel and whipped cream).

★**Jardinière**   CALIFORNIAN $$
(Map p80; ☑ 415-861-5555; www.jardiniere.com; 300 Grove St; mains $20-36; ⊙ 5-9pm Sun-Thu, to 10:30pm Fri & Sat; ☐ 5, 21, 47, 49, Ⓜ Van Ness) 🍃 *Iron Chef* winner, *Top Chef Masters*

finalist and James Beard Award–winner Traci Des Jardins champions sustainable, salacious California cuisine. She has a way with California's organic produce, sustainable meats, and seafood, slathering sturgeon with buttery chanterelles and lavishing root vegetables with truffles and honey from Jardinière's rooftop hives. Mondays bring $55 three-course dinners with wine pairings.

★**Rich Table** CALIFORNIAN $$

(Map p80; ☑415-355-9085; http://richtablesf. com; 199 Gough St; mains $17-36; ⊘5:30-10pm Sun-Thu, to 10:30pm Fri & Sat; ☐5, 6, 7, 21, 47, 49, ⓜVan Ness) 🥢 Impossible cravings begin at Rich Table, inventor of porcini doughnuts, miso-marrow-stuffed pasta and fried-chicken madeleines with caviar. Married co-chefs and owners Sarah and Evan Rich playfully riff on seasonal California fare, freestyling with whimsical off-menu amuse-bouches like trippy beet marshmallows or the Dirty Hippie: nutty hemp atop silky goat-buttermilk *pannacotta*, as offbeat and entrancing as Hippie Hill drum circles.

★**Cala** MEXICAN, CALIFORNIAN $$$

(Map p80; ☑415-660-7701; www.calarestaurant. com; 149 Fell St; ⊘5-10pm Mon-Wed, to 11pm Thu-Sat, 11am-3pm Sun, taco bar 11am-2pm Mon-Fri; ☐6, 7, 21, 47, 49, ⓜVan Ness) Like discovering a long-lost twin, Cala's Mexico Norte cuisine is a revelation. San Francisco's Mexican-rancher roots are deeply honored here: silky bone-marrow salsa and fragrant heritage-corn tortillas grace a sweet potato slow-cooked in ashes. Brace yourself with mezcal margaritas for the ultimate California surf and turf: sea urchin with beef tongue. Original and unforgettable, even before Mayan-chocolate gelato with amaranth brittle.

✕ The Castro & Noe Valley

★**Poesia** ITALIAN $$

(Map p90; ☑415-252-9325; http://poesiasf.com; 4072 18th St; mains $19-31; ⊘5-10:30pm Mon-Sat, to 10pm Sun; ⓜCastro St) An all-Italian staff flirts with diners at this unpretentious 2nd-floor bistro with a sunny yellow interior and comfy banquettes good for lingering long after a hearty dinner. Expect dishes you don't typically see at American-Italian restaurants, with standout housemade pastas and a stellar *branzino* (sea bass) cooked in parchment. Fun fact: this is where Oprah ate when she visited the Castro.

★**Frances** CALIFORNIAN $$$

(Map p90; ☑415-621-3870; www.frances-sf.com; 3870 17th St; mains $26-34; ⊘5-10pm Sun & Tue-Thu, to 10:30pm Fri & Sat; ⓜCastro St) Chef-owner Melissa Perello earned a Michelin star for fine dining, then ditched downtown to start this market-inspired neighborhood bistro. Daily menus showcase bright, seasonal flavors and luxurious textures: cloud-like sheep's-milk ricotta gnocchi with crunchy breadcrumbs and broccolini, grilled calamari with preserved Meyer lemon, and artisan wine served by the ounce, directly from Wine Country.

✕ The Mission, Dogpatch & Potrero Hill

★**La Taqueria** MEXICAN $

(Map p90; ☑415-285-7117; 2889 Mission St; items $3-11; ⊘11am-9pm Mon-Sat, to 8pm Sun; ⍊; ☐12, 14, 48, 49, Ⓑ24th St Mission) SF's definitive burrito has no saffron rice, spinach tortilla or mango salsa – just perfectly grilled meats, slow-cooked beans and tomatillo or mesquite salsa wrapped in a flour tortilla. They're purists at James Beard Award–winning La Taqueria. You'll pay extra to go without beans, because they add more meat – but spicy pickles and *crema* (sour cream) bring burrito bliss. Worth the wait, always.

★**Mitchell's Ice Cream** ICE CREAM $

(☑415-648-2300; www.mitchellsicecream.com; 688 San Jose Ave; ice cream $3.50-6; ⊘11am-11pm; ⍊; ☐14, 49, Ⓑ24th St Mission, ⓜJ) When you see happy dances break out on Mission sidewalks, you must be getting close to Mitchell's. One glance at the day's flavors induces gleeful gluttony: classic Kahlua mocha cream, exotic tropical *macapuno* (young coconut)... or *both*?! Avocado and *ube* (purple yam) are acquired tastes, but they've been local favorites for generations – Mitchell's has kept fans coming back for seconds since 1953.

★**La Palma Mexicatessen** MEXICAN $

(Map p90; ☑415-647-1500; www.lapalmasf.com; 2884 24th St; tamales, tacos & huarache $3-5; ⊘8am-6pm Mon-Sat, to 5pm Sun; ☑⍊; ☐12, 14, 27, 48, Ⓑ24th St Mission) 🥢 Follow the applause: that's the sound of organic tortilla-making in progress at La Palma. You've found the Mission mother lode of handmade tamales, *pupusas* (tortilla pockets) with potato and *chicharones* (pork crackling), *carnitas* (slow-roasted pork), *cotija* (Oaxacan cheese) and La Palma's own tangy tomatillo sauce. Get takeout, or bring a small army to finish that massive meal at sunny sidewalk tables.

★ Al's Place
CALIFORNIAN $$

(☑415-416-6136; www.alsplacesf.com; 1499 Valencia St; share plates $15-19; ☺5:30-10pm Wed-Sun; ☑; ☐12, 14, 49, Ⓜ J, Ⓑ 24th St Mission) ⬥ The Golden State dazzles on Al's plates, featuring homegrown heirloom ingredients, pristine Pacific seafood, and grass-fed meat on the side. Painstaking preparation yields sun-drenched flavors and exquisite textures: crispy-skin cod with frothy preserved-lime dip, grilled peach melting into velvety foie gras. Dishes are half the size but thrice the flavor of mains elsewhere – get two or three, and you'll be California dreaming.

Foreign Cinema
CALIFORNIAN $$$

(Map p90; ☑415-648-7600; www.foreigncinema. com; 2534 Mission St; mains $22-33; ☺5:30-10pm Sun-Wed, to 11pm Thu-Sat, brunch 11am-2:30pm Sat & Sun; ☐12, 14, 33, 48, 49, Ⓑ 24th St Mission) ⬥ Chef Gayle Pirie's acclaimed California classics such as velvety Pacific *poke* (marinated tuna) and crisp sesame fried chicken are the star attractions here – but subtitled films by Luis Buñuel and François Truffaut screening in the courtyard are mighty handy when conversation lags with first dates or in-laws. Get the red-carpet treatment with valet parking ($15) and a well-stocked oyster bar.

✗ Golden Gate Park & the Avenues

★ Cinderella Russian Bakery
RUSSIAN $

(Map p94; ☑415-751-6723; www.cinderella bakery.com; 436 Balboa St; pastries $1.50-3.50, mains $7-13; ☺7am-7pm; ☑☺; ☐5, 21, 31, 33) Fog banks and cold wars are no match for the heartwarming powers of the Cinderella, serving treats like your *baba* used to make since 1953. Join SF's Russian community in Cinderella's new parklet near Golden Gate Park for scrumptious, just-baked egg-and-green-onion piroshki, hearty borscht and decadent dumplings – all at neighborly prices.

Revenge Pies
DESSERTS $

(Map p94; www.revengepies.com; 1248 9th Ave; pies $5-8, picecreams $3-6; ☺9am-9pm; ☑; ☐6, 7, 43, 44, Ⓜ N) Living well is only the second-best revenge – a face full of pecan Revenge Pie is far more satisfying. Here's the compensation for every skimpy à la mode serving you've endured: picecream (homemade frozen custard with flakes of buttery pie crust). The chocolate-almond Revenge Pie is a crowd-pleaser – but the key-lime picecream could make, break and remake friendships. Inside San Franpsycho.

★ Dragon Beaux
DIM SUM $

(Map p94; ☑415-333-8899; www.dragonbeaux. com; 5700 Geary Blvd; dumplings $4-9; ☺11:30am-2:30pm & 5:30-10pm Mon-Thu, to 10:30pm Fri, 10am-3pm & 5:30-10pm Sat & Sun; ☑; ☐2, 38) Hong Kong meets Vegas at SF's most glamorous, decadent Cantonese restaurant. Say yes to cartloads of succulent roast meats – hello, duck and pork belly – and creative dumplings, especially XO dumplings with plump, brandy-laced shrimp in spinach wrappers. Expect premium teas, sharp service and impeccable Cantonese standards, including Chinese doughnuts, *har gow* (shrimp dumplings) and Chinese broccoli in oyster sauce.

🍷 Drinking & Nightlife

No matter what you're having, SF bars, cafes and clubs are here to oblige. But why stick to your usual, when there are California wines, Bay spirits, microbrews and local roasts to try? Adventurous drinking is abetted by local bartenders, who've been making good on gold-rush-saloon history. SF baristas take their cappuccino-foam drawings seriously and, around here, DJs invent their own software.

🍷 Downtown, Civic Center & SoMa

★ Pagan Idol
LOUNGE

(Map p86; ☑415-985-6375; www.paganidol.com; 375 Bush St; ☺4pm-1am Mon-Fri, 6pm-1:30am Sat; Ⓑ Montgomery, Ⓜ F, J, K, L, M) Volcanoes erupt inside Pagan Idol every half hour, or until there's a virgin sacrifice...what, no takers? Then order your island cocktail and brace for impact – these tiki drinks are no joke. Flirt with disaster over a Hemingway is Dead: rum, bitters and grapefruit, served in a skull. Book online to nab a hut for groups of four to six.

★ Bourbon & Branch
BAR

(Map p80; ☑415-346-1735; www.bourbonand branch.com; 501 Jones St; ☺6pm-2am; ☐27, 38) 'Don't even think of asking for a cosmo' read the House Rules at this Prohibition-era speakeasy, recognizable by its deliciously misleading Anti-Saloon League sign. For award-winning cocktails in the liquored-up library, whisper the password ('books') to be ushered through the bookcase secret passageway. Reservations required for front-room booths and Wilson & Wilson Detective Agency, the noir-themed speakeasy-within-a-speakeasy (password supplied with reservations).

★ **Bar Agricole**　　　　　　　　BAR
(Map p90; ☑ 415-355-9400; www.baragricole. com; 355 11th St; ⊙ 5-11pm Mon-Thu, 5pm-12am Fri & Sat, 10am-2pm & 6-9pm Sun; ☑ 9, 12, 27, 47) ◢ Drink your way to a history degree with well-researched cocktails: Whiz Bang with house bitters, whiskey, vermouth and absinthe scores high, but El Presidente with white rum, farmhouse curaçao and California-pomegranate grenadine takes top honors. This overachiever wins James Beard Award nods for spirits and eco-savvy design, plus popular acclaim for $1 oysters and $5 aperitifs during happy hour (5pm to 6pm, Monday to Sunday).

♉ **North Beach & Chinatown**

★ **Comstock Saloon**　　　　　　BAR
(Map p86; ☑ 415-617-0071; www.comstock saloon.com; 155 Columbus Ave; ⊙ 4pm-midnight Sun-Mon, to 2am Tue-Thu & Sat, noon-2am Fri; ☑ 8, 10, 12, 30, 45, ⬛ Powell-Mason) Relieving yourself in the marble trough below the bar is no longer advisable – Emperor Norton is watching from above – but otherwise this 1907 Victorian saloon brings back the Barbary Coast's glory days with authentic pisco punch and martini-precursor Martinez (gin, vermouth, bitters, maraschino liqueur). Reserve booths or back-parlor seating to hear on nights when ragtime-jazz bands play.

★ **Li Po**　　　　　　　　　　　BAR
(Map p86; ☑ 415-982-0072; www.lipolounge.com; 916 Grant Ave; ⊙ 2pm-2am; ☑ 8, 30, 45, ⬛ Powell-Mason, Powell-Mason) Beat a hasty retreat to red-vinyl booths where Allen Ginsberg and Jack Kerouac debated the meaning of life under a golden Buddha. Enter the 1937 faux-grotto doorway and dodge red lanterns to place your order: Tsingtao beer or a sweet, sneaky-strong Chinese mai tai made with *baijiu* (rice liquor). Brusque bartenders, basement bathrooms, cash only – a world-class dive bar.

★ **Specs**　　　　　　　　　　　BAR
(Specs Twelve Adler Museum Cafe; Map p86; ☑ 415-421-4112; 12 William Saroyan Pl; ⊙ 5pm-2am; ☑ 8, 10, 12, 30, 41, 45, ⬛ Powell-Mason) The walls here are plastered with merchant-marine memo-

rabilia, and you'll be plastered too if you try to keep up with the salty characters holding court in back. Surrounded by seafaring mementos – including walrus genitalia over the bar – your order seems obvious: pitcher of Anchor Steam, coming right up. Cash only.

★ **Caffe Trieste**　　　　　　　CAFE
(Map p86; ☑ 415-392-6739; www.caffetrieste. com; 601 Vallejo St; ⊙ 6:30am-10pm Sun-Thu, to 11pm Fri & Sat; ☎; ☑ 8, 10, 12, 30, 41, 45) Poetry on bathroom walls, opera on the jukebox, live accordion jams and sightings of Beat poet-laureate Lawrence Ferlinghetti: this is North Beach at its best, since the 1950s. Linger over legendary espresso and scribble your screenplay under the Sardinian fishing mural just as young Francis Ford Coppola did. Perhaps you've heard of the movie: *The Godfather*. Cash only.

★ **Vesuvio**　　　　　　　　　　BAR
(Map p86; ☑ 415-362-3370; www.vesuvio.com; 255 Columbus Ave; ⊙ 8am-2am; ☑ 8, 10, 12, 30, 41, 45, ⬛ Powell-Mason) Guy walks into a bar, roars and leaves. Without missing a beat, the bartender says to the next customer, 'Welcome to Vesuvio, honey – what can I get you?' Jack Kerouac blew off Henry Miller to go on a bender here, and after you've joined neighborhood characters on the stained-glass mezzanine for microbrews or Kerouacs (rum, tequila and OJ), you'll see why.

♉ **The Marina, Fisherman's Wharf & the Piers**

★ **Interval Bar & Cafe**　　　　BAR
(Map p88; www.theinterval.org; 2 Marina Blvd, Fort Mason Center, Bldg A; ⊙ 10am-midnight; ☑ 10, 22, 28, 30, 47, 49) Designed to stimulate discussion of philosophy and art, the Interval is a favorite spot in the Marina for cocktails and conversation. It's inside the Long Now Foundation, with floor-to-ceiling bookshelves, which contain the canon of Western lit, rising above a glorious 10,000-year clock – a fitting backdrop for a daiquiri, gimlet or aged Tom Collins, or single-origin coffee, tea and snacks.

★ **Buena Vista Cafe**　　　　　BAR
(Map p88; ☑ 415-474-5044; www.thebuenavista. com; 2765 Hyde St; ⊙ 9am-2am Mon-Fri, 8am-2am Sat & Sun; ☎; ☑ 19, 47, ⬛ Powell-Hyde) Warm your cockles with a prim little goblet of bitter-creamy Irish coffee, introduced to America at this destination bar that once served

SOMA GAY BARS

Sailors have cruised Polk St and Tenderloin gay/trans joints since the 1940s, Castro bars boomed in the 1970s and women into women have been hitting Mission dives since the '60s – but SoMa warehouses have been the biggest weekend gay scene for decades now. From leather bars and drag cabarets to full-time LGBTQ clubs, SoMa has it all. True, internet cruising has thinned the herd, many women still prefer the Mission and some nights are slow starters – but the following fixtures on the gay drinking scene pack at weekends.

Eagle Tavern (Map p90; www.sf-eagle.com; 398 12th St; $5-10; ⏰2pm-2am Mon-Fri, from noon Sat & Sun; 🚌9, 12, 27, 47) Legendary leather bar with Sunday beer busts.

Oasis (Map p90; 📞415-795-3180; www.sfoasis.com; 298 11th St; tickets $15-35; 🚌9, 12, 14, 47, Ⓜ Van Ness) SF's dedicated drag cabaret mounts outrageous shows, sometimes literally.

Lone Star Saloon (Map p90; 📞415-863-9999; http://lonestarsf.com; 1354 Harrison St; ⏰4pm-2am Mon-Thu, from 2pm Fri, from noon Sat & Sun; 🚌9, 12, 27, 47) The original bear bar makes manly men warm and fuzzy at happy hour.

Stud (Map p80; www.studsf.com; 399 9th St; $5-8; ⏰noon-2am Tue, 5pm-3am Thu-Sat, 5pm-midnight Sun; 🚌12, 19, 27, 47) The freaks come out at night for surreal, only-in-SF theme events.

Powerhouse (Map p80; 📞415-522-8689; www.powerhouse-sf.com; 1347 Folsom St; free-$10; ⏰4pm-2am; 🚌9, 12, 27, 47) Major men-only back-patio action.

Hole in the Wall (Map p80; 📞415-431-4695; www.holeinthewallsaloon.com; 1369 Folsom St; ⏰2pm-2am Mon-Fri, noon-2am Sat & Sun; 🚌9, 12, 47) Spiritual home to gay bikers and loudmouth punks.

Club OMG (Map p80; 📞415-896-6473; www.clubomgsf.com; 43 6th St; free-$10; ⏰5pm-2am Tue-Fri & Sun, 7pm-2am Sat; Ⓜ Powell, Ⓑ Powell) Dance in your skivvies on Skid Row.

---

sailors and cannery workers. That old Victorian floor manages to hold up carousers and families alike, served community-style at round tables overlooking the cable-car turnaround at Victoria Park.

🍸 Nob Hill, Russian Hill & Fillmore

⭐**Tonga Room**　　　　　　　LOUNGE
(Map p86; 📞reservations 415-772-5278; www.tongaroom.com; Fairmont San Francisco, 950 Mason St; cover $5-7; ⏰5-11:30pm Sun, Wed & Thu, to 12:30am Fri & Sat; 🚌1, 🚋California, Powell-Mason, Powell-Hyde) Tonight's San Francisco weather: 100% chance of tropical rainstorms every 20 minutes, but only on the top-40 band playing on the island in the middle of the indoor pool – you're safe in your grass hut. For a more powerful hurricane, order one in a plastic coconut. Who said tiki bars were dead? Come before 8pm to beat the cover charge.

Big 4　　　　　　　　　　　BAR
(Map p80; www.big4restaurant.com; 1075 California St; ⏰11:30am-midnight; 📶; 🚌1, 🚋California) A classic for swank cocktails, the Big 4 is named for the railroad barons who once

dominated Nob Hill society, and its decor pays tribute with opulence – oak-paneled walls, studded green leather and a big mahogany bar where you can order great martinis. Service isn't fab, but the room's lovely. Live piano on weekend evenings.

🍷 The Haight & Hayes Valley

⭐**Blue Bottle Coffee Kiosk**　　CAFE
(Map p80; www.bluebottlecoffee.net; 315 Linden St; ⏰7am-6pm Mon-Sat, from 8am Sun; 🚶🏻; 🚌5, 21, 47, 49, Ⓜ Van Ness) Don't mock SF's coffee geekery until you've tried the elixir emerging from this back-alley garage-door kiosk. The Bay Area's Blue Bottle built its reputation with microroasted organic coffee – especially Blue Bottle–invented, off-the-menu Gibraltar, the barista-favorite drink with foam and espresso poured together into the eponymous short glass. Expect a (short) wait and seats outside on creatively repurposed traffic curbs.

⭐**Riddler**　　　　　　　　WINE BAR
(Map p90; www.theriddlersf.com; 528 Laguna St; ⏰4-10pm Tue-Thu & Sun, to 11pm Fri & Sat; 🚌5, 6, 7, 21) Riddle me this: how can you ever thank the women in your life? As the Riddler's

all-women sommelier-chef-investor team points out, champagne makes a fine start. Bubbles begin at $12 and include Veuve Clicquot, the brand named after the woman who invented riddling, the process that gives champagne its unclouded sparkle.

★ Aub Zam Zam
BAR

(Map p94; ☑ 415-861-2545; 1633 Haight St; ⊙ 3pm-2am Mon-Fri, 1pm-2am Sat & Sun; 🚍 6, 7, 22, 33, 43, Ⓜ N) Persian arches, *One Thousand and One Nights* murals, 1930s jazz on the jukebox and top-shelf cocktails at low-shelf prices have brought Bohemian bliss to Haight St since 1941. Legendary founder Bruno used to throw people out for ordering a vodka martini, but he was a softie in the end, bequeathing his beloved bar to regulars who had become friends. Cash only.

The Castro & Noe Valley

Swirl
WINE BAR

(Map p90; ☑ 415-864-2262; www.swirloncastro. com; 572 Castro St; ⊙ 2-8pm Mon-Thu, 1-9pm Fri, noon-9pm Sat, to 8pm Sun; 🚍 33, 🚇 F, Ⓜ K, L, M) Other Castro bars are niche driven, but this wine shop–bar has universal appeal: reliably delicious wine at fair prices in friendly company. Come as you are – pinstripes or leather, gay, straight or whatever – to toast freedom with sublime bubbly, or find liquid courage for sing-alongs at the Castro Theatre in flights of bold reds.

Blackbird
GAY

(Map p90; ☑ 415-503-0630; www.blackbirdbar. com; 2124 Market St; ⊙ 3pm-2am Mon-Fri, from 2pm Sat & Sun; Ⓜ Church St) The Castro's first-choice lounge-bar draws an unpretentious mix of guys in tight T-shirts and their gal pals for seasonally changing cocktails made with bitters and tinctures, good wine and craft beer by the glass, billiards and – everyone's favorite bar amenity – the photo booth. Ideal on a Castro pub crawl, but crowded – and earsplittingly loud – at weekends.

Twin Peaks Tavern
GAY

(Map p90; ☑ 415-864-9470; www.twinpeakstav ern.com; 401 Castro St; ⊙ noon-2am Mon-Fri, from 8am Sat & Sun; Ⓜ Castro St) Don't call it the glass coffin. Show some respect: Twin Peaks was the world's first gay bar with windows open to the street. The jovial crowd skews (way) over 40, but they're not chicken hawks (or they wouldn't hang here) and they love it when happy kids show up to join the party.

The Mission, Dogpatch & Potrero Hill

★ %ABV
COCKTAIL BAR

(Map p90; ☑ 415-400-4748; www.abvsf.com; 3174 16th St; ⊙ 2pm-2am; 🚍 14, 22, Ⓑ 16th St Mission, Ⓜ J) As kindred spirits will deduce from the name (the abbreviation for 'percent alcohol by volume'), this bar is backed by cocktail crafters who know their Rittenhouse rye from their Japanese malt whisky. Top-notch hooch is served promptly and without pretension, including excellent Cali wine and beer on tap and original historically inspired cocktails like the Sutro Swizzle (Armagnac, grapefruit shrub, maraschino liqueur).

★ Trick Dog
BAR

(Map p90; ☑ 415-471-2999; www.trickdogbar.com; 3010 20th St; ⊙ 3pm-2am; 🚍 12, 14, 49) Drink adventurously with ingenious cocktails inspired by local obsessions: San Francisco muralists, Chinese diners or conspiracy theories. Every six months, Trick Dog adopts a new theme and the entire menu changes – proof that you can teach an old dog new tricks, and improve on classics like the Manhattan. Arrive early for bar stools or hit the mood-lit loft for high-concept bar bites.

★ Zeitgeist
BAR

(Map p90; ☑ 415-255-7505; www.zeitgeistsf.com; 199 Valencia St; ⊙ 9am-2am; 🚍 14, 22, 49, Ⓑ 16th St Mission) You've got two seconds flat to order from tough-gal barkeeps used to putting macho bikers in their place – but with 48 beers on draft, you're spoiled for choice. Epic afternoons unfold in the graveled beer garden, with folks hanging out and smoking at long picnic tables. SF's longest happy hour lasts 9am to 8pm weekdays. Cash only; no photos (read: no evidence).

☆ Entertainment
Live Music

★ SFJAZZ Center
JAZZ

(Map p80; ☑ 866-920-5299; www.sfjazz.org; 201 Franklin St; tickets $25-120; 🖬; 🚍 5, 6, 7, 21, 47, 49, Ⓜ Van Ness) 🖉 Jazz legends and singular talents from Argentina to Yemen are showcased at North America's newest, largest jazz center. Hear fresh takes on classic jazz albums and poets riffing with jazz combos in the downstairs Joe Henderson Lab, and witness extraordinary main-stage collaborations ranging from Afro-Cuban All Stars to roots legends Emmylou Harris, Rosanne Cash and Lucinda Williams.

★ **Chapel** LIVE MUSIC
(Map p90; ☑ 415-551-5157; www.thechapelsf.com; 777 Valencia St; cover $15-40; ☺ bar 7pm-2am; ☐ 14, 33, Ⓜ J, Ⓑ 16th St Mission) Musical prayers are answered in a 1914 California arts-and-crafts landmark with heavenly acoustics. The 40ft roof is regularly raised by shows by New Orleans brass bands, folk-YEAH! Americana groups, legendary rockers like Peter Murphy and hip-hop icons such as Prince Paul. Many shows are all ages, except when comedians like W Kamau Bell test edgy material.

★ **Bottom of the Hill** LIVE MUSIC
(☑ 415-621-4455; www.bottomofthehill.com; 1233 17th St; $5-20; ☺ shows generally 9pm Tue-Sat; ☐ 10, 19, 22) The bottom of Potrero Hill tops the list for rocking out with punk legends the Avengers, Pansy Division and Nerf Herder and newcomers worth checking out for their names alone (Summer Salt, the Regrettes, Sorority Noise). The smokers' patio is covered in handbills and ruled by a cat that prefers music to people – totally punk rock. Anchor Steam on tap; cash-only bar.

★ **Great American Music Hall** LIVE MUSIC
(Map p80; ☑ 415-885-0750; www.gamh.com; 859 O'Farrell St; shows $20-45; ☺ box office 10:30am-6pm Mon-Fri & show nights; 🚹; ☐ 19, 38, 47, 49) Everyone busts out their best sets at this opulent 1907 bordello turned all-ages venue – indie rockers like the Band Perry throw down, international legends such as Salif Keita grace the stage, and John Waters hosts Christmas extravaganzas. Pay $25 extra for dinner with prime balcony seating to watch shows comfortably, or rock out with the standing-room scrum downstairs.

Fillmore Auditorium LIVE MUSIC
(☑ 415-346-6000; http://thefillmore.com; 1805 Geary Blvd; tickets from $20; ☺ box office 10am-3pm Sun, plus 30min before doors open to 10pm show nights; ☐ 22, 38) Jimi Hendrix, Janis Joplin, the Doors – they all played the Fillmore. Now you might catch the Indigo Girls, Willie Nelson or Tracy Chapman in the historic 1250-capacity, standing-room-only theater (if you're polite and lead with the hip, you might squeeze up to the stage). Don't miss the priceless collection of psychedelic posters in the upstairs gallery.

Classical Music & Dance

★ **San Francisco Symphony** CLASSICAL MUSIC
(Map p80; ☑ box office 415-864-6000, rush-ticket hotline 415-503-5577; www.sfsymphony.org; Grove St, btwn Franklin St & Van Ness Ave; tickets $20-150; ☐ 21, 45, 47, Ⓜ Van Ness, Ⓑ Civic Center) From the moment conductor Michael Tilson Thomas bounces up on his toes and raises his baton, the audience is on the edge of their seats for another thunderous performance by the Grammy-winning SF Symphony. Don't miss signature concerts of Beethoven and Mahler, live symphony performances with such films as *Star Trek*, and creative collaborations with artists from Elvis Costello to Metallica.

★ **San Francisco Opera** OPERA
(Map p80; ☑ 415-864-3330; www.sfopera.com; War Memorial Opera House, 301 Van Ness Ave; tickets $10-350; ☐ 21, 45, 47, 49, Ⓜ Van Ness) Opera was SF's gold-rush soundtrack – and SF Opera rivals the Met, with world premieres of original works ranging from Stephen King's *Dolores Claiborne* to *Girls of the Golden West*, filmmaker Peter Sellars' collaboration with composer John Adams. Expect haute couture costumes and radical sets by painter David Hockney. Score $10 same-day standing-room tickets at 10am; check website for Opera Lab pop-ups.

San Francisco Ballet DANCE
(Map p80; ☑ tickets 415-865-2000; www.sfballet.org; War Memorial Opera House, 301 Van Ness Ave; tickets $22-141; ☺ ticket sales 10am-4pm Mon-Fri; ☐ 5, 21, 47, 49, Ⓜ Van Ness, Ⓑ Civic Center) The USA's oldest ballet company is looking sharp in more than 100 shows annually, from *The Nutcracker* (the US premiere was here) to modern originals. Performances are mostly at the War Memorial Opera House from January to May, and occasionally at the Yerba Buena Center for the Arts. Score $15-to-$20 same-day standing-room tickets at the box office (from noon Tuesday to Friday, 10am weekends).

Theater & Performing Arts

★ **American Conservatory Theater** THEATER
(ACT; Map p80; ☑ 415-749-2228; www.act-sf.org; 405 Geary St; ☺ box office 10am-6pm Mon, to curtain Tue-Sun; ☐ 8, 30, 38, 45, ☐ Powell-Mason, Powell-Hyde, Ⓑ Powell, Ⓜ Powell) Breakthrough shows launch at this turn-of-the-century landmark, which has hosted ACT's productions of Tony Kushner's *Angels in America*

and Robert Wilson's *Black Rider*, with William S Burroughs' libretto and music by Tom Waits. Major playwrights like Tom Stoppard, Dustin Lance Black, Eve Ensler and David Mamet premiere work here, while the ACT's new **Strand Theater** (Map p80; ☏415-749-2228; www.act-sf.org/home/box_office/strand. html; 1127 Market St; ⛴F, ⒷCivic Center, ⓂCivic Center) stages experimental works.

★**Oberlin Dance Collective**   DANCE
(ODC; Map p90; ☏box office 415-863-9834, classes 415-549-8519; www.odctheater.org; 3153 17th St; drop-in classes from $15, shows $20-50; ☒12, 14, 22, 33, 49, Ⓑ16th St Mission) For 45 years, ODC has been redefining dance with risky, raw performances and the sheer joy of movement. ODC's season runs from September to December, but its stage presents year-round shows featuring local and international artists. ODC Dance Commons is a hub and hangout for the dance community, offering 200-plus classes a week, from flamenco to vogue; all ages and skill levels welcome.

**Yerba Buena
Center for the Arts**   PERFORMING ARTS
(YBCA; Map p80; ☏415-978-2700; www.ybca. org; 700 Howard St; tickets free-$35; ☺box office noon-6pm Sun, Tue & Wed, to 8pm Thu-Sat, galleries closed Mon & Tue; ♿; ☒14, ⓂPowell, ⒷPowell) Rock stars would be jealous of art stars at YBCA openings, which draw overflow crowds of art-school groupies with shows ranging from cyberpunk video art to hip-hop showdowns and Indian kathak–American tap-dance fusion freestyle. Most touring dance and jazz companies perform at YBCA's main theater (across the sidewalk from the gallery).

Cinema
★**Castro Theatre**   CINEMA
(Map p90; ☏415-621-6120; www.castrotheatre. com; 429 Castro St; adult/child $11/8.50; ⓂCastro St) The Mighty Wurlitzer organ rises from the orchestra pit before evening performances and the audience cheers for the Great American Songbook, ending with: 'San Francisco open your Golden Gate/You let no stranger wait outside your door...' If there's a cult classic on the bill – say, *Whatever Happened to Baby Jane?* – expect participation. Otherwise, crowds are well behaved and rapt.

★**Alamo Drafthouse Cinema**   CINEMA
(Map p90; ☏415-549-5959; https://drafthouse. com/sf; 2550 Mission St; tickets $9-20; ♿; ☒14,

Ⓑ24th St Mission) The landmark 1932 New Mission cinema, now restored to its original Timothy Pfleuger–designed art-deco glory, has a new mission: to upgrade dinner-and-a-movie dates. Staff deliver microbrews and tasty fare to plush banquette seats, so you don't miss a moment of the premieres, cult revivals (especially Music Mondays) or SF favorites from *Mrs Doubtfire* to *Dirty Harry* – often with filmmaker Q&As.

★**Roxie Cinema**   CINEMA
(Map p90; ☏415-863-1087; www.roxie.com; 3117 16th St; regular screening/matinee $11/8; ☒14, 22, 33, 49, Ⓑ16th St Mission) This vintage 1909 cinema is a neighborhood nonprofit with an international reputation for distributing documentaries and showing controversial films banned elsewhere. Tickets to film-festival premieres, rare revivals and raucous Oscars telecasts sell out – get tickets online – but if the main show's packed, discover riveting documentaries in teensy next-door Little Roxy instead. No ads, plus personal introductions to every film.

🔒 Shopping
Union Square is the city's principal shopping district, with flagship stores and department stores, including international chains. Downtown shopping-district borders are (roughly) Powell St (west), Sutter St (north), Kearny St (east) and Market St (south), where the **Westfield mall** (Map p80; www.westfield.com/sanfrancisco; 865 Market St; ☺10am-8:30pm Mon-Sat, 11am-7pm Sun; ♿; ☒Powell-Mason, Powell-Hyde, ⓂPowell, ⒷPowell) sprawls. The epicenter of the Union Square shopping area is around Post St, near Grant Ave. Stockton St crosses Market St and becomes 4th St, flanked by flagship stores and **Metreon cinema and mall** (Map p80; ☏415-369-6201; www.amctheatres.com; 101 4th St; adult/child $14.49/11.49; ☒14, ⓂPowell, ⒷPowell). For boutique offerings, head toward **Jackson Sq** (Map p86; www.jacksonsquaresf.com; around Jackson & Montgomery Sts; ⓂEmbarcadero, ⒷEmbarcadero) and along Commercial St.

★**Recchiuti Chocolates**   FOOD & DRINKS
(Map p80; ☏415-834-9494; www.recchiuticonfec tions.com; 1 Ferry Bldg, cnr Market St & the Embarcadero; ☺10am-7pm Mon-Fri, 8am-6pm Sat, 10am-5pm Sun; ⓂEmbarcadero, ⒷEmbarcadero) No San Franciscan can resist award-winning Recchiuti: Pacific Heights parts with old money for its *fleur de sel* caramels; Noe Valley's foodie kids prefer S'more Bites to the

campground variety; North Beach toasts to the red-wine-pairing chocolate box; and the Mission approves SF-landmark chocolates designed by Creativity Explored – proceeds benefit the Mission arts-education nonprofit for artists with developmental disabilities.

★ Heath Ceramics   HOMEWARES
(Map p80; ☑415-399-9284; www.heathceramics. com; 1 Ferry Bldg, cnr Market St & the Embarcadero; ⊙10am-7pm Mon-Fri, 8am-6pm Sat, 11am-5pm Sun; Ⓜ Embarcadero, Ⓑ Embarcadero) Odds are your favorite SF meal was served on Heath Ceramics, Bay Area chefs' tableware of choice ever since Alice Waters started using Heath's modern, hand-thrown dishes at Chez Panisse. Heath's muted colors and streamlined, mid-century designs stay true to Edith Heath's originals c 1948. Pieces are priced for fine dining, except studio seconds, sold here at weekends.

★ Golden Gate
Fortune Cookie Company   FOOD & DRINKS
(Map p86; ☑415-781-3956; 56 Ross Alley; ⊙9am-6pm; ☒8, 30, 45, ☒Powell-Mason, Powell-Hyde) Make a fortune at this bakery, where cookies are stamped from vintage presses – just as they were in 1909, when fortune cookies were invented for SF's Japanese Tea Garden (p90). Write your own fortunes for custom cookies (50¢ each), or get cookies with regular or risqué fortunes (pro tip: add 'in bed' to regular ones). Cash only; 50¢ tip for photos.

ⓘ Information

DANGERS & ANNOYANCES
Keep your city smarts and wits about you, especially at night in the Tenderloin, South of Market (SoMa) and the Mission.
➡ Avoid using your smart phone unnecessarily on the street – phone-snatching is a crime of opportunity and a problem in SF.
➡ The Bayview–Hunters Point neighborhood (south of Potrero Hill, along the water) is plagued by crime and violence and isn't suitable for wandering tourists.
➡ After dark, Mission Dolores Park, Buena Vista Park and the entry to Golden Gate Park at Haight and Stanyan Sts are used for drug deals and casual sex hookups.

EMERGENCY & MEDICAL SERVICES
Before traveling, contact your health-insurance provider to learn what medical care they will cover outside your hometown (or home country). Overseas visitors should acquire travel insurance that covers medical situations in the US, where nonemergency care for uninsured patients can be very expensive.

For nonemergency appointments at hospitals, you'll need proof of insurance, or credit card or cash. Even with insurance, you'll most likely have to pay up front for nonemergency care and then wrangle afterward with your insurance company to get reimbursed. San Francisco has excellent medical facilities, plus alternative medical practices and herbal apothecaries.

San Francisco General Hopsital (Zuckerberg San Franciso General Hospital and Trauma Center; ☑ emergency 415-206-8111, main hospital 415-206-8000; www.sfdph.org; 1001 Potrero Ave; ⊙24hr; ☒9, 10, 33, 48) Best for serious trauma. Provides care to uninsured patients, including psychiatric care; no documentation required beyond ID.

University of California San Francisco Medical Center (☑415-476-1000; www.ucsfhealth. org; 505 Parnassus Ave; ⊙24hr; ☒6, 7, 43, ⓂN) ER at leading university hospital.

Haight-Ashbury Free Clinic (HealthRIGHT 360; ☑415-746-1950; www.healthright360.org; 558 Clayton St; ⊙by appointment 8:45am-noon & 1-5pm; ☒6, 7, 33, 37, 43, ⓂN) Provides substance abuse and mental health services by appointment.

San Francisco City Clinic (☑415-487-5500; www.sfcityclinic.org; 356 7th St; ⊙8am-4pm Mon, Wed & Fri, 1-6pm Tue, 1-4pm Thu) Low-cost treatment for sexually transmitted diseases (STDs), including emergency contraception and post-exposure prevention (PEP) for HIV.

Drug & Alcohol Emergency Info Line (☑415-362-3400; www.sfsuicide.org)

Trauma Recovery & Rape Treatment Center (☑24hr hotline 415-206-8125, business hours 415-437-3000; www.traumarecoverycenter. org)

INTERNET ACCESS
Apple Store (☑415-392-0202; www.apple. com/retail/sanfrancisco; 300 Post St; ⊙9am-9pm Mon-Sat, 10am-8pm Sun; ☎; ☒38, ☒Powell-Mason, Powell-Hyde, ⓂPowell) Free wi-fi and internet-terminal usage.

San Francisco Main Library (☑415-557-4400; www.sfpl.org; 100 Larkin St; ⊙10am-6pm Mon & Sat, 9am-8pm Tue-Thu, noon-6pm Fri, noon-5pm Sun; ☎; ⓂCivic Center) Free 30-minute internet-terminal usage; spotty wi-fi access.

POST
Rincon Center Post Office (Map p80; ☑800-275-8777; www.usps.gov; 180 Steuart St; ⊙7:30am-5pm Mon-Fri, 9am-2pm Sat; ⓂEmbarcadero, ⒷEmbarcadero) Postal services plus historic murals.

US Post Office (Map p80; ☑ 800-275-8777; www.usps.gov; Macy's, 170 O'Farrell St; ⊙10am-5pm Mon-Sat; ⓖ Powell-Mason, Powell-Hyde, Ⓜ Powell, Ⓑ Powell) Inside Macy's department store.

TOURIST INFORMATION

California Welcome Center (Map p88; ☑415-981-1280; www.visitcwc.com; Pier 39, 2nd fl; ⊙9am-7pm; ⓠ47, ⓖPowell-Mason, ⓂE, F) Handy resource for stroller and wheelchair rental, plus luggage storage, phone charging, and ideas for broader California travel.

San Francisco Visitor Information Center (Map p80; ☑ 415-391-2000; www.sftravel. com/visitor-information-center; lower level, Hallidie Plaza, cnr Market & Powell Sts; ⊙9am-5pm Mon-Fri, to 3pm Sat & Sun, closed Sun Nov-Apr; ⓖ Powell-Mason, Powell-Hyde, Ⓜ Powell, Ⓑ Powell) Provides practical multilingual information, sells transportation passes, publishes glossy maps and booklets, and provides interactive touch screens.

❶ Getting There & Away

If you've unlimited time, consider taking the train, instead of driving or flying, to avoid traffic hassles and excess carbon emissions.

Flights, cars and tours can be booked online at lonelyplanet.com/bookings.

AIR

The Bay Area has three international airports: **San Francisco** (SFO; www.flysfo.com; S McDonnell Rd), **Oakland (OAK**; p149) and **San Jose (SJC**; p165). Direct flights from Los Angeles take 60 minutes; Chicago, four hours; Atlanta, five hours; New York, six hours. Factor in additional transit time – and cost – to reach San Francisco proper from Oakland or San Jose, and note that what you save in airfare you may wind up spending on ground transportation. However, if schedule is most important, note that SFO has more weather-related delays than OAK.

BUS

San Francisco's intercity hub is the Transbay Transit Center. From here you can catch the following buses:

AC Transit (p149) Buses to the East Bay.

Greyhound (☑ 800-231-2222; www.greyhound. com) Buses leave daily for Los Angeles ($39 to $90, eight to 12 hours), Truckee near Lake Tahoe ($35 to $46, 5½ hours) and other major destinations.

Megabus (p165) Low-cost bus service to San Francisco from Los Angeles, Sacramento and Reno.

SamTrans Southbound buses to Palo Alto and the Pacific coast.

TRAIN

Easy on the eyes and light on carbon emissions, train travel is a good way to visit the Bay Area and beyond.

Caltrain (www.caltrain.com; cnr 4th & King Sts) connects San Francisco with Silicon Valley hubs and San Jose.

Amtrak (☑ 800-872-7245; www.amtrakcalifornia.com) serves San Francisco via stations in Oakland and Emeryville (near Oakland), with free shuttle-bus connections to San Francisco's Ferry Building and Caltrain station, and Oakland's Jack London Sq. Amtrak offers rail passes good for seven days of travel in California within a 21-day period (from $159).

CAR & MOTORCYCLE

Major car-rental operators have offices at airports and downtown.

❶ Getting Around

When San Franciscans aren't pressed for time, most walk, bike or ride Muni instead of taking a car or cab. Traffic is notoriously bad at rush hour, and parking is next to impossible in center-city neighborhoods. Avoid driving until it's time to leave town – or drive during off-peak hours.

For Bay Area transit options, departures and arrivals, call ☑ 511 or check www.511.org. A detailed *Muni Street & Transit Map* is available free online.

BART High-speed transit to East Bay, Mission St, SF airport and Millbrae, where it connects with Caltrain.

Cable cars Frequent, slow and scenic, from 6am to 12:30am daily. Single rides cost $7; for frequent use, get a Muni Passport ($21 per day).

Muni streetcar and bus Reasonably fast, but schedules vary wildly by line; infrequent after 9pm. Fares are $2.50.

Taxi Fares are about $2.75 per mile; meters start at $3.50. Add 15% to the fare as a tip ($1 minimum). For quickest service in San Francisco, download the Flywheel app for smart phones, which dispatches the nearest taxi.

TO/FROM THE AIRPORT

SamTrans (☑ 800-660-4287; www.samtrans. com) Express bus KX takes about 30 to 45 minutes to run from San Francisco International Airport to SF's **Transbay Transit Center** (Map p80; cnr Howard & Main Sts; ⓠ 5,38,41,71), and makes two stops in downtown SF (the last at the Transbay Transit Center).

Airport Express (☑ 800-327-2024; www. airportexpressinc.com) Runs a scheduled shuttle every hour from 5:30am to 12:30am between San Francisco International Airport and Sonoma ($34) and Marin ($26) counties.

BART

The fastest link between downtown and the Mission District also offers transit to SF airport (SFO; $8.95), Oakland ($3.45) and Berkeley ($4). Four of the system's five lines pass through SF before terminating at Daly City or SFO. Within SF, one-way fares start at $1.95.

BICYCLE

Contact the San Francisco Bicycle Coalition (p124) for maps, information and legal matters regarding bicyclists. Bike sharing is new in SF: racks for **Bay Area Bike Share** (☑ 855-480-2453; www.bayareabikeshare.com; 30-day membership $30) are located east of Van Ness Ave, and in the SoMa area; however, bikes come without helmets, and biking downtown without proper protection can be particularly dangerous. Bicycles can be taken on BART, but not aboard crowded trains, and never in the first car, nor in the first three cars during weekday rush hours; folded bikes are allowed in all cars at all times. On Amtrak, bikes can be checked as baggage for $5.

BOAT

With the revival of the Embarcadero and the reinvention of the Ferry Building as a gourmet dining destination, commuters and tourists alike are taking the scenic ferry across the bay.

Alcatraz

Alcatraz Cruises (Map p88; ☑ 415-981-7625; www.alcatrazcruises.com; tours day adult/child/family $37.25/23/112.75, night adult/child $44.25/26.50; Ⓜ E, F) has ferries (reservations essential) departing Pier 33 for Alcatraz every half-hour from 8:45am to 3:50pm and at 5:55pm and 6:30pm for night tours.

East Bay

Blue & Gold Fleet Ferries (Map p80; ☑ 415-705-8200; www.blueandgoldfleet.com) operates from the Ferry Building, Pier 39 and Pier 41 at Fisherman's Wharf to Jack London Sq in Oakland (one way $6.65). During baseball season, a Giants ferry service runs directly from the landing at AT&T Park's Seals Plaza entrance to Oakland and Alameda. Ticket booths are located at the Ferry Building and Piers 39 and 41.

San Francisco Bay Ferry (p149) operates from both Pier 41 and the Ferry Building to Oakland/Alameda. Fares are $6.60.

Marin County

Golden Gate Transit Ferries (Map p80; ☑ 415-455-2000; www.goldengateferry.org; ⊘ 6am-9:30pm Mon-Fri, 10am-6pm Sat & Sun) runs regular ferry services from the Ferry Building to Larkspur and Sausalito (one way $11.75).

Transfers are available to Muni bus services and bicycles are permitted. Blue & Gold Fleet Ferries also operate to Tiburon or Sausalito (one way $11.50) from Pier 41.

Napa Valley

Get to Napa car free (weekdays only) via the **Vallejo Ferry** (Map p80; ☑ 707-643-3779, 877-643-3779; http://sanfranciscobayferry.com), with departures from the Ferry Building docks about every hour from 6:30am to 7pm weekdays and roughly every 90 minutes from 10am to 9pm on weekends; bikes are permitted. However, the connecting bus from the Vallejo Ferry Terminal – Napa Valley Vine bus 29 to downtown Napa, Yountville, St Helena or Calistoga – operates only on weekdays. Fares are $13.80.

CAR

If you can, avoid driving in San Francisco: heavy traffic is a given, street parking is harder to find than true love, and meter readers are ruthless.

MUNI

Muni (Municipal Transit Agency; ☑ 511; www.sfmta.com) Operates bus, streetcar and cable-car lines. Buses and streetcars are referred to interchangeably as Muni, but when streetcars run underground beneath Market St, they're called the Muni Metro. Some areas are better connected than others, but Muni spares you the costly hassle of driving and parking – and it's often faster than driving, especially along metro-streetcar lines J, K/T, L, M and N.

Muni stops are indicated by a street sign and/or a yellow-painted stripe on the nearest lamppost, with route numbers stamped on the yellow stripe; if there is no street sign or lamppost, look on the pavement for a yellow bar with a route number painted on it. Ignore yellow circles and Xs on the pavement, or bars that do not also have route numbers; these other markings tell electric-trolley drivers when to engage or disengage the throttle; they do not indicate bus stops.

TAXI

DeSoto Cab (☑ 415-970-1300; http://flywheel|taxi.com/)

Green Cab (☑ 415-626-4733; www.greencabsf.com) Fuel-efficient hybrids; worker-owned collective.

Homobiles (☑ 415-574-5023; www.homobiles.org) Get home safely with secure, reliable, donation-based transport for the GLBT community: drivers provide 24/7 taxi service – text for fastest service.

Luxor (☑ 415-282-4141; www.luxorcab.com)

Yellow Cab (☑ 415-333-3333; www.yellowcabsf.com)

Marin County & the Bay Area

Best Places to Eat

➡ Chez Panisse (p156)

➡ Fish (p128)

➡ Hog Island Oyster
Company (p138)

➡ Sunday Marin Farmers
Market (p131)

➡ Commis (p145)

Best Places to Sleep

➡ Cavallo Point (p123)

➡ Mountain Home Inn (p133)

➡ HI Pigeon Point Lighthouse
(p169)

➡ Steep Ravine (p134)

Why Go?

The San Francisco Bay Area encompasses a bonanza of natural vistas and wildlife. Cross the Golden Gate Bridge into Marin County and visit wizened ancient redwoods body-blocking the sun and herds of elegant tule elk prancing along the bluffs of Tomales Bay. Gray whales show some fluke off the cape of the wind-scoured Point Reyes peninsula, while hawks surf the skies in the shaggy hills of the Marin Headlands.

On the cutting edge of intellectual thought, Stanford University – near the tech powerhouse of Silicon Valley and the University of California, Berkeley in the East Bay – draws academics and students from around the world. The city of Berkeley sparked the state's locavore food movement and continues to be at the forefront of environmental and left-leaning political causes. South of San Francisco, Hwy 1 traces miles of undeveloped coastline and sandy pocket beaches as it slowly winds south to Santa Cruz.

When to Go
Berkeley

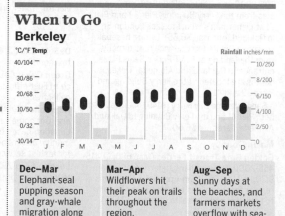

Dec–Mar
Elephant-seal pupping season and gray-whale migration along the coast.

Mar–Apr
Wildflowers hit their peak on trails throughout the region.

Aug–Sep
Sunny days at the beaches, and farmers markets overflow with seasonal goodness.

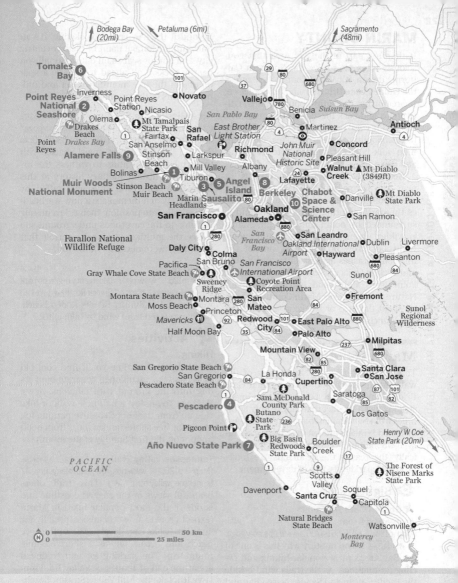

Marin County & the Bay Area Highlights

1 Gazing up at a majestic redwood canopy at **Muir Woods National Monument** (p135).

2 Spotting gray whales from the lighthouse at **Point Reyes National Seashore** (p139).

3 Ferrying over from San Francisco to bohemian **Sausalito** (p124) houseboats bobbing in the bay.

4 Touring the coastline along Hwy 1 to **Pescadero** (p168).

5 Hiking or cycling the **Angel Island** (p132) perimeter.

6 Kayaking past harbor seals in **Tomales Bay** (p140).

7 Spying on noisy elephant seals in **Año Nuevo State Park** (p169).

8 Hanging with hippies, students and passionate foodies in **Berkeley** (p150).

9 Cooling off at blissful Bass Lake, then trekking to **Alamere Falls** (p137).

10 Heading into the Oakland Hills to marvel at stars and planets in the **Chabot Space & Science Center** (p144).

MARIN COUNTY

If there's a part of the Bay Area that consciously attempts to live the Northern California dream, it's Marin County. Just across the Golden Gate Bridge from San Francisco, the region has a wealthy population that cultivates a laid-back lifestyle. Towns may look like idyllic rural hamlets, but the shops cater to cosmopolitan, expensive tastes. The 'common' folk here eat organic, vote Democrat and drive Teslas.

Geographically, Marin County is a near mirror image of San Francisco. It's a south-pointing peninsula that nearly touches the north-pointing tip of the city, and is surrounded by ocean and bay. But Marin is wilder, greener and more mountainous. Redwoods grow on the coast side of the hills, surf crashes against cliffs, and hiking and cycling trails crisscross blessedly scenic Point Reyes, Muir Woods and Mt Tamalpais. Nature is what makes Marin County such an excellent day trip or weekend escape from San Francisco.

Marin Headlands

The headlands rise majestically out of the water at the north end of the Golden Gate Bridge, their rugged beauty all the more striking given the fact that they're only a few miles from San Francisco's urban core. A few forts and bunkers are left over from a century of US military occupation – which is, ironically, the reason the headlands are today protected parklands, free of development.

⊙ Sights

★ **Golden Gate National Recreation Area**   PARK
(Map p126; ☑ 415-561-4700; www.nps.gov/goga; P ⊛) FREE It's no mystery why this is one of the Bay Area's most popular hiking and cycling destinations. As the trails wind beside the Pacific Ocean and San Francisco Bay and through the Marin Headlands, they afford stunning views of the sea, the Golden Gate Bridge and the city of San Francisco.

★ **Point Bonita Lighthouse**   LIGHTHOUSE
(Map p126; ☑ 415-331-1540; www.nps.gov/goga/ pobo.htm; ⊙ 12:30-3:30pm Sat-Mon; P) FREE This historical lighthouse is a breathtaking half-mile walk from a small parking area off Field Rd. From the tip of Point Bonita, you can see the distant Golden Gate Bridge and beyond it the San Francisco skyline. It's an uncommon vantage point of the bay-centric city, and harbor seals haul out seasonally on nearby rocks. Call ahead to reserve a spot on one of the free monthly sunset and full-moon tours of the promontory.

Nike Missile Site SF-88   HISTORIC SITE
(Map p126; ☑ 415-331-1540; www.nps.gov/goga/ nike-missile-site.htm; Field Rd; ⊙ 12:30-3:30pm Sat; P) FREE File past guard shacks with uniformed mannequins to witness the area's not-too-distant military history at this fascinating Cold War museum staffed by veterans. Watch them place a now-warhead-free missile into position, then ride a missile elevator to the cavernous underground silo to see the multikeyed launch controls that thankfully were never set in motion.

Rodeo Beach   BEACH
(Map p126; www.parksconservancy.org/visit/park sites/rodeo-beach.html; off Bunker Rd; P ⊛) At the western end of Bunker Rd sits Rodeo Beach, partly protected from wind by high cliffs.

🏃 Activities

Hiking
All along the coastline you'll find cool old battery sites – abandoned concrete bunkers dug into the ground with fabulous views. **Battery Townsley**, a half-mile walk or bike ride up from the **Fort Cronkite** parking lot, opens for free subterranean tours from noon to 4pm on the first Sunday of the month.

Tennessee Valley Trail   HIKING
(Map p126; www.nps.gov/goga/planyourvisit/ tennessee_valley.htm; ⊛) This trail offers beautiful views of the rugged coastline and is one of the most popular hikes in Marin (expect crowds on weekends), especially for families. It has easy, level access to the cove beach and ocean, and is a short 3.5-mile round-trip. The parking lot and trailhead are at the end of Tennessee Valley Rd. From Hwy 101, take the Mill Valley/Stinson Beach/ Hwy 1 exit, follow Shoreline Hwy and turn left on to Tennessee Valley Rd.

Coastal Trail   HIKING
(Map p126; www.nps.gov/goga/planyourvisit/ hiking.htm) From nearby Rodeo Beach, the Coastal Trail meanders 3.5 miles inland, past abandoned military bunkers, to intersect the Tennessee Valley Trail. It then continues almost 3 miles along the blustery headlands all the way to Muir Beach (p135).

WHY IS IT SO FOGGY?

When the summer sun's rays warm the air over the chilly Pacific, fog forms and hovers offshore. To grasp how it moves inland requires an understanding of California's geography. The vast agricultural region in the state's interior, the Central Valley, is ringed by mountains like a giant bathtub. The only substantial sea-level break in these mountains occurs at the Golden Gate to the west, which happens to be the direction from which prevailing winds blow. As the inland valley heats up and the warm air rises, it creates a deficit of air at surface level, generating wind that gets sucked through the only opening it can find: the Golden Gate. It happens fast and it's unpredictable. Gusty wind is the only indication that the fog is about to roll in. But even this is inconsistent: there can be fog at the beaches south of the Golden Gate and sun a mile to the north. Hills block fog – especially at times of high atmospheric pressure, as often happens in summer. Because of this, weather forecasters speak of the Bay Area's 'microclimates.' In July it's not uncommon for inland areas to top 100°F (38°C), while the mercury at the coast barely reaches 70°F (21°C).

Mountain Biking

The Marin Headlands have some excellent mountain-biking routes and it's an exhilarating ride across the Golden Gate Bridge to reach them.

For a good 12-mile dirt loop, choose the **Coastal Trail** west from the fork of Conzelman and McCullough Rds, bumping and winding down to Bunker Rd where it meets **Bobcat Trail**, which joins **Marincello Trail** and descends steeply into the Tennessee Valley parking area. The **Old Springs Trail** and the **Miwok Trail** take you back to Bunker Rd a bit more gently than the Bobcat Trail, though any attempt to avoid at least a couple of hefty climbs is futile.

🛏 Sleeping

There's one deluxe lodge, a cozy youth hostel and four campgrounds in the headlands. **Hawk Camp**, **Bicentennial** and **Haypress** campgrounds are inland, with free camping; sites must be reserved through the Marin Headlands Visitor Center (p124). None have water available and two campgrounds require hiking (or cycling) in from the nearest parking lot.

Kirby Cove Campground   CAMPGROUND $
(Map p126; ☑ reservations 877-444-6777; www.recreation.gov; Kirby Cove Rd; tent sites $25; ⊙ Apr-Nov; ℗) In a spectacular shady nook near the entrance to the bay, there's a small beach with the Golden Gate Bridge arching over the rocks nearby. At night you can watch the phantom shadows of cargo ships passing by (and sometimes be lulled to sleep by the dirge of a fog horn). Reserve far ahead.

HI Marin Headlands   HOSTEL $
(Map p126; ☑ 415-331-2777; www.norcalhostels. org/marin; Fort Barry, Bldg 941; r with shared bath $105-135, dm $31-40; ⊙ reception 7:30am-11:30pm; ℗ ⊖ @ 🛜) 🐾 Wake up to grazing deer and dew on the ground at this Spartan 1907 military compound snuggled in the woods. It has comfortable beds and two well-stocked kitchens, and guests can gather round a fireplace in the common room, shoot pool or play Ping-Pong. Hiking trails beckon outside.

Cavallo Point   LODGE $$$
(Map p126; ☑ 415-339-4700; www.cavallopoint. com; 601 Murray Circle; r from $399; ℗ ⊖ ❄ @ 🛜 ❄ 🐾) 🐾 Spread over 45 acres of the Bay Area's most scenic parkland, Cavallo Point lodge flaunts an eco-conscious focus with a full-service spa, restaurant and bar, and easy access to outdoor activities. Choose from richly renovated rooms in the landmark Fort Baker officers' quarters or contemporary, stylish 'green' accommodations with exquisite bay views (including a turret of the Golden Gate Bridge).

🍴 Eating

Bring a picnic lunch, trail snacks and enough water with you, since there's nowhere to eat in the Marin Headlands except at Cavallo Point lodge and the children's museum, near Sausalito.

Murray Circle   MODERN AMERICAN $$$
(Map p126; ☑ 415-339-4750; www.cavallopoint.com; 601 Murray Circle; dinner mains $25-36; ⊙ 7-11am & 11:30am-2pm Mon-Fri, 7am-2:30pm Sat & Sun, 5:30-9pm Sun-Thu, 5:30-10pm Fri & Sat; ☑ 👶) 🐾 At Cavallo Point lodge, dine on locally sourced

DON'T MISS

HIKING & CYCLING THE GOLDEN GATE BRIDGE

Walking or cycling across the Golden Gate Bridge to Sausalito is a fun way to avoid traffic, get some great ocean views and fresh air. Getting to Sausalito is a relatively easy journey, mostly flat or downhill when heading north from San Francisco. Cycling back isn't nearly as fun. The return trip involves a big climb out of Sausalito. Unless you want a work out, simply hop on a ferry back to SF.

The trip is about 4 miles from the south end of the bridge and takes less than an hour. Pedestrians have access to the bridge's east walkway between 5am and 9pm daily (until 6pm in winter). Cyclists generally use the west side, except on weekdays between 5am and 3:30pm, when they share the east side with pedestrians (who have the right-of-way). After 9pm (6pm in winter), cyclists can still cross the bridge on the east side through a security gate. Check the bridge website for changes.

For more ambitious cyclists, the Cal Park Hill Tunnel is a safe subterranean passage from Larkspur (another ferry terminus) to San Rafael.

More information and resources are available at the websites of the **San Francisco Bicycle Coalition** (☑415-431-2453; www.sfbike.org) and the **Marin County Bicycle Coalition** (MCBC; ☑415-456-3469; www.marinbike.org).

meats, seafood and produce – perhaps grass-fed organic beef burgers or Dungeness-crab BLT sandwiches – in a clubby dining room topped by a pressed-tin ceiling. Reservations recommended for dinner and weekend brunch.

ℹ Information

Information is available from the **Golden Gate National Recreation Area** (p122) and the **Marin Headlands Visitors Center** (Map p126; ☑415-331-1540; www.nps.gov/goga/marin-headlands. htm; Bunker Rd, Fort Barry; ◷9:30am-4:30pm), in an old chapel off Bunker Rd near Fort Barry.

ℹ Getting There & Away

By car, take the Alexander Ave exit just after crossing north over the Golden Gate Bridge and dip left under the freeway. Conzelman Rd, to the right, takes you up along the bluffs; you can also take Bunker Rd, which leads to the headlands through a one-way tunnel. Arrive before 2pm on weekends to avoid traffic and parking congestion, or cycle over the bridge instead.

On Saturday, Sunday and holidays, **MUNI** (☑511, 415-701-2311; www.sfmta.com) bus 76X runs every 60 to 90 minutes from San Francisco's Financial District to the Marin Headlands Visitors Center, Rodeo Beach and the Nike missile site. Buses are equipped with bicycle racks.

Sausalito

Perfectly arranged on a secure little harbor on the bay, Sausalito is undeniably lovely. Named for the tiny willows that once populated the banks of its creeks, it's famous for its colorful houseboats bobbing in the bay. Much of the well-heeled downtown has uninterrupted views of San Francisco and Angel Island, and due to the ridgeline at its back, fog generally skips it.

Sausalito is understandably a major tourist trap, jam-packed with souvenir shops and costly boutiques. It's the first town you encounter after crossing the Golden Gate Bridge from San Francisco, so daytime crowds turn up in droves and make parking difficult. Ferrying over from San Francisco makes for a more relaxing excursion.

The town sits on Richardson Bay, a smaller bay within San Francisco Bay. The commercial district is mainly one street, Bridgeway Blvd, which runs alongside the waterfront.

◉ Sights

★**Sausalito Houseboats** ARCHITECTURE
(Map p126) Bohemia still thrives along the shoreline of Richardson Bay, where free spirits inhabit hundreds of quirky homes that bobble in the waves among the seabirds and seals. Structures range from psychedelic mural-splashed castles to dilapidated salt-sprayed shacks and immaculate three-story floating mansions. You can poke around the houseboat docks located off Bridgeway Blvd between Gate 5 and Gate 6½ Rds.

It's a tight-knit community, where residents tend sprawling dockside gardens and stop to chat on the creaky wooden boardwalks as they wheel their groceries home.

Etiquette tips for visitors: no smoking, no pets, no bicycles and no loud noise.

Bay Model Visitors Center
MUSEUM
(Map p126; ☑415-332-3871; www.spn.usace. army.mil/missions/recreation/baymodelvisitor center.asp; 2100 Bridgeway Blvd; ⊙9am-4pm Tue-Sat, extended summer hours 10am-5pm Sat & Sun; P⛴) FREE One of the coolest things in town, fascinating to both kids and adults, is the Army Corps of Engineers' solar-powered visitor center. Housed in one of the old (and cold!) Marinship warehouses, it's a 1.5-acre hydraulic model of San Francisco Bay and the delta region. Self-guided tours take you over and around it as the water flows.

Bay Area Discovery Museum
MUSEUM
(Map p126; ☑415-339-3900; www.baykidsmuseum.org; 557 McReynolds Rd; $14, 1st Wed each month free; ⊙9am-4pm Tue-Fri, to 5pm Sat & Sun, also 9am-4pm some Mon; P⛴) Below the north tower of the Golden Gate Bridge, at Fort Baker, this excellent hands-on activity museum is designed for children. Multilingual exhibits include a wave workshop, a small underwater tunnel and a large outdoor play area with a shipwreck to romp around. The museum's **Bean Sprouts Café** has healthy nibbles.

🏃 Activities

Sausalito is great for **bicycling**, whether for a leisurely ride around town, a trip across the Golden Gate Bridge or a longer-haul journey. From the ferry terminal, an easy option is to head south on Bridgeway Blvd, veering left on to East Rd toward the Bay Area Discovery Museum. Another nice route heads north along Bridgeway Blvd, then crosses under Hwy 101 to Mill Valley. At Blithedale Ave, you can veer east to Tiburon; a bike path parallels parts of Tiburon Blvd.

Sea Trek
KAYAKING, SUP
(Map p126; ☑415-332-8494; www.seatrek.com; 2100 Bridgeway; kayak or SUP set per hour from $25, tours from $75; ⊙9am-5pm Mon-Fri, 8:30am-5pm Sat & Sun Apr-Oct, 9am-4pm daily Nov-Mar) On a sunny day, Richardson Bay is irresistible. Kayaks and stand up paddleboard (SUP) sets can be rented here. No experience is necessary, and lessons and group outings are also available. Guided kayaking excursions include full-moon and starlight tours and an adventurous crossing to Angel Island. May through October is the best time to paddle.

Sausalito Bike Rentals
BICYCLE RENTAL
(☑415-331-2453, 415-332-8815; www.sausalito bikerentals.com; 34a Princess St; bicycle rental per hour from $15; ⊙9:30am-6:30pm; ⛴) Rents road, mountain, hybrid, tandem and electric bicycles by the hour or the day to explore the area.

🛏 Sleeping

Most of the lodgings in town charge a pretty penny, with a two-night minimum on weekends. On the outskirts of town, midrange chain motels and hotels line the Hwy 101 corridor.

Hotel Sausalito
HISTORIC HOTEL $$
(Map p126; ☑415-332-0700; www.hotelsausalito. com; 16 El Portal St; r from $175; P⊖❄🅖) Steps away from the ferry in the middle of downtown, this grand 1915 hotel has loads of period charm, paired with modern touches such as satellite TV, DVD player and MP3-player docking station. Each guest room is decorated in Mediterranean hues and some enjoy partial bay views. Parking is $20.

Inn Above Tide
BOUTIQUE HOTEL $$$
(Map p126; ☑415-332-9535; www.innabovetide. com; 30 El Portal; r $405-695; P⊖❄@🅖) Next to the ferry terminal, ensconce yourself in one of 31 modern and spacious rooms – most with private deck and wood-burning fireplace – that practically levitate over the water. There are envy-inducing bay views from your window; scan the horizon with the in-room binoculars. Free parking and loaner bicycles.

Gables Inn
INN $$$
(Map p126; ☑415-289-1100; www.gablesinn sausalito.com; 62 Princess St; r $190-545; P⊖@🅖) Tranquil and inviting, this inn has nine guest rooms in a historic 1869 home and six in a newer building. The more expensive rooms have Jacuzzi, fireplace and balcony with spectacular views, but even the smaller, cheaper rooms are stylish and tranquil. Evening wine and cheese included. Parking is $20.

🍴 Eating

Bridgeway Blvd is packed with moderately priced cafes, a few casual budget-priced options and many more expensive bay-view seafood restaurants.

Marin County

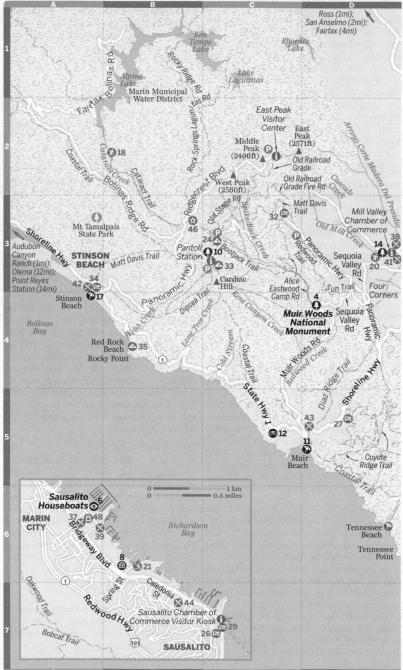

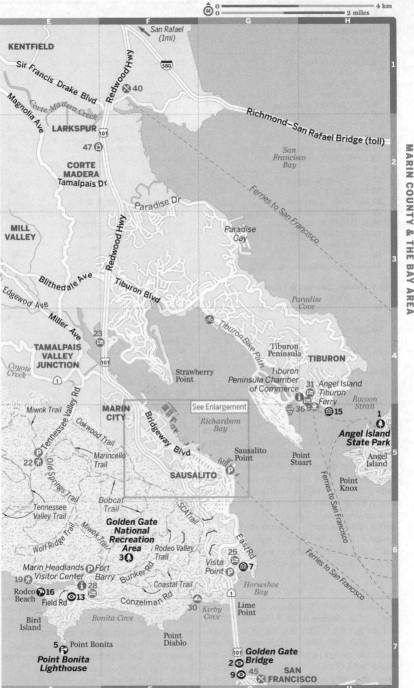

0 4 km
0 2 miles

KENTFIELD

Sir Francis Drake Blvd

Magnolia Ave

Corte Madera Creek

Redwood Hwy

San Rafael (1mi)

580

⊗ 40

Richmond–San Rafael Bridge (toll)

San Francisco Bay

LARKSPUR 101

47 🔒

Ferries to San Francisco

CORTE MADERA
Tamalpais Dr

Paradise Dr

MILL VALLEY

Paradise Cay

Redwood Hwy

Blithedale Ave

Tiburon Blvd

Paradise Cove

Edgewod Ave

Miller Ave

23

TAMALPAIS VALLEY JUNCTION

101

1

Tiburon Bike Path

Coyote Creek

Strawberry Point

Tiburon Peninsula

TIBURON

Tiburon Peninsula Chamber of Commerce

31 🚻 Angel Island Tiburon Ferry

🏛 15

Angel Island

Miwok Trail

Tennessee Valley Rd

Oakwood Trail

MARIN CITY

Bridgeway Blvd

See Enlargement

Richardson Bay

Sausalito Point

Point Stuart

Racoon Strait

1 🚶

Angel Island State Park

22 P

Marincello Trail

Old Springs Trail

SAUSALITO

P

Point Knox

Ferries to San Francisco

Tennessee Valley Trail

Bobcat Trail

Golden Gate National Recreation Area
3 🚶

SCA Trail

Wolf Ridge Trail

Miwok Trail

Rodeo Valley Trail

East Rd

25

7

Vista Point P

Ferries to San Francisco

Marin Headlands Visitor Center

P Fort Barry

Bunker Rd

Coastal Trail

Horseshoe Bay

19 🚶

🛈 28

Conzelman Rd

30

1

Lime Point

Rodeo Beach 16

Field Rd 13

Bonita Cove

Kirby Cove

Bird Island

5 🚶 Point Bonita

Point Diablo

Point Bonita Lighthouse

101 **Golden Gate Bridge**

2 ⊙

9 ◉ 45 ⊗

SAN FRANCISCO

Marin County

★ **Fish** SEAFOOD $$
(Map p126; ☎415-331-3474; www.331fish.com; 350 Harbor Dr; mains $17-36; ⊗11:30am-8:30pm; 🔊) 🅿 Chow down on seafood sandwiches, BBQ oysters or a Dungeness-crab roll at redwood picnic tables facing Richardson Bay. A local leader in promoting fresh and sustainably caught fish, this place has wonderful wild salmon in season and refuses to serve the farmed stuff. It's pricey, but so worth it. Cash only. Expect a queue. Limited menu available from 4:30pm to 5:30pm daily.

Avatar's INDIAN $$
(Map p126; ☎415-332-8083; www.enjoyavatars. com; 2656 Bridgeway Blvd; mains $13-20; ⊗11am-3pm & 5-9:30pm Mon-Sat; 🎤🔊) Boasting a cuisine of 'ethnic confusions,' the Indian-fusion dishes here incorporate Mexican, Italian and Caribbean ingredients and will bowl you over with flavor and creativity. Think Punjabi enchiladas with curried sweet potato or spinach fettucine with mild-curry tomato sauce. All diets (vegan, gluten-free etc) are graciously accommodated.

Sushi Ran JAPANESE $$$
(Map p126; ☎415-332-3620; http://sushiran.com; 107 Caledonia St; shared dishes $5-38; ⊗11:45am-2:30pm Mon-Fri, 5-10pm Sun-Thu, 5-11pm Fri & Sat) Many Marin residents claim this place is the best sushi spot around. If you didn't reserve ahead, the wine and sake bar next door eases the pain of the long wait for a table.

🛍 **Shopping**

Heath Ceramics HOMEWARES
(Map p126; ☎415-332-3732; www.heathceramics. com; 400 Gate 5 Rd; ⊗10am-6pm Mon-Wed, Fri & Sat, to 7pm Thu, 11am-6pm Sun) Near Sausalito's houseboat docks, this factory has been baking and glazing iconic dinnerware and home goods made of clay since 1959. Even chef Alice Waters adores the iconic earth-toned

place settings, which show arts-and-crafts styling. The showroom discounts overstock and seconds. Reserve ahead for free factory tours on Fridays, Saturdays and Sundays.

ℹ️ Information

Sausalito Chamber of Commerce (Map p126; ☑ 415-331-1093; www.sausalito.org; foot of El Portal St; ⊙ 10am–4pm) offers local information at a visitor kiosk by the ferry terminal.

ℹ️ Getting There & Away

Driving to Sausalito from San Francisco, take the Alexander Ave exit (the first exit after the Golden Gate Bridge) and follow the signs into downtown. There are five municipal parking lots in town, each charging varying rates; you can get three hours of free parking in the lot at the foot of Locust St, off Bridgeway Blvd. Street parking (metered or free, but time-limited) is difficult to find.

The ferry is a fun and easy way to travel to Sausalito. **Golden Gate Ferry** (☑ 415-455-2000, ☑ 511; http://goldengateferry.org) operates to and from San Francisco's Ferry Building ($11.75, 25 to 30 minutes) several times daily. **Blue & Gold Fleet** (☑ 415-705-8200; www.blueandgoldfleet.com) sails to Sausalito several times daily from the Fisherman's Wharf area in San Francisco ($11.50, 30 to 55 minutes). Both ferries operate year-round and transport bicycles for no additional charge.

Golden Gate Transit (☑ 415-455-2000, ☑ 511; www.goldengatetransit.org) bus 30 runs hourly to Sausalito from downtown San Francisco ($4.75, 40 to 55 minutes). On weekends and holidays, **West Marin Stagecoach** (☑ 415-226-0825; www.marintransit.org/stage.html) route 61 ($2) extends to Sausalito, with at least a few departures for Pantoll Station in Mt Tamalpais State Park, Stinson Beach and Bolinas. The seasonal **Muir Woods Shuttle** (Route 66F; www.marintransit.org; round-trip adult/child $5/free) connects with San Francisco ferries arriving in Sausalito before 3pm.

Tiburon

At the end of a small peninsula pointing out into the center of the bay, Tiburon is blessed with gorgeous views. The name comes from the Spanish Punta de Tiburon (Shark Point). Take the ferry from San Francisco, browse the shops on Main St, grab a bite to eat and you've seen Tiburon. The town is also a jumping-off point for nearby Angel Island.

The central part of town is comprised of Tiburon Blvd, Juanita Lane and charming Main St. Main St, which is also known as Ark Row, is where the old houseboats have taken root on dry land and metamorphosed into classy shops and boutiques.

⊙ Sights & Activities

Railroad & Ferry Depot Museum   MUSEUM
(Map p126; ☑ 415-435-1853; http://landmarkssociety.com; 1920 Paradise Dr; suggested donation $5; ⊙ 1–4pm Wed-Sun Apr-Oct) Formerly the terminus for a 3000-person ferry to San Francisco and a railroad that once reached north to Ukiah, this late 19th-century building showcases a scale model of Tiburon's commercial hub, c 1900. The restored stationmaster's quarters can be visited upstairs.

Bay Cruises   CRUISE
(Map p126; ☑ 415-435-2131; http://angelislandferry.com; 21 Main St; 90min cruise adult/child $20/10; ⊙ usually 6:30-8pm Fri & Sat mid-May–mid-Oct) The Angel Island Tiburon Ferry (p130) runs San Francisco Bay sunset cruises on weekend evenings in summer and fall. Reserve ahead and bring your own picnic dinner to enjoy outside on the deck.

🛌 Sleeping

Tiburon has only a couple of places to stay downtown. Midrange motels and chain hotels line Hwy 101.

Lodge at Tiburon   HOTEL $$
(Map p126; ☑ 415-435-3133; www.lodgeattiburon.com; 1651 Tiburon Blvd; r from $225; 🅿️ ❄️ 🐾 @ 📶 ⛱️ 🏊) 🐾 Now a stylish and comfortable contemporary hotel, concrete hallways and staircases testify to the more basic motel it once was. The best value in town, it's a short stroll to anywhere – including the ferry – and there's a pool, DVD library, tavern, rental bikes, free parking and a rooftop deck with fireplace and heady Mt Tamalpais views.

Waters Edge Hotel   BOUTIQUE HOTEL $$$
(Map p126; ☑ 415-789-5999; www.watersedgehotel.com; 25 Main St; r from $269; 🅿️ ❄️ @ 📶) 🐾 At this hotel, with its deck extending over the bay, tasteful rooms have an elegant minimalism that combines comfort and style. Rooms with rustic, high wood ceilings are quite romantic and all afford bay views. Complimentary bicycles and evening wine and cheese included. Parking is $15.

✗ Eating

Downtown, Tiburon Blvd and Main St offer several cafes and restaurants, mostly pricey and unsatisfying.

Sam's Anchor Cafe   SEAFOOD $$
(Map p126; ☑ 415-435-4527; www.samscafe.com; 27 Main St; mains $13-25; ⊘ 11am-9:30pm Mon-Fri, from 9:30am Sat & Sun; ⬛) Sam's has been slinging seafood and burgers since 1920, and though the entrance looks like a shambling little shack, the area out back has fantastic waterfront views. On a warm afternoon, you can't beat a cocktail or a tasty plate of sautéed prawns on the deck.

ⓘ Information

Tiburon Peninsula Chamber of Commerce (Map p126; ☑ 415-435-5633; www.tiburon chamber.org; 96b Main St) provides area information.

ⓘ Getting There & Away

On Hwy 101, look for the off-ramp for Tiburon Blvd/E Blithedale Ave/Hwy 131. Drive about 4 miles east to downtown, where Tiburon Blvd intersects Main St.

Golden Gate Transit (p129) commuter bus 8 runs direct between San Francisco and Tiburon ($5.50, 60 to 80 minutes) once or twice on weekdays.

Blue & Gold Fleet (p129) sails several times daily from San Francisco's Pier 41 or 39 to Tiburon ($11.50, 30 to 50 minutes). Golden Gate Ferry (p129) connects San Francisco's Ferry Building with Tiburon ($11.50, 30 minutes) during weekday commuter hours only. You can transport bicycles for free on both ferry services.

In downtown Tiburon, the smaller **Angel Island Tiburon Ferry** (Map p126; ☑ 415-435-2131; http://angelislandferry.com; 21 Main St; round-trip adult/child/bicycle $15/13/1; ⬛) departs from a nearby dock.

Sir Francis Drake Boulevard & Around

The towns along and nearby the Sir Francis Drake Blvd corridor – including Larkspur, Corte Madera, Ross, San Anselmo and Fairfax – evoke charmed small-town life, even though things get busy around Hwy 101.

Starting from the eastern section in **Larkspur**, window-shop along Magnolia Ave or explore the redwoods in nearby **Baltimore Canyon**. On the east side of the freeway is the hulking mass of **San Quentin State Penitentiary**, California's oldest and most notorious prison, founded in 1852.

Take the bicycle and pedestrian bridge from the ferry terminal across the road to the **Marin Country Mart**, a shopping center with a excellent eateries and outdoor seating. One favorite is the **Marin Brewing Company** (Map p126; ☑ 415-461-4677; www. marinbrewing.com; 1809 Larkspur Landing Cirle, Larkspur; mains $11-15; ⊘ 11:30am-midnight Sun-Thu, to 1am Fri & Sat; ⬛⬛) brewpub, where you can see the glassed-in kettles behind the bar. The head brewer, Arne Johnson, has won many awards, and the Mt Tam Pale Ale complements the menu of pizza, burgers and hearty sandwiches.

Just south, **Corte Madera** is home to one of the Bay Area's best bookstores, **Book Passage** (Map p126; ☑ 415-927-0960; www.bookpassage. com; 51 Tamal Vista Blvd; ⊘ 9am-9pm; ⬛), in the Marketplace shopping center. It has a strong travel section, and frequent readings.

West along Sir Francis Drake, **San Anselmo** is a cute downtown area along San Anselmo Ave. The attractive center of neighboring **Fairfax** has ample dining and shopping options, and cyclists congregate at **Gestalt Haus Fairfax** (☑ 415-721-7895; https://gestalthausoffairfax.com; 28 Bolinas Rd, Fairfax; ⊘ 11:30am-10pm Mon, to 11pm Tue, to midnight Wed & Thu, to 2am Fri & Sat, to 9pm Sun) for the indoor bicycle parking, board games, European draft beers and sausages.

Six miles east of Olema on Sir Francis Drake Blvd, **Samuel P Taylor State Park** (☑ 415-488-9897; www.parks.ca.gov; 8889 Sir Francis Drake Blvd, Lagunitas; per car $8; ⊘ 8am-sunset; ⓟ⬛) has beautiful, secluded campsites in redwood groves and a coveted handful of new five-person cabins with electricity and wood stoves. The park's also located on the paved **Cross Marin Trail**, with miles of creekside landscape to explore along a former railroad grade.

San Rafael

The oldest and largest town in Marin, San Rafael is slightly less upscale than most of its neighbors but doesn't lack atmosphere. It's a common stop for travelers on their way to Point Reyes. Two blocks south of the 19th-century Spanish Catholic mission that gives the town its name, San Rafael's main drag, 4th St, is lined with cafes and shops. If you follow it west out of downtown San Rafael, it meets Sir Francis Drake Blvd and continues west to the coast. Just north of San Rafael, Lucas Valley Rd heads west toward Nicasio, passing George Lucas' Skywalker Ranch.

⊙ Sights

Marin County Civic Center ARCHITECTURE
(☑415-473-3762; www.marincounty.org/depts/cu/tours; 3501 Civic Center Dr; tour adult/child $10/5; ⊘10am-6pm Mon-Fri, guided tour 10:30am Wed; [P]) Although he didn't live to see it built, this was architect Frank Lloyd Wright's final commission. He designed the horizontal hilltop buildings to flow with the natural beauty of the county's landscape, with sky-blue roofs and sand-colored walls. Show up on Wednesday morning for a one-hour guided tour or access the prerecorded audioguide and self-guiding tour brochure online anytime.

China Camp State Park PARK
(☑415-456-0766; https://friendsofchinacamp.org; San Pedro Rd; per car $5; ⊘8am-sunset; [P][⊞]) About 6 miles northeast of San Rafael, this is a pleasant place to stop for a picnic or short hike. From Hwy 101, take the N San Pedro Rd exit and continue east. A Chinese shrimp-fishing village once stood here and a small museum exhibits interesting artifacts from the 19th-century settlement.

🛏 Sleeping

Midrange motels and hotels hug Hwy 101 on the outskirts of town.

China Camp State Park Campground CAMPGROUND $
(☑reservations 800-444-7275; www.reserveamerica.com; 730 N San Pedro Rd; tent sites $35; [P]) Pretty waterfront park with 31 walk-in campsites. It has pleasant shade and coin-op hot showers.

🍴 Eating

Downtown overflows with restaurants and cafes, all within walking distance of each other. Start exploring along 4th St.

★**Sunday Marin Farmers Market** MARKET $
(☑415-472-6100; http://agriculturalinstitute.org; 3501 Civic Center Dr; ⊘8am-1pm Sun; [P][⊅][⊞]) 🍴 Nowhere else in Marin County do as many farmers, ranchers, fishers and gourmet-food makers gather than at this Sunday-morning farmers market, happening rain or shine at the Marin Civic Center off Hwy 101. Browse the season's most luscious fruit, freshest vegetables, richest honey and cheeses, aromatic

breads, colorful flowers and even handmade art, jewelry and crafts. With almost 200 vendors, it's the third-largest farmers market in California.

Sol Food PUERTO RICAN $$
(☑415-451-4765; www.solfoodrestaurant.com; 903 Lincoln Ave; mains $8-17; ⊘9am-midnight Sun-Thu, to 1am Fri & Sat) 🍴 Lazy ceiling fans, tropical plants and the pulse of Latin rhythms create a soothing atmosphere for delicious dishes such as a *jíbaro* sandwich with thinly sliced steak and other island-inspired meals concocted with plantains, organic veggies and free-range meats.

State Room CALIFORNIAN $$
(☑415-295-7929; http://stateroombrewery.com; 1132 4th St; mains $15-25; ⊘11:30am-10pm Sun & Tue-Wed, to midnight Thu-Sat) Wood-fired pizzas, fresh market salads and create-your-own burgers stacked hands high will sate your grumbling stomach at this downtown brewery, bar and kitchen. Serious cocktails and draft beers, ciders and barley wine on tap.

☆ Entertainment

Smith Rafael Film Center CINEMA
(☑415-454-1222; http://rafaelfilm.cafilm.org; 1118 4th St; tickets $8.50-11.25) Innovative art-house programming on three screens in state-of-the-art surroundings in a restored cinema.

ℹ Information

Marin Convention & Visitors Bureau (☑415-925-2060; www.visitmarin.org; 1 Mitchell Blvd; ⊘9am-5pm Mon-Fri) Provides tourist information for the entire county.

ℹ Getting There & Away

Several Golden Gate Transit (p129) buses operate between San Francisco and the San Rafael Transit Center at 3rd and Hetherton Sts ($6.75, one hour). From the transit center, local buses ($2) run by Golden Gate Transit and **Marin Transit** (☑415-455-2000, ☑511; www.marintransit.org) fan out across the county.

For ambitious cyclists, the Cal Park Hill Tunnel is a safe subterranean passage from Larkspur – a terminus for Golden Gate Ferry (p129) services from San Francisco – to San Rafael.

Mill Valley

Nestled under the redwoods at the base of Mt Tamalpais, tiny Mill Valley is one of the Bay Area's most picturesque hamlets. Mill

WORTH A TRIP

ANGEL ISLAND

Angel Island (Map p126; ☏415-435-5390; www.parks.ca.gov; ♿) **FREE**, in San Francisco Bay, has a mild climate with fresh bay breezes, which makes it pleasant for hiking and cycling. For a unique treat, picnic in a protected cove overlooking the surrounding cities. The island history is apparent in its unique buildings – it was a hunting and fishing ground for the Miwok people, served as a military base, an immigration station, a WWII Japanese internment camp and a Nike missile site. There are 12 miles of roads and trails around the island, including a hike to the summit of 781ft **Mt Livermore** (no bicycles) and a 5-mile perimeter trail.

The **Immigration Station** (USIS; ☏415-435-5537; www.aiisf.org/visit; adult/child $5/3, incl tour $7/5, cash only; ⊙11am-3pm Wed-Sun), which operated from 1910 to 1940, was the Ellis Island of the West Coast. But this facility was primarily a screening and detention center for Chinese immigrants, who were at that time restricted from entering the US under the **Chinese Exclusion Act**. Many detainees were cruelly held for long periods before ultimately being sent home. The mournful Chinese poetry etched into the barrack walls is a heartbreaking testament to their trials. The site is now a museum with excellent interpretive exhibits; tours include admission fees and can be reserved ahead or purchased on-site.

Sea Trek (p125) runs kayaking excursions around the island. You can rent bicycles (per hour/day $12.50/40) at **Ayala Cove**, and there are **tram tours** ($15) around the island. Tour schedules vary seasonally; go to www.angelisland.com for information.

You can camp on the island, and when the last ferry sails for the night, the place is your own – except for the very persistent raccoons. The dozen hike-, bicycle- or kayak-in **campsites** (☏reservations 800-444-7275; www.reserveamerica.com; tent sites from $30) are usually reserved months in advance. Near the ferry dock, there's a cafe serving sandwiches and snacks.

Getting There & Away

All ferry tickets are sold on a first-come, first-served basis.

From San Francisco's Pier 41, take a Blue & Gold Fleet (p129) ferry (one-way adult/child $9/4.75). There are at least three or four daily sailings year-round.

From Tiburon, take the Angel Island Tiburon Ferry (p130), which runs daily from April to September (weekends only November to March). As you board, pay fares (one-way adult/child $9/4.75) by cash or check only.

Valley was originally a logging town, its name stemming from an 1830s sawmill – the first in the Bay Area to provide lumber. Though the 1892 Mill Valley Lumber Company still greets motorists on Miller Ave, the town is a vastly different place today, packed with wildly expensive homes, luxury cars and pricey boutiques.

Mill Valley once served as the starting point for the scenic railway that carried visitors up Mt Tamalpais. The tracks were removed in 1940 and today the Depot Bookstore & Cafe occupies the former rail station.

🏃 Activities

⭐**Dipsea Trail**   HIKING
(Map p126; www.dipsea.org) A beloved though demanding hike, the 7-mile Dipsea Trail climbs over the coastal range and down to Stinson Beach, cutting through a corner of Muir Woods (p135). This classic trail starts at **Old Mill Park** (Map p126; ☏415-383-1370; www.cityofmillvalley.org; Throckmorton Ave & Cascade Dr; ⊙dawn-dusk; ♿) with a climb up 676 steps in three separate flights, and includes a few more ups and downs before reaching the ocean.

The few slaloms between staircases aren't well-signed, but locals can point the way. West Marin Stagecoach (p129) route-61 buses run from Stinson Beach back to Mill Valley at least a few times every day, making it a doable one-way day hike. You can refill water bottles and grab a snack at **Muir Woods Trading Company** (Map p126; ☏415-388-7059; www.muirwoodstradingcompany.com; 1 Muir Woods Rd, Mill Valley; items $2-11; ⊙8am-5pm; ♿) 🌿 cafe, about a 2-mile hike from Mill Valley, or start or end the trail there instead.

★ Festivals & Events

Mill Valley Film Festival   FILM
(☑ 415-383-5256; www.mvff.com; adult/child per film $15/10; ☺ Oct) In October look for an innovative, internationally regarded program of independent films screened in Mill Valley and San Rafael.

🛏 Sleeping

Lackluster midrange motels stand beside Hwy 101. Boutique hotels and inns shelter by the waterfront and on the forested hillsides around Mt Tamalpais.

Acqua Hotel   BOUTIQUE HOTEL $$
(Map p126; ☑ 415-380-0400; www.marinhotels.com; 555 Redwood Hwy; r from $229; ⓟ☺✴@🛜🐕) With views of the bay and Mt Tamalpais, and a lobby with a welcoming fireplace, this boutique hotel doesn't lack for eye candy. Contemporary rooms are sleekly designed with beautiful fabrics and aromatherapy bath products. Perks include free loaner bikes for guests and a morning espresso bar and evening wine service.

Mountain Home Inn   INN $$$
(Map p126; ☑ 415-381-9000; www.mtnhomeinn.com; 810 Panoramic Hwy; r $195-345; ☺🛜) Set amid redwood, spruce and pine trees on a ridge of Mt Tamalpais, this retreat is both modern and rustic. The larger (more expensive) rooms are rugged beauties, with unfinished timbers forming columns from floor to ceiling, as though the forest is shooting up through the floor. Smaller rooms are cozy dens for two. The positioning of a good local trail map on each dresser makes it clear that it's a place to breathe and unwind. West Marin Stagecoach (p129) route 61 stops at the inn.

🍴 Eating

You'll find a handful of cafes and restaurants downtown.

Depot Bookstore & Cafe   CAFE $
(Map p126; ☑ 415-383-2665; http://depotbookstore.com; 87 Throckmorton Ave; mains $5-10; ☺ cafe 7am-7pm, bookstore from 8am; 🛜) Smack in the town center, Depot serves coffee and espresso drinks, sandwiches, soups and baked goods. The bookstore sells lots of local publications, including trail guides.

Mill Valley Beerworks   GASTROPUB $$
(Map p126; ☑ 415-888-8218; www.millvalleybeerworks.com; 173 Throckmorton Ave; dinner mains $18-30; ☺ 5:30-9pm Sun & Mon, to 9:30pm Tue-Thu, to 10:30pm Fri & Sat, also 11:30am-3pm Sat & Sun) With hard-to-find bottled brews and a few of its own (from Fort Point Beer Company in San Francisco) among the dozen or so on tap, here beer-lovers can pair their favorites with the kitchen's delicious farm-to-table cooking. The unsigned seating is stark and stylish, with a pressed-tin wall and chalkboards above the bar.

ℹ Information

Mill Valley Chamber of Commerce (Map p126; ☑ 415-388-9700; www.enjoymillvalley.com; 85 Throckmorton Ave; ☺10am-4pm Tue-Sat) Offers tourist information and maps.

ℹ Getting There & Away

From San Francisco or Sausalito, take Hwy 101 north to the Mill Valley/Stinson Beach/Hwy 1 exit. Follow Hwy 1/Shoreline Hwy to Almonte Blvd (which becomes Miller Ave), then follow Miller Ave into downtown Mill Valley.

From the north, take the E Blithedale Ave exit from Hwy 101, then head west into downtown Mill Valley.

Golden Gate Transit (p129) bus 4 runs directly from San Francisco to Mill Valley ($4.75, one hour, every 20 to 60 minutes) on weekdays. Marin Transit (p131) route 17 ($2, 30 minutes, every 30 to 60 minutes) connects Mill Valley with the Sausalito ferry terminal daily.

Mt Tamalpais State Park

Standing guard over Marin County, majestic Mt Tamalpais (Mt Tam) has breathtaking 360-degree views of ocean, bay and hills rolling into the distance. The rich, natural beauty of the 2572ft mountain and its surrounding area is inspiring – especially considering it lies within an hour's drive from one of the state's largest metropolitan areas.

Mt Tamalpais State Park (Map p126; ☑ 415-388-2070; www.parks.ca.gov; per car $8; ☺7am-sunset; ⓟ♿) was formed in 1930, partly from land donated by congressman and naturalist William Kent (who also donated the land that became Muir Woods National Monument in 1907). Its 6300 acres are home to deer, foxes, bobcats and 60 miles of hiking and mountain-biking trails.

Mt Tam was a sacred place to the Coast Miwok people for thousands of years before the arrival of European and American settlers. By the late 19th century, San Franciscans were escaping the bustle of the city with all-day outings on the mountain, and in 1896 the 'world's crookedest railroad' (281 turns) was completed from Mill Valley to the summit. Though the railroad was closed in 1930, Old Railroad Grade is today one of Mt Tam's most popular and scenic hiking and cycling paths.

🏃 Activities

Panoramic Hwy climbs from Mill Valley through the park to Stinson Beach. From Pantoll Station, it's 4.2 miles by car to **East Peak Summit**; take Pantoll Rd and then panoramic Ridgecrest Blvd to the top. A 10-minute hike leads to a fire lookout at the very top and awesome sea-to-bay views.

Mountain Biking

Cyclists must stay on the fire roads (and off the single-track trails) and keep to speeds under 15mph. Rangers are prickly about these rules and a ticket can result in a steep fine.

The most popular ride is the Old Railroad Grade from Mill Valley to Mt Tam's East Peak. Alternatively, from just west of Pantoll Station, cyclists can take either the **Deer Park Fire Road**, which runs close to the Dipsea Trail through giant redwoods to the main entrance of Muir Woods, or the aptly named **Coast View Trail**, which joins Hwy 1 north of Muir Beach Overlook. Both options require a return to Mill Valley via Frank Valley/Muir Woods Rd, which climbs steadily (800ft) to Panoramic Hwy, then becomes Sequoia Valley Rd as it drops toward Mill Valley.

For more information on bicycle routes and rules, contact the Marin County Bicycle Coalition (p124); its *Marin Bicycle Map* ($10) is the gold standard for local cycling.

Old Railroad Grade   MOUNTAIN BIKING

For a sweaty, 6-mile, 2500ft climb, start in Mill Valley at the end of W Blithedale Ave and cycle up to East Peak. For a head start, begin part way up at the Mountain Home Inn instead and follow Gravity Car Rd to the Old Railroad Grade, an easy half-hour ride to the summit.

Hiking

The park map is a smart investment as there are a dozen worthwhile hiking trails, including to Cataract Falls.

From Pantoll Station, the **Steep Ravine Trail** follows a wooded creek on to the coast (about 2.1 miles each way). For a longer hike, veer right (northwest) after 1.5 miles on to the Dipsea Trail (p132), which meanders

through trees for 1 mile before ending at Stinson Beach. Grab some lunch, then walk north through town and follow signs for the **Matt Davis Trail**, which leads 2.7 miles back to Pantoll Station, making a good loop. The Matt Davis Trail continues on beyond Pantoll Station, wrapping gently around the mountain with superb views.

Cataract Falls & Alpine Lake   HIKING

(Map p126) A worthy hiking option on Mt Tam is the **Cataract Trail**, which runs along Cataract Creek. From the trailhead along Pantoll Rd, it's less than 3 miles to Alpine Lake. The last mile or so is a spectacular rooty staircase that descends alongside Cataract Falls, at its prettiest immediately after winter or spring rainfall.

🛌 Sleeping

★ Steep Ravine   CAMPGROUND, CABIN $

(Map p126; 🖉 reservations 800-444-7275; www. reserveamerica.com; tent sites $25, cabins $100; ☺ Nov-Sep; 🅿) Just off Hwy 1, about 1 mile south of Stinson Beach, this jewel has seven primitive beachfront campsites and nine rustic five-person cabins with woodstoves overlooking the ocean. Both options book up far in advance; reservations can be made up to seven months ahead.

Bootjack Campground   CAMPGROUND $

(Map p126; 🖉 info 415-388-2070; www.parks. ca.gov; Panoramic Hwy; tent sites $25; 🅿 🐾) The 15 first-come, first-served walk-in campsites are right on two of the park's best hiking trails and adjacent to Redwood Creek, with open vistas to the south. It's 0.3 miles northeast of Pantoll Station.

Pantoll Campground   CAMPGROUND $

(Map p126; 🖉 info 415-388-2070; www.parks. ca.gov; Panoramic Hwy; tent sites $25; 🅿 🐾) From the parking lot it's only a 100yd walk or cycle to the campground, with 16 first-come, first-served woodsy tent sites, fire pits, picnic tables and potable water, but no showers.

☆ Entertainment

Mountain Theater   THEATER

(Cushing Memorial Amphitheater; Map p126; 🖉 415-383-1100; www.mountainplay.org; off Pantoll Rd; adult/child $40/25; ☺ late May–mid-Jun; ♿) Built by the Civilian Conservation Corps in the 1930s, the park's natural-stone, 3750-seat theater hosts the annual 'Mountain Play' series on weekend afternoons in late spring and early summer. Free shuttles run from Mill Valley; otherwise, parking is $15 to $20.

❶ Information

Pantoll Station (Map p126; ☑ 415-388-2070; www.parks.ca.gov; 801 Panoramic Hwy; ⊙ hours vary; ⛨) The park headquarters. Detailed park maps are sold here.

East Peak Visitor Center (Map p126; www. friendsofmttam.org; off Ridgecrest Blvd; ⊙ 11am-4pm Sat & Sun) Small center with nature and historical exhibits and a gift shop.

❶ Getting There & Away

To reach Pantoll Station by car, take Hwy 1 to the Panoramic Hwy and look for the signs. Panoramic Hwy climbs from Mill Valley through the park, then winds downhill to Stinson Beach.

West Marin Stagecoach (p129) route 61 runs a few times daily on weekdays from Marin City via Mill Valley (more frequent weekend and holiday service from the Sausalito ferry terminal) to Pantoll Station ($2, 55 minutes).

Muir Woods National Monument

Walking through an awesome stand of the world's tallest trees is an experience to be had only in Northern California and a small part of southern Oregon. The old-growth redwoods at **Muir Woods** (Map p126; ☑ 415-388-2595; www.nps.gov/muwo; 1 Muir Woods Rd, Mill Valley; adult/child $10/free; ⊙ 8am-8pm mid-Mar–mid-Sep, to 7pm mid-Sep–early Oct, to 6pm Feb–mid-Mar & early Oct-early Nov, to 5pm early Nov-Jan; ℙ⛨) ⌁, just 12 miles north of the Golden Gate Bridge, make up the closest redwood stand to San Francisco. The trees were initially eyed by loggers, and Redwood Creek, as the area was known, seemed ideal for a dam. Those plans were halted when congressman and naturalist William Kent bought a section of Redwood Creek and, in 1907, donated 295 acres to the federal government. President Theodore Roosevelt made the site a national monument in 1908, the name honoring John Muir, naturalist and founder of environmental organization the Sierra Club.

Muir Woods can become quite crowded, especially on weekends. Try to come midweek, early in the morning or late in the afternoon, when tour buses are less of a problem. Even at busy times, a short hike will get you out of the densest crowds and onto trails with huge trees and stunning vistas. A lovely cafe, **Muir Woods Trading Company** (Map p126; ☑ 415-

388-7059; www.muirwoodstradingcompany.com; items $2-11; ⊙ 8am-5pm; ⛨) ⌁ serves local and organic goodies and hot drinks that hit the spot on foggy days.

🏃 Activities

The 1-mile Main Trail Loop is a gentle walk alongside Redwood Creek to the 1000-year-old trees at **Cathedral Grove**; it returns via **Bohemian Grove**, where the tallest tree in the park stands 254ft high. The **Dipsea Trail** is a good 2-mile hike up to the top of aptly named Cardiac Hill.

You can also walk down into Muir Woods by taking trails from the Panoramic Hwy, such as the **Bootjack Trail** from the Bootjack picnic area, or from Mt Tamalpais' Pantoll Station campground, along the **Ben Johnson Trail**.

❶ Getting There & Away

The parking lot is insanely full during busy periods, so consider taking the seasonal **Muir Woods Shuttle** (p129) from Sausalito, where ferries from San Francisco arrive.

To get there by car, drive north on Hwy 101, exit at Hwy 1 and continue north along Hwy 1/ Shoreline Hwy to the Panoramic Hwy (a right-hand fork). Follow that for about 1 mile to Four Corners, where you turn left on to Muir Woods Rd (there are plenty of signs).

Muir Beach

Muir Beach is a quiet hamlet with a pretty beach and superb views up and down the coast from an overlook just north of town. For visitors, it's a quick stop between visiting Muir Woods and Stinson Beach.

◉ Sights

Muir Beach Overlook   VIEWPOINT
(Map p126; www.nps.gov/goga/planyourvisit/ muirbeach.htm; Shoreline Hwy; ℙ) Just over a mile north of Pelican Inn (p136) along Hwy 1, there are superb coastal views from this overlook. During WWII scouts kept watch from the surrounding concrete lookouts for invading Japanese ships.

Muir Beach   BEACH
(Map p126; www.nps.gov/goga/planyourvisit/ muirbeach.htm; off Pacific Way; ℙ⛨) ⌁ Restored wetlands, creeks, lagoons and sand dunes provide habitat for birds, California red-legged frogs and coho salmon. In winter you might spot monarch butterflies roosting in

a small grove of Monterey pines and migratory whales swimming offshore. The turnoff from Hwy 1 is next to the coast's longest row of mailboxes at Mile 5.7, just before Pelican Inn.

🛏 Sleeping & Eating

Most people visit Muir Beach on a day trip from San Francisco.

Green Gulch LODGE $$
(Map p126; ☑415-383-3134; www.sfzc.org/green gulch; 1601 Shoreline Hwy; s $100-175, d $175-250, incl all meals; P🐾@🗟) 🍃 In the hills above Muir Beach, this Zen Buddhist retreat center's contemporary accommodations are restful. Delicious buffet-style vegetarian meals are included.

Pelican Inn PUB FOOD $$$
(Map p126; ☑415-383-6000; www.pelicaninn. com; 10 Pacific Way; dinner mains $18-36; ⊙8-11am Sat & Sun, 11:30am-3pm & 5:30-9pm daily; 🍴) The oh-so-English Pelican Inn is Muir Beach's only commercial establishment. Hikers, cyclists and families come for pub lunches inside its timbered restaurant and cozy bar, perfect for a pint, a game of darts and warming up beside the open fire. The food is nothing mind-blowing and the service is hit or miss, but the setting is magical. Upstairs are seven cozy rooms (from $225) with half-canopy beds.

Stinson Beach

Just 5 miles north of Muir Beach, Stinson Beach is positively buzzing on warm weekends. The town flanks Hwy 1 for about three blocks and is densely packed with galleries, shops, eateries and B&Bs. The beach is often blanketed with fog, and when the sun's shining it's blanketed with surfers, families and gawkers. There are views of Point Reyes and San Francisco on clear days, and the beach is long enough for an invigorating stroll.

⊙ Sights

Stinson Beach BEACH
(Map p126; ☑415-868-0942; www.nps.gov/goga; off Hwy 1; ⊙ from 9am daily, closing time varies seasonally; P🍴) Three-mile-long Stinson Beach is a popular surf spot, with swimming advised from late May to mid-September only. For updated weather and surf conditions call ☑415-868-1922. The beach is one block

west of Hwy 1. There's free parking but the lot often fills up before noon on sunny days.

Martin Griffin Preserve WILDLIFE RESERVE
(☑415-868-9244; www.egret.org; 4900 Shoreline Hwy; suggested donation $20; ⊙hours vary; P🍴) 🍃 One of four regional Audubon Canyon Ranch preserves hides in the hills above Bolinas Lagoon. It's a major nesting ground for great blue herons and great egrets; viewing scopes are set up behind blinds where you can watch these magnificent birds congregate to nest and hatch their chicks in tall redwoods. At low tide, harbor seals often doze on sandbars in the lagoon. Confirm hours, which vary seasonally, before visiting. It's 3 miles north of Stinson Beach on Hwy 1.

🛏 Sleeping & Eating

Sandpiper Lodging MOTEL, CABIN $$
(Map p126; ☑415-868-1632; www.sandpiperstin sonbeach.com; 1 Marine Way; r $165-180, cabins $220-250, cottages $350; P🍴🗟) Just off Hwy 1 and a quick stroll to the beach, these nine comfortable rooms, cabins and cottage all have gas fireplace and kitchenette, and are ensconced in a lush garden and picnic area. Two-night minimum stay on weekends and holidays between April and October.

Parkside AMERICAN, BAKERY $$
(Map p126; ☑415-868-1272; www.parksidecafe. com; 43 Arenal Ave; mains $9-28; ⊙7:30am-9pm, coffee bar from 6am; 🍴🍴) 🍃 Famous for its hearty breakfasts and lunches, this cozy eatery next to the beach serves wood-fired pizzas and excellent coastal cuisine such as Tomales Bay oysters and king salmon at dinner, when reservations are recommended. Popular with beachgoers, hikers and cyclists, Parkside's outdoor snack bar serves burgers, fruit smoothies, baked goods and ice cream.

❶ Getting There & Away

By car from San Francisco, it's nearly an hour's drive, though on weekends plan for toe-tapping traffic delays.

West Marin Stagecoach (p129) route 61 runs a few daily minibuses ($2) from Marin City (one hour), with more frequent weekend and holiday services connecting with Sausalito ferries (75 minutes).

Bolinas

For a town that is so famously unexcited about tourism, Bolinas offers some fairly tempting attractions for the visitor. Known as Jugville during the gold-rush days, the sleepy beachside community is home to writers, musicians and fisherfolk, and deliberately hard to find. The highway department used to put signs up at the turnoff from Hwy 1; locals kept taking them down, so the highway department finally gave up.

◉ Sights & Activities

Palomarin Field Station   NATURE CENTER
(☑ 415-868-0655; www.pointblue.org; 999 Mesa Rd; ☺ sunrise-sunset; ℙ ⚑) ✆ FREE Formerly Point Reyes Bird Observatory, Point Blue's Palomarin Field Station has bird-banding and netting demonstrations, an unstaffed visitor center and a nature trail. Banding demonstrations are held in the morning Tuesday to Sunday from May through late November, and on Wednesday, Saturday and Sunday the rest of the year. Show up between 8am and 11am for the best bird-watching.

★**Bass Lake & Alamere Falls Trail**   HIKING
(www.nps.gov/pore) At the end of Mesa Rd, the Palomarin parking lot accesses various hiking trails in the southern part of Point Reyes National Seashore (p139), including the easy (and popular) 3-mile trail to lovely **Bass Lake**. Continuing another 1.5 miles northwest, you'll reach an unmaintained trail to **Alamere Falls**, a fantastic flume plunging 50ft off a cliff and on to the beach.

A sweet inland spot buffered by tall trees, small Bass Lake is perfect for a swim on a toasty day. You can dive in wearing your birthday suit (or not), bring an inner tube to float about, or do a long lap all the way across.

Approaching Alamere Falls, sketchy beach access may make it more enjoyable to hike another 1.5 miles along the trail to Wildcat Beach, then backtrack a mile south on sand.

2 Mile Surf Shop   SURFING
(☑ 415-868-0264, surf report 415-868-2412; www.2milesurf.com; 22 Brighton Ave; ☺ 9am-6pm May-Oct, 10am-5pm Nov-Apr, closed Wed Jan-Mar) Surfing's popular in these parts, and this shop behind the post office rents boards and wet suits and also gives lessons.

Agate Beach County Park   BEACH
(www.marincounty.org; end of Elm Rd; ☺ dawn-dusk) Meander by tide pools along the coastline at Agate Beach, around the end of Duxbury Point. Collecting rocks, shells or marine life is prohibited.

🛏 Sleeping & Eating

Smiley's Saloon & Hotel   INN $$
(☑ 415-868-1311; http://smileyssaloon.com; 41 Wharf Rd; r $135-225; 🛜 🐾) A crusty old place dating to 1851, Smiley's has simple but decent rooms (no TV or phone), and last-minute weekday rates can be a bargain. The bar, which serves some food, has live bands on weekends and is frequented by plenty of salty dogs and grizzled deadheads.

Coast Cafe   AMERICAN $$
(☑ 415-868-2298; www.coastcafebolinas.com; 46 Wharf Rd; dinner mains $15-32; ☺ 11:30am-3pm & 5-8pm Tue-Thu, to 9pm Fri, 8am-3pm & 5-9pm Sat, to 8pm Sun; ⚑) ✆ The only 'real' restaurant in town. Everyone jockeys for outdoor seats among the flower boxes for fish-and-chips, barbecued oysters, or buttermilk pancakes with damn good coffee. Live music on Thursday and Sunday nights.

❶ Getting There & Away

By car, follow Hwy 1 north from Stinson Beach and turn west for Bolinas at the first road north of the lagoon. At the first stop sign, take another left on to Olema–Bolinas Rd and follow it 2 miles to town.

West Marin Stagecoach (p129) route 61 travels a few times daily from the Marin City transit hub (more frequent weekend and holiday service connects with the Sausalito ferry) to downtown Bolinas ($2).

Olema & Nicasio

Near the junction of Hwy 1 and Sir Francis Drake Blvd, Olema was the main settlement in west Marin in the 1860s. Back then, there was stagecoach service to San Rafael and *six* saloons. In 1875, when the railroad was built through Point Reyes Station instead of Olema, the town's importance began to fade.

About a 15-minute drive inland from Olema, at the geographic center of Marin County, is Nicasio, a tiny town with a low-key rural flavor.

The **Bolinas Ridge Trail** (www.nps.gov/goga/planyourvisit/bolinas.htm), a 12-mile series of ups and downs for hikers and bikers, starts about 1 mile west of Olema, on Sir Francis Drake Blvd. It has great views.

In the former Olema Inn, a creaky 1876 building, hyper-local **Sir & Star** (☑ 415-663-1034;

MARIN COUNTY & THE BAY AREA OLEMA & NICASIO

www.sirandstar.com; 10000 Sir Francis Drake Blvd, Olema; mains $20, Sat prix-fixe menu $85; ☺5-9pm Wed-Sun; 🐾) 🍴 restaurant delights with Marin-sourced seasonal bounty such as Tomales Bay oysters, Dungeness crab and duck 'faux' gras. Reservations recommended.

A few minutes away in Nicasio, check out the **Nicasio Valley Cheese Company** (☑415-662-6200; http://nicasiocheese.com; 5300 Nicasio Valley Rd; ☺10am-5pm), where you can get free tastings at one of Marin County's renowned cheese-making shops. Crafted on a ranch started by a Swiss immigrant family, these wheels of soft cheeses – such as the award-winning Foggy Morning *fromage blanc* – appear on chef's menus and at farmers markets around the Bay Area.

You can get a dose of local flavor at the tiny town's music venue, **Rancho Nicasio** (☑415-662-2219; www.ranchonicasio.com; 1 Old Rancheria Rd, Nicasio; tickets free-$25; ☺show schedules vary), a rustic saloon that regularly attracts local and national blues, rock and country performers.

ℹ Getting There & Away

Olema is about 13 miles northwest of Stinson Beach via Hwy 1. Nicasio is at the west end of Lucas Valley Rd, 10 miles from Hwy 101.

West Marin Stagecoach (p129) Route 68 runs several times daily to Olema from the San Rafael Transit Center, stopping at Samuel P Taylor State Park.

Point Reyes Station

Though the railroad stopped coming through in 1933 and the town is small, Point Reyes Station is nevertheless the hub of western Marin County. Dominated by dairies and ranches, the region was invaded by artists in the 1960s. Today Main St is a diverting blend of art galleries, tourist shops, restaurants and cafes. The town has a rowdy saloon and the occasional smell of cattle on the afternoon breeze.

🛏 Sleeping & Eating

Cute little cottages, cabins and B&Bs are plentiful in and around Point Reyes. The **West Marin Chamber of Commerce** (☑415-663-9232; www.pointreyes.org) and the Point Reyes Lodging Association (www.ptreyes.com) have additional listings.

Windsong Cottage Guest Yurt   YURT $$
(☑415-663-9695; www.windsongcottage.com; 25 McDonald Lane; d $195-230; 🅿🐾🛜) A

wood-burning stove, private outdoor hot tub, comfy king bed and kitchen stocked with breakfast supplies make this round skylighted abode a slice of rural heaven.

Nick's Cove   COTTAGE $$$
(☑415-663-1033; http://nickscove.com; 23240 Hwy 1, Marshall; cottages $250-850; 🅿🐾🛜🐕) Fronting a peaceful cove at Tomales Bay, these water-view and waterfront vacation cottages are expensive, but oh-so romantic. Some have wood-burning fireplace, deep soaking tub, private deck and plasma TV. Two-night minimum stay on weekends and holidays. It's about a 20-minute drive north of Point Reyes Station.

★**Hog Island Oyster Company**   SEAFOOD $
(☑415-663-9218; https://hogislandoysters.com; 20215 Hwy 1, Marshall; 12 oysters $13-16, picnic per person $5; ☺shop 9am-5pm daily, picnic area from 10am, cafe 11am-5pm Fri-Mon) Ten miles north of Point Reyes Station you'll find the salty turnout for Hog Island Oyster Company. There's not much to see: just some picnic tables and BBQ grills, an outdoor cafe and a window selling the famously silky oysters and a few other provisions. A picnic at the farm is an unforgettable lunch – and popular, so make reservations (required).

**Cowgirl Creamery at
Tomales Bay Foods**   DELI $
(☑415-663-9335; www.cowgirlcreamery.com; 80 4th St; deli items $3-10; ☺10am-6pm Wed-Sun; 🐾🐕) 🍴 An indoor deli and marketplace in an old barn sells farm-fresh picnic items, including gourmet cheeses and organic produce. Reserve in advance for an artisanal cheese-maker's demonstration and tasting ($5); watch the curd-making and cutting; then sample a half-dozen fresh and aged cheeses. The milk is local and organic, with vegetarian rennet in soft cheeses.

Bovine Bakery   BAKERY $
(☑415-663-9420; www.bovinebakeryptreyes.com; 11315 Hwy 1; most items $2-6; ☺6:30am-5pm Mon-Fri, 7am-5pm Sat, 7am-4pm Sun; 🐾🐕) 🍴 Don't leave town without sampling something buttery from this beloved country bakery. A sweet bear-claw pastry and organic coffee are a good way to kick off your morning.

Marshall Store   SEAFOOD $$
(☑415-663-1339; www.themarshallstore.com; 19225 Hwy 1, Marshall; mains $11-20; ☺10am-5pm Mon-Fri, to 6pm Sat & Sun, closes 1hr earlier Oct-Apr; 🐕) Catapulted to fame by peripatetic chef and

TV host Anthony Bourdain, this ramshackle country store lets you slurp down BBQ oysters at tables as your legs practically dangle in Tomales Bay. Smoked seafood plates and sandwiches aren't half bad either. It's a 15-minute drive north of Point Reyes Station.

ⓘ Getting There & Away

From Hwy 101 and San Rafael, it's about a 45-minute drive to Point Reyes Station. Driving the coast, it's less than 30 minutes from Bolinas. Hwy 1 becomes Main St in town, running right through the center.

West Marin Stagecoach (p129) route 68 runs to Point Reyes Station several times daily from the San Rafael Transit Center ($2, 75 minutes) via Bear Valley Visitor Center at Point Reyes National Seashore.

Inverness

The last outpost on your journey westward toward the tip of Point Reyes, this tiny town stretches out along the west side of Tomales Bay. Several great beaches are only a short drive away.

🏃 Activities

★ **Blue Waters Kayaking** KAYAKING
(☑415-669-2600; www.bluewaterskayaking.com; 12944 Sir Francis Drake Blvd; rentals/tours from $60/68; ☺usually 9am-5pm, last rental 2pm; ⊕) Long-running outfit guides tours of Tomales Bay, or you can rent a kayak and paddle to secluded beaches and rocky crevices on your own; no experience necessary. Book ahead for full-moon and bioluminescence excursions.

🛏 Sleeping

Dancing Coyote Beach Cottages COTTAGE $$$
(☑415-669-7200; www.dancingcoyotebeach.com; 12794 Sir Francis Drake Blvd; cottages $200-295; Ⓟ☺🛜🐾) Serene and comfortable, these four modern cottages back right on to Tomales Bay, with skylights and decks extending the views in all directions. Full kitchens contain locally sourced breakfast foods, and fireplaces are stocked with firewood for foggy nights.

Cottages at Point Reyes Seashore COTTAGE $$
(☑415-669-7250; www.cottagespointreyes.com; 13275 Sir Francis Drake Blvd; r $129-269; Ⓟ☺🛜🐾🐾) Hidden in the woods, this family-friendly place offers contemporary kitchenette rooms in A-frame structures and a tennis court, hot tub, croquet, horseshoe pitches, barbecue grills and saltwater pool. There's also a large garden and private nature trail.

ⓘ Getting There & Away

From Hwy 1, Sir Francis Drake Blvd heads northwest straight into Inverness. West Marin Stagecoach (p129) route 68 from San Rafael ($2) makes several daily runs here via Olema and Point Reyes Station.

Point Reyes National Seashore

Windswept Point Reyes peninsula is a rough-hewn beauty that has always lured marine mammals and migratory birds as well as scores of shipwrecks. It was here in 1579 that Sir Francis Drake landed to repair his ship, the *Golden Hind*. During his five-week stay he mounted a brass plaque near the shore claiming this land for England. In 1595 the first of scores of ships lost in these waters went down. The *San Augustine* was a Spanish treasure ship out of Manila, laden with luxury goods – to this day bits of its cargo still wash up on shore. Despite modern navigatiosan, the dangerous waters here continue to claim the odd boat.

Point Reyes National Seashore (Map p121; ☑415-654-5100; www.nps.gov/pore; Ⓟ⊕) 🆓 protects 110 sq miles of pristine ocean beaches and coastal wilderness and has excellent hiking and camping opportunities. Be sure to bring warm clothing, as even the sunniest days can quickly turn cold and foggy.

◉ Sights & Activities

For a curious view, follow the 0.6-mile **Earthquake Trail** from the picnic area opposite Bear Valley Visitor Center. The trail reaches a 16ft gap between the two halves of a once-connected fence line, a lasting testimonial to the power of the 1906 earthquake that was centered in this area. Another 0.8-mile trail leads from the visitor center around **Kule Loklo**, a reproduction of a Coast Miwok village.

Limantour Rd, off Bear Valley Rd about 1 mile north of Bear Valley Visitor Center, leads to **Limantour Beach**, where a 2-mile trail runs along Limantour Spit with Estero de Limantour on one side and Drakes

Bay on the other. The **Inverness Ridge Trail** heads from Limantour Rd for around 3 miles up to Mt Vision (1282ft), affording spectacular views of the entire national seashore. You can drive almost to the top of Mt Vision from the other side.

Northwest of the town of Inverness, Pierce Point Rd splits off to the right from Sir Francis Drake Blvd. The road lets you access two swimming beaches on Tomales Bay: seductively named **Heart's Desire**, in **Tomales Bay State Park** ([📞]415-669-1140; www.parks.ca.gov; 1100 Pierce Point Rd, Inverness; per car $8; ⊘8am-sunset; [P][♿]), is accessible by car, while **Marshall Beach** requires a 1.2-mile hike from the parking area at the end of the road.

Pierce Point Rd continues to the huge windswept sand dunes at.**Abbotts Lagoon**, full of peeping killdeer and other shore-birds. At the end of the road is historical Pierce Point Ranch, the trailhead for the 9.4-mile round-trip **Tomales Point Trail** through the **Tule Elk Reserve**. The plentiful elk are an amazing sight, standing with their big horns against the backdrop of Tomales Point, with Bodega Bay to the north, Tomales Bay to the east and the Pacific Ocean to the west.

Point Reyes Lighthouse   LIGHTHOUSE
([📞]415-669-1534; www.nps.gov/pore; end of Sir Francis Drake Blvd; ⊘10am-4:30pm Fri-Mon, lens room 2:30-4pm Fri-Mon; [P][♿]) [FREE] With wild terrain and ferocious winds, this spot feels like the end of the earth and offers the best whale-watching along the coast. The lighthouse sits below the headlands; to reach it you need to descend more than 300 stairs.

Five Brooks Ranch   HORSEBACK RIDING
([📞]415-663-1570; www.fivebrooks.com; 8001 Shoreline Hwy, Olema; trail rides $40-180; [♿]) Explore the Point Reyes landscape on horseback with a trail ride. Take a slow amble through a pasture or ascend Inverness Ridge for views of the Olema Valley. If you can stay in the saddle for six hours, ride along the coastline to Alamere Falls (p137) via Wildcat Beach.

Chimney Rock   HIKING
(www.nps.gov/pore; off Sir Francis Drake Blvd) Not far from the lighthouse, Chimney Rock is a fine short hike, especially in spring when wildflowers are blossoming. During winter, a viewing area allows you to spy on an elephant-seal colony hauled out below the cliffs.

[🛏] Sleeping

Wake up to deer nibbling under a blanket of fog at one of Point Reyes' very popular **backcountry campgrounds** ([📞]reservations 877-444-6777; www.recreation.gov; tent sites $20), or stay at the pastoral youth hostel. More inns, motels and B&Bs are found in nearby Inverness, off Sir Francis Drake Blvd.

HI Point Reyes   HOSTEL $
([📞]415-663-8811; www.norcalhostels.org/reyes; 1390 Limantour Spit Rd; r with shared bath $105-130, dm $29-38; ⊘reception 7:30-10:30am & 4:30-10pm; [P][⊕][@]) [♿] Just off Limantour Rd, this rustic hostel has bunkhouses with warm and cozy front rooms, big-view windows and outdoor areas with hill vistas. A newer building with Leadership in Energy and Environmental Design (LEED) certification has four private rooms (two-night minimum stay on weekends) and a modern kitchen. It's in a beautiful secluded valley 2 miles from the ocean and surrounded by lovely hiking trails.

[ℹ] Information

At park headquarters, a mile west of Olema, **Bear Valley Visitor Center** ([📞]415-464-5100; www.nps.gov/pore; 1 Bear Valley Rd, Point Reyes Station; ⊘10am-5pm Mon-Fri, 9am-5pm Sat & Sun; [♿]) has information and maps. You can also get information at the Point Reyes Lighthouse and the **Kenneth Patrick Center** ([📞]415-669-1250; www.nps.gov/pore; 1 Drakes Beach Rd; ⊘9:30am-4:30pm Sat, Sun & holidays late Dec-late Mar or early Apr) at Drakes Beach.

[ℹ] Getting There & Away

By car you can get to Point Reyes a few different ways. The curviest is along Hwy 1, through Stinson Beach and Olema. More direct is to exit Hwy 101 in San Rafael and follow Sir Francis Drake Blvd all the way to the tip of Point Reyes. By either route, it's less than 1½ hours to Olema from San Francisco barring weekend and rush-hour traffic jams.

Just north of Olema, where Hwy 1 and Sir Francis Drake Blvd come together, is Bear Valley Rd; turn left to reach Bear Valley Visitor Center. If you're heading to the outermost reaches of Point Reyes, follow Sir Francis Drake Blvd north toward Point Reyes Station, turning left and heading out on to the peninsula (at least a 45-minute drive).

West Marin Stagecoach (p129) route 68 from San Rafael stops several times daily at the Bear Valley Visitor Center ($2, 70 minutes) before continuing to the town of Point Reyes Station.

EAST BAY

Berkeley and Oakland are what most San Franciscans think of as the East Bay, though the area includes numerous other suburbs that swoop up from the bayside flats into exclusive enclaves in the hills. Many residents of the 'West Bay' would like to think they needn't ever cross the Bay Bridge or take a Bay Area Rapid Transit (BART) train through an underwater tunnel. But a wealth of museums and historical sites, a world-famous university, excellent restaurants and bars, a creative arts scene, offbeat shopping, woodsy parks and better weather are just some of the attractions that lure travelers from San Francisco over to the sunny side of the Bay.

Oakland

Named for the grand oak trees that once lined its streets, Oakland is to San Francisco what Brooklyn is to Manhattan. To some degree a less expensive alternative to 'the city' across the Bay, this is often where people have moved to escape skyrocketing San Francisco housing costs. An ethnically diverse city, Oakland has a strong African American community and a long labor-union history. Urban farmers raise chickens in their backyard or occupy abandoned lots to start community gardens; families find more room to stretch out; and self-satisfied residents thumb their noses at San Francisco's fog while basking in sunny weather. For visitors, the city offers a handful of diverting museums and historical sites, a vibrant arts scene, innovative restaurants and bars, vintage and boutique shops, and outdoor recreation galore – down by the waterfront, around Lake Merritt and up in the forested hills.

◉ Sights & Activities

Oakland is full of historic buildings and a growing number of colorful businesses. With such easy access from San Francisco via BART or ferry, it's worth spending part of a day exploring here on foot or by bicycle.

◉ Downtown, Chinatown & Waterfront

Pedestrianized **City Center**, between Broadway and Clay St, 12th and 14th Sts, forms the heart of downtown Oakland. Nearby **City Hall** (Map p142; ✆510-444-2489; www. oaklandnet.com; Frank H Ogawa Plaza; ◎9am-6pm Mon-Fri; ⒷL12th St Oakland City Center) is a beautifully refurbished 1914 beaux-arts building.

Old Oakland, west of Broadway between 8th and 10th Sts, is lined with restored historic buildings dating from the late 19th century. The area has a lively restaurant and after-work scene, and a farmers market every Friday from 8am until 2pm.

East of Broadway and bustling with commerce, Oakland's Chinatown centers on Franklin and Webster Sts, as it has since the 1850s. Jack London Sq is on the waterfront further south.

Oakland Museum of California MUSEUM (OMCA; Map p142; ✆510-318-8400; http://museum ca.org; 1000 Oak St; adult/child $16/7, 1st Sun each month free; ◎11am-5pm Wed-Thu, to 9pm Fri, 10am-6pm Sat & Sun; ⒫⓴; ⒷLake Merritt) Near the southern end of Lake Merritt, this museum has rotating exhibitions on artistic and scientific themes, and permanent galleries dedicated to the state's diverse ecology and history, as well as California art. Admission is steeply discounted on Friday nights (after 5pm), when DJs, food trucks and free art workshops for kids make it a fun hangout.

◉ Uptown & Lake Merritt

North of downtown Oakland, the Uptown district contains many of the city's art-deco beauties, such as the Fox Theater (p147) and Paramount Theatre (p148), and a proliferating arts, restaurant and nightlife scene. The area stretches roughly between Telegraph and Broadway, bounded by Grand Ave to the north.

Follow Grand Ave east of Broadway and you'll run into the shores of Lake Merritt. Grand Ave (north of the lake) and Lakeshore Ave (east of the lake) are pedestrian-friendly streets for local shops, restaurants, cafes and bars.

Lake Merritt LAKE (Map p142; ✆510-238-7275; www.oaklandnet.com; ⒫⓴; ⒷLake Merritt) ⌀ An urban respite, Lake Merritt is a popular place to stroll or go running (a 3.5-mile paved path circles the lake), with bonsai and botanical gardens, a children's amusement park (p143), bird sanctuary, **boathouse** (Map p142; ✆510-238-2196; www.oaklandnet.com; 568 Bellevue Ave; boat rentals per hour $12-24, cash only; ◎daily Mar-Oct, Sat & Sun only Nov-Feb; ⓴; ⎚AC Transit 12) and **gondola rides** (Map p142; ✆510-663-6603;

Central Oakland

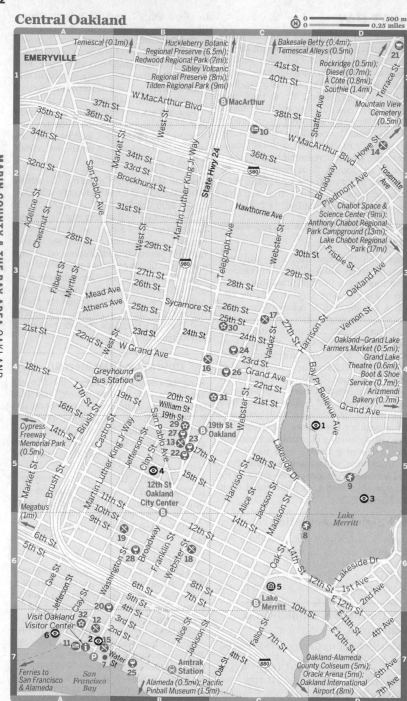

500 m
0.25 miles

EMERYVILLE

Temescal (0.1mi)

Huckleberry Botanic
Regional Preserve (6.5mi);
Redwood Regional Park (7mi);
Sibley Volcanic
Regional Preserve (8mi);
Tilden Regional Park (9mi)

Bakesale Betty (0.4mi);
Temescal Alleys (0.5mi)

Rockridge (0.5mi);
Diesel (0.7mi);
À Côte (0.8mi);
Southie (1.4mi)

Mountain View
Cemetery
(0.5mi)

41st St
40th St

W MacArthur Blvd

MacArthur

10

W MacArthur Blvd

38th St

14

35th St
37th St
36th St
34th St
32nd St

West St

State Hwy 24

Market St

San Pablo Ave

Adeline St

Chestnut St

34th St
33rd St
Brockhurst St

31st St

36th St

580

Hawthorne Ave

Broadway

Piedmont Ave

Yosemite Ave

Chabot Space &
Science Center (9mi);
Anthony Chabot Regional
Park Campground (13mi);
Lake Chabot Regional
Park (17mi)

28th St

Filbert St
Myrtle St

West St

27th St
26th St

28th St

Telegraph Ave

Webster St

30th St

29th St

Frisbie St

Oakland Ave

Vernon St

980

Mead Ave
Athens Ave

Sycamore St

25th St

26th St
25th St

30

17

Valdez St

27th St

Harrison St

Oakland–Grand Lake
Farmers Market (0.5mi);
Grand Lake
Theatre (0.6mi);
Boot & Shoe
Service (0.7mi);
Arizmendi
Bakery (0.7mi)

21st St
18th St

22nd St

23rd St

West

W Grand Ave

24th St

24th St
23rd St
Grand Ave
22nd St

24

26

16

Greyhound
Bus Station

20th St
William St
19th St

29
27
13

23

19th St
Oakland

21st St

Webster St

Bay Pl

Bellevue Ave

Grand Ave

Cypress
Freeway
Memorial Park
(0.5mi)

Market St

Brush St

17th St
16th St

19th St

Castro St

San Pablo Ave

Jefferson St

Clay St

22

17th St

31

1

Megabus
(1mi)

Martin Luther King Jr Way

11th St
10th St
9th St

Broadway

4

15th St

12th St Oakland
City Center

Harrison St

Alice St

Jackson St

Madison St

19th St

Lakeside Dr

Lake
Merritt

9

3

8

6th St
5th St

Gve St

Jefferson St

Clay St

Washington St

19

28

18

Franklin St

Webster St

12th St

14th St

Oak St

14th St

8

Lakeside Dr

20

12

32

2 15

11

7

25

Visit Oakland
Visitor Center

Water St

6th St
5th St

4th St
3rd St
2nd St

8th St
7th St

Alice St

Jackson St

Oak St

4th St

5

Lake
Merritt

10th St

Fallon St

7th St

880

1st Ave

E 12th St

E 11th St

E 10th St

2nd Ave

4th Ave

Amtrak
Station

Ferries to
San Francisco
& Alameda

San
Francisco
Bay

Alameda (0.5mi); Pacific
Pinball Museum (1.5mi)

Oakland-Alameda
County Coliseum (5mi);
Oracle Arena (5mi);
Oakland International
Airport (8mi)

6th Ave

7th Ave

Central Oakland

http://gondolaservizio.com; 1520 Lakeside Dr; 30/50min cruise $60/85; ⓑ Lake Merritt). The two main commercial streets skirting Lake Merritt are Grand Ave, running along the north shore, and Lakeshore Ave on the eastern edge of the lake.

Children's Fairyland AMUSEMENT PARK
(Map p142; ☑ 510-452-2259; http://fairyland.org; 699 Bellevue Ave; $10, child under 1yr free; ⊙ 10am-4pm Mon-Fri, to 5pm Sat & Sun Jun-Aug, off-season hours vary; ⓟ 🚼 ; 🚌 AC Transit 12) Lakeside Park, on the northern side of Lake Merritt, includes this 10-acre kiddie attraction, which dates from 1950 and has a charming fairy-tale-themed train, carousel and mini Ferris wheel.

◎ Jack London Square

Jack London Square SQUARE
(Map p142; ☑ 510-645-9292; www.jacklondonsquare.com; Broadway & Embarcadero; ⊙ 24hr, shop, restaurant & bar hours vary; ⓟ ; 🚌 Broadway Shuttle) The area where writer and adventurer Jack London once raised hell now bears his name. The pretty waterfront location is worth a stroll, especially when the Sunday **farmers market** (Map p142; ☑ 415-291-3276; www.cuesa.org; ⊙ 10am-3pm Sun; 🚲 🚼) 🟢 takes over, or get off your feet and kayak around the harbor. Contemporary redevelopment has added a cinema complex, condo development and popular restaurants and bars. A replica of Jack London's Yukon **cab-in** stands at the eastern end of the square. Oddly, people throw coins inside as if it's a fountain.

Another interesting historical stop, adjacent to the tiny cabin, is Heinold's First & Last Chance Saloon (p147). Catch a ferry from San Francisco – a worthwhile excursion in itself – and you'll land just paces away.

USS Potomac SHIP
(Map p142; ☑ 510-627-1215; www.usspotomac.org; 540 Water St; adult/child $10/free; ⊙ tours 11am-2:30pm Wed, Fri & Sun; 🚌 Broadway Shuttle) Franklin D Roosevelt's 'floating White House,' the 165ft USS *Potomac*, is moored at Clay and Water Sts by the ferry dock, and is open for dockside tours. Two-hour cruises (adult/child $55/35) are scheduled several times a month from April through November (book far ahead).

◎ Piedmont Ave, Temescal & Rockridge

North of downtown Oakland, Broadway becomes a lengthy strip of car dealerships called Auto Row. Detour a couple of blocks east to Piedmont Ave, wall-to-wall with vintage-clothing stores, coffeehouses, restaurants and an art-house cinema.

A half-dozen or so long blocks west of Broadway, Temescal wins the prize for being Oakland's artiest, hippest neighborhood.

Find unique shops, creative restaurants and happening bars on Telegraph Ave north of 40th St.

Rockridge, a lively, upscale neighborhood, is further north between Broadway and Telegraph Ave. College Ave is lined with upscale boutiques, a bookstore, pubs and cafes and quite a few fancy restaurants.

Mountain View Cemetery   CEMETERY
(☑ 510-658-2588; www.mountainviewcemetery. org; 5000 Piedmont Ave; ⊙ 6:30am-7:30pm; Ⓟ; ☐ AC Transit 12) At the northern end of Piedmont Ave, this is perhaps the most serene and lovely artificial landscape in the East Bay. Designed by Frederick Law Olmstead (the landscape architect of New York City's Central Park), it's great for walking and the views are stupendous.

⊙ Oakland Hills

The large parks of the Oakland Hills are ideal for day hiking and challenging cycling, and the **East Bay Regional Parks** (☑ 888-327-2757; www.ebparks.org; per car free-$6; ⊙ hours vary; ⊕⛹) ⚑ manages more than 1200 miles of trails in 65 regional parks, preserves and recreation areas in the Alameda and Contra Costa Counties.

Off Hwy 24, **Robert Sibley Volcanic Regional Preserve** is the northernmost of the Oakland Hills parks. It has great views of the Bay Area from its **Round Top Peak** (1761ft). From Sibley, Skyline Blvd runs south past **Redwood Regional Park** and adjacent **Joaquin Miller Park** to **Anthony Chabot Regional Park**. A hike or mountain-bike ride through the groves and along the hilltops of any of these sizable parks will make you forget you're in an urban area. At the southern end of Chabot Park is the enormous **Lake Chabot**, with an easy trail along its shore, and canoes, kayaks and other boats for rent from the **Lake Chabot Marina** (☑ 510-247-2526; www.lakechabotrecreation. com; 17936 Lake Chabot Rd, Castro Valley; rentals/ tours from $23/45; ⊙ 6am-6pm Mon-Thu, to 7pm Fri-Sun May-early Sep, off-season hours vary; ⊕).

★ **Chabot Space
& Science Center**   MUSEUM
(☑ 510-336-7300; www.chabotspace.org; 10000 Skyline Blvd; adult/child $18/14; ⊙ 10am-5pm Wed-Sun, also Tue Jun-Aug; Ⓟ⊕; ☐ AC Transit 339) ⚑ Stargazers will go gaga over this kid-oriented science and technology center in the Oakland Hills with loads of exhibits

on subjects such as space travel and eclipses, as well as cool planetarium shows. When the weather's good, check out the free Friday and Saturday evening viewings (7:30pm to 10:30pm) using a 20in refractor telescope.

Admission is just $5 on the first Friday evening of each month (6pm to 10pm), when the museum organizes hands-on activities, science demonstrations, movies and night hikes.

✳✳ Festivals & Events

Oakland First Fridays   STREET CARNIVAL
(☑ 510-361-0615; http://oaklandfirstfridays.org; Telegraph Ave; entry by donation; ⊙ 5-9:30pm 1st Fri each month; ✿; Ⓑ 19th St Oakland) A kinetic street festival takes place on the first Friday of the month, when a five-block stretch of Telegraph Ave closes to car traffic. Thousands of people turn out for food vendors, live music and performances.

🛏 Sleeping

Oakland has surprisingly few places to stay, apart from chain motels and hotels off the freeways, downtown and near the airport.

**Anthony Chabot
Regional Park**   CAMPGROUND $
(☑ reservations888-327-2757;www.reserveamerica. com; end of Marciel Rd, Castro Valley; tent sites $25, RV sites with hookups $25-35; Ⓟ✿) ⚑ In the East Bay's forested hills, this 5000-acre park has 75 campsites open year-round and hot showers.

Inn at Temescal   MOTEL $$
(Map p142; ☑ 510-652-9800; www.innattemescal. com; 3720 Telegraph Ave; r from $129; Ⓟ⊕✿☎; Ⓑ MacArthur) Though the location isn't lovely, it's a short walk to BART or Temescal's main strip. Recently renovated, the motel has exterior doors painted in avocado green and sunset orange. Clean-lined rooms come with pillow-top mattresses, wall-sized historic photos and retro accents. Expect some street noise.

Waterfront Hotel   BOUTIQUE HOTEL $$$
(Map p142; ☑ 510-836-3800; www.waterfronthotel oakland.com; 10 Washington St; r from $299; Ⓟ⊕✿@☎✿) Paddle-printed wallpaper and lamps fashioned from faux lanterns round out the playful nautical theme of this cheerful harborside hotel. A huge brass-topped fireplace warms the foyer, and comfy rooms include iPod docking stations and coffeemakers. Unless you're an avid

train-spotter, water-view rooms are preferred, as trains rattle by on the city side. Complimentary wine-and-cheese reception on weekdays. Parking is $30.

✗ Eating

Oakland's diverse eateries nearly rival those of foodie neighbor San Francisco. Take your pick of sophisticated restaurants run by top Bay Area chefs, neighborhood cafes, international kitchens or pop-up food trucks. Downtown, Old Oakland and Chinatown abound with budget-friendly local favorites. Uptown, Temescal and Rockridge attract culinary trend-spotters. West Oakland does soul food, while East Oakland has authentic taquerias.

✗ Uptown, Downtown & Jack London Square

Swan's Market　　　　　　FOOD HALL $
(Map p142; ☑510-287-5353; http://swansmarket.com; 510 9th St; most mains $8-15; ⊗9am-10pm Mon-Sat; ⛟; Ⓑ12th St Oakland City Center) Old Oakland's 100-year-old marketplace has been given new life with a gourmet food court, where the wooden tables are always full, day and night. Stop at Cosecha for Mexican fare, AS B-Dama for udon noodles and Japanese fried chicken, Delage sushi bar, the Cook & Her Farmer oyster bar and cafe, Rosamunde Sausage Grill or Miss Ollie's for Caribbean food.

Shandong Restaurant　　　　CHINESE $
(Map p142; ☑510-839-2299; http://shandongoakland.com; 328 10th St; mains $7-13; ⊗11am-3pm & 4-9pm Sun-Thu, to 9:30pm Fri & Sat; ⛟; Ⓑ12th St Oakland City Center) Not everything tastes so amazing at this crowded, family-friendly Chinatown restaurant, but that's OK because you're only here for two things: handmade sesame noodles and from-scratch pork dumplings. Expect a wait for a table.

Authentic Bagel Co　　　BAKERY, DELI $
(Map p142; ☑510-459-1201; www.abagelcompany.com; 463 2nd St; sandwiches $3-10; ⊗7am-3pm; ⛟⛟) Once upon a time two Jewish guys from Rhode Island set up shop near Jack London Sq. Today they make the Bay Area's best East Coast–style bagels while blasting Beastie Boys albums. Chow down on a 'Lox Monsta' (pumpernickel bagel with bacon, lox, avocado and cilantro curry) at sunny sidewalk tables.

Kingston 11　　　　　　　CARIBBEAN $$
(Map p142; ☑510-465-2558; http://kingston11eats.com; 2270 Telegraph Ave; mains $13-20; ⊗11am-2pm & 5-10pm Tue-Fri, 5-10pm Sat, 11am-4pm Sun; ⛟; Ⓑ19th St Oakland) The wait will be worth it at this raucous Caribbean bar with a groovy soundtrack, where oxtail stew, salt-fish fritters, fried plantains and goat curry are succulent delights. Swing by for 'Irie Hour' (5pm to 7pm Tuesday through Friday) to sip out-of-this-world cocktails such as the Rise Up (cold-brew coffee, coconut milk, spiced rum and Angostura bitters). Reservations recommended.

Mua　　　　　　　　　　CALIFORNIAN $$
(Map p142; ☑510-238-1100; https://muaoakland.com; 2442a Webster St; shared plates $7-15, mains $21-35; ⊗5:30-11pm Mon-Thu, to midnight Fri & Sat, 5-10pm Sun; ⛟; Ⓑ19th St Oakland) A warehouse-sized space in Uptown, this social gathering spot is just as good for date night as it is for groups getting ready for a night out. Peruse the long, long menu of creative shared plates like quinoa-arugula salad with nectarines and goat's cheese or beef bone-marrow toast, with a 'Stormy Oaktown' cocktail or rosemary martini in hand. Reservations recommended.

Camber Uptown　　　THAI, LAOTIAN $$
(Map p142; ☑510-663-4560; http://camberoakland.com; 1707 Telegraph Ave; mains $10-20; ⊗11:30am-2:30pm & 5-9:30pm Mon-Thu, 11:30am-11:30pm Fri, 5-11:30pm Sat; ⛟; Ⓑ19th St Oakland) While you might find cheaper and more authentic Southeast Asian kitchens in Oakland's Chinatown, Camber can't be beaten for proximity to Uptown nightlife. Fusion dishes such as the 'bouncing beef' stir-fry and garlic-basil fish with sliced jalapeño peppers are popular with the young crowd sidling up to the bar.

✗ Piedmont Ave, Temescal & Rockridge

★ Commis　　　　　　CALIFORNIAN $$$
(Map p142; ☑510-653-3902; http://commisrestaurant.com; 3859 Piedmont Ave; 8-course dinner $149, with wine & beer pairings $229; ⊗5:30-9:30pm Wed-Sat, 5-9pm Sun; 🚍AC Transit 51A) The East Bay's only Michelin-starred restaurant, the signless and discreet dining room counts a minimalist decor and some coveted counter real estate where patrons can watch chef James Syhabout and his team piece together creative and innovative dishes,

SUMMONING ALL PINBALL WIZARDS

Put down that video-game console, cast aside your latest phone app, and return to the bygone days of pinball play. Lose yourself in bells and flashing lights at **Pacific Pinball Museum** (☑510-769-1349; http://pacificpinball.org; 1510 Webster St, Alameda; all-day pass adult/child $20/10; ☺11am-9pm Tue-Thu & Sun, to 10pm Fri & Sat; 🚸; 🚌AC Transit 51A), a pinball parlor with almost 100 games dating from the 1930s to the present, and vintage jukeboxes playing hits from the past. Take AC Transit bus 51A from downtown Oakland.

maybe Monterey Bay abalone, soy-milk custard with chanterelles or a perfectly ripe peach topped with oats, beeswax creme and marigolds. Reservations essential.

Bakesale Betty SANDWICHES, BAKERY $
(☑510-985-1213; www.bakesalebetty.com; 5098 Telegraph Ave; sandwiches $9; ☺11am-2pm Tue-Sat; 🚌AC Transit 6) Aussie expat Alison Barakat has patrons licking their lips and lining up out the door and down the block for heavenly strawberry shortcake and scrumptious fried-chicken sandwiches. Rolling pins dangle from the ceiling and blissed-out locals sit down at ironing-board sidewalk tables.

Southie SANDWICHES $
(☑510-654-0100; http://southieoakland.com; 6311 College Ave; mains $9-18; ☺9am-9pm Mon-Sat, to 3pm Sun; 🚏Rockridge) Wood Tavern's side venture steals the show with its gobstopping meatball and pork-belly sandwiches. This busy storefront eatery has only a few tightly squeezed-together tables, with a half-dozen wines and craft beers on tap. Finish off with passion-fruit–buttermilk *panna cotta* or a brownie ice-cream sandwich.

✕ Lake Merritt

★**Oakland–Grand Lake Farmers Market** MARKET $
(☑415-472-6100; https://agriculturalinstitute.org; Lake Park Ave, at Grand Ave; ☺9am-2pm Sat; 🚸; 🚌AC Transit 12) A rival to San Francisco's Ferry Plaza Farmers Market, this bountiful weekly market hauls in bushels of fresh fruit, vegetables, seafood, ranched meats, artisanal cheese and baked goods from as

far away as Marin County and the Central Valley. The northern side of the market is cheek-to-jowl with food trucks and hot-food vendors – don't skip the dim-sum tent.

Arizmendi Bakery BAKERY $
(☑510-268-8849; http://arizmendilakeshore.com; 3265 Lakeshore Ave; pizza slices $2.50; ☺7am-8pm Tue-Sun; 🚸; 🚌AC Transit 12) Great for breakfast or lunch but beware: this bakery co-op is not for the weak-willed. Gourmet vegetarian pizza, chewy breads and gigantic scones, all baked fresh, are addictive.

Boot & Shoe Service PIZZA $$
(☑510-763-2668; www.bootandshoeservice.com; 3308 Grand Ave; pizzas $14-22; ☺7am-noon & 5:30-10pm Tue-Thu, 7am-noon & 5-10:30pm Fri, 10am-2pm & 5-10:30pm Sat, 10am-2pm & 5-10pm Sun; 🚸; 🚌AC Transit 12) The name plays off its former identity as a cobbler's shop, but the current patrons pack this brick-walled place for its wood-fired pizzas, original cocktails and creative antipasti made from sustainably sourced fresh ingredients.

Camino CALIFORNIAN $$$
(☑510-547-5035; www.caminorestaurant.com; 3917 Grand Ave; dinner mains $32-42; ☺5:30-9:30pm Mon, Wed & Thu, to 10pm Fri, 10am-2pm & 5:30-10pm Sat, to 9:30pm Sun; 🚸; 🚌AC Transit 12) From the culinary imagination of chef Russell Moore (a Chez Panisse alum), Camino's short daily-changing menu showcases the best of local organic produce and meats, most cooked over an open fire in slow-food-meets-California-now style. The tables are of recycled old-growth redwood and the place buzzes with bon vivants buzzed on craft cocktails and European and California wines. Reservations essential.

🍷 Drinking & Nightlife

Oakland's busiest and hippest bars are in the Uptown district, just north of downtown and a short stumble from BART. You'll find eclectic watering holes near Jack London Sq and in Old Oakland. Students hang out in Rockridge, while a mix of locals gravitate to bars around Lake Merritt, along Piedmont Ave and on Temescal's main drag.

★**Blue Bottle Coffee Company** CAFE
(Map p142; ☑510-653-3394; http://bluebottlecoffee.com; 4270 Broadway; ☺7am-6pm; 🚌AC Transit 51A) Blue Bottle's roomier cafe is inside the beautiful WC Morse Building, a 1920s truck showroom. Communal tables, lofty ceilings and minimalist white decor

invite sipping a Gibraltar – similar to a cortado (espresso with a dash of milk), but made with more milk – or a cold-brew iced coffee.

Drake's Dealership
BEER GARDEN

(Map p142; ☑ 510-568-2739; http://drinkdrakes.com/visit/dealership; 2325 Broadway; ⏱ 11:30am-11pm Sun-Wed, to 1am Thu-Sat; 🖐🎨; Ⓑ 19th St Oakland) East Bay craft brewer Drake's Brewing Company has transformed a humdrum Dodge dealership into a lively restaurant, bar and outdoor beer garden with fire pits that crackle on foggy nights. Order a pint of Black Robusto porter or Hopocalypse double IPA with a wood-oven-fired pizza. DJs spin Thursday to Saturday. Book ahead online for complimentary tours of the actual brewery, a short bus ride from San Leandro BART station.

Dogwood
COCKTAIL BAR

(Map p142; ☑ 510-444-6669; www.bardogwood.com; 1644 Telegraph Ave; ⏱ 4pm-2am; Ⓑ 19th St Oakland) A hip, tattooed young crowd hobnobs inside this red-brick-walled bar on a busy corner of Uptown. Order a creative house cocktail or classic concoction such as the Brooklyn from mixologists behind the bar. Simple sandwiches and meat-and-cheese plates keep stomachs from growling.

Make Westing
COCKTAIL BAR

(Map p142; ☑ 510-251-1400; www.makewesting.com; 1741 Telegraph Ave; ⏱ 4pm-2am; Ⓑ 19th St Oakland) On weekends, people pack this Uptown hot spot, named for a Jack London short story, for its indoor bocce courts and eclectic cocktails. Toss back a 'Garden Gimlet' (gin, cucumber, basil and lime) and satiate the munchies with cilantro-and-habañero-infused popcorn or a mason jar of homemade pickled beets.

Trappist
PUB

(Map p142; ☑ 510-238-8900; www.thetrappist.com; 460 8th St; ⏱ noon-12:30am Sun-Thu, to 1:30am Fri & Sat; Ⓑ Oakland 12th St City Center) Busting out of its original brick-and-wood-paneled shoe box into a second storefront and outdoor back patio, this place specialises in Belgian ales. Two dozen drafts rotate through the taps, and tasty charcuterie and cheese boards, salads and grilled cheese sandwiches make it easy to linger.

Heinold's First & Last Chance Saloon
BAR

(Map p142; ☑ 510-839-6761; www.heinoldsfirstandlastchance.com; 48 Webster St; ⏱ noon-11pm Sun-Thu, to 1am Fri & Sat; 🚌 Broadway Shuttle) At this 1883 bar constructed from wood scavenged from an old whaling ship, you really have to hold on to your beer. Keeled to a severe slant during the 1906 earthquake, the building's tilt might make you feel self-conscious about stumbling before you even order. Its big claim to fame is that adventure writer Jack London was a regular patron.

Café Van Kleef
BAR

(Map p142; ☑ 510-763-7711; http://cafevankleef.com; 1621 Telegraph Ave; ⏱ 4pm-2am Mon, from noon Tue-Fri, from 6pm Sat, from 7pm Sun; Ⓑ 19th St Oakland) Order a greyhound (with freshly squeezed grapefruit juice) and take a gander at the profusion of antique musical instruments, fake taxidermy heads, sprawling formal chandeliers and bizarro ephemera clinging to every surface possible. Quirky even *before* you get lit, it features live blues, jazz and the occasional rock band on weekends.

Luka's Taproom & Lounge
LOUNGE

(Map p142; ☑ 510-451-4677; www.lukasoakland.com; 2221 Broadway; ⏱ 5:30-11pm Sun-Wed, to 1am Thu, to 2am Fri & Sat; Ⓑ 19th St Oakland) Go Uptown to get down. At this long-running restaurant and lounge, DJs spin a soulful mix of hip-hop, R&B and Latin grooves Thursday to Sunday nights (cover charge $5 to $10).

Beer Revolution
BAR

(Map p142; http://beer-revolution.com; 464 3rd St; ⏱ noon-11pm Sun-Thu, to midnight Fri & Sat; 🚌 Broadway Shuttle) With 50 beers on tap and hundreds more in bottles, there's a lifetime of discovery ahead, so kick back on the sunny deck or park yourself at that barrel table embedded with bottle caps. Bonuses include a punk-rock soundtrack played at conversation-friendly levels.

☆ Entertainment

Professional sports teams play at Oakland–Alameda County Coliseum and Oracle Arena off I-880 including Golden State Warriors (p148) (NBA basketball; moving to San Francisco in 2019), Oakland Raiders (p148) (NFL football; headed to Las Vegas in 2020) or Oakland A's (p148) (American League baseball; not leaving, phew). See www.coliseum.com for upcoming concerts and events. Most of Oakland's smaller live-music and performing-arts venues are Uptown.

★ Fox Theater
THEATER

(Map p142; ☑ 510-302-2250, tickets 800-745-3000; http://thefoxoakland.com; 1807 Telegraph

Ave; tickets from $35; ⊙ hours vary; B 19th St Oakland) A phoenix arisen from the urban ashes, this restored 1928 art-deco stunner adds dazzle and neon lights to Telegraph Ave, where it's a cornerstone of the happening Uptown theater and nightlife district. Once a movie house, it's now a popular concert venue for edgy and independent Californian, national and international music acts. Buy tickets early, since many shows sell out.

★ **Golden State Warriors**　　BASKETBALL
(☑ tickets 888-479-4667; www.nba.com/warriors; 7000 Coliseum Way; tickets from $55; ⊙ Oct-Apr; 🖕; B Coliseum) If it's hoops you must have, then it's the Warriors for you. Originally from Philadelphia, this team moved across the bay from San Francisco in 1971. Today they play at Oracle Arena (next to the Coliseum). The Warriors caused quite a commotion when they won the National Basketball Association (NBA) championship playoffs in 2015. Alas, they're moving back to San Francisco in 2019.

Paramount Theatre　　THEATER, CINEMA
(Map p142; ☑ 510-465-6400; www.paramountthe atre.com; 2025 Broadway; movie/concert tickets from $7/25; ⊙ hours vary; 🚇 19th St Oakland) This massive 1931 art-deco masterpiece shows classic films a few times each month and is also home to the Oakland Symphony (www.oaklandsymphony.org) and Oakland Ballet (http://oaklandballet.org). It periodically books big-name concerts and screens classic flicks. Guided tours ($5) are given at 10am on the first and third Saturdays of the month (no reservations).

Yoshi's　　JAZZ
(Map p142; ☑ 510-238-9200; www.yoshis.com; 510 Embarcadero W; from $20; ⊙ hours vary; 🚇 Broadway Shuttle) Yoshi's has a solid jazz calendar, with talent from around the world passing through on a near-nightly basis. It's also a Japanese restaurant, so if you enjoy a sushi dinner before the show, you'll be rewarded with reserved cabaret-style seating. Otherwise, resign yourself to limited high-top tables squeezed along the back walls of this intimate club.

Grand Lake Theatre　　CINEMA
(☑ 510-452-3556; www.renaissancerialto.com; 3200 Grand Ave; tickets $5-12.50; ⊙ hours vary; 🖕; 🚇 AC Transit 12) Once a vaudeville theater and silent-movie house, this 1926 beauty near Lake Merritt lures you in with its huge corner marquee (which sometimes displays left-leaning political messages) and keeps you coming with a fun balcony and a Wurlitzer organ playing on weekends.

New Parkway Theater　　CINEMA
(Map p142; ☑ 510-658-7900; www.thenewpark way.com; 474 24th St; tickets $5-10; ⊙ hours vary; 🚇 AC Transit 6) This laid-back movie house, pub and community-events space shows second-run and throwback indie films. Reasonably priced beer, wine, sandwiches and pizza are delivered to your couch seat.

Oakland A's　　BASEBALL
(☑ 510-568-5600, tickets 877-493-2255; http:// oakland.athletics.mlb.com; 7000 Coliseum Way; tickets from $15; ⊙ Apr-Sep; 🖕; B Coliseum) When the San Francisco Giants are away, the Oakland A's are usually home, which expands the possibilities for those desperate for a summer baseball fix. The A's most recent World Series pennant came at the Giants' expense in the quake-addled 1989 series, and they remain contenders. If you want to catch them in interleague play, get tickets early.

Oakland Raiders　　FOOTBALL
(☑ 510-864-5022, tickets 800-724-3377; www. raiders.com; 7000 Coliseum Way; tickets from $40; ⊙ Sep-Jan; B Coliseum) With three Super Bowl championships, the notorious bad boys of the National Footbal League (NFL) have had ups and downs over the years, but they still have the staunchest, rowdiest fans in the western US. The team ungratefully moved to Los Angeles for 12 years, but returned in 1995 to Oakland's open arms. They're leaving again for Las Vegas in 2020.

ℹ Information

MEDIA
Oakland's daily newspaper is the *Oakland Tribune* (www.insidebayarea.com/oaklandtribune). The free weekly *East Bay Express* (www.eastbay express.com) has good Oakland and Berkeley listings.

TOURIST INFORMATION
Visit Oakland Visitor Center (Map p142; ☑ 510-839-9000; www.visitoakland.com; 481 Water St; ⊙ 9am-5pm Mon-Fri, 10am-4pm Sat & Sun) At Jack London Sq.

ℹ Getting There & Away

AIR
Oakland International Airport is less crowded and sometimes cheaper to fly into than San Francisco International Airport (SFO) across

the bay. OAK airport is connected to Oakland, Berkeley and San Francisco by frequent BART trains.

BART

Within the Bay Area, the most convenient way to get to Oakland and back is by BART (Bay Area Rapid Transit; www.bart.gov). Trains run on a set schedule approximately every 10 to 20 minutes from around 4:30am to midnight on weekdays, 6am to midnight on Saturday and 8am to midnight on Sunday.

Downtown BART stations are on Broadway at 12th and 19th Sts; other Oakland stations are on the south side of Lake Merritt, close to Chinatown; near Temescal (MacArthur station) and in Rockridge.

To get to downtown Oakland, catch a Richmond or Pittsburg/Bay Point train. The fare to Oakland's 12th or 19th St stations from any BART station in downtown San Francisco is $3.45. Rockridge is on the Pittsburg/Bay Point line, while all Berkeley stops are on the Richmond line. To Lake Merritt or the Coliseum (for connections to Oakland's airport), catch a BART train heading toward Fremont or Dublin/Pleasanton.

BUS

AC Transit (☏ 510-891-4777; www.actransit. org) runs convenient buses from San Francisco's Transbay Transit Center to downtown Oakland ($4.20, or $2.10 with purchase of $5 day pass valid on local East Bay buses). Scores of Transbay buses run during commute hours, but only the 'O' line runs both ways all day and on weekends.

After BART trains stop, late-night transportation between downtown San Francisco and downtown Oakland is with the AC Transit bus 800 line ($4.20), which runs hourly on weekdays and every 20 minutes on weekends.

Between downtown Berkeley and downtown Oakland, take fast and frequent AC Transit bus 6 along Telegraph Ave. Alternatively, take AC Transit bus 18 via Martin Luther King Jr Way and Shattuck Ave. The one way local bus fare for either is $2.10.

Greyhound operates direct buses from Oakland, including to Vallejo, San Jose, Santa Rosa, Sacramento and Los Angeles; its **bus station** (Map p142; ☏ 510-832-4730; 2103 San Pablo Ave; Ⓑ 19th St Oakland) in downtown Oakland is seedy. Discount carrier **Megabus** (☏ 877-462-6342; http://us.megabus.com) has daily service to LA, Burbank and Anaheim, departing from outside the West Oakland BART station.

CAR & MOTORCYCLE

From San Francisco by car, cross the Bay Bridge and enter Oakland via one of two ways: I-580, which leads to I-980 heading to downtown Oakland; or I-880, which curves through West Oakland and lets you off near the south end of Broadway. I-880 then continues to the Coliseum, Oakland International Airport and, eventually, San Jose. Driving back westbound from the East Bay to San Francisco, the bridge toll is $4 to $6, depending on the time and day of the week.

FERRY

From San Francisco's Ferry Building and Pier 41, **San Francisco Bay Ferry** (☏ 415-705-8291; http://sanfranciscobayferry.com) sails to Jack London Sq (one-way $6.60, 30 to 45 minutes) more frequently on weekdays than on weekends. Ferry tickets include a free transfer, which you can use on AC Transit buses.

TRAIN

Oakland is a regular stop for Amtrak trains operating up and down the coast. From Oakland's **Amtrak station** (245 2nd St; ☐ Broadway Shuttle) at Jack London Sq, catch AC Transit bus 12 or the free Broadway Shuttle to downtown Oakland, or take a ferry across the bay to San Francisco.

Amtrak passengers with reservations on to San Francisco disembark at the **Emeryville Amtrak station** (5885 Horton St), one stop north of Oakland. From there, an Amtrak bus shuttles you to San Francisco's Ferry Building stop. Emeryville is also the terminus for Amtrak's daily California Zephyr train service to/from Chicago. The free **Emery Go Round** (☏ 510-451-3862; www.emerygoround.com) shuttle runs a weekday circuit including the Emeryville Amtrak and MacArthur BART stations.

ⓘ Getting Around

The best way to get around much of central Oakland is to walk, cycle or take public buses.

TO/FROM THE AIRPORT

Flying into **Oakland International Airport** (OAK; www.oaklandairport.com; 1 Airport Dr; ☏; Ⓑ Oakland International Airport), car rentals are available from all the major agencies. Outside the terminal, free shuttle buses depart every 10 minutes for the airport's rental-car center.

BART is the easiest public transportation option. Opposite the terminal, catch a BART shuttle train to Coliseum Station, where you'll pay min the fare to your final destination when changing trains. BART trains run on weekdays between 4:30am until after midnight daily (from 6am on Saturday, 8am on Sunday).

SuperShuttle (☏ 800-258-3826; www.super shuttle.com) is one of many door-to-door shuttle services operating out of Oakland International Airport. One-way service to San Francisco destinations starts at around $60 for up to four people. East Bay service destinations are also served. Reserve ahead.

A taxi from Oakland International Airport to downtown Oakland costs about $40; to downtown San Francisco about $70.

BUS

AC Transit (p149) has a comprehensive bus network within Oakland. Local bus fares are $2.10; pay with cash (bring exact change) or a Clipper card (www.clippercard.com).

The free **Broadway Shuttle** (www.meetdowntownoak.com/shuttle.php; ☉7am-10pm Mon-Thu, to 1am Fri, 6pm-1am Sat) runs along Broadway between Jack London Sq and Lake Merritt, stopping at Old Oakland/Chinatown, downtown BART stations and the Uptown district. The lime-green buses arrive every 10 to 15 minutes.

Berkeley

Berkeley – the birthplace of the free-speech and disability-rights movements, and the home of the hallowed halls of the University of California, Berkeley (aka 'Cal') – is no bashful wallflower. A national hot spot of (mostly left-of-center) intellectual discourse and with one of the most vocal activist populations in the country, this infamous college town has an interesting mix of graying progressives and idealistic undergrads. It's easy to stereotype 'Beserkeley' for some of its recycle-or-else PC crankiness, but the city is often on the forefront of environmental and political issues that eventually go mainstream.

Berkeley is also home to a large South Asian community, as evidenced by an abundance of sari shops on University Ave and an unusually large number of Indian, Pakistani and Nepalese restaurants.

◉ Sights & Activities

◉ University of California, Berkeley

The Berkeley campus of the University of California (UCB, called 'Cal' by both students and locals) is the oldest university in the state. The decision to found the college was made in 1866, and the first students arrived in 1873. Today UCB has more than 35,000 students, more than 1500 professors and more Nobel laureates than you could point a particle accelerator at.

From Telegraph Ave, enter the campus via Sproul Plaza and Sather Gate, a center for people-watching, soapbox oration and pseudotribal drumming. Or you can enter from Center St and Oxford Lane, near the downtown BART station.

Campanile   LANDMARK

(Sather Tower; Map p152; ☑510-642-6000; http://campanile.berkeley.edu; adult/child $3/2; ☉10am-3:45pm Mon-Fri, 10am-4:45pm Sat, to 1:30pm & 3-4:45pm Sun; 👪; ⓑDowntown Berkeley) Officially called Sather Tower, the Campanile was modeled on St Mark's Basilica in Venice. The 307ft spire offers fine views of the Bay Area, and at the top you can stare up into the carillon of 61 bells, ranging from the size of a cereal bowl to that of a Volkswagen. Recitals take place on weekdays at 7:50am and at noon and 6pm Monday to Saturday, with a longer piece performed at 2pm on Sunday.

Sather Gate   GATE

(Map p152; ☑510-642-6000; www.berkeley.edu; Sather Rd; ☉24hr; 🚃AC Transit 6, 51B) The frenetic energy buzzing from the university's Sather Gate on any given day is a mixture of youthful posthippies reminiscing about days before their time and fashion-conscious hipsters and punk rockers who sneer at tie-dyed nostalgia. Political activists still hand out leaflets here at the south entrance to campus.

Bancroft Library   LIBRARY

(Map p152; ☑510-642-3781; www.lib.berkeley.edu/libraries/bancroft-library; University Dr; ☉archives 10am-4pm or 5pm Mon-Fri; ⓑDowntown Berkeley) **FREE** The Bancroft houses, among other gems, the papers of Mark Twain, a copy of Shakespeare's folios and a diary from the Donner Party. Its small public exhibits of historical Californiana include the surprisingly small gold nugget that sparked the 1849 gold rush. Rotating temporary exhibits spotlight history and art, with pieces from the library's own collections. To register to use the library, you must present a current government or academic-issued photo ID. The registration desk is on your way in.

UC Berkeley Art Museum   MUSEUM

(BAMPFA; Map p152; ☑510-642-0808; www.bampfa.berkeley.edu; 2155 Center St; adult/child $12/free; ☉11am-7pm Sun, Wed & Thu, to 9pm Fri & Sat; ⓑDowntown Berkeley) With a stainless-steel exterior wrapping around a 1930s printing plant, the museum's new location holds multiple galleries showcasing a limited number of artworks, from ancient Chinese to cutting-edge contemporary. The complex also houses a bookstore, cafe and the much-loved Pacific Film Archive (p158).

Phoebe A Hearst Museum of Anthropology MUSEUM
(Map p152; ☑510-642-3682; http://hearstmu seum.berkeley.edu; Bancroft Way, at College Ave; adult/child $6/free; ⊙11am-5pm Sun-Wed & Fri, to 8pm Thu, 10am-6pm Sat; ☑AC Transit 6, 51B) South of the Campanile in Kroeber Hall, this small museum includes exhibits from indigenous cultures around the world, including ancient Peruvian, Egyptian and African items. There's also a large collection highlighting Native Californian cultures.

UC Museum of Paleontology MUSEUM
(Map p152; ☑510-642-1821; www.ucmp.berkeley.edu; Campanile Way; ⊙8am-10pm Mon-Thu, 8am-5pm Fri, 10am-5pm Sat, 1-10pm Sun; Ⓑ Downtown Berkeley) FREE Housed in the ornate Valley Life Sciences Building (and primarily a research facility that's closed to the public), this museum has a number of fossil exhibits in the atrium, including a *Tyrannosaurus rex* skeleton.

◉ South of Campus

South of campus along College Ave is the **Elmwood District**, a charming nook of shops and restaurants that offers a calming alternative to the frenetic buzz around Telegraph Ave. Continue further south and you'll be in Rockridge, in the neighboring city of Oakland.

Telegraph Avenue STREET
(Map p152; ⊙shop & restaurant hours vary; Ⓟ; ☑AC Transit 6) Telegraph Ave has traditionally been the throbbing heart of studentville in Berkeley, the sidewalks crowded with undergrads, postdocs and youthful shoppers squeezing their way past throngs of vendors, buskers and panhandlers. Street stalls hawk everything from crystals to bumper stickers to self-published tracts. Several cafes and budget eateries cater to students.

First Church of Christ, Scientist CHURCH
(Map p152; ☑510-845-7199; www.friendsof firstchurch.org; 2619 Dwight Way; ⊙tour 12:15pm 1st Sun each month; Ⓟ; ☑AC Transit 6) FREE Bernard Maybeck's impressive 1910 church uses concrete and wood in its blend of arts-and-crafts, Asian and Gothic influences. Maybeck was a professor of architecture at UC Berkeley and designed San Francisco's Palace of Fine Arts, plus many landmark homes in the Berkeley Hills.

Free 45-minute guided tours are given on the first Sunday of every month.

Julia Morgan Theater THEATER
(Map p152; ☑510-845-8542; http://tickets. berkeleyplayhouse.org; 2640 College Ave; ⊙not open to the public, except for performances; ☑AC Transit 51B) A beautifully understated, redwood-paneled 1910 theater, this performance space (formerly a church) was created by Bay Area architect Julia Morgan. She designed several landmark Bay Area buildings and, most famously, Hearst Castle on the Central Coast.

People's Park PARK
(Map p152; 2556 Haste St; ⊙24hr; ☑AC Transit 6) This park, just east of Telegraph Ave, is a marker in local history as a political battleground between residents and the city and state government in the late 1960s. Occasional festivals do still happen here, but it's rather run-down and serves mostly as a gathering spot for Berkeley's homeless.

There's talk of redeveloping the park into university-student housing.

◉ Downtown

Berkeley's downtown, centered on Shattuck Ave between University Ave and Dwight Way, has few traces of the city's tie-dyed reputation. Today it abounds with shops, restaurants and restored public buildings.

The nearby **arts district** revolves around the acclaimed thespian stomping grounds of the Berkeley Repertory Theatre and Aurora Theatre Company and live music at the historic Freight & Salvage Coffeehouse, all on Addison St.

◉ North Berkeley & Albany

Not too far north of the university campus, North Berkeley is a neighborhood filled with lovely garden-front homes and parks. The popular **Gourmet Ghetto** stretches along Shattuck Ave north of University Ave for several blocks, anchored by acclaimed restaurant Chez Panisse (p156). Further northwest, **Solano Avenue**, which crosses from Berkeley into Albany, is lined with funky shops and family-friendly restaurants.

Berkeley Rose Garden GARDENS
(☑510-981-6700; www.ci.berkeley.ca.us; 1200 Euclid Ave; ⊙dawn-dusk; ☑AC Transit 65) FREE In North Berkeley discover the Berkeley Rose Garden, with its eight terraces of colorful explosions. Here you'll find quiet benches

Central Berkeley

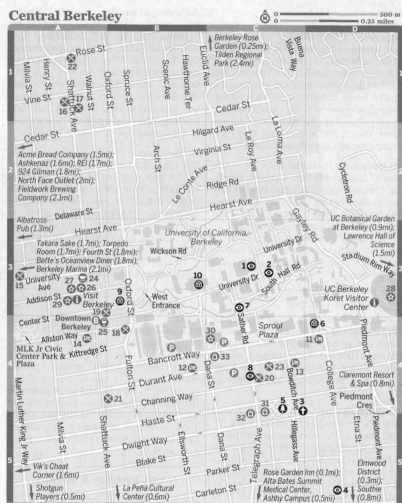

and a plethora of almost perpetually blooming roses arranged by hue. Across the street, **Cordornices Park** has a children's playground with a very fun concrete slide, about 40ft long.

◎ The Berkeley Hills

★ Tilden Regional Park   PARK
(📞 510-544-2747; www.ebparks.org/parks/tilden; ⏰ 5am-10pm; 🅿️🚼🐾; 🚍 AC Transit 67) 🎫 FREE
This 2079-acre park, up in the hills east of town, is Berkeley's best. It has nearly 40 miles of hiking and multiuse trails of var-

ying difficulty, from paved paths to hilly scrambles, including part of the magnificent Bay Area Ridge Trail. There's also a miniature steam train ($3), a children's farm and environmental education center, a wonderfully wild-looking botanical garden and an 18-hole golf course. Lake Anza is good for picnics and from spring through fall you can swim ($3.50).

AC Transit bus 67 runs to the park on weekends and holidays from Downtown Berkeley BART station, but only stops at the park entrance on weekdays.

Central Berkeley

◎ Sights
1 Bancroft Library C3
2 Campanile C3
3 First Church of Christ, Scientist C4
4 Julia Morgan Theater D5
5 People's Park C4
6 Phoebe A Hearst Museum of
  Anthropology D4
7 Sather Gate C3
8 Telegraph Avenue C4
9 UC Berkeley Art Museum B3
10 UC Museum of Paleontology B3

⬢ Sleeping
11 Bancroft Hotel D4
12 Berkeley City Club B4
13 Graduate Berkeley C4
14 Hotel Shattuck Plaza A4

✴ Eating
15 Butcher's Son A3
16 Cheese Board Collective A1
17 Chez Panisse A1
   Cream .... (see 20)

18 Gather B4
19 Ippuku A3
20 KoJa Kitchen C4
21 La Note B4
22 North Berkeley Farmers Market A1
23 Smoke's Poutinerie C4

☕ Drinking & Nightlife
24 Asha Tea House A3
   Caffe Strada .... (see 11)
25 Jupiter A4

✪ Entertainment
26 Aurora Theatre Company A3
27 Berkeley Repertory Theatre A3
28 California Memorial Stadium D3
29 Freight & Salvage Coffeehouse A3
   Pacific Film Archive .... (see 9)
30 Zellerbach Hall C4

🛍 Shopping
31 Amoeba Music C4
32 Moe's Books C5
33 University Press Books C4

UC Botanical Garden at Berkeley GARDENS
(☑ 510-643-2755; http://botanicalgarden.berkeley.edu; 200 Centennial Dr; adult/child $10/2; ◷ 9am-5pm, last entry 4:30pm, closed 1st Tue each month; ℗ 👪; 🚍 Bear Transit H) 🌿 With 34 acres and more than 10,000 types of plants, this garden in the hills above campus has one of the most varied collections in the USA. Flora from every continent except Antarctica are lovingly tended here, with special emphasis on Mediterranean species that grow in California, the Americas, the Mediterranean and southern Africa.

On weekdays, catch the university's Bear Transit H Line shuttle ($1) from campus. Limited parking across the street from the garden costs $1 per hour.

A nearby **fire trail** makes a woodsy walking loop around Strawberry Canyon, offering great views of town and the off-limits Lawrence Berkeley National Laboratory. Find the trailhead on the east side of Centennial Dr just southwest of the botanical garden; you'll emerge near the Lawrence Hall of Science.

Lawrence Hall of Science MUSEUM
(☑ 510-642-5132; www.lawrencehallofscience.org; 1 Centennial Dr; adult/child $12/10; ◷ 10am-5pm Wed-Sun, daily mid-Jun–early Sep; ℗ 👪; 🚍 AC Transit 65) Near Grizzly Peak Blvd, this science hall is named after Ernest Lawrence, who won the Nobel Prize for his invention

of the cyclotron particle accelerator. He was a key member of the WWII Manhattan Project, and he's also the name behind the Lawrence Berkeley and Lawrence Livermore national laboratories. The museum has interactive but dated exhibits for kids and adults (many closed weekdays) on subjects ranging from earthquakes to nanotechnology. Outside there's a 60ft model of a DNA molecule.

From Downtown Berkeley BART station, take AC Transit bus 65. From campus, catch the university's Bear Transit H Line shuttle ($1). On-site parking costs $1 per hour.

◎ West Berkeley

Adventure Playground PARK
(☑ 510-981-6720; www.cityofberkeley.info/adventureplayground; 160 University Ave; ◷ 11am-5pm mid-Jun–mid-Aug, Sat & Sun only rest of year; ℗ 👪; 🚍 AC Transit 81) FREE At the Berkeley Marina, this is one of the coolest play spaces in the Bay Area – a free outdoor park encouraging creativity and cooperation where supervised kids of any age can help build and paint their own structures. There's an awesome zipline too. Dress the tykes in play clothes, because they *will* get dirty.

Berkeley Marina MARINA
(☑ 510-981-6740; www.ci.berkeley.ca.us; 201 University Ave; ◷ 6am-10pm; ℗ 👪 🐕; 🚍 AC Transit

81) At the west end of University Ave is the marina, frequented by squawking seagulls, silent types fishing from the pier and, especially on windy weekends, families flying colorful kites. It offers sweeping waterfront views from paved walking, cycling and running paths.

The marina was originally built in the late 19th century, then replaced by a ferry pier in the 1920s (its unusual length dictated by the bay's extreme shallowness).

Takara Sake
MUSEUM

(☎510-540-8250; www.takarasake.com; 708 Addison St; tasting fee $5-10; ⊙noon-6pm, last tasting 5:30pm; 🚇AC Transit 51B) Stop in to see the traditional wooden tools used for making sake and a short video of the brewing process. Tours of the factory aren't offered, but you can view elements of modern production and bottling through a window. Sake flights are poured in a spacious tasting room constructed with reclaimed wood and floor tiles fashioned from recycled glass.

🛏 Sleeping

Lodging rates spike during special university events such as graduation (mid-May) and home football games. A number of older, less expensive motels along University Ave can be handy during peak demand, as can chain motels and hotels off I-80 in Emeryville or Vallejo.

Graduate Berkeley
BOUTIQUE HOTEL $$

(Map p152; ☎510-845-8981; http://graduate berkeley.com; 2600 Durant Ave; r from $160; P❄🅿@🛜🐾; 🚇AC Transit 51B) Located a block from campus, this classic 1928 hotel has been cheekily renovated to highlight the connection to the university. The lobby is adorned with embarrassing yearbook photos and a ceiling mobile of exam books, and smallish rooms have dictionary-covered shower curtains and bongs repurposed into bedside lamps. Parking is $20.

Berkeley City Club
HISTORIC HOTEL $$

(Map p152; ☎510-848-7800; www.berkeleycity club.com; 2315 Durant Ave; r/ste from $215; P❄@🛜🐾; 🚇AC Transit 51B) Designed by Julia Morgan (the architect of Hearst Castle), the 35 rooms and dazzling common areas of this refurbished 1929 historic landmark building (which is also a private club) feel like a glorious time warp into a more refined era. The hotel contains lush and serene

Italianate courtyards, gardens and terraces and a stunning indoor pool. Parking is $20.

Elegant Old World rooms contain no TV, and those with numbers ending in 4 and 8 have to-die-for views of the bay and the Golden Gate Bridge.

Hotel Shattuck Plaza
HOTEL $$

(Map p152; ☎510-845-7300; www.hotelshattuck plaza.com; 2086 Allston Way; r from $200; P❄ ✳@🛜; Ⓑ Downtown Berkeley) Following a $15-million renovation and greening of this 100-year-old downtown jewel, a foyer of red Italian glass lighting, flocked Victorian-style wallpaper – and yes, a peace sign tiled into the floor – leads to comfortable rooms with down comforters and an airy, columned restaurant serving all meals. Accommodations off Shattuck Ave are quietest, while cityscape rooms boast bay views.

Bancroft Hotel
HISTORIC HOTEL $$

(Map p152; ☎510-549-1000; http://bancrofthotel. com; 2680 Bancroft Way; r $125-230; P❄@🛜; 🚇AC Transit 51B) 🌿 A gorgeous 1928 arts-and-crafts building that was originally a women's club, the Bancroft is just across the street from campus and two blocks from Telegraph Ave (p151). It has 22 small, simply furnished rooms (some with lovely balconies) and a spectacular bay-view rooftop, though no elevator. Limited parking.

★ Claremont Resort & Spa
RESORT $$$

(☎510-843-3000; www.fairmont.com/claremont -berkeley; 41 Tunnel Rd; r from $240; P❄✳@ 🛜🏊🐾) The East Bay's classy crème de la crème, this Fairmont-owned historic hotel is a glamorous white 1915 building with elegant restaurants, a fitness center, swimming pools, tennis courts and a full-service spa. The bay-view rooms are superb. It's located at the foot of the Berkeley Hills, off Hwy 13 (Tunnel Rd) near the Oakland border. Parking is $30.

✕ Eating

Telegraph Ave is packed with cafes, pizza counters and cheap restaurants, and Berkeley's Little India runs along the University Ave corridor. Many more restaurants can be found along Shattuck Ave near the Downtown Berkeley BART station. The section of Shattuck Ave north of University Ave, nicknamed the 'Gourmet Ghetto,' is home to excellent restaurants and cafes for all budgets.

⚔ Downtown & Around Campus

KoJa Kitchen
FUSION $

(Map p152; ☑510-962-5652; www.kojakitchen. com; 2395 Telegraph Ave; items $4-10; ⊘11am-10pm; ⬚AC Transit 51B) From food truck to a brick-and-mortar shop, this Korean-Japanese fusion eatery makes addictive short-rib and braised-pork sandwiches out of garlicky fried-rice buns, with kimchi-spiked waffle fries on the side. Order ahead, or expect a wait.

Smoke's Poutinerie
FAST FOOD $

(Map p152; ☑510-540-7500; http://smokespou tinerie.com; 2518 Durant Ave; items $3-13; ⊘11am-4am; ⬚AC Transit 51B) Since California legalized recreational marijuana use, demand has only increased at this Canadian poutine shop, open till the wee hours. Get the classic Quebecois taste of cheese curds and gravy, or a wilder combination such as jerk chicken or veggie nacho.

Butcher's Son
VEGAN, DELI $

(Map p152; ☑510-984-0818; www.thebutcherve ganson.com; 1941 University Ave; mains $8-13; ⊘11am-8pm Mon & Thu-Fri, to 3pm Tue & Wed, 9am-5pm Sat & Sun; ☑; ⒷDowntown Berkeley) What could be more in tune with Berkeley's granola-crunchy, latter-day-hippie vibe than a vegan deli? Gorge yourself on imitation deli meats and cheeses that will scratch that itch for a fried mozzarella and meatball sandwich or hot turkey and roast beef on rye, all made without any animal products.

Cream
ICE CREAM $

(Map p152; ☑510-649-1000; http://creamnation. com; 2399 Telegraph Ave; items $2-4; ⊘noon-11pm Sun-Thu, to midnight Fri & Sat; ☑⬚; ⬚AC Transit 51B) With a line out the door, this corner shop smooshes together ice-cream sandwiches with creative flavors and freshly baked cookies. Otherwise, get an ice-cream sundae in a less exciting cup or cone.

North Berkeley Farmers Market
MARKET $

(Map p152; ☑510-548-3333; www.ecologycenter. org; Shattuck Ave, at Rose St; ⊘3-7pm Thu; ☑⬚; ⬚AC Transit 79) ⬤ Pick up some organic produce or tasty prepared food at North Berkeley's weekly farmers market, operating year-round.

Ippuku
JAPANESE $$

(Map p152; ☑510-665-1969; www.ippukuberkeley. com; 2130 Center St; shared plates $5-20; ⊘5-10pm Tue-Thu, to 11pm Fri & Sat; ⒷDowntown Berkeley) Japanese expats gush that Ippuku reminds them of *izakaya* (Japanese gastro-pubs) back in Tokyo. Choose from a menu of yakitori (skewered meats and vegetables) and handmade soba noodles as you settle in at one of the traditional tatami tables (no

---

WATERSPORTS ON THE BAY

As well as making for a lovely postcard or iconic snapshot, San Francisco Bay offers plenty of options for getting out on the water. Myriad outfitters provide equipment, lessons and guided tours.

California Canoe & Kayak (Map p142; ☑510-893-7833; www.calkayak.com; 409 Water St; kayak & SUP rentals per hour $25-50, tours from $50; ⊘10am-6pm Mon-Fri, 9am-6pm Sat, 9am-5pm Sun; ⬚Broadway Shuttle) Rents kayaks and stand up paddleboard (SUP) sets at Oakland's Jack London Sq. Book ahead for moonlight paddles along the waterfront.

Cal Adventures (☑510-642-4000, recorded info 510-642-7707; http://recsports.berkeley. edu/cal-adventures; 124 University Ave; rentals/classes from $20/45; ⊘hours vary; ⬚AC Transit 81) Run by the UC Aquatic Center at Berkeley Marina, it organizes sailing, windsurfing, SUP and sea-kayaking classes and rentals.

Cal Sailing Club (www.cal-sailing.org; 124 University Ave; 3-month membership $99; ⊘noon-sunset Mon-Fri, from 9am Sat & Sun; ⬚AC Transit 81) Membership-based, volunteer-run nonprofit that runs sailing and windsurfing programs at Berkeley Marina.

Boardsports California (☑415-385-1224; https://boardsportscalifornia.com; rentals/lessons from $25/49; ⊘hours vary) Offers lessons and rentals for kiteboarding, windsurfing, SUP and kayaking, with locations at Alameda in the East Bay and Coyote Point Recreation Area in San Mateo, near San Francisco International Airport.

Sea Trek (p125) In Sausalito, this long-running outfitter has kayaks and SUP sets for rent and a fabulous array of tours, including bay crossings to Angel Island.

shoes, please) or cozy booth perches. Order *shōchū*, a distilled alcohol usually made from rice or barley. Reservations essential.

La Note FRENCH **$$**
(Map p152; ☑ 510-843-1525; www.lanoterestaurant. com; 2377 Shattuck Ave; mains $10-25; ⊙ breakfast & lunch 8am-2:30pm Mon-Fri, to 3pm Sat & Sun, dinner 6-10pm Thu-Sat; B Downtown Berkeley) A rustic country-French bistro downtown, La Note serves excellent breakfasts. Wake up to a big bowl of café au lait, paired with brioche *pain perdu* or lemon-gingerbread pancakes with poached pears. Anticipate a wait on weekends.

Gather CALIFORNIAN **$$**
(Map p152; ☑ 510-809-0400; www.gatherrestaurant.com; 2200 Oxford St; dinner mains $16-30; ⊙ 11:30am-2pm & 5-9pm Mon-Thu, 11:30-2pm & 5-10pm Fri, 10am-2pm & 5-10pm Sat, 10am-2pm & 5-9pm Sun; ☑; B Downtown Berkeley) ⬤ When vegan foodies and passionate farm-to-table types dine out together, they often end up here. Inside a salvaged-wood interior punctuated by green vines streaking down over an open kitchen, dishes are created from locally sourced ingredients and sustainably raised meats. Reservations recommended.

✖ North Berkeley

Cheese Board Collective PIZZA **$**
(Map p152; ☑ 510-549-3055; www.cheeseboardcollective.coop; 1504 & 1512 Shattuck Ave; slices/half-pizzas $2.75/11; ⊙ shop 7am-1pm Mon, to 6pm Tue-Fri, to 5pm Sat, pizzeria 11:30am-3pm & 4:30-8pm Tue-Sat; ☑ ⚑; ☐ AC Transit 7) Stop in to take stock of more than 300 cheeses available at this worker-owned business and scoop up some fresh bread to make a picnic lunch. Or sit down for a slice of the crispy veggie pizza just next door, where live music's often featured.

★ Chez Panisse CALIFORNIAN **$$$**
(Map p152; ☑ cafe 510-548-5049, restaurant 510-548-5525; www.chezpanisse.com; 1517 Shattuck Ave; cafe dinner mains $22-35, restaurant prix-fixe dinner $75-125; ⊙ cafe 11:30am-2:45pm & 5-10:30pm Mon-Thu, 11:30am-3pm & 5-11:30pm Fri & Sat, restaurant seatings 5:30pm & 8pm Mon-Sat; ☑; ☐ AC Transit 7) ⬤ Foodies come to worship here at the church of Alice Waters, inventor of California cuisine. It's in a lovely arts-and-crafts house in Berkeley's 'Gourmet Ghetto,' and you can choose to pull out all the stops with a prix-fixe meal downstairs, or go less expensive and a tad less formal in the up-

stairs cafe. Reservations accepted one month ahead. The restaurant is as good and popular as it ever was, and despite its fame, the place has retained a welcoming atmosphere.

✖ West Berkeley

Vik's Chaat Corner INDIAN **$**
(☑ 510-644-4412; www.vikschaatcorner.com; 2390 4th St; mains $6-12; ⊙ 11am-6pm Mon-Thu, to 8pm Fri-Sun; ☑ ⚑; ☐ AC Transit 80) Off in West Berkeley, this longtime, popular *chaat* house gets mobbed at lunchtime by regulars that include equal numbers of hungry office workers, students and Indian families. Order samosas or a puffy *bhature* (flatbread) with *chole* (chickpea curry), an *uttapam* (savory pancake) or one of many filling *dosas* (savory crepes). Colorful Indian sweets, sold by the piece or pound, are irresistible.

Bette's Oceanview Diner AMERICAN **$$**
(☑ 510-644-3230; www.bettesdiner.com; 1807 4th St; mains $7-16; ⊙ 6:30am-2:30pm Mon-Fri, to 4pm Sat & Sun; ⚑; ☐ AC Transit 51B) ⬤ This is a buzzing breakfast spot, especially on the weekends. It dishes up baked soufflé pancakes and German-style potato pancakes with applesauce, plus eggs and sandwiches. From-scratch baked goods and a nifty diner interior make it worth the wait.

♟ Drinking & Nightlife

You'll never come up short of places to imbibe in Berkeley. Join students at bars and pubs scattered around downtown, on side streets near the university campus or along College Ave in Elmwood. Detour to industrial areas of West Berkeley to discover craft beers and a sake distillery (p154).

Fieldwork Brewing Company BREWERY
(☑ 510-898-1203; http://fieldworkbrewing.com; 1160 6th St; ⊙ 11am-10pm Sun-Thu, to 11pm Fri & Sat; ☐ AC Transit 12) Come to this industrial brewery taproom at the edge of town for outstanding craft beer and sit down on the outdoor patio with a tasting flight of IPAs or a glass of rich Mexican hot chocolate stout. It's dog-friendly, and there are racks to hang your bicycle inside the front door. There's a short menu of Mexican-Californian food too.

Asha Tea House CAFE
(Map p152; www.ashateahouse.com; 2086 University Ave; ⊙ 11am-10pm Mon-Sat, to 8pm Sun; ☎; B Downtown Berkeley) ⬤ Find your bliss in this industrial-modern tea shop, where acrylic prints of verdant tea plantations

overhang the bar. Handcrafted Indian chai, Japanese matcha and Hong Kong–style milk tea star on a connoisseur's drinks menu.

Torpedo Room   BAR
(☑510-647-3439; www.sierranevada.com/brewery/california/torpedoroom; 2031 4th St; ☺noon-9pm Tue-Fri, from 11am Sat, noon-7pm Sun; ☒AC Transit 51B) Sample a flight of tasting pours or order a pint from the 16 rotating drafts (including some rare small-batch beers) on tap at Sierra Nevada brewery's tasting room in West Berkeley.

Albatross   PUB
(☑510-843-2473; www.albatrosspub.com; 1822 San Pablo Ave; ☺6pm-2am Sun-Tue, from 4:30pm Wed-Sat; ☒AC Transit 51B) Berkeley's oldest pub is one of the most inviting and friendly in the city. Some serious darts are played here and board games get played around many of the worn-out tables. Sunday is trivia quiz night.

Jupiter   PUB
(Map p152; ☑510-843-8277; www.jupiterbeer.com; 2181 Shattuck Ave; ☺11:30am-12:30am Mon-Thu, to 1:30am Fri, noon-1:30am Sat, noon-11:30pm Sun; ☒Downtown Berkeley) This downtown pub has loads of regional microbrews, a beer garden, decent pizza and live bands most nights. Sit upstairs for a bird's-eye view of bustling Shattuck Ave.

Caffe Strada   CAFE
(Map p152; ☑510-843-5282; 2300 College Ave; ☺6am-midnight; ☺; ☒AC Transit 51B) At this popular, student-saturated hangout with an inviting shaded patio, try the strong espressos or a sweet white-chocolate mocha.

☆ Entertainment
Berkeley's arts district, centered on Addison St between Milvia St and Shattuck Ave, anchors downtown's performing-arts scene.

Berkeley also has plenty of intimate live-music venues. Cover charges usually range from $5 to $20, and several venues are all-ages or 18-and-over.

Freight & Salvage Coffeehouse   LIVE MUSIC
(Map p152; ☑510-644-2020; www.thefreight.org; 2020 Addison St; tickets $5-45; ☺shows daily; ☺; ☒Downtown Berkeley) This legendary club has almost 50 years of history and is conveniently located in the downtown arts district. It features great traditional folk, country, bluegrass and world music and welcomes all ages, with half-price tickets for patrons under 21.

924 Gilman   LIVE MUSIC
(☑510-524-8180; www.924gilman.org; 924 Gilman St; tickets from $10; ☺Sat & Sun; ☒AC Transit 12) This volunteer-run and booze-free all-ages space is a West Coast punk-rock institution. Check the online calendar for upcoming shows on weekend nights.

Ashkenaz   WORLD MUSIC, DANCE
(☑510-525-5054; www.ashkenaz.com; 1317 San Pablo Ave; free-$20; ☺hours vary; ☺; ☒AC Transit 52) Ashkenaz is a 'music and dance community center' attracting activists, hippies and fans of folk, swing, world music and more who love to dance (lessons offered).

La Peña Cultural Center   WORLD MUSIC
(☑510-849-2568; www.lapena.org; 3105 Shattuck Ave; free-$16; ☺hours vary; ☒Ashby) This fun-loving, warmhearted community center presents dynamic dance classes and musical and visual arts events with a peace and justice bent. Look for a vibrant mural outside and the on-site Mexican cafe, perfect for grabbing drinks and a preshow bite.

Berkeley Repertory Theatre   THEATER
(Map p152; ☑510-647-2949; www.berkeleyrep.org; 2025 Addison St; tickets $40-100; ☺box office noon-7pm Tue-Sun; ☒Downtown Berkeley) This highly respected company has produced bold versions of classical and modern plays since 1968. Most shows have half-price tickets for patrons under 30.

California Shakespeare Theater   THEATER
(☑510-548-9666; www.calshakes.org; 701 Heinz Ave; tickets $21-56; ☺late May-early Oct) Headquartered in Berkeley, with the fantastic outdoor Bruns Amphitheater east of the Berkeley Hills in Orinda, 'Cal Shakes' is a warm-weather tradition of alfresco Shakespeare and other classic productions.

Zellerbach Hall   PERFORMING ARTS
(Map p152; ☑510-642-9988; https://calperformances.org; off Bancroft Way; tickets from $10; ☺ticket office usually noon-5:30pm Tue-Fri, 1-5pm Sat & Sun; ☒AC Transit 51B) At the south end of campus near Bancroft Way and Dana St, Zellerbach Hall features dance events, musical concerts and performances of all types by national and international touring artists. The on-site Cal Performances Ticket Office sells tickets.

Shotgun Players   THEATER
(☑510-841-6500; www.shotgunplayers.org; 1901 Ashby Ave; tickets $20-50; ☺hours vary; ☒Downtown Berkeley) ☙ Berkeley's solar-powered

WORTH A TRIP

EAST BROTHER LIGHT STATION

Most Bay Area residents have never heard of this speck of an island off the East Bay city of Richmond, and even fewer know that the **East Brother Light Station** (☏ 510-233-2385; www.ebls.org; 1900 Stenmark Dr, Richmond; d incl breakfast & dinner $295-415; ☺ Thu-Sun; ➡) is a five-room Victorian B&B. Spend the night in the romantic lighthouse or fog-signal building (the foghorn blares from October 1 to April 1). Access is by boat; reserve ahead.

Resident innkeepers serve afternoon hors d'oeuvres and champagne, and after dinner you can stroll around the breezy 0.75-acre islet and rummage through historical photos and artifacts.

theater company stages exciting and provocative works in an intimate space.

Aurora Theatre Company   THEATER
(Map p152; ☏ 510-843-4822; www.auroratheatre.org; 2081 Addison St; tickets from $25; ☺ box office usually 1-4pm Tue-Fri; **B** Downtown Berkeley) Intimate downtown theater performs contemporary, thought-provoking plays staged with subtle aesthetics.

Pacific Film Archive   CINEMA
(PFA; Map p152; ☏ 510-642-5249; www.bampfa.berkeley.edu; 2155 Center St; adult/child from $12/8; ☺ hours vary; ♿; **B** Downtown Berkeley) A world-renowned film center with an ever-changing schedule of international and classic films – cineastes should seek out this place. The spacious theater has seats comfy enough for hours-long movie marathons. Movie tickets include same-day admission to the UC Berkeley Art Museum (p150).

🔒 Shopping

Heading south of the university campus, Telegraph Ave caters mostly to students, hawking a steady dose of urban hippie gear, handmade sidewalk-vendor jewelry and head-shop paraphernalia. Audiophiles will swoon over the music stores.

Berkeley's other shopping corridors include College Ave in the Elmwood District (on the Oakland border), 4th St (north of University Ave) and Solano Ave (heading into Albany).

Amoeba Music   MUSIC
(Map p152; ☏ 510-549-1125; www.amoeba.com; 2455 Telegraph Ave; ☺ 11am-8pm Sun-Thu, to 10pm Fri & Sat; ☐ AC Transit 51B) If you're a music junkie, you might plan on spending a few hours at the original Berkeley branch of Amoeba Music, packed with massive quantities of new and used CDs, DVDs, tapes and records (yes, lots of vinyl).

Down Home Music   MUSIC
(☏ 510-525-2129; www.downhomemusic.com; 10341 San Pablo Ave, El Cerrito; ☺ 11am-7pm Tue-Sun; ☐ AC Transit 72) North of Berkeley, this world-class store for roots, blues, folk, country, jazz and world music is affiliated with the Arhoolie record label, which has been issuing landmark recordings since the early 1960s.

University Press Books   BOOKS
(Map p152; ☏ 510-548-0585; www.universitypressbooks.com; 2430 Bancroft Way; ☺ 11am-7pm Mon-Fri, to 6pm Sat, noon-5pm Sun; ☐ AC Transit 51B) Across the street from campus, this academic and scholarly bookstore stocks works by UC Berkeley professors and other academic and museum publishers, with frequent author appearances.

REI   SPORTS & OUTDOORS
(☏ 510-527-4140; www.rei.com; 1338 San Pablo Ave; ☺ 10am-9pm Mon-Fri, to 8pm Sat, to 7pm Sun; ♿; ☐ AC Transit 52) This large and busy co-op lures in active folks for camping and mountaineering rentals, sports clothing and all kinds of nifty outdoor gear.

North Face Outlet   SPORTS & OUTDOORS
(☏ 510-526-3530; www.thenorthface.com; 1238 5th St; ☺ 10am-7pm Mon-Sat, 11am-5pm Sun; ☐ AC Transit 12) Discount store for the Bay Area–based brand of outdoor gear is just off Gilman St.

Fourth Street   HOMEWARES, FASHION
(☏ 510-644-3002; www.fourthstreet.com; ☺ store hours vary; ☐ AC Transit 51B) Hidden within an industrial section near I-80, this three-block area offers shaded sidewalks for upscale shopping or just strolling, and a few good restaurants.

Moe's Books   BOOKS
(Map p152; ☏ 510-849-2087; www.moesbooks.com; 2476 Telegraph Ave; ☺ 10am-10pm; ☐ AC Transit 51B) A long-standing local favorite, Moe's offers four floors of new, used and remaindered books for hours of browsing.

ⓘ Information

MEDICAL SERVICES

Alta Bates Summit Medical Center, Ashby Campus (☑ 510-204-4444; www.sutterhealth.org; 2450 Ashby Ave; ☺ 24hr; ☐ AC Transit 6) offers 24-hour emergency services.

TOURIST INFORMATION

UC Berkeley Koret Visitor Center (Map p152; ☑ 510-642-5215; http://visit.berkeley.edu; 2227 Piedmont Ave; ☺ 8:30am-4:30pm Mon-Fri, 9am-1pm Sat & Sun; ☐ AC Transit 36) Campus maps anad information available at the new visitor center on Goldman Plaza at California Memorial Stadium (Map p152; ☑ 510-642-2730; www.californiamemorialstadium.com; 2227 Piedmont Ave; ☺ hours vary; ♿; ☐ AC Transit 52). Free 90-minute campus walking tours usually start at 10am daily (advance reservations required).

Visit Berkeley (Map p152; ☑ 510-549-7040; www.visitberkeley.com; 2030 Addison St; ☺ 9am-1pm & 2-5pm Mon-Fri; Ⓑ Downtown Berkeley) The helpful Berkeley Convention & Visitors Bureau prints a free visitors guide, also available online.

ⓘ Getting There & Away

BART

To get to Berkeley, catch a Richmond-bound train to one of three BART (p149) stations: Ashby, Downtown Berkeley or North Berkeley. Fares between Berkeley and San Francisco cost $4.10 to $4.40, between Berkeley and downtown Oakland $1.95. After 8pm on weekdays, 6pm on Saturday and all day Sunday, there is no direct train service operating from San Francisco to Berkeley; instead, catch a Pittsburg/Bay Point train, then transfer at 19th St station in Oakland.

BUS

On AC Transit (p149), the F line leaves from the Transbay Transit Center in San Francisco for downtown Berkeley and the university campus approximately every half-hour ($4.20, 40 minutes). The Transbay bus fare is discounted to $2.10 if you also purchase a day pass ($5) valid on AC Transit's local East Bay bus routes.

Between downtown Berkeley and downtown Oakland, take fast and frequent AC Transit bus 6 along Telegraph Ave. Alternatively, take bus 18 via Martin Luther King Jr Way and Shattuck Ave. Bus 51B travels along University Ave past Downtown Berkeley BART station to the Berkeley Marina. All one-way local bus fares on AC Transit are $2.10.

CAR & MOTORCYCLE

From San Francisco, drive over the Bay Bridge and then follow either I-80 (for University Ave, Berkeley Marina, downtown Berkeley and the university campus) or Hwy 24 (for College Ave and the Berkeley Hills).

TRAIN

Amtrak does stop in Berkeley, but the platform is not staffed and direct connections are few. More convenient is Emeryville Amtrak station (p149), about 2 miles south.

To reach the Emeryville station from downtown Berkeley, take AC Transit bus F ($4.20) or ride BART to the MacArthur station ($1.95, five minutes) and then catch the free Emery Go Round (p149) shuttle bus.

ⓘ Getting Around

Local buses, cycling and walking are the best ways to get around Berkeley.

BICYCLE

By Downtown Berkeley BART station, **Bike Station** (☑ 510-548-7433; http://bikehub.com/bartbikestation; 2208 Shattuck Ave; per day/week/month $35/95/200; ☺ 7am-9pm Mon-Fri, 11am-7pm Sat) rents bicycles with a helmet and U-lock.

BUS

AC Transit (p149) operates local public buses in and around Berkeley. The one-way fare is $2.10; pay with cash (exact change required) or a Clipper card (www.clippercard.com).

The university's **Bear Transit** (☑ 510-643-7701; http://pt.berkeley.edu) runs a shuttle from Downtown Berkeley BART station to various points on campus. From Bear Transit's on-campus stop at Hearst Mining Circle, the H Line runs along Centennial Dr to the upper parts of the campus. For visitors, each ride costs $1 (bring cash).

CAR & MOTORCYCLE

Drivers should note that numerous barriers have been set up to prevent car traffic from traversing residential streets at high speeds, so zigzagging is necessary in some neighborhoods.

Downtown and near the university campus, pay-parking lots are well signed. Metered street-parking spots are rarely empty.

Mt Diablo State Park

Collecting a light dusting of snowflakes on the coldest days of winter, Mt Diablo (3849ft) is over 1200ft higher than Mt Tamalpais in Marin County. On a clear day (early on a winter morning is a good bet) the views from Diablo's summit are vast and sweeping. To the west you can see over the bay and out to the Farallon Islands; to the east you can look out over the Central Valley to the Sierra Nevada.

Most easily accessed from Danville or Walnut Creek, the **park** (☏925-837-2525; www.mdia.org; per vehicle $6-10; ⊗8am-sunset) is threaded by over 50 miles of hiking trails. You can also drive to the summit, where there's a visitor center.

⌖ Sleeping

Mt Diablo State Park Campgrounds   CAMPGROUND $

(☏reservations 800-444-7275; www.reserveameri ca.com; tent & RV sites $30) Of the park's three drive-in campgrounds, Juniper and Live Oak have showers. All campgrounds may be closed during high fire danger and water may be turned off throughout the park if water restrictions are in effect.

❶ Information

Summit Visitor Center (www.parks.ca.gov; ⊗10am-4pm) Mt Diablo State Park's small main visitor center.

John Muir National Historic Site

Naturalist John Muir's **former residence** (☏925-228-8860; www.nps.gov/jomu; 4202 Alhambra Ave, Martinez; ⊗Muir Home 10am-5pm, Mt Wanda sunrise-sunset) FREE sits in a pastoral patch of farmland in bustling, modern Martinez. Though Muir wrote of sauntering the Sierra Nevada with a sack of tea and bread, it may be a shock for those familiar with the iconic Sierra Club founder's ascetic weather-beaten appearance that this house (built by his father-in-law) is a model of Victorian Italianate refinement, with a tower cupola, a daintily upholstered parlor and splashes of white lace.

Muir's 'scribble den' has been left as it was during his life, with crumbled papers overflowing from wire wastebaskets and driedbread balls – his preferred snack – resting on the mantelpiece.

Acres of the family's fruit orchards still stand, and visitors can enjoy seasonal samples. The grounds include the 1849 Martinez Adobe, part of the ranch on which the house was built, and oak-speckled hiking trails on nearby Mt Wanda, named for one of Muir's daughters. Check the website for special campfire programs, wildflower walks and full-moon hikes. The park is just north of

Hwy 4. **County Connection** (☏925-676-7500; https://countyconnection.com) buses 16 and 98X from nearby Amtrak and BART stations stop here.

THE PENINSULA

South of San Francisco, squeezed tightly between the bay and the coastal foothills, a vast swath of suburbia continues toward San Jose. Dotted inside this area are Palo Alto, home of Stanford University, and Silicon Valley, the epicenter of the Bay Area's tech industry.

Don't bother looking for Silicon Valley on the map – you won't find it. Because silicon chips form the basis of modern microcomputers, and the Santa Clara Valley – stretching from Palo Alto through Mountain View, Sunnyvale and Cupertino to San Jose – is thought of as the birthplace of the microcomputer, it's nicknamed 'Silicon Valley.' It's hard to imagine that even after WWII this was still a wide expanse of orchards and farms.

Further west, the 70-mile stretch of coastal Hwy 1 from San Francisco to Santa Cruz is one of California's most bewitching oceanside drives. For the most part, it's winding, two-lane blacktop, passing beach after beach.

San Francisco to San Jose

South of the San Francisco peninsula, I-280 is the dividing line between the densely populated South Bay area and the rugged and lightly populated Pacific Coast. With sweeping views of hills and reservoirs, I-280 is a more scenic choice than Hwy 101, which runs through business parks. Unfortunately, these parallel north–south arteries are often both clogged with traffic.

A historic site where European explorers first set eyes on San Francisco Bay, **Sweeney Ridge** (www.nps.gov/goga/sweeney.htm; end of Sneath Lane, San Bruno) straddles a prime spot between Pacifica and San Bruno, and offers hikers unparalleled ocean and bay views. From I-280, exit at Sneath Lane and follow it 2 miles west until it dead ends at the trailhead.

Right on the bay at the northern edge of San Mateo, 4 miles south of San Francisco International Airport, is **Coyote Point Recreation Area** (☏650-573-2592; http://parks. smcgov.org; 1701 Coyote Point Dr, San Mateo; per car $6; ⊗8am-8pm Apr-Aug, to 6pm or 7pm Sep-Mar;

P ♿), a popular park and windsurfing destination. The main attraction – formerly known as the Coyote Point Museum – is **CuriOdyssey** (☑ 650-342-7755; http://curiodyssey.org; adult/child $11/8; ⊘ 10am-5pm Tue-Sun; P ♿), with innovative exhibits highlighting science and wildlife. Exit Hwy 101 at Coyote Point Dr.

Stanford University

Sprawled over 8200 leafy acres in Palo Alto, Stanford University (www.stanford.edu) was founded by Leland Stanford, one of the Central Pacific Railroad's 'Big Four' founders and a former governor of California. When the Stanfords' only child died of typhoid during a European tour in 1884, they decided to build a university in his memory. The campus was built on the site of the Stanfords' horse-breeding farm and, as a result, Stanford is still known as 'The Farm.'

◉ Sights

Main Quad   PLAZA
(☑ 650-723-2560; http://visit.stanford.edu/plan/guides/visit.html; off Palm Dr) Auguste Rodin's *Burghers of Calais* bronze sculpture marks the entrance to Stanford University's Main Quad, an open plaza where the original 12 campus buildings, a mix of Romanesque and Mission Revival styles, were joined by Memorial Church in 1903. The church is noted for its beautiful mosaic-tiled frontage, stained-glass windows and five organs with more than 8000 pipes. Free guided tours of 'MemChu' are given at 2pm every Friday and 11:15am on the first Sunday of the month.

Hoover Tower   TOWER
(☑ 650-723-2560; http://visit.stanford.edu/plan/guides/hoover.html; adult/child $4/3; ⊘ 10am-4pm, last entry 3:30pm) A campus landmark at the east of the Main Quad, the 285ft-high Hoover Tower offers superb views. The tower houses a university library, offices and part of the right-wing Hoover Institution on War, Revolution & Peace (where Donald Rumsfeld caused a university-wide stir by accepting a position after he resigned as Secretary of Defense).

Cantor Arts Center   MUSEUM
(☑ 650-498-1480; http://museum.stanford.edu; 328 Lomita Dr; ⊘ 11am-5pm Wed & Fri-Mon, to 8pm Thu; P) FREE The Cantor Center for Visual Arts is a large museum originally dating from 1894. Its collection spans works from ancient civilizations to contemporary art, sculpture and photography, and rotating exhibits are eclectic in scope. Step outside into the Rodin and Papua New Guinea sculpture gardens.

❶ Information

Stanford Visitor Center (☑ 650-723-2560; http://visit.stanford.edu; 295 Galvez St; ⊘ 8:30am-5pm Mon-Fri, 10am-5pm Sat & Sun) Offers free 70-minute walking tours of the campus at 11am and 3:15pm daily, except during academic breaks and some holidays. Special-interest tours also available.

NERD'S NIRVANA

Touted as the largest computer-history exhibition in the world, the **Computer History Museum** (☑ 650-810-1010; www.computerhistory.org; 1401 N Shoreline Blvd, Mountain View; adult $17.50, student & senior $13.50; ⊘ 10am-5pm Wed-Sun, to 8pm Fri; P) has rotating exhibits drawn from its 100,000-item collection. Artifacts range from the abacus to the iPod, including Cray-1 supercomputers, a Babbage Difference Engine (a Victorian-era automatic computing engine) and the first Google server.

Though there are no tours of the **Googleplex** (☑ 650-214-3308; www.google.com/about/company/facts/locations; 1600 Amphitheatre Pkwy, Mountain View; ⊘ store 10am-6:30pm Mon-Fri; P), visitors can stroll the campus and gawk at the public art on the leafy grounds, where scads of Googlers zoom about on primary-colored bicycles. Don't miss the 'dessert yard' outside Building 44, with lawn sculptures of Android operating systems (a cupcake! a donut! a robot!), and across the street, a toothy Tyrannosaurus rex festooned in pink flamingos next to the volleyball court.

At the Intel headquarters, the **Intel Museum** (☑ 408-765-5050; www.intel.com/museum; 2200 Mission College Blvd, Santa Clara; ⊘ usually 9am-6pm Mon-Fri, 10am-5pm Sat; P) FREE has displays on the birth and growth of the computer industry with special emphasis, not surprisingly, on microchips and Intel's involvement. Reserve ahead if you want to schedule a tour.

❶ Getting There & Away

Stanford University's free public shuttle, **Marguerite** (☑650-723-9362; http://transportation. stanford.edu/marguerite), provides service from Caltrain's Palo Alto and California Ave stations to the campus, and has bicycle racks. Parking on campus is expensive and trying.

San Jose

Though culturally diverse and historic, San Jose has always been in San Francisco's shadow, awash in Silicon Valley's suburbia. Founded in 1777 as El Pueblo de San José de Guadalupe, San Jose is California's oldest Spanish civilian settlement. Its downtown is small and scarcely used for a city of its size, though it does bustle with 20-something clubgoers on weekends. Industrial parks, high-tech computer firms and look-alike housing developments have sprawled across the city's landscape, taking over where farms, ranches and open spaces once spread between the bay and the surrounding hills.

◉ Sights

History Park   HISTORIC BUILDING
(☑408-287-2290; http://historysanjose.org; 1650 Senter Rd; ⊙noon-5pm Mon-Fri, 11am-5pm Sat & Sun, last entry 4:30pm; P🐾) FREE Historic buildings from all over San Jose have been brought together in this open-air history museum, southeast of the city center in Kelley Park. The centerpiece is a scaled-down replica of the 1881 **Electric Light Tower**. Other buildings include the 1880 **Pacific Hotel**, which has rotating art exhibits inside (closed Monday). The **Trolley Barn** restores historic trolley cars to operate on San Jose's light-rail line; on weekends you can ride a trolley along the park's own short line.

Tech Museum of Innovation   MUSEUM
(The Tech; ☑408-294-8324; www.thetech.org; 201 S Market St; adult/child $24/19, incl IMAX movie $29/23; ⊙10am-5pm; 🐾) Opposite Plaza de Cesar Chavez, San Jose's excellent technology museum examines subjects from robotics to space exploration, and genetics to virtual reality. The museum also includes an IMAX dome theater, which screens newly released films throughout the day.

MACLA   GALLERY
(Movimiento de Arte y Cultura Latino Americana; ☑408-998-2783; http://maclaarte.org; 510 S 1st St; ⊙noon-7pm Wed & Thu, to 5pm Fri & Sat) FREE A cutting-edge gallery highlighting themes by both established and emerging Latino artists, MACLA is one of the Bay Area's best community arts spaces, with open-mike performances, live-music shows, experimental theater and well-curated, thought-provoking visual-arts exhibits.

Rosicrucian Egyptian Museum   MUSEUM
(☑408-947-3635; www.egyptianmuseum.org; 1660 Park Ave; adult/child $9/5; ⊙9am-5pm Wed-Fri, 10am-6pm Sat & Sun; P) West of downtown, this unusual and educational Egyptian museum is one of San Jose's more unusual attractions. Its extensive collection includes statues, household items and mummies; there's even a two-room, walk-through reproduction of an ancient subterranean tomb.

San Jose Museum of Art   MUSEUM
(☑408-271-6840; http://sjmusart.org; 110 S Market St; adult/child $10/5; ⊙11am-5pm Tue-Sun) With a permanent collection of 20th-century works and imaginative changing exhibits, the city's central art museum is worth a quick look. The main building started life as the post office in 1892, was damaged by the 1906 earthquake and became an art gallery in 1933. A modern wing was added in 1991.

🛏 Sleeping

Budget and midrange motels and hotels cluster near freeways, especially Hwy 101 from south of San Francisco International Airport to San Jose. Upmarket hotels and motels and atmospheric lodges and inns cluster off Hwy 1 near the beaches, especially around Half Moon Bay. Off Hwy 1 is also where you'll find charming lighthouse hostels, campgrounds and cabins.

Hotel De Anza   HISTORIC HOTEL $$
(☑408-286-1000; www.destinationhotels.com/hotel-de-anza; 233 W Santa Clara St; r from $149; ➡🌂@🛜🐾) Opened during the Jazz Age, this downtown hotel is a restored art-deco beauty that pays homage to the property's history. Guest rooms offer plush comforts (those facing south are a tad larger) and there's full concierge service. Complimentary midnight snacks, in-room espresso makers and a 24-hour fitness center seal the deal.

Hotel Valencia   BOUTIQUE HOTEL $$
(☑408-551-0010; www.hotelvalencia-santanarow. com; 355 Santana Row; r from $189; P➡🌂@🛜🐾)

WINCHESTER MYSTERY HOUSE

An odd structure purposefully commissioned to be so by the heir to the Winchester rifle fortune, this ridiculous Victorian **mansion** (☑ 408-247-2101; www.winchestermysteryhouse. com; 525 S Winchester Blvd; adult/child $36/26; ◷ 9am-7pm, to 5pm early Sep-late May; Ⓟ) is filled with 160 rooms of various sizes and little utility, with dead-end hallways and a staircase that runs up to a ceiling all jammed together like a toddler playing architect. The standard hour-long guided mansion tour includes a self-guided romp through the gardens plus entry to an exhibition of guns and rifles.

Apparently, Sarah Winchester spent 38 years constructing this mammoth white elephant because the spirits of the people killed by Winchester rifles told her to. No expense was spared in the construction, the extreme results of which sprawl over 4 acres.

The house is west of central San Jose and just north of I-280, incongruously across the street from **Santana Row**, a shopping center.

A burbling lobby fountain and deep-red corridor carpeting set the tone for this tranquil 212-room contemporary hotel in the **Santana Row** (☑ 408-551-4611; www.santanarow.com; 377 Santana Row; ◷ 10am-9pm Mon-Sat, 11am-7pm Sun; 🐾) shopping complex. In-room minibars and bathrobes and an outdoor pool and hot tub create a stylish oasis of contemporary design. Parking is $24.

Westin San Jose　　　　　HISTORIC HOTEL $$
(☑ 408-295-2000; www.westinsanjose.com; 302 S Market St; r from $149; Ⓟ ❀ ✲ @ 🛜 🐾) Formerly the Sainte Claire, this atmospheric 1926 landmark hotel overlooking Plaza de Cesar Chavez has a gorgeous lobby with stretched-leather ceilings. Guest rooms are smallish, but have been remodeled. Parking is $39.

✕ Eating

San Jose is no culinary hub, but you'll find plenty of thronged restaurants downtown. Budget-friendly cafes are further east near the SJSU campus. For a more memorable meal, visit San Jose's historic Japantown, spread out along Jackson St east of 1st St, north of downtown.

Hukilau　　　　　　　　　FUSION $
(☑ 408-279-4888; www.dahukilau.com/sanjose; 230 Jackson St; mains $10-18; ◷ 11am-2pm & 5-9pm Mon-Thu & Sun, 11am-2pm & 5-10pm Fri, 11am-2.30pm & 5-10pm Sat; 🐾) Incongruously located in San Jose's tiny Japantown, this fun Hawaii-themed bar puts together incredibly filling island-style plate meals (sesame chicken is da best) and *pupus* (snacks or appetizers) such as Spam *musubi* (block of rice with a slice of fried Spam on top, wrapped with a strip of nori) and bowls of *ahi poke* (raw-fish salad). Live Hawaiian music some weekend evenings.

San Pedro Square Market　　　FOOD HALL $
(www.sanpedrosquaremarket.com; 87 N San Pedro St; most mains $6-20; ◷ usually 7am to 10pm-1am; 🖊 🐾) Always busy, this indoor/outdoor marketplace downtown showcases a few shining local food stars such as Bray Butcher Block and Bistro, Pizza Bocca Lupo, Konjoe Burger Bar and Treatbot ice cream. All seating is first-come, first-served. Live music every Friday and Saturday evening and Sunday afternoon. Some vendors validate parking in the adjacent garage.

Tofoo Com Chay　　VEGETARIAN, VIETNAMESE $
(☑ 408-286-6335; 388 E Santa Clara St; mains from $6.50; ◷ 9am-9pm Mon-Fri, 10am-6pm Sat; 🖊) Conveniently located on the border of the San Jose State University campus. Students and vegetarians queue for the Vietnamese dishes such as the fake-meat pho and the heaped combo plates.

Back A Yard　　　　　　CARIBBEAN $$
(☑ 408-294-8626; www.backayard.net/sanjose; 80 N Market St; mains $8-16; ◷ 11am-2:30pm & 4:30-8:30pm Mon-Thu, 11am-9pm Fri, from noon Sat) Jamaican-jerk chicken, pork, salmon and tofu are the house specialties of this Caribbean-barbecue kitchen, which also fries catfish, snapper and shrimp, all hot and spicy. Look for beef oxtail and curried goat on the daily specials menu, and tropically colored murals on the red-brick walls.

Original Joe's　　　　　　ITALIAN $$
(☑ 408-292-7030; www.originaljoes.com; 301 S 1st St; mains $10-33; ◷ 11am-midnight) Waiters in bow ties flit about this busy 1950s San Jose landmark, serving standard Italian dishes to locals and conventioneers. The dining room is a curious but tasteful hodgepodge of '50s

brick, contemporary wood paneling and tall Asian vases. Expect a wait.

Arcadia
STEAK, SEAFOOD $$$

(☑408-278-4555; www.michaelmina.net/restaurants; 100 W San Carlos St; mains lunch $15-23, dinner $34-64; ⊘6:30am-2pm daily, 5:30-10pm Mon-Sat) This New American steakhouse restaurant in the Marriott Hotel is run by chef Michael Mina, one of San Francisco's celebrity chefs. It's not the daring, cutting-edge style Mina is known for, but it's slick, expensive and reasonably good.

🍸 Drinking & Nightlife

Original Gravity Public House
CRAFT BEER

(☑408-915-2337; www.originalgravitypub.com; 66 S 1st St; ⊘11:30am-10:30pm Sun-Wed, to midnight Thu-Sat) Squeeze inside this crowded yet friendly pub for beer geeks and the 'craft curious.' With nearly three dozen rotating taps of brews, including ciders and meads, as well as scores of bottles, you'll be confounded by choice. Consider your options while you nosh on housemade sausage, a grilled cheese sandwich or duck-fat poutine.

Paper Plane
COCKTAIL BAR

(☑408-713-2625; www.paperplanesj.com; 72 S 1st St; ⊘4:30pm-midnight Sun-Tue, to 2am Wed-Sat) Downtown at this industrial-chic watering hole with wall-sized, backlit shelves of liquor, tattooed bartenders willingly customize your drink if nothing on the menu of old-school classics and imaginative modern mixology tempts. Share a punch bowl and appetizers with friends.

B2 Coffee
COFFEE

(www.bellanocoffee.com; 170 W St John St; ⊘7am-7pm Mon-Fri, 8am-7pm Sat & Sun) Haute coffee-roaster Bellano has opened a branch inside downtown's San Pedro Square Market (p163), serving the same rich pour-over coffee, nitro cold brew and iced almond-milk lattes mixed with from-scratch vanilla syrup.

Haberdasher
COCKTAIL BAR

(☑408-792-7356; www.haberdashersj.com; 43 W San Salvador St; ⊘5pm-midnight Sun, Tue & Wed, to 1am Thu-Sat) A cool basement lounge, where sharply dressed bartenders artfully mix cocktails (including 'House Fittings' options), with some recipes dating to before Prohibition. It's a justifiably popular place but you can (and should) book ahead for a table Friday and Saturday nights to guarantee your spot.

Hedley Club
LOUNGE

(☑408-286-1000; www.destinationhotels.com/hotel-de-anza/dining/hedley-club-lounge; 233 W Santa Clara St; ⊘hours vary) Inside the elegant 1931 Hotel De Anza, the Hedley Club is a good place for a quiet drink in swanky art-deco surroundings. Jazz combos play most nights.

⭐ Entertainment

Avaya Stadium
SPECTATOR SPORT

(1123 Coleman Rd; ⊘hours vary) Located near San Jose's airport, this is the home of the **San Jose Earthquakes** (☑408-556-7700; www.sjearthquakes.com), the city's professional soccer team (season runs from February through October).

SAN JOSE FOR CHILDREN

Children's Discovery Museum (☑408-298-5437; www.cdm.org; 180 Woz Way; $13, child under 1yr free; ⊘10am-5pm Tue-Sat, noon-5pm Sun; 🖪) Downtown, this science and creativity museum has hands-on displays incorporating art, technology and the environment, with plenty of toys and cool play-and-learn areas for tots to school-aged children. The museum is on Woz Way, named after Steve Wozniak, cofounder of Apple.

California's Great America (☑408-988-1776; www.cagreatamerica.com; 4701 Great America Pkwy, Santa Clara; adult/child under 4ft $69/48; ⊘Apr-Oct, hours vary; 🖪) If you can handle the shameless product placements, kids love the roller coasters and other thrill rides. Online tickets cost much less than walk-up prices. Parking is $15 to $25, but the park is also accessible by public transportation.

Raging Waters (☑408-238-9900; www.rwsplash.com; 2333 S White Rd; adult/child under 4ft $39/29; ⊘May-Sep, hours vary; 🖪) A water park inside Lake Cunningham Regional Park, Raging Waters has fast waterslides, a wave pool and a nifty Pirate's Cove. Buy tickets online for discounts. Parking is $6 to $10.

SAP Center   STADIUM

(☑408-287-9200; www.sapcenteratsanjose.com; 525 W Santa Clara St) The fanatically popular **San Jose Sharks** (☑800-559-2333; www.nhl. com/sharks), the city's professional hockey team, plays at this massive glass-and-metal stadium (formerly the HP Pavilion) from September through April. Megaconcerts by touring acts go on stage year-round.

California Theatre   THEATER

(☑408-792-4111;   http://sanjosetheaters.org/ theaters/california-theatre; 345 S 1st St; ☺hours vary) The absolutely stunning Spanish Colonial interior of this landmark entertainment venue is cathedral-worthy. The theater is home to Opera San Jose and Symphony Silicon Valley.

ℹ Information

San Jose Convention & Visitors Bureau (☑408-792-4511; www.sanjose.org; 408 Almaden Blvd; ☺9am-5pm Mon-Fri) Free visitor information guides and maps online.
Santa Clara Valley Medical Center (☑408-885-5000; www.scvmc.org; 751 S Bascom Ave; ☺24hr) 24-hour emergency services.

ℹ Getting There & Away

AIR

Four miles northwest of downtown between Hwy 101 and I-880, **Mineta San Jose International Airport** (SJC; ☑408-392-3600; www.flysanjose.com; 1701 Airport Blvd) has free wi-fi and mostly domestic US flights from two terminals.

BART

To access the BART (p149) system in the East Bay, VTA bus 181 runs between downtown San Jose and the Fremont BART station ($4, 35 to 45 minutes, every 15 to 20 minutes).

BUS

Greyhound buses to Los Angeles ($21 to $84, 6½ to 10½ hours) leave from San Jose's **Diridon Station** (Diridon Transit Center; 65 Cahill St). Discount carrier **Megabus** (☑877-462-6342; http://us.megabus.com) offers daily service between San Jose and Burbank, Los Angeles or Anaheim ($5 to $44, six to seven hours), with departures outside Diridon Station.

The **Santa Clara Valley Transportation Authority** (VTA; ☑408-321-2300, 800-894-9908; www.vta.org) Hwy 17 Express bus plies a handy route between Diridon Station and Santa Cruz ($7, 55 minutes, hourly).

CAR & MOTORCYCLE

San Jose is at the southern end of the San Francisco Bay, about 40 miles from Oakland (via I-880) or 50 miles from San Francisco (via Hwy 101 or I-280). Expect lots of traffic at all times of day on Hwy 101 from San Francisco; although I-280 is slightly longer, it's much prettier and usually less congested. Heading south, Hwy 17 leads over the mountains to Santa Cruz.

TRAIN

A double-decker commuter rail service operating up and down the peninsula, **Caltrain** (☑800-660-4287; www.caltrain.com) runs between San Jose and San Francisco ($9.75, 65 to 85 minutes). Trains run hourly on weekends and more frequently on weekdays. Bicycles may be brought on designated cars only. San Jose's terminal, **Diridon Station**, is just south of the Alameda.

Diridon Station also is the terminal for Amtrak trains serving Seattle, Los Angeles and Sacramento, as well as **Altamont Commuter Express** (ACE; ☑800-411-7245; www.acerail.com) trains, which run to Great America, Livermore and Stockton.

VTA runs a free weekday shuttle (known as the Downtown Area Shuttle or DASH) from Diridon Station to downtown San Jose.

ℹ Getting Around

VTA buses run all over Silicon Valley. Fares for VTA buses (except express lines) and light-rail trains are $2 for a single ride (day pass $6).

From the airport, free VTA Airport Flyer shuttles (route 10) run every 10 to 15 minutes to the Metro/Airport Light Rail station, where you can catch light rail to downtown San Jose; shuttles also go to the Santa Clara Caltrain station.

The main San Jose light-rail line runs north–south from the city center. Heading south gets you as far as Almaden and Santa Teresa. The northern route runs to Japantown, the airport and Tasman, where it connects with another line that heads west past Great America to downtown Mountain View.

In San Jose, many downtown retailers offer two-hour parking validation. Otherwise, city-owned lots and garages downtown charge a $5 flat rate after 6pm on weekdays and all day on weekends. Check www.sjdowntownparking.com for details.

Pacifica & Devil's Slide

One of the real surprises of the Bay Area is how fast the cityscape disappears along the rugged and largely undeveloped coast. The lazy beach town of Pacifica, just 15 miles from downtown San Francisco, signals the end of the urban sprawl. Most beaches along Hwy 1 are buffeted by wild and unpredictable surf, making them better suited to sunbathing (weather permitting) than swimming. Immediately south of Pacifica is the Devil's Slide, a gorgeous coastal cliff area now bypassed by a car tunnel.

Pacifica State Beach   BEACH
(Linda Mar Beach; ☑ 650-738-7381; www.parks. ca.gov; 5000 Pacific Coast Hwy; per car $5-9; ☺5am-dusk; P♿) In Pacifica, collecting a suntan or catching a wave are the main attractions at popular Pacifica State Beach, as well as Rockaway Beach just north.

Nor-Cal Surf Shop   SURFING
(☑650-738-9283; 5440 Coast Hwy, Pedro Point Shopping Center; ☺9am-6pm Sun-Thu, to 7pm Fri, 8am-7pm Sat) Rents surfboards ($19 per day), wet suits ($16.50) and SUP sets ($45) next to Pacifica State Beach. Book ahead for surf lessons (from $95).

Devil's Slide Trail   HIKING
(☑650-355-8289; http://parks.smcgov.org/devils -slide-trail; Hwy 1; ☺8am-8pm Apr-Aug, closes earlier Sep-Mar; ♿) Hikers and cyclists cruise along the Devil's Slide Coastal Trail, a paved 1.3-mile section of the old highway. Heading south or north on Hwy 1, turn off before entering the tunnels into the trailhead parking lots.

Pacifica to Half Moon Bay

Other than a string of gorgeous, wild beaches along Hwy 1, there's little to stop for on the short, but distractingly scenic drive between Pacifica and Half Moon Bay. South of historic Point Montara Lighthouse, a hidden marine reserve protects natural tide pools and harbor seals.

Montara State Beach   STATE PARK
(☑650-726-8819; www.parks.ca.gov; Hwy 1; ☺8am-sunset; P♿) FREE About 5 miles south of the town of Pacifica, this wide-open crescent is a local favorite for its pristine sand. Inland the park encompasses McNee Ranch, which has hiking and cycling trails aplenty, including a strenuous ascent to a panoramic viewpoint atop Montara Mountain (1898ft), a 7.6-mile round-trip from Hwy 1.

Ranch Corral de Tierra   PARK
(www.nps.gov/goga/rcdt.htm; off Hwy 1) FREE From the town of Montara, about 20 miles from San Francisco, trails climb from Montara State Beach to access the undeveloped 4000-acre park of Ranch Corral de Tierra, part of Golden Gate National Recreation Area.

Fitzgerald Marine Reserve   NATURE RESERVE
(☑650-728-3584; www.fitzgeraldreserve.org; 200 Nevada Ave, Moss Beach; ☺8am-8pm Apr-Aug, closes earlier Sep-Mar; P♿) FREE At Moss Beach, this marine reserve protects tide pools teeming with sea life. Walk out among the pools at low tide – wearing shoes that you can get wet – and explore the myriad crabs, sea stars, mollusks and rainbow-colored sea anemone. Note that it's illegal to remove any creatures, shells or even rocks from the marine reserve.

From Hwy 1, turn west on to Vermont Ave, which becomes Lake St and intersects Nevada Ave. SamTrans bus 17 stops along Hwy 1, only a five-minute walk or so from the reserve.

HI Point Montara Lighthouse   HOSTEL $
(☑650-728-7177; www.norcalhostels.org/montara; cnr Hwy 1 & 16th St, Montara; r with shared bath $83-128, dm $33-39; ☺reception 7:30am-10:30pm; P🐕@🛜) 🍴 Starting life as a fog station in 1875, Point Montara Lighthouse Hostel is adjacent to the current lighthouse, which dates from 1928. This very popular hostel has a living room, kitchen facilities and an international clientele. There are a few private rooms for couples or families. Reservations are a good idea anytime, but especially on weekends and in summer.

If you're not staying at the hostel, you can visit the lighthouse grounds between 9am and sunset daily (but check in at the front desk first). SamTrans bus 17 stops across the highway from the hostel.

Moss Beach Distillery   BAR
(☑650-728-5595; www.mossbeachdistillery.com; 140 Beach Way, Moss Beach; ☺noon-9pm Mon-Sat, 11am-9pm Sun) Overlooking the cove where bootleggers used to unload Prohibition-era liquor, the restaurant's heated ocean-view deck is perfectly positioned to catch sunset. In fair weather it's the best place for miles around to have a leisurely cocktail, but head elsewhere for a meal if you're hungry.

Half Moon Bay

With its long coastline and mild weather, this area has always been prime real estate. When Spanish missionaries set up shop along the coast in the late 1700s, this had been indigenous Ohlone territory for thousands of years. Developed as a beach resort in the early 1900s, Half Moon Bay today is the main coastal town between San Francisco

SCENIC DRIVE: HIGHWAY 84
....

Inland from the Pacific, vast stretches of the peninsula's hills are protected in a patchwork of parks that, just like the coast, remain remarkably untouched despite huge urban populations only a short drive away.

Heading east from Hwy 1, about 10 miles south of Half Moon Bay (p166), Hwy 84 winds its way upward through thick stands of redwood trees, passing local and state parks and open-space preserves with hiking and mountain-biking opportunities. Allow at least an hour to make the 25-mile drive to Palo Alto without stopping.

A mile in from **San Gregorio State Beach** (☑ 650-726-8819; www.parks.ca.gov; Hwy 1, San Gregorio; per car $8; ☉ 8am-sunset) on Hwy 1, kick off your shoes and stomp your feet to live bluegrass, Celtic and folk music on the weekends at the **San Gregorio General Store** (☑ 650-726-0565; www.sangregoriostore.com; 7615 Stage Rd, San Gregorio; ☉ store 10:30am-6pm Sun-Thu, to 7pm Fri, 10am-7pm Sat, to 6pm Sun). Check out the wooden bar singed by area branding irons.

Eight miles further east is the tiny township of **La Honda**, former home to *One Flew Over the Cuckoo's Nest* author Ken Kesey and the launching spot for his 1964 psychedelic bus trip immortalized in Tom Wolfe's *The Electric Kool-Aid Acid Test*. Housed in a 19th-century blacksmith's shop, **Apple Jack's** (☑ 650-747-0331; 8790 Hwy 84; ☉ noon-2am) is a rustic, down-home country-and-western bar with motorcycles lined up in a row outside.

To stretch your legs in the redwoods, **Sam McDonald County Park** (☑ 650-879-0238; http://parks.smcgov.org/sam-mcdonald-park; 13435 Pescadero Creek Rd, Loma Mar; per car $6; ☉ 8am-8pm Apr-Aug, closes earlier Sep-Mar; [P] [🔥]), 2 miles south of La Honda, has forested hiking trails and a secluded hike-to **cabin** (☑ 650-390-8411; www.sierraclub.org/loma-prieta/hikers-hut; per night adult $20-30, child $10; ☉) 🌿. From the park, it's a 20-minute winding drive downhill along Pescadero Creek Rd to visit the tiny farm town of Pescadero (p168), just inland from the coast.

Otherwise, backtrack to La Honda and continue north on Hwy 84, passing more nature preserves and viewpoints over Silicon Valley. Turn left on to Skyline Blvd to eat at **Alice's Restaurant** (☑ 650-851-0303; www.alicesrestaurant.com; 17288 Skyline Blvd, Woodside; mains $9-14; ☉ 8am-8pm Sun-Thu, to 9pm Fri-Sat) inside an early 20th-century general store. It's not the same diner made famous by 1960s folk singer Arlo Guthrie, but it's still a popular stop for bikers, cyclists and Sunday drivers, especially for weekend brunch.

Keep following Hwy 84 as it corkscrews downhill, turning right on to Sand Hill Rd, which leads east to Stanford University (p161) and downtown Palo Alto.

(29 miles north) and Santa Cruz (49 miles south). Its long stretches of beach still attract rambling weekenders and die-hard surfers.

Half Moon Bay spreads out along Hwy 1/ Cabrillo Hwy, but despite development, it's still relatively small. Downtown, the main drag is a five-block stretch of Main St lined with art galleries, antiques shops, cafes and restaurants. For aquatic pursuits and seafood restaurants, detour to Pillar Point Harbor, about 4 miles northwest of downtown, off Hwy 1.

Sea Horse Ranch   HORSEBACK RIDING
(☑ 650-726-9903;   http://seahorseranch.org; 1828 Cabrillo Hwy; trail ride $60-90; ☉ hours vary; [🔥]) Just over a mile north of the Hwy 92 junction, Sea Horse Ranch offers daily horseback rides along the beach. Minimum age for riders is seven years; weight limits and clothing restrictions apply. Book ahead.

**Half Moon Bay
Kayak Co**   WATER SPORTS, CYCLING
(☑ 650-773-6101; www.hmbkayak.com; 2 Johnson Pier; kayak or SUP set rental per hour/day $25/75, bicycle rental $25/50; ☉ 9am-5pm Wed-Mon; [🔥]) When the bay is calm, get out on the water with Half Moon Bay Kayak Co, which rents kayaks, stand up paddle surfing (SUP) sets and bicycles too. Book ahead for harbor, sunset or full-moon tours or an adventurous kayak-fishing trip. Last walk-up rental is at 3:30pm.

Mavericks SURFING

At the western end of Pillar Point is Mavericks, a serious surf break that attracts pro big-wave riders to battle its huge, steep and very dangerous waves. The invitational **Titans of Mavericks** (http://titansofmavericks.com/event) FREE surf contest, called on a few days' notice when the swells get huge, is held annually between November and March.

Half Moon Bay Art & Pumpkin Festival FOOD, CULTURAL

(☑ 650-726-9652; www.pumpkinfest.miramar events.com; Main St; ☺ mid-Oct; ♦) FREE Pumpkins are a major deal around Half Moon Bay and the pre-Halloween harvest is celebrated with this annual festival. It kicks off with the World Championship Pumpkin Weigh-Off, where some bulbous beasts bust the scales at nearly 2000lb.

Half Moon Bay Brewing Company PUB FOOD **$$**

(☑ 650-728-2739; www.hmbbrewingco.com; 390 Capistrano Rd; mains $12-25; ☺ 11:30am-9pm Mon-Thu, to 10pm Fri, 10am-10pm Sat, to 9pm Sun; 🛜 ♦ 🐾) Chomp on seafood and burgers while you swill pints from a respectable menu of local brews and gaze out at the bay from a sheltered, heated outdoor patio. Live music some weekends.

❶ Getting There & Away

SamTrans bus 294 operates hourly between the Caltrain (p165) Hillsdale station in San Mateo and Half Moon Bay ($2.25, 45 minutes). From Half Moon Bay, SamTrans bus 17 heads up the coast to Moss Beach, Montara and Pacifica ($2.25, one hour) every hour or two daily, with limited weekday service south to Pescadero ($2.25, 25 minutes).

Pescadero

A foggy speck of coastal crossroads between Half Moon Bay and Santa Cruz, 160-year-old Pescadero is a close-knit rural town of sugar-lending neighbors and community pancake breakfasts. But on weekends the tiny downtown strains its seams with long-distance cyclists panting for carbohydrates and day-trippers dive-bombing in from the oceanfront highway. They're all drawn to the winter vistas of emerald-green hills parched to burlap brown in summer, the wild Pacific beaches populated by seals and pelicans, and the unbelievably fresh food from local farms and ranches. With its cornucopia of tide-pool coves and parks of sky-blotting redwood canopy, city dwellers come here to slow down and smell the sea breeze wafting over fields of bushy artichokes.

◉ Sights

Pigeon Point Light Station State Historic Park LIGHTHOUSE

(☑ 650-879-2120; www.parks.ca.gov; 210 Pigeon Point Rd; ☺ 8am-sunset, visitor center 10am-4pm Thu-Mon; P ♦) A half-dozen miles south of Pescadero along the coast, the 115ft light station is one of the tallest lighthouses on the West Coast. The 1872 landmark had to close access to the upper tower when chunks of its cornice began to rain from the sky (future restorations are planned), but the beam still flashes brightly and the bluff is a prime though blustery spot to scan for breaching gray whales in winter. Half-hour guided history walks of the lighthouse grounds leave at 1pm (weather permitting) from the visitor center and bookstore.

Bean Hollow State Beach BEACH

(☑ 650-726-8819; www.parks.ca.gov; off Hwy 1; ☺ 8am-sunset; P ♦) 🐾 FREE Pretty sand beaches speckle the coast, though one of the most interesting places to stop is Pebble Beach, a jewel less than 2 miles south of Pescadero Creek Rd (and part of Bean Hollow State Beach). The shore is awash with bite-sized eye candy of agate, jade and carnelian, and sandstone troughs are pockmarked by groovy honeycombed formations called tafoni.

Butano State Park STATE PARK

(☑ 650-879-2040; www.parks.ca.gov; 1500 Cloverdale Rd; per car $10; ☺ sunrise-sunset; P ♦) 🐾 Five miles south of Pescadero, bobcats and coyotes reside discreetly in this pretty park's 4600 acres of dense redwood canyon and uplands laced with hiking and mountain-biking trails and shady campsites. From Pescadero Creek Rd in downtown Pescadero, follow Cloverdale Rd south for 4 miles to the turnoff.

To take the scenic route back to Hwy 1, continue south on Cloverdale Rd, turning right on to Gazos Creek Rd and winding 2 more miles to the coast.

Pescadero State Beach & Marsh Natural Preserve STATE PARK

(☑ 650-726-8819; www.parks.ca.gov; off Hwy 1; per car $8; ☺ 8am-sunset; P ♦) 🐾 Fifteen miles south of Half Moon Bay, this state beach and marshland preserve attract beachcombers and birders. Pull over and get out of the car to explore the marine-life-rich coastal tide pools on rocky outcroppings.

🛏 Sleeping & Eating

HI Pigeon Point Lighthouse   HOSTEL $
(📞650-879-0633; www.norcalhostels.org/pigeon; 210 Pigeon Point Rd; r with shared bath from $82-186, dm $26-32; ⊙reception 7:30am-10:30pm; 🅿🍴@🛜) 🧺 Not your workaday youth hostel, this highly coveted coastside lodging is all about location. Book ahead and check in early to snag a spot in the outdoor hot tub ($8 per person per 30 minutes) and contemplate roaring waves as the lighthouse beacon races through a starburst sky. It's about 6 miles south of Pescadero.

Butano State Park
Campground   CAMPGROUND $
(📞reservations 800-444-7275; www.reserveamerica.com; 1500 Cloverdale Rd; tent & RV sites $35; 🅿🐾) 🧺 Shady campsites have picnic tables and fire pits, but the most serene spots are the walk-in, tent-only sites tucked back into the forest.

Costanoa   CABIN, LODGE $$
(📞650-879-1100; www.costanoa.com; 2001 Ros si Rd; tent/cabin with shared bath from $100/200, lodge r from $200; 🅿🍴🛜) Even though this coastal resort, about 10 miles south of Pescadero, includes a campground (📞650-879-7302; http://koa.com/campgrounds/santa-cruz-north; tent/RV sites with hookups from $36/85; 🅿🛜🐾), no one can pull a straight face and declare they're actually roughing it here. Down bedding swaddles guests in canvas-sided tent bungalows and hard-sided Douglas-fir cabins. Chill-averse folks can use communal 'comfort stations' with 24-hour dry saunas, fireside patio seating, heated floors and hot showers.

Bland lodge rooms with private fireplaces and hot-tub access cater to those without such Spartan delusions. There's an expensive restaurant, bar and spa on-site. Bicycle rentals, yoga classes, horseback rides and guided bird-watching are available to guests only.

Pescadero Creek Inn   INN $$
(📞650-879-1898; www.pescaderocreekinn.com; 393 Stage Rd; d $175-250; 🅿🍴🛜) 🧺 Unwind in the private two-room cottage or one of the spotless Victorian rooms in a restored 100-year-old farmhouse with a tranquil creekside garden.

Duarte's Tavern   AMERICAN $$
(📞650-879-0464; www.duartestavern.com; 202 Stage Rd; mains $8-39; ⊙7am-8pm; 🐾) You'll rub shoulders with fancy-pants foodies, spandex-swathed cyclists and dusty cowboys at this casual, surprisingly unpretentious fourth-generation family restaurant. Duarte's is this town's culinary magnet, though some critics say it's resting on its laurels. Feast on crab cioppino and a half-and-half split of cream of artichoke and green-chili soups, then bring it home with a wedge of olallieberry pie. Except for the unfortunate lull of Prohibition, the wood-paneled bar has been hosting the locals and their honored guests since 1894. Reservations strongly recommended.

❶ Getting There & Away

By car, the town is 3 miles east of Hwy 1 on Pescadero Creek Rd, leading inland from Pescadero State Beach. On weekdays, SamTrans (📞511, 800-660-4287; www.samtrans.com) bus 17 runs twice a day to and from Half Moon Bay ($2.25, 25 minutes).

Año Nuevo State Park

Just over a dozen miles southeast of Pescadero State Beach, Año Nuevo State Park (📞park office 650-879-2025, recorded info 650-879-0227, tour reservations 800-444-4445; www.parks.ca.gov; 1 New Years Creek Rd; per car $10, 2½hr tour per person $7; ⊙8:30am-sunset Apr-Nov, tours only Dec 15–Mar 31; 🅿🐾) is home to the world's largest mainland breeding colonies of northern elephant seals. More raucous than a full-moon beach rave, thousands of boisterous animals party year-round on the dunes of Año Nuevo Point, their squeals and barks reaching fever pitch during the winter pupping season.

Northern elephant seals were just as fearless two centuries ago as they are today, but unfortunately, seal trappers were not as friendly as today's tourists. During the 19th century, northern elephant seals were driven to the edge of extinction. Only a handful survived around the Guadalupe Islands off the Mexican state of Baja California. With the availability of substitutes for seal oil and the conservationist attitudes of more recent times, northern elephant seals have come back, reappearing on the Southern

THE CULINARY COAST

Pescadero is renowned for Duarte's Tavern (p169), but loads of other tidbits are close by.

Arcangeli Grocery Company (Norm's Market; ☎ 650-879-0147; www.normsmarket.com; 287 Stage Rd; sandwiches $7-10; ⊙ 10am-6pm; ⚹ 👪) Create a picnic with made-to-order deli sandwiches, homemade artichoke salsa and a chilled bottle of California wine. Don't go breezing out the door without nabbing a crusty loaf of the famous artichoke garlic herb bread, baked fresh almost hourly.

Harley Farms Goat Dairy (☎ 650-879-0480; http://harleyfarms.com; 250 North St; ⊙ 10am-5pm Thu-Mon Apr-Dec, 11am-4pm Fri-Sun Jan-Mar; P 👪) Another local food treasure, here the split-level farm shop sells creamy artisanal goat's cheeses festooned with fruit, nuts and a rainbow of edible flowers, as well as goat's-milk bath and body products. Show up anytime to pat the heads of the goats out back, or reserve ahead for a weekend farm tour ($30) or dinner ($150) in the Victorian-era barn. The farm is less than a mile east of downtown: follow the cool wooden cutouts of the goat and the Wellington-shod girl with the faraway eyes.

Pie Ranch (☎ 650-879-9281; www.pieranch.org; 2080 Cabrillo Hwy; ⊙ noon-5pm Mon-Fri, 10am-5pm Sat & Sun; 👪) Hit the brakes for this roadside farm stand in a wooden barn to pick up fresh produce, eggs and coffee, plus amazing fruit pies (which sell out fast). The historic pie-slice-shaped farm is a nonprofit dedicated to leadership development and food education for urban youth. Check the website for volunteer work days, farm tours, potluck dinners and barn dances. It's around 11 miles south of Pescadero Creek Rd.

Swanton Berry Farm Stand & U-Pick (☎ 650-469-8804; www.swantonberryfarm.com; 25 Swanton Rd, Davenport; ⊙ 8am-8pm late May-early Sep, closes earlier rest of year; P 👪) Roll up your shirtsleeves and harvest some fruit at this organic pick-your-own farm south of Año Nuevo. It's a union outfit (operated by Cesar Chavez's United Farm Workers), with buckets of seasonal strawberries, olallieberries, blackberries and even kiwis ripe for the plucking. The farm stand sells baskets of ripe berries and berry shortcakes, pies and jams.

Bonnie Doon Vineyard Tasting Room (☎ 831-471-8031; www.bonnydoonvineyard.com; 450 Hwy 1, Davenport; tasting fee $10-20; ⊙ 11am-5pm, to 6pm Fri & Sat late May-early Sep, closed Wed early Sep-Feb; P) In the sleepy village of Davenport, round out your palate with a wine flight in the roadside tasting room of Randall Grahm's acclaimed winery, where Edison lights and rough-hewed wooden tables entice you to sample Le Cigare Volant (yes, that's a flying cigar), a Rhône-style red blend and other bottles made with lesser-known grape varietals. The tasting room is about 10 miles northwest of Santa Cruz on Hwy 1.

California coast during the 1920s. They returned to Año Nuevo Beach in 1955.

In peak season, during the mating and birthing time from mid-December to end of March, visitors are only permitted access to the reserve on guided tours. For the busiest period, from mid-January to mid-February, it's recommended you book two months ahead. Although the park office can answer general questions, tours must be arranged through ReserveAmerica (http://anonuevo. reserveamerica.com).

The rest of the year, advance reservations aren't necessary, but visitor permits from the entrance station are required; arrive before 3pm in September, October or November or 3:30pm April to August. From the ranger station it's a 3- to 5-mile round-trip hike on sand; allow two to three hours. Dogs are not allowed on-site and no visitors are permitted during the first two weeks of December.

The park is less than 7 miles southeast of Pigeon Point or over 20 miles northwest of Santa Cruz.

Napa & Sonoma Wine Country

Best Places to Eat

➡ Handline (p214)

➡ Oxbow Public Market (p181)

➡ Fremont Diner (p204)

➡ SingleThread (p228)

➡ Shed (p227)

Best Places to Sleep

➡ El Bonita (p188)

➡ Shanti Permaculture Farm (p216)

➡ Hotel Healdsburg (p226)

➡ Windhaven Cottage (p203)

➡ Brannan Cottage Inn (p194)

Why Go?

America's premier viticulture region has earned its reputation among the world's best. Despite hype about Wine Country style, it's from the land that all Wine Country lore springs. Rolling hills, dotted with century-old oaks, turn the color of lion's fur under the summer sun and swaths of vineyards carpet hillsides as far as the eye can see. Where they end, redwood forests follow serpentine rivers to the sea.

There are over 900 wineries in Napa and Sonoma Counties, but it's quality, not quantity, that distinguishes the region – especially in Napa, which competes with France and doubles as an outpost of San Francisco's top-end culinary scene. Sonoma prides itself on agricultural diversity, with goat's-cheese farms, you-pick-'em orchards and roadside fruit stands. Plan to get lost on back roads, and, as you picnic atop sun-dappled hillsides, grab a hunk of earth and know firsthand the thing of greatest meaning in Wine Country.

When to Go
Napa

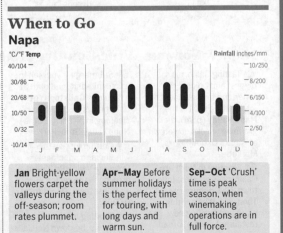

Jan Bright-yellow flowers carpet the valleys during the off-season; room rates plummet.

Apr–May Before summer holidays is the perfect time for touring, with long days and warm sun.

Sep–Oct 'Crush' time is peak season, when winemaking operations are in full force.

ℹ Getting There & Getting Away

Napa and Sonoma Counties each have an eponymous city and valley. So Sonoma town is in Sonoma County, at the southern end of Sonoma Valley. The same goes for the city, county and valley of Napa.

From San Francisco, public transportation gets you to the valleys, but it's insufficient for vineyard-hopping. For public-transit information, dial ☑ 511, or look online at www.transit.511.org.

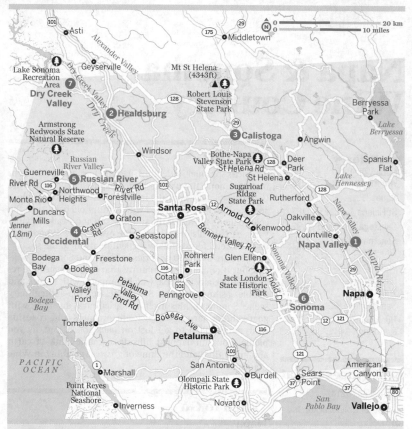

Napa & Sonoma Wine Country Highlights

❶ Tasting California's biggest and boldest red wines and falling under their intoxicating spell in the **Napa Valley** (p174), then grabbing snacks downtown at Napa's Oxbow Public Market.

❷ Feasting in Northern California's greatest food town, **Healdsburg** (p225). Then, wallet permitting, hitting up exciting new restaurant, SingleThread.

❸ Submerging yourself in a volcanic-ash mud bath at a fabulous **Calistoga** (p198) hot-springs resort, then sleeping in a yurt in Bothe-Napa Valley State Park.

❹ Getting lost on the winding and spectacular Coleman Valley Rd before arriving in the region's wackiest town, **Occidental** (p215).

❺ Floating in a canoe, kayak or tube down NorCal's natural lazy **Russian River** (p209; put-ins available at Guerneville and Healdsburg), then hopping out and drinking some wine.

❻ Picnicking in sun-dappled grass on the state's largest historic town square, **Sonoma Plaza** (p200)

❼ Pedaling between wineries along pastoral and undulating West Dry Creek Rd in **Dry Creek Valley** (p211).

Both valleys are a 90-minute drive from San Francisco. Napa, further inland, has about 500 wineries and attracts the most visitors (expect heavy traffic on summer weekends). Sonoma County has more than 425 wineries and around 40 in Sonoma Valley, which is less commercial and less congested than Napa. If you have time to visit only one, for ease go with Sonoma.

AIR

Visitors fly into either **San Francisco International Airport** (☎ 650-821-8211; www.flysfo.com; 780 S Airport Blvd) or **Sacramento International Airport** (☎ 916-929-5411; http://sacramento.aero/smf; 6900 Airport Blvd); the drive from either to Napa Valley takes about 1½ hours. San Francisco is a more attractive destination but its airport is also far busier and more crowded than Sacramento's.

BOAT

Baylink Ferry (☎ 877-643-3779; www.sanfranciscobayferry.com) Downtown San Francisco to Vallejo (adult/child $13.80/6.90, 60 minutes); connect with Napa Valley Vine bus 29 (weekdays) or bus 11 (daily).

BUS

Evans Transportation (☎ 707-255-1559; www.evanstransportation.com) Shuttles ($40) to Napa from San Francisco and Oakland airports.

Golden Gate Transit (p117) Bus from San Francisco to Petaluma (adult/youth $11.75/5.75) and Santa Rosa (adult/youth $13/6.50); board at 1st and Mission Sts. Connects with Sonoma County Transit buses.

Greyhound (☎ 800-231-2222; www.greyhound.com) Buses run from San Francisco to Santa Rosa ($21 to $38).

Napa Valley Vine Operates local bus 10 daily from downtown Napa to Calistoga ($1.60); express bus 29 Monday to Friday from the Vallejo Ferry Terminal ($3.25) and El Cerrito del Norte Bay Area Rapid Transit (BART) station via Napa to Calistoga ($5.50); and local bus 11 daily from the Vallejo Ferry Terminal to downtown Napa ($1.60).

Sonoma County Airport Express (☎ 800-327-2024, 707-837-8700; www.airportexpressinc.com) Shuttles ($34) between Sonoma County Airport (Santa Rosa) and San Francisco and Oakland airports.

CAR & MOTORCYCLE

From San Francisco, take Hwy 101 north over the Golden Gate Bridge, then Hwy 37 east to Hwy 121 north; continue to the junction of Hwy 12/121. For Sonoma Valley, take Hwy 12 north; for Napa Valley, take Hwy 12/121 east. Plan 70 minutes in light traffic, two hours during the weekday commute.

Hwy 12/121 splits south of Napa: Hwy 121 turns north and joins with Hwy 29/St Helena Hwy; Hwy 12 merges with southbound Hwy 29 toward Vallejo. Hwy 29 backs up weekdays 3pm to 7pm, slowing returns to San Francisco.

From the East Bay (or downtown San Francisco), take I-80 east to Hwy 37 west (north of Vallejo), then northbound Hwy 29.

From Santa Rosa, take Hwy 12 east to access the northern end of Sonoma Valley. From Petaluma and Hwy 101, take Hwy 116 east.

TRAIN

Amtrak (☎ 800-872-7245; www.amtrak.com) trains travel to Martinez (south of Vallejo), with connecting buses to Napa (45 minutes), Santa Rosa (1¼ hours) and Healdsburg (1¾ hours). From San Francisco, **BART Trains** (☎ 415-989-2278; www.bart.gov) connecting to Richmond station can deliver you to Amtrak.

BART also runs from San Francisco to El Cerrito del Norte ($4.45, 30 minutes). **Napa Valley Vine** bus 29 runs weekdays from that same BART stop to Calistoga, via Napa ($5.50); on Saturdays take **SolTrans** (☎ 707-648-4666; www.soltransride.com; adult/youth $5/4) from BART to Vallejo ($5, 30 minutes), then connect with Napa Valley Vine bus 11 to Napa and Calistoga ($1.60); on Sundays, there's no connecting bus service from BART.

ⓘ Getting Around

You'll need a car or bike to winery-hop. Alternatively visit tasting rooms in downtown Napa or downtown Sonoma. For more information on touring Napa and Sonoma Wine Country by bicycle, see page p175.

BICYCLE

Touring Wine Country by bicycle is a fantastic experience. The majority of trails between wineries are flat and very approachable for beginners, however crossing between the Napa and Sonoma valleys is challenging with steep roads. It's best to stick to back roads, and we particularly recommend West Dry Creek Rd.

BUS

Sonoma County Transit (☎ 800-345-7433, 707-576-7433; http://sctransit.com) buses travel around Santa Rosa, Healdsburg, Sebastopol, Petaluma, Kenwood, Glen Ellen, Russian River towns, Sonoma Valley and Geyserville. Prices range from $1.50 to $4.80 depending on how many zones you pass through on your journey. Youth prices range from $1.25 to $4.55.

Napa Valley Vine (☎ 800-696-6443, 707-251-2800; www.ridethevine.com) local bus 10 runs daily from downtown Napa to Calistoga (adult/youth $1.60/1.10).

CAR & MOTORCYCLE

Napa Valley is 30 miles long and 5 miles across at its widest point (city of Napa) and 1 mile at its narrowest (Calistoga). Two roads run north–south: Hwy 29/St Helena Hwy and the more scenic Silverado Trail, a mile east. Drive up one, down the other.

The American Automobile Association ranks Napa Valley among America's most congested rural vacation destinations. Summer and fall weekend traffic is unbearable, especially on Hwy 29 between Napa and St Helena. Plan accordingly.

Cross-valley roads linking Silverado Trail with Hwy 29 – including Yountville, Oakville and Rutherford crossroads – are bucolic and get less traffic. For scenery, the Oakville Grade and rural Trinity Rd (which leads southwest to Hwy 12 in Sonoma Valley) are narrow, curvy and beautiful – but treacherous in rainstorms. Mt Veeder Rd leads through pristine countryside west of Yountville.

Note: police watch like hawks for traffic violators. *Don't drink and drive.*

There are a number of shortcuts between the Napa and Sonoma Valleys: from Oakville, take Oakville Grade to Trinity Rd; from St Helena, take Spring Mountain Rd into Calistoga Rd; from Calistoga, take Petrified Forest Rd to Calistoga Rd.

TRAIN

The **Napa Valley Wine Train** (p179) can take you from Napa to St Helena and back in a comfy, vintage dining car. An additional winery tour is optional. Trains depart from **Napa Valley Wine Train Depot** (http://winetrain.com/getting-here; 1275 McKinstry St) on McKinstry St near 1st St.

NAPA VALLEY

The birthplace of modern-day Wine Country is famous for regal Cabernet Sauvignons, château-like wineries and fabulous food. It attracts more than three million visitors a year, many planning to wine and dine themselves into a stupor, maybe get a massage, and sleep somewhere swell with fine linens and a heated pool.

The city of Napa anchors the valley, but the real work happens up-valley. And while Napa may not be as scenic as other stops, it has some noteworthy sights, among them Oxbow Public Market and the new cooking-school campus, CIA at Copia. The prettiest towns include St Helena, Yountville and Calistoga – the latter more famous for mud and water than wine.

History

A few decades ago, Napa was a quiet agricultural valley dense with orchards, its 5-by-35-mile strip peppered with stagecoach stops. Grapes had grown here since the gold rush, but juice-sucking phylloxera bugs, Prohibition and the Great Depression reduced 140 wineries in the 1890s to around 25 by the 1960s.

In 1968 Napa was declared the 'Napa Valley Agricultural Preserve,' effectively blocking future valley development for non-ag purposes. The law prohibited the subdivision of valley-floor land under 40 acres, which helped preserve the valley's natural beauty. But when Napa wines earned top honors at a 1976 blind tasting in Paris, the wine-drinking world noticed, land values skyrocketed and only the very rich could afford to build – hence so many architecturally jaw-dropping wineries. Independent, family-owned wineries still exist – we highlight a number of them – but much of Napa Valley is now owned by global conglomerates.

Napa Valley Wineries

Cab is king in Napa. No varietal captures imaginations like the fruit of the Cabernet Sauvignon vine – Bordeaux is the French equivalent – and no wine fetches a higher price. Napa farmers can't afford *not* to grow Cabernet, and Chardonnay, which flourishes in the calcium-rich soil of cooler areas of the valley, is second. Other varietals such as Merlot and Zinfandel also thrive here.

Napa's wines merit their reputation among the world's finest – complex, with luxurious finishes. Napa wineries sell many 'buy-and-hold' wines, versus Sonoma's 'drink-now' wines.

★**Hess Collection**   WINERY, GALLERY
(☎707-255-1144; www.hesscollection.com; 4411 Redwood Rd, Napa; museum free, tasting $25 & $35, tours free; ⊙10am-5:30pm, last tasting 5pm)
⬤ Art-lovers: don't miss Hess Collection, whose galleries display mixed-media and large-canvas works, including pieces by Francis Bacon and Robert Motherwell. In the elegant stone-walled tasting room, find well-known Cabernet Sauvignon and Chardonnay, but also try the Viognier. There's garden service in the warmer months, which is lovely, as Hess overlooks the valley. Make reservations and be prepared to drive a winding road. Bottles are $30 to $100. Public tour 10:30am.

TOURING NAPA & SONOMA WINE COUNTRY

Touring Wine Country by bicycle is unforgettable. Stick to back roads. We love pastoral West Dry Creek Rd, northwest of Healdsburg, in Sonoma County. Through Sonoma Valley, take Arnold Dr instead of Hwy 12; through Napa Valley, take the Silverado Trail instead of Hwy 29. Cycling between wineries isn't demanding – the valleys are mostly flat – but crossing between the Napa and Sonoma Valleys is intense, particularly via steep Oakville Grade and Trinity Rd (between Oakville and Glen Ellen). Bicycles, in boxes, can be checked on Greyhound buses (p173) for $30 to $40; bike boxes cost $10 (call ahead). You can transport bicycles on Golden Gate Transit (p117) buses.

Bicycle Tours & Rentals

Guided tours start around $90 per day including bikes, tastings and lunch. Daily rentals cost $25 to $85; make reservations.

Getaway Adventures (☑ 800-499-2453, 707-568-3040; http://getawayadventures.com; 5½hr tour $139-175) These great guided cycling tours visit wineries and other attractions, and include a picnic lunch. They depart from Napa and Calistoga.

Backroads (☑ 800-462-2848; www.backroads.com) All-inclusive, multiday guided biking and walking.

Calistoga Bike Shop (Map p190; ☑ 707-942-9687; http://calistogabikeshop.com; 1318 Lincoln Ave; bicycle rental from $28, guided tours from $149; ⊙ 10am-6pm) Rents full-suspension mountain bikes, hybrids, road bikes and tandem models and provides reliable trail information. DIY touring packages ($110 per day) include free tastings and wine pickup.

Napa River Velo (☑ 707-258-8729; www.naparivervelo.com; 680 Main St, Napa; rentals per day $40-90; ⊙ 10am-7pm Mon-Fri, 9am-6pm Sat, to 5pm Sun) Hourly, daily and weekly rentals in downtown Napa; reservations recommended.

Spoke Folk Cyclery (☑ 707-433-7171; www.spokefolk.com; 201 Center St; hybrid bicycle rental per hour/day from $14/38; ⊙ 10am-6pm Mon-Fri, to 5pm Sat & Sun) Rents touring, racing and tandem bicycles that come with locks and helmets. Great service.

Sonoma Adventures (☑ 707-938-2080; www.sonoma-adventures.com; bicycle rental per day $30-65, tours $129-189, segway tours $129) Bicycle rentals and guided cycling tours of Sonoma Valley, Dry Creek Valley and Carneros. There's a minimum of two people for the Sonoma tours, four people for the Dry Creek Valley and Carneros tours.

Wine Country Bikes (Map p210; ☑ 707-473-0610; www.winecountrybikes.com; 61 Front St; rentals per day from $39, guided tours from $139; ⊙ 9am-5pm) Rents bikes in downtown Healdsburg and guides multiday Sonoma County tours.

Napa Valley Bike Tours (Map p185; ☑ 707-944-2953; www.napavalleybiketours.com; 6500 Washington St, Yountville; bicycle rental per day $45-75, tours $109-124; ⊙ 8:30am-5pm) Two-hour and daily rentals, as well as easy and moderately difficult tours starting in Yountville. Second location at the foot of the Vine Trail at 3259 California Blvd, you can rent in one location and drop off in the other for $10 extra.

Other Tours

Platypus Wine Tours (☑ 707-253-2723; www.platypustours.com; join-in tour per person $110) Billed as the anti-wine-snob tour, Platypus specializes in backroad vineyards and family-owned operations. There's a daily 'join-in' tour that takes in four wineries and a picnic lunch, and private tours with a dedicated driver. The Napa tours are the most popular, but Platypus also takes people to Sonoma, Russian River and Dry Creek Valleys.

Beyond the Label (☑ 707-363-4023; www.btlnv.com; per couple from $995) Personalized tours, including lunch at home with a vintner, guided by a knowledgeable Napa native.

Beau Wine Tours (Map p180; ☑ 707-938-8001, 800-387-2328; www.beauwinetours.com) Winery tours in sedans and stretch limos; charges a base rate of $65 to $205 per hour (four- to six-hour minimum), but expect to pay more for gas, tax and tip.

Magnum Tours (☑ 707-753-0088; www.magnumwinetours.com) Sedans and specialty limousines from $65 to $110 per hour (four-hour minimum, five hours Saturdays).

★ **Robert Sinskey Vineyards** WINERY
(Map p185; ☑ 707-944-9090; www.robertsinskey.
com; 6320 Silverado Trail, Napa; bar tasting $40,
seated food & wine pairings $70-175; ⊙10am-
4:30pm; P) ⬤ The fabulous hillside tasting
room, constructed of stone, redwood and
teak, resembles a small cathedral – fitting,
given the sacred status here bestowed upon
food and wine. It specializes in bright-ac-
id organic Pinot Noir, plus exceptional
aromatic white varietals, dry rosé and
Bordeaux varietals such as Merlot and Cab
Franc, all crafted for the dinner table.

Small bites accompany bar tastings, and
seated food and wine experiences are curated by chef Maria Sinskey herself. Reserve
ahead for sit-down tastings and culinary
tours. Bottles $22 to $100.

★ **Frog's Leap** WINERY
(Map p185; ☑ 707-963-4704; www.frogsleap.com;
8815 Conn Creek Rd, Rutherford; tasting $20-25,
incl tour $25; ⊙10am-4pm by appointment only;
P🖐🐾) ⬤ Meandering paths wind through
magical gardens and fruit-bearing orchards
surrounding an 1884 barn and farmstead
with cats and chickens. The vibe is casual,
with a major emphasis on *fun*. Sauvignon
Blanc is its best-known wine but the Merlot
merits attention. There's also a dry, restrained
Cabernet, atypical of Napa.All grapes are organically farmed. Bottles cost $20 to $55.

★ **Tres Sabores** WINERY
(Map p185; ☑ 707-967-8027; www.tressabores.
com; 1620 South Whitehall Lane, St Helena; tour &
tasting $40; ⊙10:30am-3pm, by appointment; 🐾)
⬤ At the valley's westernmost edge, where
sloping vineyards meet wooded hillsides,
Tres Sabores is a portal to old Napa – no fancy tasting room, no snobbery, just great wine
in a spectacular setting. Bucking the Cabernet custom, Tres Sabores crafts elegantly
structured, Burgundian-style Zinfandel and
spritely Sauvignon Blanc, which the *New
York Times* dubbed a top 10 of its kind in
California. Reservations are essential.

Pride Mountain WINERY
(☑ 707-963-4949; www.pridewines.com; 4026
Spring Mountain Rd, St Helena; tasting & tour $20-
30, summit experience $75; ⊙ by appointment only)
High atop Spring Mountain, cult-favorite
Pride straddles the Napa–Sonoma border and
bottles vintages under both appellations. The
well-structured Cabernet and heavy-hitting
Merlot are the best-known wines but there's
also an elegant Viognier (perfect with oysters)
and standout Cab Franc, available only here.
Picnicking is spectacular: choose Viewpoint
for drop-dead vistas, or Ghost Winery for
shade and the historic ruins of a 19th-century
winery, but you must first reserve a tasting.
Bottles cost $42 to $70.

Artesa WINERY
(☑ 707-254-2126; www.artesawinery.com; 1345
Henry Rd, Napa; tastings from $35, tour/glass
$45/15; ⊙10am-5pm, last pour 4:30pm) Begin or
end the day with a glass of bubbly or Pinot at
Artesa, southwest of Napa. Built into a moun-
tainside, the ultramodern Barcelona-style ar-

NAPA OR SONOMA?

Napa and Sonoma Valleys run parallel, separated by the narrow, imposing Mayacamas
Mountains. The two couldn't be more different. It's easy to mock aggressively sophisticated Napa, its monuments to ego, trophy homes and trophy wives, $1000-a-night inns,
$50-plus tastings and wine-snob visitors. Sonoma residents refer to Napa as 'the dark
side'; still, its wines are some of the world's best. Constrained by geography, Napa stretches along a single valley, making it easy to visit. Drawbacks are high prices and heavy traffic,
but there are more than 500 wineries, nearly side by side. And the valley is gorgeous.

There are three Sonomas: Sonoma town is in Sonoma Valley, which is in Sonoma
County. Think of them as Russian dolls. Sonoma County is much more down-to-earth
and politically left-leaning. Though it's becoming gentrified, Sonoma lacks Napa's chic
factor (Healdsburg notwithstanding) and locals like it that way. The wines are more approachable, but the county's 400 or so wineries are spread out. If you're here on a weekend, head to Sonoma (County or Valley), which gets less traffic, but on a weekday, see
Napa too. Ideally schedule two to four days: one for each valley and one or two additional
days for western Sonoma County.

Spring and fall are the best times to visit. Summers are hot, dusty and crowded. Fall
brings fine weather, harvest time and the 'crush,' the pressing of the grapes, but lodging
prices skyrocket.

chitecture is stunning and you can't beat the top-of-the-world vistas over San Pablo Bay. Tours run at 11am and 2pm. Recent changes include a new winemaker and increased focus on wine and food pairings. Reservations recommended. Bottles cost $28 to $85.

Cade
WINERY

(Map p190; ☎707-965-2746; www.cadewinery.com; 360 Howell Mountain Rd S, Angwin; tasting & tour $80; ⊙by appointment only) 🍷 Ascend Mt Veeder for drop-dead vistas, 1800ft above the valley, at Napa's oh-so-swank, first-ever organically farmed, Leadership in Energy and Environmental Design (LEED) gold-certified winery, partly owned by former San Francisco mayor Gavin Newsom. Hawks ride thermals at eye level as you sample bright Sauvignon Blanc and luscious Cabernet Sauvignon that's more Bordelaise in style than Californian. Reservations required. Bottles cost $44 to $80.

Vincent Arroyo
WINERY

(Map p190; ☎707-942-6995; www.vincentarroyo. com; 2361 Greenwood Ave, Calistoga; ⊙by appointment) **FREE** The tasting room is a garage, where you may even meet Mr Arroyo, known for his all-estate-grown Petite Sirah and Cabernet Sauvignon. They're distributed nowhere else and are so consistently good that 75% of production is sold before it's bottled. Tastings are free, but appointments are required. Bottles are $21 to $65.

Long Meadow Ranch
FARM

(Map p190; ☎707-963-4555; www.longmeadow ranch.com; 738 Main St, St Helena; tasting $25-40, chef's table $145; ⊙11am-6pm) 🍷 Long Meadow stands out for olive-oil tastings ($5), plus good estate-grown Cabernet, Sauvignon Blanc, Chardonnay and Pinot Noir, served inside an 1874 farmhouse surrounded by lovely gardens. It also has a whiskey flight for $30; sells housemade products such as preserves, BBQ sauce and Bloody Mary mix; and hosts chef's tables (four- to five-course meal and wine experiences) at lunch and dinner daily. Reservations for chef's table required. Bottles $20 to $50.

Twenty Rows
WINERY

(Map p185; ☎707-265-7750; www.twentyrows. com; 880 Vallejo St, Napa; tasting $20, glass $10; ⊙11am-6pm Wed-Mon, by appointment Tue) This long-standing downtown Napa winery crafts light-on-the-palate Cabernet Sauvignon ($32 a bottle). Taste in a chilly garage with fun dudes who know their wines, or sip on the newly constructed back patio. Good Sauvignon Blanc.

---

❶ BOOKING APPOINTMENTS AT WINERIES

Because of strict county zoning laws, many Napa wineries cannot legally receive drop-in visitors; unless you've come strictly to buy, you'll have to call ahead. This is *not* the case with all wineries. We recommend booking one tasting, plus a lunch or dinner reservation, and planning your day around those appointments.

Hall
WINERY

(Map p190; ☎707-967-2626; www.hallwines.com; 401 St Helena Hwy, St Helena; tasting & tour from $40; ⊙10am-5:30pm; 🅿🍽) 🍷 Co-owned by Bill Clinton's former ambassador to Austria, Hall specializes in Cabernet Sauvignon, Sauvignon Blanc and Merlot, crafted in big-fruit California style. Its dramatic tasting room has a stand-up bar with 180-degree views of vineyards and mountains through floor-to-ceiling glass, and the glorious art collection includes a giant chrome rabbit leaping over the vines. Bottles cost $24 to $170.

Schramsberg
WINERY

(Map p190; ☎707-942-2414, 800-877-3623; www. schramsberg.com; 1400 Schramsberg Rd, off Peterson Dr; tour & tasting $70, tour & sparkling-wine tasting $95, reserve wine & cheese pairing $125; ⊙by appointment at 9:30am, 10am, 10:30am, 11:30am, noon, 1:30pm, & 2:30pm) Napa's second-oldest winery, Schramsberg makes some of California's best brut sparkling wines, and in 1972 was the first domestic wine served at the White House. Blanc de Blancs is the signature. The appointment-only tasting and tour (book well ahead) is expensive, but you'll sample all the *tête de cuvées*, not just the low-end wines. Tours include a walk through the caves; bring a sweater. Bottles cost $24 to $150.

Titus
WINERY

(Map p190; ☎707-963-3235; www.titusvineyards. com; 2971 Silverado Trail N, St Helena; tasting $20; ⊙by appointment; 🏍🍽) Formerly modest Titus has gone fancy of late, opening a modern tasting facility with windows for days, surrounded by 40 acres of vineyards. It's best to call ahead to sample the winery's good-value, fruit-forward Cabernet Sauvignon and old-vine Zinfandel – rare in Napa. Afterward, take your glass outside, and relax on the expansive patio. The tasting fee is waived with a purchase; bottles are $20 to $70.

ⓘ HIGH SEASON VS LOW SEASON

Many Wine Country restaurants and hotels diminish operations in wintertime. Make reservations, especially in summertime, or you may not eat. Hotel rates jump during September and October's grape-crushing season.

Castello di Amorosa
WINERY, CASTLE

(Map p190; ☏707-967-6272; www.castellodiamorosa.com; 4045 Hwy 29, Calistoga; entry & tasting $25-35, incl guided tour $40-85; ⊙9:30am-6pm Mar-Oct, to 5pm Nov-Feb; P⊕) It took 14 years to build this perfectly replicated, 13th-century Italian castle, complete with moat, hand-cut stone walls, ceiling frescoes by Italian artisans, Roman-style cross-vault brick catacombs, and a torture chamber with period equipment. You can taste without an appointment, but this is one tour worth taking. Oh, the wine? Some respectable Italian varietals, including a velvety Tuscan blend and a Merlot that goes great with pizza. Bottles are $20 to $98.

Darioush
WINERY

(Map p185; ☏707-257-2345; www.darioush.com; 4240 Silverado Trail, Napa; tasting from $40; ⊙10:30am-5pm; P) Like a modern-day Persian palace, Darioush ranks high on the fabulosity scale, with towering columns, Le Corbusier furniture, Persian rugs and travertine walls. Though known for Cabernet Sauvignon, Darioush also bottles Chardonnay, Merlot and Shiraz, all made with 100% of their respective varietals. Call about wine-and-cheese pairings ($75). Bottles cost $40 to $95.

Mumm Napa
WINERY, GALLERY

(Map p185; ☏800-686-6272, 707-967-7700; www.mummnapa.com; 8445 Silverado Trail, Rutherford; tasting $20-50, tour $30, glass $12-15; ⊙10am-6pm; P)

Valley views are spectacular at Mumm, which makes respectable sparkling wines you can sample by the glass beneath a vineyard-side pergola or seated on a vineyard-view terrace – ideal if you want to impress conservative parents-in-law. Dodge crowds by coming early, or paying $50 for the reserve-tasting Oak Terrace (reservations required). There's also a fabulous photography gallery featuring the work of Ansel Adams. Last seating is at 5:45pm.

Regusci
WINERY

(Map p185; ☏707-254-0403; www.regusciwinery.com; 5584 Silverado Trail, Napa; tasting $50, incl tour $60; ⊙10am-5pm; P) One of Napa's oldest, Regusci dates to the late 1800s, with 160 acres of vineyards unfurling around a century-old stone winery that makes Bordeaux-style blends on the valley's quieter eastern side – good when traffic up-valley is bad. There's a lovely oak-shaded picnic area. Reservations required; tasting fee is waived with a purchase of $80 or more. Bottles cost $55 to $120.

Elizabeth Spencer
WINERY

(Map p185; ☏707-963-6067; www.elizabethspencerwinery.com; 1165 Rutherford Rd, Rutherford; tasting $25-60; ⊙10am-6pm, last tasting 5:30pm) Check in at this 1872 former post-office building and indulge in tastings tableside in the outdoor garden courtyard at this inviting small winery. Featured are monster-sized Pinot Noir, a range of white-wine varietals including Sauvignon Blanc and Chenan Blanc, structured lightbody Grenache and an array of Cabernet. Tastings are a relaxed affair; allow an hour for the alfresco experience. Bottles cost $35 to $250.

Robert Mondavi
WINERY

(Map p185; ☏707-226-1395, 888-766-6328; www.robertmondaviwinery.com; 7801 Hwy 29, Oakville; tasting/tour from $5/25; ⊙10am-5pm, store to 6pm; P⊕) ✔ Tour buses flock to this corporate-owned winery, but if you know nothing about wine and can cope with crowds, the

CALIFORNIA WILDFIRES

In October 2017 a series of wildfires burned throughout Northern California including Mendocino, Napa and Sonoma Counties. For 19 days the wildfires burned killing at least 42 people, destroying thousands of homes and prompting 100,000 people to evacuate.

The research for this book was conducted before the fires hit and the content was sent to print soon afterward, when long term effects of the fires were still unknown. This area of California is heavily reliant on tourism and most businesses were already announcing they were open for guests. Still, the state parks remained closed until further notice and many businesses and historic sites were uncertain when they would be back on their feet. Those planning to travel to Napa & Sonoma Wine Country should check official websites for the latest information.

worthwhile tours provide good insight into winemaking. Definitely skip the charcuterie plate, but do consider attending one of the glorious outdoor summer **concerts**; call for schedules. Bottles cost $35 to $165.

Napa

The valley's workaday hub was once a nothing-special city of storefronts, Victorian cottages and riverfront warehouses, but booming real-estate values caused an influx of new money that's transforming downtown into a hub of arts and food.

Napa lies between Silverado Trail and St Helena Hwy/Hwy 29. For downtown, exit Hwy 29 at 1st St and drive east. Napa's main drag, 1st St, is lined with shops and restaurants.

◉ Sights

★**di Rosa**   ARTS CENTER
(☑707-226-5991; www.dirosaart.org; 5200 Hwy 121; $5, tours $12-15; ☉10am-4pm Wed-Sun; Ⓟ) West of downtown, scrap-metal sculptures dot Carneros vineyards at the 217-acre di Rosa Art + Nature Preserve, a stunning collection of Northern California art, displayed indoors in galleries and outdoors in gardens by a giant lake. Reservations recommended for tours.

★**Oxbow Public Market**   MARKET
(Map p180; ☑707-226-6529; www.oxbowpublicmarket.com; 610 & 644 1st St; ☉9am-9pm; Ⓟ📶) 🍴 Showcasing all things culinary (produce stalls, kitchen shops and everywhere something to taste), Oxbow is foodie central with emphasis on seasonal eating and sustainability. Some vendors and restaurants open early or close late. Come hungry.

CIA at Copia   CENTER
(Map p180; ☑707-967-2500; www.ciaatcopia.com; 500 1st St; ☉10:30am-9pm) The former food museum beside Napa's famous Oxbow Public Market has been revived as a center of all things edible by the prestigious Culinary Institute of America. In its new life as Copia, the 80,000-sq-ft campus offers wine tastings, interactive cooking demos, an innovative restaurant, a massive fork statue (composed of many thousands of smaller forks) and more food-related features.

The eponymous **Restaurant at CIA Copia** takes a new approach to food service, with cart-and-tray dishes traveling around the dining room and chefs similarly on the move, answering questions from curious guests.

☞ Tours

Napa Valley Wine Train   TOURS
(Map p180; ☑800-427-4124, 707-253-2111; http://winetrain.com; 1275 McKinstry St; ticket incl dining from $146) A cushy, if touristy, way to see Wine Country, the Wine Train offers three-hour daily trips in vintage Pullman dining cars, from Napa to St Helena and back, with optional winery tours. It also offers six-hour journeys visiting multiple wineries with Napa Valley cuisine served between visits.

🛏 Sleeping

The digs here are decent, ranging from high-end spa resorts to quiet inns to comfy chain hotels but prices are high. On weekends and over summer, when rates skyrocket, consider staying in Calistoga. Archer Hotel (https://archerhotel.com/napa) and its Charlie Palmer Steakhouse are new to downtown, and everybody is talking about them.

★**Carneros Resort & Spa**   RESORT $$$
(☑888-400-9000, 707-299-4900; www.thecarnerosresort.com; 4048 Sonoma Hwy; r from $500; ❄@🛜🛑🐕) Carneros Resort & Spa's contemporary aesthetic and retro small-town agricultural theme shatter the predictable Wine Country mold. The semi-detached, corrugated-metal cottages look like itinerant housing, but inside they're snappy and chic, with cherry-wood floors, ultrasuede headboards, wood-burning fireplaces, heated-tile bathroom floors, giant tubs and indoor-outdoor showers.

ⓘ **CUTTING COSTS IN NAPA**

To avoid overspending on tasting fees, it's perfectly acceptable to pay for one tasting to share between two people. Ask in advance if fees are applicable to purchase (they usually aren't). Tour fees cannot be split. Ask at your hotel, or at visitor centers, for free- or discounted-tasting coupons, or download from www.napatouristguide.com. If you can't afford the hotels, try western Sonoma County, but if you want to be closer to Napa, try the suburban towns of Vallejo and American Canyon, about 20 minutes from downtown Napa. Both have motels for $75 to $125 in high season. Also find chains 30 minutes away in Fairfield, off I-80 exits 41 (Pittman Rd) and 45 (Travis Blvd).

Napa

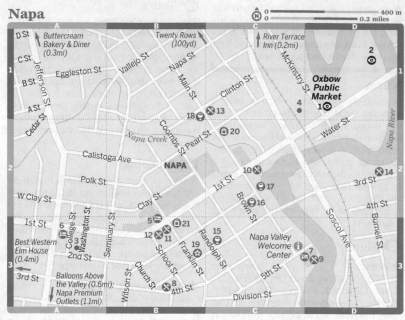

Napa

Andaz Napa   HOTEL **$$$**
(Map p180; ☎707-687-1234; www.andaznapa.com;
1450 1st St; r from $270; P🅟❄✳@🛜) Smack
downtown, the Andaz was constructed in
2009 and feels like a big-city hotel, with
business-class-fancy rooms styled in sexy
contemporary style. It's walking distance to
restaurants and bars. There's an on-site ter-

race bar with fire pits and guests have access
to an adjacent health club with indoor lap
pool, sauna and gym.

Cottages of Napa Valley   BUNGALOW **$$$**
(Map p185; ☎707-252-7810; www.napacottages.
com; 1012 Darns Lane; cottages $350-600; ✳🛜)
Eight pristine cottages of quality construc-

tion – made for romantic hideaways, with extralong soaking tubs, indoor gas fireplaces and outdoor campfire pits – surround a big garden shaded by towering pines. Cottages 4 and 8 have private porches and swinging chairs. The only drawback is noise from traffic, but interiors are quiet.

Milliken Creek Inn   INN $$$
(Map p185; ☑707-255-1197; www.millikencreekinn. com; 1815 Silverado Trail; r $295-750; ✳@ᴥ) Understatedly elegant Milliken Creek combines small-inn charm, fine-hotel service and B&B intimacy. Rooms are impeccably styled in English-colonial style and higher-end rooms have top-flight amenities, fireplace and ultrahigh-thread-count linen. Breakfast is delivered. Book a river-view room.

Blackbird Inn   B&B $$$
(Map p180; ☑707-226-2450, 888-567-9811; www. blackbirdinnnapa.com; 1755 1st St; r $250-285; ✳ᴥ) Gorgeous, eight-room arts-and-crafts-style B&B. Anticipate street noise.

Napa River Inn   HOTEL $$$
(Map p180; ☑707-251-8500, 877-251-8500; www. napariverinn.com; 500 Main St; r $300-600; ✳@ᴥᴥ) Beside the river in the 1884 Hatt Building, the inn has top-end rooms, Victoriana to modern, in three satellite buildings. Walkable distance to restaurants and bars. Dogs get special treatment.

Napa Winery Inn   HOTEL $$$
(Map p185; ☑707-257-7220; www.napawineryinn. com; 1998 Trower Ave; r Mon-Fri $179-279, Sat & Sun $229-350; ✳@ᴥᴥᴥ) Request a remodeled room at this good-value hotel, north of downtown, decorated with generic Colonial-style furniture. It has a hot tub and good service. There are complimentary wine receptions each night: weekdays 5:30pm to 6:30pm, to 7pm weekends.

River Terrace Inn   HOTEL $$$
(Map p185; ☑707-320-9000; www.riverterraceinn.com; 1600 Soscol Ave; r $189-360; ✳ᴥᴥ) Upmarket, business-class, chain-style hotel with shopping-mall-bland architecture fronting on the Napa River. The entire property was recently renovated, including a new restaurant and bar.

✖ Eating

Deliciousness abounds, but it's going to cost you. Make reservations whenever possible, and cut costs by grabbing sandwiches from Soda Canyon Store for a picnic lunch.

★**Oxbow Public Market**   MARKET $
(Map p180; ☑707-226-6529; www.oxbowpublic market.com; 610 & 644 1st St; items from $3; ⊘9am-9pm; ᴥ✚) ✐ Graze at this gourmet market and plug into the Northern California food scene. Standouts: **Hog Island Oyster Co**; comfort cooking at celeb-chef Todd Humphries' **Kitchen Door**; great Cal-Mexican tacos at **C Casa & Taco Lounge**; the India pale ales (IPAs) and sour beers at **Fieldwork Brewing Company**; espresso from **Ritual Coffee**; and **Three Twins** certified-organic ice cream.

Tuesday is locals' night (5pm to 8pm), with many discounts. Some stalls remain open to 9pm, even on Sundays, but many close earlier and some vendors open early in the morning.

Alexis Baking Company & Cafe   CAFE $
(Map p180; ☑707-258-1827; www.abcnapa.com; 1517 3rd St; mains $9-17; ⊘7am-3pm Mon-Fri, 7:30am-3pm Sat, 8am-2pm Sun; ✐✚) Our fave spot for quality egg scrambles, granola, focaccia sandwiches, big cups of joe and boxed lunches to go.

Taqueria Maria   MEXICAN $
(Map p180; ☑707-257-6925; www.taqueriamariaapa1.com; 640 3rd St; mains $8-15; ⊘8am-9pm Sun-Thu, to 9:30pm Fri & Sat; ✐✚) Reliably good Mexican cooking that won't break the bank. Also serves breakfast.

Buttercream Bakery & Diner   DINER $
(Map p185; ☑707-255-6700; www.buttercream-bakery.com; 2297 Jefferson St; breakfast $5-10, cakes $15-25; ⊘bakery 5:30am-6pm Mon-Sat, to 4pm Sun, diner 5:30am-3pm Mon-Sat, to 2:30pm Sun) This retro-flashback pink-striped diner, favored by Napa's little old ladies, has all-day breakfasts and white-bread lunches, served by matrons in heavy eye shadow. Also famous for its champagne cakes.

Soda Canyon Store   DELI $
(Map p185; ☑707-252-0285; www.sodacanyon store.com; 4006 Silverado Trail; ⊘6am-6pm Mon-Sat, 7am-5pm Sun) This roadside deli with shaded picnic area makes an easy stop while winery-hopping north of town.

Oenotri   ITALIAN $$
(Map p180; ☑707-252-1022; www.oenotri.com; 1425 1st St; brunch $13-15, dinner mains $18-34; ⊘brunch 10am-3pm Sat & Sun, 5:30-9pm Sun-Thu, to 10pm Fri & Sat) ✐ Housemade *salumi* (cured meat) and pastas, and wood-fired Naples-style pizzas are the stars at always-busy Oenotri,

which draws crowds for daily-changing, locally sourced, rustic-Italian cooking, served in a cavernous brick-walled space.

Pizza Azzuro
PIZZA **$$**

(Map p180; ☎ 707-255-5552; www.azzurropizzeria.com; 1260 Main St; mains $15-18; ⊙11:30am-9:30pm Sun-Thu, to 10pm Fri & Sat; 🖉🕅) This Napa classic gets deafeningly loud, but it's worth bearing for tender-crusted pizzas, salad-topped 'manciata' bread, good Caesar salads and pastas.

Norman Rose Tavern
PUB FOOD **$$**

(Map p180; ☎ 707-258-1516; www.normanrosenapa.com; 1401 1st St; mains $10-24; ⊙11:30am-9pm Sun-Thu, to 10pm Fri & Sat; 🕅) This happening gastropub, styled with reclaimed wood and tufted-leather banquettes, is good for a burger and beer. Great fries and plenty of seasonal favorites. Full bar.

Bounty Hunter Wine Bar & Smokin' BBQ
BARBECUE **$$**

(Map p180; ☎ 707-226-3976; www.bountyhunterwinebar.com; 975 1st St; mains $14-28; ⊙11am-10pm Sun-Thu, to midnight Fri & Sat; 🕅) Inside an 1888 grocery store, Bounty Hunter has an Old West vibe and superb barbecue, made with house-smoked meats. The standout 'beer-can chicken' is a whole chicken roasted over a can of Tecate. Libations include 40 local beers, 60 whiskeys and 400 wines (40 by the glass).

Angèle
FRENCH **$$$**

(Map p180; ☎ 707-252-8115; www.angelerestaurant.com; 540 Main St; lunch mains $14-27, dinner $26-30; ⊙11:30am-4pm & 5-9pm Sun-Thu, to 10pm Sat & Sun) Stalwart Angèle serves reliable provincial-French cooking – French onion soup, Nicoise salads and *croques mes-*

sieurs (gourmet toasted ham and cheese sandwiches) at lunch, cassoulet with duck confit at dinner – on a river-view deck or in the cozy dining room, both perfect for lingering with a good bottle of wine.

Bistro Don Giovanni
ITALIAN **$$$**

(Map p185; ☎ 707-224-3300; www.bistrodongiovanni.com; 4110 Howard Lane; mains $16-34; ⊙11:30am-10pm Sun-Thu, to 11pm Fri & Sat) This long-running favorite roadhouse serves modern-Italian pastas, crispy pizzas and wood-roasted meats. Reservations essential. Weekends get packed – and loud. Request a vineyard-view table (good luck).

Torc
CALIFORNIAN **$$$**

(Map p180; ☎ 707-252-3292; www.torcnapa.com; 1140 Main St; mains $28-46, prix-fixe menu $46; ⊙5-9:30pm Wed-Mon) Wildly popular Torc plays off the seasons with dynamic combinations of farm-fresh ingredients such as pork belly with satsuma-imo potato and choy raab, or artichoke velouté with wild mushrooms. Well-arranged for people-watching, the big stone dining room has an open-truss ceiling and pinewood tables that downplay formality. Reservations essential.

🍷 Drinking & Nightlife

There is no shortage of drinking establishments in the downtown area, including breweries, sports bars and wine-tasting rooms, which have proliferated in recent years.

Vintners' Collective
WINE BAR

(Map p180; ☎ 707-255-7150; www.vintnerscollective.com; 1245 Main St; tastings $10-40, private tastings $75 & $95; ⊙11am-7pm) Ditch the car and chill in downtown Napa at this tasting bar inside a former 20th-century brothel. It represents 20-plus high-end boutique wineries that are too small to have their own tasting rooms. There are around 140 wines to try, and the pricier the tasting, the more sought-after the wine. The $75 and $95 tastings include artisanal cheese and charcuterie.

Tannery Bend Beerworks
BREWERY

(Map p185; ☎ 707-681-5774; http://tannerybendbeerworks.com; 101 S Coombs St; ⊙noon-8pm Wed-Sun) What do you call a brewery smaller than micro? A Napa brewery stepped up to answer that question in 2017 and this nanobrewery produces just 15 gallons of beer per batch. The teeny tiny booze biz is a collaboration between a chef, a brewer and a restaurateur (same one who owns the fabulous Oenotri, p181).

A LOVELY SPOT FOR A PICNIC

Unlike Sonoma, there aren't many places to picnic legally in Napa. Here's a short list, in south–north order, but call ahead and remember to buy a bottle (or glass, if available) of your host's wine. If you don't finish it, California law forbids driving with an uncorked bottle in the car (keep it in the trunk).

➡ Regusci (p178)

➡ Napa Valley Museum (p184)

➡ Pride Mountain (p176)

➡ Casa Nuestra (p178)

With their powers combined, they've created a few delicious and locally sourced Saisons and IPAs, in addition to a rotating menu of food pairings featuring things such as grilled blue crab and deviled eggs.

Carpe Diem Wine Bar
WINE BAR

(Map p180; ☑707-224-0800; www.carpediem winebar.com; 1001 2nd St; ⊗4-9pm Mon-Thu, to 10pm Fri & Sat) This busy storefront wine bar and restaurant (mains $22–$48) makes inventive, flavorful small plates, from simple skewers and flatbreads to elaborate ostrich burgers, salumi platters and – wait for it – duck confit 'quack and cheese.'

Downtown Joe's
SPORTS BAR, BREWERY

(Map p180; ☑707-258-2337; www.downtownjoes. com; 902 Main St, at 2nd St; ⊗8am-1am Mon & Tue, to 2am Wed-Sun; 🛜) Live music Thursday to Sunday, TV sports nightly and a pet-friendly, riverfront patio. Often packed, usually messy.

Billco's Billiards & Darts
SPORTS BAR

(Map p180; www.billcos.com; 1234 3rd St; ⊗noon-2am Mon-Sat, to midnight Sun) Dudes with beards swill craft beers and throw darts inside this lively pool hall.

☆ Entertainment

Silo's Jazz Club
LIVE MUSIC

(Map p180; ☑707-251-5833; www.silosnapa.com; 530 Main St; cover varies; ⊗4-10pm Wed, 5-10pm Thu, 7-11pm Fri & Sat, varied hours Sun) A cabaret-style wine-and-beer bar, Silo's hosts free jazz on Wednesday, and varied music acts on Friday and Saturday nights. On Thursday it's good for drinks. Buy tickets ahead of time on weekends.

Uptown Theatre
THEATER

(Map p180; ☑707-259-0123, ext 6; www.uptown theatrenapa.com; 1350 3rd St) Big-name acts play this restored 1937 theater.

🔒 Shopping

Napa Valley Olive Oil Mfg Co
FOOD

(Map p180; ☑707-265-6866; 1331 1st St; ⊗10am-5:30pm) Sample 40 varieties of fine olive oil and vinegar at this downtown specialty-food boutique, which also carries fancy salts and local jam.

Betty's Girl
WOMEN'S CLOTHING, VINTAGE

(Map p180; ☑707-254-7560; www.bettysgirlnapa. com; 968 Pearl St; ⊗by appointment) Expert couturier Kim Northrup fits women with fabulous vintage cocktail dresses and custom-made designs, altering and shipping for

no additional charge. She also has an annex at 1320 2nd St.

Napa General Store
GIFTS & SOUVENIRS

(Map p180; ☑707-259-0762; www.napageneral store.com; 540 Main St; ⊗8am-6pm) Finally, cutesy Wine Country souvenirs reasonably priced. The on-site **wine bar** is convenient for nonshopping spouses.

ⓘ Information

INTERNET

Napa Library (☑707-253-4241; www.county ofnapa.org/library; 580 Coombs St; ⊗10am-9pm Mon-Thu, to 6pm Fri & Sat; 🛜) Free internet access.

TOURIST INFORMATION

Napa Valley Welcome Center (Map p180; ☑707-251-5895, 855-847-6272; www.visitna pavalley.com; 600 Main St; ⊗9am-5pm; 🚹) Lodging assistance (call ☑707-251-9188 or ☑855-333-6272), wine-tasting passes, spa deals and comprehensive winery maps.

ⓘ Getting There & Away

From San Francisco, public transportation can get you to Napa, but it's insufficient for vineyard-hopping. For public-transit information, dial ☑511, or look online at www.transit.511.org.

Downtown Napa is about an 80-minute drive from San Francisco.

ⓘ Getting Around

Pedicabs park outside downtown restaurants – especially at the foot of Main St, near the Napa Valley Welcome Center – in summer. Car-sharing service Uber (www.uber.com) operates in Napa, but plans to hire an Uber can go awry in some areas due to spotty cell reception.

Yountville

This onetime stagecoach stop, 9 miles north of Napa, is now a fine-food destination playing to the haute bourgeoisie, with more Michelin stars per capita than any other American town. A stay in Yountville means drinking at dinner without having to drive afterward, as the town is walkable, but Napa and Calistoga make for livelier bases. Most businesses are on Washington St.

◉ Sights

Ma(i)sonry GALLERY, WINERY
(Map p185; ☏707-944-0889; www.maisonry.com; 6711 Washington St; ☺10:30am-4:30pm Sun-Thu, to 5:30pm Fri & Sat; P) Ma(i)sonry occupies a free-to-browse 1904 stone house and garden, transformed into a fussy winery-collective and gallery of pricey rustic-modern *meubles* (furniture) and art, some quite cool. Reservations recommended for wine tastings.

Napa Valley Museum MUSEUM
(Map p185; ☏707-944-0500; www.napavalleymuseum.org; 55 Presidents Circle; adult/child $7/2.50; ☺11am-4pm Wed-Sun; P) Yountville's modernist 40,000-sq-ft museum chronicles cultural history and showcases local paintings. Good picnicking outside. From town, it's across Hwy 29. Second Saturdays of the month are free.

Yountville Park PARK
(Map p185; cnr Washington & Madison Sts; ☺6am-8pm) Good park for a picnic.

🛏 Sleeping

There are some lovely inns here and many are walking distance from the restaurants and shops. Budget travelers will not find suitable accommodations though.

Poetry Inn INN $$$
(Map p185; ☏707-944-0646; www.poetryinn.com; 6380 Silverado Trail; r $1100-1975; ❋🛜🐾) There's no better valley view than from this contemporary five-room inn, high on the hills east of Yountville. Decorated with posh restraint, rooms have private balcony, wood-burning fireplace, 1000-thread-count linen and enormous bath with indoor-outdoor shower. Bring a ring.

Petit Logis INN $$$
(Map p185; ☏877-944-2332, 707-944-2332; www.petitlogis.com; 6527 Yount St; r $145-325; ❋🛜) Simple, cozy and comfortable, this cedar-sided inn has five uniquely adorned rooms, each with jetted tub and gas fireplace.

🍴 Eating

Make reservations or you may not eat. Yountville Park has picnic tables and barbecue grills. Find groceries across from the post office. There's a great taco truck parked in town.

Bouchon Bakery BAKERY $
(Map p185; ☏707-944-2253; www.bouchonbakery.com; 6528 Washington St; items from $3; ☺7am-7pm; 🍴) Bouchon makes as-good-as-in-Paris French pastries and strong coffee. There's always a line and rarely a seat: get it to go.

Ottimo ITALIAN $
(Map p185; ☏707-944-0102; www.ottimo-nv.com; 6525 Washington St; pizzas $14, crescintines $8; ☺7am-6pm) Chef Michael Chiarello opened this Italian market, cafe and *mozzeria* in Yountville's V Marketplace across from his popular farm-to-table establishment Bottega in early 2017, and it quietly became a prime spot for industry folks and in-the-know tourists. Most delicious are the brick-oven pizzas and crescentines (panini-like sandwiches), along with samples of preserves (from Chiarello's family recipes) in the shop. Grab a table on the sunny outdoor patio and hit the espresso bar on your way out.

Tacos Garcia FAST FOOD $
(Map p185; ☏707-980-4896; 6764 Washington St; tacos $1.50; ☺11am-9pm) This beloved taco truck operates out of the parking lot in front of the dive bar Pancha's (p186), offering delicious tacos with fillings such as beef cheeks, *tripa* (fried intestine) and fried pork double-wrapped in a corn tortilla and topped with onion and cilantro.

Redd Wood ITALIAN $$
(Map p185; ☏707-299-5030; www.redd-wood.com; 6755 Washington St; pizzas $16-19, most mains $17-28; ☺11:30am-10pm Sun-Thu, to 11pm Fri & Sat) Celeb-chef Richard Reddington's casual Italian trattoria serves outstanding homemade pastas, *salumi* and tender-to-the-tooth pizzas from a wood-fired oven.

Addendum SOUTHERN US $$
(Map p185; ☏707-944-1565; www.adhocrestaurant.com/addendum; 6476 Washington St; box lunch $16.50; ☺11am-2pm Thu-Sat; 🍴) An offspring of parent restaurant Ad Hoc (p186), Thomas Keller's Addendum provides boxed lunches of finger-lickin' buttermilk-fried chicken, BBQ pork ribs and pulled-pork sandwiches, accompanied by Southern-style sides to go. It's simple and delicious.

Napa Valley South

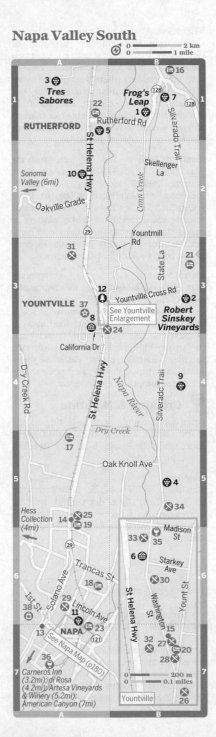

Napa Valley South

◎ Top Sights
1 Frog's Leap	B1
2 Robert Sinskey Vineyards	B3
3 Tres Sabores	A1

◎ Sights
4 Darioush	B5
5 Elizabeth Spencer	A1
6 Ma(i)sonry	B6
7 Mumm Napa	B1
8 Napa Valley Museum	A3
9 Regusci	B4
10 Robert Mondavi	A2
11 Twenty Rows	A6
12 Yountville Park	A3

⊕ Activities, Courses & Tours
13 Balloons Above the Valley	A7
14 Napa Valley Balloons	A5
15 Napa Valley Bike Tours	B7

⊜ Sleeping
16 Auberge du Soleil	B1
17 Cottages of Napa Valley	A5
18 Milliken Creek Inn	A6
19 Napa Winery Inn	A5
20 Petit Logis	B7
21 Poetry Inn	B3
22 Rancho Caymus	A1
23 River Terrace Inn	A7

⊗ Eating
Ad Hoc	(see 24)
24 Addendum	A3
25 Bistro Don Giovanni	A5
26 Bistro Jeanty	B7
27 Bouchon	B7
28 Bouchon Bakery	B7
29 Buttercream Bakery & Diner	A6
Ciccio	(see 35)
30 French Laundry	B6
31 Mustards Grill	A3
32 Ottimo	B7
33 Redd Wood	B6
Rutherford Grill	(see 22)
34 Soda Canyon Store	B5
Tacos Garcia	(see 35)

⊙ Drinking & Nightlife
35 Pancha's	B6
36 Tannery Bend Beerworks	A7

⊕ Entertainment
37 Lincoln Theater	A3

⊜ Shopping
Finesse, the Store	(see 15)
38 Napa Premium Outlets	A6

★ **French Laundry**   CALIFORNIAN $$$

(Map p185; ☑707-944-2380; www.thomaskeller.com/tfl; 6640 Washington St; prix-fixe dinner $310; ⏳seatings 11am-12:30pm Fri-Sun, 5-9pm daily) The pinnacle of California dining, Thomas Keller's French Laundry is epic, a high-wattage culinary experience on par with the world's best. Book one month ahead on the online app Tock, where tickets are released in groupings. This is the meal you can brag about the rest of your life.

★ **Ciccio**   ITALIAN $$$

(Map p185; ☑707-945-1000; www.ciccionapavalley.com; 6770 Washington St; mains $25-32; ⏳5-9pm Wed-Sun) The small, frequently changing menu at this family-owned Italian place is dependent on the season and likely to include just a couple of veggies, pastas, meat options and four to six wood-fired pizzas. But wow! You cannot go wrong, especially if you're lucky enough to show up when whole sea bass and garlicky pea tendrils are available. There's a negroni bar and many delicious wines from the owner's Altamura Ranch, along with a prix-fixe chef's dinner (by limited reservation) that includes menu and off-menu favorites for visitors to choose from.

Bouchon   FRENCH $$$

(Map p185; ☑707-944-8037; www.thomaskeller.com; 6354 Washington St; mains $19-59; ⏳11am-midnight Mon-Fri, from 10am Sat & Sun) Details at celeb-chef Thomas Keller's French brasserie are so impeccable – zinc bar to white-aproned waiters – you'd swear you were in Paris. Only the Bermuda-shorts-clad Americans look out of place. On the menu: oysters, onion soup, roasted chicken, trout with almonds, runny cheeses and perfect profiteroles.

Ad Hoc   CALIFORNIAN $$$

(Map p185; ☑707-944-2487; www.adhocrestaurant.com; 6476 Washington St; prix-fixe dinner from $55; ⏳5-10pm Thu-Sat & Mon, 9am-1:30pm &

5-10pm Sun) A winning formula by Thomas Keller, Yountville's culinary patriarch, Ad Hoc serves the master's favorite American home cooking in four family-style courses with no variations (dietary restrictions notwithstanding). The menu changes daily but regularly features pot roast, BBQ and fried chicken, which is also available (for takeout only) on weekends behind Ad Hoc at Keller's latest venture, Addendum (p184).

Mustards Grill   CALIFORNIAN $$$

(Map p185; ☑707-944-2424; www.mustardsgrill.com; 7399 St Helena Hwy; mains $16-33; ⏳11:30am-9pm Mon-Thu, to 9:30pm Fri, 11am-9:30pm Sat & Sun; 🚗) The valley's original and always-packed roadhouse makes platters of crowd-pleasing, wood-fired, California comfort food: roasted meats, lamb shanks, pork chops, hearty salads and sandwiches.

Bistro Jeanty   FRENCH $$$

(Map p185; ☑707-944-0103; www.bistrojeanty.com; 6510 Washington St; mains $21-34; ⏳11:30am-10:30pm) French bistros by classical definition serve comfort food to weary travelers and that's what French-born chef-owner Philippe Jeanty does here, with succulent cassoulet, coq au vin, *steak frites* (steak and chips), slow-roasted pork shoulder and scrumptious tomato soup.

🍷 Drinking & Nightlife

There are a couple of wine-tasting rooms in town where much of the day-drinking is done, while the smoky local dive Pancha's passes for nightlife.

Pancha's   BAR

(Map p185; ☑707-944-2125; 6764 Washington St; ⏳noon-2am) If you don't mind constant cigarette smoke, hang here and swill tequila with vineyard workers early in the night and waiters later. Cash only.

FLYING & BALLOONING

Wine Country is stunning from the air – a multihued tapestry of undulating hills, deep valleys and rambling vineyards. Make reservations.

The Vintage Aircraft Company (p203) flies over Sonoma in a vintage biplane with an awesome pilot who'll do loop-de-loops on request (add $50). Twenty-minute tours cost $175/270 for one/two adults.

Napa Valley's signature hot-air balloon flights leave early, around 6am or 7am, when the air is coolest; they usually include a champagne breakfast on landing. Adults pay about $200 to $250, and kids $150 to $175. Call **Balloons Above the Valley** (Map p185; ☑707-253-2222, 800-464-6824; www.balloonrides.com; 603 California Blvd) or **Napa Valley Balloons** (Map p185; ☑707-944-0228, 800-253-2224; www.napavalleyballoons.com; per person $239, 2-person private flight $2200), both in Yountville.

⭐ Entertainment

Lincoln Theater THEATER
(Map p185; 🖉box office 707-949-9900; www.
lincolntheater.org; 100 California Dr) Various artists, including Napa Valley Symphony, play this 1200-seat theater.

🛍 Shopping

Finesse, the Store GIFTS & SOUVENIRS
(Map p185; 🖉707-363-9552; www.finessethestore.
com; 6540 Washington St; ⊙11am-6pm Thu-Mon)
Thomas Keller disciples and fanatics can finally take a piece of the action home. The culinary guru's new gift and souvenir shop features items such as cookbooks, cookware, aprons and sauces.

ℹ Getting There & Away

For public-transit information, dial 🖉511, or look online at www.transit.511.org. Yountville is about an 80-minute drive from San Francisco.

Oakville & Rutherford

It'd be easy to drive through Oakville and never know you'd missed it. Vineyards sprawl everywhere. Rutherford is slightly more conspicuous.

🛏 Sleeping & Eating

There aren't many places to stay here and those on a budget should steer clear. North in Calistoga and south in downtown Napa there are far more choices.

The two tiny towns have between them a couple of good markets and the lip-smacking Rutherford Grill, which is essentially a Houston's.

★ Auberge du Soleil LUXURY HOTEL $$$
(Map p185; 🖉800-348-5406, 707-963-1211; www.
aubergedusoleil.com; 180 Rutherford Hill Rd, Rutherford; r $795-1500, ste $1525-5300; 🕸🛋🏊) The top splurge for a no-holds-barred romantic weekend, Auberge's hillside cottages, some of which are brand new, are second to none. A meal in its **dining room** (breakfast mains $33, lunch $31 to $42, three-/four-/six-course prix-fixe dinner $115/130/150) is an iconic Napa experience: come for a fancy breakfast, lazy lunch or will-you-wear-my-ring dinner; valley views are mesmerizing – *don't* sit inside. Make reservations; arrive before sunset.

Rancho Caymus HOTEL $$$
(Map p185; 🖉800-845-1777, 707-963-1777; www.
ranchocaymus.com; 1140 Rutherford Rd, Rutherford;

r $400-800; 🕸@🛜🏊) Styled after California's missions, this hacienda-like inn was closed for years before a recent comeback. The restored hotel features 25 large suites with oak-beamed wood ceilings, gas fireplaces and secluded patios. The steeper price reflects work put in to refurbish the entire property, including the relaxing spa, leafy courtyard and plunge pool.

Rutherford Grill AMERICAN $$
(Map p185; 🖉707-963-1792; www.rutherfordgrill.
com; 1180 Rutherford Rd, Rutherford; mains $15-38; ⊙11:30am-9:30pm Mon-Thu, to 10pm Fri, 11am-10pm Sat, to 9:30pm Sun) Yes, it's part of a chain (Houston's), but its bar at lunchtime provides a chance to rub shoulders with winemakers. The food is consistent – ribs, rotisserie chicken, good grilled artichokes – and there's no corkage, so bring that bottle you just bought.

St Helena

You'll know you're here when traffic halts. St Helena (ha-*lee*-na) is the Rodeo Dr of Napa. Fancy boutiques line the historic downtown's Main St (Hwy 29) and provide excellent window-shopping. Parking, however, is next-to-impossible on summer weekends. Tip: look behind the visitor center (p192).

⊙ Sights

Robert Louis Stevenson Museum MUSEUM
(Map p190; 🖉707-963-3757; http://stevenson
museum.org; 1490 Library Lane; ⊙noon-4pm Tue-Sat; 🅿) **FREE** This museum contains the largest displayed collection of Robert Louis Stevenson's belongings in the world. In 1880 the author – then sick, penniless and unknown – stayed in an abandoned bunkhouse at the old Silverado Mine on Mt St Helena with his wife, Fanny Osbourne; his novel the *Silverado Squatters* is based on his time there. Turn east off Hwy 29 at the Adams St traffic light and cross the railroad tracks.

Farmers Market MARKET
(Map p190; 🖉707-486-2662; www.sthelenafarm
ersmkt.org; ⊙7:30am-noon Fri May-Oct) Meets at Crane Park, half a mile south of downtown.

🎓 Courses

Culinary Institute of America at Greystone COOKING
(Map p190; 🖉707-967-1100; www.ciachef.edu/
california; 2555 Main St; 🍴) Inside an 1889 stone château, this culinary-school campus

houses a new restaurant, a gadget- and cookbook-filled culinary shop, a bakery-cafe, weekend cooking demonstrations and wine-tasting classes. Cooking demonstrations are $25 and take place at 1:30pm Saturday and Sunday. Classes start at $95.

🛏 Sleeping

Most options in St Helena are pricey, particularly on weekends and during high season. The one reasonable option is El Bonita, but it fills up fast.

★ El Bonita   MOTEL $$
(Map p190; 📞800-541-3284, 707-963-3216; www.elbonita.com; 195 Main St; r $140-325; P❄❀ @🛜🏊❄) Book in advance to secure this sought-after motel, with up-to-date rooms (quietest are in back), attractive grounds, a heated pool, hot tub and sauna.

Las Alcobas   BOUTIQUE HOTEL $$$
(Map p190; 📞707-963-7000; www.lasalcobasnapavalley.com; 1915 Main St; r from $600-2500; ❀🛜❄) A newcomer with a sister property in Mexico City, this boutique has already secured its place among Napa Valley's finest stays. The plush, modern rooms offer both vineyard vista and proximity to some of the region's best dining, shopping and wine tasting. That's if you attempt to pry yourself from the delicious hotel-restaurant Acacia, heated pool and relaxing spa.

Meadowood   RESORT $$$
(Map p190; 📞707-963-3646, 877-963-3646; www.meadowood.com; 900 Meadowood Lane; r from $850; P❄❀@🛜❄) Hidden in a wooded dell with towering pines and miles of hiking, Napa's grandest resort has cottages and rooms in satellite buildings surrounding a croquet lawn. We most like the hillside fireplace suites; lawn-view rooms lack privacy but are good for families. The vibe is Republican country club: wear linen and play *Great Gatsby*. Kids love the mammoth pool and there's also an adult pool.

Harvest Inn by Charlie Palmer   INN $$$
(Map p190; 📞800-950-8466, 707-963-9463; www.harvestinn.com; 1 Main St; r $449-899; ❀@🛜❄❄)
🏊 A former estate, this 78-room resort has rooms in satellite buildings on sprawling manicured grounds. The reception and rooms were recently repainted and redecorated; vineyard-view rooms are loveliest (each has private hot tub). The grounds contain two heated pools and two hot tubs. The Harvest Table restaurant is delish, with ostentatious flaming cocktails and locally sourced, expertly prepared New American cuisine.

Wydown Hotel   BOUTIQUE HOTEL $$$
(Map p190; 📞707-963-5100; www.wydownhotel.com; 1424 Main St; r Sun-Thu $320-370, Fri & Sat $500-550; ❀❄) Opened in 2012, this fashion-forward boutique hotel, with good service, sits smack downtown, its 12 oversized rooms smartly decorated with tufted velvet, distressed leather, subway-tile baths and California-king beds with white-on-white high-thread-count linens.

🍴 Eating

St Helena is packed with fabulous restaurants where you'll need reservations; alternatively, self-cater at the local market Sunshine Foods.

Napa Valley Olive Oil Mfg Co   MARKET $
(Map p190; 📞707-963-4173; www.oliveoilsainthelena.com; 835 Charter Oak Ave; ⏰8am-5:30pm) Before the advent of fancy-food stores, this ramshackle market introduced Napa to Italian delicacies: real prosciutto and salami, meaty olives, fresh bread, nutty cheeses and, of course, olive oil. Ask nicely and the owner will lend you a knife and a board to picnic at the rickety tables in the grass outside. Cash only.

Sunshine Foods   MARKET, DELI $
(Map p190; 📞707-963-7070; www.sunshinefoodsmarket.com; 1115 Main St; ⏰7:30am-8:30pm) Town's best grocery store; excellent deli.

Model Bakery   CAFE $
(Map p190; 📞707-963-8192; www.themodelbakery.com; 1357 Main St; dishes $8-10; ⏰6:30am-5pm Mon-Sat, 7am-5pm Sun) Good bakery with scones, muffins, salads, pizzas, sandwiches and exceptional coffee.

Cook St. Helena   ITALIAN $$
(Map p190; 📞707-963-7088; www.cookshelena.com; 1310 Main St; lunch $14-23, dinner $18-26; ⏰11:30am-10pm Mon-Sat, 4-9pm Sun) Locals crowd this tiny storefront bistro, beloved for its earthy Cal-Italian cooking: homemade pasta and risotto, crispy sole and soft polenta. Expect a wait, even with reservations. Next door, the pizzeria Cook Tavern is under the same ownership and also a good choice.

Cindy's Backstreet Kitchen   MODERN AMERICAN $$
(Map p190; 📞707-963-1200; www.cindysbackstreetkitchen.com; 1327 Railroad Ave; mains $17-29; ⏰11:30am-9pm) 🏊 The inviting retro-homey decor complements the Cal-American com-

WINE TASTING

The best way to discover the real Wine Country is to avoid factory wineries and visit family-owned boutique houses (producing fewer than 20,000 annual cases) and mid-sized houses (20,000 to 60,000 annual cases). Why does it matter? Think of it. If you were to attend two dinner parties, one for 10 people, one for 1000, which would have the better food? Small wineries maintain tighter control. Also, you won't easily find these wines elsewhere.

Tastings are called 'flights' and include four to six different wines. Napa wineries charge around $10 to $50. In Sonoma Valley, tastings cost about $5 to $20, often refundable with purchase. In Sonoma County, tastings are free or $5 to $10. You must be 21 to taste.

Do not drink and drive. The curvy roads are dangerous and police monitor traffic, especially on Napa's Hwy 29.

To avoid burnout, visit no more than three wineries per day. Most open daily 10am or 11am to 4pm or 5pm, but call ahead if your heart's set, or you absolutely want a tour, especially in Napa, where law requires that some wineries accept visitors only by appointment. If you're buying, ask if there's a wine club, which is free to join and provides discounts, but you'll have to agree to buy a certain amount annually.

NAPA & SONOMA WINE COUNTRY ST HELENA

fort food, such as avocado-and-papaya salad, a Chinatown duck burger and sautéed petrale sole. The bar makes a mean mojito.

Gott's Roadside   AMERICAN $$
(Map p190; ☎707-963-3486; http://gotts.com; 933 Main St; mains $8-16; ⊗10am-10pm May-Sep, to 9pm Oct-Apr; 🖈) 🍴 Wiggle your toes in the grass and feast on quality burgers – beef, turkey, ahi or veggie – plus Cobb salads and fish tacos at this classic roadside drive-in. Avoid weekend waits by phoning ahead or ordering online. There's another at Oxbow Public Market (p181).

Market   MODERN AMERICAN $$
(Map p190; ☎707-963-3799; www.marketsthelena. com; 1347 Main St; mains $14-22; ⊗11:30am-9pm Mon-Thu, to 10pm Fri & Sat, 10am-9pm Sun) 🍴 We love Market's big portions of simple, fresh American cooking, including hearty salads of local produce and soul-satisfying mains such as buttermilk-fried chicken. The stone-walled dining room dates to the 19th century, as does the ornate backbar, where cocktails get muddled to order. Free corkage.

Restaurant at Meadowood   CALIFORNIAN $$$
(Map p190; ☎707-967-1205; www.meadowood.com; 900 Meadowood Lane; 12-course menu $275; ⊗5:30-9:30pm Tue-Sat) If you couldn't score reservations at French Laundry, fear not: Meadowood – the valley's only other three-Michelin-star restaurant – has a slightly more sensibly priced menu, elegantly unfussy dining room and lavish haute cuisine that's not too esoteric. Auberge (p187) has better views, but Meadowood's food and service far surpass it.

Farmstead   MODERN AMERICAN $$$
(Map p190; ☎707-963-4555; www.longmeadow ranch.com; 738 Main St; mains $22-31; ⊗11:30am-9:30pm Mon-Thu, to 10pm Fri & Sat, 11am-9:30pm Sun; 🖈) 🍴 An enormous open-truss barn with big leather booths and rocking-chair porch, Farmstead draws an all-ages crowd and farms many of its own ingredients – including grass-fed beef and lamb – for an earthy menu highlighting wood-fired cooking.

Terra   CALIFORNIAN $$$
(Map p190; ☎707-963-8931; www.terrarestaurant. com; 1345 Railroad Ave; 4-/5-/6-course menu $78/93/105; ⊗6-9pm Thu-Mon) Seamlessly blending Japanese, French and Italian culinary styles, Terra is one of Wine Country's top tables – the signature meal is broiled sake-marinated black cod with shrimp dumplings in shiso broth. The adjoining bar serves small bites without reservations, but the dining room's the thing.

Archetype   FUSION $$$
(Map p190; ☎707-968-9200; http://archetype napa.com; 1429 Main St; dinner mains $25-37; ⊗11am-2:30pm Wed & Thu, 9am-2:30pm Sat & Sun, 5:30-9pm Wed-Sun) In an architect-designed dining room that breaks the Wine Country mold, Archetype effortlessly melds Asian and Mediterranean techniques with the best of California farms and foraging. Savor anything from the oak wood-burning oven and grill, or show up for sweet weekend brunch on the sunny back patio. Happy-hour drinks and bites are a steal (from just $5).

Napa Valley North

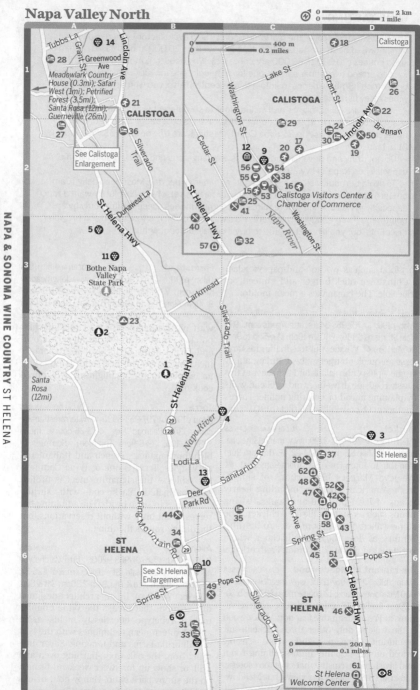

Napa Valley North

Sights
1	Bale Grist Mill State Historic Park	B4
2	Bothe-Napa Valley State Park	A4
3	Cade	D5
4	Casa Nuestra	C5
5	Castello di Amorosa	A3
6	Farmers Market	B7
7	Hall	B7
8	Long Meadow Ranch	D7
9	Olabisi Wines	C2
10	Robert Louis Stevenson Museum	B6
11	Schramsberg	A3
12	Sharpsteen Museum	C2
13	Titus	B5
14	Vincent Arroyo	A1

Activities, Courses & Tours
15	Calistoga Bike Shop	C2
16	Calistoga Spa Hot Springs	C2
	Culinary Institute of America at Greystone	(see 44)
17	Dr Wilkinson's Hot Springs Resort	C2
18	Golden Haven Hot Springs	D1
19	Indian Springs Spa	D2
20	Mount View Spa	C2
21	Oat Hill Mine Trail	B1
	Spa Solage	(see 36)

Sleeping
	Aurora Park Cottages	(see 27)
22	Best Western Plus Stevenson Manor	D1
23	Bothe-Napa Valley State Park Campground	B4
24	Brannan Cottage Inn	D2
25	Calistoga Inn	C2
26	Calistoga Motor Lodge & Spa	D1
	Calistoga Spa Hot Springs	(see 16)
27	Chanric	A2
28	Chateau De Vie	A1
29	Chelsea Garden Inn	C2
30	Cottage Grove Inn	D2
	Dr Wilkinson's Motel & Hideaway Cottages	(see 17)
31	El Bonita	B7

32	EuroSpa & Inn	C3
33	Harvest Inn by Charlie Palmer	B7
	Indian Springs Resort	(see 19)
34	Las Alcobas	B6
35	Meadowood	C6
	Mount View Hotel & Spa	(see 20)
36	Solage	B2
37	Wydown Hotel	D5

Eating
38	All Seasons Bistro	C2
39	Archetype	C5
40	Buster's Southern BBQ	B3
	Calistoga Inn & Brewery	(see 25)
41	Calistoga Kitchen	C2
42	Cindy's Backstreet Kitchen	D5
43	Cook St. Helena	D6
	Farmstead	(see 8)
44	Gatehouse Restaurant	B6
45	Goose & Gander	C6
46	Gott's Roadside	D7
47	Market	C5
48	Model Bakery	C5
49	Napa Valley Olive Oil Mfg Co	B6
	Restaurant at Meadowood	(see 35)
50	Sam's Social Club	D2
	Solbar	(see 36)
51	Sunshine Foods	D6
52	Terra	D5

Drinking & Nightlife
53	Brannan's Grill	C2
54	Hydro Grill	C2
	Solbar	(see 36)
55	Susie's Bar	C2
56	Yo El Rey	C2

Shopping
57	Calistoga Pottery	B3
	Coperfield's Books	(see 15)
58	Footcandy	D6
59	Lolo's Consignment	D6
60	Main Street Books	D5
61	Napa Soap Company	D7
	Rabbit Rabbit Fair Trade	(see 47)
62	Woodhouse Chocolates	C5

Goose & Gander   MODERN AMERICAN $$$
(Map p190; ☏707-967-8779; www.goosegander.com; 1245 Spring St; mains $19-39; ⏱11:30am-11pm Sun-Thu, to midnight Fri & Sat) Inside a converted arts-and-crafts house with cathedral ceiling and gorgeous woodwork, Goose & Gander has a clubby vibe conducive to drinking, excellent craft cocktails and an imaginative (sometimes heavy) menu with standouts such as the G&G burger. Consider the garden, although hard-drinking locals favor the basement pub.

Gatehouse Restaurant   CALIFORNIAN $$$
(Map p190; ☏707-967-1010; www.ciarestaurant group.com/gatehouse-restaurant; 2555 Main St; 3-/4-course lunch $32/$42, dinner $39/$49; ⏱11:30am-1pm & 6-8:30pm Tue-Sat) Testing skills and knowledge they've picked up in culinary school, students serve prix-fixe meals at this elegant restaurant on the Culinary Institute of America's Greystone campus. Ingredients for many dishes come from CIA's farm and herb gardens.

♀ Drinking & Nightlife

There's not a whole lot going on here after hours. Calistoga to the north offers a more vibrant bar scene.

🔒 Shopping

Main St is lined with high-end boutiques (think $100 socks), but some mom-and-pop shops remain.

Woodhouse Chocolates   FOOD
(Map p190; www.woodhousechocolate.com; 1367 Main St; ⊘11am-5:30pm) Woodhouse looks more like Tiffany than a candy shop, with housemade chocolates similarly priced, but their quality is beyond reproach.

Rabbit Rabbit Fair Trade   HOMEWARES
(🗹707-968-9182; www.rabbitrabbitfairtrade.com; 1327 Main St; ⊘11am-5pm Sun & Mon, 10am-5pm Tue-Thu, to 6pm Fri & Sat) 🥖 Handcrafted fair-trade goods including gifts, cards, toys, household items, accessories and other items.

Footcandy   SHOES
(Map p190; 🗹 707-963-2040; www.footcandyshoes. com/info/about; 1239 Main St; Manolo Blahnik pairs up to $1245; ⊘10am-6pm Mon-Sat, 10:30am-6pm Sun) A boutique shoe store that feels more like high-heel museum, with designer pairs from Christian Louboutin, Jimmy Choo and Manolo Blahnik.

Napa Soap Company   COSMETICS
(Map p190; Map p190; 🗹707-963-5010; www. napasoap.com; 655 Main St; ⊘10am-5:30pm) 🥖 Ecofriendly bath products, locally produced.

Lolo's Consignment   VINTAGE
(Map p190; 🗹 707-963-7972; www.lolosconsign ment.com; 1120 Main St; ⊘10am-4pm Mon, to 5:30pm Tue-Sat, 11am-4pm Sun) Groovy cheap dresses and cast-off cashmere.

Main Street Books   BOOKS
(Map p190; 🗹707-963-1338; 1315 Main St; ⊘10am-5:30pm Mon-Sat, 11am-3pm Sun) Good used books.

ℹ️ Information

St Helena Welcome Center (🗹707-963-4456; www.sthelena.com; 657 Main St; ⊘9am-5pm Mon-Fri, 10am-4pm Sat, 11am-5pm Sun) The visitor center has information and lodging assistance.

ℹ️ Getting There & Away

For public-transit information, dial 🗹 511, or look online at www.transit.511.org. St Helena is an 80-minute drive from San Francisco.

Calistoga & Around

Famed 19th-century author Robert Louis Stevenson said of Calistoga: 'the whole neighborhood of Mt St Helena is full of sulfur and boiling springs...Calistoga itself seems to repose on a mere film above a boiling, subterranean lake.' And indeed, it does. Calistoga is synonymous with mineral water bearing its name, bottled here since 1924, and its springs and geysers have earned it an appropriate nickname: 'Hot springs of the West.'

The least gentrified town in Napa Valley feels refreshingly simple, with an old-fashioned main street lined with quirky shops and diverse characters wandering the sidewalks. Bad hair? No problem. Fancy-pants St Helena couldn't feel further away. Many don't go this far north, but you should, if only for a spa visit to indulge in the local specialty: hot-mud baths, made with volcanic ash from nearby Mt St Helena.

◉ Sights

Safari West   ZOO
(🗹707-579-2551; www.safariwest.com; 3115 Porter Creek Rd; adult/child 4-12yr from $83/45; ⊘tours at 9am, 10am, 1pm, 2pm & 4pm; P 🚻) Giraffes in Wine Country? Whadya know. Safari West sprawls over 400 acres and protects wildebeests, zebras, cheetahs and other exotic animals, which mostly roam free. See them and some recently born giraffe and wildebeest babies on a guided 2½-hour safari in open-sided jeeps, which also includes a 30-minute hike; reservations required, no kids under four (unless you book a private wagon). Those feeling adventurous can stay overnight in nifty canvas-sided **tent cabins** (including breakfast $260 to $475) inside the preserve.

Bale Grist Mill State Historic Park   PARK
(Map p190; 🗹707-963-2236; 3369 St Helena Hwy; adult/child $5/2; ⊘10am-4pm Sat & Sun; 🚻) This park features a 36ft-high water-powered mill wheel dating to 1846 – the largest still operating in North America; on Saturdays and Sundays (and sometimes Fridays, rarely Mondays) from 10am to 4pm, it grinds flour. In early October, look for living-history festival Old Mill Days.

Robert Louis Stevenson
State Park   STATE PARK
(🗹707-942-4575; www.parks.ca.gov; 3801 Hwy 29; ⊘sunrise-sunset; P) **FREE** At this undeveloped state park 8 miles north of Calistoga,

the long-extinct volcanic cone of Mt St Helena marks Napa Valley's end and often gets snow in winter. It's a strenuous 5-mile climb to the peak's 4343ft summit, but what a view – 200 miles on a clear winter's day. Check conditions before setting out. Also consider 2.2-mile one-way **Table Rock Trail** (go south from the summit trailhead parking area) for drop-dead valley views. No dogs allowed.

Olabisi Wines   WINERY

(Map p190; ☑707-942-4472; www.olabisiwines.com; 1226 Washington St; tasting $25; ⊙11am-6pm) In downtown Calistoga, this newer tasting room run by a long-time winemaker specializes in extremely small-production wines produced with wild yeast. The big Cabs, floral Pinots and dry whites often sell out quickly, with the winery producing less than 1000 cases a year. Bottles cost $38 to $125. Tasting fee is waived with a purchase of three bottles.

Bothe-Napa Valley State Park   STATE PARK

(Map p190; ☑707-942-4575; 3801 St Helena Hwy; parking $8; ⊙8am-sunset; ⊛) A mile-long trail leads from Bale Grist Mill State Historic Park to adjacent Bothe-Napa Valley State Park, where there's a swimming pool ($5) and camping, plus hiking through redwood groves. If you're two or more adults, go first to Bothe and pay $8, instead of the per-head charge at Bale Grist.

Sharpsteen Museum   MUSEUM

(Map p190; ☑707-942-5911; www.sharpsteen museum.org; 1311 Washington St; suggested donation $3; ⊙11am-4pm; ⊛) **FREE** Across from the picturesque 1902 City Hall (originally an opera house), the Sharpsteen Museum was created by an ex-Disney animator (whose Oscar is on display) and houses a fantastic diorama of town in the 1860s, big Victorian dollhouse, full-size horse-drawn carriage and a restored cottage from entrepreneur Samuel Brannan's original resort. (The only Brannan cottage still at its original site is at 109 Wappo Ave).

Petrified Forest   FOREST

(☑707-942-6667; www.petrifiedforest.org; 4100 Petrified Forest Rd; adult/child 6-11yr/child 12-18yr $12/6/8; ⊙10am-7pm late May-early Sep, to 6pm Apr-late May & early Sep-Oct, to 5pm Nov-Mar; P⊛) Three million years ago at this now roadside-Americana attraction, a volcanic eruption at Mt St Helena blew down a stand of redwoods. The trees fell in the same direction, away from the blast, and over the millennia the mighty giants' trunks turned to stone.

Discover them on short trails through the woods and stop by the monument that marks Robert Louis Stevenson's 1880 visit, which he described in the *Silverado Squatters*. Guided tours go at 11am, 1pm and 3pm.

🏃 Activities

Find biking information and rentals at Calistoga Bike Shop (p175).

Oat Hill Mine Trail   CYCLING, HIKING

(Map p190; 2082 Oat Hill Mine Rd) One of Northern California's most technically challenging trails, this draws hard-core mountain bikers and hikers. Less experienced walkers take heart: a moderately strenuous half-mile from town, there's a bench with incredible valley views. The trailhead is at the intersection of Hwy 29 and Silverado Trail.

Spas

Calistoga is famous for hot-spring spas and mud-bath emporiums, where you're buried in hot mud and emerge feeling supple, detoxified and enlivened. (The mud is made with volcanic ash and peat; the higher the ash content, the better the bath.)

Packages take 60 to 90 minutes and cost $90 to $100. You start semisubmerged in hot mud, then soak in hot mineral water – a steam bath and blanket-wrap follow. A massage increases the cost to $130 or more.

Baths can be taken solo or, at some spas, as couples. Variations include thin, painted-on clay-mud wraps (called 'fango' baths, good for those uncomfortable sitting in mud), herbal wraps, seaweed baths and various massage treatments. Discount coupons are sometimes available from the visitors center (p197). Book ahead, especially on summer weekends. Reservations are essential everywhere. Most spas offer multi-treatment packages. Some offer discounted spa-lodging packages.

★ Indian Springs Spa   SPA

(Map p190; ☑707-709-2449; www.indiansprings calistoga.com; 1712 Lincoln Ave; ⊙by appointment 9am-9pm) California's longest continually operating spa, and original Calistoga resort, has concrete mud tubs and mines its own ash. Treatments include use of the huge, hot-spring-fed pool. Great cucumber body lotion.

Dr Wilkinson's Hot Springs Resort   SPA

(Map p190; ☑707-942-4102; www.drwilkinson.com; 1507 Lincoln Ave; mud bath from $94; ⊙by appointment 8:30am-3:45pm) For more than 60 years running, 'the doc' uses more peat in its mud.

Spa Solage
SPA

(Map p190; ☑707-266-0825; www.solage.auberge resorts.com/spa; 755 Silverado Trail; ⊗by appointment 8am-8pm) Chichi, austere, top-end spa, with couples' rooms and a fango-mud bar for DIY paint-on treatments. Also has zero-gravity chairs for blanket wraps and sex-segregated clothing-optional mineral pools.

Golden Haven Hot Springs
SPA

(Map p190; ☑707-942-8000; www.goldenhaven. com; 1713 Lake St; mud bath $99; ⊗by appointment 8am-8pm) Old-school and unfussy; offers couples' mud baths and massage.

Calistoga Spa Hot Springs
SPA

(Map p190; ☑707-942-6269, 866-822-5772; www.cal istogaspa.com; 1006 Washington St; mud bath $99; ⊗by appointment 9am-4pm Mon-Thu, to 7pm Fri-Sun) Traditional mud baths and massage at a motel complex with two huge swimming pools.

Mount View Spa
SPA

(Map p190; ☑707-942-1500; www.mountview hotel.com; 1457 Lincoln Ave; single/couple mud bath $90/110; ⊗by appointment 8:30am-7pm) Traditional full-service, five-room spa, good for clean-hands gals who prefer a mineral bath infused with lighter mud.

🛏 Sleeping

From upscale hot-springs resorts to quaint country cottages, there must be a dozen good options in and around Calistoga. Budget travelers will love the yurts and campsites in Bothe-Napa Valley State Park.

Bothe-Napa Valley State Park Campground
CAMPGROUND $

(Map p190; ☑800-444-7275; www.reserveamerica. com; 3801 Hwy 128; camping & RV sites $35, yurts $55-70, cabins $150-225; ⊛⊛) Three miles south of Calistoga, Bothe has shady camping near redwoods, coin-operated showers, and gorgeous hiking (p193). Sites 28 to 36 are most secluded.

EuroSpa & Inn
MOTEL $$

(Map p190; ☑707-942-6829; www.eurospa.com; 1202 Pine St; r $169-325; ⊛🖙⊛) Immaculate single-story motel on a quiet side street, with extras such as gas-burning fireplaces, afternoon refreshments and small on-site spa. Excellent service, but tiny pool.

Dr Wilkinson's Motel & Hideaway Cottages
MOTEL, COTTAGES $$

(Map p190; ☑707-942-4102; www.drwilkinson. com; 1507 Lincoln Ave; r $165-275, cottage $175-280; ⊛⊠@🖙⊛) This good-value vintage-1950s motel has well-kept rooms facing a swimming-pool courtyard with hot tub, three pools (one indoors) and mud baths. Also rents simple, great-value stand-alone cottages with kitchen at the affiliated Hideaway Cottages, also with pool and hot tub.

Best Western Plus Stevenson Manor
HOTEL $$

(Map p190; ☑800-528-1234, 707-942-1112; www. stevensonmanor.com; 1830 Lincoln Ave; r weekday $179-209, weekend $299-329; ⊛@🖙⊛) This entry-level business-class hotel feels generic, but has good extras, including full hot breakfast. Upstairs rooms are quietest. New elevator and exercise room.

Calistoga Spa Hot Springs
MOTEL $$

(Map p190; ☑866-822-5772, 707-942-6269; www. calistogaspa.com; 1006 Washington St; r $197-267; ⊛🖙⊛) Great for families who jam the place on weekends, this motel-resort has slightly scuffed generic rooms (request one that's been remodeled) with kitchenette, and fantastic pools: two full size, a kiddie pool with miniwaterfall and a huge adults-only Jacuzzi. Outside are barbecues and a snack bar.

Calistoga Inn
INN $$

(Map p190; ☑707-942-4101; www.calistogainn. com; 1250 Lincoln Ave; r with shared bath $169-229, cottages $229-289; 🖙) Upstairs from a busy bar, this inn has 17 clean, basic rooms with shared bath, ideal for no-fuss bargain hunters. No TV and no elevator. Bring earplugs. A newer cottage contains its own bathroom, air-conditioning and TV.

★ Brannan Cottage Inn
BOUTIQUE HOTEL $$$

(Map p190; ☑707-942-4200; https://brannancot tageinn.com; 109 Wappo Ave; r from $309; P⊛🖙) Adorable, gingerbread-style Victorian cottage amid lush grounds that in the 1860s belonged to the town's favorite entrepreneur Samuel Brannan. Recently restored to preserve its old-timey character, the cottage is listed in the National Register of Historic Places and offers six uniquely adorned rooms featuring comfy, pillow-top mattresses and modern amenities. A concierge will help plan your trip.

Solage
RESORT $$$

(Map p190; ☑707-226-0800, 866-942-7442; www. solage.aubergeresorts.com; 755 Silverado Trail; r $530-675, ste $835-1275; ⊛🖙⊛⊛) ⌀ Recently taken over by Auberge Resorts, Calistoga's top spa-hotel ups the style factor, with Ca-li-chic semidetached cottages and a glam pool surrounded by palm trees. Rooms are austere, with vaulted ceilings, zil-lion-thread-count linens and pebble-floor showers. Cruiser bikes included.

Indian Springs Resort   RESORT $$$
(Map p190; ☑707-942-4913; www.indianspringscalistoga.com; 1712 Lincoln Ave; r/cottages from $269/349; P✿🎱✳🛜🏊) The definitive old-school Calistoga resort, Indian Springs has cottages facing a central lawn with palm trees, shuffleboard, bocce and hammocks – not unlike a vintage Florida resort. Some sleep four. There are also top-end, motel-style lodge rooms (adults only). Huge hot-springs-fed swimming pool. Also has Sam's Social Club (p196).

Meadowlark Country House   B&B $$$
(☑707-942-5651; www.meadowlarkinn.com; 601 Petrified Forest Rd; r $245-450, ste $310-355; ✳🛜🏊) About a mile west of Calistoga, sitting on 20 lush acres, Meadowlark has homey rooms decorated in contemporary style, most with deck and Jacuzzi. Outside there's a hot tub, sauna and clothing-optional pool. The truth-telling innkeeper lives elsewhere, offers helpful advice, then vanishes when you want privacy. There's a fabulous cottage costing $450 for two and $640 for four. Gay friendly.

Cottage Grove Inn   BUNGALOW $$$
(Map p190; ☑707-942-8400; www.cottagegrove.com; 1711 Lincoln Ave; cottages $275-450; ✳🛜) Romantic cottages for over-40s, with wood-burning fireplaces, two-person Jacuzzis and rocking-chair front porches.

Chelsea Garden Inn   B&B $$$
(Map p190; ☑707-942-0948; www.chelseagardeninn.com; 1443 2nd St; r $195-350; ✳🛜🏊) On a quiet side street, this single-story inn has five floral-print rooms with private entrances, facing pretty gardens. Never mind the pool's rust spots.

Chateau De Vie   B&B $$$
(Map p190; ☑707-942 6446, 877-558-2513; www.cdvnapavalley.com; 3250 Hwy 128; r $269-469; ✳🛜🏊) Surrounded by vineyards, with gorgeous views of Mt St Helena, CDV has five modern, elegantly decorated B&B rooms with top-end amenities and zero froufrou. Charming owners serve wine on the sun-dappled patio, then leave you alone. Hot tub, big pool. Gay friendly.

Chanric   B&B $$$
(Map p190; ☑707-942-4535; www.thechanric.com; 1805 Foothill Blvd; r from $690; ✳🛜🏊) A converted Victorian near the road, this cushy B&B has small but smartly furnished rooms, plus many free extras including champagne on arrival and lavish three-course breakfasts. Gay friendly. No elevator.

Aurora Park Cottages   COTTAGE $$$
(Map p190; ☑707-942-6733, 877-942-7700; www.aurorapark.com; 1807 Foothill Blvd; cottages $269-349, houses $399-899; ✳🛜) Six immaculately kept, sunny-yellow cottages – with polished-wood floors, feather beds and sundeck – stand in a row beside flowering gardens. There's also a pricier rental home with a full kitchen. Though close to the road, everything's quiet by night and the innkeeper couldn't be nicer.

Mount View Hotel & Spa   HISTORIC HOTEL $$$
(Map p190; ☑707-942-6877; www.mountviewhotel.com; 1457 Lincoln Ave; r Mon-Fri $209-429, Sat & Sun $279-459; ✳🛜🏊) Smack in the middle of town, this 1917 Mission Revival hotel is decorated in vaguely mod-Italian style at odds with the vintage building – rooms are clean and fresh-looking nonetheless. Gleaming bathrooms, on-site spa, year-round heated pool. No elevator.

Calistoga Motor Lodge & Spa   MOTEL $$$
(Map p190; ☑707-942-0991; www.thesunburstcalistoga.com; 1880 Lincoln Ave; r $229-469; @🛜🏊) This single-story 1950s motor lodge got a makeover in 2017, with mid-century-modern-led aesthetics, but it's basically still a drive-to-the-door motel with upscale furnishings and thin walls.

🍴 Eating

The dining scene in Calistoga isn't as up-pity as the rest of the valley, but you can certainly procure a high-class meal at Calistoga Kitchen (p196), Solbar (p196) and the newly opened Sam's Social Club (p196). Many decent and affordable restaurants line Lincoln Ave.

Buster's Southern BBQ   BARBECUE $
(Map p190; ☑707-942-5605; www.busterssouthern bbq.com; 1207 Foothill Blvd; dishes $8-12; ⏱10am-

8pm Mon-Sat, to 7pm Sun; 🌙) The sheriff dines at this indoor-outdoor barbecue joint, which serves smoky ribs, chicken, tri-tip steak and burgers, plus beer and wine. It closes early at dinnertime.

★ Calistoga Kitchen
CALIFORNIAN $$$

(Map p190; ✆707-942-6500; www.calistogakitchen. com; 1107 Cedar St; mains lunch $12-18, dinner $20-36; ⏱5:30pm-close Thu, 11:30am-3pm & 5:30pm-close Fri & Sat, 9:30am-3pm Sun) A sparsely decorated cottage surrounded by a white picket fence, Calistoga Kitchen is especially good for lunch in the garden. The chef-owner favors simplicity, focusing on quality ingredients in a half-dozen changing dishes, such as a delicious braised rabbit. Reservations advised, especially for the patio.

Solbar
CALIFORNIAN $$$

(✆707-226-0860; www.solage.aubergeresorts. com; 755 Silverado Trail N, Calistoga; lounge menu dishes $4-16, dinner mains $26-38; ⏱7am-11:30am, 11:45am-3pm & 5:30-9pm, to 9:30pm Fri & Sat) 🌿 We like the Spartan ag-chic look of this Michelin-starred resort restaurant, the menu of which writing maximizes seasonal produce in elegant dishes, playfully composed. A chef from Italy had just been hired, but the crispy petrale sole tacos were as delectable as ever. The menu remains split for calorie-counters into light and hearty dishes. Reservations essential.

All Seasons Bistro
MODERN AMERICAN $$$

(Map p190; ✆707-942-9111; www.allseasonsnapa valley.net; 1400 Lincoln Ave; mains lunch $12-18, dinner $16-27; ⏱11:30am-2:30pm & 5:30-9pm, hours vary) 🌿 It looks like a white-tablecloth soda fountain, but All Seasons makes very fine meals, from a simple lasagna to composed dishes such as scallop, prawn, mussel and clam risotto. The salads are fresh and totally organic.

Sam's Social Club
AMERICAN $$$

(Map p190; ✆707-942-4969; http://samssocial club.com; 1712 Lincoln Ave; dinner mains $17-38; ⏱7:30am-9pm Mon-Wed, to 9:30pm Thu-Sun) Housed in the Indian Springs Resort (p195), this is Calistoga's fancy American restaurant that also brews its own beer. Colorful and expertly prepared dishes feature the freshest local ingredients, and the bacon-wrapped, Point Reyes Farmstead blue-cheese-stuffed dates are otherworldly. There's outdoor patio seating and a bright, comfortable dining room and bar. It's perfect for a relaxing feast post mud bath.

Calistoga Inn & Brewery
AMERICAN $$$

(Map p190; ✆707-942-4101; www.calistogainn. com; 1250 Lincoln Ave; dinner mains $15-38; ⏱11:30am-9:30pm Mon-Fri, from 11am Sat & Sun) Locals crowd the outdoor beer garden on Sundays. Midweek we prefer the country dining room's big oakwood tables – a homey spot for simple American cooking. Live music on summer weekends.

🍷 Drinking & Nightlife

There are a few hoppin' bars along Lincoln Ave and they'll often have live music on weekends.

Brannan's Grill
BAR

(Map p190; ✆707-942-2233; www.brannans calistoga.com; 1374 Lincoln Ave; ⏱11:30am-9pm) The mahogany bar at Calistoga's handsomest restaurant is great for martinis and microbrews, especially 7pm to 10pm Friday and Saturday, when there's live jazz.

Yo El Rey
CAFE

(Map p190; www.yoelreyroasting.com; 1217 Washington St; ⏱6:30am-5:30pm) 🌿 Hip kids favor this microroastery, which serves stellar small-batch, organic, fair-trade coffee.

Susie's Bar
BAR

(Map p190; ✆707-942-6710; 1365 Lincoln Ave; ⏱noon-2am Mon-Fri, 10am-2am Sat & Sun) Turn your baseball cap sideways, swill beer and shoot pool to a soundtrack of classic rock.

Solbar
BAR

(Map p190; Map p190; ✆707-226-0860; www.solage. aubergeresorts.com; 755 Silverado Trail; ⏱11am-9pm, to 9:30pm Fri & Sat) Sip craft cocktails beside outdoor fireplaces and a pool surrounded with palm trees at this Napa-swank resort bar.

Hydro Grill
BAR

(Map p190; ✆707-942-9777; 1403 Lincoln Ave; ⏱8:30am-10:30pm Mon-Thu, to 11:30pm Fri-Sun) Live music plays on Sundays and one Saturday a month at this hoppin' corner bar-restaurant.

🛍 Shopping

Calistoga Pottery
CERAMICS

(Map p190; ✆707-942-0216; www.calistogapottery. com; 1001 Foothill Blvd; ⏱9am-5pm Mon-Sat) Artisanal pottery, hand-thrown on-site. Ask about the pots glazed with local grapevine ash.

Coperfield's Books
BOOKS

(Map p190; ✆707-942-1616; 1330 Lincoln Ave; ⏱10am-7pm Sun-Thu, to 8pm Fri & Sat) Indie bookshop, with local maps and guides.

ℹ Information

Calistoga Visitors Center & Chamber of Commerce (☑707-942-6333; www.visitcalistoga.com; 1133 Washington St; ⊙9am-5pm) Lodging info, maps, pamphlets etc.

ℹ Getting There & Away

From San Francisco, public transportation can get you to Calistoga, though it's better to have your own wheels. For public-transit information, dial ☑511, or look online at www.transit.511.org.

Calistoga is about a 100-minute drive from San Francisco.

ℹ Getting Around

Hwys 128 and 29 split in Calistoga, where Hwy 29 turns east and becomes Lincoln Ave, continuing across Silverado Trail, toward Clear Lake. Hwy 128 continues north as Foothill Blvd.

SONOMA VALLEY

We have a soft spot for Sonoma's folksy ways. Unlike fancy Napa, nobody cares if you drive a clunker and vote Green. Locals call it 'Slow-noma.' Anchoring the bucolic 17-mile-long valley, the town of Sonoma makes a great jumping-off point for exploring Wine Country – it's an hour from San Francisco – and has a marvelous sense of place, with storied 19th-century historical sights surrounding the state's largest town square.

Halfway up-valley, tiny Glen Ellen (p206) is straight from a Norman Rockwell painting – in stark contrast to the valley's northernmost town, Santa Rosa (p222), the workaday urban center best known for traffic. If you have more than a day, explore Sonoma's quiet, rustic western side along the Russian River Valley, and continue to the sea.

Sonoma Valley Wineries

Rolling grass-covered hills rise from Sonoma Valley. Its 40-some wineries get less attention than Napa's, but many are equally good. If you love Zinfandel and Syrah, you're in for a treat.

Picnicking is allowed at Sonoma wineries. Get maps and discount coupons in the town of Sonoma or, if you're approaching from the south, the Sonoma Valley Visitors Bureau (p203) at Cornerstone Gardens.

Plan at least five hours to visit the valley from bottom to top.

OUTLET SHOPPING

Max out your credit cards on last season's closeouts.

Napa Premium Outlets (Map p185; ☑707-226-9876; www.premiumoutlets.com; 629 Factory Stores Dr; ⊙10am-8pm Mon-Thu, to 9pm Fri & Sat, to 7pm Sun) A large shopping center with fifty stores-swest of downtown Napa.

Petaluma Village Premium Outlets (☑707-778-9300; www.premiumoutlets.com; 2200 Petaluma Blvd N, Petaluma; ⊙10am-9pm) Sixty stores, Sonoma County.

Vacaville Premium Outlets (☑707-447-5755; www.premiumoutlets.com/vacaville; 321 Nut Tree Rd, Vacaville; ⊙10am-9pm) One hundred and twenty stores, northeast of Wine Country on I-80.

★**Gundlach-Bundschu Winery**   WINERY
(Map p198; ☑707-938-5277; www.gunbun.com; 2000 Denmark St, Sonoma; tasting $20-30, incl tour $30-60; ⊙11am-5:30pm May-Oct, to 4:30pm Nov-Apr; ℗) ✦ California's oldest family-run winery looks like a castle but has a down-to-earth vibe. Founded in 1858 by a Bavarian immigrant, its signatures are Gewürztraminer and Pinot Noir, but 'Gun-Bun' was the first American winery to produce 100% Merlot. Down a winding lane, it's a terrific bike-to winery with picnicking, hiking, a lake and frequent concerts, including a two-day folk-music festival in June. Tour the 1800-barrel cave by reservation only. Bottles are $20 to $50.

★**Bartholomew Park Winery**   WINERY
(Map p198; ☑707-939-3026; www.bartpark.com; 1000 Vineyard Lane, Sonoma; tasting $15; ⊙11am-4:30pm; ℗) ✦ A great bike-to winery, Bartholomew Park occupies a 375-acre nature preserve with oak-shaded picnicking and valley-view hiking. The vineyards were originally cultivated in 1857 and now yield certified-organic, citrusy Sauvignon Blanc, Cabernet Sauvignon softer in style than Napa and lush Zinfandel. There's also a new collection of reserve wines and a new private tasting experience. Bottles are $27 to $48. Tasting fee is waived with bottle purchase.

St Francis Winery & Vineyards   WINERY
(Map p198; ☑707-538-9463; www.stfranciswinery.com; 100 Pythian Rd at Hwy 12, Santa Rosa; tasting $15, wine & cheese pairing $25, wine & food pairing

$68; ⊙10am-5pm) The vineyards are scenic and all, but the real reason to visit St Francis is the much-lauded food-pairing experience. The mouthwatering, multicourse affair is hosted by amiable and informative wine experts and includes things such as braised Kurobuta pork with Okinawan sweet potatoes paired with Cab Franc, and American Wagyu strip loin and chanterelles paired with an old-vine Zin. Seatings at 11am and 1pm and 3pm, Thursday to Monday. Spots fill fast; book well in advance.

Robledo
WINERY

(Map p198; ☑707-939-6903; www.robledofamily winery.com; 21901 Bonness Rd, off Hwy 116; tasting $15-25; ⊙10am-5pm Mon-Sat, 11am-4pm Sun) Sonoma Valley's feel-good winery, Robledo was founded by a former migrant worker from Mexico who worked his way up to vineyard manager, then land owner, now vintner. His kids run the place. The wines – served at hand-carved Mexican furniture in a barn – include a nonoaked Sauvignon Blanc, spicy Cabernet and bright, fruit-forward Pinot Noir. Bottles cost $20 to $60. Appointments recommended for groups of six or more.

Little Vineyards
WINERY

(Map p198; ☑707-996-2750; www.littlevineyards. com; 15188 Sonoma Hwy, Glen Ellen; tasting $15; ⊙11am-4:30pm Thu-Mon; 🐾🧺) The name fits at this family-owned small-scale winery surrounded by grapes, with a lazy dog to greet you and a weathered, old-timey wooden bar, at which Jack London formerly drank (before it moved here). The big reds include Syrah, Petite Sirah, Zin, Cab and several delish blends. It also has a rosé and a Pinot Blanc. There's good picnicking on the vineyard-view terrace. Also rents a cottage in the vines. Bottles cost $20 to $50.

Homewood
WINERY

(Map p198; ☑707-996-6353; www.homewoodwin ery.com; 23120 Burndale Rd, Sonoma; tasting $10; ⊙10am-4pm; 🅿) Barn cats dart about at this down-home winery with several different tasting areas and a $20 wine and chocolate pairing. The winemaker crafts standout Chardonnays and Roussannes, and an array of other whites, reds and late-harvest dessert wines. Bottles are $22 to $36; tasting fee waived with purchase.

Hawkes
TASTING ROOM

(Map p202; ☑707-938-7620; www.hawkeswine. com; 383 1st St W, Sonoma; tasting $15; ⊙11am-6pm Thu-Mon) When you're in downtown

Sonoma Valley

Sonoma and don't feel like fighting traffic, Hawke's refreshingly unfussy tasting room showcases meaty Cabernet Sauvignon from family-owned vineyards in Alexander Valley, never blended with other varietals. Bottles are $30 to $70; the tasting fee is waived with a purchase over $40.

Sonoma Valley

Benziger
WINERY

(Map p198; ☑ 888-490-2739, 707-935-3000; www.benziger.com; 1883 London Ranch Rd, Glen Ellen; tasting $20-40, tours $25-50; ☺ 10am-5pm; P ᵴ) ✐ If you're new to wine, make Benziger your first stop for Sonoma's best crash course in winemaking. The worthwhile tour (11am–3:30pm; reservations recommended) includes an open-air tram ride (weather permitting) through biodynamic vineyards and a five-wine tasting. Great picnicking, excellent for families. The large-production wine is OK (head for the reserves); the tour's the thing. Bottles are $20 to $80.

Marimar Estate
WINERY

(☑ 707-823-4365; www.marimarestate.com; 11400 Graton Rd, Sebastopol; tasting $15; ☺ 11am-5pm by appointment only; 🐾) ✐ Middle-of-nowhere Marimar Estates specializes in all-organic Pinot – seven different kinds – and Spanish varietals. The hilltop tasting room has a knockout vineyard-view terrace, good for picnics. Also consider the guided tour, which includes a bottle ($95). Bottles are $49 to $59.

Cline Cellars
WINERY

(Map p198; ☑ 707-940-4030; www.clinecellars.com; 24737 Arnold Dr, Hwy 121; tasting free-$20; ☺ tasting room 10am-6pm, museum to 4pm) ✐ Balmy days are for pondside picnics and rainy ones for fireside tastings of old-vine Zinfandel and Mourvèdre inside an 1850s farmhouse. Stroll out back to the **California Mission Museum**, housing 1930s miniature replicas of California's original 21 Spanish Colonial missions.

Kunde
WINERY

(Map p198; ☑ 707-833-5501; www.kunde.com; 9825 Hwy 12, Kenwood; tasting $15-50, cave tours free; ☺ 10:30am-5pm; P) ✐ This family-owned winery on a historic ranch has vineyards that are more than a century old. It offers mountaintop tastings with impressive valley views and seasonal guided hikes (advance reservations recommended), though you can also just stop for a tasting and a tour. Elegant, 100% estate-grown wines include crisp Chardonnay and unfussy red blends, all made sustainably. Bottles $17 to $100.

NAPA & SONOMA WINE COUNTRY SONOMA VALLEY WINERIES

Loxton WINERY

(Map p198; ☑ 707-935-7221; www.loxtonwines.com; 11466 Dunbar Rd, Glen Ellen; tasting $10-20, walking tour $25; ☺ 11am-5pm) Say g'day to Chris the Aussie winemaker at Loxton, a no-frills winery with million-dollar views of the grapes you'll actually be tasting. The tasting room contains a small warehouse where racing cars were once designed, and there you can sample wonderful Syrah and Zinfandel; nonoaky, fruit-forward Chardonnay; and good port. Bottles cost $17 to $32.

Ravenswood Winery WINERY

(Map p198; ☑ 707-933-2332; www.ravenswood winery.com; 18701 Gehricke Rd, Sonoma; tasting $20-60, incl tour $25; ☺ 10am-4:30pm) With the slogan 'no wimpy wines,' this buzzing winery pours a full slate of estate Zinfandels. Novices welcome. Tours at 10:30am daily; reservations recommended.

Scribe WINERY

(Map p198; ☑ 707-939-1858; http://scribewinery. com; 2100 Denmark St, Sonoma; tasting $35, food pairing $65; ☺ 11:30am-4pm Thu-Mon, by appointment only) With Scribe, a new generation has found its place in Wine Country. Bantering groups of bespectacled, high-waisted-jeans-wearing millennials frequent this hip winery designed to resemble a French château, and at outdoor picnic tables they hold forth on the terroir-driven rosé of Pinot, the skin-fermented Chardonnay and the bold Cab. The food pairing is hit and miss.

BR Cohn WINERY

(Map p198; ☑ 707-938-4064, 800-330-4064; www. brcohn.com; 15000 Sonoma Hwy, Glen Ellen; tasting indoors $20, weekend patio tasting $30; ☺ 10am-5pm) Picnic like a rock star at always-busy BR Cohn. Its founder managed '70s superband the Doobie Brothers before moving on to make outstanding organic olive oils and fine wines. Although the winery has changed hands, it's still an excellent spot for tasting wine, slurping oysters (weekends only) and sampling olive oil in the gourmet shop. Bottles are $16 to $56.

Imagery Estate WINERY

(Map p198; ☑ 707-935-4515, 800-989-8890; www. imagerywinery.com; 14335 Sonoma Hwy, Glen Ellen; tasting $15; ☺ 10am-4:30pm Mon-Fri, to 5:30pm Sat & Sun; ℗ ␐) ✿ Imagery produces lesser-known varietals such as Legrain and Tannat, biodynamically grown, that you often can't buy anywhere else. Each bottle sports an artist-designed label, with originals on

display in the on-site gallery. Lovely gardens include a grassy picnic area with horseshoes, cornhole and bocce. Limited picnic supplies available. Bottles are $27 to $65. Kid and dog-friendly.

Sonoma & Around

Fancy boutiques may lately be replacing hardware stores, but Sonoma still retains an old-fashioned charm, thanks to the plaza – California's largest town square – and its surrounding frozen-in-time historic buildings. You can legally drink on the plaza – a rarity in California parks – but only between 11:30am and sunset.

Sonoma has a rich history. In 1846 it was the site of a second American revolution, this time against Mexico, when General Mariano Guadalupe Vallejo deported all foreigners from California, prompting outraged frontiersmen to occupy the Sonoma Presidio and declare independence. They dubbed California the Bear Flag Republic after the battle flag they'd fashioned.

The republic was short-lived. The Mexican-American War broke out a month later, and California was annexed by the US. The revolt gave California its flag, which remains emblazoned with the words 'California Republic' beneath a muscular brown bear. Vallejo was initially imprisoned but ultimately returned to Sonoma to play a major role in its development.

⊙ Sights

★Sonoma Plaza SQUARE

(Map p202; btwn Napa, Spain & 1st Sts) Smack in the center of the plaza, the Mission Revival-style city hall, built 1906–08, has identical facades on four sides, reportedly because plaza businesses all demanded City Hall face their direction. At the plaza's northeast corner, the **Bear Flag Monument** (Map p202; Sonoma Plaza) marks Sonoma's moment of revolutionary glory. The **weekly farmers market** (5:30-8pm Tues Apr-Oct) showcases Sonoma's incredible produce.

Sonoma State Historic Park HISTORIC SITE

(Map p202; ☑ 707-938-9560; www.parks.ca.gov; adult/child $3/2; ☺ 10am-5pm) This park in Sonoma is comprised of multiple sites, most side by side. Founded in 1823, Mission San Francisco Solano anchors the plaza, and was the final California mission. Sonoma Barracks houses exhibits on 19th-century life.

A WINE COUNTRY PRIMER

When people talk about Sonoma, they're referring to the *whole* county, which unlike Napa, is huge. It extends all the way from the coast, up the Russian River Valley, into Sonoma Valley and eastward to Napa Valley; in the south it stretches from San Pablo Bay (an extension of San Francisco Bay) to Healdsburg in the north. It's essential to break Sonoma down by district.

West County refers to everything west of Hwy 101 and includes the Russian River Valley and the coast. Sonoma Valley stretches north–south along Hwy 12. In northern Sonoma County, Alexander Valley lies east of Healdsburg, and Dry Creek Valley lies north of Healdsburg. In the south, Carneros straddles the Sonoma–Napa border, north of San Pablo Bay. Each region has its own particular wines; what grows where depends upon the weather.

Inland valleys get hot; coastal regions stay cool. In West County and Carneros, nighttime fog blankets the vineyards. Burgundy-style wines do best, particularly Pinot Noir and Chardonnay. Further inland, Alexander, Sonoma and much of Dry Creek Valleys (as well as Napa Valley) are protected from fog. Here Bordeaux-style wines thrive, especially Cabernet Sauvignon, Sauvignon Blanc, Merlot and other heat-loving varieties. For California's famous Cabernets, head to Napa. Zinfandel and Rhône-style varieties such as Syrah and Viognier grow in both regions, warm and cool. In cooler climes, wines are lighter and more elegant; in warmer areas they are heavier and more rustic. As you explore, notice the bases of grapevines: the fatter they are, the older. 'Old vine' grapes yield color and complexity not found in grapes from younger vines.

Some basics: wineries and vineyards aren't the same. Grapes grow in a vineyard then get fermented at a winery. Wineries that grow their own grapes are called estates, as in 'estate-grown' or 'estate-bottled,' but estates also ferment grapes from other vineyards. When vintners speak of 'single-vineyard' or 'vineyard-designate' wines, they mean the grapes all originated from the same vineyard; this allows for tighter quality control. 'Single varietal' means all the grapes are the same variety (such as 100% Merlot) but may come from different vineyards. Reserves are the vintner's limited-production wines; they're usually available only at the winery.

Don't be afraid to ask questions. Vintners love to talk. If you don't know how to taste wine, or what to look for, ask the person behind the counter to help you discover what you like. Just remember to spit out the wine; the slightest buzz will diminish your capacity to taste.

For a handy-dandy reference on the road, pick up a copy of Karen MacNeil's *The Wine Bible* (2015, Workman Publishing) or Jancis Robinson's *The Oxford Companion to Wine* (2015, Oxford University Press) to carry in the car.

The 1886 Toscano Hotel lobby is beautifully preserved – peek inside. The 1852 Vallejo's Home (p203) lies a half-mile northwest. One ticket allows same-day admission to all, including **Petaluma Adobe State Park** (707-762-4871; www.petalumaadobe.com; 3325 Adobe Rd, Petaluma; adult/child $3/2; ⊙10am-5pm; P) at General Vallejo's former ranch, 15 miles away.

Mission San Francisco Solano HISTORIC BUILDING
(Map p202; 707-938-9560; www.parks.ca.gov; 114 E Spain St; adult/child $3/2; ⊙10am-5pm) At Sonoma Plaza's northeast corner, the mission was built in 1823, partly to forestall Russians at Fort Ross from moving inland. This was the 21st and final California mission – the northernmost point on El Camino Real – and the only one built during the Mexican period

(the rest were founded during the Spanish Colonial era). Five original rooms remain. The not-to-be-missed **chapel** dates to 1840.

Toscano Hotel HISTORIC BUILDING
(Map p202; 707-938-9560; www.parks.ca.gov; 20 E Spain St; adult/child $3/2; ⊙10am-5pm) Toscano Hotel opened as a store and library in the 1850s, then became a hotel in 1886. Peek into the lobby and, except for the traffic outside, you'd swear you were peering back in time. Tours 1pm–4pm Saturday and Sunday.

Sonoma Barracks HISTORIC BUILDING
(Map p202; 707-939-9420; www.parks.ca.gov; 20 E Spain St; adult/child $3/2; ⊙10am-5pm) The adobe Sonoma Barracks was built by Vallejo between 1834 and 1841 to house Mexican troops. Today, interpretive displays describe life during the Mexican and

Sonoma

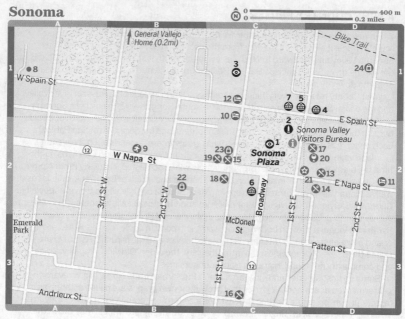

Sonoma

American periods. The barracks became the capital of a rogue nation on June 9, 1846, when American settlers of varying sobriety surprised guards and declared an independent 'California Republc' [sic] with a homemade flag featuring a blotchy bear.

Bartholomew Park   PARK
(Map p198; ☎707-938-2244; www.bartholomew park.org; 1000 Vineyard Lane; ⊙10am-4:30pm; P⊞) FREE The top near-town outdoors destination is 375-acre Bartholomew Park, off Castle Rd, where you can picnic beneath gi-

ant oaks and hike 2 miles of trails, with hilltop vistas to San Francisco. The **Palladian Villa**, at the park's entrance, is a re-creation of Count Haraszthy's original Pompeian residence, open noon to 3pm Saturdays and Sundays. There's also a good **winery**, independently operated. Last entry is at 4:30pm.

Vallejo's Home   HISTORIC BUILDING
(Map p198; ☑707-938-9559; 363 3rd St W; adult/child $3/2; ☉10am-5pm) A half-mile from the plaza, this lovely historical estate, also known as Lachryma Montis (Latin for 'Tears of the Mountain'), was built in the 1850s for General Vallejo and named for the on-site spring, which the Vallejo family made good money from by piping water to town. The Gothic-style American-Victorian home remained in the family until 1933, when the state of California purchased it, along with its original furnishings. A bicycle path leads to the house from downtown. Tours 1pm, 2pm and 3pm Saturday and Sunday.

Sonoma Valley Museum of Art   MUSEUM
(Map p202; ☑707-939-7862; www.svma.org; 551 Broadway; adult/child 14-17yr/family $10/5/15; ☉11am-5pm Wed-Sun) The 8000-sq-ft modern- and contemporary-art museum presents changing exhibitions by international and local artists, and focuses on building community around art.

Cornerstone Sonoma   GARDENS
(Map p198; ☑707-933-3010; www.cornerstone sonoma.com; 23570 Arnold Dr; ☉10am-5pm, gardens to 4pm; ℗♿) 𝗙𝗥𝗘𝗘 This roadside, Wine Country marketplace showcases 25 walk-through (in some cases edible) gardens, along with a bunch of innovative and adorable shops, wine-tasting parlors and on-site **Sonoma Valley Visitors Bureau** (Map p198; ☑707-996-1090; www.sonomavalley.com; 23570 Hwy 121, Cornerstone Gardens; ☉10am-4pm). There's a good, if pricey, cafe, and an outdoor 'test kitchen.' Look for the enormous orange Adirondack chair at road's edge.

🏃 Activities

Many local inns provide bicycles.

Willow Stream Spa at Sonoma Mission Inn   SPA
(Map p198; ☑707-938-9000; www.fairmont.com/sonoma; 100 Boyes Blvd; ☉9am-6pm Mon-Thu, to 8pm Fri-Sun) Few Wine Country spas compare with glitzy Sonoma Mission Inn. Purchasing a treatment or paying $89 (make reservations) allows use of three outdoor

and two indoor mineral pools, gym, sauna and herbal steam room at the Romanesque bathhouse. No under 18s.

Wine Country Cyclery   CYCLING
(Map p202; ☑707-966-6800; www.winecountry cyclery.com; 262 W Napa St; bicycle rental per day $30-75; ☉10am-6pm) Offers hybrids, electric bikes, road bikes and even tandem bikes. Book ahead.

Sonoma Valley Cyclery   CYCLING
(Map p198; ☑707-935-3377; www.sonomacyclery. com; 20091 Broadway/Hwy 12; bikes per day from $30; ☉10am-6pm Mon-Sat, to 4pm Sun; ♿) Sonoma is ideal for cycling – not too hilly – with multiple wineries near downtown. This place rents mountain bikes, road bikes and hybrids. Book ahead for weekends.

Vintage Aircraft Company   SCENIC FLIGHTS
(Map p198; ☑707-938-2444; www.vintageaircraft. com; 23982 Arnold Dr, Sonoma; 20min flight 1/2 people $175/270) Scenic flights in biplanes, with an option to add aerobatic maneuvers.

🍴 Courses

Ramekins Sonoma Valley Culinary School   COOKING
(Map p202; ☑707-933-0450; www.ramekins.com; 450 W Spain St; ♿) Offers excellent demonstrations and hands-on classes for home chefs, covering things such as hors d'oeuvres and cheese-and-wine pairings. The school also hosts culinary tours of local farms and dinners with vintners and chefs.

🛏 Sleeping

There are lots of historic inns and romantic cottages suitable for a midrange budget, but those counting pennies will have better luck in Santa Rosa. Off-season rates plummet. Reserve ahead and ask about parking; some inns don't have lots.

★Windhaven Cottage   COTTAGE $$
(Map p198; ☑707-938-2175, 707-483-1856; www. windhavencottage.com; 21700 Pearson Ave; cottages $165-175; ❋🐾) Great-bargain Windhaven has two units: a hideaway cottage with vaulted wooden ceilings and fireplace, and a handsome 800-sq-ft studio. We prefer the romantic cottage. Both have hot tubs. Bicycles and barbecues sweeten the deal.

Sonoma Chalet   B&B $$
(Map p198; ☑800-938-3129, 707-938-3129; www. sonomachalet.com; 18935 5th St W; r $160-190, r with shared bath $150, cottages $210-235; ℗➷) On

a historic farmstead surrounded by rolling hills, rooms in this Swiss-chalet-style house are adorned with little balconies and country-style bric-a-brac. We love the garden hot tub and the freestanding cottages; Laura's has a wood-burning fireplace. Breakfast is served on a deck overlooking a nature preserve. No air-conditioning in rooms with shared bath. No phone, no internet.

Sonoma Creek Inn MOTEL $$
(Map p198; ☑707-939-9463; www.sonomacreekinn. com; 239 Boyes Blvd; r Sun-Thu $155-195, Fri & Sat $205-240; ✪ 🛜 🐾) This cute-as-a-button motel has spotless, cheery, retro-Americana rooms, but it's not downtown. Valley wineries are a short drive. When available, last-minute bookings cost just $89.

Sonoma Hotel HISTORIC HOTEL $$
(Map p202; ☑707-996-2996, 800-468-6016; www. sonomahotel.com; 110 W Spain St; r weekday $160-248, weekend $225-248, ste $308; ✪ ✪ 🛜) Long on charm, this good-value, vintage hotel was built in 1872 and is decorated with country-style willow-wood furnishings. It sits right on the plaza and its double-pane glass blocks the noise, but there's no elevator or parking lot.

El Dorado Hotel BOUTIQUE HOTEL $$$
(Map p202; ☑707-996-3030; www.eldoradosonoma. com; 405 1st St W; r Sun-Thu $225-330, Fri & Sat $385-500; 🅿 ✪ ✪ 🛜 🐾) Stylish touches, such as high-end linens, justify rates and compensate for the rooms' compact size, as do private balconies, which overlook the plaza or rear courtyard (we prefer the plaza view, despite noise). No elevator.

El Pueblo Inn MOTEL $$$
(Map p198; ☑707-996-3651, 800-900-8844; www. elpuebloinn.com; 896 W Napa St; r $189-384; ✪ @ 🛜 🐾) One mile west of downtown, family-owned El Pueblo has surprisingly cushy rooms with great beds. The big lawns and heated pool are perfect for kids; parents appreciate the 24-hour hot tub. Check the website for discounts.

Hidden Oak Inn B&B $$$
(Map p202; ☑707-996-9863; www.hiddenoakinn. com; 214 E Napa St; r $255-315; ✪ 🛜 🐾) Three-room, 1914 arts-and-crafts B&B with lovely service.

MacArthur Place INN $$$
(Map p198; ☑707-938-2929, 800-722-1866; www.macarthurplace.com; 29 E MacArthur St; r/ste from $399/555; ✪ @ 🛜 🐾) Sonoma's top

full-service inn occupies a former estate with century-old gardens. There's also an attached steakhouse, spa, giant chess set on the lawn and a complimentary wine-and-cheese reception each night.

Sonoma's Best Guest Cottages COTTAGE $$$
(Map p198; ☑707-933-0340; www.sonomasbest cottages.com; 1190 E Napa St; cottages $199-349, q $279-395; ✪ 🛜) Each of these four colorful, inviting cottages has a bedroom, living room, kitchen and barbecue, with comfy furniture, stereo, DVDs and bicycles. It's 1 mile east of the plaza, just behind a general store under the same ownership, featuring a deli, an espresso bar and a wine-tasting room.

✕ Eating

Sonoma takes a culinary backseat to many towns in Napa Valley and Healdsburg to the north, but has some decent restaurants on the plaza plus Fremont Diner, the best diner in Wine Country.

Angelo's Wine Country Deli DELI $
(Map p198; ☑707-938-3688; 23400 Arnold Dr; sandwiches $7; ⊗9am-5pm) Look for the cow on the roof of this roadside deli south of town, a fave for fat sandwiches and homemade turkey and beef jerky (free samples!).

Pearl's Diner DINER $
(Map p198; ☑707-996-1783; 561 5th St W; mains $7-10; ⊗7am-2:30pm; 🐾) Across from Safeway's west-facing wall, greasy-spoon Pearl's serves giant American breakfasts, including standout bacon and waffles with batter enriched by melted vanilla ice cream. More of a locals joint than a tourist spot.

Sonoma Market DELI $
(Map p198; ☑707-996-3411; https://sonomamar ket.net; 500 W Napa St; sandwiches from $6; ⊗5am-9:30pm) Sonoma's best groceries and deli sandwiches.

★ Fremont Diner AMERICAN, SOUTHERN $$
(Map p198; ☑707-938-7370; www.thefremontdiner. com; 2698 Fremont Dr; mains $9-22; ⊗8am-3pm Mon-Wed, to 9pm Thu-Sun; 🐾) 🍴 Lines snake out the door at peak times at this farm-to-table roadside diner. We prefer the indoor tables but will happily accept a picnic table to feast on buttermilk pancakes with homemade cinnamon-vanilla syrup, chicken and waffles, oyster po'boys, finger-licking barbecue and skillet-baked cornbread. Arrive early or late to beat queues, or call ahead within

an hour of your arrival to put your name on the wait list.

Della Santina's ITALIAN $$
(Map p202; ☑707-935-0576; www.dellasantinas. com; 133 E Napa St; mains $14-26; ⏰11:30am-3pm & 5-9:30pm) The waiters have been here forever and the 'specials' rarely change, but Della Santina's Italian-American cooking – linguini pesto, veal parmigiana, rotisserie chickens – is consistently good and the brick courtyard is inviting on warm evenings.

Hopmonk Tavern PUB FOOD $$
(Map p202; ☑707-935-9100; www.hopmonk.com; 691 Broadway; mains $11-23; ⏰11:30am-9pm Sun-Thu, to 10pm Fri & Sat) This happening gastropub and beer garden takes its brews seriously with over a dozen of its own and guest beers on tap, served in type-appropriate glassware. Live music Friday through Sunday, open mike on Wednesday starting at 8pm.

Taste of the Himalayas INDIAN, NEPALESE $$
(Map p202; ☑707-996-1161; 464 1st St E; mains $10-20; ⏰11am-2:30 Tue-Sun, 5-10pm daily) Spicy curries, luscious lentil soup and sizzle-platter meats make a refreshing break from the usual French-Italian Wine Country fare.

Red Grape ITALIAN $$
(Map p202; ☑707-996-4103; http://theredgrape. com; 529 1st St W; mains $12-20; ⏰11:30am-9pm; 🅱) A reliable spot for an easy meal, Red Grape serves good thin-crust pizzas and big salads in a cavernous, echoey space. Good for takeout too.

★ Cafe La Haye CALIFORNIAN $$$
(Map p202; ☑707-935-5994; www.cafelahaye.com; 140 E Napa St; mains $19-25; ⏰5:30-9pm Tue-Sat) 🍴 One of Sonoma's top tables for earthy New American cooking, La Haye only uses produce sourced from within 60 miles. Its dining room gets packed cheek-by-jowl and service can border on perfunctory, but the clean simplicity and flavor-packed cooking make it many foodies' first choice. Reserve well ahead.

Girl & the Fig FRENCH $$$
(Map p202; ☑707-938-3634; www.thegirlandthefig. com; 110 W Spain St; mains $20-32; ⏰11:30am-10pm Mon-Thu, 11am-11pm Fri, 8am-11pm Sat, 10am-10pm Sun) For a festive evening, book a garden table at this French-provincial bistro, with good small plates ($14 to $16), including steamed mussels with matchstick fries or duck confit with lentils. Weekday three-course prix fixe

costs $42; add $12 for wine. Stellar cheeses. Reservations essential.

La Salette PORTUGUESE $$$
(Map p202; ☑707-938-1927; www.lasalette-restau rant.com; 452 1st St E; mains lunch $12-25, dinner $22-32; ⏰11:30am-2:30pm & 5:30-9pm Mon-Fri, 11:30am-9pm Sat & Sun) 🍴 Contemporary Portuguese cuisine is the focus at this just-off-the-plaza restaurant that serves excellent-value, proper sit-down meals, including a standout fisherman's stew. Make reservations.

El Dorado Kitchen CALIFORNIAN $$$
(Map p202; ☑707-996-3030; http://eldorado sonoma.com/restaurant; 405 1st St W; mains lunch $15-24, dinner $21-31; ⏰8-11am, 11:30am-2:30pm & 5:30-9pm Mon-Thu, to 10pm Fri & Sat) 🍴 The swank plazaside choice for contemporary California-Mediterranean cooking, El Dorado showcases seasonal-regional ingredients in dishes such as seafood paella, ahi tartare and housemade pasta, served in a see-and-be-seen dining room with a big community table at its center. The happening lounge serves good small plates ($11 to $22) and craft cocktails. Make reservations.

Harvest Moon Cafe MODERN AMERICAN $$$
(Map p202; ☑707-933-8160; www.harvestmoon cafesonoma.com; 487 1st St W; mains $19-29; ⏰5:30-9pm Sun-Mon & Wed-Thu, to 9:30pm Sat & Sun) 🍴 Inside a cozy 1836 adobe, this casual bistro uses local ingredients in its changing menu, with simple soul-satisfying dishes such as grilled Liberty Farm duck breast with dried cherry farro, cauliflower and saba sauce. Book the patio in warm weather.

🍸 Drinking & Nightlife

There's more of a late-night scene here than in other Sonoma Valley towns; **Steiner's** (Map p202; ☑707-996-3812; www.steinerstavern. com; 465 1st St W; ⏰6am-2am; 🖥) is pretty much the social hub.

Carneros Brewing Company MICROBREWERY
(Map p198; ☑707-938-1880; www.carnerosbrew ing.com; 22985 Burndale Rd; ⏰noon-5:30pm Wed-Mon) A family-owned microbrewery with seasonal craft beers and a mission-inspired tap room halfway between downtown Sonoma and Napa. On weekend afternoons the beer garden is a lively scene.

Prohibition Spirits Distillery DISTILLERY
(Map p198; ☑707-933-7507; www.prohibition-spir its.com; 23570 Arnold Dr, Sunset Gardens at Corner-stone; ⏰10am-5pm) New at Cornerstone, this

WHAT'S CRUSH?

Crush is autumn harvest, the most atmospheric time of year, when the vine's leaves turn brilliant colors and you can smell fermenting fruit on the breeze. Farmers throw big parties for the vineyard workers to celebrate their work. Everyone wants to be here and room rates skyrocket. If you can afford it, visit in autumn. To score party invitations, join your favorite winery's wine club.

hip tasting room offers sips of a California version of Italian aperitifs limoncello, orangecello and grappa, along with tasty gins made with things such as cantaloupe and elderflower, and brandy distilled from prickly pear cacti.

Murphy's Irish Pub   PUB
(Map p202; ☑707-935-0660; www.sonomapub. com; 464 1st St E; ⊙11am-9pm) Don't ask for Bud – there are only *real* brews here. Good hand-cut fries and shepherd's pie. Live music Friday and Saturday evenings.

☆ Entertainment

Free jazz concerts happen on the plaza every second Tuesday of the month, June to September, 6pm to 8:30pm; arrive early and bring a picnic.

Sebastiani Theatre   CINEMA
(Map p202; ☑707-996-2020; www.sebastianithea tre.com; 476 1st St E) The plaza's gorgeous 1934 Mission Revival cinema screens art-house and revival films, and sometimes live theater.

🔒 Shopping

Chateau Sonoma   HOMEWARES
(Map p202; ☑707-935-8553; www.chateausono ma.com; 23588 Arnold Dr; ⊙10am-5pm) France meets Sonoma in one-of-a-kind gifts and arty home-decor store, which recently relocated to Cornerstone Sonoma.

Figone's Olive Oil   FOOD
(Map p202; ☑707-282-9092; www.figoneoliveoil. com; 483 1st St W; ⊙10am-6pm Sun-Thu, to 7pm Fri & Sat) Figone's presses its own extra-virgin olive oil and infuses some with flavors such as Meyer lemon, all free to sample.

Vella Cheese Co   FOOD
(Map p202; ☑707-938-3232; www.vellacheese. com; 315 2nd St E; ⊙9:30am-6pm Mon-Fri, to 5pm Sat) Known for its jacks (made here since the 1930s), Vella specializes in dry-jack with a cocoa-powder-dusted rind. Also try Mezzo Secco, a cheese you can only find here. Staff will vacuum-pack for shipping.

Tiddle E Winks   TOYS
(Map p202; ☑707-939-6933; www.tiddleewinks. com; 115 E Napa St; ⊙10:30am-5:30pm Mon-Sat, 11am-5pm Sun; ⊕) Vintage five-and-dime, with classic mid-20th-century toys.

ℹ️ Information

Sonoma Valley Visitors Bureau (Map p202; ☑866-966-1090; www.sonomavalley.com; 453 1st St E; ⊙9am-5pm Mon-Sat, 10am-5pm Sun) Offers guides, maps, pamphlets, merchandise information on deals and events, and more. There's another at Cornerstone Sonoma (p203).

ℹ️ Getting There & Away

Public transport is not a great idea but it can be done. Find out by dialing ☑511 or looking online at www.transit.511.org. Sonoma Valley is a 90-minute drive from San Francisco.

ℹ️ Getting Around

Sonoma Hwy/Hwy 12 is lined with wineries and runs from Sonoma to Santa Rosa, then to western Sonoma County; Arnold Dr has less traffic (but few wineries) and runs parallel up the valley's western side to Glen Ellen. Plan at least five hours to visit the valley from bottom to top.

Glen Ellen & Kenwood

Sleepy Glen Ellen is a snapshot of old Sonoma, with white picket fences and tiny cottages beside a poplar-lined creek. When downtown Sonoma is jammed, you can wander quiet Glen Ellen and feel far away. It's ideal for a leg-stretching stopover between wineries or a romantic overnight – the nighttime sky blazes with stars. Glen Ellen's biggest daytime attractions are Jack London State Historic Park and Benziger winery (p199).

⊙ Sights & Activites

Jack London State Historic Park   PARK
(Map p198; ☑707-938-5216; www.jacklondonpark. com; 2400 London Ranch Rd, Glen Ellen; per car $10, cottage adult/child $4/2; ⊙9:30am-5pm; 🅿⊕)
Napa has Robert Louis Stevenson, but Sonoma has Jack London. This 1400-acre park frames that author's last years; don't miss the excellent on-site museum. Miles of **hiking trails** (some open to mountain bikes)

weave through oak-dotted woodlands, between 600ft and 2300ft elevations; an easy 2-mile loop meanders to **London Lake**, great for picnicking. On select summer evenings, the park transforms into a theater for 'Broadway Under the Stars.' Be alert for poison oak.

Changing occupations from Oakland fisher-man to Alaska gold prospector to Pacific yachtsman (and novelist on the side) London (1876–1916) ultimately took up farming. He bought 'Beauty Ranch' in 1905 and moved here in 1911. With his second wife, Charmian, he lived and wrote in a small cottage while his mansion, **Wolf House**, was under construction. On the eve of its completion in 1913, it burned down. The disaster devastated London, and although he toyed with rebuilding, he died before construction got underway. His widow, Charmian, built the **House of Happy Walls**, which has been preserved as a **museum** (open 10am to 5pm). It's a half-mile walk from there to the remains of Wolf House, passing London's grave along the way. Other paths wind around the farm to the cottage, open noon to 4pm, where he lived and worked.

Quarryhill Botanical Garden　GARDENS
(Map p198; ☑ 707-996-3166; www.quarryhillbg.org; 12841 Hwy 12; adult/child 13-17yr $12/8; ☺ 9am-4pm) Just when you thought the vineyards would stretch as far as the eye could see, out of nowhere comes a world-renowned botanical garden specializing in the flora of Asia. It's a treat to stroll the trails, observing specimens collected on yearly expeditions to countries throughout the Far East, and to relax near the pond, contemplating the artfully created woodland landscape.

Sugarloaf Ridge State Park　PARK
(Map p198; ☑ 707-833-5712; www.sugarloafpark.org; 2605 Adobe Canyon Rd, Kenwood; per car $8; P ⊕) ⏀ There are 30 miles of fantastic hiking – when it's not blazingly hot. On clear days, **Bald Mountain** has drop-dead views to the sea, while the **Brushy Peaks Trail** peers into Napa Valley. Both are moderately strenuous; plan on a three-hour round-trip. Bikes and horses can use perimeter trails seasonally. There's a small but well-stocked visitor center.

Oak Hill Farm　FARM
(Map p198; ☑ 707-996-6643; www.oakhillfarm.net; 15101 Sonoma Hwy, Glen Ellen; ☺ 9am-3pm Sat May-Dec; P ⊕) ⏀ At the southern end of Glen Ellen, Oak Hill Farm contains acres upon acres of organic flowers and produce,

hemmed in by lovely steep oak and manzanita woodland. The farm's **Red Barn Store** is a historic dairy barn filled with handmade wreaths, herbs and organic goods reaped from the surrounding fields. Try the heirloom tomatoes, pumpkins and blue plums.

Triple Creek Horse Outfit　HORSEBACK RIDING
(Map p198; ☑ 707-887-8700; www.triplecreek horseoutfit.com; 2400 London Ranch Rd; 60/90min rides $80/100; ☺ 9am-5pm Mon-Sat) Explore Jack London State Park by horseback for vistas over Sonoma Valley. Reservations required.

Morton's Warm Springs　SWIMMING
(Map p198; ☑ 707-833-5511; www.mortonswarm springs.com; 1651 Warm Springs Rd, Glen Ellen; adult/child $12/6; ☺ 10am-6pm Tue-Sun Jun-Aug, Sat, Sun & holidays May & Sep; ⊕) This old-fashioned spring-fed geothermal-pool complex and family-friendly gathering place has two mineral pools, limited hiking, volleyball and BBQ facilities. From Sonoma Hwy in Kenwood, turn west on Warm Springs Rd.

🛏 Sleeping

Couples will not regret staying in the romantic cottages and inns of Glen Ellen. Kenwood has one high-end resort and an excellent campground.

Sugarloaf Ridge State Park　CAMPGROUND $
(Map p198; ☑ 707-833-6084, 800-444-7275; www.reserveamerica.com; 2605 Adobe Canyon Rd, Kenwood; tent & RV sites $35; ⊛) Sonoma's nearest camping is north of Kenwood at this lovely hilltop park, with 48 drive-in sites, clean coin-operated showers and great hiking.

Beltane Ranch　B&B $$
(Map p198; ☑ 707-833-4233; www.beltaneranch.com; 11775 Hwy 12, Glen Ellen; d $185-375; P ☺ ☎) ⏀ Surrounded by horse pastures and vineyards, Beltane is a throwback to 19th-century Sonoma. The cheerful 1890s ranch house has double porches lined with swinging chairs and white wicker. Though it's technically a B&B, each country-Americana-style room and the cottage has a private entrance – nobody will make you pet the cat. No phone or TV means zero distraction from pastoral bliss.

Glen Ellen Cottages　BUNGALOW $$
(Map p198; ☑ 707-996-1174; www.glenelleninn.com; 13670 Arnold Dr, Glen Ellen; cottages Sun-Thu $149-175, Fri & Sat $219-275; ⊛ ☎) Hidden behind Glen Ellen Inn (p208), these five creekside cottages are designed for romance, with oversized jetted tub, steam shower and gas fireplace.

Jack London Lodge MOTEL $$
(☑707-938-8510; www.jacklondonlodge.com; 13740 Arnold Dr, Glen Ellen; r Mon-Fri $134, Sat & Sun $205; ❄️🛜🏊) An old-fashioned wood-sided motel with well-kept rooms decorated with antique repros, this is a weekday bargain. Outside there's a pool and hot tub; next door, a saloon. Two-night minimum during high-season weekends.

Gaige House Inn INN $$$
(☑707-935-0237; www.gaige.com; 13540 Arnold Dr, Glen Ellen; d/ste from $275/345; P🅿️👶@🛜🏊🐶) Among the valley's most chic inns, Gaige has 23 rooms, five inside an 1890 house decked out in Euro-Asian style. Best are the Japanese-style 'Zen suites,' with requisite high-end bells and whistles, including freestanding tubs made from hollowed-out granite boulders. Fabulous.

Kenwood Inn & Spa INN $$$
(Map p198; ☑707-833-1293, 800-353-6966; www.kenwoodinn.com; 10400 Sonoma Hwy, Kenwood; r $450-825; ❄️@🛜🏊) Lush gardens surround ivy-covered bungalows at this sexy 30-room inn, designed to resemble a Mediterranean château. Two hot tubs (one with a waterfall) and an on-site spa make it ideal for lovers, boring for singles. No kids. Book an upstairs balcony room.

✖ Eating

Italian and French establishments dominate the scene, but there are also a couple of good bakeries and a market for self-caterers. Jack London Village has some good options.

Garden Court
Cafe & Bakery CAFE $
(☑707-935-1565; www.gardencourtcafe.com; 13647 Arnold Dr, Glen Ellen; mains $9-12; ⏱8:30am-2pm Wed, Thu & Mon, 8am-2pm Sat & Sun) Basic breakfasts, sandwiches and salads.

Fig Cafe & Winebar FRENCH, CALIFORNIAN $$
(☑707-938-2130; www.thefigcafe.com; 13690 Arnold Dr, Glen Ellen; mains $12-24, 3-course dinner $36; ⏱10am-2:30pm Sat & Sun, 5-9pm Sun-Thu, 5-9:30pm Fri & Sat) The earthy California-Provençal comfort food includes flash-fried calamari with spicy lemon aioli, fig and arugula salad and *steak frites*. Good wine prices and weekend brunch give reason to return. No reservations; complimentary corkage.

Mayo Winery Reserve WINERY $$
(Map p198; ☑707-833-5504; www.mayofamilywinery.com; 9200 Sonoma Hwy, Kenwood; 7-course menu $50; ⏱by appointment 10:30am-6:30pm) Feast on a seven-course small-plates menu paired with seven wines for $50 at this roadside wine-tasting room.

Cafe Citti ITALIAN $$
(Map p198; ☑707-833-2690; www.cafecitti.com; 9049 Sonoma Hwy, Kenwood; mains $8-15; ⏱11am-3:30pm & 5-8:30pm Sun-Thu, to 9pm Fri & Sat; 👶) Locals favor this order-at-the-counter Italian-American deli, with standout roast chicken, and homemade gnocchi and ravioli. At lunchtime there's pizza and house-baked focaccia sandwiches.

Glen Ellen Inn AMERICAN $$
(☑707-996-6409; www.glenelleninn.com; 13670 Arnold Dr, Glen Ellen; mains $16-25; ⏱11:30am-9pm Thu-Tue, 5:30-9pm Wed) Oysters, martinis and grilled steaks. Lovely garden, full bar.

Glen Ellen Star CALIFORNIAN, ITALIAN $$$
(☑707-343-1384; http://glenellenstar.com; 13648 Arnold Dr, Glen Ellen; pizzas $15-20, mains $24-50; ⏱5:30-9pm Sun-Thu, to 9:30pm Fri & Sat; 👶) 🌿 Helmed by chef Ari Weiswasser, who once worked at Thomas Keller's French Laundry (p186), this petite Glen Ellen bistro shines a light on the best of Sonoma farms and ranches. Local, organic and seasonal ingredients star in dishes such as spring-lamb ragù, whole roasted fish with broccoli di cicco or golden beets with harissa crumble. Reservations recommended. Wednesdays are neighborhood nights, which means no corkage fee and a $35 two-course menu.

Aventine ITALIAN $$$
(Map p198; ☑707-934-8911; http://glenellen.aventinehospitality.com; 14301 Arnold Dr, Glen Ellen; mains $14-28; ⏱4:30-10pm Wed-Fri, 11am-10pm Sat & Sun) The Sonoma outpost of the popular San Francisco restaurant occupies an atmospheric former grist mill with a sun-dappled outdoor patio. It serves Italian-derived dishes, including house-special Aventino: mozzarella-stuffed meatball with pesto over polenta. Make reservations.

❶ Getting There & Away

Glen Ellen is an hour's drive north from San Francisco.

RUSSIAN RIVER AREA

Lesser-known western Sonoma County was formerly famous for its apple farms and vacation cottages. Lately vineyards are replacing orchards and the Russian River has taken its place among California's important wine appellations, especially for Pinot Noir.

'The River,' as locals call it, has long been a summer-weekend destination for Northern Californians who come to canoe, wander country lanes, taste wine, hike redwood forests and live at a lazy pace. In winter the river floods, and nobody's here. The Russian River begins in the mountains north of Ukiah, in Mendocino County, but the most visited sections lie southwest of Healdsburg, where the river cuts a serpentine course toward the sea.

Russian River Wineries

Sonoma County's wine-growing regions encompass several diverse areas, each famous for different reasons. Pick up the free, useful *Russian River Wine Road* map (www.wineroad.com) from tourist-brochure racks.

Russian River Valley

Nighttime coastal fog drifts up the Russian River Valley, then usually clears by midday. Pinot Noir does beautifully, as does Chardonnay, which also grows in hotter regions, but prefers the longer 'hang time' of cooler climes. The highest concentration of wineries is along Westside Rd, between Guerneville and Healdsburg.

★ **Macrostie**   WINERY
(Map p210; ☑707-473-9303; www.macrostiewinery.com; 4605 Westside Rd; tasting $20-25, with tour $55; ☺11am-5pm Mon-Thu, 10am-5pm Fri-Sun) For its creamy and crisp Chardonnays and earthy Pinots, along with top-notch service and an elegant tasting room, Macrostie is the talk of Wine Country. The sit-down tastings are relaxed and highly personal, with gorgeous views of the vineyard. Visionary winemaker Heidi Bridenhagen holds the distinction of being the youngest female on the job in Sonoma Valley. Pair your tasting with a delicious charcuterie plate that includes three local cheeses, prosciutto, olives, almonds and dried fruit.

Hartford   WINERY
(Map p210; ☑800-588-0234; www.hartfordwines.com; 8075 Martinelli Rd, Forestville; tasting $15; ☺10am-4:30pm) ☞ Surprisingly upscale for West County, Hartford sits in a pastoral valley surrounded by redwood-forested hills, on one of the area's prettiest back roads. It specializes in fine single-vineyard Pinot (13 kinds), Chardonnay and Zinfandel from old-vine fruit. Umbrella-shaded picnic tables dot the garden. Bottles are $30 to $100; the tasting fee is waived with purchase.

J Winery   WINERY
(Map p210; ☑707-431-3646, 707-431-5430; www.jwine.com; 11447 Old Redwood Hwy; tasting/tour $20/30; ☺11am-5pm) ☞ J crafts crisp sparkling wines, among Sonoma's best, but it's pricey. Make an appointment and splurge on one of the seated food-and-wine-pairing experiences. The decadent 'bubble room' tasting includes five wines paired with five locally sourced dishes prepared by chef Carl Shelton ($110 per person). The alfresco 'terrace' tasting (April to November) is also a winner, with four wines paired with four small appetizers ($55). Bottles cost $24 to $75.

De La Montanya   WINERY
(Map p210; ☑707-433-3711; www.dlmwine.com; 999 Foreman Lane, Healdsburg; tasting $10; ☺11am-4:30pm, ☎) This tiny winery, tucked amid vineyards, is known for 17 small-batch varieties made with estate-grown fruit. Viognier, Primitivo, Pinot and Cabernet are signatures; the 'summer white' and Gewürztraminer are great back-porch wines. Apple-shaded picnic area, bocce ball and horseshoes add to the fun. Bottles are $20 to $60 and the tasting fee is refundable with a purchase. Appointments suggested.

Landmark Vineyards at Hop Kiln Estate   WINERY
(Map p210; ☑707-433-6491; www.landmarkwine.com; 6050 Westside Rd; tasting $20; ☺10am-5pm) This photogenic historic landmark has a busy tasting room inside a former hop kiln; we especially like the Flocchini Chardonnay. You can build your own picnic with meats, cheeses and crackers for $40, and the winery provides wine glasses, baskets, blankets and cheese boards with knives.

Porter Creek   WINERY
(Map p210; ☑707-433-6321; www.portercreekvineyards.com; 8735 Westside Rd; tasting $15; ☺10:30am-4:30pm; ℗) ☞ Inside a vintage-1920s garage, Porter Creek's tasting bar is a former bowling-alley lane. Porter is old-school Northern California, an early

Russian River Area

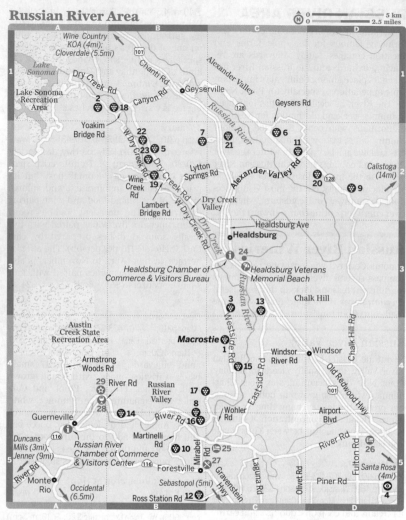

pioneer in biodynamic farming. High-acid, food-friendly Pinot Noir and Chardonnay are specialties, but there's old-vine Zinfandel and other Burgundian- and Rhône-style wines too. Tasting fee waived with purchase. Bottles cost $24 to $72.

Moshin
WINERY

(Map p210; ☎707-433-5499; www.moshinvine yards.com; 10295 Westside Rd; tasting $15, private tour & tasting by appointment only $30; ⏱11am–4:30pm; P) 🍷 Pinot Noir is a finicky grape that withers in sun and mildews in fog, yet it thrives in Russian River Valley, including

at solar-powered Moshin Vineyards. The winery also specializes in small-production Pinot Noir, Sauvignon Blanc, Chardonnay, Merlot, Petite Sirah and Zinfandel. Tasting fee waived with purchase.

Iron Horse
WINERY

(Map p210; ☎707-887-1507; www.ironhorsevine yards.com; 9786 Ross Station Rd, off Hwy 116, Sebastopol; tasting $25, incl tour $50; ⏱10am–4:30pm, last tasting 4pm; P) Atop a hill with drop-dead views over the county, Iron Horse is known for sparkling wines, which the White House often pours. The outdoor

Russian River Area

tasting room is refreshingly unfussy; when you're done with your wine, pour it in the grass. On Sundays from noon to 4pm, April through October, oysters, cheese and olive oil are served. Bottles cost $30 to $110. Reservations strongly recommended.

Korbel WINERY
(Map p210; ☎707-824-7000; www.korbel.com; 13250 River Rd, Guerneville; ◎10am-5pm; 🅿) **FREE** Gorgeous rose gardens (April to October) and a stellar on-site deli make Korbel worth a stop for a free tasting, but the sparkling wine's just OK. Try the sparkling

wine you can't get elsewhere; the rouge is particularly good.

Gary Farrell WINERY
(Map p210; ☎707-473-2909; www.garyfarrellwines.com; 10701 Westside Rd; tasting $35-75; ◎10am-3pm Mon-Fri, by appointment; 🅿) High on a hilltop overlooking the Russian River, Gary Farrell's tasting room sits perched among second-growth redwoods. The elegant Chardonnay and long-finish Pinot Noir, made by a big-name winemaker, score high marks for consistency. Bottles are $35 to $75.

Dry Creek Valley

Hemmed in by 2000ft-high mountains, Dry Creek Valley is relatively warm, ideal for Sauvignon Blanc and Zinfandel, and in some places Cabernet Sauvignon. It's west of Hwy 101, between Healdsburg and Lake Sonoma. Dry Creek Rd is the fast-moving main thoroughfare. Parallel-running West Dry Creek Road is an undulating country lane with no center stripe – one of Sonoma's great back roads, ideal for cycling.

Bella WINERY
(Map p210; ☎707-473-9171; www.bellawinery.com; 9711 W Dry Creek Rd; tasting $15; ◎11am-4:30pm; 🅿) Atop the valley's north end, always-fun Bella has cool caves built into the hillside. The estate-grown grapes include 112-year-old vines from Alexander Valley. The focus is on big reds – Zinfandel and Syrah – but there's terrific rosé (good for barbecues) and late-harvest Zinfandel (great with brownies). The wonderful vibe and dynamic staff make Bella special. Bottles are $25 to $55.

Preston WINERY
(Map p210; ☎707-433-3372; www.prestonvineyards.com; 9282 W Dry Creek Rd; tasting/tours $10/25; ◎11am-4:30pm; 🅿🚻) 🌿 An early leader in organics and recently certified bi-odynamic, Lou Preston's 19th-century farm is old Sonoma. Weathered picket fencing frames the tasting room, with candy-colored walls and tongue-in-groove ceilings setting a country mood. The signature is citrusy Sauvignon Blanc, but try the Rhône varietals and small-lot wines: Carignane, Viognier, Cinsault and cult-favorite Barbera. Preston also bakes good bread and cold-presses its own olive oil; picnic in the shade of a walnut tree. Bottles are $22 to $40. Tours by appointment.Monday to Friday, there's bocce and a new farm store sells seasonal produce adjacent to the tasting room.

Family Wineries
WINERY

(Map p210; 888-433-6555; www.familywines.com; 4791 Dry Creek Rd; tasting $10; 10:30am-4:30pm Mar-Dec, Thu-Mon Jan-Feb) Sample multiple varietals at this cooperative, which showcases six boutique wineries too small to have their own tasting rooms. Tasting fee is refundable with a purchase.

Truett Hurst
WINERY

(Map p210; 707-433-9545; www.truetthurst.com; 5610 Dry Creek Rd; tasting $10; 10am-5pm; P) Pull up an Adirondack chair and picnic creekside at Truett Hurst, one of Dry Creek's biodynamic wineries. Sample terrific old-vine Zinfandel, standout Petite Sirah and Russian River Pinot Noir at the handsome contemporary tasting room, then meander through fragrant fruit and gardens to the creek, where salmon spawn in autumn. Another good winery, VML, now shares tasting-room space with Truett Hurst. Bottles are $20 to $53.

Unti Vineyards
WINERY

(Map p210; 707-433-5590; www.untivineyards.com; 4202 Dry Creek Rd; tasting $10; 10am-4pm by appointment only;) Inside a vineyard-view tasting room, Unti pours all estate-grown varietals – Châteauneuf-du-Pape–style Grenache, compelling Syrah and superb Sangiovese – favored by oenophiles for their structured tannins and concentrated fruit. If you love small-batch wines, don't miss Unti. Bottles are $20 to $50 and the tasting fee is refundable with a purchase.

Quivira
WINERY

(Map p210; 707-431-8333, 800-292-8339; www.quivirawine.com; 4900 W Dry Creek Rd; tasting $15-30, incl tour $40, tour & estate tasting by reservation only; 11am-4pm, 10am-4:30pm Apr-Oct; P) Sunflowers, lavender, beehives and crowing roosters greet your arrival at this winery and biodynamic farm, with self-guided garden tours and a redwood grove beside the vines. Kids can giggle with pigs and chickens while you sample Rhône varietals, unusual blends and lip-smacking, award-winning Sauvignon Blanc. Bottles are $24 to $55.

Alexander Valley

Bucolic Alexander Valley flanks the Mayacamas Mountains, with postcard-perfect vistas and wide-open vineyards. Summers are hot, ideal for Cabernet Sauvignon, Merlot and warm-weather Chardonnays, but there are also fine Sauvignon Blancs and Zinfandels. For events info visit www.alexandervalley.org.

Hawkes
WINERY

(Map p210; 707-433-4295; www.hawkeswine.com; 6734 Hwy 128; tasting $15, barrel/vineyard tour $45/45; 10am-5pm; P) Hawkes makes an easy stopover while you're exploring the valley, and offers private barrel tastings in which guests sample straight from the oak before the wine is bottled or released to the market. The single-vineyard Cabernet Sauvignon is damn good, as is the Merlot; there's also a clean-and-crisp Chardonnay. Bottles are $30 to $75.

Francis Ford Coppola Winery
WINERY, MUSEUM

(Map p210; 707-857-1471; www.francisfordcoppolawinery.com; 300 Via Archimedes, Geyserville; tasting $18-25; 11am-6pm; P) The famous movie director's vineyard estate is a self-described 'wine wonderland.' Taking over historic Chateau Souverain, this hillside winery has a bit of everything: wine-tasting flights, a free museum of moviemaking memorabilia, a shameless gift shop and two modern Italian-American restaurants. Outside you'll find bocce courts by two swimming pools (Map p210; day pass adult/child $35/15; 11am-6pm daily Jun-Sep, Fri-Sun Apr, May & Oct;). The most satisfying tasting is the reserve flight ($25) upstairs. Bottles are $12 to $90. From 5pm to 9pm on Tuesdays, there's A Tavola, a multiple-course, family-style meal served by staff in elaborate costumes ($45).

Hanna
WINERY

(Map p210; 707-431-4310, 800-854-3987; www.hannawinery.com; 9280 Hwy 128; tasting $20-40; 10am-4pm; P) Abutting oak-studded hills, Hanna's tasting room has lovely vineyard views and good picnicking. At the bar, find estate-grown Sauvignon Blanc, Malbec, Cabernet Sauvignon, Chardonnay and big-fruit Zinfandel. Sit-down wine-and-cheese tastings ($40) are available with advance reservations. Bottles cost $19 to $68.

Soda Rock Winery
WINERY

(Map p210; 707-433-3303; www.sodarockwinery.com; 8015 CA 128; tasting $15; 11am-5pm) Come to Soda Rock to behold Lord Snort, a 20,000lb metal boar sculpture displayed out front, and stay for the big Bordeaux varietals, including Cabernet Savignon, Cab Franc and Petit Verdot, along with a rare and juicy Primitivo. With a sky-high ceiling and dignified brick, the lovingly restored tasting room is a former general store that now doubles as an elegant event space. Bottles cost $18 to $41. Tasting fee waived with one bottle purchase.

Trentadue WINERY
(Map p210; ☑707-433-3104, 888-332-3032; www.
trentadue.com; 19170 Geyserville Ave, Geyserville;
tasting $10-15, tour $25; ☺10am-5pm; ☻) Specializes in ports (ruby, not tawny); the chocolate port makes a great gift. The tour is good
fun and includes tastes of sparkling and still
wine as guests are towed through the vineyards by a tractor. Tasting fee waived with
four-bottle purchase or wine-club sign-up.
Bottles $15 to $38.

Foley Sonoma WINERY
(Map p210; ☑707-433-1944; www.foleysonoma.
com; 5110 Hwy 128; tasting $20, incl tour $40;
☺10am-5pm; ☑) ❧ Wow, what a view from
the hilltop concrete-and-glass tasting room
at Foley Sonoma. Winemaker Courtney Foley
specializes in Bordeaux varietals and blends,
along with Zinfandels and Pinots. An hour-
long tour takes guests through the crush pad,
barrel room and vineyard and finishes with a
tasting. Bottles are $30 to $80.

Sebastopol

Grapes have replaced apples as the new cash
crop, but Sebastopol's farm-town identity remains rooted in the apple – evidenced by the
much-heralded summertime Gravenstein
Apple Fair. The town center feels suburban
because of traffic, but a hippie tinge gives it
color. This is the refreshingly laid-back side
of Wine Country and makes a good-value
base for exploring the area.

◉ Sights

Around Sebastopol, look for family-friendly
farms, gardens, animal sanctuaries and
pick-your-own orchards. For a countywide
list, check out the Sonoma County Farm
Trails Guide (www.farmtrails.org).

★Patrick Amiot Junk Art GALLERY
(www.patrickamiot.com; Florence Ave; ☑🚻) Prepare to gawk and giggle at the wacky Patrick
Amiot sculptures gracing front yards along
Florence Ave. Fashioned from recycled materials, a hot-rodding rat, a hectic waitress
and a witch in midflight are a few of the
oversized and demented lawn ornaments
parading along the street. Keep an eye out
and you'll notice more of these scattered
throughout Sebastopol.

California Carnivores GARDENS
(☑707-824-0433; www.californiacarnivores.com;
2833 Old Gravenstein Hwy S; ☺10am-4pm Thu-

Mon) Even vegans can't help admiring these
incredible carnivorous plants (the largest
collection in the US), including specimens
from around the globe. Owner Peter D'Amato encourages visitors to BYOB (bring your
own bugs) and watch as the plants devour
them. He's also written a book with a perfect
name, *The Savage Garden*.

Spirit Works Distillery DISTILLERY
(☑707-634-4793; www.spiritworksdistillery.
com; 6790 McKinley St, 100, Barlow; tasting/tour
$18/20; ☺11am-5pm Wed-Sun) ❧ A bracing al-
ternative to wine tasting, Spirit Works crafts
superb small-batch spirits – vodka, gin,
sloe gin and (soon) whiskey – from organic
California red-winter wheat. The distillery
abides by a 'grain-to-glass' philosophy, with
milling, mashing, fermenting and distilling all done on-site. Sample and buy in the
warehouse. Tours (by reservation) happen
Friday to Sunday at 5pm and finish with a
tasting. Bottles are $27 to $36.

Barlow MARKET
(☑707-824-5600; www.thebarlow.net; cnr Sebastopol & Morris Sts; ☺hours vary; ☑🚻) ❧ The
Barlow occupies a former apple-processing
plant, repurposed into a 12-acre village of
food producers, artists, winemakers, coffee
roasters, spirits distillers and indie restaurateurs, who showcase West County's culinary
and artistic diversity. Wander shed to shed,
sample everything from house-brewed beer
to ice cream flash-frozen with liquid nitrogen and meet artisans in their workshops.
Usually on Thursdays 4pm to 8pm, from
May to October, the Barlow hosts a 'street
fair,' with live music and local vendors.

Farmers Market MARKET
(www.sebastopolfarmmarket.org; cnr Petaluma &
McKinley Aves; ☺10am-1:30pm Sun) Meets at
the downtown plaza.

✯ Festivals & Events

Apple Blossom Festival CULTURAL
(www.appleblossomfest.com; ☺Apr) Live music,
food, drink, wine, a parade and exhibits.

Gravenstein Apple Fair FOOD & DRINK
(www.gravensteinapplefair.com; ☺Aug) Arts,
crafts, food, wine, brews, games, live entertainment and farm-life activities.

🛏 Sleeping

There are only a couple of hotels in Sebastopol, but staying here is convenient to Russian River Valley, the coast and Sonoma Valley.

Sebastopol Inn
MOTEL $$

(☑800-653-1082, 707-829-2500; www.sebastopol
inn.com; 6751 Sebastopol Ave; r $119-388; ❈☎❂)
We like this independent, *non*-cookie-cutter
motel for its quiet, off-street location, usual-
ly reasonable rates and good-looking if basic
rooms. Outside are grassy areas for kids and
a hot tub.

✖ Eating

Sebastopol is a town of artists and locavores,
and while its restaurant scene reflects those
predilections, there are plenty of interna-
tional options as well. Above all, the local
produce and seafood is top-notch.

★ Handline
CALIFORNIAN $

(☑707-827-3744; www.handline.com; 935 Graven-
stein Ave; mains $9-21; ☉11am-10pm) ✐ Housed
in a former Foster's Freeze, this highly an-
ticipated seafood restaurant is over-the-
counter casual but undeniably elegant. The
stylish interior is defined by reclaimed wood
and shoji-style paneling that opens to a
tree-shaded patio. In a room designated the
tortilleria, corn tortillas are hand-molded
each day and topped with battered and fried
rockfish, pickled onion and roasted summer
squash. The oysters and ceviche are divine,
and in a nod to the previous tenant there's
organic Straus soft serve for dessert.

Slice of Life
VEGETARIAN $

(☑707-829-6627; www.thesliceoflife.com; 6970
McKinley St; mains under $10; ☉11am-9pm Tue-
Fri, 9am-9pm Sat & Sun; ♫) ✐ This good ve-
gan-vegetarian kitchen doubles as a pizzeria
and also offers plenty of Mexican dishes.
Breakfast all day. Great smoothies.

Mom's Apple Pie
DESSERTS $

(☑707-823-8330; www.momsapplepieusa.com;
4550 Gravenstein Hwy N; whole pies $7-17; ☉10am-
6pm; ✐❂) Pie's the thing at this roadside
bakery – and yum, that flaky crust. Apple is
predictably good, especially in autumn, but
the blueberry is our fave, made better with
vanilla ice cream.

Screamin' Mimi
ICE CREAM $

(☑707-823-5902; www.screaminmimisicecream.
com; 6902 Sebastopol Ave; ☉11am-10pm) Delish
homemade ice cream.

Pacific Market
MARKET $

(Pacific Market; ☑707-823-9735; www.pacificmkt.
com; 550 Gravenstein Hwy N; ☉7am-9pm Mon-Sat,
8am-8pm Sun) Excellent for groceries and pic-
nics; north of downtown.

Hopmonk Tavern
PUB FOOD $$

(☑707-829-7300; www.hopmonk.com; 230 Petaluma Ave; mains $12-23; ☉11:30am-9pm Mon-Thu,
to 10pm Fri, 11am-10pm Sat & Sun; ☎) Inside
a converted 1903 railroad station, Hop-
monk's serves 76 varieties of beer – served
in type-specific glassware – that pair with a
good menu of burgers, fried calamari, charcuterie platters and salads.

Zazu Kitchen & Farm
AMERICAN $$$

(☑707-523-4814; http://zazukitchen.com; 6770
McKinley St, 150, Barlow; mains lunch $13-18, din-
ner $24-29; ☉5-10pm Mon & Wed, 3-10pm Thu,
11:30am-midnight Fri & Sat, 9am-10pm Sun) ✐
We love the farm-to-table ethos of Zazu – it
grows its own pigs and sources everything
locally – but some dishes miss and the
industrial-style space gets crazy loud. Still,
it does excellent pizzas, salads, housemade
salumi, pork and bacon. Good breakfasts too.

K&L Bistro
FRENCH $$$

(☑707-823-6614; www.klbistro.com; 119 S Main St;
lunch $14-20, dinner $19-29; ☉11am-11pm) K&L
serves earthy provincial Cal-French bistro
cooking in a convivial bar-and-grill space
with sidewalk patio. Expect classics such as
mussels and french fries, and grilled steaks
with red-wine reduction. Reservations
essential.

❦ Drinking & Nightlife

Nightlife isn't Sebastopol's strong suit, but
there are a couple of great breweries and
tastings rooms at the Barlow (p213).

Woodfour Brewing Co
BREWERY

(☑707-823-3144; www.woodfourbrewing.com; 6780
Depot St, Barlow; ☉noon-7pm Wed & Thu, to 8pm
Fri & Sat, 11am-6pm Sun) ✐ Woodfour's solar-
powered brewery serves about a dozen
housemade beers, light on alcohol and hops,
plus several sours (high-acid beer). It also
has an exceptionally good menu of small
plates (designed to pair with beer), from simple snacks to refined, technique-driven dishes better than any we've had at a California
brewery.

Taylor Maid Farms
CAFE

(☑707-634-7129; www.taylormaidfarms.com; 6790
McKinley St, Barlow; ☉6:30am-6pm Sun-Thu, to
7pm Fri, 7am-7pm Sat) ✐ Choose your brew
method (drip, press etc) at this third-wave
coffeehouse that roasts its own organic
beans. Seasonal drinks include lavender
lattes.

Hardcore Espresso
CAFE

(☎707-823-7588; 81 Bloomfield Rd; ⊙5am-7pm Mon-Fri, 6am-7pm Sat & Sun; 🐕) ✐ Meet local hippies and artists over coffee and smoothies at this classic NorCal, off-the-grid, indoor-outdoor coffeehouse, south of downtown, that's essentially a corrugated-metal-roofed shack surrounded by umbrella tables.

🛍 Shopping

Antique shops line Gravenstein Hwy S toward Hwy 101.

Funk & Flash
CLOTHING

(☎707-829-1142; www.funkandflash.com; 228 S Main St; ⊙11am-7pm) Disco-glam party clothes, inspired by Burning Man.

Midgley's Country Flea Market
MARKET

(☎707-823-7874; www.mfleamarket.com; 2200 Gravenstein Hwy S; ⊙7:30am-4:30pm Sat, 6:30am-5:30pm Sun) The region's largest flea market.

Copperfield's Books
BOOKS

(☎707-823-2618; www.copperfields.net; 138 N Main St; ⊙10am-7pm Mon-Sat, to 6pm Sun) Indie bookshop with literary events.

Beekind
FOOD, HOMEWARES

(☎707-824-2905; www.beekind.com; 921 Gravenstein Hwy S; ⊙10am-6pm Mon-Sat, to 4pm Sun) ✐ Local honey and beeswax candles.

Antique Society
ANTIQUES

(☎707-829-1733; www.antiquesociety.com; 2661 Gravenstein Hwy S; ⊙10am-5pm) More than 125 antiques vendors under one roof.

Aubergine
VINTAGE

(☎707-827-3460; www.auberginevintageempori um.com; 755 Petaluma Ave; ⊙10:30am-6pm) Vast vintage emporium, specializing in cast-off European thrift-shop clothing.

Sumbody
COSMETICS

(☎707-823-2053; www.sumbody.com; 118 N Main St; ⊙10am-7pm Mon-Fri, to 8pm Sat, to 6pm Sun) Ecofriendly bath products made with all-natural ingredients. Also offers facials ($79) and massages ($80) at its small on-site spa.

Toyworks
TOYS

(☎707-829-2003; www.sonomatoyworks.com; 6940 Sebastopol Ave; ⊙10am-6pm Mon-Sat, 11am-5pm Sun; 🖬) ✐ Indie toy seller with phenomenal selection of quality games for kids.

❶ Information

Sebastopol Area Chamber of Commerce & Visitors Center (☎877-828-4748, 707-823-3032; www.sebastopol.org; 265 S Main St; ⊙10am-5pm Mon-Fri) Maps, information and exhibits.

❶ Getting There & Away

For public-transit information, dial ☑511, or look online at www.transit.511.org.

Sebastopol is about an 80-minute drive north from San Francisco. Hwy 116 splits downtown; southbound traffic uses Main St, northbound traffic Petaluma Ave. North of town, it's called Gravenstein Hwy N and continues toward Guerneville; south of downtown, it's Gravenstein Hwy S, which heads toward Hwy 101 and Sonoma.

Occidental & Around

Our favorite West County town is a haven of artists, back-to-the-landers and counter-culturalists. Historic 19th-century buildings line a single main street, easy to explore in an hour; continue north by car and you'll hit the Russian River in Monte Rio. At Christmas-time, Bay Area families flock to Occidental to buy trees. The town decorates to the nines and there's weekend cookie-decorating and caroling at the Union Hotel's Bocce Ballroom.

◉ Sights & Activities

Grove of the Old Trees
FOREST

(☎707-544-7284; www.landpaths.org; 17599 Fitzpatrick Lane; ⊙dawn-dusk) **FREE** Outside Occidental and up on a ridge off Fitzpatrick Lane, Grove of the Old Trees is a peaceful, 28-acre forest of old-growth redwoods. The forest and its trails are managed by a local nonprofit.

Bohème Wines
WINERY

(☎707-874-3218; www.bohemewines.com; 3625 Main St; ⊙3-5pm Thu & Fri, noon-6pm Sat & Sun) Drop in to this little tasting room in downtown Occidental for free swigs of dry Chardonnay, earthy Pinots and a big Syrah, all from the cooler climes. Bottles range from $39 to $49.

Occidental Bohemian Farmers Market
MARKET

(☎707-874-8478; www.occidentalfarmersmarket. com; 3611 Bohemian Hwy; ⊙4pm-dusk Fri Jun-Oct; 🖬) ✐ Meet the whole community at Occidental's detour-worthy farmers market, with musicians, craftspeople and – the star attraction – Gerard's Paella (www.gerardspa ella.com) of Food Network TV fame.

Osmosis SPA
(☑707-823-8231; www.osmosis.com; 209 Bohemian Hwy, Freestone; packages from $219; ⊙by appointment 9am-8pm) Tranquility prevails at this Japanese-inspired spa, which indulges patrons with dry-enzyme baths of aromatic cedar fibers paired with other treatments including outdoor massages and facials. The tea-and-meditation gardens are lovely. Make reservations.

Sonoma Canopy Tours OUTDOORS
(☑888-494-7868; www.sonomacanopytours.com; 6250 Bohemian Hwy; adult $99-109, child $69) North of town, fly through the redwood canopy on seven interconnected ziplines, ending with an 80ft-rappel descent; reservations required.

🛏 Sleeping

Occidental offers a couple of historic inns and one fantastic farmstay.

★**Shanti Permaculture Farm** FARMSTAY $$
(☑707-874-2001; www.shantioccidental.com; Coleman Valley Rd; tent & RV sites $75, cottages & yurts $199-225) Tucked back in the redwoods on scenic Coleman Valley Rd, this is the ultimate NorCal farmstay. The knowledgeable Oregonian owner educates guests about ecofriendly agricultural concepts such as biochar and hugelkultur, and shows off her chickens, ducks, goats and enormous llama. While the operation feels somewhat rustic, it is impressively MacGyvered and the one-bedroom cottage is surprisingly posh.

Near the top of the 6-acre property, a wonderfully homey yurt offers comfort and seclusion, though the llama has been known to wander up the hill to stare through a window at sleeping guests. Continuing down the hill, private campsites are ensconced in the trees, and RVs are also welcome at the bottom of the hill, where a hookup is available for a fee. Delicious farm-to-table meals are available for $15 to $20.

Valley Ford Hotel INN $$
(☑707-876-1983; www.vfordhotel.com; r $115-175) Surrounded by pastureland 8 miles southeast in Valley Ford, this 19th-century, seven-room inn has good beds, great rates and a terrific roadhouse bar and restaurant.

Inn at Occidental INN $$$
(☑800-522-6324, 707-874-1047; www.innatoccidental.com; 3657 Church St; r $259-399; 🐾) One of Sonoma's finest, this beautifully restored 18-room Victorian inn is filled with collectible antiques; rooms have gas fireplaces and cozy feather beds.

🍴 Eating & Drinking

Delicious meals and snacks abound for every budget, all in close proximity.

Wild Flour Bread BAKERY $
(☑707-874-2938; www.wildflourbread.com; 140 Bohemian Hwy, Freestone; items from $3; ⊙8:30am-6:30pm Fri-Mon; 🖋) Organic brick-oven artisan breads, giant sticky buns and good coffee.

Howard Station Cafe AMERICAN $
(☑707-874-2838; www.howardstationcafe.com; 3611 Bohemian Hwy; mains $8-14; ⊙7am-2:30pm Mon-Fri, to 3pm Sat & Sun; 🖋🐾) Big plates of comfort-food cooking and freshly squeezed juices. Cash only.

Bohemian Market DELI $
(☑707-874-3312; 3633 Main St; ⊙8am-9pm, 7am-9pm Sat & Sun) Occidental's best grocery store has a good deli which prepares sandwiches from 10am to 7pm. There's also a coffee bar open daily until 1pm.

Hazel CALIFORNIAN $$
(☑707-874-6003; www.restauranthazel.com; 3782 Bohemian Hwy; mains $15-32; ⊙5-9pm Wed-Sat, 10am-2pm & 5-9pm Sun) Occidental's newest restaurant is small, unassuming and serves absolutely delectable food. The menu only features a few starters, pizzas and mains but you cannot go wrong, particularly with the scallop ceviche (fresh mango, radishes, a delightful medley of oils and spices, delicate morsels of mollusk). Also great: fried brussels sprouts, braised pot roast and the strawberry-rhubarb crisp with vanilla ice cream.

Union Hotel ITALIAN $$
(☑707-874-3555; www.unionhoteloccidental.com; 3703 Bohemian Hwy; meals $15-26; ⊙11am-9pm, bar to 2am; 🖋) Occidental has two old-school American-Italian restaurants that serve family-style meals. The Union is slightly better and serves a delicious, complimentary bruschetta with the purchase of any main. Monday nights mean $5 pizza or pasta in-house (adults only). On a sunny day you can't beat the patio for lunch, and there's also a bakery with freshly baked cookies for $1.

Barley & Hops PUB
(☑707-874-9037; www.barleynhops.com; 3688 Bohemian Hwy; ⊙4-9pm Mon-Thu, 1-9:30pm Fri-Sun) Serving around 40 beers, sandwiches, burgers, giant salads and amazing bacon-cheddar fries. Mains $10-15.

🔒 Shopping

Hand Goods   CERAMICS
(📞707-874-2161; www.handgoods.net; 3627 Main St; ⊙10am-6pm) Collective of ceramicists, potters, jewelers, fine artists and more.

ℹ️ Getting There & Away

Occidental is about a two-hour drive from San Francisco. There's no good way to get here via public transportation.

Guerneville & Around

The Russian River's biggest vacation-resort town, Guerneville gets busy over summer weekends with party-hardy gay boys, sun-worshiping lesbians and long-haired, beer-drinking Harley riders, earning it the nickname 'Groin-ville.' Though the town is slowly gentrifying, it hasn't lost its honky-tonk vibe – fun-seeking crowds still come to canoe, hike and hammer cocktails poolside.

Downriver, some areas are sketchy (due to drugs). The local chamber of commerce has chased most of the tweakers from Main St in Guerneville, but if some off-the-beaten-path areas feel creepy – especially campgrounds – they probably are.

Four miles downriver, tiny Monte Rio has a sign over Hwy 116 declaring it 'Vacation Wonderland' – an overstatement, but the dog-friendly beach is a hit with families. Further west, idyllic Duncans Mills is home to a few dozen souls and has picture-ready historic buildings converted into cute shops. Upriver, east of Guerneville, Forestville is where farm country resumes.

◎ Sights & Activities

Look for sandy beaches and swimming holes along the river; there's good river access east of town at Sunset Beach. Fishing and watercraft outfitters operate mid-May to early October, after which winter rains dangerously swell the river. A **farmers market** (16290 5th St) meets downtown on Wednesdays, May through September, from 3pm to 7pm. On summer Saturdays, there's also one at **Monte Rio Beach**, 11am to 2pm.

Armstrong Redwoods State
Natural Reserve   FOREST
(📞info 707-869-2015, visitor center 707-869-2958; www.parks.ca.gov; 17000 Armstrong Woods Rd; per car $8; ⊙8am-1hr after sunset; 🅿️🎫) 🌲 A magnificent redwood forest 2 miles north of Guerneville, this 805-acre reserve was saved from the saw by a 19th-century lumber magnate. Short interpretive trails lead into magical forests, with old-growth redwoods 30 stories high. Beyond lie 20 miles of backcountry trails through oak woodlands in adjoining **Austin Creek State Recreation Area**, one of Sonoma County's last remaining wilderness areas. Walk or cycle in for free; pay only to park.

Sunset Beach   BEACH
(📞707-433-1625; www.sonoma-county.org/parks; 11060 River Rd, Forestville; per car $7; ⊙7am-sunset) Nice park on the water featuring paddle sports and picnicking.

Burke's Canoe Trips   CANOEING
(📞707-887-1222; www.burkescanoetrips.com; 8600 River Rd, Forestville; canoe/kayak rental incl shuttle $68/$45, cash only) You can't beat Burke's for a day on the river. Self-guided canoe and kayak trips include shuttle back to your car. Make reservations; plan for four hours. Camping in the riverside redwood grove is $10 per person.

Johnson's Beach   WATER SPORTS
(📞707-869-2022; www.johnsonsbeach.com; 16215 &16217 First St; kayak & canoe rental per hour/day $15/40; ⊙10am-6pm summer only; 🚹) **FREE** Canoe, kayak and paddleboat rental available. Beer, wine, hot dogs and burgers are for sale. Beach admission is free though it's $5 to park and closed in poor weather. You can camp (p218) here.

R3 Hotel Pool   SWIMMING
(Triple R; 📞707-869-8399; www.ther3hotel.com; 16390 4th St; ⊙9am-close) **FREE** The gay, adults-only, party-scene swimming pool at the R3 Hotel (p218) is free, provided you buy drinks. Bring your own towel. Bathing suits are mandatory, but only because state liquor-license laws require them.

Pee Wee Golf & Arcade   GOLF, CYCLING
(📞707-869-9321; 16155 Drake Rd, at Hwy 116; 18/36 holes $8/12; ⊙11am-10pm Jun-Aug, to 5pm Sat & Sun May & Sep; 🚹) Flash back to 1948 at this impeccably kept retro-kitsch 36-hole miniature golf course, just south of the Hwy 116 bridge, with brilliantly painted obstacles, including T Rex and Yogi Bear. Bring your own cocktails. It also rents gas barbecue grills.

King's Sport & Tackle   OUTDOORS
(📞707-869-2156; www.kingsrussianriver.com; 16258 Main St; ⊙8am-6pm May-Oct, hours vary Nov-Apr) *The* local source for fishing and river-condition information. Also rents kayaks

($45 to $65), stand up paddleboards (from $60) and fishing gear.

River Rider
CYCLING

(☎707-887-2453; www.riverridersrentals.com; half-/full-day rental from $35/45, delivery $20; ☉7am-7pm) Delivers bicycles, along with wine-tasting passes on request; there are discounts for multiday rentals.

✦ Festivals & Events

Naughty Nuns Bingo
LGBT

(www.rrsisters.org/bingo.html; 16255 1st St; 2 bingo cards & 5 raffle tickets $20; ☉doors 5:30pm, 2nd Sat of month) These fabulous themed bingo nights are put on by the Russian River Sisters of Perpetual Indulgence, an activist group of gender-bending performance artists who dress as ostentatious nuns.

Monte Rio Variety Show
MUSIC

(www.monterioshow.org; adult/child $30/15; ☉Jul) Members of the elite, secretive Bohemian Grove (Google it) perform publicly, sometimes showcasing unannounced celebrities.

Lazy Bear Weekend
LGBT

(www.lazybearweekend.com; ☉Aug) Read: heavy, furry gay men.

Russian River Jazz & Blues Festival
MUSIC

(www.russianriverfestivals.com; ☉Sep) A day of jazz, followed by a day of blues, with occasional luminaries such as BB King.

⌂ Sleeping

Guerneville has lovely resorts, inns and cottages, but few budget sleeps apart from campgrounds; prices drop midweek. For weekends and holidays, book ahead. Also, because the river sometimes floods, some lodgings have cold linoleum floors: pack slippers.

⌂ Guerneville

Bullfrog Pond Campground
CAMPGROUND $

(☎707-869-2015; www.stewardscr.org; sites reserved/nonreserved $35/25; ☀) Reached via a steep road from Armstrong Redwoods State Natural Reserve (p217), 4 miles from the entrance kiosk, Bullfrog Pond has forested campsites with cold water and primitive hike-in and equestrian backcountry campsites. Reserve via www.hipcamp.com or by phone.

Johnson's Beach Resort
CABIN, CAMPGROUND $

(☎707-869-2022; www.johnsonsbeach.com; 16241 1st St; tent sites $40, cabins $145-165) On the riv-

er in Guerneville, Johnson's (p217) has rustic but clean, thin-walled cabins on stilts; all have kitchen. There's camping too, but no RVs. Credit card only.

Schoolhouse Canyon Campground
CAMPGROUND $

(☎707-869-2311; www.schoolhousecanyon.com; 12600 River Rd; tent sites for 2 people & a car $40; ☀) Two miles east of Guerneville, Schoolhouse's well-tended sites lie beneath tall trees across the main road from the river. Coin-operated hot showers, clean bathrooms, quiet by night. Cash only.

Guerneville Lodge
CAMPGROUND $

(☎707-869-0102; www.guernevillelodge.com; 15905 River Rd; tent sites $40) The prettiest place to camp in downtown Guerneville is behind this retreat-center lodge on sprawling grassy lawns fronting the river. Amenities: hot clean showers, big campsites, refrigerator access, fire pits with grills. When available, lodge rooms cost $199.

R3 Hotel
RESORT $$

(Triple R; ☎707-869-8399; www.ther3hotel.com; 16390 4th St; r $125-299; ☎☀) Ground zero for party-hardy gay lads and lesbians, Triple R (as it's known) has plain-Jane, motel-style rooms surrounding a bar and pool deck that get so crowded on summer weekends that management won't allow guests to bring pets because 'they get hurt' (actual quote). Come for the scene, not for quiet (light sleepers: bring earplugs). Midweek it's mellow, wintertime dead.

Boon Hotel + Spa
BOUTIQUE HOTEL $$

(☎707-869-2721; www.boonhotels.com; 14711 Armstrong Woods Rd; tents $175-225; r $225-425; Ⓟ☉☎☀☀) ✦ Rooms surround a swimming-pool courtyard (with Jacuzzi) at this 14-room adults-only resort, gussied up in minimalist modern style. The look is austere but fresh, with organic-cotton linens and spacious rooms; most have wood-burning fireplaces. Between Memorial Day and Labor Day, 'glamping tents' and an Airstream trailer are also available. It's a 15-minute walk north of downtown.

Highlands Resort
CABIN, CAMPGROUND $$

(☎707-869-0333; www.highlandsresort.com; 14000 Woodland Dr; tent sites $40-60, r $95-180, cabins $130-215; ☎☀☀) Guerneville's mellowest gay (and straight-friendly) resort sits on a wooded hillside, walkable distance to town, and has simply furnished rooms, little

SCENIC DRIVE: COLEMAN VALLEY ROAD

Wine Country's most scenic drive isn't through the grapes, but along these 10 miles of winding West County byway, from Occidental to the sea. It's best late morning, after the fog has cleared. Drive west, not east, with the sun behind you and the ocean ahead. First you'll pass through redwood forests and lush valleys where Douglas firs stand draped in sphagnum moss – an eerie sight in the fog. The real beauty shots lie further ahead, when the road ascends 1000ft hills, dotted with gnarled oaks and craggy rock formations, with the vast blue Pacific unfurling below. The road ends at coastal Hwy 1, where you can explore Sonoma Coast State Beach (p223), then turn left and find your way to the tiny town of Bodega (not Bodega Bay) to see locales where Hitchcock shot his 1963 classic, The Birds.

cottages with porches and good camping. The large pool is clothing-optional (weekday/weekend day use $10/15).

Fern Grove Cottages
CABIN $$

(☑707-869-8105; www.ferngrove.com; 16650 River Rd; cabins $159-249, with kitchen $229-299; @ 🛜 🐾 🐕) Downtown Guerneville's cheeriest resort, Fern Grove has vintage-1930s pine-paneled cabins tucked beneath redwoods and surrounded by lush flowering gardens. Some have Jacuzzi and fireplace. The pool uses salt, not chlorine; there are concierge services and breakfast includes homemade granola.

★ Applewood Inn
INN $$$

(☑707-869-9093; www.applewoodinn.com; 13555 Hwy 116; r $250-500; 🌞 @ 🛜 🐾) A hideaway estate on a wooded hilltop south of town, cushy Applewood has marvelous 1920s-era detail, with dark wood and heavy furniture that echo the forest. Some rooms have Jacuzzi and couples' shower; some have fireplace. Amenities include a small spa and two heated pools, but the best perk is the coupon for complimentary tastings at more than 100 wineries. At the time of writing, the hotel's new Italian restaurant was about to open.

Santa Nella House
B&B $$$

(☑707-869-9488; www.santanellahouse.com; 12130 Hwy 116; r $205-249; @ 🛜 🐾) All five spotless rooms at this 1871 Victorian, south of town, have wood-burning fireplace and frilly Victorian furnishings. Upstairs rooms are biggest. Outside there's a hot tub and sauna. Best for travelers who appreciate the B&B aesthetic.

🛏 Forestville

Farmhouse Inn
INN $$$

(Map p210; ☑707-887-3300, 800-464-6642; www. farmhouseinn.com; 7871 River Rd; r $695-1495; 🌞 @ 🛜 🐾) Think love nest. The area's premier

inn was recently renovated and offers spacious rooms and cottages, styled with cushy amenities such as saunas, steam showers and wood-burning fireplaces. Small on-site spa and top-notch restaurant (Farmhouse Inn restaurant on p220). Check in early to maximize time.

Raford Inn
B&B $$$

(☑707-887-9573, 800-887-9503; http://rafordinn. com; 10630 Wohler Rd; r $225-275; 🌞 @ 🛜) 🍴 We love this 1880 Victorian B&B's secluded hilltop location, surrounded by tall palms and rambling vineyards. Rooms are big and airy, with lace and antiques; some have fireplace. And wow, those sunset views.

🛏 Monte Rio

Village Inn
INN $$

(☑707-865-2304; www.villageinn-ca.com; 20822 River Blvd; r $145-250; 🛜) 🍴 This cute, old-fashioned, 11-room inn perches beneath towering trees, right on the river. Some rooms have river views; all have fridge and microwave. No elevator.

Rio Villa Beach Resort
INN $$

(☑707-865-1143, 877-746-8455; www.riovilla.com; 20292 Hwy 116; r with kitchen $190-205, without $160-165; 🌞 🛜 🐾) Landscaping is lush at this small riverside resort with excellent sun exposure (you see redwoods, but you're not under them). Rooms are well-kept but simple (request a quiet room, not by the road); the emphasis is on the outdoors, evident by the large riverside terrace, outdoor fireplace and barbecues. Some air-conditioning.

Highland Dell
INN $$

(☑707-865-2300; www.highlanddell.com; 21050 River Blvd; r $109-179; ☉Apr-Nov; 🌞 🛜) 🍴 Built in 1906 in grand lodge style, redone in 2007, the inn fronts right on to the river. Above the giant dining room are 12 bright, fresh-looking

NAPA & SONOMA WINE COUNTRY GUERNEVILLE & AROUND

rooms with comfy beds. No elevator. Doubles as an event center.

✗ Eating

Staying downtown means you can walk to restaurants and bars. From deli sandwiches to farm-to-table feasts to Korean-diner grub, there are plenty of good options.

✗ Guerneville

Big Bottom Market MARKET, CAFE $
(☑707-604-7295; www.bigbottommarket.com; 16228 Main St; sandwiches $11-15; ⊘8am-5pm Wed-Mon) 🍴 Gourmet deli and wine shop with coffee, delicious pastries and grab-and-go picnic supplies. Supposedly the home of Oprah's favorite biscuit.

Taqueria La Tapatia MEXICAN $
(☑707-869-1821; 16632 Main St; mains $7-14; ⊘4-9pm Tue-Sun) Reasonable choice for traditional Mexican.

Garden Grill BARBECUE $
(☑707-869-3922; www.gardengrillbbq.com; 17132 Hwy 116, Guernewood Park; mains $6-12; ⊘8am-3pm) One mile west of Guerneville, this roadhouse barbecue joint, with redwood-shaded patio, serves good house-smoked meats but the fries could be better.

Food for Humans MARKET $
(☑707-869-3612; 16385 1st St; ⊘9am-8pm; 🍴) 🍴 Organic groceries; better alternative than neighboring Safeway.

Dick Blomster's Korean Diner KOREAN, AMERICAN $$
(☑707-896-8006; 16236 Main St; mains breakfast & lunch $8.50-12.50, dinner $15-20; ⊘8am-2pm & 5-9pm Sun-Thu, to 10pm Fri & Sat) By day a vintage-1940s coffee shop, by night a Korean-American diner with full bar, Dick Blomster's serves playfully tongue-in-cheek dishes, including fried peanut butter and jelly sandwiches and 'the other KFC – Korean fried crack': fried chicken with sugary-sweet brown sauce, which sure hits the spot after a night of drinking.

Seaside Metal Oyster Bar SEAFOOD $$
(☑707-604-7250; http://seasidemetal.com; 16222 Main St; dishes $8-18; ⊘5-9pm Wed, Thu & Sun, to 10pm Fri & Sat) Unexpectedly urban for Guerneville, this storefront raw bar is an offshoot of San Francisco's Bar Crudo – one of the city's best – and showcases oysters, clams, shrimp and exquisitely prepared raw-fish dishes. There's limited hot food, but it's overwrought: stick to raw. Reservations recommended.

Boon Eat + Drink CALIFORNIAN $$$
(☑707-869-0780; http://eatatboon.com; 16248 Main St; mains lunch $15-18, dinner $15-26; ⊘11am-3pm Thu-Tue, 5-9pm Sun-Thu, to 10pm Fri & Sat; 🖋) Locally sourced ingredients inform the seasonal, Cali-smart cooking at this tiny, always-packed, New American bistro, with cheek-by-jowl tables that fill every night. Serves local wine and craft beer. Show up early or expect to wait.

✗ Forestville

Canneti Roadhouse ITALIAN $$
(Map p210; ☑707-887-2232; http://cannetires taurant.com; 6675 Front St; mains lunch $12-24, dinner $16-38; ⊘5:30-9pm Tue-Wed, 11:30am-3pm & 5:30-9pm Thu-Sat, 11am-8:30pm Sun) 🍴 A Tuscan-born chef makes bona fide *cucina Italiana* using quality ingredients from local farms at this austere restaurant in downtown Forestville, worth the 15-minute drive from Guerneville. The menu ranges from simple brick-oven pizzas to an all-Tuscan, five-course tasting menu ($65; dinner only). When it's warm, sit on the patio beneath a giant redwood. Make reservations. Thursdays, three-course dinners cost $40.

★Backyard CALIFORNIAN $$$
(☑707-820-8445; www.backyardforestville.com; 6566 Front St; mains lunch & brunch $10-22, dinner mains $21-28; ⊘11am-9pm Mon & Thu, to 9:30pm Fri, 9am-9:30pm Sat, to 8:30pm Sun) This relaxing, alfresco spot gets every fruit, vegetable and animal from local farmers or fishers and the chef knows just what to do with all of it. California-inspired dishes are simple and delicious; the steak, piquillo-pepper and duck-egg hash was perhaps the world's most perfect brunch. The coffee and artisanal doughnut holes are winners.

Oh, and don't start a meal with anything other than the house pickle plate, which comes with the most delightful array of pickled, seasonal vegetables (often including cauliflower and asparagus) and house-fermented kimchi.

Farmhouse Inn MODERN AMERICAN $$$
(☑707-695-1495; www.farmhouseinn.com; 7871 River Rd; 3-/4-course dinner $99/115; ⊘5:30-8:30pm Thu-Mon) 🍴 Special-occasion worthy, Michelin-starred Farmhouse changes its seasonal Euro-Cal menu daily, using locally

raised, organic ingredients such as Sonoma lamb, wild halibut and rabbit – the latter is the house specialty. The wine pairings are exquisite, but detractors call the whole thing precious. Reservations required.

✕ Monte Rio

Rio Café   FAST FOOD $
(☑707-865-4190; www.riocafetake2.com; 20396 Bohemian Hwy; sandwiches $4-12; ☺8am-8pm Wed-Sun summer, noon-7pm Fri-Sun winter; 🛜🪑) Gourmet burgers, hot dogs and grilled sandwiches, along with breakfast options and lots of veggie choices, behind the Rio Theater. Beer and wine also served.

Village Inn   AMERICAN $$$
(☑707-865-2304; www.villageinn-ca.com; 20822 River Blvd; mains $19-26; ☺5-8pm Wed-Sun) The straightforward steaks-and-seafood menu is basic American and doesn't distract from the wonderful river views. Great local wine list, full bar.

✕ Duncans Mills

Cape Fear Cafe   AMERICAN $$
(☑707-865-9246; 25191 Main St; mains lunch $9-15, dinner $15-25; ☺10am-9pm Mon-Fri, to 9pm Sat & Sun) A country-Americana diner in a 19th-century grange, Cape Fear is visually charming, but it's erratic – except at weekend brunch when the kitchen makes excellent Benedicts. Good stopover en route to the coast.

🍷 Drinking & Nightlife

Stumptown Brewery is the town's after-hours social hub, but there are plenty of good opportunities for day-drinking – particularly at the wineries and while floating down the river in summer.

Rainbow Cattle Company   GAY
(www.queersteer.com; 16220 Main St; ☺noon-2am) This stalwart gay watering hole has pinball and shuffleboard. Tuesdays are big, with a donation-based buffet, silent auction, raffle and a percentage of sales going to various causes.

Sophie's Cellars   WINE BAR
(☑707-865-1122; www.sophiescellars.com; 25179 Main St/Hwy 116; glasses $7-15; ☺11am-5pm Thu, Sat & Sun, to 7pm Fri) The perfect stopover between river and coast, Sophie's rural wine bar pours glasses and tastes of local wine, and carries cheese, salami and a well-curated selection of bottles. Friday's

'locals happy hour' (4pm to 7pm) brings hors d'oeuvres, drink specials and a big crowd.

Stumptown Brewery   BREWERY
(Map p210; www.stumptown.com; 15045 River Rd; ☺11am-midnight Sun-Thu, to 2am Fri & Sat) Guerneville's best straight bar, 1 mile east of downtown, is gay friendly and has a foot-stompin' jukebox, billiards, riverside beer garden and several homemade brews. Pretty good pub grub includes house-smoked barbecue.

☆ Entertainment

Rio Nido Roadhouse   LIVE MUSIC
(Map p210; ☑707-869-0821; www.rionidoroadhouse.com; 14540 Canyon Two, off River Rd, Rio Nido) Raucous roadhouse bar, 4 miles east of Guerneville, with eclectic lineup of live bands. Shows start 6pm Saturday and sometimes Friday and Sunday too; check website. There's also a pool open 11am to 6pm daily, to 5pm on Saturday and water aerobics is offered. The pool was being renovated at the time of writing.

Rio Theater   CINEMA
(☑707-865-0913, 707-520-4075; www.riotheater.com; 20396 Bohemian Hwy, Monte Rio; $10-12; ♿) Dinner and a movie take on new meaning at this vintage-WWII Quonset hut converted to a cinema in 1950. In 2014 they finally added heat, but still supply blankets. Only in Monte Rio. Shows nightly (and sometimes Sunday afternoons), but call ahead, especially off-season.

Main Street Bistro   CABARET
(☑707-869-0501; www.mainststation.com; 16280 Main St; ☺4-11pm Mon-Thu, noon-11pm Fri-Sun; ♿) Hosts live acoustic-only jazz, blues and cabaret nightly in summer (weekends in winter). Families are welcome as the cabaret doubles as an American-Italian restaurant (stick to pizza).

🔒 Shopping

Eight miles west of Guerneville, tiny Duncans Mills has good shopping in a handful of side-by-side businesses within weathered 19th-century cottages.

★ Guerneville Bank Club   FOOD
(☑707- 666-9411; www.guernevillebankclub.com; 16290 Main St; ☺11am-9pm Sun-Thu, to 10pm Fri & Sat) After 30 years of abandonment, this beautifully restored 1921 bank building now contains stuff more valuable than money:

art, wine, ice cream and pie. The new collective retail and art-gallery space houses small businesses such as Chile Pies Banking Company (go for the Mexican Chocolate Pecan) and Nimble Finn's Ice Cream, which sells organic dairy products, jams, cakes etc. There's a small wine-tasting room and the old vault has been converted into a photo booth adorned in murals.

Pig Alley
JEWELRY

(☑707-865-2698; www.pigalleyshop.com; 25193 Main St; ⊙10am-5pm Mon-Fri, 9:30am-5:30pm Sat & Sun) Vast selection of hand-crafted American-made jewelry, notable for gorgeous earrings.

Mr Trombly's Tea & Table
FOOD & DRINKS

(☑707-865-9610; www.mrtromblystea.com; 25185 Main St; ⊙10am-5pm Sun-Thu, to 5:30pm Fri & Sat) Different kinds of tea and teapots, plus quality kitchen gadgets and well-priced tableware.

❶ Information

Russian River Chamber of Commerce & Visitors Center (Map p210; ☑707-869-9000; www.russianriver.com; 16209 1st St; ⊙10am-5pm Mon-Sat, plus to 3pm Sun May-Oct) Information and lodging referrals.

❶ Getting There & Away

Public transit isn't a great option, but to check bus routes dial ☑511, or look online at www. transit.511.org. The drive from San Francisco takes about two hours.

Santa Rosa

Wine Country's biggest city and the Sonoma County seat, Santa Rosa claims two famous native sons – a world-renowned cartoonist and a celebrated horticulturalist – whose legacies include museums and gardens that'll keep you busy for an afternoon. Otherwise, there isn't much to do, unless you need your car fixed or you're here in July during the **Sonoma County Fair** (www. sonomacountyfair.com), at the fairgrounds on Bennett Valley Rd.

Beyond that, Santa Rosa is mostly known for traffic and suburban sprawl, though the downtown's redwood trees make for some impressive landscaping.

Orientation

The main shopping stretch is 4th St, which abruptly ends at Hwy 101, but reemerges

across the freeway at historic Railroad Sq. Downtown parking garages (75¢ per hour, $8 maximum) are cheaper than street parking. East of town, 4th St becomes Hwy 12 into Sonoma Valley.

◉ Sights & Activities

Charles M Schulz Museum
MUSEUM

(☑707-579-4452; www.schulzmuseum.org; 2301 Hardies Lane; adult/child $12/5; ⊙11am-5pm Mon & Wed-Fri, 10am-5pm Sat & Sun; ℗♿) Charles Schulz, creator of *Peanuts* cartoons and Santa Rosa resident, was born in 1922, published his first drawing in 1937, introduced Snoopy and Charlie Brown in 1950 and produced *Peanuts* cartoons until his death in 2000. This modern museum honors his legacy with a Snoopy labyrinth, *Peanuts*-related art and a re-creation of Schulz' studio. Skip Snoopy's Gallery gift shop; the museum has the good stuff.

Farmers Market
MARKET

(www.wednesdaynightmarket.org; Old Courthouse Sq; ⊙5-8:30pm Wed mid-May–Aug) Sonoma County's largest farmers market. A second smaller market meets year-round, 9am to 1pm, Wednesdays and Saturdays at Santa Rosa Veterans Building.

Luther Burbank Home & Gardens
GARDENS

(☑707-524-5445; www.lutherburbank.org; 204 Santa Rosa Ave; grounds free, tour adult/child $10/5; ⊙gardens 8am-dusk, museum 10am-4pm Tue-Sun Apr-Oct) Pioneering horticulturist Luther Burbank (1849–1926) developed many hybrid plant species, including the Shasta daisy, here at his 19th-century, Greek-revival home. Guided tours 10am-3:30pm Tuesday-Sunday April-October. The extensive gardens are lovely. The house and adjacent **Carriage Museum** have displays on Burbank's life and work, or you can take a self-guided cellphone tour of the grounds for free.

Epicenter
CENTER

(Map p210; ☑707-708-3742; www.visitepicenter.com; 3215 Coffey Lane; ⊙11am-midnight Sun-Thu, to 2am Fri & Sat) An entertainment complex with restaurants, bars, bowling, an arcade and a trampoline park.

Children's Museum of Sonoma County
SCIENCE CENTER

(☑707-546-4069; www.cmosc.org; 1835 Steele Lane; $12; ⊙9am-4pm Mon & Wed-Sat, 11am-4pm Sun; ♿) Geared to children 10 and under, this happy learning center inspires discovery, exploration and creativity with hands-on indoor and outdoor exhibits focused on nature and science. Picnicking welcome. No adults without kids.

Redwood Empire Ice Arena
SKATING

(☎ 707-546-7147; www.snoopyshomeice.com; 1667 West Steele Lane; incl skates $5-13; ☺ hours vary; ♿) This skating rink was formerly owned and deeply loved by *Peanuts* cartoon creator Charles Schulz. It's open most afternoons (call for schedules). Bring a sweater.

🛌 Sleeping

Chain hotels abound, in addition to a couple of historic inns and a decent campground. In general, Santa Rosa offers reasonably priced accommodations and easy access to Sonoma County and Valley.

Spring Lake Park
CAMPGROUND $

(☎ 707-539-8092, reservations 707-565-2267; www.sonomacountyparks.org; 5585 Newanga Ave; sites $32; ☺ campground May-Sep, weekends only Oct-Apr; ☀) ✐ Lovely lakeside park, 4 miles from downtown; make reservations online ($8.50 fee) or by phone 10am to 3pm weekdays. The park is open year-round, with lake swimming (complete with a floating playground) in summer. Take 4th St eastbound, turn right on Farmer's Lane, pass the first Hoen St and turn left on the second Hoen St, then left on Newanga Ave.

Hillside Inn
MOTEL $

(☎ 707-546-9353; www.hillside-inn.com; 2901 4th St; s/d $78/86; ☜☀) Santa Rosa's best-value motel, Hillside is close to Sonoma Valley; add $4 for kitchens. Furnishings are dated and service peculiar, but everything is scrupulously maintained. Adjoins an excellent breakfast cafe.

Sandman
INN $$

(☎ 707-293-2100; www.sandmansantarosa.com; 3421 Cleveland Ave; r $120-300; ☀@☜☀) Once Santa Rosa's best budget choice, Sandman has been revamped by new owners to feature a Southwestern aesthetic, quirky vintage furnishings and a hot bar replete with bamboo sofas and poolside cocktail window. The pool's heated and there's a hot tub.

Hotel La Rose
HISTORIC HOTEL $$

(☎ 707-579-3200; www.hotellarose.com; 308 Wilson St; r Mon-Fri $149-199, Sat & Sun $209-269; ☀☜) ✐ At Railroad Sq, Hotel La Rose has rooms in a well-kept historic 1907 brick hotel and across the street in a 1980s-built 'carriage house,' which feels like a small condo

complex with boxy, spacious rooms. All are decorated in out-of-fashion pastels but have excellent beds with quality linens and down duvets; some have jetted tubs.

Vintners Inn
INN $$$

(Map p210; ☎ 707-575-7350, 800-421-2584; www.vintnersinn.com; 4350 Barnes Rd; r $245-495; ☀@☜) ✐ Surrounded by 92 acres of vineyards north of town (near River Rd), Vintner's Inn caters to the gated-community crowd with business-class amenities. Complimentary wine tastings in the lobby at 5pm on Fridays. Check for last-minute specials.

Flamingo Conference Resort & Spa
HOTEL $$

(☎ 707-545-8530, 800-848-8300; www.flamingoresort.com; 2777 4th St; r $179-299; ☀@☜☀☀) ✐ Sprawling over 11 acres, this mid-century modern hotel doubles as a conference center. Rooms are business-class generic, but the pool is gigantic – and kept at 82ºF (28ºC) year-round. Kids love it. On-site health club and gym. Prices double on summer weekends.

Best Western Garden Inn
MOTEL $$

(☎ 707-546-4031; www.thegardeninn.com; 1500 Santa Rosa Ave; r Mon-Fri $119-139, Sat & Sun $199-229; ☀@☜☀☀) Recently renovated motel, south of downtown, with two pools and a hot tub. Rear rooms open to grassy gardens, but you may hear kids in the pool; book up front for quiet. The street gets seedy by night but the hotel is secure, clean and comfortable.

Best Western Wine Country Inn & Suites
HOTEL $$

(☎ 707-545-9000; www.winecountryhotel.com; 870 Hopper Ave; r Sun-Thu $135-140, Sat & Sun $180-220; ☀@☜☀☀) ✐ Pretty standard midrange chain hotel, off Cleveland Ave. There's a pool and some rooms have Jacuzzi.

🍴 Eating

Santa Rosa's culinary star is on the rise, with a solid selection of long-time international and farm-to-table restaurants and plenty of ambitious openings to keep things interesting.

Criminal Baking Co
BAKERY $

(☎ 707-888-3546; www.criminalbaking.com; 463 Sebastopol Ave; baked goods $1-5; ☺ 7:30am-4pm Mon-Fri, 8am-4pm Sat & Sun) A superior Santa Rosa bakery, with delicious vegan banana-walnut cookies, three-cheese knishes and supernutritious lunches such as the 'warrior bowl,' which comes with spinach, quinoa, potatoes, artichokes, bacon and goat's cheese. Don't miss the lavender lemonade.

Taqueria Las Palmas
MEXICAN $

(☑707-546-3091; 415 Santa Rosa Ave; dishes $4-11; ☺9am-9pm; 🖉) For Mexican, this is the real deal, with standout *carnitas* (barbecued pork), homemade salsas and veggie burritos.

Jeffrey's Hillside Cafe
AMERICAN $

(☑707-546-6317; www.jeffreyshillsidecafe.com; 2901 4th St; dishes $9-13; ☺7am-2pm; 🖃) 🍷 East of downtown, near Sonoma Valley, chef-owned Jeffrey's is excellent for breakfast or brunch before wine tasting.

Tasca Tasca
TAPAS $$

(Map p202; ☑707-996-8272; www.tascatasca. com; 122 W Napa St; 3/5/7 items $15/24/32; ☺noon-midnight) Specializing in Portuguese and Mediterranean fare, this new tapas tavern in food-obsessed downtown Sonoma holds its own. Try the authentic *caldo verde* (Portugal's national soup), along with one of the fabulous cheeses and the inventive Dungeness-crab empanadas with chipotle mayo. Wash everything down with the house-red sangria, made with passion fruit.

Yeti
NEPALI $$

(☑707-521-9608; www.yeticuisine.com; 190 Farmers Lane; mains lunch $12-17, dinner $18-25; ☺11:30am-2pm & 5-9:30pm) This places serves up spectacular Indian and Nepali dishes, and offers a brunch smorgasbord every Saturday and Sunday with spicy curries, *saag paneer* (spinach and paneer curry) and tikka masala (with both meat and veggie options).

Naked Pig
CAFE $$

(☑707-978-3231; 435 Santa Rosa Ave; mains $11-14; ☺8am-3pm Wed-Sun) 🍷 This tiny cafe in a former bus depot makes everything from scratch

---

OLIVE-OIL TASTING

When you weary of wine tasting, pop by one of the following olive-oil makers and dip some crusty bread – it's free. Harvest and pressing happen in November.

➡ BR Cohn (p200)

➡ Napa Valley Olive Oil Mfg Co (p183)

➡ Long Meadow Ranch (p177)

➡ Figone's Olive Oil (p206)

---

and serves simple-delicious, farm-to-table breakfasts and lunches at communal tables.

Rosso Pizzeria & Wine Bar
PIZZA $$

(☑707-546-6317; www.rossopizzeria.com; 53 Montgomery Dr, Creekside Shopping Center; pizzas $13-17; ☺11:30am-10pm; 🖃) 🍷 Fantastic wood-fired pizzas, inventive salads and standout wines make Rosso worth seeking out.

★Flower + Bone
INTERNATIONAL $$$

(☑707-708-8529; www.flowerandbonerestaurant. com; 640 5th St; mezes $11-18, 6-course prix fixe $67; ☺11am-3pm Wed, 6-9pm Thu-Sat) From the foraging, pickling, preserving Santa Rosa couple behind the Naked Pig comes Flower + Bone. The cuisine is inspired by ancient cooking techniques, including bone broths, pasture-raised meat and housemade hooch. The prix-fixe menu, also known as 'the full story,' is epic, with everything from foraged weeds to Polish dumplings. Dessert involves a gold-dusted truffle.

Spinster Sisters
CALIFORNIAN $$$

(☑707-528-7100; www.thespinstersisters.com; 401 South A St; mains lunch $10-16, dinner $23-26; ☺8am-2:30pm Mon, to 9pm Tue-Thu, to 10pm Fri, 9am-10pm Sat, to 2:30pm Sun) 🍷 At Santa Rosa's culinary vanguard, this casual market-driven restaurant makes its own bagels, cheese and charcuterie meats. The diverse tapas-like small plates ($7 to $14) pair well with the extensive wine list.

🍷 Drinking & Nightlife

There are a few decent pubs and bars around town, but Russian River Brewing Co is the social hub of Santa Rosa, drawing visitors from all over Northern California for its double IPA.

★Russian River Brewing Co
BREWERY

(☑707-545-2337; www.russianriverbrewing.com; 729 4th St; ☺11am-midnight) Santa Rosa's justly famous brewery crafts a wildly popular double IPA called Pliny the Elder, plus top-grade sour beer aged in wine barrels. Good pizza and pub grub too.

A'Roma Roasters
CAFE

(☑707-576-7765; www.aromaroasters.com; 95 5th St, Railroad Sq; ☺6am-11pm Mon-Thu, to midnight Fri, 7am-midnight Sat, to 10pm Sun; 🖥) Town's hippest cafe serves no booze, but hosts acoustic music Saturday evenings.

ℹ Information

MEDICAL SERVICES

Santa Rosa Memorial Hospital (☑707-525-5300; www.stjoesonoma.org; 1165 Montgomery Dr; ⊙24hr) Wide range of health services; houses the region's trauma center.

TOURIST INFORMATION

California Welcome Center & Santa Rosa Visitors Bureau (☑707-577-8674, 800-404-7673; www.visitsantarosa.com; 9 4th St; ⊙9am-5pm) Same-day lodging assistance. At Railroad Sq, west of Hwy 101; take downtown exit from Hwy 12 or 101.

ℹ Getting There & Away

Sonoma County Airport Express (p173) runs shuttles ($34) between Sonoma County Airport (Santa Rosa) and San Francisco and Oakland airports.

Golden Gate Transit (p117) buses run between San Francisco and Santa Rosa (adult/youth $13/6.50); board at 1st and Mission Sts in San Fran.

Greyhound (p173) buses run from San Francisco to Santa Rosa ($21 to $38).

Healdsburg & Around

Once a sleepy ag town best known for its Future Farmers of America parade, Healdsburg has emerged as northern Sonoma County's culinary capital. Foodie-scenester restaurants and cafes, wine-tasting rooms and fancy boutiques line Healdsburg Plaza, the town's sun-dappled central square (bordered by Healdsburg Ave and Center, Matheson and Plaza Sts).

Traffic grinds to a halt on summer weekends, when second-home-owners and tourists jam downtown. Old-timers aren't happy with the Napa-style gentrification but at least Healdsburg retains its historic look, if not its once-quiet summers. It's best visited weekdays – stroll tree-lined streets, sample locavore cooking and soak up the NorCal flavor.

◉ Sights

Tasting rooms surround the plaza.

Saturday Market MARKET
(www.healdsburgfarmersmarket.org; ⊙9am-noon Sat May-Dec) Healdsburg's downtown farmers market.

Wednesday Market MARKET
(☑707-824-8717; cnr Vine & North Sts; ⊙3:30-6pm Wed Jun-Nov) Healdsburg's weekday farmers market.

Locals Tasting Room TASTING ROOM
(☑707-857-4900; www.tastelocalwines.com; Geyserville Ave & Hwy 128; ⊙11am-6pm) FREE Eight miles north of Healdsburg, tiny Geyserville is home to this indie tasting room, which represents 10 small-production wineries with free tastings.

Healdsburg Public Library LIBRARY
(☑707-433-3772; www.sonomalibrary.org; cnr Piper & Center Sts; ⊙10am-9pm Mon & Wed, to 6pm Tue, Thu & Fri, to 4pm Sat) Wine Country's leading oenology-reference library.

Healdsburg Veterans Memorial Beach BEACH
(Map p210; ☑707-433-1625; www.sonomacountyparks.org; 13839 Old Redwood Hwy; per car $7; ⊙7am-30min before sunset; P🚻) You can swim at this in-town beach between July and early September – lifeguards are on duty summer weekends. The fastidious can confirm current water quality online (www.sonoma-county.org/health/services/freshwater.asp).

Healdsburg Museum MUSEUM
(☑707-431-3325; www.healdsburgmuseum.org; 221 Matheson St; donation requested; ⊙11am-4pm Wed-Sun) Rotating exhibits include compelling installations on northern Sonoma County history, with an emphasis on Healdsburg. Pick up the walking-tour pamphlet.

🏃 Activities

After you've walked around the plaza, there isn't much to do in town. Go wine tasting in Dry Creek Valley or Russian River Valley. Bicycling on winding W Dry Creek Rd is brilliant, as is paddling the Russian River, which runs through town. Rent bikes from Spoke Folk Cyclery (p175).

River's Edge Kayak & Canoe Trips KAYAKING, CANOEING
(☑707-433-7247; www.riversedgekayakandcanoe.com; 13840 Healdsburg Ave; kayak/canoe rental & shuttle from $50/100) Rents hard-sided canoes and kayaks (single and double) for self-guided river tours that include a shuttle.

Russian River Adventures
CANOEING

(☎707-433-5599, 800-280-7627; www.russianriver adventures.com; 20 Healdsburg Ave; half-day canoe rental & shuttle adult/child from $45/25; 🖈) Paddle a secluded stretch of river in quiet inflatable canoes, stopping for rope swings, swimming holes, beaches and bird-watching. This ecotourism outfit points you in the right direction and shuttles you back at day's end. Or they'll guide your kids downriver while you go wine tasting (guides $125 per day). Reservations required.

👉 Tours

Getaway Adventures
CYCLING, KAYAKING

(☎800-499-2453; www.getawayadventures.com; tours 1-day $139-175, multiday $899-2500) Guides a variety of hiking, biking and kayaking tours in Dry Creek Valley, varying in length and difficulty. For example, a one-day tour might include spectacular morning vineyard cycling in Dry Creek Valley, followed by lunch and optional kayaking on Russian River.

🗣 Courses

Relish Culinary Adventures
COOKING

(☎707-431-9999; www.relishculinary.com; 14 Matheson St; ⊙ by appointment) Plug into the locavore food scene with culinary day trips, demo-kitchen classes or winemaker dinners.

🎉 Festivals & Events

Russian River Wine Road Barrel Tasting
WINE

(www.wineroad.com; ⊙ Mar) Sample wine, directly from the cask, before it's bottled or released for sale.

Future Farmers Parade
CULTURAL

(www.healdsburgfair.org; ⊙ May) The whole town shows up for this classic-Americana farm parade, which kicks off a country fair.

Wine & Food Affair
FOOD & DRINK

(www.wineroad.com/events/wine-food-affair; ⊙ Nov) Special food and wine pairings at over 100 wineries.

🛏 Sleeping

Healdsburg is expensive: demand exceeds supply. Rates drop winter to spring, but not significantly. Guerneville is much less expensive and just 20 minutes away. Most Healdsburg inns are within walking distance of the plaza; several B&Bs are in surrounding countryside. Find motels at Hwy 101's Dry Creek exit.

Cloverdale Wine Country KOA
CAMPGROUND $

(☎707-894-3337, 800-562-4042; www.winecoun trykoa.com; 1166 Asti Ridge Rd, Cloverdale; tent/RV sites from $50/65, 1-/2-bedroom cabins $85/95; 🛜🐕♿) Six miles from central Cloverdale (exit 520) off Hwy 101; hot showers, pool, hot tub, laundry, paddleboats and bicycles.

L&M Motel
MOTEL $$

(☎707-433-6528; www.landmmotel.com; 70 Healdsburg Ave; r $175-195; 🅿🐕❄🛜🐕♿) This simple, clean, old-fashioned motel with big lawns and barbecue grills is great for families. There's an indoor swimming pool, Jacuzzi and dry cedar sauna too. Breakfast included. Winter rates plummet.

Geyserville Inn
MOTEL $$

(☎877-857-4343, 707-857-4343; www.geyserville inn.com; 21714 Geyserville Ave, Geyserville; r Mon-Fri $160-205, Sat & Sun $269-315; 🅿🐕❄🛜♿) Eight miles north of Healdsburg, this immaculately kept upmarket motel is surrounded by vineyards. Rooms have unexpectedly smart furnishings and quality extras such as feather pillows. Request a remodeled room. There's a solar-heated pool and a hot tub.

Best Western Dry Creek
MOTEL $$

(☎707-433-0300; www.drycreekinn.com; 198 Dry Creek Rd; r Mon-Wed $143-198, Thu-Sun $187-239; ❄@🛜♿) This generic midrange motel has good service and an outdoor hot tub. New rooms have jetted tubs and gas fireplaces.

★ Hotel Healdsburg
HOTEL $$$

(☎707-431-2800; www.hotelhealdsburg.com; 25 Matheson St; r from $499; ❄@🛜♿) Smack on the plaza, the fashion-forward HH has a coolly minimalist style of concrete and velvet, with requisite top-end amenities, including sumptuous beds and extradeep tubs. There's a full-service spa. The restaurant, Dry Creek Kitchen, is run by celebchef Charlie Palmer.

Madrona Manor
HISTORIC HOTEL $$$

(☎800-258-4003, 707-433-4231; www.madrona manor.com; 1001 Westside Rd; r Mon-Fri $255-655; ❄🛜♿) The first choice of lovers of country inns and stately manor homes, the regal 1881 Madrona Manor exudes Victorian elegance. Surrounded by 8 acres of woods and gorgeous century-old gardens, the hilltop mansion is decked out with many original furnishings. A mile west of downtown, it's convenient to Westside Rd wineries.

Belle de Jour Inn   B&B $$$
(⌨707-431-9777; www.belledejourinn.com; 16276 Healdsburg Ave; r $225-295, ste $355; ❋🛜) Charming Belle de Jour's sunny, uncluttered rooms have American-country furnishings, with extras such as private entrances, sundried sheets and jetted tubs. The manicured gardens are ready-made for a moonlight tryst.

Camellia Inn   B&B $$$
(⌨707-433-8182, 800-727-8182; www.camelliainn.com; 211 North St; r $159-395; ❋🛜⊞) Elegantly furnished 1869 mansion, with (among others) a rare-for-Healdsburg budget room ($159), plus a two-bed family room ($269). There are no TVs, but iPads are provided. Also, the innkeeper is really nice.

**Healdsburg Inn
on the Plaza**   INN $$$
(⌨800-431-8663, 707-433-6991; www.healdsburginn.com; 112 Matheson St; r $295-460; ❋🛜⊞) The spiffy, clean-lined rooms, conservatively styled in khaki and beige, feel bourgeois summer-house casual, with fine linen and gas fireplace; some have jetted double tub. The plaza-front location explains the price.

H2 Hotel   HOTEL $$$
(⌨707-431-2202; www.h2hotel.com; 219 Healdsburg Ave; r Mon-Fri $269-389, Sat & Sun $399-699; P❄❋@🛜⊞⊞) ✏ Little sister to Hotel Healdsburg, H2 has the same angular concrete style, but was built LEED-gold-certified from the ground up, with a living roof, reclaimed everything and fresh-looking rooms with bamboo floors and organic-cotton linens. Also has a heated saltwater pool and free bikes. Waters, snacks and espresso are complimentary.

Haydon Street Inn   B&B $$$
(⌨707-433-5228; www.haydon.com; 321 Haydon St; r $210-350, cottages $425-450; ❋🛜) Two-story Queen Anne with big front porch and separate cottage.

Honor Mansion   INN $$$
(⌨707-433-4277, 800-554-4667; www.honormansion.com; 891 Grove St; r $450-695; ❋🛜⊞) Elegant 1883 Victorian mansion with spectacular resort-like grounds, cushy rooms and great service.

✗ Eating

Healdsburg is the gastronomic capital of Sonoma County. Your hardest decision will be choosing where to eat. Reservations essential.

★ Shed   CAFE $$
(⌨707-431-7433; www.healdsburgshed.com; 25 North St; dinner mains $15-30; ☺8am-9pm Wed-Mon, to 6pm Tue; 🖐) ✏ At the vanguard of locavore eating, the Shed integrates food at all stages of production, milling its own locally sourced grain flours, fermenting vinegars and kombucha from local fruit and growing its own produce. It comprises a cafe with wood-fired dishes, a fermentation bar with homegrown shrubs, a coffee bar with stellar pastries and a market with prepared-to-go foods.

Reason enough to visit Healdsburg, the Shed is not a restaurant per se, but a dynamic multiuse culinary center, like a modern-day grange built of glass, nudging diners to see through what they're eating and take an active role in the future of food. Events, such as movie nights, biodynamic cannabis panel discussions and sushi-making workshops, are held upstairs.

Costeaux French Bakery & Cafe   CAFE $$
(⌨707-433-1913; www.costeaux.com; 417 Healdsburg Ave; mains $10-13; ☺cafe 7am-3pm Mon-Sat, to 1pm Sun, bakery to 4pm Mon-Thu, to 5pm Sat & Sun; 🛜) This cavernous bakery-cafe is good for an easy lunch of salads and sandwiches on house-baked bread, plus all-day breakfast dishes including omelets and scrambles.

Diavola   ITALIAN, CALIFORNIAN $$
(⌨707-814-0111; www.diavolapizzera.com; 21021 Geyserville Ave, Geyserville; mains $16-29; ☺11:30am-9pm; 🖐) ✏ Ideal for lunch while wine tasting in Alexander Valley, Diavola makes outstanding *salumi* and thin-crust pizzas, served in an Old West, brick-walled space, loud enough to drown out the kids.

Healdsburg Bar & Grill   PUB FOOD $$
(⌨707-433-3333; www.healdsburgbarandgrill.com; 245 Healdsburg Ave; mains $11-23; ☺11am-9pm Mon-Fri, 9am-9pm Sat & Sun) *Top Chef Masters* winner Doug Keane's gastropub is perfect when you're famished but don't want to fuss. Expect simple classics – mac 'n' cheese, pulled-pork sandwiches, top-end burgers and truffle-parmesan fries. At breakfast, look for homemade waffles and English

muffins fresh from Costeaux Bakery. Sit in the garden.

★**Madrona Manor**   CALIFORNIAN $$$
(☑707-433-4231, 800-258-4003; www.madrona manor.com; 1001 Westside Rd; 11-course menu $165; ⊙6-9pm Wed-Sun) *⊘* You'd be hard-pressed to find a lovelier place to propose than this retro-formal Victorian mansion's garden-view verandah – though there's nothing old-fashioned about the artful haute cuisine: the kitchen churns its own butter, each course comes with a different variety of just-baked bread, courses include items such as Monterey abalone and Hokkaido-scallop crudo, and there's frozen lemon verbena for dessert. Reserve a presunset table.

★**SingleThread Farm-Restaurant-Inn**   JAPANESE $$$
(☑707-723-4646; www.singlethreadfarms.com; 131 North St; tasting menu per person $293; ⊙5:30-11pm Tue-Sun) The most ambitious project in Northern California is SingleThread, a world-class restaurant and, secondarily, an inn, where *omotenashi* (warm hospitality in Japanese) reigns and dishes from an 11-course tasting menu are prepared in handmade Japanese *donabe* (earthenware pots). The cuisine is California-Japanese and guests book tickets in advance, offering up their preferences and dietary restrictions, and the chef abides.

On arrival, guests are taken to a roof to enjoy sparkling wine, canapes and 360-degree views of the countryside before sitting down to feast. The sleek space features its own fermentation tank, which local winemakers use to craft a new vintage each year, along with a boutique **hotel** offering five sumptuous rooms starting at $800 a night. Down the road, the owners have a 5-acre organic garden where they farm specialized Japanese produce, hens and flowers.

Valette   CALIFORNIAN $$$
(☑707-473-0946; www.valettehealdsburg.com; 344 Center St; 'trust me' tasting menu per course $15, minimum 4 courses; ⊙5:30-9:30pm) If you're looking to impress somebody, Healdsburg residents suggest Valette. The sleek American restaurant is regularly packed with suits and fancy ladies making a show of swirling their local wine (corkage fee is only $20) and ordering the multicourse 'trust me' tasting menu, where the gifted chef asks what you're into then decides what to feed you.

The scallop dish, which is baked within a squid-inked puffy pastry and bathed in caviar-studded champagne beurre blanc, is otherworldly.

Barndiva   CALIFORNIAN $$$
(☑707-431-0100; www.barndiva.com; 231 Center St; mains lunch $16-24, dinner $28-38; ⊙noon-2:30pm & 5:30-9pm Wed-Sat, from 11am Sun) *⊘* Impeccable seasonal-regional cooking, happening bar, beautiful garden, but service sometimes misses.

Bravas Bar de Tapas   TAPAS $$$
(☑707-433-7700; www.starkrestaurants.com/stark-restaurant/bravas-bar-de-tapas; 420 Center St; tapas $7-16, family-style large plates $28-74; ⊙11:30am-9pm Sun-Thu, to 10pm Fri & Sat) This beloved tapas restaurant is part of the distinguished Stark restaurant chain and serves up Spanish cuisine, including the ever-popular paella, on small and large plates to share. The back patio is particularly lovely on a warm evening and the vast menu includes everything from crispy pig ears to duck-meatball sliders. Good sangria too.

Mateo's Cocina Latina   FUSION $$$
(☑707-433-1520; www.mateoscocinalatina.com; 214 Healdsburg Ave; mains lunch $12-19, dinner $14-35; ⊙11am-9pm Wed-Sun) *⊘* Here the upmarket Yucatan-inspired cooking at lunch and the California-French fusion dishes in the evening integrate fine technique and all-local ingredients for standout dishes, such as daily beef cuts and *cochinita pibil* (a pork dish cooked with annatto seed), whose subtle flavors shine through the spice. The full bar showcases rare tequilas and mescals. Make reservations; request a garden table.

Self-Catering

Downtown Bakery & Creamery   BAKERY $
(☑707-431-2719; 308a Center St; ⊙6am-5:30pm Mon-Fri, 7am-5:30pm Sat, 7am-4pm Sun) Healdsburg's classic bakery makes perfect breakfast pastries and specialty breads.

Noble Folk Ice Cream & Pie Bar   DESSERTS $
(☑707-395-4426; www.thenoblefolk.com; 116 Matheson St; items $3-6; ⊙noon-9pm; 🖼) *⊘* Hand-crafted ice cream and classic American pie, made with top-quality, all-local ingredients.

Moustache Baked Goods   BAKERY $
(☑707-395-4111; www.moustachebakedgoods.com; 381 Healdsburg Ave; cupcakes $3.50;

⊙11am-7pm) 🍴 Incredible locavore small-batch sweets (some gluten-free), including scrumptious cupcakes in unusual combos such as maple-bacon (available seasonally).

Shelton's Natural Foods Market   MARKET, DELI $
(☏707-431-0530; www.sheltonsmarket.com; 428 Center St; ⊙8am-8pm) 🍴 Indie alternative for groceries and picnic supplies; reasonably priced.

Jimtown Store   DELI, MARKET $$
(☏707-433-1212; www.jimtown.com; 6706 Hwy 128; sandwiches $8-13; ⊙7am-3pm Sun, Mon & Wed-Fri, 7:30am-4pm Sat) One of our favorite Alexander Valley stopovers, Jimtown is great for picnic supplies and sandwiches spread with housemade condiments.

Oakville Grocery   DELI $$
(☏707-433-3200; www.oakvillegrocery.com; 124 Matheson St; sandwiches $10-15; ⊙5am-5pm) Fancy sandwiches and grab-and-go gourmet picnics. It's pricey, but the plaza-view fireside terrace is ever so fun for scouting Botox blonds, while nibbling cheese and sipping vino.

🍸 Drinking & Nightlife

Healdsburg is not a party town, but there are some good craft breweries and a new cocktail bar that stays open on weekends till (gasp!) 2am.

Bear Republic Brewing Company   BREWERY
(☏707-433-2337; www.bearrepublic.com; 345 Healdsburg Ave; ⊙11am-9:30pm Sun-Thu, to 10pm Fri & Sat) Bear Republic features hand-crafted award-winning ales, non-award-winning pub grub, weekly trivia and monthly comedy nights.

Duke's Spirited Cocktails   COCKTAIL BAR
(☏707-431-1060; www.healdsburgcottages.com; 111 Plaza St; ⊙4pm-midnight Sun-Thu, 4pm-2am Fri, 2pm-2am Sat) The town's new cocktail bar is as popular for its crafty libations as it is for staying open beyond midnight on weekends, which is pretty much unheard of in Healdsburg. Also the drinks have really cute names such as 'Unicorn Tears' and 'Mr Bojangles.'

Flying Goat Coffee   CAFE
(www.flyinggoatcoffee.com; 324 Center St; ⊙7am-7pm) 🍴 See ya later, Starbucks. Flying Goat is what coffee should be – fair-trade and house-roasted – and locals line up for it every morning.

☆ Entertainment

In summer free summer concerts take place each Tuesday afternoon in the plaza.

Raven Performing Arts Theater   THEATER
(☏707-433-6335; www.ravenfilmcenter.com; 115 North St) Hosts concerts, events and first-run art-house films.

🛍 Shopping

One World   GIFTS & SOUVENIRS
(☏707-473-0880; www.oneworldfairtrade.net; 104 Matheson St; ⊙10am-6pm, to 5:30pm Sun) 🍴 Household goods with a global outlook: alpaca shawls to Vietnamese trivets to cashmere shawls from Tibet, sourced from fair-trade collectives in 58 countries.

Copperfield's Books   BOOKS
(☏707-433-9270; www.copperfieldsbooks.com; 104 Matheson St; ⊙9am-7pm Sun-Thu, to 8pm Fri & Sat) Good general-interest books.

Options Gallery   CRAFTS, JEWELRY
(☏707-431-8861; www.optionsgallery.com; 126 Matheson St; ⊙10:30am-5:30pm Mon-Sat, 11am-4pm Sun) Gifts, crafts and jewelry by local artists, including lovely earrings.

Gardener   GARDENS
(☏707-431-1063; www.thegardener.com; 516 Dry Creek Rd; ⊙10am-5pm) 🍴 Garden-shop lovers: don't miss this rural beauty.

Levin & Company   BOOKS, MUSIC
(☏707-433-1118; 306 Center St; ⊙9am-9pm Mon-Sat, 10am-6pm Sun) Fiction and CDs; co-op art gallery.

ℹ Information

Healdsburg Chamber of Commerce & Visitors Bureau (Map p210; ☏800-648-9922, 707-433-6935; www.healdsburg.com; 217 Healdsburg Ave; ⊙10am-4pm Mon-Fri, to 3pm Sat & Sun) A block south of the plaza. Has winery maps and information on ballooning, golf, tennis, spas and nearby farms; 24-hour walk-up booth.

ℹ Getting There & Away

Sonoma County Transit (p173) buses travel around Healdsburg and connect it to neighboring cities, with prices ranging from $1.50 to $4.80 depending on how many zones you pass through on your journey. Youth prices range from $1.25 to $4.55.

Healdsburg is about an 80-minute drive north from San Francisco.

North Coast & Redwoods

Best Places to Eat

➡ Saw Shop Bistro (p254)

➡ Brick & Fire (p265)

➡ Saucy Ukiah (p258)

➡ Taka's Japanese Grill (p249)

➡ Fishetarian Fish Market (p234)

Best Places to Sleep

➡ Alegria (p245)

➡ Philo Apple Farm Guest Cottages (p257)

➡ Bay Hill Mansion (p234)

➡ Elk Cove Inn & Spa (p242)

➡ Didjeridoo Dreamtime Inn (p244)

Why Go?

This is not the legendary California of the Beach Boys' song – there are no palm-flanked beaches and very few surfboards. The jagged edge of the continent is wild, scenic and even slightly foreboding, where spectral fog and an outsider spirit have fostered the world's tallest trees, most potent weed and a string of idiosyncratic two-stoplight towns. Explore hidden coves with a blanket and a bottle of local wine, scan the horizon for migrating whales and retreat at night to fire-warmed Victorians. As you travel further north, find valleys of redwood, wide rivers and mossy, overgrown forests. Expect cooler, damper weather too. Befitting this dramatic clash of land and water are its unlikely mélange of residents: timber barons and tree huggers, pot farmers and radicals of every political persuasion.

When to Go
Eureka

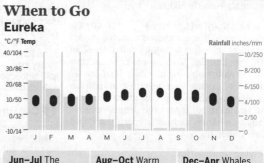

Jun–Jul The driest season in the Redwoods is spectacular for day hikes and big views.

Aug–Oct Warm weather and clear skies are the best for hiking the Lost Coast.

Dec–Apr Whales migrate off the coast. In early spring look for mothers and calves.

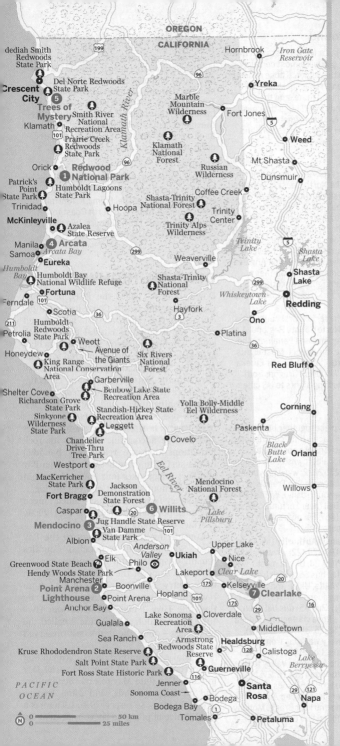

North Coast & Redwoods Highlights

1 Hiking along meandering trails of **Redwood National Park** (p279), flanked by virgin redwood forests that will give you a crick in your neck.

2 Climbing to the top of historic **Point Arena Lighthouse** (p240) for sweeping views over the extraordinary coastline.

3 Admiring the dazzle of plants and flowers at the coast-side **Mendocino Coast Botanical Gardens** (p248).

4 Sipping the samplers at brewpub **Six Rivers Brewery** (p275) near Arcata; one of the best in Northern California.

5 Indulging in some all-American roadside kitsch along Hwy 101 at **Trees of Mystery** (p282).

6 Discovering the life of early settlers via the excellent **Mendocino County Museum** (p261) in Willits.

7 Enjoying the wonderful retro experience of a drive-in movie at the classic **Lakeport Auto Movies** (p255) in Clearlake.

❶ Getting Around

Although Hwy 1 is popular with cyclists and there are bus connections, you will almost certainly need a car to explore this region. Those headed to the far north and on a schedule should take Hwy 101, the faster, inland route, and then cut over to the coast. Windy Hwy 1 hugs the coast, then cuts inland and ends at Leggett, where it joins Hwy 101. Neither Amtrak nor Greyhound serve cities on coastal Hwy 1.

AIR

Arcata-Eureka Airport (p272) is located north of McKinleyville on the North Coast, signposted west of Hwy 101. **Alaska Airlines** (☑1-800-252-722; www.alaskaair.com), **Penair** (www.penair.com), Delta, American Airlines and United Airlines are the main carriers to operate national flights to/from here but fares tend to be high. Flights come and go from several major Californian cities, including Los Angeles, San Francisco, Sacramento and San Diego. There are also regular flights from other US cities, including New York, Denver, Phoenix and Portland (Oregon).

In the far north of the region, Crescent City is home to the tiny Del Norte County Regional Airport (p284). Alaska Airlines and Penair are the main carriers to serve this airport. Most flights contact with the nearby hubs of Arcata-Eureka Airport and Portland Airport in Oregon, from where there are connecting flights to US cities further afield.

BUS

Brave souls willing to piece together bus travel through the region will face a time-consuming headache, but connections are possible to most (but certainly not all!) towns in the region. **Greyhound** (☑800-231-2222; www.greyhound.com; 🕸) runs buses between San Francisco and Ukiah ($44, three hours, daily), Willits ($44, 3½ hours, daily), Rio Dell (near Fortuna; $57, six hours, daily), Eureka ($57, 6¾ hours, daily) and Arcata ($57, seven hours, daily).

The **Mendocino Transit Authority** (MTA; ☑800-696-4682, 707-462-1422; www.mendocinotransit.org; 241 Plant Rd, Ukiah; most 1-way fares $1.50-6) operates bus 65, which travels between Fort Bragg, Willits, Ukiah and Santa Rosa daily, with an afternoon return ($26.25, three hours, four daily). Bus 95 runs between Point Arena and Santa Rosa via Jenner, Bodega Bay and Sebastopol ($8.25, 3¼ hours, daily). Bus 75 heads north every weekday from Gualala to the Navarro River junction at Hwy 128, then runs inland through the Anderson Valley to Ukiah, returning in the afternoon ($6.75, 2½ hours, daily). The North Coast route 60 goes north between Navarro River junction and Albion, Little River, Mendocino and Fort Bragg, Monday to Friday ($2.25, 1½ hours, two daily).

North of Mendocino County, the **Redwood Transit System** (☑707-443-0826; www.redwoodtransit.org) operates buses ($3) Monday through Saturday between Scotia and Trinidad (2½ hours), stopping en route at Eureka (1¼ hours) and Arcata (1½ hours). **Redwood Coast Transit** (☑707-464-9314; www.redwoodcoasttransit.org) runs buses Monday to Saturday between Crescent City, Klamath ($1.50, one hour, three daily) and Arcata ($30, two hours, three daily), with numerous stops along the way.

TRAIN

Amtrak (☑800-872-7245; www.amtrakcalifornia.com) operates the Coast Starlight between Los Angeles and Seattle. From LA, Amtrak buses connect to several North Coast towns, including Leggett ($87, 11 hours, two daily) and Garberville ($87, 11½ hours, two daily).

COASTAL HIGHWAY 1

Down south it's called the 'PCH,' or Pacific Coast Hwy, but North Coast locals simply call it 'Hwy 1.' However you label it, get ready for a fabulous coastal drive, which cuts a winding course on isolated cliffs high above the crashing surf. Compared to the famous Big Sur coast, the serpentine stretch of Hwy 1 up the North Coast is more challenging, more remote and more *real,* passing farms, fishing towns and hidden beaches. Drivers use roadside pullouts to scan the hazy Pacific horizon for migrating whales and explore a coastline dotted with rock formations that are relentlessly pounded by the surf. The drive between Bodega Bay and Fort Bragg takes four hours of daylight driving without stops. At night in the fog, it takes steely nerves and much, much longer. The most popular destination is the cliffside charmer of Mendocino.

Considering their proximity to the Bay Area, Sonoma and Mendocino Counties remain unspoiled, and the austere coastal bluffs are some of the most spectacular in the country. But the trip north gets more rewarding and remote with every mile. By the time Hwy 1 cuts inland to join Hwy 101, the land along the Pacific – called the Lost Coast – offers the state's best-preserved natural gifts.

Coastal accommodations (including campgrounds) can fill from Memorial Day to Labor Day (late May to early September) and on fall weekends, and often require two-night stays, so reserve ahead. There is a good choice of places to lay your head along the highway, although the budget conscious may find a definite lack of chain motels in these parts.

Bodega Bay

Bodega Bay is the first pearl in a string of sleepy fishing towns that line the North Coast and was the setting of Hitchcock's terrifying 1963 avian psycho-horror flick *The Birds*. The skies are free from bloodthirsty gulls today (though you'd best keep an eye on the picnic); it's Bay Area weekenders who descend en masse for extraordinary beaches, tide pools, whale-watching, fishing, surfing and seafood. Mostly a few restaurants, hotels and shops on both sides of Hwy 1, the downtown is not made for strolling, but it is a great base for exploring the endless nearby coves of the Sonoma Coast State Beach. Hwy 1 runs through town and along the east side of Bodega Bay. On the west side, a peninsula resembling a crooked finger juts out to sea, forming the entrance to Bodega Harbor.

⊙ Sights & Activities

Surfing, beachcombing and sportfishing are the main activities here – the latter requires advance booking. From December to April, the fishing boats host whale-watching trips, which are also good to book ahead. Just about everyone in town sells kites, which are great for flying at Bodega Head. The excellent **Farm Trails** (www.farmtrails.org) guide at the Sonoma Coast Visitor Center has suggestions for tours of local ranches, orchards, farms and apiaries.

Bodega Head   VIEWPOINT
(Bay Flat Rd) At the peninsula's tip, Bodega Head rises 265ft above sea level. It's great for whale-watching. Landlubbers enjoy hiking above the surf, where several good trails include a 3.75-mile trek to Bodega Dunes Campground and a 2.2-mile walk to Salmon Creek Ranch. Head west from Hwy 1 onto Eastshore Rd, then turn right at the stop sign onto Bay Flat Rd.

Ren Brown Collection Gallery   GALLERY
(☑707-875-2922; www.renbrown.com; 1781 Hwy 1; ⊙10am-5pm Wed-Sun) The renowned collection of modern Japanese prints and California works at this small gallery is a tranquil escape from the elements. Check out the Japanese garden at the back.

**Bodega Marine Laboratory
& Reserve**   SCIENCE CENTER
(☑707-875-2211; www.bml.ucdavis.edu; 2099 Westshore Rd; ⊙2-4pm Fri; P) FREE Run by University of California (UC) Davis, this spectacularly diverse teaching and research reserve surrounds the research lab, which has studied Bodega Bay since the 1920s. The 263-acre reserve hosts many marine environments, including rocky intertidal coastal areas, mudflats and sand flats, salt marsh, sand dunes and freshwater wetlands. On most Friday afternoons docents give tours of the lab and surrounds.

Chanslor Ranch   HORSEBACK RIDING
(☑707-875-3333,707-875-2721; www.horsenaround trailrides.com; 2660 N Hwy 1; rides from $125; ⊙10am-5pm; ⊕) Just north of town, this friendly outfit leads horseback expeditions along the coastline and the rolling inland hills. Ron, the trip leader, is an amiable, sun-weathered cowboy straight from central casting; he recommends taking the Salmon Creek ride or calling ahead for weather-permitting moonlight rides. The 90-minute beach rides are justifiably popular.

BLOODTHIRSTY BIRDS OF BODEGA BAY

Bodega Bay has the enduring claim to fame as the setting for Alfred Hitchcock's *The Birds*. Although special effects radically altered the actual layout of the town, you still get a good feel for the supposed site of the farm owned by Mitch Brenner (played by Rod Taylor). The once-cozy Tides Wharf & Restaurant (p235), where much avian-caused havoc occurs in the movie, is still there but since 1962 it has been transformed into a vast restaurant complex. Venture 5 miles inland to the tiny town of Bodega and you'll find two icons from the film: the schoolhouse and the church. Both stand just as they did in the movie – a crow overhead may make the hair rise on your neck.

Coincidentally, right after production of *The Birds* began, a real-life bird attack occurred in Capitola, the sleepy seaside town south of Santa Cruz. Thousands of seagulls ran amok, destroying property and attacking people.

NORTH COAST & REDWOODS BODEGA BAY

Bodega Bay

Sportfishing Center FISHING, WHALE-WATCHING
(☑707-875-3495; www.bodegacharters.com; 1410b Bay Flat Rd; fishing trips $135, whale-watching adult/child $50/35; ☻) Beside the Sandpiper Cafe, this outfit organizes full-day fishing trips and three-hour whale-watching excursions. It also sells bait, tackle and fishing licenses. Call ahead to ask about recent sightings.

Bodega Bay Surf Shack SURFING
(☑707-875-3944; www.bodegabaysurf.com; 1400 N Hwy 1, Pelican Plaza; surfboard/SUP/kayak/bike rental from $17/40/45/16) If you want to get on the water, this easygoing one-stop shop has all kinds of rentals, lessons and good local information. It also rents bikes for landlubbers.

🎉 Festivals & Events

Bodega Bay Fishermen's Festival CULTURAL
(www.bbfishfest.org; ☉ Apr) At the end of April, this festival culminates in a blessing of the fleet, a flamboyant parade of vessels, an arts-and-crafts fair, kite-flying and feasting.

Bodega Seafood, Art & Wine Festival FOOD & DRINK
(www.winecountryfestivals.com; 16855 Bodega Hwy, Watt's Ranch; ☉10am-6pm Sat, to 5pm Sun late Aug; ☻) Held over a weekend in late August, this festival of food and drink brings together the best beer- and wine-makers of the area, tons of seafood and activities for kids. It takes place in the town of Bodega.

🛌 Sleeping

There's a wide spread of options – RV and tent camping, quaint motels, B&Bs and fancy hotels. Several have lovely views of the bay and all fill up early during peak seasons and at weekends. Campers should consider heading just north of town to the state-operated sites.

Doran Regional Park CAMPGROUND $
(www.parks.sonomacounty.ca.gov; 201 Doran Park Rd; tent sites $7, RV sites without hookups $32; ☉7am-sunset; P☻) Watch for the sign if you are approaching town from the south. There are a few campsites here and easy access to the protected 2-mile Doran Beach, which has a boat launch and picnic areas.

Westside Regional Park CAMPGROUND $
(www.parks.sonomacounty.ca.gov; 2400 Westshore Rd; tent sites $7, RV sites without hookups $32; ☉7am-sunset) This park caters mainly for RVs and boaters. It has windy exposures, beaches, hot showers, fishing and boat ramps.

Chanslor Guest Ranch RANCH $$
(☑707-875-2721; www.chanslorranch.com; 2660 Hwy 1; campsites $50, r from $144) A mile north of town, this working horse ranch has rooms and options for upscale camping. Wildlife programs and guided horse tours make this one sweet place, with sweeping vistas across open grasslands to the sea.

★ **Bay Hill Mansion** B&B $$$
(☑877-468-1588; www.bayhillmansion.com; 3919 Bay Hill Rd; d $279-299; P☻🅿☻☻) A luxe B&B in a spacious, modern mansion. The decor is tasteful and the cleanliness and comfort standards are some of the best we've ever seen. Get a private yoga class or massage, then the helpful hosts, Kirtis and Kristopher, can direct you to the area's best spots. Views overlook trees with just a peek at the bay.

The daily breakfast is more like a brunch, with a vast selection of delicious fare on offer. Other perks include a complimentary bottle of wine on arrival, cocktails at dusk and Nespresso machines in all rooms.

Bodega Bay Lodge & Spa LODGE $$$
(☑707-875-3525; www.bodegabaylodge.com; Doran Beach Rd; r $190-470; P☻@☻☻) Bodega's plushest option, this small oceanfront resort has an ocean-view swimming pool, a golf course, a Jacuzzi and a state-of-the-art fitness club. In the evenings it hosts wine tastings. The more expensive rooms have commanding views, but all have balconies. The other pluses on-site include Bodega Bay's best spa and Drakes restaurant, which is the fanciest dining in town.

🍴 Eating & Drinking

For the old-fashioned thrill of seafood by the docks, there are several options where you can enjoy sea views, along with a simple menu of clam chowder, fried fish and coleslaw. There are also fish and produce markets in town where self-caterers can pick up supplies, and a fair range of other eateries specializing in everything from fast-food hotdogs to Tex-Mex and super-sophisticated offerings.

★ **Fishetarian Fish Market** CALIFORNIAN $
(☑707-480-9037; www.fishetarianfishmarket.com; 599 Hwy 1; mains from $12; ☉11am-6pm Mon-Thu & Sun, to 7pm Fri & Sat; P☻☻) A fish market,

deli and great place to eat with reggae as the soundtrack, an outdoor deck near the water and an expansive menu that includes colorful and imaginative organic salads, fried tofu (or calamari) with homemade fries, oysters, fish tacos, crab cakes and a fine clam chowder. Also serves craft beers on tap and decadent desserts.

Spud Point Crab Company SEAFOOD $
(☑707-875-9472; www.spudpointcrab.com; 1860 Westshore Rd; mains $6.75-12; ☺9am-5pm; [P][🍴]) In the classic tradition of dockside crab shacks, Spud Point serves salty-sweet crab sandwiches and *real* clam chowder (that consistently wins local culinary prizes). You can also buy a crab to take home if you fancy. Eat at picnic tables overlooking the marina. Take Bay Flat Rd to get here.

Lucas Wharf Restaurant & Bar SEAFOOD $$
(☑707-875-3522; www.lucaswharfrestaurant.com; 595 Hwy 1; mains $9-28; ☺11:30am-9pm Mon-Fri, 11am-9:30pm Sat & Sun; [P][🍴]) Located right on the water, this place specializes in sophisticated seafood options, with ingredients such as roasted cherry tomatoes accompanying dishes like Dungeness crab cakes and popcorn shrimp. Founded by a family of commercial fishers, the restaurant originated as a fish market, which is now next door, together with an upmarket deli. In other words, these folks know their seafood and you can guarantee it is flapping fresh.

Tides Wharf & Restaurant SEAFOOD $$
(☑707-875-3652; www.innatthetides.com; 835 Hwy 1; breakfast $9-24, lunch $17-30, dinner $25-38; ☺7:30am-9:30pm Mon-Thu, 7:30am-10pm Fri, 7am-10pm Sat, 7am-9:30pm Sun; [P][🍴]) Enjoy a stunning view of the bay and an upscale atmosphere. Seafood is the emphasis here, but pasta and meat dishes are also available. The black-and-white pics of the Hitchcock days add to the atmosphere and, if you're lucky, you may spy seals and dolphins from the vast picture window. The desserts are outstanding.

Terrapin Creek Cafe & Restaurant CALIFORNIAN $$
(☑707-875-2700; www.terrapincreekcafe.com; 1580 Eastshore Dr; lunch mains $12-19, dinner mains $23-30; ☺11am-2:30pm & 4:30-9pm Thu-Sun; [P][🍴][🍷]) 🌿 This upscale restaurant is run by a husband-wife team who espouse the slow-food movement and serve local dishes sourced from the surrounding area.

Comfort-food offerings such as black cod roasted in lemongrass and coconut broth are artfully executed, while the Dungeness crab salad is fresh, briny and perfect. Jazz and warm light complete the atmosphere.

Drakes CALIFORNIAN $$$
(☑888-875-2250; www.drakesbodegabay.com; 103 Hwy 1, Bodega Bay Lodge & Spa; mains $25-28, appetizers $8-17; ☺7am-10pm; [P][🍷]) This fancy spot offers a choice of dining experiences. The Drakes Sonoma Coast Kitchen offers breakfast and dinner, the latter concentrating on such classics as pan-seared duck breast and Black Angus rib-eye steak with accompaniments like orange and almond relish and Parmesan mash. The Fireside Lounge offers a relaxed setting for lighter bites, including Pacific oysters and garlic fries.

Gourmet Au Bay WINE BAR
(☑707-875-9875; www.gourmetaubay.com; 1412 Bay Flat Rd; ☺11am-6pm Thu-Tue; 🍷) This sophisticated wine bar moved to larger premises in 2017 and now offers sophisticated snacks to accompany your tipple. Head to the spacious deck where you can enjoy a salty breeze along with your wine tasting.

❶ Information

Sonoma Coast Visitor Center (☑707-875-3866; www.bodegabay.com; 850 Hwy 1; ☺9am-5pm Mon-Thu & Sat, to 6pm Fri, 10am-5pm Sun) Opposite the Tides Wharf. Stop by for the best help on the coast and for a copy of the *North Coaster*, a small-press indie newspaper of essays and brilliant insights on local culture.

Sonoma Coast State Beach

Stretching 17 miles north from Bodega Head to Vista Trail, 4 miles north of Jenner, the glorious Sonoma Coast State Beach is actually a series of beaches separated by several beautiful rocky headlands. Some beaches are tiny, hidden in little coves, while others stretch far and wide. Most of the beaches are connected by vista-studded coastal hiking trails that wind along the bluffs. Bring binoculars and your camera – the views are stunning, with rock outcrops, mini islands, inlets and shifting tides. During summer there can be morning fog, which generally burns off by midday. Exploring this area makes an excellent day-long adventure, but facilities are zero, so bring water and food, as well as a fully charged cell phone, in case of emergency. Also note that the surf is often too treacherous to wade, so keep a close eye on children.

◉ Sights & Activities

Schoolhouse Beach   BEACH
(btwn Bodega Bay & Jenner; **P**) A very pleasant beach with parking (but no other facilities); can be prone to riptides so swimmers should take care.

Goat Rock   BEACH
(5400-5900 N Hwy 1, Jenner; **P**) Famous for its colony of harbor seals, lazing in the sun at the mouth of the Russian River. Noted for its mystical-looking rock archway, as well.

Duncan's Landing   BEACH
(6947 Cliff Ave, Bodega Bay; **P**) Small boats unload near this rocky headland in the morning. A good place to spot wildflowers in the spring.

Shell Beach   BEACH
(Shell Beach Rd, Jenner; **P**) Just south of the small town of Jenner, a boardwalk and trail leads out to a stretch perfect for tide-pooling and beachcombing.

Salmon Creek Beach   BEACH
(3095 Hwy 1, Bodega Bay; **P**) Situated around a lagoon, with 2 miles of hiking and good waves for surfing.

Portuguese Beach   BEACH
(btwn Bodega Bay & Jenner; **P**) Very easy to access; sheltered coves between rocky outcroppings.

🛏 Sleeping

Unless you are willing to hammer down tent pegs (and even that is increasingly restricted; most camping is for day-use only), you will need to base yourself in Bodega Bay or Jenner. This is no real hardship, however, as both are just a few miles away either to the south or the north.

Wright's Beach Campground   CAMPGROUND $
(**☎** 800-444-7275; www.reserveamerica.com; 7095 Hwy 1; tent & RV sites $35, day use $8; **P**) Of the precious few parks that allow camping along Sonoma Coast State Beach, this is the best, even though sites lack privacy and there are no hot showers. There are just 27 sites but they can be booked six months in advance, and numbers one to 12 are right on the beach. There are BBQ pits for day use and it's a perfect launch for sea kayakers.

Bodega Dunes   CAMPGROUND $
(**☎** 800-444-7275; www.reserveamerica.com; 3095 Hwy 1, Ranch Rd, Bodega Bay; tent & RV sites $35, day use $8; **P**) The largest campground in the Sonoma Coast State Beach system of parks with close to 100 sites; it is also closest to Bodega Bay, so it gets a lot of use. Sites are in high dunes and have hot showers, but be warned – the foghorn sounds all night.

Jenner

Perched on the hills looking out to the Pacific and above the mouth of the Russian River, tiny Jenner offers access to the coast and the Russian River wine region. A **harbor-seal colony** sits at the river's mouth and pups are born here from March to August. There are restrictions about getting too close to the chubby, adorable pups – handling them can be dangerous and cause the pups to be abandoned by their mothers. Volunteers answer questions along the roped-off area where day-trippers can look on at a distance. The best way to see them is by kayak, and most of the year you will find **Water Treks Ecotours** (**☎** 707-865-2249; www.watertreks.com; kayak rental from $30; ⊙ hours vary) renting kayaks on the highway. Heading north on Hwy 1 you will begin driving on one of the most beautiful, windy stretches of California highway. You'll also probably lose cell-phone service – possibly a blessing.

🛏 Sleeping & Eating

River's End Inn   COTTAGE $$
(**☎** 707-865-2484; www.ilovesunsets.com; 11048 Hwy 1; cottages $169-279; **P**⊛) Run by the same folk who own the superb River's End Restaurant, these ocean-view cottages are wood-paneled and have no TVs, wi-fi or phones, but many do come with fireplaces, breezy decks and breathtaking ocean views, complete with harbor seals. Children under 12 years old not recommended.

★ Café Aquatica   CAFE $
(**☎** 707-865-2251; 10439 Hwy 1; pastries & sandwiches $4-10; ⊙ 8am-5pm; 🛜🌱) This is the kind of North Coast coffee shop you've been dreaming of: fresh pastries, fog-lifting organic coffee and chatty locals. The expansive view of the Russian River from the patio and gypsy sea-hut decor make it hard to leave, especially at weekends when a strumming

guitarist adds to the California dreamin' ambience.

River's End Restaurant CALIFORNIAN $$$
(☎707-865-2484; www.ilovesunsets.com; 11048 Hwy 1; lunch mains $15-26, dinner mains $26-42; ⊙noon-3:30pm & 5-9pm Fri-Mon; P 📶) Unwind in style at this picture-perfect restaurant, perched on a cliff overlooking the river's mouth and a grand sweep of the Pacific Ocean. It serves world-class meals at world-class prices, but the real reward is the view.

Fort Ross State Historic Park

A curious glimpse into Tsarist Russia's exploration of the California coast, the salt-washed buildings of **Fort Ross State Historic Park** (☎707-847-3437; www.fortross.org; 19005 Hwy 1; per car $8; ⊙10am-4:30pm) offer a fascinating insight into the pre-American Wild West. It's a quiet, picturesque place with a riveting past. If you pass by on a weekday when the fort is closed (due to budget cuts), you still may be able to walk down and have a peek inside if a school group is there.

In March 1812, a group of 25 Russians and 80 Alaskans (including members of the Kodiak and Aleutian tribes) built a wooden fort here, near a Kashaya Pomo village. The southernmost outpost of the 19th-century Russian fur trade on America's Pacific Coast, Fort Ross was established as a base for sea-otter hunting operations and trade with Alta California, and for growing crops for Russian settlements in Alaska. The Russians dedicated the fort in August 1812 and occupied it until 1842, when it was abandoned because the sea-otter population had been decimated and agricultural production had never taken off.

Fort Ross State Historic Park, an accurate reconstruction of the fort, is 11 miles north of Jenner on a beautiful point. The original buildings were sold, dismantled and carried off to Sutter's Fort during the gold rush. The visitor center has a great museum with historical displays and an excellent bookshop on Californian and Russian history. Ask about hikes to the Russian cemetery.

On Fort Ross Heritage Day, the last Saturday in July, costumed volunteers bring the fort's history to life; check www.parks.ca.gov or call the visitor center for other special events.

Sleeping

Stillwater Cove Regional Park CAMPGROUND $
(☎reservations 707-565-2267; www.sonoma-county.org/parks; 22455 N Hwy 1; tent & RV sites $28; P) Two miles north of Timber Cove, this park has hot showers and hiking under Monterey pines. Sites 1, 2, 4, 6, 9 and 10 have ocean views.

Timber Cove Inn INN $$$
(☎707-847-3231; www.timbercoveinn.com; 21780 N Hwy 1; r $230-350; P ⊖ 📶) A dramatic and quirky '60s-modern seaside inn that has been refurbished into a luxury lodge. The rustic architectural shell is stunning, and a duet of tinkling piano and crackling fire fills the vast open-plan lobby. Rooms have fireplaces and balconies or terraces. Prices vary according to the views. The Coast Kitchen restaurant offers a menu of well-prepared Californian cuisine.

Even those who don't bunk here should wander agape in the shadow of Benny Bufano's 93ft peace statue, a spectacular totem on the edge of the sea.

Salt Point State Park

Stunning 6000-acre **Salt Point State Park** (☎707-847-3221; www.parks.ca.gov; 25050 Hwy 1; per car $8; ⊙park sunrise-sunset, visitor center 10am-3pm Sat & Sun Apr-Oct; P) has sandstone cliffs that drop dramatically into the kelp-strewn sea and hiking trails that crisscross windswept prairies and wooded hills, connecting pygmy forests and coastal coves rich with tidepools. The 6-mile-wide park is bisected by the **San Andreas Fault** – the rock on the east side is vastly different from that on the west. Check out the eerily beautiful tafonis (honeycombed-sandstone formations) near Gerstle Cove. For a good roadside photo op, there's a pullout at mile marker 45.

Though many of the day-use areas have been closed off due to budget cuts, trails lead off Hwy 1 pullouts to views of the pristine coastline. The platform overlooking Sentinel Rock is just a short stroll from the Fisk Mill Cove parking lot at the park's north end. Further south, seals laze at **Gerstle Cove Marine Reserve**, one of California's first underwater parks. Tread lightly around tidepools and don't lift the rocks: even a glimpse of sunlight can kill some critters. If you're here between April and June, you must see **Kruse Rhododendron State Reserve**.

Growing abundantly in the forest's filtered light, magnificent, pink rhododendrons reach heights of over 30ft, making them the tallest species in the world; turn east from Hwy 1 onto Kruse Ranch Rd and follow the signs. Be sure to walk the short Rhododendron Loop Trail.

Sleeping

★ Ocean Cove Lodge Bar & Grill   MOTEL $
(☑ 707-847-3158;   www.oceancovelodge.com; 23255 Hwy 1; r from $89; ⊖❀🛜) Just a few minutes south of Salt Point State Park is Ocean Cove Lodge Bar & Grill, a godsend for those on a budget. It's just a basic motel but the location is fabulous, with uninterrupted ocean views (and whale-watching) beyond the sweeping lawns and hot tub. There's a surprisingly good American-style restaurant on the premises. The owner prides himself on the homemade cinnamon rolls made daily with an added hit of chili.

Salt Point State Park
Campgrounds   CAMPGROUND $
(☑ 800-444-7275; www.reserveamerica.com; Salt Point State Park; tent/RV sites $25/35; 🅿) Two campgrounds, Woodside and Gerstle Cove, both signposted off Hwy 1, have sites with cold water. Inland Woodside (closed December to March) is well protected by Monterey pines. Gerstle Cove's trees burned over a decade ago and have only grown halfway back, giving the gnarled, blackened trunks a ghostly look when the fog twirls between the branches.

Sea Ranch

Though not without its fans, the exclusive community of Sea Ranch is a sort of weather-beaten Stepford-by-the-Sea. The ritzy subdivision that sprawls 10 miles along the coast is connected with a well-watched network of private roads, with hiking trails leading to the sea and along the bluffs. Approved for construction prior to the existence of the watchdog Coastal Commission, the community was a precursor to the concept of 'slow growth,' with strict zoning laws requiring that houses be constructed of only weathered wood. Though there are some pleasant short-term rentals here, don't break any community rules – like throwing wild parties – or security will come knockin'. For supplies and gasoline, go to Gualala. North of the Sea Ranch Lodge, you'll find

the iconic nondenominational chapel; an extraordinary contemporary building surrounded by meadows of grazing cattle.

⊙ Sights

Stengel Beach   BEACH
(Hwy 1, Mile 53.96; ⊘ 6am-sunset May-Sep, from 8am Oct-Apr; 🅿🚻) One of a handful of idyllic beaches on this stretch of coastline, Stengel has a large, free car park and a short access trail lined by cypress trees that takes you to a wooden staircase leading to the beach.

Walk-On Beach   BEACH
(Hwy 1, Mile 56.53; parking per day $7; ⊘ 6am-sunset May-Sep, from 8am Oct-Apr; 🅿) A short trail passes through a large grove of cypress trees leading to a staircase down to the pristine quarter-mile beach; note that there is also wheelchair access. Walkers can follow the stunning Bluff Top Trail from here, which leads north to Gualala Point Regional Park.

Shell Beach   BEACH
(Hwy 1, Mile 55.24; parking per day $7; ⊘ 6am-sunset May-Sep, from 8am Oct-Apr; 🅿🚻) A lovely beach comprising two sandy coves divided by a rocky headland. You can park just south of Whale Bone Reach Rd from where there is an approximately 2-mile access trail to the beach via pine trees and meadows. Note that there are no facilities, aside from toilets at the car park.

Sleeping

Depending on the season, it can be surprisingly affordable to rent a house in Sea Ranch. There are several agencies that can assist you in finding a place, including **Rams Head Realty & Rentals** (☑ 707-884-1427; www.ramshead.com; 309000 Hwy 1; ⊘ 9am-6pm) and **Sea Ranch Rentals** (☑ 707-884-4235; www.searanchrentals.com; 39200 Hwy 1; ⊘ 9am-6pm), both located in the center of nearby Gualala.

Sea Ranch Lodge   HOTEL $$$
(☑ 707-785-2371; www.searanchlodge.com; 60 Sea Walk Dr; r $199-369; 🅿🛜) A marvel of '60s-modern California architecture, timber clad Sea Ranch has spacious, minimalist rooms, many with dramatic views of the ocean; some have hot tubs and fireplaces. On the downside, Sea Ranch lodge is starting to look just a little bit dated and readers have complained about a lack of insulation which can be a problem with noisy neighbors.

Gualala & Anchor Bay

Located at the mouth of the Gualala River on the Pacific Coast, Gualala (pronounced by most locals as 'Wah-la-la') is a Native American Pomo name meaning 'where the waters flow down'. It is northern Sonoma coast's hub for a weekend getaway as it sits squarely in the middle of the 'Banana Belt,' an area known for unusually sunny weather. Founded as a prosperous lumber town in the 1860s, the downtown stretches along Hwy 1 with a bustling commercial district that has a great grocery store and some cute, slightly upscale shops.

Just north, quiet Anchor Bay is the destination of choice for many visitors seeking a tranquil stay, as it is home to some exceptional accommodation choices with a string of secluded, hard-to-find beaches situated just to the north. Both Gualala and Anchor Bay are excellent jumping-off points for exploring the surrounding area.

◉ Sights & Activities

Seven miles north of Anchor Bay, pull off at mile marker 11.41 for **Schooner Gulch**. A trail into the forest leads down cliffs to a sandy beach with tide pools. Bear right at the fork in the trail to reach iconic **Bowling Ball Beach**, where low tide reveals rows of big, round rocks resembling bowling balls. Consult tide tables for Arena Cove. The forecast low tide must be lower than +1.5ft on the tide chart for the rocks to be visible.

Gualala Arts Center　　　　ARTS CENTER
(☑707-884-1138; www.gualalaarts.org; 46501 Old State Hwy, Gualala; ☺9am-4pm Mon-Fri, noon-4pm Sat & Sun; Ⓟ) Inland along Old State Hwy, at the south end of town, and beautifully built entirely by volunteers, this center hosts changing exhibitions, organizes the **Art in the Redwoods Festival** in late August, holds a range of art classes and has loads of info on local art.

🛏 Sleeping & Eating

Of the two towns, Gualala has more services than Anchor Bay, including places to stay, and is a more practical hub for exploring – there is a bunch of good motels, plus campgrounds and a handful of inns and B&Bs.

Gualala Point Regional Park　　CAMPGROUND $
(☑707-567-2267; http://parks.sonomacounty.ca.gov; 42401 Hwy 1, Gualala; tent & RV sites $35; Ⓟ) Shaded by a stand of redwoods and fragrant California bay laurel trees, a short trail connects this creek-side campground to the windswept beach. The quality of sites, including several secluded hike-in spots, makes it the best drive-in camping on this part of the coast.

Gualala River Redwood Park　　CAMPGROUND $
(☑707-884-3533; www.gualalapark.com; Gualala Rd, Gualala; day use $6, tent/RV sites $42/49; Ⓟ) Another excellent Sonoma County Park. Located inland from the Old State Hwy, you can camp and do short hikes along the Gualala River.

★St Orres Inn　　　　　　　INN $$
(☑707-884-3303; www.saintorres.com; 36601 Hwy 1, Gualala; B&B $95-135, cottages $140-445; Ⓟ🐾🛜🐕) Famous for its striking Russian-inspired architecture: dramatic rough-hewn timbers, stained glass and burnished-copper domes, there's no place quite like St Orres. On the property's fairytale-like, wild mushroom–strewn 90 acres, hand-built cottages range from rustic to luxurious. The inn's fine restaurant is worth the splurge, with inspired California cuisine in one of the coast's most romantic rooms.

North Coast Country Inn　　B&B $$
(☑707-884-4537; www.northcoastcountryinn.com; 34591 S Hwy 1, Anchor Bay; r $185-235; Ⓟ🐾🛜🐕) Perched on an inland hillside beneath towering trees and surrounded by lovely gardens, the perks of this adorable place begin with the gregarious owner and a hot tub. The six spacious, country-style rooms are decorated with lovely prints and boast exposed beams, fireplaces, board games and private entrances.

★Mar Vista Cottages　　CABIN $$$
(☑707-884-3522; www.marvistamendocino.com; 35101 Hwy 1, Anchor Bay; cottages $190-310; Ⓟ🐾🛜🐕) ✈ These elegantly renovated 1930s fishing cabins offer a simple, stylish seaside escape with a vanguard commitment to sustainability. The harmonious environment is the result of pitch-perfect details: linens are line-dried over lavender, guests browse the organic vegetable garden to harvest their own dinner and chickens cluck around the grounds laying the next morning's breakfast. It often requires two-night stays.

Trinks
CAFE $

(☑707-884-1713; www.trinkscafe.com; 39140 Hwy 1, Gualala; snacks & sandwiches $10-15; ⊗7am-4pm Mon-Tue, Fri & Sat, to 8pm Wed & Thu, 8am-4pm Sun; P🐾) Tucked into the corner of a strip of shops with a seaview terrace, the overstuffed sandwiches are great value here. Be sure to leave room for a slice of fresh fruit pie; there are generally at least four to select from. Lightweights can opt for quiche and salad, while vegetarians will rejoice over the hearty veg-filled lentil bowl.

Anchor Bay Village Market
MARKET $

(☑707-884-4245; 35513 S Hwy 1, Anchor Bay; ⊗8am-7pm Mon-Sat, to 6pm Sun; P) This grocery store specializes in organic produce and products, with a superb range including baked goods and deli items.

ℹ️ Information

Redwood Coast Visitors Center (☑707-884-1080; www.redwoodcoastchamber.com; 39150 Hwy 1, Shoreline Hwy, Gualala; ⊗noon-5pm Thu, Fri & Sun, from 11am Sat) A well-stocked tourist office with plenty of information on the area, including a free local map.

Point Arena

This laid-back little town of less than 450 residents combines creature comforts with relaxed, eclectic California living and is the first town up the coast where the majority of residents don't seem to be retired Bay Area refugees, but are rather a young, creative bunch who tout organic food, support their local theater and sell their fair share of dream catchers. The main street is part of scenic Hwy 1, with a small harbor at one end and a clutch of small arty shops, cafes and restaurants housed in pretty Victorian-era buildings running through the center of town. Peruse the shops and restaurants then follow the sign leading to the lighthouse at the north end of Main St, or head to the docks a mile west of town at Arena Cove and watch surfers mingle with fisherfolk and locals.

⊙ Sights

★**Point Arena Lighthouse**
LIGHTHOUSE

(☑707-882-2809; www.pointarenalighthouse.com; 45500 Lighthouse Rd; adult/child $7.50/1; ⊗10am-3:30pm mid-Sep–mid-May, to 4:30pm mid-May–mid-Sep; P) This 1908 lighthouse (the tallest on the US West Coast) stands 10 stories high and is the only lighthouse in California you can ascend. Check in at the museum, then climb 145 steps to the top and see the Fresnel lens and the jaw-dropping view. You can stay on-site. The turnoff is 2 miles northwest of town off Hwy 1.

Stornetta Public Lands
NATURE RESERVE

(Lighthouse Rd; P) For fabulous bird-watching, hiking on terraced rock past sea caves and access to hidden coves, head 1 mile down Lighthouse Rd from Hwy 1 and look for the Bureau of Land Management (BLM) signs on the left indicating these 1132-acre public lands. The best, most dramatic walking trail leads along the coast and also begins on Lighthouse Rd from a small parking area about a quarter-mile before the lighthouse parking area.

🛏️ Sleeping

Point Arena Lighthouse Lodging
RENTAL HOUSE $$

(☑707-882-2809; www.pointarenalighthouse.com; 45500 Lighthouse Rd; houses $150-250; P⊗🐾) True lighthouse buffs should look into staying at the plain, three-bedroom, kitchen-equipped former coast-guard homes at the lighthouse. They're quiet, windswept retreats.

Wharf Master's Inn
HOTEL $$

(☑707-882-3171; www.wharfmasters.com; 785 Iversen Ave; r $129-259; P⊗🐾🐕) This is a cluster of comfortable, spacious rooms on a cliff overlooking fishing boats and a stilt pier. Recently reformed, they are eminently comfortable; several sporting four-poster beds. Most of the rooms have private balconies with uninterrupted sea views.

🍴 Eating & Drinking

Franny's Cup & Saucer
BAKERY $

(☑707-882-2500; www.frannyscupandsaucer.com; 213 Main St; cakes from $2; ⊗8am-4pm Wed-Sat) The cutest patisserie on this stretch of coast is run by Franny and her mother, Barbara (a veteran of Chez Panisse in Berkeley). The fresh berry tarts and creative housemade chocolates seem too beautiful to eat, until you take the first bite and immediately want to order another. Once a month they pull out all the stops for a farmhouse dinner ($28).

Arena Market
ORGANIC, DELI $

(☑707-882-3663; www.arenaorganics.org; 185 Main St; soup $6.50, sandwiches $8; ⊗7am-7pm Mon-Sat, 8am-6pm Sun; P🐾) 🌿 The deli at this fully stocked organic co-op makes excellent to-go veg and gluten-free options, including sandwiches, with ingredients generally sourced from local farms. The serve-yourself soup is delicious; you can enjoy it at one of the tables out front.

Uneda CALIFORNIAN $$
(☑707-882-3800; www.unedaeat.com; 206 Main St; mains $16-25; ☺5:30-8:30pm Wed-Sat) The owners are serious about food, they travel the world sourcing recipes and have a catering business as well as a food truck. The menu changes nightly depending on what is fresh in the market that day, but is always healthy and imaginative. There are just nine tables so reserve ahead of time. Cash only.

215 Main BAR
(www.facebook.com/215Main; 215 Main St; ☺2pm-2am Tue-Sun) Head to this open, renovated historic building to drink local beer and wine. There's jazz on the weekends.

☆ Entertainment

Arena Theater CINEMA
(☑707-882-3020; www.arenatheater.org; 214 Main St) Shows mainstream, foreign and art films in a beautifully restored movie house. Sue, the ticket seller, has been in that booth for 40 years. Got a question about Point Arena? Ask Sue.

Manchester

Follow Hwy 1 north beyond Point Arena, through gorgeous rolling fields dropping down from the hills to the blue ocean, and a turnoff leads to Manchester State Beach, a long, wild stretch of sand. If you visit from October to April, you may spy gray and humpback whales during their annual migration. Part of the protected Manchester State Park (☑707-882-2463; www.parks.gov. ca; Kinney Rd; tent sites $25-35; ℗), a 111-acre camping park, the area around here is remote and beautiful, with grazing land for sheep and cattle further inland and two freshwater streams noted for their salmon and steelhead (anglers take note). The population hovers around the 200 mark so there is not much here in terms of shops and facilities (only one grocery store), but it's a quick 7-mile drive east to Point Arena with its shops, restaurants and appealing places to stay.

Based inland around 8 miles to the north and actually closer to Elk, **Ross Ranch**

TOP WHALE-WATCHING SPOTS

Watch for spouts, sounding and breaching whales and pods. Anywhere coastal will do, but the following are some of the North Coast's best:

➡ Bodega Head (p233)

➡ Mendocino Headlands State Park (p244)

➡ Jug Handle State Natural Reserve (p247)

➡ MacKerricher State Park (p250)

➡ Shelter Cove (p266) & Lost Coast (p264)

➡ Trinidad Head Trail (p277)

➡ Klamath River Overlook (p282)

(☑707-877-1834; www.rossranch.biz; 28300 Philo Greenwood Rd; rides $50-60; ⊞) organizes two-hour rides along Manchester Beach or in nearby woodlands and forest for groups of up to 10.

Toward the ocean, **Mendocino Coast KOA** (☑707-882-2375; www.manchesterbeach koa.com; 44300 Kinney Rd; tent/RV sites from $32/65, cabins $75-85; ℗☎) is an impressive private campground with tightly packed campsites beneath enormous Monterey pines, a cooking pavilion, hot showers, a hot tub, bicycles and a community campfire area. The cabins are a great option for families who want to get the camping experience without roughing it.

Elk

Itty-bitty Elk is famous for its stunning cliff-top views of 'sea stacks,' towering rock formations jutting out of the water. Otherwise, it's one of the cutest yet gentrified-looking villages before Mendocino. There is *nothing* to do after dinner, so bring a book if you're a night owl. And you can forget about the cell phone, too; reception here is nonexistent. Elk's visitor center (p242) has exhibits on the town's logging past. At the southern end of town, **Greenwood State Beach** sits where Greenwood Creek meets the sea and marks the spot where ships used to stop when carrying timber to San Francisco and China. There are some excellent walks along the cliffs offering dramatic ocean views combined with dense woods.

🛏 Sleeping & Eating

★ Elk Cove Inn & Spa · INN $$$

(☎800-725-2967; www.elkcoveinn.com; 6300 S Hwy 1; r $100-375, cottages $275-355; 🅿🐕🛏🎑🐾) Several upmarket B&Bs take advantage of the views but you simply can't beat those from Elk Cove Inn & Spa, located on a bluff with steps leading down to the driftwood-strewn beach below. Prices in the wide selection of rooms and cottages include breakfast, wine, champagne and cocktails, plus you can relax even further at the deluxe spa.

Elk Store · DELI $

(☎707-877-3544; 6101 Hwy 1, Shoreline Hwy; sandwiches from $9; ⊙9am-6pm) Make a stop here for gourmet foods, gifts, Mendocino County wines and a great deli menu with build-your-own sandwiches, burritos, bagels and wraps, and an awesomely good clam chowder.

Queenie's Roadhouse Cafe · CAFE $

(☎707-877-3285; 6061 S Hwy 1, Shoreline Hwy; mains $6-10; ⊙8am-3pm Thu-Mon; 🖉) Everyone swears by this excellent, retro-chic classic diner for a creative range of breakfast (try the wild-rice waffles) and lunch treats, including a great burger and Reuben sandwich.

ℹ Information

Elk Visitor Center (☎707-937-5804; www.mendoparks.org/greenwood-state-beach-elk-ca/; Greenwood State Beach; ⊙11am-1pm Sat & Sun mid-Mar–Oct; 🐾) This small visitor center-cum-museum provides information about the region and also has a photographic display about the history of Elk (formerly known as Greenwood) as a lumber town in the late 1800s.

Van Damme State Park

Three miles south of Mendocino, this sprawling 1831-acre **park** (☎707-937-5804; www.parks.ca.gov; 8001 N Hwy 1, Little River; per car $8; ⊙8am-9pm; 🅿) draws beachcombers, divers and kayakers to its easy-access beach, and hikers to its pygmy forest. The latter is a unique and precious place, where acidic soil and an impenetrable layer of hardpan have created a miniature forest of decades-old trees. The visitor center has nature exhibits and programs.

You can reach the forest on the moderate 3.5-mile **Fern Canyon Scenic Trail**, which crosses back and forth over Little River and

past the Cabbage Patch, a bog of skunk cabbage that's rich with wildlife.

Two pretty **campgrounds** (☎800-444-7275; www.reserveamerica.com; 8001 Hwy 1, Little River; tent/RV sites $25/35; 🅿🎑) are excellent for family car camping. They both have hot showers: one is just off Hwy 1, the other is in a highland meadow, which has lots of space for kids to run around. Nine environmental campsites (tent sites $25) lie just a 1¼-mile hike up Fern Canyon; there's untreated creek water.

For sea-cave kayaking tours contact **Kayak Mendocino** (☎707-937-0700; www.kayakmendocino.com, 8001 N Hwy 1, Little River; adult/child $60/40; ⊙tours 9am, 11:30am & 2pm).

Mendocino

Leading out to a gorgeous headland, Mendocino is the North Coast's salt-washed perfect village, with B&Bs surrounded by rose gardens, white-picket fences and New England–style redwood water towers. Bay Area weekenders walk along the headland among berry bramble and wildflowers, where cypress trees stand over dizzying cliffs. The town itself is full of cute shops – no chains – and has earned the nickname 'Spendocino,' for its upscale goods.

Built by transplanted New Englanders in the 1850s, Mendocino thrived late into the 19th century, with ships transporting redwood timber from here to San Francisco. The mills shut down in the 1930s, and the town was rediscovered in the 1950s by artists and bohemians. Today the culturally savvy, politically aware, well-traveled citizens welcome visitors, but eschew corporate interlopers – don't look for a Big Mac or Starbucks. To avoid crowds, come midweek or in the low season, when the vibe is mellower – and prices more reasonable.

◎ Sights

Mendocino is lined with all kinds of interesting galleries, which hold openings on the second Saturday of each month from 5pm to 8pm.

Kwan Tai Temple · TEMPLE

(Map p243; ☎707-937-5123; www.kwantaitemple.org; 45160 Albion St; ⊙by appointment) Peering in the window of this 1852 temple reveals an old altar dedicated to the Chinese god of war. Tours are available by appointment and provide a fascinating insight into the

Mendocino

Catch a Canoe &
Bicycles, Too! (0.8mi);
Stanford Inn by
the Sea (0.8mi);
Ravens (0.8mi);
Alhion (5mi)

Mendocino

◉ Sights
1 Kelley House Museum	C3
2 Kwan Tai Temple	A3
3 Mendocino Art Center	A2

☺ Activities, Courses & Tours
4 Mendocino Headlands State Park	B1

🛏 Sleeping
5 Alegria	D3
6 Didjeridoo Dreamtime Inn	D2
7 MacCallum House Inn	B2
8 Mendocino Coast Reservations	B2
9 Mendocino Hotel	B3
10 Packard House	B2
11 Raku House	D2

✖ Eating
12 955 Ukiah Street	C2
13 Café Beaujolais	D2
14 Farmers Market	C3
15 Flow	B3
16 Frankie's	C2
MacCallum House Restaurant	(see 7)
17 Patterson's Pub	C2
18 Tote Fête Deli & Burger Grill	C2

☕ Drinking & Nightlife
19 Dick's Place	B3

🛍 Shopping
20 Gallery Bookshop	B3
21 Harvest Market	C2
22 Mendocino Chocolate Company	C2
23 Out Of This World	B3
24 Twist	A3
25 Village Toy Store	C2

history of the area's Chinese American immigrants, dating from the mid-19th century when they worked in the lumber industry.

Point Cabrillo Light Station   LIGHTHOUSE
(☎707-937-6123; www.pointcabrillo.org; 45300 Lighthouse Rd; ⊙park sunrise-sunset, lighthouse 11am-4pm) FREE Restored in 1909, this stout lighthouse stands on a 300-acre wildlife preserve north of town, between Russian

Gulch and Caspar Beach. Guided walks of the preserve leave at 11am on Sundays from May to September. You can also stay in the lighthouse keeper's house and cottages.

Kelley House Museum   MUSEUM
(Map p243; ☎707-937-5791; www.mendocino history.org; 45007 Albion St; $2; ⊙11am-3pm Thu-Tue Jun-Sep, Fri-Mon Oct-May) Check out the research library and changing exhibits on

early California and Mendocino. The 1861 museum hosts seasonal, two-hour walking tours for $10; call for times.

Mendocino Art Center GALLERY

(Map p243; ☑707-937-5818; www.mendocinoart center.org; 45200 Little Lake St; ☉10am-5pm Apr-Oct, to 4pm Tue-Sat Nov-Mar) FREE Behind a yard of twisting iron sculpture, the city's art center takes up a whole tree-filled block, hosting exhibitions, the 81-seat Helen Schonei Theatre and nationally renowned art classes. This is also where to pick up the *Mendocino Arts Showcase* brochure, a quarterly publication listing all the happenings and festivals in town.

🏃 Activities

Wine tours, whale-watching, shopping, hiking, cycling: there's more to do in the area than a thousand long weekends could accomplish. For navigable river and ocean kayaking, launch from tiny Albion, which hugs the north side of the Albion River mouth, 5 miles south of Mendocino.

Catch a Canoe
& Bicycles, Too! CANOEING, CYCLING

(☑707-937-0273; www.catchacanoe.com; 44850 Comptche-Ukiah Rd, Stanford Inn by the Sea; 3hr kayak, canoe or bicycle rental adult/child $28/14; ☉9am-5pm; 🚼) This friendly outfit rents bikes, kayaks and canoes (including redwood outriggers) for trips up the 8-mile Big River tidal estuary. Northern California's longest undeveloped estuary has no highways or buildings, only beaches, forests, marshes, streams, abundant wildlife and historic logging sites. Bring a picnic and a camera to enjoy the ramshackle remnants of century-old train trestles and majestic blue herons.

Mendocino Headlands State Park HIKING

(Map p243; ☑707-937-5804; www.parks.ca.gov; Ford St) FREE Mendocino Headlands State Park surrounds the village, where trails crisscross bluffs and rocky coves. Ask at the visitor center (p247) about guided weekend walks, including spring wildflower explorations and whale-watching jaunts.

🎉 Festivals & Events

For a complete list of Mendocino's many festivals, check with the visitor center or www.gomendo.com.

Mendocino Whale Festival WILDLIFE

(www.mendowhale.com; ☉early Mar) Wine and chowder tastings, whale-watching and plenty of live music.

Mendocino Music Festival MUSIC

(www.mendocinomusic.com; ☉mid-Jul; 🚼) Enjoy orchestral and chamber music concerts on the headlands, children's matinees and open rehearsals.

Mendocino Wine
& Mushroom Festival FOOD & DRINK

(www.mendocino.com; ☉early Nov) Includes guided mushroom tours and symposia.

🛌 Sleeping

Standards are high in stylish Mendocino and so are prices; two-day minimums often crop up on weekends. Fort Bragg, 10 miles north, has cheaper lodgings. All B&B rates include breakfast; only a few places have TVs. For a range of cottages and B&Bs, contact **Mendocino Coast Reservations** (Map p243; ☑707-937-5033; www.mendocinovacations. com; 45084 Little Lake St; ☉9am-5pm).

Russian Gulch State Park CAMPGROUND $

(☑reservations 800-444-7275; www.reserve america.com; tent & RV sites $35; P) In a wooded canyon 2 miles north of town, with secluded drive-in sites, hot showers, a small waterfall and the Devil's Punch Bowl (a collapsed sea arch).

★ Didjeridoo Dreamtime Inn B&B $$

(Map p243; ☑707-937-6200; www.didjeridoo inn.com; 44860 Main St; r $112-160; 🖶🛜🐾) One of the town's more economical choices, rooms here are all different yet share the same homey, unpretentious atmosphere with tasteful artwork, antiques and parquet flooring. Several rooms have en suites, and a couple have mini hot tubs. The breakfast spread is excellent and on Sunday you are treated to some soothing live music. The front garden is a lovely place to sit.

MacCallum House Inn B&B $$

(Map p243; ☑707-937-0289; www.maccallum house.com; 45020 Albion St; r & cottages from $149, water-tower ste $259-359; P🖶@🛜🐾) 🌿 One of the finest B&B options in town with gardens in a riot of color. There are cheerful cottages, and a modern luxury home, but the most memorable space is within one of Mendocino's iconic, historic water towers – living quarters fill the ground floor, a sauna is on the 2nd and there's a view of the coast from the top.

Andiron Seaside Inn & Cabins   CABIN $$

(☑707-937-1543; http://theandiron.com; 6051 N Hwy 1, Little River; d $109-299; P🐕🌐📶🎱) 🏊 Styled with hip vintage decor, this cluster of 1950s roadside cottages is a refreshingly playful option amid the cabbage-rose and lace aesthetic of Mendocino. Each cabin houses two rooms with complementing themes: 'Read' has old books, comfy vintage chairs and retro eyeglasses, while the adjoining 'Write' features a huge chalkboard and a ribbon typewriter.

Lighthouse Inn at Point Cabrillo   B&B $$

(☑707-937-6124; www.pointcabrillo.org; Point Cabrillo Dr; cottages from $132, houses from $450; P🐕🌐📶🎱) On 300 acres, in the shadow of Point Cabrillo lighthouse, the stately lightkeeper's and assistant lightkeeper's houses, together with the staff's two turn-of-the-century cottages have been revamped into vacation rentals. All options have verandas and lush period decor but are not very private.

Packard House   B&B $$

(Map p243; ☑707-937-2677; www.packardhouse.com; 45170 Little Lake St; r $175-225; P🐕📶) Decked out in contemporary style, this place is Mendocino's most chic and sleek B&B choice, with beautiful fabrics, colorful minimalist paintings and limestone bathrooms.

★Alegria   B&B $$$

(Map p243; ☑707-937-5150; www.oceanfront magic.com; 44781 Main St; r $239-299; 🐕📶) A perfect romantic hideaway, beds have views over the coast, decks have ocean views and all rooms have wood-burning fireplaces; outside, a gorgeous path leads to a big, amber-gray beach. Ever-so-friendly innkeepers whip up amazing breakfasts served in the sea-view dining area. Less-expensive rooms are available across the street at bright and simple **Raku House** (Map p243; ☑800-780-7905; 998 Main St; r $109-139; P🐕📶).

★Stanford Inn by the Sea   INN $$$

(☑707-937-5615; www.stanfordinn.com; 44850 Comptche-Ukiah Rd; r $211-299; 🐕@📶🚣🎱) 🏊 This masterpiece of a lodge standing on 10 lush acres has wood-burning fireplaces, knotty-pine walls, original art, stereos and top-quality mattresses in every room. Take a stroll in the organic gardens, where they har-

vest food for the excellent on-site restaurant, and a dip in the solarium-enclosed pool and hot tub, and it's a sublime getaway.

Brewery Gulch Inn   B&B $$$

(☑707-937-4752; www.brewerygulchinn.com; 9401 N Hwy 1; d $245-495; 🐕📶) 🏊 Just south of Mendocino, this bright, woodsy place has 10 modern rooms (all with flat-screen televisions, gas fireplaces and spa bathtubs), and guests enjoy touches like feather beds and leather reading chairs. The hosts pour heavily at the complimentary wine hour and leave out sweets for midnight snacking. Made-to-order breakfast is served in a small dining room overlooking the distant water.

Glendeven   B&B $$$

(☑707-937-0083; www.glendeven.com; 8205 Hwy 1, Shoreline Hwy; r $216-280; P🐕📶) 🏊 This historic 1860s estate 2 miles south of town has organic gardens, grazing llamas (with daily feedings at dusk), chickens for those breakfast eggs, forest and oceanside trails and a wine bar serving only Mendocino wines – and that's just the start. Romantic rooms have neutral tones, soothing decor, fireplaces and top-notch linens. Farm-to-table dinners are available at the bistro.

✕ Eating

With quality to rival Napa Valley, the influx of Bay Area weekenders has fostered an excellent dining scene that enthusiastically espouses organic, sustainable principles. Make reservations. Gathering picnic supplies is easy at Harvest Market (p247) organic grocery store (with deli) and the **farmers market** (Map p243; cnr Howard & Main St; ⏱noon-2pm Fri May-Oct).

Tote Fête Deli & Burger Grill   BURGERS $

(Map p243; ☑707-937-3383; 10450 Lansing St; burgers $9-15, mains $12-15; ⏱11:30am-7:30pm Mon, Tue & Thu-Sat, to 5pm Sun) Dine in or take away at this serious burger place with its all-natural, grass-fed beef and 11 choices, including veggie and portobello-mushroom options. Also on the menu are seafood dishes, such as fish tacos, calamari and coconut shrimp, plus steaks, gourmet salads and sandwiches. The atmosphere is laid back; this is not the place for a romantic dinner.

Frankie's   PIZZA $

(Map p243; ☑707-937-2436; www.frankies mendocino.com; cnr Ukiah & Lansing Sts; pizza $13-16; ⏱11am-9pm; 🍴) 🏊 There is no Sicilian-style simplicity to these pizzas, they are pure Californian with piled-high organic ingredients such as cremini mushrooms, Canadian bacon, roasted red peppers and pineapple (not combined, fortunately). It also serves healthy fare such as quinoa kale cakes and gluten-free falafel, plus soups, salads and Fort Bragg's famous Cowlick's ice cream.

Flow
CALIFORNIAN $$
(Map p243; ☑707-937-3569; www.mendocino flow.com; 45040 Main St; mains $14-20; ⊗8am-10pm; ☜⚑) Run by the Mendocino Cafe, this very busy place has the best views of the ocean in town from its 2nd-story perch. Brunch is a specialty as are Mexican-inspired small plates, artisan pizzas and a sublime local Dungeness crab chowder. Gluten-free and vegan options are available.

Ledford House
MEDITERRANEAN $$
(☑707-937-0282; www.ledfordhouse.com; 3000 N Hwy 1, Albion; mains $14-30; ⊗5-8pm Wed-Sun; ℗) Watch the water pound the rocks and the sun set out of the Mendocino hubbub (8 miles south) at this friendly Cal-Med bistro. Try the cassoulet or the gnocchi. It's a local hangout and gets hoppin' with live jazz most nights.

Patterson's Pub
PUB FOOD $$
(Map p243; www.pattersonspub.com; 10485 Lansing St; mains $13-16; ⊗10am-midnight, food to 11pm) If you pull into town late and hungry, you'll thank your lucky stars for this place; it serves quality pub grub – fish and chips, burgers and dinner salads – with cold beer. The only traditional Irish pub ambience spoiler is the plethora of flat-screen TVs. A busy brunch is served on Saturday and Sunday mornings from 10am to 2pm.

★ Café Beaujolais
CALIFORNIAN $$$
(Map p243; ☑707-937-5614; www.cafebeaujolais. com; 961 Ukiah St; lunch mains $10-18, dinner mains $23-38; ⊗11:30am-2:30pm Wed-Sun, dinner from 5:30pm daily; ℗) ✿ Mendocino's iconic, beloved country-Cal–French restaurant occupies an 1893 farmhouse restyled into a monochromatic urban-chic dining room, perfect for holding hands by candlelight. The refined, inspired cooking draws diners from San Francisco, who make this the centerpiece of their trip. The locally sourced menu changes with the seasons, but the Petaluma duck confit is a gourmand's delight.

955 Ukiah Street
CALIFORNIAN $$$
(Map p243; ☑707-937-1955; www.955restaurant. com; 955 Ukiah St; mains $18-37; ⊗from 6pm Thu-Sun) One of those semi-secret institutions, the menu here changes with what's available locally. When we visited, that meant wondrous things such as a roasted cauliflower, feta and caramelized-onion appetizer. The dimly lit, bohemian setting overlooks rambling gardens. Check the website for the excellent-value, three-course meal with wine for $25 every Thursday, and other events.

Don't miss the paintings by Emmy Lou Packard, who lived round the corner during the '60s and was famously both a communist and an assistant to Mexican painter and muralist, Diego Rivera.

MacCallum House Restaurant
CALIFORNIAN $$$
(Map p243; ☑707-937-0289; www.maccallum house.com; 45020 Albion St; cafe dishes $12-18, mains $25-42; ⊗8:15-10am Mon-Fri, to 11am Sat & Sun, plus 5:30-9pm daily; ℗) ✿ Sit on the veranda or fireside for a romantic dinner of all-organic game, fish or risotto primavera. Chef Alan Kantor makes *everything* from scratch and his commitment to sustainability and organic ingredients is nearly as visionary as his menu. The cafe menu, served at the Grey Whale Bar, is one of Mendocino's few four-star bargains.

Ravens
CALIFORNIAN $$$
(☑707-937-5615; www.ravensrestaurant.com; Stanford Inn by the Sea, Comptche-Ukiah Rd; breakfast $11-15, mains $24-30; ⊗8am-10pm; ℗⚑) ✿ Ravens brings haute-contemporary concepts to a completely vegetarian and vegan menu. Produce comes from the idyllic organic gardens of the Stanford Inn by the Sea (p245) and the bold menu takes on everything from sea-palm strudel and portabella sliders to decadent (guilt-free) desserts.

🍷 Drinking & Nightlife

Have cocktails at the **Mendocino Hotel** (Map p243; ☑707-937-0511; www.mendocinohotel.com; 45080 Main St; ℗⊜☜) or the Grey Whale Bar at the MacCallum House Inn (p244). For boisterousness and beer head straight to Patterson's Pub.

Dick's Place
BAR
(Map p243; ☑707-937-6010; 45080 Main St; ⊗11:30am-2am) A bit out of place among the fancy-pants shops downtown, but an

excellent spot to check out the *other* Mendocino and do shots with rowdy locals. And don't miss the retro experience of dropping 50¢ in the jukebox to hear that favorite tune.

🔒 Shopping

Mendocino's walkable streets are great for shopping, and the ban on chain stores ensures unique, often upscale gifts. There are many small galleries in town where one-of-a-kind artwork is for sale.

Twist CLOTHING
(Map p243; ☑707-937-1717; www.mendocino twist.com; 45140 Main St; ⊙11am-5pm Mon-Fri, 10:30am-5:30pm Sat & Sun) ∅ Twist stocks eco-friendly, natural-fiber clothing and lots of locally made clothing and toys.

Mendocino Chocolate Company CHOCOLATE
(Map p243; ☑800-722-1107; www.mendocino-chocolate.com; 10466 Lansing St; ⊙10am-5:30pm) This company has been around for 30 years in Fort Bragg, so it know its cocoa beans. This newer second outlet adds a sweet touch to Mendocino's shopping scene. Check out the exquisite handmade seashells in marbled white, milk and dark chocolate.

Harvest Market FOOD & DRINK
(Map p243; ☑707-937-5879; www.harvestmarket. com; 10501 Lansing St; ⊙7:30am-10pm) ∅ The town's biggest grocery store has legit organic credentials, an excellent cold-food bar and great cheese and meat.

Village Toy Store TOYS
(Map p243; ☑707-937-4633; www.mendotoystore. com; 10450 Lansing St; ⊙10am-6pm) Get a kite or browse the old-world selection of wooden toys and games that you won't find in the chains – hardly anything requires batteries.

Gallery Bookshop BOOKS
(Map p243; ☑707-937-2665; www.gallerybook shop.com; 319 Kasten St; ⊙9:30am-6pm) Stocks a great selection of books on local topics, titles from California's small presses and specialized outdoor guides.

Out of This World SPORTS & OUTDOORS
(Map p243; ☑707-937-3335; www.outofthis worldshop.com; 45100 Main St; ⊙10am-5:30pm) Birders, astronomy buffs and science geeks head directly to this telescope, binocular and science-toy shop.

ⓘ Information

Ford House Museum & Visitor Center (Map p243; ☑707-537-5397; www.mendoparks. org; 45035 Main St; ⊙11am-4pm) Enjoy maps, books, information and exhibits, including a scale model of 1890 Mendocino, plus a historical setting with original Victorian-period furniture and decor.

Jug Handle State Reserve

Between Mendocino and Fort Bragg, **Jug Handle** (☑707-937-5804; www.parks.ca.gov; Hwy 1, Caspar; ⊙sunrise-sunset; ▣⚠) ∅ FREE preserves an **ecological staircase** that you can view on a 5-mile (round-trip) self-guided nature trail. The reserve is also a good spot to stroll the headlands, whale-watch or lounge on the beach; you can pick up a printed guide detailing the area's geology, flora and fauna from the parking lot. Note that it's easy to miss the entrance; watch for the turnoff, just north of Caspar.

Five wave-cut terraces ascend in steps from the seashore, each 100ft and 100,000 years removed from the previous one, and each with its own distinct geology and vegetation. One of the terraces has a **pygmy forest**, similar to the better known example at Van Damme State Park, 9 miles south.

Jug Handle Creek Farm & Nature Center (☑707-964-4630; www.jughandlecreek farm.com; 15501 N Hwy 1; tent sites $14, r & cabins adult/student $45/38; ⊙9am-8pm; ▣☺☻) is a nonprofit 39-acre farm with rustic cabins and hostel rooms in a 19th-century farmhouse. Call ahead about work-stay discounts. Drive 5 miles north of Mendocino to Caspar; the farm is on the east side of Hwy 1. Take the second driveway after Fern Creek Rd.

Fort Bragg

In the past, Fort Bragg was Mendocino's ugly stepsister, home to a lumber mill, a scrappy downtown and blue-collar locals who gave a cold welcome to outsiders. Since the mill closure in 2002, the town has started to reinvent itself, slowly warming to a tourism-based economy, with the downtown continuing to develop as a wonderfully unpretentious alternative to Mendocino (even if the southern end of town is hideous). Unlike the *entire* franchise-free 180-mile stretch of Coastal Hwy 1 between here and the Golden Gate, in Fort Bragg you can get a

Big Mac, grande latte or any of a number of chain-store products whose buildings blight the landscape. Don't fret. In downtown you'll find better hamburgers and coffee, old-school architecture and residents eager to show off their little town.

By car, twisting Hwy 20 provides the main access to Fort Bragg from the east, and most facilities are near Main St, a 2-mile stretch of Hwy 1. The Mendocino Transit Authority (p232) operates bus 65, which travels between Fort Bragg, Willits, Ukiah and Santa Rosa daily, with an afternoon return ($23, three hours, four daily). Monday to Friday, the North Coast route 60 goes north between Navarro River junction and Albion, Little River, Mendocino and Fort Bragg ($2.25, 1½ hours, two daily).

◉ Sights & Activities

Fort Bragg has the same banner North Coast activities as Mendocino – beachcombing, surfing, hiking – but basing yourself here is much cheaper and arguably less quaint and pretentious. The wharf lies at Noyo Harbor – the mouth of the Noyo River – south of downtown. Here you can find whale-watching cruises and deep-sea fishing trips.

★ Mendocino Coast Botanical Gardens   GARDENS
(☎707-964-4352; www.gardenbythesea.org; 18220 N Hwy 1; adult/child/senior $14/5/10; ⊙9am-5pm Mar-Oct, to 4pm Nov-Feb; 🅿) 🌿 This gem of Northern California displays native flora, rhododendrons and heritage roses. The succulent display alone is amazing and the organic garden is harvested by volunteers to feed area residents in need. The serpentine paths wander along 47 seafront acres south of town. Primary trails are wheelchair accessible.

Northcoast Artists Gallery   GALLERY
(www.northcoastartists.org; 362 N Main St; ⊙10am-6pm) An excellent local arts cooperative where 20 full-time members work in photography, glass, woodworking, jewelry, painting, sculpture, textiles and printmaking. Openings are on the first Friday of the month. Visit www.mendocino.com for a comprehensive list of galleries throughout Mendocino County.

Glass Beach   BEACH
(Elm St) Named for (what's left of) the sea-polished glass in the sand, remnants of its days as a city dump, this beach is now part of MacKerricher State Park (p250). Take the headlands trail from Elm St, off Main St, but leave the glass – visitors are not supposed to pocket souvenirs.

Triangle Tattoo & Museum   MUSEUM
(☎707-964-8814; www.triangletattoo.com; 356b N Main St; ⊙noon-7pm) FREE This one-off museum has an excellent exhibition of international tattoo art and explains the history in various cultures. You can also get a tattoo done here if you fancy.

★ Skunk Train   HISTORIC TRAIN
(☎707-964-6371; www.skunktrain.com; 100 W Laurel St; adult/child $84/42; ⊙9am-3pm; 🚸) Fort Bragg's pride and joy, the vintage train got its nickname in 1925 for its stinky gas-powered steam engines, but today the historic steam and diesel locomotives are odorless. Passing through redwood-forested mountains, along rivers, over bridges and through deep mountain tunnels, the trains run from both Fort Bragg and Willits (p261) to the midway point of Northspur, where they turn around.

If you want to go to Willits, plan to spend the night. The depot is downtown at the foot of Laurel St, one block west of Main St.

All-Aboard Adventures   FISHING, WHALE-WATCHING
(☎707-964-1881; www.allaboardadventures.com; 32400 N Harbor Dr; fishing trips $80, whale-watching $40) Captain Tim leads five-hour crabbing and salmon-fishing trips and two-hour whale-watching explorations during the whale migration.

✦ Festivals & Events

Fort Bragg Whale Festival   WILDLIFE
(www.mendowhale.com; ⊙Mar) Held on the third weekend in March, with microbrew tastings, crafts fairs and whale-watching trips.

Paul Bunyan Days   CARNIVAL
(www.paulbunyandays.com; ⊙Sep) Held on Labor Day weekend in September, celebrate California's logging history with a logging show, square dancing, parade and fair.

🛌 Sleeping

Fort Bragg's lodging is cheaper than Mendocino's, but most of the motels along noisy Hwy 1 don't have air-conditioning, so you'll hear traffic through your windows. The best of the motel bunch is **Colombi Motel**

(☑707-964-5773; www.colombimotel.com; 647 E Oak St; 1-/2-bedroom units with kitchenette from $80/85; ❂❧), which is in town. Most B&Bs do not have TVs and they all include breakfast.

Country Inn B&B $$

(☑707-964-3737; www.bcourguests.com; 632 N Main St; r $125-170; P❂❧❦) This gingerbread-trimmed B&B in the middle of town is an excellent way to dodge the chain motels for a good-value stay. The lovely family hosts are welcoming and easygoing and can offer good local tips. Breakfast can be delivered to your room and at night you can soak in a hot tub out back. There is a minimum two-night stay at weekends.

Grey Whale Inn B&B $$

(☑707-964-0640; www.greywhaleinn.com; 615 N Main St; r $110-172; P❂❧) Situated in a historic (some say haunted!) building and former hospital on the north side of town (walking distance from downtown and glass beach), this comfortable, family-run inn has simple, straightforward rooms that are good value for families. Expect a warm welcome, especially from Sweetpea, the resident cat.

Shoreline Cottages MOTEL, COTTAGE $$

(☑707-964-2977; www.shoreline-cottage.com; 18725 Hwy 1; d $129-149; P❂❧❦) Low-key, four-person rooms and cottages with kitchens surround a central, tree-filled lawn. The family rooms are a good bargain, and suites feature modern artwork and clean sight lines. All rooms have microwaves, cable TV, snacks and access to a library of DVDs, plus there's a communal hot tub.

Weller House Inn B&B $$$

(☑707-964-4415; www.wellerhouse.com; 524 Stewart St; r $200-310; P❂❧) Rooms in this beautifully restored 1886 mansion have down comforters, underfloor heating, good mattresses and fine linens. The water tower is the tallest structure in town – and it has a hot tub at the top! Breakfast is in the massive redwood ballroom.

✕ Eating

Similar to the lodging scene, the food in Fort Bragg is less spendy than Mendocino, but there are a number of truly excellent options, mainly located on or around Main St. Self-caterers should try the farmers market (p250) downtown or the **Harvest Market** (☑707-964-7000; cnr Hwys 1 & 20; ◷5am-11pm) for the best groceries.

★ Taka's Japanese Grill JAPANESE $

(☑707-964-5204; 250 N Main St; mains $10.50-17; ◷11:30am-3pm & 4:30-9pm; P) Although it may look fairly run of the mill, this is an exceptional Japanese restaurant. The owner is a former grader at the Tokyo fish market so the quality is tops and he makes a weekly run to San Francisco to source freshly imported seafood. Sushi, teriyaki dishes, noodle soups and pan-fried noodles with salmon, beef or chicken are just a few of the options.

Los Gallitos MEXICAN $

(☑707-964-4519; 130 S Main St; burritos $5.50-6.50; ◷11am-8pm Mon-Sat, from 10am Sun) A packed hole-in-the-wall that serves the best Mexican on the coast. Chips are homemade, the guacamole is chunky and the dishes, from the fresh fish tacos to homemade pork tamales and generous soups, are consistently flavorful and well beyond the standard glob of refried beans. It's located across the parking lot from the CVS.

Cowlick's Handmade Ice Cream ICE CREAM $

(☑707-962-9271; www.cowlicksicecream.com; 250b N Main St; scoops from $1.85; ◷11am-9pm) Just great ice cream in fun flavors, from classics such as mocha almond fudge to the very unusual, such as candy cap mushroom (tastes like maple syrup but better), ginger or blackberry chocolate chunk. The sorbets (try the grapefruit Campari) are also delish.

Headlands Coffeehouse CAFE $

(☑707-964-1987; www.headlandscoffeehouse. com; 120 E Laurel St; mains $4-8; ◷7am-10pm Mon-Sat, to 7pm Sun; ❧✐) The town's best cafe is in the middle of the historic downtown, with high ceilings and lots of atmosphere. The menu gets raves for the Belgian waffles, homemade soups, veggie-friendly salads, panini and lasagna.

Silver's at the Wharf CALIFORNIAN $

(☑707-964-4283; www.silversatthewharf.com; 32260 N Harbor Dr; mains $10-15; ◷11am-9:30pm; P♿) Given its position, overlooking the docks, you would expect this to be a swanky oysters-and-champagne sort of place. Far from it. The decor is stuck in the '60s and the cuisine is well prepared but solidly traditional, with a vast selection that includes pasta, rib-eye steak, Mexican fare and seafood, such as Pacific

NORTH COAST BEER TOUR

The craft breweries of the North Coast don't mess around – bold hop profiles, Belgian-style ales and smooth lagers are regional specialties, and they're produced with style. Some breweries are better than others, but the following tour makes for an excellent long weekend of beer tasting in the region.

➡ Anderson Valley Brewing Company (p255), Boonville

➡ North Coast Brewing Company (p250), Fort Bragg

➡ Six Rivers Brewery (p275), near Arcata

➡ Eel River Brewing (p268), Fortuna

Bay shrimp and calamari steak. Ideal for families.

Farmers Market   MARKET $
(cnr E Laurel & N Franklin Sts; ⊙3:30-6pm Wed May-Oct) This is an above-average farmers market with an excellent array of fresh produce, plus breads, preserves and locally produced cheese.

★ Piaci Pub & Pizzeria   ITALIAN $$
(☑707-961-1133; www.piacipizza.com; 120 W Redwood Ave; mains $8-20; ⊙11am-9:30pm Mon-Thu, to 10pm Fri & Sat, 4-9:30pm Sun) Fort Bragg's must-visit pizzeria is known for its sophisticated wood-fired, brick-oven pizzas as much as for its long list of microbrews. Try the 'Gustoso' – with chèvre, pesto and seasonal pears, all carefully orchestrated on a thin crust. It's tiny, loud and fun, with much more of a bar atmosphere than a restaurant. Expect to wait at peak times.

North Coast Brewing Company   AMERICAN $$
(☑707-964-2739; www.northcoastbrewing.com; 455 N Main St; mains $17-25; ⊙restaurant 4-10pm Sun-Thu, to 11pm Fri & Sat, bar from 2pm daily; 🐾) Though thick, rare slabs of steak and a list of specials demonstrate that they take the food as seriously as the bevvies, it's the burgers and garlic fries that soak up the fantastic selection of handcrafted brews. A great stop for serious beer lovers.

★ Cucina Verona   ITALIAN $$$
(☑707-964-6844; www.cucinaverona.com; 124 E Laurel St; mains $26-30; ⊙9am-9pm) A real-deal Italian restaurant with no-fail traditional dishes, plus a few with a Californian tweak, such as butternut-squash lasagne and artichoke bruschetta. The atmosphere is as comforting as the cuisine, with dim lighting, a warm color scheme and unobtrusive live music most evenings. There is an extensive microbrewery selection on offer, as well as local and imported wines.

☆ Entertainment

Gloriana Musical Theater   THEATER
(Eagles Hall Theater; ☑707-964-7469; www.gloriana.org; 210 N Corry St; tickets from $12; ⊙hours vary) Since 1976 this company has been staging high-standard musical theater and operettas.

🛍 Shopping

There's plenty of window-shopping in Fort Bragg's compact downtown, including a string of antique shops along Franklin St.

Fractalize Eco Boutique   FASHION & ACCESSORIES
(☑707-672-2208; www.fractalizeecoboutique.com; 107 E Laurel St; ⊙11am-5pm Wed-Sun) Sells a fabulous array of women's fashions in rich earth colors made with all-natural fabrics, including hemp and bamboo.

Outdoor Store   SPORTS & OUTDOORS
(☑707-964-1407; www.mendooutdoors.com; 247 N Main St; ⊙10am-5:30pm Mon-Sat, to 5pm Sun) If you're planning on camping on the coast or exploring the Lost Coast, this is the best outfitter in the region, stocking detailed maps of the region's wilderness areas, fuel for stoves and high-quality gear.

ℹ Information

Fort Bragg-Mendocino Coast Chamber of Commerce (☑707-961-6300; www.mendocinocoast.com; 332 S Main St; ⊙10am-5pm Mon-Fri, to 3pm Sat; 🐾) The chamber of commerce has lots of helpful information about this stretch of coast and what's on. Its online guide is also worth checking out.

MacKerricher State Park

Three miles north of Fort Bragg, the MacKerricher State Park (☑707-964-9112; www.parks.ca.gov) preserves 9 miles of pristine rocky headlands, sandy beaches, dunes and tidepools.

The visitor center sits next to the whale skeleton at the park entrance. Hike the

Coastal Trail along dark-sand beaches and see rare and endangered plant species. **Lake Cleone** is a 30-acre freshwater lake stocked with trout and visited by over 90 species of birds. At nearby **Laguna Point** an interpretive boardwalk (accessible to visitors with disabilities) overlooks harbor seals and, from December to April, migrating whales. **Ricochet Ridge Ranch** (☑707-964-7669; www.horse-vacation.com; 24201 N Hwy 1; per hr/day $60/330; ☉9am-6:30pm) offers horseback-riding trips through redwoods or along the beach.

Just north of the park is **Pacific Star Winery** (☑707-964-1155; www.pacificstarwinery.com; 33000 Hwy 1; tastings $5; ☉noon-5pm Thu-Mon), in a dramatic, rub-your-eyes-in-disbelief-beautiful location on a bluff over the sea. The wines don't get pros excited but they are very drinkable, the owners are friendly and you're encouraged to picnic at one of the many coast-side tables, stroll some of the short coastal trails along the cliffs and generally enjoy yourself (which isn't hard).

Popular **campgrounds** (☑800-444-2725; www.reserveamerica.com; tent & RV sites $35), nestled in pine forest, have hot showers and water; the first-choice reservable tent sites are numbers 21 to 59. Ten superb, secluded walk-in tent sites (numbers 1 to 10) are first-come, first-served.

Westport

If sleepy Westport feels like the peaceful edge of nowhere, that's because it is. The last hamlet before the Lost Coast, on a twisting 15-mile drive north of Fort Bragg, it is the last town before Hwy 1 veers inland on the 22-mile ascent to meet Hwy 101 in Leggett. The population here is around 60 and the town today consists of little more than a couple of choice places to stay, a fine pub, a small grocer and deli, and a couple of gas pumps. Westport dates from 1877 when it was called Beall's Landing after a (long-gone) timber loading facility built by Samuel Beall, the town's first white settler.

Head 1.5 miles north of town for the ruggedly beautiful **Westport-Union Landing State Beach** (☑707-937-5804; 40501 Hwy 1; tent sites $25; 🅿🚻), which extends for 3 miles on coastal bluffs. A rough hiking trail leaves the primitive campground and passes by tidepools and streams, accessible at low tide.

🛌 Sleeping & Eating

Westport Inn INN $
(☑707-964-5135; www.westportinnca.com; 37040 Hwy 1, Shoreline Hwy; r from $80; 🅿😊🐾) Dating from the 1970s, this simple place to stay has beach access and recently refurbished, pleasant rooms with fresh flowers and nice art work. The owner is charming and can provide meals on request.

★**Westport Hotel & Old Abalone Pub** INN $$
(☑877-964-3688; www.westporthotel.us; 38921 Hwy 1, Shoreline Hwy; r $150-245; 🅿😊📶) Westport Hotel & Old Abalone Pub is quiet enough to have a motto that brags 'You've finally found nowhere.' The rooms are sumptuous – feather duvets, hardwood furniture, plush carpeting – with excellent views. The classy historic pub downstairs is the only option for dinner, so be thankful it's a delicious sampling of whimsical California fusions and hearty, expertly presented pub food.

Howard Creek Ranch CABIN $$
(☑707-964-6725; www.howardcreekranch.com; 40501 N Hwy 1, Shoreline Hwy; r $90-198, cabins $105-198; 🅿😊📶🐾) Howard Creek Ranch, sitting on 60 stunning acres of forest and farmland abutting the wilderness, has accommodations in an 1880s farmhouse or a few cabins including a carriage barn, whose way-cool redwood rooms have been expertly handcrafted by the owner. Rates include full breakfast. Bring hiking boots, not high heels.

ALONG HIGHWAY 101

To get into the most remote and wild parts of the North Coast on the quick, eschew winding Hwy 1 for inland Hwy 101, which runs north from San Francisco as a freeway, then as a two- or four-lane highway north of Sonoma County, occasionally pausing under the traffic lights of small towns.

Know that escaping the Bay Area at rush hour (weekdays between 4pm and 7pm) ain't easy. You might sit bumper-to-bumper through Santa Rosa or Willits, where trucks bound for the coast turn onto Hwy 20.

Although Hwy 101 may not look as enticing as the coastal route, it's faster and less winding, leaving you time along the way to detour into Sonoma and Mendocino Counties' wine regions (Mendocino claims to be the greenest wine region in the country), explore pastoral Anderson Valley, splash about Clear Lake or soak at hot-springs resorts outside Ukiah – time well spent indeed!

Hopland

Apparently using the most solar power per capita in the world, Hopland flaunts its eco-geek, green-living ways at every turn with more organic produce available than you can shake a carrot stick at, plus a sustainable-living demonstration site, complete with a bio-fuel pump that recycles vegetable oil from local restaurants! Hops were first grown here in 1866, but Prohibition brought the industry temporarily to a halt. Today, with its location as a gateway to Mendocino County's wine country, booze drives Hopland's economy again, with wine tasting the primary draw. Most of the tasting rooms are conveniently located right on Hwy 101, which runs through the center of town, and are generally small, boutique-style operations offering an enjoyable personalized experience.

◉ Sights

For an excellent weekend trip, use Hopland as a base for exploring the regional wineries. More information about the constantly growing roster of wineries is available at www.destinationhopland.com. Find a map to the wine region at www.visitmendocino.com.

Brutocao Cellars TASTING ROOM
(✆800-433-3689; www.brutocaocellars.com; 13500 S Hwy 101; ◷10am-5pm; P) FREE
Located in a former 1920s schoolhouse in central Hopland, this fourth-generation family-owned winery has bocce courts, bold red wines and chocolate – a perfect combo. There is also, refreshingly, no charge for wine tasting here (although there is generally a limit to how much tippling you can do!). The gift shop specializes in gourmet goodies, great for gifts.

Real Goods Solar Living Center MUSEUM
(✆707-742-2460; www.solarliving.org; 13771 S Hwy 101; self-guided tour free, guided tour per person/family $3/5, wine tasting $5; ◷center 9am-6pm daily, tours 11am & 3pm Sat & Sun Apr-Oct; P🖼) ⌀ This progressive, futuristic 12-acre campus is largely responsible for

the area's bold green initiatives. The Real Goods Store, run by the same company that sold the first solar panel in the US in 1978, is an impressive straw-bale-house showroom. You can also enjoy an exhibition on permaculture and a demonstration of solar-powered water systems. Plus, on the off chance your car runs on bio-diesel, you can fill up your tank here.

Graziano Family of Wines WINERY
(✆707-744-8466; www.grazianofamilyofwines.com; 13251 S Hwy 101; ◷10am-5pm; P) FREE
The Italian Graziano family is one of the oldest grape-growing families in Mendocino County and specializes in 'Cal-Ital' wines – including Primitivo, Dolcetto, Barbera and Sangiovese – at some great prices. Wine tasting is complimentary.

Saracina Vineyards WINERY
(✆707-670-0199; www.saracina.com; 11684 S Hwy 101; tasting & tour $15; ◷11am-5pm; P) ⌀ The highlight of a tour here is the descent into the cool caves. Sensuous whites are all bio-dynamically and sustainably farmed.

🛏 Sleeping & Eating

Piazza de Campovida INN $$
(✆707-744-1977; www.piazzadecampovida.com; 13441 S Hwy 101; ste $185-220; P🐕🖼📶) Modern Californian meets Italian at this very comfortable inn where all of the spacious suites have Jacuzzis, fireplaces and private balconies. The homey taverna and pizzeria in front have big tables for communal dining and fantastic artisanal pizzas, craft beer and wine.

Burger My Way BURGERS $
(✆707-744-8762; 13600 Mountain House Rd, 76 Gas Station; burgers $6-8; ◷8am-9pm; P🖼) Look beyond the surroundings (this place is attached to a gas station) and instead concentrate on the quality of burgers, with some 17 varieties, including vegetarian, turkey and salmon. The fries are hand cut and crispy and there are non-burger options too, including a selection of Mexican dishes, sandwiches and salads. But it's the burgers that will have you salivating...

Bluebird Cafe DINER $
(✆707-744-1633; 13340 S Hwy 101; breakfast $11-13, lunch mains $10-15; ◷7am-2pm Mon-Thu, to 7pm Fri-Sun; 🖼) This classic American diner serves hearty breakfasts and homemade pie (the summer selection of peach-blueberry pie is dreamy). For a more

exciting culinary adventure, try the wild-game burgers, such as elk, with a bite of horseradish.

Clear Lake

With over 100 miles of shoreline and 68 square miles of surface area, Clear Lake is the largest naturally occurring freshwater lake in California (Tahoe is bigger, but crosses the Nevada state line). In summer the warm water thrives with algae, giving it a murky green appearance and creating a fabulous habitat for fish, especially bass and catfish, so you can expect plenty of anglers here, particularly on weekends. Mt Konocti, a 4200ft-tall dormant volcano, lords over the scene. The lake is ringed by small, tasteful resorts with places to stay, dine and kick back enjoying the lake views. You can also rent boats, kayaks, paddleboards and just about anything else that floats on the water at one of several marinas. On a more somber note, the area was devastated by fire in the summer of 2015 with Middletown, in particular, being badly affected; a vigorous rebuilding program continues.

Locals refer to the northwest portion as 'upper lake' and the southeast portion as 'lower lake.' Likeable and well-serviced Lakeport (population 4695) sits on the northwest shore, a 45-minute drive east of Hopland along Hwy 175 (off Hwy 101); tiny, Old West style Kelseyville (population 3353) is 7 miles south. Clearlake, off the southeastern shore, is the biggest town.

Hwy 20 links the relatively bland north-shore hamlets of Nice (the northernmost town) and Lucerne, 4 miles southeast. Middletown, a cute village, lies 20 miles south of Clearlake at the junction of Hwys 175 and 29, 40 minutes north of Calistoga.

◉ Sights

Clear Lake State Park STATE PARK
(☑707-279-2267, 707-279-4293; www.clearlake statepark.org; 5300 Soda Bay Rd, Kelseyville; per car $8; ⊙sunrise-sunset; Ⓟ⛺) Four miles from Kelseyville, on the lake's southern shore, this park is idyllic and gorgeous, with hiking trails, fishing, boating and camping. The bird-watching is extraordinary. The visitor center has natural history and cultural diorama exhibits.

🛏 Sleeping & Eating

For the greatest range of places to stay, head to Lakeport, where most accommodations are conveniently located on and around Main St. Be sure to make reservations ahead on weekends and during summer, when people flock to the cool water. There

---

TOP CLEAR LAKE WINERIES

These four wineries are the best; some offer tours by appointment.

Kaz Winery (☑707-833-2536; www.kazwinery.com; 1435 Big Valley Rd, Lakeport; tasting $5-10; ⊙11am-5pm Sat or by appointment; Ⓟ) A cult favorite, supercool Kaz is about blends: whatever is in the organic vineyards goes into the wine – and they're blended at crush, not during fermentation. Expect lesser-known varietals like Tannat and Lenoir, and worthwhile cabernet-merlot blends. Bottles cost $26 to $45.

Brassfield Estate (☑707-998-1895; www.brassfieldestate.com; 10915 High Valley Rd, Clearlake Oaks; tasting $5; ⊙11am-5pm May-Nov, from noon Dec-Apr; Ⓟ) Remote, stunning Tuscan villa in the unique High Valley appellation surrounded by magnificent landscaped gardens.

Wildhurst (☑707-279-4302; www.wildhurst.com; 3855 Main St, Kelseyville; ⊙10am-5pm; Ⓟ) Looking like a Western movie set, downtown Kelseyville is where family-owned winery tasting rooms such as Wildhurst (tasting free) rustle beside hardware stores, soda fountains and cafes.

Langtry Estate Vineyards (☑707-995-7521; www.langtryestate.com; 21000 Butts Canyon Rd, Middletown; tasting $5, tours from $60; ⊙11am-5pm; Ⓟ) This winery has a stunning location on a hilltop overlooking the lake with picnic tables available for anyone who wants to pack a lunch. Visitors can opt for a wine tasting of six wines, a tasting plus tour, a vineyard tour or a historical tour that includes a wine tasting with appetizers at the nearby Lillie Langry mansion; the famous late actress owned the vineyard and house from 1888 until 1906.

are several campsites close to the lake, although be aware that they can flood if there are heavy rains, so always check in advance. For the budget conscious, Lakeport also has the most affordable options.

Clearlake

Visto del Lago Lakehouse
CABIN $$

(707-356-9721; www.vdlresort.com; 14103 Lakeshore Dr, Clearlake; cottages $75-179; P☺♠) Located right on the main road, so handy for shops and restaurants, these clean-as-a-whistle cottages are a delight. Sizes and facilities vary greatly, but all have well-equipped kitchenettes and are comfortably furnished. Other options may include hot tubs, fireplaces and Netflix; one cabin even has its own pool table. There is an outside Jacuzzi, swing chair and barbecue right on the lake.

Lakeport & Kelseyville

There are a number of motels along the main drags in Kelseyville and Lakeport, but if you want fresh air, Clear Lake State Park has four **campgrounds** (800-444-7275; www.reserveamerica.com; State Park Rd; tent & RV sites $35; ☺year round; P⚞⚟) with showers. The weekly **farmers market** (www.clearlakefarmersmarket.com/; Hwy 29 & Thomas Dr; ☺8:30am-noon Sat Jun-Oct) is in Kelseyville.

★Lakeport English Inn
B&B $$

(707-263-4317; www.lakeportenglishinn.com; 675 N Main St, Lakeport; r $185-210, cottages $210; P☺✳♠) The finest B&B at Clear Lake is an 1875 Carpenter Gothic with 10 impeccably furnished rooms, styled with a nod to the English countryside and with such quaint names as the Prince of Wales or (wait for it) Roll in the Hay. Weekends take high tea (nonguests welcome by reservation), with scones and real Devonshire cream.

★Angelina's Bakery & Espresso
CAFE $

(707-263-0391; www.angelinas365.com; 365 N Main St, Lakeport; sandwiches from $5; ☺7am-5pm Mon-Fri, 8am-2pm Sat; ♠) The best baked goodies in Clear Lake, especially the giant decadent muffins and gooey cinnamon rolls. Also makes sandwiches to order and serves savory pastries. The coffee is the real McCoy, with a caffeine kick that should set you up for the day.

Park Place
AMERICAN $

(707-263-0444; www.parkplacelakeport.com; 50 3rd St, Lakeport; mains $7-11; ☺11am-9pm Tue-Sun, to 3pm Mon; P) Simple but right on the waterfront, come to this bright and completely unpretentious eatery for basics like pasta, burgers and pizza made from sustainable, local produce at great prices. A local favorite.

Studebaker's Coffee House
DELI $

(707-279-8871; 3990 Main St, Kelseyville; sandwiches from $6; ☺6am-4pm Mon-Fri, 7am-4pm Sat, 7am-2pm Sun) A friendly, old-style diner with plenty of character, from black-and-white checker linoleum floors to old photos on the wall. Great sandwiches, including vegetarian options, plus Mexican fare such as quesadillas and burritos; the coffee's good too.

★Saw Shop Bistro
CALIFORNIAN $$

(707-278-0129; www.sawshopbistro.com; 3825 Main St, Kelseyville; small plates $10-16, mains $15-26; ☺11:30am-10pm Tue-Sat; ♠) The best restaurant in Lake County serves a California-cuisine menu of wild salmon and rack of lamb, as well as a small-plates menu of sushi, lobster tacos, Kobe-beef burgers and flatbread pizzas. Laid-back atmosphere, too. Reservations recommended.

Northshore

Tallman Hotel
HISTORIC HOTEL $$

(information 707-275-2244, reservations 707-275-2245; www.tallmanhotel.com; 9550 Main St, Upper Lake; r $185-265; P☺✳♠) The centerpiece may be the smartly renovated historic hotel – tile bathrooms, warm lighting, thick linens – but the rest of the property's lodging, including the shady garden, walled-in swimming pool, brick patios and porches, exudes timeless elegance. Some garden rooms come with outdoor Japanese soaking tubs heated by an energy-efficient geothermal-solar system.

Featherbed Railroad Co
HOTEL $$

(707-274-8378; www.featherbedrailroad.com; 2870 Lakeshore Blvd, Nice; cabooses $175-220; ☺✳⚞) A treat for train buffs and kids, Featherbed has 10 comfy, real cabooses on a grassy lawn. Some of the cabooses straddle the border between kitschy and tacky (the 'Easy Rider' has a Harley-Davidson headboard and a mirrored ceiling), but they're great fun if you keep a sense of humor. There's a tiny beach across the road.

Sea Breeze Resort COTTAGE **$$**
(☑707-998-3327; www.seabreezeresort.net; 9595 Harbor Dr, Glenhaven; cottages $125-180; ⊗Apr-Oct; P😊❄🐾) Just south of Lucerne on a small peninsula, lush green gardens surround seven spotless lakeside cottages. All but one have full kitchens.

🍷 Drinking & Nightlife

Library Park, in Lakeport, has free lakeside Friday-evening summer concerts, with blues and rockabilly tunes to appeal to road-trippers.

Kelsey Creek Brewing BREWERY
(☑707-279-2311; www.kelseycreekbrewing.com; 3945 Main St, Kelseyville; ⊗2-8pm Mon-Fri, noon-8pm Sat, noon-6pm Sun) A 'hop'-ping fun local's scene with excellent craft beer, peanut shells on the floor and a bring-your-own-food, bring-your-dog kind of laid-back vibe.

☆ Entertainment

Lakeport Auto Movies CINEMA
(www.lakeportautomovies.com; 52 Soda Bay Rd, Lakeport; 1/2/3 people per car $10/18/25; ⊗Fri & Sat Apr-Sep; 🐾) Lakeport is home to one of the few surviving and wonderfully nostalgic drive-in movie theaters, with showings on Friday and Saturday nights.

ℹ Information

Lake County Visitor Information Center
(☑800-525-3743; www.lakecounty.com; 255 N Forbes St, Lakeport; ⊗9am-5pm Mon-Sat, noon-4pm Sun) Has complete information and an excellent website, which allows potential visitors to narrow their focus by interests.

ℹ Getting Around

Lake Transit (☑707-994-3334, 707-263-3334; www.laketransit.org; 9240 Highway 53, Lower Lake) Operates weekday routes between Middletown, Calistoga and St Helena ($5, 35 minutes, three daily). Buses serve Ukiah ($8, two hours, four daily), from Clearlake via Lakeport ($5, 1¼ hours, seven daily). Since piecing together routes and times can be difficult, it's best to phone ahead.

Anderson Valley

A one-time redwood-logging community, rolling hills surround pocket-size Anderson Valley, more famous today for the apple orchards, vineyards, pastures and its general air of tranquility. Visitors come primarily to winery-hop; the winery scene here has been compared to the Napa Valley some 30 years ago. Most of the wineries are clustered between Boonville and Navarro, but you'll also find good hiking and cycling in the hills and the chance to escape civilization (although weekends can get busy with San Franciscans escaping the clamor of the city). Other things to check out include the craft breweries and the farmstead cheeses; look for signs on the roadside. Cheese is also sold at several of the vineyards and agreeably available for tasting along with the wine. Traveling through the valley is the most common route to Mendocino and Fort Bragg from San Francisco.

Boonville (population 1488) and Philo (population 349) are the valley's principal towns. From Ukiah, winding Hwy 253 heads 20 miles south to Boonville. Equally scenic Hwy 128 twists and turns 60 miles between Cloverdale on Hwy 101, south of Hopland, and Albion on coastal Hwy 1.

◎ Sights & Activities

Philo Apple Farm FARM
(☑707-895-2333; www.philoapplefarm.com; 18501 Greenwood Rd, Philo; ⊗10am-5pm; P🐾) 🍃 For the best fruit, skip the obvious roadside stands and head to this gorgeous farm for organic preserves, chutneys, heirloom apples and pears, as well as a tasteful array of homeware and furniture. For overnight guests, the farm also hosts **cooking classes**. You can make a weekend out of it by staying in one of the Philo Apple Farm Guest Cottages (p257).

Anderson Valley Brewing Company BREWERY
(☑707-895-2337; www.avbc.com; 17700 Hwy 253, Boonville; tasting from $2, tours & disc-golf course free; ⊗11am-6pm Sat-Thu, to 7pm Fri; P🐾) 🍃 East of the Hwy 128 crossroads, this solar-powered brewery crafts award-winning beers in a Bavarian-style brewhouse. You can also toss around a Frisbee on the **disc-golf course** while enjoying the brews, but, be warned, the sun can take its toll. Tours leave at 1:30pm daily (no reservations).

Anderson Valley Historical Society Museum MUSEUM
(☑707-895-3207; www.andersonvalleymuseum.org; 12340 Hwy 128, Boonville; ⊗1-4pm Sat & Sun Feb-Nov; P) **FREE** Situated in a tastefully renovated red schoolhouse west of Boonville, this museum displays historical artifacts, including an interesting display centered on

the Pomos (an indigenous Native American tribe who once populated this region and were famed for their beautiful woven baskets). You can examine the works here, ranging from 4ft-to-5ft storage baskets to tiny intricate examples barely the size of a finger tip.

✨ Festivals & Events

Pinot Noir Festival   WINE
(☎707-895-9463; www.avwines.com; Goldeneye Winery, Philo; ☺May) One of Anderson Valley's many wine celebrations; held over four days toward the end of May.

Sierra Nevada World Music Festival   MUSIC
(www.snwmf.com; Mendocino County Fairgrounds, 14400 Hwy 128, Boonville; ☺mid-Jun) In the middle of June, over three days, the sounds of reggae and roots fill the air, co-mingling with the scent of Mendocino County's *other* cash crop.

Mendocino County Fair
& Apple Show   FAIR
(www.mendocountyfair.com; Mendocino County Fairgrounds, 14400 Hwy 128, Boonville; adult/child $9/6; ☺mid-Sep; ✋) A county classic autumnal fair with wine tasting, a rodeo and lively parades.

🛏 Sleeping

Overall the accommodation options are in the midrange to high-end categories, catering to San Franciscan weekenders seeking a self-pampering break with wine tasting, vineyard views and Egyptian-cotton sheets thrown in. If you are looking for somewhere more family and budget friendly, there are some excellent campsites in the valley, some with cabin accommodation available. The Anderson Valley Chamber of Commerce can advise on places to stay throughout the region.

Hendy Woods State Park   CAMPGROUND $
(☎707-937-5804, reservations 800-444-7275; www.reserveamerica.com; Hwy 128; tent & RV sites $40, cabins $60; ℗) Bordered by the Navarro River on Hwy 128, west of Philo, this lovely park has hiking, picnicking and a forested campground with hot showers.

Other Place   COTTAGE $$
(Sheep Dung Properties; ☎707-895-3979; www.sheepdung.com; 14655 CA-128, Boonville; cottages $190-350; ℗☺🔊🏕) Located outside of town on a ridge with blissful panoramic and vineyard views, the 500 acres of ranch land here surround private, fully equipped hilltop cottages. The owners also hire out a cottage in downtown Boonville that shares access to the ranch with its picturesque views and walking trails.

★ Boonville Hotel   BOUTIQUE HOTEL $$$
(☎707-895-2210; www.boonvillehotel.com; 14050 Hwy 128, Boonville; d $295-365; ℗☀🏕🔊) Decked out in a contemporary American country feel with sea-grass flooring, pastel colors and fine linens, this historic hotel's rooms and suites are safe for urbanites who refuse to abandon style just because they've gone to the country. The rooms are all different and there are agreeable extras, including hammocks and fireplaces.

TOP ANDERSON VALLEY WINERIES

The valley's cool nights yield high-acid, fruit-forward, food-friendly wines. Pinot Noir, Chardonnay and dry Gewürtztraminer flourish. Most wineries (www.avwines.com) sit outside Philo. Many are family-owned and offer free tastings; some give tours. The following are particularly noteworthy:

Navarro Vineyards (☎707-895-3686; www.navarrowine.com; 5601 Hwy 128, Philo; ☺8am-6pm Mon-Fri, to 5pm Sat & Sun; ℗) The best option around with award-winning Pinot Noir and dry Gewürztraminer; has twice-daily free tours (reservations accepted) and picnicking facilities.

Husch Vineyards (☎707-462-5370; www.huschvineyards.com; 4400 Hwy 128, Philo; ☺10am-6pm, to 5pm Nov-Mar; ℗) The oldest vineyard in the valley serves exquisite tastings inside a rose-covered cottage.

Bink Wines (☎707-895-2940; www.binkwines.com; 9000 Hwy 128, Philo; ☺11am-5pm Wed-Mon; ℗) This winery produces small-batch artisanal wines that get rave reviews. Bink is located within the Med-style Madrones complex, which houses a total of four local vintners, as well as a hotel, restaurant and gift shop.

★**Philo Apple Farm Guest Cottages**　　　COTTAGE $$$
(☑707-895-2333; www.philoapplefarm.com; 18501 Greenwood Rd, Philo; d $250-300; P☺) ✿ Set within the orchard, guests of bucolic Philo Apple Farm (p255) choose from four exquisite cottages, each built with reclaimed materials. With bright, airy spaces, polished plank floors, simple furnishings and views of the surrounding trees, each one is an absolute dream.

Red Door cottage is a favorite because of the bathroom – you can soak in the slipper tub, or shower on the private deck under the open sky. The cottages often get booked with participants of the farm's cooking classes, so book well in advance. For a swim, the Navarro River is within walking distance.

Madrones　　　HOTEL $$$
(☑707-895-2955; www.themadrones.com; 9000 Hwy 128, Philo; r $175-350; P☺☎) Tucked off the back of the Madrones Mediterranean-inspired complex that includes a restaurant and the wonderful Bink Wines tasting room, the spacious 'guest quarters' here are modern-country-luxe, with a tinge of Tuscany. Above all, they are eminently comfortable with plush furnishings, marshmallow-soft pillows, soft carpeting and a soothing color scheme.

✗ **Eating**

Boonville restaurants seem to open and close as they please, so expect hours to vary based on season and whims. There are several places along Hwy 128 which can supply a picnic with fancy local cheese and fresh bread. Locally grown produce is the norm in these parts, so you can expect organic seasonal veg and a pleasing lack of fast-food options. Nope, gourmet burgers don't count.

Paysanne　　　ICE CREAM $
(☑707-895-2210; www.sweetpaysanne.com; 14111 Hwy 128, Boonville; ice cream from $2.50; ☺10am-6pm Sun-Thu; ✎☀) Boonville's fantastic sweets shop serves the innovative flavors of Three Twins Ice Cream, whose delightful choices include Lemon Cookie and Strawberry Je Ne Sais Quoi (which has a hint of balsamic vinegar); it's the best ice cream to be found in the Anderson Valley according to the locals – and they know best.

Boonville General Store　　　DELI $
(☑707-895-9477; 17810 Farrer Lane, Boonville; dishes $7-14; ☺7:30am-3pm Mon-Thu, 7:30am-3pm & 5:30-8pm Fri, 8:30am-3pm Sat & Sun; P☀) ✿ Opposite the Boonville Hotel, this superb deli is good to stock up for picnics, offering gourmet sandwiches on homemade bread, thin-crust pizzas and organic cheeses. It also serves hearty homemade soups if you feel like grabbing a pew, as well as scrumptious breakfasts. Organic produce is used as far as possible and there are plenty of vegetarian options.

★**Table 128**　　　CALIFORNIAN $$
(☑707-895-2210; www.boonvillehotel.com; 14050 Hwy 128, Boonville; lunch mains $10-14, dinner mains $19-31; ☺6-8pm Thu-Mon Apr–mid-Jun, from 4:30pm mid-Jun–mid-Oct; P☎) Food-savvy travelers love the constantly changing New American menu here, featuring simple dishes done well, like Alaskan turbot, grilled local lamb, and cheesecake. The family-style service makes dinner a freewheeling, elegant social affair, with big farm tables and soft lighting. It's got great wines, craft beers, scotch and cocktails.

ⓘ **Information**

Anderson Valley Chamber of Commerce (☑707-895-2379; www.andersonvalley chamber.com; 9800 Hwy 128, Boonville; ☺9am-5pm Mon-Fri) Has tourist information and a complete schedule of annual events, plus can also advise on places to stay, including campsites.

Ukiah

As the county seat and Mendocino's largest city, Ukiah is mostly a utilitarian stop for travelers to refuel the car and get a bite. But, if you have to stop here for the night, you could do much worse: the town is a friendly place that's gentrifying. There is a plethora of cookie-cutter hotel chains, some cheaper mid-century motels and a handful of very good dining options. The coolest attractions, a pair of thermal springs and a sprawling campus for Buddhist studies complete with 10,000 golden Buddha statues, lie outside the city limits. There are also some excellent wineries and tasting rooms within easy access from the center; the helpful **Chamber of Commerce** (☑707-462-4705; www.gomendo.com; 200 S School St; ☺9am-5pm Mon-Fri) can point you in the right direction. Ukiah has a pleasant, walkable shopping district along School St near the courthouse, where you can find some idiosyncratic small shops and larger chains.

◉ Sights

Grace Hudson Museum & Sun House
MUSEUM

(☑707-467-2836; www.gracehudsonmuseum.org; 431 S Main St; $4; ⊘10am-4:30pm Wed-Sat, from noon Sun) One block east of State St, the collection's mainstays are paintings by Grace Hudson (1865-1937). Her sensitive depictions of Pomo people and other indigenous groups complement the ethnological work and Native American baskets collected by her husband, John Hudson. The lovely 1911 Sun House, adjacent to the museum, was the former Hudson home and is typical of the arts-and-crafts style of that era; docent-guided tours are available.

✷ Festivals & Events

Redwood Empire Fair
FAIR

(☑707-462-3884; www.redwoodempirefair.com; 1055 N State St; ⊘Jun & Aug; ⋒) There are two major fairs held here: the Redwood Empire Spring Fair, held over a weekend in early June, and the Redwood Empire Fair, held over a weekend in early August. Both have loads of events, ranging from quilt exhibitions to garden expos.

Ukiah Country PumpkinFest
CULTURAL

(www.cityofukiah.com; ⊘late Oct; ⋒) In late October, with an arts-and-crafts fair, children's carnival and a fiddle contest.

⨭ Sleeping

Hampton Inn
MOTEL $$

(☑707-462-6555; www.hamptoninn3.hilton.com; 1160 Airport Park Blvd; r $125-175; P❋✿❄✉) The best of the chain gang in Ukiah, with a whiff of a Hilton about it (Hampton is now part of the Hilton portfolio). Expect excellent amenities, including a fitness center and comprehensive offerings for the business bunch. The recently updated rooms may still be hotel-chain bland but are comfortable, carpeted and spacious.

✗ Eating

It'd be a crime to eat the fast-food junk located off the highway; Ukiah has a burgeoning food scene that pairs nicely with the surrounding wine country.

★ Schat's Bakery & Cafe
CAFE $

(☑707-462-1670; www.schats.com; 113 W Perkins St; lunch mains $5-8, dinner mains $8-14; ⊘5:30am-6pm Mon-Fri, to 5pm Sat) Founded by Dutch bakers, Schat's makes a dazzling array of chewy, dense breads, sandwiches, wraps, big salads, dee-lish hot mains, full breakfasts and homemade pastries.

Kilkenny Kitchen
CAFE $

(☑707-462-2814; www.kilkennykitchen.com; 1093 S Dora St; sandwiches $8; ⊘10am-3pm Mon-Fri; ✍⋒) Tucked into a neighborhood south of downtown, county workers love this chipper yellow place for the fresh rotation of daily soups and sandwich specials (a recent visit on a blazing-hot day found a heavenly, cold spinach and dill soup). The salads – like the cranberry, spinach with pecans and feta cheese – are also fantastic, and there's a kid's menu.

★ Saucy Ukiah
PIZZA $$

(☑707-462-7007; www.saucyukiah.com; 108 W Standley St; pizzas $14-19, mains $13-19; ⊘11:30am-9pm Mon-Thu, to 10pm Fri, noon-10pm Sat) Yes there are arty pizzas with toppings like organic fennel pollen and almond basil pesto but there are also amazing soups, salads, pastas and starters – Nana's meatballs are to die for and the 'kicking' minestrone lives up to its name. The small-town ambience is mildly chic but fun and informal at the same time.

Oco Time
JAPANESE $$

(☑707-462-2422; www.ocotime.com; 111 W Church St; lunch mains $7-10, dinner mains $8-19; ⊘11:15am-2:30pm Tue-Fri, 5:30-8:30pm Mon-Sat; ✍) Shoulder your way through the locals to get Ukiah's best sushi, noodle bowls and oco (a delicious combo of seaweed, grilled cabbage, egg and noodles). The 'Peace Café' has a great vibe, friendly staff and interesting special rolls. Downside? The place gets mobbed, so reservations are a good idea.

Patrona
MODERN AMERICAN $$

(☑707-462-9181; www.patronarestaurant.com; 130 W Standley St; lunch mains $10-16, dinner mains $15-34; ⊘11am-9pm Sun-Thu, to 10pm Fri & Sat) ⌘ Foodies flock to excellent Patrona for earthy, flavor-packed, seasonal and regional organic cooking in super stylish surrounds. The unfussy menu includes dishes such as roasted chicken, brined-and-roasted pork chops and housemade pasta, as well as local wines. Reservations recommended at weekends.

Ukiah Garden Cafe   CALIFORNIAN $$
(☑707-462-1221; 1090 S State St; mains $17-24; ◷11am-9pm Tue-Fri, from 4pm Mon & Sat; P) Meat lovers will be swooning at the top-quality steaks, roast prime rib and lamb and pork chops here. The chicken dishes are also winners but vegetarians will have to stick to the appetizers: think homemade fried mozzarella sticks or crispy zucchini with a creamy dip.

Himalayan Cafe   NEPALI $$
(☑707-467-9900; www.thehimalayancafe.com; 1639 S State St; mains $15-18; ◷5-9pm Mon,11am-3pm Tue-Sat) South of downtown, find delicately spiced Nepalese cooking – think tandoori breads and curries, including plenty of vegetarian options. Some Sundays there's a Nepalese buffet at 4pm.

🍷 Drinking & Nightlife

Dive bars and scruffy cocktail lounges line State St, especially to the north of town. For a wider and marginally classier selection, head to S State St and the surrounding streets.

Black Oak Coffee Roasters   CAFE
(☑866 390-1427; www.blackoakcoffee.com; 476 N State St; ◷6:30am-6pm Mon-Fri, 7am-5pm Sat & Sun; 🛜) A big modern coffee house that roasts its own beans with some interesting and delicious choices such as a *café borgia latté* with artisan chocolate and orange essence or, for tea lovers, a *matcha chia* milkshake. Light breakfasts and lunches are also on offer.

ℹ Information

Army Corps of Engineers (☑707-462-7581; www.spn.usace.army.mil/mendocino; 1160 Lake Mendocino Dr; ◷8am-4pm Mon-Fri May-Sep) The visitor center here can provide information about Lake Mendocino, including hiking and biking trails, as well as boating and campsites.
Bureau of Land Management (☑707-468-4000; www.blm.gov; 2550 N State St; ◷10am-5pm Mon-Fri) Maps and information on backcountry camping, hiking and biking in wilderness areas.

ℹ Getting Around

Mendocino Transit Authority (☑707-462-1422; www.mendocinotransit.com; 241 Plant Rd) The Mendocino Transit Authority runs a sparse bus service covering major towns in the Mendocino region.

Around Ukiah

Vichy Springs Resort

This **spa resort** (☑707-462-9515; www.vichysprings.com; 2605 Vichy Springs Rd; s $175-235, d $235-285, ste s/d $255/315, cottages from $325; P☻✳🛜▨) offers a tranquil retreat with a choice of rooms and suites in a historic 1870s inn with a shared terrace overlooking sweeping lawns. The cottages are airy and light with floral fabrics and light pine decor and a fully equipped kitchen. Guests can enjoy the spa facilities as well as hiking trails on the 700-acre property.

Vichy is the oldest continuously operating mineral-springs spa in California. The water's composition perfectly matches that of its famous namesake in Vichy, France. A century ago, Mark Twain, Jack London and Robert Louis Stevenson traveled here for the water's restorative properties, which ameliorate everything from arthritis to poison oak.

Today, the historic resort has the only warm-water, naturally carbonated mineral baths in North America. Unlike others, Vichy requires swimsuits (rentals $3). Day use (for guests and non-guests) costs $35 for two hours, $65 for a full day.

Facilities include a swimming pool, outdoor mineral hot tub, 14 indoor and outdoor tubs with natural 100°F (38°C) waters, and a grotto for sipping the effervescent waters. Massages and facials are available. The resort's hiking trails lead to a 40ft waterfall, an old cinnabar mine and 1100ft peaks – great for sunset views.

Orr Hot Springs

A soak in the thermal waters of the rustic **Orr Hot Springs resort** (☑707-462-6277; www.orrhotsprings.org; 13201 Orr Springs Rd; day-use adult/child $30/25; ◷by appointment 10am-10pm) is heavenly. While it's not for the bashful, the clothing-optional resort is beloved by locals, back-to-the-land hipsters, backpackers and liberal-minded tourists. Still, you don't have to let it all hang out. Enjoy the private tubs, a sauna, a spring-fed, rock-bottomed swimming pool, steam room, massage and magical gardens. Soaking in the rooftop stargazing tubs on a clear night is magical. Make reservations.

You can stay here in one of the elegantly rustic **accommodations** (☑707-462-6277; www.orrhotsprings.org; 13201 Orr Springs Rd; tent site per adult/child $70/25, r & yurt $210, cottages $280; (P⊝⊛). Accommodations include use of the spa and communal kitchen, while some share bathrooms; cottages have their own kitchens. There are also six yurts tucked into the woods here, offering total privacy.

Orr Hot Springs can be tricky to find. Drive south on Hwy 101 and take exit 551 for N State St. Turn left and head approximately a quarter mile north, turning left onto Orr Springs Rd. Follow the paved road over the hills for approximately 12 miles until you reach the signposted hot springs.

Ukiah Wineries

You'll notice the acres of grapes stretching out in every direction on your way into town. Winemakers around Ukiah enjoy many of the same climatic conditions that made Napa so famous. Pick up a wineries map from the Ukiah Chamber of Commerce (p257). Tasting fees are generally around $5.

Nelson Family Vineyards   WINERY
(☑707-462-3755; www.nelsonfamilyvineyards. com; 550 Nelson Ranch Rd; ⊙10am-5pm; (P)(♣)) Just north of Ukiah, this winery, vineyard and pear, olive and Christmas-tree farm with wondrous views over the valley is a great place to picnic (in a redwood grove), make friends and sip not-too-sweet Chardonnay and luscious red blends. Just one aside – it is a popular venue for weddings, which can affect visits by the public.

Parducci Wine Cellars   WINERY
(☑707-463-5357; www.parducci.com; 501 Parducci Rd; wine tasting $5; ⊙10am-5pm; (P)) ∅ Sustainably grown, harvested and produced, 'America's Greenest Winery' offers affordable, bold, earthy reds. The tasting room, lined in brick with low ceilings and soft lights, is a perfect little cave-like environment to get out of the summer heat, sip wine and chat about sustainability practices. Or head for the terrace overlooking the vineyards and organic gardens, complete with contented chickens.

Montgomery Woods State Natural Reserve

Two miles west of Orr Hot Springs, this 2743-acre **reserve** (☑707-937-5804; www. parks.ca.gov; 15825 Orr Springs Rd; (P)) ∅ FREE

protects five old-growth virgin redwood groves, which are some of the best groves within a day's drive from San Francisco. The 2-mile loop **trail**, starting near the picnic tables and toilets, crosses the creek, winding through the serene groves. It's out of the way, so visitors are likely to have it mostly to themselves.

The trees here are impressive – some are up to 14ft in diameter – but remember to admire them from the trail, both to protect the root systems of the trees and to protect yourself from poison oak, which is all over the park.

City of Ten Thousand Buddhas

The showpiece at the **City of Ten Thousand Buddhas** (☑707-462-0939; www.cttbusa.org; 4951 Bodhi Way; ⊙8am-6pm; (P)) is the beautiful temple with its 10,000 golden Buddha statues. Elsewhere enjoy pretty courtyards, lush landscaping and decorative peacocks. This Buddhist monastery and college is home to both nuns and monks and runs courses on Buddhism; check the website for more information. There is an interesting gift shop with souvenirs as well as literature on Buddhism.

The excellent **Jyun Kang Vegetarian Restaurant** (4951 Bodhi Way; mains $8-12; ⊙11:30am-3pm Wed-Mon; ∅) will have vegetarians (and vegas) swooning over the superb Asian-influenced dishes.

Willits

Twenty miles north of Ukiah, Willits mixes NorCal dropouts with loggers and ranchers (the high school has a bull-riding team). Lamp posts on the main drag are decorated with cowboys and similar, while the heart of the place has a small-town atmosphere with an appealing clutch of idiosyncratic small shops and some solid eating choices.

Though ranching, timber and manufacturing may be its mainstays, tie-dye and gray ponytails are de rigueur. For visitors, Willits has a couple of claims to fame: it is the eastern terminus of the Skunk Train and is also home to the oldest continuous rodeo in California. Willits Frontier Days & Rodeo, held annually here in July, attracts bucking bronco fans from all over the US. Fort Bragg is about 35 miles away on the coast; allow an hour to navigate twisty Hwy 20.

◉ Sights & Activities

Ten miles north of Willits, Hwy 162/Covelo Rd makes for a superb drive following the route of the Northwestern Pacific Railroad along the Eel River and through the **Mendocino National Forest**. The trip is only about 30 miles, but plan on taking at least an hour on the winding road, passing exquisite river canyons and rolling hills. Eventually, you'll reach **Covelo**, known for its unusual round valley.

★**Mendocino County Museum**   MUSEUM
(☑707-459-2736; www.mendocinomuseum.org; 400 E Commercial St; adult/child $4/1; ☺10am-4:30pm Wed-Sun; ℗) Among the best community museums in this half of the state, this puts the lives of early settlers in excellent historical context – much drawn from old letters – and there's an entire 1920s soda fountain and barber shop inside. You could spend an hour perusing Pomo and Yuki basketry and artifacts, or reading about local scandals and countercultural movements.

Outside, the **Roots of Motive Power** (www.rootsofmotivepower.com) exhibit occasionally demonstrates steam logging and machinery.

Ridgewood Ranch   HISTORIC SITE
(☑reservations 707-459-7910; www.seabiscuitheritage.org; 16200 Hwy 101; group/private tours $25/40; ☺9:30am 1st & 3rd Sat May-Oct) Willits' most famous resident was the horse Seabiscuit, who grew up here. Three-hour tours for eight or more people are available by reservation and there are other events listed on the website; private tours are also available. Docent-led nature tours of the surrounding natural area are free with advance reservations.

Skunk Train   HISTORIC TRAIN
(☑707-964-6371; www.skunktrain.com; E Commercial St; adult/child $54/34) This heritage railroad has its depot on E Commercial St, three blocks east of Hwy 101. Trains run between Willits and Fort Bragg (p248), passing through some lush redwood country en route.

**Jackson Demonstration
State Forest**   HIKING
(www.stateparks.com; Fort Bragg-Willits Rd) Fifteen miles west of Willits on Hwy 20, the forest offers day-use recreational activities, including hiking trails and mountain-biking. You can also camp here. A demonstration forest is so named as it is used for forestry education, research and sustainable felling techniques. Seek out the Chamberlain Creek Waterfall on the Chamberlain Creek Trail and Camellia Trail if you can. These beautiful falls are situated in a lush canyon surrounded by redwoods and ferns.

✯ Festivals & Events

Willits Frontier Days & Rodeo   RODEO
(www.willitsfrontierdays.com; adult/child $15/5; ☺early Jul) Dating from 1926, Willits has the oldest continuous rodeo in California, occurring in the first week in July.

⌔ Sleeping

Quality accommodations are pretty sparse here. Some of the in-town motels – and there seems to be about a hundred of them – are dumps, so absolutely check out the room before checking in. Ask about Skunk Train packages. For only the most desperate campers, there are a couple of crowded, loud RV parks on the edges of town.

★**Old West Inn**   MOTEL $
(☑707-459-4201; www.theoldwestinn.com; 1221 S Main St; r $79; ℗☺❋☎) The facade looks like a mock up of an Old West main street and each room has a theme, from the 'Stable' to the 'Barber Shop.' The decor is simple and comfy with just enough imagination to make it interesting. Besides that this is the cleanest, friendliest and most highly recommended place in town.

Baechtel Creek Inn & Spa   BOUTIQUE HOTEL $$
(☑707-459-9063; www.baechtelcreekinn.com; 101 Gregory Lane; d $125-165; ℗☺❋☎☎☎) As Willits' only upscale option, this place draws an interesting mix: Japanese bus tours, business travelers and wine-trippers. The standard rooms are nothing too flashy, but they have top-notch linens, iPod docks and tasteful art. Custom rooms come with local wine and more space. The immaculate pool and lovely egg breakfast on the patio are perks.

✕ Eating

La Siciliana   ITALIAN $
(☑707-459-5626; www.lasicilianawillits.com; 1611 S Main St; mains $11-13; ☺11am-9pm Tue-Sun; ☝) The *sugo* (sauce) is pure Sicilian, the pesto is rich with basil and pine nuts, the olive oil is extra virgin and the pizza crust is crisp and thin. There is no dreaded ping of the microwave and everything is freshly made

in-house. That said, the prices are low and the atmosphere no-fuss and family friendly.

Aztec Grill
MEXICAN $

(781 S Main St; burritos $5-8; ⊙5am-9pm) Yes this is in the Chevron Gas Station, but the unanimous vote from locals is that this is, hands down, the best Mexican food in town. Cheap too.

Loose Caboose Cafe
SANDWICHES $

(✆707-459-1434; www.loosecaboosewillits.com; 10 Wood St; sandwiches $7-11; ⊙7:30am-3pm) People tend to get a bit flushed when talking about the sandwiches at the Loose Caboose, which gets jammed at lunch. The Reuben and Sante Fe chicken sandwiches are two savory delights. Look for a ramshackle entrance complete with a historic rail crossing sign.

Adam's Restaurant
CALIFORNIAN $$$

(✆707-409-4378; 50 N Main St; mains $22-27; ⊙5-9pm Tue-Sun; 🐾) Willits' swankiest address is known for its crab cakes and special occasion-worthy mains like big New York steaks, lamb osso buco or cajun chicken pasta, perhaps finished off with a blueberry crème brûlée. The ambience is simple and the service stellar. Check out its Facebook page.

🍷 Drinking & Nightlife

The main street through town is home to a couple of cafes, as well as a pub with regular live music and a dimly-lit bar (or two).

Shanachie Pub
PUB

(✆707-459-9194; 50 N Main St; ⊙3pm-1am Mon-Sat) This is a friendly little garden-side dive with tons on tap and regular live music.

☆ Entertainment

Willits Community Theatre
THEATER

(✆707-459-0895; www.willitstheatre.org; 37 W Van Lane; ⊙hours vary) Stages award-winning plays, poetry readings and comedy.

🛍 Shopping

JD Redhouse & Co
CLOTHING, HOMEWARES

(✆707-459-1214; www.jdredhouse.com; 212 S Main St; ⊙9am-6pm Mon-Fri, from 10am Sat & Sun) Family-owned and operated, this central mercantile is a good reflection of Willits itself, balancing cowboy essentials – boots and grain, tools and denim – with treats for the weekend tourist. The Cowlick's counter (with excellent Mendocino-made ice cream)

is a good place to cool off when the heat on the sidewalk gets intense.

Mariposa Market
FOOD & DRINK

(✆707-459-9630; www.mariposamarket.com; 600 S Main St; ⊙8am-7pm Mon-Fri, from 9am Sat & Sun) Willits' natural-food grocery market has plenty of organic fresh fruit and veg, plus a juice bar and baked-goods section.

SOUTHERN REDWOOD COAST

There's some real magic in the loamy soil and misty air 'beyond the redwood curtain'; it yields the tallest trees and most potent herb on the planet. North of Fort Bragg, Bay Area weekenders and antique-stuffed B&Bs give way to lumber wars, pot farmers and an army of carved bears. The 'growing' culture here is palpable and the huge profit it brings to the region has evident cultural side effects – an omnipresent population of transients who work the harvests, a chilling respect for 'No Trespassing' signs and a political culture that is an uneasy balance between gun-toting libertarians, ultra-left progressives and typical college-town chaos. Nevertheless, the reason to visit is to soak in the magnificent landscape, which runs through a number of pristine, ancient redwood forests.

ⓘ Information

Redwood Coast Heritage Trails (www.redwoods.info) gives a nuanced slant on the region, with itineraries based around lighthouses, Native American culture, the timber and rail industries, and maritime life.

Leggett

Leggett marks the redwood country's beginning and Hwy 1's end. There's not much going on here, aside from a single gas station, a grocery store, a small restaurant and a post office, however, fear not, there is plenty to do and see close by.

Visit 1000-acre **Standish-Hickey State Recreation Area** (✆707-925-6482; www.parks.ca.gov; 69350 Hwy 101; per car $8; 🅿), 1.5 miles to the north, for picnicking, swimming and fishing in the Eel River and hiking trails among virgin and second-growth redwoods.

Chandelier Drive-Thru Tree Park (☑707-925-6464; www.drivethrutree.com; 67402 Drive Thru Tree Rd; per car $5; ⊗8:30am-9pm Jun-Aug, closes earlier Sep-May; ℙ♿) has 200 private acres of virgin redwoods with picnicking and nature walks. And yes, there's a redwood with a square hole carved out, which cars can drive through. Only in America.

The 1949 tourist trap of **Confusion Hill** (☑707-925-6456; www.confusionhill.com; 75001 N Hwy 101; Gravity House adult/child $5/4; ⊗9am-6pm May-Sep, 10am-5pm Oct-Apr; ♿) is an enduring curiosity and the most elaborate of the old-fashioned stops that line the route north.

Richardson Grove State Park

Fifteen miles to the north of Leggett, and bisected by the Eel River, serene **Richardson Grove** (☑707-247-3318; www.parks.ca.gov; 1600 Hwy 101, Garberville; per car $8) occupies 1400 acres of virgin forest. Many trees are over 1000 years old and 300ft tall, but there aren't many hiking trails. In winter, there's good fishing for silver and king salmon. For the last few years, CalTrans has been considering widening the road through Richardson Grove, which has sparked an intense protest.

The **visitor center** (⊗9am-2pm May-Sep) sells books inside a 1930s lodge, which often has a fire going during cool weather. The park is primarily a **campground** (☑reservations 800-444-7275; www.reserveamerica.com; 1600 Hwy 101; tent & RV sites $35; ℙ), with three separate areas and hot showers; some remain open year-round. Summer-only Oak Flat on the east side of the river is shady and has a sandy beach.

Garberville

The main supply center for southern Humboldt County is the primary jumping-off point for both the Lost Coast, to the west, and the Avenue of the Giants, to the north. There's an uneasy relationship between the old-guard loggers and the hippies, many of whom came in the 1970s to grow sinsemilla (potent, seedless marijuana) after the feds chased them out of Santa Cruz. More recently there has also been a troubling number of homeless on the streets, especially during the warm summer months. Reggae

Southern Redwood Coast

fans note that there is a popular music festival here in July attracting some top names in the genre. Two miles west, Garberville's ragtag sister, Redway, has fewer services. Garberville is about four hours north of San Francisco, one hour south of Eureka.

✸ Festivals & Events

The **Mateel Community Center** (www. mateel.org), in Redway, is the nerve center for many of the area's long-running annual festivals, which celebrate everything from hemp to miming.

**Harley-Davidson
Redwood Run**   MOTORCYCLE RALLY
(www.redwoodrun.com; ☺mid-Jun) The redwoods rumble with the sound of hundreds of shiny bikes in mid-June.

Reggae on the River   MUSIC
(www.reggaeontheriver.com;   657   Hwy   101;
☺mid-Jul) In mid-July, this fest draws huge crowds for reggae, world music, arts-and-craft fairs, camping and swimming in the river.

🛌 Sleeping

Humboldt Redwoods Inn   MOTEL $
(☑707-923-2451;   www.humboldtredwoodsinn. com; 987 Redwood Dr; r $65-110; P ⊖ ❋ 🛜 ⛉)
A reliable low-budget option with spacious rooms, although they could do with a lick of paint. That said, the inn has the added plus of a pool.

★ **Benbow Historic Inn**   HISTORIC HOTEL $$$
(☑707-923-2124; www.benbowinn.com; 445 Lake Benbow Dr, Garberville; d $175-475; P ⊖ ❋ 🛜 ⛉ 🐾) This inn is a monument to 1920s rustic elegance; the Redwood Empire's first luxury resort is a national historic landmark. Hollywood's elite once frolicked in the Tudor-style resort's lobby, where you can play chess by the crackling fire, and enjoy complimentary afternoon tea and scones. Note that the inn is currently undergoing a massive expansion project.

Rooms have top-quality beds, antique furniture and crystal sherry decanters (including complimentary sherry). The window-lined **dining room** (breakfast and lunch $10 to $15, dinner mains $22 to $32) serves excellent meals; the rib eye earns rave reviews.

🍴 Eating

Expect a small but varied choice of eateries, including some healthy options, as well as Mexican and down-home USA. Just about all the restaurants and cafes are located on Redwood Dr running through the center of town and essentially part of Hwy 101.

Woodrose Café   BREAKFAST, AMERICAN $
(☑707-923-3191;   www.woodrosecafe.com;   911
Redwood Dr; mains $9-18; ☺8am-2pm; 🍴🚻)
🍴 Garberville's beloved cafe serves organic omelets, veggie scrambles and buckwheat pancakes with *real* maple syrup in a cozy room. Lunch brings crunchy salads, sandwiches with all-natural meats and good burritos. Plenty of gluten-free options.

Bon Bistro & Bakery   BAKERY $
(☑707-923-2509; 867 Redwood Dr; sandwiches from $5; ☺7am-3pm Mon-Fri, 8am-2pm Sat & Sun)
At the southern, quieter end of town backed by lofty trees, this cozy spot has a cottage feel with its warm wood paneling and lacy curtains. Enjoy freshly baked breads, bagels and sandwiches with such tasty, unusual fillings as cashew chicken.

Cecil's New Orleans Bistro   CAJUN $$
(☑707-923-7007; www.garbervillebistro.com; 733 Redwood Dr; mains $18-28; ☺5-9pm Thu-Mon)
This 2nd-story eatery overlooks Main St and serves ambitious dishes that may have minted the California-Cajun style. Start with fried green tomatoes before launching into the smoked-boar gumbo. Check the website for music events.

ℹ Information

Find out what's really happening by tuning in to amazing community radio KMUD FM91 (www. kmud.org).
Garberville-Redway Area Chamber of Commerce (☑707-923-2613; www.garberville.org; 784 Redwood Dr; ☺10am-4pm daily May-Aug, 10am-4pm Mon-Fri Sep-Apr) Located inside the Redwood Drive Center, with plenty of information about the town including where to stay and what is on.

Lost Coast

The North Coast's superlative backpacking destination is a mystifying coastal stretch where narrow dirt trails ascend rugged coastal peaks. Here you'll find volcanic beaches of black sand and ethereal mist hovering above the roaring surf as majestic Roosevelt elk graze the forests. The King Range boldly rises 4000ft within 3 miles of the coast between where Hwy 1 cuts inland north of Westport to just south of Ferndale. The coast became 'lost' when the state's highway system deemed the region impassable in the early 20th century. The area north of the King Range is more accessible, if less dramatic.

In autumn, the weather is clear and cool. Wildflowers bloom from April through May and gray whales migrate from December through April. The warmest, driest months are June to August, but days are foggy. Note the weather can quickly change.

Aside from a few one-horse villages, Shelter Cove is the only option for services.

❶ Information

The area is a patchwork of government-owned land and private property; visit the **Bureau of Land Management** (BLM; ☑707-825-2300, 707-986-5400; www.blm.gov; 768 Shelter Cove Rd; ☺8am-4:30pm Mon-Sat Sep-May, 8am-4:30pm Mon-Fri Jun-Aug) office for information, permits and maps. There are few circuitous routes for hikers, and rangers can advise on reliable (if expensive) shuttle services in the area.

For information about the flora and fauna stop by the **Needle Rock Visitor Center** (☑707-986-7711; www.parks.ca.gov; Bear Harbor Rd; per car $6; ☺hours vary).

A few words of caution: lots of weed is grown around here and it's wise to stay on trail and to respect 'no trespassing' signs, lest you find yourself at the business end of someone's right to bear arms. And pot farmers don't pose the only threat: you'll want to check for ticks (Lyme disease is common) and keep food in bear-proof containers, which are required for camping.

Sinkyone Wilderness State Park

Named for the Sinkyone people who once lived here, this 7367-acre wilderness extends south of Shelter Cove along pristine coastline. The **Lost Coast Trail** passes through here for 22 miles, from Whale Gulch south to Usal Beach Campground. It takes at least three days to walk as it meanders along high ridges, providing bird's-eye views down to deserted beaches and the crashing surf (side trails descend to water level).

To get to Sinkyone, drive west from Garberville and Redway on Briceland-Thorn Rd, 21 miles through Whitethorn to Four Corners. Turn left (south) and continue for 3.5 miles down a very rugged road to the ranch house; it takes 1½ hours.

North of the **Usal Beach Campground** (☑707-247-3318; www.parks.ca.gov; tent sites $25; ☎), Usal Rd (County Rd 431) is much rougher and recommended only if you have a high-clearance 4WD and a chainsaw. Seriously.

King Range National Conservation Area

Stretching over 35 miles of virgin coastline, with ridge after ridge of mountainous terrain plunging to the surf, the 60,000-acre area tops out at namesake King's Peak (4087ft). The wettest spot in California, the range receives over 120in – and sometimes as much as 240in – of annual rainfall, causing frequent landslides; in winter, snow falls on the ridges. (By contrast, nearby sea-level Shelter Cove gets only 69in of rain and no snow.) Two-thirds of the area is awaiting wilderness designation. Note that for overnight hikes, you will need a backcountry-use permit, which can be obtained from the Bureau of Land Management.

Fire restrictions begin July 1 and last until the first soaking rain, usually in November. During this time, there are no campfires allowed outside developed campgrounds.

North of the King Range

Though it's less of an adventure, you can reach the Lost Coast's northern section year-round via paved, narrow Mattole Rd.

HIKING THE LOST COAST

The best way to see the Lost Coast is to hike, and the best hiking is through the southern regions within the Sinkyone and Kings Range wilderness areas. Some of the best trails start from Mattole Campground, just south of Petrolia, which is on the northern border of the Kings Range. It's at the ocean end of Lighthouse Rd, 4 miles from Mattole Rd (sometimes marked as Hwy 211), southeast of Petrolia.

Both Wailaki and Nadelos have developed **campgrounds** (tent sites $8) with toilets and water. There are another four developed campgrounds around the range, with toilets but no water (except Honeydew, which has purifiable creek water). There are multiple primitive walk-in sites. You'll need a bear canister and backcountry permit, both available from the Bureau of Land Management (p265).

Plan on three hours to navigate the sinuous 68 miles from Ferndale in the north to the coast at Cape Mendocino, then inland to Humboldt Redwoods State Park and Hwy 101. Don't expect redwoods: the vegetation is grassland and pasture. It's beautiful in spots – lined with sweeping vistas and wildflowers that are prettiest in spring.

You'll pass two tiny settlements, both 19th-century stage-coach stops. **Petrolia** has an all-in-one store that rents bear canisters, and sells supplies for the trail, good beer and gasoline. **Honeydew** also has a general store. The drive is enjoyable, but the Lost Coast's wild, spectacular scenery lies further south in the more remote regions.

Shelter Cove

The only sizable community on the Lost Coast, Shelter Cove is surrounded by the King Range National Conservation Area and abuts a large south-facing cove. It's a tiny seaside subdivision with an airstrip in the middle – indeed, many visitors are private pilots. Fifty years ago, Southern California swindlers subdivided the land, built the airstrip and flew in potential investors, fast-talking them into buying seaside land for retirement. But they didn't tell buyers that a steep, winding, one-lane dirt road provided the *only* access and that the seaside plots were eroding into the sea. Today, the large number of 'For Sale' plaques are a sobering sign of the times.

Today, there's still only one route, but now it's paved. Cell phones barely work here: this is a good place to disappear. A short drive brings you to the stunning Black Sands Beach stretching for miles northward.

🛏 Sleeping

Oceanfront Inn   INN $$
(✆707-986-7002; www.sheltercoveoceanfrontinn. com; 10 Seal Ct; r $180-235, ste $250; 🅿😑😑🛜) The recently renovated big, bright rooms here all have private balconies, fridges, microwaves, coffeemakers and phenomenal sea views, and the owners provide a basket of goodies; provisions are pretty scarce in this town. There is one suite complete with a full kitchen (minimum two-night stay). The nine-hole golf course across the street is within putting distance of the sea. The on-site Cove Restaurant is one of the top dining options in town.

Inn of the Lost Coast   INN $$
(✆707-986-7521; www.innofthelostcoast.com; 205 Wave Dr, Shelter Cove; r from $225, ste from $240; 🅿😑😑🛜🐾) Shelter Cove's most family-friendly hotel has a choice of rooms and suites; the latter including options with a full kitchen, private hot tub and sauna and/ or fireplace. The double rooms are spacious, with picture windows to maximize the breathtaking ocean views; most have private balconies.

Downstairs the Delgada Pizzeria & Bakery serves decent pizza, while the Fish Tank Cafe is a good stop for coffee, pastries and sandwiches.

Tides Inn   HOTEL $$
(✆707-986-7900; www.sheltercovetidesinn.com; 59 Surf Pt; r $170, ste $195-390; 🅿😑🛜) Perched above tide pools teeming with starfish and sea urchins, the squeaky-clean rooms here offer excellent views (go for the mini suites on the 3rd floor with their fireplaces and full kitchens). The suite options are good for families, and kids are greeted warmly with an activity kit by the innkeeper.

Spy Glass Inn   INN $$$
(✆707-986-4030; www.spyglassinnsheltercove. com; 118 Dolphin Dr; ste $345-375; 🅿😑🛜) Up on a hill a short walk from town, the four luxurious suites here all have sea-view Jacuzzi tubs, full kitchens, private decks and windows lit up by the expansive shoreline beyond. Note that there is a minimum two-night stay at weekends.

🍴 Eating

Shelter Cove General Store   SUPERMARKET $
(✆707-986-7733; 7272 Shelter Cove Rd) For those who are self-catering, Shelter Cove General Store is 2 miles beyond town. Get groceries and gasoline here.

Cove Restaurant   AMERICAN $$
(✆707-986-1197; www.sheltercoveoceanfrontinn. com; 10 Seal Ct; mains $10-44; ☺5-9pm Thu-Sun; 🅿) The first-choice place to eat, located at the Oceanfront Inn, this restaurant has everything from artichoke-mushroom lasagna to New York steaks.

Humboldt Redwoods State Park & Avenue of the Giants

Don't miss this magical drive through California's largest redwood park, **Humboldt Redwoods State Park** (✆707-946-2409;

www.parks.ca.gov; Hwy 101; P 🚻) 🏷️**FREE**, which covers 53,000 acres – 17,000 of which are old-growth – and contains some of the world's most magnificent trees. It also boasts three-quarters of the world's tallest 100 trees. Tree huggers take note: these groves rival (and some say surpass) those in Redwood National Park, which is a long drive further north, although the landscapes here are less diverse.

Exit Hwy 101 when you see the 'Avenue of the Giants' sign, take this smaller alternative to the interstate; it's an incredible, 32-mile, two-lane stretch. You'll find free driving guides at roadside signboards at both the avenue's southern entrance, 6 miles north of Garberville, near Phillipsville, and at the northern entrance, south of Scotia, at Pepperwood; there are access points off Hwy 101.

Three miles north, the **California Federation of Women's Clubs Grove** is home to an interesting four-sided hearth designed by renowned San Franciscan architect Julia Morgan in 1931 to commemorate 'the untouched nature of the forest.'

Primeval **Rockefeller Forest**, 4.5 miles west of the avenue via Mattole Rd, appears as it did a century ago. It's the world's largest contiguous old-growth redwood forest, and contains about 20% of all such remaining trees. Walk the 2.5-mile Big Trees Loop (note that at the time of research a footbridge had been taken out and you'll have to walk across a fallen tree to cross the river where the trail starts). You quickly walk out of sight of cars and feel like you have fallen into the time of dinosaurs.

In **Founders Grove**, north of the visitor center, the Dyerville Giant was knocked over in 1991 by another falling tree. A walk along its gargantuan 370ft length, with its wide trunk towering above, helps you appreciate how huge these ancient trees are.

The park has over 100 miles of trails for hiking, mountain biking and horseback riding. Easy walks include short nature trails in Founders Grove, Rockefeller Forest and **Drury-Chaney Loop Trail** (with berry picking in summer). Challenging treks include the popular **Grasshopper Peak Trail**, south of the visitor center, which climbs to the 3379ft fire lookout.

Humboldt Redwoods
State Park Campgrounds   CAMPGROUND **$**
(🖉information 707-946-2263, reservations 800-444-7275; www.reserveamerica.com; tent & RV

sites $20-35; P 🐾) The park runs three seasonal campgrounds with hot showers, one environmental camp, a hike/bike camp and primitive trail camps. Of the developed spots, Burlington Campground is beside the visitor center and near a number of trailheads; Hidden Springs Campground is 5 miles south along Avenue of the Giants; and Albee Creek Campground is on Mattole Rd past Rockefeller Forest.

Miranda Gardens Resort   RESORT **$$**
(🖉707-943-3011; www.mirandagardens.com; 6766 Avenue of the Giants, Miranda; cottages $125-300; P ⊖ 🐾 🐕) The best indoor stay along the avenue. The cozy, dark, slightly rustic cottages have redwood paneling, some with fireplaces and kitchens, and are spotlessly clean. The grounds – replete with outdoor Ping Pong, a seasonal swimming pool and a play area for kids amid swaying redwoods – have wholesome appeal for families.

Riverbend Cellars   WINERY **$$**
(🖉707-943-9907; www.riverbendcellars.com; 12990 Avenue of the Giants, Myers Flat; ⊘ noon-6pm) For something a bit posh, pull over here. The El Centauro red – named for Pancho Villa – is an excellent estate-grown blend.

ℹ️ Information

Humboldt Redwoods Visitor Center (🖉707-946-2263; www.humboldtredwoods.org; Avenue of the Giants; ⊘9am-5pm Apr-Oct, 10am-4pm Nov-Mar) Located 2 miles south of Weott, a volunteer-staffed visitor center shows videos (three in total), sells maps and also has a small exhibition center about the local flora and fauna.

Scotia

For years, Scotia was California's last 'company town,' entirely owned and operated by the Pacific Lumber Company, which built cookie-cut houses and had an open contempt for long-haired outsiders who liked to get between their saws and the big trees. The company went belly up in 2006, sold the mill to another redwood company and, though the town still has a creepy *Twilight Zone* vibe, you no longer have to operate by the company's posted 'Code of Conduct.'

As you drive along Hwy 101 and see what appears to be a never-ending redwood forest, understand that this 'forest' sometimes consists of trees only a few rows deep – called a 'beauty strip' – a carefully crafted illusion for tourists. Most old-growth trees have been cut.

There are dingy diners and a couple of bars in Rio Dell, across the river. Back in the day, this is where the debauchery happened: because it wasn't a company town, Rio Dell had bars and hookers. In 1969 the freeway bypassed the town and it withered. Upon entering the town from the north, there is a Hoby's Market and Deli located in the Scotia Center (a small shopping center).

The best reason to pull off here is the **Eel River Brewing Company Taproom & Grill** (☑702-725-2739; http://eelriverbrewing.com; 1777 Alamar Way, Fortuna; ⊙11am-11pm) 🍴, where a breezy beer garden and excellent burgers ($11 to $15) accompany all-organic brews.

Ferndale

The North Coast's most charming town is stuffed with impeccable Victorians – known locally as 'butterfat palaces' because of the dairy wealth that built them. There are so many, in fact, that the entire place is a state and federal historical landmark. Dairy farmers built the town in the 19th century and it's still run by the 'milk mafia': you're not a local till you've lived here 40 years. A stroll down Main St offers a taste of super wholesome, small-town America, from galleries to old-world emporiums and soda fountains. Although Ferndale relies on tourism, it has avoided becoming a tourist trap and has no chain stores. Though a lovely place to spend a summer night, folk close the shutters early in winter and it may be hard to find a bite to eat late evening time, let alone a pint of something frothy.

⊙ Sights

Fern Cottage HISTORIC BUILDING
(☑707-786-4835; www.ferncottage.org; 2121 Centerville Rd; group tours per person $10; ⊙11am-3pm Thu-Sat) This 1866 Carpenter Gothic grew to a 32-room mansion. Only one family ever lived here, so the interior is completely, and charmingly, preserved. Tours are held at 11am, noon and 2pm.

✸ Festivals & Events

This wee town has a packed social calendar, especially in the summer. If you're planning a visit, check the events page at www.victorianferndale.com.

Tour of the Unknown Coast SPORTS
(www.tuccycle.org; ⊙May) A challenging one-day event in late May, in which participants in the 100-mile bicycle race climb nearly 10,000ft. Widely recognized as being California's toughest cycle race.

Humboldt County Fair FAIR
(www.humboldtcountyfair.org; Humboldt County Fairgrounds; ⊙mid-Aug) Held in mid-August, the longest-running county fair in California.

🛏 Sleeping & Eating

Victorian Inn HISTORIC HOTEL $$
(☑707-786-4949; www.victorianvillageinn.com; 400 Ocean Ave; r $125-250; ❀🛜) The bright, sunny rooms inside this venerable, two-story former bank building (1890) are comfortably furnished with thick carpeting, period-style wallpaper, good linens and antiques.

Shaw House B&B $$
(☑707-786-9958; www.shawhouse.com; 703 Main St; r $129-175, ste $225-275; ❀🛜🐾) Shaw House, an emblematic 'butterfat palace,' was the first permanent structure in Ferndale, completed by founding father Seth Shaw in 1866. Today, it's California's oldest B&B, set back on extensive grounds. Original details remain, including painted wooden ceilings. Most of the rooms have private entrances, and three have private balconies overlooking the large garden with its magnificent shady trees and suitably situated benches.

Hotel Ivanhoe HISTORIC HOTEL $$
(☑707-786-9000; www.ivanhoe-hotel.com; 315 Main St; r $95-145; ❀🛜) Ferndale's oldest hostelry opened in 1875. It has four antique-laden rooms and an Old West–style, 2nd-floor gallery, perfect for morning coffee. The adjoining saloon with dark wood and lots of brass is an atmospheric place for a nightcap, while the adjacent restaurant is a reliable choice for a meal.

★ Gingerbread Mansion B&B $$$
(☑707-786-4000; www.gingerbread-mansion.com; 400 Berding St; r $175-495; 🅿❀🛜) This is the cream of dairyland elegance, an 1898 Queen Anne–Eastlake that's unsurprisingly the town's most photographed building. And the inside is no less extravagant, with each room having its own unique (and complex) mix of floral wallpaper, patterned carpeting, grand antique furniture and perhaps a fireplace, wall fresco, stained-glass window or Greek statue thrown in for kicks.

✕ Eating

★ Lost Coast Cafe
VEGETARIAN $
(☑707-786-5330; 468 Main St; mains $7-10; ☺10:30am-4pm Thu-Mon; ✍) Step into a homey kitchen, where the soups, sandwiches, salads and baked goods are easily the best vegetarian choices north of Fort Bragg. The owner, Mario, is a wonderful, friendly character and passionate about his cooking and Ferndale. Organic coffee is on the house. Cash only.

Humboldt Sweets
BAKERY $
(☑707-786-4683; 614 Main St; scones $5; ☺8am-5pm Fri-Sun) This cute-as-a-button small place is recommended for coffee and cake; favorites include coconut cream and carrot. Or opt for one of the giant buttery scones, including jalapeño, and cheddar cheese with spring onions. It also makes its own truffles and toffees for the ultimate sugar rush.

No Brand Burger Stand
BURGERS $
(☑707-786-9474; 989 Milton Ave; burgers $7; ☺11am-4pm; P) Hiding near the entrance to town by an industrial building, this hole-in-the-wall turns out a juicy jalapeño double cheeseburger that ranks easily as the North Coast's best burger. The shakes – so thick your cheeks hurt from pulling on the straw – are about the only other thing on the menu.

Farmhouse on Main Restaurant
CALIFORNIAN $$
(☑707-786-9222; 460 Main St; mains $18-23; ☺11am-2pm & 5-9pm Thu-Sun; ☎) This light-filled dining space is one of Ferndale's latest culinary hits with a menu of no-fuss favorites like rib-eye steak, pork cutlets, lamb shanks and braised beef served with appetizing sides such as a creamy polenta. Lightweights can opt for the salads and homemade soups, plus housemade artisan breads, quiches and similar.

☆ Entertainment

Ferndale Repertory Theatre
THEATER
(☑707-786-5483; www.ferndale-rep.org; 447 Main St) This top-shelf community company produces excellent contemporary theater in the historic Hart Theatre Building.

🔓 Shopping

Main St is a great place to shop. Look for the handful of secondhand stores selling vintage cowboy boots and used designer jeans at reasonable prices.

Blacksmith Shop & Gallery
METAL GOODS
(☑707-786-4216; www.ferndaleblacksmith.com; 455 & 491 Main St; ☺9:30am-5pm) From wrought-iron art to sculpture and jewelry, this is the largest collection of contemporary blacksmithing in the US. Note that there are two venues here: the shop and the gallery, two doors apart, and it is well worth checking them both out.

Ferndale Arts Gallery
ARTS & CRAFTS
(☑707-786-9634; www.ferndaleartgallery.com; 580 Main St; ☺10am-5pm) This artists' co-operative runs a large gallery space selling prints, paintings, pottery, photography and greeting cards that showcase local artists from Humboldt County.

Humboldt Bay National Wildlife Refuge

This pristine **wildlife refuge** (☑707-733-5406; www.fws.gov/refuge/humboldt_bay; 1020 Ranch Rd, Loleta; ☺8am-5pm; P🕭) ✦FREE protects wetland habitats for more than 200 species of birds migrating annually along the Pacific Flyway. Between the fall and early spring, when Aleutian geese descend en masse to the area, more than 25,000 geese might be seen in a cackling gaggle outside the visitor center.

The peak season for waterbirds and raptors runs September to March; for black brant geese and migratory shorebirds it's mid-March to late April. Gulls, terns, cormorants, pelicans, egrets and herons come year-round. Look for harbor seals offshore; bring binoculars. If it's open, drive out South Jetty Rd to the mouth of Humboldt Bay for a stunning perspective.

Pick up a map from the **Richard J Guadagno Headquarters & Visitor Center.** Exit Hwy 101 at Hookton Rd, 11 miles south of Eureka, turn north along the frontage road, on the freeway's west side. In April, look for the Godwit Days festival, a celebration of the spring bird migration.

Eureka

One hour north of Garberville, on the edge of the giant Humboldt Bay, lies Eureka, the largest bay north of San Francisco. With a strip-mall sprawl surrounding a lovely historic downtown, it wears its role as the county seat a bit clumsily. Despite a diverse and interesting community of artists, writers, pagans and other free-thinkers, Eureka's wild side slips out only occasionally – the Redwood Coast Jazz Festival has events all over town, and summer concerts rock out the F Street Pier – but mostly, Eureka goes to bed early. Make for Old Town, a small historic district with good shopping and a revitalized waterfront. For nightlife, head to Eureka's livelier sister up the road, Arcata.

Eureka was a major logging town in the late 19th century, and Victorian lumberbaron mansions dot the town; an impressive 16% or so of the city's Old Town buildings have been catalogued as important historical structures.

◉ Sights

The free *Eureka Visitors Map*, available at tourist offices, details walking tours and scenic drives, focusing on architecture and history. **Old Town**, along 2nd and 3rd Sts from C St to M St, was once down-and-out, but has been refurbished into a buzzing pedestrian district. The F Street Plaza and Boardwalk runs along the waterfront at the foot of F St. Gallery openings fall on the first Saturday of every month.

Romann Gabriel Wooden
Sculpture Garden   GARDENS
(315 2nd St) The coolest thing to gawk at downtown is this collection of whimsical outsider art that's enclosed by aging glass. For 30 years, wooden characters in Gabriel's front yard delighted locals. After he died in 1977, the city moved the collection here.

Morris Graves Museum of Art   MUSEUM
(☑707-442-0278; www.humboldtarts.org; 636 F St; $5; ☺noon-5pm Wed-Sun; ♦) Across Hwy 101, this excellent museum shows rotating Californian artists and hosts performances inside the 1904 **Carnegie library**, the state's first public library. If you are around for a while it also hosts art workshops and classes for adults and kids.

Sequoia Park   PARK
(☑707-441-4263; www.sequoiaparkzoo.net; 3414 W St; park free, zoo adult/child $5/3; ☺zoo 10am-5pm May-Sep, 10am-5pm Tue-Sun Oct-Apr; ℗♦) A 77-acre old-growth redwood grove is a surprising green gem in the middle of a residential neighborhood. It has biking and hiking trails, a children's playground and picnic areas, and a small **zoo**, the oldest in California.

Kinetic Museum Eureka   MUSEUM
(☑707-786-3443; http://kineticgrandchampionship. com/kinetic-museum-eureka; 518 A St; admission by donation; ☺2:15-6:30pm Fri-Sun, also 6-9pm 1st Sat of month; ♦) Come see the fanciful, astounding, human-powered contraptions used in the annual Kinetic Grand Championship (p274) race from Arcata to Ferndale. Shaped like giant fish and UFOs, these colorful piles of junk propel racers over roads, water and marsh during the May event.

🏃 Activities

Harbor Cruise   CRUISE
(Madaket Cruises; ☑707-445-1910; www.humboldt baymaritimemuseum.com; 1st St; narrated cruises adult/child $22/18; ☺1pm, 2:30pm & 4pm Wed-Sat, 1pm & 2:30pm Sun-Tue mid-May–mid-Oct; ♦) Board the 1910 *Madaket*, the USA's oldest continuously operating passenger vessel, and learn the history of Humboldt Bay. Docked at the foot of C St, it originally ferried mill workers and passengers until the Samoa Bridge opened in 1971. The $10 sunset cocktail cruise serves from the smallest licensed bar in the state, and there's also a 75-minute wildlife cruise.

Hum-Boats Sail,
Canoe & Kayak Center   BOATING
(☑707-443-5157; www.humboats.com; 601 Startare Dr; kayak tours from $55; ☺9am-5pm Mon-Fri, to 6pm Sat & Sun Apr-Oct, to 2:30pm Nov-Mar) At Woodley Island Marina, this outfit rents kayaks and sailboats, offering lessons, tours, charters, sunset sails and full-moon paddles.

👉 Tours

Blue Ox Millworks
& Historic Park   HISTORIC BUILDING
(☑707-444-3437; www.blueoxmill.com; 1 X St; adult/child 6-12yr $10/5; ☺9am-5pm Mon-Fri year-round, plus 9am-4pm Sat Apr-Nov; ♦) One of only a few of its kind in the US, here antique tools and mills are used to produce authentic gingerbread trim for Victorian buildings. One-hour self-guided tours take you through the mill and historical buildings, including a blacksmith shop and 19th-century skid camp. Kids love the oxen. Be sure to leave time to peruse the gift shop.

🛌 Sleeping

Every brand of chain hotel is along Hwy 101. Room rates run high midsummer; you can sometimes find cheaper options in Arcata, to the north, or Fortuna, to the south. There is also a handful of motels that cost from $55 to $100 and have no air-conditioning; choose places set back from the road. The cheapest options are south of downtown on the suburban strip.

Inn at 2nd & C　　　　HISTORIC HOTEL **$$**
(✆707-444-3344; www.theinnat2ndandc.com; 139 2nd St; r from $129, ste from $209; ❁ ⊛) Formerly the Eagle House Inn, but reopened under new ownership in May 2017, this glorious Victorian hotel has been tastefully restored to combine Victorian-era decor with every possible modern amenity. The magnificent turn-of-the-century ballroom is used for everything from theater performances to special events. There is also a yoga studio and spa room. Breakfast, tea and complimentary cocktails are additional perks.

Although the hotel is non-smoking, the owners have thoughtfully designated an outside secluded area for smokers (with a bay view, no less!).

Cornelius Daly Inn　　　　B&B **$$**
(✆707-445-3638; www.dalyinn.com; 1125 H St; r with/without bathroom $185/130; ⊛) This impeccably maintained 1905 Colonial Revival mansion has individually decorated rooms with turn-of-the-20th-century European and American antiques. Guest parlors are trimmed with rare woods; outside are century-old flowering trees. The breakfasts reflect co-owner Donna's culinary skills with such gourmet offerings as apple-stuffed French toast.

Eureka Inn　　　　HISTORIC HOTEL **$$**
(✆707-497-6903; www.eurekainn.com; cnr 7th & F Sts; r from $119; ❁ 🛜) This majestic and enormous historic hotel with its mock Tudor frontage has been renovated. The style is cozy, in an early-20th-century-lodge, vaguely Wild West sort of way, the staff are extremely friendly and there's a decent bar and restaurant on the premises.

Carter House Inns　　　　B&B **$$$**
(✆707-444-8062; www.carterhouse.com; 301 L St; r $184-384; P ❁ 🛜) Constructed in period style, this aesthetically remodeled hotel is a Victorian lookalike. Rooms have all modern amenities and top-quality linens; suites have in-room Jacuzzis and marble fireplaces. The same owners operate four other sumptuously decorated lodgings: a single-level house, two honeymoon hideaway cottages and a

replica of an 1880s San Francisco mansion, which the owner built himself, entirely by hand.

✖ Eating

You won't go hungry in this town, and health-conscious folk are particularly well catered to with two excellent natural-food grocery stores – **North Coast Co-op** (✆707-443-6027; www.northcoast.coop; cnr 4th & B Sts; ⊙6am-9pm) and **Eureka Natural Foods** (✆707-442-6325; www.eurekanaturalfoods.com; 1626 Broadway St; ⊙7am-9pm Mon-Sat, 8am-8pm Sun) – and two weekly farmers markets – one **street market** (cnr 2nd & F Sts; ⊙10am-1pm Tue Jun-Oct) and one at the **Henderson Center** (✆707-445-3101; 2800 F St; ⊙10am-1pm Thu Jun-Oct). The vibrant dining scene is focused in the Old Town district and has an excellent array of foodie options and price categories.

★ Cafe Nooner　　　　MEDITERRANEAN **$**
(✆707-443-4663; www.cafenooner.com; 409 Opera Alley; mains $10-14; ⊙11am-4pm Sun-Wed, to 8pm Thu-Sat; 🖔) Exuding a cozy bistro-style ambience with red-and-white checkered tablecloths and jaunty murals, this perennially popular restaurant serves natural, organic and Med-inspired cuisine with choices that include a Greek-style *meze* platter, plus kebabs, salads and soups. There's a healthy kid's menu, as well.

Ramone's Bakery & Cafe　　　　BAKERY, DELI **$**
(✆707-443-6027; www.ramonesbakery.com; 2297 Harrison Ave; mains $6-10; ⊙7am-6pm Mon-Sat, 8am-4pm Sun; 🛜) Come here for delicious cakes, tarts, pies and pastries, as well as baguette sandwiches and salads; there are four other branches in town.

★ Brick & Fire　　　　CALIFORNIAN **$$**
(✆707-268-8959; www.brickandfirebistro.com; 1630 F St, Eureka; dinner mains $14-23; ⊙11:30am-9pm Mon & Wed-Fri, 5-9pm Sat & Sun; 🛜) Eureka's best restaurant is in an intimate, warm-hued, bohemian-tinged setting that is almost always busy. Choose from thin-crust pizzas, delicious salads (try the pear and blue cheese) and an ever-changing selection of appetizers and mains that highlight local produce and wild mushrooms. There's a weighty wine list and servers are well-versed in pairings.

Kyoto　　　　JAPANESE **$$**
(✆707-443-7777; 320 F St; sushi $4-6, mains $15-27; ⊙11:30am-3pm & 5:30-9:30pm Wed-Sat) Renowned as the best sushi in Humboldt

County, dine in a tiny, packed room, where conversation with the neighboring table is inevitable. A menu of sushi and sashimi is rounded out by grilled scallops and fern-tip salad. North Coast travelers who absolutely need sushi should phone ahead for a reservation.

Jack's SEAFOOD $$
(☎707-273-5273; www.jacksseafoodeureka.com; 4 C St; mains $16-24; ⊙11am-9pm; P🅿🛜♿) Grab a pew by the large picture window overlooking the birds, the boats and Humboldt Bay. The seafood menu here includes all the classics, like steamer clams in a white wine broth and Dungeness crab cakes. Oysters are served three ways: smokey, traditional and raw. There are several pasta dishes, as well, and the salads are huge.

★Restaurant 301 CALIFORNIAN $$$
(☎707-444-8062; www.carterhouse.com; 301 L St; mains $24-40; ⊙5-8:30pm) 🍴 Part of the excellent Carter House Inn, Eureka's top table, romantic, sophisticated 301 serves a contemporary Californian menu, using produce from its organic gardens (tours available). The five-course tasting menu ($62, with wine pairings $107) is a good way to taste local seasonal food in its finest presentation.

🍸 Drinking & Nightlife

Eureka has some fine old bars and pubs, including live music venues, mainly located in and around the historic center. The annual jazz festival attracts some top musicians and also includes blues concerts (unfortunately the Blues on the Bay annual festival has been suspended in recent years).

Old Town Coffee & Chocolates CAFE
(☎707-445-8600; www.oldtowncoffeeeureka.com; 211 F St; ⊙7am-9pm; 🛜♿) You'll smell roasting coffee blocks before you see this place. It's a local hangout in a historic building and has board games, local art on the wall and baked goods that include savory choices like bagels with hummus, and wraps.

Speakeasy BAR
(☎707-444-2244; 411 Opera Alley; ⊙4-11pm Sun-Thu, to 2am Fri & Sat) Squeeze in with the locals at this New Orleans–inspired bar with regular live blues and an infectious convivial atmosphere.

2 Doors Down WINE BAR
(☎707-268-8959; www.2doorsdownwinebar.com; 1626 F St; ⊙4:40-9:30pm Wed-Mon) Wonderfully cozy and inviting, this Victorian-feeling wine bar lets you create your own flights and will open any bottle on their list of 80-plus wines if you're getting two or more glasses from it. Plenty of snacks are available for order from Brick & Fire (p271) a couple of doors down.

Shanty BAR
(☎707-444-2053; 213 3rd St; ⊙noon-2am; 🛜) The coolest spot in town is grungy and fun. Play pool, Donkey Kong, Ms Pac-Man or Ping-Pong, or kick it on the back patio with local 20- and 30-something hipsters.

☆ Entertainment

Morris Graves Museum of Art PERFORMING ARTS
(☎707-442-0278; www.humboldtarts.org; 636 F St; suggested donation $5) Hosts performing-arts events between September and May, usually on Saturday evenings and Sunday afternoons, but sometimes on other days as well.

🛍 Shopping

Eureka's streets lie on a grid: numbered streets cross lettered streets. For the best window-shopping, head to the 300, 400 and 500 blocks of 2nd St, between D and G Sts. The town's low rents and cool old spaces harbor lots of indie boutiques.

❶ Information

Eureka Chamber of Commerce (☎707-442-3738; www.eurekachamber.com; 2112 Broadway; ⊙8:30am-5pm Mon-Fri; 🛜) The main visitor information center is on Hwy 101.

❶ Getting There & Around

Arcata-Eureka Airport (Humboldt County Airport; ☎707-839-5401; www.humboldtgov.org/1396/Aviation; 3561 Boeing Ave) The Arcata-Eureka Airport (ACV) is located north of McKinleyville on the North Coast, signposted west of Hwy 101 and with regular services to major cities in California and Oregon, as well as further afield. Several carriers operate from this airport including Penair (p232), United Airlines, Delta, American Airlines, United Airlines and Alaska Airlines (p232), though prices tend to be high.

Eureka Transit Service (☎707-443-0826; www.eurekatransit.org; Humboldt Transit Authority, 133 V St; single fare $1.70) Runs four routes throughout Eureka: the red, gold, green and purple routes. Fares may be paid on the bus and day or monthly passes are also available.

Samoa Peninsula

Grassy dunes and windswept beaches extend along the half-mile-wide, 7-mile long Samoa Peninsula. Stretches of it are spectacular, particularly the dunes, which are part of a 34-mile-long dune system – the largest in Northern California – and the wildlife viewing is excellent.

At the peninsula's south end, **Samoa Dunes Recreation Area** (☐707-825-2300; www.blm.gov; ☺sunrise-sunset; P) **FREE** is good for picnicking and fishing. For wildlife, head to **Mad River Slough & Dunes**; from Arcata, take Samoa Blvd west for 3 miles, then turn right at Young St, the Manila turnoff. Park at the community center lot, from where a trail passes mudflats, salt marsh and tidal channels. There are over 200 species of birds: migrating waterfowl in spring and fall, songbirds in spring and summer, shorebirds in fall and winter, and waders year-round.

These undisturbed dunes reach heights of over 80ft. Because of the environment's fragility, access is by guided tour only. **Friends of the Dunes** (www.friendsofthedunes.org) leads free guided walks.

The **Samoa Cookhouse** (☐707-442-1659; www.samoacookhouse.net; 908 Vance Ave; all-you-can-eat meals per adult $13-17, child $5-9; ☺7am-3pm & 5-8pm; P♿) is the dining hall of an 1893 lumber camp. Hikers, hippies and lumberjacks get stuffed while sharing long, red-checked oilcloth-covered tables. There is no menu but you can guarantee that anything you order will be freshly made that day. Think fried chicken, pork ribs and bumper breakfasts. Vegetarians should call ahead.

Arcata

The North Coast's most progressive town, Arcata surrounds a tidy central square that fills with college students, campers, transients and tourists. Sure, it occasionally reeks of patchouli and its politics lean far left, but its earnest embrace of sustainability has fostered some of the most progressive civic action in America. Here, garbage trucks run on biodiesel, recycling gets picked up by tandem bicycle, wastewater gets filtered clean in marshlands and almost every street has a bike lane. Predictably enough, organic products and produce are the norm, art-and-craft markets are rampant and vegans are well catered to.

Founded in 1850 as a base for lumber camps, today Arcata is defined as a magnet for 20-somethings looking to expand their minds: either at Humboldt State University (HSU), and/or on the local highly potent marijuana. Since a 1996 state proposition legalized marijuana for medical purposes, the economy of the region has become inexorably tied to the crop.

◉ Sights

Around Arcata Plaza are two National Historic Landmarks: the 1857 **Jacoby's Storehouse** (☐707-826-2426; www.facebook.com/pages/Jacoby-Storehouse; Arcata Plaza; ☺hours vary) and the 1915 **Hotel Arcata** (☐707-826-0217; www.hotelarcata.com; 708 9th St). Another great historic building is the 1914 **Minor Theatre** (☐707-822-3456; www.minortheatre.com; 1013 10th St; ☺hours vary), which some local historians claim is the oldest theater in the US built specifically for showing films.

Arcata Marsh & Wildlife Sanctuary WILDLIFE RESERVE
(www.cityofarcata.org; Klopp Lake) On the shores of Humboldt Bay, this sanctuary has 5 miles of walking trails and outstanding birding. The **Redwood Region Audubon Society** (☐707-826-7031; www.rras.org; donation welcome) offers guided walks on Saturdays at 8:30am, rain or shine, from the parking lot at I St's south end. Friends of Arcata Marsh offer guided tours Saturdays at 2pm from the Arcata Marsh Interpretive Center (p276).

Humboldt State University UNIVERSITY
(HSU; ☐707-826-3011; www.humboldt.edu; 1 Harpst Dr; P) ✈ The university on the northeastern side of town holds the Campus Center for Appropriate Technology (CCAT; www.ccathsu.com), a world leader in developing sustainable technologies. On Tuesday at 10am and Friday at 3pm you can take a tour of CCAT's house, a converted residence that uses only 4% of the energy of a comparably sized dwelling.

🏃 Activities

Finnish Country Sauna and Tubs SPA
(☐707-822-2228; http://cafemokkaarcata.com; 495 J St; per 30min adult/child $9.75/2; ☺noon-11pm Sun-Thu, to 1am Fri & Sat; ♿) Like some kind of Euro-crunchy bohemian dream, these private, open-air redwood hot tubs and sauna are situated around a small frog pond. The staff is easygoing, and the facility

is relaxing, simple and clean. Reserve ahead, especially on weekends.

HSU Center Activities OUTDOORS
(☑707-826-3357; www.humboldt.edu/center activities; Humboldt State University, 1 Harpst Dr; ⊘10am-4pm Mon-Fri) An office on the 2nd floor of the University Center, beside the campus clock tower, sponsors myriad workshops, outings and sporting-gear rentals; non-students welcome.

☆☆ Festivals & Events

Kinetic Grand Championship ART, SPORTS
(☑707-786-3443; www.kineticgrandchampionship. com; ⊘late May; ☝) ☝ Arcata's most famous event is held Memorial Day weekend: people on amazing self-propelled contraptions travel 42 miles from Arcata to Ferndale over a period of three days.

Arcata Bay Oyster Festival FOOD & DRINK
(www.oysterfestival.net; 8th St; ⊘mid-Jun) A magical celebration of oysters and beer held on a Saturday in mid-June.

North Country Fair FAIR
(www.sameoldpeople.org; Arcata Plaza; ⊘Sep) A fun September street fair, where bands with names like the Fickle Hillbillies jam.

🛏 Sleeping

Arcata has affordable but limited lodgings. A cluster of hotels – Comfort Inn, Hampton Inn etc – is just north of town, off Hwy 101's Giuntoli Lane. There's cheap camping further north at Clam Beach. One of the best situated hotels is the old fashioned **Hotel Arcata** (☑707-826-0217; www.hotelarcata.com; 708 9th St; r $97-167; P♿🐾📶🏊), right on the city's main square.

Fairwinds Motel MOTEL $
(☑707-822-4824; www.fairwindsmotelarcata.com; 1674 G St; s $70-75, d $80-90; 📶) Serviceable rooms in a standard-issue motel, with some noise from Hwy 101. It's more expensive than the chain motels but has the advantage of being in town and also having an adjacent, reasonable (in price and quality) restaurant.

Lady Anne Inn INN $$
(☑707-822-2797; www.ladyanneinn.com; 902 14th St; r $115-220; P♿📶) Dating from 1983, this eco inn is owned by the former mayor of Arcata, so he knows a fair bit about the town. The front garden is a dazzle of roses and native flowers and, while the rooms all

differ, they continue the floral theme with decorative wallpaper and pastel paintwork. Dark wood antiques complete the look.

A couple of rooms have a claw-foot tub in the bedroom.

Arcata Stay ACCOMMODATION SERVICES $$
(☑707-822-0935; www.arcatastay.com; 814 13th St; apt from $169; ⊘11am-5pm) A network of excellent and centrally situated apartments, B&Bs and cottage rentals. There is a two-night minimum and prices go down the longer you stay.

✗ Eating

Great food abounds in restaurants throughout Arcata, almost all casual and most promoting organic produce and ingredients; vegetarians and vegans will have no problem in this town.

There are fantastic farmers markets, at the **Arcata Plaza** (www.humfarm.org; btwn 8th & 9th Sts; ⊘9am-2pm Sat Apr-Nov, from 10am Dec-Mar) and in the parking lot of Wildberries Market. Just a few blocks north of downtown, there is a cluster of the town's best restaurants on G St, near Hwy 101.

Slice of Humboldt Pie CALIFORNIAN $
(☑707-630-5100; 828 I St; pies $4.50-7.50; ⊘11am-10pm Mon-Thu, to 11pm Fri & Sat) Pies and cider are the mainstays here, ranging from chicken pot pie to cottage, steak and mushroom and savory *empanadas*, including chicken coconut curry and Thai chicken with satay sauce. Sweet pastry treats include peanut-butter fudge and traditional apple, while the ciders cover imports and local varieties. The decor is pure industrial chic with exposed pipes and soft gray paintwork.

T's Cafe CAFE $
(☑707-826-2133; 860 10th St; breakfast $8-13; ⊘7am-2pm; 📶) Housed in a wonderful early-20th-century mansion, try and grab the table on the front porch if you can. Inside, two cavernous rooms with mismatched furniture, local art, books, toys and magazines provide an informal kickback space for enjoying delicious breakfast classics such as eggs with corned beef hash, stuffed French toast and the specialty: seven choices of eggs Benedict.

Cafe Brio CAFE $
(☑707-822-5922; www.cafebrioarcata.com; 791 G St; mains $12-15; ⊘7am-5pm Mon, Tue & Thu, to 6pm Wed, to 9pm Fri & Sat) Occupying an ace

THE ECONOMICS OF THE HUMBOLDT HERB

With an estimated one-fifth of Humboldt County's population farming its world-famous weed, a good chunk of the economy here has run, for decades, as bank-less, tax-evading and cash only – but it's also been prosperous enough to strongly support many local businesses. Back in the 1990s farmers could expect to get around $6000 a pound for their crops but since medical marijuana has become legal the price has dropped radically, to just above $1000 per pound. In November 2016 a further law was passed legalizing recreational cannabis use in the state, which some feel may lead to prices plummeting still further and the possibility of large farms and corporations putting the small farmers out of business.

position on the corner of this central square, the patisserie here serves sumptuous cakes, breakfasts are delish and the lunch salads, sandwiches and pies are a notch above the norm. There is also a coffee-cum-wine-bar for suppin'.

Japhy's Soup & Noodles NOODLES $
(☑707-826-2594; www.japhys.com; 1563 G St; mains $7.50-9; ⊙11:30am-8pm Mon-Fri) Big salads, tasty coconut curry, cold noodle salads with a vast choice of sauces and homemade soups – and cheap!

★**Folie Douce** MODERN AMERICAN $$$
(☑707-822-1042; www.foliedoucearcata.com; 1551 G St; dinner mains $28-37, pizzas $17 24; ⊙11am-2pm Mon, 11am-2pm & 5:30-9pm Tue-Thu, 11am-2pm & 5:30-10pm Fri & Sat) 🍴 Just a slip of a place, but with an enormous reputation. The short but inventive menu features seasonally inspired bistro cooking, from Asian to Mediterranean, with an emphasis on local organics. Wood-fired pizzas are renowned and desserts are pretty special, as well. A slice of artichoke-heart cheesecake perhaps? Dinner reservations essential.

🍷 Drinking & Nightlife

Dive bars and cocktail lounges line the plaza's northern side. Arcata is awash with coffeehouses and brewpubs.

★**Six Rivers Brewery** MICROBREWERY
(☑707-839-7580; www.sixriversbrewery.com; 1300 Central Ave, McKinleyville; ⊙11:30am-11:30pm Sun & Tue-Thu, to 12:30am Fri & Sat, from 4pm Mon) One of the first female-owned breweries in California, the 'brew with a view' kills it in every category: great beer, amazing community vibe, occasional live music and delicious hot wings. The spicy chili-pepper ale is amazing. At first glance the menu might seem like ho-hum pub grub, but portions

are fresh and huge. They also make a helluva pizza.

Redwood Curtain Brewing Company MICROBREWERY
(☑707-826-7222; www.redwoodcurtainbrewing. com; 550 S G St; ⊙noon-11pm Sun-Tue, to midnight Wed-Sat) This tiny gem of a brewery has a varied collection of rave-worthy craft ales and live music or DJs some nights. Plus it offers free wheat thins and goldfish crackers to munch on.

Cafe Mokka CAFE
(☑707-822-2228; www.cafemokkaarcata.com; cnr 5th & J Sts; ⊙noon 11pm Sun-Thu, to 1am Fri & Sat) Bohos head to this cafe at Finnish Country Sauna & Tubs (p273) for a mellow, old-world vibe, good coffee drinks and homemade cookies.

Humboldt Brews BAR
(☑707-826-2739; www.humbrews.com; 856 10th St; ⊙11:30am-midnight Sat-Thu, to 2am Fri) This popular dimly-lit beer house has a huge range of carefully selected beer taps, fish tacos, buffalo wings and for veggies, smoked tofu (pub grub $11 to $13). Regular live music and a pool table add to the entertainment.

☆ Entertainment

Center Arts PERFORMING ARTS
(☑tickets 707-826-3928; www.humboldt.edu/ centerarts; Humboldt State University, 1 Harpst Dr; ⊙hours vary) Hosts events on campus and you'd be amazed at who shows up. The place to buy tickets is at the University Ticket Office in the HSY Bookstore on the 3rd floor of the University Center.

Arcata Theatre CINEMA
(☑707-822-1220; www.arcatatheater.com; 1036 G St) An exquisite remodeling has revived this classic movie house, which shows art films,

Northern Redwood Coast

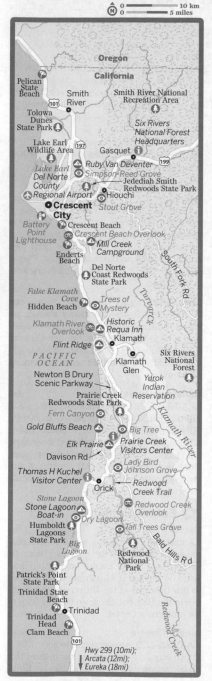

N 0 —— 10 km
0 —— 5 miles

Oregon
California

Pelican State Beach
Smith River
Smith River National Recreation Area
Tolowa Dunes State Park
Six Rivers National Forest Headquarters
Lake Earl Wildlife Area
Gasquet
Lake Earl
Ruby Van Deventer
Del Norte County
Simpson-Reed Grove
Jedediah Smith Redwoods State Park
Regional Airport
Hiouchi
Crescent City
Stout Grove
Battery Point Lighthouse
Crescent Beach
Crescent Beach Overlook
Enderts Beach
Mill Creek Campground
Del Norte Coast Redwoods State Park
South Fork Rd
False Klamath Cove
Hidden Beach
Trees of Mystery
Turwar Ck
Klamath River Overlook
Historic Requa Inn
Flint Ridge
Klamath
PACIFIC OCEAN
Klamath Glen
Six Rivers National Forest
Newton B Drury Scenic Parkway
Yurok Indian Reservation
Prairie Creek Redwoods State Park
Fern Canyon
Klamath River
Gold Bluffs Beach
Big Tree
Elk Prairie
Prairie Creek Visitors Center
Davison Rd
Lady Bird Johnson Grove
Thomas H Kuchel Visitor Center
Orick
Redwood Creek Trail
Stone Lagoon
Redwood Creek Overlook
Stone Lagoon Boat-in
Dry Lagoon
Tall Trees Grove
Humboldt Lagoons State Park
Big Lagoon
Redwood National Park
Bald Hills Rd
Patrick's Point State Park
Trinidad State Beach
Trinidad
Trinidad Head
Clam Beach
Hwy 299 (10mi);
Arcata (12mi);
Eureka (18mi)
Redwood Creek

rock documentaries, silent films and more. Plus, it serves beer.

ⓘ Information

Arcata Marsh Interpretive Center (☏707-826-2359; www.humboldt.edu/arcatamarsh; 569 South G St; ⊙9am-5pm Tue-Sun, from 1pm Mon; ⊞) Staffed by the Friends of Arcata Marsh (FOAM), who give free guided tours on Saturday afternoons.

California Welcome Center (☏707-822-3619; www.arcatachamber.com; ⊙9am-5pm) At the junction of Hwys 299 and 101; has area info.

ⓘ Getting There & Around

Alaska Airlines, Penair, Delta, American Airlines and United Airlines are the main carriers to operate national flights to/from the Arcata-Eureka Airport (p272) but fares tend to be high. Flights come and go from several major Californian cities, including Los Angeles, San Francisco, Sacramento and San Diego. There are also regular flights from other US cities, including New York, Denver, Phoenix and Portland (Oregon).

Greyhound (p232) serves Arcata from San Francisco ($57, seven hours, daily). Redwood Transit System (p232) serves Arcata and Eureka on the Trinidad–Scotia routes Monday to Saturday ($3, 2½ hours).

Arcata city buses stop at the **Arcata & Mad River Transit Center** (☏707-825-8934; www.arcatatransit.org; 925 E St at 9th St). For shared rides, read the bulletin board at the North Coast Co-op.

Life Cycle Bike Shop (☏707-822-7755; www.lifecyclearcata.com; 1593 G St; per day $25; ⊙9am-6pm Mon-Sat) rents, services and sells bicycles.

Only in Arcata: borrow a bike from **Library Bike** (www.arcata.com/greenbikes; 865 8th St; deposit $20; ⊙hours vary). They're beaters, but they ride.

NORTHERN REDWOOD COAST

Congratulations, traveler, you've reached the middle of nowhere, or at least the top of the middle of nowhere. Here, the trees are so large that the tiny towns along the road seem even smaller. The scenery is pure drama: cliffs and rocks, native lore, legendary salmon runs, mammoth trees, wild elk and RVing retirees. Leave time to dawdle and bask in the haunting natural grandeur of it all and, even though there are scores of mid-century motels, try and make an effort to sleep outdoors if possible. Then, as you gaze skywards, ponder the fact that giant redwoods once covered some 5000 square miles of coast here, before the brutal mass logging that took place around the turn of the 20th century (apparently some 95% of the trees were felled). Fortunately, conservation measures are now firmly in place to protect these magnificent trees that can live for thousands of years.

Trinidad

Cheery, tiny Trinidad perches prettily on the side of the ocean, combining upscale mid-century homes with a mellow surfer vibe. Somehow it feels a bit off-the-beaten-path even though tourism augments fishing to keep the economy going. Trinidad is also a big hit with ornithologists; it's home to one of the most diverse seabird colonies in California. The town gained its name when Spanish sea captains arrived on Trinity Sunday in 1775 and named the area La Santisima Trinidad (the Holy Trinity); later it was the site of bloody battles and raids against the local Native Americans during the Civil War. Around this period, it also experienced a boom, becoming an important port for miners. If you can, check out the superb beaches and rocky coves and stop for a seafood meal overlooking the water.

◉ Sights & Activities

Trinidad is small: approach via Hwy 101 or from the north via Patrick's Point Dr (which becomes Scenic Dr further south). To reach town, take Main St.

The free town map at the information kiosk (p278) shows several fantastic hiking trails, most notably the **Trinidad Head Trail** with superb coastal views and excellent for **whale-watching** (December to April). Stroll along an exceptionally beautiful cove at **Trinidad State Beach**; take Main St and bear right at Stagecoach, then take the second turn left (the first is a picnic area) into the small lot.

Scenic Dr twists south along coastal bluffs, passing tiny coves with views back toward the bay. It peters out before reaching the broad expanses of **Luffenholtz Beach** (accessible via the staircase) and serene white-sand **Moonstone Beach**. Exit Hwy 101 at 6th Ave/Westhaven to get there.

Further south Moonstone becomes **Clam Beach County Park**.

Surfing is good year-round, but potentially dangerous: unless you know how to judge conditions and get yourself out of trouble – there are no lifeguards here – surf in better-protected Crescent City.

HSU Telonicher
Marine Laboratory   AQUARIUM
(☑ 707-826-3671; www.humboldt.edu/marinelab; 570 Ewing St; $1; ☺ 9am-4:30pm Mon-Fri year-round, plus 10am-5pm Sat & Sun mid-Sep–mid-May; P🚻)
 Near Edwards St, this marine lab has a touch tank, several aquariums (look for the giant Pacific octopus), an enormous whale jaw and a cool 3D map of the ocean floor. You can join a naturalist on **tide-pooling expeditions** (per person $3, minimum $20). All tours are by appointment only so call ahead and be sure to ask about conditions.

🛏 Sleeping

Most of the inns and motels line Patrick's Point Dr, north of town, and are family owned and welcoming, with fabulous ocean views. In the center, choices are limited to a cute B&B which gets booked up fast at weekends. **Trinidad Retreats** (www.trinidadretreats.com) and **Redwood Coast Vacation Rentals** (www.redwoodcoastvacationrentals.com) can also help you find a bed for the night.

View Crest Lodge   LODGE $$
(☑ 707-677-3393; www.viewcrestlodge.com; 3415 Patrick's Point Dr; 1- & 2-bedroom cottages $95-240; P☺🛜) On a hill above the ocean on the inland side, these well-maintained, modern and terrific-value cottages all have ocean views and added extras like fireplaces and hot tubs. They range from one to two bedroom and breakfast is included in the price.

Trinidad Inn   INN $$
(☑ 707-677-3349; www.trinidadinn.com; 1170 Patrick's Point Dr; r $100-245; P☺🛜🍳) Sparklingly clean and attractively decorated rooms fill this upmarket, gray-shingled motel under tall trees. The accommodations vary considerably; some rooms have sitting rooms, fireplaces and fully equipped kitchens, others are straightforward double rooms with a TV and desk.

★ **Lost Whale Inn**   B&B $$$
(☑ 707-677-3425; www.lostwhaleinn.com; 3452 Patrick's Point Dr; r $199-325, ste $408-750;

P ⊕ ⑤) Perched atop a grassy cliff, high above crashing waves and braying sea lions, this spacious, modern, light-filled B&B has stunning views out to the sea. The lovely gardens have a 24-hour hot tub and other perks include the superb breakfast and complimentary tea that is served at 4pm. The owner is Portuguese and family antiques feature in every room.

Turtle Rocks Oceanfront Inn
B&B $$$

(☑707-677-3707; www.turtlerocksinn.com; 3392 Patrick's Point Dr; r $295-335; P ⊕ ⑤) Enjoy truly stunning sea vistas from every room at this plush, modern place on three peaceful, windswept acres. Rooms are spacious with terraces; number 3 comes particularly recommended with its warm blue decor. A complimentary buffet is served from 3pm to 6pm.

Trinidad Bay B&B
B&B $$$

(☑707-677-0840; www.trinidadbaybnb.com; 560 Edwards St; r $200-350; P ⊕ ⑤) Opposite the lighthouse, this light-filled Cape Cod–style home overlooks the harbor and Trinidad Head. Breakfast may be delivered to your uniquely styled room and in the afternoon the house fills with the scent of freshly baked cookies. The Trinity Alps room has a kitchenette and is well set up for families.

✖ Eating

Trinidad is home to superb beaches and hideaway coves where packing a picnic is always a tempting option (thankfully the town has a solid choice of delis and supermarkets). Trinidad State Beach also has excellent picnicking facilities. The restaurants here are, unsurprisingly, centered on seafood and fish; several have coastal views to enhance that ocean-inspired dining experience.

Katy's Smokehouse & Fishmarket
SEAFOOD $

(www.katyssmokehouse.com; 740 Edwards St; ⊙9am-6pm) ✔ Makes its own chemical-free and amazingly delicious smoked and canned fish, using line-caught, sushi-grade seafood; the tuna has been voted number one in the US, no less. There's no restaurant, just grab some for a picnic.

Beachcomber Café
CAFE $

(☑707-677-0106; 363 Trinity St; breakfast from $4; ⊙7am-4pm Mon-Fri, 8am-4pm Sat & Sun; ⑤ ⑧) Head here for the best breakfast in these parts, ranging from a hearty bowl of organic black beans with avocado and poached egg

to moist and delicious homemade muffins. Also has plenty of newspapers and mags to peruse. Bring your own cup if you want a drink to go.

Lighthouse Café
CALIFORNIAN $

(☑707-677-0390; 355 Main St; mains $6-9; ⊙11am-7pm Tue-Sun; ⑧) ✔ Across from the Chevron, this fun little arty joint makes good food fast, using mostly organic ingredients – try the creative soups, fish and chips with hand-cut fries, local grass-fed beef burgers and homemade ice cream. Order at the counter and then sit inside or out.

Larrupin Cafe
CALIFORNIAN $$$

(☑707-677-0230; www.thelarrupin.com; 1658 Patrick's Point Dr; mains $22-42; ⊙5-9pm Tue-Sun; P) Everybody loves Larrupin, where Moroccan rugs, chocolate-brown walls, gravity-defying floral arrangements and deep-burgundy Oriental carpets create a moody atmosphere perfect for a lovers' tryst. On the menu, expect consistently good mesquite-grilled seafood and meats – the smoked beef brisket is amazing. In the summer, book a table on the garden patio for live music some nights.

❶ Information

Information Kiosk (www.trinidadcalif.com; cnr Patrick's Point Dr & Main St; ⊙11am-5pm Jun-Sep, shorter hours Oct-May) Just west of the freeway. Pick up the pamphlet *Discover Trinidad* from here – it has an excellent map.

Trinidad Chamber of Commerce (☑707-667-1610; www.trinidadcalif.com) Information on the web, but no visitor center.

Patrick's Point State Park

Coastal bluffs jut out to sea at this 640-acre state park, where sandy beaches abut rocky headlands. Easy access to dramatic coastline makes this is a great bet for families, but any age will find a feast for the senses as they climb rock formations, search for breaching whales, carefully navigate tide pools and listen to barking sea lions and singing birds.

Sumêg is an authentic reproduction of a Yurok village, with hand-hewn redwood buildings where Native Americans gather for traditional ceremonies. In the native plant garden you'll find species for making traditional baskets and medicines.

On Agate Beach look for stray bits of jade and sea-polished agate. Follow the signs to tide pools. The 2-mile Rim Trail, an old

Yurok trail around the bluffs, circles the point with access to huge rocky outcrops. Don't miss Wedding Rock, one of the park's most romantic spots. Other trails lead around unusual formations like Ceremonial Rock and Lookout Rock.

The park's three well-tended **campgrounds** (ℹ️information 707-677-3570, reservations 800-444-7275; www.reserveamerica.com; 4150 Patrick's Point Dr; tent/RV sites $35/45; P⊗) have coin-operated showers and clean bathrooms. Penn Creek and Abalone campgrounds are more sheltered than Agate Beach.

Humboldt Lagoons State Park

Stretching out for miles along the coast, Humboldt Lagoons has long, sandy beaches and a string of coastal lagoons. **Big Lagoon** and the even prettier **Stone Lagoon** are both excellent for kayaking and bird-watching. Sunsets are spectacular, with no artificial structures in sight. Picnic at Stone Lagoon's north end. The Stone Lagoon Visitor Center, on Hwy 101, has closed due to staffing shortages, but there's a toilet and a bulletin board displaying information.

A mile north, **Freshwater Lagoon** is also great for birding. South of Stone Lagoon, tiny **Dry Lagoon** (a freshwater marsh) has a fantastic day hike and good agate hunting. Park at Dry Lagoon's picnic area and hike north on the unmarked trail to Stone Lagoon; the trail skirts the southwestern shore and ends up at the ocean, passing through woods and marshland rich with wildlife. Mostly flat, it's about 2.5 miles one way – and nobody takes it because it's unmarked.

You will have to sleep under canvas in these parts. All campsites are first-come, first-served. The park runs two **environmental campgrounds** (tent sites $20; ⏱Apr-

Oct; P); bring water. Stone Lagoon has six boat-in environmental campsites.

Humboldt County Parks also operates a lovely cypress-grove picnic area and campground: the **Big Lagoon County Park Campground** (☎707-445-7651; http://co.humboldt.ca.us; off Hwy 101; tent sites $20; P⊗) beside Big Lagoon, a mile off Hwy 101, with flush toilets and cold water, but no showers.

Redwood National & State Parks

This richly forested region can be a little confusing regarding which park is where and what they all offer. The main parks in this jigsaw of mighty redwoods are: the Redwood National Park; Prairie Creek Redwoods State Park; Del Norte Coast Redwoods State Park and Jedediah Smith Redwoods State Park (famed for being a backdrop in the original *Star Wars* movie). Interspersed among the parks are a number of small towns, while to the south lies Orick (population 650), which offers a few storefronts, a gas station and an excellent visitor center. All the parks are an International Biosphere Reserve and World Heritage Site, yet they remain little visited when compared to their southern brethren, like the Sequoia National Park. It is worth contemplating that some of these trees have been standing here for time immemorial, predating the Roman Empire by over 500 years. Prepare to be impressed.

Redwood National Park

This park is the southernmost of a patchwork of state and federally administered lands under the umbrella of Redwood **National & State Parks** (☎707-465-7335; www.nps.gov/redw; Hwy 101, Orick; P♿) 🍃**FREE**. After picking up a map at the **visitor center**, you'll have a suite of choices for hiking. A few miles north along Hwy 101, a

THE ENDANGERED MARBLED MURRELET

Notice how undeveloped the Redwood National and State Parks have remained? Thank the marbled murrelet, a small white and brown-black auk that nests in old-growth conifers. Loss of nesting territory due to logging has severely depleted the bird's numbers but Redwood National Park scientists have discovered that corvid predators (ravens, jays etc) are also to blame. Because corvids are attracted to food scraps left by visitors, the number of snacking, picnicking or camping humans in the park greatly affects predation on the marbled murrelet. Restrictions on development to prevent food scraps and thus protect the birds are so strict that it's nearly impossible to build anything new.

trip inland on Bald Hills Rd will take you to Lady Bird Johnson Grove, with its 1-mile, kid-friendly loop trail, or get you lost in the secluded serenity of Tall Trees Grove.

To protect the Tall Trees Grove, a limited number of cars per day are allowed access; get permits at the visitor center. This can be a half-day trip itself, but you're well rewarded after the challenging approach (a 6-mile rumble on an old logging road behind a locked gate, then a moderately strenuous 4-mile round-trip hike). Another recommended hike is to Trillium Falls – a 2½-mile trail leading to a small waterfall, accessed from Davidson Rd at Elk Meadow.

Note that during the winter, several foot bridges crossing the Redwood Creek are removed due to the high waters. If you are hiking at this time of year, be sure to check with a ranger regarding the current situation before striding out.

Elk Meadow Cabins
CABIN $$$

(✆ 866-733-9637; www.redwoodadventures.com; 7 Valley Green Camp Rd, Orick; cabins $239-289; P 🎧 📶 🐾) These spotless and bright cabins with equipped kitchens and all the mod-cons are in a perfect mid-parks location – they're great if you're traveling in a group and the most comfy choice even if you're not. Expect to see elk on the lawn in the mornings. Cabins sleep six to eight people and there's an additional $65 cleaning fee.

ℹ Information

Unlike most national parks, there are no fees and no highway entrance stations at Redwood National Park, so it's imperative to pick up the free map at the park headquarters in Crescent City (p284) or at the information center in Orick. Rangers here issue permits to visit Tall Trees Grove and loan bear-proof containers for backpackers.

For in-depth redwood ecology, buy the excellent official park handbook. The **Redwood Parks Association** (www.redwoodparksassociation.org) provides good information on its website, including detailed descriptions of all the park hikes.

Prairie Creek Redwoods State Park

Famous for some of the world's best virgin redwood groves and unspoiled coastline, this 14,000-acre section (www.parks.ca.gov; Newton B Drury Scenic Pkwy; per car $8; P 🎧) 🌿 of Redwood National & State Parks has

spectacular scenic drives and 70 miles of mainly shady hiking trails, many of which are excellent for children. Kids of all ages will enjoy the magnificent herd of elk here, which can generally be spied grazing at the Elk Prairie, signposted from the highway; the best times to be sure of seeing the elk are early morning and around sunset.

There are 28 **mountain-biking** and **hiking trails** through the park, from simple to strenuous. Only a few of these will appeal to hard-core hikers, who should take on the Del Norte Coast Redwoods. A few easy nature trails start near the visitor center, including Revelation Trail and Elk Prairie Trail. Stroll the recently reforested logging road on the Ah-Pah Interpretive Trail at the park's north end. The most challenging hike in this corner of the park is the spectacular 11.5-mile Coastal Trail which goes through primordial redwoods and is part of the California Coastal Trail (www.californiacoastaltrail.info).

Just past the Gold Bluffs Beach Campground the road deadends at Fern Canyon, the second busiest spot in the park, where 60ft fern-covered sheer-rock walls are so unusual that they were used in scenes from Steven Spielberg's *Jurassic Park 2: The Lost World*, as well as *Return of the Jedi*. This is one of the most photographed spots on the North Coast – damp and lush, all emerald green – and totally worth getting your toes wet to see.

Newton B Drury Scenic Parkway
DRIVING

(Hwy 101, Orick; ♿) Just north of Orick is the turnoff for the 8-mile parkway, which runs parallel to Hwy 101 through untouched ancient redwood forests. This is a not-to-miss short detour off the freeway where you can view the magnificence of these trees. Numerous trails branch off from roadside pullouts, including family-friendly options and trails that fit ADA (American Disabilities Act) requirements, such as Big Tree Wayside and Revelation Trail.

★ Gold Bluffs Beach
CAMPGROUND $

(tent sites $35) This gorgeous campground sits between 100ft cliffs and wide-open ocean, but there are some windbreaks and solar-heated showers. Look for sites up the cliff under the trees. No reservations.

Elk Prairie Campground
CAMPGROUND $

(✆ reservations 800-444-7275; www.reserveamerica.com; Prairie Creek Rd; tent & RV sites $35; P 🐾) Elk roam this popular campground,

SMITH RIVER NATIONAL RECREATION AREA

West of Jedediah Smith Redwoods State Park, the Smith River, the state's last remaining undammed waterway, runs right beside Hwy 199. Originating high in the Siskiyou Mountains, its serpentine course cuts through deep canyons beneath thick forests. Chinook salmon (October to December) and steelhead trout (December to April) annually migrate up its clear waters. Camp (there are four developed campgrounds), hike (75 miles of trails), raft (145 miles of navigable white water) and kayak here, but check regulations if you want to fish. Stop by the **Six Rivers National Forest Headquarters** (☎707-457-3131; www.fs.fed.us/r5/sixrivers; 10600 Hwy 199, Gasquet; ☺8am-4:30pm daily May-Sep, 8am-4:30pm Mon-Fri Oct-Apr) to get your bearings. Pick up pamphlets for the **Darlingtonia Trail** and **Myrtle Creek Botanical Area**, both easy jaunts into the woods, where you can see rare plants and learn about the area's geology.

where you can sleep under redwoods or at the prairie's edge. There are hot showers, some hike-in sites and a shallow creek to splash in. Sites one to seven and 69 to 76 are on grassy prairies and get full sun; sites eight to 68 are wooded. To camp in a mixed redwood forest, book sites 20 to 27.

Del Norte Coast Redwoods State Park

Marked by steep canyons and dense woods north of Klamath, half the 6400 acres of this **park** (☎707-465-7335; www.parks.ca.gov; Mill Creek Rd; per car $8; P) 🐾 are virgin redwood forest, crisscrossed by 15 miles of hiking trails, some of which pass by branches of Mill Creek (bring your fishing rod). The park also fronts 8 miles of rugged coastline.

Hwy 1 winds in from the coast at dramatic Wilson Beach, and traverses the dense forest, with groves stretching as far as you can see. Picnic on the sand at False Klamath Cove. Heading north, tall trees cling precipitously to canyon walls that drop to the rocky, timber-strewn coastline. Unfortunately, it is impossible to hike to the water – as of April 2017, the trail bridge located 1.75 miles in from the parking lot on Damnation Creek Trail was closed until further notice.

Serious hikers will be most greatly rewarded by the Damnation Creek Trail. It's only 4 miles long, but the 1100-ft elevation change and cliff-side red- wood makes it the park's best hike. The unmarked trailhead starts from a parking area off Hwy 101 at Mile 16.

Crescent Beach Overlook and picnic area has superb wintertime whale-watching. At the park's north end,

watch the surf pound at Crescent Beach, just south of Crescent City via Enderts Beach Rd.

Mill Creek Campground (☎reservations 800-444-7275; www.reserveamerica.com; Mill Creek Rd; tent & RV sites $35; ☺mid-May–Oct; P) has hot showers and 145 sites in a redwood grove, 2 miles east of Hwy 101 and 7 miles south of Crescent City. Sites 1-74 are woodsier; sites 75-145 sunnier. Hike-in sites are prettiest.

Pick up maps and inquire about guided walks at the Crescent City Information Center (p284) or the **Thomas H Kuchel Visitor Center** (☎707-465-7765; www.nps.gov/redw; Hwy 101, Orick; ☺9am-5pm Apr-Oct, to 4pm Nov Mar; ♿) in Orick.

Jedediah Smith Redwoods State Park

The northernmost park, Jedediah Smith is 9 miles northeast of Crescent City (via Hwy 101 north to Hwy 199 east). The redwood stands are so thick that few trails penetrate the park, but the outstanding 11-mile **Howland Hill Rd scenic drive** cuts through otherwise inaccessible areas (take Hwy 199 to South Fork Rd; turn right after crossing two bridges). It's a rough road, impassable for RVs, but if you can't hike, it's the best way to see the forest.

Stop for a stroll under enormous trees in **Simpson-Reed Grove**. There's a swimming hole and picnic area near the park entrance. An easy half-mile trail, departing from the far side of the campground, crosses the Smith River via a summer-only footbridge, leading to Stout Grove, the park's most famous grove. The visitor center sells hiking maps and nature guides.

Klamath

Giant metal-cast golden bears stand sentry at the bridge across the Klamath River, announcing Klamath, one of the tiny settlements that break up Redwood National & State Parks between Prairie Creek Redwoods State Park and Del Norte Coast Redwoods State Park. With a gas station/market, diner and a casino, Klamath is basically a wide spot in the road with some seriously great roadside kitsch at its edges. The Yurok Tribal Headquarters is in the town center and the entire settlement and much of the surrounding area is the tribe's ancestral land. The Yuroks are the largest group of Native Americans in the state of California.

Klamath is roughly an hour north of Eureka and is popular with hikers, campers and anglers; the river is famed for its wild freshwater salmon and is one of California's last free-flowing rivers after a proposal to build a dam here was thwarted in 1994.

◉ Sights & Activities

The mouth of the **Klamath River** is a dramatic sight. Marine, riparian, forest and meadow ecological zones all converge and the birding is exceptional. For the best views, head north of town to Requa Rd and the **Klamath River Overlook** and picnic on high bluffs above driftwood-strewn beaches. On a clear day, this is one of the most spectacular viewpoints on the North Coast, and one of the best whale-watching spots in California (this is one of the mammal's first feeding stops as they come south from Alaska). For a good hike, head north along the Coastal Trail. You'll have the sand to yourself at **Hidden Beach**; access the trail at the northern end of Motel Trees.

Just south of the river, on Hwy 101, the scenic **Coastal Drive**, a narrow, winding country road, traces extremely high cliffs over the ocean. Due to erosion a 3.3-mile section of the 9.5-mile loop (between Carruther's Cove trailhead and the intersection of the Coastal Drive with Alder Camp Rd) has been closed to motor traffic since 2011, but it's still walkable.

🛏 Sleeping

Woodsy Klamath is cheaper than Crescent City, but there aren't as many places to eat or buy groceries, and there's nothing to do at night but play cards. There are ample private RV parks in the area.

Flint Ridge Campground   CAMPGROUND
(☎707-464-6101) **FREE** Four miles from the Klamath River Bridge via Coastal Dr, this tent-only, hike-in campground sits among a wild, overgrown meadow of ferns and moss. It's a 10-minute walk (half a mile) east, uphill from the parking area. There's no water, plenty of bear sightings (bear boxes on-site) and you have to pack out trash. But, hey, it's free.

Ravenwood Motel   MOTEL $
(☎707-482-5911; www.ravenwoodmotel.com; 131 Klamath Blvd; r/ste with kitchen $95/140; P❂☎) The spotlessly clean rooms are individually decorated with furnishings and flair you'd expect in a city hotel, not a small-town motel. The same could be said of the surrounding attractions – there is a casino virtually next door!

★ Historic Requa Inn   HISTORIC HOTEL $$
(☎707-482-1425; www.requainn.com; 451 Requa Rd; r $119-199; P❂☎) 🍃 A woodsy country lodge on bluffs overlooking the mouth of the Klamath, the creaky and bright 1914 Requa Inn is a North Coast favorite and – even better – it's a carbon-neutral facility. Many of the charming, old-timey Americana rooms have mesmerizing views over the misty river, as does the dining room, which serves locally sourced, organic New American cuisine.

TREES OF MYSTERY

It's hard to miss the giant statues of Paul Bunyan and Babe the Blue Ox towering over the parking lot at **Trees of Mystery** (☎707-482-2251; www.treesofmystery.net; 15500 Hwy 101; museum free, gondola adult/child $16/8; ◷8:30am-6:30pm Jun-Aug, 9am-6pm Sep & Oct, 9:30am-4:30pm Nov-May; P🚗), a shameless tourist trap with a gondola running through the redwood canopy and a fun 'Tall Tales Forest' where chainsaw sculptures tell the tale of Paul Bunyan. It's perfect for families. The surprisingly wonderful **End of the Trail Museum** located behind the gift shop has an outstanding collection of Native American arts and artifacts, and it's free.

Crescent City

Crescent City is California's last big town north of Arcata. Founded as a thriving seaport and supply center for inland gold mines in the mid-19th century, the town's history was quite literally washed away in 1964, when half the town was swallowed by a tsunami. Of course, it was rebuilt (though mostly with the utilitarian ugliness of ticky-tacky buildings), but its marina was devastated by effects of the 2011 Japan earthquake and tsunami, when the city was evacuated. The economy depends heavily on shrimp and crab fishing, hotel tax and on Pelican Bay maximum-security prison, just north of town, which adds tension to the air and lots of cops to the streets.

Hwy 101 splits into two parallel one-way streets, with the southbound traffic on L St, northbound on M St. To see the major sights, turn west on Front St toward the lighthouse. Downtown is along 3rd St.

◉ Sights

If you're in town in August, the **Del Norte County Fair** features a rodeo, and lots of characters.

North Coast Marine Mammal Center   SCIENCE CENTER
(☏707-465-6265; www.northcoastmmc.org; 424 Howe Dr; ◷10am-5pm; 🏛) *✐* Just east of Battery Point, this is the ecologically minded foil to the garish Ocean World. The clinic treats injured seals, sea lions and dolphins and releases them back into the wild. There is an interesting gift shop.

Battery Point Lighthouse   LIGHTHOUSE
(☏707-467-3089; www.delnortehistory.org; South A St; adult/child $3/1; ◷10am-4pm Wed-Sun Apr-Sep) The 1856 lighthouse still operates on a tiny, rocky island that you can easily reach at low tide. You can also get a tour of the on-site museum for $3. Note that the listed hours are subject to change due to tides and weather.

Beachfront Park   PARK
(Howe Dr; 🅿🏛) Between B and H Sts, this park has a harborside beach with no large waves, making it perfect for little ones. Further east on Howe Dr, near J St, you'll come to **Kidtown**, with slides and swings and a make-believe castle.

🛌 Sleeping

Most people stop here for one night while traveling; motels are overpriced, but you'll pass a slew of good midrange hotels on the main arteries leading into and out of town, and you will generally have no problem finding a room, whatever the season. The county operates two excellent first-come, first-served campgrounds just outside of town and a couple of B&Bs have more recently opened up in town.

Curly Redwood Lodge   MOTEL $
(☏707-464-2137; www.curlyredwoodlodge.com; 701 Hwy 101 S; r $79-107; 🅿🈁❄🛜) The motel is a marvel: it's entirely built and paneled from a single curly redwood tree that measured over 18ft thick in diameter. Progressively restored and polished into a gem of mid-20th-century kitsch, the inn is like stepping into a time capsule and a delight for retro junkies. Rooms are clean, large and comfortable (request one away from the road).

Florence Keller Park   CAMPGROUND $
(☏707-464-7230; www.co.del-norte.ca.us; 3400 Cunningham Lane; tent sites $10; 🅿) County-run Florence Keller Park has 50 sites in a beautiful grove of young redwoods (take Hwy 101 north to Elk Valley Cross Rd and follow the signs). There are limited facilities at this campground: toilets, but no showers.

Bay View Inn   HOTEL $
(☏800-742-8439; www.ccbvi.com; 310 Hwy 101 S; s/d $55/99; 🅿🛜🛜) Bright, modern, updated rooms with microwaves and refrigerators fill this centrally located, independent hotel. It may seem a bit like a better-than-average highway-exit chain, but colorful bedspreads and warm hosts add necessary homespun appeal. The rooms upstairs in the back have views of the lighthouse and the harbor.

Anna Wulf Bed & Breakfast   B&B $$
(☏707-464-5340; www.annawulfhousebedand breakfast.com; 622 J St; r/ste $100/150; 🅿🛜🛜) Nice, Victorian-style B&B built in 1896. It's not as frilly inside as the lavender exterior would predict. The Honeymoon Suite has an inviting clawfoot tub. Check-out time is civilized (noon) – refreshing in these parts.

★Scopa at the Sea   B&B $$$
(☏541-944-4156; www.scopaproperties.com; 344 N Pebble Beach Dr; r from $250; 🅿🛜🛜) The Cape Cod–style architecture twinned with deluxe contemporary decor make this a

good option for those weary of motel chains. Furnished in warm earth colors with a design eye for detail, the en suites have tubs, as well as showers, while the front terrace is ideally placed for whale-watching. The breakfast highlights are the homemade breads and pastries made by innkeeper Deborah.

✖ Eating

Crescent City has plenty of restaurants, including a large number of fast-food options located on Hwy 101. For fresh seafood, there are a couple of aptly located restaurants near the water that specialize in fresh shrimp and crab. There is an excellent farmers market held every Saturday from June to October at the Del Norte County Fairgrounds.

Good Harvest Cafe   AMERICAN $
(☑707-465-6028; 575 Hwy 101 S; mains $7-16; ☺7:30am-9pm Mon-Sat, from 8am Sun; 🍴👶) This popular family owned cafe is in a spacious location across from the harbor. It's got a bit of everything – all pretty good – from soups and sandwiches to full meals and smoothies. Fine beers, a crackling fire and loads of vegetarian options make this among the best dining spots in town.

North Coast Ocean Sports & Grill   GRILL $
(☑707-465-1465; www.northcoastoceansportsandgrill.com; 110 Anchor Way; mains $11-15; ☺11am-8pm; 🅿🛜) A young, informal vibe, a no-frills sound menu of seafood, burgers and salads and exceptional ice cream mean this place is always packed out, especially in summer when folk spill out onto the front deck across from the ocean. It also rents out surf boards, kayaks and bikes.

Enoteca   ITALIAN, AMERICAN $
(960 3rd St; mains $7-12; ☺11am-7pm Mon-Wed & Sat, to 8pm Thu, to 10pm Fri; 🛜) Stop in for salads, pasta, sandwiches or jazz on Friday nights. Hands down the most happening place downtown.

Chart Room   SEAFOOD $$
(☑707-464-5993; www.ccchartroom.com; 130 Anchor Way; dinner mains $10-28; ☺7am-7pm Wed-Thu & Sun, to 8pm Fri & Sat, 11am-4pm Tue; 🅿👶) At the tip of the South Harbor pier, this joint is renowned far and wide for its fish and chips: batter-caked golden beauties that deliver on their reputation. It's often a hive of families, retirees, Harley riders and fisherfolk, so grab a beer at the small bar and wait for a table. Other recommendations include the creamy clam chowder.

ℹ Information

Crescent City Information Center (☑707-465-7335; www.nps.gov/redw; 1111 2nd St; ☺9am-5pm Apr-Oct, to 4pm Nov-Mar) On the corner of K St; you'll find rangers here and information about all four parks under its jurisdiction.

Crescent City-Del Norte Chamber of Commerce (☑707-464-3174; www.exploredelnorte.com; 1001 Front St; ☺9am-5pm daily May-Aug, 9am-5pm Mon-Fri Sep-Apr) A helpful office that can provide local information, as well as a map.

ℹ Getting There & Around

Alaska Airlines (p232) and Penair (p232) fly into tiny **Del Norte County Regional Airport** (CEC; ☑707-464-7288; www.flycrescentcity.com; 250 Dale Rupert Rd, Crescent City; ☺5am-7:30pm), located 3 miles northwest of town. There are frequent flights to Eureka as well as Portland, Redding and North Bend in Oregon.

Redwood Coast Transit (p232) serves Crescent City with local buses ($1), and runs buses Monday to Saturday to Klamath ($1.50, one hour, three daily) and Arcata ($30, two hours, three daily), with stops in between. Have the exact fare, the driver carries no change.

Drivers may experience delays on Hwy 101 between Klamath and Crescent City as corrosion continues to affect the highway, particularly after heavy rains.

Tolowa Dunes State Park & Lake Earl Wildlife Area

Two miles north of Crescent City, this **state park and wildlife area** (☑707-464-6101, ext 5112; Kellogg Rd; ☺sunrise-sunset) encompasses 10,000 acres of wetlands, dunes, meadows and two lakes – **Lake Earl** and **Lake Tolowa**. This major stopover on the Pacific Flyway route brings over 250 species of birds here. Listen for the whistling, warbling chorus. On land, look for coyotes and deer, angle for trout, or hike or ride 20 miles of trails; at sea, spot whales, seals and sea lions.

The park and wildlife area are a patchwork of lands administered by California State Parks and the Department of Fish and Game (DFG). The DFG focuses on single-species management, hunting and fishing; the State Parks' focus is on ecodiversity and recreation. You might be hiking a vast expanse of pristine dunes, then suddenly hear a shotgun or a whining 4WD. Strict regulations limit where and when you can hunt and drive; trails are clearly marked.

To get here from Crescent City, take Northcrest Dr north off of Hwy 101, which becomes Lake Earl Dr. Turn left on Lower Lake Rd to Kellogg Rd, which leads to the park.

Pelican State Beach

The northernmost beach in California and the most northern spot on the California Coastal Trail, never-crowded **Pelican State Beach** (☑707-464-6101, ext 5151; Gilbert Way, Hwy 101; Ⓟ) occupies 5 coastal acres just south of the Oregon border. There are no facilities and due to its easy-to-miss access, this beach has been described as the loneliest beach in California, but it's great for walking, beachcombing and kite flying; pick one up at one of the kite specialty shops just over the border in Oregon.

The beach is around 2 miles east of Pelican Bay State Prison; the only so-called super maximum security facility in California and a world away, one imagines, from the tranquility of this beautiful unspoiled beach.

Clifford Kamph Memorial Park CAMPGROUND $
(☑707-464-7230; 15100 Hwy 101; tent sites $10) Pitch a tent by the ocean (no windbreaks) at Clifford Kamph Memorial Park; no RVs. It's a steal for the beachside location and, even though sites are exposed in a grassy area and there isn't much privacy, all have BBQs.

Casa Rubio BOUTIQUE HOTEL $$
(☑707-487-4313; www.casarubio.com; 17285 Crissey Rd; r $98-178; Ⓟⓞⓡⓢ) The best reason to visit Pelican State Beach is to stay at secluded, charming Casa Rubio, where three of the four ocean-view rooms have kitchens. Surrounded by tropical gardens, a short path leads directly to the beach.

Central Coast

Best Places to Eat

➡ Assembly (p294)

➡ Ember (p344)

➡ Foremost Wine Co (p338)

➡ Thomas Hill Organics (p336)

➡ La Cosecha Bar & Restaurant (p333)

Best Places to Sleep

➡ Post Ranch Inn (p318)

➡ Jabberwock (p304)

➡ Cass House Inn (p325)

➡ Avila La Fonda (p341)

➡ Summerwood Inn (p333)

Why Go?

Too often forgotten or dismissed as 'flyover' country between San Francisco and LA, this fairy-tale stretch of California coast is packed with wild beaches, misty redwood forests where hot springs hide, and rolling golden hills of fertile vineyards and farm fields.

Coastal Hwy 1 pulls out all the stops, scenery-wise. Flower-power Santa Cruz and the historic port town of Monterey are gateways to the rugged wilderness of the bohemian Big Sur coast. It's an epic journey snaking down to vainglorious Hearst Castle, past lighthouses and edgy cliffs atop which endangered condors soar.

Get acquainted with California's agricultural heartland along inland Hwy 101, called El Camino Real (the King's Highway) by Spanish conquistadors and Franciscan friars. Colonial missions still line the route, which passes through Paso Robles' flourishing wine and craft-beer country. Then soothe your nature-loving soul in collegiate San Luis Obispo, ringed by sunny beach towns and volcanic peaks.

When to Go
Santa Cruz

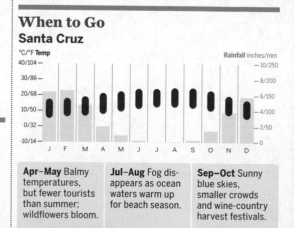

Apr–May Balmy temperatures, but fewer tourists than summer; wildflowers bloom.

Jul–Aug Fog disappears as ocean waters warm up for beach season.

Sep–Oct Sunny blue skies, smaller crowds and wine-country harvest festivals.

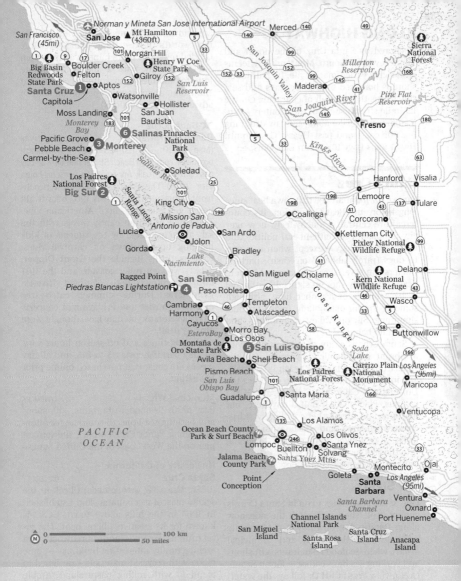

Central Coast Highlights

1 Learning to surf, and scaring yourself silly on the Giant Dipper along the famed beach boardwalk in **Santa Cruz** (p288).

2 Cruising Hwy 1, where the sky touches the sea along the rocky coastline of mystical **Big Sur** (p313).

3 Being mesmerized by aquatic denizens of the 'indoor ocean' at the superb aquarium in **Monterey** (p299).

4 Marveling at the jawdropping grandiosity of Hearst Castle in **San Simeon** (p321) after meeting the neighbors: ginormous elephant seals.

5 Chilling out in easygoing college town **San Luis Obispo** (p335), surrounded by beaches, vineyards and mountains.

6 Exploring **Salinas** (p329) and the blue-collar world of Nobel Prize–winning, down-to-earth novelist John Steinbeck.

ALONG HIGHWAY 1

Anchored by Santa Cruz to the north and Monterey to the south, Monterey Bay teems with richly varied marine life. Its half-moon shore is bordered by wild beaches and seaside towns that are full of character. On the 125-mile stretch south of the Monterey Peninsula, you'll snake along the jaw-dropping Big Sur coast and past Hearst Castle until Hwy 1 joins Hwy 101 in San Luis Obispo.

Santa Cruz

Santa Cruz has marched to its own beat since long before the Beat Generation. It's counterculture central, a touchy-feely, new-agey city famous for its leftie-liberal politics and easygoing ideology – except when it comes to dogs (rarely allowed off-leash), parking (meters run seven days a week) and Republicans (allegedly shot on sight). It's still cool to be a hippie or a stoner here, although some of the far-out-looking freaks are just slumming Silicon Valley millionaires and trust-fund babies.

Santa Cruz is a city of madcap fun, with a vibrant but chaotic downtown. On the waterfront is the famous beach boardwalk, and in the hills redwood groves embrace the University of California, Santa Cruz (UCSC) campus. Plan at least half a day here, but to appreciate the aesthetic of jangly skirts, crystal pendants and Rastafarian dreadlocks, stay longer and plunge headlong into the rich local brew of surfers, students, punks and eccentric characters.

⊙ Sights

One of the best things to do in Santa Cruz is simply stroll, shop and watch the sideshow along **Pacific Ave** downtown. A 15-minute walk away is the beach and Municipal Wharf, where seafood restaurants, gift shops and barking sea lions compete for attention. Ocean-view **West Cliff Dr** follows the waterfront southwest of the wharf, paralleled by a paved recreational path.

★**Seymour Marine Discovery Center** MUSEUM
(Map p298; ☑ 831-459-3800; http://seymourcenter. ucsc.edu; 100 Shaffer Rd; adult/child 3-16yr $8/6; ⊙10am-5pm Tue-Sun; P ⓙ) ⊘ By Natural Bridges State Beach, this kids' educational center is part of UCSC's Long Marine Laboratory. Interactive natural-science exhibits include tidal touch pools and aquariums, while outside you can gawk at the world's largest blue-whale skeleton. Guided one-hour tours happen at 1pm, 2pm and 3pm daily, with a special 30-minute tour for families with younger children at 11am; sign up for tours in person an hour in advance (no reservations).

★**Santa Cruz Beach Boardwalk** AMUSEMENT PARK
(Map p290; ☑ 831-423-5590; www.beach boardwalk.com; 400 Beach St; per ride $4-7, all-day pass $37-82; ⊙ daily Apr-early Sep, seasonal hours vary; P ⓙ) The West Coast's oldest beachfront amusement park, this 1907 boardwalk has a glorious old-school Americana vibe. The smell of cotton candy mixes with the salt air, punctuated by the squeals of kids hanging upside down on carnival rides. Famous thrills include the **Giant Dipper**, a 1924 wooden roller coaster, and the 1911 **Looff carousel**, both National Historic Landmarks. During summer, catch free midweek movies and Friday-night concerts by rock veterans you may have thought were already dead.

Closing times and off-season hours vary. All-day parking costs $5 to $15, and all-day passes are cheaper if purchased online prior to visiting.

Municipal Wharf LANDMARK
(Map p290) Seafood restaurants, gift shops and barking sea lions all compete for attention along Santa Cruz's wharf, the longest pier on the West Coast of the United States.

University of California, Santa Cruz UNIVERSITY
(UCSC; Map p298; www.ucsc.edu) Check it: the school mascot is a banana slug! Established in 1965 in the hills above town, UCSC is known for its creative, liberal bent. The rural campus has fine stands of redwoods and architecturally interesting buildings – some made with recycled materials – designed to blend in with rolling pastureland. Amble around the peaceful **arboretum** (Map p298; ☑ 831-502-2998; www.arboretum.ucsc.edu; cnr High St & Arboretum Rd; adult/child 6-17yr $5/2, free 1st Tue of each month; ⊙9am-5pm) and picturesquely decaying 19th-century structures from Cowell Ranch, upon which the campus was built.

Museum of Art & History MUSEUM
(Map p290; ☑ 831-429-1964; www.santacruzmah. org; McPherson Center, 705 Front St; adult/child 12-17yr $10/8, free 1st Fri of each month; ⊙11am-5pm

DON'T MISS

TOP SANTA CRUZ BEACHES

Sun-kissed Santa Cruz has warmer beaches than San Francisco or Monterey. *Baywatch* it isn't, but 29 miles of coastline reveal a few Hawaii-worthy beaches, craggy coves, some primo surf spots and big sandy stretches where your kids will have a blast. Fog may ruin many a summer morning; it often burns off by the afternoon.

West Cliff Dr is lined with scramble-down-to coves and plentiful parking. If you don't want sand in your shoes, park yourself on a bench and watch enormous pelicans dive for fish. You'll find bathrooms and showers at the lighthouse parking lot.

Locals favor less-trampled East Cliff Dr beaches, which are bigger and more protected from the wind, meaning calmer waters. Except at a small metered lot at 26th Ave, parking is by permit only on weekends (buy a $8 per-day permit at 9th Ave).

Main Beach (Map p290) *The* scene in Santa Cruz, with a huge sandy stretch, volleyball courts and swarms of people. Park on E Cliff Dr and walk across the *Lost Boys* trestle to the beach boardwalk (p288).

Its Beach (Map p298; 🐾) The only official off-leash beach for dogs (before 10am and after 4pm) in Santa Cruz is just west of the lighthouse. The field across the street is another good romping ground.

Natural Bridges State Beach (Map p298; ☎831-423-4609; www.parks.ca.gov; 2531 W Cliff Dr; per car $10; ⏲8am-sunset; P 👪) Best for sunsets, this family favorite has lots of sand, tide pools and monarch butterflies from mid-October through mid-February. It's at the far western end of W Cliff Dr.

Seacliff State Beach (☎831-685-6442; www.parks.ca.gov; State Park Rd, Aptos; per car $10; ⏲8am-sunset) Seacliff State Beach harbors a 'cement boat,' a quixotic freighter built of concrete that floated OK, but ended up here as a coastal fishing pier. During huge storms in February 2017, the boat actually broke apart but remains *in situ*.

Manresa State Beach (☎831-724-3750; www.parks.ca.gov; San Andreas Rd, Watsonville; per car $10; ⏲8am-sunset) Near Watsonville, the La Selva Beach exit off Hwy 1 leads here to this sparsely populated beach.

Moran Lake County Park (Map p298; E Cliff Dr; ⏲8am-sunset) With a good surf break and bathrooms, this pretty all-around sandy spot is further east of 26th Ave off E Cliff Dr.

Cowell's Beach (Map p290) Popular Santa Cruz surfing beach off WCliff Dr.

Sunset State Beach (☎831-763-7062; www.parks.ca.gov; San Andreas Rd, Watsonville; per car $10; ⏲8am-sunset) The La Selva Beach exit off Hwy 1, near Watsonville, brings you here, where you can have miles of sand and surf almost all to yourself.

Tue-Thu & Sat & Sun, to 9pm Fri) In Santa Cruz's downtown, rotating displays by contemporary California artists and exhibits that dive into local history are worth a quick look. Recent renovations include an adjacent courtyard with cafes and restaurants.

Sanctuary Exploration Center MUSEUM
(Map p290; ☎831-421-9993; www.montereybay.noaa.gov; 35 Pacific Ave; ⏲10am-5pm Wed-Sun; 👪) FREE Operated by the Monterey Bay National Marine Sanctuary, this educational museum near the beach boardwalk is an interactive multimedia experience that teaches kids and adults about the bay's marine treasures, watershed conservation and high-tech underwater exploration for scientific research.

Santa Cruz Surfing Museum MUSEUM
(Map p298; ☎831-420-6289; www.santacruzsurfingmuseum.org; 701 W Cliff Dr; by donation; ⏲10am-5pm Wed-Mon Jul 4-early Sep, noon-4pm Thu-Mon early Sep-Jul 3; 👪) A mile southwest of the wharf along the coast, this tiny museum inside an old lighthouse is packed with memorabilia, including vintage redwood surfboards. Fittingly, Lighthouse Point overlooks two popular surf breaks.

Mystery Spot LANDMARK
(☎831-423-8897; www.mysteryspot.com; 465 Mystery Spot Rd; $8; ⏲10am-4pm Mon-Fri, to 5pm Sat & Sun Sep-May, 10am-6pm Mon-Fri, 9am-7pm Sat & Sun Jun-Aug; P 👪) A kitschy, old-fashioned tourist trap, Santa Cruz's Mystery Spot has scarcely changed since it opened in 1940. On

Santa Cruz

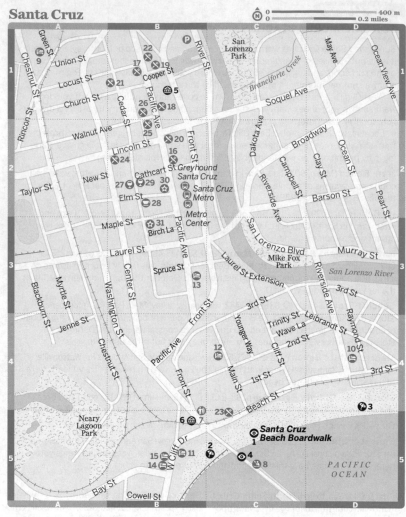

a steeply sloping hillside, compasses seem to point crazily, mysterious forces push you around and buildings lean at silly angles. Make reservations, or risk getting stuck waiting for a tour. It's about 4 miles northeast of downtown: take Water St to Market St north and continue on Branciforte Dr into the hills. Parking costs $5. Don't forget your bumper sticker!

**Santa Cruz Museum
of Natural History**   MUSEUM
(Map p298; ☎831-420-6115; www.santacruz
museum.org; 1305 E Cliff Dr; adult/child under
18yr $4/free, free 1st Fri of each month; ◷11am-

4pm Tue-Fri & 10am-5pm Sat-Sun; ⊕) The collections at this pint-sized museum include stuffed-animal mounts, Native Californian cultural artifacts and a touch-friendly tide pool that shows off sea critters living by the beach right across the street.

🏃 Activities

★ **Santa Cruz Food Tour**   FOOD
(☎866-736-6343; www.santacruzfoodtour.com;
per person $59; ◷2:30-6pm Fri & Sat) Combining Afghan flavors, a farm-to-table bistro, vegan cupcakes and artisan ice cream, these highly recommended walking tours

Santa Cruz

also come with a healthy serving of local knowledge and interesting insights into Santa Cruz history, culture and architecture. Sign up for a tour when you first arrive in town to get your bearings in the tastiest way possible.

Slow Adventure   WALKING
(☑831-332-7923; www.slowadventure.us; per person $1495; ⊙Apr-Oct) ⏎ Well-traveled Santa Cruz local Margaret Leonard arranges self-guided walking adventures around Monterey Bay. The full itinerary from Santa Cruz to Monterey takes six days and five nights, covering from 40 to 50 miles in total, and overnighting in very comfortable ocean-view accommodations along the way. Luggage is transferred independently, and highlights include birdlife, marine mammals and superb coastal views. Shorter four-day/three-night coastal adventures to the north and south of Santa Cruz are also available (per person $995 to $1095).

DeLaveaga Disc Golf Club   GOLF
(Map p298; www.facebook.com/groups/Dela DDGC; Upper Park Rd; 👪) FREE Touring pros and families with kids toss discs across this challenging hillside layout that peaks at Hole No 27, nicknamed 'Top of the World.' It's a couple of miles northeast of downtown Santa Cruz, off Branciforte Dr.

SUP Shack   WATER SPORTS
(Map p298; ☑831-464-7467; www.supshacksanta cruz.com; 2214 E Cliff Dr; rental/lessons from $20/59) Based in the calm waters of Santa Cruz Harbor, SUP Shack offers paddleboarding lessons and rentals. Kayaks and body boards are also available for rental.

Surfing
Year-round, water temperatures average under 60°F, meaning that without a wetsuit, body parts quickly turn blue. Surfing is incredibly popular, especially at experts-only **Steamer Lane** and beginners' Cowell's (p289), both off W Cliff Dr. Other favorite surf spots include **Pleasure Point Beach**, on E Cliff Dr toward Capitola, and Manresa State Beach (p289) off Hwy 1 southbound.

O'Neill Surf Shop   SURFING
(Map p298; ☑831-475-4151; www.oneill.com; 1115 41st Ave; wetsuit/surfboard rental from $15/25; ⊙9am-8pm Mon-Fri, from 8am Sat & Sun) Head east toward Pleasure Point to worship at this internationally renowned surfboard-maker's flagship store, with branches on the beach boardwalk and downtown.

Richard Schmidt Surf School   SURFING
(Map p298; ☑831-423-0928; www.richard schmidt.com; 849 Almar Ave; 2hr group/1hr private lesson $90/120; 👪) Award-winning,

time-tested surf school can get you out there, all equipment included. Summer surf camps hook adults and kids alike.

Cowell's Beach Surf Shop
SURFING

(Map p290; ☑831-427-2355; www.cowellssurf shop.com; 30 Front St; 2hr group lesson $90; ⊙8am-6pm, to 5pm Nov-Mar; 📦) Rent surfboards, boogie boards, wetsuits and other beach gear near the wharf, where veteran staff offer local tips and lessons.

Kayaking

Kayaking lets you discover the craggy coastline and kelp beds where sea otters float.

Kayak Connection
WATER SPORTS

(Map p298; ☑831-479-1121; www.kayakconnection. com; Santa Cruz Harbor, 413 Lake Ave; kayak rental/tour from $35/50; ⊙10am-5pm Mon, Wed & Fri, 9am-5pm Sat-Sun; 📦) Rents kayaks and offers lessons and tours, including whale-watching, sunrise, sunset and full-moon trips. Also rents stand-up paddle boarding (SUP) sets (from $35), wetsuits ($10) and boogie boards ($10).

Venture Quest
KAYAKING

(Map p290; ☑831-427-2267, 831-425-8445; www. kayaksantacruz.com; Municipal Wharf; kayak rental/tour from $35/56; ⊙10am-7pm Mon-Fri, from 9am Sat & Sun late May–late Sep, hours vary late Sep–mid-May) Convenient rentals on the wharf, plus whale-watching and coastal sea-cave tours, moonlight paddles and kayak-sailing trips. Book ahead for kayak-surfing lessons.

Whale-Watching & Fishing

Winter whale-watching trips run from December through April, though there's plenty of marine life to see on a summer bay cruise.

Many fishing trips depart from Santa Cruz's wharf, where a few shops rent fishing tackle and poles, if you're keen to join locals waiting patiently for a bite.

Stagnaro's
BOATING

(Map p298; ☑info 831-427-0230, reservations 888-237-7084; www.stagnaros.com; 1718 Brommer St; adult/child under 14yr cruise from $22/15, whale-watching tour from $50/36) Longstanding tour operator offers scenic and sunset cruises around Monterey Bay during spring and summer, and whale-watching tours year-round.

✿ Festivals & Events

Woodies on the Wharf
CULTURAL

(www.santacruzwoodies.com; ⊙late June) Classic-car show features vintage surf-style station wagons on Santa Cruz's Municipal Wharf (p288).

Open Studio Art Tour
ART

(www.firstfridaysantacruz.com) Step inside local artists' creative workshops over three weekends in October. The arts council also sponsors 'First Friday' art exhibitions on the first Friday of each month, including access to artists' ateliers at the heritage Tannery Arts Center located just north of downtown.

🛏 Sleeping

Santa Cruz does not have enough beds to satisfy demand: expect high prices at peak times for nothing-special rooms. Places near the beach boardwalk (p288) range from friendly to frightening. For a decent motel, cruise Ocean St inland or Mission St (Hwy 1). Several new hotels scheduled to open from late 2017 will improve the city's accommodations options. Contact the visitor center (p296) for details.

HI Santa Cruz Hostel
HOSTEL $

(Map p290; ☑831-423-8304; www.hi-santacruz. org; 321 Main St; dm $28-31, r $85-140, all with shared bath; ⊙check in 5-10pm; @🅰) Budget overnighters dig this cute hostel at the century-old Carmelita Cottages surrounded by flowering gardens, just two blocks from the beach. Cons: midnight curfew, daytime lockout (11am to 5pm) and three-night maximum stay. Reservations are essential. Street parking costs $2.

California State Park
Campgrounds
CAMPGROUND $

(☑reservations800-444-7275;www.reserveamerica. com; tent & RV sites $35-65) Book well ahead to camp at state beaches off Hwy 1 south of Santa Cruz or up in the foggy Santa Cruz Mountains off Hwy 9. Family-friendly campgrounds include Henry Cowell Redwoods State Park in Felton and New Brighton State Beach in Capitola.

★ Adobe on Green B&B
B&B $$

(Map p290; ☑831-469-9866; www.adobeongreen. com; 103 Green St; r $179; P🐾🅰) 🐾 Peace and quiet are the mantras at this place, a short walk from Pacific Ave. The hosts are practically invisible, but their thoughtful touches are everywhere, from boutique-hotel amenities in spacious, stylish and solar-powered rooms to breakfast spreads from their organic gardens.

Carousel Beach Inn
MOTEL $$

(Map p290; ☑831-425-7090; www.carousel-beach -inn.com; 110 Riverside Ave; r $159-229; P🅰) Colorful decor and bright artwork feature at this recently renovated motel that is the closest accommodations to the attractions of the Santa Cruz boardwalk. Prices surge in summer, but it's worth checking online for off-peak and seasonal discounts.

Seaway Inn   MOTEL $$
(Map p290; ☑831-471-9004; www.seawayinn. com; 176 W Cliff Dr; r $139-150; 🅿☻🕏) Good value and welcoming accommodations just a short walk uphill from the Santa Cruz Municipal Wharf. Try and stay on a weekday as prices surge on weekends.

Hotel Paradox   HOTEL $$
(Map p298; ☑831-425-7100; www.thehotelparadox. com; 611 Ocean St; r from $229; @🕏🏊) This downtown boutique hotel brings the great outdoors inside, with nature prints on the walls, textured wood panels and earth-toned furnishings. Relax in a cabana by the pool or next to an outdoor fire pit. Weekday rates can be reasonable, but summer weekends are ridiculously high-priced. Parking is $10.

Mission Inn   MOTEL $$
(Map p298; ☑831-425-5455; www.mission-inn. com; 2250 Mission St; r $139-179; 🏊🕏) Perfectly serviceable two-story motel with a garden courtyard, hot tub and complimentary continental breakfast. It's on busy Hwy 1 near the UCSC campus, away from the beach.

Pelican Point Inn   INN $$
(Map p298; ☑831-475-3381; www.pelicanpoint innsantacruz.com; 21345 E Cliff Dr; ste $139-229; 🅿☻🕏🏊) Ideal for families, these roomy apartments near a kid-friendly beach come with everything you'll need for a lazy vacation, including kitchenettes. Weekly rates available. Pet fee $25.

Pacific Blue Inn   B&B $$$
(Map p290; ☑831-600-8880; www.pacificblueinn. com; 636 Pacific Ave; r $189-289; 🅿☻🕏🏊) ⌗ This downtown courtyard B&B is an eco-conscious gem, with water-saving fixtures and renewable and recycled building materials. Refreshingly elemental rooms have pillowtop beds, electric fireplaces and flat-screen TVs with DVD players. Free parking and loaner bikes. Pet fee $50.

Babbling Brook Inn   B&B $$$
(Map p298; ☑831-427-2437; www.babblingbrookinn. com; 1025 Laurel St; r $229-329; 🕏) Built around a running stream with meandering gardens, the inn has cozy rooms decorated in French-provincial style. Most have gas fireplaces, some have Jacuzzis and all have featherbeds. There's afternoon wine and hors d'oeuvres, plus a full breakfast.

Dream Inn   HOTEL $$$
(Map p290; ☑831-426-4330; www.dreaminn santacruz.com; 175 W Cliff Dr; r $279-576; 🅿☻❀ @🕏🏊) Overlooking the wharf from a hillside perch, this chic hotel offers some of Santa Cruz's most stylish accommodations. Newly renovated rooms all have ocean views, while the beach and the revamped swimming pool area are just steps away. Don't miss having an end-of-day cocktail in the Jack O'Neill Lounge, named after Santa Cruz's iconic pioneer of surfing culture.

West Cliff Inn   INN $$$
(Map p290; ☑831-457-2200; www.westcliffinn. com; 174 W Cliff Dr; r $210-425; 🅿🕏) In a classy Victorian house west of the wharf, this boutique inn's quaint rooms mix seagrass wicker, dark wood and jaunty striped curtains. The most romantic suites have gas fireplaces and let you spy on the breaking surf. Rates include a breakfast buffet and afternoon wine, tea and snacks.

🍴 Eating

Downtown Santa Cruz is packed with casual cafes. If you're looking for seafood, wander the wharf's takeout counter joints. Mission St, near UCSC, and 41st Ave offer cheaper eats.

★Penny Ice Creamery   ICE CREAM $
(Map p290; ☑831-204-2523; www.thepenny icecreamery.com; 913 Cedar St; snacks $3-5; ⊙noon-11pm; 🖲) ⌗ With a cult following, this artisan ice-cream shop crafts zany flavors such as bourbon-candied ginger, lemon-verbena–blueberry and ricotta apricot all from scratch using local, organic and wild-harvested ingredients. Even plain old vanilla is special: it's made using Thomas Jefferson's original recipe. Also at a **downtown kiosk** (Map p290; 1520 Pacific Ave; snacks $3-5; ⊙noon-6pm; 🖲) ⌗ and near **Pleasure Point** (Map p298; 820 41st Ave; snacks $3-5; ⊙noon-9pm Sun-Thu, to 10pm Fri & Sat; 🖲) ⌗.

★Santa Cruz Farmers Market   MARKET $
(Map p290; ☑831-454-0566; www.santacruz farmersmarket.org; cnr Lincoln & Center Sts; ⊙1:30-6:30pm Wed; 🖋🖲) ⌗ Organic produce, baked goods and arts-and-crafts and food booths all give you an authentic taste of the local vibe. Shorter fall and winter hours.

Akira

JAPANESE $

(Map p298; 831-600-7093; www.akirasantacruz.com; 1222 Soquel Ave; sushi & sashimi $10-15; 11am-11pm;) Head northeast of downtown Santa Cruz to Soquel Ave's restaurant strip for Akira's modern take on sushi, sashimi and other Japanese flavors. Combining sake, craft brews and a surf-town ambience, Akira's menu harnesses briny-fresh tuna, salmon, eel and shellfish for a huge variety of sushi. Bento boxes for lunch ($10 to $14) are good value, and there's a wide range of vegetarian options.

Buttercup Cakes

CAFE $

(Map p290; 831-466-0373; www.facebook.com/scbuttercupcakes; 1141 Pacific Ave; snacks from $3; 10am-9pm;) Vegan and organic ingredients all feature, but there's absolutely no trade-off in flavor with Buttercup's cupcakes and desserts. The downtown location is a handy coffee stop, too.

Walnut Ave Cafe

BREAKFAST $

(Map p290; 831-457-2804; www.walnutavenuecafe.com; 106 Walnut Ave; mains $9-12; 7am-3pm Mon-Fri, 8am-4pm Sat & Sun;) Line up at this clean, well-lit breakfast spot for fluffy Belgian waffles, blackened ahi tuna eggs benny, Mexican huevos rancheros with pulled pork and all kinds of veggie scrambles. Lunch brings less-exciting sandwiches, salads and soups. Dogs are welcome on the outdoor patio.

New Leaf Community Market

SUPERMARKET $

(Map p290; 831-425-1793; www.newleaf.com; 1134 Pacific Ave; 8am-9pm;) Organic and local produce, natural-foods groceries and deli take-out meals in the middle of downtown Santa Cruz.

Picnic Basket

DELI $

(Map p290; 831-427-9946; www.facebook.com/pg/thepicnicbasketsc; 125 Beach St; snacks $6-11; 7am-9pm;) Across the street from the beach boardwalk, this locavorian kitchen puts together creative sandwiches such as beet with lemony couscous or 'fancy pants' grilled cheese with fruit chutney, plus homemade soups, breakfast burritos and baked goods. Service can be standoffish, but ice-cream treats are sweet. It's open shorter hours in the off season.

★ Assembly

CALIFORNIAN $$

(Map p290; 831-824-6100; www.assembly.restaurant; 1108 Pacific Ave; brunch & lunch $12-16, dinner mains $22-28; 11:30am-9pm Mon & Wed-Thu, to 10pm Fri, 10am-10pm Sat-Sun;) Farm-to-table and proudly regional flavors feature at this excellent bistro in downtown Santa Cruz. Assembly's Californian vibe belies real culinary nous in the kitchen, and the seasonal menu could include dishes such as chicken breast with crispy pancetta or a truffle-laced asparagus risotto. Don't miss trying the Scotch olives and meatballs with a tasting flight of local craft beers.

Soif

BISTRO $$

(Map p290; 831-423-2020; www.soifwine.com; 105 Walnut Ave; small plates $5-17, mains $19-25; 5-9pm Sun-Thu, to 10pm Fri & Sat;) Following a recent makeover, one of Santa Cruz's more established restaurants is now better than ever, and the chic and cosmopolitan decor showcases a stunning wine list – including tasting flights ($20.50) of local Santa Cruz varietals – and a well-curated menu with standouts like slow-roasted pork and scallops wrapped in bacon. Wine-matching suggestions are available for all dishes.

An on-site **wine shop** (noon-8pm Tue-Sun, 5-8pm Mon) also features many Californian wines.

Jaguar

MEXICAN $$

(Map p298; 831-600-7428; www.jaguarrestaurantinc.com; 1116 Soquel Ave; mains $14-22; 5-10pm Thu-Tue) Regional Mexican flavors feature at this bricks-and-mortar expansion of a popular long-standing Santa Cruz food stall. A strong adherence to organic ingredients shines in dishes like a delicious chicken mole (a Mexican dish with a rich spicy sauce), and a delicate ceviche packed with fresh seafood. Wines from local Santa Cruz vineyards partner well with the robust flavors.

Bantam

CALIFORNIAN, ITALIAN $$

(Map p298; 831-420-0101; www.bantam1010.com; 1010 Fair Ave; shared plates $11-23, pizza $11-20; 5-9pm Mon-Thu, to 9:30pm Fri-Sat;) Another opening in the up-and-coming dining scene in Santa Cruz's West End, Bantam's versatile space is often packed with SC locals enjoying wood-fired pizza, a savvy cocktail, the wine and craft-beer list, and moreish shared plates including squid, meatballs and pork belly. No reservations, but the informal and easygoing ambience means tables are turned over fairly promptly.

Laili

AFGHANI $$

(Map p290; 831-423-4545; www.lailirestaurant.com; 101b Cooper St; mains $14-26; 11:30am-2:30pm & 5-9pm Tue-Sun;) A chic downtown

TOP SANTA CRUZ BREWERIES & BEER BARS

We asked Derek Wolfgram, home brewer and local beer columnist, to share a few of his favorite places for a pint:

Boulder Creek Brewery Outpost (☑831-338-7882; www.facebook.com/bouldercreek brewery; 13101 Hwy 9, Boulder Creek; ☺noon-9pm) High up in the mountains in the village of Boulder Creek, these guys brew amber 'Redwood Ale' and 'Dragon's Breath' American IPA. After a fire in 2016, they've relocated just across the road to this pop-up location while they rebuild.

Sante Adairius Rustic Ales (Map p298; ☑831-462-1227; www.rusticales.com; 103 Kennedy Dr; ☺3-8pm Tue-Thu, from noon Fri-Sun) Off Hwy 1 east of Santa Cruz, Belgian-inspired and barrel-aged beers are a beer geek's dream.

Discretion Brewing (Map p298; ☑831-316-0662; www.discretionbrewing.com; 2703 41st Ave, Soquel; ☺11:30am-9pm; 🍴) Rye IPA, English ales and traditional Belgian and German brews are always on tap, off Hwy 1. The raffish beer garden is dog-friendly, and ramen noodles and risotto both come with a proudly Californian farm-to-table accent.

Santa Cruz Mountain Brewing (Map p298; ☑831-425-4900; www.scmbrew.com; 402 Ingalls St, Ingalls St Courtyard; ☺11:30am-10pm; 🍴) An essential part of the eating and drinking scene in the Ingalls St Courtyard on Santa Cruz's Westside, Santa Cruz Mountain Brewing is a rustic spot to combine brews and a burger. Crowd into the compact tasting room or share an outside table with friendly locals and their well-behaved canine pals. Our favorite beer is the robust Devout Scout.

From Friday to Sunday, adjacent urban wine-tasting rooms are also open, often offering live music.

Santa Cruz Ale Works (Map p298; ☑831-425-1182; www.santacruzaleworks.com; 150 Du Bois St; ☺11am-6pm; 🍴) Hefeweizen and 'Dark Night' oatmeal stout are commendable at this dog-friendly brewpub with a deli. The beers are good, but the location in an office park lacks ambience.

dining oasis, family-owned Laili invites diners in with an elegant high-ceilinged dining room and garden patio. Share apricot-chicken flatbread, tart pomegranate eggplant, roasted cauliflower with saffron, succulent lamb kebabs and more. Reservations for dinner advised.

Engfer Pizza Works PIZZA $$
(Map p298; ☑831-429-1856; www.engferpizza works.com; 537 Seabright Ave; pizzas $11-27; ☺4-9:30pm Tue-Sun; 🍴🚼) Detour to find this old factory, where wood-fired oven pizzas are made from scratch with love – the no-name specialty is like a giant salad on roasted bread. Play Ping-Pong and down craft beers from local breweries while you wait. Try the Hot Hawaiian pizza with a Santa Cruz Ale Works Hefeweizen.

El Palomar MEXICAN $$
(Map p290; ☑831-425-7575; www.elpalomar santacruz.com/; 1336 Pacific Ave; mains $10-22; ☺11:30am-10pm Mon-Fri, 10am-10pm Sat-Sun; 🚼) Always packed and consistently good (if not great), El Palomar serves tasty Mexican

staples – try the ceviches – and fruity margaritas. Tortillas are made fresh by charming women in the covered courtyard.

🍸 Drinking & Nightlife

Santa Cruz's downtown overflows with bars, lounges and coffee shops. Heading west on Mission St (Hwy 1), craft breweries and wine-tasting rooms fill the raffish industrial ambience of the Smith St and Ingalls St courtyards.

Lupulo Craft Beer House CRAFT BEER
(Map p290; ☑831-454-8306; www.lupulosc. com; 233 Cathcart St; ☺11:30am-10pm Sun-Thu, to 11:30pm Fri-Sat) Named after the Spanish word for hops, Lupulo Craft Beer House is an essential downtown destination for traveling beer fans. Modern decor combines with an ever-changing taplist – often including seasonal brews from local California breweries – and good bar snacks such as empanadas, tacos and charcuterie plates. Almost 400 bottled and canned beers create delicious panic for the indecisive drinker.

If you're a fan of hard-to-find Belgian beers, you'll be in hoppy heaven.

515
COCKTAIL BAR

(Map p290; ☑831-425-5051; www.515santacruz.com; 515 Cedar St; ☺5pm-late Mon-Fri, 10am-late Sat-Sun) Superior cocktails and eclectic food feature at this cosmopolitan spot near Santa Cruz's main drag. Settle into a huge armchair amid vintage-chic decor and enjoy cocktails based on the American classics – think Sazeracs, Negronis and Whisky Sours – or a cold craft brew from the well-curated tap list. 515 is open to 1:30am from Friday to Saturday.

Verve Coffee Roasters
CAFE

(Map p290; ☑831-600-7784; www.vervecoffee.com; 1540 Pacific Ave; ☺6:30am-9pm; ☜) To sip finely roasted artisan espresso or a cup of rich pour-over coffee, join the surfers and hipsters at this industrial-zen cafe. Single-origin brews and house blends rule. it's been so successful around their home patch that it's also opened satellite cafes in Los Angeles and Tokyo.

West End Tap & Kitchen
CRAFT BEER

(Map p298; ☑831-471-8115; www.westendtap.com; 334d Ingalls St, Ingalls St Courtyard; ☺11:30am-9:30pm Sun-Thu, to 10pm Fri-Sat) Another recent opening amid the gathering of brewpubs, cafes and wine-tasting rooms in the Ingalls St Courtyard, West End Tap & Kitchen combines beers from Hermitage Brewing in San Jose – often including zingy sour beers – and a full menu including Mediterranean-style flatbreads and hearty steaks, pasta and burgers. Try Hermitage's Ale of the Imp 8% Imperial IPA.

Caffe Pergolesi
CAFE

(Map p290; ☑831-426-1775; www.theperg.com; 418 Cedar St; ☺11am-9pm Mon-Sat, 11am-8pm Sun; ☜) Discuss conspiracy theories over stalwart coffee, tea or beer at this landmark Victorian house with a big ol' tree-shaded veranda. There's live music some evenings.

☆ Entertainment

Free tabloid *Good Times* (http://goodtimes.sc/) covers the music, arts and nightlife scenes in Santa Cruz.

Kuumbwa Jazz Center
LIVE MUSIC

(Map p290; ☑831-427-2227; www.kuumbwajazz.org; 320 Cedar St; admission varies by gig) Hosting jazz luminaries since 1975, this nonprofit theater is for serious jazz cats snapping their fingers for famous-name performers in an electrically intimate room.

Moe's Alley
LIVE MUSIC

(Map p298; ☑831-479-1854; www.moesalley.com; 1535 Commercial Way; admission varies by gig) In a way-out industrial wasteland, this joint puts on live sounds almost every night: jazz, blues, reggae, roots, salsa and acoustic world-music jams.

Catalyst
LIVE MUSIC

(Map p290; ☑831-423-1338; www.catalystclub.com; 1011 Pacific Ave; admission varies by gig) Over the years, this stage for local bands has seen big-time national acts perform, from Queens of the Stone Age to Snoop Dogg. Expect loads of punk attitude and look forward to gigs ranging from classic reggae acts to the occasional Ned Flanders–inspired thrash-metal band (c'mon down Okilly Dokilly...).

🔒 Shopping

Stroll Pacific Ave and downtown side streets to find Santa Cruz's one-of-a-kind, locally owned boutiques. For vintage clothing and surf shops, amble 41st Ave around Portola Dr.

Bookshop Santa Cruz
BOOKS

(Map p290; ☑831-423-0900; www.bookshopsantacruz.com; 1520 Pacific Ave; ☺9am-10pm Sun-Thu, to 11pm Fri & Sat) Vast selection of new books, a few used ones, popular and unusual magazines, and 'Keep Santa Cruz Weird' bumper stickers.

Donnelly Fine Chocolates
FOOD

(Map p298; ☑831-458-4214; www.donnellychocolates.com; 1509 Mission St; ☺10:30am-6pm Tue-Fri, from noon Sat & Sun) The Willy Wonka of Santa Cruz makes stratospherically priced chocolates on par with the big city. Try the cardamom or chipotle truffles. Pricey, but worth it we reckon.

ℹ Information

Public Library (☑831-427-7707; www.santacruzpl.org; 224 Church St; ☺10am-7pm Mon-Thu, 10am-5pm Fri & Sat, 1-5pm Sun; ☜) Free wi-fi and public internet terminals for California public-library cardholders (out-of-state visitors $10).

Santa Cruz Post Office (Map p298; ☑800-275-8777; www.usps.com; 850 Front St; ☺9am-5pm Mon-Fri)

Santa Cruz Visitor Center (Map p298; ☑831-425-1234; www.santacruzca.org; 303 Water St; ☺9am-noon & 1-4pm Mon-Fri, 11am-3pm Sat & Sun) Free public internet terminal, plus maps and brochures.

❶ Getting There & Around

Greyhound Santa Cruz (Map p290; ☑ 800-231-2222; www.greyhound.com; Metro Center, 920 Pacific St) Greyhound has a few daily buses to San Francisco, Salinas, Santa Barbara and Los Angeles.

Santa Cruz Airport Shuttles (☑ 831-421-9883; www.santacruzshuttles.com) Santa Cruz Airport Shuttles runs shared shuttles to/from the airports at San Jose ($50), San Francisco ($80) and Oakland ($80), with a $5 cash discount; the second passenger pays $10.

Santa Cruz Metro (Map p290; ☑ 831-425-8600; www.scmtd.com; 920 Pacific Ave; single-ride/day pass $2/6) Local and regional buses converge on downtown's Metro Center. Destinations include San Jose, Capitola and Watsonville.

Santa Cruz Trolley (www.santacruztrolley. com; per ride 25¢) From late May through early September, the trolley shuttles between downtown and the beach from 11am until 9pm daily.

Around Santa Cruz

Santa Cruz Mountains

Winding between Santa Cruz and Silicon Valley, Hwy 9 is a 40-mile backwoods byway through the Santa Cruz Mountains, passing tiny towns, towering redwood forests and fog-kissed vineyards. The Santa Cruz Mountains Winegrowers Association (www. scmwa.com) publishes a free winery map, available at tasting rooms, including those that have opened more convenient tasting rooms in Santa Cruz.

Heading north from Santa Cruz, it's 7 miles to **Felton**, where there is forest ziplining adventures and also hiking in the **Henry Cowell Redwoods State Park** (☑ info 831-335-4598, reservations 800-444-7275; www.parks. ca.gov; 101 N Big Trees Park Rd; entry per car $10, campsites $35; ☉ sunrise-sunset; ℗ ⍟) ⌀. Also in Felton is the pioneer-era fun and spectacle of **Roaring Camp Railroads** (☑ 831-335-4484; www.roaringcamp.com; 5401 Graham Hill Rd; adult/child 2-12yr from $29/22, parking $8; ⍟). Seven miles further north on Hwy 9, stop in **Boulder Creek** for a bite and a cold beer at Boulder Creek Brewery Outpost (p295).

Follow Hwy 236 northwest for a further nine twisting miles from Boulder Creek to **Big Basin Redwoods State Park** (Map p42; ☑ 831-338-8860; www.parks.ca.gov; 21600 Big Basin Way; entry per car $10, campsites $35; ☉ sunrise-sunset; ℗ ⍟) ⌀ for excellent hiking. A 12.5-mile

one-way section of the **Skyline to the Sea Trail** ends at Waddell Beach, almost 20 miles northwest of Santa Cruz on Hwy 1. On weekends between mid-March and mid-December, you can usually ride **Santa Cruz Metro** (☑ 831-425-8600; www.scmtd.com) bus 35A up to Big Basin in the morning and get picked up by bus 40 at the beach in the afternoon.

Capitola

Six miles east of Santa Cruz, the diminutive beach town of Capitola nestles quaintly between ocean bluffs. Show up for mid-September's **Capitola Art & Wine Festival**, or the famous **Begonia Festival** (www.begonia festival.com), held over Labor Day weekend, with floral floats along Soquel Creek.

By the beach, downtown is laid out for strolling, where cute shops and touristy restaurants inhabit seaside houses. Drop by family-friendly **Capitola Beach Company** (Map p298; ☑ 831-462-5222; www.capitolabeachcompany. com; 131 Monterey Ave; surfboard/SUP rental from $12/20, surfing & SUP lessons from $85; ☉ 10am-6pm) or **Capitola Surf & Paddle** (Map p298; ☑ 831-435-6503; www.capitolasurfandpaddle.com; 208 San Jose Ave; surfboard/SUP rental from $10/20, surfing & SUP lessons $65-75; ☉ 10am-6pm) to rent water-sports gear or, if you book ahead, take surfing and stand-up paddleboarding lessons.

Catch an organic, fair-trade java buzz at **Mr Toots Coffeehouse** (Map p298; ☑ 831 475-3679; www.facebook.com/MrTootsCoffeehouse; 2nd fl, 231 Esplanade; ☉ 7am-10pm; 🖥) ⌀, which has an art gallery, live music and ocean-view deck. Head inland to **Gayle's Bakery & Rosticceria** (Map p298; ☑ 831-462-1200; www.gaylesbakery. com; 504 Bay Ave; dishes $4-11; ☉ 6:30am-8:30pm; ⍟), which has a deli to stock up for a beach picnic. A few miles east in Aptos, **Aptos St BBQ** (☑ 831-662-1721; www.aptosstbbq.com; 8059 Aptos St; mains $10-32; ☉ 11am-9pm) pairs smoked tri-tip beef and pulled pork with California craft beers and live music.

The **Capitola Chamber of Commerce** (Map p298; ☑ 800-474-6522; www.capitolacham ber.com; 716G Capitola Ave; ☉ 10am-4pm) offers travel tips. Driving downtown can be a nightmare in summer and on weekends; use the parking lot behind City Hall, off Capitola Ave by Riverview Dr.

Moss Landing & Elkhorn Slough

Hwy 1 swings back toward the coast at Moss Landing, just south of the Santa Cruz County line, almost 20 miles north of Monterey.

Around Santa Cruz

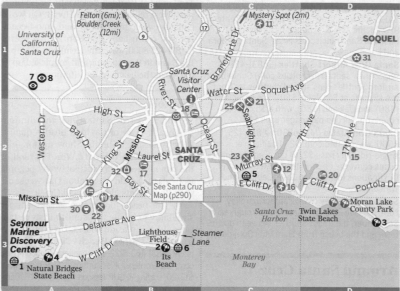

Around Santa Cruz

From the working fishing harbor, **Sanctuary Cruises** (ℐinfo 831-917-1042, tickets 888-394-7810; www.sanctuarycruises.com; 7881 Sandholdt Rd; tours $45-55; ▣) ✎ operates whale-watching and dolphin-spotting cruises year-round aboard biodiesel-fueled boats (reservations are essential). Devour dock-fresh seafood at warehouse-sized **Phil's Fish**

Map labels:
- 0 — 2 km
- 0 — 1 mile
- Seacliff State Beach (1.2mi); Aptos (3mi); Manresa State Beach (6mi); Sunset State Beach (11.5mi)
- Soquel Dr
- CAPITOLA
- Capitola Chamber of Commerce
- Capitola Ave
- Capitola Rd
- Bay Ave
- Park Ave
- New Brighton State Beach
- 41st Ave
- Pleasure Point Beach
- E Cliff Dr
- PACIFIC OCEAN

Around 10 miles north of Moss Landing on the edge of **Watsonville** are a couple of interesting shops to stop at en route north or south.

Monterey

Working-class Monterey is all about the sea. What draws many visitors is a world-class aquarium overlooking **Monterey Bay National Marine Sanctuary**, which protects dense kelp forests and a sublime variety of marine life, including seals and sea lions, dolphins and whales. The city itself possesses the best-preserved historical evidence of California's Spanish and Mexican periods, with many restored adobe buildings. An afternoon's wander through downtown's historic quarter promises to be more edifying than time spent in the tourist ghettos of Fisherman's Wharf and Cannery Row.

◉ Sights

★**Monterey Bay Aquarium**   AQUARIUM
(Map p302; ☑info 831-648-4800, tickets 866-963-9645; www.montereybayaquarium.org; 886 Cannery Row; adult/child 3-12yr/youth 13-17yr $50/30/40; ⊙10am-6pm; ♠) ✔ Monterey's most mesmerizing experience is its enormous aquarium, built on the former site of the city's largest sardine cannery. All kinds of aquatic creatures are featured, from kid-tolerant sea stars and slimy sea slugs to animated sea otters and surprisingly nimble 800lb tuna. The aquarium is much more than an impressive collection of glass tanks – thoughtful placards underscore the bay's cultural and historical contexts.

Every minute, up to 2000 gallons of seawater are pumped into the three-story **kelp forest**, re-creating as closely as possible the natural conditions you see out the windows to the east. The large fish of prey are at their charismatic best during mealtimes; divers hand-feed at 11am. More entertaining are the sea otters, which may be seen basking in the **Great Tide Pool** outside the aquarium, where they are readied for reintroduction to the wild.

Even new-agey music and the occasional infinity-mirror illusion don't detract from the astounding beauty of jellyfish in the **Jellies Gallery**. To see marine creatures – including hammerhead sharks, ocean sunfish and green sea turtles – that outweigh kids many times over, ponder the awesome

Market (☑831-633-2152; www.philsfishmarket.com; 7600 Sandholdt Rd; mains $10-26; ⊙10am-9pm; ♠) or, after browsing the antiques shops, lunch at **Haute Enchilada** (☑831-633-5483; www.hauteenchilada.com; 7902 Moss Landing Rd; mains $13-26; ⊙11am-9pm) ✔, an inspired Mexican restaurant inside an art gallery.

On the eastern side of Hwy 1, **Elkhorn Slough National Estuarine Research Reserve** (☑831-728-2822; www.elkhornslough.org; 1700 Elkhorn Rd, Watsonville; adult/child under 16yr $4/free; ⊙9am-5pm Wed-Sun; 🅿♠) ✔ is popular with bird-watchers and hikers, and can also be explored by cruising on an electric boat with **Whisper Charters** (☑800-979-3370; www.whispercharters.com; 2370 Hwy 1, Moss Landing; 2hr tour adult/child under 12yr $49/39; ♠) ✔. Kayaking and SUP are also fantastic ways to see the slough, though not on a windy day or when the tides are against you. Reserve ahead for kayak or SUP rentals, guided tours and paddling instruction with **Kayak Connection** (☑831-724-5692; www.kayakconnection.com; 2370 Hwy 1, Moss Landing; kayak & SUP rental from $35, tours adult/child from $50/40; ⊙9am-5pm; ♠) ✔ or **Monterey Bay Kayaks** (☑831-373-5357; www.montereybaykayaks.com; 2390 Hwy 1, Moss Landing; kayak & SUP rental/tour from $30/55; ♠) ✔.

Open Sea tank. Upstairs and downstairs you'll find **touch pools**, where you can get close to sea cucumbers, bat rays and tidepool creatures. Younger kids love the **Splash Zone**, with interactive bilingual exhibits in English and Spanish, and penguin feedings at 10:30am and 3pm.

To avoid long lines in summer and on weekends and holidays, buy tickets in advance. A visit can easily become a full-day affair, so get your hand stamped and break for lunch. Metered on-street parking is limited. Parking lots offering daily rates are plentiful just uphill from Cannery Row.

★**Monterey State**
Historic Park HISTORIC SITE
(Map p302; ☑info 831-649-7118; www.parks. ca.gov) FREE Old Monterey is home to an extraordinary assemblage of 19th-century brick and adobe buildings, administered as Monterey State Historic Park, and all found along a 2-mile self-guided walking tour portentously called the 'Path of History.' You can inspect dozens of buildings, many with charming gardens; expect some to be open while others aren't, according to a capricious schedule dictated by unfortunate state-park budget cutbacks.

➡ Pacific House
(Map p302; ☑831-649-7118; www.parks.ca.gov; 20 Custom House Plaza; walking tour adult/child $5/ free; ◷10am-4pm, closed Mon-Wed Nov-Mar; ☝) Find out what's currently open at Monterey State Historic Park, grab a free map and buy tickets for guided walking tours inside this 1847 adobe building, where fascinatingly in-depth exhibits cover the state's early Spanish, Mexican and American eras. Walking tours run at 10:30am, 12:30pm & 2pm Thursday to Sunday.

Nearby are some of the state park's historical highlights, including an old whaling station (Map p302; ◷10am-2pm Tue-Fri) and California's first theater (Map p302). A 10-minute walk south is the old Monterey jail (Map p302; ☑831-646-5640; www.monterey. org; Dutra St; ◷10am-4pm) FREE featured in John Steinbeck's novel *Tortilla Flat*.

➡ Custom House
(Map p302; ☑831-649-7111; www.parks.ca.gov; Custom House Plaza; ◷10am-4pm; ☝) FREE In 1822, a newly independent Mexico ended the Spanish trade monopoly and stipulated that any traders bringing goods to Alta (Upper) California must first unload their cargoes here for duty to be assessed. In 1846, when the US flag was raised over the Custom House, *voilà*! California was formally annexed from Mexico. Restored to its 1840s appearance, today this adobe building displays an exotic selection of goods that traders once brought to exchange for California cowhides.

➡ Stevenson House
(Map p302; ☑831-649-7118; www.parks.ca.gov; 530 Houston St; ◷10am-4pm Thu-Sun) FREE Scottish writer Robert Louis Stevenson came to Monterey in 1879 to court his wife-to-be, Fanny Van de Grift Osbourne. This building, then the French Hotel, was where he stayed while reputedly devising his novel *Treasure Island*. The boarding-house rooms were primitive and Stevenson was still a penniless unknown. At the time of writing, the house was only open for private tours.

Cannery Row HISTORIC SITE
(Map p302; ☝) John Steinbeck's novel *Cannery Row* immortalized the sardine-canning business that was Monterey's lifeblood for the first half of the 20th century. A bronze **bust** of the Pulitzer Prize–winning writer sits at the bottom of Prescott Ave, just steps from the unabashedly touristy experience that the famous row has devolved into. The historical **Cannery Workers Shacks** (Map p302) at the base of flowery Bruce Ariss Way provide a sobering reminder of the hard lives led by Filipino, Japanese, Spanish and other immigrant laborers.

Back in Steinbeck's day, Cannery Row was a hardscrabble, working-class melting pot, which the novelist described as 'a poem, a stink, a grating noise, a quality of light, a tone, a habit, a nostalgia, a dream.' Sadly, there's precious little evidence of that era now, as overfishing and climatic changes caused the sardine industry's collapse in the 1950s.

Dali17 GALLERY
(Map p302; ☑831-372-2608; www.dali17.com; 5 Custom House Plaza, Museum of Monterey; adult/ child $20/10; ◷10am-5pm Sun-Thu, 10am-7pm Fri-Sat) Escaping WWII in Europe, Spanish surrealist artist Salvador Dalí lived and worked in the Monterey and Carmel area in the 1940s. Comprising over 300 Dalí etchings, mixed media, lithographs and sculptures, this permanent exhibition in the Museum of Monterey is named after Carmel's 17-Mile Drive (p311), where the artist lived at Pebble Beach from 1943 to 1948.

Monterey Museum of Art MUSEUM
(MMA; www.montereyart.org; adult/child $10/
free; ⊘11am-5pm Thu-Mon) Downtown, **MMA
Pacific Street** (Map p302; ☑831-372-5477;
559 Pacific St; adult/child $10/free; ⊘11am-5pm
Thu-Mon, to 8pm 1st Fri of month; P⊕) is particularly strong in California contemporary
art and modern landscape painters and
photographers, including Ansel Adams and
Edward Weston. Southeast of downtown,
MMA La Mirada (Map p302; ☑831-372-3689;
720 Via Mirada), a silent-film star's villa, has
humble adobe origins that are exquisitely
concealed. It is now only used for special
museum events, and not generally open to
the public. Check the website to see if anything is scheduled.

**Royal Presidio Chapel
& Heritage Center Museum** CHURCH
(Map p302; ☑831-373-2628; www.sancarlos
cathedral.org; 500 Church St; donations accepted;
⊘10am-noon Wed, to 3pm Fri, to 2pm Sat, 1-3pm
Sun, also 10am-noon & 1:15-3:15pm 2nd & 4th Mon
of month; P⊕) Built of sandstone in 1794,
this graceful chapel is California's oldest
continuously functioning parish and first
stone building. The original 1770 mission
church stood here before being moved to
Carmel. As Monterey expanded under Mexican rule in the 1820s, older buildings were
gradually destroyed, leaving behind this National Historic Landmark as the strongest
reminder of the defeated Spanish colonial
presence. On-site docents are happy to provide tours during opening hours.

🏃 Activities

Like its larger namesake in San Francisco,
Monterey's **Fisherman's Wharf** is a tacky
tourist trap, but also a jumping-off point for
deep-sea fishing trips and whale-watching
cruises. A short walk east at workaday **Municipal Wharf 2**, fishing boats bob and sway
in the bay.

Dennis the Menace Park PLAYGROUND
(Map p302; www.monterey.org; 777 Pearl St;
⊘10am-dusk, closed Tue Sep-May; ⊕) FREE
The brainchild of Hank Ketcham, the crea-
tor of the classic *Dennis the Menace* comic
strip, this ain't your standard dumbed-down
playground suffocated by Big Brother's safety regulations. With lightning-fast slides, a
hedge maze, a suspension bridge and towering climbing walls, even some adults can't
resist playing here.

Whale-Watching
You can spot whales off the coast of Monterey Bay year-round. The season for blue
and humpback whales runs from April to
early December, while gray whales pass by
from mid-December through March. Tour
boats depart from Fisherman's Wharf and
Moss Landing (p298). Reserve trips at least
a day in advance; be prepared for a bumpy,
cold ride.

Monterey Whale Watching BOATING
(Map p302; ☑831-372-2203; www.monterey
whalewatching.com; 96 Fisherman's Wharf; 2½hr
tour adult/child 5-11yr $45/35) Several daily de-
partures; no children under age five or preg-
nant women allowed.

Monterey Bay Whale Watch BOATING
(Map p302; ☑831-375-4658; www.montereybay
whalewatch.com; 84 Fisherman's Wharf; 3hr tour
adult/child 4-12yr from $44/29; ⊕) Morning and
afternoon departures; young children and
well-behaved dogs are welcome on board.

Diving & Snorkeling
Monterey Bay offers world-renowned diving
and snorkeling, including off **Lovers Point**
in Pacific Grove and at Point Lobos State
Natural Reserve (p310) south of Carmel-by-
the-Sea. You'll want a wetsuit year-round.
In summer, upwelling currents carry cold
water from the deep canyon below the bay,
sending a rich supply of nutrients up toward
the surface level to feed the bay's diverse marine life. These frigid currents also account
for the bay's chilly water temperatures and
the summer fog that blankets the peninsula.

Aquarius Dive Shop DIVING
(☑831-375-1933; www.aquariusdivers.com; 2040
Del Monte Ave; snorkel/scuba-gear rental $35/65,
dive tours from $65; ⊘9am-6pm Mon-Fri, 7am-
6pm Sat-Sun) Talk to this five-star PADI operation for gear rentals, classes and guided
dives into Monterey Bay.

Monterey Bay Dive Charters DIVING
(☑831-383-9276; www.mbdcscuba.com; scuba-
gear rental $75, shore/boat dives from $65/85)
Arrange shore or boat dives and rent a
full scuba kit with wetsuit from this well-
reviewed outfitter.

Kayaking & Surfing
Monterey Bay Kayaks KAYAKING
(Map p302; ☑831-373-5357; www.montereybay
kayaks.com; 693 Del Monte Ave; kayak or SUP set
rental per day from $35, tours from $45; ⊘8:30am-
5pm, extended hours in summer) Rents kayaks

Monterey

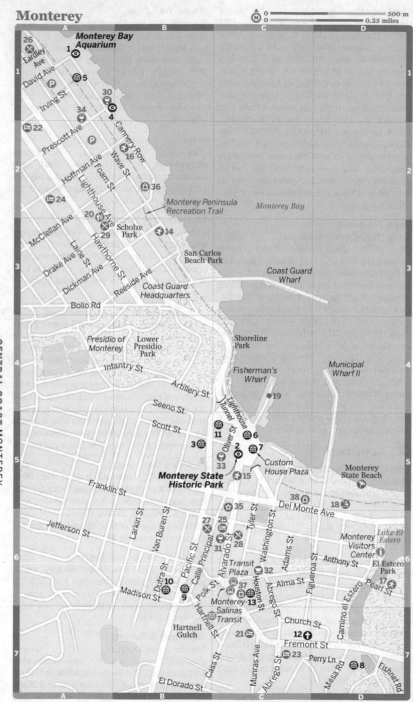

Monterey

and SUP equipment, offers paddling lessons and leads guided tours of Monterey Bay, including full-moon and sunrise trips.

Sunshine Freestyle Surf & Sport   SURFING
(Map p302; ☏831-375-5015; www.facebook.com/SunshineFreestyle; 443 Lighthouse Ave; surfboard/wetsuit/body board rental from $20/10/7; ⊙10am-6pm Mon-Sat, 11am-5pm Sun) Monterey's oldest surf shop rents and sells all the surfing gear you'll need.

Cycling & Mountain Biking

Along an old railway line, the **Monterey Peninsula Recreational Trail** travels for 18 car-free miles along the waterfront, passing Cannery Row en route to Lovers Point in Pacific Grove. Road-cycling enthusiasts can make the round trip to Carmel along the 17-Mile Drive (p311). Mountain-bikers head to **Fort Ord National Monument** to pedal over 80 miles of single-track and fire roads; the **Sea Otter Classic** (www.seaotterclassic.com) races there in mid-April.

Adventures by the Sea   CYCLING, KAYAKING
(Map p302; ☏831-372-1807; www.adventuresbythesea.com; 299 Cannery Row; rental per day kay-

ak or bicycle $35, SUP set $50, kayak tours from $60; ⊙9am-5pm, to 8pm in summer; ⊕) Beach cruisers, electric bikes and water-sports gear rentals and tours available at multiple locations on Cannery Row and **downtown** (Map p302; 210 Alvarado St; ⊙9am-5pm, to 8pm in summer; ⊕).

Bay Bikes   CYCLING
(Map p302; ☏831-655-2453; www.baybikes.com; 585 Cannery Row; bicycle rental per hour/day from $9/36, tours from $70; ⊙9am-5pm Sun-Thu, to 6pm Fri, to 6:30pm Sat; ⊕) Cruiser, tandem, hybrid and road-bike rentals near the aquarium and also **downtown** (Map p302; 486 Washington St; ⊙10am-5pm Sun-Mon, 10am-6pm Tue-Fri, 9am-6pm Sat; ⊕). Check out its handy free maps detailing local bike routes. Tours taking in Cannery Row, Pacific Grove or local wine-tasting are also available.

🎆 Festivals & Events

Castroville Artichoke
Food & Wine Festival   FOOD & DRINK
(☏831-633-2465; www.artichokefestival.org; ⊙late May/early Jun) Head 15 miles north of Monterey for 3D 'agro art' sculptures, cooking

demos, a farmers market and field tours. A recent addition is a wine-and-beer garden with tasty beverages from around the region.

Monterey County Fair
CARNIVAL, FOOD
(www.montereycountyfair.com; ⊙ late Aug & early Sep) Old-fashioned fun, carnival rides, horseback riding and livestock competitions, wine tasting and live music.

★Monterey Jazz Festival
MUSIC
(www.montereyjazzfestival.org; ⊙ mid-Sep) One of the world's longest-running jazz festivals (since 1958) showcases big-name headliners over a long spring weekend.

🛏 Sleeping

Book ahead for special events, on weekends and in summer. To avoid the tourist congestion and jacked-up prices of Cannery Row, look to Pacific Grove. Cheaper motels line Munras Ave, south of downtown, and N Fremont St, east of Hwy 1.

HI Monterey Hostel
HOSTEL $
(Map p302; ☏831-649-0375; www.montereyhostel. org; 778 Hawthorne St; with shared bathdm $30-40; ⊙ check in 4-10pm; @ 🛜) Four blocks from Cannery Row and the aquarium, this simple, clean hostel houses single-sex and mixed dorms, as well as private rooms accommodating up to five people (check online for rates). Budget backpackers stuff themselves silly with make-your-own-pancake breakfasts. Reservations strongly recommended. Take MST bus 1 from downtown's Transit Plaza (p306).

Veterans Memorial Park Campground
CAMPGROUND $
(Map p308; ☏831-646-3865; www.monterey. org; Veterans Memorial Park; tent & RV sites $30) Tucked into the forest, this municipal campground has 40 grassy, non-reservable sites near a nature preserve's hiking trails. Amenities include coin-op hot showers, flush toilets, drinking water and barbecue fire pits. Three-night maximum stay.

Inn by the Bay
MOTEL $$
(Map p308; ☏831-372-5409; www.innbythebay monterey.com; 936 Munras Ave; d from $110; P ⊖ 🛜) An easy walk downhill to downtown Monterey, Inn on the Bay is the quiet achiever along the Munras Ave motel strip. Recent renovations have modernized the interiors, there are flat-screen TVs in the rooms, and a location set back from the street means it is uniformly quiet. A young, switched-on team

at reception offer plenty of tips for enjoying Monterey and around.

Hotel Abrego
BOUTIQUE HOTEL $$
(Map p302; ☏831-372-7551; www.hotelabrego.com; 755 Abrego St; r from $144; 🛜❄) At this downtown Monterey boutique hotel, most of the spacious, clean-lined contemporary rooms have gas fireplaces and chaise longues. Work out in the fitness studio, take a dip in the recently redeveloped outdoor pool or warm up in the hot tub. A new fire pit is a cozy addition for cooler Monterey evenings.

Casa Munras
BOUTIQUE HOTEL $$
(Map p302; ☏831-375-2411; www.hotelcasamunras. com; 700 Munras Ave; r from $140; P ⊖ @ 🛜 ❄❅) Built around an adobe hacienda once owned by a 19th-century Spanish colonial don, chic modern rooms come with lofty beds and some have gas fireplaces, all inside two-storey motel-esque buildings. Splash in a heated outdoor pool, unwind at the tapas bar or take a sea-salt scrub in the tiny spa. Pet fee $50.

Monterey Hotel
HISTORIC HOTEL $$
(Map p302; ☏831-375-3184; www.montereyhotel. com; 406 Alvarado St; r $131-275; 🛜) In the heart of downtown and a short walk from Fisherman's Wharf, this 1904 edifice harbors five-dozen smallish but renovated rooms and suites with Victorian-styled furniture and plantation shutters. No elevator. A recently added boutique spa offers massage and beauty treatments.

★Jabberwock
B&B $$$
(Map p302; ☏831-372-4777; www.jabberwockinn. com; 598 Laine St; r $249-339; @ 🛜) Barely visible through a shroud of foliage, this 1911 arts-and-crafts house hums a playful *Alice in Wonderland* tune through seven immaculate rooms, a few with fireplaces and Jacuzzis. Over afternoon tea and cookies or evening wine and hors d'oeuvres, ask the genial hosts about the house's many salvaged architectural elements. Weekends are more expensive and have a two-night minimum.

Also available is Tumtum Tree, a stand-alone cottage cradled by Monterey Cypress trees, and accommodating up to four guests.

Sanctuary Beach Resort
HOTEL $$$
(☏831-883-9478; www.thesanctuarybeachresort. com; 3295 Dunes Dr, Marina; r from $260; ❄ @ 🛜 ❅❆) Be lulled to sleep by the surf at this low-lying retreat hidden in the sand dunes north of Monterey. Reached via golf carts, townhouses harbor petite rooms with gas

fireplaces and binoculars for whale-watching. Sunset bonfires bring out s'mores. The beach is an off-limits nature preserve, but there are public beaches and walking trails nearby. Pet fee $50.

✕ Eating

Uphill from Monterey's Cannery Row, Lighthouse Ave features casual, budget-friendly eateries including Hawaiian barbecue and Thai flavors, through to sushi and Middle Eastern kebabs. Downtown around Alvarado St also features cafes and pub dining.

Zab Zab   NORTHERN THAI $
(Map p302; 831-747-2225; www.zabzabmonterey. com; 401 Lighthouse Ave; mains $11-15; 11am-2:30pm & 5-9pm Tue-Fri, noon-9pm Sat-Sun;) Our pick of Lighthouse Ave's ethnic eateries, Zab Zab channels the robust flavors of northeast Thailand. The bijou cottage interior is perfect in cooler weather, but during summer the best spot is on the deck surrounded by a pleasantly overgrown garden. For fans of authentic Thai heat, go for the Kai Yang grilled chicken. Lunch boxes ($11 to $13) are good value.

Tricycle Pizza   PIZZA $
(Map p308; www.tricyclepizza.com; 899 Lighthouse Ave; pizza $11-13; 3-9pm Wed-Fri, noon-9pm Sat) One of Monterey's favorite food trucks has graduated to a bricks-and-mortar location along Lighthouse Ave. Tricycle's crusty wood-fired pizza is still cooked in the original truck on-site, but there's now the option of takeout or dining in a hip, industrial space nearby. Try the sausage and mushroom with organic oregano, wood-fired mushrooms and fennel sausage.

Old Monterey Marketplace   MARKET $
(Map p302; www.oldmonterey.org; Alvarado St, btwn Del Monte Ave & Pearl St; 4-7pm Tue Sep-May, to 8pm Jun-Aug;) Rain or shine, head downtown on Tuesdays for farm-fresh fruit and veggies, artisan cheeses, international food stalls and a scrumptious 'baker's alley.'

First Awakenings   AMERICAN $
(Map p302; 831-372-1125; www.firstawakenings. net; American Tin Cannery, 125 Oceanview Blvd; mains $9-13; 7am-2pm Mon-Fri, to 2:30pm Sat & Sun;) Sweet and savory, all-American breakfasts and lunches and bottomless pitchers of coffee merrily weigh down outdoor tables at this cafe uphill from the aquarium. Try the unusual 'bluegerm' pancakes or a spicy Sonoran frittata.

Monterey's Fish House   SEAFOOD $$
(831-373-4647; www.montereyfishhouse.com; 2114 Del Monte Ave; mains $11-25; 11:30am-2:30pm Mon-Fri & 5-9:30pm daily) Watched over by photos of Sicilian fishermen, dig into oak-grilled or blackened swordfish, barbecued oysters or, for those stout of heart, the Mexican squid steak. Reservations are essential (it's so crowded), but the vibe is island-casual: Hawaiian shirts seem to be de rigueur for men.

Montrio Bistro   CALIFORNIAN $$$
(Map p302; 831-648-8880; www.montrio.com; 414 Calle Principal; shared plates $12-30, mains $25-44; 4:30-10pm Sun-Thu, to 11pm Fri & Sat) Inside a 1910 firehouse, Montrio combines leather walls and iron trellises, and the tables have butcher paper and crayons for kids. The eclectic seasonal menu mixes local, organic fare with Californian, Asian and European flair, including tapas-style shared plates and mini desserts. Well-priced bar snacks and happy-hour prices from 4:30pm daily are a fine end-of-the-day option.

🍷 Drinking & Nightlife

Prowl downtown Monterey's Alvarado St, touristy Cannery Row and locals-only Lighthouse Ave for watering holes.

★ Alvarado Street Brewery   CRAFT BEER
(Map p302; 831-655-2337; www.alvaradostreet brewery.com; 426 Alvarado St; 11:30am-10pm Sun-Wed, to 11pm Thu-Sat) Vintage beer advertising punctuates Alvarado Street's brick walls, but that's the only concession to earlier days at this excellent craft-beer pub. Innovative brews harness new hop strains, sour and barrel-aged beers regularly fill the taps, and superior bar food includes Thai-curry mussels and truffle-crawfish mac 'n' cheese. In summer, adjourn to the alfresco beer garden out back.

Peter B's Brewpub   BREWERY
(Map p302; 831-649-2699; www.facebook.com/ PeterBsBrewpub; 2 Portola Plaza; 11am-11pm Sun-Thu, to midnight Fri-Sat) Often heaving with locals and tourists, Peter B's combines huge meals – the burgers are really good value – with a solid array of craft beers brewed on-site. Students crowd in to watch live sports on big-screen TVs, while visiting beer buffs work their way through beer sampling trays. Peter B's seasonal one-off brews are always worth trying.

A Taste of Monterey   WINE BAR
(Map p302; www.atasteofmonterey.com; 700 Cannery Row; tasting flights $14-22; 11am-6pm

Sun-Thu, to 8pm Fri-Sat) Sample medal-winning Monterey County wines from as far away as the Santa Lucia Highlands while soaking up dreamy sea views, then peruse thoughtful exhibits on barrel-making and cork production. Shared plates, including crab cakes and smoked salmon, provide a tasty reason to linger.

Sardine Factory Lounge LOUNGE
(Map p302; ☑831-373-3775; www.sardinefactory. com; 701 Wave St; ⊙5pm-midnight) The legendary restaurant's fireplace lounge pours wines by the glass, delivers filling appetizers to your table and has a live piano player most nights.

East Village Coffee Lounge CAFE, LOUNGE
(Map p302; ☑831-373-5601; www.facebook.com/ eastvillagemonterey; 498 Washington St; ⊙6am-10pm Mon-Fri, from 7am Sat & Sun; 🕿) Downtown Monterey coffee shop on a busy corner brews with fair-trade, organic beans. At night, it pulls off a big-city lounge vibe with film, open-mike and live-music nights and an all-important booze license. Check the Facebook page for event listings.

☆ Entertainment

For comprehensive entertainment listings, browse the free tabloid *Monterey County Weekly* (www.montereycountyweekly.com).

Osio Cinema CINEMA
(Map p302; ☑831-644-8171; http://osiotheater. com; 350 Alvarado St; adult $10, before 6pm $7; 🕿) Downtown Monterey cinema screens indie dramas, cutting-edge documentaries and offbeat Hollywood films. Drop by its Cafe Lumiere for locally roasted coffee, loose-leaf tea, decadent cheesecake and wi-fi.

Sly McFly's Fueling Station LIVE MUSIC
(Map p302; ☑831-649-8050; www.slymcflys monterey.com; 700 Cannery Row; ⊙11:30am-midnight Sun-Thu, to 2am Fri & Sat) Waterfront dive showcases live local blues, jazz and rock bands nightly after 8:30pm or 9pm. Skip the food, though.

🛍 Shopping

Cannery Row is jammed with claptrap shops, while downtown Monterey's side streets hide more one-of-a-kind finds.

Wharf Marketplace FOOD & DRINKS
(Map p302; ☑831-649-1116; www.thewharf marketplace.com; 290 Figueroa St; ⊙7am-7pm) 🍸

Inside an old railway station, this gourmet-food emporium carries bountiful farm goodness, artisanal products and wine from Monterey County and beyond. It's a good spot for a leisurely breakfast, too.

**Monterey Peninsula
Art Foundation Gallery** ART
(Map p302; ☑831-655-1267; www.mpaf.org; 425 Cannery Row; ⊙11am-5pm) Taking over a cozy sea-view house, more than 30 local artists sell plein-air paintings and sketches alongside contemporary works in all media.

Old Capitol Books BOOKS
(Map p302; ☑831-333-0383; www.oldcapitolbooks. com; 559 Tyler St; ⊙10am-6pm Wed-Mon, to 7pm Tue) Tall shelves of new, used and antiquarian books, including rare first editions, California titles and John Steinbeck's works.

ℹ Information

Doctors on Duty (☑831-649-0770; www. doctorsonduty.com; 501 Lighthouse Ave; ⊙8am-8pm Mon-Sat, to 6pm Sun) Walk-in, non-emergency medical clinic.

Monterey Public Library (☑831-646-3933; www.monterey.org/library; 625 Pacific St; ⊙noon-8pm Mon-Wed, 10am-6pm Thu-Sat, 1-5pm Sun; 🕿) Free wi-fi and public internet terminals.

Monterey Visitors Center (Map p302; ☑831-657-6400; www.seemonterey.com; 401 Camino el Estero; ⊙9am-6pm Mon-Sat, to 5pm Sun, closes 1hr earlier Nov-Mar) Free tourist brochures and accommodations booking service; ask for a *Monterey County Literary & Film Map*.

Post Office (Map p302; ☑800-275-8777; www.usps.com; 565 Hartnell St; ⊙8:30am-5pm Mon-Fri, 10am-2pm Sat) Located just south of downtown Monterey.

ℹ Getting There & Away

Monterey is 43 miles south of Santa Cruz and 177 miles north of San Luis Obispo.

AIR

A few miles east of downtown off Hwy 68, **Monterey Regional Airport** (☑831-648-7000; www. montereyairport.com; 200 Fred Kane Dr) has flights with United (LA, San Francisco), American (Phoenix), Alaska (San Diego and LA) and Allegiant Air (Las Vegas). A taxi from downtown is around $20 (10 minutes), and to get here by public transport, catch buses 7, 56 or 93 ($2.50) from Monterey's **Transit Plaza** (Map p302; cnr Pearl & Alvarado Sts).

The **Monterey Airbus** (☑831-373-7777; www. montereyairbus.com; 🕿) shuttle service links Monterey with international airports in San Jose

($40, 1½ hours) and San Francisco ($50, 2½ hours) almost a dozen times daily; book online for discounts.

BUS

Monterey-Salinas Transit (MST; Map p302; ☑888-678-2871; www.mst.org; Jules Simmoneau Plaza; single-ride fares $1.50-3.50, day pass $10) operates local and regional buses; routes converge on downtown's Transit Plaza, including routes to Pacific Grove, Carmel and Big Sur. From late May until early September, MST's free trolley loops around downtown, Fisherman's Wharf and Cannery Row between 10am and 7pm or 8pm daily.

Pacific Grove

Founded as a tranquil Methodist summer retreat in 1875, Pacific Grove (or PG) maintained its quaint, holier-than-thou attitude well into the 20th century. The selling of liquor was illegal up until 1969, making it California's last 'dry' town. Today, leafy streets are lined by stately Victorian homes and a charming, compact downtown orbits Lighthouse Ave.

◉ Sights & Activities

Pacific Grove's aptly named **Ocean View Blvd** affords views from Lovers Point Park west to Point Pinos, where it becomes **Sunset Dr**, offering tempting turnouts where you can stroll by pounding surf, rocky outcrops and teeming tide pools all the way to Asilomar State Beach. This seaside route is great for cycling, too – some say it rivals the famous 17-Mile Drive for beauty and, even better, it's free.

Asilomar State Beach   BEACH
(Map p308; Sunset Dr) Negotiate a 1-mile trail boardwalk through rugged sand dunes. Note this beach is known for riptides and unpredictable surf, and care must be taken when swimming here.

Point Pinos Lighthouse   LIGHTHOUSE
(Map p308; ☑831-648-3176; www.pointpinoslighthouse.org; 80 Asilomar Ave; suggested donation adult/child 6-12yr $4/2; ⊙1-4pm Thu-Mon) The West Coast's oldest continuously operating lighthouse has been warning ships off the hazardous tip of the Monterey Peninsula since 1855. Inside are modest exhibits on the lighthouse's history and, alas, its failures – local shipwrecks.

Monarch Grove Sanctuary   PARK
(Map p308; www.cityofpacificgrove.org/visiting; 250 Ridge Rd; ⊙dawn-dusk; ⍾) *FREE* Between November and February, over 25,000 migratory monarch butterflies cluster in this thicket of tall eucalyptus trees, secreted inland. During peak season, volunteer guides answer all of your questions between noon and 3pm, weather permitting.

Pacific Grove Golf Links   GOLF
(Map p308; ☑831-648-5775; www.playpacificgrove.com; 77 Asilomar Blvd; green fees $43-64) Can't afford to play at famous Pebble Beach? This historic 18-hole municipal course, where deer freely range, has impressive sea views, and it's a lot easier (not to mention cheaper) to book a tee time here.

⍾ Sleeping

Antique-filled B&Bs have taken over many stately Victorian homes around downtown Pacific Grove and by the beach. Motels cluster at the peninsula's western end, off Lighthouse and Asilomar Aves.

Asilomar Conference Grounds   LODGE $$
(Map p308; ☑831-372-8016; www.visitasilomar.com; 800 Asilomar Ave; r from $188; @🛜⍾) This state-park lodge sprawls by sand dunes in pine forest. Skip ho-hum motel rooms and opt for historic houses designed by early-20th-century architect Julia Morgan (of Hearst Castle fame) – the thin-walled, hardwood-floored rooms may be small, but they share a fireplace lounge. Head to the lodge lobby for Ping-Pong, pool tables and wi-fi. Bike rentals available.

Sunset Inn   MOTEL $$
(Map p308; ☑831-375-3529; www.gosunsetinn.com; 133 Asilomar Blvd; r $99-235; 🛜) At this small motor lodge near the golf course and the beach, attentive staff hand out keys to crisply redesigned rooms that have hardwood floors, king-sized beds with cheery floral-print comforters and sometimes a hot tub and a fireplace.

✕ Eating

Downtown PG teems with European-style bakeries, coffee shops and neighborhood cafes.

Jeninni Kitchen & Wine Bar MEDITERRANEAN $$
(Map p308; ☑831-920-2662; www.jeninni.com; 542 Lighthouse Ave; mains $18-32; ⊙4pm-late Thu-Tue, 9:30am-1:30pm Sun) Happy-hour

Monterey Peninsula

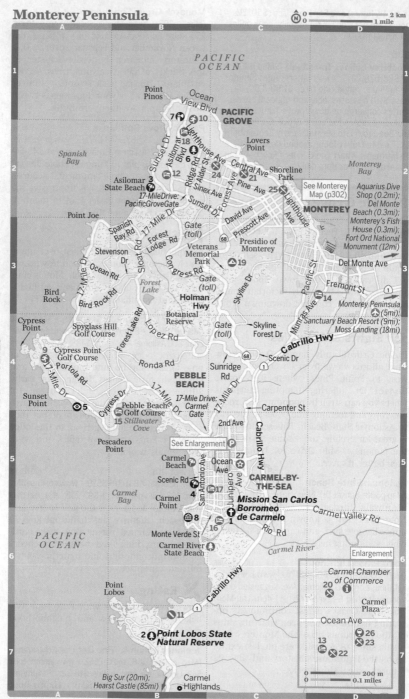

N 0 — 2 km
0 — 1 mile

PACIFIC OCEAN

Point Pinos
Ocean View Blvd
PACIFIC GROVE
7
10
Lighthouse Ave
18
Asilomar Blvd
6
Alder St
Ridge Rd
Sunset Dr
12
24
Sinex Ave
Lovers Point
Central Ave
21
Pine Ave
Forest Ave
Shoreline Park
25
Lighthouse Ave
Spanish Bay
Asilomar State Beach
3
17-MileDrive: PacificGroveGate
17-Mile Dr
Sunset Dr
David Ave
Prescott Ave
Gate (toll)
68
Presidio of Monterey
See Monterey Map (p302)
MONTEREY
Monterey Bay
Aquarius Dive Shop (0.2mi); Del Monte Beach (0.3mi); Monterey's Fish House (0.3mi); Fort Ord National Monument (12mi)
Point Joe
Spanish Bay Rd
Sloat Rd
Forest Lodge Rd
Veterans Memorial Park
19
Stevenson Dr
Ocean Rd
17-Mile Dr
Congress Rd
Gate (toll)
Skyline Dr
Del Monte Ave
Pacific St
Fremont St
14
Monterey Peninsula (5mi); Sanctuary Beach Resort (9mi); Moss Landing (18mi)
Bird Rock
Bird Rock Rd
Forest Lake
Holman Hwy
Botanical Reserve
Gate (toll)
Skyline Forest Dr
Cabrillo Hwy
Munras Ave
Cypress Point
Spyglass Hill Golf Course
Forest Lake Rd
Lopez Rd
9
Cypress Point Golf Course
Portola Rd
Ronda Rd
PEBBLE BEACH
Sunridge Rd
68
1
Scenic Dr
Sunset Point
5
17-Mile Dr
Cypress Dr
17-Mile Dr: Carmel Gate
17-Mile Dr
17-Mile Dr
Carpenter St
Pescadero Point
Pebble Beach Golf Course
15
Stillwater Cove
2nd Ave
Cabrillo Hwy
See Enlargement
P
Carmel Beach
Carmel Bay
Scenic Rd
4
San Antonio Ave
Ocean Ave
17
27
Junipero Ave
CARMEL-BY-THE-SEA
Mission San Carlos Borromeo de Carmelo
Carmel Point
8
16
1
PACIFIC OCEAN
Monte Verde St
Carmel River State Beach
Rio Rd
Carmel Valley Rd
Carmel River
Point Lobos
11
1
2
Point Lobos State Natural Reserve
Big Sur (20mi); Hearst Castle (85mi)
Carmel Highlands

Enlargement
Carmel Chamber of Commerce
20
Carmel Plaza
Ocean Ave
13
26
23
22
0 — 200 m
0 — 0.1 miles

Monterey Peninsula

snacks from 4pm to 6pm segue to dinner at this bistro featuring the flavors of the Med. Housemade charcuterie and shared plates, such as crispy octopus, create a convivial ambience, while larger mains featuring venison, duck or lamb partner well with an informed wine list. On balmy summer nights, dine on the front patio watching Pacific Grove's passing parade.

Passionfish   SEAFOOD $$$
(Map p308; ☑ 831-655-3311; www.passionfish.net; 701 Lighthouse Ave; mains $21-42; ☺ 5-9pm Sun-Thu, to 10pm Fri & Sat; ☑) ✔ Fresh, sustainable seafood is artfully presented in any number of inventive ways, and a seasonally inspired menu also carries slow-cooked meats and vegetarian dishes spotlighting local farms. The earth-tone decor is spare, with tables squeezed conversationally close together. An ambitious world-ranging wine list is priced near retail, and there are as many Chinese teas as wines by the glass.

Reservations strongly recommended.

♟ Drinking & Nightlife

Pacific Grove is largely a daytime destination, so make the short journey to Monterey for better after-dark action.

① Information

Pacific Grove Chamber of Commerce (Map p308; ☑ 831-373-3304; www.pacificgrove.

org; 584 Central Ave; ☺ 9:30am-5pm Mon-Fri, 10am-3pm Sat)

① Getting There & Around

MST (p307) bus 1 connects downtown Monterey and Cannery Row with Pacific Grove, continuing to Asilomar ($2.50, 15 minutes, every 30 to 60 minutes).

Carmel-by-the-Sea

With borderline fanatical devotion to its canine citizens, quaint Carmel has the well-manicured feel of a country club. Watch the parade of behatted ladies toting fancy-label shopping bags to lunch and dapper gents driving top-down convertibles along Ocean Ave, the village's slow-mo main drag.

Founded as a seaside resort in the 1880s – fairly odd, given that its beach is often blanketed in fog – Carmel quickly attracted famous artists and writers, such as Sinclair Lewis and Jack London, and their hangers-on. Artistic flavor survives in over 100 galleries that line downtown's immaculate streets, but sky-high property values have long obliterated any salt-of-the-earth bohemia.

Dating from the 1920s, Comstock cottages, with their characteristic stone chimneys and pitched gable roofs, still dot the town, making it look vaguely reminiscent of the English countryside. Even payphones, garbage cans and newspaper vending boxes are quaintly shingled.

⦿ Sights & Activities

Escape downtown Carmel's harried shopping streets and stroll tree-lined neighborhoods on the lookout for domiciles charming and peculiar. The Hansel and Gretel houses on Torres St, between 5th and 6th Avenues, are just how you'd imagine them. Another eye-catching house in the shape of a ship, made from local river rocks and salvaged ship parts, is on Guadalupe St near 6th Ave.

★ Point Lobos
State Natural Reserve   STATE PARK
(Map p308; ☑ 831-624-4909; www.pointlobos.org; Hwy 1; per car $10; ☺ 8am-7pm, to 5pm early Nov–mid-Mar; P ♿) ✐ They bark, they bathe and they're fun to watch – sea lions are the stars here at Punta de los Lobos Marinos (Point of the Sea Wolves), almost 4 miles south of Carmel, where a dramatically rocky coastline offers excellent tide-pooling. The full perimeter hike is 6 miles, but shorter walks take in wild scenery too, including Bird Island, shady cypress groves, the historical Whaler's Cabin and the Devil's Cauldron, a whirlpool that gets splashy at high tide.

The kelp forest at Whalers Cove is popular with snorkelers and scuba divers. Don't skip paying the entry fee by parking outside the park gates on the highway shoulder – California's state parks are chronically underfunded and need your help.

➜ Whalers Cove
(Map p308) Without donning a wetsuit, you can still get an idea of the underwater terrain with a 3D model located by the parking lot. Reserve snorkeling, scuba-diving, kayaking and SUP permits ($10 to $30) up to two months in advance online.

★ Mission San Carlos
Borromeo de Carmelo   CHURCH
(Map p308; ☑ 831-624-1271; www.carmelmission. org; 3080 Rio Rd; adult/child 7-17yr $6.50/2; ☺ 9:30am-7pm; ♿) Monterey's original mission was established by Franciscan friar Junípero Serra in 1770, but poor soil and the corrupting influence of Spanish soldiers forced the move to Carmel two years later. Today this is one of California's most strikingly beautiful missions, an oasis of solemnity bathed in flowering gardens. The mission's adobe chapel was later replaced with an arched basilica made of stone quarried in the Santa Lucia Mountains. Museum exhibits are scattered throughout the meditative complex.

The spartan cell attributed to Serra looks like something out of *The Good, the Bad and the Ugly*, while a separate chapel houses his memorial tomb.

Don't overlook the gravestone of 'Old Gabriel,' a Native American convert whom Serra baptized, and whose dates put him at 151 years old when he died. People say he smoked like a chimney and outlived seven wives. There's a lesson in there somewhere.

Tor House   HISTORIC BUILDING
(Map p308; ☑ 844-285-0244; www.torhouse. org; 26304 Ocean View Ave; adult/child 12-17yr $12/7; ☺ tours hourly 10am-3pm Fri & Sat) Even if you've never heard of 20th-century poet Robinson Jeffers, a pilgrimage to this house built with his own hands offers fascinating insights into both the man and the bohemian ethos of Old Carmel. A porthole in the Celtic-inspired Hawk Tower reputedly came from the wrecked ship that carried Napoleon from Elba. The only way to visit the property is to reserve a tour (children under 12 years old not allowed), although the tower can be glimpsed from the street.

Carmel Beach City Park   BEACH
(Map p308; off Scenic Rd; ♿ 🐾) Not always sunny, Carmel Beach is a gorgeous blanket of white sand, where pampered pups excitedly run off-leash. South of 10th Ave, bonfires crackle after sunset (until 10pm Monday through Thursday only).

✷ Festivals & Events

Pebble Beach Food & Wine   FOOD & DRINK
(☑ 866-907-3663; www.pbfw.com) Excellent four-day gastronomy-focused festival sponsored by the prestigious *Food & Wine* magazine. Held in mid- to late-April.

Carmel International Film Festival   FILM
(www.carmelfilmfest.com; ☺ mid-Oct) Live music and over 100 independent film screenings. Animation, documentaries, features and short films are all covered.

🛏 Sleeping

Shockingly overpriced boutique hotels, inns and B&Bs fill up quickly in Carmel-by-the-Sea, especially in summer. Ask the chamber of commerce (p313) about last-minute deals.

For better-value lodgings, head north to Monterey.

Mission Ranch
INN **$$**

(Map p308; ☑ 831-624-6436; www.missionranch carmel.com; 26270 Dolores St; r $140-340; 🐾) If woolly sheep grazing on green fields by the beach doesn't convince you to stay here, maybe knowing that Hollywood icon Clint Eastwood restored this historic ranch will. Accommodations are shabby-chic, even a tad rustic.

Sea View Inn
B&B **$$**

(Map p308; ☑ 831-624-8778; www.seaviewinn carmel.com; El Camino Real, btwn 11th & 12th Aves; r $145-295; 🐾) Retreat from downtown Carmel's hustle to fireside nooks tailor-made for reading. The cheapest rooms with slanted ceilings are short on cat-swinging space. Rates include afternoon wine and noshes on the front porch.

Lodge at Pebble Beach
RESORT **$$$**

(Map p308; ☑ 831-624-3811; www.pebblebeach. com; 1700 17-Mile Drive; r from $815; ✳@🐾🏊) The luxurious Lodge at Pebble Beach includes a spa and designer shops where the most demanding of tastes are catered to. Even if you're not a trust-fund baby, you can still soak up the rich atmosphere in the resort's art-filled public spaces and bay views from the cocktail lounge.

Cypress Inn
BOUTIQUE HOTEL **$$$**

(Map p308; ☑ 831-624-3871; www.cypress-inn. com; cnr Lincoln St & 7th Ave; r/ste from $279/499; P🍴🐾🏊) Done up in Spanish Colonial style, this 1929 inn is co-owned by movie star Doris Day. Airy terracotta hallways with colorful tiles give it a Mediterranean feel, while sunny rooms face the courtyard. Pet fee $30.

✗ Eating

Carmel's dining scene has traditionally been more about old-world atmosphere, but a few recent openings have added a more modern, cosmopolitan sheen.

Cultura Comida y Bebida
MEXICAN **$$**

(Map p308; ☑ 831-250-7005; www.culturacarmel. com; Dolores St btwn 5th & 6th Aves; mains $19-32; ⏰11:30am-midnight Thu-Sun, 5pm-midnight Mon-Tue) Located near art galleries in a brick-lined courtyard, Cultura Comida y Bebida is a relaxed bar and eatery inspired by the food of Oaxaca in Mexico. Pull up a seat at the elegant bar and sample a vertical tasting of mezcal, or partner Monterey squid tostadas

CENTRAL COAST CARMEL-BY-THE-SEA

17-MILE DRIVE

What to See

Pacific Grove and Carmel are linked by the spectacularly scenic, if overhyped, **17-Mile Drive** (Map p308; www.pebblebeach.com; per car/bicycle $10/free), which meanders through Pebble Beach, a wealthy private resort. It's no chore staying within the 25mph limit – every curve in the road reveals another postcard vista, especially when wildflowers are in bloom. Cycling the drive is enormously popular: try to do it during the week, when traffic isn't as heavy, and ride with the flow of traffic from north to south.

Using the self-guided touring map you'll receive at the toll gate, you can pick out landmarks such as **Spanish Bay**, where explorer Gaspar de Portolá dropped anchor in 1769; treacherously rocky **Point Joe**, which was often mistaken for the entrance to Monterey Bay and thus became the site of shipwrecks; and **Bird Rock**, also a haven for harbor seals and sea lions. The pièce de résistance is the trademarked **Lone Cypress** (Map p308), which has perched on a seaward rock for possibly more than 250 years.

Besides the coastal scenery, star attractions at Pebble Beach include world-famous golf courses, where a celebrity and pro tournament happens every February. The luxurious **Lodge at Pebble Beach** (p311) has a spa and designer shops.

The Route

Operated as a toll road by the Pebble Beach Company, the 17-Mile Drive is open from sunrise to sunset. The toll can be refunded later as a discount on a $30 minimum food purchase at local restaurants.

Time & Mileage

There are five separate gates for the 17-Mile Drive; how far you drive and how long you take is up to you. To take advantage of the most scenery, enter on Sunset Dr in Pacific Grove and exit onto San Antonio Ave in Carmel-by-the-Sea.

WORTH A TRIP

CARMEL VALLEY

Where sun-kissed vineyards rustle beside farm fields, Carmel Valley is a peaceful side trip, just a 20-minute drive east of Hwy 1 along eastbound Carmel Valley Rd. At organic **Earthbound Farm Stand** (☑ 805-625-6219; www.ebfarm.com; 7250 Carmel Valley Rd; ⊙ 8am-6:30pm Mon-Sat, 9am-6pm Sun; 🖷) 🍃, sample homemade soups and salads or harvest your own herbs from the garden. Several wineries further east offer tastings – don't miss the Pinot Noir bottled by **Boekenoogen** (Map p314; ☑ 831-659-4215; www.boekenoogen wines.com; 24 W Carmel Valley Rd; tasting flights $10-15; ⊙ 11am-5pm; 🅿). Afterwards, stretch your legs in the village of Carmel Valley, chock-a-block with genteel shops and bistros.

Corkscrew Cafe (Map p314; ☑ 831-659-8888; www.corkscrewcafe.com; 55 W Carmel Valley Rd; mains $15-26; ⊙ noon-9pm Wed-Mon) Just possibly Carmel Valley's coziest eatery, the Corkscrew Cafe combines a rustic wine-country vibe and a Mediterranean-influenced menu – think wood-fired salmon, pizza, and mushroom and lamb pasta – with a stellar local wine list. Relax into a Carmel Valley evening under the market umbrellas in the pleasant garden, and don't leave without checking out the quirky corkscrew museum.

Valley Greens Gallery (Map p314; ☑ 831-620-2985; www.valleygreensgallery.com; 16e E Carmel Valley Rd; 4-beer tasting flights $12; ⊙ 3-9pm Mon-Tue, 3-10pm Wed-Thu, 1-11pm Fri-Sat, 1-9pm Sun) One part funky art gallery and two parts craft-beer bar, Valley Greens is a stand-out destination amid Carmel Valley's laid-back main drag. Four rotating beer taps deliver some real surprises from smaller Californian breweries, old-school reggae and foosball tables create a fun ambience, and open-mike night from 6pm on Tuesdays is always worth catching.

and oak-roasted trout with cilantro, lime and garlic with Californian and French wines.

Mundaka
TAPAS $$

(Map p308; ☑ 831-624-7400; www.mundakacarmel.com; San Carlos St, btwn Ocean & 7th Aves; small plates $8-15; ⊙ 5-9pm Sun-Thu, to 10pm Fri-Sat) This stone courtyard hideaway is a svelte escape from Carmel's stuffy 'newly wed and nearly dead' crowd. Taste Spanish tapas and housemade sangria while world beats spin. Partner the garlic prawns or grilled octopus with a chilled glass of local wine.

La Bicyclette
FRENCH, ITALIAN $$

(Map p308; ☑ 831-622-9899; www.labicyclette restaurant.com; cnr Dolores St & 7th Ave; dinner mains $18-31; ⊙ 8am-10pm) 🍃 Rustic European comfort food using seasonal local ingredients packs canoodling couples into this bistro, with an open kitchen baking wood-fired-oven pizzas. Excellent local wines by the glass. It's also a top spot for a breakfast or lunch.

🍷 Drinking & Entertainment

Winery tasting rooms dot Carmel's compact and well-kept centre, and the best option for late-night drinks is the cool and energetic scene at Barmel.

Barmel
WINE BAR

(Map p308; ☑ 831-626-2095; www.facebook.com/BarmelByTheSea; San Carlos St, btwn Ocean & 7th Aves; ⊙ 2pm-2am Mon-Fri, 1pm-2am Sat-Sun) Shaking up Carmel's conservative image and adding a dash of after-dark fun is this cool little Spanish-themed courtyard bar. There's live music from 7pm to 9pm from Thursday to Saturday, robust cocktails and an energetic, younger vibe.

Scheid Vineyards
WINE BAR

(Map p308; ☑ 831-656-9463; www.scheidvineyards.com; San Carlos St, at 7th Ave; tasting flights $10-20; ⊙ noon-7pm Sun-Thu, to 8pm Fri & Sat) Pop into Scheid Vineyards' wine-tasting room to sip a prodigious range of grape varietals, all grown in Monterey County. Red wine varietals including Merlot, Pinot Noir and Cabernet Sauvignon are local stars.

Forest Theater
THEATER

(Map p308; ☑ box office 831-622-0100; www.foresttheatercarmel.org; cnr Mountain View Ave & Santa Rita St) At this 1910 venue, community-theater musicals, dramas and comedies as well as film screenings take place under the stars by flickering fire pits.

ℹ Information

Carmel Chamber of Commerce (Map p308; ☑ 831-624-2522; www.carmelcalifornia.org; San Carlos St, btwn 5th & 6th Aves; ⊙ 10am-5pm)

ℹ Getting There & Away

Carmel is about 5 miles south of Monterey via Hwy 1. There's free parking (no time limit) in a **municipal lot** (Map p308; cnr 3rd & Junípero Sts) behind the Vista Lobos building.

MST (☑ 888-678-2871; www.mst.org) 'Grapevine Express' bus 24 ($2.50, hourly) connects Monterey's Transit Plaza with downtown Carmel, the mission and Carmel Valley. Bus 22 ($3.50) stops in downtown Carmel and at the mission en route to/from Point Lobos and Big Sur three times daily between late May and early September, and twice daily on Saturday and Sunday only the rest of the year.

Big Sur

Big Sur is more a state of mind than a place to pinpoint on a map, and when the sun goes down, the moon and the stars are the area's natural streetlights. (That's if summer's fog hasn't extinguished them.) Raw beauty and an intense maritime energy characterize this land shoehorned between the Santa Lucia Range and the Pacific Ocean, and a first glimpse of the craggy, unspoiled coastline is a special moment.

In the 1950s and '60s, Big Sur – named by Spanish settlers living on the Monterey Peninsula, who referred to the wilderness as *el país grande del sur* ('the big country to the south') – became a retreat for artists and writers, including Henry Miller and Beat Generation visionaries such as Lawrence Ferlinghetti. Today Big Sur attracts self-proclaimed artists, new-age mystics, latter-day hippies and city slickers seeking to unplug and reflect more deeply on this emerald-green edge of the continent.

◎ Sights

At Big Sur's state parks, your parking fee ($10) receipt is valid for same-day entry to all except Limekiln. Please don't skip paying the entry fee by parking illegally outside the parks along Hwy 1 – California's state parks have suffered severe budget cutbacks, and every dollar helps.

Garrapata State Park   PARK
(Map p314; ☑ 831-624-4909; www.parks.ca.gov; off Hwy 1; 🅿) **FREE** Over 4 miles south of Point Lobos on Hwy 1, pull over to hike coastal headlands, where you might spot whales cruising by offshore during winter, or into canyons of wildflowers and redwood trees. *Garrapata* is Spanish for 'tick', of which there are many in the canyon and woods, so wearing long sleeves and pants is smart. Leashed dogs are allowed on the beach only.

Bixby Bridge   LANDMARK
(Map p314) Less than 15 miles south of Carmel, this landmark spanning Rainbow Canyon is one of the world's highest single-span bridges. Completed in 1932, it was built by prisoners eager to lop time off their sentences. There's a perfect photo-op pull-off on the bridge's north side. Before Bixby Bridge was constructed, travelers had to trek inland on what's now called the **Old Coast Rd**, a rough dirt route that reconnects after 11 miles with Hwy 1 near Andrew Molera State Park. When the weather is dry enough, the old road is usually navigable by 4WD or a mountain bike.

ℹ HIGHWAY 1 ROAD CLOSURES

At the time of writing, temporary road closures have shuttered a 23 mile stretch along Hwy 1 through Big Sur. To the north, the Pfeiffer Canyon Bridge has been condemned after the eroding hillside undermined the support columns. In the southern part of the region, mudslides have covered the road at Mud Creek, significantly changing the landscape and making the area inaccessible via car. The Pfeiffer Canyon Bridge is scheduled to reopen in September 2017. However, the California Department of Transportation has a larger challenge with the landslides. A plan was put forward in August 2017 to realign the highway across the landslide, but the enormous undertaking had no set date of completion at that time.

Until the road reopens, travelers can detour around Big Sur on Hwy 101 (p328). You'll miss out on some coastal views, but between stunning views of the California countryside, quaint towns and world-class wine tasting, it's a detour worth taking on its own merit.

Big Sur

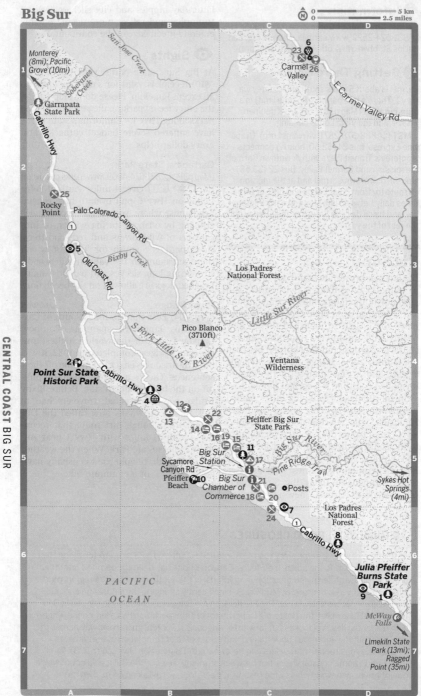

N
0 ——————— 5 km
0 ——————— 2.5 miles

Monterey (8mi); Pacific Grove (10mi)

Garrapata State Park

San Jose Creek

Soberanes Creek

Carmel Valley
23 6
26

E Carmel Valley Rd

Cabrillo Hwy

25
Rocky Point

Palo Colorado Canyon Rd

1

5
Old Coast Rd

Bixby Creek

Los Padres National Forest

Little Sur River

Pico Blanco (3710ft)

S Fork Little Sur River

Ventana Wilderness

2
Point Sur State Historic Park

Cabrillo Hwy

3
4
12
13
14
16 19 15
22
11
17

Pfeiffer Big Sur State Park

Big Sur River

Pine Ridge Trail

Big Sur Station

Sycamore Canyon Rd
Pfeiffer Beach
10
Big Sur Chamber of Commerce
18 20
21
Posts

24
1 Cabrillo Hwy
7

Sykes Hot Springs (4mi)

Los Padres National Forest

8

Julia Pfeiffer Burns State Park

9 1

PACIFIC OCEAN

McWay Falls

Limekiln State Park (13mi); Ragged Point (35mi)

★**Point Sur State Historic Park** LIGHTHOUSE
(Map p314; ☑831-625-4419; www.pointsur.org; off
Hwy 1; adult/child 6-17yr from $12/5; ☺tours usu-
ally at 1pm Wed, 10am Sat & Sun Oct-Mar; 10am &
2pm Wed & Sat, 10am Sun Apr-Sep, also 10am Thu
Jul & Aug) FREE A little over 6 miles south of
Bixby Bridge (p313), Point Sur rises like a
velvety green fortress out of the sea. It looks
like an island, but is actually connected to
land by a sandbar. Atop the volcanic rock
sits an 1889 stone light station, which was
staffed until 1974. During three-hour guided tours, ocean views and tales of the lighthouse keepers' family lives are engrossing.
Meet your tour guide at the locked farm gate
0.25-miles north of Point Sur Naval Facility.

Special monthly moonlight tours are giv-
en between April and September. Call ahead
to confirm all tour schedules. Show up early
because space is limited (no reservations;
some credit cards accepted).

Andrew Molera State Park STATE PARK
(Map p314; ☑831-667-2315; www.parks.ca.gov;
Hwy 1; per car $10; ☺30min before sunrise-30min
after sunset; P ⊞) ✿ Named after the farmer who first planted artichokes in California, this oft-overlooked park is a trail-laced
pastiche of grassy meadows, ocean bluffs
and rugged sandy beaches offering excellent
wildlife watching. Look for the entrance just
over 8 miles south of Bixby Bridge.

South of the parking lot, you can learn
all about endangered California condors
and long-term species recovery and moni-
toring programs inside the **Big Sur Discovery Center** (Map p314; ☑831-624-1202; www.
ventanaws.org/discovery_center; ☺10am-4pm Sat
& Sun late May–early Sep; P ⊞) ✿ FREE.

From the main parking lot, a short walk
along the beach-bound trail passes through
a first-come-first-serve campground, from
where a gentle spur trail leads to the 1861
redwood **Cooper Cabin**, Big Sur's oldest
building. Keep hiking on the main trail out
toward a wild beach where the Big Sur River
runs into the ocean; condors may be spotted circling overhead and migrating whales
sometimes cruise by offshore.

Pfeiffer Big Sur State Park PARK
(Map p314; ☑831-667-2315; www.parks.ca.gov;
47225 Hwy 1; per car $10; ☺30min before sun-
rise-30min after sunset; P ⊞) ✿ Named after
Big Sur's first European settlers who arrived
in 1869, this is Big Sur's largest state park,
where hiking trails loop through stately
redwood groves. The most popular hike –
to 60ft-high **Pfeiffer Falls**, a delicate cascade hidden in the forest, which usually
runs from December to May – is a 2-mile
round-trip. Built in the 1930s by the Civilian
Conservation Corps (CCC), rustic **Big Sur
Lodge** (Map p314; ☑831-667-3100; www.bigsur
lodge.com; 47225 Hwy 1; d $309-439; P ⊖ ☎ ☒)

stands near the park entrance, about 13 miles south of Bixby Bridge (p313).

★ **Julia Pfeiffer Burns State Park**　PARK
(☑ 831-667-2315; www.parks.ca.gov; Hwy 1; per car $10; ☺ 30min before sunrise-30min after sunset; ℗ 🖼) 🍃 If you're chasing waterfalls, swing into this state park named for a Big Sur pioneer. From the parking lot, the 1.3-mile round-trip **Overlook Trail** rushes downhill toward the ocean, passing through a tunnel underneath Hwy 1. Everyone comes to photograph 80ft-high **McWay Falls**, which tumbles year-round over granite cliffs and freefalls into the sea – or the beach, depending on the tide. The park entrance is on the east side of Hwy 1, about 8 miles south of Nepenthe restaurant (p319). McWay Falls is the classic Big Sur postcard shot, with tree-topped rocks jutting above a golden beach next to swirling blue pools and crashing white surf. From trailside benches, you might spot migrating whales during winter.

Pfeiffer Beach　BEACH
(Map p314; ☑ 831-667-2315; www.fs.usda.gov/lpnf; end of Sycamore Canyon Rd; per car $10; ☺ 9am-8pm; ℗ 🖼🐕) This phenomenal, crescent-shaped and dog-friendly beach is known for its huge double-rock formation, through which waves crash with life-affirming power. It's often windy, and the surf is too dangerous for swimming. But dig down into the wet sand – it's purple! That's because manganese garnet washes down from the craggy hillsides above. To get here from Hwy 1, make a sharp right onto Sycamore Canyon Rd, marked by a small yellow sign that says 'narrow road' at the top. From the turnoff, which is a half-mile south of Big Sur Station on the ocean side of Hwy 1, it's two narrow, twisting miles down to the beach (RVs and trailers prohibited).

Henry Miller Memorial Library　ARTS CENTER
(Map p314; ☑ 831-667-2574; www.henrymiller.org; 48603 Hwy 1; donations accepted; ☺ 10am-5pm) FREE Novelist Henry Miller was a Big Sur denizen from 1944 to 1962. More of a beatnik memorial, alt-cultural venue and bookshop, this community gathering spot was never Miller's home. The house belonged to Miller's friend, painter Emil White, until his death and is now run by a nonprofit group. Stop by to browse and hang out on the front deck. It's 0.4 miles south of Nepenthe restaurant (p319).

Inside are copies of all of Miller's written works, many of his paintings and a collection of Big Sur and Beat Generation material, including copies of the top 100 books Miller said most influenced him. Check the online calendar for upcoming events.

Partington Cove　BEACH
(off Hwy 1) FREE This is a raw, breathtaking spot where crashing surf salts your skin. On the steep, half-mile dirt hike down to the cove, you'll cross a cool bridge and go through an even cooler tunnel. The cove's water is unbelievably aqua and within it grow tangled kelp forests. Look for the unmarked trailhead turnoff inside a hairpin turn on the ocean side of Hwy 1, about 6 miles south of Nepenthe restaurant (p319) and 2 miles north of Julia Pfeiffer Burns State Park.

The trail starts just beyond the locked vehicle gate. There's no real beach access and ocean swimming isn't safe, but some people scamper on the rocks and look for tide pools as waves splash ominously. Originally used for loading freight, Partington Cove allegedly became a landing spot for Prohibition-era bootleggers.

Limekiln State Park　PARK
(☑ 831-434-1996; www.parks.ca.gov; 63025 Hwy 1; per car $10; ☺ 8am-sunset) Two miles south of Lucia, this park gets its name from the four remaining wood-fired kilns originally built here in the 1880s to smelt quarried limestone into powder, a key ingredient in cement building construction from Monterey to San Francisco. Tragically, pioneers chopped down most of the steep canyon's old-growth redwoods to fuel the kilns' fires. A 1-mile round-trip trail leads through a redwood grove to the historic site, passing a creekside spur trail to a delightful 100ft-high waterfall.

Los Padres National Forest　FOREST
(☑ 805-968-6640; www.fs.usda.gov/lpnf; Hwy 1, almost opp Plaskett Creek Campground; 🐕) The tortuously winding 40-mile stretch of Hwy 1 south of Lucia to Hearst Castle is sparsely populated, rugged and remote, mostly running through national forest lands. Around 5 miles south of Kirk Creek Campground (p319) and Nacimiento-Fergusson Rd, almost opposite Plaskett Creek Campground (p319), is **Sand Dollar Beach** (http://campone.com; Hwy 1; per car $10, free with local USFS campground fee; ☺ 9am-8pm; 🐕). From the picnic area, it's a five-minute walk to southern Big Sur's longest sandy

VENTANA WILDERNESS

The 240,000-acre Ventana Wilderness is Big Sur's wild backcountry. It lies within the northern Los Padres National Forest, which straddles the Santa Lucia Range running parallel to the coast. Most of this wilderness is covered with oak and chaparral, though canyons cut by the Big Sur and Little Sur Rivers support virgin stands of coast redwoods and the rare endemic Santa Lucia fir, which grows on steep, rocky slopes too.

Now regenerating after devastating wildfires in 2008, Ventana Wilderness is popular with adventurous backpackers. A much-trammeled overnight destination is Sykes Hot Springs, natural 100°F (35°C) mineral pools framed by redwoods. It's a moderately strenuous 10-mile, one-way hike along the Pine Ridge Trail, starting from Big Sur Station (p320), where you can get free campfire permits and pay for overnight trailhead parking ($5). Don't expect solitude on weekends during peak season (April through September) and always follow Leave No Trace (www.lnt.org) principles.

beach, a crescent-shaped strip of sand protected from winds by high bluffs. Nearby is **Jade Cove** (http://campone.com; Hwy 1; ☉sunrise-sunset; 🐾) **FREE** and it's a short drive south to Salmon Creek Falls.

Heading south before leaving Lucia, make sure you've got at least enough fuel in the tank to reach the expensive gas stations at Gorda, about 11 miles south of Limekiln State Park, or Ragged Point, another 12 miles further south.

Ragged Point　　　　　　　LANDMARK
(19019 Hwy 1) Your last – or first – taste of Big Sur's rocky grandeur comes at this craggy cliff outcropping with fabulous views of the coastline in both directions, about 15 miles north of Hearst Castle (p322). Once part of the Hearst empire, it's now taken over by a sprawling, ho-hum lodge with a pricey gas station. Heading south, the land grows increasingly wind-swept as Hwy 1 rolls gently down to the water's edge.

Salmon Creek Falls　　　　　WATERFALL
(www.fs.usda.gov/lpnf; Hwy 1; 🅿🐾🐕) **FREE** Take a short hike to splash around in the pools at the base of this double-drop waterfall, tucked uphill in a forested canyon. The falls usually run from December through May, and the trail is dog-friendly. In a hairpin turn of Hwy 1, the roadside turnoff is marked only by a small brown trailhead sign, about 8 miles south of Gorda.

🏃 Activities

Esalen Hot Springs　　　　HOT SPRINGS
(☎831-667-3047; www.esalen.org; 55000 Hwy 1; per person $30; ☉by reservation) At the private **Esalen Institute** (☎831-667-3000),

clothing-optional baths fed by a natural hot spring sit on a ledge above the ocean. We're confident you'll never take another dip that compares scenery-wise, especially on stormy winter nights. Only two small outdoor pools perch directly over the waves, so once you've stripped and taken a quick shower, head outside immediately. Credit cards only.

Advance reservations are required. The signposted entrance is on Hwy 1, about 3 miles south of Julia Pfeiffer Burns State Park (p316).

Molera Horseback Tours　　HORSEBACK RIDING
(Map p314; ☎831-625-5486; www.molerahorseback tours.com; Hwy 1; per person $58-96; 🐎) Across Hwy 1 from Andrew Molera State Park (p315), Molera offers guided trail rides on the beach and through redwood forest. Walk-ins and novices are welcome; children must be at least six years old, with most rides recommended for ages 12 and up.

🛏 Sleeping

With few exceptions, Big Sur's lodgings do not have TVs and rarely have telephones. This is where you come to escape the world. There aren't a lot of rooms overall, so demand often exceeds supply and prices can be steep. Bigger price tags don't necessarily buy you more amenities either. In summer and on weekends, reservations are essential everywhere, from campgrounds to deluxe resorts.

Ripplewood Resort　　　　　CABIN $$
(Map p314; ☎831-667-2242; www.ripplewood resort.com; 47047 Hwy 1; cabins $140-250; ☉🐕) North of Pfeiffer Big Sur State Park (p315), Ripplewood has gotten behind fiscal equality by charging the same rates year-round.

Throwback Americana cabins mostly have kitchens and sometimes even wood-burning fireplaces. Quiet riverside cabins are surrounded by redwoods, but roadside cabins can be noisy. Wi-fi in restaurant only.

★ Post Ranch Inn   RESORT $$$

(Map p314; ☑ 831-667-2200; www.postranchinn. com; 47900 Hwy 1; d from $925; P 🐾 ❄ @ 🛜 🏊) The last word in luxurious coastal getaways, the exclusive Post Ranch pampers demanding guests with slate spa tubs, wood-burning fireplaces, private decks and walking sticks for coastal hikes. Ocean-view rooms celebrate the sea, while treehouses lack views and have a bit of sway. Paddle around the clifftop infinity pool after a shamanic-healing session or yoga class in the spa. No children allowed.

Panoramic sea-view Sierra Mar restaurant requires reservations for lunch and dinner; the gourmet breakfast buffet is served to guests only.

Ventana Inn & Spa   RESORT $$$

(Map p314; ☑ 831-667-2331; www.ventanainn.com; 48123 Hwy 1; d from $596; 🛜 🏊) 🍃 Almost at odds with Big Sur's hippie-alternative vibe, Ventana injects a little soul into its deluxe digs. Honeymooning couples and paparazzi-fleeing celebs pad from tai chi class to the Japanese baths and outdoor pools (one is famously clothing-optional), or hole up all day next to the wood-burning fireplace in their own private villa, hot-tub suite or ocean-view cottage.

Treebones Resort   CABIN $$$

(☑ 877-424-4787; www.treebonesresort.com; 71895 Hwy 1; campsites $95, d with shared bath from $320; ⊖ 🛜 🏊) Don't let the word 're-sort' throw you. Yes, it has an ocean-view hot tub, heated pool and massage treatments. But a unique woven 'human nest' and canvas-sided yurts with polished pine floors, quilt-covered beds, sink vanities and redwood decks are more like glamping, with little privacy. Communal bathrooms and showers are a short stroll away. Wi-fi in main lodge only.

Basic walk-in campsites (no vehicle access) are also available. Children must be at least six years old. Look for the signposted turnoff a mile north of Gorda, at the southern end of Big Sur.

Glen Oaks Motel   MOTEL, CABIN $$$

(Map p314; ☑ 831-667-2105; www.glenoaksbigsur. com; 47080 Hwy 1; d $300-475; P ⊖ 🛜) 🍃 At this 1950s redwood-and-adobe motor lodge, rustic rooms and cabins seem effortlessly chic. Dramatically transformed by eco-conscious design, snug romantic hideaway rooms all have gas fireplaces. Woodsy cabins in a redwood grove have kitchenettes and share outdoor fire pits, or retreat to the one-bedroom house with a full kitchen.

Public Campgrounds

Camping is currently available at four of Big Sur's state parks and two United States Forest Service (USFS) campgrounds along Hwy 1.

CALIFORNIA'S COMEBACK CONDORS

When it comes to endangered species, one of the state's biggest success stories is the California condor (*Gymnogyps californianus*). These gigantic, prehistoric birds weigh over 20lb with a wingspan of up to 10ft, letting them fly great distances in search of carrion. They're easily recognized by their naked pink head and large white patches on the underside of each wing.

This big bird became so rare that in 1987 there were only 27 left in the world, and all were removed from the wild to special captive-breeding facilities. Read the whole gripping story in journalist John Moir's book *Return of the Condor: The Race to Save Our Largest Bird from Extinction*.

There are over 400 California condors alive today, with increasing numbers of captive birds being released back into the wild. It's hoped they will begin breeding naturally, although it's an uphill battle. Wild condors are still dying of lead poisoning caused by hunters' bullets in the game carcasses that the birds feed on.

The Big Sur coast and Pinnacles National Park (p331) offer excellent opportunities to view this majestic bird. In Big Sur, the Ventana Wildlife Society (www.ventanaws.org) occasionally leads two-hour guided condor-watching tours ($50) using radio telemetry to track the birds; for sign-up details, check the website or ask at the Big Sur Discovery Center (p315).

Big Sur Campground & Cabins
CABIN, CAMPGROUND **$$**

(Map p314; ☑831-667-2322; www.bigsurcamp.
com; 47000 Hwy 1; tent/RV sites from $63/73, cabins $175-430; P◉) On the Big Sur River and shaded by redwoods, cozy cabins sport full kitchens and fireplaces, while canvas-sided tent cabins share bathroom facilities. The riverside campground, where neighboring sites have little privacy, is popular with RVs. There are hot showers and a coin-op laundry, playground and general store.

Pfeiffer Big Sur State Park Campground
CAMPGROUND **$**

(Map p314; ☑reservations 800-444-7275; www.
reserveamerica.com; 47225 Hwy 1; tent & RV sites $35-50; P▨) Best for novice campers and families with young kids, here over 200 campsites nestle in a redwood-shaded valley. Facilities include drinking water, fire pits and coin-op hot showers and laundry.

Julia Pfeiffer Burns State Park Campground
CAMPGROUND **$**

(Map p314; ☑831-667-2315; www.parks.ca.gov; Hwy 1; tent sites $30) Two small walk-in campsites sit up on a semi-shaded ocean bluff, with fire pits and vault toilets but no water. All campers must check in first at Pfeiffer Big Sur State Park (p315), 11 miles north.

Andrew Molera State Park Campground
CAMPGROUND **$**

(Map p314; www.parks.ca.gov; Hwy 1; tent sites $25) Two-dozen primitive tent sites (no reservations) in a grassy meadow come with fire pits and drinking water, but no ocean views. The campground is a 0.3-mile walk from the parking lot.

Limekiln State Park Campground
CAMPGROUND **$**

(Map p314; ☑805-434-1996; www.parks.ca.gov; 63025 Hwy 1; tent & RV sites $35; ▨) In southern Big Sur, this quiet state park has two-dozen campsites huddled under a bridge next to the ocean. Drinking water, fire pits and coin-op hot showers are available.

USFS Kirk Creek Campground
CAMPGROUND **$**

(☑reservations 877-444-6777; www.recreation.
gov; Hwy 1; tent & RV sites $35) Over 30 exposed ocean-view blufftop campsites with drinking water and fire pits cluster close together, nearly 2 miles south of Limekiln State Park (p316).

USFS Plaskett Creek Campground
CAMPGROUND **$**

(Map p42; ☑reservations 877-477-6777; www.rec
reation.gov; Hwy 1; tent & RV sites $35) Nearly 40 spacious, shady campsites with drinking water and vault toilets circle a forested meadow near Sand Dollar Beach (p317) in southern Big Sur.

✖ Eating

Like Big Sur's lodgings, some restaurants and cafes alongside Hwy 1 can be overpriced and underwhelming, but stellar views at some locations do offset any mediocrity.

Big Sur Roadhouse
CALIFORNIAN **$**

(Map p314; ☑831-667-2370; www.bigsurroadhouse.
com; 47080 Hwy 1; snacks & mains $7-15; ◎8am-2:30pm; ☎) This modern roadhouse glows with color-splashed artwork and an outdoor fire pit. At riverside tables, fork into upscale California-inspired pub grub like spicy wings, pork sliders and gourmet burgers, with craft beer on tap. It's also a top spot for coffee and cake.

Big Sur Deli & General Store
DELI **$**

(Map p314; ☑831-667-2225; www.bigsurdeli.com; 47520 Hwy 1; snacks $2-12; ◎7am-8pm) With the most reasonable prices in Big Sur, this family-owned deli slices custom-made sandwiches and piles up tortillas with carne asada, pork *carnitas*, veggies or beans and cheese. The small market carries camping food, snacks, beer and wine.

Rocky Point
CALIFORNIAN, SEAFOOD **$$**

(Map p314; ☑831-624-2933; www.rockypoint
restaurant.com; 36700 Hwy 1; mains $18-36; ◎11:30am-8pm Thu-Tue) Come for the hillside ocean-view terrace, where cocktails and Californian wines are served all day long, and the steak and seafood menu includes on-the-road treats like scallops, paella and crab cakes. The spectacularly located restaurant is 2.5 miles north of Bixby Bridge (p313).

Nepenthe
CALIFORNIAN **$$$**

(Map p314; ☑831-667-2345; www.nepenthebig
sur.com; 48510 Hwy 1; mains $18-50; ◎11:30am-4:30pm & 5-10pm; ☑) Nepenthe comes from a Greek word meaning 'isle of no sorrow,' and indeed, it's hard to feel blue while sitting by the fire pit on this aerial terrace. Just-okay California cuisine (try the renowned Ambrosia burger) takes a backseat to the views and Nepenthe's history – Orson Welles and Rita Hayworth briefly owned a cabin here in the 1940s. Reservations essential.

ℹ DRIVING HIGHWAY 1

Driving this narrow two-lane highway through Big Sur and beyond is very slow going. Allow about three hours to cover the distance between the Monterey Peninsula and San Luis Obispo, much more if you want to explore the coast. Traveling after dark can be risky and more to the point, it's futile, because you'll miss out on the seascapes. Watch out for cyclists and make use of signposted roadside pullouts to let faster-moving traffic pass.

Downstairs, cheaper but still expensive Café Kevah delivers coffee, baked goods, light brunches and head-spinning ocean views on its outdoor deck (closed during winter and bad weather).

Big Sur Bakery & Restaurant CALIFORNIAN $$$
(Map p314; ☎831-667-0520; www.bigsurbakery.com; 47540 Hwy 1; bakery items $3-14, mains $20-36; ⊙bakery from 8am daily, restaurant 9:30am-2pm Mon-Fri, 10am-2:30pm Sat & Sun, 5:30pm-late Wed-Sat) Behind the Shell station, this warmly lit, funky house has seasonally changing menus, on which wood-fired pizzas share space with rustic dishes like grilled swordfish or wood-roasted chicken. Fronted by a pretty patio, the bakery makes addictive cinnamon buns and super-stuffed sandwiches. Expect longish waits and standoffish service. Dinner reservations are essential.

Big Sur River Inn AMERICAN $$$
(Map p314; ☎831-667-2700; www.bigsurriverinn.com; 46840 Hwy 1; breakfast & lunch $15-20, dinner $15-40; ⊙8am-9pm; 🐾🚻) Woodsy restaurant with a deck, overlooking a creek teeming with throaty frogs. The food is standard American (seafood, grilled meats and pastas, plus vegetarian options), but diner-style breakfasts and lunches such as berry pancakes and BLT sandwiches satisfy. Rooms (starting at $150), a general store, and gas are also available.

🍷 Drinking & Entertainment

Californian craft beers are a Big Sur highlight at the Big Sur Taphouse and the Maiden Publick House, while there are excellent wine lists at clifftop restaurants with rugged Pacific Ocean vistas.

Big Sur Taphouse BAR
(Map p314; ☎831-667-2225; www.bigsurtaphouse.com; 47520 Hwy 1; ⊙noon-10pm Mon-Fri, 10am-midnight Sat, to 10pm Sun; 🐾) Down California craft beers and regional wines on the back deck or by the fireplace inside this high-ceilinged wooden bar with board games, sports on the TVs and pub grub from the next-door deli.

Maiden Publick House PUB
(Map p314; ☎831-667-2355; Village Center Shops, Hwy 1; ⊙3pm-2am Mon-Thu, from 1pm Fri & from 11am Sat-Sun) Just south of the Big Sur River Inn, this dive has an encyclopedic beer bible and motley local musicians jamming, mostly on weekends. Sixteen rotating taps and three pages of bottled brews create havoc for the indecisive drinker.

Henry Miller Memorial Library PERFORMING ARTS
(Map p314; ☎831-667-2574; www.henrymiller.org; 48603 Hwy 1; ⊙10am-5pm & longer hours for specific events; 🐾) Just south of Nepenthe (p319), this nonprofit alternative space hosts a bohemian carnival of live-music concerts, author readings, open-mike nights and indie-film screenings outdoors, especially during summer.

ℹ Information

Visitors often wander into businesses along Hwy 1 and ask, 'How much further to Big Sur?' In fact, there is no town of Big Sur as such, though you may see the name on maps. Commercial activity is concentrated along the stretch north of Pfeiffer Big Sur State Park. Sometimes called 'the Village,' this is where you'll find most of the lodgings, restaurants and shops.

Big Sur Chamber of Commerce (Map p314; ☎831-667-2100; www.bigsurcalifornia.org; Hwy 1; ⊙9am-1pm Mon, Wed & Fri)

Big Sur Station (Map p314; ☎831-667-2315; www.bigsurcalifornia.org/contact.html; 47555 Hwy 1; ⊙9am-4pm) About 1.5 miles south of Pfeiffer Big Sur State Park, this multiagency ranger station has information and maps for state parks, the Los Padres National Forest and Ventana Wilderness. The location is also one of the spots along Big Sur where there is more reliable cellphone coverage.

ℹ Getting There & Around

Big Sur is best explored by car, since you'll be itching to stop frequently and take in the rugged beauty and vistas that reveal themselves after every hairpin turn. Even if your driving skills are up to these narrow switchbacks, others' aren't:

expect to average 35mph or less along the route. Parts of Hwy 1 are battle-scarred, evidence of a continual struggle to keep them open after landslides and washouts. Check current highway conditions with CalTrans (☑800-427-7623; www.dot.ca.gov) and fill up your gas tank beforehand.

MST (☑888-678-2871; www.mst.org) bus 22 ($3.50, 1¼ hours) travels from Monterey via Carmel and Point Lobos as far south as Nepenthe restaurant (p319), stopping en route at Andrew Molera State Park (p315) and the Big Sur River Inn. Buses run three times daily between late May and early September, and twice daily on Saturdays and Sundays only the rest of the year.

Point Piedras Blancas

Many lighthouses still stand along California's coast, but few offer such a historically evocative seascape. Federally designated an outstanding natural area, the jutting, windblown grounds of this 1875 light station (☑805-927-7361; www.piedrasblancas.gov; off Hwy 1; tours adult/child 6-17yr $10/5; ☉tours 9:45am Mon-Tue & Thu-Sat mid-Jun–Aug, 9:45am Tue, Thu & Sat Sep–mid-Jun) have been replanted with native flora. Everything looks much the way it did when the first lighthouse keepers helped ships find safe harbor at San Simeon Bay. Guided tours meet at the old Piedras Blancas Motel, 1.5 miles north of the lighthouse gate on Hwy 1. No reservations are taken; call ahead to check tour schedules.

At a signposted vista point, around 4.5 miles north of Hearst Castle, you can observe a colony of northern elephant seals bigger than the one at Año Nuevo State Reserve near Santa Cruz. During peak winter season, about 18,000 seals seek shelter in the coves and beaches along this stretch of coast. On sunny days the seals usually 'lie around like banana slugs,' in the words of one volunteer. Interpretive panels along a beach boardwalk and blue-jacketed Friends of the Elephant Seal (www.elephantseal.org) guides demystify the behavior of these giant beasts.

Mission San Antonio De Padua

Remote and evocative, this historical mission sits in the Valley of the Oaks, once part of the sprawling Hearst Ranch landholdings and now inside the boundaries of the US Army's Fort Hunter Liggett. Around the grounds, you can inspect the remains of a grist mill and irrigation system with aqueducts. It's seldom crowded, and you may have this vast site all to yourself, except during Mission Days in late April and La Fiesta on the second Sunday of June.

The mission was founded in 1771 by Franciscan priest Junípero Serra. Built with Native Californian labor, the church has been restored to its early-19th-century appearance, with a wooden pulpit, canopied altar and decorative flourishes on whitewashed walls. A creaky door leads to a cloistered garden anchored by a fountain. The museum has a small collection of utilitarian items such as an olive press and a weaving loom once used in the mission's workshops.

You may be asked for photo ID and proof of your vehicle's registration at a nearby military checkpoint. From the north, take the Jolon Rd exit off Hwy 101 before King City and follow Jolon Rd (County Rte G14) about 18 miles south to Mission Rd. From the south, take the Jolon Rd (County Rte G18) exit off Hwy 101 and drive 22 miles northwest to Mission Rd.

San Simeon

Little San Simeon Bay sprang to life as a whaling station in 1852, by which time California sea otters had been hunted almost to extinction by Russian fur traders. Shoreline whaling was practiced to catch gray whales migrating between Alaskan feeding grounds and birthing waters in Baja California. In 1865 Senator George Hearst purchased 45,000 acres of ranch land and established a small settlement beside the sea. Designed by architect Julia Morgan, the historic 19th-century houses today are rented to employees of the Hearst Corporation's 82,000-acre free-range cattle ranch.

◉ Sights & Activities

William Randolph Hearst Memorial State Beach   BEACH
(www.parks.ca.gov; Hwy 1; ☉dawn-dusk) FREE
Across from Hearst Castle (p322), this bayfront beach is a pleasantly sandy stretch punctuated by rock outcroppings, kelp forests, a wooden pier (fishing permitted) and picnic areas with barbecue grills.

Kayak Outfitters   KAYAKING
(☑805-927-1787; www.kayakcambria.com; Hwy 1; single/double kayak rentals from $20/40, tours

CENTRAL COAST POINT PIEDRAS BLANCAS

$50-110; ⊙10am-4pm or later mid-Jun–early Sep, call for off-season hours) Right on San Simeon's beach, you can rent sea kayaks, wetsuits, stand-up paddle boarding (SUP) sets, bodyboards and surfboards, or take a kayak-fishing trip or a guided paddle around San Simeon Cove. Sea kayaking along the famed Moonstone Beach south at Cambria is another excellent option.

🍴 Sleeping & Eating

Modern San Simeon is nothing more than a strip of unexciting motels and lackluster restaurants. There are better-value places to stay and eat in Cambria and beach towns further south, such as Cayucos and Morro Bay.

Hearst San Simeon
State Park Campground　　CAMPGROUND $
(✒reservations 800-444-7275; www.reserve america.com; Hwy 1; tent & RV sites $25) About 5 miles south of Hearst Castle are two state-park campgrounds: **San Simeon Creek**, with coin-op hot showers and flush toilets; and undeveloped **Washburn**, located along a dirt road. Drinking water is available at both.

Morgan　　MOTEL $$
(✒805-927-3828; www.hotel-morgan.com; 9135 Hearst Dr; r from $179; 🛜🐾🍳) Although rates are high for these revamped motel-style accommodations, the oceanfront setting makes up for a lot, as do gas fireplaces in deluxe rooms. Complimentary continental breakfast and board games to borrow. Pet fee $25.

Sebastian's　　AMERICAN $
(✒805-927-3307; www.facebook.com/Sebastians SanSimeon; 442 SLO–San Simeon Rd; mains $9-14; ⊙11am-4pm Tue-Sun) Down a side road across Hwy 1 from Hearst Castle, this tiny historic market sells cold drinks, Hearst Ranch beef burgers, giant deli sandwiches and salads for beach picnics at San Simeon Cove. Hearst Ranch Winery tastings are available at the copper-top bar.

Hearst Castle

Perched high on a hill, **Hearst Castle** (✒info 805-927-2020, reservations 800-444-4445; www.hearstcastle.org; 750 Hearst Castle Rd; tours) is a wondrous, historic, over-the-top homage to material excess. The estate sprawls across acres of lushly landscaped gardens, accentuated by shimmering pools and fountains, statues from ancient Greece and Moorish Spain and the ruins of what was in Hearst's day the world's largest private zoo (look for zebras grazing on the hillsides of neighboring Hearst Ranch). To see anything of this historic monument, you have to take a tour (try to book ahead).

The most important thing to know about William Randolph Hearst (1863–1951) is that he did not live like Citizen Kane. Not that Hearst wasn't bombastic, conniving and larger than life, but the moody recluse of Orson Welles' movie? Definitely not. Hearst also didn't call his 165-room estate a castle, preferring its official name, La Cuesta Encantada ('The Enchanted Hill'), or more often calling it simply 'the ranch.'

EYEING ELEPHANT SEALS

The elephant seals that visit coastal California each year follow a precise calendar. In November and December, bulls (adult males) return to their colony's favorite California beaches and start the ritual struggles to assert superiority. Only the largest, strongest and most aggressive 'alpha' males gather a harem of females. In January and February, adult females, already pregnant from last year's beach antics, give birth to pups and soon mate with the dominant males, who promptly depart on their next feeding migration. The bulls' motto is 'love 'em and leave 'em.'

At birth an elephant seal pup weighs about 75lb; while being fed by its mother, it puts on about 10lb a day. Female seals leave the beach in March, abandoning their offspring. For up to two months the young seals, now known as 'weaners,' lounge around in groups, gradually learning to swim, first in tidal pools, then in the ocean. The weaners depart by May, having lost 20% to 30% of their weight during a prolonged fast.

Between June and October, elephant seals of all ages and both sexes return in smaller numbers to the beaches to molt. Always observe elephant seals from a safe distance (minimum 25ft) and do not approach or otherwise harass these unpredictable wild animals, who surprisingly can move faster on the sand than you can!

From the 1920s into the '40s, Hearst and Marion Davies, his longtime mistress (Hearst's wife refused to grant him a divorce), entertained a steady stream of the era's biggest movers and shakers. Invitations were highly coveted, but Hearst had his quirks – he despised drunkenness, and guests were forbidden to speak of death.

California's first licensed woman architect Julia Morgan based the main building, Casa Grande, on the design of a Spanish cathedral, and over the decades she catered to Hearst's every design whim, deftly integrating the spoils of his fabled European shopping sprees, including artifacts from antiquity and pieces of medieval monasteries.

Much like Hearst's construction budget, the castle will devour as much of your time and money as you let it. In peak summer months, show up early enough and you might be able to get a same-day tour ticket, but it's always better to make reservations in advance.

Tours (adult/child 5-12yr from $25/12; daily except Thanksgiving, Christmas & New Year's Day, closing time varies) usually depart starting at 9am daily, with the last leaving the visitor center for the 10-minute ride to the hilltop by 4pm (later in summer). There are three main tours: the guided portion of each lasts about an hour, after which you're free to wander the gardens and terraces and soak up the views. Best of all are Christmas holiday and springtime evening tours, featuring living-history re-enactors who escort you back in time to the castle's 1930s heyday. For holiday and evening tours, book at least two weeks to a month beforehand.

Dress in plenty of layers: gloomy fog at the sea-level visitor center can turn into sunny skies at the castle's hilltop location, and vice versa. At the visitor center, a five-story-high theater shows a 40-minute historical film (free admission included with daytime tour tickets) about the castle and the Hearst family. Other facilities are geared for industrial-sized mobs of visitors. Before you leave, take a moment to visit the often-overlooked museum area at the back of the center.

RTA (☎805-541-2228; www.slorta.org) bus 15 makes a few daily round-trips to Hearst Castle via Cambria and Cayucos from Morro Bay ($23, 55 minutes), where you can transfer to bus 12 to San Luis Obispo.

Note that at the time of writing the famed Neptune Pool had been emptied for repairs, and restoration was expected to be completed by early- to mid-2018.

Cambria

With a whopping dose of natural beauty, the coastal idyll of Cambria is a lone pearl cast along the coast. Built on lands that once belonged to Mission San Miguel, one of the village's first nicknames was Slabtown, after the rough pieces of wood that pioneer buildings were constructed from. Today, just like at neighboring Hearst Castle, money is no object in this wealthy community, whose motto 'Pines by the Sea' is affixed to the back of BMWs that toodle around town.

◉ Sights & Activites

Although its milky-white moonstones are long gone, Moonstone Beach still attracts romantics to its oceanfront boardwalk and truly picturesque rocky shoreline. For more solitude, take the Windsor Blvd exit off Hwy 1 and drive down to where the road dead-ends, then follow a 2-mile round-trip blufftop hiking trail across Fiscalini Ranch Preserve.

A 10-minute drive south of Cambria, past the Hwy 46 turnoff to Pasa Robles' wine country, tiny Harmony (population 18) is an easygoing slice of Americana where an 1865 creamery houses artists' workshops, and a charming winery sits on a nearby hillside. A few miles further south there's good hiking at **Harmony Headlands State Park** (www.parks.ca.gov; Hwy 1; ◎6am-sunset) FREE.

🛏 Sleeping

Cambria's choicest motels and hotels line Moonstone Beach Dr, while quaint B&Bs cluster around the village.

Bridge Street Inn GUESTHOUSE $
(☎805-215-0724; www.bsicambria.com; 4314 Bridge St; r $50-90, vans $30; 🛜) Inside a 19th-century parsonage and surrounded by a pleasant garden, this European-style guesthouse has a quaint, raffish charm. There's a communal kitchen and five rooms with shared bathroom facilities, and the BBQ area is well-used by international guests. One additional room has a separate toilet and washbasin. There's parking outside for one smaller campervan, but you'll need to book ahead.

CENTRAL COAST CAMBRIA

Van guests can use the kitchen, bathroom and lounge facilities, and also jump on Bridge Street's wi-fi network.

Blue Dolphin Inn
MOTEL $$

(☎805-927-3300; www.cambriainns.com; 6470 Moonstone Beach Dr; r from $188; 🛜🐾) This sand-colored, two-story, slat-sided building may not look as upscale as other oceanfront motels, but rooms have romantic fireplaces, pillowtop mattresses and to-go breakfast picnics to take to the beach. Pet fee $25.

Fogcatcher Inn
HOTEL $$$

(☎805-927-1400; www.fogcatcherinn.com; 6400 Moonstone Beach Dr; r from $204; 🛜🏊🐾) Moonstone Beach Dr hotels are nearly identical, but this one stands out with its pool and hot tub. Faux English Tudor–style cottages harboring quietly luxurious modern rooms, some with fireplaces and ocean views. Pet fee $75.

✖ Eating & Drinking

It's a short walk between cutesy cafes and interesting restaurants in Cambria's East Village.

Linn's Easy as Pie Cafe
AMERICAN $

(☎805-927-0371; www.linnsfruitbin.com; 4251 Bridge St; dishes $6-12; ⊙10am-7pm Mon-Thu, to 8m Fri-Sat; 👶) If you don't have time to visit Linn's original farm stand on Santa Rosa Creek Rd (a 20-minute drive east via Main St), you can fork into its famous olallieberry pie at this take-out counter that delivers soups, salads, sandwiches and comfort fare such as chicken pot pie to a sunny deck.

Robin's
INTERNATIONAL $$

(☎805-927-5007; www.robinsrestaurant.com; 4095 Burton Dr; lunch $13-19, dinner $24-33; ⊙11am-9pm Sun-Thu, to 9:30pm Fri-Sat; 🅿) Global flavors from Asia and India feature on the wide-ranging menu at Robin's. Relax under the shaded arbor canopy in the rustic courtyard and graze on Indian flatbreads or Vietnamese spring rolls, or tuck into surprising lamb-curry burritos. A stellar wine list is equally cosmopolitan, with labels from Australia, New Zealand, Spain and France complementing Californian favorites.

Harmony Cellars
BAR

(☎805-927-1625; www.harmonycellars.com; 3255 Harmony Valley Rd, Harmony; tasting fee $7; ⊙10am-5pm, to 5:30pm Jul & Aug) This popular hillside winery is strong on robust reds including Syrah, Cabernet Sauvignon and Zin-

fandel, and cheese and charcuterie platters ($30 to $48, must be ordered 24 hours in advance) are also available.

927 Beer Company
CRAFT BEER

(☎805-203-5265.; www.927beer.com; 821 Cornwall St; ⊙noon-7pm Mon-Sat, to 6pm Sun) Enlivened by colorful music posters – 927's friendly owner is a big fan of Pearl Jam – this nano-brewery tucked away behind Main St in the West Village features a relaxed neighborhood tasting room that's a real hit with locals and their canine companions. Our favorite brews are the Mudhoney Oatmeal Stout and the zesty Belgian-style Saison.

❶ Information

Cambria Chamber of Commerce (☎805-927-3624; www.cambriachamber.org; 767 Main St; ⊙9am-5pm Mon-Fri, noon-4pm Sat & Sun) Staffed by a friendly crew ready to dispense maps and information.

❶ Getting There & Away

Cambria is 140 miles south of Monterey and 39 miles north of San Luis Obispo. From San Luis Obispo, RTA (p339) bus 15 makes a few daily trips from Morro Bay via Cayucos to Cambria ($3, 35 minutes), stopping along Main St and Moonstone Beach Dr. Most buses continue north to Hearst Castle (p322).

Cayucos

With its historic storefronts housing antiques shops and eateries, the main drag of amiable, slow-paced Cayucos recalls an Old West frontier town. Just one block west of Ocean Ave, surf's up by the recently renovated pier.

◉ Sights & Activities

Fronting a broad white-sand beach, Cayucos' long wooden pier is popular with fishers. It's also a sheltered spot for beginner surfers.

Estero Bluffs State Park
PARK

(☎805-772-7434; www.parks.ca.gov; Hwy 1; ⊙sunrise-sunset) FREE Ramble along coastal grasslands and pocket beaches at this small state park, accessed from unmarked roadside pulloffs north of Cayucos. Look among the scenic sea stacks to spot harbor seals hauled out on tide-splashed rocks.

Good Clean Fun
WATER SPORTS

(☎805-995-1993; www.goodcleanfuncalifornia.com; 136 Ocean Front Ln; group surfing lesson or kayak tour from $75) By the beach, this friendly surf shop has all kinds of rental gear – wetsuits, body boards, surfboards, SUP sets and kayaks. Book in advance for surfing lessons and kayak (or kayak-fishing) tours.

Cayucos Surf Company SURFING
(☑805-995-1000;www.faccbook.com/CayucosSurf; 95 Cayucos Dr; 1hr private/2hr group lesson $90/100; ☺10am-5pm Sun-Thu, to 6pm Fri & Sat) Near the pier, this landmark local surf shop rents surfboards, body boards and wetsuits. Call ahead for learn-to-surf lessons.

🛏 Sleeping

Cayucos doesn't lack for motels or beach-front inns. If there's no vacancy or prices look too high, head 6 miles south to Morro Bay (p326).

Shoreline Inn on the Beach HOTEL $$
(☑805-995-3681; www.cayucosshorelineinn.com; 1 N Ocean Ave; r $159-249; 🐾) There are few beachside lodgings on Hwy 1 where you can listen to the surf from your balcony for such a reasonable price tag. Standard-issue rooms are spacious and perked up by sea-foam painted walls. It's also dog-friendly (pet fee $35)

Seaside Motel MOTEL $$
(☑805-995-3809; www.seasidemotel.com; 42 S Ocean Ave; d $80-170; 🕾) Expect a superwarm welcome from the hands-on owners of this vintage motel with a pretty garden featuring Cape Cod chairs and ocean views. Country-kitsch rooms may be on the small side, though some have kitchenettes. Cross your fingers for quiet neighbors.

★Cass House Inn INN $$$
(☑805-995-3669; www.casshousecayucos.com; 222 N Ocean Ave; d $265-345; ➰❄🕾) Inside a charmingly renovated 1867 Victorian inn, five boutique rooms beckon, some with ocean views, deep-soaking tubs and antique fireplaces to ward off chilly coastal fog. All rooms have plush beds, flat-screen TVs with DVD players and tasteful, romantic accents. The best eating and drinking in town is most pleasantly on-site.

🍴 Eating & Drinking

The versatile dining scene at Cacuyos stretches from excellent barbecue and fish tacos to fine dining in a heritage inn.

Brown Butter Cookie Co BAKERY $
(☑805-995-2076; www.brownbuttercookies.com; 98 N Ocean Ave; snacks from $2.50; ☺9am-6pm; 🐾) Seriously addictive cookies are baked in all sorts of flavors including almond, citrus, cocoa, coconut-lime and original butter. Buy a bagful to provide tasty sustenance as you negotiate a stroll along Cayucos' recently restored 1872 pier.

Ruddell's Smokehouse SEAFOOD $
(☑805-995–5028; www.smokerjim.com; 101 D St; dishes $4-13; ☺11am-6pm; 🐾🐕) 'Smoker Jim' transforms fresh-off-the-boat seafood into succulently smoked slabs, sandwiches topped with spicy mustard and fish tacos slathered in a unique apple-celery relish. Squeeze yourself in the door to order. Dogs are allowed at the sidewalk tables. If you're lucky, you might chance upon the Ruddell's food truck on summer weekends at craft breweries around the region.

Cass House Grill CALIFORNIAN, FRENCH $$
(☑805-995-1014; www.casshousecayucos.com; Cass House Inn, 222 N Ocean Ave; mains $13-32; ☺11am-3pm & 4-8:30pm Thu-Sun mid-Sep late May, plus Wed during summer) 🍴 The Grill's wood-fired oven is harnessed for pizza, empanadas and grilled prawn and lamb, and a lighter touch is evident in roast salmon and a delicate fettucine crammed with seasonal produce. Many of the ingredients are sourced locally and from Cass House's own gardens, and the wine and beer list both offer Californian provenance. See www.casshousecayucosevents.com for special winemaker dinners.

The adjacent Cass House Bakery is open from 7am Thursday to Sunday for coffee, scones and muffins.

Schooners Wharf BAR
(www.schoonerswharf.com; 171 N Ocean Ave; ☺11am-midnight) Come for drinks on the ocean-view deck, rather than the fried seafood. The cocktails are punchy and there's an OK selection of draft beers from central Californian breweries. Vistas of Cayucos' heritage pier come free of charge.

ℹ Getting There & Away

Cayucos is 15 miles south of Cambria and 19 miles north of San Luis Obispo. **RTA** (☑805-541-2228; www.slorta.org) bus 15 travels three to five times daily from Morro Bay ($2, 15 minutes) to Cayucos, continuing north to Cambria ($2, 20 minutes) and Hearst Castle ($2, 35 minutes).

Morro Bay

Home to a commercial fishing fleet, Morro Bay's biggest claim to fame is Morro Rock, a volcanic peak jutting dramatically from the ocean floor. It's one of the Nine Sisters, a 21-million-year-old chain of rocks stretching all the way south to San Luis Obispo. The town's less boast-worthy landmark comes courtesy of the power plant, whose three cigarette-shaped smokestacks mar the bay views. Along this humble, working-class stretch of coast you'll find fantastic opportunities for kayaking, hiking and camping.

◉ Sights & Activities

This town harbors natural riches that are easily worth a half-day's exploration. The bay itself is a deep inlet separated from the ocean by a 5-mile-long sand spit. South of Morro Rock is the Embarcadero, a small waterfront boulevard jam-packed with souvenir shops and eateries.

Morro Rock   LANDMARK
Chumash tribespeople are the only people legally allowed to climb this volcanic rock, now the protected nesting ground of peregrine falcons. You can laze at the small beach on the rock's north side, but you can't drive all the way around it. Instead, rent a kayak to paddle the giant estuary, inhabited by two-dozen threatened and endangered species, including brown pelicans, snowy plovers and sea otters.

Morro Bay Skateboard Museum   MUSEUM
(☏805-610-3565; www.mbskate.com; Embarcadero, Marina Sq; donations appreciated; ☺noon-5pm Mon-Wed & Fri, from 10am Sat-Sun; ⊕) With exhibits, posters and more than 200 skateboards from the 1930s to the 21st century, this excellent privately operated museum is essential for anyone who's ever fallen under the spell of zipping along on four urethane wheels. Look forward to damn fine souvenir T-shirts and merchandise, too.

Morro Bay Whale Watching   WHALE WATCHING
(☏805-772-9463; www.morrobaywhalewatching.com; 699 Embarcadero; adult/child/student $45/35/40; ☺tours 9am & 12:30pm; ⊕) Humpback whales visit the Morro Bay area from May to October, and then from December to May more than 20,000 gray whales pass by on their annual migration. Other species often seen include minke whales, dolphins, porpoises, sea lions and sea otters. Bring along binoculars for coastal and pelagic birdlife. Excursions take place on an open catamaran, so dress warmly. Tours only depart with a minimum of six passengers.

Kayak Shack   WATER SPORTS
(☏805-772-8796; www.morrobaykayakshack.com; 10 State Park Rd; kayak/SUP rental from $14/16; ☺usually 9am-4pm late May-Jun, to 5pm Jul-early Sep, 9am-4pm Fri-Sun mid-Sep–late May) No one gets you out on the water faster than this laid-back kayak, canoe and SUP rental spot by the marina in Morro Bay State Park. A no-frills DIY operation, this is a calmer place to start paddling than the Embarcadero. Guided kayak tours are also offered in conjunction with Central Coast Outdoors.

⟲ Tours

Sub-Sea Tours   BOATING
(☏805-772-9463; www.subseatours.com; 699 Embarcadero; 45min tour adult/child 3-12yr $18/10; ☺hourly departures usually 11am-5pm; ⊕) For pint-sized views of kelp forests and schools of fish, take the kids on a spin around the bay in a yellow semi-submersible with underwater viewing windows. Departures may be limited to twice daily outside of the peak season.

Central Coast Outdoors   TOURS
(☏805-528-1080; www.centralcoastoutdoors.com; tours $65-150) Leads kayaking tours (including sunset and full-moon paddles), guided hikes and cycling trips along the coast and to Paso Robles and Edna Valley vineyards.

✹ Festivals & Events

Morro Bay Winter Bird Festival   OUTDOORS
(☏805-234-1170; www.morrobaybirdfestival.org; ☺Jan) Bird-watchers flock here for guided hikes, kayaking tours and naturalist-led field trips, during which over 200 species can be spotted along the Pacific Flyway.

⌁ Sleeping

Dozens of motels cluster along Hwy 1 and around Harbor and Main Sts, between downtown Morro Bay and the Embarcadero.

California
State Park Campgrounds   CAMPGROUND $
(☏reservations 800-444-7275; www.reserveamerica.com; tent & RV sites $25-50; ⊕) In Morro Bay State Park, over 240 campsites are fringed by eucalyptus and cypress trees; amenities include coin-op hot showers and an RV dump station.

At the north end of town off Hwy 1, **Morro Strand State Beach** (☑ reservations 800-444-7275; www.reserveamerica.com; tent & RV sites $25-50) has 75 simpler oceanfront campsites.

456 Embarcadero Inn & Suites   HOTEL **$$**
(☑ 805-772-2700; www.embarcaderoinn.com; 456 Embarcadero; r from $200; P ⊗) Located at the quieter southern end of the Embarcadero, this recently renovated property features 33 chic and spacious rooms, some with excellent views of the estuary and Morro Rock. Decor is more modern than at a few other local accommodation spots, and online midweek discounts are good value. Ease into the Jacuzzi after an afternoon's kayaking.

Pleasant Inn Motel   MOTEL **$$**
(☑ 805-772-8521; www.pleasantinnmotel.com; 235 Harbor St; r $169-229; ⊗ ⊗) Two blocks uphill from the Embarcadero, this spiffy motel has nautical-esque rooms (some with compact kitchens) sporting sailboat photos on the walls, open-beam wooden ceilings and blue-and-white rugs underfoot. A recent renovation makes it one of the most welcoming places in town, and the team at reception have plenty of good restaurant advice. Pet fee $25.

Beach Bungalow Inn & Suites   MOTEL **$$**
(☑ 805-772-9700; www.morrobaybeachbungalow.com; 1050 Morro Ave; d $180-230; P ⊗ ⊗) This butter-yellow motor court's chic, contemporary rooms are dressed up with hardwood floors, plush rugs, pillowtop mattresses and down comforters for foggy nights. Cape Cod chairs circle a compact fire pit in the middle of the complex. Complimentary breakfasts are delivered to guests' rooms and the pet fee is $30.

★ Anderson Inn   INN **$$$**
(☑ 805-772-3434; www.andersoninnmorrobay.com; 897 Embarcadero; d $269-349; ⊗) Like a small boutique hotel, this waterfront inn has just a handful of spacious, soothingly earth-toned rooms. If you're lucky, you'll get a gas fireplace, spa tub and harbor views. The friendly owners infuse the whole property with an easygoing Californian cool. Weekday rates offer the best value.

✗ Eating

Predictably touristy seafood shacks line the Embarcadero, and a few other worthwhile eateries are scattered around Morro Bay.

Flavor Factory   BURGERS **$**
(☑ 805-772-4040; www.facebook.com/FlavorFactoryMB; 420 Quintana Rd; soup & burgers $9-13; ⊗ 11am-8pm Fri-Tue) ✔ Superlative gourmet burgers make this place located in a compact shopping mall worth seeking out. Classics like beef and bacon share the menu with ritzy combos with blue cheese or stuffed green chillies, and the concise list of six rotating craft beers is equally surprising. Even the seasonal soups and salad bar crammed with local produce prepared onsite are winners.

Giovanni's Fish Market & Galley   SEAFOOD **$**
(☑ 877-521-4467; www.giovannisfishmarket.com; 1001 Front St; mains $5-15; ⊗ market 9am-6pm, restaurant from 11am; ⊗) At this family-run joint on the Embarcadero, folks line up for batter-fried fish and chips and killer garlic fries. You'll have to dodge beggar birds on the outdoor deck. Inside there's a market with all the fixin's for a beach campground fish-fry.

The Galley Seafood Grill & Bar   SEAFOOD **$$$**
(☑ 805-772-7777; www.galleymorrobay.com; 899 Embarcadero; mains $24-48; ⊗ 11:30-10pm) Our pick of Morro Bay's Embarcadero restaurants, The Galley combines an absolute waterfront location and expert renditions of classic American dishes with a briny touch of the ocean. There's definitely nothing groundbreaking about the menu, but when you're hankering for crab cakes and fresh oysters, or perfectly grilled fish and a glass of white wine, this is where to come.

☕ Drinking & Nightlife

Explore the Embarcadero for good wine and craft beer, or head up the hill to Morro Bay's Main St for live music and the occasional DJ.

★ Libertine Pub   PUB
(☑ 805-772-0700; www.libertinebrewing.com; 801 Embarcadero; ⊗ noon-11pm Mon-Thu, 11am-11pm Fri-Sat, 10am-10pm Sun) Stroll down to the Embarcadero for barrel-aged and sour beers from one of California's most interesting breweries. Lots more excellent American craft beers are on the 48 taps, and entertainment comes from the bartenders spinning vintage vinyl, or occasional live gigs. Taster glasses make it easy for the traveling beer geek to dive in and explore some very special brews.

The Siren LOUNGE

(☎805-772-8478; www.thesirenmorrobay.com; 900 Main St; ⏰11am-2am Tue-Sat, from 9am Sun) A laidback spot for a quiet drink or game of pool during the week, The Siren is transformed into a rockin' live-music venue on Friday and Saturday nights. Beats range from blues and Americana through to indie rock and reggae, and crowding onto the dance floor is definitely encouraged after a few nine-buck cocktails or tasty craft brews.

ℹ️ Information

Morro Bay Visitor Center (☎805-225-1633; www.morrobay.org; 695 Harbor St; ⏰10am-5pm) Located a few blocks uphill from the Embarcadero, in the less touristy downtown area.

ℹ️ Getting There & Away

Morro Bay is 142 miles south of Monterey and 13 miles northwest of San Luis Obispo. From San Luis Obispo, **RTA** (☎805-541-2228; www.slorta.org) bus 12 travels hourly on weekdays and a few times daily on weekends along Hwy 1 to Morro Bay ($2.50, 25 minutes). Three to five times daily, bus 15 heads north to Cayucos ($2, 15 minutes), Cambria ($2, 35 minutes) and Hearst Castle ($2, 55 minutes).

From late May through early October, a **trolley** (single ride $1, day pass $3) loops around the waterfront, downtown and north Morro Bay, operating varying hours (no service Tuesday to Thursday).

Montaña de Oro State Park

In spring the hillsides are blanketed by bright California native poppies, wild mustard and other wildflowers, giving this **park** (Map p42; ☎805-528-0513; www.parks.ca.gov; 3550 Pecho Valley Rd, Los Osos; ⏰6am-10pm; P🅿️) *FREE* its Spanish name, meaning 'mountain of gold.'

Wind-tossed coastal bluffs with wild, wide-open sea views make it a favorite spot with hikers, mountain bikers and horseback riders. The northern half of the park features sand dunes and an ancient marine terrace visible due to seismic uplifting.

Once used by smugglers, **Spooner's Cove** is now a postcard-perfect sandy beach and picnic area. If you go tidepooling, avoid disturbing the marine creatures and never remove them from their aquatic homes. You can hike along the grassy ocean bluffs, or drive uphill past the visitor center inside a historic ranch house to the start of the exhilarating 7-mile loop trail tackling **Valencia Peak** (1346ft) and **Oats Peak** (1347ft).

🛏️ Sleeping

Montaña de Oro State Park Campground CAMPGROUND $

(☎reservations800-444-7275;www.reserveamerica.com; Montaña de Oro State Park; tent & RV sites $25) Tucked into a small canyon, this minimally developed campground has pleasantly cool drive-up and environmental walk-in sites. Limited amenities include vault toilets, drinking water and fire pits.

ℹ️ Getting There & Away

To reach Montaña de Oro State Park by private car from the north, exit Hwy 1 in Morro Bay at South Bay Blvd; after 4 miles, turn right onto Los Osos Valley Rd (which runs into Pecho Valley Rd) for 6 miles. From the south, exit Hwy 101 in San Luis Obispo at Los Osos Valley Rd, then drive northwest for around 16 miles.

ALONG HIGHWAY 101

Driving inland along Hwy 101 is a quicker way to travel between the Bay Area and Southern California. Although it lacks the striking scenery of coastal Hwy 1, the historic El Camino Real (King's Highway), established by Spanish conquistadors and missionaries, has a beauty of its own. Along the way are plenty of sights worth stopping for – from oak-dappled golden hills and ghostly missions to jaw-dropping sights in Pinnacles National Park and sprawling wineries.

San Juan Bautista

In atmospheric old San Juan Bautista, where you can practically hear the whispers of the past, California's 15th mission is fronted by the state's only remaining original Spanish plaza. In 1876 the railroad bypassed the town, which has been a sleepy backwater ever since. Along 3rd St, evocative historic buildings mostly shelter antiques shops and petite garden restaurants. Hark! That cock you hear crowing is one of the town's roosters, which are allowed by tradition to stroll the streets at will.

◉ Sights

Mission San Juan Bautista   CHURCH
(☑831-623-4528; www.oldmissionsjb.org; 406 2nd St; adult/child 5-17yr $4/2; ⊙9:30am-4:30pm; ♿) Founded in 1797, this mission claims the largest church among California's original 21 missions. Unknowingly built directly atop the San Andreas Fault, the mission has been rocked by earthquakes. Bells hanging in the tower today include chimes that were salvaged after the 1906 San Francisco earthquake toppled the original mission. Scenes from Alfred Hitchcock's thriller *Vertigo* were shot here, although the bell tower in the movie's climactic scene was just a special effect.

Below the mission cemetery, you can spy a section of El Camino Real, the Spanish colonial road built to link California's first missions.

**San Juan Bautista
State Historic Park**   PARK
(☑831-623-4881; www.parks.ca.gov; 2nd St, btwn Mariposa & Washington Sts; museum adult/child $3/free; ⊙10am-4:30pm) Buildings around the old Spanish plaza opposite the mission anchor this small historical park. Cavernous **stables** hint at San Juan Bautista in its 1860s heyday as a stagecoach stop. The 1858 **Plaza Hotel**, which started life as a single-story adobe building, now houses a little historical **museum**. Next door to the hotel, the **Castro-Breen Adobe** once belonged to Mexican general and governor José Castro. In 1848 it was bought by the Breen family, survivors of the Donner Party disaster.

🛏 Sleeping & Eating

San Juan Bautista features a few B&Bs but is conveniently visited as a day trip from Santa Cruz or Monterey.

**Fremont Peak
State Park Campground**   CAMPGROUND $
(☑reservations800-444-7275;www.reserveamerica. com; San Juan Canyon Rd; tent & RV sites $25) A pretty but primitive 25-site campground with vault toilets (no water) is shaded by oak trees on a hilltop with distant views of Monterey Bay.

Vertigo Coffee   CAFE $
(☑831-623-9533;www.facebook.com/vertigocoffee; 81 4th St; dishes $4-12; ⊙7am-7pm Tue-Fri, from 8am Sat & Sun) Rich espresso and pour-over brews, wood-fired pizzas and garden salads make this coffee-roaster's shop a real find.

Rotating exhibitions from local artists often fill the whitewashed walls, and seven taps of craft beer feature surprising brews from around the central Californian coast. Ask if anything from Brewery Twenty Five based in nearby Hollister is available.

❶ Getting There & Away

San Juan Bautista is on Hwy 156, a few miles east of Hwy 101, about a 20-minute drive south of Gilroy. Public transport is very limited, and the town is best visited with your own transport. Further south, Hwy 101 enters the sun-dappled eucalyptus grove that James Stewart and Kim Novak drove through in *Vertigo*.

Gilroy

About 30 miles south of San Jose, the self-proclaimed 'garlic capital of the world' hosts the jam-packed **Gilroy Garlic Festival** (www.gilroygarlicfestival.com) over the last full weekend in July. Show up for the chow – garlic fries, garlic ice cream and more – and cooking contests under the blazing-hot sun.

Unusual **Gilroy Gardens** (☑408-840-7100; www.gilroygardens.org; 3050 Hecker Pass Hwy; adult/child 3-10yr $50/40; ⊙11am-5pm Mon-Fri early Jun–mid-Aug, plus 10am-6pm Sat & Sun early Apr-Nov; ♿) is a nonprofit family-oriented theme park focused on food and plants. You've got to really love flowers, fruit and veggies to get your money's worth, though. Most rides such as the 'Mushroom Swing' are tame. Buy tickets online to save. From Hwy 101, follow Hwy 152 west; parking is $12.

Heading east on Hwy 152 toward I-5 **Casa de Fruta** (☑408-842-7282; www.casadefruta. com; 10021 Pacheco Pass Hwy; per ride $2.50-4; ⊙seasonal hours vary; ♿) **FREE** is a commercialized farm stand with an old-fashioned carousel and choo-choo train rides for youngsters.

Salinas

Best known as the birthplace of John Steinbeck and nicknamed the 'Salad Bowl of the World,' Salinas is a working-class agricultural center with down-and-out streets. It makes a thought-provoking contrast with the affluence of the Monterey Peninsula, a fact of life that helped shape Steinbeck's novel *East of Eden*. Historic downtown stretches along Main St, with the National Steinbeck Center capping off its northern end.

◉ Sights

★ National Steinbeck Center
MUSEUM

(☑ 831-775-4721; www.steinbeck.org; 1 Main St; adult/child 6-17yr $13/7; ⊙ 10am-5pm; 🚹) This museum will interest almost anyone, even if you don't know anything about Salinas' Nobel Prize–winning native son, John Steinbeck (1902–68), a Stanford University dropout. Tough, funny and brash, he portrayed the troubled spirit of rural, working-class Americans in novels like *The Grapes of Wrath*. Interactive exhibits and short video clips chronicle the writer's life and works in an engaging way. Gems include Rocinante, the camper in which Steinbeck traveled around the USA while researching *Travels with Charley*.

Take a moment and listen to Steinbeck's Nobel acceptance speech – it's grace and power combined.

Steinbeck House
HISTORIC BUILDING

(☑ 831-424-2735; www.steinbeckhouse.com; 132 Central Ave; ⊙ restaurant 11:30am-2pm Tue-Sat, gift shop to 3pm) Steinbeck was born and spent much of his boyhood in this house, four blocks west of the museum. It's now a twee lunch cafe, which we're not sure he'd approve of. Guided tours are given on select summer Sundays; check online for details.

✪ Festivals & Events

Steinbeck Festival
CULTURAL

(www.steinbeck.org; ⊙ early May) This three-day festival features films, lectures, live music and guided bus and walking tours.

California Rodeo Salinas
RODEO

(www.carodeo.com; ⊙ late Jul) Bull riding, calf roping, cowboy poetry and carnival rides.

California International Airshow
OUTDOORS

(www.salinasairshow.com; ⊙ late Sep) Professional stunt flying and vintage and military aircraft take wing.

🛏 Sleeping

Salinas has plenty of motels off Hwy 101, including at the Market St exit.

Laurel Inn
MOTEL $

(☑ 831-449-2474; www.laurelinnsalinas.com; 801 W Laurel Dr; r from $95; 🅿 ❄ 🛜 🐾) If chain motels don't do it for you, this sprawling, family-owned cheapie has cozy rooms that are nevertheless spacious.

✕ Eating

Cafes and restaurants feature in downtown Salinas, and at the time of research, spacious heritage buildings near the National Steinbeck Center were being repurposed to house new eating and drinking openings. Let us know what you discover.

First Awakenings
AMERICAN $

(☑ 831-784-1125; www.firstawakenings.net; 171 Main St; mains $8-13; ⊙ 7am-2pm; 🚹) Fork into diner-style breakfasts of fruity pancakes, crepes and egg skillets, or turn up later in the day for handcrafted sandwiches and market-fresh salads. Try the Sonoran frittata, an open-faced omelet crammed with spicy chorizo.

Giorgio's at 201
MEDITERRANEAN, PIZZA $$

(☑ 831-800-7573; www.201complex.com; 201 Main St; mains $15-37; ⊙ 4-9pm Mon-Thu, to 11pm Fri-Sat, 10am-3pm Sun) In a stately, high-ceilinged former bank, Giorgio's at 201 is the lead address in an expanding if compact enclave of restaurants and terrace cafes. Drop in for excellent pizza, pasta and Mediterranean cuisine – with occasional diversions into Asian flavors – and then check out what new eating, drinking or live-music destinations have been added since we last visited.

🍷 Drinking & Nightlife

Downtown Salinas has a compact selection of good pubs and bars, and the Alvarado Street Brewery & Tasting Room is definitely worth the short journey from central Salinas for craft-beer fans.

Farmers Union Pour House
CRAFT BEER

(☑ 831-975-4890; www.facebook.com/FarmersUnionPourHouse; 217 Main St; ⊙ 2-10pm Tue-Thu & Sun, to midnight Fri-Sat) Brick-lined walls and wooden floors combine with a thoroughly modern big screen displaying the 24 different beers on tap. Food options include cheese and charcuterie boards, or you can order pizza and full meals from the separate restaurant next door. Up to 15 Californian wines are also available.

Alvarado Street Brewery & Tasting Room
CRAFT BEER

(☑ 831-800-3332; www.alvaradostreetbrewery.com/salinas-brewery; 1315 Dayton St; ⊙ 3-8pm Tue-Fri, from 1pm Sat-Sun) This Salinas offshoot of the Monterey-based craft brewery is another excellent recent addition to the growing beer scene around Salinas.

Location-wise, it's in an industrial park around 3 miles south of downtown. Ask if the stonking 10.5% Triple IPA is on tap.

ℹ Information

Salinas 411 (☑ 831-594-1799; www.salinas411. org; 222 Main St, ☺ 11am-8pm)

ℹ Getting There & Away

Salinas is 106 miles south of San Francisco and 126 miles north of San Luis Obispo.

Amtrak (☑ 800-872-7245; www.amtrak.com; 11 Station Pl) runs daily *Coast Starlight* trains north to Oakland ($18, three hours) and south to Paso Robles ($20, two hours), San Luis Obispo ($28, 3¼ hours), Santa Barbara ($41, 6¼ hours) and LA ($58, 9¼ hours).

Greyhound (☑ 800-231-2222; www.greyhound. com; Station Pl) has a few daily buses north to Santa Cruz ($16, 65 minutes) and San Francisco ($21, 3½ to five hours), and south to Santa Barbara ($40, 4¾ hours). Buses depart from the Salinas railway station.

From the nearby **Salinas Transit Center** (110 Salinas St), **MST** (☑ 888-678-2871; www.mst. org) bus 20 goes to Monterey ($3.50, one hour, every 30 to 60 minutes).

Pinnacles National Park

Named for the towering spires that rise abruptly out of the chaparral-covered hills east of Salinas Valley, this off-the-beaten-path park protects the remains of an ancient volcano. The best time to visit Pinnacles National Park (☑ 831-389-4486; www.nps.gov/ pinn; per car $15; ℙ ♿) *✎* is during spring or fall; summer heat is extreme.

◉ Sights & Activites

Besides rock climbing (for route information, visit www.pinnacles.org), the park's biggest attractions are its two talus caves, formed by piles of boulders. Balconies Cave is almost always open for exploration. Scrambling through it is not an exercise recommended for claustrophobes, as it's pitch-black inside, making a flashlight essential. Be prepared to get lost a bit too. The cave is found along a 2.5-mile hiking loop from the west entrance. Nearer the east entrance, Bear Gulch Cave is closed seasonally, so as not to disturb a resident colony of Townsend's big-eared bats.

To really appreciate Pinnacles' stark beauty, you need to hike. Moderate loops of varying lengths and difficulty ascend into the High Peaks and include thrillingly narrow clifftop sections. In the early morning or late afternoon, you may spot endangered California condors soaring overhead. Get an early start to tackle the 9-mile round-trip trail to the top of Chalone Peak, granting panoramic views.

Rangers lead guided full-moon hikes and star-gazing programs on some weekend nights, usually in spring or fall. Reservations are required: call ☑ 831-389-4485 in advance or check for last-minute vacancies at the visitor center.

🛏 Sleeping & Eating

The **Pinnacles Campground Store** (☑ 831-389-4538; ☺ 3-4pm Mon-Thu, noon-6pm Fri, 9am-6pm Sat & Sun) sells water, drinks and basic snacks and supplies, but you're best to stock up for self-catering in supermarkets in King City or Salinas.

Pinnacles National Park Campground   CAMPGROUND **$**
(☑ 877-444-6777; www.recreation.gov; tent/RV sites $23/36; ⛺ ♿) On the park's east side, this popular family-oriented campground has over 130 sites (some with shade), drinking water, coin-op hot showers, fire pits and an outdoor pool (usually closed from October to March).

ℹ Information

Pinnacles National Park Visitor Center (☑ 831-389-4485; ☺ 9:30am-5pm daily, to 8pm Fri late Mar-early Sep) Information, maps and books are available on the park's east side from the small NPS visitor center inside the campground store.

ℹ Getting There & Away

There is no road connecting the two sides of Pinnacles National Park. To reach the less-developed **west entrance** (☺ 7:30am-8pm), exit Hwy 101 at Soledad and follow Hwy 146 northeast for 14 miles. The **east entrance** (☺ 24hr), where you'll find the visitor center and campground, is accessed via lonely Hwy 25 in San Benito County, southeast of Hollister and northeast of King City.

San Miguel

Founded in 1797, **Mission San Miguel Arcángel** (☑ 805-467-3256; www.mission sanmiguel.org; 775 Mission St; adult/child 5-17yr $3/2; ☺ 10am-4:30pm) suffered heartbreaking damage during a 2003 earthquake.

Although repairs are still underway, the church, cemetery, museum and gardens are open. An enormous cactus out front was planted during the early days of the mission.

Hungry? Look for a couple of no-name Mexican delis, where the limited options include massive shrimp burritos.

Paso Robles

In northern San Luis Obispo County, Paso Robles is the heart of a historic agricultural region where grapes are now the biggest money-making crop. Scores of wineries along Hwy 46 produce a brave new world of more-than-respectable bottles. The Mediterranean climate and laidback lifestyle is yielding other bounties as well, and olive oil, craft beer and artisan distilleries are growing in popularity. Paso's historic downtown centers on Park and 12th Sts, where boutique shops and wine-tasting rooms await.

◉ Sights & Activities

Around Paso Robles, you could spend days wandering country back roads off Hwy 46, running east and west of Hwy 101. Most wineries have tasting rooms and a few offer vineyard tours. For dozens more wineries and olive-oil farms to visit, browse www.pasowine.com.

Studios on the Park   GALLERY
(☑805-238-9800; www.studiosonthepark.org; 1130 Pine St; ⊘noon-4pm Mon-Wed, to 6pm Thu & Sun, to 9pm Fri-Sat) Artists from around the Central Coast work and display their art at this collection of open studios on the eastern edge of Paso Robles' town square. Up to 15 different artists work from six studios, and other facilities include art galleries and an excellent fine art shop. Check the website for always-interesting special exhibitions and what interactive classes are scheduled.

◉ Eastside

J Lohr Vineyards & Wines   WINERY
(☑805-239-8900; www.jlohr.com; 6169 Airport Rd; tastings free-$10; ⊘10am-5pm) A Central Coast wine pioneer, J Lohr owns vineyards in Napa Valley, Monterey's Santa Lucia Highlands and Paso's pastoral countryside. Knowledgeable staff guide you through a far-reaching wine list.

Tobin James Cellars   WINERY
(☑805-239-2204; www.tobinjames.com; 8950 Union Rd; ⊘10am-6pm) Anti-serious Old West saloon pours bold reds, including an outlaw 'Ballistic' Zinfandel and 'Liquid Love' dessert wine. No tasting fee.

Eberle Winery   WINERY
(☑805-238-9607; www.eberlewinery.com; 3810 E Hwy 46; tastings free-$10; ⊘10am-5pm) Offers lofty vineyard views and tours of its wine caves every half-hour from 10:30am to 5pm. Sociable tastings run the gamut of white and red varietals and Rhône blends.

◉ Westside

Tablas Creek Vineyard   WINERY
(☑805-237-1231; www.tablascreek.com; 9339 Adelaida Rd; tastings from $10; ⊘10am-5pm) ✔ Breathe easy at this organic estate vineyard reached via a pretty winding drive up into the hills. Known for Rhône varietals, the signature blends also rate highly. Free tours at 10:30am and 2pm daily (reservations necessary).

Castoro Cellars   WINERY
(☑805-238-0725; www.castorocellars.com; 1315 N Bethel Rd; tasting fee $5; ⊘10am-5:30pm) Husband-and-wife team produces 'dam fine wine' (the mascot is a beaver, get it?), including from custom-crushed and organic grapes. Outdoor vineyard concerts happen during summer.

Thacher Winery   WINERY
(☑805-237-0087; www.thacherwinery.com; 8355 Vineyard Rd; tastings $10; ⊘11am-5pm Thu-Mon) Breathe deeply as you drive up the dirt road to this historic ranch that makes memorable Rhône blends – 'Controlled Chaos' is a perennial fave.

✪ Festivals & Events

Wine Festival   WINE, FOOD
(www.pasowine.com; ⊘mid-May) Oenophiles come for Paso's premier Wine Festival in mid-May, but the Vintage Paso weekend, focusing on Zinfandel wines, in mid-March and the Harvest Wine Weekend in mid-October are just as much fun.

California Mid-State Fair   CARNIVAL, MUSIC
(www.midstatefair.com; ⊘mid-Jul) Twelve days of live rock and country-and-western concerts, farm exhibits, carnival rides and a rodeo draw huge crowds.

🛏 Sleeping

Adelaide Inn MOTEL **$$**
(📞 805-238-2770; www.adelaideinn.com; 1215 Ysabel Ave; r $104-161; 🅿️ @ 🛜 🏊) Fresh-baked cookies, muffins for breakfast, mini golf and a fitness room keep families happy at this motel just off Hwy 101.

⭐**Summerwood Inn** B&B **$$$**
(📞 805-227-1111; www.summerwoodwine.com; 2175 Arbor Rd; d from $300; 🚾🛜) 🅿️ Along Hwy 46 within an easy drive of dozens of wineries, this gorgeous inn renovated in cool neutral tones mixes vintage and modern elements. Each of the nine rooms is named after a wine varietal and has a gas fireplace and balcony overlooking the vineyards. Indulge with the chef's gourmet breakfast, afternoon hors d'oeuvres and evening desserts.

⭐**Hotel Cheval** BOUTIQUE HOTEL **$$$**
(📞 805-226-9995; www.hotelcheval.com; 1021 Pine St; d $330-475; 🚾🛜) Near downtown Paso Robles, this European-style boutique hotel has 16 rooms arrayed around a sheltered inner courtyard. Spacious guest accommodation features flat-screen TVs and fireplaces, and rates include breakfast. Stylish shared spaces incorporate a library – decked out with sumptuous leather couches – and the Pony Bar, serving Californian wines, and featuring live music from 5pm on Friday and Saturday. Rates are around $60 cheaper on weekdays.

Inn Paradiso B&B **$$$**
(📞 805-239-2800; www.innparadiso.com; 975 Mojave Ln; ste $395-425; 🛜🏊) An intimate B&B pulls off no-fuss luxury with four suites decorated with art and antiques, and perhaps a fireplace, a deep soaking tub, a canopy king-sized bed or French balcony doors. Breakfast generously overflows with local and organic produce. Pet fee $50.

🍴 Eating

⭐**La Cosecha Bar**
& Restaurant LATIN AMERICAN, SPANISH **$$**
(📞 805-237-0019; www.lacosechabr.com; 835 12th St; pizza $14-15, mains $21-30) The Honduran heritage of chef and owner Santos MacDonal shines through at this cosmopolitan bar and bistro translating from Spanish into 'the harvest.' That means a strong focus on local and seasonal produce crafted into dishes with a Latin American and Iberian flair. Combine one of Paso's best wine and beer lists with delicate Ecuadorian shrimp, paella or wood-fired pizza.

Check the website for regular dinner events partnering with local winemakers.

The Hatch Rotisserie & Bar AMERICAN **$$**
(📞 805-221-5727; www.hatchpasorobles.com; 835 13th St; mains $15-23; ⏰ 3-9pm Mon-Wed, to 10pm Thu, to 11pm Fri-Sat) Wood-fired treats in this heritage location combining shimmering chandeliers and rustic bricks include grilled octopus, rotisserie chicken and creamy bone marrow, and a sly sophistication is added to American comfort food including shrimp and grits and buttermilk fried chicken. Regular smoked-meat specials, craft beer and cocktails, and Paso Robles wine on tap all make The Hatch an essential destination.

Artisan CALIFORNIAN **$$$**
(📞 805-237-8084; www.artisanpasorobles.com; 843 12th St; shared plates $14-16, mains $17-36; ⏰ 4:30pm-9pm Mon-Thu, to 10pm Fri-Sat, 10am-2:30pm & 4:30-9pm Sun) 🅿️ Chef Chris Kobayashi often ducks out of the kitchen just to make sure you're loving his impeccable contemporary renditions of modern American cuisine, featuring sustainably farmed meats, wild-caught seafood and artisan California cheeses. Impressive wine, beer and cocktail menus. Reservations essential.

🍸 Drinking & Nightlife

Paso Robles is home to several excellent craft breweries, and the up-and-coming Tin City area south of the city also features cider bars, urban distilleries and wine-tasting rooms.

⭐**Tin City Cider Co** CIDER
(📞 805-293-6349; www.tincitycider.com; 3005a Limestone Way, Tin City; tastings $12; ⏰ 1-7pm Tue-Thu, 1-8pm Fri, 11am-6pm Sat-Sun) Joining the tangle of breweries, distilleries and wine-tasting rooms in Paso Robles' Tin City neighborhood, Tin City Cider's thoroughly modern tasting room showcases tart and tangy tipples crafted from apples. Their standard range is crisp and refreshing, and more complex flavors underpin innovative variations fermented with Belgian brewers' yeast, enlivened with passionfruit, or aged bourbon barrels or French oak.

Silva Brewing CR
(📞 805-369-2337; www.silvabrewing.com St; ⏰ 2-7pm Wed-Fri, noon-5pm Sat-S Silva is US brewing aristocrac

> **DON'T MISS**
>
> ## JAMES DEAN MEMORIAL
>
> In Cholame, about 25 miles east of Paso Robles via Hwy 46, there's a memorial near the spot where *Rebel Without a Cause* star James Dean fatally crashed his Porsche on September 30, 1955, at the age of 24. Ironically, the actor had recently filmed a public-safety campaign TV spot, in which he said, 'The road is no place to race your car. It's real murder. Remember, drive safely. The life you save might be mine.'
>
> Look for the shiny stainless-steel memorial wrapped around an oak tree outside the truck-stop Jack Ranch Cafe, which has old photographs and movie-star memorabilia inside.

previously with Green Flash Brewing in San Diego – and now he's crafting his own brews in a compact space in Paso Robles. Look forward to bold, hop-forward styles and also Belgian-influenced beers. Just through an adjoining door (literally!) is a separate craft-beer pub, so make a night of it.

Wine Shine DISTILLERY
(☎805-286-4453; www.wineshine.com; 3064 Limestone Way, Tin City; ☺1-5pm Fri-Sun) Grape juice sourced from Paso Robles wineries is the versatile basis for the innovative spirits crafted by Wine Shine. Sample brandies tinged with mango, ginger or cinnamon and aged in oak barrels, or try Wine Shine's Manhattan Project whiskey that is a tribute to the classic days of American cocktails.

BarrelHouse Brewing Co BREWERY
(☎805-296-1128; www.barrelhousebrewing.com; 3055 Limestone Way, Tin City; ☺2-8pm Wed-Thu, 11am-9pm Fri & Sat, to 8pm Sun) Detour south of downtown, where locals chill in the outdoor beer garden with ales, stouts, zingy sour beers and fruity Belgian-style brews. Live bands frequently play, and most evenings there's a local food truck in attendance.
an afternoon of it.
tours run on a first-come, first-
?pm from Friday to Sunday.
sed-toe shoes for safe-

525 Pine
Chuck
he was

DISTILLERY
www.refinddistillery.com;
11am-5pm) Paso Robles'
ry makes crisp botanical

brandy (gin) and also whiskey and flavored vodkas. Scores of lemons were being zested when we dropped by. Try all the spirits in the rustic and rural tasting room, and ask how the plans are going to open an urban tasting room in Paso Robles' iconic Fox Theater on the edge of downtown.

For more on the Paso Robles distillery scene see www.pasoroblesdistillerytrail.com, and download a touring map listing 10 different distilleries.

🔒 Shopping

Around Paso Robles' downtown square, side streets are full of wine-country boutiques.

Pasolivo FOOD & DRINKS
(☎805-227-0186; www.pasolivo.com; 8530 Vineyard Dr; ☺11am-5pm) Located on a pleasantly winding back road in Paso Robles wine country, Pasolivo's olive-oil tasting room features bold and earthy oils flavored with basil, citrus and rosemary. The laid-back ranch-style surroundings make a pleasant break from wine-tasting, and the attached shop sells excellent artisan foods and olive oil–based soaps and beauty products.

Paso Robles General Store FOOD, GIFTS
(☎805-226-5757; www.generalstorepr.com; 841 12th St; ☺10am-7pm) 🥐 Stock up on picnic provisions such as California-made pistachio butter, fresh local baguettes, fruit jams and more, plus home goods like lavender soap. Many of the products are locally sourced, organic and sustainable. Also an excellent source of gifts and homewares.

ℹ️ Information

Paso Robles Chamber of Commerce (☎805-238-0506; www.travelpaso.com; 1225 Park St; ☺8:30am-5pm Mon-Fri, 9am-5pm Sat, 10am-2pm Sun)

ℹ️ Geting There & Away

From an unstaffed **Amtrak station** (☎800-872-7245; www.amtrak.com; 800 Pine St), daily *Coast Starlight* trains head north to Salinas ($20, two hours) and Oakland ($32, 4¾ hours) and south to Santa Barbara ($29, 4¼ hours) and LA ($43, 7½ hours). Several daily Thruway buses link to more-frequent regional trains, including the *Pacific Surfliner*.

RTA (☎805-541-2228; www.slorta.org) bus 9 travels between San Luis Obispo and Paso Robles ($3, 70 minutes) hourly Monday to Friday, and a few times daily on weekends.

San Luis Obispo

Almost midway between LA and San Francisco, at the junction of Hwys 101 and 1, San Luis Obispo is a popular overnight stop for road-trippers. With no must-see attractions, SLO might not seem to warrant much of your time. Even so, this low-key town has an enviably high quality of life – in fact, it has been named America's happiest city. CalPoly university students inject a healthy dose of hubbub into the city's streets, bars and cafes throughout the school year. Nestled at the base of the Santa Lucia foothills, SLO is just a grape's throw from Edna Valley wineries, too.

◉ Sights

San Luis Obispo Creek, once used to irrigate mission orchards, flows through downtown. Uphill from Higuera St, **Mission Plaza** is a shady oasis with restored adobe buildings and fountains overlooking the creek. Look for the **Moon Tree**, a coast redwood grown from a seed that journeyed on board *Apollo 14*'s lunar mission.

Mission San Luis Obispo de Tolosa   CHURCH
(Map p337; ☑805-543-6850; www.missionsanluis obispo.org; 751 Palm St; suggested donation $5; ⊙9am-5pm late Mar-Oct, to 4pm Nov–mid-Mar; ⊞) Those satisfyingly reverberatory bells heard around downtown emanate from this active parish dating from 1772. The fifth California mission founded by Padre Junípero Serra, it was named for a 13th-century French saint. The modest **church** has an unusual L-shape and whitewashed walls decorated with Stations of the Cross. An adjacent building contains an old-fashioned **museum** about daily life during the Chumash tribal and Spanish colonial periods. Interesting guided tours of the mission take place most days at 1:15pm.

San Luis Obispo Museum of Art   MUSEUM
(Map p337; ☑805-543-8562; www.sloma.org; 1010 Broad St; ⊙11am-5pm, closed Tue early Sep-early Jul) FREE By the creek, this small gallery showcases the work of local painters, sculptors, printmakers and fine-art photographers, as well as traveling California art exhibitions.

🏃 Activities & Tours

For hiking with ocean views, head to Montaña de Oro State Park (p328), not far away from San Luis Obispo.

Margarita Adventures   ZIPLINING, KAYAKING
(☑805-438-3120; www.margarita-adventures.com; 22719 El Camino Real, Santa Margarita; adult/child zip-line tour $119/89; ⊙8am-4:30pm Thu-Tue; ⊞) Whoosh down five zip lines across the vineyards beneath the Santa Lucia Mountains at this historic ranch, about a 10-mile drive northeast of SLO via Hwy 101. Reservations are required and trips leave from Margarita Adventures' office in the main street of sleepy Margarita. Ziplining experiences are ten bucks cheaper from Monday to Friday.

Hop On Beer Tours   FOOD & DRINK
(☑855-554-6766; www.hoponbeertours.com; per person $30) Jump aboard these sociable minibus tours to explore the San Luis Obispo and Paso Robles craft-beer scenes. Tours visit up to four different breweries. Check the website for timings of Social Tours open to the public – usually on Friday, Saturday or Sunday nights, two to four times per month – as Hop On also runs private tours.

Tours depart from downtown San Luis Obispo. Note that beer needs to be purchased separately.

🎉 Festivals & Events

SLO International Film Festival   FILM
(www.slofilmfest.org; ⊙mid-Mar) This annual six-day celebration of film has been a mainstay of the SLO cultural calendar since 1993. Events and screenings are held around the greater San Luis Obispo County area, including in Paso Robles and Pismo Beach.

Concerts in the Plaza   MUSIC, FOOD
(www.downtownslo.com; ⊙Fri nights, Jun-Sep) Downtown's Mission Plaza rocks out with local bands and food vendors.

🛏 Sleeping

Motels cluster off Hwy 101 in San Luis Obispo, especially off Monterey St northeast of downtown and around Santa Rosa St (Hwy 1). A slew of interesting new openings has increased the range of accommodation in town.

HI Hostel Obispo   HOSTEL $
(Map p337; ☑805-544-4678; www.hostelobispo. com; 1617 Santa Rosa St; dm $32-39, r from $65, all with shared bath; ⊙check in 4:30-10pm; @🖂) On a tree-lined street near SLO's train station, this solar-empowered, avocado-colored hostel inhabits a converted Victorian, which gives it a bit of a B&B feel. Amenities include a kitchen, bike rentals (from $10 per day)

and complimentary sourdough pancakes and coffee for breakfast. BYOT (bring your own towel).

The Butler DESIGN HOTEL $$
(Map p337; ☑805-548-1884; www.thebutlerhotel. com; 1511 Monterey St; r $229-249; ☻☜) Just six stylish rooms fill this unique property that used to be an automotive workshop. There's definitely no grease and grime now evident in the rooms decked out with colorful artwork and featuring stellar bathrooms. Shared spaces include a lounge with design books, a record player (including plenty of vintage jazz vinyl), and a compact kitchen with drinks and snacks available.

Note that guest access is via a key code and there are no hotel staff resident at the property.

San Luis Creek Lodge HOTEL $$
(☑805-541-1122; www.sanluiscreeklodge.com; 1941 Monterey St; r $159-229; ❄@☜) Rubbing shoulders with neighboring motels, this boutique inn has fresh, spacious rooms with divine beds (and some have gas fireplaces and jetted tubs) inside three whimsically mismatched buildings built in Tudor, California arts-and-crafts, and Southern plantation styles. DVDs, chess sets and board games are free to borrow.

Madonna Inn HOTEL $$
(☑805-543 3000; www.madonnainn.com; 100 Madonna Rd; r $209-329; ❄@☜☒) The fantastically campy Madonna Inn is a garish confection visible from Hwy 101. Japanese tourists, vacationing Midwesterners and irony-loving hipsters adore the 110 themed rooms – including Yosemite Rock, Caveman and hot-pink Floral Fantasy (check out photos online). The urinal in the men's room is a bizarre waterfall. But the best reason to stop here? Old-fashioned cookies from the storybook bakery.

SLO Brew Lofts APARTMENT $$$
(Map p337; ☑805-543-1843; www.slobrew.com; 738 Higuera St; apts from $250; ☜) Located above a brewpub and live-music venue, SLO Brew Lofts offer a unique urban stay in downtown. Apartments range from one to three bedrooms – the lofts are suitable for families or friends – and stylish decor is partnered by cool touches like a refrigerator stocked with SLO Brew's fine products, and record players with stacks of vintage vinyl. Expect some noise from downstairs, especially on weekends.

✖ Eating

Downtown SLO has several excellent restaurants, befitting the area's farm-to-fork focus and wine-country heritage.

★**San Luis Obispo Farmers Market** MARKET $
(Map p337; ☑805-541-0286; www.downtownslo. com; Higuera St; ☻6-9pm Thu; ☒⊞) ☞ The county's biggest and best weekly farmers market turns downtown SLO's Higuera St into a giant street party, with smokin' barbecues, overflowing fruit and veggie stands, live music and free sidewalk entertainment, from salvation peddlers to wackadoodle political activists. Rain cancels it.

★**Thomas Hill Organics** BISTRO $$
(Map p337; ☑805-457-1616; www.thomashill organics.com; 858 Monterey St; mains $22-40; ☻11am-late Mon-Sat, from 10am Sun; ☒) ☞ More contemporary than its original namesake eatery in Paso Robles, Thomas Hill's San Luis Obispo opening presents seasonal menus amid a stylish combination of chandeliers and whitewashed walls. Secure a spot at the bar and combine Central Coast wines with a delicate salad of beets, burrata and pistachios, or devour a sausage-and-mushroom pizza with a zingy draft cider. For Sunday brunch and on warm summer evenings, the outside patio is the place to be.

Guiseppe's Cucina Rustica ITALIAN $$
(Map p337; ☑805-541-9922; www.giuseppes restaurant.com; 849 Monterey St; pizza & sandwiches $13-16, mains $21-36; ☻11:30am-11pm) ☞ Visit Guiseppe's for a leisurely downtown lunch dining on excellent salads, pizza and antipasti, or to grab a take-out meatball or Caprese sandwich from the deli counter out the front. Out the back, the facade of the heritage Sensheimer Brothers building looks over a shaded courtyard that's equally suited to long dinners of slow-roasted chicken and SLO County wines.

Luna Red FUSION $$
(Map p337; ☑805-540-5243; www.lunaredslo.com; 1023 Chorro St; shared plates $6-20, mains $20-39; ☻11:30am-9:30pm Mon-Thu, to midnight Fri, 9am-11:30pm Sat, to 9pm Sun; ☒) ☞ Local bounty from the land and sea, artisan cheeses and farmers-market produce pervade the chef's Californian, Asian and Mediterranean small-plates menu. Cocktails and glowing lanterns enhance a sophisticated ambience indoors, or

San Luis Obispo

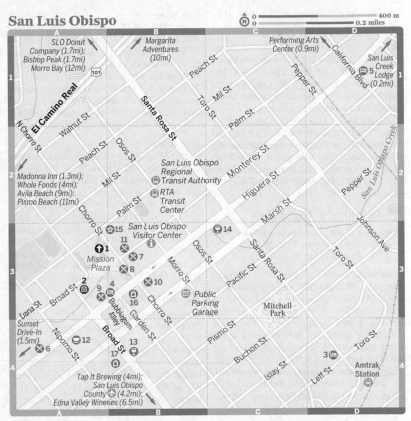

San Luis Obispo

⊙ Sights
1 Mission San Luis Obispo de
   Tolosa A3
2 San Luis Obispo Museum of Art A3

🛏 Sleeping
3 HI Hostel Obispo D4
4 SLO Brew Lofts B3
5 The Butler D1

🍴 Eating
6 Foremost Wine Co A4
7 Guiseppe's Cucina Rustica B3
8 Luna Red B3
9 Novo A3

10 San Luis Obispo Farmers Market B3
11 Thomas Hill Organics B3

🍷 Drinking & Nightlife
12 Kreuzberg A4
13 Libertine Brewing Company B4
14 Luis Wine Bar C3
   SLO Brew .... (see 4)

☆ Entertainment
15 Palm Theatre B3

🛍 Shopping
16 Hands Gallery B3
17 The Mountain Air B4

linger over brunch on the mission-view garden patio. Reservations recommended.

Novo   FUSION $$
(Map p337; ☏805-543-3986; www.novorestaurant.com; 726 Higuera St; mains $18-36; ⊙11am-9pm Mon-Thu, to 1am Fri & Sat, 10am-9pm Sun) 🖋 Novo spins out moreish European, Latin and Asian-inspired tapas with an artistic eye towards classy presentation. Pick from dozens of international beers, wines or sakes, then savor the view from tables on the

creekside deck. Reservations essential. It's a top spot for a leisurely Sunday brunch, too.

★ Foremost Wine Co
BISTRO $$$

(Map p337; ☑ 805-439-3410; www.foremostslo. com; 570 Higuera St; mains $24-32; ☺ 4-10pm Tue-Sat, 10am-2pm Sun; ☑) ✔ Ease into the warehouse interior softened by rustic tables crafted from repurposed timber, and experience some of San Luis Obispo's best farm-to-table dining. Intensely seasonal menus and regular wine-matching events showcase the absolute best of the region. Ask if the lamb biryani or crispy potato tacos are available, and don't leave without browsing the on-site wine shop.

⬤ Drinking & Nightlife

Downtown in SLO, Higuera St is littered with college-student-jammed bars, and for craft-beer fans there is plenty to look forward to.

Libertine Brewing Company
CRAFT BEER

(Map p337; ☑ 805-548-2337; www.libertinebrewing. com; 1234 Broad St; ☺ 11am-10pm Sun-Thu, to 11pm Fri-Sat) Barrel-aged and sour beers are the standout brews at this recent opening on the edge of downtown SLO. Saisions, kettle sours, goses and grisettes all appeal to the traveling beer geek, but the ambience is still welcoming and inclusive. When we visited, the finishing touches were being added to a spacious dining hall and live-music venue.

SLO Brew
BAR

(Map p337; ☑ 805-543-1843; www.slobrew.com; 736 Higuera St; ☺ 11:30am-2am Tue-Sat, to midnight Sun-Mon) SLO Brew's versatile setup incorporates an on-site brewery with good pub meals – combine the Red Reggae wheat beer with the Yard Bird roast-chicken pizza – and it's also a rocking live-music venue with regular gigs. Past performers have included The Strokes and Lee 'Scratch' Perry, so it's definitely worth checking out who's playing.

Tap It Brewing
BREWERY

(☑ 805-545-7702; www.tapitbrewing.com; 675 Clarion St; ☺ noon-6pm Sun, to 7pm Tue, to 8pm Wed, to 10pm Thu-Sat) Head out toward the airport to this upstart brewery's tap room, where cacti grow inside an old Jeep and live bands sometimes rock on the patio. Order up a beer-tasting rack, chill with the brewery's regular posse of visiting hounds, and look forward to being surprised by Tap It's always interesting seasonal brews.

Luis Wine Bar
WINE BAR

(Map p337; ☑ 805-762-4747; www.luiswinebar.com; 1021 Higuera St; ☺ 3-11pm Sun-Thu, to midnight Fri-Sat) Evincing style and sophistication, this downtown wine bar has wide-open seating, a strong craft-beer list of more than 70 brews, and small plates including cheese and charcuterie platters. Welcome to an urbane but unpretentious alternative to SLO's more raucous student-heavy bars and pubs.

Kreuzberg
CAFE

(Map p337; ☑ 805-439-2060; www.kreuzberg california.com; 685 Higuera St; ☺ cafe 7:30am-10pm daily, lounge 6-11pm Wed-Sat; ☏) ✔ This shabby-chic coffeehouse and roaster has earned a fervent following with its comfy couches, sprawling bookshelves and local art. Look forward to occasional live music partnered with craft beer and comfort food – think gourmet burgers, mac 'n' cheese and parmesan-risotto balls – in the adjacent lounge from Wednesday to Saturday.

☆ Entertainment

Sunset Drive-In
CINEMA

(☑ 805-544-4475; www.facebook.com/sunsetdrivein; 255 Elks Ln; adult/child 5-11yr $9/4; ⬤) Recline your seat, put your feet up on the dash and munch on bottomless bags of popcorn at this classic Americana drive-in. Sticking around for the second feature (usually a B-list Hollywood blockbuster) doesn't cost extra. It's about 2 miles southwest of downtown SLO off Higuera St.

Palm Theatre
CINEMA

(Map p337; ☑ 805-541-5161; www.thepalmtheatre. com; 817 Palm St; tickets $5-9) ✔ This small-scale movie house showing foreign and indie flicks just happens to be the USA's first solar-powered cinema. Seats are a bargain $5 on Mondays. Look for the SLO International Film Festival (p335) in March.

🔒 Shopping

For shopping fans to San Luis Obispo, downtown Higuera and Marsh Sts, along with all of the arcades and cross streets in between, are full of unique boutiques.

Hands Gallery
ARTS & CRAFTS

(Map p337; ☑ 805-543-1921; www.handsgallery. com; 777 Higuera St; ☺ 10am-6pm Mon-Wed, to 8pm Thu-Sat, 11am-5pm Sun) Brightly lit downtown shop sells vibrant contemporary pieces by California artisans, including jewelry, fiber arts, sculptures, ceramics and blown glass.

The Mountain Air
SPORTS & OUTDOORS

(Map p337; ☑805-543-1676; www.themountainair. com; 667 Marsh St; ☺10am-6pm Mon-Sat, to 8pm Thu, 11am-4pm Sun) At this local outdoor outfitter, pick up anything from campstove fuel and tents to brand-name clothing and hiking boots.

❶ Information

San Luis Obispo Visitor Center (Map p337; ☑805-781-2777; www.visitslo.com; 895 Monterey St; ☺10am-5pm Sun-Wed, to 7pm Thu-Sat)

Mission San Luis Obispo Post Office (Map p337; ☑800-275-8777; www.usps.com; 893 Marsh St; ☺10am-5pm Mon-Fri, to 2pm Sat) Centrally located in downtown SLO.

San Luis Obispo Library (☑805-781-5991; www.slolibrary.org; 995 Palm St; ☺10am-5pm Wed-Sat, to 8pm Tue; ☎) Free wi-fi and public internet terminals.

French Hospital (☑805-543-5353; www. frenchmedicalcenter.org; 1911 Johnson Ave; ☺24hr) Emergency-room services.

❶ Getting There & Away

Amtrak (☑800-872-7245; www.amtrak.com; 1011 Railroad Ave) runs daily Seattle–LA *Coast Starlight* and twice-daily SLO–San Diego *Pacific Surfliner* trains. Both routes head south to Santa Barbara ($35, 2¾ hours) and Los Angeles ($57, 5½ hours). The *Coast Starlight* connects north via Paso Robles to Salinas ($28, 3 hours) and Oakland ($41, six hours). Several daily Thruway buses link to more regional trains.

Off Broad St, over 3 miles southeast of downtown, **San Luis Obispo County Regional Airport** (☑805-781-5205; www.sloairport.com; 903 Airport Dr) has scheduled flights with United (San Francisco and LA), American Airlines (Phoenix) and Alaska Airlines (Seattle). A new four-gate terminal opened at the airport in 2017.

There's no public bus transport to the airport and a taxi from downtown is around $18.

San Luis Obispo Regional Transit Authority (RTA; Map p337; ☑805-541-2228; www.slorta. org; single-ride fares $1.50-3, day pass $5) operates daily county-wide buses with limited weekend services. All buses are equipped with bicycle racks. Lines converge on downtown's **transit center** (Map p337; cnr Palm & Osos Sts).

Avila Beach

Quaint, sunny Avila Beach lures crowds with its strand of golden sand and a shiny seafront commercial district of restaurants, cafes and shops. Explore the arcades behind Front St for art galleries and winery tasting rooms. Two miles west of downtown, Port San Luis is a working fishing harbor with a rickety old pier.

◉ Sights & Activities

For a lazy summer day at Avila Beach, you can rent beach chairs and umbrellas, surfboards, boogie boards and wetsuits underneath **Avila Pier**, off downtown's waterfront promenade. Over by the port, the beach has bonfire pits and the barking of sea lions accompanies your stroll atop **Harford Pier**, one of the Central Coast's most authentic fishing piers.

★ **Point San Luis Lighthouse**　LIGHTHOUSE
(Map p340; ☑guided hike reservations 805-528-8758, trolley tour reservations 805-540-5771; www. pointsanluislighthouse.org; lighthouse $5, incl trolley tour adult/child 3-12yr $20/15; ☺guided hikes 8:45am-1pm Wed & Sat, trolley tours noon & 1pm Wed & Sat) Just getting to this scenic 1890 lighthouse, overshadowed by Diablo Canyon nuclear power plant, is an adventure. The cheapest way to reach the lighthouse is via a rocky, crumbling, 3.75-mile round-trip hiking trail, for which guided-hike reservations are required. If you'd rather take it easy and ride out to the lighthouse, join an afternoon trolley tour (reservations also required). Inside the lighthouse you can inspect an original Fresnel lens and authentic Victorian-period furnishings.

The **Pecho Coast Trail** to the lighthouse is open only for guided hikes led by Pacific Gas & Electric (PG&E) docents, weather permitting. These guided hikes are free; children under nine years old are not allowed. Make reservations online at least two weeks in advance and bring plenty of water.

Avila Valley Barn　FARM
(Map p340; ☑805-595-2816; www.avilavalleybarn. com; 560 Avila Beach Dr; ☺9am-6pm mid-Mar–late Dec, to 5pm Thu-Mon Jan–mid-Mar; ☝) At this rural farmstand and pick-your-own berry farm, park alongside the sheep and goat pens, lick an ice-cream cone, then grab a basket and walk out into the fields to harvest jammy olallieberries in late spring and early summer, mid-summer peaches and nectarines, or autumn apples and pumpkins. During summer, the kids can jump aboard tractor rides or pony rides.

San Luis Obispo Bay

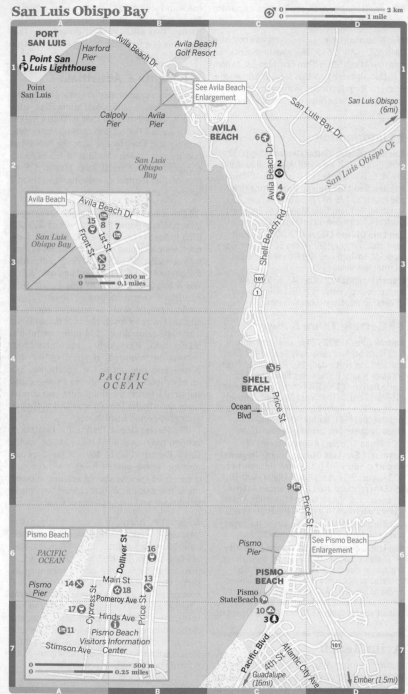

San Luis Obispo Bay

Sycamore Mineral Springs　　　SPA
(Map p340; ☑805-595-7302; www.sycamore springs.com; 1215 Avila Beach Dr; 1hr per person $15-20; ⊙8am-midnight) Make time for a therapeutic soak in one of these private redwood hot tubs discreetly laddered up a woodsy hillside. Call in advance for reservations, especially during summer and after dark on weekends. Last reservation time is 10:30pm.

Avila Hot Springs　　　HOT SPRINGS
(Map p340; ☑805-595-2359; www.avilahotsprings. com; 250 Avila Beach Dr; adult/child under 16yr $12/10; ⊙usually 8am-9pm Sun-Tue & Thu, to 10pm Wed, Fri & Sat; 🐾) Slightly sulfuric, lukewarm public swimming pool has kiddie waterslides that are usually open from noon to 5pm on Saturday and Sunday.

🛏 Sleeping

Accommodation in Avila Beach ranges from simple RV parking to a very comfortable boutique hotel.

★**Avila La Fonda**　　　INN $$$
(Map p340; ☑805-595-1700; www.avilalafonda. com; 101 San Miguel St; d from $269; @🛜) Downtown, this small boutique hotel is a harmonious mix of Mexican and Spanish colonial styles, with hand-painted tiles, stained-glass windows, wrought iron and rich wood. Gather around the fireplace for nightly wine and hors d'oeuvres. Complimentary beach gear to borrow for guests.

Avila Lighthouse Suites　　　HOTEL $$$
(Map p340; ☑805-627-1900; www.avilalighthouse suites.com; 550 Front St; ste from $359; ❄@🛜🛝) Any closer to the ocean and your bed would actually be sitting on the sand. With families

in mind, this apartment-style hotel offers suites and villas with kitchenettes. But it's the giant heated outdoor pool, Ping-Pong tables, putting green and life-sized checkers board that keep kids amused. Ask about steep off-season discounts. Reception is off First St.

✖ Eating & Drinking

Avila's Front St promenade features cafes and upscale restaurants. At Port San Luis, Harford Pier is home to seafood shops that sell fresh catch right off the boats.

Avila Beach Farmers Market　　　MARKET $
(Map p340; ☑805-801-1349; www.facebook.com/ AvilaBeachFarmersMarket; Front St; ⊙4-8pm Fri early Apr-late Sep) 🌿 With local farmers, food booths and rockin' live music, this outdoor street party takes over downtown's oceanfront promenade weekly from spring to fall.

PierFront Wine & Brew　　　WINE BAR
(Map p340; ☑805-439-3400; www.pierfrontwine andbrew.com; 480 Front St; ⊙noon-7pm Sun-Thu, to 9pm Fri-Sat; 🛜🐾) Californian craft beers and West Coast wines come with a side order of stellar sunset views of Avila's pier at this recent opening. Relax on a comfortable sofa in the eclectic interior or secure a sun-dappled spot under market umbrellas on the compact patio. Well-behaved dogs are welcomed as regulars, and PierFront's concise food menu includes flatbreads and cheese boards.

ⓘ Getting There & Away

Avila is around 10 miles south of San Luis Obispo and 8 miles northwest of Pismo Beach.

Between 10am and 4pm on Saturdays and Sundays from late March until mid-October, a free **trolley** (SCT; ☑ 805-781-4472; www.slorta. org) loops from Pismo Beach around downtown Avila Beach to Port San Luis; from early June to early September, extended hours are 10am to 6pm Thursday through Sunday. There's no public transportation offered between mid-October and late March.

Pismo Beach

Backed by a wooden pier that stretches toward the setting sun, Pismo Beach is where James Dean once trysted with Pier Angeli. Fronted by an invitingly wide, sandy beach, this 1950s-retro town feels like somewhere straight out of *Rebel Without a Cause* or *American Graffiti*. If you're looking for a sand-and-surf respite from coastal road tripping, break your journey here.

Pismo likes to call itself the 'Clam Capital of the World,' but these days the beach is pretty much clammed out. You'll have better luck catching something fishy off the pier, where you can rent rods. To rent a wetsuit, body board or surfboard, cruise nearby surf shops.

◎ Sights & Activities

Pismo Beach

Monarch Butterfly Grove PARK
(Map p340; ☑805-773-5301; www.monarch butterfly.org; Hwy 1; ☺sunrise-sunset; ⊕) ✔ FREE
From November through February, over 25,000 black-and-orange monarchs make their winter home here. Forming dense clusters in the tops of eucalyptus trees, they might easily be mistaken for leaves. Between 10am and 4pm during the roosting season, volunteers can tell you all about the insects' incredible journey, which outlasts any single generation of butterflies. Look for a gravel parking pull-out on the ocean side of Pacific Blvd (Hwy 1), just south of Pismo State Beach's **North Beach Campground** (399 S Dolliver St; tent & RV sites $40; ⊛).

Central Coast Kayaks KAYAKING
(Map p340; ☑805-773-3500; www.centralcoast kayaks.com; 1879 Shell Beach Rd, Shell Beach; kayak or SUP set rental $20-25, classes $60-75, tours $60-120; ☺9am-4:30pm Mon-Tue & Thu-Fri, to 5pm Sat-Sun) Paddle out among sea otters and seals and through mesmerizing sea caves, rock grottos, arches and kelp forests. Wetsuits, paddle jackets and booties available (small surcharge applies) with kayak rentals.

★ Festivals & Events

Wine, Waves & Beyond CULTURAL, FOOD
(www.winewavesandbeyond.com; ☺early Jun) Surfing competitions, surf-themed movies, wine tasting and a big bash on the beach with live music and food.

Clam Festival FOOD & DRINK
(www.pismochamber.com; ☺mid-Oct) Celebrate the formerly abundant and still tasty mollusc with a clam dig, chowder cookoff, food vendors and live music.

⌁ Sleeping

Pismo Beach has dozens of motels, but rooms fill up quickly and prices skyrocket in summer, especially on weekends. Resorts and hotels roost on cliffs north of town via Price St and Shell Beach Rd, while motels cluster near the beach and along Hwy 101.

Pismo Lighthouse Suites HOTEL $$
(Map p340; ☑805-773-2411; www.pismolighthouse suites.com; 2411 Price St; ste from $239; ▣⊖⊛ ⊛⊛) With everything a vacationing family needs – from kitchenettes to a life-sized outdoor chessboard, a putting green, table tennis and badminton courts – this contemporary all-suites hotel right on the beach is hard to tear yourself away from. Ask about off-season discounts and check out the onsite spa services. Pet fee $50.

Sandcastle Inn HOTEL $$$
(Map p340; ☑805-773-2422; www.sandcastleinn. com; 100 Stimson Ave; r $305; ☎) Many of these Eastern Seaboard-styled rooms are mere steps from the sand. The top-floor ocean-view patio is perfect for cracking open a bottle of wine at sunset or after dark by the fireplace.

✗ Eating

Good restaurants – including cheaper seafood joints – feature in downtown Pismo Beach, especially along Price St, and the nearby adjoining town of Arroyo Grande also has good eating.

Doc Burnstein's Ice Cream Lab ICE CREAM $
(☑805-474-4068; www.docburnsteins.com; 114 W Branch St, Arroyo Grande; snacks $4-12; ☺11am-9:30pm Sun-Thu, to 10:30pm Fri & Sat, reduced hours in winter; ⊕) In Pismo's neighboring Arroyo Grande, Doc's scoops up fantastical flavors like Merlot raspberry truffle and the 'Elvis Special' (peanut butter with banana swirls). Live ice-cream lab shows start at

SCENIC DRIVE: HWY 1 SOUTH OF PISMO BEACH

What to See

Hwy 1 ends its fling with Hwy 101 at Pismo Beach, veering off toward the coast. Some truly wild, hidden beaches beckon along this back-door route to Santa Barbara.

Guadalupe Dunes

You almost expect to have to dodge tumbleweeds as you drive into the agricultural town of Guadalupe. Five miles further west at **Rancho Guadalupe Dunes Preserve** (www.countyofsb.org/parks/day-use/rancho-guadalupe-dunes.sbc; off Hwy 166; ⊙7am-sunset; **P**) **FREE**, enormous Egyptian-esque film sets from Cecil B DeMille's 1923 Hollywood epic *The Ten Commandments* still lie buried in the sand. Learn more about the 'Lost City of DeMille,' the ecology of North America's largest coastal dunes, and the mystical Dunites who lived here during the 1930s back at downtown Guadalupe's small **Dunes Center** (☑805-343-2455; www.dunescenter.org; 1055 Guadalupe St; adult/child $5/free; ⊙10am-4pm Wed-Sun) museum.

Surf & Ocean Beaches

These wind-whipped beaches, one surf beach with a lonely Amtrak train whistlestop platform station, cozy up to the Vandenberg Air Force Base. On the 10-mile drive west of Lompoc and Hwy 1 (take Hwy 246/W Ocean Ave), you'll pass odd-looking structures supporting spy and commercial satellite launches. Between March and September, both Surf Beach and **Ocean Beach** (www.countyofsb.org/parks/day-use/ocean-beach.sbc; Ocean Park Rd, off Hwy 246; ⊙8am-sunset Oct-Feb) **FREE** may be closed to protect endangered Snowy Plovers during their nesting season.

Jalama Beach

Leaving Hwy 1 about 5 miles east of Lompoc, Jalama Rd follows 14 miles of twisting tarmac across ranch- and farmlands before arriving at utterly isolated **Jalama Beach County Park** (☑recorded info 805-736-3616; www.countyofsb.org/parks/jalama; Jalama Beach Rd, Lompoc; per car $10). To stay overnight, reserve a cabin in advance or arrive by 8am to get on the waiting list for a campsite in the crazily popular **campground** (☑805-568-2460; www.countyofsb.org/parks/jalama.sbc; 9999 Jalama Rd, Lompoc; tent/RV sites from $25/40, cabins $120-220; **P**🐾) – look for the 'campground full' sign back near Hwy 1 to avoid a wasted trip. There is a local general store selling basics, but it's recommended to bring your food and drink supplies.

The Route

Heading south of Pismo Beach, Hwy 1 slowly winds along, passing through Guadalupe and Lompoc, where you can detour to **La Purísima Mission State Historic Park** (☑805-733-3713; www.lapurisimamission.org; 2295 Purísima Rd, Lompoc; per car $6; ⊙9am-5pm, tours at 1pm Wed-Sun & public holidays Sep-Jun, daily Jul & Aug; **P**♿) 🗲. Past Lompoc, Hwy 1 curves east to rejoin Hwy 101 south of Santa Barbara's wine country, near Gaviota.

Time & Mileage

With all of the detours described above, it's a 165-mile drive from Pismo Beach to Santa Barbara. The drive takes at least 3½ hours without any stops or traffic delays.

7pm sharp on Wednesday. From Hwy 101 southbound, exit at Grand Ave.

Frutiland La Casa Del Sabor MEXICAN **$$**
(☑805-541-3663; www.facebook.com/frutiland.frutiland; 803 E Grand Ave, Arroyo Grande; mains $8-14; ⊙10am-6pm) Oversized, overstuffed Mexican *tortas* (sandwiches) will feed two, and there are two dozen varieties to choose from. Or order a platter of blue-corn-tortilla fish tacos with a mango or papaya *agua fresca* (fruit drink). To find this taco shack in Arroyo Grande, exit Hwy 101 southbound at Halcyon Rd.

Cracked Crab SEAFOOD **$$**
(Map p340; ☑805-773-2722; www.crackedcrab.com; 751 Price St; mains $16-59; ⊙11am-9pm Sun-

Thu, to 10pm Fri & Sat; ⊕) Fresh seafood and regional wines are the staples at this super-casual, family-owned grill. When the famous bucket o'seafood, full of flying bits of fish, Cajun sausage, red potatoes and cob corn, gets dumped on your butcher-paper-covered table, make sure you're wearing one of those silly-looking plastic bibs. No reservations, but the wait is worth it.

★ **Ember**   CALIFORNIAN $$$
(☑ 805-474-7700; www.emberwoodfire.com; 1200 E Grand Ave, Arroyo Grande; shared dishes $12-26, mains $26-36; ☺4-9pm Wed-Thu & Sun, to 10pm Fri & Sat) ✐ Chef Brian Collins, who once cooked at Alice Waters' revered Chez Panisse, has returned to his roots in SLO County. Out of this heart-warming restaurant's wood-burning oven come savory flatbreads, artfully charred squid and hearty red-wine-smoked short ribs. No reservations, so show up at 4pm or after 7:30pm, or be prepared for a very long wait for a table.

Sociable seating in the bar, where you can order off the full menu, is first-come, first-served. Look forward to being surprised with a different seasonal menu each month. The restaurant is west of Hwy 101 (southbound exit Halcyon Rd) in Arroyo Grande.

Oyster Loft   CALIFORNIAN, SEAFOOD $$$
(Map p340; ☑ 805-295-5104; www.oysterloft.com; 101 Pomeroy Ave; mains $20-45; ☺5-9pm Sun-Thu & to 10pm Fri-Sat) Delve into the appetizers menu – including crab cakes or orange-glazed octopus – or kick off with tuna tataki or fresh oysters from the crudo raw bar. Mains including pan-fried halibut are still seafood-heavy, but do venture successfully into steaks and chicken. Look forward to excellent views of the surf and the Pismo Beach pier from the restaurant's elevated position. Reservations recommended although walk-in diners can sit at the bar.

🍷 **Drinking & Nightlife**

Pismo Beach has a standout craft-beer bar, and downtown Arroyo Grande along W Branch St has welcoming pubs, bistros and wine-tasting rooms.

The Boardroom   BAR
(Map p340; ☑ 805-295-6222; www.theboardroompismobeach.com; 160 Hinds Ave; ☺2-10pm Mon-Wed, noon-10pm Sun & Thu, noon-1am Fri-Sat; 🎧) An exemplary range of craft beers – mainly from the West Coast of the US – combines with knowledgeable and friendly bartenders at this easygoing bar with a surfing ambience. Get to know the locals over a game of darts, maximize your travel budget during happy hour from 4pm to 6pm, and fill up on pizza, salads and panini.

Taste of the Valleys   WINE BAR
(Map p340; ☑ 805-773-8466; www.pismowineshop.com; 911 Price St; ☺noon-9pm Mon-Sat & to 8pm Sun) Inside a wine shop stacked floor to ceiling with hand-picked vintages from around California and beyond, ask for a taste of anything they've got open, or sample from a quite astounding list of more than 1000 wines poured by the glass.

☆ **Entertainment**

Pismo Bowl   BOWLING
(Map p340; ☑ 805-773 2482; www.pismobeachbowl.com; 277 Pomeroy Ave; game per person $4.25, shoe rental $3.25; ☺noon-10pm Sun-Thu, to midnight Fri & Sat; ⊕) Epitomizing Pismo Beach's retro vibe, this old-fashioned bowling alley is just a short walk uphill from the pier. Blacklight 'cosmic' and karaoke bowling rule Friday and Saturday nights.

ⓘ **Information**

Pismo Beach Visitors Information Center
(Map p340; ☑ 805-773-4382; www.classiccalifornia.com; 581 Dolliver St; ☺9am-5pm Mon-Fri, 10am-2pm Sat) Free maps and brochures. A smaller kiosk on the pier is open from 11am to 4pm on Sunday.

ⓘ **Getting There & Around**

Hourly from Monday to Friday, and a few times daily on weekends, **RTA** (☑ 805-541-2228; www.slorta.org) bus 10 links San Luis Obispo with Pismo's Premium Outlets mall ($2, 30 minutes), a mile from the beach, before continuing to downtown Arroyo Grande ($1.50, 15 minutes).

Santa Barbara County

Best Places to Eat

➡ Santa Barbara Shellfish Company (p361)

➡ Mesa Verde (p361)

➡ Bouchon (p362)

➡ Knead (p381)

➡ Yoichi's (p362)

Best Places to Sleep

➡ Belmondo El Encanto (p358)

➡ Pacific Crest Hotel (p357)

➡ Inn of the Spanish Garden (p359)

➡ Landsby (p374)

➡ Hotel Californian (p357)

Why Go?

Frankly put, this area is damn pleasant to putter around. Low-slung between lofty mountains and the shimmering Pacific, chic Santa Barbara's red-tiled roofs, white stucco buildings and Mediterranean vibe give credence to its claim of being the 'American Riviera.' It's an enticing place to loll on the beach, eat and drink extraordinarily well, shop a bit and push all your cares off to another day. The city's car-free campaign has brought electric shuttle buses, urban bike trails and earth-friendly wine tours. Mother Nature returns the love with hiking, biking, surfing, kayaking, scuba-diving and camping opportunities galore, from offshore Channel Islands National Park to arty Ojai, in neighboring Ventura County. Meanwhile, winemaking is booming in the bucolic Santa Ynez Mountains, west of Santa Barbara, where over a hundred wineries vie for your attention.

When to Go
Santa Barbara

Apr Balmy temperatures, fewer tourists than in summer. Wildflowers bloom on Channel Islands.

Jun Summer vacation and beach season begin. Summer Solstice Celebration parade.

Oct Sunny blue skies and smaller crowds. Wine Country harvest festivities.

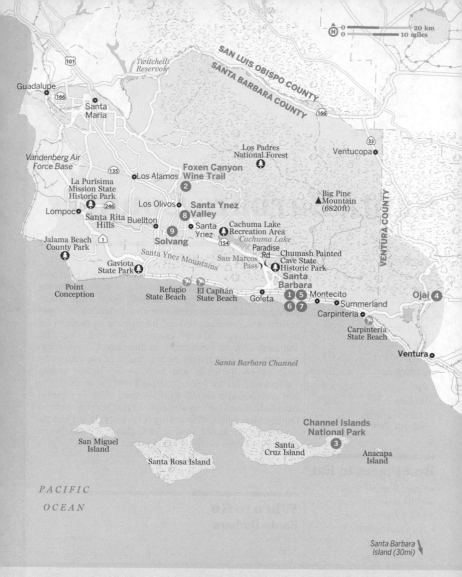

Santa Barbara County Highlights

1 Eyeing panoramic views atop the *Vertigo*–esque clock tower of the **Santa Barbara County Courthouse** (p347).

2 Following the **Foxen Canyon Wine Trail** (p367) to taste top-rated Pinot Noir.

3 Kayaking sea caves, hiking windswept cliffs and watching for whales in **Channel Islands National Park** (p384).

4 Rejuvenating your body and soul in **Ojai** (p379).

5 Strolling out to sea along **Stearns Wharf** (p348), California's oldest pier.

6 Ambling between wine-tasting rooms, hip bars and eateries, art galleries and unique shops in Santa Barbara's **Funk Zone** (p355).

7 Exploring Spanish-colonial history at **Mission Santa Barbara** (p347).

8 Pedaling past vineyards and organic farms through the **Santa Ynez Valley** (p371).

9 Eating *aebleskivers* (pancake popovers) by a kitschy windmill in the Danish village of **Solvang** (p373).

SANTA BARBARA

Perfect weather, beautiful buildings, excellent bars and restaurants, and activities for all tastes and budgets make Santa Barbara a great place to live (as the locals will proudly tell you) and a must-see place for visitors to Southern California. Check out the Spanish mission church first, then just see where the day takes you.

History

For hundreds of years before the arrival of the Spanish, Chumash tribespeople thrived in this region, setting up trade routes between the mainland and the Channel Islands and constructing redwood canoes known as *tomols*. In 1542 explorer Juan Rodríguez Cabrillo sailed into the channel and claimed it for Spain – then quickly met his doom (from a gangrenous leg injury) on a nearby island.

The Chumash had little reason for concern until the permanent return of the Spanish in the late 18th century. Catholic priests established missions up and down the coast, ostensibly to convert Native Americans to Christianity. Spanish soldiers often forced the Chumash to construct the missions and presidios (military forts) and provide farm labor; they also rounded up the tribespeople on the Channel Islands and forced them to leave. Back on the mainland, the indigenous population shrank dramatically, as many Chumash died of European diseases and ill treatment.

Mexican ranchers arrived after their country won independence in 1821. Easterners began migrating en masse after California's gold rush kicked off in 1849. By the late 1890s, Santa Barbara was an established SoCal vacation spot for the wealthy. After a massive earthquake in 1925, laws were passed requiring much of the city to be rebuilt in a faux-but-attractive Spanish Colonial–style,with white-stucco buildings and red-tiled roofs.

⊙ Sights

★MOXI   MUSEUM
(Wolf Museum of Exploration + Innovation; Map p356; ☑805-770-5000; www.moxi.org; 125 State St; adult/child $14/10; ⊙10am-5pm; 🐾) Part of the regeneration of this neglected strip of State St, Moxi's three floors filled with hands-on displays covering science, arts and technology themes will tempt families in, even when it's not raining outside. If all

MEETING MONARCHS

If you're here in late fall or winter, ask at the Outdoors Santa Barbara Visitors Center (p366) about the best places to see migratory monarch butterflies roosting in the trees – an extraordinary sight.

that interactivity gets too much, head to the roof terrace for views across Santa Barbara and a nerve-challenging walk across a glass ceiling.

Highlights include booths where you re-create sound effects from famous movie scenes, the 'mind ball' game where you use just your calm thoughts to move a metal ball against an opponent, and workshops that feature different make-and-learn activities.

Weekends get very busy with waits for many of the exhibits, so try to come during the week when it's quieter.

★Santa Barbara
County Courthouse   HISTORIC BUILDING
(Map p356; ☑805-962-6464; http://sbcourthouse.org; 1100 Anacapa St; ⊙8am-5pm Mon-Fri, 10am-5pm Sat & Sun) FREE Built in Spanish-Moorish Revival style in 1929, the courthouse features hand-painted ceilings, wrought-iron chandeliers, and tiles from Tunisia and Spain. On the 2nd floor, step inside the hushed mural room depicting Spanish-colonial history, then head up to El Mirador, the 85ft clock tower, for arch-framed panoramas of the city, ocean and mountains.

You can explore on your own, but you'll get a lot more out of a free, one-hour docent-guided tour: 2pm daily, plus 10:30am Monday to Friday.

★Mission Santa Barbara   CHURCH
(☑805-682-4713; www.santabarbaramission.org; 2201 Laguna St; adult $9, child 5-17yr $4; ⊙9am-5pm, last entry 4:15pm; 🅿🐾) California's 'Queen of the Missions' reigns above the city on a hilltop perch over a mile north of downtown. Its imposing Ionic facade, an architectural homage to an ancient Roman chapel, is topped by an unusual twin bell tower. Inside the mission's 1820 stone church, notice the striking Chumash artwork. In the cemetery the elaborate mausoleums of early California settlers stand out, while the graves of thousands of Chumash lie largely forgotten.

The self-guided tour starts in the pretty garden before heading to the cemetery (where Juana María, the Chumash girl made famous in *Island of the Blue Dolphins*, was buried). Next up is the church itself, followed by a series of rooms turned into a museum and exhibiting Chumash baskets, a missionary's bedroom and time-capsule black-and-white photos showing the last Chumash residents of the Mission and the damage done to the buildings after the 1925 earthquake. Docent-guided tours are usually given at 11am on Tuesday, Thursday and Friday, 10:30am on Saturday, and 12:30pm on Sunday; no reservations are taken.

The mission was established on December 4 (the feast day of St Barbara), 1786, as the 10th California mission. Of California's original 21 Spanish-colonial missions, it's the only one that escaped secularization under Mexican rule. Continuously occupied by Catholic priests since its founding, the mission is still an active parish church.

From downtown, take MTD bus 6 or 11, then walk five blocks uphill.

Santa Barbara Zoo
ZOO

(☑805-962-6310; www.sbzoo.org; 500 Ninos Dr; adult $17, child under 13 $10; ☺10am-5pm; Ⓟ❹) Small (so it's perfect for young kids) Santa Barbara Zoo has 146 species covering all creatures great and small, including several not found in many other zoos. Asian elephants Little Mac and Sujatha have been together here since 1972 and are hugely popular, as are the adorable meerkats. Don't miss the chance to see endangered California condors – probably your best bet for seeing them in the whole state – and giant anteaters. The antics of the Humboldt penguins always raise a smile.

Information panels give details on the animals and their habitats, plus tips for visitors on how to help preserve the creatures' natural environments (don't buy unsustainable palm oil, for example).

Parking is available (weekdays $7, weekends $10) or take the Waterfront shuttle for just 50¢.

Shoreline Park
PARK

(Shoreline Dr; ☺8am-sunset; Ⓟ❂) FREE For great views across the city, mountains and ocean (with the chance to spot whales in season and dolphins year-round), come to Shoreline Park, southwest of Santa Barbara. There are restrooms, picnic tables and a children's playground, and dogs are welcome.

Santa Barbara Museum of Natural History
MUSEUM

(☑805-682-4711; www.sbnature.org; 2559 Puesta del Sol; adult $12, child 2-12yr $7, youth 13-17yr $8, incl planetarium show $16/12/12; ☺10am-5pm; Ⓟ❹) The huge whale skeleton by the entrance whets the appetite for the city's natural history museum. The usual dioramas of stuffed animals are on display in dimly lit rooms (the bird collection is especially good on local species), but the joy of this place is that once you've learned about nature inside, you can head outside to the 'Museum's Backyard', a trail through woods by a creek, and engage with the real thing.

Santa Barbara Historical Museum
MUSEUM

(Map p356; ☑805-966-1601; www.santabarbara museum.com; 136 E De La Guerra St; ☺10am-5pm Tue-Sat, from noon Sun) FREE Embracing a romantic cloistered adobe courtyard, this peaceful little museum tells the story of Santa Barbara. Its endlessly fascinating collection of local memorabilia ranges from the simply beautiful, such as Chumash woven baskets and Spanish-colonial-era textiles, to the intriguing, such as an intricately carved coffer that once belonged to Junípero Serra. Learn about the city's involvement in toppling the last Chinese monarchy, among other interesting lessons in local history.

Stearns Wharf
WATERFRONT

(Map p356; www.stearnswharf.org; ☺open daily, hours vary; Ⓟ❹) FREE The southern end of State St gives way to Stearns Wharf, a rough wooden pier lined with souvenir shops, snack stands and seafood shacks. Built in 1872, it's the oldest continuously operating wharf on the West Coast, although the actual structure has been rebuilt more than once. During the 1940s it was co-owned by tough-guy actor Jimmy Cagney and his brothers. If you have kids, take them inside the Sea Center (Map p356; ☑805-962-2526; www.sb nature.org; 211 Stearns Wharf; adult $8.50, child 2-12yr $6, youth 13-17yr $7.50; ☺10am-5pm; Ⓟ❹).

Santa Barbara Botanic Garden
GARDENS

(☑805-682-4726; www.sbbg.org; 1212 Mission Canyon Rd; adult $12, child 2-12yr $6, youth 13-17yr $8; ☺9am-6pm Mar-Oct, to 5pm Nov-Feb; Ⓟ❹❂) Take a soul-satisfying jaunt around this 40-acre botanic garden, devoted to California's native flora. Miles of partly wheelchair-accessible trails meander past cacti, redwoods and wildflowers and by the old mission dam, originally built by Chumash tribespeople to irrigate the mission's fields.

TOP 10 BEACHES IN SANTA BARBARA

Although Santa Barbara's beaches are beauty-pageant prize winners, don't expect sunsets over the ocean because most of this coast faces south.

East Beach (Map p356; www.santabarbaraca.gov/gov/depts/parksrec; E Cabrillo Blvd; 🚹) Santa Barbara's largest and most popular beach is a long, sandy stretch sprawling east of Stearns Wharf, with volleyball nets for pick-up games, a children's play area and a snack bar. On Sunday afternoons, artists set up booths along the sidewalk, near the bike path.

Butterfly Beach (Channel Dr) No facilities but quite a high chance of celebrity spotting (the nearby Four Seasons Biltmore hotel is a popular destination for the rich and famous) at this small beach.

West Beach (Map p356; W Cabrillo Blvd; 🚹) Central, palm-tree-backed stretch of sand, right next to Stearns Wharf and the harbor (swimming isn't advisable). It's also the setting for large outdoor city events such as Fourth of July celebrations.

Leadbetter Beach (☏ 805-564-5418; Shoreline Dr, at Loma Alta Dr; per vehicle $2; P 🚹) One of Santa Barbara's most popular beaches, always busy with surfers, wind- and kite-surfers, joggers and sunbathers. Facilities include reservable picnic areas and showers.

Goleta Beach County Park (www.countyofsb.org/parks/day-use/goleta-beach.sbc; Sandspit Rd, Goleta; ⊙ 8am-sunset; P) Good beach for sunbathing, swimming and picnicking (nab a prized shaded spot if you can), or strolling the 1500ft-long pier for views out to the Channel Islands.

Arroyo Burro Beach County Park (Hendry's; ☏ 805-568-2460; www.countyofsb.org/parks; Cliff Dr, at Las Positas Rd; ⊙ 8am-sunset; P 🚹 🐾) Swim (lifeguards on duty), stroll or just picnic on this gem of a stretch of sand, also known as Hendry's Beach, 5 miles southwest of Santa Barbara. It's flat, wide, away from tourists and great for kids, who can go tide-pooling. It's also a popular local surf spot and the eastern section is dog-friendly (there's even a dog wash in the parking lot).

El Capitán State Beach (Map p50; ☏ 805-968-1033; www.parks.ca.gov; El Capitan State Beach Rd, Goleta; $10 per vehicle; ⊙ 8am-sunset; P 🚹) Head down from the low cliffs to enjoy swimming (confident bathers only), surfing and fishing from this pebbly beach, overlooked by native sycamore and oak trees. The seasonal beach store opens April to mid-September and sells basic groceries and camping supplies.

Thousand Steps Beach (Shoreline Dr, southern end of Santa Cruz Blvd; ⊙ sunrise-10pm) Descend the cliffs on a historic staircase (don't worry, there aren't actually a thousand steps) for some windy beachcombing and tide-pooling (only at low tide), but no swimming. The beach is also accessible from Shoreline Park (p348) – head west along Shoreline Dr from the park and take a left on Santa Cruz Blvd.

Carpinteria State Beach (p378) Calm waters and tide pools make this idyllyic stretch of beach an ideal spot for families. Also a good location to see harbor seals and sea lions during winter.

Guided tours (included with admission) depart at 11am and 2pm on Saturday and Sunday, and 2pm on Monday. Leashed, well-behaved dogs are welcome.

If you're driving, head north from the mission to Foothill Blvd/Hwy 192, turn right and then left to continue on Mission Canyon Rd.

Santa Barbara Maritime Museum MUSEUM (Map p356; ☏ 805-962-8404; www.sbmm.org; 113 Harbor Way; adult $8, child 6-17yr $5; ⊙ 10am-5pm Thu-Tue; P 🚹) On the harborfront, this jam-packed, two-story exhibition hall celebrates the town's briny history with nautical artifacts, memorabilia and hands-on exhibits, including a big-game fishing chair from which you can 'reel in' a trophy marlin. Take a virtual trip through the Santa Barbara Channel, stand on a surfboard or watch deep-sea-diving documentaries in the theater. There's 90 minutes of free parking in the public lot or take the Lil' Toot water taxi (p367) from Stearns Wharf.

Southern California's Best Beaches

Hundreds of miles of Pacific beaches edge SoCal's golden coast – which makes choosing just one to visit almost impossible. Take your pick depending on what you prefer doing: launching your surfboard onto a world-famous break; snapping on a snorkel mask and peeking at colorful marine life; or just lazing on the sand.

1. Santa Monica (p397)

A carnival pier with a solar-powered Ferris wheel and a tiny aquarium for the kiddos sits atop this idyllic, 3-mile long strand, where LA comes to play.

2. Malibu (p397)

Celebrity residents aren't keen to share their paradisiacal pocket beaches, but with persistence and some insider tips, you too can share these million-dollar views.

3. Huntington Beach (p441)

Officially 'Surf City, USA,' Huntington Beach is everything you imagined SoCal beach life to be, from surfing by the pier to sunset bonfires on the sand.

4. Mission Beach (p464)

A day trip to San Diego's most fun-crazed beach should begin with a ride on the Giant Dipper wooden roller coaster and end with sunset along Ocean Front Walk.

5. Crystal Cove State Park (p449)

Tired of manicured beaches crowded with beach towels? Escape instead to this wilder, undeveloped Orange County gem for beachcombing and scuba diving.

6. Coronado (p464)

Pedal a beach cruiser along the Silver Strand, or frolic like Marilyn Monroe did on the golden sand fronting San Diego's landmark Hotel del Coronado.

7. East Beach (p349)

Next to historic Stearns Wharf, where Santa Barbara meets the sea, this easy-access beach fills with swimmers, volleyball players and even sea kayakers in summer.

8. Carpinteria State Beach (p378)

Even tots can get their feet wet or poke around the tide pools at this Santa Barbara County classic, where palm trees wave above soft sands.

MAREMAGNUM/GETTY IMAGES ©

LAGUNATICPHOTO/SHUTTERSTOCK ©

GAGLIARDIIMAGES/SHUTTERSTOCK ©

GERI LAVROV/GETTY IMAGES ©

VENTURE MEDIA GROUP/GETTY IMAGES ©

Santa Barbara Museum of Art   MUSEUM
(Map p356; ☎805-963-4364; www.sbmuseart. org; 1130 State St; adult $10, child 6-17yr $6, all free 5-8pm Thu; ☉11am-5pm Tue-Wed & Fri-Sun, to 8pm Thu; ♿) This thoughtfully curated, bite-sized art museum displays European and American masters – including Monet, Van Gogh and Degas – along with photography, classical antiquities and Asian artifacts and thought-provoking temporary exhibits. At the time of writing, some galleries were closed while the museum is retrofitted for earthquake protection.

Highlight tours of current exhibitions start at 1pm daily and are included in admission. It also has an interactive children's space, a museum shop and a cafe.

**El Presidio de Santa Barbara
State Historic Park**   HISTORIC SITE
(Map p356; ☎805-965-0093; www.sbthp.org; 123 E Canon Perdido St; adult $5, child under 17yr free; ☉10:30am-4:30pm) Founded in 1782 to defend the mission, this adobe-walled fort built by Chumash laborers was Spain's last military stronghold in Alta California. But its purpose wasn't solely to protect – the presidio also served as a social and political hub, and as a stopping point for traveling Spanish military. Today this small urban park harbors some of the city's oldest structures. On a self-guided walking tour, be sure to stop at the chapel, its interior radiant with rich hues.

🏃 Activities

Cycling
A paved **recreational path** stretches 3 miles along the waterfront in both directions from Stearns Wharf, west to Leadbetter Beach beyond the harbor and east just past East Beach. For more pedaling routes, Santa

---

> ### ℹ️ DIY WALKING TOURS
>
> Santa Barbara's self-guided, 12-block **Red Tile walking tour** is a convenient introduction to downtown's historical highlights. The tour's name comes from the half-moon-shaped red clay tiles covering the roofs of many Spanish Revival–style buildings. You can download a free map of this walking tour, as well as other paths including along the waterfront, from Santa Barbara Car Free (www.santabarbaracarfree.org). For a lazy stroll between wine-tasting rooms, follow the city's Urban Wine Trail (p363).

Barbara Bikes to Go offers free downloadable DIY cycling tours of the city, mountains and Wine Country, along with links to bicycle rentals and specialty shops.

Wheel Fun Rentals   CYCLING
(Map p356; ☎805-966-2282; http://wheelfun rentalssb.com; 23 E Cabrillo Blvd; ☉8am-8pm; ♿) Hourly rentals of beach cruisers ($9.95), mountain bikes ($10.95) and two-/four-person surreys ($28.95/38.95), with discounted half-day and full-day rates. A second, seasonal branch is in the Fess Parker Double Tree Hotel at 633 E Cabrillo Blvd.

Santa Barbara Bikes To-Go   CYCLING
(Map p356; ☎805-628-2444; www.sbbikestogo. com; 1 N Calle Cesar Chavez; bike rental per day $35-105; ☉9am-5pm) Delivers top-quality road and hybrid mountain bikes to wherever you're staying in Santa Barbara. Rentals include helmets and emergency-kit saddle bags. Discounts for multiday, weekly and monthly rentals; reservations essential.

Kayaking & Boating
Paddle the calm waters of Santa Barbara's harbor or the coves of the Gaviota coast, or hitch a ride to the Channel Islands for awesome sea caves.

Some tour companies offer year-round whale-watching boat trips, mostly to see grays in winter and spring, and humpbacks and blues in summer.

**Santa Barbara
Adventure Company**   KAYAKING
(Map p356; ☎805-884-9283; www.sbadventureco. com; 32 E Haley St; ☉office 8am-5pm Mon-Sat; ♿) The name says it all: if you want a company that provides a whole host of well-organized adventures then you've come to the right place. It offers everything from Channel Island kayaking ($179) to surf lessons ($89), and bike tours (from $119) to horseback riding ($150).

Paddle Sports Center   KAYAKING
(Map p356; ☎805-617-3425; http://paddlesports ca.com; 117b Harbor Way; SUP/kayak rental from $20/12; ☉usually 8am-6pm) Long-established, friendly outfitter offering year-round kayak and SUP rentals from Santa Barbara harbor and Goleta Beach. Walk-ins are welcome but reduced rates are available if you book online in advance.

Santa Barbara Sailing Center   CRUISE, SAILING
(Map p356; ☎805-962-2826; www.sbsail.com; Marina 4, off Harbor Way; ☉9am-6pm, to 5pm winter;

SANTA BARBARA COUNTY IN...

One Day

Spend your first morning exploring Santa Barbara's historic mission (p347) before visiting downtown's museums, landmarks and shops along **State St**, stopping at the county courthouse (p347) for 360-degree views from its clock tower. Grab lunch on State St and then soak up some rays at the city's East Beach (p349), walking out on to Stearns Wharf (p348) and down by the harbor for sunset. After dark, head to the **Funk Zone** for dinner and drinks in Santa Barbara's coolest neighborhood.

Two Days

Head up to Santa Barbara's Wine Country. Enjoy a do-it-yourself vineyards tour by car, motorcycle or bicycle along a scenic wine trail – Foxen Canyon (p367) and the Santa Rita Hills (p370) are exceptionally beautiful. Pack a picnic lunch or grab a bite in charming Los Olivos (p372) or Danish-esque Solvang (p373).

Three Days

Spend the morning cycling along the coast, surfing or sea-kayaking on the Pacific, or hiking in the Santa Ynez foothills. In the afternoon, drive to posh Montecito (p377) for shopping and people-watching, or hang loose in Carpinteria (p378), a retro beach town.

Four Days

Head east for a stop in arty Ojai (p379), up in the mountains and known for its hot springs and spas, or book a day trip from Ventura (p382) by boat to explore one of the rugged Channel Islands (p384).

) Climb aboard the *Double Dolphin*, a 50ft sailing catamaran, for a two-hour coastal or sunset cruise ($35). Seasonal whale-watching trips ($40) and quick half-hour spins around the harbor to view marine life ($18) are more kid-friendly. It also offers kayak and SUP rentals and tours.

Condor Express   CRUISE
(Map p356; 805-882-0088; www.condorcruises. com; 301 W Cabrillo Blvd; 2½/4½hr cruises adult from $50/99, child 5-12yr from $30/50;) Take a whale-watching excursion aboard the high-speed catamaran *Condor Express*. Whale sightings are guaranteed, so if you miss out the first time, you'll get a free voucher for another cruise.

Sunset Kidd's Sailing Cruises   CRUISE
(Map p356; 805-962-8222; www.sunsetkidd.com; 125 Harbor Way; cruises $40) Float in an 18-passenger sailboat on a 2½-hour whale-watching trip or a two-hour morning, after-noon, sunset-cocktail or full-moon cruise. Reservations recommended.

Surfing

Unless you're a novice, conditions are too mellow in summer – come back in winter when ocean swells kick back up. Santa Barbara's **Leadbetter Point** is best for beginners. Experts-only **Rincon Point** awaits just outside Carpinteria.

Surf-n-Wear's Beach House   SURFING
(Map p356; 805-963-1281; www.surfnwear. com; 10 State St; rental per hour/day wetsuit $4/16, bodyboard $4/16, surfboard $10/35, SUP set per day $50; 9am-6pm Sun-Thu, to 7pm Fri & Sat) Not far from Stearns Wharf, you can rent soft (foam) boards, bodyboards, wetsuits and SUP sets from this 1960s surf shop. It also sells modern and vintage surfboards, unique T-shirts and hoodies, colorful bikinis, shades, beach bags and flip-flops.

Hiking

Gorgeous day hikes await in the foothills of the Santa Ynez Mountains and elsewhere in the Los Padres National Forest. Most trails cut through rugged chaparral and steep canyons – sweat it out and savor jaw-dropping coastal views. Spring and fall are the best seasons for hiking, when temperatures are moderate. Always carry plenty of extra water and watch out for poison oak.

To find even more local trails to explore, browse Santa Barbara Hikes online (www. santabarbarahikes.com) or visit the Los Padres National Forest Headquarters (p365), west of the airport.

SANTA BARBARA FOR CHILDREN

Santa Barbara abounds with family-friendly fun for kids of all ages, from tots to tweens.

MOXI (p347) Santa Barbara's newest hands-on, kid-friendly attraction.

Santa Barbara Museum of Natural History (p348) Giant skeletons, an insect wall and a pitch-dark planetarium captivate kids' imaginations. It's a 0.5-mile drive uphill from the mission.

Santa Barbara Maritime Museum (p349) Peer through a periscope, reel in a virtual fish, watch underwater films or check out the model ships.

Santa Barbara Sailing Center (p352) Short sails around the harbor let young 'uns see sea lions up close.

Sea Center (p348) From touch tanks full of tide-pool critters and crawl-through aquariums to whale sing-alongs, it's interactive and educational. Hourly parking on the wharf costs $2.50.

Lil' Toot water taxi (p367) Take a joyride along the waterfront on this tiny yellow boat.

Chase Palm Park (Map p356; www.santabarbaraca.gov/gov/depts/parksrec; 323 E Cabrillo Blvd; ⊙ sunrise-10pm; 🚹) **FREE** Antique-carousel rides ($2, cash only) plus a shipwreck-themed playground decked out with seashells and a miniature lighthouse.

Arroyo Burro Beach County Park (p349) A wide, sandy beach, away from the tourists but not too far from downtown.

🕝 Tours

★ Architectural Foundation of Santa Barbara
WALKING

(📞 805-965-6307; www.afsb.org; adult $10, child under 12yr free; ⊙ 10am Sat & Sun weather permitting) Take time out of your weekend for a fascinating 90-minute guided walking tour of downtown's art, history and architecture. No reservations required; call or check the website for meet-up times and places.

Santa Barbara Trolley
BUS

(Map p356; 📞 805-965-0353; www.sbtrolley.com; adult $22, child 3-12yr $8; ⊙ 10am-3pm; 🚹) 🚐 Biodiesel-fueled trolleys make a narrated 90-minute one-way loop stopping at 14 major tourist attractions around the city, including the mission and the zoo. They start from the visitor center (hourly departures 10am to 3pm) and the hop-on, hop-off tickets are valid all day (and one consecutive day) – pay the driver directly, or buy discounted tickets online in advance.

Land & Sea Tours
TOURS

(Map p356; 📞 805-683-7600; www.out2seesb. com; 99 W Cabrillo Blvd; adult $30, child 2-9yr $15; ⊙ noon & 2pm, also 4pm daily May-Oct; 🚹) If you dig James Bond–style vehicles, take a narrated tour of the city on the *Land Shark,* an amphibious vehicle that drives right into the water. Trips depart from Stearns Wharf; buy tickets onboard (no reservations).

★★ Festivals & Events

To find out what's happening now, check the events calendars at www.santabarbaraca. com and www.independent.com.

Santa Barbara International Film Festival
FILM

(📞 805-963-0023; http://sbiff.org; 1528 Chapala St, Suite 203; from $60; ⊙ late Jan-early Feb) Film buffs and Hollywood A-list stars show up for screenings of more than 200 independent US and foreign films.

I Madonnari Italian Street Painting Festival
ART, FOOD

(www.imadonnarifestival.com; ⊙ Memorial Day weekend, generally last weekend in May; 🚹; 🚌 6, 11) **FREE** Colorful chalk drawings adorn Mission Santa Barbara's sidewalks over Memorial Day weekend, with Italian-food vendors and arts-and-crafts booths too.

★ Summer Solstice Celebration
FESTIVAL

(📞 805-965-3396; www.solsticeparade.com; ⊙ late Jun) **FREE** Kicking off summer, this wildly popular and wacky float parade down State St feels like something out of Burning Man. Live music, kids' activities, food stands, a wine-and-beer garden and an arts-and-craft show happen all weekend long.

Santa Barbara County Fair FAIR

(📞805-925-8824; www.santamariafairpark.com; Santa Maria Fairpark, 937 S Thornburg St, Santa Maria; adult/child $10/8, child under 5yr free; ⊙mid-Jul; ♿) This old-fashioned county fair combines agriculture exhibits, carnival rides and lots of food and wine. The fairgrounds are in Santa Maria, over an hour's drive northwest of Santa Barbara via Hwy 101.

French Festival CULTURE, ART

(📞805-963-8198; www.frenchfestival.com; Oak Park; ⊙mid-Jul; 🐾; 🚌3) FREE California's biggest Francophile celebration has lots of food and wine, world music and dancing, a mock Eiffel Tower and Moulin Rouge and even a poodle parade.

★**Old Spanish Days Fiesta** CULTURE, ART

(www.oldspanishdays-fiesta.org; ⊙late Jul-early Aug) FREE The entire city fills up for this long-running – if slightly overblown – festival celebrating Santa Barbara's Spanish and Mexican colonial heritage. Festivities include outdoor bazaars and food markets, live music, flamenco dancing, horseback and rodeo events and a big ole parade.

🛏 Sleeping

Prepare for sticker shock; even basic motel rooms by the beach command over $200 in summer. Don't arrive without reservations and expect to find anything reasonably priced, especially not on weekends. A good selection of renovated motels are tucked between the harbor and the 101 freeway, just about walking distance to everything. Cheaper motels cluster along upper State St and Hwy 101 northbound to Goleta and southbound to Carpinteria, Ventura and Camarillo.

★**Santa Barbara Auto Camp** CAMPGROUND $$

(📞888-405-7553; http://autocamp.com/sb; 2717 De La Vina St; d $175-215; 🅿❄🛜📺) 🐾 Ramp up the retro chic and bed down with vintage style in one of five shiny metal Airstream trailers parked near upper State St, north of downtown. All five architect-designed trailers have unique perks, such as a claw-foot tub or extra twin-size beds for kiddos, as well as full kitchen and complimentary cruiser bikes to borrow.

Book ahead; two-night minimum may apply. Pet fee $25.

Agave Inn MOTEL $$

(📞805-687-6009; www.agaveinnsb.com; 3222 State St; r from $119; 🅿❄🛜) While it's still just a motel at heart, this boutique-on-a-budget property's 'Mexican pop meets modern' motif livens things up with a color palette from a Frida Kahlo painting. Flat-screen TVs, microwaves, minifridges and air-con make it a standout option. Family-sized rooms have a kitchenette and pull-out sofa beds. It's a little north of town so a car is a necessity, or good walking shoes.

Castillo Inn MOTEL $$

(Map p356; 📞800-965-8570; www.sbcastilloinn. com; 22 Castillo St; r from $175; 🅿@🛜) Minutes from West Beach, the harbor and Stearns Wharf, you can't get better priced accommodations in central Santa Barbara than at the Castillo Inn. The simply decorated rooms at this spruced-up motel are large and bright and a continental breakfast (just fruit and muffins) is included in the rate. Some rooms have terraces.

Harbor House Inn MOTEL $$

(Map p356; 📞805-962-9745; www.harborhouse inn.com; 104 Bath St; r from $180; 🅿❄🛜) Down by the harbor, this friendly, converted motel offers brightly lit studios with hardwood floors and a beachy design scheme. Most have full kitchen and one has a fireplace. Rates include a welcome basket of breakfast goodies (with a two-night minimum stay) and beach towels, chairs, umbrellas and three-speed bicycles to borrow.

Hotel Indigo BOUTIQUE HOTEL $$

(Map p356; 📞805-966-6586; www.indigosanta barbara.com; 121 State St; r from $180; 🅿❄@🛜📺) 🐾 Poised between downtown and the beach, this petite Euro-chic boutique hotel has all the right touches: curated contemporary-art displays, outdoor terraces

---

ⓘ **SANTA BARBARA ART WALKS**

Prime time for downtown gallery hopping is **First Thursday** (www.santa barbaradowntown.com), from 5pm to 8pm on the first Thursday of every month, when art galleries on and off State St throw open their doors for new exhibitions, artists' receptions, wine tastings and live music, all free. Closer to the beach but similar in aim is the **Funk Zone Art Walk** (http://funkzone. net), happening on a bimonthly basis from 5pm to 8pm and featuring free events and entertainment at offbeat art galleries, bars and restaurants.

Downtown Santa Barbara

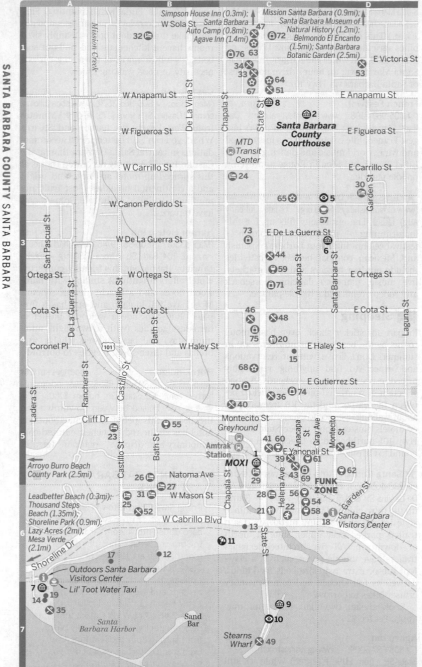

Simpson House Inn (0.3mi);
Santa Barbara
Auto Camp (0.8mi);
Agave Inn (1.4mi)

Mission Santa Barbara (0.9mi);
Santa Barbara Museum of
Natural History (1.2mi);
Belmondo El Encanto
(1.5mi); Santa Barbara
Botanic Garden (2.5mi)

W Sola St

E Victoria St

32

76
63
47
72

34
33

64
51

67

W Anapamu St

E Anapamu St

8

W Figueroa St

2

Santa Barbara County Courthouse

E Figueroa St

MTD Transit Center

W Carrillo St

E Carrillo St

30

24

W Canon Perdido St

65
5

57

73

E De La Guerra St

6

W De La Guerra St

44

W Ortega St

59

E Ortega St

71

Cota St

W Cota St

46

48

E Cota St

75

20

W Haley St

E Haley St

15

68

70

E Gutierrez St

36
74

40

Cliff Dr

Montecito St
Greyhound

55

23

Amtrak Station

41
60
45

1

E Yanonali St

MOXI

39
61

29

62

Natoma Ave

43
69

FUNK ZONE

26

W Mason St

28

56

27

31

25

22
54

52

58
18

W Cabrillo Blvd

21

13

Santa Barbara Visitors Center

11

Arroyo Burro Beach County Park (2.5mi)

Leadbetter Beach (0.3mi);
Thousand Steps
Beach (1.35mi);
Shoreline Park (0.9mi);
Lazy Acres (2mi);
Mesa Verde
(2.1mi)

17

12

Outdoors Santa Barbara
Visitors Center

Lil' Toot Water Taxi

7

19

9

14

35

Santa
Barbara Harbor

Sand Bar

10

Stearns
Wharf
49

and ecofriendly green-design elements. Peruse local-interest and art-history books in the library nook, or retreat to your room and wrap yourself up in a plush bathrobe. Parking $30. Pet fee $40.

Marina Beach Motel MOTEL **$$**
(Map p356; 📞805-963-9311; www.marinabeach motel.com; 21 Bath St; r from $155; P✳🛜🐾) Family-owned since 1942, this whitewashed, one-story motor lodge that wraps around a grassy courtyard is worth a stay just for the location. Right by the beach, tidy remodeled rooms are comfy enough and some have kitchenette. Complimentary beach-cruiser bikes to borrow. Small pets OK (fee $15).

Franciscan Inn MOTEL **$$**
(Map p356; 📞805-963-8845; www.franciscaninn. com; 109 Bath St; r $155-215; P✳🛜🏊) Settle into the relaxing charms of this Spanish Colonial two-story motel just over a block from the beach. Rooms differ in shape and decor, but some have kitchenette and all evince French-country charm. Embrace the friendly vibe, afternoon cookies and outdoor pool.

Motel 6 Santa Barbara-Beach MOTEL **$$**
(📞805-564-1392; www.motel6.com; 443 Corona del Mar; r $100-210; P✳🛜🏊🐾) The very first Motel 6 to 'leave the light on for you' has been remodeled with IKEA-esque contemporary design, flat-screen TVs and multimedia stations. It fills nightly; book ahead. Wi-fi costs $3 extra every 24 hours. Pet fee $10.

⭐**Hotel Californian** BOUTIQUE HOTEL **$$$**
(Map p356; www.thehotelcalifornian.com; 36 State St; r from $400; P✳🛜🏊) Hotel Californian is the new kid on the once-rundown block that is the lower end of State St. Spearheading the area's rehabilitation, it would be worth staying just for the prime location (next to the beach, Stearns Wharf and the Funk Zone) but its appeal goes way beyond geography. A winning architectural mix of Spanish Colonial and North African Moorish styles set a glamorous tone.

⭐**Pacific Crest Hotel** BOUTIQUE HOTEL **$$$**
(📞805-966-3103; www.pacificcrestsantabarbara. com; 433 Corona del Mar Dr; r from $235; P🛜🏊) 🐾 Wonderfully friendly Greg and Jennifer make sure all guests feel at home at their boutique motel, close to East Beach and the zoo. Landscaped grounds welcome you, rooms are spacious (bathrooms are small but plans are afoot to enlarge them) and come in cool, neutral tones that provide a soothing experience.

★ **Belmondo El Encanto** LUXURY HOTEL **$$$** (☑805-845-5800; www.elencanto.com; 800 Alvarado Pl; r from $475; P❄@☎☰☀) Triumphantly reborn in 2013, this 1908 icon of Santa Barbara style is a hilltop hideaway for travelers who demand the very best of everything. An infinity pool gazes out at the Pacific, while flower-filled gardens, fireplace lounges, a full-service spa and private bungalows with sun-drenched patios concoct the glamorous atmosphere perfectly fitted to SoCal socialites.

CAMPING & CABINS AROUND SANTA BARBARA

You won't find a campground anywhere near downtown Santa Barbara, but less than a half-hour drive west via Hwy 101, right on the ocean, are **El Capitán & Refugio State Beaches** (☑reservations 800-444-7275; www.reserveamerica.com; off Hwy 101; tent & RV drive-up sites $35, hike-&-bike tent sites $10; P❀). You'll also find family-friendly campgrounds with varying amenities in the mountainous **Los Padres National Forest** (☑877-444-6777; www.recreation.gov; Paradise Rd, off Hwy 154; campsites $30) and at **Cachuma Lake Recreation Area** (Map p38; ☑info 805-686-5055, reservations 805-568-2460; http://reservations.sbparks.org; 2225 Hwy 154; campsites $25-45, yurts $65-90, cabins $110-140; P❀), closer to Santa Barbara's Wine Country.

★**Inn of the**
Spanish Garden   BOUTIQUE HOTEL $$$
(Map p356; ☑805-564-4700; www.spanishgarden inn.com; 915 Garden St; r from $309; P♋❀ @❀❀) At this Spanish Colonial–style inn, casual elegance, first-rate service and a romantic central courtyard will have you lording about like the don of your own private villa. Rooms have a balcony or patio, beds have luxurious linens and bathrooms have oversized tubs. The concierge service is topnotch. Palms surround a small outdoor pool, or unwind with a massage in your room.

Simpson House Inn   B&B $$$
(☑805-963-7067; www.simpsonhouseinn.com; 121 E Arrellaga St; r $325-610; P❀❀) Whether you book an elegant room with a claw-foot bathtub or a sweet cottage with a fireplace, you'll be pampered at this Victorian-era estate ensconced by English-style gardens. From gourmet vegetarian breakfasts through to evening wine, hors d'oeuvres and sweets receptions, you'll be well fed too. In-room mod cons include Netflix. Complimentary bicycles and beach gear to borrow.

The hotel is perfect for a romantic break and is for adults only.

Canary Hotel   BOUTIQUE HOTEL $$$
(Map p356; ☑805-884-0300; www.canary santabarbara.com; 31 W Carrillo St; r $325-575; P❀@❀❀❀) 🖉 On a busy block downtown, this grand multistory hotel has a rooftop pool and sunset-watching perch for cocktails. Stylish accommodations show off four-poster beds and all mod cons. In-room spa services, Saturday yoga classes and bathroom goodies will soothe away stress, but ambient street noise may leave you sleepless (ask for an upper floor). Complimentary fitness-center access and cruiser bicycles.

Hungry? Taste local farm goodness at the hotel's downstairs restaurant, Finch & Fork.

Parking is $35; pets are welcome and stay for free.

White Jasmine Inn   B&B $$$
(Map p356; ☑805-966-0589; www.whitejasmine innsantabarbara.com; 1327 Bath St; r $170-350; P❀) Tucked behind a jasmine-entwined wooden fence, this cheery inn stitches together an arts-and-crafts bungalow and two quaint cottages. Rooms all have private bath and fireplace, most are air-conditioned and come with Jacuzzi. Full breakfast basket delivered daily to your door. No children under 12 years old allowed.

Brisas del Mar   HOTEL $$$
(Map p356; ☑805-966-2219; http://brisasdelmar inn.com; 223 Castillo St; r from $210; P❀@❀❀) Kudos for all the freebies (DVDs, continental breakfast, afternoon wine and cheese, evening milk and cookies), the newer Mediterranean-style front section and the helpful staff. The outdoor pool and mountain-view sun decks are great for winding down after a day of sightseeing. It's on a noisy street three blocks north of the beach, so ask for a room in the back.

✖ Eating

Restaurants abound along downtown's State St and by the waterfront, where you'll find a few gems among the touristy claptrap. More creative kitchens are found in the Funk Zone, while east of downtown, Milpas St has great taco shops. It's wise to book well in advance (a couple of weeks) for popular places or somewhere you're particularly keen to eat.

★**Corazon Cocina**   MEXICAN $
(Map p356; ☑805-845-0282; www.facebook.com/ sbcorazoncocina; 38 W Victoria St; ◷11am-9pm Tue-Sat, to 8pm Sun & Mon) The usual Mexican crowd-pleasers are all here (tacos *al pastor,* quesadillas, agua fresca) but made to such

perfection that previous versions pale in comparison. Head into the Santa Barbara Public Market and prepare to get food drunk (and to wait a while – it's popular).

★ **La Super-Rica Taqueria** MEXICAN $
(Map p356; ☑805-963-4940; 622 N Milpas St; ⊙11am-9pm Thu-Mon) It's small, there's usually a line and the decor is basic, but all that's forgotten once you've tried the most authentic Mexican food in Santa Barbara. The fish tacos, tamales and other Mexican staples have been drawing locals and visitors here for decades, and were loved by TV chef and author Julia Childs.

★ **Lucky Penny** PIZZA $
(Map p356; ☑805-284-0358; www.luckypennysb. com; 127 Anacapa St; pizzas $10-16; ⊙11am-9pm Sun-Thu, to 10pm Fri & Sat; ☑) Shiny exterior walls covered in copper pennies herald a brilliant pizza experience inside this Funk Zone favorite, right beside the Lark (p362). Always jam-packed, it's worth the wait for a crispy pizza topped with a variety of fresh ingredients, many vegetarian-friendly, or a wood-oven-fired lamb-and-pork-meatball sandwich. The coffee is taken seriously too.

★ **McConnell's Fine Ice Creams** DESSERTS $
(Map p356; ☑805-324-4402; www.mcconnells. com; 728 State St; pints from $10; ⊙11am-10pm Sun-Thu, to 11pm Fri & Sat; 🖤) Just try walking past this place on State St if you have a sweet tooth. A Santa Barbara institution since 1949, McConnell's uses local milk and other ingredients to produce an array of flavors, from the classics such as chocolate and vanilla to the adventurous like Turkish coffee and cardamom and gingersnaps.

★ **Arigato Sushi** JAPANESE $
(Map p356; ☑805-965-6074; www.arigatosb.com; 1225 State St; rolls from $7; ⊙5:30-10pm Sun-Thu, to 10:30pm Fri & Sat; 🖤☑) Phenomenally popular Arigato Sushi always has people milling around waiting for a table (no reservations taken) but it's worth the wait. Traditional and more unusual sushi, including lots of vegetarian options, plus salads and a dizzying array of hot and cold starters will make you order a sake pronto just to help you get through the menu.

It's noisy and bustling so not the place for a romantic dinner, unless you nab a table on the small patio on State St. Diners at the bar get to see the chefs in action right in front of them.

Dawn Patrol BREAKFAST $
(Map p356; ☑805-962-2889; www.dawnpatrolsb. com; 324 State St; breakfast $6-13; ⊙7:30am-2pm; ☑) Bright and colorful decor helps wake you up, and the option to build your own hash breakfast ($12.50) sets you up for exploring Santa Barbara. Bread is housemade and other ingredients are locally sourced. Add a coffee, smoothie or a mimosa (go on, you're on vacation) and you have a great start to the day.

Shop Cafe BREAKFAST $
(Map p356; ☑805-845-1696; 730 N Milpas St; breakfast $6.50-15; ⊙8am-3pm; 🖤) Away from the hustle of State St, the Shop still gets crowded thanks to its top-quality breakfast offerings. The poached eggs on toast are on the healthier end of the menu spectrum. In the opposite direction are the Yolo (fried chicken, biscuit and gravy) and the Tugboat (eggs Benedict with your choice of protein).

Los Agaves MEXICAN $
(Map p356; ☑805-564-2626; www.los-agaves. com; 600 N Milpas St; mains $9.25-16.95; ⊙11am-9pm Mon-Fri, 9am-9pm Sat & Sun) In the heart of east Santa Barbara's Mexican culinary scene, Los Agaves stands out for its well-cooked food and hacienda-style decor. Start with the zucchini-blossom quesadillas if they're in season and then take your pick from the mostly seafood and meat dishes. There's always a wait but that allows you time to peruse the menu carefully.

El Buen Gusto MEXICAN $
(Map p356; ☑805-962-2200; 836 N Milpas St; dishes $2-8; ⊙8am-9pm; ☑) At this red-brick strip-mall joint, order authentic south-of-the-border tacos, tortas, quesadillas and burritos with an agua fresca (fruit drink) or cold Pacifico beer. Mexican music videos and soccer games blare from the TVs. *Menudo* (tripe soup) and *birria* (spicy meat stew) are weekend specials.

Metropulos DELI $
(Map p356; ☑805-899-2300; www.metrofine foods.com; 216 E Yanonali St; dishes $2-10; ⊙8:30am-5pm Mon-Fri, 10am-5pm Sat) Before a day at the beach, pick up custom-made sandwiches and fresh salads at this gourmet deli in the Funk Zone. Artisan breads, imported cheeses, cured meats, and California olives and wines will be bursting out of your picnic basket.

Lilly's Taquería MEXICAN $
(Map p356; ☑805-966-9180; http://lillystacos.
com; 310 Chapala St; items from $1.60; ⊙10:30am-
9pm Sun, Mon, Wed & Thu, to 10pm Fri & Sat)
There's almost always a line roping around
this downtown taco shack at lunchtime.
But it goes fast, so you'd best be snappy
with your order – the *adobada* (marinated
pork) and *lengua* (beef tongue) are standout
choices. Second location in Goleta, west of
the airport, off Hwy 101.

Loquita TAPAS $
(Map p356; ☑805-880-3380; http://loquitasb.
com; 202 State St; mains from $11; ⊙5-10pm Sun-
Wed, to midnight Thu-Sat, 10am-2pm Sun brunch;
☑) Spanish tapas done the Spanish way –
simply and with top-quality ingredients. The
wine list is a curated best-of-Spain selection,
too, so pair your *pulpo* (octopus) with a
crisp Albariño and eat with a smile on your
face. Or loosen your belt for one of the best
paellas this side of the Atlantic. Sunday's
popular flamenco brunch is great fun.

⭐**Mesa Verde** VEGAN $$
(☑805-963-4474;http://mesaverderestaurant.com;
1919 Cliff Dr; mains $15-21; ⊙11am-9pm; ☑) 🌿
Perusing the menu is usually a quick job for
vegetarians – but not at Mesa Verde. There
are so many delicious, innovative all-vegan
dishes on offer here (the tacos with jackfruit
are a highlight) that meat-avoiding pro-
crastinators will be in torment. If in doubt,
pick a selection and brace yourself for fla-
vor-packed delights. Meat-eaters welcome
(and possibly converted).

Desserts are equally inspired – don't
hesitate to try the chocolate ganache if it's
available.

The location is in a residential neighbor-
hood west of the action, but it's a quick drive
to get here and most definitely worth the
effort.

⭐**Santa Barbara
Shellfish Company** SEAFOOD $$
(Map p356; ☑805-966-6676; http://shellfishco.
com; 230 Stearns Wharf; dishes $4-19; ⊙11am-
9pm; 🐾🦞) 'From sea to skillet to plate' sums
up this end-of-the-wharf seafood shack
that's more of a buzzing counter joint than
a sit-down restaurant. Chase away the seagulls as you chow down on garlic-baked
clams, crab cakes and coconut-fried shrimp
at wooden picnic tables outside. Awesome
lobster bisque, ocean views and the same
location for almost 40 years.

Boathouse CALIFORNIAN $$
(☑805-898-2628; http://boathousesb.com; 2981
Cliff Dr; mains from $14; ⊙7:30am-close; ☑🐾)
Water views and ocean air accompany your
healthy dining at the Boathouse, right on
Arroyo Burro Beach (p349). The outdoor pa-
tio is great for enjoying a cocktail and fancy
salad with other beachgoers, while the walls
inside display photos paying homage to the
area's surfing and rowing heritage.

Opal CALIFORNIAN $$
(Map p356; ☑805-966-9676; http://opalrestaurant
andbar.com; mains $16-30; ⊙11:30am-2:30pm
Mon-Sat, 5-10pm Sun-Thu, 5-11pm Fri & Sat; ☑)
Start with a cocktail (martinis are a specialty) and take your time choosing from
the inventive dishes on this Californian-
cuisine-meets-French-bistro-style restaurant
at the top end of State St. Strong flavors are
brought together and work well in things
like the homemade basil fettuccine with tiger
shrimp or lemongrass salmon with Thai curry. Wine pairings are suggested for each dish.

Depending on how you're feeling, you'll
either find the large open-plan dining space
buzzing or noisy.

Toma MEDITERRANEAN $$
(Map p356; ☑805-962-0777; www.tomarestaurant.
com; 324 W Cabrillo Blvd; ⊙5pm-close) Enjoy a
glass of wine or a cocktail before tucking
into some tasty pasta, flat breads or meat
and seafood dishes at one of Santa Barbara's
most popular restaurants. The decor's not
the most exciting but the food more than
compensates. Book well in advance.

Olio Pizzeria ITALIAN $$
(Map p356; ☑805-899-2699; www.oliopizzeria.
com; 11 W Victoria St; shared plates $5-24, pizzas
$15-21; ⊙11:30am-10pm; ☑) Just around the
corner from State St, this high-ceilinged
pizzeria with a happening wine bar proffers
crispy, wood-oven-baked pizzas, platters of
imported cheeses and meats, garden-fresh
insalate (salads), savory traditional Italian
antipasti and sweet *dolci* (desserts). The entrance is off the parking-lot alleyway.

Palace Grill CAJUN, CREOLE $$
(Map p356; ☑805-963-5000; http://palacegrill.
com; 8 E Cota St; mains lunch $10-22, dinner $17-
32; ⊙11:30am-3pm daily, 5:30-10pm Sun-Thu,
5:30-11pm Fri & Sat; 🐾) With all the exuber-
ance of Mardi Gras, this N'awlins-style grill
makes totally addictive baskets of house-
made muffins and breads, and ginormous
(if so-so) plates of jambalaya, gumbo ya-ya,

blackened catfish and pecan chicken. Stiff cocktails and indulgent desserts make the grade. Act unsurprised when the staff lead the crowd in a rousing sing-along.

Brophy Brothers
SEAFOOD $$

(Map p356; ☑ 805-966-4418; www.brophybros. com; 119 Harbor Way; mains $19-26; ⊙ 11am-10pm; ℗) ✐ A longtime favorite for its fresh-off-the-dock fish and seafood, rowdy atmosphere and salty harborside setting. Slightly less claustrophobic tables on the upstairs deck are worth the long wait – they're quieter and have the best ocean views. Or skip the long lines and start knocking back oyster shooters and Bloody Marys with convivial locals at the bar.

★ Yoichi's
JAPANESE $$$

(Map p356; ☑ 805-962-6627; www.yoichis.com; 230 E Victoria St; set 7-course menu $100; ⊙ 5-10pm Tue-Sun) Headline: *kaiseki* (traditional Japanese multicourse dining) comes to Santa Barbara and wows locals. It might have limited hours, take a chunk out of your wallet and need to be booked way in advance, but none of that has stopped Yoichi's being hailed as one of Santa Barbara's best (and slightly hidden away) eating experiences.

The set menu consists of seven courses, divided into different types of dishes (soup, sashimi, grilled and so on), each of which delivers on both flavor and presentation thanks to chef Yoichi's culinary skills and the beautiful, handmade, ceramic plates on which he serves his creations. And of course there's top quality and some unusual sakes to try too. It's tucked away on a quiet residential road a few blocks northeast of State St.

★ Lark
CALIFORNIAN $$$

(Map p356; ☑ 805-284-0370; www.thelarksb.com; 131 Anacapa St; shared plates $7-17, mains $19-48; ⊙ 5-10pm Tue-Sun, bar to midnight) ✐ There's no better place in Santa Barbara County to taste the bountiful farm and fishing goodness of this stretch of SoCal coast. Named after an antique Pullman railway car, this chef-run restaurant in the Funk Zone morphs its menu with the seasons, presenting unique flavor combinations such as crispy Brussels sprouts with dates or harissa and honey chicken. Make reservations. The cocktails and beer deserve serious consideration too.

★ Bouchon
CALIFORNIAN $$$

(Map p356; ☑ 805-730-1160; www.bouchonsanta barbara.com; 9 W Victoria St; mains $26-36; ⊙ 5-9pm Sun-Thu, to 10pm Fri & Sat) ✐ The perfect, unhurried, follow up to a day in the Wine Country is to feast on the bright, flavorful California cooking at pretty Bouchon (meaning 'wine cork'). A seasonally changing menu spotlights locally grown farm produce and ranched meats that marry beautifully with almost three-dozen regional wines available by the glass. Lovebirds, book a table on the candlelit patio.

Somerset
CALIFORNIAN $$$

(Map p356; ☑ 805-845-7112; http://somersetsb. com; 7 E Anapamu St; mains from $28; ⊙ 5:30pm-close Mon-Fri, from 5pm Sat & Sun) ✐ The decor has an art-deco-meets-the-'70s wow factor and the olive-tree patio is as romantic as it gets at this relative newcomer to Santa Barbara's upscale dining scene. Chef Lauren Hermann is cooking up innovative dishes similar to those that earned her James Beard awards at two LA restaurants, using only local ingredients in creative ways. Book in advance – it's one of the hottest places in town despite some mixed reviews for the food.

Lazy Acres
SUPERMARKET

(☑ 805-564-4410; www.lazyacres.com; 302 Meigs Rd; ⊙ 7am-11pm Mon-Sat, to 10pm Sun; ℗ ☑) ✐ High-quality supermarket standards, plus a salad and soup bar. It's a short drive southwest of town, follow W Carrillo St which turns into Meigs Rd.

🍷 Drinking & Nightlife

On lower State St, most of the boisterous watering holes have happy hours, tiny dance floors and rowdy college nights. The Funk Zone's eclectic mix of bars and wine-tasting rooms provides a trendier, more sophisticated alternative.

★ Brass Bear
CRAFT BEER

(Map p356; ☑ 805-770-7651; www.brassbear brewing.com; 28 Anacapa St; ⊙ noon-9pm Wed & Sun-Mon, to 10pm Thu, to 11pm Fri & Sat; 🖈 🐾) Large glasses of wine and beer and a great grilled cheese make this cozy place, located up an alley off Anacapa (follow the murals), a worthy detour. Friendly staff add to the convivial atmosphere. Just be careful not to drink too much and end up taking some of the for-sale art on the walls home with you.

★ Good Lion
COCKTAIL BAR

(Map p356; ☑ 805-845-8754; www.goodlion cocktails.com; 1212 State St; ⊙ 4pm-1am) Grab a cocktail at the beautiful, blue-tiled bar, then grab a book from the shelves and settle into

DON'T MISS

URBAN WINE TRAIL

No wheels to head up to Santa Barbara's Wine Country? No problem. Ramble between over a dozen wine-tasting rooms (and microbreweries, too) downtown and in the Funk Zone near the beach. Pick up the Urban Wine Trail (www.urbanwinetrailsb.com) anywhere along its route. Most tasting rooms are open every afternoon or sometimes into the early evening. On weekends, join the beautiful people rubbing shoulders as they sip outstanding glasses of regional wines and listen to free live music.

For a sociable scene, start at Municipal Winemakers or Corks n' Crowns, both on Anacapa St. Then head up to Yanonali St, turning left for Riverbench Winery Tasting Room; Cutler's Artisan Spirits distillery, a storefront where you can sample bourbon whiskey, vodka and apple liqueur; and Figueroa Mountain Brewing Co. Walk further west to find more wine-tippling spots.

Or turn right on Yanonali St and stop at the Valley Project (p364) for a liquid education about Santa Barbara's five distinct wine-growing regions. A couple of blocks east on Santa Barbara St, Waterline has the Fox Wine tasting room, housed in a cool, multipurpose complex that offers beer and food too.

a leather banquette in this petite place that has a cool Montmartre-turn-of-the-20th-century feel (candles on the tables and absinthe in many of the cocktails helps with the Parisian atmosphere).

★**Municipal Winemakers**   BAR
(Map p356; ☑805-931-6864; www.municipalwine makers.com; 22 Anacapa St; tastings $12; ⊙11am-8pm Sun-Wed, to 11pm Thu-Sat; 🖲) Dave, the owner of Municipal Winemakers, studied the vine arts in Australia and France before applying his knowledge in this industrially decorated tasting room and bar. Pale Pink rosé is a staple and hugely popular – enjoy a bottle on the large patio. For food, you can't beat the cheese plate, or at weekends a burger van parks outside.

★**Figueroa Mountain Brewing Co**   BAR
(Map p356; ☑805-694-2252; www.figmtnbrew. com; 137 Anacapa St; ⊙11am-11pm Sun-Thu, to midnight Fri & Sat) Father and son brewers have brought their gold-medal-winning hoppy IPA, Danish red lager and double IPA from Santa Barbara's Wine Country to the Funk Zone. Knowledgeable staff will help you choose before you clink glasses on the taproom's open-air patio while acoustic acts play. Enter on Yanonali St.

Test Pilot   COCKTAIL BAR
(Map p356; ☑805-845-2518; www.testpilotcocktails. com; 211 Helena Ave; ⊙4pm-1am Mon-Thu, 4pm-2am Fri, 2pm-2am Sat, 2pm-1am Sun) Any actual test pilot would be grounded after one of the strong but delicious cocktails at this tiki bar in the Funk Zone. The decor follows a nautical theme; the drinks ($9 to $12) keep it simple

with interesting twists on traditional concoctions. Expect foliage in your piña colada.

Waterline   BREWERY
(Map p356; ☑805-845-1482; www.waterlinesb. com; 116-120 Santa Barbara St; ⊙varies; 🖲) Extending the Funk Zone a little further east is no bad thing, and Waterline's combination of two taprooms (Topa Topa and Lama Dog), a restaurant (the Nook) serving elevated bar food, a wine-tasting room (Fox Wine) and a clothing, art and accessories section (Guilded Table), means you might happily spend longer here than planned.

Riverbench Winery Tasting Room   WINE BAR
(Map p356; ☑805-324-4100; www.riverbench. com; 137 Anacapa St; tastings $10; ⊙11am-6pm) Tasting room in the Funk Zone for the Santa Maria Valley vineyard of the same name. Amiable staff can guide you through a selection of Chardonnay and Pinot Noir, or a newer sparkling wine.

Corks n' Crowns   BAR
(Map p356; ☑805-845-8600; www.corksand crowns.com; 32 Anacapa St; tastings $7-20; ⊙11am-late, last call for tastings 6pm; 🖲) Sit on the sunny porch or inside the rustic-feel hut by the fire and try out the wines and beers from Santa Barbara in general and a few international destinations too. Tastings come in a flight of three for wine and four for beer – pours are generous. Board games are available – try Jenga after a tasting for added fun.

Cutler's Artisan Spirits   DISTILLERY
(Map p356; ☑805-845-4040; http://cutlers artisan.com; 137 Anacapa St; tastings $10; ⊙1-6pm Thu-Sun) Family-run craft distillers pro-

ducing whiskey, vodka, gin and apple pie (liqueur) since before (and during) Prohibition. The spirits are hard to find in stores so this is your chance to taste and then purchase up to three bottles (the maximum under local law) of their specialty liquors. The gin in particular is highly prized.

Valley Project
BAR

(Map p356; ☑805-453-6768; www.thevalley projectwines.com; 116 E Yanonali St; tastings $12; ⊙noon-7pm Mon-Thu, to 8pm Fri-Sun) From the sidewalk, passersby stop just to peek through the floor-to-ceiling glass windows at a wall-sized map of Santa Barbara's Wine Country, all hand-drawn in chalk. Inside, wine lovers lean on the tasting bar while sipping flights of locally grown reds and whites.

Press Room
PUB

(Map p356; ☑805-963-8121; 15 E Ortega St; ⊙11am-2am) This tiny pub can barely contain the college students and European travelers who cram the place to its seams. Pop in to catch soccer games, stuff the jukebox with quarters and enjoy jovial banter with the bartender.

Hollister Brewing Company
BREWERY

(☑805-968-2810; www.hollisterbrewco.com; Camino Real Marketplace, 6980 Marketplace Dr, Goleta; ⊙11am-10pm) With over a dozen microbrews on tap, this place draws serious beer geeks out to Goleta, near the UCSB campus, off Hwy 101. IPAs are the permanent attractions, along with nitrogenated stout. Skip the food, though.

Handlebar Coffee Roasters
CAFE

(Map p356; www.handlebarcoffee.com; 128 E Canon Perdido St; ⊙7am-5pm; 🐾) Bicycle-themed coffee shop brewing rich coffee and espresso drinks from small-batch roasted beans. Sit and sip yours on the sunny patio.

Brewhouse
BREWERY

(Map p356; ☑805-884-4664; www.sbbrewhouse. com; 229 W Montecito St; ⊙11am-midnight; 🛜🐾) Down by the railroad tracks, the boisterous Brewhouse crafts its own unique small-batch beer (Saint Barb's Belgian-style ales rule), serves wines by the glass, dishes up surprisingly good bar food and has cool art and rockin' live music Wednesday to Saturday nights.

☆ Entertainment

Santa Barbara's appreciation of the arts is evidenced not only by the variety of performances available on any given night, but

also its gorgeous, often historic venues. For a current calendar of live music and special events, check www.independent.com or www.newspress.com/top/section/scene.

Santa Barbara Bowl
LIVE MUSIC

(Map p356; ☑805-962-7411; http://sbbowl.com; 1122 N Milpas St; most tickets $35-125) Built by Works Progress Administration (WPA) artisans during the 1930s Great Depression, this naturally beautiful outdoor stone amphitheater has ocean views from the highest cheap seats. Kick back in the sunshine or under the stars for live rock, jazz and folk concerts in summer. Big-name acts like Brian Wilson, Radiohead and local graduate Jack Johnson have all taken the stage here.

Zodo's Bowling & Beyond
BOWLING

(☑805-967-0128; www.zodos.com; 5925 Calle Real, Goleta; bowling lane per hour $22-55, shoe rental $4.50; ⊙8:30am-1:30am Wed-Sat, to midnight Sun-Tue; 🐾) With over 40 beers on tap, pool tables and a video arcade (Skee-Ball!), this bowling alley near UCSB is good ol' family fun. Call ahead to get on the wait list and for schedules of open-play lanes and 'Glow Bowling' black-light nights with DJs. From Hwy 101 west of downtown, exit Fairview Ave north.

Arlington Theatre
THEATRE

(Map p356; ☑805-963-4408; www.thearlington theatre.com; 1317 State St; ⊙box office 10am-6pm Mon-Sat, to 4pm Sun) Harking back to 1931, this Mission Revival–style movie palace has a Spanish courtyard and a star-spangled ceiling. It's a drop-dead gorgeous place to attend a film-festival screening, and has a series of high-profile performers throughout the year.

Velvet Jones
MUSIC, COMEDY

(Map p356; ☑805-965-8676; http://velvet-jones. com; 423 State St; most tickets $10-25) Long-running downtown punk and indie dive for rock, hip-hop, comedy and 18-plus DJ nights for the city's college crowd. Many bands stop here between gigs in LA and San Francisco.

Granada Theatre
THEATER, MUSIC

(Map p356; ☑805-899-2222; www.granadasb. org; 1214 State St; ⊙box office 10am-5:30pm Mon-Sat, noon-5pm Sun) This beautifully restored 1930s Spanish Moorish–style theater is home to the city's symphony, ballet and opera, as well as touring Broadway shows and big-name musicians.

Lobero Theatre
THEATER, MUSIC

(Map p356; ☑805-963-0761; www.lobero.org; 33 E Canon Perdido St) One of California's oldest theaters (founded in 1873) presents modern dance, chamber music, jazz and world-music touring acts and stand-up comedy nights.

Soho
LIVE MUSIC

(Map p356; ☑805-962-7776; www.sohosb.com; suite 205, 1221 State St; most tickets $8-50) One unpretentious brick room plus live music almost nightly equals Soho, upstairs inside a downtown office complex behind McDonald's. Lineups range from indie rock, jazz, folk and funk to world beats. Some all-ages shows.

🛍 Shopping

Downtown's **State St** is packed with shops of all kinds, and even chain stores conform to the red-roofed architectural style. The lower (beach) end has budget options, with quality and prices going up as the street does. For more local art galleries and indie shops, dive into the **Funk Zone**, east of State St, tucked in south of Hwy 101.

REI
SPORTS & OUTDOORS

(Map p356; ☑805-560-1938; www.rei.com; 321 Anacapa St; ⊘10am-9pm Mon-Fri, to 7pm Sat, to 6pm Sun) If you forgot your tent or rock-climbing carabiners at home, the West Coast's most popular independent co-op outdoor retailer is the place to pick up outdoor recreation gear, active clothing, sport shoes and topographic maps.

Santa Barbara Public Market
MARKET

(Map p356; ☑805-770-7702; http://sbpublicmarket. com; 38 W Victoria St; ⊘7:30am-10pm Mon-Wed, 7:30am-11pm Thu & Fri, 8am-11pm Sat, 8am-10pm Sun) 🍴 Noodles, cupcakes, ice cream and Mexican magic from Corazon Cocina (p359) are just some of the tempting food options available at this central market, handy for a break from sightseeing or for takeout picnic provisions. Stop by too for coffee and wine, and have a break in the Garden, where dozens of beers come on tap.

Chocolate Maya
CHOCOLATE

(Map p356; ☑805-965-5956; www.chocolatemaya. com; 15 W Gutierrez St; ⊘10am-6pm Mon-Fri, to 5pm Sat, to 4pm Sun) Personally sourced, fair-trade cacao from around the world means the chocolates on offer here not only taste good but make you feel good about yourself for buying them. Truffles are a specialty and ingredients are sometimes unusual (tarragon and pineapple, anyone?). Be adventurous or ask for recommendations.

Santa Barbara Farmers Market
MARKET

(Map p356; ☑805-962-5354; www.sbfarmers market.org; 500 & 600 blocks of State St; ⊘4-7:30pm Tue mid-Mar–early Nov, 3-6:30pm Tue mid-Nov–mid-Mar, 8:30am-1pm Sat year-round; 👪) 🌿 Stock up on fresh fruits and veggies, cheese, nuts and honey at the Tuesday Santa Barbara Farmers Market, which also happens again on Saturday morning at the corner of Santa Barbara and Cota Sts.

Diani
CLOTHING

(Map p356; ☑805-966-7175; www.dianiboutique. com; 1324 State St, Arlington Plaza; ⊘10am-6pm Mon, 10am-7pm Tue-Sat, 11am-6pm Sun) Carries high-fashion, Euro-inspired designs, with a touch of funky California soul thrown in for good measure. Think Humanoid dresses, Rag & Bone skinny jeans and Stella McCartney sunglasses. A few doors down, Diani has expanded into shoes and homewares.

Channel Islands Surfboards
SPORTS & OUTDOORS

(Map p356; ☑805-966-7213; www.cisurfboards. com; 36 Anacapa St; ⊘10am-7pm Mon-Sat, 11am-5pm Sun) Are you ready to take home a handcrafted, Southern California–born surfboard? Down in the Funk Zone, this surf shack is the place for innovative pro-worthy board designs, as well as surfer threads and beanie hats.

CRSVR Sneaker Boutique
SHOES, CLOTHING

(Map p356; ☑805-962-2400; www.crsvr.com; 632 State St; ⊘11am-7pm) Check out this sneaker boutique run by DJs, not just for limited-edition Nikes and other athletic-shoe brands, but also T-shirts, jackets, hats and more urban styles for men.

Paseo Nuevo
MALL

(Map p356; ☑805-963-7147; www.paseonuevoshop ping.com; 651 Paseo Nuevo; ⊘10am-9pm Mon-Fri, 10am-8pm Sat, 11am-7pm Sun) This busy open-air mall is anchored by Macy's and Nordstrom department stores and offers all the usual clothing, accessories and beauty chains you could want, plus a few dining options.

ℹ Information

Los Padres National Forest Headquarters

(☑805-968-6640; www.fs.usda.gov/lpnf; 6750 Navigator Way, Goleta; ⊘8am-12pm & 1-4:30pm Mon-Fri) HQ for the whole Los Padres National Forest. Pick up maps, recreation passes etc.

Outdoors Santa Barbara Visitors Center

(Map p356; ☑805-456-8752; http://outdoorsb. sbmm.org; 4th fl, 113 Harbor Way; ⊘11am-5pm) Inside the same building as the maritime museum, this volunteer-staffed visitor center offers info on Channel Islands National Park and a harbor-view deck.

Santa Barbara Central Library (☑805-564-5608; www.sbplibrary.org; 40 E Anapamu St; ⊙10am-7pm Mon-Thu, 10am-5:30pm Fri & Sat, 1-5pm Sun; 🛜) Free internet access for up to two hours (photo ID required). Reserve in advance or try a walk-in.

Santa Barbara Visitors Center (Map p356; ☑805-568-1811, 805-965-3021; www.santa barbaraca.com; 1 Garden St; ⊙9am-5pm Mon-Sat, 10am-5pm Sun, closes 1hr earlier Nov-Jan) Pick up maps and brochures while consulting with the helpful but busy staff. The website offers free downloadable DIY touring maps and itineraries, from famous movie locations to wine trails, art galleries and outdoors fun. Self-pay metered parking lot nearby.

❶ Getting There & Away

Small **Santa Barbara Airport** (www.flysba.com; 500 Fowler Rd, Goleta; 🛜), 9 miles west of downtown via Hwy 101, has scheduled flights to/from LA, San Francisco and other western US cities.

Amtrak (☑800-872-7245; www.amtrak.com; 209 State St) trains run south to LA ($31, 2½ hours) via Carpinteria, Ventura and Burbank's airport, and north to San Luis Obispo ($22, 2¾ hours) and Oakland ($43, 8¾ hours), with stops in Paso Robles, Salinas and San Jose.

Greyhound (Map p356; ☑805-965-7551; www.greyhound.com; 224 Chapala St) operates a few direct buses daily to LA ($15, three hours), Santa Cruz ($42, six hours) and San Francisco ($40, nine hours).

Vista (☑800-438-1112; www.goventura.org) runs frequent daily 'Coastal Express' buses between Santa Barbara and Carpinteria ($3, 25 to 30 minutes) and Ventura ($3, 40 to 70 minutes); check online or call for schedules.

If you're driving on Hwy 101, take the Garden St or Carrillo St exits for downtown.

❶ Getting Around

TO/FROM THE AIRPORT

A taxi to downtown or the waterfront costs about $30 to $35 plus tip. Car-rental agencies with airport lots include Alamo, Avis, Budget, Enterprise, Hertz and National; reserve in advance.

Santa Barbara Airbus (☑805-964-7759; www.sbairbus.com) shuttles between Los Angeles International Airport (LAX) and Santa Barbara ($49/94 one-way/round-trip, 2½ hours, eight departures daily). The more people in your party, the cheaper the fare. For more discounts, prepay online.

BICYCLE

For bicycle rentals, Wheel Fun Rentals (p352) has two locations close to Stearns Wharf.

GO GREEN IN SANTA BARBARA

Santa Barbara's biggest eco-travel initiative is **Santa Barbara Car Free** (www.santa barbaracarfree.org). Browse the website for tips on seeing the city without your car, plus valuable discounts on accommodations, vacation packages, rail travel and more. Still don't believe it's possible to tour Santa Barbara without a car? Let us show you how to do it.

From LA, hop aboard the *Pacific Surfliner* or *Coast Starlight* for a memorably scenic, partly coastal ride to Santa Barbara's Amtrak station (around 2½ hours), a few blocks from the beach and downtown. Then hoof it or catch one of the electric shuttles that zips north–south along State St and east–west along the waterfront. MTD buses 6 and 11 connect with the shuttle halfway up State St and will get you within walking distance of the famous mission (get off at Los Olivos St and walk uphill). For a DIY cycling tour, **Wheel Fun Rentals** (p352) is a short walk from the train station.

Even Santa Barbara's Wine Country is getting into the sustainable swing of things. More and more vineyards are implementing biodynamic farming techniques and following organic guidelines. Many vintners and oenophiles are starting to think that the more natural the growing process, the better the wine, too. **Sustainable Vine Wine Tours** (p372) whisks you around family-owned sustainable vineyards. Minimize your carbon footprint even further by following Santa Barbara's Urban Wine Trail (www.urbanwine trailsb.com) on foot. If you love both wine and food, *Edible Santa Barbara* magazine (http://ediblecommunities.com/santabarbara) publishes insightful articles about vineyards and restaurants that are going green. It's available free at many local markets, restaurants and wineries.

Santa Barbara County abounds with ecofriendly outdoor activities, too. Take your pick of hiking trails, cycling routes, ocean kayaking, swimming, surfing or stand up paddle boarding (SUP). If you're going whale-watching, ask around to see if there are any alternative-fueled tour boats with trained onboard naturalists.

CAR
Downtown street parking or parking in any of a dozen municipal lots is free for the first 75 minutes; each additional hour costs $1.50.

LOCAL BUS
Local buses operated by the **Metropolitan Transit District** (MTD; ☎805-963-3366; www.sbmtd.gov) cost $1.75 per ride (exact change, cash only). Equipped with front-loading bike racks, these buses travel all over town and to adjacent communities; ask for a free transfer upon boarding. **MTD Transit Center** (Map p356; ☎805-963-3366; www.sbmtd.gov/passenger-information/transit-center.html; 1020 Chapala St; ⊘6am-7pm Mon-Fri, 9am-5pm Sat & Sun) has details about routes and schedules.

BUS	DESTINATION	FREQUENCY
5	Arroyo Burro Beach	hourly
11	State St, UCSB campus	every 30min
20	Montecito, Summerland, Carpinteria	hourly

SHUTTLE
MTD's electric **Downtown Shuttle** buses run along State St down to Stearns Wharf at 9am and 9:30am, and then every 15 minutes from 10am to 6pm daily. A second **Waterfront Shuttle** travels from Stearns Wharf west to the harbor and east to the zoo every 30 minutes from 10am to 6pm daily. Between Memorial Day (late May) and Labor Day (early September), both routes run every 10 to 15 minutes, including from 6pm to 9pm on Fridays and Saturdays. The fare is 50¢ per ride; transfers between routes are free.

TAXI
Taxis are metered around $3 at flagfall, with an additional $3 to $4 for each mile.

WATER TAXI
Lil' Toot water taxi (Map p356; ☎805-465-6676; www.celebrationsantabarbara.com; 113 Harbor Way; 1-way fare adult/child $5/1; ⊘usually noon-6pm Apr-Oct, hours vary Nov-Mar; ⊛) provides an ecofriendly, biodiesel-fueled ride between Stearns Wharf and the harbor, docking in front of the maritime museum. Look for ticket booths on the waterfront. Trips run every half-hour, weather permitting.

SANTA BARBARA WINE COUNTRY

Oak-dotted hillsides, winding country lanes, rows of grapevines stretching as far as the eye can see – it's hard not to gush about the Santa Ynez and Santa Maria Valleys and the Santa Rita Hills wine regions.

This is an area made for do-it-yourself exploring. Locals here are friendly, from long-time landowners and farmers displaying small-town graciousness to vineyard owners who've fled big cities to follow their passion and who will happily share their knowledge and intriguing personal histories in intimate vineyard tasting rooms.

With around 100 local wineries, visiting can seem daunting, but the Santa Ynez Valley's five small towns – Los Olivos, Solvang, Buellton, Santa Ynez and Ballard – are all clustered within 10 miles of one another, so it's easy to stop, shop and eat whenever and wherever you like. Don't worry about sticking to a plan – instead, be captivated by the scenery and pull over wherever looks welcoming.

Wineries

The big-name appellations for Santa Barbara's Wine Country are the Santa Ynez Valley, Santa Maria Valley and Santa Rita Hills, plus smaller Happy Canyon and upstart Ballard Canyon. Wine-tasting rooms abound in Los Olivos and Solvang, handy for anyone with limited time.

The Santa Ynez Valley, where you'll find most of the wineries, lies south of the Santa Maria Valley. Hwy 246 runs east–west, via Solvang, across the bottom of the Santa Ynez Valley, connecting Hwy 101 with Hwy 154. North–south secondary roads bordered by vineyards include Alamo Pintado Rd from Hwy 246 to Los Olivos, and Refugio Rd between Santa Ynez and Ballard.

If you can't stay a night or two, then a half-day trip will allow you to see one winery or tasting room, have lunch and return to Santa Barbara. Otherwise make it a full day and plan to have lunch and possibly dinner before returning to the city.

Foxen Canyon Wine Trail

The scenic Foxen Canyon Wine Trail runs north from Hwy 154, just west of Los Olivos, deep into the heart of the rural Santa Maria Valley. It's a must-see for oenophiles or anyone wanting to get off the beaten path. For the most part, it follows Foxen Canyon Rd, though a couple of top spots lie close to Santa Maria town.

★**Foxen** WINERY
(Map p368; ☎805-937-4251; www.foxenvineyard.com; 7200 & 7600 Foxen Canyon Rd, Santa Maria; tastings $15-20; ⊘11am-4pm; ℗) ✦ On what was once a working cattle ranch, Foxen crafts

Santa Barbara Wine Country

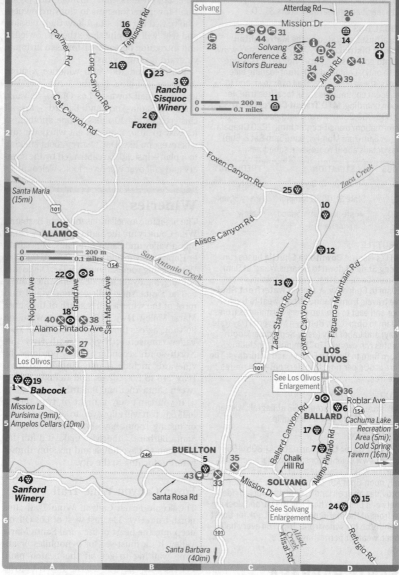

full-fruited Pinot Noir, warm Syrah, steel-cut Chardonnay and rich Rhône-style wines, all sourced from standout vineyards. The newer tasting room (for the Rhône-style tasting) is solar-powered, while the old 'shack' – a former blacksmith's with a corrugated-metal roof, funky-cool decor and leafy patio – pours Bordeaux-style and Cal-Ital varietals.

★ **Rancho Sisquoc Winery** WINERY
(Map p368; ☎ 805-934-4332; www.ranchosisquoc. com; 6600 Foxen Canyon Rd; tastings $10; ☺ 10am-

Santa Barbara Wine Country

4pm Mon-Thu, to 5pm Fri-Sun) This tranquil gem is worth the extra mileage, not just for the award-winning small-batch reds and whites, but for the delightfully rustic tasting room surrounded by pastoral views. The grounds are perfect for a picnic (fittingly, 'sisquoc' is Chumash for 'gathering place') so bring your own supplies or grab some of the on-site snacks, cheese and salami.

Turn right off Foxen Canyon Rd when you spot **San Ramon Chapel** (Map p368; ☑805-937-1334; www.sanramonchapel.org; Foxen Canyon Rd; ☉grounds 6:30am-6:30pm; ⓟ) FREE, look out for the 'Winery' sign and follow the narrow, partly olive-tree-lined road for a mile or two.

Demetria Estate WINERY
(Map p368; ☑805-686-2345; www.demetria estate.com; 6701 Foxen Canyon Rd, Los Olivos; tastings $25; ☉by appointment; ⓟ) 🌿 This hilltop retreat has the curving arches and thick wooden doors of your hospitable Greek uncle's country house, with epic views of vine-yards and rolling hillsides. Tastings are by appointment only, but are worth it just to sample the biodynamically farmed Chardonnay, Syrah and Viognier, plus rave-worthy Rhône-style red blends.

Zaca Mesa Winery WINERY
(Map p368; ☑805-688-9339; www.zacamesa. com; 6905 Foxen Canyon Rd, Los Olivos; tastings $15-25, tours $30; ☉10am-4pm daily year-round, to 5pm Fri & Sat late May-early Sep; ⚐) Stop by this barn-style tasting room for a rustic, sipping-on-the-farm ambience. Santa Barbara's highest-elevation winery, Zaca Mesa specializes in Syrah, but is also known for its estate-grown Rhône varietals and signature Z Cuvée red blend and Z Blanc white blend. An outsized outdoor chessboard and a tree-shaded picnic area that's dog-friendly add to the laid-back atmosphere.

Firestone Vineyards WINERY
(Map p368; ☑805-688-3940; www.firestonewine. com; 5017 Zaca Station Rd; tastings $10-15, incl tour $20; ☉10am-5pm; ⓟ) Founded in the 1970s,

Firestone is Santa Barbara's oldest estate winery. Sweeping views of the vineyard from the sleek, wood-paneled tasting room are nearly as satisfying as the value-priced Cabernet Sauvignon and Bordeaux-style blends for which it's best known. Arrive in time for a winery tour, daily at 11:15am and 1:15pm, plus 3:15pm weekends (no reservations).

Kenneth Volk Vineyards WINERY
(Map p368; ☑ 805-938-7896; www.volkwines. com; 5230 Tepusquet Rd, Santa Maria; tastings $10; ⊙ 10:30am-4:30pm Thu-Mon, by appointment Tue & Wed) Only an established cult winemaker could convince oenophiles to drive so far out of their way to taste rare heritage varietals such as floral-scented Malvasia and inky Negrette, as well as standard-bearing Pinot Noir, Chardonnay, Cabernet Sauvignon and Merlot.

Riverbench Vineyard & Winery WINERY
(Map p368; ☑ 805-937-8340; www.riverbench. com; 6020 Foxen Canyon Rd, Santa Maria; tastings $15; ⊙ 10am-4pm) Riverbench has been creating prized Pinot Noir and Chardonnay since the early 1970s, and sparkling wines more recently. The rural tasting room is inside a butter-yellow arts-and-crafts farmhouse with panoramic views across the Santa Maria Valley. Out back is a picnic ground and bocce-ball court. Tours, cheese and chocolate pairings and other events available.

You can also sample its wines on Santa Barbara's Urban Wine Trail (p363).

Fess Parker Winery & Vineyard WINERY
(Map p368; ☑ 800-841-1104; www.fessparker wines.com; 6200 Foxen Canyon Rd; tastings $14; ⊙ 10am-5pm) Besides its on-screen appearance as Frass Canyon in the movie *Sideways,* the winery's other claim to fame is its late founder Fess Parker, best known for playing Davy Crockett on TV. Fess has now passed on, but you can still enjoy his winery's award-winning Chardonnay and Pinot Noir on the newly extended patio, and buy a souvenir coonskin-cap-etched glass.

Santa Rita Hills Wine Trail

When it comes to country-road scenery, eco-conscious farming practices and top-notch Pinot Noir, the less-traveled Santa Rita Hills (www.staritahills.com) region holds its own. Almost a dozen tasting rooms line an easy driving loop west of Hwy 101 via Santa Rosa Rd and Hwy 246. Be prepared to share the roads with cyclists and an occasional John Deere tractor. More artisan winemak-

ers hide out in the industrial warehouses of Buellton near Hwy 101 and further afield in Lompoc, where you can combine a visit to La Purísima (p374) mission with an exploration of the town's 'Wine Ghetto,' a concentration of tasting rooms centered on Industrial Way, located on the eastern edge of the town, generally open only at weekends. See www.lom poctrail.com for more information.

★Babcock WINERY
(Map p368; ☑ 805-736-1455; www.babcock winery.com; 5175 E Hwy 246; tastings $15-18; ⊙ 11am-5:30pm; P) Hillside, family-owned vineyards overflowing with different grape varietals – Chardonnay, Sauvignon Blanc, Pinot Gris, Pinot Noir, Syrah, Cabernet Sauvignon and more – that let innovative small-lot winemaker Bryan Babcock be the star: 'Slice of Heaven' and 'Ocean's Ghost' Pinot Noirs alone are worthy of a pilgrimage. The eccentrically furnished tasting room offers vintage vinyl for sale and elevated views alongside the wine.

★Sanford Winery WINERY
(Map p368; ☑ 800-426-9463; www.sanfordwinery. com; 5010 Santa Rosa Rd; tastings $20-25; ⊙ 10am-4pm) Be enchanted by this romantic tasting room built of stone and handmade bricks, embraced by estate vineyards on historic Rancho La Rinconada. Watch the sun sink over the vineyards from the patio with a silky Pinot Noir or citrusy Chardonnay in hand. Hour-long winery tours are given at 11am daily ($50, book at least 48 hours in advance).

Alma Rosa Winery & Vineyards WINERY
(Map p368; ☑ 805-688-9090; www.almarosawinery. com; 181 Industrial Way; tastings $15; ⊙ noon-6:30pm Mon-Fri, from 11am Sat & Sun; P) ✐ Richard Sanford left the powerhouse winery bearing his name to start this new winery with his wife, Thekla, using sustainable, organic farming techniques. The vineyard is closed to visitors at the moment, but tastings are held in the stylish, wood-heavy tasting room in Buellton; Pinot Noir, Chardonnay, Pinot Blanc and Pinot Gris are poured.

Ampelos Cellars TASTING ROOM
(☑ 805-736-9957; www.ampeloscellars.com; 312 N 9th Ave, Lompoc; tastings $10; ⊙ 11am-5pm Thu-Sun, to 4pm Mon) ✐ Danish grower Peter Work and wife Rebecca display their passion for the vine through biodynamic farming techniques and encyclopedic knowledge of their lots. Their Pinot Noir, Syrah and Grenache shine – you can sample them in Lom-

poc's 'Wine Ghetto,' an industrial area on the eastern edge of the town.

Melville   WINERY
(Map p368; ☑805-735-7030; www.melvillewinery. com; 5185 E Hwy 246, Lompoc; tastings $10-20; ⊙11am-4pm Sun-Thu, to 5pm Fri & Sat; P) ✐ This beautiful Mediterranean hillside villa gives tastes of estate-grown, small-lot bottled Pinot Noir, Syrah and Chardonnay made by folks who believe in talking about pounds per plant, not tons per acre. Don't think there isn't variety though, with seven different clones of Pinot Noir alone grown. 'Vineyard to Bottle' tours are available noon and 2pm weekends ($25, 75 minutes).

Santa Ynez Valley
One of California's top viticulture regions, the Santa Ynez Valley is a compact area comprising a handful of small towns and dozens of vineyards. Put on the map back in 2004 by the movie *Sideways,* the area still draws the crowds and it's a hugely pleasant place to stay in upmarket lodgings, eat at high-quality restaurants and, of course, enjoy the many fine wines produced here. Los Olivos is the cutest town, Buellton the most down-to-earth, with incongruous Danish Solvang and tiny Santa Ynez and Ballard in between. Popular wineries cluster between Los Olivos and Solvang along Alamo Pintado Rd and Refugio Rd, south of Roblar Ave and west of Hwy 154.

Beckmen Vineyards   WINERY
(Map p368; ☑805-688-8664; www.beckmen vineyards.com; 2670 Ontiveros Rd, Solvang; tastings $20; ⊙11am-5pm; P🐾🧺) ✐ Bring a picnic to one of the pond-side gazebos at this tranquil winery, where estate-grown Rhône varieties flourish on the unique terroir of Purisima Mountain. Biodynamic farming principles mean natural methods are used to prevent pests. To sample superb Syrah and a cuvée blend with Grenache, Syrah, Mourvèdre and Counoise, follow Roblar Ave west of Hwy 154 to Ontiveros Rd. Vineyard tours are offered at 11am daily ($25 including tasting; reservations required).

Lincourt Vineyard   WINERY
(Map p368; ☑805-688-8554; www.lincourtwines. com; 1711 Alamo Pintado Rd, Solvang; tastings from $10; ⊙10am-5pm) ✐ Respected winemaker Bill Foley, who also owns Firestone Vineyards (p369) in Foxen Canyon, founded this vineyard in the 1990s on a former dairy farm. Today, the attractive, original 1926 farmhouse

ⓘ BEST SANTA BARBARA WINERIES FOR PICNICS

You won't have any problem finding picnic fare in Santa Barbara's Wine Country. The region is chock-full of local markets, delis and bakeries serving up portable sandwiches and salads. When picnicking at a winery, remember it's polite to buy a bottle of wine before spreading out your feast.

➡ Beckmen Vineyards (p371)

➡ Sunstone Vineyards & Winery (p371)

➡ Zaca Mesa Winery (p369)

➡ Lincourt Vineyard (p371)

➡ Rancho Sisquoc Winery (p368)

(built from a Sears catalog kit) is home to the tasting room: sip finely crafted Chardonnay and Pinot Noir and a dry French-style rosé, all made from locally grown grapes.

Sunstone Vineyards & Winery   WINERY
(Map p368; ☑805-688-9463; www.sunstonewinery. com; 125 N Refugio Rd, Santa Ynez; tastings $18; ⊙11am-5pm) ✐ Wander inside what looks like an 18th-century stone farmhouse from Provence and into a cool hillside cave housing wine barrels. Sunstone crafts Bordeaux-style wines made from 100% organically grown grapes. Bring a picnic to eat in the courtyard beneath gnarled oaks. Groups (eight or more) can order a wine-paired gourmet lunch to accompany their tasting ($30).

Kalyra Winery   WINERY
(Map p368; ☑805-693-8864; www.kalyrawinery. com; 343 N Refugio Rd, Santa Ynez; tastings $12-14; ⊙11am-5pm Mon-Fri, from 10am Sat & Sun; P) Australian Mike Brown traveled halfway around the world to combine his two loves: surfing and winemaking. Try his full-bodied red blends, unusual white varietals or sweet dessert wines (the orange muscat is a crowd-pleaser), all in bottles with Aboriginal-art-inspired labels. Kalyra also pours at Helix, a smaller venue on Buellton's Industrial Way (noon to 5pm Friday to Sunday; $15), close to several other tasting rooms.

Buttonwood Farm Winery & Vineyard   WINERY
(Map p368; ☑805-688-3032; www.buttonwood winery.com; 1500 Alamo Pintado Rd, Solvang; tastings $10-15; ⊙11am-5pm; 🐾🧺) ✐ Bordeaux

SANTA BARBARA WINE COUNTRY 101

Although large-scale winemaking has only been happening here since the 1980s, the climate of Santa Barbara's Wine Country has always been perfect for growing grapes. Two parallel, transverse mountain ranges – Santa Ynez and San Rafael – cradle the region and funnel coastal fog eastward off the Pacific into the valleys between. The further inland you go, the warmer it gets.

To the west, fog and low clouds may hover all day, keeping the weather crisp even in summer, while only a few miles inland, temperatures approach 100°F in July. These delicately balanced microclimates support two major types of grapes. Nearer the coast in the cooler Santa Maria Valley, Pinot Noir – a particularly fragile grape – and other Burgundian varietals such as Chardonnay thrive. Inland in the hotter Santa Ynez Valley, Rhône-style grapes do best, including Syrah and Viognier.

and Rhône varieties do well in the sun-dappled limestone soil at this friendly winery best for wine-tasting neophytes and dog owners. The trellised back patio, bordering a fruit-tree orchard, is a pleasant spot to relax with a bottle of zingy Sauvignon Blanc.

☞ Tours

Full-day wine-tasting tours average $120 to $160 per person; most leave from Santa Barbara, and some require a minimum number of participants. The website www.sbcountywines.com has a detailed list.

★ **Sustainable Vine Wine Tours** TOURS
(☑805-698-3911; www.sustainablevinewinetours.com; tours from $150) ✒ Biodiesel-van tours of wineries implementing organic and sustainable agricultural practices. Tours include stops at three tasting rooms, behind-the-scenes visits and organic picnic lunches. Pick-ups from any location in the Santa Barbara/Wine Country region.

Wine Edventures TOURS
(☑805-965-9463; www.welovewines.com; tours $120) Serves up a fun-lovin' side dish of local history and behind-the-scenes wine education on its shuttle-driven tasting tours, one of which visits a microbrewery, too. Price includes a picnic lunch and a bottle of local wine. Pick-ups from just about anywhere in the local area, including many Santa Barbara and Solvang hotels, are free.

Santa Barbara Wine Country Cycling Tours CYCLING
(Map p368; ☑805-686-9490; www.winecountrycycling.com; 1693 Mission Dr; tours from $170 per person; ⊙9am-6pm Mon-Fri, to 5pm Sat, to 4pm Sun) Guided and DIY bike rides start from the same building as Dr J's (p374) and come in easy to moderate versions – except the

Epic Cycling Tours which cover up to 65 miles around the Santa Ynez Valley and out to Jalama Beach (p343). Multiday trips also available.

Los Olivos

The posh ranching town of Los Olivos is many visitors' first stop when exploring Santa Barbara's Wine Country. Its four-block-long main street has rustic wine-tasting rooms, bistros and boutiques seemingly air-lifted straight out of Napa.

◉ Sights

Clairmont Farms FARM
(Map p368; ☑805-688-7505; www.clairmontfarms.com; 2480 Roblar Ave; ⊙11am-5pm Wed-Mon Apr-Oct, to 4pm Thu-Mon Nov-Mar; 🅿🍴) ✒ Natural beauty awaits just outside Los Olivos at this friendly, organic, family-owned farm, where purple lavender fields bloom like a Monet masterpiece, usually peaking mid-June to late July. Cruise the olive-tree-lined drive to the tiny shop selling bath and body products, and enjoy a lavender-scented picnic outside.

🛏 Sleeping & Eating

Options are limited and choices aren't cheap around these parts, but the quality is high.

Fess Parker Wine Country Inn & Spa SPA HOTEL $$$
(Map p368; ☑805-688-7788; www.fessparkerinn.com; 2860 Grand Ave; r from $395; ❄@🛜🏊) Spacious rooms and suites, done out in calming, contemporary design, set the scene at this luxurious spa hotel in the center of Los Olivos. Fireplaces are standard, there's a heated pool and a decent-size gym, and breakfast and a wine tasting are included in the price.

Los Olivos Grocery DELI $

(Map p368; 805-688-5115; www.losolivosgro
cery.com; 2621 W Hwy 154; 7am-9pm;)
Eat in for breakfast or lunch (grab a table
on the covered porch) or get sandwiches,
artisan breads, salads, specialty cheeses,
pickles and everything else you'll need for
a vineyard picnic to go. Everything's produced inhouse or locally. It's a couple of
minutes southeast of central Los Olivos,
just off Hwy 154.

Panino SANDWICHES $

(Map p368; 805-688-9304; http://panino
restaurants.com; 2900 Grand Ave; sandwiches $10-
12.50; 10am-4pm;) Take your pick from
a huge range of gourmet deli sandwiches
and salads: curry chicken is a perennial
fave, but there are robust vegetarian options
too. Order at the counter, then eat outside at
an umbrella-covered table. There are other
branches around Santa Barbara County, including in nearby Solvang and Santa Ynez.

**Los Olivos Wine
Merchant & Café** CALIFORNIAN, MEDITERRANEAN $$

(Map p368; 805-688-7265; www.winemerchant
cafe.com; 2879 Grand Ave; mains breakfast $9-12,
lunch & dinner $13-29; 11:30am-8:30pm daily, also
8-10:30am Sat & Sun) This wine-country land-
mark (as seen in *Sideways*) swirls up a casual-
chic SoCal ambience with its wisteria-covered
trellis entrance. It stays open between lunch
and dinner for antipasto platters, hearty sal-
ads and crispy pizzas, and wine flights at the
bar. Sit inside in the elegant dining room or
outside on the covered patio.

★ **Sides Hardware & Shoes** AMERICAN $$$

(Map p368; 805-688-4820; http://sidesrestaurant.
com; 2375 Alamo Pintado Ave; mains lunch $14-18,
dinner $26-35; 11am-2:30pm daily, 5-8:30pm
Sun-Thu, to 9pm Fri & Sat;) Behind its historic
storefront, this bistro delivers haute country
cooking. For lunch you can't beat the burgers,
though there are lighter salads and tacos too.
In the evenings (book ahead) start with the
bacon steak (exactly what it says), followed by
the fried chicken with garlicky kale or housemade vegetarian pasta. Sit out on the porch or
in the open-plan dining room.

Drinking

Bring a book and buy a bottle of wine during your day-time vineyard visits if you want
something to while away your Los Olivos
evenings.

Los Olivos Tasting Room TASTING ROOM

(Map p368; 805-688-7406; http://site.thelos
olivostastingroom.com; 2905 Grand Ave; tastings
$10; 11am-5pm) Inside a rickety 19th-century
general store, this tasting room stocks rare
vintages you won't find anywhere else. Well-
oiled servers are by turns loquacious and
gruff, but refreshingly blunt in their opinions
about local wines, and pours are generous.

Saarloos + Sons TASTING ROOM

(Map p368; 805-688-1200; http://saarloos
andsons.com; 2971 Grand Ave; tasting fee $10-15;
11am-5pm, last pour 4:30pm) Wine snobs are
given the boot at this shabby-chic tasting
room pouring estate-grown, small-lot Syrah,
Grenache Noir, Cabernet Sauvignon and
Sauvignon Blanc. Pair your wine flight with
a mini-cupcake and watch Los Olivos go by
from the large outdoor deckchairs.

**Carhartt Vineyard
Tasting Room** TASTING ROOM

(Map p368; 805-693-5100; www.carhartt
vineyard.com; 2990a Grand Ave; tasting fee $15;
11am-6pm) An unpretentious tasting room
inside a red-trimmed wooden shack that leads
on to a shady garden patio out back, where a
fun-loving younger crowd sips unfussy Zinfandel, Merlot and 'Not-So Petite' Syrah.

Solvang

Statues of the Little Mermaid and Hans
Christian Andersen in the middle of Wine
Country can only mean one thing: Solvang.
A Danish village founded in 1911 on what
was once a 19th-century Spanish-colonial
mission, this Santa Ynez Valley town holds
tight to its Danish heritage. With its knick-
knack stores and cutesy motels, the town is
almost as sickly sweet as the Scandinavian
pastries sold to the crowds of day-trippers.
But a few new businesses are toning down
the kitsch and upping the modern-Scandi
cool, plus the town has the best sleeping
and eating options in the valley, making it a
great base for exploration.

Sights

Hans Christian Andersen Museum MUSEUM

(Map p368; 805-688-2052; www.solvangca.
com/museum; 2nd fl, 1680 Mission Dr; 10am-
5pm;) FREE If you remember childhood
fairy tales with fondness, stop by this tiny
two-room museum. A larger-than-life bust
of Denmark's favorite storyteller welcomes
you to a mix of original letters, 1st-edition

WORTH A TRIP

MISSION LA PURÍSIMA

One of the most evocative of Southern California's missions, La Purísima was founded in 1787 and completely restored in the 1930s by the Civilian Conservation Corps (CCC). Today it's a **state historic park** (✆805-733-3713; www.lapurisimamission.org; 2295 Purísima Rd, Lompoc; per car $6; ⊙9am-5pm, tours at 1pm Wed-Sun & public holidays Sep-Jun, daily Jul & Aug; P⊕) ⚲ with buildings furnished just as they were during Spanish-colonial times. The mission's fields still support livestock, while outdoor gardens are planted with medicinal plants and trees once used by Chumash tribespeople.

Start in the excellent visitor center, where exhibits tell stories of the Chumash, the Spanish missionaries and the work of the CCC. Self-guided visits are the usual way to explore the buildings themselves, though guided tours, lasting 1½ to 2 hours, are available too. The mission is just outside Lompoc, about 16 miles west of Hwy 101 (take Hwy 246 west from Buellton).

copies of his illustrated books, and a model of Andersen's childhood home. It's upstairs in the Book Loft (p376) building.

Elverhøj Museum of History & Art MUSEUM (Map p368; ✆805-686-1211; www.elverhoj.org; 1624 Elverhoy Way; suggested donation adult $5, child under 13yr free; ⊙11am-4pm Wed-Sun; ⊕) South of downtown, tucked away on a residential side street, this delightful little museum has modest but thoughtful exhibits on Solvang's Danish heritage, as well as Danish culture, art and history.

Old Mission Santa Ínes CHURCH (Map p368; ✆805-688-4815; www.missionsantaines.org; 1760 Mission Dr; adult $5, child under 12yr free; ⊙9am-4:30pm; P⊕) Off Hwy 246 just east of Solvang's Alisal Rd, this historic Catholic mission (founded in 1804) was one of the settings for the Chumash revolt in 1824 against Spanish-colonial cruelty. A self-guided tour takes you through a small, dated museum, into the restored church, and through the pretty gardens to the cemetery. It's still an active parish today.

🤽 Activities

Solvang is best known by cyclists for the **Solvang Century races** (www.bikescor.com) in March. For self-guided cycling tours, visit www.solvangusa.com and www.bike-santa barbara.org and rent a bike from **Dr J's Bicycle Shop** (Map p368; ✆805-688-6263; www.drjsbikeshop.com; 1693 Mission Dr; day rates $45-85; ⊙9am-6pm Mon-Fri, 9am-5pm Sat, 10am-4pm Sun).

🛌 Sleeping

Choices are the best in the region but sleeping in Solvang isn't cheap, not even at older motels with faux-Danish exteriors. On week-

ends, rates skyrocket and rooms fill fast, so book ahead.

★**Landsby** BOUTIQUE HOTEL $$ (Map p368; ✆805-688-3121; www.thelandsby.com; 1576 Mission Dr; r from $149; @🛜) Forget Solvang's cheesy Danish side, the Landsby is all about slick contemporary Scandinavian style. The principal decorative themes in this new arrival on the town's sleeping scene are white and wood, but cool design doesn't mean there's not a warm atmosphere. Start your day with the complimentary breakfast and finish it with a drink at the popular lobby bar.

The in-house Mad & Vin restaurant (meaning 'food and wine' in Danish) has similarly chic surroundings and a good menu of classic American dishes (mains $16 to $34).

Hamlet Inn MOTEL $$ (Map p368; ✆805-688-4413; www.thehamletinn. com; 1532 Mission Dr; r $99-229; P⊖❄🛜) This remodeled motel is to wine-country lodging what IKEA is to interior design: a budget-friendly, trendy alternative. Crisp, modern rooms have bright Danish-flag bedspreads and iPod docking stations. Free loaner bicycles and a bocce-ball court for guests add to the appeal.

Hadsten House BOUTIQUE HOTEL $$ (Map p368; ✆805-688-3210; www.hadstenhouse. com; 1450 Mission Dr; r $140-270; P⊖❄🛜❄) This revamped motel has luxuriously updated just about everything, except for its routine exterior. Inside, rooms are surprisingly plush, with flat-screen TVs, comfy duvets and high-end bath products. Spa suites come with jet tubs. There's a good in-house restaurant (Tuesday to Saturday).

Hotel Corque
BOUTIQUE HOTEL **$$$**

(Map p368; ☑805-688-8000; www.hotelcorque. com; 400 Alisal Rd; r $179-409; ❄@🛜🐾) This clean-lined hotel is a relief from all things Danish. Overpriced rooms may look anonymous, but they're quite spacious. Amenities include an outdoor swimming pool and hot tub, plus access to the next-door fitness center, where you can work off all those Danish butter rings.

✗ Eating

When it comes to eating, the emphasis is most definitely on Danish dishes, with pastry-producing bakeries abounding. A couple of non-Danish standouts provide a break from the sweet stuff though, with innovative menus showing off the rich local produce.

Paula's Pancake House
DANISH **$**

(Map p368; ☑805-688-2867; www.paulaspancake house.com; 1531 Mission Dr; pancakes from $6.50; ☺6am-3pm; 🖍) *God Morgen!* Start the day Danish-style with a warm welcome and a hearty breakfast in which, clue in the name, pancakes feature heavily – over 30 years beating batter means Paula knows her stuff. The lunch menu ventures into burgers and sandwiches territory, but with breakfast served all day, there's no wrong time to put away some pancakes.

It's hugely popular and lines are long so prepare to either get here as soon as it opens or to wait a while.

Solvang Restaurant
BAKERY **$**

(Map p368; ☑805-688-4645; www.solvang restaurant.com; 1672 Copenhagen Dr; items from $4; ☺6am-3pm or 4pm Mon-Fri, to 5pm Sat & Sun; 🖉🖍) Duck around the Danish-inscribed beams with decorative borders to order *aebleskivers* – round pancake popovers covered in powdered sugar and raspberry jam. They're so popular there's even a special takeout window, and if you develop a fondness for them you can buy all the ingredients (and the special pan) to make your own.

Solvang Bakery
BAKERY **$**

(Map p368; www.solvangbakery.com; 438 Alisal Rd; items from $3.50; ☺7am-6:30pm Sun-Thu, to 8pm Fri & Sat; 🖍) Gingerbread is a specialty here (have a personalized holiday creation made for you) but that doesn't mean other bestsellers like the almond-butter ring and the jalapeño-cheese bread sit on the shelves for long either. The decor is exactly how you'd want this kind of place's decor to be.

★ First & Oak
CALIFORNIAN **$$**

(Map p368; ☑805-688-1703; www.firstandoak. com; 409 First St, Mirabelle Inn; mains $12-23; ☺5:30-8:45pm) Rich, innovative small plates in an elegant but cozy setting make First & Oak Solvang's best dining experience. The menu changes with the seasons but you can expect unusual takes on California cuisine, such as baked beets with bee pollen and whipped goat's cheese or linguini with softshell crab and yuzu emulsion. Inventive desserts round off a memorable meal.

★ Succulent Café
CALIFORNIAN **$$**

(Map p368; ☑805-691-9444; www.succulentcafe. com; 1555 Mission Dr; mains breakfast & lunch $5-15, dinner $16-36; ☺10am-3pm & 5-9pm Mon & Wed-Sun, from 8:30am Sat & Sun; 🖉🖍) 🌿 An inspired menu allows farm-fresh ingredients to speak for themselves at this family-owned gourmet cafe and market. Fuel up on breakfast biscuits with fried chicken, pulled pork and artisan grilled-cheese sandwiches for lunch, or pumpkin-seed-crusted lamb for dinner. On sunny days, eat outside on the patio, where dogs are welcome (they even have their own menu).

Aly's
MODERN AMERICAN **$$$**

(Map p368; ☑805-697-7082; http://alysbyalebru. com; 451 2nd St; ☺5-8:45pm Thu-Mon) Fine cuisine isn't usually associated with Solvang, but Aly's meat- and fish-focused dishes hit the mark. The low-lit, simply furnished dining room complements the rich, flavorful food that is sourced locally and prepared with skill. If you're struggling to choose, go with the chef's tasting menu and pair it with carefully selected wines.

Root 246
AMERICAN **$$$**

(Map p368; ☑805-686-8681; www.root-246.com; 420 Alisal Rd; mains $26-39, brunch buffet adult $27, child 6-12yr $11; ☺5-9pm Tue-Thu, 5-10pm Fri & Sat, 10am-2pm & 5-9pm Sun) 🌿 Next to Hotel Corque, chef Bradley Ogden's creative farm-to-table cuisine shows an artful touch. It's hard to beat the chicken and steaks, or come for the Sunday brunch buffet. Make reservations or seat yourself in the sleek fireplace lounge to sip California wines by the glass after 4pm. Service can be hit and miss.

🍸 Drinking & Nightlife

After dinner this town is deader than an ancient Viking, with a couple of notable exceptions, listed below.

Copenhagen Sausage Garden BEER GARDEN
(Map p368; ☎805-697-7354; www.csg-solvang.
com; 1660 Copenhagen Dr; ☺10am-midnight)
Another sign of Solvang's attempts to stay
up late, CSG keeps the beers (and wine)
flowing well into the evening on its outdoor
patio. Sausages from around the world (little flags on the menu help you choose the
country you want, from Spain and Italy to
Denmark and the US) provide the snacks,
and occasional live music provides the
entertainment.

Solvang Brewing Company BREWERY
(Map p368; ☎805-688-2337; http://solvang
brewing.com; 1547 Mission St; ☺11am-midnight or
later, from 4pm Wed) If you're done with wine
but not with alcohol then the Brewing Company is the place to head. A decent selection
of beers (including a stout and a couple of
wheat ales) is complemented by filling pub
grub and live music (usually Wednesday to
Sunday). Plus it's one of the few places in
town that stays open past sundown.

🛍 Shopping

Downtown Solvang's notoriously kitschy
shops cover a half-dozen blocks south of
Mission Dr/Hwy 246 between Atterdag Rd
and Alisal Rd. For Danish cookbooks, hand-
crafted quilts and other homespun items,
visit the Elverhøj Museum (p374).

★Copenhagen House DESIGN
(Map p368; ☎805-693-5000; http://thecopenhagen
house.com; 1660 Copenhagen Dr; ☺10am-5.30pm
Mon-Fri, to 6pm Sat & Sun) The name stays true
to Solvang's Danish roots but the eclectic
mix of top-quality design goods, all from the
motherland, couldn't be further from the
town's usual tourist tat. Keep kids happy with
some Lego, treat yourself to exquisite Pandora
jewelry or a Bering watch, or buy some stylish
home- and kitchenwares that make you feel
cooler just looking at them.

Book Loft BOOKS
(Map p368; ☎805-688-6010; www.bookloftsolvang.
com; 1680 Mission Dr; ☺9am-8pm Tue-Thu, to 9pm
Fri & Sat, to 6pm Sun & Mon) Long-running, independent bookshop carrying antiquarian
and Scandinavian titles and children's story-
books. The Hans Christian Andersen Museum (p373) is upstairs.

ℹ Information

Solvang Conference & Visitors Bureau (Map
p368; ☎805-688-6144; www.solvangusa.com;
1639 Copenhagen Dr; ☺9am-5pm) Pick up free
tourist brochures and winery maps at this kiosk
in the town center, by the municipal parking lot
and public restrooms.

ℹ Getting There & Away

Santa Ynez Valley Transit (☎805-688-5452;
www.syvt.com; $1.50 each way; ☺7am-7pm)
runs local buses equipped with bike racks on
a loop around Buellton, Solvang, Santa Ynez,
Ballard and Los Olivos. Buses operate roughly between 7am and 7pm Monday through Saturday;
one-way rides cost $1.50 (exact change only).

Buellton

Tiny Buellton was once best known for Andersen's Pea Soup Restaurant, and you can
still get heaping bowls of the green stuff,
a tradition going back almost 100 years.
If split-pea soup doesn't appeal, then the
growing drinking (beer as well as wine) and
eating scene on Industrial Way, just south of
Hwy 246, should do the trick instead.

🍴 Eating

★Industrial Eats AMERICAN $
(Map p368; ☎805-688-8807; http://industrialeats.
com; 181 Industrial Way; mains $9-15; ☺10am-
9pm) Hugely and justifiably popular locals'
hangout, housed in an eclectically decorated
warehouse on Buellton's coolest street. Pizzas have traditional to what-the? toppings
(eg duck and pistachio); the small plates are
huge, innovative and eminently shareable;
and the wine and beer are top-notch. On a
changing menu perennial favorites include
the shrimp and pancetta on toast combo
and the beef-tongue Reuben.

Ellen's Danish Pancake House BREAKFAST $
(Map p368; ☎805-688-5312; www.ellensdanish
pancakehouse.com; 272 Ave of Flags; mains $10-
15; ☺6am-8pm, to 2pm Mon; ℗) West of Hwy
101, just off Hwy 246, this old-fashioned, always-busy diner is where locals congregate
for friendly service and the Wine Country's
best Danish pancakes and sausages. Breakfast served all day.

Hitching Post II STEAK $$$
(Map p368; ☎805-688-0676; www.hitchingpost2.
com; 406 E Hwy 246; mains $26-55; ☺5-9:30pm
Mon-Fri, from 4pm Sat & Sun; 🐾) As seen in the
movie *Sideways*, this dark-paneled chop-
house offers oak-grilled steaks, pork ribs,
smoked duck breast and rack of lamb. Every
old-school meal comes with a veggie tray,

garlic bread, shrimp cocktail or soup, salad and potatoes. The Hitching Post makes its own Pinot Noir, and it's damn good (wine tastings at the bar start at 4pm).

📍 Drinking & Nightlife

Bottlest Winery, Bar & Bistro WINE BAR
(Map p368; ☑805-686-4742; http://avantwines.com; 35 Industrial Way; ⊗11am-9pm, dinner from 5pm) Small plates ($13–24) and dozens of wines come together in this 'winery restaurant,' formerly called Terravant. Step up to the Wine Wall to take your pick from 52 options and then add some crab cakes, pork belly or garden greens with burrata to the mix. Larger, meat and fish meals ($21–39) are also available. Happy hour (3pm to 5pm daily) brings prices down.

Figueroa Mountain Brewing Co BREWERY
(Map p368; ☑805-694-2252; www.figmtnbrew.com; 45 Industrial Way; ⊗11am-9pm; 🐾) Fig Mountain's original brewpub gives you a break from the wine with its award-winning, inhouse-brewed beers: Hoppy Poppy, Danish red lager and Davy Brown ale are three favorites. Soak them up with some great pub grub and enjoy the frequent live music and comedy nights. Or sit outside in the pet-friendly beer garden.

🛈 Getting There & Around

Central Coast Shuttle (☑805-928-1977; www.cclax.com; 1-way/round-trip LA–Buellton $70/128; ⊗info line 8am-7:30pm Mon-Fri, 9:30am-5:30pm Sat & Sun) will bus you from LAX to Buellton (book in advance online to avoid a non-prepaid small additional cost). Amtrak provides a couple of daily connecting Thruway buses to and from Solvang, but only if you're catching a train (or arriving on one) in Santa Barbara.

Santa Ynez Valley Transit runs local buses equipped with bike racks on a loop around Buellton, Solvang, Santa Ynez, Ballard and Los Olivos. You'll need exact change for the fare.

AROUND SANTA BARBARA

Can't quit your day job to follow your bliss? Don't despair: a long weekend in the mountains, valleys and beaches between Santa Barbara and LA will keep you inspired until you can. In this land of daydreams, perfect waves beckon off Ventura's coast, shady trails wind skyward in the Los Padres National Forest and spiritual Zen awaits you in Ojai Valley. Surf, stroll, seek – if outdoor rejuvenation is your goal, this is the place.

And then there's Channel Islands National Park, a biodiverse chain of islands shimmering just off the coast where you can kayak majestic sea caves, scuba dive in wavy kelp forests, wander fields of wildflower blooms or simply disappear from civilization at a remote wilderness campsite.

Montecito

Well-heeled, leafy Montecito, just east of Santa Barbara in the Santa Ynez foothills, is not just home to the rich and famous but to the obscenely rich and the uber-famous.

Though many homes hide behind manicured hedges these days, a taste of the Montecito lifestyle of yesteryear can be experienced by taking a tour of **Casa del Herrero** (☑805-565-5653; http://casadelherrero.com; 1387 E Valley Rd; 90min tour $25; ⊗10am & 2pm Wed & Sat, reservations 9am-5pm Mon-Sat; 🅿). The town's cafe- and boutique-filled main drag is Coast Village Rd (exit Hwy 101 at Olive Mill Rd).

Most visitors base themselves in Santa Barbara and visit Montecito (a 15-minute drive away) as a day trip. Upmarket, beachside Four Seasons Biltmore is an option if money is no object.

From Santa Barbara, MTD (p367) buses 14 and 20 run to and from Montecito ($1.75, 20 minutes, every 40 to 60 minutes); bus 20 also connects Montecito with Summerland and Carpinteria.

Summerland

This drowsy seaside community was founded in the 1880s by HL Williams, a real-estate speculator. Williams was also a spiritualist, whose followers believed in the power of mediums to connect the living with the dead. Spiritualists were rumored to keep hidden rooms for séances – a practice that earned the town the indelicate nickname of 'Spookville.'

Today, those wanting to connect to the past wander the town's antique shops, where you won't find any bargains, but you can ooh and aah over beautiful furniture, jewelry and art from decades or even centuries gone by.

To find the beach, turn south off exit 91 and cross the railroad tracks to cliffside **Lookout Park** (www.countyofsb.org/parks; Lookout Park Rd; ⊙8am-sunset; 🅿) **FREE** which has a kids' playground, picnic tables, barbecue grills and access to a wide, relatively quiet stretch of sand (leashed dogs OK).

Grab breakfast or brunch at the Victorian seaside-style **Summerland Beach Café** (☑805-969-1019; www.summerlandbeachcafe.com; 2294 Lillie Ave; mains $7-14; ⊙7am-3pm Mon-Fri, to 4pm Sat & Sun; 🅿🍴🅿), known for its fluffy omelets, and enjoy the ocean breezes on the patio. Or walk over to **Tinker's** (☑805-969-1970; 2275 Ortega Hill Rd; items $5-10; ⊙11am-8pm; 🍴), an eat-out-of-a-basket burger shack that delivers seasoned curly fries and old-fashioned milkshakes.

From Santa Barbara, MTD bus 20 runs to Summerland ($1.75, 25 minutes, hourly) via Montecito, continuing to Carpinteria.

Carpinteria

Lying 11 miles east of Santa Barbara, the time-warped beach town of Carpinteria – so named because Chumash carpenters once built seafaring canoes here – is a laid-back place. You could easily spend an hour or two wandering in and out of antiques shops and beachy boutiques along Linden Ave, downtown's main street. To gawk at the world's largest vat of guacamole, show up for the California Avocado Festival in early October.

⊙ Sights & Activities

If you're an expert surfer, **Rincon Point** has long, glassy, right point-break waves. It's about 3 miles southeast of downtown, off Hwy 101 (exit Bates Rd).

Carpinteria State Beach   BEACH
(☑805-968-1033; www.parks.ca.gov; end of Linden Ave; per car $10; ⊙7am-sunset; 🍴) An idyllic, mile-long strand where kids can splash around in calm waters and go tide-pooling along the shoreline. In winter, you may spot harbor seals and sea lions hauled out on the sand, especially if you hike over a mile south along the coast to a bluff-top overlook.

Surf Happens   SURFING
(Map p356; ☑805-966-3613; http://surfhappens.com; 13 E Haley St; 2hr private lesson from $160; 🍴) Welcoming families, beginners and 'Surf Happens Sisters,' these highly reviewed classes and camps led by expert staff incorporate the Zen of surfing. In summer, you'll

begin your spiritual wave-riding journey. Make reservations in advance. The office is based in downtown Santa Barbara.

✦✦ Festivals & Events

California Avocado Festival   FOOD & DRINK
(www.avofest.com; 800 Linden Ave; ⊙early Oct) **FREE** Still going strong after 30 years, the annual California Avocado Festival is one of the state's largest free events, held in downtown Carpinteria. Bands play, avocado recipes are judged and the world's largest vat of guacamole makes a guest appearance.

🛏 Sleeping

Carpinteria's cookie-cutter chain motels and hotels are unexciting, but usually less expensive than those in nearby Santa Barbara.

Carpinteria State Beach Campground   CAMPGROUND $
(☑800-444-7275; www.reserveamerica.com; 205 Palm Ave; tent & RV drive-up sites $45-70, hike-&-bike tent sites $10) Often crowded, this oceanfront campground offers lots of family-friendly amenities including flush toilets, hot showers, picnic tables and barbecue grills. Book ahead (reservations are taken up to seven months in advance).

✗ Eating & Drinking

Tacos Don Roge   MEXICAN $
(☑805-566-6546; www.facebook.com/tacosdonroge; 751 Linden Ave; items from $1.50; ⊙10am-9pm) This Mexican taqueria stakes its reputation on a rainbow-colored salsa bar with up to a dozen different sauces to drizzle on piquant meat-stuffed, double-rolled corn tortillas – try the jalapeño or pineapple versions. If the spiciness gets you, grab an ice cream from Rainbows next door.

Padaro Beach Grill   AMERICAN $
(☑805-566-9800; http://padarobeachgrill.com; 3765 Santa Claus Lane; mains $7-11; ⊙usually 10:30am-8pm Mon-Fri, from 11am Sat & Sun; 🅿🍴) Off Hwy 101 west of downtown, this oceanfront grill makes darn good burgers (including vegan versions), grilled-fish tacos, sweet-potato fries and thick, hand-mixed milkshakes. The palm-tree-shaded garden is a relaxing place to devour them.

Corktree Cellars   CALIFORNIAN $$
(☑805-684-1400; www.corktreecellars.com; 910 Linden Ave; small plates $7.50-14; ⊙usually 11:30am-9pm Tue-Thu & Sun, to 9:30pm Fri & Sat) Downtown's contemporary wine bar and

DON'T MISS

LOTUSLAND

In 1941 the eccentric opera singer and socialite Madame Ganna Walska bought the 37 acres that make up **Lotusland** (☑ info 805-969-3767, reservations 805-969-9990; www. lotusland.org; 695 Ashley Rd; adult $45, child 3-18yr $20; ⊙ tours by appt 10am & 1:30pm Wed-Sat mid-Feb–mid-Nov; [P]) with her lover and yoga-guru Theos Bernard. After marrying and then divorcing Bernard, she retained control of the gardens and spent the next four decades tending and expanding this incredible collection of rare and exotic plants from around the world; there are over 140 varieties of aloe alone. Come in summer when the lotuses bloom, typically during July and August.

Reservations are required for tours, but the phone is only attended from 9am to 5pm weekdays, to 1pm Saturday.

bistro offers tasty California-style tapas, charcuterie and cheese plates, and a good number of wine flights ($14).

Rincon Brewery CRAFT BEER
(☑ 805-684-6044; http://rinconbrewery.com; 5065 Carpinteria Ave; ⊙ 11am-9:30pm Sun-Thu, to 11pm Fri & Sat) Swap ocean waves for 'waves of grain' (their words) and knock back Belgian-style craft beers (among others) and a long menu of standard but tasty pub grub that keeps this place busy most nights of the week.

Island Brewing Co BREWERY
(☑ 805-745-8272; www.islandbrewingcompany. com; 5049 6th St, off Linden Ave; ⊙ noon-9pm Mon-Thu, noon-10pm Fri, 11am-10pm Sat, 11am-9pm Sun; ☺) Wanna hang loose with friendly beach bums and drink bourbon-barrel-aged brews? Find this locals-only, industrial space with an outdoor, dog-friendly patio by the railroad tracks – look for the Island sign.

ⓘ Getting There & Away

Carpinteria is 11 miles east of Santa Barbara via Hwy 101 (southbound exit Linden Ave, north-bound Casitas Pass Rd). From Santa Barbara, take MTD (p367) bus 20 ($1.75, 40 minutes, at least hourly) via Montecito and Summerland.
Amtrak (☑ 800-872-7245; www.amtrak.com; 475 Linden Ave) has an unstaffed platform downtown; buy tickets online or by phone before catching one of five daily *Pacific Surfliner* trains west to Santa Barbara ($8.50, 15 to 20 minutes) and south to Ventura ($11, 25 minutes) or LA ($29, 2½ hours).

Ojai

Hollywood director Frank Capra chose the Ojai Valley to represent a mythical Shangri-la in his 1937 movie *Lost Horizon*. Today Ojai ('*OH*-hi', from the Chumash word for 'moon') attracts artists, organic farmers, spiritual

seekers and anyone ready to indulge in day-spa pampering. Bring shorts and flip-flops: Shangri-la sure gets hot in summer.

⊙ Sights & Activities

Ojai Olive Oil Company FARM
(☑ 805-646-5964; www.ojaioliveoil.com; 1811 Ladera Rd; ⊙ 9am-4pm Mon-Fri, 10am-4pm Sat) FREE
Outside town, family-owned Ojai Olive Oil Company has a tasting room open six days a week, and offers free talks and tours on Wednesdays (1pm to 4pm) and Saturdays (10am to 4pm). It also sells at the Ojai Farmers Market (p382) on Sundays. Dip bread into the various oils (and balsamic vinegars from Modena, its home) – the milder Provençale variety is the most popular.

Meditation Mount VIEWPOINT
(☑ 805-646-5508; https://meditationmount.org; 10340 Reeves Rd; ⊙ 8:30am-sunset Wed-Sun) FREE Ojai is famous for the rosy glow that emanates from its mountains at sunset (some days) – the so-called 'Pink Moment.' The ideal vantage point for catching the show is the peaceful lookout atop Meditation Mount. Head east of downtown on Ojai Ave/Hwy 150 for about 2 miles, turn left at Boccali's farm-stand restaurant and drive another 2.5 miles on Reeves Rd (there's some signage) until it heads uphill and dead-ends at a parking lot and meditation center.

As well as the view, the gardens are a scented delight and, in keeping with the name, meditation is available (8:30am guided classes, from 9am until close for private meditation).

Ojai Vineyard Tasting Room WINERY
(☑ 805-798-3947; www.ojaivineyard.com; 109 S Montgomery St; tastings $15; ⊙ noon-6pm) Inside downtown's historic firehouse, Ojai Vineyard pours tastes of its delicate, small-batch

wines. It's best known for standard-bearing Chardonnay, Pinot Noir and Syrah, but the crisp Sauvignon Blanc, dry Riesling and zippy rosé are also worth sampling.

Ojai Valley Trail   HIKING
(www.traillink.com/trail/ojai-valley-trail.aspx) FREE Running beside the highway, the 9-mile Ojai Valley Trail, converted from defunct railway tracks, is popular with walkers, runners, cyclists and equestrians. Pick it up downtown two blocks south of Ojai Ave, off Bryant St, then head west through the valley.

Mob Shop   CYCLING
(☎805-272-8102; www.themobshop.com; 110 W Ojai Ave; bicycle rental per hour $12, day $25-50; ☉10am-5pm Mon & Wed-Fri, 9am-5pm Sat, 9am-4pm Sun) Bike rental (including electric and kid versions) for DIY, two-wheel exploration of Ojai, plus organized tours of the city and surrounding area. Mountain bikers can sign up for a descent of nearby Sulphur Mountain.

Spa Ojai   SPA
(☎855-697-8780; www.ojairesort.com/spa-ojai; Ojai Valley Inn & Spa, 905 Country Club Rd) For the ultimate in relaxation, book a day at top-tier Spa Ojai in the Ojai Valley Inn, where nonresort guests pay an extra $20 to access swimming pools, a workout gym and mind/body fitness classes.

Day Spa of Ojai   SPA
(☎805-640-1100; www.thedayspa.com; 209 N Montgomery St; treatments $21-190; ☉10:30am-5:30pm) Soothing everyday cares away for two decades now, this family-run operation is the place to come for facials, body wraps and hot-rock treatments for men and women. It specializes in Swedish massages, starting from $88.

🛏 Sleeping

Pricey but excellent quality would best describe the local accommodations scene. Book well in advance, especially for weekends.

★ Lavender Inn   B&B $$
(☎805-646-6635; http://lavenderinn.com; 210 E Matilija St; r from $145; P🖥📶🐾) For a central location in a historic 1874 schoolhouse building, you can't beat the Lavender Inn. Room decor ranges from quaint to modern; a hearty, healthy breakfast can be enjoyed on the porch overlooking the pretty garden; and the evening tapas and wine are nice touches.

An on-site spa sees to your relaxation needs, while the in-house cookery courses can satisfy any culinary aspirations. Just remember you *are* allowed to leave to explore Ojai itself, a short walk away.

Ojai Retreat   B&B $$
(☎805-646-2536; www.ojairetreat.com; 160 Besant Rd; r $90-295; 🖥@📶) On a hilltop on the outskirts of town, this peaceful place has a back-to-nature collection of 12 country arts-and-crafts-style guest rooms and cottage suites, all perfect for unplugging. Find a quiet nook for reading or writing (no TVs), ramble through the wonderful grounds, or practice your downward dog in a yoga class.

Emerald Iguana Inn   BOUTIQUE HOTEL $$
(☎805-646-5277; www.emeraldiguana.com; 108 Pauline St; ☉r/ste from $179/249; P🖥📶🏊) Sister property of the Blue Iguana Inn, the Emerald Iguana is oriented more toward adults looking for a getaway but within walking distance of downtown Ojai. Local art hangs on the walls, in-room spa treatments can be arranged, and packages include romantic touches (wine, roses and chocolate). Two-bed cottages, complete with full kitchen, are available alongside comfortable standard rooms.

A two-night minimum is usually required. Book well in advance for weekends.

Ojai Rancho Inn   MOTEL $$
(☎805-646-1434; http://ojairanchoinn.com; 615 W Ojai Ave; r $120-200; 🖥📶🏊🐾) At this low-slung motel next to the highway, pine-paneled rooms each have a king bed. Cottage rooms come with fireplaces, and some have Jacuzzis and kitchenettes. Besides competitive rates, the biggest bonuses of staying here are a small pool and sauna, shuffleboard, fire pit, and bicycles to borrow for the half-mile ride to downtown. Pet fee $20.

Blue Iguana Inn   INN $$
(☎805-646-5277; www.blueiguanainn.com; 11794 N Ventura Ave; r/ste from $139/169; 📶🏊🐾) Artsy iguanas lurk everywhere at this funky architect-designed inn – on adobe walls around Mediterranean-tiled fountains and anywhere else that reptilian style could bring out a smile. Roomy bungalow and cottage suites are unique, and the pool is a social scene for LA denizens. Rates include continental breakfast; two-night minimum stay on weekends. Some pets allowed with prior approval only.

For a more central location and romantic atmosphere, try the sister Emerald Iguana Inn, just north of downtown.

Ojai Valley Inn & Spa RESORT $$$
(☑ 805-646-1111, 855-697-8780; www.ojairesort.com; 905 Country Club Rd; r from $349; 🅿❄@🛜♨🐾) At the west end of town, this pampering resort has landscaped gardens, tennis courts, swimming pools, a championship golf course and a fabulous spa. Luxurious rooms are outfitted with all mod cons, and some sport a fireplace and balcony. Recreational activities run the gamut from kids' camps and complimentary bikes to full-moon yoga and astrological readings. Nightly 'service' surcharge is $35.

If the resort's size puts you off, don't worry – a free golf-cart shuttle will whisk you to wherever you want to be.

On-site restaurant Olivella (p382) is one of the best in town.

🍴 Eating

You can guarantee top-quality ingredients in Ojai. Organic, sustainable and local are part of everyday culinary life here, and in keeping with the city's bohemian, hippie vibe, vegetarians and vegans will revel in the options available. The main drag, Ojai Ave, has plenty of places serving excellent food, but equally good choices are in out-of-the-way but worth-seeking-out locations around town.

★ Knead BAKERY, CAFE $
(☑ 310-770-3282; http://kneadbakingcompany.com; 469 E Ojai Ave; items $3.50-16; ⊙8am-2pm Wed-Sun) Family-run artisan bakery mixing batters with the best of Ojai's fresh fruit, herbs, honey and nuts. Get a slice of sweet tart (the lemon ricotta is sensational), a savory quiche or a made-to-order breakfast sandwich. Saturday's sticky buns fly off the shelves. Enjoy a mimosa, wine or beer too. No credit cards.

HiHo! BURGERS $
(☑ 805-640-4446; http://hihoburger.com; 401 E Ojai Ave; burgers from $10.95; ⊙11:30am-8pm Wed-Sun) Sometimes even health-conscious Ojai residents just want a burger, fries and a cola. HiHo! in the heart of downtown scratches that itch. It's a simple menu: wagyu-beef patties (vegetarian burgers available) served 'classic' (lettuce, cheese, ketchup) or 'HIHO' (same but with pickles and onion jam). Sit under the umbrellas and forget kale salads exist.

Bonnie Lu's Country Cafe BREAKFAST $
(☑805-646-0207; www.facebook.com/bonnielus; 328 E Ojai Ave; mains from $8; ⊙7am-2:30pm Thu-Tue) Central, and therefore busy (expect to wait at weekends), diner where all your breakfast favorites are available, including a variety of eggs Benedict, pancakes and biscuits with gravy. Not the place for a light start to the day.

Hip Vegan VEGAN $
(☑805-646-1750; www.hipvegancafe.com; 928 E Ojai Ave; mains $9.50-15; ⊙11am-5pm Mon & Thu, to 7pm Fri-Sun; 🍴🐾) 🌿 Tucked back from the street in a tiny garden (look for the arrow on the wall), this locals' kitchen stays true to Ojai's granola-crunching hippie roots with Mexican-leaning salads and sides, Asian-influenced sandwiches and classic SoCal date shakes and teas. The interior is spartan so grab a shaded picnic table outside.

Farmer & the Cook MEXICAN, VEGETARIAN $$
(☑805-640-9608; www.farmerandcook.com; 339 W Roblar Ave; mains $8.50-14.50; ⊙8:30am-8:30pm; 🍴🐾) 🌿 Flavorful, organic, vegetarian (some vegan) homemade Mexican cooking bursts out of this roadside market, which has its own farm nearby. Come for the squash and goat's-cheese tacos or the highly rated *huarache* (tortilla, potatoes, onions, pepper, feta and more), or, at dinner Thursday to Sunday, creative pizzas and a salad bar. Smoothies are available throughout the day.

Boccali's ITALIAN $$
(☑805-646-6116; http://boccalis.com; 3277 Ojai-Santa Paula Rd; mains $10-19; ⊙4-9pm Mon & Tue, from noon Wed-Sun; 🍴🐾) This roadside farm stand with red-and-white-checkered tablecloths does simple, big-portion Italian cooking. Much of the produce is grown behind the restaurant and the fresh tomato salad is often still warm from the garden. The real draws are the wood-oven pizzas and the seasonal strawberry shortcake. It's over 2 miles east of downtown via Ojai Ave.

★ Suzanne's Cuisine INTERNATIONAL $$$
(☑805-640-1961; www.suzannescuisine.com; mains $18-36; ⊙11:30am-2:30pm & 5:30pm-close Mon & Wed-Sun) The eclectic menu in this Ojai locals' favorite ranges from French-inspired snails and hearty pasta dishes to healthy salads and excellent meat, fish and seafood options. It's a family-run affair with an attention to detail that reflects the dedication

of the eponymous Suzanne. In summer ask for a table on the outside patio overlooking the charming garden.

Olivella
CALIFORNIAN $$$
(📞855-697-8780; www.ojairesort.com/dining/olivella-restaurant; 905 Country Club Rd; mains $35-55; ⊙5:30-9pm Wed-Sun; 🅿) In the Ojai Valley Inn & Spa, this worth-getting-dressed-up-for (though you don't have to) restaurant is *the* place in Ojai for a special meal. Meat and pasta are the stars of the menu (the Bolognese sauce is a 19th-century chef-family recipe) but salads and fish dishes are equally tasty. Or push the boat out (and loosen the belt) with the four-course experience.

Service is friendly but can be disorganized.

🛍 Shopping

★ Bart's Books
BOOKS
(📞805-646-3755; www.bartsbooksojai.com; 302 W Matilija St; ⊙9:30am-sunset) One block north of Ojai Ave, this charming, unique indoor-outdoor space sells new and well-loved tomes. It's been going for well over a half century so demands at least a half-hour browse and a purchase or two – just don't step on the lurking but surprisingly nimble cat.

Ojai Farmers Market
MARKET
(📞805-698-5555; www.ojaicertifiedfarmersmarket.com; 300 E Matilija St; ⊙9am-1pm Sun) It's no surprise that in an agriculturally blessed region, Ojai's farmers market is a beauty. There are the usual high-quality fruit and vegetables on offer each Sunday, plus seafood, meat, breads, chocolate, flowers and plants.

Ojai Clothing
CLOTHING
(📞805-640-1269; http://ojaiclothing.com; 325 E Ojai Ave; ⊙noon-5pm Mon & Wed-Thu, noon-5:30pm Fri, 10am-5:30pm Sat, 11am-5pm Sun) Equally comfy for doing an interpretive dance or just hanging out, these earth-toned and vibrantly patterned casual pieces for women and men are made from soft cotton knits and woven fabrics.

Human Arts Gallery
ARTS & CRAFTS
(📞805-646-1525; www.humanartsgallery.com; 246 E Ojai Ave; ⊙11am-5pm Mon-Sat, noon-5pm Sun) Browse the colorful handmade jewelry, sculpture, woodcarvings, glassworks, folk-art furnishings and more from over 150 American artists. A custom-design service is also available if you want a unique souvenir of your Ojai visit.

ℹ Information

Ojai Library (📞805-646-1639; www.vencolibrary.org/locations/ojai-library; 111 E Ojai Ave; ⊙10am-8pm Mon-Thu, noon-5pm Fri-Sun; 🛜) Free online computer terminals and wi-fi for public use.

Ojai Ranger Station (📞805-646-4348; www.fs.usda.gov/detail/lpnf; 1190 E Ojai Ave; ⊙8am-4:30pm Mon-Fri) Camping tips and trail maps for hiking to hot springs, waterfalls and mountaintop viewpoints in the Los Padres National Forest.

Ojai Visitors Bureau (📞805-640-3606; www.ojaivisitors.com; 109 N Blanche St; ⊙8am-4pm Mon-Fri) Provides brochures and other material to visitors.

ℹ Getting There & Away

Ojai is around 33 miles east of Santa Barbara via scenic Hwy 150, or 15 miles inland (north) from Ventura via Hwy 33. **Gold Coast Transit** (📞805-487-4222; www.goldcoasttransit.org) bus 16 runs from Ventura (including a stop near the Amtrak station) to downtown Ojai ($1.50, 45 minutes, hourly).

Ventura

The primary pushing-off point for Channel Island boat trips, the beach town of San Buenaventura may not look to be the most enchanting coastal city, but it has seaside charms, especially on the historic pier and downtown along Main St, north of Hwy 101 via California St.

⊙ Sights

South of Hwy 101 via Harbor Blvd, **Ventura Harbor** is the main departure point for boats to Channel Islands National Park.

Museum of Ventura County
MUSEUM
(📞805-653-0323; www.venturamuseum.org; 100 E Main St; adult $5, child 6-17yr $1; ⊙11am-5pm Tue-Sun; 🚻) This tiny downtown museum has an excellently eclectic collection that includes exhibits on the local Chumash people and rotating exhibitions of local artists. The highlight though is the George Stuart Historical Figures gallery. An Ojai resident, Stuart made models of famous people from the past to help bring to life historical lectures he gave around the country. Look out for emperor Nero, Vlad Tepes (aka Dracula), Henry VIII (with, sadly, just two of his wives), Hitler and Putin.

San Buenaventura State Beach   BEACH
(☑ 805-968-1033; www.parks.ca.gov; enter off San
Pedro St; per car $10; ⊙ dawn-dusk; ⑭) Along
the waterfront off Hwy 101, this long white-
sand beach is ideal for swimming, surfing
or just lazing on the sand. A recreational
cycling path connects to nearby **Emma
Wood State Beach**, another popular spot
for swimming, surfing and fishing.

Mission San Buenaventura   CHURCH
(☑ 805-643-4318; www.sanbuenaventuramission.
org; 211 E Main St; adult/child $4/2; ⊙ 10am-5pm,
from 9am Sat) Ventura's Spanish-colonial
roots go back to this last mission founded by
Junípero Serra in California in 1782. A stroll
around the mellow parish church leads you
through a garden courtyard and a small museum, past statues of saints, centuries-old
religious paintings and unusual, unique
wooden bells.

✗ Eating

In downtown Ventura, Main St is chockablock with Mexicali taco shops, casual cafes
and globally flavored kitchens.

★ Paradise Pantry   DELI $
(☑ 805-641-9440; www.paradisepantry.com; 222
E Main St; sandwiches $12-16; ⊙ 11am-8:30pm
Tue-Thu, to 9:30pm Fri & Sat, Sun hours vary; ☑)
On the cafe side of Paradise Pantry you can
grab a sandwich, soup, cheese or meat plate
in a quietly buzzing atmosphere. On the
deli side, you can stock up on supplies for a
beach or Channel Island picnic (sandwiches
can be made to go) and even grab some wine
or beer to wash it all down.

Jolly Oyster   SEAFOOD $
(☑ 805-798-4944; www.thejollyoyster.com; 911 San
Pedro St; items $5-16; ⊙ 11am-5pm Sat & Sun; ⑭)
✎ At San Buenaventura State Beach, the
Jolly Oyster sells its own farm-raised oysters and clams. The main option is shucking
your own (seat yourself at the nearby picnic
tables) though their licensed truck prepares
oysters on the half shell, baked and fried
oysters, clam steamers and a bay-scallop
ceviche. One-hour parking free.

Ventura Certified Farmers Market   MARKET $
(☑ 805-529-6266; http://vccfarmersmarkets.com;
cnr Santa Clara & Palm Sts; ⊙ 8:30am-noon Sat;
☑⑭) ✎ Over 45 farmers and food vendors
show up each week, offering fresh fruits and
vegetables, home-baked bread and ready-
made meals – Mediterranean, Mexican and
more. Another farmers market sets up at

midtown's Pacific View Mall from 9am to
1pm on Wednesdays.

★ Lure Fish House   SEAFOOD $$$
(☑ 805-567-4400; www.lurefishhouse.com; 60 S
California St; mains $17-37; ⊙ 11:30am-9pm Sun-
Thu, to 10pm Fri & Sat; ⑭) ✎ For seafood any
fresher, you'd have to catch it yourself off
Ventura pier. Go nuts ordering off a stalwart
menu of sustainably caught seafood, organic
regional farm produce and California wines.
Make reservations or turn up at the bar dur-
ing happy hour (4pm to 6pm Monday to
Friday, 11:30am to 6pm Sunday) for strong
cocktails, fried calamari and charbroiled
oysters.

♀ Drinking & Nightlife

You'll find plenty of rowdy dives down by
the harbor and a couple of excellent craft-
beer places around town.

★ Topa Topa Brewing Company   CRAFT BEER
(☑ 805-628-9255; http://topatopa.beer; 104 E
Thompson Blvd; ⊙ noon-9pm Mon-Thu, noon-
10pm Fri & Sat, 11am-8pm Sun; ⑭☺) Between
the freeway and downtown Ventura is not
exactly the most salubrious location, but
the beer here makes up for the surround-
ings. Chief Peak IPA takes the medal but
all the quality brewed-on-site options are
worth trying. Food trucks (a different one
every night, see the website for details) feed
the hungry.

Surf Brewery   BREWERY
(☑ 805-644-2739; http://surfbrewery.com; suite
A, 4561 Market St; ⊙ 4-9pm Tue-Thu, from 1pm Fri,
noon-9pm Sat, noon-7pm Sun) Operating since
2011, Surf Brewery makes big waves with
its hoppy and black IPAs and rye American
pale ale. Beer geeks and food trucks gath-
er at the sociable taproom in an industrial
area, about 5 miles from downtown (take
Hwy 101 southbound, exit Donlon St).

🔒 Shopping

★ Copperfield's   GIFTS & SOUVENIRS
(☑ 805-667-8198; www.facebook.com/copper
fieldsvta; 242 E Main St; ⊙ 10am-6pm Mon-Sat,
from 11am Sun) Part standard gift shop, part
what can only be described as emporium of
ephemera, this is the kind of place where
you can buy a birthday card one day and
an infra-compunctive resonance perversion
ray gun the next (your guess is as good as
ours). Quirky souvenirs don't come better
than this.

Rocket Fizz
FOOD & DRINKS

(☎805-641-1222; www.rocketfizz.com; 315 E Main St; ⊙10:30am-8pm Mon-Thu, to 9pm Fri & Sat, to 7pm Sun) Part of a national retro-style soda-pop and old-fashioned candy-store chain, this is the place for stocking your cooler with all types of so-bad-but-so-good sweets and drinks before a day at the beach.

B on Main
GIFTS & SOUVENIRS

(☎805-643-9309; www.facebook.com/b-on-main; 446 E Main St; ⊙10:30am-6pm Mon-Thu, 10am-7pm Fri & Sat, 11am-5pm Sun) For coastal living, B sells nifty reproductions of vintage surf posters, shabby-chic furnishings, SoCal landscape art, locally made jewelry and beachy clothing for women.

Ormachea
JEWELRY

(☎805-652-0484; www.ormacheajewelry.com; 451 E Main St; ⊙11am-5:30pm Mon-Fri, to 6pm Sat, to 5pm Sun) Run by a third-generation Peruvian jewelry craftsman, Ormachea skillfully hammers out one-of-a-kind, handmade rings, pendants and bangles in a downtown studio.

ARC Foundation Thrift Store
VINTAGE

(☎805-650-861; www.arcvc.org; 265 E Main St; ⊙9am-6pm Mon-Thu, 9am-7pm Fri & Sat, 10am-6pm Sun) Loads of thrift stores, antiques malls and secondhand and vintage shops cluster downtown. Most are on Main St, west of California St, where ARC is always jam-packed with bargain hunters.

❶ Information

Ventura Visitors & Convention Bureau
(☎805-648-2075; www.ventura-usa.com; 101 S California St; ⊙9am-5pm Mon-Sat, 10am-4pm Sun) Downtown visitor center handing out free maps and tourist brochures. It also contains a gift shop.

❶ Getting There & Away

Ventura is about 30 miles southeast of Santa Barbara via Hwy 101. **Amtrak** (☎800-872-7245; www.amtrak.com; Harbor Blvd, at Figueroa St) operates five daily trains north to Santa Barbara ($15, 45 minutes) via Carpinteria and south to LA ($24, 2¼ hours). Amtrak's platform station is unstaffed; buy tickets in advance online or by phone. **VCTC** (Ventura County Transportation Commission; ☎800-438-1112; www.goventura. org) runs several daily 'Coastal Express' buses between downtown Ventura and Santa Barbara ($3, 40 to 70 minutes) via Carpinteria; check online or call for schedules.

Channel Islands National Park

Don't let this off-the-beaten-path **national park** (Map p38; ☎805-658-5730; www.nps. gov/chis) 🖉 FREE loiter for too long on your lifetime to-do list. It's easier to access than you might think, and the payoff is immense. Imagine hiking, kayaking, scuba diving, camping and whale-watching, and doing it all amid a raw, end-of-the-world landscape. Rich in unique flora and fauna, tide pools and kelp forests, the islands are home to 145 plant and animal species found nowhere else in the world, earning them the nickname 'California's Galapagos.'

Geographically, the Channel Islands are an eight-island chain off the Southern California coast, stretching from Santa Barbara to San Diego. Five of them – San Miguel, Santa Rosa, Santa Cruz, Anacapa and tiny Santa Barbara – comprise Channel Islands National Park.

Originally the Channel Islands were inhabited by Chumash tribespeople, who were forced to move to mainland Catholic missions by Spanish military forces in the early 1800s. The islands were subsequently taken over by Mexican and American ranchers during the 19th century and the US military in the 20th, until conservation efforts began in the 1970s and '80s.

◉ Sights & Activities

Anacapa and Santa Cruz, the park's most popular islands, are within an hour's boat ride of Ventura. Both are doable day trips, though much larger Santa Cruz is a good overnight camping option. Bring plenty of water, because none is available on either island except at Scorpion Campground on Santa Cruz.

Most visitors arrive during summer, when island conditions are hot, dusty and bone-dry. Better times to visit are during the spring wildflower bloom or in early fall, when the fog clears. Winter can be stormy, but it's also great for wildlife-watching, especially whales.

Before you shove off from the mainland, stop by Ventura Harbor's NPS Visitor Center (p377) for educational natural-history exhibits, a free 25-minute nature film and on weekends and holidays, family-friendly activities and ranger talks.

Santa Cruz Island   ISLAND
(www.nps.gov/chis/planyourvisit/santa-cruz-island.htm) Santa Cruz, the Channel Islands' largest at 96 sq miles, claims two mountain ranges and the park's tallest peak, Mt Diablo (2450ft). The western three-quarters is mostly wilderness, managed by the Nature Conservancy and only accessible with a permit (www.nature.org/cruzpermit). The rest, managed by the National Park Service, is ideal for an action-packed day trip or laid-back overnight stay. Boats land at either Prisoners Harbor or Scorpion Anchorage, a short walk from historic Scorpion Ranch.

You can swim, snorkel, dive and kayak here, and there are plenty of hiking options too, starting from Scorpion Anchorage. It's a 1-mile climb to captivating Cavern Point. Views don't get much better than from this windy spot. For a longer jaunt, continue 1.5 miles west, along the North Bluff Trail, to Potato Harbor. The 4.5-mile Scorpion Canyon Loop heads uphill to an old oil well and fantastic views, then drops through Scorpion Canyon to the campground. Alternatively, follow Smugglers Rd all the way to the pebble beach at Smugglers Cove, a strenuous 7.5-mile round-trip. From Prisoners Harbor there are several more strenuous trails including the 18-mile round-trip China Pines hike – your efforts will be rewarded by the chance to see the rare Bishop pine.

There's little shade on the island (so avoid midday summer walks), bring plenty of water (available at Scorpion Anchorage only) and make sure you're at the harbor in plenty of time to catch your return boat, otherwise you'll be stuck overnight.

Anacapa Island   ISLAND
(www.nps.gov/chis/planyourvisit/anacapa.htm) Actually three separate islets totaling just over 1 sq mile, Anacapa gives a memorable introduction to the Channel Islands' ecology. It's also the best option if you're short on time. Boats dock year-round on the East Island where, after a short climb, you'll find 2 miles of trails offering fantastic views of island flora, a historic lighthouse, and rocky Middle and West Islands. You're bound to see western gulls too – the world's largest breeding colony is here.

Kayaking, diving, tide-pooling and watching seals and sea lions are popular outdoor activities, while inside the museum at the small visitor center, divers with video cameras occasionally broadcast images to a TV monitor you can watch during spring and summer.

Santa Rosa   ISLAND
(www.nps.gov/chis/planyourvisit/santa-rosa-island.htm) The indigenous Chumash people called Santa Rosa 'Wima' (driftwood) because of the redwood logs that often came ashore here, with which they built plank canoes called *tomols*. This 84-sq-mile island has rare Torrey pines, sandy beaches and hundreds of plant and bird species. Beach, canyon and grasslands hiking trails abound, but high winds can make swimming, diving and kayaking tough for anyone but experts.

San Miguel   ISLAND
(www.nps.gov/chis/planyourvisit/san-miguel-island.htm) While 14-sq-mile San Miguel can guarantee solitude and a remote wilderness experience, its westernmost location in the Channel Islands chain means it's often windy and shrouded in fog. Some sections are off-limits to protect the island's fragile ecosystem, which includes a caliche forest (hardened calcium-carbonate castings of trees and vegetation) and seasonal colonies of seals and sea lions. Peregrine falcons have been reintroduced, and some of the archeological sites from when the Chumash lived here date back almost 12,000 years.

Santa Barbara   ISLAND
(www.nps.gov/chis/planyourvisit/santa-barbara-island.htm) Currently closed because of storm damage to its landing pier, Santa Barbara, only 1 sq mile and the smallest of the islands, is normally a jewel-box for nature lovers. Big, blooming coreopsis, cream cups

---

ISLAND OF THE BLUE DOLPHINS

For bedtime reading around the campfire, pick up Scott O'Dell's Newbery Medal–winning *Island of the Blue Dolphins*. This young-adult novel was inspired by the true-life story of a girl from the Nicoleño tribe who was left behind on San Nicolas Island during the early 19th century, when her people were forced off the Channel Islands. Incredibly, the girl survived mostly alone on the island for 18 years, before being discovered and brought to the mainland by a hunter in 1853. However, fate was not on her side, and she died just seven weeks later.

and chicory are just a few of the island's memorable plant species. You'll also find the humongous northern elephant seal here as well as Scripps's murrelets, a bird that nests in cliff crevices.

Get more information from the island's small visitor center. For the latest information on when it might open, check the website.

Tours

Most trips require a minimum number of participants, and may be canceled due to high surf or weather conditions.

Aquasports KAYAKING
(☑805-968-7231; www.islandkayaking.com) Aquasports offers day and overnight kayaking trips to Santa Cruz, Anacapa and along the coast near Santa Barbara, led by professional naturalists. Prices vary from $89 to $495, depending on the length of trip and whether you bring your own camping gear and arrange the ferry to the islands yourself.

Raptor Dive Charters DIVING
(☑805-650-7700; www.raptordive.com; 1559 Spinnaker Dr, Ventura) Certified and experienced divers can head out for some underwater action, including night dives, off Anacapa and Santa Cruz Islands. Prices start at $120; equipment rentals are available for a surcharge; and plenty of snacks, sandwiches and drinks are available on board.

Truth Aquatics OUTDOORS
(Map p356; ☑805-962-1127; www.truthaquatics.com; 301 W Cabrillo Blvd, Santa Barbara) Based in Santa Barbara, this long-running outfitter organizes seasonal (usually April to Octo-

ber) diving, kayaking and hiking day trips and three-day, all-inclusive excursions to the Channel Islands aboard specially designed dive boats.

Island Packers CRUISE
(☑805-642-1393; http://islandpackers.com; 1691 Spinnaker Dr, Ventura; Channel Island day trips from $59, wildlife cruises from $68) Main provider of boats for Channel Islands visits, with day trips and overnight camping excursions available. Boats mostly set out from Ventura but a few go from nearby Oxnard. It also offers wildlife cruises year-round, including seasonal whale-watching from late December to mid-April (gray whales) and mid-May through mid-September (blue and humpback whales).

Channel Islands Kayak Center KAYAKING
(☑805-984-5995; www.cikayak.com; 1691 Spinnaker Dr, Ventura; ☉by appointment only) Book ahead to rent kayaks (from $12.50) and SUPs (from $25) or arrange a private guided kayaking tour of Santa Cruz or Anacapa (from $180 per person, two-person minimum).

Sleeping

Each island has a primitive year-round **campground** (☑reservations 877-444-6777; www.recreation.gov; tent sites $15) with pit toilets and picnic tables. Water is only available on Santa Cruz Island. You must pack everything in and out, including trash. Due to fire danger, campfires aren't allowed, but enclosed, gas campstoves are OK. Advance reservations are required for all island campsites.

CHANNEL ISLANDS NATIONAL PARK CAMPGROUNDS

CAMPGROUND	NUMBER OF SITES	ACCESS FROM BOAT LANDING	DESCRIPTION
Anacapa	7	0.5-mile walk with over 150 stairs	High, rocky, sun-exposed and isolated
Santa Barbara	10	Steep 0.25-mile walk uphill	Large, grassy and surrounded by trails
Santa Cruz (Scorpion Ranch)	31	Flat 0.5-mile walk	Popular with groups, often crowded and partly shady
San Miguel	9	Steep 1-mile walk uphill	Windy, often foggy with volatile weather
Santa Rosa	15	Flat 1.5-mile walk	Eucalyptus grove in a windy canyon

CALIFORNIA'S CHANNEL ISLANDS: PARADISE LOST & FOUND

Human beings have left a heavy footprint on the Channel Islands. Erosion was caused by overgrazing livestock and rabbits fed on native plants. The US military even used San Miguel as a practice bombing range. In 1969 an offshore oil spill engulfed the northern islands in an 800-sq-mile slick, killing thousands of seabirds and mammals. Meanwhile, deep-sea fishing has caused the destruction of three-quarters of the islands' kelp forests, which are key to the marine ecosystem.

Despite past abuses, the future isn't all bleak. Brown pelicans – decimated by the effects of DDT and reduced to one surviving chick in 1970 – have rebounded and are now off the endangered list, with healthy populations on West Anacapa and Santa Barbara Islands. On San Miguel Island, native vegetation has returned a half century after overgrazing sheep were removed. On Santa Cruz Island, the National Park Service and the Nature Conservancy have implemented multiyear plans to eliminate invasive plants and feral pigs.

❶ Information

Channel Islands National Park Visitor Center (Robert J Lagomarsino Visitor Center; ☑805-658-5730; www.nps.gov/chis; 1901 Spinnaker Dr, Ventura; ☺8:30am-5pm; ♿) Trip-planning information, books and maps are available on the mainland at the far end of Ventura Harbor. A free video, *A Treasure in the Sea,* gives some background on the islands, and weekends and holidays see ranger-led free programs at 11am and 3pm.

❶ Getting There & Away

You can access the national park by taking a boat from Ventura or Oxnard or a plane from Camarillo. Trips may be canceled anytime due to high surf or weather conditions. Reservations are essential for weekends, holidays and summer trips.

The open seas on the boat ride out to the Channel Islands may feel choppy to landlubbers. To avoid seasickness, sit outside on the lower deck, keep away from the diesel fumes in the back, and focus on the horizon. The outbound trip is typically against the wind and a bit bumpier than the return. Over-the-counter motion-sickness pills (eg Dramamine) can make you drowsy. Boats usually brake when dolphins or whales are spotted – always a welcome distraction from any nausea.

AIR

If you're prone to seasickness or just want a memorable way to get to the Channel Islands, you can take a scenic flight to Santa Rosa or San Miguel with **Channel Islands Aviation** (☑805-987-1301; www.flycia.com; 305 Durley Ave, Camarillo). Half-day packages include hiking or a guided 4WD tour, while overnight camping excursions are more DIY.

BOAT

Island Packers offers regularly scheduled boat services to all islands, mostly from Ventura, but with a few sailings from Oxnard too. Anacapa and Santa Cruz are closer to the mainland and so less expensive to visit than other islands. Day trips are possible; overnight campers pay an additional surcharge. Be forewarned: if you do camp and seas are rough the following day, you could get stuck for an extra night or more.

Los Angeles

POP 10.1 MILLION

Best Places to Eat

➡ Cassia (p414)

➡ Bestia (p409)

➡ Otium (p409)

➡ Gjelina (p414)

➡ Joss Cuisine (p411)

Best Places to Sleep

➡ Palihouse (p406)

➡ Chateau Marmont (p404)

➡ Hotel Indigo (p403)

➡ Petit Ermitage (p404)

Why Go?

LA runs deeper than her blond beaches, bosomy hills and ubiquitous beemers would have you believe. She's a myth. A beacon for countless small-town dreamers, rockers and risk-takers, an open-minded angel who encourages her people to live and let live without judgment or shame. She has given us Quentin Tarantino, Jim Morrison and Serena and Venus Williams, spawned skateboarding and gangsta rap, popularized implants, electrolysis and spandex, and has nurtured not just great writers, performers and directors, but also the ground-breaking yogis who first brought Eastern wisdom to the Western world.

LA is best defined by those simple life-affirming moments. A cracked-ice, jazz-age cocktail on Beverly Blvd, a hike high into the Hollywood Hills sagebrush, a pink-washed sunset over a thundering Venice Beach drum circle, the perfect taco. And her night music. There is always night music.

When to Go

Los Angeles

°C/°F **Temp**   Rainfall Inches/mm

Dec–Feb
Good hotel deals, though demand is high in February due to the Academy Awards.

Mar–May
An ideal time to visit. Decent hotel deals are still available.

Sep–Nov
The summer crowds have thinned, though temperatures remain warm.

◉ Sights & Activities

◉ Downtown Los Angeles & Boyle Heights

Downtown Los Angeles is historical, multi-layered and fascinating. It's a city within a city, alive with young professionals, designers and artists who have snapped up stylish lofts in rehabbed art-deco buildings. The growing gallery district along Main and Spring Sts draws thousands to its monthly art walks.

★ **Broad**   MUSEUM

(Map p394; ☑213-232-6200; www.thebroad.org; 221 S Grand Ave; ⊙11am-5pm Tue & Wed, to 8pm Thu & Fri, 10am-8pm Sat, to 6pm Sun; P�"🛜; MRed/Purple Lines to Civic Center/Grand Park) The Broad (rhymes with 'road') is a must-visit for contemporary-art fans. It houses the world-class collection of local philanthropist and real-estate billionaire Eli Broad and his wife Edythe, with more than 2000 postwar pieces by the likes of Cindy Sherman, Jeff Koons, Andy Warhol, Roy Lichtenstein, Robert Rauschenberg, Keith Haring and Kara Walker.

★ **Walt Disney Concert Hall**   NOTABLE BUILDING

(Map p394; ☑ 323 850 2000; www.laphil.org; 111 S Grand Ave; ⊙ guided tours usually noon & 1:15pm Thu-Sat, 10am & 11am Sun; P; MRed/Purple Lines to Civic Center/Grand Park) FREE A molten blend of steel, music and psychedelic architecture, this iconic concert venue is the home base of the Los Angeles Philharmonic, but has also hosted contemporary bands such as Phoenix and classic jazz men such as Sonny Rollins. Frank Gehry pulled out all the stops: the building is a gravity-defying sculpture of heaving and billowing stainless steel.

★ **MOCA Grand**   MUSEUM

(Museum of Contemporary Art; Map p394; ☑213-626-6222; www.moca.org; 250 S Grand Ave; adult/child $15/free, 5-8pm Thu free; ⊙11am-6pm Mon, Wed & Fri, to 8pm Thu, to 5pm Sat & Sun) MOCA's superlative art collection focuses mainly on works created from the 1940s to the present. There's no shortage of luminaries, among them Mark Rothko, Dan Flavin, Willem de Kooning, and David Hockney, their creations housed in a postmodern building by award-winning architect Arata Isozaki. Galleries are below ground, yet sky-lit bright.

★ **Grammy Museum**   MUSEUM

(Map p394; ☑213-765-6800; www.grammymuseum. org; 800 W Olympic Blvd; adult/child $13/11;

⊙10:30am-6:30pm Mon-Fri, from 10am Sat & Sun; P🚼) It's the highlight of LA Live (Map p394; ☑866-548-3452, 213-763-5483; www.lalive.com; 800 W Olympic Blvd; P🚼). Music lovers will get lost in interactive exhibits, which define, differentiate and link musical genres. Spanning three levels, the museum's rotating exhibitions might include threads worn by the likes of Michael Jackson, Whitney Houston and Beyonce, scribbled words from the hands of Count Basie and Taylor Swift and instruments once used by world-renowned rock deities.

Union Station   NOTABLE BUILDING

(Map p394; www.amtrak.com; 800 N Alameda St; P) Built on the site of LA's original Chinatown, Union Station opened in 1939 as America's last grand rail station. The marble-floored main hall, with cathedral ceilings, original leather chairs and 3000-pound chandeliers, is breathtaking. The station's Traxx Bar was once the telephone room, complete with operator to place customers' calls. The LA Conservancy runs 2½-hour walking tours of the station on Saturdays at 10am (book online).

◉ Hollywood

No other corner of LA is steeped in as much mythology as Hollywood. It's here that you'll find the Hollywood Walk of Fame, the Capitol Records Tower and Grauman's Chinese Theatre, where the hand- and footprints of entertainment deities are immortalized in concrete. Look beyond the tourist-swamped landmarks of Hollywood Blvd and you'll discover a nuanced, multifaceted neighborhood where industrial streets are punctuated by edgy galleries and boutiques and where steep, sleepy streets harbor the homes of long-gone silver-screen stars.

★ **Grauman's Chinese Theatre**   LANDMARK

(TCL Chinese Theatres; Map p400; ☑ 323-461-3331; www.tclchinesetheatres.com; 6925 Hollywood Blvd; guided tour adult/senior/child $16/13.50/8; 🚼; MRed Line to Hollywood/Highland) Ever wondered what it's like to be in George Clooney's shoes? Just find his footprints in the forecourt of this world-famous movie palace. The exotic pagoda theater – complete with temple bells and stone heaven dogs from China – has shown movies since 1927.

★ **Hollywood Museum**   MUSEUM

(Map p400; ☑ 323-464-7776; www.thehollywood museum.com; 1660 N Highland Ave; adult/child $15/5; ⊙10am-5pm Wed-Sun; MRed Line to Hollywood/Highland) For a taste of Old

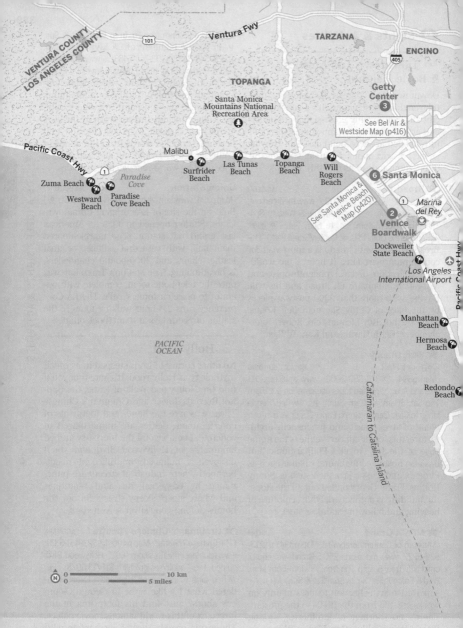

Los Angeles Highlights

1 Checking out LA's oldest buildings, its most glorious movie palaces and many of its hottest restaurants, bars and boutiques **downtown** (p409).

2 Strutting your stuff on **Venice Boardwalk** (p398) – one long, eclectic runway flanked by soaring palms, street artists and bulging Schwarzenegger wannabes.

3 Feeling your spirits soar surrounded by art, architecture, views and gardens at the **Getty Center** (p395).

4 Joining an obligatory stop for culture vultures at the **Los Angeles County Museum**

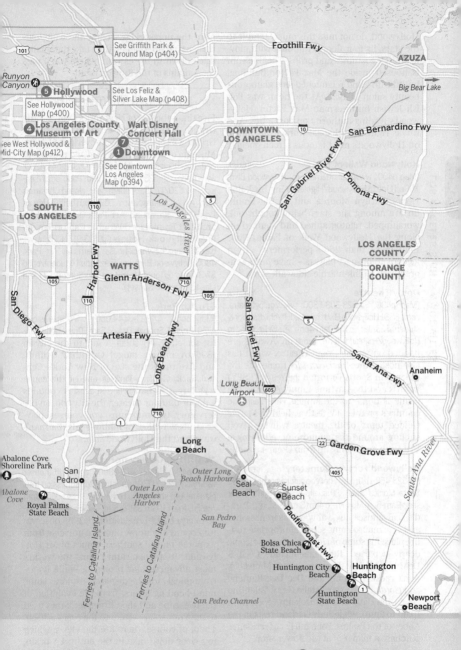

101 **5** See Griffith Park &
Around Map (p404)

Foothill Fwy

AZUZA

Runyon
Canyon
Big Bear Lake

5 **Hollywood**
See Los Feliz &
Silver Lake Map (p408)

See Hollywood
Map (p400)

4 **Los Angeles County**
Museum of Art
Walt Disney
Concert Hall

See West Hollywood &
Mid-City Map (p412)
7
1 **Downtown**

DOWNTOWN
LOS ANGELES

10 San Bernardino Fwy

San Gabriel River Fwy

Pomona Fwy

See Downtown
Los Angeles
Map (p394)
5

Los Angeles River

SOUTH
LOS ANGELES

110

LOS ANGELES
COUNTY

ORANGE
COUNTY

WATTS

Harbor Fwy

Glenn Anderson Fwy

110
710

105
105

San Gabriel Fwy

5

Santa Ana Fwy

San Diego Fwy

Artesia Fwy

Long Beach Fwy

Long Beach
Airport

605

Anaheim

710

1

Long
Beach

22 Garden Grove Fwy

Abalone Cove
Shoreline Park
San
Pedro

Outer Long
Beach Harbour

Seal
Beach

Sunset
Beach

405

Santa Ana River

Outer Los
Angeles Harbor

Abalone
Cove
Royal Palms
State Beach

San Pedro
Bay

Pacific Coast Hwy

Ferries to Catalina Island

Ferries to Catalina Island

Bolsa Chica
State Beach

Huntington City
Beach
70

Huntington
Beach

San Pedro Channel

Huntington
State Beach

1

Newport
Beach

of Art (p393), the largest art
museum in the western US and
home to 100,000-plus works..

5 Hitting **Hollywood** (p415)
bars and clubs for a night of

tabloid-worthy decadence and
debauchery.

6 Learning to surf, riding a
solar-powered Ferris wheel or
dipping your toes in the ocean
in **Santa Monica** (p397).

7 Marveling at Pritzker
Prize–winning architect Frank
Gehry's **Walt Disney Concert
Hall** (p389) with its undulating
steel forms evoking the
movement of music itself.

Hollywood, do not miss this musty temple to the stars, its four floors crammed with movie and TV costumes and props. The museum is housed inside the Max Factor Building, built in 1914 and relaunched as a glamorous beauty salon in 1935. At the helm was Polish-Jewish businessman Max Factor, Hollywood's leading authority on cosmetics. And it was right here that he worked his magic on Hollywood's most famous screen queens.

Hollywood Walk of Fame   LANDMARK
(Map p400; www.walkoffame.com; Hollywood Blvd; Ⓜ Red Line to Hollywood/Highland) Big Bird, Bob Hope, Marilyn Monroe and Aretha Franklin are among the stars being sought out, worshipped, photographed and stepped on along the Hollywood Walk of Fame. Since 1960 more than 2600 performers – from legends to bit-part players – have been honored with a pink-marble sidewalk star.

Dolby Theatre   THEATER
(Map p400; ☑ 323-308-6300; www.dolbytheatre. com; 6801 Hollywood Blvd; tours adult/child, senior & student $23/18; ⊙ 10:30am-4pm; Ⓟ; Ⓜ Red Line to Hollywood/Highland) The Academy Awards are handed out at the Dolby Theatre, which has also hosted the *American Idol* finale, the Excellence in Sports Performance Yearly (ESPY) awards and the Daytime Emmy Awards. The venue is home to the annual PaleyFest, the country's premier TV festival, held in March. Guided tours of the theatre will have you sniffing around the auditorium, admiring a VIP room and nosing up to an Oscar statuette.

Hollywood Forever Cemetery   CEMETERY
(☑ 323-469-1181; www.hollywoodforever.com; 6000 Santa Monica Blvd; ⊙ usually 8:30am-5pm, flower shop 9am-5pm Mon-Fri, to 4pm Sat & Sun; Ⓟ) Paradisiacal landscaping, vainglorious tombstones and epic mausoleums set an appropriate resting place for some of Hollywood's most iconic dearly departed. Residents include Cecil B DeMille, Mickey Rooney, Jayne Mansfield, punk rockers Johnny and Dee Dee Ramone and *Golden Girls* star Estelle Getty. Valentino lies in the Cathedral Mausoleum (open from 10am to 2pm), while Judy Garland rests in the Abbey of the Psalms. For a full list of residents, purchase a map ($5) at the flower shop.

★ Runyon Canyon   HIKING
(www.runyoncanyonhike.com; 2000 N Fuller Ave; ⊙ dawn-dusk) A chaparral-draped cut in the Hollywood Hills, this 130-acre public park is as famous for its buff runners and exercising celebrities as it is for the panoramic views from the upper ridge. Follow the wide, partially paved fire road up then take the smaller track down to the canyon, where you'll pass the remains of the Runyon estate.

◉ Los Feliz & Griffith Park

Five times the size of New York's Central Park, Griffith Park is home to the world-famous Griffith Observatory, the oft-overlooked Autry Museum of the American West and the take-it-or-leave-it city zoo (Map p404; ☑ 323-644-4200; www.lazoo.org; 5333 Zoo Dr, Griffith Park; adult/senior/child $20/17/15; ⊙ 10am-5pm, closed Christmas Day; Ⓟ ♿). Rising above the southern edge of Los Feliz, Barnsdall Art Park is crowned by architect Frank Lloyd Wright's Californian debut, **Hollyhock House** (☑ 323-913-4031; www. barnsdall.org/hollyhock-house; Barnsdall Art Park, 4800 Hollywood Blvd, Los Feliz; adult/student/child $7/3/free; ⊙ tours 11am-4pm Thu-Sun; Ⓟ; Ⓜ Red Line to Vermont/Sunset).

Griffith Park   PARK
(Map p404; ☑ 323-644-2050; www.laparks.org; 4730 Crystal Springs Dr; ⊙ 5am-10pm, trails sunrise-sunset; Ⓟ ♿) FREE A gift to the city in 1896 by mining mogul Griffith J Griffith, and five times the size of New York's Central Park, Griffith Park is one of the country's largest urban green spaces. It contains a major outdoor theater, the city zoo, an observatory, two museums, golf courses, playgrounds, 53 miles of hiking trails, Batman's caves and the Hollywood sign.

★ Griffith Observatory   MUSEUM
(Map p404; ☑ 213-473-0890; www.griffithobser vatory.org; 2800 E Observatory Rd; admission free, planetarium shows adult/child $7/3; ⊙ noon-10pm Tue-Fri, from 10am Sat & Sun; Ⓟ ♿; ⬛ DASH Observatory) FREE LA's landmark 1935 observatory opens a window onto the universe from its perch on the southern slopes of Mt Hollywood. Its planetarium claims the world's most advanced star projector, while its astronomical touch displays explore some mind-bending topics, from the evolution of the telescope and the ultraviolet x-rays used to map our solar system to the cosmos itself. Then, of course, there are the views, which (on clear days) take in the entire LA basin, surrounding mountains and Pacific Ocean.

◉ Silver Lake & Echo Park

Pimped with stencil art, inked skin and skinny jeans, Silver Lake and Echo Park are the epicenter of LA hipsterdom. Silver Lake is the

UNIVERSAL STUDIOS HOLLYWOOD

Although **Universal** (Map p404; ☑800-864-8377; www.universalstudioshollywood.com; 100 Universal City Plaza, Universal City; admission from $99, child under 3yr free; ⊙daily, hours vary; P ⛟; M Red Line to Universal City) is one of the world's oldest continuously operating movie studios, the chances of seeing any filming action here, let alone a star, are slim to none. But never mind. This theme park on the studio's back lot presents an entertaining mix of thrill rides, live-action shows and a tram tour.

First-timers should head straight for the 45-minute narrated **Studio Tour** aboard a multi-car tram that drives around the sound stages in the front lot then heads to the back lot past the crash site from War of the Worlds, vehicles from Jurassic Park and the spooky Bates Motel from Psycho. Also prepare to brave a flash flood, survive a shark attack, a spitting dino and an 8.3-magnitude earthquake, before facing down King Kong in a new 3-D exhibit created by Peter Jackson. It's a bit hokey, but fun.

Newly opened, the phenomenally popular **Wizarding World of Harry Potter** is the park's biggest attraction. Climb aboard the Flight of the Hippogriff roller coaster and the 3-D ride Harry Potter and the Forbidden Journey.

more upwardly mobile of the pair, home to revitalized modernist homes, sharing-plate menus and obscure fashion labels on boutique racks. To the southeast lies grittier Echo Park, one of LA's oldest neighborhoods. Despite its own ongoing gentrification, it continues to offer a contrasting jumble of rickety homes, Mexican *panderias* (bakeries), indie rock bars, vintage stores, design-literate coffee shops and the serenity of its namesake lake, featured in Polanski's *Chinatown*.

Silver Lake and Echo Park are more about the vibe than ticking off sights. Consider starting your explorations at Silver Lake Junction (the intersection of Sunset and Santa Monica Blvds), grabbing coffee and exploring the well-curated stores that dot Sunset Blvd. The Echo Park stretch of Sunset Blvd is home to its own booty of small galleries and cool shops. When fatigue kicks in, retire to Echo Park Lake, where you can chill on the well-tended lawns or on the water itself in a pedal boat.

Neutra VDL House　　ARCHITECTURE
(www.neutra-vdl.org; 2300 Silver Lake Blvd, Silver Lake; adult/senior/child $15/10/free; ⊙guided tours 11am-3pm Sat, last tour commences 2:30pm) Built in 1932, burnt to a crisp in 1963 then subsequently rebuilt, the light-washed former home and laboratory of modernist architect Richard Neutra is a leading example of mid-century Californian design. Indeed, the site was declared a National Historic Landmark in 2017. Thirty-minute guided tours of the property run most Saturdays, shedding light on the Austrian-born architect's theories and stylistic evolution. Reservations not required. Always check the website as tours are not run some weeks.

⊙ West Hollywood & Mid-City

Welcome to West Hollywood (WeHo), an independent city with way more personality (some might say, frivolity) than its 1.9-sq-mile frame might suggest. Upscale and low-rent (but rising), gay fabulous and Russian-ghetto chic, this is a bastion of LA's fashionista best and home to some of the trashiest shops you'll ever see.

Mid-City, to the south and east, encompasses the Miracle Mile (home to some of the best museums in the west), the Orthodox-Jewish-meets-hipster Fairfax district and the legendary rock, punk and vintage shopping strip of Melrose Ave.

★**Original Farmers Market**　　MARKET
(Map p412; ☑323-933-9211; www.farmersmarketla.com; 6333 W 3rd St, Fairfax District; ⊙9am-9pm Mon-Fri, to 8pm Sat, 10am-7pm Sun; P ⛟) Long before the city was flooded with farmers markets, there was *the* farmers market. Fresh produce, roasted nuts, doughnuts, cheeses, blini – you'll find them all at this 1934 landmark. Casual and kid friendly, it's a fun place for a browse, snack or for people-watching.

★**Los Angeles County Museum of Art**　　MUSEUM
(LACMA; Map p412; ☑323-857-6000; www.lacma.org; 5905 Wilshire Blvd, Mid-City; adult/child $15/free, 2nd Tue each month free; ⊙11am-5pm Mon, Tue & Thu, to 8pm Fri, 10am-7pm Sat & Sun; P; ☐Metro lines 20, 217, 720, 780 to Wilshire & Fairfax) The depth and wealth of the collection at the largest museum in the western US is stunning. LACMA holds all the major players – Rembrandt, Cézanne, Magritte, Mary

Downtown Los Angeles

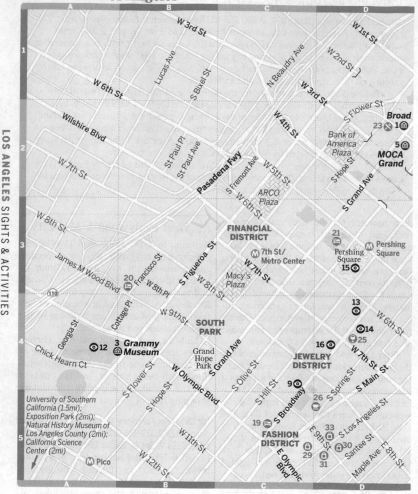

Cassat, Ansel Adams – plus millennia worth of Chinese, Japanese, pre-Columbian and ancient Greek, Roman and Egyptian sculpture. Recent acquisitions include massive outdoor installations such as Chris Burden's *Urban Light* (a surreal selfie backdrop of hundreds of vintage LA streetlamps) and Michael Heizer's *Levitated Mass,* a surprisingly inspirational 340-ton boulder perched over a walkway.

★ **Petersen Automotive Museum** MUSEUM
(Map p412; ☎ 323-930-2277; www.petersen.org; 6060 Wilshire Blvd, Mid-City; adult/senior & student/child $15/12/7; ☉10am-6pm; P ♿; ☐ Metro lines

20, 217, 720, 780 to Wilshire & Fairfax) A four-story ode to the auto, the Petersen Automotive Museum is a treat even for those who can't tell a piston from a carburetor. A futuristic makeover (by Kohn Pederson Fox) in late 2015 left it fairly gleaming from the outside; the exterior is undulating bands of stainless steel on a hot-rod-red background. The once-dowdy inside is now equally gripping, with floors themed for the history, industry and artistry of motorized transportation.

La Brea Tar Pits & Museum MUSEUM
(Map p412; www.tarpits.org; 5801 Wilshire Blvd, Mid-City; adult/student & senior/child $12/9/5,

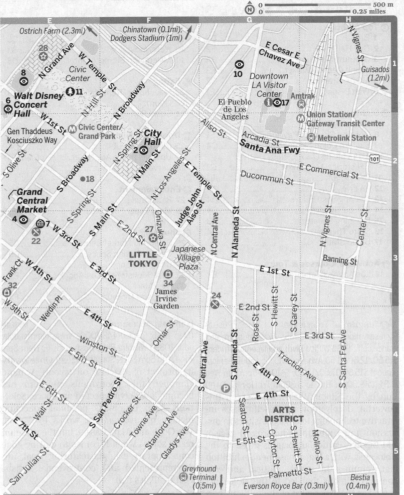

1st Tue of month Sep-Jun free; ⊙9:30am-5pm; P 🚶) Mammoths, saber-toothed cats and dire wolves used to roam LA's savannah in prehistoric times. We know this because of an archaeological trove of skulls and bones unearthed at the La Brea Tar Pits, one of the world's most fecund and famous fossil sites.

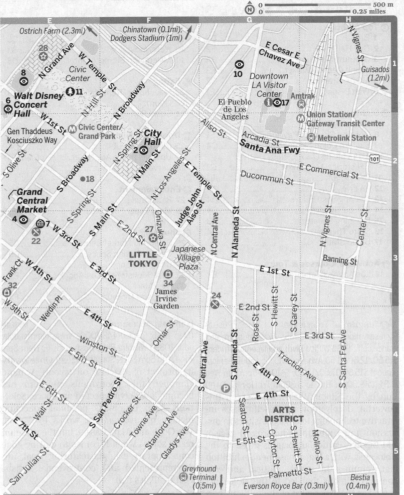 **Beverly Hills, Bel Air, Brentwood & Westwood**

A triptych of megamansions, luxury wheels and tweaked cheekbones, Beverly Hills, Bel Air and Brentwood encapsulate the LA of international fantasies.

★ **Getty Center** MUSEUM
(☏310-440-7300; www.getty.edu; 1200 Getty Center Dr, off I-405 Fwy; ⊙10am-5:30pm Tue-Fri & Sun, to 9pm Sat; P🚶; 🚍734, 234) FREE In its billion-dollar, in-the-clouds perch, high above the city grit and grime, the Getty Center presents triple delights: a stellar art collection (everything from medieval triptychs to baroque sculpture and impressionist brushstrokes), Richard Meier's cutting-edge architecture, and the visual splendor of seasonally changing gardens. Admission is free, but parking is $15 ($10 after 3pm).

Downtown Los Angeles

★ **Museum of Tolerance** MUSEUM
(✓reservations 310-772-2505; www.museumoftol erance.com; 9786 W Pico Blvd; adult/senior/student $15.50/12.50/11.50, Anne Frank Exhibit adult/senior/ student $15.50/13.50/12.50; ⊙10am-5pm Sun-Wed & Fri, to 9:30pm Thu, to 3:30pm Fri Nov-Mar; ℗) Run by the Simon Wiesenthal Center, this powerful, deeply moving museum uses interactive technology to engage visitors in discussion and contemplation around racism and bigotry. Particular focus is given to the Holocaust, with a major basement exhibition that examines the social, political and economic conditions that led to the Holocaust as well as the experience of the millions persecuted. On the museum's 2nd floor, another major exhibition offers an intimate look into the life and effect of Anne Frank.

**University of California,
Los Angeles** UNIVERSITY
(UCLA; Map p416; www.ucla.edu; ℗) Founded in 1919, the alma mater of Jim Morrison, Kareem Abdul Jabbar and Jackie Robinson ranks among the nation's top universities. The campus is vast: walking briskly from one end to the other takes at least 30 minutes. You could easily spend a couple of hours exploring its manicured, sycamore-shaded lawns, profuse gardens, Romanesque Revival architecture and cultural assets.

Hammer Museum MUSEUM
(Map p416; ✓310-443-7000; www.hammer.ucla. edu; 10899 Wilshire Blvd, Westwood; ⊙11am-8pm Tue-Fri, to 5pm Sat & Sun; ℗) FREE Once a vanity project of the late oil tycoon Armand Hammer, this eponymous museum has become a widely respected art space. Selections from Hammer's personal collection include relatively minor works by Monet, Van Gogh and Mary Cassat, but the museum really shines when it comes to cutting-edge contemporary exhibits featuring local, under-represented and controversial artists. Best of all, it's free.

**Westwood Village Memorial
Park Cemetery** CEMETERY
(Map p416; ✓310-474-1579; 1218 Glendon Ave, Westwood; ⊙8am-6pm; ℗) You'll be spending quiet time with entertainment heavyweights at this compact cemetery, hidden behind Wilshire Blvd's wall of high-rise towers. The northeast mausoleum houses Marilyn Monroe's simple crypt, while just south of it, the Sanctuary of Love harbors Dean Martin's crypt. Beneath the central lawn lie a number of iconic names, including actress Natalie Wood, pin-up Bettie Page and crooner Roy Orbison (the latter lies in an unmarked grave to the left of a marker labeled 'Grandma Martha Monroe').

Skirball Cultural Center MUSEUM
(📞310-440-4500; www.skirball.org; 2701 N Sepulveda Blvd; adult/student & senior/under 13yr $12/9/7, Thu free; 🕙noon-5pm Tue-Fri, 10am-5pm Sat & Sun; P♿) Although it is, technically speaking, the country's largest Jewish museum and cultural center, the Skirball has something for all. The preschool set can board a gigantic wooden Noah's Ark, while grown-ups gravitate to the permanent exhibit, an engagingly presented romp through 4000 years of history, traditions, trials and triumphs of the Jewish people.

👁 **Malibu & Pacific Palisades**

Malibu enjoys near-mythical status thanks to its large celebrity population (it's been celebrity central since the 1930s) and the incredible beauty of its 27 miles of coastal mountains, pristine coves, wide sweeps of golden sand and epic waves. Despite its wealth and star quotient, the best way to appreciate Malibu is through its natural assets, so grab your sunscreen and a towel and head to the beach.

⭐**El Matador State Beach** BEACH
(📞818-880-0363; 32215 Pacific Coast Hwy, Malibu; P) Arguably Malibu's most stunning beach, where you park on the bluffs and stroll down a trail to sandstone rock towers that rise from emerald coves. Topless sunbathers stroll through the tides, and dolphins breech the surface beyond the waves. It's been impacted by coastal erosion, but you can still find a sliver of dry sand tucked against the bluffs.

⭐**Getty Villa** MUSEUM
(📞310-430-7300; www.getty.edu; 17985 Pacific Coast Hwy, Pacific Palisades; 🕙10am-5pm Wed-Mon; P♿; 🚌line 534 to Coastline Dr) FREE Stunningly perched on an ocean-view hillside, this museum in a replica 1st-century Roman villa is an exquisite, 64-acre showcase for Greek, Roman and Etruscan antiquities. Dating back 7000 years, they were amassed by oil tycoon J Paul Getty. Galleries, peristiles, courtyards and lushly landscaped gardens ensconce all manner of friezes, busts and mosaics, millennia-old cut, blown and colored glass and brain-bending geometric configurations in the Hall of Colored Marbles. Other highlights include the Pompeii fountain and Temple of Herakles.

Zuma Beach BEACH
(30000 Pacific Coast Hwy, Malibu; P; 🚌MTA 534) Zuma is easy to find, and thanks to the wide sweep of blonde sand that has been attracting valley kids to the shore since the 1970s, it gets busy on weekends and summer afternoons. Pass around Point Dume to Westward Beach (6800 Westward Rd, Malibu; P; 🚌MTA 534).

Will Rogers State Historic Park MONUMENT, PARK
(📞310-454-8212; www.parks.ca.gov; 1501 Will Rogers State Park Rd, Pacific Palisades; parking $12; 🕙8am-sunset, ranch house tours hourly 11am-3pm Thu & Fri, 10am-4pm Sat & Sun; P; 🚌MTA lines 2 & 302) This park sprawls across ranch land once owned by Will Rogers (1875–1935), an Oklahoma-born cowboy turned humorist, radio-show host and movie star (in the early 1930s he was the highest-paid actor in Hollywood). In the late '20s, he traded his Beverly Hills manse for a 31-room ranch house (📞tours 310-454-8212 x103; www.parks.ca.gov/?page_id=26257; 1501 Will Rogers State Park Rd, Pacific Palisades, Will Rogers State Historic Park; 🕙tours hourly 11am-3pm Thu & Fri, 10am-4pm Sat & Sun) and lived here until his tragic 1935 death in a plane crash.

Topanga Canyon SCENIC DRIVE
(Topanga Canyon Rd) Take this sinuous road from the sea and climb into a primordial canyon cut deep in the Santa Monica Mountains. The drive lays bare naked boulders and reveals jagged chaparral-covered peaks from every hairpin turn. The road is shadowed by lazy oaks and glimmering sycamores, and the whole thing smells of wind-blown black sage and 'cowboy cologne' (artemisia).

👁 **Santa Monica**

Santa Monica is LA's cute, alluring, hippie-chic little sister, its karmic counterbalance and, to many, its salvation. Surrounded by LA on three sides and the Pacific on the fourth, SaMo is a place where real-life Lebowskis sip White Russians next to martini-swilling Hollywood producers, celebrity chefs dine at family-owned taquerias, and soccer moms and career bachelors shop at abundant farmers markets. All the while, kids, out-of-towners and those who love them flock to wide beaches and the pier, where the landmark Ferris wheel and roller coaster welcome one and all.

Once the very end of the mythical Route 66, and still a tourist love affair, the **Santa**

Monica Pier (Map p420; ☏310-458-8901; www.santamonicapier.org; ♿) dates back to 1908, is stocked with rides and arcade games and blessed with spectacular views, and is the city's most compelling landmark. After a stroll on the pier, hit the **beach** (Map p420; ☏310-458-8411; www.smgov.net/portals/beach; ☐Big Blue Bus 1). We like the stretch just north of Ocean Park Blvd. Or rent a bike or some skates from **Perry's Café** (Map p420; ☏310-939-0000; www.perryscafe.com; Ocean Front Walk; bikes per hour/day from $10/30, boogie boards $7/20; ⊙9am-7:30pm Mon-Fri, from 8:30am Sat & Sun) and explore the 22-mile **South Bay Bicycle Trail** (Map p420; ⊙sunrise-sunset; ♿).

⊙ Venice

If you were born too late, and have always been a little jealous of the hippie heyday, come down to the Boardwalk and inhale a (not just) incense-scented whiff of Venice, a boho beach town and longtime haven for artists, new agers, road-weary tramps, freaks and free spirits. This is where Jim Morrison and the Doors lit their fire, where Arnold Schwarzenegger pumped himself to stardom, and the place the late Dennis Hopper once called home. These days, even as tech titans move in, the Old Venice spirit endures.

★**Venice Boardwalk**   WATERFRONT
(Ocean Front Walk; Map p420; Venice Pier to Rose Ave) Life in Venice moves to a different rhythm and nowhere more so than on the famous Venice Boardwalk, officially known as Ocean Front Walk. It's a freak show, a human zoo and a wacky carnival alive with Hula-hoop magicians, old-timey jazz combos, solo distorted garage rockers and artists (good and bad) – as far as LA experiences go, it's a must.

★**Abbot Kinney Boulevard**   AREA
(Map p420; ☐Big Blue Bus line 18) Abbot Kinney, who founded Venice in the early 1900s, would probably be delighted to find that one of Venice's best-loved streets bears his name. Sort of a seaside Melrose with a Venetian flavor, the mile-long stretch of Abbot Kinney Blvd between Venice Blvd and Main St is full of upscale boutiques, galleries, lofts and sensational restaurants. A few years back, GQ named it America's coolest street, and that cachet has only grown since.

★**Venice Skatepark**   SKATEBOARDING
(Map p420; www.veniceskatepark.com; 1500 Ocean Front Walk, Venice; ⊙dawn-dusk) Long the desti-

nation of local skate punks, the concrete at this skate park has now been molded and steel-fringed into 17,000 sq ft of vert, tranny and street terrain with unbroken ocean views. The old-school-style skate run and the world-class pool are most popular for high flyers and gawking spectators. Great photo opps, especially as the sun sets.

★**Muscle Beach**   GYM
(Map p420; ☏310-399-2775; www.musclebeach.net; 1800 Ocean Front Walk, Venice; per day $10; ⊙8am-7pm Mon-Sat, 10am-4pm Sun Apr-Sep, shorter hours rest of year) Gym rats with an exhibitionist streak can get a tan and a workout at this famous outdoor gym right on the Venice Boardwalk, where Arnold Schwarzenegger and Franco Columbo once bulked up.

Venice Boardwalk
Bike Rental   CYCLING, SKATING
(Map p420; ☏310-396-2453; 517 Ocean Front Walk, Venice; 1hr/2hr/day bikes $7/12/20, surfboards $10/20/30, skates $7/12/20) Located in the Gingerbread Court complex, which was built by Charlie Chaplin, are a few shops, a cafe, some apartments above and this reliable Venice outfitter.

⊙ Long Beach & San Pedro

Along LA County's southern shore and adjacent to Orange County, the twin ports of Long Beach and San Pedro provide attractions from ship to hip. Ramble around the art deco ocean liner *Queen Mary*, scramble around the *Battleship Iowa*, or immerse yourself in the Aquarium of the Pacific. Then go for retro shopping and coastal cliff views.

★**Aquarium of the Pacific**   AQUARIUM
(☏tickets 562-590-3100; www.aquariumofpacific.org; 100 Aquarium Way, Long Beach; adult/senior/child $30/27/19; ⊙9am-6pm; [P]♿) Long Beach's most mesmerizing experience, the Aquarium of the Pacific is a vast, high-tech indoor ocean where sharks dart, jellyfish dance and sea lions frolic. More than 11,000 creatures inhabit four re-created habitats: the bays and lagoons of Baja California, the frigid northern Pacific, tropical coral reefs and local kelp forests.

★**Museum of Latin American Art** MUSEUM
(☏562-437-1689; www.molaa.org; 628 Alamitos Ave, Long Beach; adult/senior & student/child $10/7/free, Sun free; ⊙11am-5pm Wed, Thu, Sat & Sun, to 9pm Fri; [P]) This gem of a museum is the only one in the US to present

SOUTH BAY BEACHES

When you've had all the Hollywood ambition, artsy pretension, velvet ropes and mind-numbing traffic you can take, head south of the airport, where this string of beach towns along Santa Monica Bay will soothe that mess from your psyche in one sunset. Buff volleyballers brush elbows with well-to-do University of Southern California (USC) alumni and an increasingly interesting restaurant scene.

It all starts with Manhattan Beach, just 15 minutes from LAX. A bastion of surf music and the birthplace of beach volleyball, Manhattan Beach has also gone chic. Its downtown area along Manhattan Beach Blvd has seen an explosion of trendy restaurants, boutiques and hotels. Yet, even with this Hollywood-ification, it remains a serene seaside enclave with prime surf on either side of the pier. To its south, Hermosa Beach is indeed *muy hermosa* (Spanish for 'very beautiful') – long, flat and dotted with permanent volleyball nets – and probably the funkiest of the three towns. Next up, Redondo Beach is a working-class beach town and the most ethnically diverse of the three.

As the coast winds to the south end of Santa Monica Bay you can follow it uphill to the Palos Verdes Peninsula. It's a revelation of sand-swept silver bays and the shadows of Catalina Island whispering through a fog rising from cold Pacific blue. Long, elegant and perfectly manicured lawns front sprawling mansions, and to the north, south and east there's nothing but layered jade hills forming the headland that cradles the bay's southernmost reach, before it turns a corner east toward Long Beach.

art created since 1945 in Latin America and in Latino communities in the US, in important temporary and traveling exhibits. Blockbuster shows have recently included Caribbean art and the works of LA's own Frank Romero.

★ **Battleship Iowa** MUSEUM, MEMORIAL
(📞877-446-9261; www.pacificbattleship.com; Berth 87, 250 S Harbor Blvd, San Pedro; adult/senior/child $20/17/12; ⏰10am-5pm, last entry 4pm; 🅿🚻; 🚇Metro Silver Line) This WWII to Cold War–era battleship is now permanently moored in San Pedro Bay and open to visitors as a museum. It's massive - 887ft long (that's 5ft longer than *Titanic*) and about as tall as an 18-story building. Step onto the gangway and download the app to take a self-guided audio tour of everything from the stateroom where FDR stayed to missile turrets and the enlisted men's galley, which churned out 8000 hot meals a day during WWII.

Retro Row AREA
(www.4thstreetlongbeach.com; 4th St btwn Junipero St & Cherry Ave, Long Beach) This blocks-long stretch of 4th St is a fab destination for retro fashion, fun cafes and restaurants and an awesome art-house theater.

Queen Mary SHIP
(📞877-342-0738; www.queenmary.com; 1126 Queens Hwy, Long Beach; tours adult/child from $27/17.50; ⏰tours 10am-6pm or later; 🅿🚻;

🚇Passport, ⛴AquaBus, AquaLink) Long Beach's 'flagship' attraction is this grand - and supposedly haunted! – British luxury liner. Larger and more luxurious than even the *Titanic*, she transported royals, dignitaries, immigrants, WWII troops and vacationers between 1936 and 1966 and has been moored here since 1967. Sure it's a tourist trap, but spend time with the memorabilia and you may envision dapper gents escorting ladies in gowns to the art deco lounge for cocktails, or to the sumptuous Sir Winston's for dinner.

Point Fermin Park & Around PARK
(San Pedro) Locals come to this grassy community park on the bluffs to jog, picnic, watch wind- and kitesurfers, cool off in the shade of spreading magnolias, gaze at the silhouette of Catalina Island, wonder at never-ending waves pounding a rugged crescent coastline and enjoy live jazz on balmy summer Sundays.

👁 Exposition Park & South LA

The world's oldest beings (dinosaur skeletons) and space-age technology (the Space Shuttle Endeavour) come together under one roof at the California Science Center, one of a trio of great museums in 'Expo Park,' a quick train ride from Downtown LA and a straight shot on the same train to Santa Monica. Several miles away, you may be equally inspired by Watts Towers, a masterpiece of folk art 33 years in the making, and

Hollywood

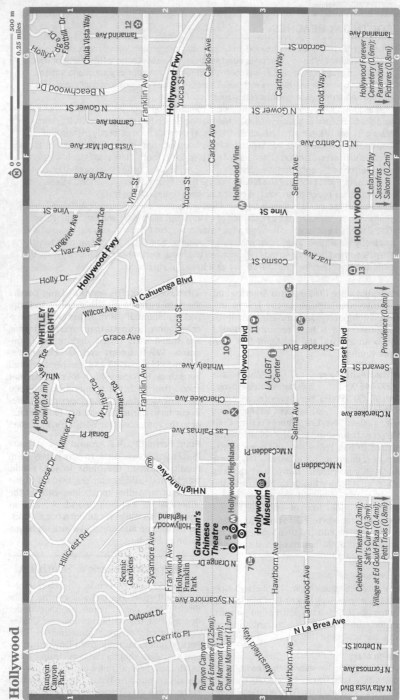

Hollywood

by the spirit of Leimert Park, the heart of LA's African-American community.

**Natural History Museum of
Los Angeles**   MUSEUM
(☏ 213-763-3466; www.nhm.org; 900 Exposition Blvd, Exposition Park; adult/student & senior/child $12/9/5; ⊙9:30am-5pm; ℗⊞; Ⓜ Expo Line to Expo/Vermont) Dinos to diamonds, bears to beetles, hissing roaches to African elephants – this museum will take you around the world and back, through millions of years in time. It's all housed in a beautiful 1913 Spanish Renaissance–style building that stood in for Columbia University in the first Toby McGuire *Spider-Man* movie – yup, this was where Peter Parker was bitten by the radioactive arachnid. There's enough to see here to fill several hours.

California Science Center   MUSEUM
(☏ film schedule 213-744-2019, info 323-724-3623; www.californiasciencecenter.org; 700 Exposition Park Dr, Exposition Park; IMAX movie adult/child $8.50/5.25; ⊙10am-5pm; ⊞) FREE Top billing at the Science Center goes to the Space Shuttle Endeavour, one of only four space shuttles nationwide, but there's plenty else to see at this large, multistory, multimedia museum filled with buttons to push, lights to switch on and knobs to pull. A simulated earthquake, baby chicks hatching and a giant techno-doll named Tess bring out the kid in everyone. Admission is free, but special exhibits, experiences and IMAX movies cost extra.

**California African American
Museum**   MUSEUM
(☏ 213-744-7432; www.caamuseum.org; 600 State Dr, Exposition Park; ⊙10am-5pm Tue-Sat, from 11am Sun; ℗⊞) FREE CAAM does an excellent job of showcasing African-American artists and the African-American experience, with a special focus on California and LA. Exhibits change a few times each year in galleries around a sunlit atrium.

Los Angeles Memorial Coliseum   STADIUM
(☏ 213-741-0410; www.lacoliseum.com; 3911 S Figueroa St, Exposition Park; guided/self-guided tours $25/10; ⊙self-guided tours 10am-4pm Wed-Sun, guided tours 10:30am & 1:30pm Wed-Sun; Ⓜ Expo Line to Exposition Park/USC) Built in 1923, this grand stadium hosted the 1932 and 1984 Summer Olympic Games, the 1959 baseball World Series and two Super Bowls, and is the temporary home stadium for the **Los Angeles Rams** (www.therams.com) and permanent home of University of Southern California Trojans (American) football teams. Informative guided tours dish the history and take you inside locker rooms, press box, the field and more (blackout dates apply).

★ **Watts Towers**   LANDMARK
(☏ 213-847-4646; www.wattstowers.us; 1761-1765 E 107th St, Watts; adult/child 13-17yr & senior/child under 13yr $7/3/free; ⊙tours 11am-3pm Thu & Fri, 10:30am-3pm Sat, noon-3pm Sun; ℗; Ⓜ Blue Line to 103rd St) The three Gothic spires of the fabulous Watts Towers rank among the world's greatest monuments of folk art. In 1921 Italian immigrant Simon Rodia set out 'to make something big' and then spent 33 years cobbling together this whimsical free-form sculpture from concrete, steel and a motley assortment of found objects: green 7-Up bottles to sea shells, tiles, rocks and pottery.

◎ Pasadena & the San Gabriel Valley

One could argue that there's more blue-blood, meat-eating, robust Americana in Pasadena than in all other LA neighborhoods combined. Here you'll find a community with a preppy old soul, a historical perspective, an appreciation for art and jazz and a progressive undercurrent. The Rose Parade and Rose Bowl football game may have given Pasadena its long-lasting fame, but it's the spirit of this genteel city and its location beneath the lofty San Gabriel Mountains that make it a charming and attractive place to visit year-round.

★ **Huntington Library, Art Collections & Botanical Gardens** MUSEUM, GARDEN
(☑626-405-2100; www.huntington.org; 1151 Oxford Rd, San Marino; adult weekday/weekend & holidays $23/25, child $10, 1st Thu each month free; ⊙10am-5pm Wed-Mon; ℗) One of the most delightful, inspirational spots in LA, the Huntington is rightly a highlight of any trip to California thanks to a world-class mix of art, literary history and over 120 acres of themed gardens (any one of which would be worth a visit on its own), all set amid stately grounds. There's so much to see and do that it's hard to know where to begin; allow three to four hours for even a basic visit.

Norton Simon Museum MUSEUM
(www.nortonsimon.org; 411 W Colorado Blvd, Pasadena; adult/child $12/free; ⊙noon-5pm Mon, Wed & Thu, 11am-8pm Fri & Sat, 11am-5pm Sun; ℗) Rodin's *Burghers of Calais* standing guard by the entrance is only a mind-teasing overture to the full symphony of art in store at this exquisite museum. Norton Simon (1907–93) was an entrepreneur with a Midas touch and a passion for art who parlayed his millions into an admirable collection of Western art and Asian sculpture. Meaty captions really help tell each piece's story.

Los Angeles County Arboretum & Botanic Garden GARDENS
(www.arboretum.org; 301 N Baldwin Ave, Arcadia; adult/student & senior/child 5-12yr $9/6/4, 3rd Tue of month free; ⊙9am-4:30pm) It's easy to spend hours amid the global vegetation, waterfalls, spring-fed lake and historic buildings of this fantastic, rambling, 127-acre park. Originally the private estate of real-estate tycoon Elias 'Lucky' Baldwin, it's so huge there's even a tram to haul those who are foot-weary.

San Gabriel Mission LANDMARK
(☑626-457-3035; www.sangabrielmission.org; 428 S Mission Dr, San Gabriel; adult/child 6-17yr $6/3; ⊙9am-4:30pm Mon-Sat, 10am-4pm Sun; ℗🚻) In 1781, settlers departed from this mission to found El Pueblo de Los Angeles in today's Downtown area. Set about 3 miles southeast of Pasadena in the city of San Gabriel, it's the fourth in the chain of 21 missions in California and is one of the prettiest.

☞ Tours

★ **Paramount Pictures** TOURS
(☑323-956-1777; www.paramountstudiotour.com; 5555 Melrose Ave; tours from $55; ⊙tours 9:30am-5pm, last tour 3pm) *Star Trek, Indiana Jones* and *Shrek* are among the blockbusters that originated at Paramount, the country's second-oldest movie studio and the only one still in Hollywood proper. Two-hour tours of the studio complex are offered year-round, taking in the back lots and sound stages. Guides are usually passionate and knowledgeable, offering fascinating insight into the studio's history and the movie-making process in general.

★ **Esotouric** BUS
(☑213-915-8687; www.esotouric.com; tours $58) Discover LA's lurid and fascinating underbelly on these offbeat, insightful and entertaining walking and bus tours themed around famous crime sites (Black Dahlia anyone?), literary lions (Chandler to Bukowski) and more.

★ **Los Angeles Conservancy** WALKING
(☑213-623-2489; www.laconservancy.org; adult/child $15/10) Downtown LA's intriguing historical and architectural gems – from an art deco penthouse to a beaux-arts ballroom and a dazzling silent-movie theater – are revealed on this nonprofit group's 2½-hour walking tours. To see some of LA's grand historic movie theaters from the inside, the conservancy also offers the Last Remaining Seats film series, screening classic movies in gilded theaters.

TMZ Celebrity Tour BUS
(Map p400; ☑844-869-8687; www.tmz.com/tour; 6925 Hollywood Blvd; adult/child $54/44; ⊙tours departing Hard Rock Cafe Hollywood 12:15pm, 3pm & 5:30pm Thu-Tue, 12:15pm & 3pm Wed; Ⓜ Red Line to Hollywood/Highland) Cut the shame; we know you want to spot celebrities, glimpse their homes and laugh at their dirt. Join this super-fun tour imagined by the paparazzi made famous. Tours run for two hours, and you'll likely meet some of the TMZ stars...and perhaps even celebrity guests on the bus.

Melting Pot Food Tours WALKING
(☑424-247-9666; www.meltingpottours.com; adult/child from $59/45) Duck into aromatic alleyways, stroll through fashionable shopping districts and explore LA landmarks

while tasting some of the city's best ethnic eats in Pasadena, Mid-City and East LA.

✨ Festivals & Events

Tournament of Roses Parade
PARADE

(www.tournamentofroses.com; viewing stands $50-95, sidewalk viewing free; ☺ Jan 1) Presented annually since 1890, this parade along Colorado Blvd through downtown Pasadena calls itself 'America's New Year Celebration.' The highlight: masterfully decorated floats covered entirely with flowers and plant material – seeds to fruit to fronds. Can't make it to the parade? Check out the Showcase of Floats nearby for the couple days afterwards. Standing and seated viewing available. Held on January 2 if January 1 is a Sunday.

Night on Broadway
CULTURAL

(http://nightonbroadway.la; Broadway; ☺ Jan) A pumping, one-night-only arts and music festival on Broadway, with both emerging and established bands, DJs, performance art, food trucks and no shortage of DTLA cool.

Smorgasburg
FOOD & DRINK

(http://la.smorgasburg.com/info; Alameda Produce Market, 746 Market Ct, Downtown; ☺ 10am-5pm Sun) This weekly, hipster-chic, open-air food fest originated in Brooklyn, but it's held there only half the year since Brooklyn's weather, well, kinda sucks the other half. Sunny DTLA to the rescue, with this year-round spin off. Dozens of food purveyors get ridonkulously creative (Filipino stews, berry kombucha, coconut bowls, raindrop cake etc), alongside stalls selling crafts, apparel, vintage goods and more.

Venice Art Walk
ART

(www.theveniceartwalk.org; tickets $50; ☺ mid-May) Each May the Venice Family Clinic sponsors this art auction and studio tour to help raise funds for the clinic, which brings health care to 24,000 under-served men, women and children each year. With a ticket, you receive a map and pass that grants entry into more than 50 local studios featuring hundreds of original pieces, whether you plan on bidding or not.

🛏 Sleeping

From rock-and-roll Downtown digs to fabled Hollywood hideaways, LA serves up a dizzying array of slumber options. The key is to plan well ahead. Do your research and find out which neighborhood is most convenient for your plans and best appeals to your style and interests. Trawl the internet for deals, and consider visiting between January and April, when room rates and occupancy are usually at their lowest (Oscars week aside).

🛏 Downtown Los Angeles & Boyle Heights

★ Hotel Indigo
HOTEL $$$

(Map p394; ☑ 877-270-1392; www.ihg.com; 899 Francisco St, Downtown; d from $229; P❋⬆☎➠; ⓂRed/Purple Lines to 7th St/Metro Center) This freshly minted, 350-room property celebrates Downtown's colorful backstory: wagon-shaped lobby lights pay tribute to the Fiesta de Las Flores, blown-up paparazzi shots around the elevators nod to vaudeville and early movie days, while the restaurant's tunnel-like booths allude to speakeasies. Rooms are plush and svelte, with city-themed splashbacks and deco-inspired bathrooms that pay tribute to early film star Anna May Wong.

Ace Hotel
HOTEL $$$

(Map p394; ☑ 213-623-3233; www.acehotel.com/losangeles; 929 S Broadway; lofts from $400; P❋⬆☎➠) The ever-hip, buzzy, 182-room Ace is big on quirky details: Haas Brothers murals in the lobby and restaurant, whimsically themed cocktails at the rooftop bar and retro-inspired rooms with boxer-style robes, blank music sheets and, in many cases, record players or guitars. Small rooms can feel tight, so consider opting for a medium. Valet parking is $36 a night.

🛏 Hollywood

★ Mama Shelter
BOUTIQUE HOTEL $$

(Map p400; ☑ 323-785-6666; www.mamashelter.com; 6500 Selma Ave; r from $179; ❋@⬆☎; ⓂRed Line to Hollywood/Vine) Hip, affordable Mama Shelter keeps things playful with its lobby gumball machines, foosball table and live streaming of guests' selfies and videos. Standard rooms are small but cool, with quality beds and linen and subway-tiled bathrooms with decent-sized showers. Quirky in-room touches include movie scripts, masks and Apple TVs with free Netflix. The rooftop bar is one of LA's best.

★ Dream
BOUTIQUE HOTEL $$$

(Map p400; ☑ 323-844-6417; www.dreamhotels.com; 6417 Selma Ave; r from $382; P❋⬆☎➠; ⓂRed Line to Hollywood/Vine) This 179-room complex is inspired by mid-century style and designed by the acclaimed Rockwell Group.

Griffith Park & Around

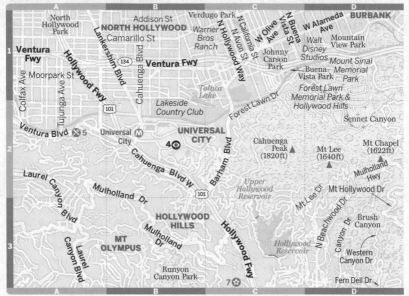

It's a hip, sceney spot, with a massive rooftop pool area and a branch of legendary New York bar Beauty & Essex. Entry-level rooms aren't especially strong on space, though all offer floor-to-ceiling windows and pared-back elegance in neutral, hangover-friendly hues.

★**Hollywood Roosevelt Hotel**   HISTORIC HOTEL **$$$**
(Map p400; ☑323-856-1970; www.thehollywood-roosevelt.com; 7000 Hollywood Blvd; d from $282; P※@☎☀; MRed Line to Hollywood/Highland) Roosevelt heaves with Hollywood lore: Shirley Temple learned to tap dance on the stairs off the lobby, Marilyn Monroe shot her first print ad by the pool (later decorated by David Hockney) and the ghost of actor Montgomery Clift can still be heard playing the bugle. Poolside rooms channel a modernist, Palm Springs vibe, while those in the main building mix contemporary and 1920s accents.

🛏 West Hollywood & Mid-City

★**Petit Ermitage**   BOUTIQUE HOTEL **$$$**
(Map p412; ☑310-854-1114; www.petitermitage. com; 8822 Cynthia St, West Hollywood; ste from $315; P※@☎☀) Bohemian-chic environs with Turkish rugs, old-world antiques, rooftop bars and fine booze set apart this intimate, one-of-a-kind hotel. No two of its 79 suites are

the same, but all feature Venetian-style plaster walls, fireplaces, fun minibar snacks, and some have wet bar and kitchenette. Guests have exclusive access to an impressive art collection lining the halls, lots of chill spaces, and the rooftop bar/butterfly sanctuary.

★**Mondrian**   HOTEL **$$$**
(Map p412; ☑323-650-8999, reservations 800-606-6090; www.mondrianhotel.com; 8440 Sunset Blvd, West Hollywood; r/ste from $329/369; P@☎☀) This chic, sleek tower has been an LA showplace since the 1990s. Giant doors facing the Sunset Strip frame the entrance, opening to a lobby of minimalist elegance: white walls, blond woods, billowy curtains and mood-good-looking staff. Upstairs, mood-lit hallways with tiny light boxes (by famed light artist James Turrell) lead to rooms with chandeliers, rain showers and down duvets.

★**Chateau Marmont**   HOTEL **$$$**
(☑323-656-1010; www.chateaumarmont.com; 8221 W Sunset Blvd, Hollywood; r $450, ste from $820; P⊖※☎☀) The French-flavored indulgence may look dated, but this faux castle has long lured A-listers with its hilltop perch, five-star mystique and legendary discretion. Howard Hughes used to spy on bikini beauties from the same balcony suite that became the favorite of U2's Bono. If nothing

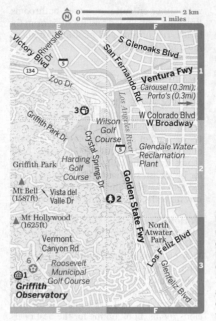

Griffith Park & Around

◎ **Top Sights**
1 Griffith Observatory E3

◎ **Sights**
2 Griffith Park F2
3 Los Angeles Zoo & Botanical
 Gardens E1
4 Universal Studios Hollywood B2

✕ **Eating**
5 Daichan A2

✪ **Entertainment**
6 Greek Theatre E3
7 Hollywood Bowl C3

else, it's worth stopping by for a cocktail at Bar Marmont (p417).

🛏 Beverly Hills, Bel Air, Brentwood & Westwood

★**Montage** HOTEL $$$
(☑ 888-860-0788; www.montagebeverlyhills.com; 225 N Canon Dr, Beverly Hills; r/ste from $695/1175; ▣@◈❋▦) Drawing on-point eye candy and serious wealth, the 201-room Montage balances elegance with warmth and affability. Models and moguls lunch by the gorgeous rooftop pool, while the property's sprawling five-star spa is a marvel, with both single-sex and unisex plunge pools. Rooms are classically styled, with custom mattresses, dual marble basins, spacious showers and deep-soaking tubs.

Beverly Hills Hotel LUXURY HOTEL $$$
(☑ 310-276-2251; www.beverlyhillshotel.com; 9641 Sunset Blvd, Beverly Hills; r/bungalows from $525/715; ▣❋@◈▦❋) The revered 'Pink Palace' packs more Hollywood lore than any other hotel in town. Slumber in one of 208 elegantly appointed hotel rooms or live like the stars in one of 23 discreet, self-contained bungalows. Interiors in the latter are inspired by the stars who've stayed there, from Liz Taylor in number 5 to Frank Sinatra in 22.

Hotel Bel-Air HOTEL $$$
(Map p416; ☑ 310-472-1211; www.hotelbelair. com; 701 Stone Canyon Rd, Bel Air; r from $525; ▣❋◈▦) This tranquil, 12-acre Spanish Colonial estate is a popular hideaway for royalty – Hollywood or otherwise. Leafy and low-key (we love the outdoor fireplaces), it exudes intimacy and restrained luxury, from the plush, living-room-style lobby with central fireplace to the dark, slinky bar and discreet alcoves of Wolfgang Puck's outstanding Californian restaurant. The pink-stucco rooms come with private entrances and French furnishings.

🛏 Malibu & Pacific Palisades

Point Mugu State Park Campground CAMPGROUND $
(☑ 800-444-7275; www.reserveamerica.com; 9000 Pacific Coast Hwy, Malibu; campsite $45, day use $12; ▣) You have two choices here: the creekside campsites shaded by gnarled, native sycamores and oaks, or the windswept beachside spots that are visible (and well within carshot) from the highway. All are within walking distance of flush toilets and coin-operated hot showers.

★**Malibu Beach Inn** INN $$$
(☑ 310-651-7777; www.malibubeachinn.com; 22878 Pacific Coast Hwy, Malibu; r from $595; ▣❋◈) This intimate, adult-oriented hacienda was recently given a four-star upgrade by Waldo Hernandez, celebrity designer who has done work for the likes of the former Brangelina. The look is ocean-friendly grays and blues, and you might just find yourself face-to-face with well-curated art pieces by the likes of Jasper Johns and Andy Warhol.

Santa Monica

HI Los Angeles-Santa Monica   HOSTEL $

(Map p420; 310-393-9913; www.hilosangeles. org; 1436 2nd St; dm low season $27-45, May-Oct $40-55, r with shared bath $109-140, with private bath $160-230; M Expo Line to Downtown Santa Monica) Near the beach and Promenade, this hostel has an enviable location and recently modernized facilities that rival properties charging many times more. Its approximately 275 beds in single-sex dorms are clean and safe, private rooms are decorated with hipster chic, and public spaces (courtyard, library, TV room, dining room, communal kitchen) let you lounge and surf.

★Palihouse   BOUTIQUE HOTEL $$$

(Map p420; 310-394-1279; www.palihousesanta monica.com; 1001 3rd St; r/studios from $315/350;) LA's grooviest hotel brand (not named Ace) occupies the 38 rooms, studios and one-bedroom apartments of the 1927 Spanish-Colonial Embassy Hotel, with antique-meets-hipster-chic style. Each comfy room is slightly different, but look for picnic-table-style desks, and wallpaper with intricate sketches of animals. Most rooms have full kitchens.

Casa del Mar   HOTEL $$$

(Map p420; 310-581-5533; www.hotelcasadel mar.com; 1910 Ocean Way; r from $525;) This mid-1920s beachfront building has alluring Spanish-Mediterranean style and 129 rooms and suites in whites and pale blues designed by Michael Smith, who did the Obama family's private residence. Room rates basically correlate with best views. 'Casa' is most definitely not a thumping pool-party scene, but there is a beach concierge for bikes, blades and umbrellas. It's across the street from **Shutters** (Map p420; 310-458-0030; www.shuttersonthebeach.com; 1 Pico Blvd; r $525;), its sister hotel. Parking is $45.

Venice

Samesun   HOSTEL $

(Map p420; 310-399-7649, reservations 888-718-8287; www.samesun.com; 25 Windward Ave, Venice; dm $39-60, r with shared/private bath from $110/150;) This hostel in a refurbished 1904 building has spectacular rooftop views of Venice Beach, bright, beachy swatches of color and four- to eight-person dorms, as well as some private rooms with either en suite or shared bathrooms. Breakfast is included and it's steps from the beach, restaurants and nightlife. All guests must present a passport.

Rose Hotel   INN $$

(Map p420; 310-450-3474; www.therosehotel venice.com; 15 Rose Ave, Venice; r from $185, ste $450-485;) This intimate, low-slung, pension-style inn was built in 1908 and recently refurbished with beach-cottage cool. It's on a quiet street just off the beach and offers small (150-sq-ft) rooms with bathrooms down the hall, coffee and croissants for breakfast, surfboards for loan and bikes for rent. Larger, family-friendly suites have private baths, kitchens and living rooms.

★Hotel Erwin   BOUTIQUE HOTEL $$$

(Map p420; 310-452-1111; www.hotelerwin.com; 1697 Pacific Ave, Venice; r from $280;) This old motor inn has been dressed up, colored and otherwise funkified in retro style. Think eye-popping oranges, yellows and greens, framed photos of graffiti art, flat-screen TVs and ergo sofas in the spacious rooms. Book online for the best deals. Whether or not you stay here, the High (p417) rooftop lounge is a wonderful place for a sundowner.

Long Beach & San Pedro

★Hotel Maya   BOUTIQUE HOTEL $$

(562-435-7676; www.hotelmayalongbeach.com; 700 Queensway Dr, Long Beach; r from $179;) West of the *Queen Mary*, this boutique property hits you with hip immediately upon entering the rusted-steel, glass and magenta paneled lobby. The feel continues in the 199 rooms (coral tile, river-rock headboards, Mayan-icon accents), set in four 1970s-era hexagons with views of downtown Long Beach that are worth the upcharge.

Queen Mary Hotel   SHIP $$

(877-342-0738; www.queenmary.com; 1126 Queens Hwy, Long Beach; r from $99; Passport) There's an irresistible romance to ocean liners, and this nostalgic retreat time warps you to a long-gone, slower-paced era. Yes, the rooms are small, but hallways are lined with bird's-eye maple veneer, period artwork and display cases of memorabilia from the Cunard days. First-class staterooms are atmospherically refurbished with original art-deco details.

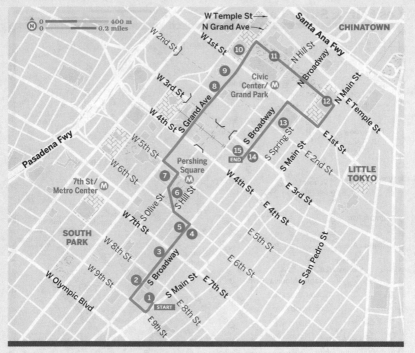

🏃 City Walk
Downtown Revealed

START VERVE
END GRAND CENTRAL MARKET
LENGTH 2.5 MILES; 2½ TO THREE HOURS

Grab a coffee at **1 Verve** then head one block northwest along 9th St to Broadway. Dominating the intersection is the **2 Eastern Columbia Building**, an art-deco beauty with a spectacular entrance. Head north on Broadway through the old theater district. Its heady soup of beaux-arts architecture and trendy new enterprises sums up the Downtown rennaisance in just a few short blocks. Take note of the **3 State Theatre**, **4 Palace Theatre** and **5 Los Angeles Theatre**. The Palace made a cameo in Michael Jackson's *Thriller* music video.

Turn left at 6th St and continue along for two blocks, passing **6 Pershing Square** on your way to the historic **7 Millennium Biltmore Hotel**; its cameos include *Fight Club* and *Mad Men*. Step inside for a look at its opulent interiors and to ask for directions to the Historical Corridor to scan the fascinating

photograph of the 1937 Academy Awards, held on this very site.

Head right into Grand Ave, which will lead you to one of Downtown's most extraordinary contemporary buildings: modern-art museum **8 Broad** (p389). The courtyard is home to hot-spot restaurant Otium, featuring a mural by artist Damian Hirst. On the other side of the Broad is Frank Gehry's showstopping **9 Walt Disney Concert Hall** (p389), home to the LA Philharmonic. Beside it is the LA Phil's former home, **10 Dorothy Chandler Pavilion**. Across the street is **11 Grand Park**, a good spot to catch your breath.

Soaring at the end of the park is **12 City Hall**. Head up its tower for stunning (and free) views and take in the building's breathtaking rotunda on level three. Done, head south along Main St, turning right into 1st St and passing the art-deco headquarters of the **13 Los Angeles Times**. Turn left onto Broadway, eyeing up the beautiful atrium inside the **14 Bradbury Building** before lunch at **15 Grand Central Market**.

Los Feliz & Silver Lake

Los Feliz & Silver Lake

⊗ Eating
1 HomeState	A2
2 Jeni's Splendid Ice Creams	B1
3 Night + Market Song	C4
4 Sqirl	B4

🍷 Drinking & Nightlife
5 Virgil	B3

🎭 Entertainment
6 Cavern Club Theater	C2

🛏 Pasadena & the San Gabriel Valley

★ **Bissell House B&B**　　　　　B&B $$
(☑ 626-441-3535; www.bissellhouse.com; 201 S Orange Grove Ave, South Pasadena; r from $159; P 🐕 🛜 🏊) Antiques, hardwood floors and a crackling fireplace make this secluded Victorian (1887) B&B on 'Millionaire's Row' a bastion of warmth and romance. The hedge-framed garden feels like a sanctuary, and there's a pool for cooling off on hot summer days. The Prince Albert room has gorgeous wallpaper and a claw-foot tub. All seven rooms have private baths.

★ **Langham**　　　　　　　RESORT $$$
(☑ 626-568-3900; www.pasadena.langhamhotels. com; 1401 S Oak Knoll Ave, Pasadena; r from $289; P 🐕 ✴ @ 🛜 🏊) Opened as the Huntington Hotel in 1906, this place spent several decades as the Ritz-Carlton before recently donning the robes of Langham. But some things don't change, and this incredible 23-acre, palm-dappled, beaux-arts country estate – complete with rambling gardens, giant swimming pool and covered picture bridge – has still got it. Rooms would cost hundreds more elsewhere in town.

Eating

Downtown Los Angeles & Boyle Heights

★**Mariscos 4 Vientos** MEXICAN **$**
(☎323-266-4045; www.facebook.com/Mariscos4 Vientos; 3000 E Olympic Blvd; dishes $2.25-14; ⊙9am-5:30pm Mon-Thu, to 6pm Fri-Sun) You'll find the greatest shrimp taco of your life at no-frills Mariscos 4 Vientos. Order from the truck (if you're in a hurry) or grab a table inside the bustling dining room. Either way, surrender to corn tortillas folded and stuffed with fresh shrimp, then fried and smothered in *pico de gallo* (fresh salsa).

★**Guisados** TACOS **$**
(☎323-264-7201; www.guisados.co; 2100 E Cesar Chavez Ave, Boyle Heights; tacos from $2.75; ⊙10:30am-8pm Mon-Thu, to 9pm Fri, 9am-9pm Sat, 9am-5pm Sun; Ⓜ Gold Line to Mariachi Plaza) Guisados' citywide fame is founded on its *tacos de guisados;* warm, thick, nixtamal tortillas made to order and topped with sultry, smoky, slow-cooked stews. Do yourself a favor and order the sampler plate ($7.25), a democratic mix of six mini tacos. The *chiles torreados* (blistered, charred chili) taco is a must for serious spice-lovers. The gourmet coffee isn't bad either.

★**Maccheroni Republic** ITALIAN **$$**
(Map p394; ☎213-346-9725; www.maccheroni republic.com; 332 S Broadway; mains $11-18; ⊙11:30am-2:30pm & 5:30-10pm Mon-Thu, 11:30am-2:30pm & 5:30-10:30pm Fri, 11:30am-10:30pm Sat, 11:30am-9pm Sun) Tucked away on a still-ungentrified corner is this gem with a leafy heated patio and tremendous Italian slow-cooked food. Don't miss the *polpettine di gamberi* (flattened ground shrimp cakes fried in olive oil), and its range of delicious housemade pastas. Perfectly al dente, the pasta is made using organic semolina flour and served with gorgeous crusty bread to mop up the sauce.

★**Bestia** ITALIAN **$$$**
(☎213-514-5724; www.bestiala.com; 2121 7th Pl; pizzas $16-19, pasta $19-29, mains $28-120; ⊙5-11pm Sun-Thu, to midnight Fri & Sat; Ⓟ) Years on, this loud, buzzing, industrial dining space remains the most sought-after reservation in town (book at least a week ahead). The draw remains its clever, produce-driven takes on Italian flavors, from pizzas topped with housemade '*nduja* (a spicy Calabrian paste), to a sultry stinging-nettle raviolo with egg,

mixed mushrooms, hazelnut and ricotta. The wine list celebrates the boutique and obscure.

★**Otium** MODERN AMERICAN **$$$**
(Map p394; ☎213-935-8500; http://otiumla. com; 222 S Hope St, Downtown; dishes $15-45; ⊙11:30am-2:30pm & 5:30-10pm Tue-Thu, 11:30am-2:30pm & 5:30-11pm Fri, 11am-2:30pm & 5:30-11pm Sat, 11am-2:30pm & 5:30-10pm Sun; 🛜) In a modernist pavilion beside the Broad is this fun, of-the-moment hot spot helmed by chef Timothy Hollingsworth. Prime ingredients conspire in unexpected ways, from the crunch of wild rice and amaranth in an eye-candy salad of avocado, beets and pomegranate, to a twist of lime and sake in flawlessly al dente whole-wheat bucatini with Dungeness crab.

★**Sushi Gen** JAPANESE **$$$**
(Map p394; ☎213-617-0552; www.sushigen.org; 422 E 2nd St; sushi $11-23; ⊙11:15am-2pm & 5:30-9:45pm Tue-Fri, 5-9:45pm Sat; Ⓟ; Ⓜ Gold Line to Little Tokyo/Arts District) Come early to grab a table at this classic sushi spot, where bantering Japanese chefs carve thick slabs of melt-in-your-mouth salmon, buttery *toro* (tuna belly), Japanese snapper and more. At lunch, perch yourself at the sushi counter for à la carte options, or queue for a table in the dining room, where the sashimi lunch special ($17) is a steal. You'll find the place in Honda Plaza.

Hollywood

★**Petit Trois** FRENCH **$$**
(☎323-468-8916; http://petittrois.com; mains $14-36; ⊙noon-10pm Sun-Thu, to 11pm Fri & Sat; Ⓟ) Good things come in small packages...like tiny, no-reservations Petit Trois! Owned by acclaimed TV chef Ludovic Lefebvre, its two long counters are where food-lovers squeeze in for smashing, honest, Gallic-inspired grub, from a ridiculously light Boursin-stuffed omelette to a showstopping double cheeseburger served with a standout foie gras–infused red-wine bordelaise.

★**Salt's Cure** MODERN AMERICAN **$$**
(☎323-465-7258; http://saltscure.com; 1155 N Highland Ave; mains $17-34; ⊙11am-11pm Mon-Thu, to midnight Fri, 10am-midnight Sat, 10am-11pm Sun) Wood-paneled, concrete-floored Salt's Cure is an out, proud locavore. From the in-season vegetables to the house-butchered and cured meats, the menu celebrates all things Californian. Expect sophisticated takes on rustic comfort grub, whether it's capicollo with chili paste or tender duck

breast paired with impressively light oat-meal griddle cakes and blackberry compote.

★ **Musso & Frank Grill**　　STEAK $$
(Map p400; ☑323-467-7788; www.mussoand
frank.com; 6667 Hollywood Blvd; mains $15-52;
☺11am-11pm Tue-Sat, 4-9pm Sun; P; MRed
Line to Hollywood/Highland) Hollywood histo-
ry hangs in the thick air at Musso & Frank
Grill, Tinseltown's oldest eatery (since 1919).
Charlie Chaplin used to knock back vodka
gimlets, Raymond Chandler penned scripts
in the high-backed booths, and movie deals
were made on the old phone at the back (the
booth closest to the phone is favored by Jack
Nicholson and Johnny Depp).

★ **Providence**　　MODERN AMERICAN $$$
(☑323-460-4170; www.providencela.com; 5955
Melrose Ave; lunch mains $40-45, tasting menus
$120-250; ☺noon-2pm & 6-10pm Mon-Fri, 5:30-
10pm Sat, 5:30-9pm Sun; P) The top restaurant
pick by preeminent LA food critic Jonathan
Gold for four years running, this two-starred
Michelin darling turns superlative seafood
into arresting, nuanced dishes that might
see abalone paired with eggplant, turnip
and nori, or spiny lobster conspire dec-
adently with macadamia nut and earthy
black truffle. À la carte options are available
at lunch only.

✗ Los Feliz & Griffith Park

★ **HomeState**　　TEX-MEX $
(Map p408; ☑323-906-1122; www.myhomestate.
com; 4624 Hollywood Blvd, Los Feliz; tacos $3.50,
dishes $7-10; ☺8am-3pm; MRed Line to Ver-
mont/Sunset) Texan expat Briana Valdez
is behind this rustic ode to the Lone Star
State. Locals queue patiently for authentic breakfast tacos such as the Trinity, a
handmade flour tortilla topped with egg,
bacon, potato and cheddar. Then there's
the *queso* (melted cheese) and our lunchtime favorite, the brisket sandwich, a coax-
ing combo of tender meat, cabbage slaw,
guacamole and pickled jalapeños in pil-
low-soft white bread.

★ **Jeni's Splendid Ice Creams**　　ICE CREAM $
(Map p408; ☑323-928-2668; https://jenis.
com; 1954 Hillhurst Ave, Los Feliz; 2/3/4 flavors
$5.50/6.50/7.50; ☺11am-11pm) Rarely short
of a queue, this Ohio import scoops some
of the city's creamiest, most inventive ice
cream. Forget plain vanilla. Here, signature
flavors include brown butter almond brittle
and a riesling poached-pear sorbet.

✗ Silver Lake & Echo Park

★ **Sqirl**　　CAFE $
(Map p408; ☑323-284-8147; http://sqirlla.
com; 720 N Virgil Ave; dishes $5-15; ☺6:30am-
4pm Mon-Fri, from 8am Sat & Sun; ☺✐; MRed
Line to Vermont/Santa Monica) Despite its
somewhat-obscure location, this tiny, sub-
way-tiled cafe is forever pumping thanks to
its top-notch, out-of-the-box breakfast and
lunch offerings. Join the queue to order
made-from-scratch wonders such as long-
cooked chicken and rice porridge served
with dried lime, ginger, turmeric, carda-
mon ghee and tomato, or the cult-status
ricotta toast, a symphony of velvety housemade ricotta, thick-cut 'burnt' brioche and
Sqirl's artisanal jams.

★ **Night + Market Song**　　THAI $
(Map p408; ☑323-665-5899; www.nightmarket
la.com; 3322 Sunset Blvd; dishes $7-15; ☺noon-
3pm Mon-Fri, 5-11pm Mon-Sat; ✐) After cultivat-
ing a cult following in WeHo, this gleefully
garish temple to real-deal Thai and Cambodian street food is killing it in the hipster
heartlands. Invigorate the taste buds with
spicy larb (minced-meat salad), proper pad
Thai and harder-to-find specialties such as
Isaan-style fermented pork sausage.

★ **Ostrich Farm**　　MODERN AMERICAN $$
(☑213-537-0657; http://ostrichfarmla.com; 1525
Sunset Blvd; dinner mains $19-29; ☺10am-2pm
Tue-Fri, to 3pm Sat & Sun, also 5:30-10pm Mon-
Thu, 5:30-11pm Fri & Sat) Flickering tea lights
and charming, competent barkeeps crank
up the charm at this intimate, convivial
space, owned and run by a husband-and-
wife team. You won't find ostrich on the
menu (the name refers to a former railway
that reached Griffith Park), just honest
takes on American classics, many of them
cooked over the kitchen's wood-fired grill.

✗ West Hollywood & Mid-City

★ **Night + Market**　　THAI $
(Map p412; ☑310-275-9724; www.nightmarketla.
com; 9043 W Sunset Blvd, West Hollywood; dishes
$8-15; ☺11:30am-2:30pm Tue-Thu, 5-10:30pm Tue-
Sun) Set behind Talésai, a long-running Thai
joint, this related kitchen pumps out out-
standing Thai street food and Thai-inspired
hybrids such as catfish tamales. Pique the
appetite with *larb lanna* (chopped pork sal-
ad), push the envelope with rich *pork toro*
(grilled pork collar).

LA'S FASHION DISTRICT DEMYSTIFIED

Bargain hunters love the 100-block warren of fashion in southwestern Downtown that is the Fashion District. Deals can be amazing, but first-timers are often bewildered by the district's size and immense selection. For orientation, check out www.fashiondistrict.org.

Basically, the area is subdivided into several distinct retail areas, with womens wear and accessories constituting the bulk of the offerings:

➡ Women – Santee St between 9th St and Pico Blvd; Pico Blvd between Main and Santee Sts; Wall and Maple Sts between Olympic Blvd and 12th St.

➡ Children – 12th St and Pico Blvd between Maple Ave and San Julian St.

➡ Men – Main, Los Angeles and Santee Sts, between Pico Blvd and 16th St, plus Los Angeles St between 7th and 9th Sts.

➡ Textiles – The blocks bordered by 8th St, Olympic Blvd, Maple Ave and San Julian St.

➡ Jewelry and accessories – Santee Alley, Olympic Blvd between Main St and Wall St, plus Main and Santee Sts between Olympic and Pico Blvds.

Shops are generally open from 10am to 5pm daily, with Saturday being the busiest day because that's when many wholesalers open up to the public. Around a third of the shops are closed on Sunday. Cash is king and haggling may get you 10% or 20% off, especially when buying multiple items. Refunds or exchanges are a no-no, so choose carefully and make sure items are in good condition. Most stores don't have dressing rooms. Sample sales are usually held on the last Friday of every month, with popular showrooms including the **California Market Center** (Map p394; ☑ 213-630-3600; www.california marketcenter.com; 110 E 9th St), **Cooper Design Space** (Map p394; ☑ 213-627-3754; www. cooperdesignspace.com; 860 S Los Angeles St), **New Mart** (Map p394; ☑ 213-627-0671; www. newmart.net; 127 E 9th St) and the **Gerry Building** (Map p394; www.gerrybuilding.com; 910 S Los Angeles St). Upcoming sales are posted on the LA Fashion District Facebook page (www.facebook.com/LAFashionDist).

★ **Gracias Madre** VEGAN, MEXICAN **$$**
(Map p412; ☑ 323-978-2170; www.graciasmadre weho.com; 8905 Melrose Ave, West Hollywood; mains lunch $10-13, dinner $12-18; ⊘11am-11pm Mon-Fri, from 10am Sat & Sun; ⌗) Gracias Madre shows just how tasty organic, plant-based Mexican cooking can be. Sit on the gracious patio or in the cozy interior and feel good as you eat healthy: sweet-potato flautas, coconut 'bacon,' plantain 'quesadillas,' plus salads and bowls.

Canter's DELI **$$**
(Map p412; ☑ 323-651-2030; www.cantersdeli. com; 419 N Fairfax Ave, Mid-City; ⊘24hr; ℗) As old-school delis go, Canter's is hard to beat. A fixture in the traditionally Jewish Fairfax district since 1931, it serves up the requisite pastrami, corned beef and matzo-ball soup with a side of sass by seen-it-all waitresses, in a rangy room with deli and bakery counters up front.

★ **Ray's** MODERN AMERICAN **$$$**
(Map p412; ☑ 323-857-6180; www.raysandstark bar.com; 5905 Wilshire Blvd, Los Angeles County Museum of Art; mains $17-36; ⊘11:30am-8pm Mon-Tue & Thu, to 10pm Fri, 10am-8pm Sat & Sun;

℗; ⊒MTA 20) Seldom does a restaurant blessed with as golden a location as this one – on the plaza of LACMA (p393) – live up to the address. Ray's does. Menus change seasonally and often daily with farm-to-table fresh ingredients – some grown in the restaurant's own garden. You can expect some form of burrata, kale salad and pizzas to be on the menu.

Beverly Hills, Bel Air, Brentwood & Westwood

★ **Joss Cuisine** CHINESE **$$**
(☑310-277-3888; www.josscuisine.com; 9919 S Santa Monica Blvd, Beverly Hills; dishes $15-30; ⊘noon-3pm Mon-Fri, 5:30-10pm daily) With fans including Barbra Streisand, Gwenyth Paltrow and Jackie Chan, this warm, intimate nosh spot serves up superlative, MSG-free Chinese cuisine at noncelebrity prices. Premium produce drives a menu of exceptional dishes, from flawless dim sum and ginger fish broth, to crispy mustard prawns and one of the finest Peking ducks you'll encounter this side of East Asia. Reservations recommended.

West Hollywood & Mid-City

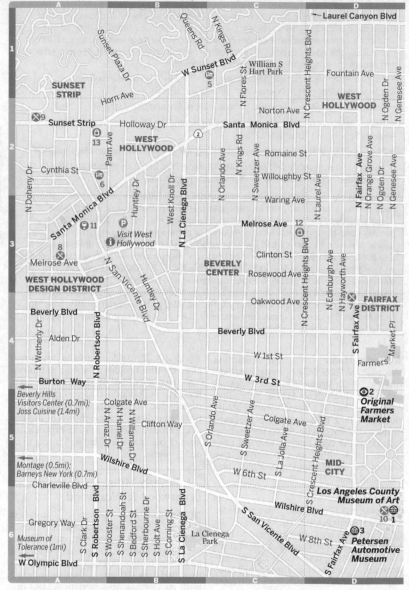

✕ Malibu & Pacific Palisades

★ **Saddle Peak Lodge**   AMERICAN **$$$**
(☎ 818-222-3888; www.saddlepeaklodge.com;
419 Cold Canyon Rd, Calabasas; appetizers $14-
23, mains $34-62; ☺ 5-9pm Mon-Fri, to 10pm Sat,
10:30am-2pm & 7-9pm Sun; 🅿) Rustic as a

Colorado mountain lodge, and tucked into
the Santa Monica Mountains with a creek
running beneath, Saddle Peak Lodge serves
up elk, venison, buffalo and other game in
a setting watched over by mounted versions
of the same. Though the furnishings are rus-
tic timber, this is fine dining, so don't come

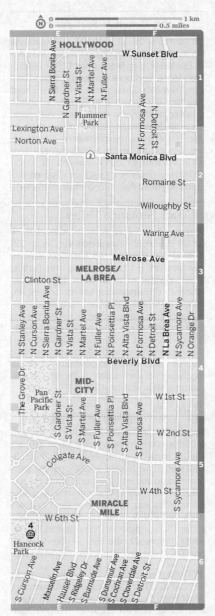

West Hollywood & Mid-City

◎ Top Sights
1 Los Angeles County Museum of
Art.. D6
2 Original Farmers Market.................... D5
3 Petersen Automotive Museum.......... D6

◎ Sights
4 La Brea Tar Pits & Museum................ E6

◎ Sleeping
5 Mondrian...C1
6 Petit Ermitage.................................... A2

◎ Eating
7 Canter's.. D4
8 Gracias Madre A3
9 Night + Market................................... A2
10 Ray's.. D6

◎ Drinking & Nightlife
11 The Abbey.. A3

◎ Shopping
12 Fred Segal C3
13 Mystery Pier Books............................ A2

$12-19, dinner $23-44; ⊙10am-3pm & 5:30-10pm; 🅿📋) 🍴 If you lived through the 1960s, you might experience flashbacks at this new-agey hideaway in an impossibly idyllic creekside setting in Topanga Canyon. It grills hanger steaks and roast lamb belly, but it also bubbles soba noodles and makes a nice squid-ink pasta, all served on elegant white tablecloths.

★**Nobu Malibu**   JAPANESE $$$
(📞310-317-9140; www.noburestaurants.com; 22706 Pacific Coast Hwy, Malibu; dishes $8-46; ⊙noon-10pm Mon-Thu, 9am-11pm Fri & Sat, to 10pm Sun; 🅿) Chef Nobu Matsuhisa's empire of luxe Japanese restaurants began in LA, and the Malibu outpost is consistently one of LA's hot spots. East of the pier, it's a cavernous, modern wood chalet with long sushi bar and a dining room that spills onto a patio overlooking the swirling sea. Remember, it's the cooked food that built the brand.

🍴 Santa Monica

★**Santa Monica Farmers Markets** MARKET $
(Map p420; www.smgov.net/portals/farmers market; Arizona Ave, btwn 2nd & 3rd Sts; ⊙Arizona Ave 8:30am-1:30pm Wed, 8am-1pm Sat, Main St 8:30am-1:30pm Sun; 🚸) 🍴 You haven't really experienced Santa Monica until you've explored one of its weekly outdoor farmers markets stocked with organic fruits, vegetables, flowers, baked goods and freshly

here after a day on the trail. The 6-mile drive up Malibu Canyon is nothing short of inspirational – and occasionally hair-raising.

★**Inn of the Seventh Ray**   ORGANIC $$$
(📞310-455-1311; www.innoftheseventhray.com; 128 Old Topanga Canyon Rd, Topanga; mains lunch

shucked oysters. The mack daddy is the Wednesday market, around the intersection of 3rd and Arizona – it's the biggest and arguably the best for fresh produce, and often patrolled by local chefs.

★**Milo & Olive** ITALIAN $$
(☏310-453-6776; www.miloandolive.com; 2723 Wilshire Blvd; dishes $7-20; ☺7am-11pm) We love this place for its small-batch wines, incredible pizzas, terrific breakfasts (creamy polenta and poached eggs anyone?), breads and pastries, all of which you may enjoy at the marble bar or shoulder to shoulder with new friends at one of two common tables. It's a cozy neighborhood joint so it doesn't take reservations.

★**Cassia** SOUTHEAST ASIAN $$$
(Map p420; ☏310-393-6699; 1314 7th St; appetizers $12-24, mains $18-77; ☺5-10pm Sun-Thu, to 11pm Fri & Sat; ℗) Ever since it opened in 2015, open, airy Cassia has made about every local and national 'best' list of LA restaurants. Chef Bryant Ng draws on his Chinese-Singaporean heritage in dishes such as *kaya* toast (with coconut jam, butter and a slow-cooked egg), 'sunbathing' prawns, and the encompassing Vietnamese *pot au feu:* short-rib stew, veggies, bone marrow and delectable accompaniments.

✗ Venice

★**Butcher's Daughter** VEGETARIAN, CAFE $$
(Map p420; ☏310-981-3004; www.thebutchers daughter.com; 1205 Abbot Kinney Blvd, Venice; dishes $10-22; ☺8am-10pm) Find yourself a seat around the central counter or facing busy Abbot Kinney to tuck in to stone-oven pizzas, handmade pastas and veggie faves such as whole roasted cauliflower and butternut-squash risotto. It's Aussie-owned, meaning great coffee. Light, airy and fun. Welcome to California!

★**Gjelina** AMERICAN $$$
(Map p420; ☏310-450-1429; www.gjelina.com; 1429 Abbot Kinney Blvd, Venice; veggies, salads & pizzas $10-18, large plates $15-45; ☺8am-midnight; ☝; ☒Big Blue Bus line 18) If one restaurant defines the new Venice, it's this. Carve out a slip on the communal table between the hipsters and yuppies, or get your own slab of wood on the elegant stone terrace, and dine on imaginative small plates (raw yellowtail spiced with chili and mint and drenched in olive oil and blood orange) and sensational thin-crust, wood-fired pizza.

✗ Long Beach & San Pedro

★**Fourth & Olive** ALSATIAN $$
(☏562-269-0731; www.4thandolive.com; 743 E 4th St, East Village, Long Beach; mains $15-29; ☺4:30-10pm Mon & Tue, 11am-10pm Wed, Thu & Sun, 11am-11pm Fri & Sat) There's much to love about this new Cal-French bistro: farmers-market produce, small-farm-raised beef and pork, housemade sausages, classic dishes such as *steak frites* and *choucroute garnie,* and low-key service, all under a high-raftered roof with generous windows to watch the world go by. *And* many of its staff are disabled veterans, so you're doing good while eating well.

✗ San Fernando Valley

Porto's CUBAN, BAKERY $
(☏818-956-5996; www.portosbakery.com; 315 N Brand Blvd, Glendale; ☺6:30am-8pm Mon-Sat, 7am-6pm Sun; ☝) Locals obsess over Porto's. There always seems to be a queue somewhere in this sprawling bakery-cafe, where different stations dispense hearty sandwiches, luscious cakes and obsession-worthy *pasteles* (small pastries). Deep-fried potato balls filled with meat or cheese and jalapeño define comfort food, as do flaky guava-cheese pastries and meaty sandwiches such as *medianoche* and Cuban. There's simple cafeteria-style seating. Olé, y'all!

★**Daichan** JAPANESE $$
(Map p404; ☏818-980-8450; 11288 Ventura Blvd, Studio City; mains $8-20; ☺11:30am-3pm & 5:30-9pm Mon-Fri, noon-3pm & 5-9pm Sat; ℗) Tucked away in an unassuming mini-mall, and stuffed with knickknacks, pasted with posters and staffed by a sunny, sweet owner-operator, this offbeat, home-style Japanese diner offers some of the best (and tastiest) deals on Sushi Row. Fried seaweed tofu *gyōza* (dumplings) are divine and so are the bowls – especially the *negitoro* bowl, which puts fatty tuna over rice, lettuce and seaweed.

★**Carousel** MIDDLE EASTERN $$
(☏818-246-7775; www.carouselrestaurant.com; 304 N Brand Blvd, Glendale; mezes $6.75-11, mains lunch $12-18.50, dinner $15.50-28; ☺11am-9:30pm Tue-Thu, to 10:30pm Fri & Sat, to 8:30pm Sun; ℗) Carousel may call itself a Lebanese restaurant, but this huge place has a commensurately huge following among Glendale's Armenian community. We can see why: succulent shawarma and kebabs, mounds of *mezzas* (small plates, hummus to steak

tartare) and desserts made with *ashta* (condensed milk) and honey are knockouts.

⚔ Pasadena & the San Gabriel Valley

★ Din Tai Fung
CHINESE $

(☎ 626-574-7068; www.dintaifungusa.com; 1108 S Baldwin Ave, Arcadia; dumplings $10-14, dishes $4.50-11.50; ⊙ 11am-9:30pm Mon-Fri, 10am-9:30pm Sat, 10am-9pm Sun; [P]) It's a testament to the SGV's ethnic Chinese community that Taiwan's most esteemed dumpling house opened its first US outpost here. The menu of dumplings, greens, noodles, desserts, teas and smoothies is as long as the phone directory at a medium-size corporation, but everyone orders pork *xiaolongbao* – steamed dumplings juicy with rich broth. Expect long waits – it's worth it.

NBC Seafood
DIM SUM $

(☎ 626-282-2323; www.nbcrestaurant.com; 404-A Atlantic Blvd, Monterey Park; dim sum $3-7, mains $10-17; ⊙ 8am-10pm, dim sum until 3pm; [P]) Behind the rotunda facade, this SGV dim-sum institution seats 388 at a time. At peak hours (roughly 10am to 1pm on weekends) all seats are full, with a line out the door. Shrimp *har gao,* pan fried leek dumplings and addictive shrimp on sugarcane are worth the wait.

★ Union
ITALIAN $$

(☎ 626-795-5841; www.unionpasadena.com; 37 E Union St, Pasadena; dishes $14-38; ⊙ 5-11pm Mon-Fri, from 4pm Sat & Sun) A cheerful, sophisticated energy animates James Beard–nominated chef Bruce Kalman's restaurant, offering California interpretations of northern Italian cuisine. The menu changes daily, but standards include pork meatballs, squid-ink pasta, fish caught from the waters of nearby Santa Barbara and a subtle and delicious olive-oil cake for dessert. Everything's made in-house, from breads to pastas to cheeses.

🍷 Drinking & Nightlife

🍷 Downtown Los Angeles & Boyle Heights

★ Everson Royce Bar
COCKTAIL BAR

(☎ 213-335-6166; www.erbla.com; 1936 E 7th St; ⊙ 5pm-2am) Don't be fooled by the unceremonious grey exterior. Behind that wall lies a hopping Arts District hangout, with a buzzy, bulb-strung outdoor patio. The barkeeps here are some of the city's best, using

craft liquor to concoct drinks such as the prickly-pear Mateo Street Margarita.

★ Clifton's Republic
COCKTAIL BAR

(Map p394; ☎ 213-627-1673; www.cliftonsla.com; 648 S Broadway; ⊙ 11am-midnight Tue-Thu, to 2am Fri, 10am-2:30am Sat, 10am-midnight Sun; 🛜; [M] Red/Purple Lines to Pershing Sq) Opened in 1935 and back after a $10-million renovation, multilevel, mixed-crowd Clifton's defies description. You can chow retro-cafeteria classics (meals around $14.75) by a forest waterfall, order drinks from a Gothic church altar, watch burlesque performers shimmy in the shadow of a 40ft faux redwood, or slip through a glass-paneled door to a luxe tiki paradise.

★ Upstairs at the Ace Hotel
BAR

(Map p394; www.acehotel.com/losangeles; 929 S Broadway, Downtown; ⊙ 11am-2am) What's not to love about a rooftop bar with knockout Downtown views, powerful cocktails and a luxe, safari-inspired fit out? Perched on the 14th floor of the Ace Hotel, this chilled, sophisticated space has on-point DJs and specially commissioned artworks that include an installation made using Skid Row blankets.

🍷 Hollywood

★ Sassafras Saloon
BAR

(☎ 323-467-2800; www.sassafrashollywood.com; 1233 N Vine St; ⊙ 5pm-2am) You'll be pining for the bayou at the hospitable Sassafras Saloon, where hanging moss evokes sultry Savannah. Cocktails include a barrel-aged Sazerac, while themed nights include live jazz on Sunday and Monday, brass bands and acrobatics on Tuesday, burlesque and blues on Wednesday, karaoke on Thursday, and DJ-spun tunes on Friday and Saturday.

★ Sayers Club
CLUB

(Map p400; ☎ 323-871-8233; www.facebook.com/TheSayersClub; 1645 Wilcox Ave; cover varies; ⊙ 9pm-2am Tue & Thu-Sat; [M] Red Line to Hollywood/Vine) When established stars such as the Black Keys, and even movie stars such as Joseph Gordon-Levitt, decide to play secret shows in intimate environs, they come to the back room at this brick-house Hollywood nightspot, where the booths are leather, the lighting moody and the music satisfying.

★ No Vacancy
BAR

(Map p400; ☎ 323-465-1902; www.novacancyla.com; 1727 N Hudson Ave; ⊙ 8pm-2am; [M] Red Line to Hollywood/Vine) If you prefer your cocktail sessions with plenty of wow factor, make a

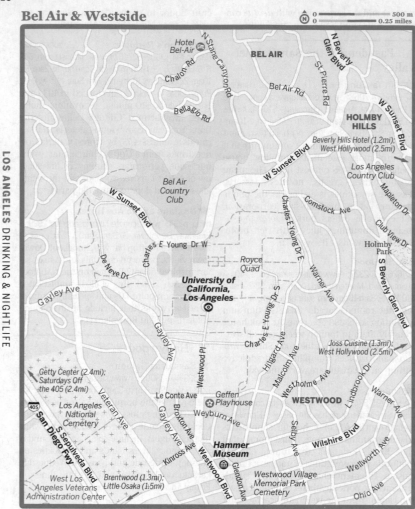

reservation online, style up (no sportswear, shorts or logos) and head to this old shingled Victorian. A vintage scene of dark timber panels and elegant banquettes, it has bars in nearly every corner, tended by clever barkeeps while burlesque dancers and a tightrope walker entertain the droves of party people.

Silver Lake & Echo Park

★ **Virgil**   BAR

(Map p408; ☑ 323-660-4540; www.thevirgil.com; 4519 Santa Monica Blvd, Silver Lake; ☺ 7pm-2am) An atmospheric, vintage-styled neighborhood hangout serving quality cocktails to local hipsters and arty types. A stocked calendar of entertainment includes top-notch live-comedy nights, with hilarious, subversive erotic fan-fiction improv on the third Sunday of the month. Other rotating events include booze-fueled spelling bees, storytelling events, bands and themed club nights, including '80s-themed Funkmosphere on Thursdays. Did we mention the jukebox?

Red Lion Tavern   BEER HALL

(☑ 323-662-5337; http://redliontavern.net; 2366 Glendale Blvd, Silver Lake; ☺ 11am-2am, beer garden to 11pm Sun-Thu & 1am Fri & Sat; ☎) Chipped, worn and armed with retro cigarette vending machine, this old-school beer dive has been pouring German suds since 1959. The snug, woody downstairs bar feels like a Teutonic version of *Cheers,* while upstairs is an even cozier bar and a super-popular beer garden. Beer flights are $10 and edibles include fantastic pretzels and a sausage platter large enough for two.

West Hollywood & Mid-City

★ **Abbey**   GAY & LESBIAN
(Map p412; ☑ 310-289-8410; www.theabbeyweho. com; 692 N Robertson Blvd, West Hollywood; ☺ 11am-2am Mon-Thu, from 10am Fri, from 9am Sat & Sun) It's been called the best gay bar in the world, and who are we to argue? Once a humble coffee house, the Abbey has expanded into WeHo's bar/club/restaurant of record. Always a party, it has so many different flavored martinis and mojitos that you'd think they were invented here, plus a full menu of upscale pub food (mains $14 to $21).

★ **Bar Marmont**   BAR
(☑ 323-650-0575; www.chateaumarmont.com; 8171 Sunset Blvd, Hollywood; ☺ 6pm-2am) Elegant, but not stuck up; been around, yet still cherished. With high ceilings, molded walls and terrific martinis, the famous and the wish-they-weres still flock here. If you time it right you might see celebs – the Marmont doesn't share who (or else they'd stop coming – get it?). Come midweek. Weekends are for amateurs.

Santa Monica

★ **Bungalow**   LOUNGE
(Map p420; www.thebungalowsm.com; 101 Wilshire Blvd, Fairmont Miramar Hotel; ☺ 5pm-2am Mon-Fri, noon-2am Sat, noon-10pm Sun) A Brent Bolthouse nightspot, the indoor-outdoor lounge at the Fairmont Miramar was one of the hottest nights out in LA when it burst onto the scene a couple of years ago. It's since settled down, and like most Westside spots can be too dude-centric late in the evening, but the setting is elegant, and there's still beautiful mischief to be found here.

★ **Basement Tavern**   BAR
(Map p420; www.basementtavern.com; 2640 Main St; ☺ 5pm-2am) A creative speakeasy, housed in the basement of the Victorian, and our favorite well in Santa Monica. We love it for its craftsman cocktails, cozy booths, island bar and nightly live-music calendar that features blues, jazz, bluegrass and rock bands.

It gets way too busy on weekends for our taste, but weeknights can be special.

Venice

★ **High**   ROOFTOP BAR
(Map p420; ☑ 424-214-1062; www.highvenice.com; 1697 Pacific Ave, Hotel Erwin, Venice; ☺ 3-10pm Mon-Thu, to midnight Fri, noon-midnight Sat, noon-10pm Sun) Venice's only rooftop bar is quite an experience, with 360-degree views from the shore to the Santa Monica Mountains – if you can take your eyes off the beautiful people. High serves creative seasonal cocktails (blood-orange julep, lemon apple hot toddy, Mexican hot chocolate with tequila) and dishes like beef or lamb sliders, meze plates and crab dip. Reservations recommended.

Intelligentsia Coffeebar   CAFE
(Map p420; ☑ 310-399-1233; www.intelligentsia coffee.com; 1331 Abbot Kinney Blvd, Venice; ☺ 6am-8pm Mon-Thu, to 10pm Fri, 7am-10pm Sat, 7am-8pm Sun; ☏; ☐ Big Blue Bus line 18) In this hip, industrial, minimalist monument to the coffee gods, perfectionist baristas – who roam the central bar and command more steaming machines than seems reasonable – never short you on foam or caffeine, and the Cake Monkey scones and muffins are addictive.

☆ Entertainment

★ **Hollywood Bowl**   CONCERT VENUE
(Map p404; ☑ 323-850-2000; www.hollywoodbowl. com; 2301 N Highland Ave; rehearsals free, performance costs vary; ☺ Jun-Sep) Summers in LA just wouldn't be the same without alfresco melodies under the stars at the Bowl, a huge natural amphitheater in the Hollywood Hills. Its annual season – which usually runs from June to September – includes symphonies, jazz bands and iconic acts such as Blondie, Bryan Ferry and Angélique Kidjo. Bring a sweater or blanket as it gets cool at night.

★ **Blue Whale**   JAZZ
(Map p394; ☑ 213-620-0908; www.bluewhalemu sic.com; 123 Onizuka St, Suite 301; cover $5-20; ☺ 8pm-2am, closed 1st Sun of month; Ⓜ Gold Line to Little Tokyo/Arts District) An intimate, concrete-floored space on the top floor of Weller Court in Little Tokyo, Blue Whale serves topnotch jazz nightly from 9pm. The crowd is eclectic, the beers craft and the bar bites decent. Acts span emerging and edgy to established, and the acoustics are excellent. Note: bring cash for the cover charge.

★**Greek Theatre** LIVE MUSIC
(Map p404; ☑844-524-7335; www.lagreekthe atre.com; 2700 N Vermont Ave; ⊙Apr-Oct) The 'Greek' in the 2010 film *Get Him to the Greek* is this 5900-capacity outdoor amphitheater, tucked into a woodsy Griffith Park hillside. A more intimate version of the Hollywood Bowl, it's much loved for its vibe and variety – recent acts include PJ Harvey, John Legend and Pepe Aguilar. Parking (cash only) is stacked, so plan on a postshow wait.

★**Saturdays Off the 405** LIVE MUSIC
(www.getty.edu; Getty Center; ⊙6-9pm Sat May-Sep) From May to September, the Getty Center courtyard fills with evening crowds for a delicious collision of art, brilliant live acts and beat-pumping DJ sets.

★**Geffen Playhouse** THEATER
(Map p416; ☑310-208-5454; www.geffenplay house.com; 10886 Le Conte Ave, Westwood) American magnate and producer David Geffen forked over $17 million to get his Mediterranean-style playhouse back into shape. The center's season includes both American classics and freshly minted works, and it's not unusual to see well-known film and TV actors treading the boards.

★**Mark Taper Forum** THEATER
(Map p394; ☑213-628-2772; www.centertheatre group.org; 135 N Grand Ave) Part of the Music Center, the Mark Taper is one of the three venues used by the Center Theatre Group, SoCal's leading resident ensemble and producer of Tony-, Pulitzer- and Emmy-winning plays. It's an intimate space with only 15 rows of seats arranged around a thrust stage, so you can see every sweat pearl on the actors' faces.

★**Comedy & Magic Club** LOUNGE
(www.comedyandmagicclub.com; 1018 Hermosa Ave; ⊙Tue-Sun) Live music and comedy right on the Hermosa strip. It has something going almost every night, including some big names: David Spade, Arsenio Hall, Alonzo Bodden, Jon Lovitz, and 10 – count 'em, 10! – comedians most Fridays and Saturdays. Sunday means Jay Leno live and up close; he's the place's big draw.

★**Upright Citizens Brigade Theatre** COMEDY
(Map p400; ☑323-908-8702; http://franklin. ucbtheatre.com; 5919 Franklin Ave; tickets $5-12) Founded in New York by *Saturday Night Live* alums Amy Poehler and Ian Roberts along with Matt Besser and Matt Walsh, this sketch-comedy group cloned itself in Hollywood in 2005. With numerous nightly shows spanning anything from stand-up comedy to improv and sketch, it's arguably the best comedy hub in town. Valet parking costs $7.

🔒 Shopping

🔒 Downtown Los Angeles

★**Last Bookstore in Los Angeles** BOOKS
(Map p394; ☑213-488-0599; www.lastbookstorela. com; 453 S Spring St; ⊙10am-10pm Mon-Thu, to 11pm Fri & Sat, to 9pm Sun) What started as a one-man operation out of a Main St storefront is now California's largest new-and-used bookstore, spanning two levels of an old bank building. Eye up the cabinets of rare books before heading upstairs, home to a horror-and-crime book den, a book tunnel and a few art galleries to boot.

★**Raggedy Threads** VINTAGE
(Map p394; ☑213-620-1188; www.raggedythreads. com; 330 E 2nd St; ⊙noon-8pm Mon-Sat, to 6pm Sun; Ⓜ Gold Line to Little Tokyo/Arts District) A tremendous vintage Americana store just off the main Little Tokyo strip. There's plenty of beautifully ragged denim, with a notable collection of pre-1950s workwear from the US, Japan and France. You'll also find a good number of Victorian dresses, soft T-shirts and a wonderful turquoise collection at decent prices.

🔒 Hollywood

Amoeba Music MUSIC
(Map p400; ☑323-245-6400; www.amoeba.com; 6400 W Sunset Blvd; ⊙10:30am-11pm Mon-Sat, 11am-10pm Sun) When a record store not only survives but thrives in this techno age, you know it's doing something right. Flip through 500,000 new and used CDs, DVDs, videos and vinyl at this granddaddy of music stores, which also stocks band-themed T-shirts, music memorabilia, books and comics. Handy listening stations and the store's outstanding *Music We Like* booklet keep you from buying lemons.

🔒 West Hollywood & Mid-City

WeHo and Mid-City are by far the best and most diverse shopping territory in a city that often feels like it's built by and for shopaholics. Melrose Ave, between La Brea and Fairfax Aves, gets most of the buzz, thanks to the boutiques stuck together like block-long hedgerows. Most of their gear is rather low-brow and low-end, with some unique gems and fab vintage stores. If you want the high-end stuff, make your way west of Fairfax on Melrose or 3rd St. Both Beverly Blvd and La Brea Ave are stocked with gorgeous interiors showrooms and galleries, with the occasional fashion boutique mixed in. Fairfax Ave, between Beverly and Melrose, is where hip-hop and skate culture collide.

Then there are the megamalls: the Beverly Center and its smaller sister, Beverly Connection, across the street, and the Grove, each with dozens of high-to-middle-end shops and department stores, and often big hangout spots in their own right.

★**Fred Segal**   FASHION & ACCESSORIES
(Map p412; ☑323-651-4129; www.fredsegal.com; 8100 Melrose Ave, Mid-City; ⊙10am-7pm Mon-Sat, noon-6pm Sun) Celebs and beautiful people circle for the very latest from Babakul, Aviator Nation and Robbi & Nikki at this warren of high-end boutiques under one impossibly chic but slightly snooty roof. The only time you'll see bargains (sort of) is during the two-week blowout sale in September.

★**Mystery Pier Books**   BOOKS
(Map p412; www.mysterypierbooks.com; 8826 W Sunset Blvd, West Hollywood; ⊙11am-7pm Mon-Sat, noon-5pm Sun) An intimate, hidden-away courtyard shop that specializes in selling signed shooting scripts from past blockbusters, and 1st editions from Shakespeare ($2500 to $4000), Salinger ($21,000) and JK Rowling ($30,000 and up).

🔒 Beverly Hills & the Westside

Downtown Beverly Hills is the area's retail heartland, heaving with both well-known and more obscure luxury fashion and jewelry brands from mainly Europe and the US. The most famous (and most expensive) strip is Rodeo Dr, with boutiques also on the surrounding streets. Among these is N Beverly Dr, dotted with higher-end midrange fashion and lifestyle brands. To the south, Wilshire Blvd offers high-end department stores, including fashion-forward Barneys.

Barneys New York   DEPARTMENT STORE
(☑310-276-4400; www.barneys.com; 9570 Wilshire Blvd; ⊙10am-7pm Mon-Wed, Fri & Sat, to 8pm Thu, 11am-6pm Sun; 🛜) The Beverly Hills branch of New York's most fashion-forward department store delivers four floors of sharply curated collections for women and men. Expect

interesting pieces from luxe Euro brands as well as unique pieces from homegrown labels like 3.1 Philip Lim and Warm.

🔒 Venice

Abbot Kinney Blvd has become one of LA's top shopping destinations. Bargains are few and far between here, but there's a lot of tantalizing stuff – clothing, gifts, accessories and more. As rents have risen, there has been spillover to surrounding streets.Along the Venice Boardwalk, shops and stalls sell everything from cheap sunglasses and microbikinis to incense and the inevitable tacky T-shirts.

Linus   SPORTS & OUTDOORS
(Map p420; ☑310-301-1866; www.linusbike.com; 1817 Lincoln Blvd, Venice; ⊙11am-7pm; 🚌Big Blue Bus line 3) You've learned to eat, talk and appreciate art like a Venetian; now get around like one. The ultimate Venice bike shop assembles sturdy, steel-frame bikes such as the Dutchi and the Roadster. You can't carry a bike home with you, you say? It also sells enviable accessories such as bike bags, baskets, cup holders and even beer holsters.

Alexis Bittar   JEWELRY
(Map p420; ☑310-452-6901; www.alexisbittar.com; 1612 Abbot Kinney Blvd, Venice; ⊙11am-7pm Mon-Sat, noon-6pm Sun) High-end women's jewelry known for Bittar's use of lucite, which is hand carved and painted in his Brooklyn studio. Some of it looks like stone. He started by selling it on the streets in Manhattan, where he was picked up by the MoMA store.

ℹ Information

INTERNET ACCESS

Cybercafes are a dying breed in LA, though free public wi-fi is proliferating, with hot spots including LAX, Pershing Sq and Grand Central Market in Downtown, Echo Park Lake, the Griffith Observatory, the Hollywood & Highland mall, Beverly Canon Gardens in Beverly Hills, Venice Beach and Santa Monica Pier.

POST

Call the **toll-free line** (☑310-247-3470; www. usps.com; 325 N Maple Dr; ⊙9am-5pm Mon-Fri, 9:30am-1pm Sat) for the nearest post-office branch.

TOURIST INFORMATION

Beverly Hills Visitors Center (☑310-248-1015; www.lovebeverlyhills.com; 9400 S Santa Monica Blvd, Beverly Hills; ⊙9am-5pm Mon-Fri, from 10am Sat & Sun; 🛜) Sightseeing, activities, dining and accommodations information focused on the Beverly Hills area.

Downtown LA Visitor Center (Map p394; www.discoverlosangeles.com; Union Station, 800 N Alameda St; ⊗9am-5pm; Ⓜ Red/Purple/Gold Lines to Union Station) Maps and general tourist information in the lobby of Union Station.

Long Beach Area Convention & Tourism Bureau (☑ 562-628-8850; www.visitlongbeach.com; 3rd fl, One World Trade Center, 301 E Ocean Blvd, Long Beach; ⊗11am-7pm Sun-Thu, 11:30am-7:30pm Fri & Sat Jun-Sep, 10am-4pm Fri-Sun Oct-May) Tourist office located in downtown Long Beach.

Marina del Rey (☑ 310-305-9545; www.visit marinadelrey.com; 4701 Admiralty Way, Marina del Rey; ⊗9am-5pm Mon-Fri, 10am-4pm Sat & Sun) Maps and information on sights, activities, events and accommodations in the Marina del Rey area.

Visit Pasadena (☑ 626-795-9311; www.visitpasadena.com; 300 E Green St, Pasadena; ⊗8am-5pm Mon-Fri, 10am-4pm Sat) Visitor information with a focus on Pasadena attractions and events.

Santa Monica Visitor Information Center (Map p420; ☑800-544-5319; www.santamonica.com; 2427 Main St) The main tourist information center in Santa Monica, with free guides, maps and helpful staff.

Visit West Hollywood (Map p412; www.visitwesthollywood.com; Pacific Design Center Blue Bldg, 8687 Melrose Ave, Suite M60, West Hollywood; ⊗9am-5pm Mon-Fri; 🛜) Information on attractions, accommodations, tours and more in the West Hollywood area.

ⓘ Getting There & Away

AIR

The main LA gateway is Los Angeles International Airport (p527). Its nine terminals are linked by the free LAX Shuttle A, leaving from the lower (arrival) level of each terminal. Cabs and hotel and car-rental shuttles stop here as well. A free minibus for travelers with disabilities can be ordered by calling ☑ 310-646-6402. Ticketing and check-in are on the upper (departure) level.

The hub for most international airlines is the Tom Bradley International Terminal.

Some domestic flights operated by Alaska, American Eagle, Delta Connection, JetBlue, Southwest and United also arrive at **Burbank Hollywood Airport** (BUR, Bob Hope Airport; www.burbankairport.com; 2627 N Hollywood Way, Burbank), which is handy if you're headed for Hollywood, Downtown or Pasadena.

To the south, on the border with Orange County, the small **Long Beach Airport** (www.lgb.org; 4100 Donald Douglas Dr, Long Beach) is convenient for

Santa Monica & Venice Beach

Santa Monica & Venice Beach

Disneyland and is served by Alaska, JetBlue and Southwest.

BUS

The main bus terminal for **Greyhound** (☑ 213-629-8401; www.greyhound.com; 1716 E 7th St) is in an industrial part of Downtown, so try not to arrive after dark. Take bus 18, 60, 62 or 760 to the 7th St/Metro Center metro station, from where metro trains head to Hollywood (Red Line), Koreatown (Purple Line), Culver City and Santa Monica (Expo Line) and Long Beach (Blue Line). Both the Red and Purple Lines reach Union Station, from where you can catch the Metro Gold Line (for Highland Park and Pasadena).

CAR & MOTORCYCLE

If you're driving into LA, there are several routes by which you might enter the metropolitan area.

From San Francisco and Northern California, the fastest route to LA is on I-5 through the San Joaquin Valley. Hwy 101 is slower but more picturesque, while the most scenic – and slowest – route is via Hwy 1 (Pacific Coast Hwy, or PCH).

From San Diego and other points south, I-5 is the obvious route. Near Irvine, I-405 branches off I-5 and takes a westerly route to Long Beach and Santa Monica, bypassing Downtown LA entirely and rejoining I-5 near San Fernando.

From Las Vegas or the Grand Canyon, take I-15 south to I-10 then head west into LA. I-10 is the main east–west artery through LA and continues on to Santa Monica.

TRAIN

Amtrak (www.amtrak.com) trains roll into Downtown's historic **Union Station** (☑ 800-872-7245; www.amtrak.com; 800 N Alameda St). Interstate trains stopping in LA are the daily *Coast Starlight*

to Seattle, the daily *Southwest Chief* to Chicago and the thrice-weekly *Sunset Limited* to New Orleans. The *Pacific Surfliner* travels numerous times daily between San Diego, Santa Barbara and San Luis Obispo via LA.

❶ Getting Around

TO/FROM THE AIRPORT

LAX FlyAway (☑ 866-435-9529; www.lawa.org/FlyAway) runs to Union Station (Downtown), Hollywood, Van Nuys, Westwood Village near UCLA, and Long Beach. A one-way ticket costs $9.75.

For scheduled bus services, catch the free shuttle bus from the airport toward parking lot C. It stops by the LAX City Bus Center hub for buses serving all of LA County. For Santa Monica or Venice, change to the Santa Monica Big Blue Bus lines 3 or Rapid 3 ($1.25). If you're headed for Culver City, catch Culver City bus 6 ($1). For Manhattan, Hermosa or Redondo Beaches, hop aboard Beach Cities Transit 109 ($1). Taxis are readily available.

BICYCLE

Most buses have bike racks, and bikes ride for free, although you must securely load and unload them yourself. Bicycles are also allowed on Metro Rail trains at all times.

LA has a number of bike-sharing programs. The following are especially useful for visitors:

Metro Bike Share (https://bikeshare.metro.net) Has more than 60 self-serve bike kiosks in the Downtown area, including Chinatown, Little Tokyo and the Arts District. Pay using your debit or credit card ($3.50 per 30 minutes) or TAP card, though you will first need to register it on the Metro Bike Share website. The

LGBTQ LOS ANGELES

LA is one of the country's gayest cities, and has made a number of contributions to gay culture. Your gaydar may well be pinging throughout the county, but the rainbow flag flies especially proudly in Boystown, along Santa Monica Blvd in West Hollywood, which is flanked by dozens of high-energy bars, cafes, restaurants, gyms and clubs. Most cater to gay men, although there's plenty for lesbians and mixed audiences. Thursday through Sunday nights are prime time.

Beauty reigns supreme among the buff, bronzed and styled of Boystown. Elsewhere the scene is considerably more laid-back and less body conscious. The crowd in Silver Lake is more mixed-age and runs from cute hipsters to leather-and-Levi's, while Downtown's burgeoning scene is an equally eclectic mix of hipsters, East LA Latinos, general counterculture types and business folk. Venice and Long Beach have the most relaxed, neighborly scenes.

If nightlife isn't your scene, there are plenty of other ways to meet, greet and engage. Outdoor options include the **Frontrunners** (www.lafrontrunners.com) running club and the **Great Outdoors** (www.greatoutdoorsla.org) hiking club. The latter runs day and night hikes, as well as neighborhood walks. For insight into LA's fascinating queer history, book a walking tour with **Out & About Tours** (www.thelavendereffect.org/tours; tours from $30).

There's gay theater all over town, but the **Celebration Theatre** (☑ 323-957-1884; www.celebrationtheatre.com; 6760 Lexington Ave, Hollywood) ranks among the nation's leading stages for LGBTQ plays. The **Cavern Club Theater** (Map p408; www.cavernclub theater.com; 1920 Hyperion Ave, Silver Lake) pushes the envelope, particularly with uproarious drag performers; it's downstairs from Casita del Campo restaurant. If you're lucky enough to be in town when the **Gay Men's Chorus of Los Angeles** (www.gmcla.org) is performing, don't miss out: this amazing group has been doing it since 1979.

The **LA LGBT Center** (Map p400; ☑ 323-993-7400; www.lalgbtcenter.org; 1625 Schrader Blvd; ☉ 9am-9pm Mon-Fri, to 1pm Sat) is a one-stop service and health agency, and its affiliated **Village at Ed Gould Plaza** (☑ 323-993-7400; https://lalgbtcenter.org; 1125 N McCadden Pl, Hollywood; ☉ 6-10pm Mon-Fri, 9am-5pm Sat; Ⓟ) offers art exhibits, theater and film screenings throughout the year.

The festival season kicks off in mid- to late May with the **Long Beach Pride Celebration** (☑ 562-987-9191; www.longbeachpride.com; 450 E Shoreline Dr, Long Beach; parade free, festival admission adult/child & senior $25/free; ☉ mid-May) and continues with the three-day **LA Pride** (www.lapride.org) in mid-June with a parade down Santa Monica Blvd. On Halloween (October 31), the same street brings out 500,000 outrageously costumed revelers of all persuasions.

smartphone app offers real-time bike and rack availability.

Breeze Bike Share (www.santamonicabike share.com; per hour $7, monthly/annually $25/99) Runs self-serve kiosks all over Santa Monica, Venice and Marina del Rey.

CAR & MOTORCYCLE

Unless time is no factor – or money is extremely tight – you're going to want to spend some time behind the wheel, although this means contending with some of the worst traffic in the country.

Parking at motels and cheaper hotels is usually free, while fancier ones charge anywhere from $8 to around $45 for the privilege.

The usual international car-rental agencies have branches at LAX and throughout LA. For Harley rentals, go to Route 66. Rates start from $149 per six hours, or $185 for one day. Discounts are available for longer rentals.

PUBLIC TRANSPORTATION

Most public transportation is handled by **Metro** (☑ 323-466-3876; www.metro.net), which offers maps, schedules and trip-planning help through its website.

To ride Metro trains and buses, buy a reusable TAP card. Available from TAP vending machines at Metro stations with a $1 surcharge, the cards allow you to add a preset cash value or day passes. The regular base fare is $1.75 per boarding, or $7 for a day pass with unlimited rides. Both single-trip tickets and TAP cards loaded with a day pass are available on Metro buses (ensure you have the exact change). When using a TAP card, tap the card against the sensor at station entrances and aboard buses.

TAP cards are accepted on DASH and municipal bus services and can be reloaded at vending machines or online on the TAP website (www.taptogo.net).

Metro Buses

Metro operates about 200 bus lines across the city and offers three types of bus services:

➡ Metro Local buses (painted orange) make frequent stops along major thoroughfares throughout the city.

➡ Metro Rapid buses (painted red) stop less frequently and have special sensors that keep traffic lights green when a bus approaches.

➡ Commuter-oriented Metro Express buses (painted blue) connect communities with Downtown LA and other business districts and usually travel via the city's freeways.

Metro Rail

The Metro Rail network consists of two subway lines, four light-rail lines and two express bus lines. Six lines converge in Downtown.

Red Line The most useful for visitors. A subway linking Downtown's Union Station to North Hollywood (San Fernando Valley) via central Hollywood and Universal City; connects with the Blue and Expo Lines at the 7th St/Metro Center station in Downtown and the Metro Orange Line express bus at North Hollywood.

Blue Line Light-rail line running from Downtown to Long Beach; connects with the Red and Expo Lines at 7th St/Metro Center station and the Green Line at Willowbrook/Rosa Parks station.

Expo Line Light-rail line linking USC and Exposition Park with Culver City and Santa Monica to the west and Downtown LA to the northeast, where it connects with the Red Line at 7th St/Metro Center station.

Gold Line Light-rail line running from East LA to Little Tokyo/Arts District, Chinatown and Pasadena via Union Station, Mt Washington and Highland Park; connects with the Red Line at Union Station.

Green Line Light-rail service between Norwalk and Redondo Beach; connects with the Blue Line at Willowbrook/Rosa Parks.

Orange Line Express bus linking the west San Fernando Valley to North Hollywood, from where the Red Line subway shoots south to Hollywood and Downtown LA.

Purple Line Subway line between Downtown LA, Westlake and Koreatown; shares six stations with the Red Line.

Silver Line Express bus linking the El Monte regional bus station to the Harbor Gateway Transit Center in Gardena via Downtown LA. Some services continue to San Pedro.

Most lines run from around 4:30am to 1am Sunday to Thursday, and until around 2:30am on Friday and Saturday nights. Frequency ranges from up to every five minutes in rush hour to every 10 to 20 minutes at other times. Schedules for all lines are available at www.metro.net.

Municipal Buses

Santa Monica–based **Big Blue Bus** (☑310-451-5444; www.bigbluebus.com) serves much of western LA, including Santa Monica, Venice, Westwood and LAX ($1.25). Its express bus 10 runs from Santa Monica to Downtown ($2.50, one hour).

The **Culver City Bus** (www.culvercity.org/enjoy/culver-city-bus) runs services throughout Culver City and the Westside. This includes a service to Aviation/LAX station on the metro Green Line ($1), from where a free shuttle connects to LAX.

Long Beach Transit (www.lbtransit.com; $1.25 per ride) serves Long Beach and surrounding communities. All three municipal bus companies accept payment by TAP card.

AROUND LOS ANGELES

Ditch the congestion, crowds and smog, and use LA as a hub to all the natural glory of California. Get an early start to beat the traffic, point the compass across the ocean or up into the mountains.

Catalina Island

Mediterranean-flavored Santa Catalina Island is a popular getaway for harried Angelenos drawn by fresh air, seemingly endless sunshine, seaside fun and excellent hiking in a unique microclimate.

Originally the home of Tongva native people, Catalina has gone through stints as a hangout for Spanish explorers, Franciscan friars, sea-otter poachers, smugglers and Union soldiers. In 1919 it was snapped up by chewing-gum magnate William Wrigley Jr (1861–1932), who had buildings constructed in the Spanish Mission style and for years sent his Chicago Cubs baseball team here for spring training. Apart from its human population (about 4100), Catalina's highest-profile residents are a herd of bison, brought here for a movie shoot and who ended up breeding.

Today most of the island is owned by the **Catalina Island Conservancy** (☑310-510-2595; www.catalinaconservancy.org; 125 Clarissa Ave, Avalon; biking/hiking permits $35/free), and 88% of the island's 75 square miles is a nature preserve requiring (easily available) permits for access to hiking and cycling.

Even if Catalina sinks under the weight of day-trippers in summer and whenever cruise ships anchor offshore, if you stay overnight you may well feel the ambience go from frantic to, as the song says, 'romance, romance, romance, romance.'

Commercial activity is concentrated in the town of Avalon (population about 3775), which is small enough to be explored in an hour or two, so there's plenty of time for hiking, swimming and touring.

The only other settlement is Two Harbors (population about 300) on the remote west coast, which has a general store, a dive and kayak center, a snack bar and a lodge.

Avalon lodging has long been pretty dowdy, but recent renovations are upgrading rooms while preserving the island's traditional charm. Rates soar on weekends and between May and September; they're about 30% to 60% lower at other times. For camping information, see www.visitcatalina island.com/avalon/camping.php.

🏃 Activities

There are plenty of activities right in Avalon and on the harbor, as well as hiking, mountain biking and ziplining inland with the chance to spot eagles and bison. If you're going into the backcountry, there's very little shade, so take a hat, sunscreen and plenty of water.

In Avalon you can hang out on the privately owned Descanso Beach (☑310-510-7410; www.visitcatalinaisland.com/activities-adven tures/descanso-beach-club; 1 St Catherine Way, Avalon). There's good snorkeling at Lovers' Cove and at Casino Point (Avalon Underwater Park), a marine reserve that's also the best shore dive. Another way to escape the throngs is by kayaking to the quiet coves along Catalina's rocky coastline. Catalina Island Expeditions (Descanso Beach Ocean Sports; ☑310-510-1226; www.kayakcatalinaisland. com; Descanso Beach Club; single/double kayak rental per hour $22/30, per day $52/72, SUP per hour/day from $24/60, 2hr tours per person $48) rents snorkeling gear, SUP kits and kayaks, and also runs guided kayaking tours and kayak camping trips.

To get into the protected backcountry, hop on the Safari Bus (☑310-510-4205; www.visit catalinaisland.com/activities-adventures/two-har bors/safari-bus; ☺mid-Jun–early Sep), which goes all the way to Two Harbors. You must book in advance and get a permit (and maps) from the Catalina Island Conservancy if you're going to be hiking or mountain biking.

Alternatively, you could just hop on an air-conditioned tour bus and let someone else show you around. Both Catalina Ad-

venture Tours (☑877-510-2888; www.catalina adventuretours.com; Green Pier, Avalon; tours adult/child & senior from $45/42) and Discovery Tour Plaza (☑800-626-1496; www.visit catalinaisland.com/island-info/tour-plaza; 10 Island Plaza, Avalon; tours $19-124) operate historical Avalon itineraries and jaunts further out with memorable views of the rugged coast, deep canyons and sandy coves, and possible encounters with eagles and a herd of bison.

Snorkelers and certified scuba divers can rent equipment at Descanso Beach to glimpse local shipwrecks and kelp forests. Two Harbors Dive and Recreation Center (☑310-510-4272; www.visitcatalinaisland.com/ activities-adventures/two-harbors/dive-recrea tion-center; 1 Banning House Rd, Two Harbors; guided trips from $99; ☺9am-5pm) accesses pristine dive sites off the island's less developed coast.

ℹ️ Getting There & Away

A few companies operate ferries to Avalon and Two Harbors. Reservations are recommended at any time and especially during summer. The use of cars on Catalina is restricted, so there are no vehicle ferry services.

Catalina Express (☑800-613-1212; www. catalinaexpress.com) Ferries to Avalon from San Pedro, Long Beach and Dana Point in Orange County, and to Two Harbors from San Pedro. It takes one to 1½ hours, with up to three ferries daily. You'll ride free on your birthday...true story.

Catalina Flyer (☑800-830-7744; www.catalina ferries.com) Catamaran to Avalon and Two Harbors from Balboa Harbor in Newport Beach (one to 1½ hours).

Big Bear Lake

Big Bear Lake is a low-key, family-friendly mountain resort (elevation 6750ft) about 110 miles northeast of LA. Snowy winters lure scores of ski bunnies and boarders to its two mountains, while summer brings hikers, mountain bikers and watersports enthusiasts wishing to escape the stifling heat down in the basin. Even getting here via the spectacular, curvy, panorama-filled Rim of the World Scenic Byway (Hwy 18) is a treat.

The purchase of Big Bear's two mountains – Snow Summit and Bear Mountain – by the owners of Mammoth Mountain ski resort in the Eastern Sierra has injected the town not only with money but also with new energy. The vibe has especially picked up in the downtown area, the Village, where upscale bars, restaurants and shops have opened.

Around Los Angeles

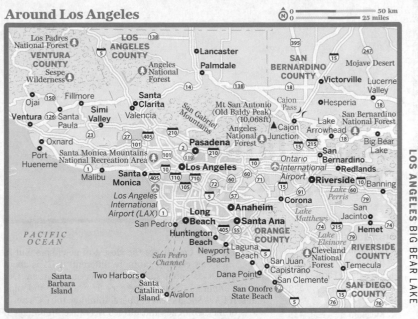

🏃 Activities

Big Bear's two ski mountains are jointly managed by **Big Bear Mountain Resorts** (📞844-462-2327; www.bigbearmountainresorts.com; 2-park lift ticket adult/child $56/46; ⊘ usually Dec-Apr; 🚹). The higher of the two, **Bear Mountain** (8805ft) is nirvana for freestyle freaks with more than 150 jumps, 80 jibs, and two pipes including a 580ft in-ground superpipe. **Snow Summit** (8200ft) is more about traditional downhill and has trails for everyone. Altogether the mountains are served by 26 lifts and crisscrossed by more than 55 runs.

🛏 Sleeping & Eating

On snowy winter weekends, demand often exceeds capacity, so plan ahead. The two hostels offer the cheapest digs, private villas the priciest and in between you'll find plenty of aging motels along the main highway and 2000 private cabins tucked into the woods.

For cheap sleeps tuck into the clean and friendly **Big Bear Hostel** (📞909-866-8900; www.bigbearhostel.com; 527 Knickerbocker Rd; dm $20-40, d $45-68; 🅿@🛜). **Switzerland Haus** (📞909-866-3729, 800-335-3729; www.switzerlandhaus.com; 41829 Switzerland Dr; r $125-249; @🛜) offers comfy rooms with mountain-view patios and a Nordic sauna. **Himalayan** (📞909-866-2907; www.himalayan bigbear.com; 672 Pine Knot Ave; mains $10-19;

⊘11am-9pm Sun-Tue, to 10pm Fri & Sat; 🚹🚹) is a popular Nepali and Indian kitchen with speedy service.

ℹ Information

Big Bear Discovery Center (📞909-382-2790; http://mountainsfoundation.org; 409/1 N Shore Dr/Hwy 38, Fawnskin; ⊘8am-4:30pm, closed Wed & Thu mid-Sep–mid-May) Nonprofit visitor center dispenses information and maps on all outdoor-related activities around Big Bear, including camping. Also sells the National Forest Adventure Pass.

Big Bear Visitors Center (📞909-866-7000; www.bigbear.com; 630 Bartlett Rd; ⊘9am-5pm; 🛜) Has lots of free flyers, maps and wi-fi, and sells trail maps and the National Forest Adventure Pass.

ℹ Getting There & Away

Big Bear is on Hwy 18, an offshoot of Hwy 30 in San Bernardino. A quicker approach is via Hwy 330, which starts in Highland and intersects with Hwy 18 in Running Springs. If you don't like serpentine mountain roads, pick up Hwy 38 near Redlands, which is longer, but easier on the queasy. Less traffic too, handy on peak weekends.

Mountain Transit (📞909-878-5200; http://mountaintransit.org) buses connect Big Bear with the Greyhound and Metrolink stations in San Bernardino at least twice daily ($10, 1¼ hours).

Disneyland & Orange County

Best Places to Eat

➡ Walt's Wharf (p440)

➡ Napa Rose (p434)

➡ Driftwood Kitchen (p453)

➡ Ramos House Café (p455)

Best Places to Sleep

➡ Paséa (p443)

➡ Disney's Grand Californian Hotel & Spa (p432)

➡ Montage (p453)

➡ Crystal Cove Beach Cottages (p450)

Why Go?

LA and Orange County are the closest of neighbors, but in some ways they couldn't be more different. If LA is about stars, the OC is about surfers. LA: ever more urban, OC: proudly *sub*urban, built around cars, freeways and shopping malls. If LA is SoCal's seat of liberal thinking, the OC's heritage is of megachurches and ultraconservative firebrands. If LA is Hollywood glam, the OC is *Real Housewives*.

Tourism is dominated by Disneyland in Anaheim in northern OC, and beach communities promising endless summer – and very different lifestyles as you progress down the coast from Seal Beach to Huntington Beach, Newport Beach to Laguna Beach.

While there's some truth to those stereotypes of life behind the 'Orange Curtain,' this diverse county's 789 sq miles, 34 cities and 3.15 million people create deep pockets of individuality and beauty, while cool, urbanesque spots keep the OC 'real,' no matter one's reality.

When to Go
Anaheim

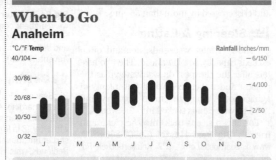

May Visitation dips from spring break to Memorial Day. Mostly sunny, balmy temperatures.

Jul & Aug Summer vacation and beach season peak. Surfing and art festivals by the coast.

Sep Blue skies, cooler temperatures inland, fewer crowds. Tall Ships Festival at Dana Point.

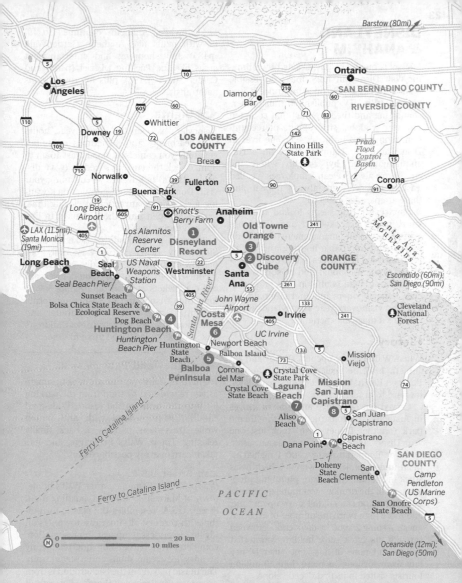

Disneyland & Orange County Highlights

1 Screaming your head off on Space Mountain before catching the fireworks show at **Disneyland Resort** (p428).

2 Fighting outrageous bed hair inside the eye of a hurricane in Santa Ana's **Discovery Cube** (p438).

3 Shopping for vintage treasures and slurping milkshakes in **Old Towne Orange** (p438).

4 Building a beach bonfire after a day of surfing waves at **Huntington Beach** (p441).

5 Cycling past Newport Beach's as-seen-on-TV sands on **Balboa Peninsula** (p444).

6 Discovering Orange County's alternative side at the Lab and the Camp 'antimalls' in **Costa Mesa** (p448).

7 Watching the sun dip below the horizon at **Laguna Beach** (p450).

8 Being awed by the Spanish colonial history and beauty of **Mission San Juan Capistrano** (p454).

DISNEYLAND & ANAHEIM

Mickey is one lucky guy. Created by animator Walt Disney in 1928, this irrepressible mouse caught a ride on a multimedia juggernaut (film, TV, publishing, music, merchandising and theme parks) that rocketed him into a global stratosphere of recognition, money and influence. Plus, he lives in Disneyland, the 'Happiest Place on Earth,' an 'imagineered' hyper-reality where the streets are always clean, employees – called 'cast members' – are always upbeat and there are parades every day.

Sure, every ride seems to end in a gift store, prices are sky-high and there are grumblings that management could do more about affordable housing and health insurance for employees – but even determined grouches should find reason to grin. For the more than 14 million kids, grandparents, honeymooners and international tourists who visit every year, Disneyland Resort remains a magical experience.

History

When Walt Disney opened Disneyland on July 17, 1955, he declared it the 'Happiest Place on Earth.' Over six decades years later, it's hard to argue.

Carved out of orange and walnut groves in Anaheim, the construction of the 'theme park' (another Disney term) took just one year. Disneyland's opening day was a disaster, however. Temperatures over 100°F melted asphalt underfoot, leaving women's high heels stuck in the tar. There were plumbing problems: all of the drinking fountains quit working. Hollywood stars didn't show up on time, and more than twice the number of expected guests – some 28,000 by day's end – crowded through the gates, some holding counterfeit tickets. But none of this kept eager Disney fans away for long, as more than 50 million tourists visited in its first decade alone.

During the 1990s, Anaheim undertook a staggering $4.2 billion revamp and expansion, cleaning up rundown stretches and establishing the first tourist police force in the US. In 2001 a second theme park, Disney's California Adventure (DCA), was added, designed to salute the state's most famous natural landmarks and cultural history. More recently added was Downtown Disney, an outdoor pedestrian mall. The ensemble is called Disneyland Resort.

Meanwhile, Anaheim continues to fill in with malls like Anaheim GardenWalk (p435) and shopping and entertainment areas like the Packing District (p436) and Center Street (p436), plus improved roads and transit.

◉ Sights

Disneyland is open 365 days a year; hours vary seasonally and sometimes daily, but generally you can count on at least 10am to 8pm. Check the current schedule (www.disneyland.com) in advance when timing your visit. Don't worry about getting stuck waiting for a ride or attraction at closing time. Parks stay open until the last guest in line has had their fun.

There is a multitude of ticket options. Single day ticket prices vary daily but on low-traffic days (typically Monday to Wednesday in the off or shoulder season) one-day tickets start at adult/child $97/91 for either Disneyland or Disney California Adventure, and a variety of multiday and 'park-hopper' passes are available. Children's tickets apply to kids aged three to nine.

◉ Disneyland Park

It's hard to deny the change in atmosphere as you're whisked by tram from the parking lot into the heart of the resort. Wide-eyed children lean forward with anticipation while stressed-out parents sit back, finally relaxing. Uncle Walt's in charge, and he's taken care of every possible detail.

Main Street, U.S.A. AREA
(Map p430; [♿]) Fashioned after Walt's hometown of Marceline, Missouri, bustling Main Street, U.S.A. resembles the classic turn-of-the-20th-century, all-American town. It's an idyllic, relentlessly upbeat representation, complete with barbershop quartet, penny arcades, ice-cream shops and a steam train. The music playing in the background is from American musicals, and there's a flag-retreat ceremony every afternoon.

Great Moments with Mr. Lincoln
(Map p430; https://disneyland.disney.go.com/attractions/disneyland/disneyland-story; [♿]), a 15-minute Audio-Animatronics presentation on Honest Abe, sits inside the fascinating **Disneyland Story** exhibit. Nearby, kids love seeing old-school Disney cartoons like *Steamboat Willie* inside **Main Street Cinema**.

Main Street ends in the **Central Plaza** (Map p430; 🎡). Lording over the plaza is **Sleeping Beauty Castle** (Map p430; https://disneyland.disney.go.com/attractions/disneyland/sleeping-beauty-castle-walkthrough; 🎡), the castle featured on the Disney logo. Inside the iconic structure (fashioned after a real 19th-century Bavarian castle), dolls and big books tell the story of Sleeping Beauty.

Tomorrowland
AREA

(Map p430; 🎡) How did 1950s imagineers envision the future? As a galaxy-minded community filled with monorails, rockets and Googie-style architecture, apparently. In 1998 this 'land' was revamped to honor three timeless futurists: Jules Verne, HG Wells and Leonardo da Vinci. These days, though, the *Star Wars* franchise gets top billing. **Hyperspace Mountain** (Map p430; https://disneyland.disney.go.com/attractions/disneyland/hyperspace-mountain; 🎡), Tomorrowland's signature attraction and one of the USA's best roller coasters, hurtles you into complete darkness at frightening speed, and **Star Wars Launch Bay** (Map p430; https://disneyland.disney.go.com/attractions/disneyland/star-wars-launch-bay; 🎡) shows movie props and memorabilia.

Meanwhile, **Star Tours** (Map p430; https://disneyland.disney.go.com/attractions/disneyland/star-tours; 🎡) clamps you into a Starspeeder shuttle for a wild 3D ride through the desert canyons of Tatooine on a space mission.

If it's retro high-tech you're after, the **monorail** glides to a stop in Tomorrowland, its rubber tires traveling a 13-minute, 2.5-mile round-trip route to Downtown Disney. Just outside Tomorrowland station, kiddies will want to shoot laser beams on **Buzz Lightyear Astro Blaster** (Map p430; https://disneyland.disney.go.com/attractions/disneyland/buzz-lightyear-astro-blasters; 🎡) and drive their own miniature cars in the classic **Autopia** (Map p430; https://disneyland.disney.go.com/attractions/disneyland/autopia; 🎡) ride. Then jump aboard the **Finding Nemo Submarine Voyage** (Map p430; 🎡) to look for the world's most famous clownfish from within a refurbished submarine and rumble through an underwater volcanic eruption.

Fantasyland
AREA

(Map p430; 🎡) Fantasyland is filled with the characters of classic children's stories. If you only see one attraction here, visit **"it's a small world,"** (Map p430; 🎡) a boat ride past hundreds of Audio-Animatronics dolls of children from different cultures all singing an earworm of a theme song.

Another classic, the **Matterhorn Bobsleds** (Map p430; https://disneyland.disney.go.com/attractions/disneyland/matterhorn-bobsleds; 🎡) is a steel-frame roller coaster that mimics a bobsled ride down a mountain. Fans of old-school attractions will also get a kick out of *The Wind in the Willows*–inspired **Mr. Toad's Wild Ride** (Map p430; 🎡), a loopy jaunt through London.

Younger kids love whirling around the **Mad Tea Party** (Map p430; 🎡) teacup ride and **King Arthur Carrousel** (Map p430; https://disneyland.disney.go.com/attractions/disneyland/king-arthur-carrousel; 🎡), then cavorting with characters in nearby **Mickey's Toontown** (Map p430; 🎡), a topsy-turvy minimetropolis where kiddos can traipse through Mickey and Minnie's houses and dozens of storefronts.

DISNEYLAND & ORANGE COUNTY DISNEYLAND & ANAHEIM

DISNEYLAND IN...

One Day

Get to **Disneyland Park** early. Stroll Main Street, U.S.A. toward **Sleeping Beauty Castle**. Enter Tomorrowland to ride **Hyperspace Mountain**. In Fantasyland don't miss the classic **"it's a small world"** ride or race down the **Matterhorn Bobsleds**. Grab a FASTPASS for the **Indiana Jones™ Adventure** or the **Pirates of the Caribbean** before lunching in **New Orleans Square**. Plummet down **Splash Mountain**, then visit the **Haunted Mansion** before the **fireworks** begin.

Two Days

On the second day, at **Disney California Adventure**, take a virtual hang-gliding ride on **Soarin' Around the World** and let kids tackle the **Redwood Creek Challenge Trail** before having fun at **Paradise Pier** with its roller coaster, Ferris wheel and carnival games. Watch the **Pixar Play Parade**, then ride the **Radiator Springs Racers** in Cars Land or cool off – fast! – on the **Grizzly River Run**. After dark, drop by **World of Color** show.

Disneyland Resort

Frontierland

AREA

(Map p430; ⬛) This Disney 'land' is a salute to old Americana: the Mississippi-style paddle-wheel **Mark Twain Riverboat** (Map p430; https://disneyland.disney.go.com/attractions/disneyland/mark-twain-riverboat; ⬛), the 18th-century replica **Sailing Ship Columbia** (Map p430; https://disneyland.disney.go.com/attractions/disneyland/sailing-ship-columbia; ⬛), a rip-roarin' Old West town with a shooting gallery and the **Big Thunder Mountain Railroad** (Map p430; https://disneyland.disney.go.com/attractions/disneyland/big-thunder-mountain-railroad; ⬛), a mining-themed roller coaster. The former Tom Sawyer Island – the

only attraction in the park personally designed by Uncle Walt – has been reimagined in the wake of the *Pirates of the Caribbean* movies and renamed the **Pirate's Lair on Tom Sawyer Island** (Map p430; https://disneyland.disney.go.com/attractions/disneyland/pirates-lair-on-tom-sawyer-island; ⬛).

Adventureland

AREA

(Map p430; ⬛) Loosely deriving its jungle theme from Southeast Asia and Africa, Adventureland has a number of attractions, but the hands-down highlight is the safari-style **Indiana Jones™ Adventure** (Map p430; https://disneyland.disney.go.com/attractions/

Disneyland Resort

disneyland/indiana-jones-adventure; ♿). Nearby, little ones love climbing the stairways of **Tarzan's Treehouse** (Map p430; https://disneyland.disney.go.com/attractions/disneyland/tarzans-treehouse; ♿). Cool down on the **Jungle Cruise** (Map p430; https://disneyland.disney.go.com/attractions/disneyland/jungle-cruise; ♿), viewing exotic Audio-Animatronics animals from rivers of South America, India, Africa and Southeast Asia. And the classic **Enchanted Tiki Room** (Map p430; https://disneyland.disney.go.com/attractions/disneyland/enchanted-tiki-room; ♿) features carvings of Hawaiian gods and goddesses and a show of singing, dancing Audio-Animatronics birds and flowers.

Pirates of the Caribbean   RIDE
(Map p430; https://disneyland.disney.go.com/attractions/disneyland/pirates-of-the-caribbean; New Orleans Sq; ♿) Pirates of the Caribbean is the longest ride in Disneyland (17 minutes) and one of the longest running, opened in 1967. That's half a century of folks hearing Audio-Animatronics pirates singing 'Yo-ho, yo-ho, a pirate's life for me' as they cruise by on a boat. You'll float through the subterranean haunts of tawdry pirates, where dead buccaneers perch atop their mounds of booty and Captain Jack Sparrow pops up occasionally.

Critter Country   AREA
(Map p430; ♿) Critter Country's main attraction is **Splash Mountain** (Map p430; https://

disneyland.disney.go.com/attractions/disneyland/splash-mountain; ⬆️), a flume ride through the story of Brer Rabbit and Brer Bear, based on the controversial 1946 film *Song of the South*. Just past Splash Mountain, hop in a mobile beehive on **The Many Adventures of Winnie the Pooh** (https://disneyland.disney.go.com/attractions/disneyland/many-adventures-of-winnie-the-pooh; ⬆️). Nearby on the Rivers of America, you can paddle **Davy Crockett's Explorer Canoes** (https://disneyland.disney.go.com/attractions/disneyland/davy-crocketts-explorer-canoes; ⬆️) on summer weekends.

👁 Disney California Adventure

Across the plaza from Disneyland's monument to fantasy is Disney California Adventure (DCA), an ode to California's geography, history and culture – or at least a sanitized G-rated version. DCA, which opened in 2001, covers more acres than Disneyland and feels less crowded, and it has more modern rides and attractions inspired by coastal amusement parks, the inland mountains and redwood forests, the magic of Hollywood, and car culture by way of the movie *Cars*.

Cars Land   AREA

(Map p430; ⬆️) This land gets kudos for its incredibly detailed design based on the popular Disney•Pixar *Cars* movies. Top billing goes to the wacky **Radiator Springs Racers** (Map p430; https://disneyland.disney.go.com/attractions/disney-california-adventure/radiator-springs-racers), a race-car ride that bumps around a track painstakingly decked out like the Great American West.

Grizzly Peak   AREA

(⬆️) Grizzly Peak is broken into sections highlighting California's natural and human achievements. Its main attraction, **Soarin' Around the World** (Map p430; https://disneyland.disney.go.com/attractions/disney-california-adventure/soarin ⬆️), is a virtual hang-gliding ride using Omnimax technology that 'flies' you over famous landmarks. Enjoy the light breeze as you soar, keeping your nostrils open for aromas blowing in the wind.

Grizzly River Run (Map p430; ⬆️) takes you 'rafting' down a faux Sierra Nevada river – you will get wet, so come when it's warm. While flat-hatted park rangers look on, kids can tackle the Redwood Creek Challenge Trail, with its 'Big Sir' redwoods, wooden towers and lookouts, and rock slide and climbing traverses.

Paradise Pier   AREA

(Map p430; ⬆️) If you like carnival rides, you'll love Paradise Pier, designed to look like a combination of all the beachside amusement piers in California. The state-of-the-art **California Screamin'** (Map p430; https://disneyland.disney.go.com/attractions/disney-california-adventure/california-screamin; ⬆️) roller coaster resembles an old wooden coaster, but it's got a smooth-as-silk steel track: it feels like you're being shot out of a cannon. Just as popular is **Toy Story Midway Mania!** (Map p430; https://disneyland.disney.go.com/attractions/disney-california-adventure/toy-story-mania) – a 4-D ride where you earn points by shooting at targets while your carnival car swivels and careens through an oversize, old-fashioned game arcade.

Hollywood Land   AREA

(Map p430; ⬆️) California's biggest factory of dreams is presented here in miniature, with soundstages, movable props, and – of course – a studio store. A new *Guardians of the Galaxy*–themed ride is one of the top attractions; another is a one-hour live stage version of *Frozen*, at the Hyperion Theater (p436).

🏃 Activities

Redwood Creek Challenge Trail   CLIMBING

(Map p430; Grizzly Peak) At this attraction in Disney California Adventure, more-active kids of all ages can tackle the Redwood Creek Challenge Trail, climbing rock faces, sliding down a rock slide and walking through the 35ft 'Big Sir' redwood stump. Flat-hatted faux park rangers look on.

🛏 Sleeping

🏨 Disneyland Resort

For the full-on Disney experience, there are three different hotels within Disneyland Resort, though there are less-expensive options just beyond the Disney gates in Anaheim. If you want a theme-park hotel for less money, try Knott's Berry Farm (p437).

⭐ Disney's Grand Californian Hotel & Spa   RESORT $$$

(Map p430; ✍️info 714-635-2300, reservations 714-956-6425; https://disneyland.disney.go.com/grand-californian-hotel; 1600 S Disneyland Dr; d from $360; P ❄ @ 🛜 ♨) Soaring timber beams rise above the cathedral-like lobby of the six-story Grand Californian, Disney's homage to the

DISNEYLAND TO-DO LIST

→ Make area hotel reservations or book a Disneyland vacation package.

→ Sign up for online resources including blogs, e-newsletters and resort updates, such as Disney Fans Insider.

→ Check the parks' opening hours, live show and entertainment schedules online.

→ Make dining reservations for sit-down restaurants or special meals with Disney characters.

→ Buy print-at-home tickets and passes online.

→ Recheck the next day's opening hours and Anaheim Resort Transportation (p437) or hotel shuttle schedules.

→ Pack a small day pack with sunscreen, hat, sunglasses, swimwear, change of clothes, jacket or hoodie, lightweight plastic rain poncho, and extra batteries and memory cards for digital and video cameras.

→ Fully charge your electronic devices, including cameras and phones.

→ Download the Disneyland app to your smartphone.

arts-and-crafts movement. Rooms have triple-sheeted beds, down pillows, bathrobes and all-custom furnishings. Outside there's a faux-redwood waterslide into the pool. At night, kids wind down with bedtime stories by the lobby's giant stone hearth.

Disneyland Hotel　　　　　HOTEL $$$
(Map p430; ☑714-778-6600; www.disneyland.com; 1150 Magic Way, Anaheim; r $210-395; P@☎☎☎)
Built in 1955, the year Disneyland opened, the park's original hotel has been rejuvenated with a dash of bibbidi-bobbidi-boo. There are three towers with themed lobbies (adventure, fantasy and frontier), and the 972 good-sized rooms now boast Mickey-hand wall sconces in bathrooms and headboards lit like the fireworks over Sleeping Beauty Castle (p429).

Disney's Paradise Pier Hotel　　　HOTEL $$$
(Map p430; ☑info 714-999-0990, reservations 714-956-6425; http://disneyland.disney.go.com/paradise-pier-hotel; 1717 S Disneyland Dr, Anaheim; d from $240; P☀@☎☎) Sunbursts, surfboards and a giant superslide are all on deck at the Paradise Pier Hotel, the smallest (472 rooms), cheapest and maybe the most fun of the Disney hotel trio. Kids will love the beachy decor and game arcade, not to mention the pool and the tiny-tot video room filled with mini Adirondack chairs.

🛏 Anaheim

While the Disney resorts have their own hotels, there are a number of worthwhile hotels just off-site or a few miles away, and every stripe of chain hotel you can imagine. Generally Anaheim's hotels are good value relative to those in the OC beach towns.

Ayres Hotel Anaheim　　　　HOTEL $$
(☑714-634-2106; www.ayreshotels.com/anaheim; 2550 F Katella Ave; r incl breakfast $139-219; P☎☀@☎☎) This well-run minichain of business hotels delivers solid-gold value. The 133 recently renovated rooms have microwaves, minifridges, safes, wet bar, pillow-top mattresses and design inspired by the Californian arts-and-crafts movement. Fourth-floor rooms have extra-high ceilings. Rates include a full breakfast and evening social hours Monday to Thursday with beer, wine and snacks.

**Residence Inn Anaheim Resort/
Convention Center**　　　　HOTEL $$
(Map p430; ☑714-782-7500; www.marriott.com; 640 W Katella Ave; r from $179; P☎☀@☎☎☎) This new hotel near the convention center, yet only about 10 minutes on foot to Disneyland, shines with sleek linens, marble tables and glass walls within in-room kitchens, big windows and a sweet rooftop pool deck with Jacuzzi and a splash zone for kids. Rates include full breakfast, and there's also a gym and laundry machines.

Hotel Indigo Anaheim　　BOUTIQUE HOTEL $$
(Map p430; ☑714-772-7755; www.ihg.com; 435 W Katella Ave; r from $170; P☎@☎☎☎) This friendly, professional 104-room hotel has a clean, mid-century modernist look with hardwood floor and pops of color, fitness center, pool and guest laundry. Mosaic murals are modeled after the walnut trees that

ℹ FASTPASS

Disneyland and Disney California Adventure's FASTPASS system can significantly cut your wait times.

➡ Walk up to a FASTPASS ticket machine – located near the entrance to select theme-park rides – and insert your park entrance ticket or annual passport. You'll receive a slip of paper showing the 'return time' for boarding (it's always at least 40 minutes later).

➡ Show up within the window of time on the ticket and join the ride's FASTPASS line. There'll still be a wait, but it's shorter (typically 15 minutes or less). Hang on to your FASTPASS ticket until you board the ride.

➡ If you're running late and miss the time window printed on your FASTPASS ticket, you can still try joining the FASTPASS line, although showing up before your FASTPASS time window is a no-no.

You're thinking, what's the catch, right? When you get a FASTPASS, you will have to wait at least two hours before getting another one (check the 'next available' time printed at the bottom of your ticket).

So, make it count. Before getting a FASTPASS, check the display above the machine, which will tell you what the 'return time' for boarding is. If it's much later in the day, or doesn't fit your schedule, a FASTPASS may not be worth it. Ditto if the ride's current wait time is just 15 to 30 minutes.

once bloomed here. It's about 15 minutes' walk or a quick drive to Disneyland and steps from shops and restaurants at Anaheim GardenWalk.

✖ Eating

From stroll-and-eat Mickey-shaped pretzels ($4) and jumbo turkey legs ($10) to deluxe, gourmet dinners (sky's the limit), there's no shortage of eating options, though mostly pretty expensive and targeted to mainstream tastes. Phone **Disney Dining** (☑714-781-3463; http://disneyland.disney.go.com/dining) to make reservations up to 60 days in advance. Restaurant hours vary seasonally, sometimes daily. Check the Disneyland app or Disney Dining website for same-day hours. Driving just a couple miles into Anaheim will expand the offerings and price points considerably.

✖ Disneyland Park

Blue Bayou　　　　　SOUTHERN US **$$$**
(Map p430; ☑714-781-3463; https://disneyland. disney.go.com/dining/disneyland/blue-bayou-res taurant; New Orleans Sq; mains lunch $28-41, dinner $30-48; ⏰lunch & dinner; ✚) Surrounded by the 'bayou' inside the Pirates of the Caribbean (p431) attraction, this is the top choice for sit-down dining in Disneyland Park and is famous for its Creole and Cajun specialties at dinner. Order fresh-baked pecan pie topped by a piratey souvenir for dessert (*ahh*, then *argh!*).

Jolly Holiday Bakery Cafe RESTAURANT, BAKERY **$**
(Map p430; https://disneyland.disney.go.com/dining/ disneyland/jolly-holiday-bakery-cafe; Main Street, U.S.A.; mains $8.50-11; ⏰breakfast, lunch & dinner; ✚) At this Mary Poppins–themed restaurant, the Jolly Holiday combo (grilled cheese and tomato basil soup for $9) is a decent deal and very satisfying. The cafe does other sandwiches on the sophisticated side, like the mozzarella caprese or turkey on ciabatta. Great people-watching from outdoor seating.

✖ Downtown Disney & Hotels

★**Napa Rose**　　　　　CALIFORNIAN **$$$**
(Map p430; ☑714-300-7170; https://disneyland. disney.go.com/dining; Grand Californian Hotel & Spa; mains $38-48, 4-course prix-fixe dinner from $100; ⏰5:30-10pm; ✚) High-back arts-and-crafts style chairs, leaded-glass windows and towering ceilings befit Disneyland Resort's top-drawer restaurant. On the plate, seasonal 'California Wine Country' (read: NorCal) cuisine is as impeccably crafted as Sleeping Beauty Castle. Kids' menu available. Reservations essential. Enter the hotel from Disney California Adventure or Downtown Disney.

Steakhouse 55　　　　　AMERICAN **$$$**
(Map p430; ☑714-781-3463; 1150 Magic Way, Disneyland Hotel; mains breakfast $14-25, dinner $31-57; ⏰7am-11pm & 5-10:30pm) Nothing at Disneyland is exactly a secret, but this clubby, grown-up hideaway comes pretty darn close. Dry-rubbed, bone-in rib eye, Australi-

an lobster tail, heirloom potatoes and green beans with applewood-smoked bacon uphold a respectable chophouse menu. There's also a full bar, good wine list and (we hope well-behaved) kids' menu.

✕ Disney California Adventure

Pacific Wharf Cafe   FOOD HALL $
(Map p430; https://disneyland.disney.go.com/din ing/disney-california-adventure/pacific-wharf-cafe; mains $10-11.50; ⊙breakfast, lunch & dinner; 🖬) This counter-service collection of restaurants shows off some of California's ethnic cuisines (Chinese, Mexican etc) as well as hearty soups in sourdough bread bowls, farmers-market salads and deli sandwiches. We like to eat at umbrella-covered tables by the water.

Wine Country Trattoria   ITALIAN $$
(Map p430; https://disneyland.disney.go.com/din ing/disney-california-adventure/wine-country-trat toria; Pacific Wharf; mains lunch $15-21, dinner $17-23; ⊙lunch & dinner; 🖬) If you can't quite swing the Napa Rose or Carthay Circle, this sunny Cal-Italian terrace restaurant is a fine backup. Fork into Italian pastas, salads or veggie paninis, washed down with Napa Valley wines.

★ Carthay Circle   AMERICAN $$$
(Map p430; https://disneyland.disney.go.com/din ing/disney-california-adventure/carthay-circle res taurant; Buena Vista St; mains lunch $24-34, dinner $32-45; ⊙lunch & dinner; 🖬) Decked out like a Hollywood country club, new Carthay Circle is the best dining in either park, with seasonal steaks, seafood, pasta, smart service and a good wine list. Your table needs at least one order of fried biscuits, stuffed with white cheddar, bacon, and jalapeño and served with apricot honey butter.

✕ Anaheim

Most restaurants on the streets surrounding Disneyland are chains, though **Anaheim GardenWalk** (www.anaheimgardenwalk.com; 400 W Disney Way; ⊙11am-9pm; 🖬) has some upscale ones. It's about a 10-minute walk from Disneyland's main gate.

★ Olive Tree   MIDDLE EASTERN $$
(☑714-535-2878; 512 S Brookhurst St; mains $8-16; ⊙10am-9pm Mon-Sat, to 8pm Sun) In Little Arabia, this simple restaurant in a nondescript strip mall ringed by flags of Arab nations has earned accolades from local papers to *Saveur* magazine. You *could* get

standards like falafel and kebabs, but daily specials are where it's at; Saturday's *kabseh* is righteous, fall-off-the-bone lamb shank over spiced rice with currants and onions.

Umami Burger   BURGERS $$
(☑714-991-8626; www.umamiburger.com; 338 S Anaheim Blvd; mains $11-15; ⊙11am-11pm Sun-Thu, to midnight Fri & Sat) The Anaheim outpost of this LA-based mini-chain sets the right tone for the Packing District (p436). Burgers span classic to truffled. Try the Hatch burger with roasted green chilies or the Manly with beer cheddar and bacon lardons. Get 'em with deep-fried 'smushed' potatoes with house-made ketchup, and top it off with a salted chocolate ice-cream sandwich. Full bar.

🍷 Drinking

You can't buy alcohol in Disneyland, but you can at Disney California Adventure, Downtown Disney and Disney's trio of resort hotels (p432). Downtown Disney offers bars, live music, a 12-screen cinema and more. Some restaurants and bars stay open as late as midnight on Fridays and Saturdays.

Golden Vine Winery   BAR
(Map p430; Pacific Wharf, Disney California Adventure) This centrally located terrace is a great place for relaxing and regrouping in Disney California Adventure. Nearby at Pacific Wharf, walk-up window **Rita's Baja Blenders** whips up frozen cocktails like marga – you know – ritas, and nonalcoholic blended strawberry and lemon drinks.

☆ Entertainment

It's tiki to the max and good, clean fun at **Trader Sam's Enchanted Tiki Lounge** (Map p430; https://disneyland.disney.go.com/ dining/disneyland-hotel/trader-sams; 1150 Magic Way, Disneyland Hotel; ⊙11:30am-1:30am). You can also hear big-name acts at **House of Blues** (☑714-778-2583; www.houseofblues.com/ anaheim; 400 W Disney Way, Anaheim Garden Walk; ⊙hours vary) or jazz at **Ralph Brennan's New Orleans Jazz Kitchen** (Map p430; ☑714-776-5200; http://rbjazzkitchen.com; Downtown Disney; mains lunch/dinner $14-19/$24.50-38.50; ⊙8am-10pm Sun-Thu, to 11pm Fri & Sat; 🖬).

★ World of Color   LIVE PERFORMANCE
(Map p430; https://disneyland.disney.go.com/enter tainment/disney-california-adventure/world-of-color; Paradise Pier) Disney California Adventure's premier show is the 22-minute *World of Color*, a dazzling nighttime display of lasers,

ANAHEIM PACKING DISTRICT & CENTER STREET

The **Anaheim Packing District** (www.anaheimpackingdistrict.com; S Anaheim Bl) launched in 2013 around a long-shuttered 1925 Packard dealership and the 1919 orange packing house a couple miles from Disneyland, near the city's actual downtown.

It relaunched in 2013–14 with chic new restaurants like **Umami Burger** (p435), the **Anaheim Brewery** (www.anaheimbrew.com; 336 S Anaheim Blvd; 5-9pm Tue-Thu, 5-11pm Fri, noon-11pm Sat, 1-7pm Sun), an evolving collection of shops and a park for events.

About a quarter-mile from here is **Center Street** (www.centerstreetanaheim.com; W Center St), a quietly splashy redeveloped neighborhood with an ice rink designed by starchitect Frank Gehry, and a couple of blocks of hip shops. Dining offerings include the fabulous food hall of the **Packing House** (714-533-7225; www.anaheimpackingdistrict. com; 440 S Anaheim St; opens 9am, closing hours vary), and the creative vegan dishes at **Healthy Junk** (714-772-5865; www.thehealthyjunk.com; 201 Center St Promenade; mains $4-10; 10am-9pm Mon-Fri, 11am-9pm Sat, 11am-5pm Sun;).

lights and animation projected over Paradise Bay. It's so popular, you'll need a FASTPASS ticket. Otherwise, several of the restaurants around DCA offer meal-and-ticket packages. Failing that, space is available without a ticket on a first-come, first-served basis.

Hyperion Theater THEATER
(Map p430; https://disneyland.disney.go.com/ entertainment/disney-california-adventure/frozen-live-at-hyperion; Hollywood Land) A live stage version of the animated movie musical *Frozen* is presented here, with actors, the hit songs and Broadway-style costumes, sets and lighting.

Shopping

Each 'land' has its own shopping, appropriate to its particular theme, whether the Old West, Route 66 or a seaside amusement park. There's no shortage of ways to spend on souvenirs, clothing and Disneyana and plenty other non-Disney goods. For collectors, **Disney Gallery** (Map p430; https://disneyland.disney.go.com; Main Street USA) and **Off the Page** (Map p430; Hollywood Land, Disney California Adventure) sell high-end art and collectibles like original sketches and vintage reproduction prints.

There are plenty of opportunities to drop cash in stores of **Downtown Disney** (not just Disney stuff either), restaurants and entertainment venues. Apart from the Disney merch, a lot of it is shops you can find elsewhere, but in the moment it's still hard to resist. Most shops here open and close with the parks.

Information

Before you arrive, visit **Disneyland Resort** (live assistance 714-781-7290, recorded info 714-781-4565; www.disneyland.com) for more information. You can also download the Disneyland Explorer app for your mobile device.

LOCKERS

Self-service lockers with in-and-out privileges cost $7 to $15 per day. You'll find them on Main Street, U.S.A. (p428; Disneyland), in **Sunshine Plaza** (Disney California Adventure) and at the **picnic area** just outside the theme park's main entrance, near Downtown Disney.

MEDICAL SERVICES

You'll find first-aid facilities at Disneyland (Main Street USA), Disney California Adventure (Pacific Wharf) and Downtown Disney (next to Ralph Brennan's Jazz Kitchen).

Anaheim Urgent Care (714-533-2273; 831 S State College Blvd, Anaheim; 8am-8pm Mon-Fri, 9am-5pm Sat & Sun) Walk-in nonemergency medical clinic.

Anaheim Global Medical Center (657-230-0265; www.anaheim-gmc.com; 1025 S Anaheim Blvd, Anaheim; 24hr) Hospital emergency room.

MONEY

Disneyland's City Hall offers foreign-currency exchange. In Disney California Adventure, head to the guest relations lobby. Multiple ATMs are found in both theme parks and at Downtown Disney.

Travelex (714-687-7977; 100 West Lincoln Ave, inside US Bank, Anaheim; 9am-5pm Mon-Fri, to 1pm Sat) Also exchanges foreign currency near Anaheim City Hall.

TOURIST INFORMATION

For information or help inside the parks, just ask any cast member or visit Disneyland's **City Hall** (Map p430; 714-781-4565; Main Street, U.S.A.) or Disney California Adventure's guest relations lobby.

Visit Anaheim (Map p430; 855-405-5020; http://visitanaheim.org; 800 W Katella Ave, Anaheim Convention Center) The city's official tourism bureau has information on lodging, dining and transportation, during events at the Convention Center.

❶ Getting There & Away

Disneyland and Anaheim can be reached by car (off the I-5 Fwy) or Amtrak or Metrolink trains at Anaheim's **ARTIC** (Anaheim Regional Transportation Intermodal Center; 2150 E Katella Ave, Anaheim) transit center. From here it's a short taxi, ride share or Anaheim Resort Transportation shuttle to Disneyland proper. The closest airport is Orange County's **John Wayne Airport** (SNA; www.ocair.com; 18601 Airport Way, Santa Ana).

AIR

Most international travelers arrive at Los Angeles International Airport (LAX), but for easy-in, easy-out domestic travel, the manageable John Wayne Airport in Santa Ana is served by all major US airlines and Canada's WestJet. It's near the junction of Hwy 55 and I-405 (San Diego Fwy).

CAR & MOTORCYCLE

Disneyland Resort is just off I-5 (Santa Ana Fwy), about 30 miles southeast of Downtown LA. Take the Disneyland Dr exit if you're coming from the north, or the Katella Ave/Disney Way exit from the south. Arriving at Disneyland Resort is like arriving at an airport. Giant, easy-to-read overhead signs indicate which ramps you need to take for the theme parks, hotels or Anaheim's streets.

TRAIN

Amtrak (☑ 800-872-7245; www.amtrak.com; 2626 E Katella Ave, ARTIC) has almost a dozen daily trains to/from LA's Union Station ($15, 40 minutes) and San Diego ($28, 2¼ hours). Less frequent **Metrolink** (☑ 800-371-5465; www.metrolinktrains.com; 22150 E Katella Ave, Anaheim, ARTIC) commuter trains connect Anaheim to LA's Union Station ($8.75, 50 minutes), Orange ($2.50, six minutes), San Juan Capistrano ($8.50, 40 minutes) and San Clemente ($10, 50 minutes).

SHUTTLE

Anaheim Resort Transportation operates some 20 shuttle routes between Disneyland and area hotels, convention centers, malls, stadiums and the transit center, saving traffic jams and parking headaches. Shuttles typically start running an hour before Disneyland opens, operating from 7am to midnight daily during summer. Departures are typically two to three times per hour, depending on the route. Purchase single or multiday ART passes at kiosks near ART shuttle stops or online in advance.

Many hotels and motels offer their own free shuttles to Disneyland and other area attractions; ask when booking.

❶ Getting Around

CAR & MOTORCYCLE

All-day parking at Disneyland Resort costs $20 ($25 for oversize vehicles). Enter the 'Mickey & Friends' parking structure from southbound Disneyland Dr, off Ball Rd. Walk outside and follow the signs to board the free tram to Downtown Disney and the theme parks. The parking garage opens one hour before the parks do.

SHUTTLE

Anaheim Resort Transportation (ART; ☑ 888-364-2787; www.rideart.org; adult/child fare $3/1, day pass $5.50/2, multiple-day passes available) ART connects the Disney resorts with hotels and other locations around Anaheim and nearby. Day passes can be purchased at hotels or via the ART Ticketing app (www.rideart.org/fares-and-passes).

TRAIN & MONORAIL

With an admission ticket to Disneyland, you can ride the monorail between Tomorrowland and the far end of Downtown Disney, near the Disneyland Hotel. It sure beats walking both ways along crowded Downtown Disney.

AROUND DISNEYLAND

Within 10 easy miles of the Mouse House you'll find a big scoopful of sights and attractions that are worth a visit in their own right.

Knott's Berry Farm

America's oldest theme park, **Knott's** (☑ 714-220-5200; www.knotts.com; 8039 Beach Blvd, Buena Park; adult/child 3-11yr $75/42; ⊙ from 10am, closing hours vary 5-11pm; 🅿 👪) is smaller and less frenetic than Disneyland, but it can be more fun, especially for thrill-seeking teens, roller-coaster fanatics and younger kids.

The park opened in 1932, when Walter Knott's boysenberries (a blackberry-raspberry hybrid) and his wife Cordelia's fried-chicken dinners attracted crowds of local farmhands. Mr Knott built an imitation ghost town to keep them entertained, and eventually hired local carnival rides and charged admission.

Today Knott's keeps the Old West theme alive and thriving with shows and demonstrations at **Ghost Town**, but it's the thrill rides that draw the big crowds. The **Sierra Sidewinder** roller coaster rips through banks and turns while rotating on its axis. The suspended, inverted **Silver Bullet** screams through a corkscrew, a double spiral and an outside loop. Xcelerator is a 1950s-themed roller coaster that blasts you from 0mph to 82mph in under 2½ seconds with a hair-raising twist at the top. Perilous Plunge whooshes at 75mph down a 75-degree angled water chute that's almost as tall as Niagara Falls.

Opening hours vary seasonally, and online savings can be substantial (eg $10 off adult admission for buying print-at-home tickets).

Next door to Knott's Berry Farm is the affiliated water park Soak City (☑714-220-5200; www.soakcityoc.com; 8039 Beach Blvd, Buena Park; adult/child 3-11yr $43/38; ⊙10am-5pm, 6pm or 7pm mid-May–mid-Sep; P➕), boasting a 750,000-gallon wave pool and dozens of high-speed slides, tubes and flumes. You must have a bathing suit without rivets or metal pieces to go on some slides. Bring a beach towel and a change of dry clothes.

🛏 Sleeping & Eating

Knott's Berry Farm Hotel (☑714-995-1111, 866-752-2444; www.knottshotel.com; 7675 Crescent Ave, Buena Park; r $79-169; P@🛜🏊) is a high-rise with bland rooms, outdoor pool, fitness center and tennis and basketball courts. For young Charlie Brown fans, ask about Camp Snoopy rooms, where kids are treated to *Peanuts*-themed decor (doghouse headboards? Awesome!), telephone bedtime stories and a goodnight 'tuck-in' visit from Snoopy himself.

The park has plenty of carnival-quality fast food, but the classic meal is the button-busting fried chicken and mashed potato dinner at the nuthin'-fancy Mrs Knott's Chicken Dinner Restaurant (☑714-220-5055; 8039 Beach Blvd, Buena Park; chicken dinner lunch $17, dinner $22; ⊙11am-9pm Mon-Fri, 8am-10pm Sat, 7am-9pm Sun; ➕).

Discovery Cube

Follow the giant 10-story cube – balanced on one of its points – to the Discovery Cube (☑714-542-2823; www.discoverycube.org; 2500 N Main St, Santa Ana; adult/child 3-14yr & senior $16/13, 4-D movies $2 extra; ⊙10am-5pm; P➕), the county's best educational kiddie attraction. About 100 hands-on displays await, covering everything from dinosaurs to robotics, rockets to the water supply, the environment to hockey. In the Grand Hall of Science, you might learn the science of tornadoes or the physics of pulleys, while the Discovery Theater screens 4-D movies.

Elsewhere, step into the eye of a hurricane or grab a seat in the Shake Shack to virtually experience a magnitude 6.4 quake. Special science-themed exhibits, like the annual Bubblefest, are fun too. There was a 44,000-sq-ft expansion of the facilities in 2015.

Best allow a good four hours here, more if your kids are budding scientists. It's about 5 miles southeast of Disneyland via the I-5.

Bowers Museum & Kidseum

From its stately, Spanish Colonial–style shell, the Bowers Museum (☑714-567-3600; www.bowers.org; 2002 N Main St, Santa Ana; Tue-Fri adult/child 12-17yr & senior $13/10, Sat & Sun $15/12, special exhibit surcharge varies; ⊙10am-4pm Tue-Sun; 🚌53,83) explodes onto the scene every year or so with remarkable exhibits that remind LA-centric museum-goers that the Bowers, too, is a local and national power player. Permanent exhibits are equally impressive, a rich collection of pre-Columbian, African, Chinese and Native American art, plus California art from the missions to Laguna Beach–style plein air painting. Our favorite: the Spirits and Headhunters gallery, showing jewelry, armaments, masks and religious articles of the Pacific Islands.

Docent-guided gallery tours are given every afternoon, and the airy cafe Tangata serves great lunches and California wines by the glass.

Admission to the Bowers also covers the affiliated Kidseum (☑714-480-1520; 1802 N Main St, Santa Ana; $8, child 2yr & younger free; ⊙10am-4pm Sat & Sun, 10am-4pm Tue-Fri during school holidays; 🚌; 🚌53, 83), a quick walk away; check in advance for its opening hours, which are more limited.

The museum is 6 miles southeast of Disneyland, off I-5 in Santa Ana. Admission is free on the first Sunday of each month. Public parking costs $6.

Old Towne Orange

The city of Orange, 7 miles southeast of Disneyland, retains its charming historical center, called Old Towne Orange. It's where locals go, and visitors will find it well worth the detour for antiques and vintage clothing shops, smart restaurants and pure SoCal nostalgia.

Orange was originally laid out by Alfred Chapman and Andrew Glassell, who in 1869 received the 1-sq-mile piece of real estate in lieu of legal fees. Orange became California's only city laid out around a central plaza, a traffic circle where present-day Glassell St and Chapman Ave meet, and it remains pleasantly walkable today.

✗ Eating

★ Linx
HOT DOGS $

(📞714-744-3647; www.linxdogs.com; 238 W Chapman Ave; mains $5.50-14; ⊙11am-10pm Mon-Wed, to 11pm Thu & Fri, 10am-11pm Sat, 10am-10pm Sun) First things first: they're not hot dogs, they're 'haute' dogs, homemade and topped with your choice of combinations (the BBQ, Bacon and Blues comes with barbecue sauce, bacon marmalade and blue cheese bacon aioli). Burgers come with fries. There's a daily-changing craft-beer selection, and bread pudding for dessert with chocolate ganache and strawberries.

Burger Parlor
BURGERS $

(📞714-602-8220; www.burgerparlor.com; 149 N Glassell St; mains $8-11; ⊙11am-9pm Sun-Wed, to 11pm Thu-Sat; 🖐) Chef Joseph Mahon has parlayed his work at a Michelin-starred restaurant into gourmet burgers that have been named the OC's best. The cheerily contemporary counter service Orange location dishes up the same award-winning Smokey and Parlor burgers, plus fries and onion rings. Bonus: you can get any burger on lettuce instead of a bun (because California).

★ Watson Soda Fountain Café
DINER $$

(📞714-202-2899; www.watsonscafe.com; 116 E Chapman Ave; mains $8-18; ⊙7am-9pm Sun-Wed, to 10pm Thu, to midnight Fri & Sat) Established 1899, this former drugstore was recently refurbished to a period design (check out the old safe, apothecary cabinets and telephone switchboard). It offers old-fashioned soda-fountain treats such as malts, milkshakes and sundaes, as well as burgers, fries, fried pickle chips and breakfast all day.

Haven Gastropub
GASTROPUB $$

(📞714-221-0680; www.havengastropub.com; 190 S Glassell St; items $8-27; ⊙11am-2am Mon-Fri, from 9am Sat & Sun) Come with your sweetie or a group to share plates like beef poutine with cheese curds and sous vide egg, Brussels sprouts with flash-fried prosciutto or mac and cheese with truffle béchamel, and the burger is so good you'll probably want to

share that too. There's a great, ever-changing craft-beer list and lots of windows to watch the scene.

🛍 Shopping

Shops line up primarily north and south, and to a lesser extent east and west, of Old Towne's **plaza** (cnr Chapman Ave & Glassell St), where you can find the OC's most concentrated collection of antiques, collectibles and vintage and consignment shops. It's fun to browse and some are very well curated. That said, real bargains are rare and you'll want to make sure the pieces are authentic.

Joy Ride
VINTAGE

(📞714-771-7118; www.joyridevintage.com; 109 W Chapman Ave; ⊙11am-7pm) The brother shop of Elsewhere Vintage, Joy Ride has a similar vibe only with men's clothing: 1950s bowling shirts to immaculately maintained wool blazers, plus vintage cameras, straight-edge razors and other manly pursuits. It even has a hat repair clinic.

Elsewhere Vintage
VINTAGE

(📞714-771-2116; www.elsewherevintage.com; 105 W Chapman Ave; ⊙11am-7pm) A hipster's love affair, this ladies' vintage store hangs sundresses next to hats, leather handbags and fabulous costume jewelry, all with a special emphasis on the 1920s to the '60s.

❶ Getting There & Away

The drive from Anaheim takes under 20 minutes: take I-5 south to Hwy 22 east, then drive north on Grand Ave, which becomes Glassell St, for just over a mile. Both **Amtrak** (📞800-872-7245; www.amtrak.com) and **Metrolink** (📞800-371-5465; www.metrolinktrains.com) commuter trains stop at Orange's **train station** (191 N Atchison St), a few blocks west of the plaza with connections to Anaheim and LA's Union Station. **OCTA** (p440) bus line 59 also runs from Anaheim.

ORANGE COUNTY BEACHES

Orange County's 42 miles of beaches are a land of gorgeous sunsets, prime surfing, just-off-the-boat seafood and serendipitous discoveries. Whether you're learning to surf the waves at Seal Beach, piloting a boat around Newport Harbor, or spotting whales on a cruise out of yacht-filled Dana Point harbor, you'll discover each town has a distinctive charm.

Seal Beach

The OC's first beach town driving south from LA County, 'Seal' is one of the last great California beach towns and a refreshing alternative to the more crowded coast further south. Its 1.5 miles of pristine beach sparkle like a crown, and that's without mentioning three-block Main St, a stoplight-free zone with mom-and-pop restaurants and indie shops that are low on 'tude and high on charm.

Although the town's east side is dominated by the sprawling retirement community Leisure World and the huge US Naval Weapons Station (look for grass-covered bunkers), all that fades away along the charming Main St and the oceanfront.

◉ Sights & Activities

Amble Main St and check out the laid-back local scene – barefoot surfers, friendly shopkeepers and silver-haired foxes scoping the way-too-young beach bunnies. Where Main St ends, walk out onto **Seal Beach Pier**, extending 1865ft over the ocean.

M&M Surfing School SURFING
(☑714-846-7873; www.surfingschool.com; 802 Ocean Ave; 1hr/3hr group lesson $77/85; ☺lessons 8am-noon early Sep–mid-Jun and Sat & Sun all year, to 2pm Mon-Fri mid-Jun–early Sep; 🖰) Offers group and private lessons that include surfboard and wet-suit rental, for students age five and up. Look for its van in the parking lot just north of the pier, off Ocean Ave at 8th St.

✖ Eating

★**Walt's Wharf** SEAFOOD $$$
(☑562-598-4433; www.waltswharf.com; 201 Main St; mains lunch $13-29, dinner $17-40; ☺11am-9pm) Everybody's favorite for fresh fish (some drive in from LA), Walt's packs them in on weekends. You can't make reservations for dinner (though they're accepted for lunch), but it's worth the wait for the oak-fire-grilled seafood and steaks in the many-windowed ground floor or upstairs in captain's chairs. Otherwise, eat at the bar.

★**Mahé** SUSHI, FUSION $$$
(☑562-431-3022; www.eatatmahe.com; 1400 Pacific Coast Hwy; mains lunch $15-20, dinner $15-39; ☺opens 4pm Mon-Thu, 3pm Fri, 11:30am Sat, 10am Sun, closing hours vary) Raw-fish fans gather barside at this beach-chic sushi bar with live bands some nights in the back room. Baked scallop parmesan, ahi *tataki* wraps, and fi-

let mignon with Gorgonzola cream all hang out on the Cal-Japanese menu. It's about five blocks from Main St but worth the walk.

🍷 Drinking

On Main St you'll find a surprising number of Irish pubs, alongside coffee bars, though we're particularly fond of cozy Bogart's, right across from the ocean.

Bogart's Coffee House CAFE
(☑562-431-2226; www.bogartscoffee.com; 905 Ocean Ave; ☺6am-9pm Mon-Thu, to 10pm Fri, 7am-10pm Sat, 7am-9pm Sun; 🖰) Around the corner from Main St, sip organic espresso drinks on the leopard-print sofa and play Scrabble as you watch the surf roll in on the beach across the street. Bogart's hosts live music Friday and Saturday nights, plus a regular open mike on Tuesdays.

☆ Entertainment

Jazz, folk and bluegrass bands play by the pier at the foot of Main St from 6pm to 8pm every Wednesday during July and August for the annual **Summer Concerts in the Park** (http://sealbeachchamber.org; Eisenhower Park; ☺6pm Wed Jul & Aug). The rest of the time, Main St is the kind of place where you'll find sidewalk musicians.

🔒 Shopping

Harbour Surfboards SPORTS & OUTDOORS
(☑562-430-5614; www.harboursurfboards.com; 329 Main St; ☺9am-7pm, to 6pm Sun) This place has been making surfboards since 1959, but it's also about the surf-and-skate lifestyle, man. Eavesdrop on local surfers talking about their wax as you pillage the racks of hoodies, wet suits, beach T-shirts and beanie hats.

Tankfarm & Co. FASHION & ACCESSORIES
(☑562-594-4800; www.tankfarmco.com; 212 Main St; ☺10am-6pm Sun-Thu, to 8pm Fri & Sat) On a street dominated by women's clothing and beachwear, Seal Beach–based Tankfarm carries duds for dudes craving the outdoor lifestyle: board shorts, hoodies, flannels and blankets from brands like Herschel and Deus Ex Machina, plus its own cool tees, woven shirts and accessories from pomade to enamel mugs reading 'coffee, whiskey or beer.' Worthy goals all.

❶ Getting There & Around

Orange County Transport Authority (OCTA; ☑714-560-6282; www.octa.net; ride/day pass

RICHARD NIXON LIBRARY & MUSEUM

The **Nixon Library** (☑714-993-5075; www.nixonfoundation.org; 18001 Yorba Linda Blvd, Yorba Linda; adult/child 5-11yr/student/senior $16/6/10/12; ◎10am-5pm Mon-Sat, 11am-5pm Sun; Ⓟ) offers a fascinating walk though America's modern history and that of this controversial native son of Orange County (1913–94), who served as president from 1969 to 74. Noteworthy exhibits include a full-size replica of the White House East Room, recordings of conversations with *Apollo 11* astronauts on the moon, access to the ex-presidential helicopter – complete with wet bar and ashtrays – and excerpts from landmark TV appearances including the Kennedy-Nixon debates and Nixon's famous self-parody on the *Laugh-In* comedy show. Exhibits about Watergate, the infamous scandal that ultimately brought down Nixon's administration, also figure prominently.

The library is in the residential community of Yorba Linda in northeastern Orange County, about 10 miles northeast of Anaheim. To get here, take Hwy 57 north and exit east on Yorba Linda Blvd, then continue straight and follow the signs.

$2/5) bus 1 connects Seal Beach with the OC's other beach towns and LA's Long Beach every hour; the one-way fare is $2 (exact change). Long Beach Transit lines 131 and 171 also stop in Seal Beach.

There's two-hour free parking along Main St between downtown Seal Beach and the pier, but it's difficult to find a spot in summer. Public parking lots by the pier cost $3 per two hours, $6 all day. Free parking along residential side streets is subject to posted restrictions.

Huntington Beach

'No worries' is the phrase you'll hear over and over in Huntington Beach, the town that goes by the trademarked nickname 'Surf City USA.' In 1910 real-estate developer and railroad magnate Henry Huntington hired Hawaiian-Irish surfing star George Freeth to give demonstrations. When legendary surfer Duke Kahanamoku moved here in 1925, that solidified its status as a surf destination. Buyers for major retailers come here to see what surfers are wearing, then market the look.

Long considered a low-key, not-quite-fashionable beach community with its share of sidewalk-surfing skate rats and hollering late-night barflies, its downtown has undergone a couple of makeovers, first along **Main Street** and then at the sparkling new **Pacific City** (www.gopacific city.com; 21010 Pacific Coast Hwy; ◎hours vary) shopping center.

Still, HB remains a quintessential spot to celebrate the hang-loose SoCal coastal lifestyle: consistently good waves, surf shops, a surf museum, bonfires on the sand, a canine-friendly beach, and hotels and restaurants with killer views.

◉ Sights

Bolsa Chica State Beach BEACH
(www.parks.ca.gov; Pacific Coast Hwy, btwn Seapoint & Warner Aves; parking $15; ◎6am-10pm; Ⓟ) A 3-mile-long strip of sand favored by surfers, volleyball players and fishers, Bolsa Chica State Beach stretches alongside Pacific Coast Hwy between **Huntington Dog Beach** (www. dogbeach.org; 100 Goldenwest Street; ◎5am-10pm; Ⓟ) to the south and Sunset Beach to the north. Even though it faces a monstrous offshore oil rig, Bolsa Chica (meaning 'Little Pocket' in Spanish) gets mobbed on summer weekends. You'll find picnic tables, fire rings and beach showers, plus a bike path running north to Anderson Ave in Sunset Beach and south to Huntington State Beach.

Huntington City Beach BEACH
(www.huntingtonbeachca.gov; ◎5am-10pm; Ⓟ♿) One of SoCal's best beaches, the sand surrounding the pier at the foot of Main St gets packed on summer weekends with surfers, volleyball players, swimmers and families. Bathrooms and showers are located north of the pier at the back of the snack-bar complex. In the evening volleyball games give way to beach bonfires.

Huntington Beach Pier HISTORIC SITE
(cnr Main St & Pacific Coast Hwy; ◎5am-midnight) The 1853ft Huntington Pier is one of the West Coast's longest. It has been here – in one form or another – since 1904, though the mighty Pacific has damaged giant sections or completely demolished it multiple times since then. The current concrete structure was built in 1983 to withstand 31ft waves or a 7.0-magnitude earthquake, whichever hits HB first. On the pier you can rent fishing gear from **Let's Go Fishing**

TOP BEACHES IN ORANGE COUNTY

➡ Seal Beach (p440) ·

➡ Bolsa Chica State Beach (p441)

➡ Huntington City Beach (p441)

➡ Balboa Peninsula (p444)

➡ Crystal Cove State Beach (p449)

➡ Aliso Beach County Park (p452)

➡ Doheny State Beach (p456)

(☑714-960-1392; 21 Main Street, Huntington Beach Pier; fishing sets per hour/day $6/15; ☻ hours vary) bait and tackle shop.

Huntington State Beach   BEACH
(☑714-536-1454; www.parks.ca.gov; ☻6am-10pm; Ⓟ) Want even more surf and sand? South of the pier, Huntington State Beach extends 2 miles from Beach Blvd (Hwy 39) to the Santa Ana River and Newport Beach boundary. All-day parking costs $15.

International Surfing Museum   MUSEUM
(☑714-960-3483; www.surfingmuseum.org; 411 Olive Ave; adult/child $2/1; ☻noon-5pm Tue-Sun) The world's biggest surfboard (in the *Guinness World Records*) fronts this small museum, an entertaining stop for surf-culture enthusiasts. Temporary exhibits chronicle the sport's history with photos, vintage surfboards, movie memorabilia and surf music. For the best historical tidbits, spend a minute chatting with the all-volunteer staff.

🏃 Activities

Huntington is a one-stop shop for outdoor pleasures by OC beaches. If you forgot to pack beach gear, you can rent umbrellas, beach chairs, volleyballs and other essentials from **Zack's** (☑714-536-0215; www.zackssurf city.com; 405 Pacific Coast Hwy; group lessons $85, surfboard rentals per hour/day $12/35, wetsuits $5/15), just north of the pier. Just south of the pier on the Strand, friendly **Dwight's Beach Concession** (☑714-536-8083; www. dwightsbeachconcession.com; 201 Pacific Coast Hwy; surfboard rentals per hour/day $10/40, bicycle rentals from $10/30; ☻9am-5pm Mon-Fri, to 6pm Sat & Sun), around since 1932, rents bikes, boogie boards, umbrellas and chairs. **Huntington Surf & Sport** (www.hsssurf.com; 300 Pacific Coast Hwy; ☻8am-9pm Sun-Thu, to 10pm Fri & Sat) also rents boards and wetsuits.

Vans Off the Wall Skatepark   OUTDOORS
(☑714-379-6666; 7471 Center Dr; helmet & pad set rentals $5; ☻9am-8pm daily) **FREE** This custom-built facility by the OC-based sneaker and skatewear company has plenty of ramps, bowls, dips, boxes and rails for boarders to catch air. BYOB (board). Helmets and pads required for visitors under 18. The biggest drawback is the location, about 6 miles from Huntington Beach Pier on the north side of town, so you'll need your own transport.

🎊 Festivals & Events

Every Tuesday brings **Surf City Nights** (www.surfcitynights.com; 1st 3 blocks Main St; ☻5-9pm Tue), a street fair with a petting zoo and bounce house for the kids, crafts, sidewalk sales for the grown-ups, and live music and farmers-market goodies for everyone.

Car buffs, get up early on Saturday mornings for the **Donut Derelicts Car Show** (www.donutderelicts.com; cnr Magnolia St & Adams Ave; ☻Sat mornings), a weekly gathering of woodies, beach cruisers and pimped-out street rods at the corner of Magnolia St and Adams Ave, 2.5 miles inland from Pacific Coast Hwy.

Vans US Open of Surfing   SURFING
(www.usopenofsurfing.com; Huntington Beach Pier; ☻late Jul & early Aug) This six-star competition lasts more than a week and draws more than 600 world-class surfers. Other festivities include beach concerts, motocross shows and skateboard jams.

Huntington Harbor Cruise
of Lights   CHRISTMAS
(www.cruiseoflights.org; 16889 Algonquin St; adult/child $19/12; ☻mid- to late Dec) If you're here for the Christmas holidays, don't miss the evening boat tour past harborside homes twinkling with holiday lights. Run by the Philharmonic Society, cruise proceeds go to support youth music education programs.

🛏 Sleeping

Huntington Surf Inn   MOTEL $$
(☑714-536-2444; www.huntingtonsurfinn.com; 720 Pacific Coast Hwy; r $119-209; Ⓟ👄❄🛜) You're paying for location at this two-story 1960s era motel just north of Main St and across from the beach. Smallish rooms are individually decorated with surf and skateboard art – cool, brah – with firm mattresses and fridges, and microwaves on request. There's a small common deck area with a beach view.

★ **Paséa** RESORT $$$
(☑ 888-674-3634; http://meritagecollection.com/
paseahotel; 21080 Pacific Coast Hwy; r from $359;
P😊✳@🛜🏊) This hotel is slick and se-
rene, with tons of light and air. Floors are
themed for shades of blue from denim to
sky, and each of its 250 shimmery, minimal-
ist, high-ceilinged rooms has an ocean-view
balcony. As if the stunning pool, gym and
Balinese-inspired spa weren't enough, it
connects to Pacific City. (p441)

★ **Shorebreak Hotel** BOUTIQUE HOTEL $$$
(☑ 714-861-4470; www.shorebreakhotel.com; 500
Pacific Coast Hwy; r from $269; P😊✳@🛜🏊)
Stow your surfboard (lockers provided) as
you head inside HB's hippest hotel, a stone's
throw from the pier. The Shorebreak has
'surf ambassadors,' a wetsuit mural in the
lobby, pseudo-steampunk fitness center with
climbing wall, and hardwood furniture and
surfboard headboards in geometric-patterned
rooms. Minibars stock surfboard wax, in case
you, you know, forgot yours.

✖ **Eating**

★ **Lot 579** FOOD HALL
(www.gopacificcity.com/lot-579; Pacific City, 21010
Pacific Coast Hwy; ⊘ hours vary; P🛜♿) The food
court at HB's stunning new ocean-view mall
offers some unique and fun restaurants for
pressed sandwiches (Burnt Crumbs – the spa-
ghetti grilled cheese is so Instagrammable),
Aussie meat pies (Pie Not), coffee (Portola)
and ice cream (Han's). For best views, take
your takeout to the deck, or eat at American
Dream (brewpub) or Bear Flag Fish Company.

★ **Sancho's Tacos** MEXICAN $
(☑ 714-536-8226; www.sanchostacos.com; 602 Pacific Coast Hwy; mains $3-10; ⊘ 8am-9pm Mon-Sat,
to 8pm Sun; P) There's no shortage of taco
stands in HB, but locals are fiercely dedicated
to Sancho's, across from the beach. This two-
room shack with patio grills flounder, shrimp
and tri-tip to order.

Cucina Alessá ITALIAN $$
(☑ 714-969-2148; http://cucinaalessarestaurants.
com; 520 Main St; mains lunch $9-13, dinner $12-
25; ⊘ 11am-10pm) Every beach town needs
its favorite go-to Italian kitchen. Alessa wins
hearts and stomachs with classics like Nea-
politan lasagna, butternut-squash ravioli and
chicken marsala. Lunch brings out panini,
pizzas and pastas, plus breakfasts including
frittata and 'famous' French toast. Get side-
walk seating, or sit behind big glass windows.

🍸 **Drinking & Nightlife**

★ **Bungalow** CLUB
(☑ 714-374-0399; www.thebungalow.com/hb;
Pacific City, 21058 Pacific Coast Hwy, Suite 240;
⊘ 5pm-2am Mon-Fri, noon-2am Sat, noon-10pm
Sun) This Santa Monica landmark of cool
has opened a second location here in Pacif-
ic City, and with its combination of lounge
spaces, outdoor patio, cozy, rustic-vintage
design, specialty cocktails, DJs who know
how to get the crowd going and – let's not
forget – ocean views, it's already setting
new standards for the OC. The food menu's
pretty great too.

Saint Marc BAR
(☑ 714-374-1101; www.saintmarcusa.com; Pacific
City, 21058 Pacific Coast Hwy; ⊘ 11am-midnight
Mon-Wed, to 2am Thu & Fri, 10am-2am Sat, to 10pm
Sun) Indoor-outdoor Saint Marc is techni-
cally a restaurant, but it's just so darn much
fun as a bar: giant beer-pong table, beer
bombers, wine on draft, infused vodkas,
red Solo Cup cocktails and, um, jello shots!
Should you get hungry, food ranges from
cheese boards to New Orleans–inflected
meals, or just go for bacon by the slice from
the bacon bar.

ℹ **Information**

Visit Huntington Beach Information Kiosk
(☑ 714-969-3492, 800-729-6232; www.surf
cityusa.com; Pier Plaza, 325 Pacific Coast Hwy;
⊘ 10:30am-7pm Mon-Fri, from 10am Sat & Sun,
shorter hrs in winter) Visitor information kiosk
by the pier.

ℹ **Getting There & Around**

Pacific Coast Hwy (PCH) runs alongside the
beach. Main St intersects PCH at the pier. Head-
ing inland, Main St ends at Hwy 39 (Beach Blvd),
which connects north to I-405.

Public parking lots by the pier and beach
– when you can get a spot – are 'pay and dis-
play' for $1.50 per hour, $15 daily maximum.
Self-service ticket booths scattered across the
parking lot take dollars or coins. More municipal
lots alongside PCH and around downtown cost
at least $15 per day in summer, typically with
an evening flat rate of $5 after 5pm. On-street
parking meters cost $1 per 40 minutes.

OCTA (p440) bus 1 connects HB with the rest
of OC's beach towns every hour; one-way/day
pass $2/5, payable on board (exact change).
When we passed through, a free **Surf City USA
Shuttle** (www.surfcityusashuttle.com; ⊘ 10am-
10pm Fri & Sat, 10am-8pm Sun, mid-Jun–early
Sep) was making a loop around beach and inland
areas.

Newport Beach

There are really three Newport Beaches: paradise for wealthy Bentley- and Porsche-driving yachtsmen and their trophy wives; perfect waves and beachside dives for surfers and stoners; and glorious sunsets and seafood for the rest of the folk, trying to live the day-to-day. Somehow, these diverse communities all seem to live – mostly – harmoniously.

For visitors, the pleasures are many: just-off-the-boat seafood, boogie-boarding the human-eating waves at the Wedge, and the ballet of yachts in the harbor. Just inland, more lifestyles of the rich and famous revolve around Fashion Island (p447), a posh outdoor mall and one of the OC's biggest shopping centers.

◉ Sights

★ **Orange County Museum of Art** MUSEUM
(Map p446; ☑ 949-759-1122; www.ocma.net; 850 San Clemente Dr; adult/student & senior/child under 12yr $10/7.50/free; ◷ 11am-5pm Wed-Sun, to 8pm Fri; P ♿) This engaging museum highlights California art and cutting-edge contemporary artists, with exhibitions rotating through two large spaces. Recent exhibitions have included the California-Pacific Triennial and works by Robert Rauschenberg. There's also a sculpture garden, eclectic gift shop and a theater screening classic, foreign and art-related films.

**Upper Newport Bay
Ecological Preserve** NATURE RESERVE
(☑ 949-640-1751; www.ocparks.com/parks/newport; 2301 University Dr; ◷ 7am-sunset; P) ⓯ FREE The brackish water of this 752-acre reserve, where runoff from the San Bernardino Mountains meets the sea, supports more than 200 species of birds. This is one of the few estuaries in Southern California that has been preserved, and it's an important stopover on the Pacific Flyway migration route. There are also trails for jogging and cycling.

Discovery Cube's Ocean Quest MUSEUM
(Map p446; ☑ 949-675-8915; www.oceanquestoc.org; 600 E Bay Ave; adult/child 2 & under $5/free; ◷ hours vary; P ♿) In the **Balboa Fun Zone** (Map p446; www.thebalboafunzone.com; 600 E Bay Ave; Ferris wheel $4; ◷ Ferris wheel 11am-6pm Sun-Thu, to 9pm Fri, to 10pm Sat; ♿), this newly refurbished museum was recently taken over by Santa Ana's Discovery Cube (p438) and runs educational programs for local schools

and field trips. When not hosting school groups, it opens to the public and shows traveling exhibits. Check the website for opening hours, what's on and for occasional whale-watching trips.

🏃 Activities

Balboa Peninsula AREA
(Map p446) Four miles long but less than a half-mile wide, the Balboa Peninsula has a white-sand beach on its ocean side and countless stylish homes, including the 1926 **Lovell Beach House** (Map p446; 1242 W Beach Front). It's just inland from the paved beach-front **recreational path**, across from a small **playground**. Hotels, restaurants and bars cluster around the peninsula's two famous piers: **Newport Pier** near the western end and **Balboa Pier** at the eastern end. The two-mile oceanfront strip between them teems with beachgoers; people-watching is great.

Near Newport Pier, several shops rent umbrellas, beach chairs, volleyballs and other necessities. For swimming, families will find a more relaxed atmosphere and calmer waves at 10th St and 18th St. The latter beach, also known as **Mothers Beach** (Map p446; Marina Park, 18th St, ♿), has a lifeguard, restrooms and a shower.

At the very tip of Balboa Peninsula, by the West Jetty, the **Wedge** (Map p446) is a bodysurfing, bodyboarding and knee-boarding spot for experts; newcomers should head a few blocks west. Park on Channel Rd or E Ocean Blvd and walk through tiny West Jetty View Park.

Spa Gregorie's SPA
(Map p446; ☑ 949-644-6672; www.spagregories.com; 200 Newport Center Dr, Suite 100; 1hr massage from $109, facial from $119) After power shopping at Fashion Island (p447), indulge yourself at Spa Gregorie's. After you've been rejuvenated by the quiet room, step in to your massage, facial or body treatment.

Surfing

Surfers flock to the breaks at the small jetties surrounding the Newport Pier between 18th and 56th streets. Word of warning: locals can be territorial. For lessons, try Huntington Beach or Laguna Beach instead.

Rent surf, bodysurfing and stand-up paddleboard equipment and gear at **15th Street Surf & Supply** (Map p446; ☑ 949-751-7867; https://15thstsurfsupply.com; 103 15th St; boogie boards per hour/day $7/15, surfboards $15/40; ◷ 9am-7pm).

Boating

Take a boat tour or rent your own kayak, sailboat or outboard motorboat. Even better, rent a flat-bottomed electric boat that you pilot yourself and cruise with up to 12 friends. Find boats at Duffy Electric Boat Rentals or **Balboa Boat Rentals** (Map p446; ✆949-673-7200; http://boats4rent.com; 510 E Edgewater Pl; per hr kayaks from $18, pontoon boats $105, powerboats from $75, electric boats from $80; ⏲10am-7pm, extended hrs in summer).

Duffy Electric Boat Rentals   BOATING
(Map p446; ✆949-645-6812; www.duffyofnew portbeach.com; 2001 W Coast Hwy; first 2hr $199; ⏲10am-8pm) These heated electric boats with canopies are a Newport tradition. Bring tunes, food and drinks for a fun evening toodling around the harbor like a local. No boating experience required; maps provided.

Cycling & Skating

To experience fabulous ocean views, ride a bike along the paved **recreational path** that encircles almost the entire Balboa Peninsula. Inland cyclists like the paved **scenic loop** around Upper Newport Bay Nature Preserve. There are many places to rent bikes near Newport and Balboa Piers.

Diving

There's terrific diving just south of Newport Beach at the underwater park at Crystal Cove State Park (p449), where divers can check out reefs, anchors and an old military plane-crash site.

☞ Tours

Davey's Locker   BOATING
(Map p446; ✆949-673-1434; www.daveyslocker. com; 400 Main St; per adult/child 3-12yr & senior 2½hr whale-watching cruise from $32/26, half-day sportfishing $41.50/34) At **Balboa Pavilion** (Map p446; www.balboapavilion.com; 400 Main St); offers whale-watching and sportfishing trips.

Fun Zone Boat Co   BOATING
(Map p446; ✆949-673-0240; www.funzoneboats. com; 700 Edgewater Pl; 45min cruise per adult/ child 5-11yr/senior from $14/7/11) Sea lion–watching and celebrity home tours depart from the Fun Zone.

✯ Festivals & Events

Newport Beach Film Festival   FILM
(www.newportbeachfilmfest.com; ⏲mid-Apr) Roll out the red carpet for screenings of over 350 mostly new independent and foreign films. Some films shown here, such as *Crash*, *Waitress*, *(500) Days of Summer* and *Chef* have gone on to become classics, while earlier classics like *Sunset Boulevard* get anniversary screenings.

Christmas Boat Parade   CHRISTMAS
(www.christmasboatparade.com; ⏲Dec) The week before Christmas brings thousands of spectators to Newport Harbor to watch a century-old tradition. The 2½-hour parade of up to 150 boats, including some fancy multi-million-dollar yachts all decked out with Christmas lights and holiday cheer, begins at 6:30pm. Watch for free from the Fun Zone or **Balboa Island** (Map p446; http://explorebalboaisland.com; P), or book ahead for a harbor boat tour.

🛏 Sleeping

A Newport stay ain't cheap, but outside of the peak season rates often drop 40% or more. Otherwise, to save some dough, you'll find chain hotels and motels further inland, especially around John Wayne Airport, in Costa Mesa, and around the triangle junction of Hwy 55 (Costa Mesa Fwy), toll road Hwy 73 and I-405 (San Diego Fwy).

**Newport Dunes
Waterfront Resort**   CABIN, CAMPGROUND $
(Map p446; ✆949-729-3863; www.newport-dunes.com; 1131 Back Bay Dr; campsite from $64, cottage/1-bedroom cottage from $90/165; P@🛜🏊🐾) RVs and tents aren't required for a stay at this upscale campground: two dozen tiny, well-kept A-frames and picket-fenced one-bedroom cottages are available, all within view of Newport Bay. A fitness center and walking trails, kayak rentals, board games, family bingo, ice-cream socials, horseshoe and volleyball tournaments, an outdoor pool and playground, and summertime movies on the beach await. Wheelchair-accessible.

★ Newport Beach Hotel   BOUTIQUE HOTEL $$
(Map p446; ✆949-673-7030; www.thenewport beachhotel.com; 2306 W Oceanfront Blvd; r/stes from $235/425; P🐾❄🛜) There's charm to spare in this intimate, 20-room beachfront inn, built in 1904 and updated with beach-chic style. Relax over tea, fruit and cookies in the ocean-view lobby with rattan chairs and white wainscoting, then head upstairs where rooms of different sizes are done up with clean whites and pastel blues, some with spa tubs and ocean views.

Newport Beach

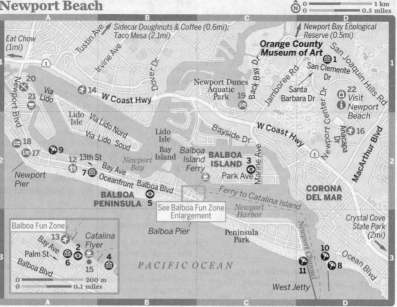

Newport Beach

Doryman's Oceanfront Inn   B&B **$$$**
(Map p446; ☑ 949-675-7300; www.dorymansinn.
com; 2102 W Oceanfront; r $299-399; 🅿 ➓ ❄ 🛜)
This 2nd-floor oceanfront B&B was built
in 1891 and retains that Victorian country
style. Each of the 11 rooms is unique, and
some boast ocean views and fireplaces. It
has a great location by Newport Pier (view
it from the roof deck), although it can get

loud in summer with the 24-hour activities.
Parking and breakfast (quiche, bagels, fruit
and more) included.

✗ Eating

Dozens of restaurants and pubs throughout
Newport offer fish dinners (as you'd expect),
plus nouveau Japanese and modern Mexican.

★ **Bear Flag Fish Company**   SEAFOOD $
(Map p446; ☑949-673-3474; www.bearflagfishco.
com; 3421 Via Lido; mains $10-16; ☺11am-9pm Tue-
Sat, to 8pm Sun & Mon; ⓓ) This is *the* place for
generously sized, grilled and *panko*-bread-
ed fish tacos, ahi burritos, spankin' fresh
ceviche and oysters. Pick out what you want
from the ice-cold display cases, then grab a
picnic-table seat. About the only way this
seafood could be any fresher is if you caught
and hauled it off the boat yourself!

Dory Deli   DELI $
(Map p446; ☑949-220-7886; www.dorydeli.com;
2108 W Oceanfront; mains $7-12; ☺6am-8pm Sun-
Thu, to 9pm Fri & Sat) This hip new beachfront
storefront does hot and cold sandwiches
like the Rubinstein, Lifeguard Club and the
steak-filled Rocky Balboa, plus fresh-caught
fish-and-chips. For breakfast, you could be
good and get the yoga pants burrito, or sin a
little with chicken and waffles. Full bar too!
Sure, we'll stop in after surfing...

Eat Chow   CALIFORNIAN $$
(☑949-423-7080; www.eatchownow.com; 211
62nd St; mains $9-18; ☺8am-9pm Mon-Thu, to
10pm Fri, 7am-10pm Sat, 7am-9pm Sun) Hidden
a block behind W Coast Hwy, Eat Chow's
crowd is equal parts tatted hipsters and
ladies who lunch, which makes it very New-
port indeed. They all queue happily for rib-
eye Thai beef salads, grilled-salmon tacos
with curry slaw, and bodacious burgers like
the Chow BBQ burger with homemade bar-
becue sauce, smoked Gouda, crispy onions
and more. Groovy indie-rock soundtrack.

🍸 Drinking

★ **Alta Coffee Warehouse**   COFFEE
(Map p446; www.altacoffeeshop.com; 506 31st St;
☺6am-10pm Mon-Fri, from 7am Sat & Sun) Hid-
den on a side street, this cozy coffeehouse in
a beach bungalow with a covered patio lures
locals with live music and poetry readings,
art on the brick walls and honest baristas
who dish the lowdown on the day's soups,
savories, popular comfort food and baked
goods like carrot cake and cheesecake. It's
the kind of place that keeps a shelf of mugs
for frequent customers, of whom there are
many. The kitchen closes at 9:30pm.

★ **Muldoon's**   BAR
(Map p446; ☑949-640-4110; www.muldoonspub.
com; 202 Newport Center Dr; ☺opens 11:30am
Mon-Sat, 10am Sun, closing hours vary) At upscale,
upbeat, much-admired Muldoon's, choose

from indoor, outdoor (under a leafy tree) and
bar seating and enjoy decent, if pricey, Irish
pub grub, 10 beers on tap and live acoustic
sounds Thursday through Saturday nights
and many Sunday afternoons.Our only com-
plaint: it's a drive from the beach, in an office
park by Fashion Island.

🛍 Shopping

Fashion Island (Map p446; ☑949-721-2000,
855-658-8527; www.shopfashionisland.com; 401
Newport Center Dr; ☺10am-9pm Mon-Fri, to 7pm
Sat, 11am-6pm Sun), inland from the beach, is
Newport's biggest, most established shop-
ping center (over 200 shops), but the new
Lido Marina district is gearing up to give
it a run for its money on a smaller scale:
about two dozen establishments including
stylish boutiques and casual indoor-outdoor
dining. On Balboa Island, **Marine Avenue**
is lined with darling shops in an old-fash-
ioned village atmosphere, a good place to
pick up something for the kids, unique gifts
and beachy souvenirs, or jewelry, art and an-
tiques for yourself.

ℹ️ Information

Visit Newport Beach (Map p446; www.visit
newportbeach.com; 401 Newport Center Dr,
Fashion Island, Atrium Court, 2nd fl; ☺10am-
9pm Mon-Fri, to 7pm Sat, to 6pm Sun) The
city's official visitor center hands out free
brochures and maps.

Balboa Branch Library (www.city.newport
-beach.ca.us/nbpl; 100 E Balboa Blvd; ☺9am-
6pm Tue & Thu-Sat, to 9pm Mon & Wed; 📶)
Near the beach; ask for a free internet-terminal
guest pass.

ℹ️ Getting There & Around

BUS
OCTA (p440) bus 1 connects Newport Beach
and Fashion Island mall with the OC's other
beach towns, including Corona del Mar just
east, every 30 minutes to one hour. From the
intersection of Newport Blvd and Pacific Coast
Hwy, bus 71 heads south along the Balboa
Peninsula to Main Ave every hour or so. On all
routes, the one-way fare is $2 (exact change).

BOAT
The West Coast's largest passenger catamaran,
the **Catalina Flyer** (Map p446; ☑949-673-
5245; www.catalinainfo.com; 400 Main St;
round-trip adult/child 3-12yr/senior $70/53/65,
per bicycle $7), makes a daily round-trip to
Catalina Island, taking 75 minutes each way. It

leaves Balboa Pavilion around 9am and returns before 6pm; check online for discounts.

Balboa Island Ferry (Map p446; www.balboa islandferry.com; 410 S Bay Front; adult/child $1/50¢, car incl driver $2; ⊙6:30am-midnight Sun-Thu, to 2am Fri & Sat)

CAR & MOTORCYCLE

Frequently jammed from dawn till dusk, Hwy 55 (Newport Blvd) is the main access road from I-405 (San Diego Fwy); it intersects with Pacific Coast Hwy near the shore. In town, Pacific Coast Hwy is called W Coast Hwy or E Coast Hwy, both in mailing addresses and conversationally by locals.

The municipal lot beside Balboa Pier costs 50¢ per 20 minutes, or $15 per day. Street parking meters on the Balboa Peninsula cost 50¢ to $1 per hour. Free parking on residential streets, just a block or two from the sand, is time-limited and subject to other restrictions. In summer expect to circle like a hawk for a space.

Around Newport Beach

Costa Mesa

So close to Newport Beach that they're often lumped together, Costa Mesa at first glance looks like just another landlocked suburb transected by the I-405, but top venues attract some 24 million visitors each year. South Coast Plaza is SoCal's largest mall – properly termed a 'shopping resort' – while Orange County's cultural heart is steps away in the performing-arts venues Segerstrom Center for the Arts and South Coast Repertory, lending the city's slogan, City of the Arts.

If that all sounds rather hoity-toity, a pair of 'anti-malls' called the Lab and the Camp brings hipster cool, while strip malls throughout town reveal cafes serving surprisingly tasty dishes, ethnic-food holes-in-the-wall, bars and clubs. A new food hall, the OC Mix, is shaking it up even more. There's some distance between all of these destinations, but combined they make Costa Mesa one of the OC's most interesting enclaves.

✖ Eating

★**Taco Mesa**　　　　　　MEXICAN $
(☑949-642-0629; www.tacomesa.net; 647 W 19th St; mains $3-13; ⊙7am-11pm; ▣) ✎ Brightly painted in Mexican Day of the Dead art, this out-of-the-way stand is a local institution for fresh, healthy, sustainably farmed tacos of steak, beer-battered fish and more, with an awesome salsa bar. We like the tacos black-

ened, with cheese, chipotle sauce, cabbage relish and *crema fresca*. The *niños* (kids) menu offers quesadillas and such.

Sidecar Doughnuts & Coffee　　DESSERTS $
(☑949-873-5424; www.sidecardoughnuts.com; 270 E 17th St; doughnuts from $2.75; ⊙6:30am-4pm Sun-Thu, to 9pm Fri & Sat; ▣) It may be in the back corner of a nondescript strip mall, but Sidecar's a landmark nonetheless. Crowds line up out the door (especially on weekends) for what are billed as the 'world's freshest doughnuts.' Changing out daily and monthly, Sidecar bakes one-of-a-kind flavors like black velvet, Saigon cinnamon crunch, maple bacon, huckleberry, and butter and salt.

OC Mix　　　　　　FOOD HALL $
(www.socoandtheocmix.com; 3303 Hyland Ave; ⊙10am-9pm, individual shop hours vary) Costa Mesa's newest food destination brings together purveyors of coffees, cheeses, oysters and more. Also here is Taco Maria, whose Michelin-starred chef started with a food truck and was recently named *Food & Wine* magazine's best new chef. It's in the middle of the SOCO outdoor mall, where foodies will also want to flock to Surfas cooking store.

Memphis　　　　　SOUTHERN US $$
(☑714-432-7685; www.memphiscafe.com; 2920 Bristol St; mains brunch $7-17, dinner $14-28; ⊙8am-9:30pm Sun-Wed, to 11pm Thu-Sat) Inside a vintage mid-century-modern building, this fashionable eatery is all about down-home flavor – think pulled-pork sandwiches, popcorn shrimp, gumbo and buttermilk-battered fried chicken. There's brunch daily, happy hour at the bar, and weeknight dinner specials cost a mere $10.

🍷 Drinking

Milk + Honey　　　　　　CAFE
(☑714-708-0092; www.milkandhoneycostamesa. com; the Camp, 2981 Bristol St; ⊙7am-10pm Mon-Thu, 8am-11pm Fri & Sat, 8am-10pm Sun; ⊚) This minimalist cool cafe takes fair-trade, shade-grown and organic coffee a little further, with unusual flavor combinations that (mostly) work: Spanish latte, lavender latte, plus chai tea, fruit smoothies, seasonal fro-yo flavors and Japanese-style shave ice with flavors like strawberry, red bean and almond. There's a small menu of sandwiches and delectable snacks like macarons and peanut butter cookie sandwiches.

Ruin
BAR

(☎714-884-3189; http://theruinbar.com; the Lab, 2930 Bristol St; ⊙4pm-1am Tue & Wed, noon-1am Thu-Sat) This intimate, eclectic bar is decorated kind of like grandma's attic...if grandma collected faux buffalo heads, piano fronts and a ski gondola, and crocheted her trees in yarn. There's a constantly changing selection of beers on tap and cocktails made from soju, the Korean distilled spirit. It's on the southern side of the Lab.

☆ Entertainment

Segerstrom Center for the Arts
THEATER, CONCERT HALL

(☎714-556-2787; www.scfta.org; 600 Town Center Dr) The county's main performance venue is home to the Pacific Symphony, Philharmonic Society of Orange County and Pacific Chorale and draws international performing-arts luminaries and Broadway shows, in three main theaters. Check the website for the wide-ranging calendar.

South Coast Repertory
THEATER

(☎714-708-5555; www.scr.org; 655 Town Center Dr) Next to Segerstrom Center, South Coast Rep was started by a band of plucky theater grads in the 1960s and has evolved into a multiple Tony Award–winning company. It's managed to hold true to its mission to 'explore the most urgent human and social issues of our time' with groundbreaking, original plays from fall through to spring.

🔒 Shopping

★Camp
MALL

(☎714-966-6661; www.thecampsite.com; 2937 Bristol St; ⊙11am-8pm Mon-Sat, to 5pm Sun, individual shop hours vary) 🌿 Vegans, treehuggers and rock climbers, lend me your ears. The Camp offers one-stop shopping for all your outdoor and natural-living needs. **Active Ride Shop** and **Seed People's Market** for outdoor gear and fair-trade home goods are among the stores clustered along a leafy outdoor walkway. Parking spaces are painted with inspirational quotes like 'Show Up for Life.' If the parking spaces are full, there's valet parking.

Among the several dining and drinking options here are **Native Foods** (www.nativefoods.com; the Camp, 2937 Bristol St; mains $8-10; ⊙11am-10pm; ☑🐾) 🌿, Milk + Honey and **Wine Lab** (☎714-850-1780; www.winelabcamp.com; the Camp, 2937 Bristol St, Suite A101B; ⊙noon-10pm Tue-Thu, to 11pm Fri & Sat, to 9pm Sun, 4-9pm Mon).

★Lab
MALL

(☎714-966-6661; www.thelab.com; 2930 Bristol St; ⊙10am-9pm Sun-Thu, to 10pm Fri & Sat, individual shop hours vary; 🐾) Sister property to the Camp cross the street, this outdoor, ivy-covered 'anti-mall' is the original in-your-face alternative to **South Coast Plaza** (☎800-782-8888; www.southcoastplaza.com; 3333 Bristol St; ⊙10am-9pm Mon-Fri, to 8pm Sat, 11am-6:30pm Sun), even if nowadays more (cool) national chains have moved in. Sift through vintage clothing, unique sneakers and trendy duds for teens, tweens and 20-somethings. For short attention spans, contemporary art exhibitions are displayed in shipping containers at ARTery.

Dining options here include **Habana** (☎714-556-0176; www.habanacostamesa.com; the Lab, 2930 Bristol St; mains lunch $13-20, dinner $20-30; ⊙11am-1am Sun-Thu, 11:30am-2am Fri & Sat), Ruin and more. Fun fact: the Lab is in a former goggle factory.

Corona del Mar

Just south of Balboa Peninsula is Corona del Mar, a ritzy bedroom community on the privileged eastern flanks of the Newport Channel with plenty of upscale stores and restaurants and some of SoCal's most celebrated ocean views from the bluffs, not to mention postcard-perfect beaches with rocky coves and child-friendly tide pools.

A half-mile long, **Main Beach** (Corona del Mar State Beach; Map p446; ☎949-644-3151; www.newportbeachca.gov; off E Shore Ave; ⊙6am-10pm; 🅿🐾) lies at the foot of rocky cliffs. There are restrooms, fire rings (arrive early to snag one) and volleyball courts. All-day parking costs $15, but spaces fill by 9am on weekends. Scenes from the classic TV show *Gilligan's Island* were shot at waveless, family-friendly **Pirate's Cove** (Map p446; 🐾); take the nearby stairs off the north end of the Main Beach parking lot.

Crystal Cove State Park

A few miles of open beach and 2400 acres of undeveloped woodland at this **state park** (Map p38; ☎949-494-3539; www.parks.ca.gov; 8471 N Coast Hwy; per car $15; ⊙6am-sunset; 🅿🐾) 🌿 let you forget you're in a crowded metropolitan area, at least once you get past the parking lots and stake out a place on the sand. Overnight guests can stay in the dozens of vintage cottages (reserve well in advance), and anyone can stop for a meal or cocktails at the landmark Beachcomber restaurant.

Crystal Cove is also an underwater park. Scuba enthusiasts can check out two historic anchors dating from the 1800s as well as the crash site of a Navy plane that went down in the 1940s. Alternatively you can just go tide-pooling, fishing, kayaking and surfing along the undeveloped shoreline. On the park's inland side, miles of hiking and mountain-biking trails await.

🛌 Sleeping & Eating

Crystal Cove State Park Campground
CAMPGROUND $
(☑ 800-444-7275; www.reserveamerica.com; 8471 N Coast Hwy, Laguna Beach; tent & RV sites $25-75; P) The Moro Campground of this beachside park accommodates both campers and/or tents and has toilets, showers and more. Heartier campers might opt for a variety of simpler, environmentally friendly and undeveloped 'primitive' campsites (no drinking water or showers) accessible only via a strenuous 3-mile hike.

★ Crystal Cove Beach Cottages
CABIN $$
(☑ reservations 800-444-7275; www.crystalcovealliance.org; 35 Crystal Cove, Crystal Cove State Park Historic District; r with shared bath $35-140, cottages $171-249; ⊙ check-in 4-9pm; P) Right on the beach, these two dozen preserved cottages (circa 1930s to '50s) now host guests for a one-of-a-kind stay. Each cottage is different, sleeping between two and eight people in a variety of private or dorm-style accommodations. To snag one, book on the first day of the month seven months before your intended stay – or pray for cancellations.

Beachcomber Café
AMERICAN $$
(☑ 949-376-6900; www.thebeachcombercafe.com; 15 Crystal Cove; mains breakfast $9-19, lunch $14-21, dinner $20-47; ⊙ 7am-9:30pm) The atmospheric Beachcomber Café lets you soak up the vintage 1950s beach vibe as you tuck into macadamia-nut pancakes, roasted turkey club sandwiches or more serious surf-and-turf. Sunset is the magic hour for Polynesian tiki drinks by the sea.

Laguna Beach

It's easy to love Laguna: secluded coves, romantic cliffs, azure waves and waterfront parks imbue the city with a Riviera-like feel. But nature isn't the only draw. From public sculptures and art festivals to free summer shuttles, the city has taken thoughtful steps to promote tourism while discreetly maintaining its moneyed quality of life (MTV's reality show Laguna Beach being one drunken, shameless exception).

◉ Sights

With 30 public beaches sprawling along 7 miles of coastline, Laguna Beach is perfect for do-it-yourself exploring. There's always another stunning view or hidden cove just around the bend. Although many of the coves are blocked from street view by multi-million-dollar homes, a good local map or sharp eye will take you to stairways leading from the Pacific Coast Hwy down to the beach. Just look for the 'beach access' signs, and be prepared to pass through people's backyards to reach the sand. Unlike its neighbors to the north, Laguna doesn't impose a beach curfew. You can rent beach chairs, umbrellas and boogie boards from **Main Beach Toys** (Map p451; ☑ 949-494-8808; 150 Laguna Ave; chairs/umbrellas/boards per day $10/10/15; ⊙ 9am-9pm).

Pacific Marine Mammal Center
NATURE CENTER
(☑ 949-494-3050; www.pacificmmc.org; 20612 Laguna Canyon Rd; donations welcome; ⊙ 10am-4pm; P ♿) ✦ FREE A nonprofit organization dedicated to rescuing and rehabilitating injured or ill marine mammals, this center northeast of town has a small staff and many volunteers who help nurse Orange County's rescued pinnipeds – mostly sea lions and seals – before releasing them back into the wild. Visitors can view outdoor pools and holding pens – but remember, this is a rescue center, not SeaWorld. Still, it's educational and heartwarming. Admission is free, but donations and gift-shop purchases (say, a stuffed animal) help.

Laguna Art Museum
MUSEUM
(Map p451; ☑ 949-494-8971; www.lagunaartmuseum.org; 307 Cliff Dr; adult/student & senior/child under 13yr $7/5/free, 5-9pm 1st Thu of month free; ⊙ 11am-5pm Fri-Tue, to 9pm Thu) This breezy museum has changing exhibitions featuring contemporary California artists, and a permanent collection heavy on California landscapes, vintage photographs and works by early Laguna bohemians. Free guided tours are usually given at 11am Tuesday, Thursday and Saturday, and there's a unique gift shop. Hours may be extended during some exhibitions.

Laguna Beach

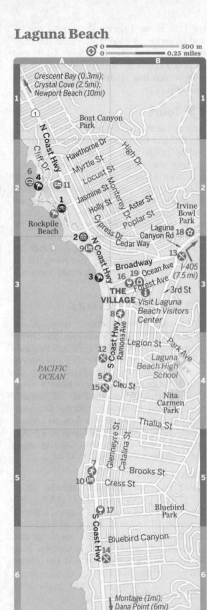

Laguna Beach

at Picnic Beach, it's too rocky to surf; tide pooling is best. Pick up a tide table at the visitors bureau.

Above **Picnic Beach** (Map p451), the grassy, bluff-top **Heisler Park** (Map p451; 375 Cliff Dr) offers vistas of craggy coves and deep-blue sea. Bring your camera – with its palm trees and bougainvillea-dotted bluffs, the scene is definitely one for posterity. A scenic walkway also connects Heisler Park to Main Beach.

North of downtown, Crescent Bay has big hollow waves good for bodysurfing, but parking is difficult; try the bluffs atop the beach. The views here are reminiscent of the Amalfi Coast.

◎ Central Beaches

Near downtown's village, **Main Beach** (Map p451; 🛝) has volleyball and basketball courts, a playground and restrooms. It's Laguna's best beach for swimming. Just north

◎ Southern Beaches

About 1 mile south of downtown, secluded **Victoria Beach** (Victoria Dr) has volleyball courts and La Tour, a Rapunzel's-tower-like structure from 1926. Skimboarding (at the south end) and scuba diving are popular here. Take the stairs down Victoria Dr; there's limited parking along Pacific Coast Hwy.

Further south, **Aliso Beach County Park** (☑ 949-923-2280; http://ocparks.com/beaches/ aliso; 31131 S Pacific Coast Hwy; parking per hr $1; ◷ 6am-10pm; P ⊞) is popular with surfers, boogie boarders and skimboarders. With picnic tables, fire pits and a play area, it's also good for families. Pay-and-display parking costs $1 per hour, or drive south and park on Pacific Coast Hwy for free.

Jealously guarded by locals, **Thousand Steps Beach** (off 9th Ave) is hidden about 1 mile south of Aliso Beach. Just past Mission Hospital, park along Pacific Coast Hwy or residential side streets. At the south end of 9th St, more than 200 steps (OK, so it's not 1000) lead down to the sand. Though rocky, the beach is great for sunbathing, surfing and bodysurfing.

🏃 Activities

With its coves, reefs and rocky outcroppings, Laguna is one of the best SoCal beaches for diving and snorkeling. Check weather and surf conditions with the city's **marine safety forecast line** (☑ 949-494-6573) beforehand, as drownings have happened. The visitors bureau has tide charts.

Divers Cove   SNORKELING
(Map p451) Down below Heisler Park (p451) is Divers Cove, a deep, protected inlet popular with snorkelers and, of course, divers. It's part of the Glenn E Vedder Ecological Reserve, an underwater park stretching to the northern border of Main Beach (p451).

La Vida Laguna   WATER SPORTS
(Map p451; ☑ 949-275-7544; www.lavidalaguna. com; 1257 S Coast Hwy; 2hr guided tour from $85) Take a guided kayaking tour of the craggy coves of Laguna's coast and you might just see a colony of sea lions. Make reservations online.

Hiking
Surrounded by a green belt – a rarity in SoCal – Laguna has great nature trails for hikes. If you love panoramic views, take the short, scenic drive to **Alta Laguna Park**, a locals-only park, up-canyon from town. There, the moderate **Park Avenue Nature Trail**, a 1.25-mile one-way hike, takes you through fields of spring wildflowers. Open to hikers and mountain bikers, the 2.5-mile **West Ridge Trail** follows the ridgeline of

the hills above Laguna. Both trails are in-and-out trips, not loops. To reach the trailheads, take Park Ave from town to its end at Alta Laguna Blvd then turn left to the park, which has restrooms and a drinking fountain.

☞ Tours

Stop by the visitors center (p454) to pick up brochures detailing self-guided tours on foot and by public bus. The *Heritage Walking Companion* is a tour of the town's architecture with an emphasis on Laguna's many bungalows and cottages, most dating from the 1920s and '30s. Laguna also overflows with public art, from well-placed murals to freestanding sculptures in unlikely locations. The free *Public Art Brochure* has color photos of all of Laguna's public-art pieces and a map to help you navigate. Or you can just swing by Heisler Park to see almost a dozen sculptures.

✷ Festivals & Events

⭐ **Pageant of the Masters**   PERFORMING ARTS
(☑ 800-487-3378; www.foapom.com; 650 Laguna Canyon Rd; tickets from $15; ◷ 8:30pm daily mid-Jul–Aug) Hey, did that painting just move? Welcome to the Pageant of the Masters, in which elaborately costumed humans step into painstaking re-creations of famous paintings on an outdoor stage. The pageant began in 1933 as a sideshow to Laguna Beach's Festival of Arts and has been a prime attraction ever since. Our favorite part: watching the paintings deconstruct.

Festival of Arts   ART
(www.foapom.com; 650 Laguna Canyon Rd; admission $7-10; ◷ usually 10am-11:30pm Jul & Aug; ⊞) A two-month celebration of original artwork in almost all its forms. About 140 exhibitors display works ranging from paintings and hand-crafted furniture to scrimshaw, plus kid-friendly art workshops and live music and entertainment daily.

🛏 Sleeping

⭐ **Ranch at Laguna Beach**   RESORT $$$
(☑ 949-499-2271, reservations 800-223-3309; www.theranchlb.com; 31106 S Coast Hwy; r from $399; P ⊞ ❋ ⊜ ☲) Laguna's newest resort is secluded away in Aliso Creek Canyon on the south side of town. Ninety-seven rooms, casitas and town homes are in multiple buildings spread across the 87-acre property, sporting a subtle, rustic refinement

with board-and-batten construction and Mexican-tile bathrooms.

★**Montage**　RESORT $$$
(☑949-715-6000; www.montagelagunabeach.com; 30801 S Coast Hwy; r from $595; P @ 🛜 🛳) You'll find nowhere more indulgent on the OC's coast than this over-the-top luxury waterside resort, especially if you hide away with your lover in a secluded bungalow. Even the most basic of its 248 rooms are plush and generous, offering California craftsman style, marble bathrooms, lemon verbena bath products and unobstructed ocean views.

★**Laguna Beach House**　HOTEL $$$
(Map p451; ☑949-497-6645; www.thelaguna beachhouse.com; 475 N Coast Hwy; r $205-419; P ☕ ✳ 🛜 🛳 🐕) Be it good feng shui, friendly staff or proximity to the beach, this 36-room courtyard inn feels right. From the surfboards in the lobby to colorful throw pillows and clean white walls and linens, the decor is contemporary, comfy and clean. Settle into the outdoor heated Jacuzzi with a glass of wine as the sun drops over the ocean.

Inn at Laguna Beach　HOTEL $$$
(Map p451; ☑949-497-9722; www.innatlaguna beach.com; 211 N Coast Hwy; r $250-500; P ✳ 🛜 🛳 🐕) Pride of place goes to this three-story white, modern hotel, at the north end of Main Beach (p451). Its 70 keen rooms were recently renovated with rattan furniture, blond woods, marble, French blinds and pillow-top beds. Some have balconies overlooking the water. Extras include DVD and CD players, bathrobes, beach gear to borrow and nightly ocean-view wine reception.

You can step from the pool deck directly into Heisler Park (p451). Our favorite part is the terrace where you can bring your own lunch or dinner and enjoy 270-degree views. Staff are welcoming and professional. A $15 resort fee covers wi-fi, those wine hours, cookies and milk, and morning coffee. Parking $30.

🍴 **Eating**

Laguna Beach Farmers Market　MARKET $
(Map p451; ☑714-573-0374; www.facebook.com/lagunabeachfm; 505 Forest Ave; ⊘8am-noon Sat) Local farmers and merchants sell their wares each Saturday, an ever-changing seasonal selection of both produce and prepared foods.

> **ℹ TIDE-POOL ETIQUETTE**
> Tread lightly on dry rocks only and don't pick anything up that you find living in the water or on the rocks.

Orange Inn　DINER $
(Map p451; ☑949-494-6085; www.orangeinncafe.com; 703 S Coast Hwy; mains $7-13; ⊘5:30am-5:30pm) Birthplace of the smoothie (in the *Guinness World Records*), this little shop from 1931 continues to pack in surfers fueling up before hitting the waves. It also serves date shakes, big omelets and breakfast burritos, homemade muffins and deli sandwiches on whole-wheat or sourdough bread.

The namesake Orange Inn smoothie ($6) contains strawberries, blueberries, bananas, dates, juice and bee pollen. Orange you glad you heard about it?

★**Driftwood Kitchen**　AMERICAN $$$
(Map p451; ☑949-715-7700; www.driftwoodkitchen.com; 619 Sleepy Hollow Lane; mains lunch $15-36, dinner $24-39; ⊘9-10:30am & 11am-2:30pm Mon-Fri, 5-9:30pm Sun-Thu, to 10:30pm Fri & Sat, 9am-2:30pm Sat & Sun) Ocean views and ridonkulous sunsets alone ought to be enough to bring folks in, but gourmet Driftwood steps up the food with seasonal menus centered around fresh, sustainable seafood, plus options for landlubbers. Inside it's all beachy casual, whitewashed and pale woods. And the cocktails are smart and creative.

Speaking of cocktails, there's a less-expensive sandwich- and salad-focused menu (mains $9-19) at the adjacent Stateroom bar.

Mozambique　AFRICAN $$$
(Map p451; ☑949-715-7777; www.mozambiqueoc.com; 1740 S Coast Hwy; dinner mains $18-44; ⊘11am-10pm Mon-Thu, to midnight Fri & Sat, 10am-10pm Sun) Macaws and toucans welcome you to this trendy, sophisticated, three-level ode to exotically spiced dishes from southern Africa – peri-peri prawns, chicken pops, grilled pineapple to soaring steaks and seafood, in small plates to pricey surf and turf ($68). Who knows, you might see a *Real Housewives* cast member hiding out in the rooftop bar. There's live music nightly; Sunday reggae gets jammed.

DON'T MISS

FIRST THURSDAYS

Once a month, downtown Laguna Beach gets festive during the **First Thursdays Gallery Art Walk** (☎949-683-6871; www.firstthursdaysartwalk.com; ⊙6-9pm 1st Thu of month). You can make the rounds of 30 local galleries and the Laguna Art Museum (p450) via free shuttles circling Laguna's art gallery districts.

🍷 Drinking & Nightlife

There are almost as many watering holes in downtown's village as there are art galleries. Most cluster along S Coast Hwy and Ocean Ave, making for an easy pub crawl. If you drink, don't drive; local cops take driving under the influence (DUI) very seriously.

Although Laguna has one of SoCal's largest gay populations, the once-thriving gay nightlife has virtually vanished. The one remaining gay bar, **Main Street** (Map p451; ☎949-494-0056; www.mainstreet-bar.com; 1460 S Coast Hwy; ⊙4pm-2am Tue-Sat, to 10pm Sun; closing hours vary), is hit or miss.

Laguna Beach Brewery & Grille
MICROBREWERY

(Map p451; ☎949-497-3381; www.lagunabeach brewery.net; 237 Ocean Ave; ⊙11:30am-10:30pm Tue-Thu, to 11:30pm Fri & Sat, 10am-9pm Sun) For pub grub and microbrews after a day of surfing, this place lines up copper vats behind the bar, pouring its own Miel de Laguna blond and Solar amber ales to go with regional Mexican cooking: homemade tortillas, Rosarito-style lobster tacos and ceviche. Kick back on the outdoor patio for primo people-watching. Live music Wednesdays to Saturdays.

Rooftop Lounge
BAR

(Map p451; www.rooftoplagunabeach.com; 1289 S Coast Hwy; ⊙11:30am-9pm Mon-Thu, to 10pm Fri & Sat, 10:30am-9pm Sun) Perched atop La Casa del Camino this bar, with 270-degree coastal views and a friendly vibe, has locals singing hallelujahs. Mango and wild berry mojitos add some spice to the cocktail menu, and you can snack on plates like meatballs in guava barbecue sauce. Enter through the hotel's lobby and take the elevator to the top.

⭐ Entertainment

Laguna Playhouse
THEATER

(Map p451; ☎949-497-2787; www.lagunaplay house.com; 606 Laguna Canyon Rd) Orange County's oldest continuously operating community theater stages lighter plays in summer, more serious works in winter.

🛍 Shopping

Downtown's village is a shopper's paradise, with hidden courtyards and eclectic little bungalows that beg further exploration. Forest Ave has the highest concentration of chic boutiques, but south of downtown, Pacific Coast Hwy has its fair share of fashionable and arty shops where you can balance your chakras or buy vintage rock albums and posters.

Hobie Surf Shop
SPORTS & OUTDOORS

(Map p451; ☎949-497-3304; www.hobiesurfshop. com; 294 Forest Ave; ⊙9am-7pm) Hobart 'Hobie' Alter started his internationally known surf line in his parents' Laguna Beach garage in 1950. Today, this is one of only a handful of logo retail shops where you can stock up on surfboards and beachwear (love those flip-flops in rainbow colors!) for both babes and dudes.

ℹ Information

Visit Laguna Beach Visitors Center (Map p451; ☎949-497-9229; www.lagunabeachinfo. com; 381 Forest Ave; ⊙10am-5pm; 🛜) Helpful staff, bus schedules, restaurant menus and free brochures on everything from hiking trails to self-guided walking tours.

ℹ Getting There & Away

From I-405, take Hwy 133 (Laguna Canyon Rd) southwest. If you're coming from along the coast, Hwy 1 goes by several names in Laguna Beach: south of Broadway, downtown's main street, it's called South Coast Hwy; north of Broadway it's North Coast Hwy. Locals also call it Pacific Coast Hwy (PCH).

OCTA (p440) bus 1 heading along the coast connects Laguna Beach with Orange County's other beach towns, including Dana Point heading south, every 30 to 60 minutes. The one-way fare is $2 (exact change).

Around Laguna Beach

San Juan Capistrano

Famous for its swallows that fly back to town every year on March 19 (though sometimes they're just a bit early), San Juan Capistrano is home to the 'jewel of the California missions'. California missions were

Roman Catholic outposts established in the late 18th and early 19th centuries. Amid that photogenic mission streetscape of adobe, tile-roofed buildings, and historic wood-built cottages, there's enough history and charm here to make almost a day of it.

'San Juan Cap' is a little town, just east of Dana Point and just over 10 miles southeast of downtown Laguna Beach.

◎ Sights

★ **Mission San Juan Capistrano**   CHURCH
(☑ 949-234-1300; www.missionsjc.com; 26801 Ortega Hwy; adult/child $9/6; ☺ 9am-5pm; ☑) Plan on spending at least an hour poking around the sprawling mission's tiled roofs, covered arches, lush gardens, fountains and courtyards – including the padre's quarters, soldiers' barracks and the cemetery. Admission includes a worthwhile free audio tour with interesting stories narrated by locals. The mission is at the corner of Ortega Hwy and Camino Capistrano.

Particularly moving are the towering remains of the **Great Stone Church**, almost completely destroyed by a powerful earthquake on December 8, 1812. The **Serra Chapel** – whitewashed outside with restored frescoes inside – is believed to be the oldest existing building in California (1782). It's certainly the only one still standing in which Junípero Serra (the founder of the mission) gave Mass. Serra founded the mission on November 1, 1776, and tended it personally for many years.

There's a special audio tour for the elementary-school set, called Saved by the Mission Bell, included in children's admission.

Los Rios Historic District   HISTORIC SITE
One block southwest of the mission, next to the Capistrano train depot, this peaceful assemblage of a few dozen historic cottages and adobes now mostly houses cafes and gift shops. To see 1880s-era furnishings and decor, as well as vintage photographs, stop by the tiny **O'Neill Museum** (31831 Los Rios St; adult/child $1/50¢; ☺ 9am-noon & 1-4pm Tue-Fri, noon-3pm Sat & Sun).

✕ Eating & Drinking

★ **El Campeon**   MEXICAN $
(31921 Camino Capistrano, El Adobe Plaza; items $2-9; ☺ 6:30am-9pm; ☑) For real-deal Mexican food, in a strip mall south of the mission, try this multiroom restaurant, *panadería* (bakery) and *mercado* (grocery store). Look for

tacos, tostadas and burritos in freshly made tortillas, *posole* (hominy stew) and pork carnitas served cafeteria-style, and *aguas frescas* (fruit drinks) in flavors like watermelon, strawberry and grapefruit.

★ **Ramos House Café**   CALIFORNIAN $$
(☑ 949-443-1342; www.ramoshouse.com; 31752 Los Rios St; weekday mains $17-21, weekend brunch $44; ☺ 8:30am-3pm) The best spot for breakfast or lunch in the Los Rios Historic District, this Old West–flavored, wood-built house from 1881 (with brick patio) does organically raised comfort food flavored with herbs grown on-site: blueberry *pain perdu* (French toast) with lemon curd, apple-cinnamon beignets, basil-cured salmon lox or spicy crab-cake salad with smoked chili rémoulade. Breads are baked in-house daily.

El Adobe de Capistrano   MEXICAN $$
(www.eladobedecapistrano.com; 31891 Camino Capistrano; mains lunch $11-24, dinner $16-38; ☺ 11am-9pm Mon-Thu, to 10pm Fri & Sat, 10am-9pm Sun) In a building that traces its origins to 1797, this sprawling, beam-ceilinged 'Mexican steakhouse' and bar does a big business in the standards (enchiladas, fajitas) through to blackened fish or lobster tacos, garlic shrimp and grilled steaks. It was a favorite of President Nixon, who lived in nearby San Clemente, which might be good or bad depending on your outlook.

Coach House   CLUB
(☑ 949-496-8930; www.thecoachhouse.com; 33157 Camino Capistrano; ☺ hours vary) Long-running live-music venue featuring a roster of local and national rock, indie, alternative and tribute bands; expect a cover charge of $15 to $40, depending on who's playing. Recent performers include classic rockers like Blue Öyster Cult, rockers Los Lonely Boys, plus comedy acts like Louie Anderson. Check the website for show times.

❶ Getting There & Around

From Laguna Beach, ride OCTA (p440) bus 1 south to Dana Point. At the intersection of Pacific Coast Hwy and Del Obispo St, catch bus 91 northbound toward Mission Viejo, which drops you near the mission. Buses run every 30 to 60 minutes. The trips takes about an hour. You'll have to pay the one-way fare ($2, exact change) twice.

Drivers should take I-5 exit 82 (Ortega Hwy), then head west about 0.25 miles. There's free three-hour parking on streets and in municipal lots.

WORTH A TRIP

TRESTLES SURF BREAK

Surfers won't want to miss world-renowned **Trestles**, in protected **San Onofre State Beach** (☑949-492-4872; www.parks.ca.gov; parking per day $15; ℗), just southeast of San Clemente. This beach is famous for its natural surf break that consistently churns out perfect waves, even in summer. There are also rugged bluff-top walking trails, swimming beaches and a developed inland **campground** (☑949-361-2531, reservations 800-444-7275; www.reserveamerica.com; San Mateo Campground, 830 Cristianitos Rd, San Onofre State Beach; San Mateo sites $40-65, bluff sites $40; ℗).

Trestles is a great success story for environmentalists and surfers, who for over a decade fought the extension of a nearby toll road. Visit savetrestles.surfrider.org to learn more.

To reach the beach, exit I-5 at Basilone Rd, then hoof to Trestles along the nature trail.

The **Amtrak** (☑800-872-7245; www.amtrak.com; 26701 Verdugo St) depot is one block south and west of the mission. You could arrive by train from LA ($21, 75 minutes) or San Diego ($22, 90 minutes) in time for lunch, visit the mission and be back in the city for dinner. A few daily **Metrolink** (☑800-371-5465; www.metrolinktrains.com) commuter trains link San Juan Capistrano to Orange ($8, 45 minutes), with limited connections to Anaheim.

Dana Point

Dana Point was once called 'the only romantic spot on the coast.' Too bad that quote dates from seafarer Richard Dana's voyage here in the 1830s. Its built-up, parking-lotted harbor detracts from the charm its neighbors have, but it still gets a lot of visitors to its lovely beaches and port for whale-watching, sportfishing and the like.

◉ Sights & Activities

Doheny State Beach   BEACH
(Map p50; ☑949-496-6171; www.dohenystatebeach.org; 25300 Dana Point Harbor Dr; per car $15; ◷park 6am-10pm, visitor center 10am-4pm Wed-Sun; ℗🅷) Adjacent to the southern border of Dana Point Harbor, this mile-long beach is great for swimmers, surfers, surf fishers and tide-poolers. You'll also find picnic tables with grills, volleyball courts and a butterfly exhibit at the 62-acre coastal park. Stop by the park's **visitor center** to check out the five aquariums, mounted birds and 500-gallon simulated tide pool. Free wi-fi at the snack bar.

Salt Creek Beach   BEACH
(☑949-923-2280; www.ocparks.com/beaches/salt; 33333 S Pacific Coast Hwy, off Ritz Carlton Dr; ◷5am-midnight; ℗) Just south of the Laguna Beach boundary, this 18-acre county-run park is popular with surfers, sunbathers, bodysurfers and tide-poolers. Families make the most of the park's picnic tables, grills, restrooms and showers – all sprawling beneath the elegant bluff-top Ritz-Carlton resort. Open in summer, a beach concession stand rents boogie boards, beach chairs and umbrellas. Pay-and-display parking costs $1 per hour.

Wheel Fun Rentals   CYCLING
(☑949-496-7433; www.wheelfunrentals.com; 25300 Dana Point Harbor Dr; cruiser rental per hour/day $10/28; ◷9am-sunset daily late May-early Sep, Sat & Sun early Sep-late May) Wheel Fun covers the basic beach cruisers all the way up to choppers and four-seater surreys.

Capo Beach Watercraft Rentals   BOATING
(☑949-661-1690; www.capobeachwatercraft.com; 34512 Embarcadero Pl; jet ski before/after 11:30am per hour Mon-Fri $85/105, Sat & Sun $100/120) This place rents kayaks and jet skis. Go through the gate and look for the small blue building.

Pure Watersports Dana Point   BOATING
(Dana Point Jet Ski & Kayak Center; ☑949-661-4947; www.danapointjetski.com; 34671 Puerto Pl; rentals per hr kayak and SUP from $15, jet ski from $95; ◷10am-6pm Mon-Fri, from 9am Sat & Sun) This friendly outfit rents jet skis and kayaks.

Beach Cities Scuba   WATER SPORTS
(☑949-443-3858; www.beachcitiesscuba.com; 34283 Pacific Coast Hwy; rentals without/with snorkeling gear $65/95, dive boat trips $120; ◷hours vary) Rents scuba equipment.

☞ Tours

Capt Dave's Dolphin &
Whale Safari BOATING
(☑949-488-2828; www.dolphinsafari.com; 34451 Ensenada Pl; adult/child 3-12yr from $65/45) This popular outfit runs year-round dolphin- and whale-watching trips on a catamaran equipped with underwater viewing pods and a listening system for you to hear what's going on below the surface.

Dana Wharf Sportfishing BOATING
(☑888-224-0603; www.danawharf.com; 34675 Golden Lantern St; sportfishing trips adult/child 3-12yr/senior from $46/29/41, whale-watching tours from $45/29/35) Half-day sportfishing trips are best for beginners. Whale-watching tours for families operate both winter and summer.

✲✲ Festivals & Events

Festival of Whales STREET CARNIVAL, CULTURAL
(www.dpfestivalofwhales.com; ⊘early–mid-Mar) For two weekends, a parade, street fair, nature walks and talks, canoe races, surfing clinics, art exhibitions, live music, and surf 'woody' wagon and hot-rod show make up the merriment.

Doheny Blues Festival MUSIC
(www.omegaevents.com/dohenyblues; Doheny State Beach; ⊘mid-May) Blues, rock and soul legends perform alongside up-and-comers over a weekend of funky live-music performances and family fun at Doheny State Beach. Recent headliners have included Joe Walsh, Melissa Etheridge, Mavis Staples and Chris Isaak.

🛏 Sleeping & Eating

Mostly chain midrange motels and luxury resorts are what you'll find along Pacific Coast Hwy. Restaurants around Dana Point Harbor serve straight-off-the-boat seafood.

Doheny State Beach CAMPGROUND $
(☑800-444-7275; www.reserveamerica.com; 25300 Dana Point Harbor Dr; inland/beachfront campsites from $40/60; ℗❀🐾) Regularly voted the county's best campground, Doheny State Beach offers picnic tables, fire rings, restrooms and showers, but little shade.

Ritz-Carlton Laguna Niguel RESORT $$$
(☑949-240-2000; www.ritzcarlton.com; 1 Ritz-Carlton Dr; r from $599; ℗❀❄@🛜🏊) A longtime OC favorite, this five-star property is perched on a 150ft cliff above the ocean – lovely strolling paths take you there. Sea-blue carpets and crisp white linens in rooms seem to enhance the fabulous views of the coast and ocean. Six dining and drinking options, a spa and daily activities round out the experience for well-heeled travelers.

Turk's GRILL $$
(☑949-496-9028; 34683 Golden Lantern St; mains $5-16; ⊘8am-2am, shorter hrs winter) At Dana Wharf, this trapped-in-amber dive bar is so dark it feels like you're drinking while jailed in the brig of a ship, but never mind. There's plenty of good pub grub (including burgers and fish-and-chips), Bloody Marys and beers, a mellow crowd and a groovy jukebox.

ℹ Information

Dana Point Chamber of Commerce & Visitor Center (☑949-248-3501; www.danapoint.org; cnr Golden Lantern & Dana Point Harbor Dr; ⊘9am-4pm Fri-Sun late May-early Sep) Stop at this tiny booth for tourist brochures and maps. Gung-ho volunteers sure love their city.

ℹ Getting There & Around

From the harbor, **Catalina Express** (☑800-481-3470; www.catalinaexpress.com; 34675 Golden Lantern St; round-trip adult/child 2-11yr/senior $76.50/70/61) makes daily round-trips to Catalina Island, taking 90 minutes each way.

OCTA (p440) bus 1 connects Dana Point with the OC's other beach towns every 30 to 60 minutes. The one-way fare is $2 (exact change).

Four-hour public parking at the harbor is free, or pay $5 per day (overnight $10).

San Diego & Around

POP 1,394,928

Why Go?

New York has its cabbie, Chicago its bluesman and Seattle its coffee-drinking boho. San Diego has its surfer dude, with his tousled hair, great tan and gentle enthusiasm; he looks like he's on a perennial vacation, and when he wishes you welcome, he really means it.

San Diego calls itself 'America's Finest City' and its breezy confidence and sunny countenance filter down even to folks you encounter every day on the street. It feels like a collection of villages each with their own personality, but it's the nation's eighth-largest city and we're hard-pressed to think of a place of any size that's more laid-back.

What's not to love? San Diego bursts with world-famous attractions for the entire family, including the zoo, Legoland and the museums of Balboa Park, plus a bubbling Downtown, beautiful hikes for all, more than 60 beaches and America's most perfect weather.

Best Places to Eat

➡ Clayton's Coffee Shop (p475)

➡ The Patio on Lamont (p476)

➡ Pacific Beach Fish Shop (p476)

➡ Big Kitchen (p471)

Best Places to Sleep

➡ Hotel del Coronado (p469)

➡ La Valencia (p484)

➡ USA Hostels San Diego (p468)

➡ US Grant Hotel (p468)

When to Go
San Diego

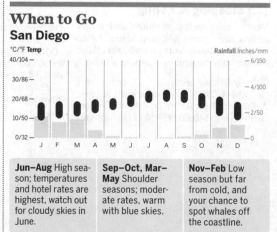

°C/°F Temp
Rainfall Inches/mm

Jun–Aug High season; temperatures and hotel rates are highest, watch out for cloudy skies in June.

Sep–Oct, Mar–May Shoulder seasons; moderate rates, warm with blue skies.

Nov–Feb Low season but far from cold, and your chance to spot whales off the coastline.

CENTRAL & COASTAL SAN DIEGO

Whoosh – here comes a skateboarder. And there goes a wet-suited surfer toting his board to the break, while a Chanel-clad lady lifts a coffee cup off a porcelain saucer. Downtown San Diego and its nearby coastal communities offer all that and more.

San Diego's Downtown is the region's main business, financial and convention district. Whatever intense urban energy Downtown generally lacks, it makes up in spirited shopping, dining and nightlife in the historic Gaslamp Quarter, while the East Village and North Park are hipster havens. The waterfront Embarcadero is good for a stroll,

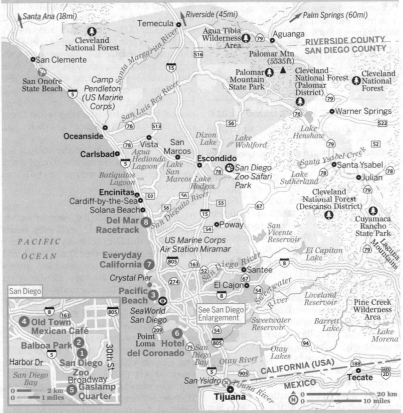

See San Diego Enlargement

San Diego & Around Highlights

1 Cooing at koalas and pandering to pandas at **San Diego Zoo** (p460).

2 Museum hopping in **Balboa Park** (p460), then sampling fish tacos or the next great taste in Hillcrest and North Park.

3 Sunning and skating on the **Pacific Beach** (p464)

boardwalk and catching an epic sunset on the pier.

4 Eating tortillas and swilling margaritas in a legendary the **Old Town Mexican Café** (p473).

5 Downtown pub-crawling and a dueling piano show at **Shout House** (p479) in the Gaslamp Quarter.

6 Marveling at the history and architecture at one of San Diego's prominent landmarks, **Hotel del Coronado** (p464).

7 Kayaking with **Everyday California** (p484) at La Jolla.

8 Mingling with Southern California's hoi polloi at **Del Mar Racetrack** (p487).

SAN DIEGO & AROUND CENTRAL & COASTAL SAN DIEGO

and in the northwestern corner of Downtown, vibrant Little Italy is full of good eats, and Old Town is the seat of local history.

The city of Coronado, with its landmark 1888 Hotel del Coronado (p464) and top-rated beach, sits across San Diego Bay from Downtown. At the entrance to the bay, Point Loma has sweeping views across sea and city from the Cabrillo National Monument (p464). Mission Bay, northwest of Downtown, has lagoons, parks and recreation from waterskiing to camping and the world-famous SeaWorld. The nearby coast – Ocean, Mission and Pacific beaches – epitomizes the SoCal beach scene.

◉ Sights

◉ San Diego Zoo & Balboa Park

San Diego Zoo is a highlight of any trip to California and should be a high priority for first-time visitors. The zoo occupies some prime real estate in Balboa Park, which itself is packed with museums and **gardens** (Map p466; ☑ 619-239-0512; www.balboapark.org/in-the-park/Gardens; Balboa Park). To visit all the park's sights would take days; plan your trip at the **Balboa Park Visitors Center** (Map p466; ☑ 619-239-0512; www.balboapark.org; House of Hospitality, 1549 El Prado; ⊙ 9:30am-4:30pm). Pick up a park map (suggested donation $1) and the latest opening schedule.

Discount admission coupons are widely available in local publications and at hotels and information-center kiosks. The **multi-day explorer pass** (adult/child $97/62) covers admission to Balboa Park's 17 museums and one day at the zoo; it's valid for seven days. A **one-day pass** ($46/27) excludes zoo entry, but includes five museums in one day.

The **Go San Diego** card offers up to 55 per cent off big-ticket attractions. The three-day pass (adult/child $189/169) includes San Diego Zoo, many of Balboa Park's museums, SeaWorld, Legoland, the USS *Midway* Museum and San Diego Zoo Safari Park.

Free tours depart Balboa Park's Visitors Center. To uncover the park's architectural heritage nature and history, led by volunteers and rangers, see www.balboapark.org/explore/tours for timings.

Balboa Park is easily reached from Downtown on bus 7 along Park Blvd. By car, Park Blvd provides easy access to free parking. El Prado is a pedestrian road running through the park and between museums; visitors can access it via Laurel St, then cross Cabrillo Bridge with the Cabrillo Fwy (CA 163) 120ft below; hanging greenery here makes it look like a rainforest gorge.

The free **Balboa Park Tram** bus makes a continuous loop around the park; however, it's easiest and most enjoyable to walk.

★ San Diego Zoo   ZOO

(Map p466; ☑ 619-231-1515; http://zoo.sandiego.org; 2920 Zoo Dr; 1-day pass adult/child from $52/42; 2-visit pass to zoo &/or safari park adult/child $83.25/73.25; ⊙ 9am-9pm mid-Jun–early Sep, to 5pm or 6pm early Sep–mid-Jun; 𝗣 ⊙ 🐾) 🍃
This justifiably famous zoo is one of SoCal's biggest attractions, showing more than 3000 animals representing more than 650 species in a beautifully landscaped setting, typically in enclosures that replicate their natural habitats. Its sister park is San Diego Zoo Safari Park (p489) in northern San Diego County.

Arrive early, as many of the animals are most active in the morning – though many perk up again in the afternoon. Pick up a map at the zoo entrance.

Balboa Park Museums   MUSEUM
(Map p466; ☑ 800-310-7106; www.balboapark.org/explorer; Balboa Park; multi-entry tickets from $46 adult, $27 child; 𝗣 ⊙) Balboa Park is a 1200-acre space with 17 museums and cultural institutions, including key attractions **San Diego History Center** (Map p466; ☑ 619-232-6203; www.sandiegohistory.org; 1649 El Prado, Suite 3; donation recommended; ⊙ 10am-5pm Tue-Sun) 𝗙𝗥𝗘𝗘, **San Diego Air & Space Museum** (Map p466; ☑ 619-234-8291; www.sandiegoairandspace.org; 2001 Pan American Plaza; adult/youth/child under 2 $19.75/$10.75/free; ⊙ 10am-4:30pm; ⊙), **San Diego Museum of Art** (SDMA; Map p466; ☑ 619-232-7931; www.sdmart.org; 1450 El Prado; adult/child $15/free; ⊙ 10am-5pm Mon, Tue & Thu-Sat, from noon Sun), **San Diego Museum of Man** (Map p466; ☑ 619-239-2001; www.museumofman.org; Plaza de California, 1350 El Prado; adult/child/teen $13/6/8; ⊙ 10am-5pm; ⊙) and **San Diego Natural History Museum** (Map p466; ☑ 877-946-7797; www.sdnhm.org; 1788 El Prado; adult/youth 3-17/child under 2 $19/12/free; ⊙ 10am-5pm; ⊙). All attractions are easily walkable, or jump aboard the park's tram to whizz around them all at speed.

★ New Children's Museum   MUSEUM
(Map p470; ☑ 619-233-8792; www.thinkplaycreate.org; 200 W Island Ave; $13; ⊙ 10am-4pm Mon, Wed,

FREE STUFF

Balboa Park Gardens A number of gardens, reflecting different horticultural styles and environments.

Hotel del Coronado (p464) Forever associated with Marilyn Monroe and *Some Like It Hot*.

Old Town San Diego State Historic Park (p463) Surrounded by trees and period buildings housing museums, shops and restaurants.

Spreckels Organ Pavilion Said to be the world's largest outdoor musical instrument.

Botanical Building Each season gives this stunning structure a different look.

Mission & Pacific Beaches (p464) Home to Ocean Front Walk and plenty of other distractions.

Coronado Municipal Beach (p464), consistently ranked in America's top 10.

Thu & Sat, 9.30am-4pm Fri, noon-4pm Sun; 🚼) This interactive children's museum offers interactive art meant for kids. Installations are designed by artists, so tykes can learn principles of movement and physics while simultaneously being exposed to art and working out the ants in their pants. Exhibits change every 18 months or so, so there's always something new.

Spreckels Organ Pavilion NOTABLE BUILDING (Map p466; 📞 619-702-8138; http://spreckelsorgan.org; Balboa Park) FREE Going south from Plaza de Panama, you can't miss the circle of seating and the curved colonnade in front of the band shell housing the organ said to be the world's largest outdoor pipe organ. Donated by the Spreckels family of sugar fortune and fame, the pipe organ came with the stipulation that San Diego must always have an official organist. Make a point of attending the free **concerts**, held throughout the year at 2pm Sundays and on Monday evenings in summer (7.30pm to 9.30pm).

Botanical Building GARDENS (Map p466; www.balboapark.org/tours/botanical-bldg; 1549 El Prado; ⊙10am-4pm) FREE The Botanical Building looks lovely from El Prado, where you can see it reflected in the large lily pond that was used for hydrotherapy in WWII when the navy took over the park. The building's central dome and two wings are covered with redwood lattice panels, which let filtered sunlight into the collection of tropical plants and ferns. The planting changes every season; in December there's a particularly beautiful poinsettia display.

⊙ Little Italy

Little Italy was settled in the mid-19th century by Italian immigrants, mostly fishermen and their families, who lived off a booming fish industry and whiskey trade.

Over the last few years, the Italian community has been joined by exciting contemporary architecture, galleries, gourmet restaurants, and design and architecture businesses. Fun bars and restaurants have made this one of San Diego's hippest neighborhoods.

⊙ Gaslamp Quarter

Gaslamp Museum & William Heath Davis House MUSEUM (Map p470; 📞 619-233-4692; www.gaslampquarter.org; 410 Island Ave; adult/senior & student $5/4, walking tour $10/8; ⊙10am-5pm Tue-Sat, noon-4pm Sun) This house, a prefab affair brought from Maine in 1850, contains a small museum with 19th-century furnishings, plus historic newspaper clippings in the basement. From here, the Gaslamp Quarter Historical Foundation leads a weekly, 90-minute **walking tour** of the neighborhood on Thursdays at 1pm ($20 per person), which includes admission to the house.

⊙ Old Town

Under the Mexican government, which took power in San Diego in 1821, any settlement with a population of 500 or more was entitled to become a 'pueblo,' and the area below the Presidio became the first official civilian Mexican settlement in California – the Pueblo de San Diego.

Metropolitan San Diego

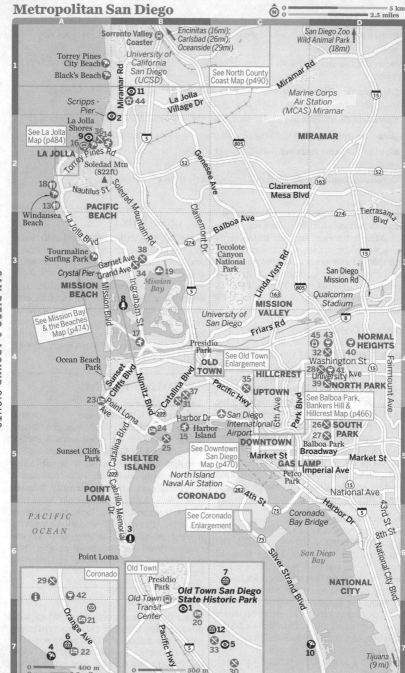

0 ———— 5 km
0 ———— 2.5 miles

Sorrento Valley Coaster

Encinitas (16mi);
Carlsbad (26mi);
Oceanside (29mi)

San Diego Zoo
Wild Animal Park
(18mi)

Torrey Pines
City Beach
Black's Beach

University of
California
San Diego
(UCSD)

See North County
Coast Map (p490)

La Jolla
Village Dr

Miramar Rd

Marine Corps
Air Station
(MCAS) Miramar

MIRAMAR

Scripps
Pier

La Jolla Shores

See La Jolla
Map (p484)

LA JOLLA

Torrey Pines Rd

Soledad Mtn
(822ft)

Nautilus St

Windansea
Beach

PACIFIC
BEACH

Genesee Ave

Clairemont
Mesa Blvd

Clairemont Dr

Balboa Ave

Tierrasanta
Blvd

Tourmaline
Surfing Park

Crystal Pier

Garnet Ave
Grand Ave

Soledad Mountain Rd

MISSION
BEACH

Ingraham St

Mission Blvd

Mission Bay

See Mission Bay
& the Beaches
Map (p474)

Tecolote
Canyon
National
Park

University
of San Diego

MISSION
VALLEY

San Diego
Mission Rd

Qualcomm
Stadium

Friars Rd

Presidio
Park

OLD
TOWN

See Old Town
Enlargement

HILLCREST

UPTOWN

Washington St

University Ave

NORMAL
HEIGHTS

NORTH PARK

See Balboa Park,
Bankers Hill &
Hillcrest Map (p466)

Ocean Beach
Park

Sunset Cliffs Blvd

Nimitz Blvd

Catalina Blvd

Pacific Hwy

Harbor Dr

San Diego
International
Airport

Harbor
Island

Point Loma Ave

Sunset Cliffs
Park

Cabrillo Memorial Dr

SHELTER
ISLAND

See Downtown
San Diego
Map (p470)

DOWNTOWN

Market St

Broadway

GAS
LAMP

Imperial Ave

Balboa Park

SOUTH
PARK

Market St

Petco
Park

National Ave

POINT
LOMA

North Island
Naval Air Station

CORONADO

4th St

See Coronado
Enlargement

Coronado
Bay Bridge

Harbor Dr

43rd St

8th St

National City Blvd

PACIFIC
OCEAN

Point Loma

Silver Strand Blvd

San Diego
Bay

NATIONAL
CITY

Tijuana
(9 mi)

Coronado

29

42

21

Orange Ave

4

6

22

0 ———— 400 m
0 ———— 0.2 miles

Old Town

Presidio
Park

Old Town
Transit
Center

Pacific Hwy

7

Old Town San Diego
State Historic Park

1

20

12

33

5

30

10

0 ———— 500 m
0 ———— 0.25 miles

Metropolitan San Diego

In 1968 the area was named **Old Town San Diego State Historic Park** (Map p462; ☑619-220-5422; www.parks.ca.gov; 4002 Wallace St; ☺visitor center & museums 10am-5pm daily; Ⓟ♿) FREE, archaeological work began, and the few surviving original buildings were restored. Now it's a pedestrian district of trees, a large open plaza, and shops and restaurants.

There's the park visitor center and an excellent history museum in the Robinson-Rose House at the southern end of the plaza. The **Whaley House** (Map p462; ☑619-297-7511; www.whaleyhouse.org; 2476 San Diego Ave; adult/child before 5pm $8/6, after 5pm $13/8; ☺10am-9:30pm daily summer, 10am-4:30pm Sun-Tue, to 9:30pm Thu-Sat rest of the year) is the city's oldest brick building and nearby is **El Campo Santo** (Map p462; San Diego Ave, btwn Arista & Conde Sts), a notable 1849 cemetery. The **Junípero Serra Museum** (Map p462; ☑619-232-6203; www.sandiegohistory.org/serra_museum; 2727 Presidio Dr; by donation; ☺10am-4pm Fri-Sun early Jun-early Sep, 10am-5pm Sat

& Sun early Sep-early Jun; Ⓟ♿) is named for the Spanish padre who established the first Spanish settlement in California, in 1769, and has artifacts of the city's mission and rancho periods.

⊙ Embarcadero & the Waterfront

South and west of the Gaslamp Quarter, San Diego's well-manicured waterfront **promenades** stretch along Harbor Dr, and are perfect for strolling or jogging. Southwest of the ship museums is Seaport Village (p479), with restaurants and gift shops, and the convention center (1989), with its sail-inspired roof that stretches for a half mile. Another gathering place is the former police headquarters (p479), now a shopping center.

USS Midway Museum MUSEUM
(Map p470; ☑619-544-9600; www.midway.org; 910 N Harbor Dr; adult/child $20/$10; ☺10am-

5pm, last admission 4pm; ⓟ 🖐) The giant aircraft carrier USS *Midway* was one of the navy's flagships from 1945 to 1991, last playing a combat role in the first Gulf War. On the flight deck of the hulking vessel, walk right up to some 29 restored aircraft including an F-14 Tomcat and F-4 Phantom jet fighter. Admission includes an audio tour along the narrow confines of the upper decks to the bridge, admiral's war room, brig and 'pri-fly' (primary flight control; the carrier's equivalent of a control tower). Parking costs $10.

★ **Maritime Museum** MUSEUM
(Map p470; ☎ 619-234-9153; www.sdmaritime.org; 1492 N Harbor Dr; adult/child $16/8; ⊙ 9am-9pm late May-early Sep, to 8pm early Sep-late May; 🖐) This museum is easy to find: look for the 100ft-high masts of the iron-hulled square-rigger *Star of India*. Built on the Isle of Man and launched in 1863, the tall ship plied the England–India trade route, carried immigrants to New Zealand, became a trading ship based in Hawaii and, finally, ferried cargo in Alaska. It's a handsome vessel, but don't expect anything romantic or glamorous on board.

⊙ Coronado

Across the bay from downtown San Diego, Coronado is a civilized escape from the jumble of the city and the chaos of the beaches. After crossing the bay by ferry or via the elegantly curved 2.12-mile-long Coronado Bay Bridge, follow the tree-lined, manicured median strip of Orange Ave a mile or so toward the commercial center, Coronado Village. Then park your car; you won't need it again until you leave.

As an alternative to ferries, water taxis and bike rentals, bus 901 from downtown San Diego runs along Orange Ave to the Hotel del Coronado. The Old Town Trolley (p467) tour stops in front of **Mc P's Irish Pub** (Map p462; ☎ 619-435-5280; www.mcpspub.com; 1107 Orange Ave; ⊙ 11am-late Mon-Sat, 10am-late Sun; 🏵).

The story of Coronado is in many ways the story of the **Hotel del Coronado** (Map p462; ☎ 619-435-6611; www.hoteldel.com; 1500 Orange Ave, Coronado; ⓟ🖐), opened in 1888 by John D Spreckels, the millionaire who bankrolled the first rail line to San Diego, took over Coronado and turned the island into one of the West Coast's most fashionable getaways. The **beach** (Map p462; www.coronado.ca.us; ⓟ🖐) is consistently ranked in America's top 10.

⊙ Point Loma

On maps Point Loma looks like an elephant's trunk guarding the entrance to San Diego Bay. Highlights are the Cabrillo National Monument (at the end of the trunk), the shopping and dining of Liberty Station (at its base) and harborside seafood meals.

Cabrillo National Monument MONUMENT
(Map p462; ☎ 619-557-5450; www.nps.gov/cabr; 1800 Cabrillo Memorial Dr; per car $10; ⊙ 9am-5pm; ⓟ🖐) 🌿 Atop a steep hill at the tip of the peninsula, this is San Diego's finest locale for history, views and nature walks. It's also the best place in town to see the gray-whale migration (January to March) from land. You may forget you're in a major metropolitan area.

The **visitor center** has a comprehensive, old-school presentation on Portuguese explorer Juan Rodríguez Cabrillo's 1542 voyage up the California coast, plus exhibits on early Native Californian inhabitants and the area's natural history.

⊙ Ocean Beach

San Diego's most Bohemian seaside community is a place of seriously scruffy haircuts, facial hair and body art. You can get tattooed, shop for antiques and walk into a restaurant barefoot and shirtless without anyone batting an eyelid. **Newport Avenue**, the main drag, runs perpendicular to the beach through a compact business district of bars, surf shops, music stores, used-clothing stores and antiques consignment stores.

⊙ Mission Bay, Mission Beach & Pacific Beach

The big ticket attraction around Mission Bay is SeaWorld, while the nearby Mission, Ocean and Pacific Beaches are the SoCal of the movies.

Mission & Pacific Beaches BEACH
(Map p474) FREE Central San Diego's best beach scene is concentrated in a narrow strip of land between the ocean and Mission Bay. There's amazing people-watching is on the **Ocean Front Walk**, the boardwalk that connects the two beaches. From South Mission Jetty to Pacific Beach Point, it's crowded with joggers, in-line skaters and cyclists any time of the year. On warm summer weekends, oiled bodies, packed like sardines, cover the beach from end to end and cheer the setting sun.

While there's lots to do here, perhaps the best use of an afternoon is to walk along the boardwalk, then spread a blanket or kick back over cocktails and take in the scenery.

A block off Mission Beach, Mission Blvd (the main north–south road), is lined with surf, smoke and swimwear shops. **Cheap Rentals** (Map p474; ☑ 800-941-7761, 858-488-9070; 3689 Mission Blvd, Pacific Beach; foam surfboards from $7 per hour; ⊙ 10am-6pm) loans bikes, skates and surfboards.

In Pacific Beach, to the north, activity extends inland, particularly along Garnet (pronounced gar-*net*) Ave, lined with bars, restaurants and shops, mostly targeted at a 20-something crowd. At the ocean end of Garnet Ave, **Crystal Pier** is a mellow place to fish or gaze out to sea.

At peak times these beaches can get supercrowded: parking around noon is just not gonna happen.

Belmont Park   AMUSEMENT PARK
(Map p474; ☑ 858-228-9283; www.belmontpark.com; 3146 Mission Blvd; per ride $3-6, all-day pass adult/child $30/20; ⊙ from 11am daily, closing times varies; ⓟ) This old-style family-amusement park at the southern end of Mission Beach has been here since 1925. There's a large indoor pool, known as the **Plunge**, and a classic wooden roller coaster named the **Giant Dipper**, plus adventure golf, a new escape-room game, a carousel and other classics. More modern attractions include wave machines like **Flowrider** (Map p474; WaveHouse Beach Club, 3125 Ocean Front Walk; wave-riding per hour $30) **FREE**, for simulated surfing. Even if it sits on dry land, Belmont is to San Diego what the Santa Monica Pier amusement park is to LA. During winter months check for closures due to ride maintenance.

Mission Bay   PARK
(Map p462; www.sandiego.gov/park-and-recreation; ⓟ ⓰) Just east of Mission and Pacific Beaches is this 7-sq-mile playground, with 27 miles of shoreline and 90 acres of parks on islands, coves and peninsulas. Sailing, windsurfing and kayaking dominate northwest Mission Bay, while waterskiers zip around **Fiesta Island**. Kite flying is popular in **Mission Bay Park**, beach volleyball is big on Fiesta Island, and there's delightful cycling and inline skating on the miles of bike paths.

Although hotels, boat yards and other businesses dot about one-quarter of the land, it feels wide open. Fun fact: Spanish explorers called this expanse at the mouth

of the San Diego River 'False Bay' – it formed a shallow bay when the river flowed and a marshy swamp when it didn't. After WWII, a combination of civic vision and coastal engineering turned it into a recreational area.

🏃 Activities

There are plenty of hikes in San Diego, but most outdoor activities involve the ocean. These waters are a dream for surfers, paddleboarders, kayakers and boaters.

Surfing

A good number of residents moved to San Diego just for the surfing, and boy, is it good. Even beginners will understand why.

Fall brings strong swells and offshore Santa Ana winds. In summer swells come from the south and southwest, and in winter from the west and northwest. Spring brings more frequent onshore winds, but the surfing can still be good. For the latest beach, weather and surf reports, call **San Diego County Lifeguard Services** (☑ 619-221-8824).

Beginners should head to Mission or Pacific Beach, for beach breaks (soft-sand bottomed). North of Crystal Pier, **Tourmaline Surfing Park** is a crowded, but good, improvers spot for those comfortable surfing reef.

Rental rates vary depending on the quality of the equipment, but figure on soft boards from around $15/45 per hour/full day; wet suits cost $7/28. Packages are available.

Diving & Snorkeling

Off the coast of San Diego County, divers will find kelp beds, shipwrecks (including the *Yukon*, a WWII destroyer sunk off Mission Beach in 2000) and canyons deep enough to host bat ray, octopus and squid. For current conditions, call San Diego County Lifeguard Services.

Fishing

The most popular public fishing piers are Imperial Beach Pier, Embarcadero Fishing Pier, Shelter Island Fishing Pier, Ocean Beach Pier

Balboa Park, Bankers Hill & Hillcrest

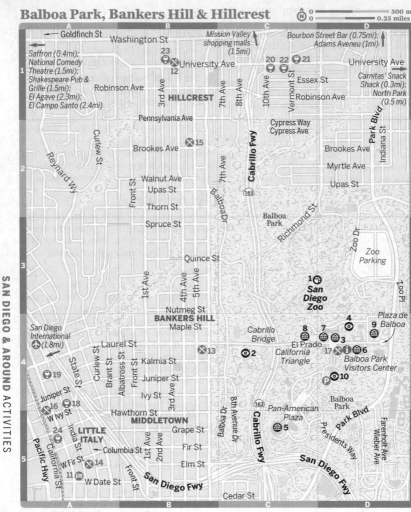

and Crystal Pier at Pacific Beach. Generally the best pier fishing is from April to October, and no license is required. For offshore fishing, catches can include barracuda, bass and yellowtail and, in summer, albacore tuna. A state fishing license is required for people over 16 for offshore fishing; visit www.wildlife.ca.gov for details or book a daily fishing trips with a tour company like **Point Loma Sport Fishing** (Map p462; ✆619-223-1627; www.pointlomasportfishing.com; 1403 Scott St, Point Loma; half-day trips from $45) including those around Coronado and Point Loma.

Boating

San Diego offers rental of powerboats (from $130 per hour), sailboats (from $30 per hour), and kayaks (from $18 per hour) and canoes on Mission Bay from **Mission Bay Sportcenter** (Map p474; ✆858-488-1004; www.missionbaysportcenter.com; 1010 Santa Clara Pl; rentals $3-230).

Kayaking

Ocean kayaking is a good way to observe sea life, and explore cliffs and caves inaccessible from land. Guided tours and lessons are available from **Family Kayak** (✆619-277-1169; www.familykayak.com; adult/child from $45/20; 👪).

Balboa Park, Bankers Hill & Hillcrest

Sailing

Experienced sailors are able to charter boats ranging from catamarans to yachts. Prices start at about $105 for four hours at **Harbor Sailboats** (Map p462; ☎800-854-6625, 619-291-9568; www.harborsailboats.com; 2040 Harbor Island Dr, Suite 104; lessons for nonmembers from $350, plus port fee) and rise steeply. Other charter operators can be found around **Shelter and Harbor Islands** (on the west side of San Diego Bay near the airport).

Whale-Watching

Gray whales pass San Diego from mid-December to late February on their way south to Baja California, and again in mid-March on their way back up to Alaskan waters. Their 12,000-mile round-trip journey is the longest migration of any mammal on earth.

Cabrillo National Monument (p464) is the best place to see the whales from land, where you'll also find exhibits, whale-related ranger programs and a shelter from which to watch the whales breach (bring binoculars).

Half-day whale-watching boat trips are offered by most of the companies that run daily fishing trips, like **Seaforth Sportfishing** (Map p462; ☎619-224-3383; www.seaforthlanding. com; 1717 Quivira Rd, Mission Bay; trips from $24-300). The trips generally cost $24 per adult excursion, sometimes with a guaranteed sighting or a free ticket. Look for coupons and special offers at tourist kiosks and online.

⌖ Tours

Brewery Tours of San Diego BREWERY
(☎619-961-7999; www.brewerytoursofsandiego. com; per person $75-95) San Diego has one of America's best craft-brew scenes, with doz-
ens of small breweries. To leave the driving to someone else, this outfits offers a variety of bus tours each week to an assortment of breweries. Price varies by amount and type of drink and food provided.

San Diego Food Tours FOOD & DRINK
(☎619-233-8687; http://sodiegotours.com/san -diego-food-tours/; from $50) Walking tours showcase the city's gastronomic treasures from Gaslamp, Little Italy and the Old Town, with some enthusiastic native San Diegan guides. Come hungry.

Old Town Trolley Tours & Seal Tours TOURS
(☎855-396-7433; www.trolleytours.com; adult/ child $40/25) Not to be confused with the municipal San Diego Trolley, this outfit operates hop-on-hop-off, open-air buses decorated like old-style streetcars, looping around the main attractions of Downtown and Coronado in about two hours, leaving every 30 minutes or so. The main trolley stand is in Old Town, but you can start or stop at any of the well-marked trolley-tour stops. It also operates 90-minute amphibious **Seal Tours** which depart from Seaport Village (p479) and tour the bay via Shelter Island.

✷ Festivals & Events

San Diego Crew Classic SPORTS
(www.crewclassic.org; ⊙late Mar/early Apr) The national college rowing regatta takes place in Mission Bay.

San Diego Rock 'n' Roll Marathon SPORTS
(www.runrocknroll.competitor.com; ⊙early Jun) Live bands perform at each mile mark of this 26.2-mile race, with a big concert at the finish line.

San Diego County Fair FAIR
(www.sdfair.com; Del Mar Fairgrounds; ☺early
Jun-early Jul) More than a million people
watch headline acts, enjoy hundreds of carnival rides and shows, and pig out on 'fair
fare' (plus some healthier options).

San Diego LGBT Pride LGBT
(www.sdpride.org; ☺mid-Jul) The city's gay
community celebrates in Hillcrest and Balboa Park at the month's end, with parades,
parties, performances, art shows and more.

Opening Day at Del Mar Racetrack SPORTS
(www.dmtc.com; ☺mid- to late Jul) Outrageous
hats, cocktails and general merriment kick off
the horse-racing season, 'where the turf meets
the surf.' Racing through early September.

Comic-Con International CONVENTION
(www.comic-con.org; San Diego Convention Center;
☺late Jul) America's largest event for collectors
of comic, pop-culture and movie memorabilia
has gone from geek chic to trendmaker.

Fleet Week MILITARY
(www.fleetweeksandiego.org; ☺early Oct) The US
military shows its pride in events including
a sea and air parade, special tours of ships,
the Miramar Air Show and the Coronado
Speed Festival (featuring vintage cars).

Little Italy Festa FOOD & DRINK, CULTURAL
(www.littleitalysd.com; ☺early Oct) Come for the
tastes and aromas of old Italia, and stay for
Gesso Italiano, chalk-art drawn directly onto
the streets.

San Diego Beer Week BEER, FOOD & DRINK
(http://sdbw.org; ☺early Nov) Celebrating all
things hoppy: take part in beer-tasting
breakfast, dinners with beer pairing, and
roam around the giant beer garden with dozens of San Diego's best breweries and chefs.

**San Diego Bay Wine
& Food Festival** FOOD & DRINK
(www.sandiegowineclassic.com;
☺mid-Nov)
Cooking classes, wine-tasting parties, gourmet food stands and more.

Harbor Parade of Lights HOLIDAY FESTIVAL
(www.sdparadeoflights.org; ☺Dec) Dozens of
decorated, illuminated boats float in proces-
sion on San Diego's harbor on two Sunday
evenings in December.

December Nights HOLIDAY FESTIVAL
(www.balboapark.org/decembernights; ☺early
Dec) This festival in Balboa Park includes
crafts, carols and a candlelight parade.

🛏 Sleeping

We list high-season (summer) rates for
single- or double-occupancy rooms. Prices
drop significantly between September and
June, but whatever time of year, ask about
specials, suites and package deals. San Diego Tourism runs a **room-reservation line**
(☎800-350-6205; www.sandiego.org).

For camping try **Campland on the Bay**
(Map p462; ☎858-581-4260, 800-422-9386; www.
campland.com; 2211 Pacific Beach Dr, Mission Bay;
RV & tent sites $55-432, beachfront from $225;
🅿🐶🐾) or **KOA** (☎800-562-9877, 619-427-
3601; www.sandiegokoa.com; 111 N 2nd Ave, Chula
Vista; tent sites from $55, RV sites with hookups
from $66, cabins from $95, deluxe cabins from $210;
🅿@🛜🐶🐾), about 8 miles south, with good
camping facilities for families like a pool,
bike rental, Jacuzzi and off-leash dog park;
deluxe cabins include linens, private bathrooms and pots and pans.

🛏 Downtown San Diego

Downtown is San Diego's most convenient
place to stay, for its wealth of restaurants
and hotels and its easy access to transit.

★**USA Hostels San Diego** HOSTEL $
(Map p470; ☎619-232-3100, 800-438-8622; www.
usahostels.com; 726 5th Ave; dm/r with shared bath
from $32/80; ✳@🛜) Lots of charm and color
at this convivial hostel in a former Victorian-era hotel. Look for cheerful rooms, a full
kitchen, and a communal lounge. Rates include linens, lockers and bagels for breakfast.
Surrounded by bars, it's smack-bang in the
middle of Gaslamp's nightlife scene, so bring
earplugs if you're a light sleeper.

★**La Pensione Hotel** BOUTIQUE HOTEL $$
(Map p466; ☎619-236-8000, 800-232-4683;
www.lapensionehotel.com; 606 W Date St; r from
$145-200; 🅿✳🛜) Despite the name, Little
Italy's La Pensione isn't a pension but an
intimate, friendly, recently renovated hotel
of 67 rooms with queen-size beds and pri-
vate bathrooms. It's set around a frescoed
courtyard and is just steps to the neighbor-
hood's dining, cafes and galleries, and walk-
ing distance to most Downtown attractions.
There's an attractive cafe downstairs, and a
recently introduced spa. Parking is $20.

★**US Grant Hotel** LUXURY HOTEL $$$
(Map p470; ☎800-237-5029, 619-232-3121;
www.starwood.com; 326 Broadway; r from $211;
🅿✳@🛜) This 11-stories high 1910 hotel

was built as the fancy city counterpart to the Hotel del Coronado (p464) and hosted everyone from Albert Einstein to Harry Truman. Today's quietly flashy lobby combines chocolate-brown and ocean-blue accents, and rooms boast original artwork on the headboards. It's owned by members of the Sycuan tribe of Native Americans. Parking costs $48.

Old Town

Base yourself in San Diego's Old Town, and you may not need a car. Many lodgings offer free airport shuttles, and there are convenient transit links on the other side of the state park.

Cosmopolitan Hotel   B&B $$
(Map p462; 619-297-1874; http://oldtowncosmopolitan.com; 2660 Calhoun St; r $139-195; front desk 9am-9pm; P) Right in Old Town State Park, this creaky, 10-room hotel is restored to its 1870 glory and has oodles of charm, antique furnishings and is possibly haunted (!). There's a **restaurant** downstairs for lunch and dinner, with live music on Fridays and Saturday evenings. Breakfast is a simple affair centered on coffee and scones. Free wi-fi and free parking.

Coronado

A stay in Coronado Village – around the Hotel del Coronado – puts you close to the beach, shops and restaurants. The northern end is an easy walk to the ferry. Or get away from it all near the deserted **Silver Strand Beach**; a car is advisable here if you're looking to explore further afield.

El Cordova Hotel   HISTORIC HOTEL $$
(Map p462; 800-229-2032, 619-435-4131; www.elcordovahotel.com; 1351 Orange Ave; r from $189; @) This exceedingly cozy Spanish-style former mansion from 1902 has rooms and suites around an outdoor courtyard of shops, restaurants, pool, hot tub and barbecue grills. Rooms are charming in an antiquey sort of way, though nothing fancy; they include TVs with free HBO.

⭐ **Hotel del Coronado**   LUXURY HOTEL $$$
(Map p462; 800-468-3533, 619-435-6611; www.hoteldel.com; 1500 Orange Ave; r from $297; P @) San Diego's iconic hotel provides the essential Coronado experience: over a century of history (p464), a pool, full-service spa, shops, restaurants, manicured grounds, a white-sand beach and an

ice-skating rink during Christmas season. Even the basic rooms have luxurious marbled bathrooms. Note: half the accommodations are not in the main Victorian-era hotel (368 rooms) but in an adjacent seven-story building constructed in the 1970s. For a sense of place, book a room in the original hotel. Self-parking is $39.

Point Loma Area

Although it's a bit out of the way, Point Loma boasts some fun accommodations. Head to **Shelter Island** for tiki-style hotels.

Pearl   MOTEL $$
(Map p462; 619-226-6100, 877-732-7573; www.thepearlsd.com; 1410 Rosecrans St; r $125-199; P) The mid-century-modern Pearl feels more Palm Springs than San Diego. The 23 rooms in its 1959 shell have soothing blue hues, trippy surf motifs and fishbowls. There's a lively pool scene (including '**dive-in' movies** on Wednesday nights), or play Jenga or Parcheesi in the groovy, shag-carpeted lobby. Light sleepers: request a room away from busy street traffic.

Ocean Beach

Ocean Beach (OB) is a happening hippy 'hood, but it is also under the outbound flight path of San Diego airport. Light sleepers might prefer to stay elsewhere or bring earplugs.

Ocean Beach International Hostel   HOSTEL $
(Map p474; 619-223-7873, 800-339-7263; www.californiahostel.com; 4961 Newport Ave; dm $29-45, r from $110;) Central OB's cheapest option is easy to spot with its psychedelic colored exterior and peace sign on the top of the building. Only a couple of blocks from the ocean, it's a simple but friendly and fun place reserved for international travelers, with free wi-fi and breakfast. Entertainment comes in the form of music nights and board games.

Inn at Sunset Cliffs   INN $$
(Map p462; 619-222-7901, 866-786-2453; www.innatsunsetcliffs.com; 1370 Sunset Cliffs Blvd; r/ste from $175/289; P @) At the south end of Ocean Beach, wake up to the sound of surf crashing onto the rocky shore. This low-key 1950s charmer wraps around a flower-bedecked courtyard with a small heated pool. Its 24 breezy rooms are compact, but most have attractive stone-and-tile bathrooms, and some suites have full kitchens.

Downtown San Diego

Downtown San Diego

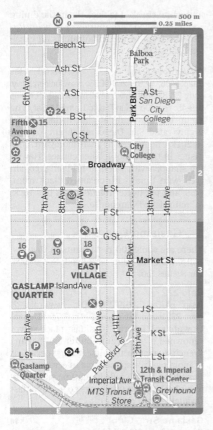

Mission Bay, Mission Beach & Pacific Beach

Just east of Mission Beach, Mission Bay has waterfront lodging at lower prices than accommodations on the ocean.

Catamaran Resort Hotel   RESORT $$
(Map p474; ☑ 800-422-8386, 858-488-1081; www.catamaranresort.com; 3999 Mission Blvd; r from $139; P@🐾🛜🏊) Tropical landscaping and tiki decor fill this resort backing onto Mission Bay (there's a luau on some summer evenings!). A plethora of activities make it a perfect place for families (sailing, kayaking, tennis, biking, skating, spa-ing, etc), or board the **Bahia Belle** (Map p474; www.sternwheelers.com; 998 W Mission Bay Dr; $10) here. Rooms are in low-rise buildings or in a 14-story tower; some have views and full kitchens.

Tower 23   BOUTIQUE HOTEL $$$
(Map p474; ☑ 858-270-2323, 866-869-3723; www.t23hotel.com; 723 Felspar St, Pacific Beach; r from $270; P🅿🐾@🛜🏊) If you like your ocean-front stay with contemporary cool style, this modernist place has an awesome location, minimalist decor, lots of teals and mint blues, water features and a sense of humor. There's no pool, but dude, you're right on the beach. Parking is $30.

Crystal Pier Hotel & Cottages   COTTAGE $$$
(Map p474; ☑ 800-748-5894; www.crystalpier.com; 4500 Ocean Blvd, Pacific Beach; d $185-525; P🐾🐾🛜) Charming, wonderful and unlike any other place in San Diego, Crystal Pier has cottages built right on the pier above the water. Almost all 29 cottages have full ocean views and kitchens; most date from the 1930s. Newer, larger cottages sleep up to six. Book eight to 11 months in advance for summer reservations. Minimum-stay requirements vary by season. No air-conditioning. Rates include parking.

🍴 Eating

San Diego has a thriving dining culture, with an emphasis on Mexican, Californian and seafood. San Diegans eat dinner early, usually around 6pm or 7pm, and most restaurants are ready to close by 10pm. Breakfast is a big affair, and there's a growing locavore and gourmet scene, especially in North Park. Less-expensive options are fun and satisfying. Reservations are recommended.

🍴 Balboa Park & Around

Big Kitchen   BREAKFAST $
(Map p462; ☑ 619-234-5789; www.bigkitchencafe.com; 3003 Grape St, South Park; mains $5-13.50; ⏱7:30am-2:30pm; 🖥) Here since the '70s, this neighborhood joint is decorated with bric-a-brac, progressive bumper stickers, homages to The Beatles and pictures of Whoopi Goldberg – she once worked here as a dishwasher. The kitchen serves American classics like stacks of pancakes, 10 different types of burgers and big-bowl specialties; chili, soup and mac 'n' cheese.

★ Nomad Donuts   DESSERTS $
(Map p462; ☑ 619-431-5000; https://nomaddonuts.com; 4504 30th St; doughnuts from $4; ⏱6am-2pm Mon-Fri, 8am-2pm Sat & Sun) 🍩 If you think you know donuts, think again. This artisanal doughnut shop is headed up by pastry chef Kristianna Zabala, who hand

crafts every batch using cage-free, organic eggs and other ingredients from farmers markets. The menu changes daily, and when they're gone they're gone. Our faves include bacon flavor, charred blueberry–cream cheese, and the ube taro coconut doughnut.

★ **Buona Forchetta** ITALIAN $$
(Map p462; ☑ 619-381-4844; www.buonaforchettasd. com; 3001 Beech St; small plates $6-15, pizzas $8-25; ☺ noon-3pm Tue-Fri, 5-10pm Mon-Thu, to 11pm Fri, noon-11pm Sat, noon-10pm Sun; 🐾) A gold-painted brick wood-fired oven imported from Italy delivers authentic Neapolitan pizzas straight to jammed-together family-sized tables at this South Park trattoria with a dog-friendly patio. No reservations.

★ **Prado** CALIFORNIAN $$$
(Map p466; ☑ 619-557-9441; www.pradobalboa. com; 1549 El Prado; lunch $8-19, dinner $8-37; ☺ 11:30am-3pm Mon, 11am-10pm Tue-Thu, 11:30am-9:30pm Sat, 11am-9pm Sun; 🐾) In one of San Diego's more beautiful dining rooms, feast on Cal-eclectic cooking by one of San Diego's most renowned chefs: bakery sandwiches, lobster bucatini, and thyme-roasted Jidori half-chicken. Go for a civilized lunch on the verandah or for afternoon cocktails and appetizers in the bar.

✕ Little Italy

Little Italy is – surprise! – happy hunting ground for Italian cooking and cafes on India St and around Date St, and some non-Italian newcomers are rounding out the scene. Ballast Point Tasting Room & Kitchen (p477) also does some great dishes.

Valentine's MEXICAN $
(Map p470; ☑ 619-234-8256; 1157 6th Ave; tacos & mains $3-10; ☺ 8am-midnight Sun-Thu, to 3am Fri & Sat) There's nothing urbane about this home-style Mexican joint, but it's a local institution. Apart from the usual tacos and burritos, the carne asada fries (french fries topped like nachos with grilled beef, sour cream, guacamole and such) are messy, coronary-inducing and oh so *bueno*. Late weekend hours mean it's great after a rager.

Filippi's Pizza Grotto PIZZA, DELI $$
(Map p466; ☑ 619-232-5094; www.realcheese pizza.com; 1747 India St; dishes $10-24; ☺ 11am-10pm Sun & Mon, to 10:30pm Tue-Thu, to 11:30pm Fri & Sat; 🐾) There are often lines out the door for Filippi's old-school Italian cooking (pizza, spaghetti and ravioli) served on red-

and-white-checked tablecloths in the dining room festooned with murals of *la bella Italia*. The front of the restaurant is an excellent Italian **deli**.

★ **Juniper & Ivy** CALIFORNIAN $$$
(Map p466; ☑ 619-269-9036; www.juniperandivy. com; 2228 Kettner Blvd; small plates $10-23, mains $19-45; ☺ 5-10pm Sun-Thu, to 11pm Fri & Sat) The menu changes daily at chef Richard Blais' highly rated San Diego restaurant, opened in 2014. The molecular gastronomy includes dishes in the vein of lobster congee, Hawaiian snapper with Valencia Pride mango, ahi (yellowfin tuna) with creamed black trumpets, and pig-trotter *totelloni*. It's in a rockin' refurbished warehouse.

✕ Gaslamp Quarter

There are some 100 restaurants in the Gaslamp, many of them very good. Some have bar scenes too.

Café 222 BREAKFAST $
(Map p470; ☑ 619-236-9902; www.cafe222. com; 222 Island Ave; mains $7-11; ☺ 7am-1:45pm) Downtown's favorite breakfast place serves renowned peanut-butter-and-banana French toast; buttermilk, orange-pecan or granola pancakes; and eggs in scrambles or Benedicts. It also sells lunchtime sandwiches and salads, but we always go for breakfast (available until closing).

Gaslamp Strip Club STEAK $$
(Map p470; ☑ 619-231-3140; www.gaslampsteak. com; 340 5th Ave; mains $17-27; ☺ 5-10pm Sun-Thu, to midnight Fri & Sat) Pull your own bottle from the wine vault, then char your own favorite cut of steak, chicken or fish on the open grills in the retro-Vegas dining room at Downtown's most novel steak house. No steak costs more than $27. Fab, creative martinis and 'pin-up' art by Alberto Vargas. Tons of fun. No one under 21 allowed. Happy hour 5pm-7pm Sunday-Thursday.

Oceanaire SEAFOOD $$$
(Map p470; ☑ 619-858-2277; www.theoceanaire. com; 400 J St; mains $30-65; ☺ 5-10pm Sun-Thu, to 11pm Fri & Sat) The look is art-deco ocean liner, and the service is just as elegant, with an oyster bar and creations like chicken-fried lobster with truffled honey, and California sole Florentine stuffed with crab meat. If you don't feel like a total splurge, look out for happy-hour deals with bargain-priced oysters and fish tacos in the bar (times vary).

✖ East Village

Neighborhood   PUB FOOD **$$**
(Map p470; ☑ 619-446-0002; www.neighborhood
sd.com; 777 G St; mains $7-14; ☺ noon-midnight)
Lit with filament bulbs and decorated with
exposed beams, pipework overhead and
a big mural of Downtown San Diego, this
place is often used as a hangout while peo-
ple are waiting to get entry to the next-door
speakeasy Noble Experiment (p478), but it's
a great spot in its own right, serving dozens
of craft ales and hipster pub eats.

Basic   PIZZA **$$**
(Map p470; ☑ 619-531-8869; www.barbasic.com;
410 10th Ave; small/large pizzas from $14/32;
☺ 11:30am-2am) East Village hipsters feast
on fragrant thin-crust, brick-oven-baked
pizzas under Basic's high ceiling (it's in a
former warehouse). Small pizzas have a
large footprint but are pretty light. Toppings span the usual to the newfangled,
like the mashed pie with mozzarella,
mashed potatoes and bacon. Wash them
down with beers (craft, naturally) or one of
several cocktails.

Café Chloe   FRENCH **$$$**
(Map p470; ☑ 619-232-3242; www.cafechloe.
com; 721 9th Ave; dinner $9-31; ☺ 8am-10pm
Mon-Sat, 8:30am-9:30pm Sun) This delightful
corner French bistro has a simple style and
gets the standards perfect, and everything
else as well. Classics include onion tart,
French toast, *moules* (mussels) or steak
frites (steak and chips) served with herb
butter and salad. There's also trout salad,
and wonderful egg dishes for weekend
brunch.

✖ Bankers Hill & Old Town

The restaurant scene is booming here.

★**Old Town Mexican Café**   MEXICAN **$$**
(Map p462; ☑ 619-297-4330; www.oldtownmexcafe.
com; 2489 San Diego Ave; mains $5-17; ☺ 7-11pm
weekdays, to midnight weekends; ④) Other restaurants come and go, but this place has been
in this busy adobe with hardwood booths
since the 1970s. While you wait to be seated,
watch the staff turn out tortillas. Then enjoy
machacas (shredded pork with onions and
peppers), carnitas and Mexican ribs. For
breakfast: *chilaquiles* (tortilla chips with
salsa or mole, broiled or grilled with cheese).

★**Cucina Urbana**   CALIFORNIAN, ITALIAN **$$$**
(Map p466; ☑ 619-239-2222; www.urbankitchen
group.com/cucina-urbana-bankers-hill/; 505 Laurel
St, Bankers Hill; mains lunch $15-23, dinner $12-31;
☺ 11:30am-2pm Tue-Fri, 5-9pm Sun & Mon, 5-10pm
Tue-Thu, 5pm-midnight Fri & Sat) In this corner
place with modern rustic ambience, busi-
ness gets done, celebrations get celebrated
and friends hug and kiss over refined yet af-
fordable Cal-Ital cooking. Look for short-rib
pappardelle, pizzas like spicy coppa pork and
pineapple or pear and Gorgonzola with cara-
melized onion, and smart cocktails and local
'brewskies.' Reservations recommended.

El Agave   MEXICAN **$$$**
(Map p462; ☑ 619-220-0692; www.elagave.com;
2304 San Diego Ave; mains lunch $10-20, dinner
$11-33; ☺ 11am-10pm; ℗) Candlelight flickers
in this romantic 2nd-floor, white-tablecloth,
high-end place catering to cognoscenti. The
mole is superb (nine types to choose from),
and there are a whopping 1500 different tequilas covering just about every bit of wall.

SAN DIEGO & AROUND EATING

LGBTQ SAN DIEGO

San Diego's main LGBTQ-friendly area is Hillcrest, which has a large concentration of
bars, restaurants, cafes and shops flying the rainbow flag. The scene is more casual,
friendly and unpretentious than neighboring LA or San Francisco. The premier lesbian
bar is **Gossip Grill** (Map p466; ☑ 619-260-8023; www.thegossipgrill.com; 1220 University Ave;
☺ noon-2am Mon-Fri, 10am-2am Sat & Sun), while **Flicks** (Map p466; ☑ 619-297-2056; www.
sdflicks.com; 1017 University Ave; ☺ 9am-late Sun, 4pm-late Mon, Wed & Thu, 2pm-late Tue & Fri,
noon-late Sat), **Rich's** (Map p466; ☑ 619-295-2195; www.richssandiego.com; 1051 University
Ave; ☺ 10pm-2am Wed-Sun) and **Urban Mo's** (Map p466; ☑ 619-491-0400; www.urbanmos.
com; 308 University Ave, Hillcrest; ☺ 9am-1:30am) are mixed, host various themed nights
and are always lively spots to grab a drink. For current LGBTQ events and news visit the
Gay San Diego website (http://gay-sd.com) or pick up a paper copy, distributed in
newspaper racks around town.

✕ North Park & Hillcrest

Hillcrest is well established and North Park is a hub of innovation.

★ Carnitas' Snack Shack
CALIFORNIAN, MEXICAN $

(Map p462; ☑ 619-294-7665; http://carnitassnack shack.com; mains $8-13; ⊙ 11am-midnight; ⊕) Eat honestly priced, pork-inspired slow food in a cute outdoor patio with natural wooden features. Wash dishes like the triple-threat pork sandwich (with schnitzel, bacon, pepperoncini, pickle relish, shack aioli and an Amish bun) down with local craft ales. Happy hour runs from 3pm–6pm Monday-Friday with $5 tacos, $5 drafts and $6 wines.

Bread & Cie
BAKERY, CAFE $

(Map p466; ☑ 619-683-9322; www.breadandcie. com; 350 University Ave, Hillcrest; mains $6-11; ⊙ 7am-7pm Mon-Fri, to 6pm Sat, 7:30am-6pm Sun; ℗) Aside from crafting some of San Diego's best artisan breads (including anise and fig, black olive, and walnut and raisin), this wide-open bakery-deli makes fabulous sandwiches with fillings such as curried-chicken salad and ham and Swiss cheese. Boxed lunches cost $11.50. Great pastries too.

★ Hash House a Go Go
AMERICAN $$

(Map p466; ☑ 619-298-4646; www.hashhousea gogo.com; 3628 5th Ave, Hillcrest; breakfast $10-22, dinner mains $15-29; ⊙ 7.30am-2.30pm Mon, 7:30am-2pm & 5:30-9pm Tue-Thu, to 2:30pm and 9:30pm Fri-Sun; ⊕) This buzzing bungalow makes biscuits and gravy straight outta Indiana, towering Benedicts, large-as-your-head pancakes and – wait for it – hash seven different ways. Eat your whole breakfast, and you won't need to eat the rest of the day. It's worth coming back for the equally massive burgers, sage-fried chicken and award-winning meatloaf sandwich. No wonder it's called 'twisted farm food.'

★ Urban Solace
CALIFORNIAN $$

(Map p462; ☑ 619-295-6464; www.urbansolace. net; 3823 30th St, North Park; mains lunch $12-22, dinner $14-27; ⊙ 11am-9pm Mon-Tue, to 9:30pm Wed-Thu, to 10:30pm Fri, 10:30am-10:30pm Sat, 9:30am-2:30pm & 4-9pm Sun) North Park's young hip gourmets revel in creative comfort food here: quinoa-veg burger; 'duckaroni' (mac 'n' cheese with duck confit); and pulled chicken and dumplings. The setting's surprisingly chill for such great eats; maybe it's the creative cocktails.

Mission Bay & the Beaches

Mission Bay & the Beaches

✕ Mission Hills

Mission Hills is the neighborhood north of Little Italy and west of Hillcrest. On India St, where it meets Washington St, there's a block of well-regarded eateries.

Saffron   THAI $$
(Map p462; ☎619-574-7737; www.saffronsandiego.com; 3731 India St; mains $7-15; ⊙10:30am-10pm Mon-Sat, 11am-10pm Sun) This multi-award-winning, hole-in-the-wall is actually two shops – **Saffron Thai Grilled Chicken** and **Noodles & Saté**, but you can get both at either shop and enjoy it in the noodle shop. Chicken is cooked over a charcoal grill and comes with a choice of sauces, salad, jasmine rice and a menu of finger foods.

Shakespeare Pub & Grille   PUB FOOD $$
(Map p462; ☎619-299-0230; www.shakespearepub.com; 3701 India St; dishes $6-15; ⊙10:30am-midnight Mon-Thu, to 1am Fri, 8am-1am Sat, 8am-midnight Sun) One of San Diego's most authentic English ale houses, Shakespeare is the place for darts, soccer by satellite, beer on tap and pub grub, including fish-and-chips, and bangers and mash. One thing they don't have in Britain: a great sundeck. On weekends, load up with a British breakfast: bacon, mushrooms, black and white pudding and more.

✕ Embarcadero & the Waterfront

★**Puesto at the Headquarters**   MEXICAN $$
(Map p470; ☎610-233-8880; www.eatpuesto.com; 789 W Harbor Dr, The Headquarters; mains $11-19; ⊙11am-10pm) This eatery serves Mexican street food that knocked our *zapatos* off: innovative takes on traditional tacos like chicken (with hibsicus, chipotle, pineapple and avocado) and some out-there fillings like zucchini and cactus. Other highlights: crab guacamole, the lime-marinated shrimp ceviche, and the grilled Baja striped bass.

✕ Coronado

★**Clayton's Coffee Shop**   DINER $
(Map p462; ☎619-435-5425; www.facebook.com/claytonscoffeeshop; 979 Orange Ave; mains $7-13; ⊙6am-10pm; ⊞) Some diners only look old-fashioned. This one is the real deal from the 1940s, with red leatherette swivel stools and booths with mini jukeboxes. It does famous all-American breakfasts and some Mexican specialties like *machaca* with eggs and cheese, and it's not above panini and croque monsieur sandwiches. For dessert: mile-high pie from the counter.

1500 Ocean   CALIFORNIAN $$$
(Map p462; ☎619-435-6611; www.hoteldel.com/1500-ocean; Hotel del Coronado, 1500 Orange Ave; mains $38-52; ⊙5:30-10pm Tue-Sat, plus Sun summer; ⓟ) It's hard to beat the romance of supping at the Hotel del Coronado (p464), especially at a table overlooking the sea from the verandah of its first-class dining room, where silver service and coastal cuisine with local ingredients set the perfect tone for popping the question or feting an important anniversary.

✕ Point Loma Area

A hot spot for seafood restaurants, plus the recently opened Liberty Public Market (p476) with more than 30 local artisan vendors touting their flavors – you can easily spend a hour or so wandering around sampling them all.

★ Point Loma Seafoods
SEAFOOD $

(Map p462; ☑619-223-1109; www.pointlomaseafoods.com; 2805 Emerson St; mains $7-16; ⏰9am-7pm Mon-Sat, 10am-7pm Sun; Ⓟ⛟) For off-the-boat-fresh seafood sandwiches, salads, sashimi, fried dishes and icy-cold beer, order at the counter at this fish-market-cum-deli and grab a seat at a picnic table on the upstairs, harbor-view deck. It also does great sushi and takeout dishes from ceviche to clam chowder.

★ Liberty Public Market
MARKET $

(Map p462; ☑619-487-9346; http://libertypublicmarket.com; 2820 Historic Decatur Rd; ⏰7am-10pm) What the Ferry Building Marketplace is to San Francisco, the newly opened Liberty Public Market is to San Diego. Inside this converted old Navy building are more than 30 hip artisan vendors such as Baker & Olive, Wicked Maine Lobster, Mastiff Sausage Company, Mama Made Thai, Le Parfait Paris, Cecilia's Taqueria and FishBone Kitchen.

Stone Brewing World Bistro & Gardens
PUB FOOD $$

(Map p462; ☑619-269-2100; www.stonebrewing.com/visit/bistros/liberty-station; Liberty Station, 2816 Historic Decatur Rd; mains lunch $15-24, dinner $16-28; ⏰11:30am-9pm Mon-Fri, until 10pm Sat & Sun; Ⓟ) Local brewer Stone has transformed the former mess hall of the naval training center at **Liberty Station** (Map p462; www.libertystation.com; 2640 Historic Decatur Rd) into a temple to local craft beer. Tuck into standard-setting, spin-the-globe dishes – beer-battered fish tacos, *yakisoba* (Japanese stir-fried noodles) bowls with Jidori chicken, and spicy lamb sausage rigatoni – at long tables or comfy booths under its tall beamed ceiling, or beneath twinkling lights in its courtyard.

Bali Hai
POLYNESIAN $$$

(Map p462; ☑619-222-1181; www.balihairestaurant.com; 2230 Shelter Island Dr; dishes lunch $8-19, dinner $19-29, small plates from $10, Sun brunch adult/child $35/17; ⏰11:30am-9pm Mon-Thu, to 10pm Fri & Sat, 9:30am-9pm Sun; Ⓟ) Near the tiki-themed hotels of Point Loma, this long-time, special-occasion restaurant serves Hawaiian-themed meals like tuna *poke* (cubed raw fish mixed with shōyu, sesame oil, salt, chili pepper and other condiments), *pupus* (small plates), chicken of the gods (with tangy orange-chili and a coconut–brown

rice cake) and a massive Sunday champagne-brunch buffet. The best part: views clear across San Diego Bay through its circular wall of windows.

🍴 Ocean Beach

★ Hodad's
BURGERS $

(Map p474; ☑619-224-4623; www.hodadies.com; 5010 Newport Ave; dishes $4-15; ⏰11am-10pm) Since the flower-power days of 1969, OB's legendary burger joint has served great shakes, massive baskets of onion rings and succulent hamburgers wrapped in paper. The walls are covered in license plates, grunge/surf-rock plays (loud!) and your bearded, tattooed server might sidle into your booth to take your order. No shirt, no shoes, no problem, dude.

Ocean Beach People's Market
VEGETARIAN $

(Map p474; ☑619-224-1387; www.obpeoplesfood.coop; 4765 Voltaire St; dishes $8, salads per pound from $7.89; ⏰8am-9pm; ⛟) 🌿 For strictly vegetarian groceries and fabulous prepared meals and salads north of central Ocean Beach, this organic cooperative does bulk foods, and excellent counter-service soups, sandwiches, salads and wraps.

Sundara
INDIAN $$

(Map p474; ☑619-889-0639; www.sundaracuisine.com; 1774 Sunset Cliffs Blvd; mains $11-12; ⏰5-9.30pm Sun-Thu, to 10pm Fri & Sat; ⛟) This little, modern, neat-as-a-pin place has a tiny but well-chosen menu of curries and tandoori chicken, and a much longer menu of craft and bottled beers from as far away as India. It's adorned with simple black-and-white photos of Indian street scenes.

🍴 Pacific Beach

★ Pacific Beach Fish Shop
SEAFOOD $

(Map p462; ☑858-483-1008; www.thefishshop-pb.com; 1775 Garnet Ave; tacos/fish plates from $4.50/15.50; ⏰11am-10pm) You can't miss this fishy-themed joint with its enormous swordfish hanging outside. Inside, it's a casual, communal bench affair. Choose from more than 10 types of fresh fish at the counter, from ahi to red snapper, then pick your marinade (garlic butter to chipotle glaze), then select your style – fish plate with rice and salad, taco or sandwich perhaps?

★ The Patio on Lamont
AMERICAN $$

(Map p462; ☑858-412-4648; www.thepatioonlamont.com; 4445 Lamont St; dishes $7-26;

⊘9am-midnight) Popular local hangout serving beautifully prepared New American small plates and cocktails. Try the crab and ahi tower or crispy artichoke with goat's cheese in a cozy fairy-lit patio area (with outside heaters in winter). Daily happy hours on selected beers and cocktails ($5/6) run from 3pm to 6pm and 10pm to midnight.

JRDN CALIFORNIAN **$$$**
(Map p474; ✆858-270-5736; www.t23hotel.com/ dine; Tower 23 Hotel, 723 Felspar St; breakfast & lunch dishes $11-21, dinner mains $28-49; ⊘9am to 4pm Mon-Fri, 5pm to 9:30pm Sun-Thu, to 10pm Fri & Sat; ❇) 🍴 A big heaping dose of chic amid PB's congenital laid-back feel. There's both an ocean view and a futuristic interior (and most excellent bar scene). Sustainably farmed meats and seafood join local veggies to create festivals on the plate. Try dishes like farmers-market apple salad, day-boat scallops, oysters on the half shell or local yellowtail.

🍷 Drinking & Nightlife

San Diego's bar scene is diverse, ranging from live-music pubs and classic American pool bars, to beach bars with tiki cocktails, gay clubs offering drag shows, and even a few hidden speakeasies. It's easy to find a local craft beer in town, or you can venture out to one of the 100 breweries or vineyards in the Temecula area.

🍷 Little Italy

El Camino LOUNGE
(Map p466; ✆619-685-3881; www.elcaminosd. com; 2400 India St; ⊘5pm-late Mon-Sat, from 11am Sun) We're not sure what it means that this buzzy watering hole has a Día de los Muertos (Mexican Day of the Dead holiday) theme in the flight path of San Diego Airport – watch planes land from the outdoor patio – but whatever, dude. The clientele is cool, design mod, the cocktails strong and the Mexican victuals *fabuloso*.

Waterfront BAR
(Map p466; ✆619-232-9656; www.waterfrontbarandgrill.com; 2044 Kettner Blvd; ⊘6am-2am) San Diego's first liquor license was granted to this place in the 1930s (it was on the waterfront until the harbor was filled and the airport built). A room full of historic bric-a-brac, big windows looking onto the street and the spirits of those who went before make this a wonderful place to spend the afternoon or evening.

Ballast Point Tasting Room & Kitchen PUB
(Map p466; ✆619-255-7213; www.ballastpoint. com; 2215 India St; ⊘11am-11pm) This San Diego–based brewery does 4oz tasters of its beers for just $5, which could be the best deal in town. Enjoy them with a full menu including housemade pretzels, beer-steamed mussels, salads or a truffle burger.

🍷 Gaslamp Quarter

The Gaslamp has the city's highest concentration of nightlife venues. Many do double (even triple) duty as restaurants, bars and clubs.

★Bang Bang BAR
(Map p470; ✆619-677-2264; www.bangbangsd. com; 526 Market St; cocktails $14-26; ⊘5-10:30pm Wed-Thu, to 2am Fri & Sat) Beneath lantern light, the Gaslamp's hottest new spot brings in local and world-renowned DJs and serves sushi and Asian small plates like dumplings and *panko*-crusted shrimp to accompany the imaginative cocktails (some in giant goblets meant for sharing with your posse). Plus, the bathrooms are shrines to Ryan Gosling and Hello Kitty: in a word, awesome. At the weekend and for special events, the place turns into a club: expect a cover charge later in the evening.

Dublin Square IRISH PUB
(Map p470; www.dublinsquareirishpub.com; 544 4th Ave; ⊘11:30am-2am weekdays, from 9am Sat & Sun) Guinness? Check. Corned beef? Check. But what sets this rambling pub apart are its long happy hours (lasting five hours early in the week) and its live music, usually in the form of a lively covers band; check the website for the schedule. Brunch is served between 9am and 2pm on weekends, and lunch and dinner from 11:30am to 10.30pm daily.

Star Bar BAR
(Map p470; ✆619-234-5575; 423 E St; ⊘6am-2am) When you've had it with gentrified style and you're looking for a historic dive, head to this old-school bar (decorated year-round with Christmas lights) for possibly the cheapest drinks in Gaslamp. It's open 20 hours a day, 365 days a year.

🍷 East Village

While out-of-towners frolic happily in the Gaslamp Quarter, San Diego locals and hipsters instead head east to these more insider-y bars.

SAN DIEGO & AROUND DRINKING & NIGHTLIFE

Noble Experiment
BAR

(Map p470; ☑ 619-888-4713; http://nobleexperimentsd.com; 777 G St; ☺ 7pm-2am Tue-Sun) This place is literally a find. Open a secret door and enter a contemporary speakeasy with miniature gold skulls on the walls, classical paintings on the ceilings and inventive cocktails on the list (from $12). The hard part: getting in. Text for a reservation, and they'll tell you if your requested time is available and how to find it; it's also possible to turn up to the bar upstairs (Neighborhood) (p473) and put your name on a waiting list.

East Village Tavern & Bowl
SPORTS BAR

(Map p470; ☑ 619-677-2695; www.tavernbowl.com; 930 Market St; ☺ 11am-12am Sun-Thu, to 2am Sat & Sun) This large sports bar a few blocks from baseball stadium **Petco Park** (Map p470; ☑ 619-795-5011; www.padres.com; 100 Park Blvd; tours adult/child/senior $15/10/10; ☺ 10:30am & 12:30pm Sun-Fri, 3pm Sat; ♿) has six bowling lanes (thankfully, behind a wall for effective soundproofing). Pub menu (dishes $5 to $14; bacon-jam sliders, mac 'n' cheese balls) is served all day.

North Park & Hillcrest

Hillcrest has the greatest concentration of bars, particularly gay spots, while North Park has a cool, hipster vibe.

★Coin-Op Game Room
BAR, GAME ROOM

(Map p462; ☑ 619-255-8523; www.coinopsd.com; 3926 30th St, North Park; ☺ 4pm-1am Mon-Fri, noon-1am Sat & Sun) Dozens of classic arcade games – pinball to Mortal Kombat, Pac-Man and Big Buck Safari to Master Beer Bong – line the walls of this hipster bar in North Park. All the better to quaff craft beers and cocktails like The Dorothy Mantooth (gin, Giffard Violette, lime, cucumber, Champagne) and chow on truffle-parm tots, fried-chicken sandwiches or fried oreos.

★Polite Provisions
COCKTAIL BAR

(Map p462; ☑ 619-677-3784; www.politeprovisions. com; 4696 30th St, North Park; ☺ 3pm-2am Mon-Thu, 11:30am-2am Fri-Sun) With a French-bistro feel and plenty of old-world charm, Polite Provisions' hip clientele sip cocktails and, in a beautifully designed space, complete with vintage cash register, wood-paneled walls and tiled floors. Many cocktail ingredients, syrups, sodas and infusions are homemade and displayed in apothecary-esque bottles.

Blind Lady Ale House
PUB

(Map p462; ☑ 619-225-2491; http://blindlady.blogspot.com; 3416 Adams Ave; ☺ 5pm-midnight Mon-Thu, from 11:30am Fri-Sun) A superb neighborhood pub, with creative decor like beer cans piled floor to ceiling and longboard skateboards attached to the walls. It sells craft ales on pump and prepares fresh pizza (from $7). Vegetarians should try the meat-free Mondays offering pies with inventive flavors.

Coronado to Pacific Beach

Pacific Beach (PB) is party central on the coast, with mostly 20-somethings on a beach bar bender (drivers: watch for tipsy pedestrians). If you've been there/done that, you might prefer one of the quieter coffeehouses or restaurant bars, or head to Ocean Beach or Coronado.

Jungle Java
CAFE

(Map p474; ☑ 619-224-0249; http://daniellemarie-hargis.wixsite.com/jungle-java/home; 5047 Newport Ave, Ocean Beach; coffees from $2; ☺ 7am-6pm Mon-Sun; ☎) Funky-dunky, canopy-covered cafe and plant shop, also crammed with crafts and art treasures. A chilled place to sip on a coffee, smoothie or chai latte, tuck into a pastry and surf the free wi-fi.

Coaster Bar and Grill
BAR

(Map p474; ☑ 858-488-4438; http://thecoasterbarandgrill.com; 744 Ventura Pl, Mission Beach; ☺ 10am-2am Mon-Fri, 8am-2am Sat & Sun) Old-fashioned neighborhood dive bar with views of the Belmont Park roller coaster. It draws an unpretentious crowd and has more than 50 beers on tap; good margaritas too.

The Grass Skirt
COCKTAIL BAR

(Map p474; ☑ 858-412-5237; http://thegrassskirt. com; 910 Grand Ave; ☺ 5pm-2am) Through a secret doorway, disguised as a refrigerator in the next-door **Good Time Poke** cafe, you'll step into a lost Hawaiian world with Polynesian wood carvings, thatched verandahs, fire features and tiki-girl figurines made into lamps. Sipping on your daiquiri or pina colada there are more surprises to come...listen out for immersive weather sounds and lighting effects.

☆ Entertainment

Check out the San Diego *City Beat* or *UT San Diego* for the latest movies, theater, galleries and music gigs around town. **Arts Tix** (Map p470; ☑ 858-437-9850; www.sdartstix.com; 28 Horton Plaza; ☺ 10am-4pm Tue-Thu, to 6pm Fri & Sat, to 2pm Sun), in a kiosk near Westfield

Horton Plaza (next to Balboa Theatre), has half-price tickets for same-day evening or next-day matinee performances and offers discounted tickets to other events. **Ticketmaster** (📞800-653-8000; www.ticketmaster.com) and House of Blues sell tickets to other gigs around the city.

Prohibition Lounge
LIVE MUSIC

(Map p470; http://prohibitionsd.com; 548 5th Avenue; ☺8:00pm-1:30am Wed-Sat) Find the unassuming doorway on 5th Ave with 'Eddie O'Hare's Law Office' on it, then flip the light switch on to alert the doorman, who'll guide you into a dimly lit basement serving craft cocktails, with patrons enjoying live jazz (music from 9:30pm). Come early as it gets busy fast; at weekends expect a waitlist.

Shout House
LIVE MUSIC

(Map p470; 📞619-231-6700; www.theshouthouse.com; 655 4th Ave; cover free-$10) Good, clean fun at this cavernous Gaslamp bar with dueling pianos. Talented players have an amazing repertoire, including classics, rock and more. The lively crowd ranges from college age to conventioneers.

House of Blues
BLUES

(Map p470; 📞619-299-2583; www.houseofblues.com/sandiego; 1055 5th Ave; ☺4-11pm) Live blues music, DJs, rock bands, karaoke, trivia nights and more. Free shows on certain nights with dinner. Scheduled gigs are priced individually depending on the popularity of the artist.

San Diego Symphony
CLASSICAL MUSIC

(Map p470; 📞619-235-0800; www.sandiegosymphony.com; 750 B St, Jacobs Music Center; from $20; ☺show times vary) This accomplished orchestra presents classical and family concerts at **Jacobs Music Center**. Look for summer concerts at Embarcadero Marina Park South.

Winston's
LIVE MUSIC

(Map p474; 📞619-222-6822; www.winstonsob.com; 1921 Bacon St, Ocean Beach; ☺1pm until late) Bands play most nights, and each night has a different happening: open mike, karaoke, comedy, cover bands, local artists etc.

🔒 Shopping

San Diego is chock-full of shops selling everything from local-pride souvenirs to Mexican gifts, adventure goods, beachwear and antiques. Keep your eyes peeled in neighborhood streets for independent shops and boutiques trading in local wares. Farmers markets are also a big hit around town. Plus, there

SURF & SUDS

There are now more than 100 craft breweries operating in the San Diego area. The **San Diego Brewers Guild** (www.sandiegobrewersguild.org) counts some 40-plus member establishments. Go to the guild's website for a map or pick up one of its pamphlets around town, and start planning your brewery-hopping tour. To leave the driving to someone else, Brewery Tours of San Diego (p467) offers bus tours to different breweries for a variety of tastes. Tour price varies by timing and whether a meal is served.

Check our recommendations to get you started, and see also Stone Brewing (p476) and Ballast Point Tasting Room & Kitchen (p477)..

are plenty of slightly-out-of-town malls for everyday big brands and luxury fashion items.

Headquarters at Seaport District
MALL

(Map p470; 📞619-235-4013; www.theheadquarters.com; ☺10am-9pm Mon-Sat, to 8pm Sun) San Diego's fairly new shopping center (opened 2013) is also one of its oldest buildings: the 1939 former police headquarters has turned into some 30 shopping, dining and entertainment options. There's a small exhibit of vintage handcuffs, badges and jail cells for you and up to 15 of your friends.

Seaport Village
SHOPPING DISTRICT

(Map p470; 📞619-235-4014; www.seaportvillage.com; 849 West Harbor Dr; ☺10am-10pm Jun-Aug, to 9pm Sep-May; 🚻) Neither seaport nor village, this 14-acre collection of novelty shops and restaurants has a faux New England theme. It's touristy and twee but good for souvenir shopping and casual eats.

Galactic
COMICS

(Map p474; 📞619-226-6543; 4981 Newport Ave; ☺11am-8pm) Lose time perusing the shelves of this cubbyhole comic-book store. It also rents new DVDs and has a bunch of retro arcade games to play inside.

Adams Avenue
ANTIQUES

(Map p462; www.adamsaveonline.com; Adams Ave) This is San Diego's main 'antique row,' featuring dozens of shops selling furniture, art and antiques from around the world. Take a rest from all the shopping at the Blind Lady Ale House, serving pizzas and craft beers.

TRAVELING TO TIJUANA

Just beyond the busiest land border in the western hemisphere, Tijuana, Mexico (population around 1.7 million) was for decades a cheap, convivial escape for hard-partying San Diegans, Angelenos, sailors and college kids. A decade ago, a double whammy of drug-related violence and global recession turned once-bustling tourist areas into ghost towns, but *tijuanenses* (as the locals call themselves) have been slowly but surely reclaiming their city. The difference from squeaky-clean San Diego is palpable from the moment you cross the border, but so are many signs of new life for those who knew TJ in the bad old days.

Avenida Revolución (aka La Revo) is the main tourist drag, though its charm is marred by cheap clothing and souvenir stores, strip joints, pharmacies selling bargain-priced medications to Americans, and touts best rebuffed with a firm 'no.' It's a lot more appealing just beyond La Revo, toward and around **Avenida Constitución**, where sightseeing highlights include **Catedral de Nuestra Señora de Guadalupe** (Cathedral of our Lady of Guadalupe; cnr Av Niños Héroes & Calle 2a), Tijuana's oldest church, **Mercado El Popo** (cnr Calle 2a & Av Constitución), an atmospheric market hall selling wares from tamarind pods to religious iconography and **Pasaje Rodríguez** (Av Revolución, btwn Calles 3a & 4a; ⊙noon- 10pm), an arcade filled with hipster coffee shops, local design shops and colorful street art.

A short ride away, **Museo de las Californias** (Museum of the Californias; ☑ from US 011-52-664-687-9600; www.cecut.gob.mx; Centro Cultural Tijuana, cnr Paseo de los Héroes & Av Independencia; adult/child under 12yr M\$27/free; ⊙10am-6pm Tue-Sun; Ⓟ🖿), inside the architecturally daring **Centro Cultural Tijuana** (CECUT; ☑ from US 011-52-664-687-9600; www. cecut.gob.mx; cnr Paseo de los Héroes & Av Independencia; ⊙9am-7pm Mon-Fri, 10am-7pm Sat & Sun; 🖿), aka El Cubo (the Cube), offers an excellent history of the border region from prehistory to the present; there's signage in English. If you're in town on a Friday night, check

❶ Information

INTERNET ACCESS

All public libraries and most coffeehouses and hotel lobbies in San Diego offer free wi-fi. Libraries also offer computer terminals for access.

San Diego Main Library (☑ 619-236-5800; www.sandiego.gov/public-library; 330 Park Blvd; ⊙9:30am-7pm Mon-Thu, to 6pm Fri & Sat, noon-6pm Sun; 🛜) The city's new main library branch is a dazzler architecturally and has all the services you could want (including wi-fi).

MEDIA

Free listings magazines *Citybeat* (http://sdcitybeat.com) and *San Diego Reader* (www.sdreader. com) cover the active music, art and theater scenes. Find them in shops and cafes.

KPBS 89.5 FM (www.kpbs.org) National Public Radio station.

San Diego Magazine (www.sandiegomagazine. com) Glossy monthly.

UT San Diego (www.utsandiego.com) The city's major daily.

POST

For post-office locations, call ☑ 800-275-8777 or log on to www.usps.com.

Coronado Post Office (Map p462; ☑ 619-435-1142; www.usps.com; 1320 Ynez Pl; ⊙8:30am-5pm Mon-Fri, 9am-noon Sat)

Downtown Post Office (Map p470; ☑ 800-275-8777; www.usps.com; 815 E St; ⊙9am-5pm Mon-Fri)

TOURIST INFORMATION

Coronado Visitors Center (Map p462; ☑ 619-437-8788, 866-599-7242; www.coronadovisitorcenter.com; 1100 Orange Ave; ⊙9am-5pm Mon-Fri, 10am-5pm Sat & Sun)

International Visitor Information Center (Map p470; ☑ 619-236-1242; www.sandiego.org; 1140 N Harbor Dr; ⊙9am-5pm Jun-Sep, to 4pm Oct-May) Across from the B St Cruise Ship Terminal, helpful staff offer very detailed neighborhood maps, sell discounted tickets to attractions and maintain a hotel-reservation hotline.

❶ Getting There & Away

AIR

Most flights to **San Diego International Airport-Lindbergh Field** (SAN; Map p462; ☑ 619-400-2404; www.san.org; 3325 N Harbor Dr; 🛜) are domestic. The airfield sits just 3 miles west of Downtown; plane-spotters will thrill watching jets come in over Balboa Park for landing. Coming from overseas, you'll likely change flights – and clear US customs – at one of the major US gateway airports, such as LA, San Francisco, Chicago, New York or Miami.

The standard one-way fare between LA and San Diego is about \$115 and takes about 35 minutes;

out a **lucha libre** (Mexican wrestling; ☎ from US 011-52-664-250-9015; Blvd Díaz Ordaz 12421, Auditorio Municipal Fausto Gutierrez Moreno; US$8-35) match at the Auditorio Municipal Fausto Gutiérrez Moreno, where oversized men in gaudy masks do Mexican wrestling.

Turista Libre (www.turistalibre.com) runs a variety of public and private tours in English, led by an American expat with endless enthusiasm for the city and its lesser-known nooks and crannies.

A passport is required to cross the border, and to reenter the US. By car, take I-5 south and look for either signs to Mexico or for the last US exit, where you can park at one of the many lots in the area (from $10 for five hours, from $20 for 24 hours). If traveling by taxi from the Mexican side of the border, be sure to take a taxi with a meter. Uber is also available for travelers with internet service on their phones. By public transport from San Diego, the **San Diego Trolley** (☎ 619-233-3004; www.sdmts.com) runs from Downtown to **San Ysidro border crossing** (☎ 619-690-8900; www.cbp.gov; 720 E San Ysidro Blvd; ⏰ 24hr). To cross the border on foot, follow the signs to Mexico, and a turnstile, which you walk through into Mexico. Follow signs reading 'Centro Downtown.' Be aware, there can be long waits to reenter the US by foot.

Driving into Mexico is easy for those with their own cars, but you will need to purchase extra road insurance for the time you are in Mexico, and international road-side assistance is advisable. Exercise caution when driving around northern Baja California. Nighttime smash-and-grab theft does happen, and there have been instances of carjackings in Mexico. It is sensible to avoid traveling at night and to use toll roads where possible. Visit government travel-advice websites for more information. Visit https://bwt.cbp.gov for updated border wait times.

unless you're connecting through LA, you're usually better off driving or taking the train.

To/from other US cities, San Diego flights are generally up to about $140 more expensive than those to LA. All major US airlines serve San Diego, plus Air Canada, British Airways, Mexico's Volaris and the Canadian carrier WestJet.

BUS

Greyhound (Map p470; ☎ 619-515-1100, 800-231-2222; www.greyhound.com; 1313 National Ave; ⏰ ticket office 5am-11:59pm) serves San Diego from cities across North America from its Downtown location. Inquire about discounts and special fares, many available only online.

Buses depart frequently for LA; standard fares (one-way/round-trip) start at $14 and the trip takes 2½ to four hours. There are several daily departures to Anaheim (singles from $12, about 2¼ hours).

Buses to San Francisco (from $59, 12 hours, about seven daily) require a transfer in Los Angeles; round-trip airfares often cost about the same. Most buses to Las Vegas (one-way from $23, eight to nine hours, about eight daily) require a transfer in LA or San Bernardino.

CAR & MOTORCYCLE

Allow at least two hours to reach San Diego from LA in nonpeak traffic. If there are two or more passengers in your car you can use the high-occupancy vehicle lanes.

TRAIN

Amtrak (☎ 800-872-7245; www.amtrak.com; 1050 Kettner Blvd) runs the *Pacific Surfliner* several times daily to Anaheim (two hours), Los Angeles (2¾ hours) and Santa Barbara (6½ hours) from the historic **Union Station** (Santa Fe Depot; ☎ 800-872-7245; 1050 Kettner Blvd; ⏰ 3am-11:59pm). Trains run to stations in Oceanside, Carlsbad, Encinitas, Solana Beach, Sorrento Valley, Old Town and Downtown. Fares start from around $30, and the coastal views are enjoyable.

ℹ Getting Around

While most people get around San Diego by car, it's possible to have an entire vacation here using municipal buses and trolleys run by the Metropolitan Transit System and your own two feet. Most buses/trolleys cost $2.25/2.50 per ride. Transfers are not available, so purchase a day pass if you're going to be taking more than two rides in a day; a refillable **Compass Card** ($2 one-time purchase) will save hassles. The **MTS Transit Store** (Map p470; ☎ 619-234-1060; www.sdmts.com; 1255 Imperial Ave; ⏰ 8am-5pm Mon-Fri) is one-stop shopping for route maps, tickets and one-/two-/three-/four-day passes ($5/9/12/15). Same-day passes are also available from bus drivers. At trolley stations, purchase tickets from vending machines.

BICYCLE

While in San Diego, mostly flat Pacific Beach, Mission Beach, Mission Bay and Coronado are all great places to ride a bike. Visit **iCommute** (www.icommutesd.com) for maps and information about biking in the region. Public buses are equipped with bike racks.

A few outfits rent bicycles, from mountain and road bikes to kids' bikes and cruisers. In general, expect to pay about $8 per hour, $15–$22 per half-day (four hours) and $25–$30 per day.

BOAT

Flagship Cruises (Map p470; ☑ 619-234-4111; www.flagshipsd.com; 990 N Harbor Dr; tours adult/child from $24/12; 👪) operates the hourly **Coronado Ferry** (Map p470; ☑ 800-442-7847; www.flagshipsd.com; 990 N Harbor Dr; 1 way $4.75; ⊗ 9am-10pm) shuttling between San Diego's **Broadway Pier** (1050 N Harbor Dr) on the Embarcadero and the ferry landing at the foot of B Ave in Coronado, two blocks south of Orange Ave. Bikes are permitted on board at no extra charge. Flagship also operates a water taxi, serving mostly Downtown and Coronado.

BUS

MTS (p481) covers most of San Diego's metropolitan area, North County, La Jolla and the beaches. It's most convenient if you're based Downtown and not staying out late.

Useful routes to/from Downtown:

BUS ROUTE NUMBER	STOPS IN SAN DIEGO
3	Balboa Park, Hillcrest, UCSD Medical Center
7	Gaslamp, Balboa Park, Zoo, Hillcrest, North Park
8/9	Old Town, Pacific Beach, SeaWorld
30	Gaslamp, Little Italy, Old Town, Pacific Beach, La Jolla, University Town Center
35	Old Town, Ocean Beach
901	Gaslamp, Coronado, Imperial Beach

CAR

All the big-name car-rental companies have desks at the San Diego airport (p480); lesser-known companies may be cheaper. Shop around – prices vary widely, even from day to day within the same company. The airport has free direct phones to a number of car-rental companies. Rental rates tend to be comparable to LA ($30 to $80 per day plus insurance fees). Smaller agencies include **West Coast Rent a Car** (☑ 619-544-0606; http://westcoastrenta-car.net; 834 W Grape St; ⊗ 9am-6pm Mon-Sat, to 5pm Sun), in Little Italy.

METROPOLITAN TRANSIT SYSTEM (MTS)

The Metropolitan Transit System runs buses and trolleys throughout central San Diego and beyond. For route and fare information, call ☑ 619-233-3004 or ☑ 800-266-6883; operators are available 5:30am to 8:30pm Monday to Friday, and 8am to 5pm Saturday and Sunday (note that the 800 number works only within San Diego). For 24-hour automated information, call ☑ 619-685-4900. Visit www.sdmts.com/schedules-real-time to plan your route online.

One paying adult may travel with up to two children aged 5 and under for free on buses with a valid MTS ticket. On Saturdays and Sundays up to two children (age 12 and under) may ride for free with one fare-paying adult (age 18 or older) on all MTS routes.

TAXI & RIDESHARE

Taxi fares vary, but plan on about $12 for a 3-mile journey. Established companies include **Orange Cab** (☑ 619-223-5555; www.orange-cabsandiego.net) and **Yellow Cab** (☑ 619-444-4444; www.driveu.com). Recently app-based ride-share companies such as **Uber** (www.uber.com) and **Lyft** (www.lyft.com) have entered the market with lower fares.

TROLLEY

Municipal trolleys, not to be confused with **Old Town Trolley tourist buses** (p467), operate on three main lines in San Diego. From the transit center across from the Santa Fe Depot, **Blue Line** trolleys go south to San Ysidro (on the Mexico border) and north to **Old Town Transit Center** (Map p462; www.amtrak.com; 4009 Taylor St). The **Green Line** runs from Gas Lamp to Old Town east through Mission Valley. The **Orange Line** connects the Convention Center and Seaport Village with Downtown, but otherwise it's less useful for visitors. Trolleys run between about 4:15am and 1am daily at 15-minute intervals during the day, and every 30 minutes in the evening. Fares are $2.50 per ride, valid for two hours from the time of purchase at vending machines on the station platforms.

LA JOLLA & NORTH COUNTY COAST

Immaculately landscaped parks, white-sand coves, upscale boutiques, top restaurants, and cliffs above deep, clear-blue waters make it easy to understand why 'La Jolla' translates from Spanish as 'The Jewel.' Pronounced la-*hoy*-yah, the name may actually date from Native Americans who inhabited the area from 10,000 years ago to the mid-19th century, and called the place 'mut la hoya, la hoya' – the place of many caves.

Northward from La Jolla, North County's coast evokes the San Diego of 40 years ago. Pretty Del Mar continues through low-key Solana Beach, Encinitas and Carlsbad (home of Legoland), before hitting Oceanside, home to Camp Pendleton Marine Base. All the beaches are terrific, and the small seaside towns are great for days of soaking up the laid-back SoCal scene and working on your tan. All that, and only about a half-hour's drive from Downtown San Diego.

La Jolla

⊙ Sights

★ Children's Pool
BEACH

(La Jolla seals; Map p484; 850 Coast Blvd) Built in the 1930s, La Jolla's Children's Pool was created as a family beach space, but since then it's been descended on by herds of seals and sea lions. Despite the pinnipeds' particularly pungent odor, tourists come in droves to see them larking around, swimming, fighting and mating. Visitors can get extremely close via a concrete platform surrounding the cove, and the seals don't seem to mind – but there's strictly no touching, feeding or selfies to be taken with the seals.

The future of the seals remains in debate, as divers and swimmers claim their presence increases bacteria levels in the water, yet animal-rights groups want to protect the cove and make it an official seal rookery. At the time of writing, courts ruled that the beach was to remain closed to swimmers, to protect the mums, pups and baby seals during pupping season (December 15 to May 15) when they are most vulnerable. But the future of the Children's Pool remains to be seen.

Birch Aquarium at Scripps
AQUARIUM

(Map p462; ☑ 858-534-3474; www.aquarium.ucsd. edu; 2300 Expedition Way; adult/child $18.50/14; ⊙9am-5pm; P ♿) ✒ Marine scientists were working at the Birch Aquarium at Scripps Institution of Oceanography (SIO) as early as 1910 and, helped by donations from the Scripps family, the institute has grown to be one of the world's largest marine research institutions. It is now a part of University of California (UC) San Diego. Off N Torrey Pines Rd, the aquarium has brilliant displays. The **Hall of Fishes** has more than 60 fish tanks, simulating marine habitats from the Pacific Northwest to tropical seas.

★ Cave Store
CAVE

(Map p484; ☑ 858-459-0746; www.cavestore. com; 1325 Coast Blvd; adult/child $5/3; ⊙10am-4:30pm Mon-Fri, to 5pm Sat & Sun; ♿) Waves have carved a series of caves into the sandstone cliffs east of La Jolla Cove. The largest is called **Sunny Jim Cave**, which you can access via this store. Taller visitors, watch your head as you descend the 145 steps.

Athenaeum
LIBRARY

(Map p484; ☑ 858-454-5872; www.ljathenaeum. org; 1008 Wall St; ⊙10am-5:30pm Tue-Sat, to 8:30pm Wed) Housed in a graceful Spanish renaissance structure, this space is devoted exclusively to art and music. Its reading room is a lovely place to relax and flick through a book, and it hosts a series of lectures plus live music, from classical to jazz.

San Diego-La Jolla Underwater Park Ecological Reserve
DIVING, SNORKELING

(Map p462) Look for the white buoys offshore from Point La Jolla north to Scripps Pier that mark this protected zone with a variety of marine life, kelp forests, reefs and canyons. Waves have carved caves into the sandstone cliffs east of the cove.

University of California San Diego
UNIVERSITY

(UCSD; Map p462; ☑ 858-534-2230; http://ucsd. edu; 9500 Gilman Dr) UCSD was established in 1960 and now has more than 30,000 students and a strong reputation, particularly for mathematics and science. It lies on rolling coastal hills in a parklike setting, surrounded by tall, fragrant eucalyptus. Its most distinctive structure is the **Geisel Library**, an upside-down pyramid named for children's author Theodor Geisel, aka Dr Seuss of *Cat in the Hat* fame; there's a collection of his drawings and books. Download a map of UCSD's excellent collection of public art at http://stuartcollection.ucsd.edu.

🏃 Activities

★ Torrey Pines State Natural Reserve
HIKING

(Map p490; ☑ 858-755-2063; https://torreypine. org/parks/trails.html; 12600 North Torrey Pines Rd; ⊙7:15am-sunset, visitors center 9am-6pm) FREE Walkers and hikers explore 8 miles of **trails** in 2000 acres of well-trodden coastal state park. Choose from routes of varying difficulties, including the 0.7-mile Guy Fleming Trail, with panoramic sea views and paths through wildflowers, ferns and cacti, or the 1.4-mile

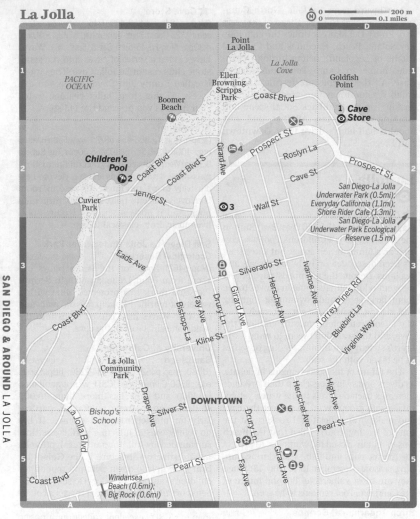

La Jolla

La Jolla

◉ Top Sights
1 Cave Store...D1
2 Children's Pool B2

◉ Sights
3 Athenaeum...C2

◉ Sleeping
4 La Valencia...C2

◎ Eating
5 George's at the Cove C2

6 Harry's Coffee Shop C4

◉ Drinking & Nightlife
7 Pannikin...C5

◉ Entertainment
8 Comedy Store C5

◉ Shopping
9 DG Wills...C5
10 Warwick's..C3

Razor Point Trail with a good whale-spotting lookout during winter months.

Everyday California   ADVENTURE SPORTS
(Map p462; 858-454-6195; www.everydaycalifornia.com; 2246 Avenida de la Playa; kayak tours from $50; 9am-5pm) This adventure outfit offers paddleboard hire, kayak hire (during summer), snorkel sets and kayaking tours year-round along La Jolla's coastline and ecological reserve. On the 90-minute tours there's a good chance of spotting sea lions and seals in the water, and if you're lucky dolphins and whales (in winter). When sea conditions are safe, kayakers can venture into **Emerald Cave**.

La Jolla Beaches   BEACH
Some of the county's best beaches are north of the Shores in Torrey Pines City Park, between the **Salk Institute** (Map p490; 858-453-4100; www.salk.edu; 10010 N Torrey Pines Rd; tours $15; tours by reservation 11:45am Mon-Fri;) and **Torrey Pines State Natural Reserve** (Map p490; 858-755-2063; www.torreypine.org; 12600 N Torrey Pines Rd; 7:15am-sunset, visitor center 10am-4pm Oct-Apr, 9am-6pm May-Sep;) FREE. Hanggliders and paragliders launch into the sea breezes rising over the cliffs at **Torrey Pines Gliderport** (Map p490; 858-452-9858; www.flytorrey.com; 2800 Torrey Pines Scenic Dr; 20min paragliding $175, hang-gliding tandem flight per person $225), at the end of Torrey Pines Scenic Dr. It's a beautiful sight – tandem flights are available if you can't resist trying it. La Jolla Shores and Black's Beach are popular surfing spots.

San Diego-La Jolla Underwater Park   SNORKELING, DIVING
(Map p462) Some of California's best and most accessible diving is in this reserve, accessible from La Jolla Cove. With an average depth of 20ft, the 6000 acres of look-but-don't-touch underwater real estate are great for snorkeling too. Ever-present are the spectacular, bright-orange Garibaldi fish – California's official state fish and a protected species (there's a hefty fine for poaching one).

Sleeping

★ Lodge at Torrey Pines   LUXURY HOTEL $$$
(Map p490; 858-453-4420; www.lodgetorreypines.com; 11480 N Torrey Pines Rd; r from $359;) Inspired by the architecture of Greene & Greene, the turn-of-the-20th-century arts-and-crafts masters who designed the Gamble House (www.gamblehouse.org) in Pasadena,

the lodge's discreetly luxurious rooms have Mission oak-and-leather furniture à la Stickley, Tiffany-style lamps, plein air paintings and basket-weave bathroom-floor tiling in marble. There's a stellar full-service spa and a croquet lawn. Parking costs $25.

La Valencia   HISTORIC HOTEL $$$
(Map p484; 858-454-0771, 800-451-0772; www.lavalencia.com; 1132 Prospect St; r from $314;) This 1926 pink-walled, Mediterranean-style landmark was designed by William Templeton Johnson. Among its 115 rooms, those in the main building are rather compact while the villas are spacious, but the property wins for its Old Hollywood romance. Even if you don't stay, consider lifting a toast – and a pinkie – to the sunset from its Spanish Revival lounge, La Sala. Parking is $30.

Eating

★ Shore Rider Cafe   CALIFORNIAN $
(Map p462; 858-412-5308; www.shoreridersd.com; 2168 Avenida de la Playa; dishes $9-15; 11am-10pm Mon-Thu, to 11pm Fri, 9am-11pm Sat, to 10pm Sun) For tasty eats in a surf vibe right near the beach, head to Shore Rider's new mellow open-air patio, where they play California rock and serve beer on tap and lunch plates like mahimahi and shrimp ceviche, blue cheese and bacon fries and SoCal salads. For weekend brunch (9-1pm Saturday-Sunday): shrimp ranchero, French toast or 'dinosaur eggs.'

Harry's Coffee Shop   DINER $
(Map p484; 858-454-7381; http://harryscoffeeshop.com/; 7545 Girard Ave; dishes $5-13; 6am-3pm;) This classic 1960 coffee shop has a posse of regulars from blue-haired socialites to sports celebs. The food is American at its best – pancakes, tuna melts, burgers (and a local concession, breakfast burritos). Wash it down with mimosas, Greyhound cocktails, Bloody Marys or beer, and soak up the special aura of the place.

★ George's at the Cove   CALIFORNIAN $$$
(Map p484; 858-454-4244; www.georgesatthecove.com; 1250 Prospect St; mains $16-46; 11am-10pm Sun-Thu, to 11pm Fri & Sat) The Euro-Cal cooking is as dramatic as the oceanfront location, thanks to the bottomless imagination of chef Trey Foshee. George's has graced just about every list of top restaurants in California, and indeed the USA. Four venues allow you to enjoy it at different price points: Ocean Terrace, George's

California Modern and the no-reservations Level 2 and Modern Bar.

🍷 Drinking & Nightlife

Pannikin   CAFE
(Map p484; 🗹 858-454-5453; https://pannikincoffeeandtea.com/; 7467 Girard Ave; drinks from $2; ☺ 6am-6pm; 🛜) A few blocks from the water, this clapboard shack of a cafe with a generous balcony is popular for its organic coffees, Italian espresso and Mexican chocolate. Like all the Pannikins, it's a North County institution. Also sells sandwiches, pastries and salads.

☆ Entertainment

Comedy Store   COMEDY
(Map p484; 🗹 858-454-9176; http://lajolla.thecomedystore.com; 916 Pearl St; ☺ show times vary) One of the area's most established comedy venues, the Comedy Store also serves popcorn, drinks and barrels of laughs. Expect a cover charge (from $10 on weekdays and $20 on weekends, with a two-drink minimum), and some of tomorrow's big names. Look out for free open-mike nights.

La Jolla Playhouse   THEATER
(Map p462; 🗹 858-550-1010; www.lajollaplayhouse.org; 2910 La Jolla Village Dr; tickets $20-75) Inside the Mandell Weiss Center for the Performing Arts, this theater has sent dozens of productions to Broadway, including *Jersey Boys*, *Peter and the Starcatcher* and 2010 Tony winner *Memphis*.

🛍 Shopping

La Jolla's skirt-and-sweater crowd pays retail for cashmere sweaters and expensive tchotchkes downtown: paintings, sculpture and decorative items. Small boutiques fill the gaps between Talbot's, Banana Republic, Ralph Lauren and Jos. A. Bank.

    DG Wills (Map p484; 🗹 858-456-1800; www.dgwillsbooks.com; 7461 Girard Ave; ☺ 10am-7pm Mon-Sat, 11am-5pm Sun) and **Warwick's** (Map p484; 🗹 858-454-0347; www.warwicks.com; 7812 Girard Ave; ☺ 9am-6pm Mon-Sat, 10am-5.30pm Sun) have good book selections and host readings and author events.

ℹ Getting There & Away

Bus number 30 connects La Jolla with Bird Rock, Pacific Beach, Mission Bay Park and the **Old Town Transit Center** (p482). There's a bus stop at Silverado St and Herschel St in La Jolla. The full journey takes around 45 minutes and costs $2.25 one way.

By car, via I-5 from Downtown San Diego, take the La Jolla Pkwy exit and head west toward Torrey Pines Rd, from where it's a right turn onto Prospect St.

Del Mar

The ritziest of North County's seaside suburbs, with a Tudor aesthetic that somehow doesn't feel out of place, Del Mar boasts good (if pricey) restaurants, unique galleries, high-end boutiques and, north of town, the West Coast's most renowned horse-racing track, also the site of the annual county fair. Downtown Del Mar (sometimes called 'the village') extends for about a mile along Camino del Mar. At its hub, where 15th St crosses Camino del Mar, the tastefully designed **Del Mar Plaza** (Map p490; 🗹 858-847-2284; http://delmarplaza.com; 1555 Camino Del Mar) shopping center has restaurants, boutiques and upper-level terraces that look out to sea.

⊙ Sights & Activities

Seagrove Park   PARK
(Map p490; Coast Blvd) At the end of 15th St, this park abuts the beach and overlooks the ocean. This little stretch of well-groomed lawn is a community hub and perfect for a picnic.

★ Los Penasquitos Canyon Trail   HIKING
(Map p490; 🗹 county ranger 858-538-8066; www.sandiego.gov/park-and-recreation/parks/osp/lospenasquitos; entry via Park Village Rd & Celome Way; ☺ sunrise-sunset) 🆓 A 20-minute drive inland is a series of wonderful, mostly flat, shady and sunny paths snaking through a lush valley and past a cascading waterfall surrounded by volcanic rock. The main 7-mile pathway is moderately trafficked with runners, walkers and mountain bikers. Lookout for butterflies, mule deer and bobcats. Stay alert when exploring – rattlesnakes also favor these arid pathways.

California Dreamin'   BALLOONING
(🗹 800-373-3359; www.californiadreamin.com; per person from $298) Brightly colored hot-air balloons are a trademark of the skies above Del Mar, on the northern fringe of the San Diego metropolitan area. For flights, contact California Dreamin', which also serves Temecula.

🛏 Sleeping & Eating

Hotel Indigo San Diego
Del Mar   BOUTIQUE HOTEL **$$**
(Map p490; ☑ 858-755-1501, 877-846-3446; www.
hotelindigosddelmar.com; 710 Camino Del Mar; r
from $165; P⊖❇@🛜🐾🐕) This collection
of whitewashed buildings with gray clay-
tiled roofs has two outdoor heated pools, a
spa, and new fitness and business centers.
Rooms have hardwood floors, mosaic-tile ac-
cents and beach-inspired motifs. Some units
have kitchenettes and distant ocean views.
The hotel's **Ocean View Bar & Grill** serves
breakfast and dinner. Free parking.

L'Auberge Del Mar Resort & Spa   RESORT **$$$**
(Map p490; ☑ 858-259-1515, 800-245-9757; www.
laubergedelmar.com; 1540 Camino Del Mar; r from
$299; P❇@🛜🐾🐕) Rebuilt in the 1990s
on the grounds of the historic Hotel del Mar,
where 1920s Hollywood celebrities once frol-
icked, L'Auberge continues a tradition of European-style elegance with luxurious linens,
a spa and lovely grounds. It feels so intimate
and the service is so individual, you'd never
know there are 120 rooms. Parking is $25.

Americana   MODERN AMERICAN **$$**
(Map p490; ☑ 858-794-6838; 1454 Camino del Mar;
dishes breakfast & lunch $7-14, dinner $9-25; ⊙ 7am-
late) This quietly chichi and much-loved local
landmark serves a diverse lineup of regional
American cuisine: cheese grits to chicken
Reubens, sesame salmon on succotash or
seared duck breast with Israeli couscous, plus
artisan cocktails, all amid checkerboard lino-
leum floors, giant windows and homey wain-
scoting. Breakfast served until 3pm.

Brigantine   SEAFOOD **$$$**
(Map p490; ☑ 858-481-1166; www.brigantine.com;
3263 Camino del Mar; lunch $9-17, dinner $16-32;
⊙ 11:30am-2:30pm Mon-Sat, 5pm-8:30pm Sun-
Thur, 5pm-9pm Fri-Sat) Try San Diego–style
surf 'n' turf at this posh seafood joint. Menu
items include wok-charred ahi, classic filet
mignon, Parmesan-crusted sautéed sand
dabs, and macadamia-crusted fresh ma-
himahi. There's an oyster bar and happy
hour (all night $1 off well drinks, and $2 off
bar-menu items) on Mondays and between
4pm and 6pm Tues through Sun.

⭐ Entertainment

Del Mar Racetrack
& Fairgrounds   HORSE RACING
(Map p490; ☑ 858-792-4242; www.dmtc.com; 2260
Jimmy Durante Blvd; from $6; ⊙ race season mid-
Jul–early Sep) Del Mar's biggest draw during
summer months was founded in 1937 by a
prestigious group which included Bing Crosby. It's worth trying to brave the crowds on
opening day (tickets from $10), if nothing else
to see the amazing spectacle of ladies wearing over-the-top hats. The rest of the season,
enjoy the visual perfection of the track's lush
gardens and pink, Mediterranean-style architecture. On opening day, the racetrack runs
free double-decker shuttle buses to and from
the **Solana Beach train station** (Solana
Beach Transit Center; 105 N Cedros Ave).

ℹ Getting There & Away

The 101 bus runs between La Jolla and Oceanside, stopping at Camino Del Mar and15th St.
Route takes approximately one hour, one-way
fares $1.75.

By car, N Torrey Pines Rd from La Jolla is the
most scenic approach from the south. Heading
north, the road (S21) changes its name from Camino del Mar to Coast Hwy 101 to Old Hwy 101. If
you're in a hurry or headed out of town, the faster
I-5 parallels it to the east. Traffic can snarl everywhere during rush hour and race or fair season.

Solana Beach

Solana Beach is the next town north from Del
Mar – it's not as posh, but it has good beaches and lots of contemporary style. Don't miss
the **Cedros Design District** (Map p490; www.
shopcedros.com; Cedros Ave), four blocks on
Cedros Ave where interior designers from
all over the region come for inspiration and
merchandise from buttons to bathrooms,
paint to photographs and even garden supplies. Aside from a beautiful coastline, this
kind of shopping is a Solana highlight.

Belly Up (Map p490; ☑ 858-481-8140; www.
bellyup.com; 143 S Cedros Ave; tickets $10-45;
⊙ show times vary) is a converted warehouse
and bar that consistently books good bands
from jazz to funk, and big names from Jimmy Buffett and Aimee Mann to Merle Haggard and tribute bands. There's also a new
microbrewery (Map p490; ☑ 858-345-1144;
https://culturebrewingco.com/; 111 S Cedros Ave,
Suite 200; pints from $5; ⊙ noon-9pm Mon-Sun) a
few doors down.

ℹ Getting There & Away

The 101 bus route (running from La Jolla to
Oceanside roughly every hour) stops at Hwy 101
and Lomas Santa Fe Dr. The route takes around
one hour and costs $1.75 per single journey.

It takes roughly 25 minutes by car to reach Solana from Downtown San Diego, heading north on the I-5.

Coaster (www.gonctd.com) commuter trains run in the morning and evening between Oceanside and downtown San Diego via Solana Beach, with fares from $8 around three daily Amtrak *Surfliner* (www.amtrak.com). Trains run through Solana Beach, with fares starting from $10. Check the websites for timetables.

Cardiff-by-the-Sea

Beachy Cardiff is good for surfing and popular with a laid-back crowd. The town center has the perfunctory supermarkets and everyday shops along San Elijo Ave, about 0.25 miles from the ocean and across the railroad tracks, but the real action is the miles of restaurants, cafes and surf shops along Hwy 101.

🛏 Sleeping & Eating

The best option if you want to spend the night is the **San Elijo State Beach Campground** (Map p490; ☑760-753-5091; reservations 800-444-7275; www.parks.ca.gov; 2050 S Coast Hwy 101; summer tent/RV sites from $35/60; P🛜). Sitting right next to the beach, it has the best views in town. For dinner, head for **Las Olas** (Map p490; ☑760-942-1860; www.lasolasmex.com; 2655 S Coast Hwy 101; mains $9-19; ☺11am-9pm Mon-Thu, to 9:30pm Fri, 10am-9:30pm Sat, to 9pm Sun; 🖟), which serves fish tacos with a sea view. Lobster is served in the style of legendary Baja California lobster village Puerto Nuevo. House cocktails include pineapple and chili margaritas and drinks made with RIP (rum infused with pineapple). **Ki's Restaurant** (Map p490; ☑760-436-5236; www.kisrestaurant.com; 2591 S Coast Hwy 101; mains breakfast $6-15, lunch $9-15, dinner $6-24; ☺8am-9pm Sun-Thu, to 8:30pm Fri & Sat; P🖉) ✐ is also a solid option. Upstairs, there's a great ocean view from the sit-down restaurant and bar, where from 4:30pm daily fancier dishes like Jidori chicken or macadamia-coated mahimahi with Thai peanut sauce are served with ingredients from nearby family farms.

ℹ Getting There & Away

The easiest way to reach Cardiff is by car, as it's a short 20- to 30-minute drive from central San Diego. However, the **North County Transit District (NCTD)** (NCTD; ☑760-966-6500; www.gonctd.com) runs bus route 101, connecting UC San Diego with Torrey Pines, Del Mar, Cardiff and Encinitas. In Cardiff, it stops near **San Elijo State Beach** (Map p490; P) and the adjacent campground. There's another stop further south in Cardiff, outside Ki's Restaurant and **Cardiff State Beach** (Map p490; ☑760-753-5091; www.parks.ca.gov; ☺7am-sunset; P). It runs roughly every hour and takes an hour from start to finish. Fares cost $1.75.

Encinitas

Peaceful Encinitas has a decidedly down-to-earth surf vibe and a laid-back, beach-town main street, perfect for a relaxing day trip or weekend escape. North of central Encinitas, yet still part of the city, is **Leucadia**, a leafy stretch of N Hwy 101 with a hippie vibe of used-clothing stores and taco shops.

◉ Sights

Self-Realization Fellowship Retreat RELIGIOUS SITE
(Map p490; ☑760-436-7220; http://encinitastemple.org; 215 K St; ☺meditation garden 9am-5pm Tue-Sat, from 11am Sun, hermitage 2-4pm Sun) FREE Yogi Paramahansa Yogananda founded his center here in 1937, and the town has been a magnet for holistic healers and natural-lifestyle seekers ever since. The gold lotus domes of the hermitage – conspicuous on South Coast Hwy 101 – mark the southern end of Encinitas and the turn-out for **Swami's Beach**, a powerful reef break surfed by territorial locals. The fellowship's compact but lovely **Meditation Garden** has wonderful ocean vistas, a stream and a koi pond.

San Diego Botanic Garden GARDENS
(Map p490; ☑760-436-3036; www.sdbgarden.org; 230 Quail Gardens Dr; adult/child/senior $14/8/10; ☺9am-5pm; P🖟) This 37-acre garden has a large collection of California native plants as well as flora of different regions of the world, including Australia and Central America. There are special activities in the children's garden (10am Tuesday to Thursday); check the website for a schedule. Parking $2.

☆ Entertainment

La Paloma Theatre CINEMA
(Map p490; ☑760-436-7469; www.lapalomatheatre.com; 471 S Coast Hwy 101) Built in 1928, this landmark – and central Encinitas' main venue – shows arthouse movies nightly and *The Rocky Horror Picture Show* on Fridays at midnight, and stages occasional concerts.

SAN DIEGO ZOO SAFARI PARK

Since the early 1960s, the San Diego Zoological Society has been developing this 1800-acre, open-range **zoo** (760-747-8702; www.sdzsafaripark.org; 15500 San Pasqual Valley Rd, Escondido; 1-day adult/child $52/42, 2-visit pass to zoo and/or safari park adult/child $83.25/73.25; 8am-6pm, to 7pm late Jun–mid-Aug; P) where herds of giraffes, zebras, rhinos and other animals roam the open valley floor. For an instant safari feel, board the Africa Tram ride, which tours you around the second-largest continent in under half an hour.

Elsewhere, animals are in enclosures so naturalistic it's as if the humans are guests, and there's a petting krall and animal shows; pick up a map and schedule. Additional 'safaris,' like ziplining, a chance to observe a cheetah whizz by while chasing a mechanical rabbit, and even sleepovers (yowza!) are available with reservations and additional payment.

The park's just north of Hwy 78, 5 miles east of I-15 from the Via Rancho Parkway exit. Plan on 45 minutes transit by car from San Diego, except in rush hour when that figure can double. For bus information contact **North County Transit District** (NCTD; 760-966-6500; www.gonctd.com)..

⊨ Sleeping

Leucadia Beach Inn   MOTEL **$**
(Map p490; 760-943-7461; www.leucadiabeach-inn.org; 1322 N Coast Hwy; r $85-145; P) All the sparkling-clean rooms in this charming 1920s courtyard motel have tile floors and bright paint jobs, and many have kitchenettes. The beach is a few blocks' walk. It's across Hwy 101 from the train tracks, so light sleepers should pack earplugs.

✕ Eating

★ Fish 101   SEAFOOD **$**
(Map p490; 760-634-6221; www.fish101restaurant.com; 1468 N Coast Hwy 101; mains $10-14) In this casual grown-up fish shack, order at the counter, sidle up to a butcher-block table, sip craft beer or Mexican coke from a mason jar and tuck into albacore-tuna *poke*, clam chowder, shrimp po'boy or fish-and-chips. Simple grilling techniques allow the catch's natural flavors to show through, and healthy rice-bran oil is used for frying.

Eve   VEGAN **$**
(Map p490; 760-230-2560; www.eveencinitas.com; 575 S Coast Hwy 101; Buddha bowls $12; 8am-9pm; ✔) ✆ One part coffee shop, one part lounge and one part restaurant, this new vegan eatery serves hearty salad bowls heaped with goodness. Opt for a superfood smoothie, local kombucha or Buddha bowl. Our fave is the Legendary Hero flavor with braised kale, sprouts, beets, carrots, brown rice, hemp seed, walnuts, cranberries and tahini sauce.

★ Trattoria I Trulli   ITALIAN **$$**
(Map p490; 760-943-6800; www.trattoriaitrullisd.com; 830 S Coast Hwy 101; mains lunch $9-19, dinner $9-28; 11am-2:30pm daily, 5-9.30pm Sun-Thu, to 10pm Fri & Sat) Country-style seating indoors and great peoople-watching on the sidewalk. Just one taste of the homemade ravioli or lasagna, salmon with arugula, capers and red onion, or *pollo uno zero uno* (101; chicken stuffed with cheese, spinach and artichokes in mushroom sauce) and you'll know why this mom-and-pop Italian trattoria is always packed. Reservations are recommended.

East Village Asian Diner   FUSION **$$**
(Map p490; 760-753-8700; www.eateastvillage.com; 628 S Coast Hwy 101; mains $9-12; 11:30am-2:30pm & 5-10pm Mon-Sat, to 9pm Sun; ✔) This cool diner-decorated eatery fuses mostly Korean cooking with Western and other Asian influences (witness the 'super awesome' beef-and-kimchi burrito). Try noodle dishes (Thai peanut, beef and broccoli etc), or build your own 'monk's stone pot,' a superheated rice bowl to which you can add ingredients from pulled pork to salmon. Sauces are made in-house.

ⓘ Getting There & Away

The 101 bus, costing $1.75 for a single one-zone fare, travels between La Jolla and Oceanside, stopping at Encinitas Station roughly every 45 minutes. The entire bus route takes around one hour, depending on traffic. It takes half an hour to drive to Encinitas by car from Downtown San Diego. Roughly three Amtrak *Surfliner* trains stop at **Encinitas Station** (25 E D St) per day, with fares from around $10. The NCTD *Coaster*, with single fares from $8, also goes through here, running approximately every hour during rush-hour periods.

North County Coast

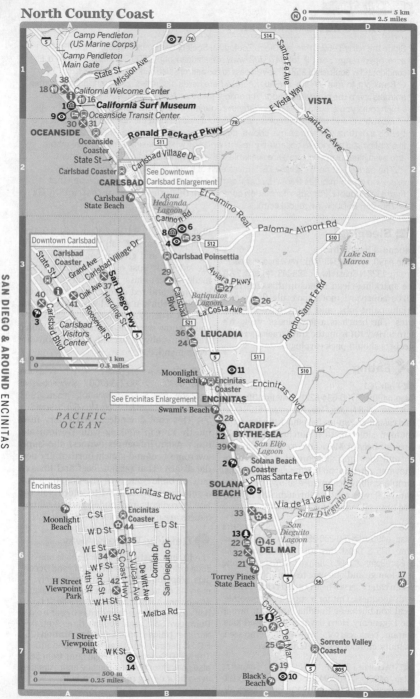

Camp Pendleton
(US Marine Corps)

Camp Pendleton
Main Gate

State St
Mission Ave

VISTA

E Vista Way

Santa Fe Ave

Santa Fe Ave

38
18
California Welcome Center
1
16
California Surf Museum
9
Oceanside Transit Center
30 31
OCEANSIDE
Oceanside
Coaster
State St
Carlsbad Coaster

Ronald Packard Pkwy

Carlsbad Village Dr

CARLSBAD

See Downtown
Carlsbad Enlargement

Carlsbad
State Beach

Agua
Hedionda
Lagoon

Cannon Rd

El Camino Real

Palomar Airport Rd

Lake San
Marcos

8 6
4 23
Carlsbad Poinsettia

29

Aviara Pkwy
27

Batiquitos
Lagoon
La Costa Ave

26

Carlsbad
Blvd

Rancho Santa Fe Rd

36
24
LEUCADIA

Moonlight
Beach
Encinitas
Coaster
ENCINITAS
Swami's Beach

11

Encinitas Blvd

28
12
**CARDIFF-
BY-THE-SEA**
39

San Elijo
Lagoon

2
Solana Beach
Coaster
5
**SOLANA
BEACH**
Lomas Santa Fe Dr

Via de la Valle

San Dieguito River

33 43
13
22 45
DEL MAR
32
21

San
Dieguito
Lagoon

Torrey Pines
State Beach

17

15
20
25
Sorrento Valley
Coaster

Camino Del Mar

19 10
Black's
Beach

Downtown Carlsbad

Carlsbad
Coaster
State St
Grand Ave
Carlsbad Village Dr
40 37
Oak Ave
41
Roosevelt St
Harding St
San Diego Fwy
3
Carlsbad
Visitors
Center
Carlsbad Blvd

1 km
0.5 miles

Encinitas

Encinitas Blvd

Moonlight
Beach
C St
Encinitas
Coaster
W D St 44
E D St
35
W E St
34
W F St 42
S Coast Hwy
S Vulcan Ave
De Witt Ave
Cornish Dr
San Dieguito Dr
4th St
3rd St
H Street
Viewpoint
Park
W H St
W I St
Melba Rd

I Street
Viewpoint
Park
W K St
14

500 m
0.25 miles

**PACIFIC
OCEAN**

7 76

S14

Santa Fe Ave

78

S11

S12

S10

S21

S11

S10

S9

S56

5

805

56

North County Coast

SAN DIEGO & AROUND CARLSBAD

Carlsbad

Most visitors come to Carlsbad for Legoland and head right back out, and that's too bad because they've missed the charming, intimate Carlsbad Village with shopping, dining and beaching nearby. It's bordered by I-5 and Carlsbad Blvd, which run north–south and are connected by Carlsbad Village Dr running east–west.

Carlsbad came into being with the railroad in the 1880s. John Frazier, an early homesteader, sank a well and found water that had a high mineral content, supposedly identical to that of spa water in Karlsbad, Bohemia (now in the Czech Republic). He built a grand Queen Anne–style spa hotel, which prospered until the 1930s and is now a local landmark.

If you've come looking for the Carlsbad Caverns, you're outta luck. Those are in New Mexico.

◉ Sights

Legoland California Resort   AMUSEMENT PARK
(Map p490; ☏760-918-5346; www.legoland.com/california; 1 Legoland Dr; adult/child 3-12yr from $95/89; ⊙hours vary, at least 10am-5pm year-round; ℗ ⊕) A fantasy environment built largely of those little colored plastic blocks from Denmark. Many rides and attractions are targeted to elementary schoolers: a junior 'driving school' a jungle cruise lined with Lego animals, wacky 'sky cruiser' pedal cars on a track, and fairy-tale-, princess-, pirate-, adventurer- and dino-themed escapades. If you have budding scientists (age 10 and over) with you, sign them up on arrival at the park for an appointment for **Mindstorms**, where they can make computerized Lego robots. There are also lots of low-thrill activities like face-painting and princess-meeting.

Carlsbad Coast   BEACH
(Map p490; ℗) Carlsbad's long, sandy beaches are great for walking and searching for seashells. Good access is from Carlsbad Blvd,

two blocks south of Carlsbad Village Dr, where there's a boardwalk, restrooms and free parking.

Carlsbad Ranch Flower Fields GARDENS
(Map p490; ☑ 760-431-0352; www.theflowerfields. com; 5704 Paseo del Norte; adult/child 3-10yr $14/7; ⊙ usually 9am-6pm Mar–mid-May; P ♿) The 50-acre flower fields of Carlsbad Ranch are ablaze in a sea of the carmine, saffron and snow-white blossoms of giant tecolote ranunculus. Take the Palomar Airport Rd exit off of I-5, head east and turn left on Paseo del Norte. It takes roughly 30 minutes from Downtown San Diego.

Museum of Making Music MUSEUM
(Map p490; www.museumofmakingmusic.org; 5790 Armada Dr; adult/child under 3 yr/student $10/ free/7; ⊙ 10am-5pm Tue-Sun) Historical exhibits and listening stations of 450 instruments from the 1890s to the present, from manufacturing to the distribution of popular music.

🛏 Sleeping
If you're looking for a budget stay in Carlsbad, there's camping on the beach. Those in search of luxury have come to the right place: Carlsbad is home to fancy golf resorts and spa stays.

Legoland Hotel HOTEL $$$
(Map p490; ☑ 877-534-6526, 760-918-5346; www. legoland.com/california; 5885 The Crossings Dr; r from $328; P ♨ ❄ @ ❀ ✿) Lego designers were let loose on this hotel, just outside Legoland's main gate. Thousands of Lego models (dragons to surfers) populate the property, and the elevator turns into a disco between floors. Each floor has its own theme (pirate, adventure, kingdom), down to the rooms' wallpaper, props, even the shower curtains.

South Carlsbad State Park Campground CAMPGROUND $
(Map p490; ☑ 760-438-3143, reservations 800-444-7275; www.reserveamerica.com; 7201 Carlsbad Blvd; ocean-/streetside tent & RV sites $50/35, ocean/inland tent & RV sites with hookups $75/60; P) Three miles south of town and sandwiched between Carlsbad Blvd and the beach, this campground has more than 200 tent and RV sites; all spaces accommodate both tents and RVs.

🍴 Eating & Drinking
State St (just north of Carlsbad Village Dr) is Carlsbad's most charming stretch, with a number of restaurants worth browsing.

For a luxury experience, also check out the restaurants at **Omni La Costa Resort & Spa** (Map p490; ☑ 800-854-5000, 760-438-9111; www.lacosta.com; 2100 Costa Del Mar Rd; r from $322; P @ ❀ ✿ 🐾) ✈ and **Park Hyatt Aviara Resort** (Map p490; ☑ 760-603-6800; www.parkhyattaviara.com; 7100 Aviara Resort Dr; r from $349; P @ ❀ ✿ 🐾). At the other end of the scale are the brewpub Pizza Port, and the local branch of Mexican **Las Olas** (Map p490; ☑ 760-434-5850; www.lasolasmex. com; 2939 Carlsbad Blvd; ⊙ 11am-9pm Mon-Thu, to 9:30pm Fri, 10am-9:30pm Sat, to 9pm Sun).

French Bakery Cafe BAKERY, CAFE $
(Map p490; ☑ 760-729-2241; www.carlsbadfrench-pastrycafe.com/; 1005 Carlsbad Village Dr; mains $6; ⊙ 7am-7pm Mon-Sat, 7.30am-5pm Sun; 🐾) Its location may be in a drab-looking shopping center just off I-5, but it's the real deal for croissants and brioches (baked daily) and kick-start espresso, plus omelets, salads and sandwiches.

Pizza Port PIZZA $$
(Map p490; ☑ 760-720-7007; www.pizzaport. com; 571 Carlsbad Village Dr; pizzas $7-24; ⊙ 11am-10pm Mon-Thu, to midnight Fri & Sat, 10am-11pm Sun; ♿) Rockin' and raucous local brewpub chain with surf art, rock music and 'anti-wimpy' pizzas to go with the signature Sharkbite Red Ale. Multiple locations.

ℹ Information
Carlsbad Visitors Center (Map p490; ☑ 760-434-6093; www.visitcarlsbad.com; 400 Carlsbad Village Dr; ⊙ 10am-5pm Mon-Fri, to 4pm Sat, to 3pm Sun.) Housed in the original 1887 Santa Fe train depot.

ℹ Getting There & Away
The 101 bus route runs between La Jolla's Westfield UTC shopping center and Oceanside, stopping at Carlsbad Village Station en route. Fares are $1.75 one way; the full bus journey takes roughly one hour.

Coaster and *Pacific Surfliner* trains run from Downtown's Santa Fe Depot (p481) along the breadth of the coastline, stopping at **Carlsbad Village Station** (☑ 800-872-7245; 2775 State St). *Coasters* (www.gonctd.com) run nearly every hour in the morning and evenings and start from $8 for a single one-zone journey; *Surfliner* (https://tickets.amtrak.com) trains run roughly three times a day, with fares from $10.

TEMECULA WINE REGION

Temecula has become a popular short-break destination for its Old West Americana main street, nearly two dozen wineries and California's largest casino, Pechanga.

Temecula means 'Place of the Sun' in the language of the native Luiseño people, who were present when Father Fermín Lasuén became the first Spanish missionary to visit in 1797. In the 1820s the area became a ranching outpost for the Mission San Luis Rey, in present-day Oceanside. Later, Temecula became a stop on the Butterfield stagecoach line (1858–61) and the California Southern railroad.

But it's Temecula's late 20th-century growth that's been most astonishing, from 2700 people in 1970 – the city didn't get its first traffic light until 1984 – to some 106,700 residents today. Between Old Town and the wineries is an off-putting, 3-mile buffer zone of suburban housing developments and shopping centers. Ignore that and you'll do fine.

Sample plenty of creative wines in the Temecula area, including the almond champagne at **Wilson Creek** (www.wilsoncreekwinery.com; 35960 Rancho California Rd; tasting $20; ☉10am-5pm; P). Get a designated driver to ferry you around the vineyards during the afternoon (many tasting rooms close at 5pm) or book on a tasting tour with **Grapeline Temecula** (☑888-894-6379; www.gogrape.com; shuttle service/tours from $69/89).

Of an evening, artisan restaurant and bar **Crush & Brew** (☑951-693-4567; www.crushnbrew.com; 28544 Old Town Front St, Suite 103; ☉11:30am-10pm Sun-Thu, to midnight Fri & Sat) serves hand-crafted cocktails, or line-dancing dive the **Temecula Stampede** (☑951-695-1761; www.thetemeculastampede.com; 28721 Old Town Front Street; $5-10 cover Fri & Sat; ☉Mon, Fri & Sat 6pm-2am, Thu 8pm-2am) is open for a late-night drink.

Many Temecula-area wineries offer entertainment, from guitar soloists to chamber concerts. Check at the **visitors center** (☑888-363-2852, 951-491-6085; www.visittemeculavalley.com; 28690 Mercedes St; ☉9am-5pm Mon-Sat) or **Visit Temecula Valley** (www.visittemeculavalley.com) for upcoming events. If you fancy a bit of line dancing or mechanical bull-riding, try the **Temecula Stampede** (p493).

Temecula is just off the I-15 freeway, which begins in San Diego. Either of the Rancho California Rd or Rte 79 exits will take you to Old Town Front St. Allow 60 minutes from San Diego, 70 from Anaheim, 80 from Palm Springs or 90 from LA.

Greyhound (☑800-231-2222, 951-676-9768; www.greyhound.com; 28464 Old Town Front St) routes head to central San Diego twice daily (from $11 one way, when purchased in advance online). Journeys take roughly one hour and thirty minutes with no traffic.

Oceanside

The largest North County town, Oceanside is home to many who work at giant Camp Pendleton Marine Base just to the north. The huge military presence mixes with an attractive natural setting, surf shops, head (marijuana) shops and a downtown that's slowly revitalizing.

Little remains from the 1880s streetscape, when the new Santa Fe coastal railway came through Oceanside, but a few buildings designed by Irving Gill and Julia Morgan still stand. The Welcome Center (p494) has a pamphlet describing a self-guided history walk.

◉ Sights & Activities

★ **California Surf Museum**　MUSEUM
(Map p490; ☑760-721-6876; www.surfmuseum.org; 312 Pier View Way; adult/child/student $5/ free/3, first Tue of month free; ☉10am-4pm Fri-Wed, to 8pm Thu; ♿) It's easy to spend an hour in this heartfelt museum of surf artifacts, from a timeline of surfing history to surf-themed art and a radical collection of boards, including the one chomped by a shark when it ate the arm of surfer Bethany Hamilton. Special exhibits change frequently along different themes (eg Women of Surfing and Surfers of the Vietnam War).

Mission San Luis
Rey de Francia　HISTORIC SITE
(Map p490; ☑760-757-3651; www.sanluisrey.org; 4050 Mission Ave; adult/child 5yr & under/youth 6-18yr/senior $7/free/3/5; ☉9:30am-5pm) About 4.5 miles inland from central Oceanside, this was the largest California mission and the most successful in recruiting Native American converts. At one point some 3000 neophytes lived and worked here. After the Mexican government secularized the missions, San Luis

fell into ruin; the adobe walls of the church, from 1811, are the only original parts left. Inside are displays on work and life in the mission, with some original religious art and artifacts.

Oceanside Pier
PIER

(Map p490) This wooden pier extends more than 1900ft out to sea. Bait-and-tackle shops rent poles to the many anglers who line its wooden fences (per hour/day $5/15). Two major surf competitions – the West Coast Pro-Am and the National Scholastic Surf Association (NSSA) – take place near the pier each June.

Surfcamps USA
SURFING

(Map p490; ☑760-889-8984; www.surfcampsusa. com; 1202 N Pacific St; lessons per person from $55; ⊞) Newbies and not-so newbies can take two-hour private or group lessons from this popular operator. All equipment is included.

Asylum Surf
SURFING

(Map p490; ☑760-722-7101; www.asylumboard-shop.com; 310 Mission Ave; surfboards 3hr/day $15/25, wetsuits $10/15) Surfers can rent equipment here.

🛏 Sleeping & Eating

Good rates can be found on rooms in Oceanside, where accommodation mainly consists of chain hotels and motels. The Springhill Suites by Marriott is a favorite: right next to the beach, in the center of the action and with dreamy views of the Pacific Ocean.

★ Springhill Suites Oceanside Downtown
HOTEL $$

(Map p490; ☑760-722-1003; www.shsoceanside. com; 110 N Myers St; r $149-379; 🅿⊖@🛜🏊) This modern, six-story, ocean-view hotel is awash in summery yellows and sea blues in the lobby. Rooms have crisp lines and distressed-wood headboards, and ocean- and pier-view rooms have balconies or patios. Best views are from the pool and hot tub on the top floor, where there's also a fitness center. Hot breakfast buffet included. Parking is $26.

101 Café
DINER $

(Map p490; ☑760-722-5220; http://101cafe.net; 631 S Coast Hwy; mains $6-10; ⊗7am-7pm Mon-Thu, to 9pm Fri-Sun; 🅿⊞) This tiny, streamlined modern diner (1928) serves all-American classics from omelets and burgers to chicken-fried steak with country gravy, or steak and eggs and hash browns. Check out the local historic

photos on the wall. If you're lucky, you'll catch the owner and can quiz him about local history.

Harbor Fish & Chips
SEAFOOD $

(Map p490; ☑760-722-4977; 276 Harbor Dr S; mains $8-16; ⊗11am-7pm Mon-Thu, to 8pm Fri & Sat; 🅿⊞) There's nothin' fancy about this harborside chippie from the '60s, but when the fish is fried to a deep crackle and you eat it at a picnic table on the dock while classic pop tunes play on the radio, you'll feel pretty good. There's a large local following and taxidermied catches on the walls.

That Boy Good
BARBECUE $$

(TBG; Map p490; ☑760-433-4227; www.tbgbbq. com; 207 N Coast Hwy; mains $9-25; ⊗from 4pm Mon, from 11am Tue-Sun) This shrine to the Mississippi Delta serves belly-busting portions of fried chicken and waffles, dirty fries (piled with chili) and Cajun catfish. Wash it all down with a craft or canned beer or the BBQ Bloody Mary, topped with a rib.

Ruby's Diner
DINER $$

(Map p490; ☑760-433-7829; www.rubys.com; 1 Oceanside Pier; mains $9-14; ⊗7am-9pm Sun-Thu, to 10pm Fri & Sat; ⊞) This '50s-style diner has good burgers and milkshakes, big breakfasts and a full bar. Yes, it's a chain, but it's right at the end of the pier.

ⓘ Information

California Welcome Center (Map p490; ☑760-721-1101, 800-350-7873; www.visitoceanside. org; 928 N Coast Hwy; ⊗9am-5pm) Helpful, informative staff dispense coupons for local attractions, as well as maps and information for the San Diego area, plus help booking lodgings in Oceanside. It's just off the freeway exit.

ⓘ Getting There & Away

Local buses and trains stop at the **Oceanside Transit Center** (Map p490; 235 S Tremont St).

Coaster (www.gonctd.com) trains run almost an hour apart in the morning and evenings and fares start from $8 for a single one-zone journey. There are around three *Surfliner* (https://tickets. amtrak.com) trains a day, with fares from $10.

The 101 bus route (running from La Jolla to Oceanside) runs approximately every hour. It costs $1.75 per single, and takes roughly an hour from the start of the route to the end.

Traveling by car via I-5 from Downtown San Diego, take the La Jolla Pkwy exit, and head west toward Torrey Pines Rd, from where it's a right turn to Oceanside's Prospect St.

Palm Springs & the Deserts

Includes ➡

Best Places to Eat

➡ La Copine (p514)

➡ Workshop Kitchen
+ Bar (p506)

➡ Cheeky's (p505)

➡ Red Ocotillo (p521)

➡ Inn Dining Room (p533)

Best Places to Sleep

➡ El Morocco Inn & Spa (p503)

➡ La Casa del Zorro (p520)

➡ Rimrock Ranch
Cabins (p515)

➡ L'Horizon (p502)

➡ Sacred Sands (p514)

Why Go?

There's something undeniably artistic in the way the landscape unfolds in the California desert. Weathered volcanic peaks stand sentinel over singing sand dunes and mountains shimmering in hues from mustard yellow to vibrant pink. Hot mineral water spurts from the earth's belly to feed palm oases and soothe aching muscles in stylish spas. Tiny wildflowers push up from the hard-baked soil to celebrate springtime.

The riches of the desert soil have lured prospectors and miners, while its beauty and spirituality have tugged at the hearts of artists, visionaries and wanderers. Eccentrics, misfits and the military are drawn by its vastness and solitude. Hipsters and celebs come for the climate and retro flair, especially in unofficial desert capital, Palm Springs. Through it all threads iconic Route 66, lined with moodily rusting roadside relics. No matter what your trail, the desert will creep into your consciousness and never fully leave.

When to Go
Palm Springs

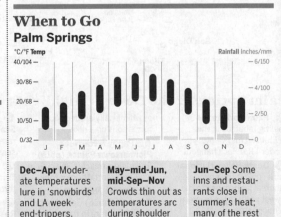

Dec–Apr Moderate temperatures lure in 'snowbirds' and LA weekend-trippers.

May–mid-Jun, mid-Sep–Nov Crowds thin out as temperatures arc during shoulder season.

Jun–Sep Some inns and restaurants close in summer's heat; many of the rest offer great deals.

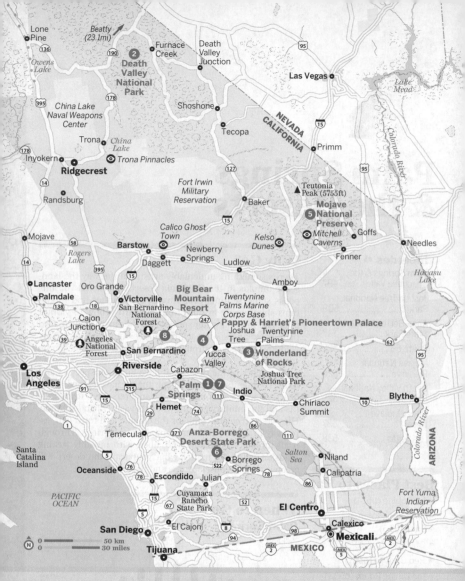

Palm Springs & the Deserts Highlights

1 Palm Springs (p497) Feeling fabulous in this revitalized mid-Century Modern Rat Pack hangout.

2 Death Valley National Park (p529) Traversing ethereal landscapes to the lowest point in the western hemisphere.

3 Wonderland of Rocks (p509) Marveling at whimsically eroded rock formations on a hike.

4 Pappy & Harriet's Pioneertown Palace (p515) Spending a rollickin' evening in a quintessential honky-tonk.

5 Mojave National Preserve (p526) Camping out under the stars in this starkly beautiful desert.

6 Anza-Borrego Desert State Park (p517) Hunting rare elephant trees and scrambling around wind caves.

7 Palm Springs Aerial Tramway (p499) Ascending through five zones in 10 minutes.

8 Big Bear Mountain Resort (p425) Schussing down the mountain in SoCal's premier ski resort.

Palm Springs & the Coachella Valley

The Rat Pack is back, baby, or at least its hangout is. In the 1950s and '60s, Palm Springs, some 100 miles east of LA, was the swinging getaway of Sinatra, Elvis and other Hollywood stars. Once the Rat Pack packed it in, though, Palm Springs surrendered to golfing retirees. However, in the mid-1990s, new generations discovered the city's retro-chic vibe and elegant mid-Century Modern structures built by famous architects. Today, retirees and snowbirds mix comfortably with hipsters, hikers and a sizeable LGBT community, on getaways from LA or from across the globe.

Palm Springs is the principal city of the Coachella Valley, a string of desert towns ranging from ho-hum Cathedral City to glamtastic Palm Desert and Coachella, home of the star-studded music festival, all linked by Hwy 111. North of Palm Springs, scruffy Desert Hot Springs draws visitors with chic boutique hotels built on top of soothing springs.

History

Cahuilla (ka-wee-ya) tribespeople have lived in the canyons on the southwest edge of the Coachella Valley for over 1000 years. Early Spanish explorers called the hot springs beneath Palm Springs *agua caliente* (hot water), which later became the name of the local Cahuilla tribe.

In 1876 the federal government carved the valley into a checkerboard of various interests. The Southern Pacific Railroad received odd-numbered sections, while the Agua Caliente were given even-numbered sections as their reservation. Casinos have made the tribes quite wealthy today.

In the town of Indio, about 20 miles southeast of Palm Springs, date palms were imported from French-held Algeria in 1890 and have become the valley's major crop, along with citrus and table grapes.

◉ Sights

Most sights are in Palm Springs proper but there are a few blue-chip destinations such as Sunnylands (p503) or the Living Desert Zoo & Gardens (p500) worth the drive down valley.

◉ Palm Springs

★ **Palm Springs Art Museum** MUSEUM
(Map p498; ✆760-322-4800; www.psmuseum.org; 101 Museum Dr, Palm Springs; adult/student $12.50/ free, all free 4-8pm Thu; ◉10am-5pm Sun-Tue & Sat, noon-9pm Thu & Fri; P) Art fans should not miss this museum which presents changing exhibitions drawn from its stellar collection of international modern and contemporary painting, sculpture, photography and glass art. The permanent collection includes works by Henry Moore, Ed Ruscha, Mark di Suvero, Frederic Remington and many more heavy hitters. Other highlights are glass art by Dale Chihuly and William Morris and a collection of pre-Columbian figurines.

Palm Springs Art Museum, Architecture & Design Center MUSEUM
(✆760-423-5260; www.psmuseum.org/architecture-design-center; 300 S Palm Canyon Dr, Palm Springs; ◉10am-5pm Sat-Tue, noon-9pm Thu & Fri) FREE
Showcasing changing exhibits drawn from the Palm Springs Art Museum's architecture and design collection, the center occupies an iconic and spiffily restored 1961 mid-Century Modern bank building by E Stewart Williams.

McCallum Adobe NOTABLE BUILDING
(Map p498; ✆760-323-8297; www.pshistoricalsociety.org; 221 S Palm Canyon Dr, Palm Springs; adult/child $1/free; ◉10am-4pm Mon & Wed-Sat, noon-3pm Sun) The town's oldest building, the 1884 McCallum Adobe, was built for John McCallum, the first permanent white settler. Today, the Palm Springs Historical Society presents changing exhibits of photos and memorabilia on the region's storied past, complemented by an engaging 24-minute video.

Agua Caliente Cultural Museum MUSEUM
(Map p498; ✆760-778-1079; www.accmuseum.org; 219 S Palm Canyon Dr, Village Green Heritage Center; ◉10am-5pm Wed-Sun Sep-May, Fri-Sun Jun-Aug) FREE This museum showcases the history and culture of the Agua Caliente band of Cahuilla people through permanent and changing exhibits and special events.

Ruddy's 1930s General Store Museum MUSEUM
(Map p498; ✆760-327-2156; www.palmsprings.com/points/heritage/ruddy.html; 221 S Palm Canyon Dr; adult/child 95¢/free; ◉10am-4pm Thu-Sun Oct-Jun, Sat & Sun Jul-Sep) This original 1930s general store shows amazingly preserved original products from groceries to

Palm Springs

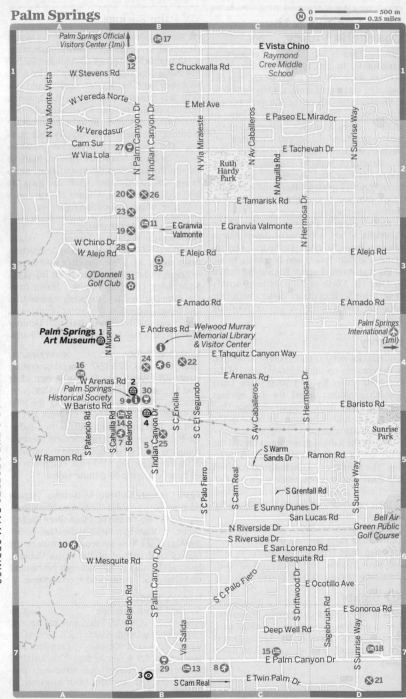

Palm Springs

medicines, beauty aids to clothing and hardware, with period showcases and signage.

Palm Springs Air Museum   MUSEUM
(Map p504; ☎760-778-6262; www.palmsprings airmuseum.org; 745 N Gene Autry Trail, Palm Springs; adult/child $16.50/9.50; ⊙10am-5pm; ℗) Adjacent to the airport, this museum has an exceptional collection of WWII aircraft and flight memorabilia, a movie theater and occasional flight demonstrations. You can even climb inside functioning Boeing B17 Flying Fortress, a bomber extensively used against German industrial and military sites during WWII.

Moorten Botanical Gardens   GARDENS
(Map p498; ☎760-327-6555; www.moortenbotanic algarden.com; 1701 S Palm Canyon Dr, Palm Springs; adult/child $5/2; ⊙10am-4pm Thu-Tue Oct-May, Fri-Sun only Jun-Sep) Chester 'Cactus Slim' Moorten, one of the original Keystone Cops, and his wife Patricia channeled their passion for plants into this compact garden founded in 1938. Today, this stroll through this enchanting symphony of cacti, succulents and other desert flora is balm for eyes and soul.

◎ Around Palm Springs

★**Palm Springs Aerial Tramway**   CABLE CAR
(Map p504; ☎760-325-1391, 888-515-8726; www. pstramway.com; 1 Tram Way, Palm Springs; adult/child $26/17, parking $5; ⊙1st tram up 10am Mon-Fri, 8am Sat & Sun, last tram down 9:45pm daily, varies seasonally; ℗👶) This rotating cable car climbs nearly 6000 vertical feet and covers five different vegetation zones, from the Sonoran desert floor to pine-scented Mt San Jacinto State Park, in 10 minutes during its 2.5-mile journey. From the mountain station (8561ft), which is 30°F to 40°F (up to 22°C) cooler than the desert floor, you can enjoy stupendous views, dine in two restaurants (ask about ride 'n' dine passes), explore over 50 miles of trails or visit the natural-history museum.

The valley station is about 3.5 miles off Hwy 111; the turnoff is about 3 miles north of downtown Palm Springs. Cars depart every 30 minutes and more frequently during peak times. Online tickets are available from six weeks to 24 hours in advance and highly recommended to avoid often horrendous wait times.

★ **Living Desert Zoo & Gardens** ZOO
(Map p504; ☑760-346-5694; www.livingdesert.
org; 47900 Portola Ave, Palm Desert; adult/child
$20/10; ⊙9am-5pm Oct-May, 8am-1:30pm Jun-
Sep; P ♠) ♪ This amazing animal park
showcases desert plants and animals alongside exhibits on regional geology and Native American culture. Highlights include a
walk-through wildlife hospital and an Afri-
can-themed village with a fair-trade market
and storytelling grove. Camel rides, giraffe
feeding, a spin on the endangered species
carousel, and a hop-on, hop-off shuttle cost
extra. It's educational, fun and worth the 15-
mile drive down-valley.

Shields Date Garden GARDENS
(Map p504; ☑760-347-7768; www.shieldsdate
garden.com; 80-225 Hwy 111, Indio; ⊙9am-5pm;
P ♠) FREE In business since 1924, this kooky
roadside attraction is where you can watch
the 15-minute documentary, *Romance and
Sex Life of the Date,* try a date shake, stock
up on plump blondes and brunettes (dates,
that is) and, incongruously, tour a garden
accented with biblical statuary.

🏃 Activities

★ **Indian Canyons** HIKING
(Map p504; ☑760-323-6018; www.indian-canyons.
com; 38520 S Palm Canyon Dr, Palm Springs; adult/
child $9/5, 90min guided hike $3/2; ⊙8am-5pm
Oct-Jun, Fri-Sun only Jul-Sep) Streams flowing
from the San Jacinto Mountains sustain
rich plant varieties in oases around Palm
Springs. Home to Native American communities for centuries, these canyons are a
hiker's delight. Follow the Palm Canyon trail

WHAT THE...?

World's Biggest Dinosaurs (☑951-
922-8700; www.cabazondinosaurs.com;
50770 Seminole Dr, Cabazon; adult/child
$10/9; ⊙10am-4:30pm Mon-Fri, 9am-
6:30pm Sat & Sun; P ♠) West of Palm
Springs, you may do a double take when
you glimpse 'Dinny the Dinosaur' and
'Mr Rex' from the I-10. Claude K Bell, a
sculptor for Knott's Berry Farm, spent
over a decade crafting these concrete
behemoths in the 1980s. Today you can
pan for dino fossils, climb inside Rex's
mouth, marvel at dozens of dinosaur
models and stock up on dino souvenirs
in the gift shop.

---

to the world's largest oasis of fan-palm trees,
the Murray Canyon trail to a seasonal waterfall or the Andreas Canyon trail to rock
formations along a year-round creek.

From downtown Palm Springs, head south
on Palm Canyon Dr (continue straight when
the main road turns east) for about 2 miles
to the reservation entrance. From here, it's 3
miles up to the trading post and ticket booth.

Tahquitz Canyon HIKING
(Map p498; ☑760-416-7044; www.tahquitzcanyon.
com; 500 W Mesquite Ave, Palm Springs; adult/child
$12.50/6; ⊙7:30am-5pm Oct-Jun, Fri-Sun only Jul-
Sep) A historic and sacred centerpiece for the
Agua Caliente people, this canyon featured
in the 1937 Frank Capra movie *Lost Horizon*.
The visitor center has natural- and cultural-
history exhibits and shows a video about the
legend of Tahquitz, a shaman of the Cahuilla
people. A 2-mile fairly steep and rocky trail
loops around to a 60ft waterfall.

Bring a picnic, water and be sure to wear
sneakers or hiking boots. Self-hiking is
available until 3:30pm. Alternatively, join a
2½-hour ranger-led hike offered four times
daily; reserve in advance.

In the 1960s the canyon was taken over by
teenage squatters and soon became a point of
contention between tribespeople, law-en-
forcement agencies and the squatters themselves. After the latter were booted out, it took
the tribe years to haul out trash, erase graffiti
and restore the site to its natural state.

Mt San Jacinto State Park HIKING
(Map p510; ☑951-659-2607; www.parks.ca.gov)
♪ FREE The wilderness beyond the Palm
Springs Aerial Tramway mountain station
is crisscrossed by 54 miles of hiking trails,
including the mile-long Discovery Trail and
a nontechnical but strenuous 11-mile round-
trip up Mt San Jacinto (10,834ft). Free day-
use wilderness permits are available at the
ranger station near the tram terminal.

Applications for overnight trips cost $5
per person and can be sent in up to eight
weeks in advance. See the website for the
form and instructions.

Wet 'n' Wild Palm Springs WATER PARK
(Map p504; ☑760-327-0499; www.wetnwildpalm
springs.com; 1500 S Gene Autry Trail, Palm Springs;
adult $40, child & senior $30; ⊙Apr–mid-Oct; ♠)
To keep cool on hot days, Wet 'n' Wild boasts
a massive wave pool, thunderous water
slides, tube rides and Flowrider surfing sim-
ulator. Some have minimum height require-

ments. Call or check the website for current opening hours. Parking costs $10.

Smoke Tree Stables HORSEBACK RIDING
(Map p504; ☑760-327-1372; www.smoketree stables.com; 2500 S Toledo Ave, Palm Springs; 1/2hr guided ride $50/120; ☉1hr rides hourly 8am-3pm, 2hr rides 9am, 11am & 1pm; ⚐) Near the Indian Canyons, this outfit offers public one-hour guided horse rides along the base of the mountains and two-hour tours into palm-lined Murray Canyon. Both are geared toward novice riders. Reservations are not needed but call to confirm departure times. Private tours are available by arrangement.

Stand By Golf GOLF
(☑760-321-2665; www.standbygolf.com; ☉7am-7pm) Golf is huge here, with more than 100 public, semiprivate, private and resort golf courses scattered around the valley. This outfit books tee times for discounted same-day or next-day play at a few dozen local courses. Golf-club rentals and online bookings available.

Winter Adventure Center SKIING, SNOWSHOEING
(☑general info 760-325-1449; www.pstramway. com/winter-adventure-center.html; snowshoe/skis rental per day $18/21; ☉open seasonally 10am-4pm Thu-Fri & Mon, from 9am Sat & Sun, last rentals 2:30pm) Outside the Palm Springs Aerial Tramway mountain station, this outfit gets you into the snowy backcountry on snowshoes and cross-country skis, available on a first-come, first-served basis.

☞ Tours

★**Desert Tasty Tours** TOURS
(☑760-870-1133; www.deserttastytours.com; tours $65; ☉11am Mon-Sat) Get the inside scoop of Palm Springs' rejuvenated dining scene on three-hour walking tours of Palm Canyon Dr. A snack is served at each of the seven stops. Also available along El Paseo in Palm Desert.

★**Palm Springs Modern Tours** TOURS
(☑760-318-6118; www.palmspringsmoderntours. com; tours $85; ☉9:30am & 1:30pm) Three-hour minivan tour of mid-Century Modern architectural jewels by such masters as Albert Frey, Richard Neutra and John Lautner. Reservations required since the group size is restricted to a maximum of six. Private tours available.

Historical Walking Tours TOURS
(Map p498; ☑760-323-8297; www.pshistorical society.org; 221 S Palm Canyon Dr, Palm Springs; tours $20) The Palm Springs Historical Soci-

ELVIS HONEYMOON HIDEAWAY

Elvis Honeymoon Hideaway (Map p504; ☑760-322-1192; www.elvishoneymoon. com; 1350 Ladera Circle, Palm Springs; per person $30; ☉tours 1pm & 3:30pm or by appointment) Elvis and Priscilla Presley had stayed at the iconic 1960 Alexander Estate in 1966 and liked it so much that Elvis carried his new bride over the threshold to begin their honeymoon on May 1, 1967. Nicknamed the 'House of Tomorrow,' it consists of three floors of four concentric circles accented with glass and stone throughout. Book ahead for a chance to walk in the footsteps of the king (and even sit on his honeymoon bed!).

ety (PSHS) runs this bouquet of seven tours lasting between one and 2½ hours and covering history, architecture, Hollywood stars and more. Check the website for the schedule and to purchase advance tickets. Tickets are also sold at the PSHS office.

Best of the Best Tours TOURS
(Map p498; ☑760-320-1365; www.thebestof thebesttours.com; 471 S Indian Canyon Dr, Palm Springs; tours $40-100) Established company offers tours of the Indian Canyons ($50), celebrity homes ($40), the windmills ($40) and a combination of all three ($100). Tickets must be bought in advance. Small discounts for children and seniors.

Desert Adventures TOURS
(☑760-340-2345; www.red-jeep.com; tours $135-200) This outfit runs Jeep tours where you get to straddle the San Andreas Fault, explore the Indian Canyons or crisscross Joshua Tree National Park.

✸ Festivals & Events

Palm Springs and the other Coachella towns have a busy schedule of events and festivals, especially in winter. Rooms usually book out during the biggest ones such as the Coachella Music & Arts Festival (p501) and the Stagecoach Festival (p502).

★**Coachella Music & Arts Festival** MUSIC
(☑855-771-3667; www.coachella.com; 81800 Ave 51, Indio; general/VIP $399/899; ☉Apr) Held at Indio's Empire Polo Club over two weekends in April, this is one of the hottest indie-music festivals of its kind featuring

major headliners and the stars of tomorrow. Get tickets early or forget about it.

Desert Trip
MUSIC

(http://deserttrip.com; ⊗ mid-Oct) Debuted in 2016 and held at the same venue as Coachella (p501), albeit in autumn, this two-weekend festival has been nicknamed 'Oldchella' for the OG rockers gigged in: the Rolling Stones, Bob Dylan, Styx, Kansas and more.

Stagecoach Festival
MUSIC

(www.stagecoachfestival.com; $329) Held at Indio's Empire Polo Club, this festival celebrates new and established country-music artists.

Palm Springs International Film Festival
FILM

(☏ 760-322-2930; www.psfilmfest.org; ⊗ early Jan) January brings a Hollywood-star-studded two-week film festival, showing more than 200 films from around the world. A short-film festival follows in June.

Modernism Week
CULTURAL

(www.modernismweek.com; ⊗ mid-Feb) Ten-day celebration of all things mid-Century Modern: architecture and home tours, films, lectures, design show and lots of parties. There are more than 250 events but tickets to some sell out quickly.

Villagefest
FOOD & DRINK

(http://villagefest.org; S Palm Canyon Dr; ⊗ 6-10pm Thu Oct-May, 7-10pm Jun-Sep) FREE Every Thursday night locals and visitors alike flock to downtown Palm Springs for this street fair with food stalls, craft vendors, music and entertainment. It runs for three blocks south of Tahquitz Canyon Way.

🛏 Sleeping

Palm Springs and the Coachella Valley offer an astonishing variety of lodging, including fine vintage-flair boutique hotels, full-on luxury resorts and chain motels. Some places don't allow children. Campers should head to Joshua Tree National Park or into the San Jacinto Mountains (via Hwy 74).

★ Arrive Hotel
BOUTIQUE HOTEL $$

(Map p498; ☏ 760-507-1650; www.arrivehotels.com; 1551 N Palm Canyon Dr, Palm Springs; studio from $179; P❄☀☎❤⛱🐾) ❤ Ecofriendly rusted steel, wood and concrete are the main design ingredients of this new adult-only lair where the bar doubles as the reception. The 32 rooms (some with patio) tick all the requisite hipster boxes such as rain shower, Apple TV and fancy bath products. The poolside restaurant, coffee shop, ice-cream parlor and craft-beer bar score high among locals.

★ L'Horizon
BOUTIQUE HOTEL $$

(Map p498; ☏ 760-323-1858; http://lhorizonpalmsprings.com; 1050 E Palm Canyon Dr, Palm Springs; r $169-249; P❄☎❤⛱🐾) The intimate William F Cody–designed retreat that saw Marilyn Monroe and Betty Grable lounging poolside has been rebooted as sleek and chic adult-on-

---

TOP THREE SPAS

Get your stressed-out self to these pampering shrines to work out the kinks and turn your body into a glowing lump of tranquility. Reservations are de rigueur.

Estrella Spa at Avalon Palm Springs (Map p498; ☏ 760-318-3000; www.avalon-hotel.com/palm-springs/estrella-spa; 415 S Belardo Rd, Palm Springs; 1hr massage $145; ⊗ 9am-6pm Sun-Thu, to 10pm Fri & Sat) A tranquil vibe permeates this stylish retreat whose menu includes such holistic treatments as the Desert Rhythms massage or the Milk Y Way manicure/pedicure that starts with a warm fresh-milk soak.

Two Bunch Palms Spa Resort (Map p504; ☏ 760-676-5000; www.twobunchpalms.com/spa; 67425 Two Bunch Palms Trail, Desert Hot Springs; day-spa package from $195; ⊗ by reservation 9am-7pm Tue-Thu, 9am-8:30pm Fri, 8am-8:30pm, 8am-7pm Sun & Mon) Tim Robbins enjoyed a mud bath at this whisper-only oasis retreat in Robert Altman's film *The Player* and so can you. Nonresort guests can book (weeks in advance, please) a day-spa package that includes one healing 60-minute treatment, lunch and a soak in the hot mineral springs of the famous 'grotto.'

Feel Good Spa (Map p498; ☏ 760-866-6188; www.acehotel.com/palmsprings/feel-good-spa; 701 E Palm Canyon Dr, Palm Springs; 1hr massage $110-135; ⊗ by appointment 9am-6pm Sun-Thu, to 8pm Fri & Sat) At the hip Ace Hotel & Swim Club, this low-key spa offers the gamut of treatments to guests and the public, including a detoxifying hot-stone massage so you feel less guilty when bellying up to the pool bar afterwards.

SUNNY LIVING AT SUNNYLANDS

Sunnylands Center & Gardens (Map p504; ☑760-202-2222; www.sunnylands.org; 37977 Bob Hope Dr, Rancho Mirage; tours $20-45, center & gardens free; ☺9am-4pm Thu-Sun, closed early Jun–mid-Sep; 🅿) Sunnylands is the mid-century modern winter retreat of Walter and Leonore Annenberg, one of America's 'first families.' It was here that they entertained seven US presidents, royalty, Hollywood celebrities and heads of state. The only way to get inside is on a guided 90-minute tour ($45) which must be booked far in advance via the website. No reservations are required to see the film and exhibits at the new visitor center, surrounded by magnificent desert gardens.

House-tour tickets are released at 9am on the 15th of the preceding month and usually sell out the same day. Two other types of tours are also available. The Open-Air Experience is a 45-minute first-come, first-served shuttle tour of the grounds and golf course ($20) that runs from September to April. With prior reservation, you can also join a bird tour ($35) offered Thursdays at 9:15am from November to April. Neither of these tours gives access to the house. See the website for the schedule and to buy tickets.

ly desert resort with 25 bungalows scattered across generous grounds for maximum privacy. Treat yourself to alfresco showers, a chemical-free swimming pool and private patio.

★ **El Morocco Inn & Spa** BOUTIQUE HOTEL **$$** (Map p504; ☑888-288-9905, 760-288-2527; http://elmoroccoinn.com; 66810 4th St, Desert Hot Springs; r $199-219; 🅿☺🌸🛜☒) Heed the call of the casbah at this drop-dead gorgeous hideaway where the scene is set for romance. Twelve exotically furnished rooms wrap around a pool deck where your enthusiastic hosts serve free 'Morocco-tinis' during happy hour. The on-site spa offers such tempting massages as 'Moroccan Rain' using an essential oil to purge the body of toxins.

Ace Hotel & Swim Club HOTEL **$$** (Map p498; ☑760-325-9900; www.acehotel.com/palmsprings; 701 E Palm Canyon Dr, Palm Springs; r $180-230, ste $300-679, $31 daily resort fee; 🅿☺🌸🛜☒☒) Palm Springs goes Hollywood – with all the sass, sans the attitude – at this former Howard Johnson motel turned hipster hangout. The 176 rooms (many with patio) sport a glorified tent-cabin look and such lifestyle essentials as big flat-screen TVs and MP3 plug-in radios. Happening pool scene, low-key spa, an on-site restaurant and bar to boot.

Orbit In BOUTIQUE HOTEL **$$** (Map p498; ☑760-323-3585, 877-966-7248; www.orbitin.com; 562 W Arenas Rd, Palm Springs; r $169-269; 🅿☺🌸🛜☒) Swing back to the '50s – pinkie raised and all – with free 'Orbitinis' during cocktail hour at this fabulously retro property, with high-end mid-Century Modern furniture (Eames, Noguchi et al) in only nine rooms set around a quiet saline pool

with Jacuzzi and fire pit. The long list of freebies includes bike rentals and poolside refreshments. Adults only.

Alcazar BOUTIQUE HOTEL **$$** (Map p498; ☑760-318-9850; www.alcazarpalmsprings.com; 622 N Palm Canyon Dr; r from $119-399; 🅿🌸@🛜☒☒) A fashionable (but not party) crowd makes new friends poolside before retiring to one of the 34 elegantly minimalist rooms around a pool. Some have Jacuzzi, patio, fireplace or all three. The daily $12 resort fee includes parking, bike rental, wi-fi and light breakfast. Must be 21 to check in. Two-night minimum on weekends.

Saguaro HOTEL **$$** (Map p498; ☑760-323-1711; www.thesaguaro.com; 1800 E Palm Canyon Dr, Palm Springs; r $129-189, ste $209-279; 🅿🌸🛜☒☒) The hot colors of a desert blooming with wildflowers animate this updated mid-Century Modern hotel (pronounced Sah-wa-ro). Three stories of rooms look over a generous pool deck. The restaurant bar does great tacos and other south-of-the-border munchies.

Riviera Palm Springs RESORT **$$** (Map p498; ☑760-327-8311; www.psriviera.com; 1600 Indian Canyon Dr, Palm Springs; r/ste from $119/175, resort fee $35; 🅿🌸@🛜☒☒) This Rat Pack playground has been given a boho-cool makeover and sparkles brighter than ever. Expect the full range of mod-cons in nearly 400 rooms amid luscious gardens; two pools, hot tubs, restaurants and bars, a luxe spa and state-of-the-art fitness center.

The $35 resort fee includes a yoga class and bike rental, among other benefits.

Coachella Valley

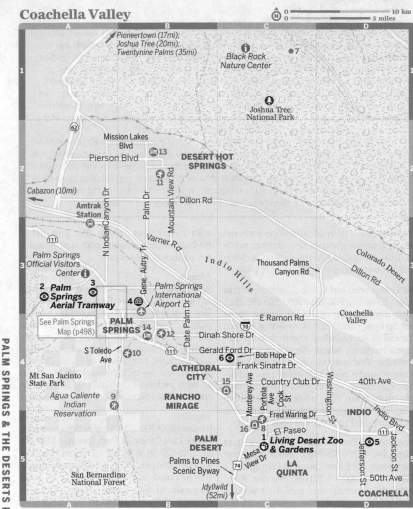

N
0 — 10 km
0 — 5 miles

Pioneertown (17mi);
Joshua Tree (20mi);
Twentynine Palms (35mi)

Black Rock
Nature Center

7

Joshua Tree
National Park

62

Mission Lakes
Blvd
Pierson Blvd
13

DESERT HOT
SPRINGS

Cabazon (10mi)
11
Dillon Rd

Amtrak
Station

Palm Dr

Mountain View Rd

111
Varner Rd

Gene. Autry. Tr

Indio Hills

Colorado Desert

Dillon Rd

Palm Springs
Official Visitors
Center
2 Palm
Springs
Aerial Tramway
3
4
Palm Springs
International
Airport

Thousand Palms
Canyon Rd

N Indian Canyon Dr

Date Palm Dr

See Palm Springs
Map (p498)

PALM
SPRINGS
14
12

Dinah Shore Dr

10
E Ramon Rd

Coachella
Valley

S Toledo
Ave
10

111

CATHEDRAL
CITY

Gerald Ford Dr
6
Bob Hope Dr
Frank Sinatra Dr

Mt San Jacinto
State Park

RANCHO
MIRAGE

15
Country Club Dr
40th Ave

Agua Caliente
Indian
Reservation
9

Monterey Ave

Portola Ave

Cook St

Washington St

INDIO

Indio Blvd

16
8
Fred Waring Dr
El Paseo

PALM
DESERT
1 Living Desert Zoo
& Gardens
5

Jefferson St

Jackson St

111

San Bernardino
National Forest
Palms to Pines
Scenic Byway

74
Mesa View Dr

LA
QUINTA
50th Ave

Idyllwild
(52mi)
COACHELLA

Coachella Valley

Del Marcos Hotel
BOUTIQUE HOTEL **$$**

(Map p498; 800-676-1214, 760-325-6902; www.delmarcoshotel.com; 225 W Baristo Rd, Palm Springs; r $200-350; P❉❆⛱☀) At this 1947 gem, designed by William F Cody, groovy lobby tunes usher you to a saltwater pool and ineffably chic mid-Century Modern rooms. The pricier ones have different bonus touches such as an Eames-style kitchen, a private redwood deck or an oversized shower.

Avalon Hotel
BOUTIQUE HOTEL **$$**

(Map p498; 760-320-4117; www.avalon-hotel.com/palm-springs; 415 S Belardo Rd, Palm Springs; r $159-259; P❉❆⛱☀) Wear a Pucci dress and blend right in at this Spanish-style minire-sort with 13 bungalows done up in sleek black-and-white Hollywood Regency style. After a day of lounging by the pool or getting pummeled in the spa, unwind on the patio or by the gas-burning fireplace. The on-site restaurant serves spirited California cuisine.

Caliente Tropics
MOTEL **$$**

(Map p498; 800-658-6034, 760-327-1391; www.calientetropics.com; 411 E Palm Canyon Dr, Palm Springs; r $99-225; P❉❆⛱☀) Elvis and the Rat Pack once frolicked poolside at this premier budget pick, a nicely spruced-up 1964 tiki-style motor lodge. Drift off to dreamland on quality mattresses in spacious rooms dressed in warm colors.

Parker Palm Springs
RESORT **$$$**

(Map p504; 760-770-5000; www.theparkerpalmsprings.com; 4200 E Palm Canyon Dr, Palm Springs; r from $295; P❋❉@❆⛱☀) This posh resort highlights whimsical decor by Jonathan Adler in public areas and rooms that include a villa once owned by Gene Autry. Stroll the lovely gardens, kick back in a hammock or try your hand at croquet and pétanque. The $30 resort charge covers parking, wi-fi and spa access.

✖ Eating

A new line-up of zeitgeist-capturing restaurants has seriously elevated the level of dining in Palm Springs. The most exciting newcomers, including several with eye-catching design, flank N Palm Canyon Dr in the Uptown design district.

★ Cheeky's
CALIFORNIAN **$**

(Map p498; 760-327-7595; www.cheekysps.com; 622 N Palm Canyon Dr, Palm Springs; mains $9-14; ⊗8am-2pm Thu-Mon, last seating 1:30pm; ❉) Waits can be long and service only so-so at this breakfast and lunch spot, but the farm-to-table menu dazzles with witty in-ventiveness. The kitchen tinkers with the menu on a weekly basis but perennial faves such as custardy scrambled eggs and grass-fed burger with pesto fries keep making appearances.

The Bloody Mary – served in a cowboy-boot-shaped glass – is an eye-opener.

Sherman's Deli & Bakery
DELI **$**

(Map p498; 760-325-1199; www.shermansdeli.com; 401 E Tahquitz Canyon Way, Palm Springs; sandwiches $8-18; ⊗7am-9pm; ♿☀) Every community with a sizeable retired contingent needs a good Jewish deli. Sherman's is it. With a breezy sidewalk patio, it pulls in an all-ages crowd with its 40 sandwich varieties (great hot pastrami!), finger-lickin' rotisserie chicken, lox and bagels and to-die-for pies. Walls are festooned with head shots of celebrity regulars. Gets megabusy on weekends.

Native Foods
VEGAN **$**

(Map p498; 760-416-0070; www.nativefoods.com; Smoke Tree Village, 1775 E Palm Canyon Dr, Palm Springs; mains $8-11; ⊗11am-9pm; ❉✦♿) From this humble mall base, Native Foods has helped pioneer America's vegan scene and now has branches all over the country. Its tempeh and seitan are made in-house and injected with complex flavors that satisfy even finicky eaters. Perennial crowd-pleasers include the 'Native nachos' with cashew cheese and the 'soul bowl' with faux chicken.

Tyler's Burgers
BURGERS **$**

(Map p498; 760-325-2990; www.tylersburgers.com; 149 S Indian Canyon Dr, Palm Springs; burgers & sandwiches $6.50-10; ⊗11am-4pm Mon-Sat; ♿) In a historic 1936 shack, owner Diana serves the same freshly ground yummy burgers on toasted buns her mom used to sell at her burger stand on the Venice Beach board-walk. Avoid the lunchtime rush or plan on catching up on your reading at the well-stocked magazine rack. Patio seating.

Trio
CALIFORNIAN **$$**

(Map p498; 760-864-8746; www.triopalmsprings.com; 707 N Palm Canyon Dr, Palm Springs; mains lunch $13-16, dinner $15-30; ⊗11am-10pm Sun-Thu, to 11pm Fri & Sat; ❆) The winning formula in this '60s modernist space: updated American comfort food (awesome Yankee pot roast!) amid eye-catching artwork and picture windows. The $19 prix-fixe three-course dinner (served until 6pm) is a steal, and the all-day daily happy hour lures a rocking after-work crowd with bar bites and cheap drinks.

Eight4Nine   AMERICAN $$

(Map p498; ☑760-325-8490; http://eight4nine.
com; 849 N Palm Canyon Dr, Palm Springs; mains
$18-38; ☺11am-3pm & 5-9pm Mon-Thu, 11am-3pm
& 5-11pm Fri, 9am-3pm & 5-11pm Sat, 9am-3pm &
5-9pm Sun; P❀ᐧ) Hot pink accents the all-
white high-ceilinged lounge and dining room
at this popular hangout in a converted post
office. Come hungry for fare that is both com-
forting and exciting with many dishes driven
by the seasons. If you're feeling just a little
peckish, sidle up to the backlit white onyx bar
and order from the $9 'happy days' menu.

King's Highway   CALIFORNIAN $$

(Map p498; ☑760-325-9900; www.acehotel.com/
palmsprings/kings-highway; 701 E Palm Canyon Dr,
Ace Hotel & Swim Club; mains $14-27; ☺7am-11pm;
P❀ᐧ) A fine case of creative recycling, this
former Denny's is now a diner for the 21st
century where the tagliatelle is handmade,
the sea bass wild-caught, the beef grass-fed,
the vegetables heirloom and the cheeses artisanal. Great breakfast, too.

Wang's in the Desert   ASIAN $$

(Map p498; ☑760-325-9264; www.wangsinthe
desert.com; 424 S Indian Canyon Dr, Palm Springs;
mains $18-28; ☺5-9pm Mon-Thu, 5-10pm Fri & Sat,
3-9pm Sun, lounge from 3pm) This mood-lit local
fave with indoor koi pond delivers creatively
crafted classics from around Asia – *tom ka
gai* to tempura shrimp and mandarin pork –
but also draws a thirsty crowd with its five-
times-weekly happy hour that gets especially
boisterous during Friday's 'boys night out.'
On weekend nights, there's live entertain-
ment in on-site **Venue Music Lounge**.

★ **Workshop Kitchen + Bar**   AMERICAN $$$

(Map p498; ☑760-459-3451; www.workshoppalm
springs.com; 800 N Palm Canyon Dr, Palm Springs;
mains $26-45; ☺5-10pm Mon-Sun, 10am-2pm Sun;
❀) Hidden away in the back of the ornate
1920s El Paseo building, a large patio with
olive trees leads to this starkly beautiful
space centered on a lofty concrete tunnel
flanked by mood-lit booths. The kitchen
crafts market-driven American classics rein-
terpreted for the 21st century and the bar is
among the most happening in town.

Copley's   AMERICAN $$$

(Map p498; ☑760-327-9555; www.copleyspalm
springs.com; 621 N Palm Canyon Dr, Palm Springs;
mains $22-40; ☺from 5:30pm daily Oct–mid-Jun,
Tue-Sun mid-Jun–Sep; P❀) After stints in the
UK, Australia and Hawaii, chef Andrew Copley
now concocts swoon-worthy American fare in

Cary Grant's former guesthouse. Go for a clas-
sic New York steak or test the chef's imagina-
tion by ordering the Muscovy duck breast with
foie-gras crème brûlée or the lavender-scented
pound cake with basil ice cream.

🍷 Drinking & Nightlife

Drinking has always been in style in Palm
Springs and many bars and restaurants have
hugely popular happy hours that sometimes
run all day. A handful of speakeasy bars have
spiced up the cocktail scene and craft beer
continues to be big as well. The big night out
for the gay crowd is Fridays.

Palm Springs Koffi North   CAFE

(Map p498; ☑760-416-2244; www.kofficoffee.
com; 515 N Palm Canyon Dr, Palm Springs; snacks &
drinks $3-6; ☺5:30am-7pm; ᐧ) Tucked among
the Uptown art galleries, this is the original
branch of this much-beloved local chain of
hip coffeehouses. The java is organic and
there are muffins, bagels and other baked
goods to feed sugar cravings.

Birba   BAR

(Map p498; ☑760-327 5678; www.birbaps.com;
622 N Palm Canyon Dr, Palm Springs; ☺5-11pm Sun
& Wed-Thu, to midnight Fri & Sat; ᐧ) On a balmy
night, Birba's hedge-fringed patio with twin-
kle lights and sunken fire pit is perfect for
unwinding with a glass of wine or smooth li-
bations like the tequila-based Heated Snake.
Get a plate of *cicchetti* (Italian bar snacks)
to stave off the blur or order modern pizza
or pasta from the full menu.

Village Pub   PUB

(Map p498; ☑760-323-3265; www.palmsprings
villagepub.com; 266 S Palm Canyon Dr, Palm
Springs; ☺11am-2am Mon-Fri, 10am-2am Sat &
Sun; ᐧ) Kick back with a cold one on the me-
andering patio, cheer on your favorite team
on the big screen or dance til the wee hours
at this all-purpose fun and charmingly divey
venue in downtown Palm Springs.

☆ Entertainment

Annenberg Theater   PERFORMING ARTS

(Map p498; ☑760-325-4490; www.psmuseum.
org; 101 Museum Dr, Palm Springs) This intimate
theater at the Palm Springs Art Museum
(p497) has great acoustics and presents an
eclectic schedule of films, lectures, theater,
ballet and music performances.

Georgie's Alibi Azul   PERFORMING ARTS

(Map p498; ☑760-325-5533; www.alibiazul.com;
369 N Palm Canyon Dr, Palm Canyon; ☺11am-11pm

SHHHH...TOP 3 SPEAKEASIES

It's been nearly a century since Prohibition spurred the proliferation of underground bars called speakeasies, but these days clandestine libation stations are making a big – voluntary – comeback. Palm Springs now fields its own contenders, including these prime picks.

Counter Reformation (Map p504; ☑760-770-5000; www.theparkerpalmsprings.com/dine/counter-reformation.php; 4200 E Palm Canyon Dr, Palm Springs; ☺3-10pm Mon, Thu & Fri, noon-10pm Sat & Sun) If you worship at the altar of Bacchus (the Roman god of wine), you'll be singing his praises in this dimly lit clandestine boite at the **Parker Palm Springs resort** (p505). The handpicked menu features just 17 reds, whites and champagne from small vineyards around the world.

Bootlegger Tiki (Map p498; ☑760-318-4154; www.bootleggertiki.com; 1101 N Palm Canyon Dr, Palm Springs; ☺4pm-2am) Crimson light bathes even pasty-faced hipsters into a healthy glow, as do the killer crafted cocktails at this teensy speakeasy with blowfish lamps and rattan walls. The entrance is via the Ernest coffee shop.

Seymour's (Map p498; ☑760-892-9000; www.facebook.com/seymourspalmsprings; 233 E Palm Canyon Dr, Palm Springs; ☺6pm-midnight Sun & Tue-Thu, to 2am Fri & Sat) In the back of the updated steakhouse Mr Lyons hides this furtive libation station named in honor of owner and entertainment lawyer Tara Lazar's dad. The eye-candy decor, mixing her old law books with exotic art, is easy fodder to kindle any conversation. So are the expertly shaken and stirred cocktails, including a mean martini.

or later; ☎) 🍴 This video bar, nightclub and cafe in an old telephone exchange regales patrons with a rainbow of daily drinks specials plus events such as Sunday Disco Brunch and charity bingo. It's above the Azul tapas bar.

🛍 Shopping

Central Palm Springs has two main shopping districts along N Palm Canyon Dr, divided by Alejo Rd. North of Alejo, Uptown is more for art-and-design-inspired shops, while Downtown (south of Alejo) is ground zero for souvenirs and casual clothing. Given the city's demographic, vintage-clothing stores flourish here like few other places. West of town are two megapopular outlet malls.

Desert Hills Premium Outlets MALL
(☑951-849-6641; www.premiumoutlets.com/outlet/desert-hills; 48400 Seminole Dr, Cabazon; ☺10am-9pm Mon-Sat, to 8pm Sun; ☎) Bargain hunters, make a beeline for dozens of outlet stores: Gap to Gucci, Polo to Prada, Off 5th to Barneys New York. Wear comfortable shoes – this mall is huge! It's off I-10 (exit at Fields Rd), 20 minutes west of Palm Springs.

Collectors Corner VINTAGE
(Map p504; ☑760-346-1012; www.facebook.com/emccollectorscorner; 71280 Hwy 111, Rancho Mirage; ☺9am-5pm Mon-Sat) It's a trek from central Palm Springs (about 12 miles), but this two-story shop is oh so worth it for its bevy of antiques, vintage clothing, jewelry and furniture. Proceeds benefit the Eisenhower Medical Center.

Angel View Resale Store THRIFT SHOP
(Map p498; ☑760-320-1733; www.angelview.org; 462 N Indian Canyon Dr, Palm Springs; ☺9am-6pm Mon-Sat, 10am-5pm Sun) At this well-established thrift store, today's hipsters can shop for clothes and accessories as cool today as when they were first worn a generation or two ago.

Proceeds benefit children and adults with a disability. There are other branches throughout the Coachella Valley – see the website for locations.

Cabazon Outlets MALL
(☑951-922-3000; www.cabazonoutlets.com; 48750 Seminole Dr, Cabazon; ☺10am-9pm) Though smaller than the adjacent Desert Hills Premium Outlets (p507), this mall still flaunts covetable brands such as Adidas, Columbia and Guess.

El Paseo Shopping District MALL
(Map p504; www.elpaseo.com; El Paseo, Palm Desert) Elegant and flower-festooned El Paseo shopping strip in Palm Desert has been dubbed the 'Rodeo Drive of the Desert.' Although it does a handful of blue-chip brands such as Escada and Gucci, most retailers are actually more in the Lululemon and Banana Republic league.

ⓘ Information

Palm Springs Official Visitor Center (☎760-778-8418, 800-347-7746; www.visitpalm springs.com; 2901 N Palm Canyon Dr, Palm Springs; ☺9am-5pm) Well-stocked and well-staffed visitor center in a 1965 Albert Frey–designed gas station at the Palm Springs Aerial Tram turnoff, 3 miles north of downtown.

Welwood Murray Memorial Library & Visitor Center (☎760-323-8296; www.visitpalm springs.com; 100 S Palm Canyon Dr, Palm Springs; ☺9am-9pm) Small downtown branch of the regional tourist office. Also houses a historical research library and free public computers in a renovated 1941 library building.

Palm Springs Historical Society (☎760-323-8297; www.pshistoricalsociety.org; 221 S Palm Canyon Dr, Palm Springs; ☺10am-4pm Mon & Wed-Sat, noon-3pm Sun) Volunteer-staffed nonprofit organization. Maintains two museums and offers guided tours focusing on local history, architecture and celebrities.

ⓘ Getting There & Away

Ask if your hotel provides free airport transfers. Otherwise, a taxi to downtown Palm Springs costs about $12 to $15, including a $2.50 airport surcharge. If you're staying in another Coachella Valley town, a ride on a shared shuttle van, such as **Sky Cap Shuttle Service** (☎760-272-5988; www.skycapshuttle.com), might work out cheaper. **SunLine** (☎800-347-8628; www.sun line.org; ticket $1, day pass $3) bus 24 stops by the airport and goes most (though, frustratingly, not all) of the way to downtown Palm Springs.

AIR

Palm Springs International Airport (☎760-318-3800; www.palmspringsairport.com; 3400 E Tahquitz Canyon Way, Palm Springs) This regional airport is served year-round by 10 airlines, including United, American, Virgin, Delta and Alaska and has flights throughout North America.

CAR & MOTORCYCLE

Palm Springs is just over 100 miles east of Los Angeles via I-10 and 140 miles northeast of San Diego via I-15 and I-10.

ⓘ Getting Around

BICYCLE

Central Palm Springs is pancake-flat, and more bike lanes are being built all the time. Many hotels have loaner bicycles.

Bike Palm Springs (Map p498; ☎760-832-8912; www.bikepsrentals.com; 194 S Indian Canyon Dr, Palm Springs; standard/kids/electric/tandem bikes half-day from $23/15/40/40, full-day $30/20/50/50; ☺9am-5pm)

Funseekers (Map p504; ☎760-340-3861; www.palmdesertbikerentals.com; 73-865 Hwy 111, Palm Desert; bicycle 24hr from $25, 3 days from $50, week from $70, delivery & pick up $30)

BUS

SunLine (p508) Alternative-fuel-powered public buses travel around the valley, albeit slowly. Bus 111 links Palm Springs with Palm Desert (one hour) and Indio (1½ hours) via Hwy 111. Buses have air-con, wheelchair lifts and a bicycle rack. Cash only (bring exact change).

Buzz Trolley (www.new.buzzps.com; ☺11am-1am Thu-Sun) This free shuttle runs more or less every 15 minutes on a loop covering N Palm Canyon Dr from Via Escuela as far as Smoketree on E Palm Canyon and then back up Indian Canyon Dr.

CAR & MOTORCYCLE

Though you can walk to most sights in downtown Palm Springs, you'll need a car to get around the valley. Travel on Hwy 111 linking the Coachella Valley towns can be extremely slow thanks to countless of traffic lights. Depending on where you're headed, it may be quicker to take I-10.

Major rental-car companies have airport desks. Also consider two-wheelers as an alternative to getting around.

Scoot Palm Springs (☎760-413-2883; www.scootpalmsprings.com; 701 East Palm Canyon Dr, Palm Springs; half-/full-day from $80/130) From its base at the Ace Hotel & Swim Club, Scoot rents Buddy scooters made by the Genuine Scooter Company for tooling around the desert roads. Rentals include helmet, one tank of gas and unlimited mileage.

Eaglerider (☎866-464-7368, 760-718-3327; www.eaglerider.com; 74855 Country Club Dr, Palm Desert; Harley per day from $119; ☺9am-5pm) At the JW Marriot Desert Spring Hotel, the valley branch of this national chain has a big fleet of Harleys, BMW and Honda motorcycles as well as touring bikes such as the Indian Chief Vintage.

Joshua Tree National Park

Taking a page from a Dr Seuss book, the whimsical Joshua trees (actually tree-sized yuccas) welcome visitors to this 794,000-acre park (Map p510; ☎760-367-5500; www.nps.gov/jotr; 7-day entry per car $25; ☺24hr; Pﾊ) ⌀ at the transition zone of two deserts: the low and dry Colorado and the higher, moister and slightly cooler Mojave.

Rock climbers know 'JT' as the best place to climb in California, hikers seek out hidden, shady, desert-fan-palm oases fed by natural springs and small streams, and mountain bikers are hypnotized by the desert vistas.

In springtime, the Joshua trees send up a huge single cream-colored flower. It was Mormon settlers who named the trees because the branches stretching up toward heaven reminded them of the Biblical prophet Joshua pointing the way to the promised land. The mystical quality of this stark, boulder-strewn landscape has inspired many artists, most famously the band U2, who named their 1987 album the *Joshua Tree*.

◉ Sights & Activities

Joshua Tree has three park entrances. Access the west entrance from the town of Joshua Tree, the north entrance from Twentynine Palms and the south entrance from I-10. The park's northern half harbors most of the attractions, including all the Joshua trees.

Oasis of Mara   OASIS
(Map p510; ☑760-367-5500; www.nps.gov/jotr; Utah Trail, Twentynine Palms; ℗) Behind the park HQ and Oasis Visitor Center, this natural oasis encompasses the original 29 palm trees that gave Twentynine Palms its name. They were planted by native Serranos who named this 'the place of little springs and much grass.' The Pinto Mountain Fault, a small branch of the San Andreas, runs through the oasis, as does a 0.5-mile, wheelchair-accessible nature trail with labeled desert plants.

★Wonderland of Rocks   NATURAL FEATURE
(☑760-367-5500; www.nps.gov/jotr; ℗) This striking rock labyrinth extends roughly from Indian Cove in the north to Park Blvd in the south and is predictably a popular rock climbers' haunt. For a quick impression, try the 0.5-mile Indian Cove Trail or the 1-mile Barker Dam Trail. The 7-mile Willow Hole Trail and the 8-mile Boy Scout Trail present more challenging treks and should not be attempted in hot weather.

Indian Cove   LANDMARK
(Map p510; ☑ 760-367-5500; www.nps.gov/jotr; ℗) Rock hounds love the hulking caramel-colored formations in this northern corner of the park, while birders are drawn by feathered friends hiding out among the yuccas and shrubs along the half-mile Indian Cove nature trail. There's a campground for tenters and RVs with potable water.

★Keys View   VIEWPOINT
(Map p510; ☑760-367-5500; www.nps.gov/jotr; Keys View Rd; ℗) From Park Blvd, it's an easy 20-minute drive up to Keys View (5185ft), where breathtaking views take in the entire Coachella Valley and extend as far as the Salton Sea. Looming in front of you are Mt San Jacinto (10,834ft) and Mt San Gorgonio (11,500ft), two of Southern California's highest peaks, while below you can spot a section of the San Andreas Fault.

Keys Ranch   HISTORIC SITE
(Map p510; ☑760-367-5500; www.nps.gov/jotr; tour adult/child $10/5; ⊙tour schedules vary; ℗♿) Old West history buffs will delight in the 90-minute ranger-led tour of this ranch named after its builder, William Keys and his family. They built a homestead here on 160 acres in 1917 and turned it into a full working ranch, school, store and workshop. The buildings stand much as they did when Keys died in 1969. Check the website's calendar page for upcoming tour dates. Tickets must be purchased on the day at the Oasis Visitor Center (p516).

Cottonwood Spring   NATURAL FEATURE
(Map p510; ☑760-367-5500; www.nps.gov/jotr; ℗) Cottonwood Spring is an oasis with a natural spring that Cahuilla tribespeople depended on for centuries. Look for *morteros* – rounded depressions in the rocks used by Native Americans for grinding seeds. Miners came searching for gold here in the late 19th century.

Hiking
Leave the car behind to appreciate Joshua Tree's trippy lunar landscapes. Staff at the visitor centers can help match your time and fitness level to the perfect trail.

Boy Scout Trail   HIKING
(Map p510; ☑760-367-5500; www.nps.gov/jotr) For an immersion into the Wonderland of Rocks (p509) embark on this 8-mile one-way trail linking Indian Cove and Park Blvd (near Quail Springs picnic area). Most people prefer to start at the latter. Arrange for pick-up at the other end or plan on camping overnight. Part of the trail is unmarked and hard to follow.

Ryan Mountain Trail   HIKING
(Map p510; ☑760-367-5500; www.nps.gov/jotr) For bird's-eye park views, tackle this popular 3-mile in-and-out hike up 5458ft-high Ryan Mountain. Be sure to pack water and stamina – although not terribly long, the 1000ft elevation gain will likely make your thighs burn.

Lost Palms Oasis Trail   HIKING
(Map p510; ☑760-367-5500; www.nps.gov/jotr; Cottonwood Spring Rd) Reach this remote canyon filled with desert-fan palms on a moderately strenuous 7.5-mile hike starting

Joshua Tree National Park

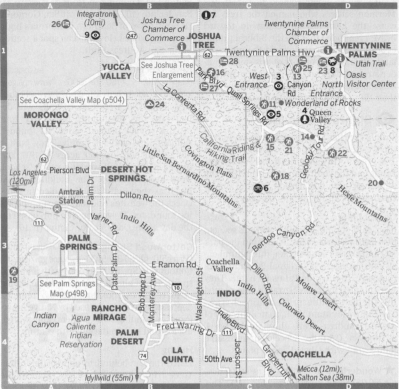

from Cottonwood Spring. There's no shade, so bring lots of water and don't head out in intense summer heat.

Hidden Valley Trail   HIKING
(Map p510; ☑760-367-5500; www.nps.gov/jotr; Park Blvd) Some 8 miles south of the West Entrance, this whimsically dramatic cluster of rocks is a bouldering mecca, but just about anyone can enjoy a clamber on the giant rocks. An easy 1-mile trail loops around and back to the parking lot and picnic area.

Skull Rock Trail   HIKING
(Map p510; ☑760-367-5500; www.nps.gov/jotr; Park Blvd) Pick up this easy 1.7-mile trail around evocatively eroded rocks – one of them shaped like a skull – at **Jumbo Rocks campground** (Map p510; ☑760-367-5500; www.nps.gov/jotr; Park Blvd; per site $15).

Fortynine Palms Oasis Trail   HIKING
(Map p510; ☑760-367-5500; www.nps.gov/jotr; Canyon Rd) Escape the crowds on this moderate 3-mile, up-and-down trail to a fan-palm oasis scenically cradled by a canyon. The trailhead is at the end of Canyon Rd that veers off 29 Palms Hwy/Hwy 62, just east of the Indian Cove turnoff.

Mastodon Peak Trail   HIKING
(Map p510; ☑760-367-5500; www.nps.gov/jotr; Cottonwood Spring) Enjoy views of the Eagle Mountains and Salton Sea from an elevation of 3371ft on this 3-mile loop past an old gold mine from Cottonwood Spring.

Lost Horse Mine Trail   HIKING
(Map p510; ☑760-367-5500; www.nps.gov/jotr; Keys View Rd) A moderately strenuous in-and-out 4-mile climb that visits the remains of an authentic Old West silver and gold mine, in operation until 1931.

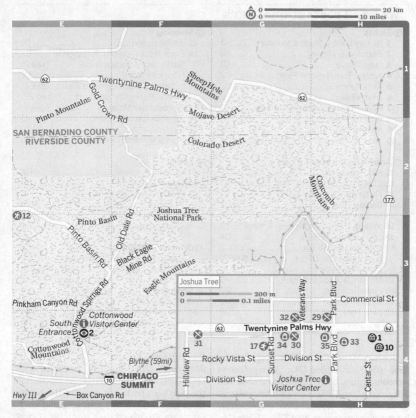

Cholla Cactus Garden Trail   HIKING
(Map p510; ☏760-367-5500; www.nps.gov/jotr;
Pinto Basin Rd) This quarter-mile loop leads
through a dense grove of 'teddy bear' cholla cactus and ocotillo plants just west of the
main north–south road in the heart of the
park. Wear sturdy shoes to guard against
cactus spines.

Cycling

Bikes are only allowed on public paved and
dirt roads that are also open to vehicles,
including 29 miles of backcountry. They
are not permitted on hiking trails. Popular routes include challenging **Pinkham
Canyon Rd**, starting from the Cottonwood
visitor center, and the long-distance **Black
Eagle Mine Rd**, which starts 6.5 miles further north. **Queen Valley** has a gentler set
of trails with bike racks found along the
way, so people can lock up their bikes and
go hiking, but it's busy with cars, as is the

bumpy, sandy and steep Geology Tour Rd
(p512). There's also a wide-open network of
dirt roads at Covington Flats (p512).

Rock Climbing

JT's rocks are famous for their rough,
high-friction surfaces; from boulders to
cracks to multipitch faces, there are more
than 8000 established routes. Some of the
most popular climbs are in the Hidden Valley area.

Shops catering to climbers with quality
gear, advice and tours include **Joshua Tree
Outfitters** (Map p510; ☏760-366-1848; www.josh
uatreeoutfitters.com; 61707 29 Palms Hwy/Hwy 62,
Joshua Tree; ⊙9am-5pm Thu-Tue), **Nomad Ventures** (Map p510; ☏760-366-4684; www.nomad
ventures.com; 61795 29 Palms Hwy/Hwy 62, Joshua
Tree; ⊙8am-6pm Mon-Thu, to 8pm Fri-Sun Oct-Apr,
9am-7pm daily May-Sep) and **Coyote Corner**
(Map p510; ☏760-366-9683; www.jtcoyotecorner.
com; 6535 Park Blvd, Joshua Tree; ⊙9am-6pm).

Joshua Tree National Park

◉ Sights

⊕ Activities, Courses & Tours

⊜ Sleeping

⊗ Eating

⊕ Drinking & Nightlife

⊛ Shopping

Joshua Tree Rock Climbing School (Map p510; ☑760-366-4745; www.joshuatree rockclimbing.com; 63439 Doggie Trail, Joshua Tree; 1-day course from $195), **Vertical Adventures** (☑949-854-6250, 800-514-8785; www.vertica ladventures.com; courses from $155; ☉Sep-May) and **Joshua Tree Uprising** (Map p510; ☑888-254-6266; www.joshuatreeuprising.com; 61693 29 Palms Hwy/Hwy 62, Joshua Tree; 4/6/8hr-course from $90/100/120; ☉8am-5pm) offer guided climbs and climbing instruction starting at $120 for a one-day introduction.

☞ Tours

Geology Tour Rd
DRIVING TOUR

(Map p510; ☑760-367-5500; www.nps.gov/jotr) On this 18-mile backcountry drive around Pleasant Valley, the forces of erosion, earthquakes and ancient volcanoes have played out in stunning splendor. There are 16 markers along the route – pick up a self-guided interpretive brochure and an update on road conditions at any park visitor center.

Passenger cars can usually handle the first 5 miles, but beyond Squaw Tank (marker 9) a 4WD is necessary. Pick up the road on Park Blvd about 2 miles west of Jumbo Rock campground.

Covington Flats
DRIVING TOUR

(Map p504; ☑760-367-5500; www.nps.gov/jotr; La Contenta Rd) Joshua trees grow throughout the northern park, but some of the biggest trees are found in this area accessed via La Contenta Rd, which runs south off Hwy 62 between Yucca Valley and Joshua Tree. For photogenic views, follow the dirt road 3.8 miles up Eureka Peak (5516ft) from the picnic area.

Pinto Basin Rd
DRIVING TOUR

(Map p510; ☑760-367-5500; www.nps.gov/jotr) To see the natural transition from the high Mojave Desert to the low Colorado Desert, wind down to Cottonwood Spring, a 30-mile drive from Hidden Valley passing by the Cholla Cactus Garden en route.

⊨ Sleeping

Unless you're day-tripping from Palm Springs, set up camp inside the park or base yourself in the desert communities linked by 29 Palms Hwy/Hwy 62 along the park's northern perimeter. Twentynine Palms and Yucca Valley have mostly national chain motels, while pads in Joshua Tree have plenty of charm and character.

Harmony Motel MOTEL $
(Map p510; 760-367-3351, 760-401-1309; www.
harmonymotel.com; 71161 29 Palms Hwy/Hwy 62,
Twentynine Palms; r $65-85; ⓟ☺❄🔊🏊) This
well-kept 1950s motel, run by the charming
Ash, was where U2 stayed while working on
the *Joshua Tree* album. It has a small pool
and seven large, cheerfully painted rooms
(some with kitchenette) set around a tidy
desert garden with serenely dramatic views.
A light breakfast is served in the communal
guest kitchen.

★ **Kate's Lazy Desert** INN $$
(845-688-7200; www.lazymeadow.com; 58380
Botkin Rd, Landers; Airstream $175 Mon-Thu, $200
Fri & Sat; ⓟ☺❄🔊🏊) Owned by Kate Pier-
son of the B-52s, this desert camp has a coin-
sized pool (May to October) and half a dozen
Airstream trailers to sleep inside. Sporting
names such as 'Tinkerbell,' 'Planet Air' and '
Hot Lava,' each is kitted out with matching
fantasia-pop design and a double bed and
kitchenette.

Spin & Margie's Desert Hide-a-Way INN $$
(Map p510; 760-366-9124, 760-774-0850; www.
deserthideaway.com; 64491 29 Palm Hwy/Hwy
62; d $145-185; ⓟ☺❄🔊) This handsome
hacienda-style inn is perfect for restoring
calm after a long day on the road. The five
boldly colored suites are an eccentric symphony of corrugated tin, old license plates
and cartoon art. Each has its own kitchen
and flat-screen TV with DVD and CD player.
Knowledgeable, gregarious owners ensure a
relaxed visit.

Hicksville Trailer Palace MOTEL $$
(310-584-1086; www.hicksville.com; Joshua Tree;
trailer $75-225; ⓟ❄🔊🏊) Fancy sleeping
among glowing wig heads, in an Airstream
or a horse stall? Then check into one of nine
wackily decorated vintage trailers (and one
cabin) set around a saltwater pool (March
to November). All but three share facilities.
There's also a tipi with fire pit and a hot tub.
Directions provided after making reserva-
tions (to keep out looky-loos).

TOP 4 OFFBEAT ATTRACTIONS NEAR JT

The California desert is full of bizarre roadside attractions and hidden surprises, but the
area north of JT seems to harbor a disproportionate share, including these kooky gems.

Noah Purifoy Desert Art Museum (Map p510; www.noahpurifoy.com; 63030 Blair Lane,
Joshua Tree; ☺dawn-dusk; ⓟ) The 'Junk Dada' sculptures and installations of African
American artist Noah Purifoy (1917–2004) are collected by the world's finest museums,
but some of his coolest works can be seen for free at his former outdoor desert studio
north of Joshua Tree. Toilets, tires, monitors, bicycles and beds are among the eclectic
castoffs he turned variously into political statements, social criticism or just plain non-
sense. Pick up a pamphlet for a self-guided tour.

Integratron (760-364-3126; www.integratron.com; 2477 Belfield Blvd, Landers; sound baths
weekdays/weekends $30/35; ☺Wed-Mon; ⓟ) It may look just like a white-domed structure,
but in reality it's an electrostatic generator for time travel and cell rejuvenation. Yup! At
least that's what its creator, former aerospace engineer George Van Tassel believed when
building the place in the 1950s after receiving telepathic instructions from extraterrestri-
als. Today, you can pick up on the esoteric vibes during a 60-minute 'sound bath' in the
wooden dome whose special design and location on a geomagnetic vortex generate an
extra-strong magnetic field.

Beauty Bubble Salon & Museum (Map p510; 760-366-9000; www.facebook.com/
beautybubblesalonandmuseum; 61855 29 Palms Hwy/Hwy 62, Joshua Tree; museum free;
☺10am-6pm Tue-Thu & Sat; ⓟ) Jeff Hafler loves hair and everything to do with it, which is
why his *Steel Magnolias*–type home salon brims with related vintage beauty parapher-
nalia he's collected for about a quarter century. Have him do your tresses up in a beehive
while surrounded by perm machines, curlers and wigs, some over 100 years old.

World-Famous Crochet Museum (Map p510; www.sharielf.com/museum.html; 61855
29 Palms Hwy/Hwy 62, Joshua Tree; ☺24hr) An old lime-green photo booth is the home of
Bunny, Buddy and hundreds of their crocheted friends collected by Shari Elf. The artist,
singer, fashion designer, raw-food chef and life coach has not mastered the art of cro-
cheting herself.

CAMPING IN JT

Of the park's eight campgrounds, only **Cottonwood** (Map p510; ☑760-367-5500; www. nps.gov/jotr; Pinto Basin Rd; per site $20) and **Black Rock** (Map p510; ☑760-367-5500, reservations 877-444-6777; www.nps.gov/jotr; Joshua Lane; per site $20; P) have potable water, flush toilets and dump stations. **Indian Cove** (Map p510; ☑760-367-5500, reservations 877-444-6777; www.nps.gov/jotr; Indian Cove Rd; per site $20) and Black Rock accept reservations from October through May. The others are first-come, first-served and have pit toilets, picnic tables and fire grates. None have showers, but there are some at Coyote Corner (p511) in Joshua Tree. Details are available at www.nps.gov/jotr or 760-367-5500.

Between October and May, campsites fill by Thursday noon, especially during the springtime bloom. If you arrive too late, there's overflow camping on Bureau of Land Management (BLM) land north and south of the park as well as in private campgrounds. For details, download http://go.nps.gov/jtnpoverflow.

Backcountry camping is allowed 1 mile from any road or 500ft from any trailhead. There is no water in the park, so bring one to two gallons per person per day for drinking, cooking and personal hygiene. Campfires are prohibited to prevent wildfires and damage to the fragile desert floor. Free self-registration is required at a backcountry board inside the park, where you can also leave your car. For full details, download the official backcountry camping guide at http://go.nps.gov/jtnpbackcountry.

29 Palms Inn   INN $$
(Map p510; ☑760-367-3505; www.29palmsinn. com; 73950 Inn Ave, Twentynine Palms; r $170-260; P❄@🔊🐾🏊) 🍴 History oozes from every nook and cranny in this old-timey inn on the ancient Oasis of Mara (p509). Choose from air-conditioned 1934 adobe bungalows, outfitted with fireplace and patio, 1950s wood-frame cabins with private deck, or two-bedroom guesthouses with kitchen. Rates include breakfast and weekend walking tours around the oasis.

★ **Sacred Sands**   B&B $$$
(Map p510; ☑760-424-6407; www.sacredsands. com; 63155 Quail Springs Rd, Joshua Tree; north/west r $329/359, 2-night minimum; P❄❉🔊) 🍴 In an isolated, pin-drop-quiet spot, these two desert-chic suites are the ultimate romantic retreat, each with a private outdoor shower, hot tub, sundeck, 2ft-thick earthen straw-bale walls and sleeping terrace under the stars. There are astounding views across the desert hills and into the National Park. Owners Scott and Steve are gracious hosts and killer breakfast cooks.

It's 4 miles south of 29 Palms Hwy (via Park Bl), 1 mile west of the park entrance.

✗ Eating

There's no food available inside the park, but the communities along Hwy 62 have big supermarkets convenient for stocking up on supplies (especially Yucca Valley). Restaurants range from mom-and-pop-run greasy spoons to organic delis, funky diners to ethnic eats. On Saturday mornings, locals gather for gossip and groceries at the **farmers market** (Map p510; ☑760-420-7529; www.joshuatree farmersmarket.com; 61705 29 Palms Hwy/Hwy 62, Joshua Tree; ⊙8am-1pm Sat; P) in Joshua Tree.

★ **La Copine**   AMERICAN $
(www.lacopinekitchen.com; 848 Old Woman Rd, Flamingo Heights; mains $10-16; ⊙9am-3pm Thu-Sun; P❉) It's a long road from Philadelphia to the high desert, but that's where Nikki and Claire decided to take their farm-to-table brunch cuisine from pop-up to brick and mortar. Their roadside bistro serves zeitgeist-capturing dishes such as the signature salad with smoked salmon and poached egg, homemade crumpets and gold milk turmeric tea. Expect a wait on weekends.

Country Kitchen   AMERICAN $
(Map p510; ☑760-366-8988; 61768 29 Palms Hwy/Hwy 62, Joshua Tree; mains $4-10; ⊙6:30am-3pm Wed-Mon; P❉) Now run by Sarah and Dennis, this been-here-forever roadside shack gets a big thumbs up for its scrumptious home cookin'. Lines can be extra-long for breakfast on weekends, but the killer pancakes, breakfast burrito with homemade salsa and egg dishes are worth the wait. Also serves lunch.

Pie for the People   PIZZA $
(Map p510; ☑760-366-0400; www.pieforthepeople. com; 61740 29 Palms Hwy/Hwy 62, Joshua Tree; pizza $8-26; ⊙11am-9pm Sun-Thu, to 10pm Fri & Sat; ❉) This neighborhood-adored lair is in the

business of thin-crust pizzas ranging from classics to creatives like the David Bowie: white pizza with mozzarella, Guinness-caramelized onions, jalapeños, pineapple, bacon and sweet plum sauce.

Crossroads Cafe AMERICAN $
(Map p510; ☎760-366-5414; www.crossroadscafejtree.com; 61715 29 Palms Hwy/Hwy 62, Joshua Tree; mains $6-12; ⏲7am-9pm Mon-Sat, to 8pm Sun; P📶) This JT institution is the go-to place for carb-loaded breakfast, dragged-through-the-garden salad and fresh sandwiches that make both omnivores (burgers, Reuben sandwich) and vegans ('Fake Philly' with seitan) happy.

Restaurant at 29 Palms Inn AMERICAN $$$
(Map p510; ☎760-367-3505; www.29spalmsinn.com; 73950 Inn Ave, Twentynine Palms; mains lunch $8-14, dinner $16-44; ⏲11am-2pm Mon-Sat, 9am-2pm Sun, 5-9pm Sun-Thu, 5pm-9:30pm Fri & Sat; 📶) This well-respected restaurant has its own organic garden and does burgers and salads at lunchtime, and grilled meats and toothsome pastas for dinner. No reservations.

Drinking & Nightlife

Joshua Tree has a couple of artsy watering holes, often with live music featuring local and regional talent, although the most atmospheric place to steer toward after dark is Pappy & Harriet's (p515) in Pioneertown. Bars in Twentynine Palms cater mostly to marines.

Shopping

Vintage and antiques lovers should head to the cluster of well-curated shops around the Pioneertown Rd turnoff on Hwy 62. Otherwise, Yucca Valley has mostly national chain supermarkets and big box stores along Hwy 62. Joshua Tree plays up its artistic pedigree with quirky shops and galleries in the blocks flanking Park Blvd, the main road into Joshua Tree National Park.

Information

MEDICAL SERVICES

Hi-Desert Medical Center (☎760-366-3711; www.hdmc.org; 6601 White Feather Rd, Joshua Tree; ⏲24hr) The main hospital in the Morongo Basin with 24-hour emergency care.

TELEPHONE

Cell-phone reception is extremely spotty inside the park – don't count on it! There are emergency phones at the ranger station in Indian Cove and at the Intersection Rock parking area near Hidden Valley Campground.

TURN BACK THE CLOCK AT PIONEERTOWN

Turn north off Hwy 62 onto Pioneertown Rd in Yucca Valley and drive 5 miles straight into the past. Looking like an 1870s frontier town, **Pioneertown** (Map p510; www.pioneertown.com; P👪) FREE was actually built in 1946 as a Hollywood Western movie set. Gene Autry and Roy Rogers were among the original investors and more than 50 movies and several TV shows were filmed here in the 1940s and '50s. These days, it's fun to stroll around the old buildings and drop into the local honky-tonk for refreshments. Mock gunfights take place on 'Mane St' at 2:30pm every second and fourth Saturday, April to October.

For local color, toothsome BBQ, cheap beer and kick-ass live music, drop in at **Pappy & Harriet's Pioneertown Palace** (Map p510; ☎760-365-5956; www.pappyandharriets.com; 53688 Pioneertown Rd, Pioneertown; mains $6-15; ⏲11am-2am Thu-Sun, from 5pm Mon), a textbook honky-tonk. Monday's open-mike nights (admission free) are legendary and often bring out astounding talent. From Thursday to Saturday, local and national talent takes over the stage.

Within staggering distance is the atmospheric **Pioneertown Motel** (Map p510; ☎760-365-7001; www.pioneertown-motel.com; 5040 Curtis Rd, Pioneertown; r from $155; P❄📶🐾), where yesteryear's silver-screen stars once slept during filming and whose rooms are now filled with eccentric Western-themed memorabilia; some have kitchenettes.

Some movie stars also stayed in the knotty-pine huts reimagined as **Rimrock Ranch Cabins** (Map p510; ☎760-228-1297; www.rimrockranchcabins.com; 50857 Burns Canyon Rd, Pioneertown; cabins $120-220, 2-day minimum on weekends; P⊖❄🐾), a soulful desert hideaway 4.5 miles north of Pioneertown. All have Old West decor, kitchen facilities, DVD player and private patio. For extra kookiness, book into the Airstream trailer; for stylish comfort book the Hatch House bungalow.

SALTON SEA: THE DISAPPEARING LAKE

Driving along Hwy 111 southeast of Indio, you'll come across a most unexpected sight: the Salton Sea – California's largest lake in the middle of its largest desert. As you can quickly tell by the postapocalyptic mood hanging over the place, it's a troubled spot with a fascinating past, complicated present and uncertain future.

The Salton Sea is very much an 'accidental sea,' created in 1905 when high spring flooding breached irrigation canals built to bring water from the Colorado River to the farmland in the Imperial Valley. The water rushed uncontrollably into the nearest low spot – the Salton Sink – for 18 months until 1500 workers and 500,000 tons of rock managed to put a halt to the flooding. With no natural outlet, the water was here to stay: the Salton Sea – about 35 miles long and 15 miles wide – was born.

By midcentury the desert lake was stocked with fish and marketed as the 'California Riviera;' vacation homes lined its shores. The fish, in turn, attracted birds, and the sea became a prime bird-watching spot. To this day, it provides habitat for around 400 species of migratory and endangered species such as snow geese, eared grebes, ruddy ducks, white and brown pelicans, bald eagles and peregrine falcons. It is one of the most important stopovers along the Pacific Flyway.

But their survival is threatened by rising salinity from decades of phosphor and nitrogen in agricultural runoff. With hardly any rainfall and little freshwater inflow, it has increased to 56 grams per liter (versus 35 grams in the Pacific Ocean), making it impossible for most fish species to survive, tilapia being an exception. Fewer fish, in turn, make the area less attractive for birds.

Efforts to rescue the Salton Sea go back to 2003 when the California State Legislature passed the Salton Sea Restoration Act but has since failed to earmark funds for it. It did manage to talk the Imperial Irrigation District into selling some of its Colorado River water to the San Diego district in order to dilute the agricultural runoff and replenish the sea with freshwater.

Since the agreement expires in late 2017, lawmakers are scrambling to prevent an imminent ecological disaster. In March 2017, the California Natural Resources Agency unveiled a 10-year plan to restore the area and control toxic dust storms resulting from shrinking water levels by building a series of ponds and water-transfer systems. The state legislature earmarked $80.5 million for the rescue effort. It remains to be seen if it's just a drop in the bucket.

TOURIST INFORMATION

Entry permits ($25 per vehicle) are valid for seven days and come with a map and the seasonally updated *Joshua Tree Guide*.

Joshua Tree Visitor Center (www.nps.gov/jotr; 6554 Park Blvd, Joshua Tree; ⊙8am-5pm; 🛜🚻) The busiest visitor center has exhibits, books and souvenirs and is just south of 29 Palms Hwy (Hwy 62) on the northern perimeter.

Oasis Visitor Center (www.nps.gov/jotr; 74485 National Park Dr, Twentynine Palms; ⊙8:30am-5pm; 🚻) The easternmost visitor center is attached to the park HQ.

Black Rock Nature Center (www.nps.gov/jotr; 9800 Black Rock Canyon Rd, Yucca Valley; ⊙8am-4pm Sat-Thu, to 8pm Fri Oct-May; 🚻) The westernmost visitor center is located at **Black Rock Canyon Campground** (p514).

Cottonwood Visitor Center (www.nps.gov/jotr; Cottonwood Springs; ⊙8:30am-4pm; 🚻) The southern visitor center is 8 miles north of I-10.

Joshua Tree Chamber of Commerce (📋760-366-3723; www.joshuatreechamber.org; 6448 Hallee Rd, Suite 10, Joshua Tree; ⊙9am-noon Wed-Sat) Info about hotels, restaurants and shops in the town of Joshua Tree, just north of Hwy 62.

Twentynine Palms Chamber of Commerce (📋760-367-6197; www.visit29.org; 73484 29 Palms Hwy/Hwy 62, Twentynine Palms; ⊙10am-4pm Mon-Fri, 9am-2pm Sat & Sun; 🛜) Visitor center with gallery, gift shop, books, free wi-fi and electric-car charging station.

ⓘ Getting There & Around

Joshua Tree National Park is flanked by I-10 in the south and Hwy 62 (Twentynine Palms Hwy) in the north. The park is about 140 miles east of LA via I-10 and 29 Palms Hwy (Hwy 62) and 175 miles from San Diego via I-15 and I-10. From Palm Springs it takes about an hour to reach the park's west (preferable) or south entrances.

Bus 1, operated by **Morongo Basin Transit Authority** (☎760-366-2395; www.mbtabus.com), runs hourly between 6am and 10pm along 29 Palms Hwy (Hwy 62), linking Yucca Valley and Joshua Tree with the Marine Base in Twentynine Palms. Single tickets cost $2.50, a day pass is $3.75. Cash only, exact fare required. Buses are equipped with bike racks.

Anza-Borrego Desert State Park

Shaped by an ancient sea and tectonic forces, enormous and little-developed Anza-Borrego (Map p518; ☎760-767-4205; www.parks.ca.gov; parking visitor center $5, day use in developed campgrounds $10; P ⊞) ⚡FREE covers 640,000 acres, making it the largest state park in California. Human history here goes back more than 10,000 years, as recorded by Native American pictographs and petroglyphs. The park is named for Spanish explorer Juan Bautista de Anza, who arrived in 1774, pioneering a colonial trail from Mexico and no doubt running into countless *borregos,* the wild bighorn sheep that once ranged as far south as Baja California. (Today only a few hundred of these animals survive due to drought, disease, poaching and off-highway driving.) In the 1850s Anza-Borrego became a stop along the Butterfield Stagecoach line, which delivered mail between St Louis and San Francisco.

◉ Sights & Activities

Anza-Borrego's commercial hub, Borrego Springs (population 3429), has restaurants, lodgings, stores, ATMs and gas stations. Nearby are the park visitor center and easy-to-reach sights, such as Borrego Palm Canyon and Fonts Point, that are fairly representative of the park as a whole. The Split Mountain area, east of Ocotillo Wells, is popular with off-highway vehicles (OHVs), but also contains interesting geology and spectacular wind caves. The desert's southernmost region is the least visited and, aside from Blair Valley, has few developed trails and facilities.

Many of the trailheads are accessible only by dirt roads. To find out which roads require high-clearance or 4WD vehicles, or are currently impassable, check with the park visitor center (p521).

Fonts Point VIEWPOINT
(Map p518; ☎760-767-4205; www.parks.ca.gov; Anza-Borrego Desert State Park, off Rte S22) FREE East of Borrego Springs, a 4-mile dirt road, sometimes passable without 4WD, diverges south from County Rte S22 out to Fonts Point (1249ft). From up here a spectacular panorama unfolds over the Borrego Valley to the west and the Borrego Badlands to the south.

Vallecito County Park HISTORIC SITE
(Map p518; ☎760-765-1188; www.sdparks.org; 37349 Great South Stage Rte 1849/County Rte S2, Julian; per car $3; ◷9.30am-5pm Mon-Fri, to sunset on weekends Sep-May; P) This pretty little park in a refreshing valley on the southern edge of Anza-Borrego Desert State Park centers on a replica of a historic **Butterfield Stage Station.** Its 44 primitive campsites are a handy staging ground for desert explorations.

It's 36 miles south of Borrego Springs via County Rte S2.

Agua Caliente Regional Park SWIMMING
(Map p518; ☎760-765-1188; www.sdparks.org; 39555 Great Southern Overland Stage Route of 1849/County

EASY HIKES IN ANZA-BORREGO

Kenyon Overlook (Map p518; ☎760-767-4205; www.parks.ca.gov; Yaqui Pass Rd/County Rte S3, Anza-Borrego Desert State Park) An easy 1-mile trail loops from the parking lot up to this viewpoint over the Vallecito Mountain and the Mescal Bajada. Views are at their golden-hued best at sunrise and sunset.

Yaqui Well Trail (Map p518; ☎760-767-4205; www.parks.ca.gov; Yaqui Pass Rd/County Rte S3, Anza-Borrego Desert State Park) A 1.7-mile round-trip, this easy trail passes creosote, cactus, mesquite and a natural water hole that attracts a rich variety of birds. Starts opposite Tamarisk Grove Campground.

Cactus Loop Trail (Map p518; ☎760-767-4205; www.parks.ca.gov; Yaqui Pass Rd/County Rte S3, Anza-Borrego Desert State Park; ◷dawn-dusk) Short but rocky and with a steep climb built into it, this 1-mile interpretive loop takes you past a great variety of cacti while delivering sweeping views of San Felipe Wash. Wear sturdy shoes. Starts across from Tamarisk Grove Campground.

Anza-Borrego State Park

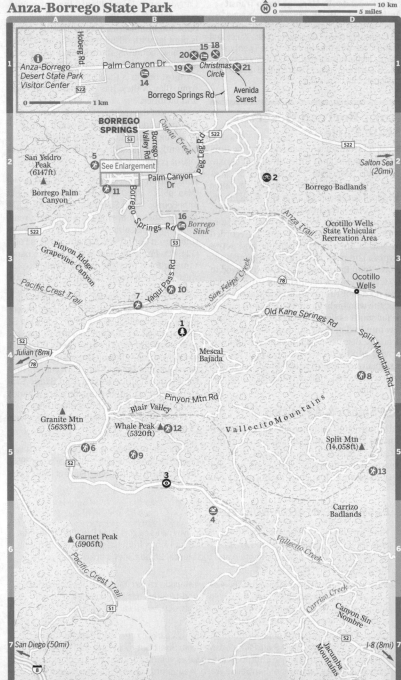

N

0 ——— 10 km
0 ——— 5 miles

Anza-Borrego Desert State Park Visitor Center

Hoberg Rd

Palm Canyon Dr

S22

20 ✕
15 ✕ 18 ✕
19 ✕   *Christmas Circle* 21 ✕
14

Borrego Springs Rd

Avenida Surest

0 ——— 1 km

BORREGO SPRINGS

S3

Borrego Valley Rd

Coyote Creek

Borrego Springs Rd

S22

San Ysidro Peak (6147ft) ▲

5 🚶
See Enlargement

11 🚶

Palm Canyon Dr

2 ✕

Salton Sea (20mi)

Borrego Badlands

Borrego Palm Canyon

S22

Pinyon Ridge Grapevine Canyon

Borrego Springs Rd

16
Borrego Sink

S3

Yaqui Pass Rd

Anza Trail

Ocotillo Wells State Vehicular Recreation Area

Pacific Crest Trail

7 🚶
10

San Felipe Creek

78

Ocotillo Wells

Old Kane Springs Rd

Split Mountain Rd

S2

Julian (8mi)
78

1

Mescal Bajada

Granite Mtn (5633ft) ▲

Blair Valley

Pinyon Mtn Rd

Vallecito Mountains

8 🚶

Whale Peak (5320ft) ▲ 12 🚶

6 🚶

S2

9

3 ◎

Split Mtn (14,058ft) ▲

13 🚶

Carrizo Badlands

Garnet Peak (5905ft) ▲

4

Pacific Crest Trail

Vallecito Creek

S1

7 *San Diego (50mi)*
8

Carrizo Creek

Canyon Sin Nombre

S2

I-8 (8mi)

Jacumba Mountains

Anza-Borrego State Park

Rte S2; per car $3; ⏰9:30am-5pm Mon-Fri, to sunset weekends Sep-May) In a lovely camping park on the southern edge of Anza-Borrego Desert State Park you can take a dip in two outdoor and one indoor pool fed by hot natural mineral springs. The indoor spa is heated to 102 degrees, outfitted with therapeutic Jacuzzi jets and open only to those 14 years or older.

Hiking

Borrego Palm Canyon Trail HIKING
(Map p518; ☎760-767 4205; www.parks.ca.gov; 200 Palm Canyon Dr, Borrego Springs; day-use parking $10; ⏰dawn-dusk) FREE This popular 3-mile loop trail starts at the top of Borrego Palm Canyon Campground, 1 mile north of the visitor center, and goes past a grove of shaggy fan palms and little waterfalls, a delightful oasis in the dry, rocky desertscape. Birds love it here and even the elusive bighorn sheep might come down for a drink.

Box Canyon HIKING
(Map p518; ☎760-767-4205; www.parks.ca.gov; off County Rte S2) FREE A short hike takes you down into a narrow canyon where, in 1847, the Mormon Battalion (a unit of the US Army) used only hand tools to hack a wagon road through the rocks to widen the Southern Emigrant Trail, one of the most important routes for pioneer settlers to California. Past the canyon, the trail continues to a dry waterfall.

Elephant Tree Trail HIKING
(Map p518; ☎760-767-4205; www.parks.ca.gov; Split Mountain Rd, Anza-Borrego Desert State Park) FREE The rare elephant trees get their name from their stubby trunks, thought to resemble elephant legs. Unfortunately only

one living elephant tree remains along this 1-mile loop trail but it's still a nice, easy hike through a rocky wash. You'll need a high-clearance 4WD to get to the trailhead.

The turnoff is on Split Mountain Rd, about 6 miles south of Hwy 78 and Ocotillo Wells.

Pictograph/Smuggler's Canyon Trail HIKING
(Map p518; ☎760-767-4205; www.parks.ca.gov; Blair Valley, off County Rte S2, Anza-Borrego Desert State Park) FREE In Blair Valley, this 3-mile round-trip trail skirts boulders covered in Native American pictographs and ends at a dry waterfall and a nice view of the Vallecito Valley. Take the Blair Valley turnoff on County Rte S2 and continue on the dirt road for about 3.6 miles.

Wind Caves Trail HIKING
(Map p518; ☎760-767-4205; www.parks.ca.gov; off Split Mountain Rd, Anza-Borrego Desert State Park) FREE This steep 1-mile in-and-out trail leads up to delicate wind caves carved into sandstone outcrops. Pick it up by taking Split Mountain Rd to the dirt-road turnoff for Fish Creek and following the wash for 4 miles.

Maidenhair Falls Trail HIKING
(Map p518; ☎760-767-4205; www.parks.ca.gov; Montezuma Valley Rd, Anza-Borrego Desert State Park) FREE This plucky 6-mile round-trip trail starts from the Hellhole Canyon Trailhead, 2 miles west of the Borrego Springs visitor center on County Rte S22 and climbs for 3 miles past several palm oases to a seasonal waterfall that supports birdlife and a variety of plants. Wear sturdy shoes as some rock scrambling is required.

PALM SPRINGS & THE DESERTS ANZA-BORREGO DESERTSTATE PARK

SALVATION MOUNTAIN

Salvation Mountain (☏760-624-8754; www.salvationmountaininc.org; 603 E Beal Rd, Niland; donations accepted; ☺dawn-dusk; P) Salvation Mountain is a mighty strange sight indeed: a 100ft-high hill of hand-mixed adobe and straw slathered in paint and decorated with flowers, waterfalls, birds and religious messages. This work of Leonard Knight (1931–2014), a passionately religious man from Vermont, was 28 years in the making. It has become one of the great works of American folk art and has even been recognized as a national treasure in the US Senate.

You'll find it in Niland, about 3 miles off Hwy 111, via Main St/Beal Rd and past train tracks and trailer parks.

Ghost Mountain Trail HIKING
(Map p518; ☏760-767-4205; www.parks.ca.gov; Blair Valley, off County Rte S2, Anza-Borrego Desert State Park) FREE A steep 2-mile round-trip trail climbs to the sparse remains of the 1930s adobe homestead built by desert recluse Marshall South and his family. The trailhead is in the southern section of Blair Valley, at the end of a 3-mile dirt road off County Rte S2.

🛏 Sleeping

A handful of motels and hotels cluster in and around Borrego Springs, but not all are open year-round. Otherwise, camping is the only mode to spend the night in the park. Besides developed campgrounds, free backcountry camping is permitted anywhere. Note that all campfires must be in metal containers and that gathering vegetation (dead or alive) is strictly prohibited.

Vallecito County Park
Campground CAMPGROUND $
(Map p518; ☏reservations 858-565-3600; www.sdparks.org; 37349 Great South Stage Route 1849/County Rte S2; tent & RV sites $22; ☺Sep-May; P) This rustic campground has 44 tent and nonhookup RV sites in a cool, green-valley refuge set around a replica of the Butterfield Stage Station. Sites come with tables, fire rings and barbecue pits. The closest supply store is at the Agua Caliente County Park, about 4 miles southeast.

Agua Caliente County Park
Campground CAMPGROUND $
(Map p518; ☏reservations 858-565-3600; www.sdparks.org; 39555 Great Southern Overland Stage Route of 1849/County Rte S2; tent sites $24, RV sites with partial/full hookups $29/33, cabins $70; ☺Sep-May; P) On the southern edge of Anza-Borrego Desert State Park, this campground comes with the added bonus of natural hot-spring pools and easy access to hiking trails. It offers the gamut of camping options, including seven new glamper-friendly cabins with air-con and private bathrooms.

Borrego Palm Canyon
Campground CAMPGROUND $
(Map p518; ☏800-444-7275; www.reserveamerica.com; 200 Palm Canyon Dr, Borrego Springs; tent/RV sites $25/35; P☺) Near the Anza-Borrego Desert State Park visitor center (p521), this campground has award-winning toilets, campsites that are close together and an amphitheater with ranger programs.

Hacienda del Sol COTTAGES $
(Map p518; ☏760-767-5442; www.haciendadelsolborrego.com; 610 Palm Canyon Dr, Borrego Springs; r/duplex/cottages $85/145/175; P☺❄☎☀) Bask in the retro glow of this indie hotel where you can choose from cottages with fireplace and kitchen, spacious duplexes perfect for families or no-frills motel rooms. The pool is great for chilling or socializing.

Palms Hotel BOUTIQUE HOTEL $$
(Map p518; ☏760-767-7788; www.thepalmsatindianhead.com; 2200 Hoberg Rd, Borrego Springs; r $149-249; P❄☀) This former haunt of Cary Grant, Marilyn Monroe and other old-time celebs has been reborn as a chic mid-Century Modern retreat. Connect with the era over martinis and filet mignon at the on-site steakhouse while enjoying mesmerizing desert views. Rooms are comfortable but uncluttered, with most facing the pool.

★La Casa del Zorro RESORT $$$
(Map p518; ☏760-767-0100; www.lacasadelzorro.com; 3845 Yaqui Pass Rd; r $224-350; P❄☎☀☀) After a top-to-bottom facelift, this venerable 1937 resort is again the region's grandest stay. The ambience exudes desert romance in 67 elegantly rustic poolside rooms and family-sized casitas sporting vaulted ceilings and marble bathtubs. A staggering 28 pools and Jacuzzi are scattered across the 42 landscaped acres, and there's a spa, five tennis courts, fun bar and gourmet restaurant.

Borrego Valley Inn   INN $$$

(Map p518; ☎760-767-0311; www.highwaywestva cations.com; 405 Palm Canyon Dr, Borrego Springs; r $243-330; ⓟ☻✳☂☃) At this rustically elegant inn, you can wrap your days tucked into rooms filled with Southwestern knickknacks and Native American weavings or into a rocking chair on your private patio. Oversized rooms orbit a courtyard filled with desert plants; some have kitchenette. Between October and May, rates include breakfast and there's a two-night minimum on weekends.

✖ Eating

Borrego Springs has a few restaurants but don't expect any culinary flights of fancy. The best supermarket is **Center Market** (Map p518; ☎760-767-3311; www.centermarket-borrego.com; 590 Palm Canyon Dr, Borrego Springs; ☺7am-8pm; ⓟ) in Borrego Springs. In summer many places keep shorter hours or have closing days.

Carmelita's Bar & Grill   MEXICAN $

(Map p518; ☎760-767-5666; kfdorado@gmail.com; 575 Palm Canyon Dr, Mall; mains $5.50-18; ☺10am-9pm; ⓟ☃) This lively joint with its cheerful decor serves the best Mexican food in town, including delicious huevos rancheros. The bar staff knows how to whip up a good margarita.

★ Red Ocotillo   BREAKFAST $$

(Map p518; ☎760-767-7400; www.facebook.com/pg/redocotillo; 721 Avenida Sureste; mains $10-20; ☺7am-8:30pm; ☂☃☃) Empty tables are as rare as puddles in Anza-Borrego State Park at this charmer that serves quality java, all-day breakfast (try the smoked-salmon eggs Benedict) and bulging burgers and sandwiches, all at a quality standard you'd not expect out in the desert.

Carlee's   AMERICAN $$

(Map p518; ☎760-767-3262; www.carleesplace.com; 660 Palm Canyon Dr, Borrego Springs; mains lunch $7-14, dinner $13-27; ☺11am-9pm, bar to 10pm Sun-Thu, midnight Fri & Sat; ⓟ) The menu is as long as a Tolstoy novel but the choices are good-old-fashioned Americana, hopscotching from burgers to pizza, steak to ribs, salads to pasta. It's popular with locals and visitors alike, not in the least for its full bar, pool table and live music on Saturdays.

❶ Information

Anza-Borrego Desert State Park Visitor Center (☎760-767-4205; www.parks.ca.gov; 200 Palm Canyon Dr, Borrego Springs; ☺9am-5pm daily mid-Oct–mid-May, Sat, Sun & holidays only mid-May–mid-Oct) Built partly underground, the stone walls of the park visitor center blend beautifully with the mountain backdrop, while inside are top-notch displays and audiovisual presentations. It's surrounded by a desert garden with a pupfish pond. The center is 1.5 miles west of central Borrego Springs.

❶ Getting There & Away

There is no public transport to Anza-Borrego Desert State Park. From Palm Springs it's 86 miles to Borrego Springs; take I-10 to Indio, then Hwy 86 south along the Salton Sea and west on to County Rte S22. From LA (150 miles) and Orange County (130 miles), take I-15 south to Hwy 79 to County Rtes S2 and S22. From San Diego (90 miles), I-8 to County Rte S2 is easiest, but if you want a more scenic ride, take twisty Hwy 79 from I-8 north through Cuyamaca Rancho State Park and into Julian, then head east on Hwy 78.

Around Anza-Borrego

Julian

The mountain hamlet of Julian, with its three-block main street, is a favorite getaway for city folk who love its quaint 1870s streetscape, gold-mining lore and famous apple pies. Prospectors, including many Confederate veterans, arrived here after the Civil War, but the population did not explode until the discovery of flecks of gold in 1869. Today, apples are the new gold with thousands of trees in the orchards flanking Hwy 178 outside town. Make sure you taste a slice of delicious apple pie, sold at bakeries all over town.

◉ Sights

Eagle Mining Co   HISTORIC SITE

(☎760-765-0036; www.theeaglemining.com; 2320 C St; adult/child $10/5; ☺10am-4pm Mon-Fri, to 5pm Sat & Sun; ⓟ☃) Pan for gold and be regaled with tales of the hardscrabble life of the town's early pioneers during an hourlong underground tour through the former Eagle and High Peak gold mines.

🛏 Sleeping & Eating

Julian Gold Rush Hotel   B&B $$

(☎760-765-0201; www.julianhotel.com; 2032 Main St; d $95-185; ⓟ☻✳☂) At this 1897 antique-filled B&B, lace curtains, claw-foot tubs and other paraphernalia painstakingly evoke a bygone era. Rates include two-course breakfast and afternoon tea in the historic parlor, once visited by James Joyce.

Julian Pie Company BAKERY $
($ 760-765-2449; www.julianpie.com; 2225 Main St; slices $3.50-4.50, whole pies $13-18; ⊘ 9am-5pm; ⊛) This famous bakery's classic apple pie is definitely crave-worthy but variations such as apple-berry crumb or the peach apple are just as tempting, especially when topped with ice cream. Buy them by the slice or take home the whole thing.

ⓘ Getting There & Away

Julian sits at the junction of Hwys 78 and 79. It's about 60 miles from San Diego (via I-8 east to Hwy 79 north) and 30 miles from Borrego Springs (via Hwy 78 west).

Route 66

Completed in 1926, iconic Route 66 connected Chicago and Los Angeles across the heartland of America. During the Great Depression, thousands of migrants escaped the Dust Bowl by slogging westward in beat-up old jalopies. After WWII Americans took their newfound wealth and convertible cars on the road and headed west.

In California, Route 66 mostly follows the National Trails Hwy, prone to potholes and dangerous bumps. From the beach in Santa

DRIVING DIRECTIONS LA TO BARSTOW
....
This stretch of Route 66 is about 200 miles long. From its western terminus at the Santa Monica Pier, follow Santa Monica Blvd east, turn right on Sunset Blvd and pick up the I-10 north to Pasadena. Take exit 31B and drive north, then turn right on Colorado Blvd. Continue east to Colorado Pl which turns into Huntington Dr E, which you'll follow to 2nd Ave, where you turn north, then east on Foothill Blvd through Monrovia. Jog south on S Myrtle Ave and hook a left on E Huntington Dr through Duarte. In Azusa, Huntington turns into E Foothill Blvd. Continue east through Rancho Cucamonga, Fontana and Rialto, then head north on N East St, turn left on W Highland Ave and pick up the I-215 to I-15. Drive downhill to Victorville, exiting at 7th St. Follow 7th St, then turn left at South D St and head north under I-15 where it turns into the National Trails Hwy, which runs straight into Barstow.

Monica, it rumbles through the LA basin, crosses over the Cajon Pass to the railway whistle-stop towns of Victorville and Barstow and runs a gauntlet of Mojave Desert ghost towns, arriving in Needles near the Nevada state line.

In larger towns, Mother Road relics may require a careful eye amid more contemporary architecture, but as you head toward Nevada, wide-open vistas and the occasional landmark remain barely changed from the days of road-trippers.

Los Angeles to Barstow

Kicking off at Route 66's western terminus in Santa Monica means first braving LA's urban and suburban sprawl. There are only a few photogenic vintage landmarks left in Pasadena, Rialto and Rancho Cucamonga, including a classic soda fountain, an orange-shaped juice stand, three retro steakhouses and a tipi hotel. Past the Cajon Pass, the route enters the vast open spaces of the Mojave. Stop to check out the sights in Victorville and Oro Grande before arriving in Barstow.

⊙ Sights

Aztec Hotel HOTEL
($ 626-358-3231; 311 W Foothill Blvd, Monrovia) **FREE** This supposedly haunted hotel built in 1925 sports elaborate Mayan Revival–style detail and once housed a speakeasy where Hollywood celebs knocked 'em back en route to the Santa Anita racetrack.

Giant Orange HISTORIC BUILDING
(15395 Foothill Blvd, Fontana; ⊘ closed to public; P) Cruising through Fontana, birthplace of the Hells Angels biker club, pause for a photo by the Giant Orange, a now-boarded-up 1930s orange-shaped juice stand of the kind that was once a fixture alongside SoCal's citrus groves. It used to offer weary Route 66 travelers 'all the juice you could drink' for a mere 10 cents.

First McDonald's Museum MUSEUM
($ 909-885-6324; www.facebook.com/firstoriginal mcdonaldsmuseum; 1398 N E St, San Bernardino; by donation; ⊘ 10am-5pm; P⊛) Half of the unofficial First McDonald's Museum has exhibits devoted to Route 66, with particularly interesting photographs and maps. It was first opened as a barbecue restaurant in 1940 by brothers Dick and Mac McDonald. Eventually Ray Kroc bought the rights to the name and built an empire. Today, the

building is owned by Albert Okura, founder of the Juan Pollo chain of chicken shacks.

California Route 66 Museum MUSEUM
(☎760-951-0436; www.califrt66museum.org; 16825 South D St, Victorville; donations welcome; ☺10am-4pm Thu-Sat & Mon, 11am-3pm Sun; P⛡) FREE
Inside the old Red Rooster Cafe opposite the railroad tracks, this nostalgic collection features a kitchen sink's worth of yesteryear's treasures, including old signs and roadside memorabilia. It's worth a quick look.

Elmer's Bottle Tree Ranch PUBLIC ART
(24266 National Trails Hwy, Oro Grande; ☺outside 24hr; P) FREE Colorful as a box of crayons, this roadside folk-art collection is a forest of over 200 'bottle trees' made from recycled soda and beer containers, telephone poles and weathered railroad signs.

🛏 Sleeping & Eating

Wigwam Motel MOTEL $
(☎909-875-3005; www.wigwammotel.com; 2728 W Foothill Blvd, Rialto; r with bath $73-110; P⛡🗶🗟🗟🗟) Get your kitsch on Route 66: stay snug in one of 19 30ft-tall concrete tipis. Built in 1949, they're equipped with nice furniture and have motel-type mod-cons. A kidney-shaped pool sits out the back.

Fair Oaks Pharmacy DINER, ICE CREAM $
(☎626-799-1414; www.fairoakspharmacy.net; 1526 Mission St, South Pasadena; mains $6-11; ☺9am-9pm Mon-Sat, 10am-7pm Sun; ⛡) Get your kicks at this original 1915 soda fountain right on Route 66. Slurp an old-fashioned 'phosphate' (flavored syrup, soda water and 'secret potion') while waiting for a heaping sandwich or hamburger or stocking up on classic candy in the gift shops. It's touristy, sure, but fun nonetheless.

The Hat SANDWICHES $
(☎626-857-0017; www.thehat.com; 611 W Alosta Ave/Rte 66, Glendora; mains $3-9; ☺10am-11pm Sun-Wed, to 1am Thu-Sat; ⛡) The classic sign featuring a chef's toque and the words 'World Famous Pastrami' greets hungry diners at the original Hat in Glendora where they've been piling up hot-pastrami sandwiches since 1951. Thinly sliced and generously salted, they're served on French rolls topped with au jus or gravy for dipping.

Iron Hog Restaurant & Saloon AMERICAN $$
(☎760-843-0609; 20848 National Trails Hwy, Oro Grande; steaks $17-50; ☺8am-10pm Sun-Thu, to 2am Fri & Sat; P) Roy Rodgers and Johnny

ℹ TIPS FOR DRIVING THE MOTHER ROAD

Sleeping
Barstow, with its chain motels, is the logical place to break the journey for a good night's sleep.

Eating
There's no shortage of eateries as you drive through the LA Basin, but as you enter the Mojave, options get thinner, with practically no pit stops between Barstow and Needles. Stock up on snacks in either town.

Navigating
For Route 66 enthusiasts who want to drive every mile of the old highway, a free turn-by-turn driving guide is available online at www.historic66.com. Also go to www.route66ca.org for more historical background, photos and info about special events.

Cash came by and scenes from *Easyrider* were filmed at this old-timey honky-tonk dripping with memorabilia and character(s). It's hugely popular with bikers and serves large portions of rib-stickers, including rattlesnake to help you connect with your inner macho. Save 2 bucks if you cook your own steak.

Magic Lamp Inn AMERICAN $$
(☎909-981-8659; www.themagiclampinn.com; 8189 Foothill Blvd, Rancho Cucamonga; mains lunch $11-17, dinner $15-42; ☺11am-10pm Mon-Thu, 11am-2am Fri, 4:30pm-2am Sat) Easily recognized by its fabulous neon Aladdin's lamp, this 1955 Route 66 dining shrine sparkles with shiny dark woods and stained-glass windows. It serves up old-school sandwiches and steaks, including a mighty Chateaubriand carved table-side. There's music nightly and a champagne brunch on Sundays.

Sycamore Inn STEAK $$$
(☎909-982-1104; www.thesycamoreinn.com; 8318 Foothill Blvd, Rancho Cucamonga; mains $30-55; ☺5-9pm Mon-Thu, to 10pm Fri & Sat, 4-8:30pm Sun; P🗶) This storied Route 66 landmark has fed its juicy steaks to generations of meat lovers, including A-listers such as Marilyn Monroe. The menu brims with old-school faves such as oysters Rockefeller, crab cakes and shrimp cocktails to start things off before tucking into the aged

and hard-carved cuts, including a 22oz porterhouse.

Barstow

At the junction of I-40 and I-15, nearly halfway between LA and Las Vegas, Barstow has been a desert travelers' crossroads for centuries. In 1776 Spanish colonial priest Francisco Garcés caravanned through, and in the mid-19th century the Old Spanish Trail passed nearby, with pioneer settlers on the Mojave River selling supplies to California immigrants. Meanwhile, mines were founded in the hills outside town. Barstow, named after a railway executive, got going as a railroad junction after 1886. After 1926 it became a major rest stop for motorists along Route 66 (Main St). Today it exists to serve nearby military bases and is still a busy pit stop for travelers.

◉ Sights

Route 66 'Mother Road' Museum MUSEUM
(☏ 760-255-1890; www.route66museum.org; 681 N 1st St; ◷ 10am-4pm Fri & Sat, 11am-4pm Sun, or by appointment; Ⓟ 🚹) FREE Inside the beautifully restored **Casa del Desierto**, a 1911 Harvey House (architecturally significant railway inns named for their originator Fred Harvey), this museum documents life along the historic highway with some great old black-and-white photographs alongside eclectic relics, including a 1915 Ford Model T, a 1913 telephone switchboard and products made from locally mined minerals.

Western America Railroad Museum MUSEUM
(WARM; ☏ 760-256-9276; www.barstowrailmuseum. org; 685 N 1st St; ◷ 11am-4pm Fri-Sun; Ⓟ) FREE Rail buffs make a beeline to the Casa del Desierto to marvel at a century's worth of railroad artifacts, including old timetables, uniforms, china and the Dog Tooth Mountain model railroad in this small museum. Outside you can see historic locomotives, bright-red cabooses and even a car used to ship racehorses.

Main Street Murals PUBLIC ART
(Main St, btwn 1st & 6th Sts; ◷ 24hr) FREE Barstow's Main St is well known for its history-themed murals that spruce up often empty and boarded-up buildings. Pick up a map at the Chamber of Commerce (p525).

Calico Ghost Town AMUSEMENT PARK
(☏ 800-862-2542; www.calicotown.com; 36600 Ghost Town Rd, Yermo; adult/child $8/5; ◷ 9am-

5pm; Ⓟ 🚹) This endearingly hokey Old West attraction consists of a cluster of pioneer-era buildings amid the ruins of a 1881 silver-mining town, reconstructed nearly a century later by Walter Knott (founder of Knott's Berry Farm). Note that optional activities such as gold panning, a mine tour and access to the 'mystery shack' are $3 extra each (or $7.50 for all). Trips on a narrow-gauge railway are $4.50. Old-timey heritage celebrations include Civil War reenactments and a bluegrass 'hootenanny.'

Take the Ghost Town Rd exit off I-15; it's about 3.5 miles uphill. There's also a **campground** (tent/RV sites with full hookup $30/40).

🛏 Sleeping & Eating

Only when the Mojave freezes over will there be no rooms left in Barstow. Just drive along E Main St and take your pick from the string of national chain motels, many with doubles from $40.

Oak Tree Inn MOTEL $
(☏ 888-456-8733, 760-254-1148; www.oaktreeinn. com; 35450 Yermo Rd, Yermo; r from $56; Ⓟ ❄ 🏊 🚹) Rooms are snug but modern and come with black-out draperies and triple-paned windows at this 65-room motel near the freeway. There's a pool and small gym for stretching after a day on the road and a 24-hour 1950s-style diner next door. It's about 10 miles east of Barstow (exit Ghost Town Rd off I-15). Kids under 12 stay free.

Peggy Sue's DINER $
(☏ 760-254-3370; www.peggysuesdiner.com; 35654 Yermo Rd, Yermo; mains $7.50-13; ◷ 6am-10pm; Ⓟ ❄ 🚹) Built in 1954 as a simple, nine-stool, three-booth diner, Peggy Sue's has since grown into a miniempire with ice-cream shop, pizza parlor, a park out back with metal sculptures of 'diner-saurs' and kitschy-awesome gift shop. Many meals – burger to ham steak – are named after Hollywood artists. It's about 10 miles north of Barstow; take the Ghost Town Rd exit off I-15.

Lola's Kitchen MEXICAN $
(☏ 760-255-1007; 1244 E Main St; mains $7-9.50; ◷ 4am-7:30pm Mon-Fri, to 4:30pm Sat; Ⓟ 🚹) Interstate truckers, blue-collar workers and Vegas-bound hipsters all gather at this simple, colorful Mexican *cocina,* tucked away inside a strip mall and run by two sisters who make the full spectrum of honest-to-goodness Mexican faves, from quesadillas and

tortas to carne asada and chile relleno. No alcohol. It's across from the Rodeway Inn.

Idle Spurs Steakhouse   STEAK $$
(📞760-256-8888; www.thespurs.us; 690 Old Hwy 58; mains lunch $9-24, dinner $12-45; ☺11am-9pm Tue-Fri, from 4pm Sat & Sun; 🅿🍴) In the saddle since 1950, this Western-themed spot, ringed around an atrium and a full bar, is a fave with locals and Route 66 travelers. Surrender to your inner carnivore with slow-roasted prime rib, hand-cut steaks and succulent lobster tail. Kids menu available.

ℹ Information

Barstow Area Chamber of Commerce (📞760-256-8617; www.barstowroute66.com; 229 E Main St; ☺10am-4pm Mon-Thu, to 2pm Fri; 📶)

Barstow to Needles

From Barstow, Route 66 crosses the Mojave Desert on the National Trails Hwy that runs mostly parallel to the I-40. Instagrammable landmarks include the Bagdad Cafe in Newberry Springs, Roy's Motel & Cafe in Amboy and the schoolhouse in Goffs.

Bring a picnic since the eateries along here, such as they are, are good for a cold drink only.

◉ Sights

Stone Hotel   HISTORIC BUILDING
(35630 Santa Fe St, Daggett; ☺no public entry; 🅿) Pay your respects to early desert adventurers at the old Stone Hotel. Built in 1875 of adobe and stone, it once housed miners, desert explorers and wanderers, including Sierra Nevada naturalist John Muir and desert-adventurer Death Valley Scotty.

The hotel is in Daggett, site of the harsh California inspection station faced by Dust Bowl refugees in *Grapes of Wrath*. Today, there isn't much action, but it's a windswept picturesque place nonetheless.

Bagdad Cafe   LANDMARK
(📞760-257-3101; www.bagdadcafethereal.com; 46548 National Trails Hwy, Newberry Springs; ☺7am-7pm) This grizzled cafe was the main filming location of Percy Adlon's eponymous 1987 classic cult flick starring CCH Pounder and Jack Palance. The interior is chockablock with posters, movie stills and memorabilia while outside the old water tower and Airstream trailer are slowly rusting away. There's food but don't bother.

DRIVING DIRECTIONS BARSTOW TO NEEDLES

This stretch of Route 66 is about 180 miles long. Leave Barstow on I-40 east and exit at Daggett. Drive north on A St, cross the railroad tracks and turn right on Santa Fe St. Continue on Santa Fe, take your first right, then turn left to pick up the National Trails Hwy going east. It runs parallel to I-40, crosses it at Lavic and continues north of I-40. This potholed, crumbling backcountry stretch crawls through ghostly desert towns. In Ludlow turn right on Crucero Rd, cross I-40 again and turn left. Beyond Ludlow, the Mother Road veers away from the freeway, leaves the National Trails Hwy past Essex and heads north on Goffs Rd through Fenner, where it once more crosses I-40. Follow Goffs Rd to I-40 and head east to Needles.

Roy's Motel & Cafe   HISTORIC SITE
(www.rt66roys.com; National Old Trails Hwy, Amboy; ☺7am-8pm, seasonal variations; 🅿) **FREE** In the ghost town of Amboy, this beautifully kept landmark was for decades a popular watering hole for Route 66 travelers. If you believe the lore, Roy once cooked his famous Route 66 double cheeseburger on the hood of a '63 Mercury. Although the motel is abandoned, the gas station and store are usually open.

Amboy Crater   VOLCANO
(📞760-326-7000; www.blm.gov/ca; ☺sunrise-sunset; 🅿) **FREE** Amboy Crater, off National Trails Hwy, 2 miles west of Amboy, is a 250ft-high, almost perfectly symmetrical volcanic cinder cone. You can hike to the top for great views over the lava fields where NASA engineers field-tested the Mars Rover. The 3-mile round-trip hike doesn't have a stitch of shade, so avoid heading out midday or in summer.

Goffs Schoolhouse   HISTORIC SITE
(📞760-733-4482; www.mdhca.org; 37198 Lanfair Rd, Essex; ☺9am-4pm Sat-Mon Oct-Jun, call to confirm; 🅿) **FREE** The shade of cottonwood trees makes the 1914 Spanish Mission–style Goffs Schoolhouse a soothing stop along this sun-drenched stretch of highway. It stands as part of the best-preserved pioneer settlement in the Mojave Desert. Browsing the black-and-white photographs of hardscrabble Dust Bowl migrants gives an evocative glimpse

into the tough life on the edge of the Mojave. A self-guided tour pamphlet is available.

Old Trails Bridge
BRIDGE

(⊘ no public access) East of the California–Arizona state line, south of I-40, the arched Old Trails Bridge welcomes the Mother Road to California under endless blue skies. You might recognize the bridge: the Great Depression–era Joad family used it to cross the Colorado River in the movie version of John Steinbeck's novel *Grapes of Wrath*.

Mojave National Preserve

If you're on a quest for the 'middle of nowhere,' you'll find it in the wilderness of the **Mojave National Preserve** (☎ 760-252-6100; www.nps.gov/moja; btwn I-15 & I-40; ℗) ✦ FREE, a 1.6-million-acre jumble of sand dunes, Joshua trees, volcanic cinder cones and habitats for bighorn sheep, desert tortoises, jackrabbits and coyotes. Solitude and serenity are the big draws. Daytime temperatures hover above 100°F (37°C) during summer, then plummet to around 50°F (10°C) in winter, when snowstorms are not unheard of. Strong winds will practically knock you over in spring and fall. No gas is available within the preserve.

⊙ Sights & Activities

Kelso Dunes
DUNES

(☎ 760-252-6108; www.nps.gov/moja; off Kelbaker Rd; ℗) FREE Rising to 700ft, these beautiful dunes are the country's third-tallest sand dunes. Under the right conditions they emanate low humming sounds that are caused by shifting sands. Running downhill some-times jump-starts the effect. The trailhead to the dunes is about 3 miles on a graded dirt road west of Kelbaker Rd, 7 miles south of the Kelso Depot Visitor Center.

Cima Dome
MOUNTAIN

(Map p528; ☎ 760-252-6108; www.nps.gov/moja; Cima Rd) FREE Visible to the south from I-15, Cima Dome is a 1500ft hunk of granite spiked with volcanic cinder cones and crusty outcrops of basalt left by lava. Its slopes are smothered in Joshua trees that collectively make up the largest such forest in the world. For close-ups, tackle the 3-mile round-trip hike up **Teutonia Peak** (5755ft), starting on Cima Rd, 5 miles northwest of Cima.

White Horse Canyon Rd
DRIVING

(☎ 760-252-6108; www.nps.gov/moja) FREE This incredibly scenic 9.5-mile backcountry drive up to Mid Hills starts at Hole-in-the-Wall. Ask about current conditions at the visitor center before setting out.

Hole-in-the-Wall
HIKING, DRIVING

(☎ 760-252-6108; www.nps.gov/moja; Black Canyon Rd) FREE These vertical walls of rhyolite tuff (pronounced toof), which look like Swiss-cheese cliffs made of unpolished marble, are the result of a powerful prehistoric volcanic eruption that blasted rocks across the landscape. Learn how the site got its name by hiking the 0.5-mile **Rings Loop Trail** where metal rings lead down through a narrow slot-canyon once used by Native Americans to escape 19th-century ranchers.

Hole-in-the-Wall lies east of Kelso-Cima Rd via the unpaved Cedar Canyon Rd. Coming from I-40, exit at Essex Rd.

SLOW: DESERT TORTOISE X-ING

The Mojave is the home of the desert tortoise, which can live for up to 80 years, munching on wildflowers and grasses. Its canteen-like bladder allows it to go for up to a year without drinking. Using its strong hind legs, it burrows to escape the summer heat and freezing winter temperatures and also to lay eggs. The sex of the hatchlings is determined by temperature: cooler for males, hotter for females.

Disease and shrinking habitat have decimated the desert-tortoise population. They do like to rest in the shade under parked cars (take a quick look around before just driving away) and are often hit by off-road drivers. If you see a tortoise in trouble (eg stranded in the middle of a road), call a ranger.

It's illegal to pick one up or even approach too closely and for good reason: a frightened tortoise may urinate on a perceived attacker, possibly dying of dehydration before the next rains come.

🛏 Sleeping & Eating

Camping is the only way to overnight in the preserve. Baker, on the northwestern edge along I-15, has plenty of cheap, charmless motels. Coming from the north, the casino hotels in Primm on the Nevada border offer slightly better options. If you're traveling on the I-40, Needles is the closest town to spend the night.

The only place in the park to get a bite is at the old-fashioned lunch counter in the Kelso Visitor Center. Baker is the closest town with restaurants and grocery stores.

🛏 Camping

First-come, first-served sites with pit toilets and potable water are available at Hole-in-the-Wall and Mid Hills campgrounds. There's also free backcountry camping as long as you're at least 0.5 miles from developed areas and roads and 0.25 miles from any water source. Roadside camping is permitted in areas already used for the purpose. Check www.nps.gov/moja for locations or ask for details and directions at the visitor center. No permits required.

ℹ Information

Hole-in-the-Wall Visitor Center (📞760-928-2572, 760-252-6104; Black Canyon Rd; ⊙9am-3pm Fri-Sun) Has seasonal ranger programs, backcountry information and road-condition updates. It's about 20 miles north of I-40 via Essex Rd.

Kelso Depot Visitor Center (📞760-252-6108; www.nps.gov/moja; Kelbaker Rd, Kelso; ⊙10am-5pm) The preserve's main visitor center is in a gracefully restored, 1920s Spanish Mission–style railway depot. The knowledgeable rangers can help you plan your day. There are also nicely presented natural- and cultural-history exhibits, a small gift store and an old-fashioned **lunch counter** (dishes $3.50 to $8.50).

ℹ Getting There & Away

There is no public transport to or within Mojave National Preserve, which is hemmed in by I-15 in the north and I-40 in the south. The main entrance off I-15 is at Baker. From there it's 35 miles south to the central Kelso Depot Visitor Center via Kelbaker Rd, which links to I-40 after another 23 miles. Cima Rd and Morning Star Mine Rd near Nipton are two other northern access roads. From I-40, Essex Rd leads to the Black Canyon Rd and Hole-in-the-Wall.

Around Mojave National Preserve

Nipton

Hugging the northeastern edge of the Mojave National Preserve, this isolated Old West outpost started out in 1900 as a gold-miners' camp and soon after began seeing the railroad pass through en route from Salt Lake City to Los Angeles. Practically a ghost town today (albeit with its own solar plant!), it was sold in August 2017 for close to $5 million to American Green, an Arizona-based marijuana-focused technology and growing company that plans to turn Nipton into a destination for pot aficionados.

Primm

Driving east on I-15 at night, the desert darkness is brightened at the Nevada state line by Primm and its three garishly blinking casino resorts. It's worth stopping if you want to fold a little gambling action into your desert getaway or need a decent and cheapish place to crash for the night. A fashion outlet mall and a nearby 18-hole golf course provide additional diversions. Coming from the east, it's a handy stopover if you're headed for Death Valley or the Mojave National Preserve.

🛏 Sleeping & Eating

Whiskey Pete's CASINO HOTEL **$**
(📞702-386-7867; www.primmvalleyresorts.com; 100 W Primm Blvd; r from $39, resort fee $15; ᴘ❄🛜🏊) This is probably the best of the trio of badly aging casino hotels in Primm, providing you stay in one of the newly renovated rooms with pillow-top beds, big LCD TV and small fridge. The outdoor pool is only open during warmer months.

GP's STEAK **$$$**
(📞702-679-5170; www.primmvalleyresorts.com; 31900 Las Vegas Blvd; mains $23-44; ⊙5-9pm; ᴘ) The best among the largely poor or mediocre eateries in Primm, GP's trains the spotlight on quality meats and seafood, prepared in classic fashion. Kick things off with old-school continental classics such as lobster bisque or oysters Rockefeller and wrap up with the luscious cheesecake.

Death Valley & Around

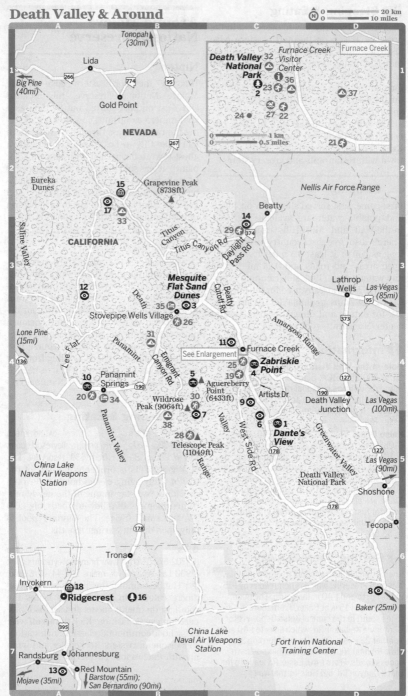

Tonopah
(30mi)

Death Valley 32
National Furnace Creek
Park Visitor
Center
23 36
2
24 27 22
21

Furnace Creek

37

0 ⎯⎯ 1 km
0 ⎯⎯ 0.5 miles

Lida

Big Pine
(40mi)

266
774
95

Gold Point

NEVADA

267

Eureka
Dunes

Grapevine Peak
(8738ft)

15
17
33

Beatty

CALIFORNIA

Nellis Air Force Range

Titus
Canyon

Titus Canyon Rd

14
29
374

Daylight Pass Rd

Saline Valley

12

**Mesquite
Flat Sand
Dunes**

Death

35 3
26

Beatty
Cutoff Rd

Lathrop
Wells

Las Vegas
(85mi)

95

373

Stovepipe Wells Village

Amargosa Range

Lone Pine
(15mi)

31

Lee Flat

Panamint

136

11
See Enlargement
Furnace Creek

25
19 4
**Zabriskie
Point**

10
Panamint
Springs

190

20 34

5

Emigrant Canyon Rd

Aguereberry
Point
(6433ft)

30

9
Artists Dr

127

Death Valley
Junction

Las Vegas
(100mi)

Wildrose
Peak (9064ft)

38

7

6

1

**Dante's
View**

Greenwater Valley

127

Las Vegas
(90mi)

28
Telescope Peak
(11049ft)

West Side Rd

178

Panamint

Valley

Range

**China Lake
Naval Air Weapons
Station**

Death Valley
National Park

Shoshone

178

Tecopa

178

Trona

Inyokern
18
Ridgecrest

16

8

Baker (25mi)

395

Randsburg Johannesburg

13 Red Mountain
Barstow (55mi);
San Bernardino (90mi)

Mojave (35mi)

**China Lake
Naval Air Weapons
Station**

Fort Irwin National
Training Center

Death Valley & Around

Death Valley National Park

The very name evokes all that is harsh, hot and hellish – a punishing, barren and lifeless place of Old Testament severity. Yet closer inspection reveals that in **Death Valley** (Map p528; ☑760-786-3200; www.nps.gov/deva; 7-day-pass per car $25; ⊙24hr; ⓟ🚹) nature is putting on a truly spectacular show: singing sand dunes, water-sculpted canyons, boulders moving across the desert floor, extinct volcanic craters, palm-shaded oases, stark mountains rising to 11,000ft and plenty of endemic wildlife. This is a land of superlatives, holding the US records for hottest temperature (134°F/57°C), lowest point (Badwater, 282ft below sea level) and largest national park outside Alaska (over 5000 sq miles).

Furnace Creek is Death Valley's commercial hub, with the park's main visitor center, a general store, gas station, post office, ATM, wi-fi, golf course, lodging and restaurants.

Park entry permits ($25 per vehicle) are valid for seven days and available from self-service pay stations at the park's access roads and at the visitor center.

◉ Sights & Activities

Families can pick up a free fun-for-all-ages *Junior Ranger Activity Booklet* at the Furnace Creek visitor center (p534), which has info-packed handouts on all kinds of activities, including hiking trails and mountain-biking routes.

◉ Furnace Creek & Around

Borax Museum   MUSEUM
(Map p528; ☑760-786-2345; www.furnacecreekresort.com; Hwy 190, Ranch at Furnace Creek; ⊙9am-9pm Oct-May, variable summer; ⓟ🚹) FREE
On the grounds of the Ranch at Furnace Creek (p532), this museum explains the history of borax in Death Valley, with alluring samples of local borate minerals and their uses. Out back there's a large collection of pioneer-era mining and transportation equipment.

Ranch at Furnace Creek
Swimming Pool   SWIMMING

(Map p528; 760-786-2345; www.furnace creekresort.com; Hwy 190, Ranch at Furnace Creek; nonguests $5; ⊗8am-11pm) This huge spring-fed pool is kept at a steady 84°F (29°C) and cleaned with a nifty flow-through system that uses minimal chlorine. It's primarily for Ranch at Furnace Creek guests, but a limited number of visitor passes are available at reception.

Furnace Creek Golf Course   GOLF

(Map p528; 760-786-3373; www.furnace creekresort.com/activities/golfing; Hwy 190, Furnace Creek; greens fees 9/18 holes $30/60; ⊗year-round) For novelty's sake, play a round at the world's lowest-elevation golf course (214ft below sea level, 18 holes, par 70), redesigned by Perry Dye in 1997. It's also been certified by the Audubon Society for its environment-friendly management.

Harmony Borax Works   HISTORIC SITE

(Map p528; 760-786-3200; www.nps.gov/deva; Hwy 190) FREE Just north of Furnace Creek, a 0.5-mile interpretive trail follows in the footsteps of late-19th-century Chinese laborers and through the adobe ruins of Harmony Borax Works, which operated from 1883–88. Follow up with a side trip through twisting Mustard Canyon.

⊙ South of Furnace Creek

★Zabriskie Point   VIEWPOINT

(Map p528; 760-786-3200; www.nps.gov/deva; Hwy 190; P) Early morning is the best time to visit Zabriskie Point for spectacular views across golden badlands eroded into waves, pleats and gullies. It was named for a manager of the Pacific Coast Borax Company and also inspired the title of Michelangelo Antonio's 1970s movie. The cover of U2's *Joshua Tree* album was also shot here.

★Dante's View   VIEWPOINT

(Map p528; 760-786-3200; www.nps.gov/deva; Dante's View Rd, off Hwy 190; P) At 5475ft, the view of the entire southern Death Valley basin from the top of the Black Mountains is absolutely brilliant, especially at sunrise or sunset. On very clear days, you can simultaneously see the highest (Mt Whitney) and lowest (Badwater) points in the contiguous USA.

Allow about 1½ hours for the 26-mile round-trip from the turnoff at Hwy 190, east of Furnace Creek.

Golden Canyon   HIKING

(Map p528; 760-786-3200; www.nps.gov/deva; Hwy 178) Narrow canyons winding through a wonderland of golden rocks is the ammo of this trail network between Hwy 178 and Zabriskie Point. Several routes can be combined for longer treks. The most popular is a 3-mile out-and-back trek from the main trailhead off Hwy 178 to the oxidized iron cliffs of Red Cathedral. Combining it with the Gower Gulch Loop adds another mile.

★Artists Drive   SCENIC DRIVE

(Map p528; 760-786-3200; www.nps.gov/deva; off Hwy 190) About 9 miles south of Furnace Creek, the 9-mile, one-way Artists Drive scenic loop offers 'wow' moments around every turn; it's best done in the late afternoon when exposed minerals and volcanic ash make the hills erupt in fireworks of color.

Badwater Basin   NATURAL FEATURE

(Map p528; Hwy 190; P) The lowest point in North America (282ft below sea level) is an eerily beautiful landscape of crinkly salt flats. Here you can walk out on to a constantly evaporating bed of salty, mineralized water that's otherworldly in its beauty. It's about 17 miles south of Furnace Creek.

Devil's Golf Course   NATURAL FEATURE

(Map p528; 760-786-3200; www.nps.gov/deva; Hwy 178; P) Some 15 miles south of Furnace Creek, salt has piled up into saw-toothed miniature mountains in what was once a major lake that evaporated about 2000 years ago. You're free to explore this bizarre landscape, but don't expect to tee up.

⊙ Stovepipe Wells & Around

★Mesquite Flat
Sand Dunes   NATURAL FEATURE

(Map p528; 760-786-3200; www.nps.gov/deva; Hwy 190) The most accessible dunes in Death Valley are an undulating sea of sand rising up to 100ft high next to the highway near Stovepipe Wells Village. They're at their most photogenic at sunrise or sunset when bathed in soft light and accented by long, deep shadows. Keep an eye out for animal tracks. Full-moon nights are especially magical.

Mosaic Canyon Trail   HIKING

(Map p528; 760-786-3200; www.nps.gov/deva; Mosaic Canyon Rd, off Hwy 190, Stovepipe Wells Village) West of Stovepipe Wells Village, a 2.3-mile gravel road leads to Mosaic Canyon, where you can hike and scramble past smooth multihued rock walls. Colors are sharpest at midday.

About 1.3 miles into the hike, passage is blocked by a pile of massive boulders but it's possible to squeeze by on the left and continue the trek. Budget about 2½ hours for the 4-mile round-trip.

◉ Northern Park

Racetrack Playa   NATURAL FEATURE

(Map p528; ☑760-786-3200; www.nps.gov/deva; Racetrack Rd) Past the northern end of Hwy 190, it's slow going for 27 miles on a tire-shredding dirt road (high-clearance and 4WD usually required) to the eerie Racetrack, where hundreds of sizeable rocks have etched tracks into the dry lake bed. In 2014, a group of researchers finally lifted the mystery when they actually observed the stones being moved by thin sheets of ice that were pushed by gentle winds across the desert floor. Read all about it at www.racetrackplaya.org.

Ubehebe Crater   NATURAL FEATURE

(Map p528; www.nps.gov/deva; Hwy 190) Hwy 190 ends at 600ft-deep Ubehebe Crater, formed some 300 years ago by the meeting of fiery magma and cool groundwater. As the water turned into steam, it expanded until the pressure gave way to a cataclysmic explosion. The result is easily appreciated from the parking lot, but you can also walk down to the bottom or loop around the perimeter of the half-mile-wide crater.

Scotty's Castle   HISTORIC BUILDING

(Map p528; ☑760-786-3200; www.nps.gov/deva; ⊘closed) Closed due to flood damage and not likely to reopen until at least 2019, this whimsical castle was the desert home of Walter E Scott, alias 'Death Valley Scotty,' a quintessential tall-tale teller who captivated people with his stories of gold. His most lucrative friendship was with Albert Johnson, a wealthy insurance magnate from Chicago, who bankrolled this elaborate desert oasis in the 1920s.

◉ Towards Beatty

Titus Canyon Rd   SCENIC DRIVE

(Map p528; ☑760-786-3200; www.nps.gov/deva; off Hwy 374) About 2 miles outside the park boundary is the turnoff to the spectacular one-way backcountry road, Titus Canyon Rd, leading to Hwy 190 in 27 miles of rough track. The road climbs, dips and winds to a crest in the Grapevine Mountains, then

slowly descends back to the desert floor past a ghost town, petroglyphs and canyon narrows.

The best light conditions are in the morning. High-clearance vehicles are highly recommended. Check road conditions at the visitor center (p534).

Goldwell Open Air Museum   MUSEUM

(Map p528; ☑702-870-9946; www.goldwellmuseum.org; off Hwy 374; ⊙park 24hr, visitor center 10am-4pm Mon-Sat, to 2pm summer; P) FREE Near the ghost town of Rhyolite, just east of Death Valley National Park, this outdoor sculpture park was begun in 1984 by Belgian artist Albert Szukalski (1945–2000) with his haunting version of DaVinci's *Last Supper*. Other Belgian friends soon joined him and added other, often bizarre, sculptures. Today there are seven sculptures as well as a visitor center and small store.

Rhyolite   GHOST TOWN

(Map p528; off Hwy 374; P) FREE Just outside the Death Valley eastern park boundary, Rhyolite epitomizes the hurly-burly, boom-and-bust story of Western gold-rush mining towns in early 1900s. Hard to imagine today that during its peak years between 1904–16, it had 8000 residents. Highlights among the skeletal remains of houses are the Spanish Mission–style train station, a three-story bank building and a house made from 50,000 beer bottles by miner Tom Kelly.

◉ Panamint Springs & Emigrant Canyon Rd

Father Crowley Vista   VIEWPOINT

(Map p528; ☑760-786-3200; www.nps.gov/deva; off Hwy 190, Panamint Springs) This viewpoint peers deep into Rainbow Canyon, created by lava flows and scattered with multihued volcanic cinders. It's worth a quick stop on your way in or out of Death Valley. The turnoff is about 8 miles west of Panamint Springs.

Darwin Falls   HIKING

(Map p528; ☑760-786-3200; www.nps.gov/deva; Hwy 190, Panamint Springs) This natural-spring-fed year-round cascade plunges into a gorge, embraced by willows that attract migratory birds. Look for the (unmarked) turnoff about 0.75 miles west of Panamint Springs, then follow the dirt road for 2.5 miles to the parking area. The 1-mile hike to the first waterfall requires some climbing over rocks and crossing small streams.

Charcoal Kilns
HISTORIC SITE

(Map p528; ☑760-786-3200; www.nps.gov/deva; Emigrant Canyon Rd) Emigrant Canyon Rd climbs steeply over Emigrant Pass for the turnoff to Wildrose Canyon Rd and a lineup of 10 large beehive-shaped charcoal kilns made of stone and once used by miners to make fuel for smelting silver and lead ore. The landscape is subalpine, with forests of piñon pine and juniper; it can be covered with snow, even in spring.

Aguereberry Point
VIEWPOINT

(Map p528; www.nps.gov/deva; off Emigrant Canyon Rd) Named for a lucky French miner who struck gold at the nearby Eureka Mine, Aguereberry Point sits at a lofty 6433ft above the desert floor and delivers fantastic views into the valley and out to the colorful Funeral Mountains. The best time to visit is late afternoon. The 6.5-mile road is quite rough and a high-clearance vehicle is highly recommended.

Wildrose Peak
HIKING

(Map p528; ☑760-786-3200; www.nps.gov/deva; Wildrose Canyon Rd) This moderate-to-strenuous trail begins near the charcoal kilns off Wildrose Canyon Rd and ascends to Wildrose Peak (9064ft). The 8.4-mile round-trip hike is best in spring or fall. The elevation gain is 2200ft, but great views start about halfway up.

Telescope Peak
HIKING

(Map p528; ☑760-786-3200; www.nps.gov/deva; Wildrose Canyon Rd) The park's most demanding summit is Telescope Peak (11,049ft), with views that plummet to the desert floor,

---

CALLING DEATH VALLEY HOME

Timbisha Shoshone tribespeople lived in the Panamint Range for centuries, visiting the valley every winter to gather acorns, hunt waterfowl, catch pupfish in marshes and cultivate small areas of corn, squash and beans. After the federal government created Death Valley National Monument in 1933, the tribe was forced to move several times and was eventually restricted to a 40-acre village site near Furnace Creek, where it still lives. In 2000 President Clinton signed an act transferring 7500 acres of land back to the Timbisha Shoshone tribe, creating the first Native American reservation inside a US national park. Learn more at www.timbisha.com.

---

which is as far below as two Grand Canyons deep! The 14-mile round-trip trail climbs 3000ft above Mahogany Flat, off upper Wildrose Canyon Rd. Summiting in winter requires ice-axe, crampons and winter-hiking experience. By June, the trail is usually free of snow. Get full details from the visitor center (p534) before setting out.

Tours

Death Valley Jeep Tours
DRIVING

(Map p528; www.farabeejeeps.com; Hwy 190, Furnace Creek; tours from $145, 2-person minimum; ☺Sep-May) If you want to venture into the background, but don't want to go it alone, sign up for a Jeep tour with this local company. Options include a trip down Titus Canyon ($145), out to Racetrack Playa ($280), into Echo Canyon ($150) or the more general Death Valley Experience ($195). There's a two-person minimum.

Furnace Creek Stables
HORSEBACK RIDING

(Map p528; ☑760-614-1018; www.furnacecreekstables.net; Hwy 190, Furnace Creek; 1/2hr rides $55/70; ☺mid-Oct–mid-May; 🐴) Saddle up to see what Death Valley looks like from the back of a horse on guided trail rides. The one-hour ride stays on the sunbaked desert floor while the two-hour rides venture into the foothills of the Funeral Mountains for great valley views. Monthly full-moon rides are the most memorable, while 45-minute carriage rides are safe and relaxing fun for all.

Festivals & Events

Death Valley '49ers
CULTURAL

(www.deathvalley49ers.org; ☺early/mid-Nov) Furnace Creek hosts this weeklong historical encampment, featuring cowboy poetry, campfire sing-alongs, a gold-panning contest and a Western art show. Show up early to watch the pioneer wagons come thunderin' in.

Sleeping

Camping is plentiful but if you're looking for a place with a roof, in-park options are limited, pricey and often booked solid in springtime. Alternative bases are the gateway towns of Beatty (40 miles from Furnace Creek), Lone Pine (40 miles), Death Valley Junction (30 miles) and Tecopa (70 miles). Options a bit further afield include Ridgecrest (120 miles) and Las Vegas (140 miles).

Ranch at Furnace Creek
RESORT $$

(Map p528; ☑760-786-2345; www.furnacecreekresort.com; Hwy 190, Furnace Creek; cabin/r from $140/180; (P ⊖ ✳ ⧴ ☰) Tailor-made for families, this rambling resort with multiple, motel-style buildings has received a vigorous facelift, resulting in spiffy rooms swathed in desert colors, updated bathrooms and French doors leading to porches with comfortable patio furniture. The grounds encompass a playground, spring-fed swimming pool, tennis courts, golf course, restaurants, shops and the Borax Museum (p529).

Stovepipe Wells Village Hotel   MOTEL $$
(Map p528; ☎760-786-2387; www.deathvalley hotels.com; 51880 Hwy 190, Stovepipe Wells; RV sites $33.30, r $140-210; (P ⊖ ✳ @ ⧴ ☰) The 83 rooms at this private resort have beds draped in quality linens and accented with cheerful Native American–patterned blankets. The small pool is cool and the on-site cowboy-style restaurant serves breakfast and dinner daily, with lunch available in the next-door saloon. Wi-fi is spotty but the new business center has two public computers and a printer.

Panamint Springs Resort   MOTEL $$
(☎775-482-7680; www.panamintsprings.com; Hwy 190, Panamint Springs; r $79-129, cabins $94-205; (P ✳ ⧴ ☰) Elsewhere 'off-grid' is a state of mind, but it's a statement of fact at this low-key, family-run motel with rustic cabins on the park's western border. A generator creates electricity, limited internet access comes via satellite, and phone service is dicey at best (reserve via the website).

It's part of a village that also has a restaurant-bar, a campground, a gas station and a general store.

Inn at Furnace Creek   HOTEL $$$
(Map p528; ☎760-786-2345; www.furnace creekresort.com; Hwy 190; d from $450; ⊙mid-Oct–mid-May; (P ⊖ ✳ @ ⧴ ☰) Roll out of bed and count the colors of the desert as you pull back the curtains in your room at this 1927 Spanish Mission–style hotel. After a day of sweaty touring, enjoy languid valley views while lounging by the spring-fed swimming pool, cocktail in hand. It's the classiest place in Death Valley, but rooms would benefit from updating.

✗ Eating & Drinking

There are restaurants and stores for stocking up on basic groceries and camping supplies in Furnace Creek, Stovepipe Wells Village and Panamint Springs. Generally speaking, restaurants are expensive and mediocre. Hours vary seasonally; some close in summer.

Toll Road Restaurant   AMERICAN $$
(Map p528; ☎760-786-2387; www.deathvalley hotels.com; 51880 Hwy 190, Stovepipe Wells; mains $12.50-34; ⊙7-10am & 5:30-9pm; (P ⧴) Above-par cowboy cooking happens at this ranch house, which gets Old West flair from a rustic fireplace and rickety wooden chairs and tables. Many of the mostly meaty mains are made with local ingredients, such as mesquite honey, prickly pear and piñons. Many dishes are named after Death Valley landmarks (eg Scotty's Chicken Wings).

Panamint Springs Resort   AMERICAN $$
(Map p528; ☎775-482-7680; www.panamintsprings. com; Hwy 190, Panamint Springs; burgers $10-18, pizza $15-35; ⊙7am-9pm; (P) It may look funky but this outback cafe serves some of the best Angus burgers, crispy salads and pizza (in three sizes) in Death Valley. Toast the panoramic views from the front porch with one of its 150 bottled beers from around the world.

Corkscrew Saloon   AMERICAN $$
(Map p528; ☎760-786-2345; www.furnace creekresort.com/dining; Hwy 190, Ranch at Furnace Creek; mains $12-20; ⊙11am-11pm, seasonal variations; (P ⧴) This gregarious joint has darts, draft beer and dynamite barbecue at dinner time, as well as pretty good, but pricey pizzas and pub grub such as onion rings and burgers. There's Badwater Ale on tap and a jukebox for entertainment. No reservations.

★ Inn Dining Room   INTERNATIONAL $$$
(Map p528; ☎760-786-2345; www.furnace creekresort.com/dining; Inn at Furnace Creek, off Hwy 190; breakfast $10-17, mains lunch $10-14, dinner $27-58; ⊙7-10:30am & noon-2pm Mon-Sat, 7-10am & 5:30-9pm Sun mid-Oct–mid-May; (P ⧴) This formal restaurant delivers continental cuisine with stellar views of the Panamint Mountains. For a more chilled ambience, enjoy breakfast, lunch or cocktails on the patio. Reservations are key for dinner when a 'no shorts or tank tops' policy kicks in, although you could always belly up to the bar and eat there. The Sunday brunch is a gourmet gut-buster ($35).

ℹ Information

MONEY
There are ATMs at the Ranch at Furnace Creek and in Stovepipe Wells.

TELEPHONE
Cell towers provide service at Furnace Creek and Stovepipe Wells but there's little to no coverage elsewhere in the park.

TOURIST INFORMATION

Furnace Creek Visitor Center (☑760-786-3200; www.nps.gov/deva; ☺8am-5pm; ☎⚐) The modern visitor center has engaging exhibits on the park's ecosystem and indigenous tribes as well as a gift shop, clean toilets, (slow) wi-fi and friendly rangers to answer questions and help you plan your day. First-time visitors should watch the gorgeously shot 20-minute movie *Seeing Death Valley*. Check the schedule for ranger-led activities.

❶ Getting There & Away

The park's main roads (Hwys 178 and 190) are paved and in great shape, but if your travel plans include dirt roads, a high-clearance vehicle and off-road tires are highly recommended and essential on many routes. 4WD is often necessary after rains. Always check with the **visitor center** (p534) for current road conditions, especially before heading to remote areas.

Gas is available 24/7 at Furnace Creek and Stovepipe Wells Village and from 7am to 9:30pm in Panamint Springs. Prices are much higher than outside the park, especially at Panamint.

❶ Getting Around

Furnace Creek Bike Rentals (Map p528; ☑760-786-3371; Hwy 190, Ranch at Furnace Creek; per 1/5/24hr $15/34/49; ☺Oct-Apr) The general store at the Ranch at Furnace Creek rents 24-speed mountain bikes. Cycling is allowed on designated bike trails as well as paved and dirt roads that are also open to public car traffic. Bikes are not allowed on hiking trails, closed roads and service roads. Pick up route suggestions at the park's visitor center.

Farabee's Jeep Rentals (Map p528; ☑760-786-9872; www.deathvalleyjeeprentals.com; Hwy 190; 2-/4-door Jeep incl 200 miles $250/300; ☺Sep-May) Rent a Jeep Wrangler from this outfit to explore Death Valley's backcountry. You must be over 25 years old, have a US driver's license, credit card and proof of insurance. International visitors must purchase CDW at $60 per day. The four-door Jeeps seat up to five people. Rates include water and a GPS spot unit in case of emergency.

Around Death Valley National Park

Shoshone

Just a blip on the map, Shoshone stakes its existence on being an early-20th-century railroad stop with lodging, eating and other businesses. The railroad disappeared in 1941, but the village still caters to travelers with a gas station, store, restaurant and lodging, as well as visitor information.

◉ Sights

Shoshone Museum MUSEUM
(Hwy 127; by donation; ☺9am-3pm Wed-Mon) A rusted Chevy parked next to antique gas pumps and other flotsam and jetsam from yesteryear are the highlights of this quirky place, so don't fret if doors are closed – unless you want to drop by the visitor center that's also housed inside.

🛏 Sleeping & Eating

Shoshone RV Park & Campground CAMPING $
(☑760-852-4569; http://shoshonevillage.com/shoshone-rv-park.html; Hwy 178; RV site with full hookup $40; ᴘ☎≋) This RV park on the northern end of the village has 25 full hookup sites as well as shaded tent spaces. Facilities include a pool and a laundromat.

Shoshone Inn MOTEL $$
(☑760-852-4335; www.shoshonevillage.com; 113 Old Hwy 127; d $125-150; ☺check-in noon-10pm; ᴘ☺✳☎≋) This roadside motel has 17 contemporary rooms with dark furniture, laminate floors and comfy beds set around a shaded courtyard. Five come with kitchenette and there's also a bungalow with full kitchen. Bonus: a small, warm spring-fed pool.

Crowbar Cafe & Saloon AMERICAN $$
(☑760-852-4224; www.shoshonevillage.com; 112 N Hwy 127; mains $10-24; ☺8am-9:30pm; ᴘ✳☎⚐) Shoshone's only restaurant is a 1920 roadhouse next to the visitor center. Its main stocks in trade are burgers and sandwiches, but it also serves breakfast, Mexican dishes, steaks and something called 'rattlesnake' chili (sorry, there are no actual snakes in it). The attached saloon can get lively on weekend nights.

❶ Information

Visitor Center (☑760-852-4524; ☺9am-3pm; ☎) Information about Death Valley National Park and the surrounding area.

Tecopa

En route to Death Valley, the old mining town of Tecopa was named after a peacemaking Paiute chief. It is home to hot natural mineral springs, a hidden date-palm oasis and a surprisingly artistic bunch of locals.

⊙ Sights & Activities

China Ranch Date Farm   FARM
(☑760-852-4415; www.chinaranch.com; China Ranch Rd; ⊙9am-5pm; P⋒) Fed by the mostly belowground Armagosa River and at the end of a narrow canyon, this family-run, organic date farm is a lush oasis in the middle of the blistering desert. You can go hiking or bird-watching, stock up on luscious dates or try the yummy date-nut bread. The location is well-signed from Tecopa.

Tecopa Hot Springs Campground & Pools   HOT SPRINGS
(☑760-852-4377; www.tecopahotspringscampground.com; 400 Tecopa Hot Springs Rd; per 24hr $7; ⊙24hr) Men and women 'take the waters' separately in two bathhouses where nude bathing is compulsory. Private baths are available for modest types. Facilities are also used by guests of the affiliated campground (RVs and tents) across the street.

Delight's Hot Springs Resort   HOT SPRINGS
(☑760-852-4343; www.delightshotspringsresort.com; 368 Tecopa Hot Springs Rd; hot springs day pass 8am-5pm $15, VIP day pass 8am-10pm $20; ⊙8am-10pm) This place has four private pools – two enclosed, two open to the sky – filled with water bubbling up from the local mineral springs at a temperature between 99°F and 104°F. There's a patio for sunning or lounging and vintage motel rooms in case you wish to spend the night.

Tecopa Hot Springs Resort   HOT SPRINGS
(☑760-852-4420; www.tecopahotsprings.org; 860 Tecopa Hot Springs Rd; bathing $8; ⊙1-5pm) There are only two lockable skylit soaking tubs in this hilltop bathhouse. The water is clean but the facilities are pretty grubby. Guests at the resort campground have free 24-hour access.

🛏 Sleeping & Eating

★ Villa Anita   B&B $$
(☑760-852-4595; www.villaanitadv.com; 10 Sunset Rd; r from $160; P❋⚲) Staying at this

---

CAMPING IN DEATH VALLEY

The **national park service** (www.nps.gov/deva; campsites free-$36) operates nine campgrounds, including four tucked into the Panamint Mountains. Only Furnace Creek accepts reservations and only from mid-October to mid-April. All other campgrounds are first-come, first-served. At peak times, such as weekends during the spring wildflower bloom, campsites fill by midmorning. On those days, vast Sunset campground is your best bet for snagging a last-minute spot, plus there's always the option of free backcountry camping.

Private campgrounds catering mostly to RVers can be found in Stovepipe Wells Village (p533), Ranch at Furnace Creek (p532) and Panamint Springs Resort (p533).

Furnace Creek Ranch and Stovepipe Wells Village offer public showers ($5, including swimming-pool access). Pay at reception.

CAMPGROUND	SEASON	LOCATION	FEE	CHARACTERISTICS
Furnace Creek	year-round	valley floor	$22	pleasant grounds, some shady sites
Sunset	Oct-Apr	valley floor	$14	huge, RV-oriented
Texas Springs	Oct-Apr	valley floor	$16	good for tents
Stovepipe Wells	Oct-Apr	valley floor	$14	parking-lot style, close to dunes
Mesquite Springs	year-round	1800ft	$14	close to Ubehebe Crater
Emigrant	year-round	2100ft	free	tents only
Wildrose	year-round	4100ft	free	seasonal water
Thorndike	Mar-Nov	7400ft	free	may need 4WD, no water, closed in winter
Mahogany Flat	Mar-Nov	8200ft	free	may need 4WD, no water, closed in winter

Free backcountry camping (no campfires) is allowed along dirt roads at least 1 mile away from paved roads and developed and day-use areas, and 100yd from any water source. Park your car next to the roadway and pitch your tent on a previously used campsite to minimize your impact. For a list of areas that are off-limits to backcountry camping, as well as additional regulations, check www.nps.gov/deva or stop by the visitor center (p534) where you can also pick up a free voluntary permit.

LIFE AT DEATH VALLEY JUNCTION

An opera house in the middle of nowhere? Yes, thanks to the vision of New York dancer Marta Beckett who fell in love with the 1920s colonnaded adobe building when her car broke down nearby in 1967. For decades she entertained the curious with dance, music and mime shows at the **Amargosa Opera House** (☑760-852-4441; www.amargosaopera house.com; Hwys 127, 178 & 190, Death Valley Junction; tours/shows $5/20; ☺tours 9:30am-4pm, shows 7pm Fri & Sat, 2pm Sun; ℗). Marta sadly passed away on January 30, 2017, but visiting performers continue to keep her legacy alive.

Tours focus on the auditorium whose walls Marta personally adorned with fanciful murals showing an audience she imagined might have attended an opera in the 16th century, including nuns, gypsies and royalty. Check at the adjacent **motel** (☑760-852-4441; www.amargosa-opera-house.com; Hwys 190 & 178, Death Valley Junction; r $70-80; ℗☺@) about tours and upcoming shows.

Should you choose to spend the night, don't come looking for luxury. With no TV, no wi-fi and soft mattresses, it may lack even in basic comforts but instead delivers buckets of kookiness thanks to eccentric staff, muraled rooms and a resident ghost or two. There's a communal kitchenette. Bring supplies as there is no store and, while serving great breakfasts, healthy sandwiches and Saturday dinners, the attached farm-to-table **cafe** (☑760-852-4432; www.amargosacafe.org; Death Valley Junction; mains $9-19, pie per slice $5; ☺8am-3pm Mon, Fri, Sat & Sun, 6:30-9pm Sat; ℗✷) ⚐ does keep erratic hours. The nearest full-time restaurant is across the Nevada border about 7 miles away.

artist-run three-room B&B feels much like bunking with good friends. Using recycled materials whenever possible, Carlo and David have fashioned one room from two boats and used bottles to build another, creating eccentric but supremely comfortable spaces to relax and reflect in. Their wacky sculptures decorate the garden where their lovely dogs like to romp.

Cynthia's　　　　　　　　　　　INN $$
(☑760-852-4580; www.discovercynthias.com; 2001 Old Spanish Trail Hwy; dm $25, r $98-138, tipi $165; ℗☺✷☎) This congenial inn helmed by the friendly Cynthia has hostel-style bunks and eclectically decorated rooms in vintage trailers, all with private bathroom. Alternatively, you can go glamping in Native American–style tipis with thick rugs and comfy beds tucked into the nearby date-palm oasis at China Ranch. Here, bathrooms are shared. Check-in is at the inn.

McNeal's BBQ　　　　　　　BARBECUE $
(☑760-852-4343; westmcneal@gmail.com; 420 Tecopa Springs Rd; meals $7-18; ☺8am-7pm seasonal; ℗) Stop by here for finger-lickin' brisket, pulled pork or ribs served with a side of toothsome coleslaw or a fresh summer salad. It's not always open, so call ahead or take your chances.

Upper Mojave Desert

The Mojave Desert is the driest desert in the US and covers a vast region, from urban areas on the northern edge of LA County to the remote unpopulated Mojave National Preserve and into southern Nevada. It's a harsh, alien landscape with sporadic mining settlements, ghost towns and vast areas set aside for weapons and aerospace testing. Historic Route 66 also traverses the Mojave whose signature plant is the endemic Joshua tree.

Mojave

Driving north on Hwy 14, Mojave is the first stop on the 'Aerospace Triangle' that also includes Boron and Ridgecrest. The modest service town is home to a huge airforce base as well as the country's first commercial space port, and has witnessed major moments in air- and space-flight history.

Being a service town, Mojave has plenty of competitively priced national motel chains along Hwys 14 and 58.

⦿ Sights

Mojave Air & Space Port　　NOTABLE BUILDING
(☑661-824-2433; www.mojaveairport.com; 1434 Flightline, Bldg 58; ☺7:30am-4:30pm Mon-Fri) **FREE** This port made history in 2003 with the launch of SpaceShipOne, the first privately funded human space flight, thus lay-

ing the groundwork for commercial space tourism. A replica of SpaceShipOne is on display in the airport's small Legacy Park, along with a scale model of the Voyager aircraft and an original Rotary Rocket Roton, a manned spacecraft intended to deliver small satellites into space. The Voyager Cafe has some great old photographs. Enter from Airport Blvd, off Hwy 58.

Part of the airport is a huge airplane graveyard (off-limits to visitors) where retired commercial airplanes roost in the dry desert air waiting to be scavenged for spare parts.

Edwards Air Force Base NOTABLE BUILDING
(☑661-277-3511; www.edwards.af.mil/tours; ⊙tours 9:30am 1st Fri of month) FREE Storied Edwards Air Force Base is a flight-test facility for the US Air Force, NASA and civilian aircraft, and a training school for test pilots with the 'right stuff.' It was here that Chuck Yeager piloted the world's first supersonic flight, and the first space shuttles glided in after their missions. Free five-hour tours are offered on the first Friday of the month. Reservations are essential and tours fill up quickly months in advance. The website has details.

Ridgecrest & Around

Ridgecrest is a service town where you can find gas, supplies, information and cheap lodging en route to Death Valley or the Eastern Sierra Nevada. Its main raison d'être is the China Lake US Naval Air Weapons Station that sprawls for a million acres (one third the size of Delaware!) north of the town.

◎ Sights

US Naval Museum of Armament & Technology MUSEUM
(Map p528; ☑760-939-3530; www.chinalake museum.org; 1 Pearl Harbor Way, China Lake; ⊙10am-4pm Mon-Sat) FREE Touch a Tomahawk missile or mug with a 'Fat Man' (atomic bomb, that is) at this museum on a classified US Navy base. The weapons collection will likely fascinate technology, flight, history and military buffs – and perhaps even utter pacifists. Until its relocation to a new building that's under construction at 130 E Las Flores in downtown Ridgecrest, access is restricted to US citizens; bring driver's license and proof of car insurance and prepare to spend two hours for clearance.

Trona Pinnacles NATURE RESERVE
(Map p528; Pinnacle Rd, Trona; ℗) FREE What do the movies *Battlestar Galactica, Star Trek V: the Final Frontier* and *Planet of the Apes* have in common? They were all filmed at Trona Pinnacles, an eerily beautiful natural landmark where some 500 calcium carbonate spires (tufa) rise up to 140ft out of an ancient lake bed in otherworldly fashion. The site sits at the end of a 5-mile dirt road off Hwy 178, about 18 miles east of Ridgecrest. Check locally for current road conditions.

Randsburg GHOST TOWN
(Map p528; ℗) FREE About 20 miles south of Ridgecrest, off US Hwy 395, Randsburg is a 'living ghost town,' an abandoned and now (somewhat) reinhabited gold-mining town circa 1895. You can visit a tiny historical museum, antiques shops, saloon, jailhouse and general store with soda fountain. Most places close on weekdays.

Las Vegas

It's three in the morning in a smoky casino when you spot an Elvis lookalike sauntering by arm in arm with a glittering showgirl just as a bride in a white dress shrieks 'Blackjack!'

Vegas, baby: It's the only place in the world you can see ancient hieroglyphics, the Eiffel Tower, the Brooklyn Bridge and the canals of Venice in a few short hours. Sure, they're all reproductions, but in a desert metropolis that has transformed itself into one of the most lavish getaway destinations on the planet, nothing is executed halfway – not even the illusions.

Las Vegas is the ultimate escape. Time is irrelevant here. There are no clocks, just never-ending buffets and ever-flowing drinks. This city has been constantly reinventing itself since the days of the Rat Pack. Today

DESERT BREWS

In the middle of nowhere, **Death Valley Brewing** (☑760-852-4273; www. deathvalleybrewing.com; 102 Old Spanish Trail; ⊙noon-6pm Fri-Sun Nov-Apr) is not a mirage but the pint-sized operation of artist and brewer Jon Zellhoefer in a restored railroad tie house. He usually has nine to 12 small-batch cold ones on tap, from IPAs to Belgian ales, stouts to wheat beers, all made with water from the local mineral springs.

its pull is all-inclusive: Hollywood bigwigs gyrate at A-list ultralounges, while college kids seek cheap debauchery and grandparents whoop it up at the hot, hot penny slots. Welcome to the dream factory.

◉ Sights

Vegas' sights are primarily concentrated along the 4.2-mile stretch of Las Vegas Blvd anchored by Mandalay Bay to the south (at Russell Rd) and the **Stratosphere** (Map p540; ☎702-380-7777; www.stratospherehotel. com; 2000 S Las Vegas Blvd; tower entry adult/child $20/10, all-day pass incl unlimited thrill rides $40; ☉casino 24hr, tower & thrill rides 10am-1am Sun-Thu, to 2am Fri & Sat, weather permitting; ᴘ♿) to the north (at Sahara Ave) and in the Downtown area around the intersection of Las Vegas Blvd (N Las Vegas Blvd at this point) and Fremont St. Note that while the street has the same name, there's an additional 2 miles between Downtown and the northern end of the Strip, with not much of interest in-between. It might look close if you decide to walk between the two, but you'll probably find yourself cursing in the desert heat if you do so. Ride-shares, the Monorail and Deuce bus services are by far the easiest ways to get around this spaced-out (in more ways than one) city.

◉ The Strip

★ Mandalay Bay
CASINO

(Map p540; ☎702-632-7700; www.mandalaybay. com; 3950 S Las Vegas Blvd; ☉24hr; ᴘ♿) Since opening in 1999, in place of the former '50s-era Hacienda, Mandalay Bay has anchored the southern Strip. Its theme may be tropical, but it sure ain't tacky, nor is its 135,000-sq-ft casino. Well-dressed sports fans find their way to the upscale race and sports book near the high-stakes poker room. Refusing to be pigeonholed, the Bay's standout attractions are many and include the multilevel **Shark Reef Aquarium** (Map p540; ☎702-632-4555; www.sharkreef.com; 3950 S Las Vegas Blvd, Mandalay Bay; adult/child $25/19; ☉10am-8pm Sun-Thu, to 10pm Fri & Sat; ᴘ♿), decadent day spas, oodles of signature dining and the unrivaled **Mandalay Bay Beach** (Map p540; ☎877-632-7800; www.mandalaybay.com/en/amenities/beach.html; Mandalay Bay; ☉pool 8am-5pm, Moorea Beach Club 11am-6pm; ♿).

★ CityCenter
LANDMARK

(Map p540; www.citycenter.com; 3780 S Las Vegas Blvd; ᴘ) We've seen this symbiotic relationship before (think giant hotel anchored by a mall 'concept') but the way that this futuristic-feeling complex places a small galaxy of hypermodern, chichi hotels in orbit around the glitzy **Shops at Crystals** (Map p540; www.crystalsat citycenter.com; 3720 S Las Vegas Blvd, CityCenter; ☉10am-11pm Sun-Thu, to midnight Fri & Sat) is a first. The uberupscale spread includes the subdued, stylish **Vdara** (Map p540; ☎702-590-2111; www.vdara.com; 2600 W Harmon Ave, CityCenter; weekday/weekend ste from $129/189; ᴘ♿✲@ 🛜☕🐾) 🍴, the hush-hush opulent **Mandarin Oriental** (Map p540; ☎702-590-8888; www.man darinoriental.com; 3752 S Las Vegas Blvd, CityCenter; r/ste from $239/469; ✲🛜☕) and the dramatic architectural showpiece **Aria** (Map p540; ☎702-590-7111; www.aria.com; 3730 S Las Vegas Blvd, CityCenter; ☉24hr; ᴘ), whose sophisticated casino provides a fitting backdrop to its many drop-dead-gorgeous restaurants. CityCenter's hotels have in excess of 6700 rooms!

★ Cosmopolitan
CASINO

(Map p540; ☎702-698-7000; www.cosmopolitan lasvegas.com; 3708 S Las Vegas Blvd; ☉24hr; ᴘ) Hipsters who thought they were too cool for Vegas finally have a place to go where they don't need irony to endure – or enjoy – the aesthetics of the Strip. Like the new Hollywood 'It' girl, the Cosmopolitan casino looks absolutely fabulous at all times. A steady stream of ingenues and entourages parade through the lobby (with some of the coolest design elements we've seen) along with anyone else who adores contemporary art and design.

★ Bellagio
CASINO

(Map p540; ☎888-987-6667; www.bellagio.com; 3600 S Las Vegas Blvd; ☉24hr; ᴘ🐾) The Bellagio experience transcends its decadent casino floor of high-limit gaming tables and in excess of 2300 slot machines; locals say odds here are less than favorable. A stop on the World Poker Tour, Bellagio's tournament-worthy poker room offers kitchen-to-gaming-table delivery around-the-clock. Most, however, come for the property's stunning architecture, interiors and amenities, including the **Conservatory & Botanical Gardens** (Map p540; Bellagio; ☉24hr; ᴘ♿) FREE, **Gallery of Fine Art** (Map p540; ☎702-693-7871; Bellagio; adult/child under 12yr $18/free; ☉10am-8pm, last entry 7:30pm; ᴘ♿), unmissable **Fountains of Bellagio** (Map p540; www.bellagio.com; Bellagio; ☉shows every 30min 3-8pm Mon-Fri, noon-8pm Sat, 11am-7pm Sun, every 15min 8pm-midnight Mon-Sat, from 7pm Sun; ᴘ♿) FREE and the 2000-plus hand-blown glass flowers embellishing the hotel (p543) lobby.

★**Paris Las Vegas** CASINO

(Map p540; ☑877-603-4386; www.parislasvegas.com; 3655 S Las Vegas Blvd; ⊘24hr; P) This mini-inversion of the French capital might lack the charm of the City of Light, but its efforts to emulate Paris' landmarks, including a 34-story Hotel de Ville and facades from the Opera House and Louvre, make it a fun stop for families and anyone yet to see the real thing. Its vaulted casino ceilings simulate sunny skies above myriad tables and slots, while its high-limit authentic French roulette wheels, sans 0 and 00, slightly improve your odds.

★**Caesars Palace** CASINO

(Map p540; ☑866-227-5938; www.caesarspalace.com; 3570 S Las Vegas Blvd; ⊘24hr; P) Caesars Palace claims that its smartly renovated casino floor has more million-dollar slots than anywhere in the world, but its claims to fame are far more numerous than that. Entertainment's heavyweights Celine Dion and Elton John 'own' its custom-built **Colosseum** (Map p540; ☑866-227-5938; www.thecolosseum.com; Caesars Palace; tickets $55-500) theater, fashionistas saunter around the **Shops at Forum** (Map p540; www.simon.com/mall/the-forum-shops-at-caesars-palace/stores; Caesars Palace; ⊘10am-11pm Sun-Thu, to midnight Fri & Sat), while Caesars hotel guests quaff cocktails in the **Garden of the Gods Pool Oasis**. By night, megaclub **Omnia** (Map p540; www.omnianightclub.com; Caesars Palace; cover female/male $20/40; ⊘10pm-4am Tue & Thu-Sun) is the only place to get off your face this side of Ibiza.

★**LINQ Promenade** STREET

(Map p540; www.caesars.com/linq; ⊘24hr; P⊞) You'll be delighted by the fun vibe of the Strip's newest outdoor pedestrian promenade, where you can browse the latest LA fashions, gorge yourself on cupcakes, jaburritos (where sushi rolls meet burritos!) and fish and chips, go bowling, ride the High Roller (p539), rock out to live music, or sip pints on lazy patios beneath the desert sun.

High Roller LANDMARK

(Map p540; ☑702-322-0591; www.caesars.com/linq; LINQ Promenade; adult/child from $22/9, after 5pm $32/19; ⊘11:30am-2am; P⊞; ⊕Flamingo or Harrah's/Linq) The world's largest observation wheel towers 550ft above LINQ Promenade (p539). Each of the 28 air-conditioned passenger cabins is enclosed by handcrafted Italian glass. Outside, 2000 colorful LED lights glow from dusk until dawn. One revolution takes about 30 minutes and each pod can hold 40 guests. From 4pm to 7pm, select pods host the adults-only (21-plus) 'happy half hour' ($35, or $47 after 5pm) with an open bar (read all-you-can-drink) shared between your fellow riders. Things can get messy, fast.

★**Venetian** CASINO

(Map p540; ☑702-414-1000; www.venetian.com; 3355 S Las Vegas Blvd; ⊘24hr; P) The Venetian's regal 120,000-sq-ft casino has marble floors, hand-painted ceiling frescoes and 120 table games, including a high-limit lounge and an elegant no-smoking poker room, where women are especially welcome (unlike at many other poker rooms in town). When combined with its younger, neighboring sibling **Palazzo** (Map p540; ☑702-607-7777; www.palazzo.com; 3325 S Las Vegas Blvd; ⊘24hr; P), the properties claim the largest casino space in Las Vegas. Unmissable on the Strip, a highlight of this miniature replica of Venice is to take a **gondola ride** (Map p540; ☑702-414-4300; www.venetian.com/resort/attractions/gondola-rides.html; Venetian; shared ride per person $29, child under 3yr free, private 2-passenger ride $116; ⊘indoor 10am-11pm Sun-Thu, to midnight Fri & Sat, outdoor rides 11am-10pm, weather permitting; ⊞) down its Grand Canal.

★**Wynn & Encore Casinos** CASINO

(Map p540; ☑702-770-7000; www.wynnlasvegas.com; 3131 S Las Vegas Blvd; ⊘24hr; P) Steve Wynn's signature casino hotel (literally – his name is emblazoned across the top) **Wynn** (Map p540; ☑702-770-7000; www.wynnlasvegas.com; 3131 S Las Vegas Blvd; weekday/weekend r from $199/259; P✱@🛜🏊) and its younger sibling **Encore** (Map p540; ☑702-770-7100; www.wynnlasvegas.com; 3131 S Las Vegas Blvd; r/ste from $199/259; P✱@🛜🏊) are a pair of curvaceous, copper-toned twin towers, whose entrances are obscured by high fences and lush greenery. Each hotel is unique, but their sprawling subterranean casinos converge to form the Strip's second-largest and arguably most elegant gaming floor, whose popular poker rooms lure pros around the clock and labyrinth of slot machines range from a penny to $5000 per pull!

◎ **Downtown & Off-Strip**

★**Mob Museum** MUSEUM

(☑702-229-2734; www.themobmuseum.org; 300 Stewart Ave; adult/child $24/14; ⊘9am-9pm; P; 🚌Deuce) It's hard to say what's more impressive: the museum's physical location in a historic federal courthouse where mobsters sat for federal hearings in 1950–51, the fact

Las Vegas Strip

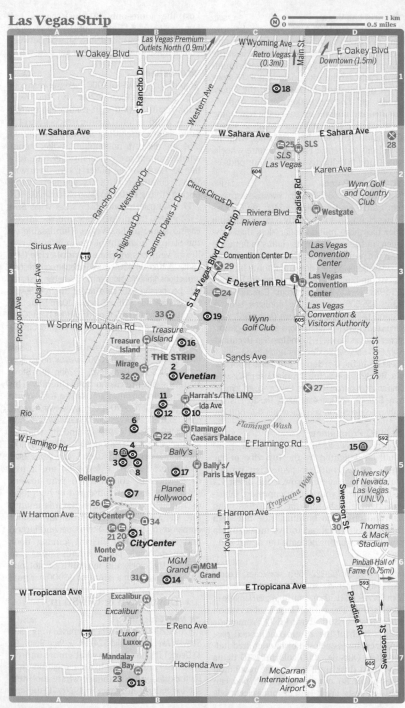

Las Vegas Strip

that the board of directors is headed up by a former FBI special agent, or the thoughtfully curated exhibits telling the story of organized crime in America. In addition to hands-on FBI equipment and mob-related artifacts, the museum boasts a series of multimedia exhibits featuring interviews with real-life Tony Sopranos.

★ **Fremont Street Experience**   STREET
(☑702-678-5600; www.vegasexperience.com; Fremont St Mall; ☺shows hourly dusk-midnight or 1am; ☐Deuce, SDX) FREE A five-block pedestrian mall, between Main St and N Las Vegas Blvd, topped by an arched steel canopy and filled with computer-controlled lights, the Fremont Street Experience has brought life back Downtown. Every evening, the canopy is transformed by light-and-sound shows enhanced by 550,000 watts of wraparound sound and a larger-than-life screen lit up by 12.5-million synchronized LEDs. Soar through the air on zip lines strung underneath the canopy from **Slotzilla** (www.vegas experience.com/slotzilla-zip-line; Fremont St Mall, Fremont Street Experience; lower line $25, upper line $45; ☺1pm-1am Sun-Thu, to 2am Fri & Sat; ☒; ☐Deuce, SDX), a 12-story, slot-machine-themed platform. Gaudy, yes. Weird, yes. Busy: always.

Neon Museum – Urban Gallery   TOURS
(☑702-387-6366; www.neonmuseum.org; 450 Fremont St E, Neonopolis; ☺24hr; ☐Deuce, SDX)

FREE Plaques tell the story of each restored vintage neon sign at these open-air galleries. Look for the flashy 40ft-tall cowboy on horseback, Aladdin's sparkling genie lamp, a glowing martini glass, a flaming steakhouse sign and more. The biggest assemblages are inside the Neonopolis and on the 3rd St cul-de-sac just north of the Fremont Street Experience (p542).

★ **Golden Nugget** CASINO
(☑702-385-7111; www.goldennugget.com; 129 Fremont St E; ☺24hr; P⍮; ⌨Deuce, SDX) Check out the polished brass and white-leather seats in the casino: day or night, the Golden Nugget is downtown's poshest address. With classy eateries and a swimming pool famous for its shark tank, the Golden Nugget outshines its competition. This swank-carpet joint rakes in a moneyed crowd with a 38,000-sq-ft casino populated by table games and slot machines with the same odds as at Strip megaresorts. The nonsmoking poker room hosts daily tournaments.

★ **Container Park** CULTURAL CENTER
(☑702-359-9982; http://downtowncontainerpark.com; 707 Fremont St E; ☺11am-9pm Mon-Thu, 10am-10pm Fri & Sat, to 8pm Sun) An incubator for up-and-coming fashion designers and local artisans, the edgy Container Park stacks pop-up shops on top of one another. Wander along the sidewalks and catwalks while searching out handmade jewelry, contemporary art and clothing at a dozen or so specialty boutiques, eateries and art installations. When the sun sets, the container bars come to life and host regular themed events and movie nights. It's adults only (21-plus) after 9pm.

★ **National Atomic Testing Museum** MUSEUM
(Map p540; ☑702-794-5151; www.nationalatomictestingmuseum.org; 755 Flamingo Rd E, Desert Research Institute; adult/child $22/16; ☺10am-5pm Mon-Sat, noon-5pm Sun; ⌨202) Fascinating multimedia exhibits focus on science, technology and the social history of the 'Atomic Age,' which lasted from WWII until atmospheric bomb testing was driven underground in 1961 and a worldwide ban on nuclear testing was declared in 1992. View footage of atomic testing and examine southern Nevada's nuclear past, present and future, from Native American ways of life to the environmental legacy of atomic testing. Don't miss the ticket booth (how could you?); it's a Nevada Test Site guard-station replica.

★ **Pinball Hall of Fame** MUSEUM
(☑702-597-2627; www.pinballmuseum.org; 1610 E Tropicana Ave; per game 25¢-$1; ☺11am-11pm Sun-Thu, to midnight Fri & Sat; ⍮; ⌨201) You may have more fun at this no-frills arcade than playing slot machines back on the Strip. Tim Arnold shares his collection of 200-plus vintage pinball and video games with the public. Take time to read the handwritten curatorial cards explaining the unusual history behind these restored machines.

★ **Hard Rock** CASINO
(Map p540; ☑702-693-5000; www.hardrockhotel.com; 4455 Paradise Rd; ☺24hr; ⌨108) The world's original rock-and-roll casino houses what may be the most impressive collection of rock-star memorabilia ever assembled under one roof. Priceless items being watched over by security guards suited up like bouncers are concert attire worn by Elvis, Britney Spears and Prince; a display case filled with Beatles mementos; Jim Morrison's handwritten lyrics to one of the Doors' greatest hits; and dozens of leather jackets and guitars formerly owned by everyone from the Ramones to U2.

🛏 Sleeping

With over 150,000 hotel rooms and consistently high occupancy rates, prices in Vegas fluctuate constantly. Sometimes the best deals are found in advance; other times, at the last minute. As a general rule, if you find a good price on a place you love, nab it. Decent rooms Downtown start from as low as $29, while the swankiest digs on the Strip can fetch upwards of $10,000 per night!

🛏 The Strip

★ **Aria Las Vegas Resort** CASINO HOTEL $$
(Map p540; ☑702-590-7111; www.arialasvegas.com; 3730 S Las Vegas Blvd, CityCenter; r weekday/weekend from $129/189; P✳@☎☀) Aria's (p539) sleek resort hotel at CityCenter (p538) has no theme, unlike the Strip's other megaproperties. Instead, its 4000-plus deluxe rooms (520 sq ft) and 560 tower suites (920-plus sq ft) are all about soothing design, spaciousness and luxury, and every room has a corner view. If you've cash to burn, **Aria Sky Suites & Villas** (Map p540; ☑702-590-7111; www.aria.com; Aria; ste/villa from $340/3000), a hotel-within-a-hotel, might be for you.

★**Cromwell Las Vegas**   BOUTIQUE HOTEL **$$**
(Map p540; ✆702-777-3777; www.caesars.com/cromwell; 3595 S Las Vegas Blvd; r/ste from $199/399; [P][✳][@][⊛][≋][⊠]) If you're 20- to 30-something, can hold your own with the cool kids, or you're just effortlessly stylish whatever your demographic, there are a few good reasons to choose Cromwell, the best being its location and frequently excellent rates on sassy, entry-level rooms. The others? You've got your sites set on partying at Drai's (p546) or dining downstairs at **Giada** (Map p540; ✆855-442-3271; www.caesars.com; Cromwell Las Vegas; mains $25-58; ⊙8am-11pm).

★**LINQ Hotel**   CASINO HOTEL **$$**
(Map p540; ✆800-634-6441; www.caesars.com/linq; 3535 S Las Vegas Blvd; d/ste from $109/209; [P][✳][⊛][≋][⊠]) Launching onto the Las Vegas Strip in late 2014, LINQ, formerly the Quad, has cemented its position as a solid all-rounder. Its fresh, white rooms have fun splashes of color and sleek Euro-styled furniture, there's a wealth of available amenities (this being part of the Caesars group) and it has an enviable location at the center of its eponymous promenade (p539).

★**Mandalay Bay**   CASINO HOTEL **$$**
(Map p540; ✆702-632-7700; www.mandalaybay.com; 3950 S Las Vegas Blvd; weekday/weekend r from $119/229; [P][✳][⊛][≋]) Anchoring the south Strip, upscale Mandalay Bay's (p538) same-named hotel (p543) has a cache of classy rooms worthy of your attention in their own right, not to mention the exclusive **Four Seasons Hotel** (Map p540; ✆702-632-5000; www.fourseasons.com/lasvegas; Mandalay Bay; weekday/weekend r from $229/289; [P][✳][@][⊛][≋][⊠]) and boutique **Delano** (Map p540; ✆877-632-7800; www.delanolasvegas.com; Mandalay Bay; r/ste from $69/129; [P][✳][@][⊛][≋][⊠]) within its bounds and a diverse range of noteworthy attractions and amenities, not least of which is Mandalay Bay Beach (p538).

★**Cosmopolitan**   CASINO HOTEL **$$$**
(Map p540; ✆702-698-7575, 702-698-7000; www.cosmopolitanlasvegas.com; 3708 S Las Vegas Blvd; r/ste from $250/300; [P][✳][@][⊛][≋][⊠]; ☐Deuce) With at least eight distinctively different and equally stylish room types to choose from, Cosmo's digs are the hippest on the Strip. Ranging from oversized to decadent, about 2200 of its 2900 or so rooms have balconies (all but the entry-level category), many sport sunken Japanese tubs and all feature plush

furnishings and design quirks you'll delight in uncovering.

If you've got cash to spare and look the part, you're going to love exploring Cosmopolitan's (p539) playground for a worldly, style-conscious and design-smart generation that's got youth on its side.

★**Bellagio**   CASINO HOTEL **$$$**
(Map p540; ✆888-987-6667; www.bellagio.com; 3600 S Las Vegas Blvd; weekday/weekend r from $179/249; [P][✳][@][⊛][≋][⊠]) When it opened in 1998, Bellagio was the world's most expensive hotel. Aging gracefully, it remains one of America's finest. Its sumptuous oversized guest rooms fuse classic style with modern amenities and feature palettes of platinum, indigo and muted white-gold, or rusty autumnal oranges with subtle splashes of *matcha* green. Cashmere throws, mood lighting and automatic drapes complete the picture.

Downtown & Off-Strip

★**El Cortez**   CASINO HOTEL **$**
(✆702-385-5200; www.elcortezhotelcasino.com; 651 E Ogden Ave; weekday/weekend r from $40/80; [P][✳][@][⊛]) A wide range of rooms with all kinds of vibes are available at this fun, retro property close to all the action on Fremont St. Rooms are in the 1980s tower addition to the heritage-listed 1941 **El Cortez** (✆702-385-5200; www.elcortezhotelcasino.com; 600 Fremont St E; ⊙24hr; ☐Deuce) casino and the modern, flashier El Cortez Suites, across the street. Rates offered are generally great value, though don't expect the earth.

★**Hard Rock**   CASINO HOTEL **$**
(Map p540; ✆702-693-5000; www.hardrockhotel.com; 4455 Paradise Rd; weekday/weekend r from $45/89; [P][✳][@][⊛][≋]) Sexy, oversized rooms and HRH suites underwent a bunch of refurbishments in 2016 and 2017, making this party palace for music lovers a great alternative to staying on the Strip – there's even a free shuttle to take you there and bring you back.

★**Golden Nugget**   CASINO HOTEL **$**
(✆702-385-7111; www.goldennugget.com; 129 Fremont St E; weekday/weekend r from $45/85; [P][✳][@][⊛][≋]) Pretend to relive the fabulous heyday of Vegas in the 1950s at this swank Fremont St address. Rooms in the Rush Tower are the best in the house.

❶ TOP TIPS ON DOING VEGAS RIGHT

➡ The Strip runs for miles: don't assume you can easily walk from point A to B. Consult a map first and note that pedestrian crossings are punctuated with sky bridges and escalators. Take advantage of free trams between casinos whenever possible.

➡ Meeting locals is a great way to get to know a city, but in a place of itinerants like Vegas, they're hard to find and even harder to hold. Don't be surprised if the locals are a little reserved at first: they'll be the first to tell you that nobody trusts anybody here. If that's the dominant discourse, it's a good idea to keep your own guard up a little.

➡ Areas either side of Las Vegas Blvd (especially to the east and north) can be dangerous, even during daylight hours. Exercise caution when on foot.

➡ Single women travelers should be wary of wandering too far from the Strip and avoid walking alone at night.

➡ Ride-share where possible – these services are by far the most convenient way to get around the city. Rates are great and you'll never wait long.

✖ Eating

The Strip has been studded with celebrity chefs for years. All-you-can-eat buffets and $10 steaks still exist, but today's high-rolling visitors demand ever more sophisticated dining experiences, with meals designed – although not personally prepared – by famous taste-makers. Flash enough cash and you can taste the same cuisine served at revered restaurants from NYC to Paris to Shanghai.

✖ The Strip

★ Tacos El Gordo   MEXICAN $
(Map p540; ☎702-251-8226; www.tacoselgordobc.com; 3049 S Las Vegas Blvd; small plates $3-12; ⏱10am-2am Sun-Thu, to 4am Fri & Sat; 🅿🚲🚶; 🚌Deuce, SDX) This Tijuana-style taco shop from SoCal is just the ticket when it's way late, you've got almost no money left and you're desperately craving carne asada (beef) or *adobada* (chile-marinated pork) tacos in hot, hand-made tortillas. Adventurous eaters

order the authentic *sesos* (beef brains), *cabeza* (roasted cow's head) or tripe variations.

★ Umami Burger   BURGERS $
(Map p540; ☎702-761-7614; www.slslasvegas.com/dining/umami-burger; SLS, 2535 S Las Vegas Blvd; burgers $12-15; ⏱11am-10pm; 🅿) SLS (Map p540; ☎702-761-7000; www.slslasvegas.com; 2535 S Las Vegas Blvd; d from $79; 🅿❄🏊🐾) burger offering is one of the best on the Strip, with its outdoor beer garden, extensive craft-beer selection and juicy boutique burgers made by the chain that won *GQ* magazine's prestigious 'burger of the year' crown.

★ Burger Bar   AMERICAN $$
(Map p540; ☎702-632-9364; www.burger-bar.com; Shoppes at Mandalay Place; mains $10-60; ⏱11am-11pm Sun-Thu, to 1am Fri & Sat; 🅿❄🐾) Since when can a hamburger be worth $60? When it's built with Kobe beef, sautéed foie gras and truffle sauce: it's the Rossini burger, the signature sandwich of chef Hubert Keller. Most menu options are more down-to-earth – diners select their own gourmet burger toppings and pair them with skinny fries and a liquor-spiked milkshake or beer float.

★ Grand Wok   CHINESE $$
(Map p540; ☎702-891-7879; www.mgmgrand.com/en/restaurants.html; MGM Grand; mains $12-28; ⏱11am-10pm Sun-Thu, to 11pm Fri & Sat) Come to Grand Wok, in business for over 25 years serving some of the best pan-Asian dishes you'll find this side of the Far East. Try the garlic shrimp fried rice with dried scallops. Sensational.

★ Guy Fieri's Vegas Kitchen & Bar   AMERICAN $$
(Map p540; ☎702-794-3139; www.caesars.com; LINQ Casino; mains $12-28; ⏱9am-midnight) *Diners, Drive-ins and Dives* celebrity chef Guy Fieri has opened his first restaurant on the Strip at LINQ Casino (Map p540; ☎800-634-6441; www.caesars.com/linq; 3535 S Las Vegas Blvd; ⏱24hr; 🅿), dishing out an eclectic menu of his own design, inspired by so many years journeying America's back roads for the best and fairest down-home cooking.

★ Eiffel Tower Restaurant   FRENCH $$$
(Map p540; ☎702-948-6937; www.eiffeltowerrestaurant.com; Paris Las Vegas; mains lunch $14-32, dinner $32-89, tasting menu without/with wine pairings $125/205; ⏱11:30am-10pm Mon-Fri, 11am-11pm Sat & Sun) At this haute eatery midway up its namesake tower, the Francophile wine list is vast, the chocolate soufflé is unforgettable,

and views of the Strip and Bellagio's fountains are breathtaking. Contemporary renditions of French classics are generally well executed. Lunch is your best bet, but it's more popular to come for sunset. Reservations essential.

★ **Joël Robuchon**   FRENCH **$$$**
(Map p540; ☑702-891-7925; www.joel-robuchon. com/en; MGM Grand; tasting menus $120-425; ☺5-10pm) The acclaimed 'Chef of the Century' leads the pack in the French culinary invasion of the Strip. Adjacent to the **MGM Grand's** (Map p540; ☑877-880-0880; www.mgmgrand.com; 3799 S Las Vegas Blvd; ☺24hr; P🖘) high-rollers' gaming area, Robuchon's plush dining rooms, done up in leather and velvet, feel like a dinner party at a 1930s Paris mansion. Complex seasonal tasting menus promise the meal of a lifetime – and they often deliver.

Reservations are essential for dinner here, as well as at the slightly less-expensive **L'Atelier de Joël Robuchon** (Map p540; ☑702-891-7358; www.joel-robuchon.com/en; MGM Grand; mains $41-97, tasting menu without/with wine pairings $159/265; ☺5-10:30pm; ☑) next door, where bar seats front an exhibition kitchen.

⚔ Downtown & Off-Strip

★**eat.**   BREAKFAST **$**
(☑702-534-1515; http://eatdtlv.com; 707 Carson Ave; mains $7-14; ☺8am-3pm Mon-Fri, to 2pm Sat & Sun; ☑) ✿ Community spirit and creative cooking provide reason enough to venture off Fremont St to find this cafe. With a concrete floor and spare decor, it can get loud as folks chow down on truffled egg sandwiches, cinnamon biscuits with strawberry compote, shrimp po'boy sandwiches and bowls of New Mexican green-chile chicken *pozole.*

Metered parking is available on the street, or take the Deuce bus to the Fremont Street Experience (p542), then walk two blocks east on Fremont and one block south on 7th, to Carson Ave.

★**Park on Fremont**   GASTROPUB **$**
(☑702-834-3160; www.parkonfremont.com; 506 Fremont St E; light meals $9-14; ☺11am-3am) The best thing about this gorgeous little oasis away from the Fremont St frenzy are its outdoor patio and courtyard areas. OK, the burgers are great too, but not as exciting as the crispy brussels sprouts and cheesy garbage fries. It's a great place to just sit and sip a margarita and watch the crowds go by.

★**Culinary Dropout**   AMERICAN **$$**
(Map p540; ☑702-522-8100; www.hardrockhotel. com; Hard Rock; mains brunch $8-14, lunch & dinner $14-32; ☺11am-11pm Mon-Thu, 11am-midnight Fri, 9am-midnight Sat, 9am-11pm Sun; ☑108) With a pool-view patio and live bands rocking on weekends, there's no funkier gastropub around. Dip warm pretzels in provolone fondue or homemade potato chips in onion dip, then bite into fried chicken and honey biscuits. Weekend brunch (9am to 3pm on Saturday and Sunday) gives you the hair of the dog with bacon Bloody Marys. Reservations essential on weekends.

★**Firefly**   TAPAS **$$**
(Map p540; ☑702-369-3971; www.fireflylv.com; 3824 Paradise Rd; shared plates $5-12, mains $15-20; ☺11:30am-1am Mon-Thu, to 2am Fri & Sat, 10am-1am Sun; ☑108) Firefly is always packed with a fashionable local crowd, who come for well-prepared Spanish and Latin American tapas, such as *patatas bravas,* chorizo-stuffed empanadas and vegetarian bites like garbanzo beans seasoned with chili, lime and sea salt. A back-lit bar dispenses the house specialty sangria – red, white or sparkling – and fruity mojitos. Reservations strongly recommended.

Show up for happy hour from 3pm to 6pm Monday through Thursday (till 5pm on Friday).

★**Lotus of Siam**   THAI **$$**
(Map p540; ☑702-735-3033; www.lotusofsiamlv. com; 953 E Sahara Ave; mains $9-30; ☺11am-2:30pm Mon-Fri, 5:30-10pm daily; ☑; ☑SDX) Saipin Chutima's authentic northern Thai cooking has won almost as many awards as her distinguished European and New World wine cellar. Critics have suggested this might be America's best Thai restaurant and we're sure it's up there with the best. Although the strip-mall hole-in-the-wall may not look like much, foodies flock here. Reservations essential.

★**Carson Kitchen**   AMERICAN **$$**
(☑702-473-9523; www.carsonkitchen.com; 124 S 6th St; tapas & mains $8-22; ☺11:30am-11pm Thu-Sat, to 10pm Sun-Wed; ☑ Deuce) This tiny eatery with an industrial theme of exposed beams, bare bulbs and chunky share tables hops with downtowners looking to escape the mayhem of Fremont St or the Strip's high prices. Excellent shared plates include rainbow cauliflower, watermelon and feta salad and decadent mac 'n' cheese, and there's a creative 'libations' menu.

★ **Grotto** ITALIAN $$

(☑702-386-8341; www.goldennugget.com; 129 Fremont St E, Golden Nugget; pizza $12-15, mains $19-35; ⊙11:30am-midnight Sun-Thu, to 1am Fri & Sat; 🚍Deuce, SDX) At this Italian trattoria covered in painted murals, you'll be drawn to the sunlight-filled patio next to the Nugget's shark-tank waterslide and swimming pool. Wood-oven-fired, thin-crust pizzas, heavy pastas, and chicken, fish, veal and steak dishes are accompanied by a 200-bottle list of Italian wines. Happy hour runs 2pm to 6pm daily.

★ **Andiamo Steakhouse** STEAK $$$

(☑702-388-2220; www.thed.com; 301 Fremont St E, The D; mains $24-79; ⊙5-11pm; 🚍Deuce, SDX) Of all the old-school steakhouses inside Downtown's carpet joints, the current front-runner is Joe Vicari's Andiamo Steakhouse. Upstairs from the casino, richly upholstered half-moon booths and impeccably polite waiters set the tone for a classic Italian steakhouse feast of surf-and-turf platters and housemade pasta, followed by a rolling dessert cart. Extensive Californian and European wine list. Reservations recommended.

🍷 Drinking & Nightlife

You don't need us to tell you that Las Vegas is party central – the Strip is ground zero for some of the country's hottest clubs and most happening bars, where you never know who you'll be rubbing shoulders with. What you might not know is that Downtown's Fremont East Entertainment District is the go-to place for Vegas' coolest nonmainstream haunts.

🍸 The Strip

★ **Hakkasan** CLUB

(Map p540; ☑702-891-3838; www.hakkasanlv. com; MGM Grand; cover $20-75; ⊙10pm-4am Wed-Sun) At this lavish Asian-inspired nightclub, international jet-set DJs like Tiësto and Steve Aoki rule the jam-packed main dance floor bordered by VIP booths and floor-to-ceiling LED screens. More offbeat sounds spin in the intimate Ling Ling Club, revealing leather sofas and backlit amber glass. Bouncers enforce the dress code: upscale nightlife attire (no athletic wear, collared shirts required for men).

★ **Drai's Beachclub & Nightclub** CLUB

(Map p540; ☑702-777-3800; www.draislv.com; Cromwell Las Vegas; nightclub cover $20-50; ⊙nightclub 10pm-5am Thu-Sun, beach club 11am-6pm Fri-Sun) Feel ready for an after-hours party scene straight outta Hollywood? Or maybe you just wanna hang out all day poolside, then shake your booty on the petite dancefloor while DJs spin hip-hop, mash-ups and electronica? This multivenue club has you covered pretty much all day and night. Dress to kill: no sneakers, tank tops or baggy jeans.

★ **Jewel** CLUB

(Map p540; ☑702-590-8000; www.jewelnight club.com; Aria; cover female/male from $20/30; ⊙10:30am-4am Fri, Sat & Mon) From the creators of Hakkasan (p546), long-awaited Jewel replaces its predecessor Haze, which failed to dazzle. Boasting five VIP suites (because it's all about being seen) and over 1400 sq ft of shimmering LED ribbon lighting, Jewel, despite accommodating up to 2000 revelers, is pitched as an 'intimate' alternative to the Strip's megaclubs. Monday nights offer locals free admission.

★ **Chandelier Lounge** COCKTAIL BAR

(Map p540; ☑702-698-7979; www.cosmopolitan lasvegas.com/lounges-bars/chandelier; Cosmopolitan; ⊙24hr; 🚍Deuce) Towering high in the center of Cosmopolitan (p539), this ethereal cocktail bar is inventive yet beautifully simple, with three levels connected by romantic curved staircases, all draped with glowing strands of glass beads. The second level is headquarters for molecular mixology (order a martini made with liquid nitrogen), while the third specializes in floral and fruit infusions.

★ **Nine Fine Irishmen** PUB

(Map p540; ☑702-740-6463; www.ninefineirish men.com; New York–New York; ⊙11am-11pm, live music from 9pm; 🛜) Built in Ireland and shipped piece by piece to America, this pub has cavernous interior booths and outdoor patio tables beside NYNY's Brooklyn Bridge. Genuine stouts, ales, ciders and Irish whiskeys are always stocked at the bar. Live entertainment is a mix of Celtic rock and traditional Irish country tunes, occasionally with sing-alongs and a champion Irish dancer.

★ **Skyfall Lounge** BAR

(Map p540; ☑702-632-7575; www.delanolasvegas. com; Delano; ⊙5pm-midnight Sun-Thu, to 1:30am Fri & Sat) Enjoy unparalleled views of the southern Strip from this rooftop bar atop Mandalay Bay's Delano (p543) hotel. Sit and sip cocktails as the sun sets over the Spring Mountains to the west, then dance the night away to mellow DJ beats, spun from 9pm.

Downtown & Off-Strip

★ Beauty Bar   BAR
(☑702-598-3757; www.thebeautybar.com; 517 Fremont St E; cover free-$10; ☺9pm-4am; ☐Deuce) Swill a cocktail or just chill with the cool kids inside the salvaged innards of a 1950s New Jersey beauty salon. DJs and live bands rotate nightly, spinning everything from tiki lounge tunes, disco and '80s hits to punk, metal, glam and indie rock. Check the website for special events like 'Karate Karaoke.' There's often no cover charge.

★ Commonwealth   BAR
(☑702-445-6400; www.commonwealthlv.com; 525 Fremont St E; ☺7pm-late Tue-Sat; ☐Deuce) It might be a little too cool for school but, whoa, that Prohibition-era interior is worth a look: plush booths, softly glowing chandeliers, Victorian-era bric-a-brac and a saloon bar. Imbibe your old-fashioned cocktails on the rooftop patio overlooking the Fremont East scene. They say there's a secret cocktail bar within the bar, but you didn't hear that from us.

★ Double Down Saloon   BAR
(Map p540; ☑702-791-5775; www.doubledown saloon.com; 4640 Paradise Rd; ☺24hr; ☐108) This dark, psychedelic gin joint appeals to the lunatic fringe. It never closes, there's never a cover charge, the house drink is called 'ass juice' and it claims to be the birthplace of the bacon martini. When live bands aren't terrorizing the crowd, the jukebox vibrates with New Orleans jazz, British punk, Chicago blues and surf-guitar king Dick Dale.

★ Gold Spike   BAR
(☑702-476-1082; www.goldspike.com; 217 N Las Vegas Blvd; ☺24hr) Gold Spike, with its playroom, living room and backyard, is many things: bar, nightclub, performance space, work space; sometime host of roller derbies, discos, live bands or dance parties; or just somewhere to soak up the sun with a relaxed crew and escape mainstream Vegas. Australians will think it's very Melburnian and feel right at home.

☆ Entertainment

That sensory overload of blindingly bright neon lights means you've finally landed on Las Vegas Blvd. The infamous Strip has the lion's share of gigantic casino hotels, all flashily competing to lure you (and your wallet) inside, with larger-than-life production shows, celebrity-filled nightclubs and burlesque cabarets. Head off-Strip to find jukebox dive bars, arty cocktail lounges, strip clubs and more.

★ Le Rêve the Dream   THEATER
(Map p540; ☑702-770-9966; http://boxoffice. wynnlasvegas.com; Wynn; tickets $105-205; ☺shows at 7pm & 9:30pm Fri-Tue) Underwater acrobatic feats by scuba-certified performers are the centerpiece of this intimate 'aqua-in-the-round' theater, which holds a one-million-gallon swimming pool. Critics call it a less-inspiring version of Cirque's *O*, while devoted fans find the romantic underwater tango, thrilling high dives and visually spectacular adventures to be superior. Beware: the cheapest seats are in the 'splash zone.'

★ O   THEATER
(Map p540; ☑888-488-7111; www.cirquedusoleil. com; Bellagio; tickets $99-185; ☺7pm & 9:30pm Wed-Sun) Phonetically speaking, it's the French word for water *(eau)*. With a lithe international cast performing in, on and above water, Cirque du Soleil's *O* tells the tale of theater through the ages. It's a spectacular feat of imagination and engineering, and you'll pay dearly to see it – it's one of the Strip's few shows that rarely sells discounted tickets.

Beatles LOVE   THEATER
(Map p540; ☑702-792-7777; www.cirquedusoleil. com; Mirage; tickets $79-180; ☺7pm & 9:30pm Thu-Mon; ⓓ) Another smash hit from Cirque du Soleil, *Beatles LOVE* started as the brainchild of the late George Harrison. Using *Abbey Road* master tapes, the show psychedelically fuses the musical legacy of the Beatles with Cirque's high-energy dancers and signature aerial acrobatics. Come early to photograph the trippy, rainbow-colored entryway and grab drinks at Abbey Road bar, next to Revolution Lounge.

ⓘ TICKET DEALS

Tix 4 Tonight (Map p540; ☑877-849-4868; www.tix4tonight.com; 3200 S Las Vegas Blvd, Fashion Show Mall; ☺10am-8pm) Offers half-price tix for a limited lineup of same-day shows and small discounts on 'always sold-out' shows. It's located outside Neiman Marcus department store. Check the website for other locations around the Strip.

GETTING AROUND LAS VEGAS

Walking The Strip is 4.2 miles long – don't assume you can walk easily between casino hotels, even those that appear to be close together.

Bus Day passes on the 24-hour Deuce and faster (though not 24-hour and not servicing all casinos) SDX buses are an excellent way to get around.

Monorail Expensive, inconveniently located on the east side of the Strip and with a limited route, but great views and regular services.

Tram Operates between some casinos. Free and slow.

Taxi Expensive. Tips are expected.

Ride-share By far the best way to get around Vegas in most circumstances, and even cheaper when traveling with others.

★ **Michael Jackson ONE**   THEATER
(Map p540; ☑702-632-7580; www.cirquedusoleil. com; Mandalay Bay; tickets from $69; ☺7pm & 9:30pm Fri-Tue) Cirque du Soleil's musical tribute to the King of Pop blasts onto Mandalay Bay's (p538) stage with showstopping dancers and lissome acrobats and aerialists all moving to a soundtrack of MJ's hits, moon-walking all the way back to his breakout platinum album *Thriller*. No children under five years old allowed.

🛍 Shopping

★ **Las Vegas Premium Outlets North**   MALL
(☑702-474-7500; www.premiumoutlets.com/ vegasnorth; 875 S Grand Central Pkwy; ☺9am-9pm Mon-Sat, to 8pm Sun; 🖬; 🚌 SDX) Vegas' biggest-ticket outlet mall features 120 mostly high-end names such as Armani, Brooks Brothers, Diane Von Furstenberg, Elle Tahari, Kate Spade, Michael Kors, Theory and Tory Burch, alongside casual brands like Banana Republic and Diesel.

Retro Vegas   VINTAGE
(☑702-384-2700; www.retro-vegas.com; 1131 S Main St; ☺11am-6pm Mon-Sat, noon-5pm Sun; 🚌108, Deuce) Near Downtown's 18b Arts District, this flamingo-pink-painted antiques shop is a primo place for picking up mid-20th-century modern and swingin' 1960s and '70s gems, from artwork to home decor, as well as vintage Vegas souvenirs like casino-hotel ashtrays. Red Kat's secondhand clothing, handbags and accessories are also found here.

ℹ Information

Harmon Medical Center (☑702-796-1116; www.harmonmedicalcenter.com; 150 E Harmon Ave; ☺8am-8pm Mon-Fri) Discounts for uninsured patients; limited translation services available.

Las Vegas Convention & Visitors Authority (LVCVA; ☑702-892-7575; www.lasvegas.com; 3150 Paradise Rd; ☺8am-5:30pm Mon-Fri; 🚌Las Vegas Convention Center)

ℹ Getting There & Around

McCarran International Airport (LAS; ☑702-261-5211; www.mccarran.com; 5757 Wayne Newton Blvd; 🚖)

The easiest and cheapest way to get to your hotel is by airport shuttle (one-way to Strip/downtown hotels from $7/9) or a shared ride-share service (from $10). As you exit baggage claim, look for shuttle-bus kiosks lining the curb; prices and destinations are clearly marked.

Northern Mountains

Best Places to Eat

➡ Red Onion Grill (p562)

➡ Café Maddalena (p573)

➡ Cafe at Indian Creek (p579)

➡ Pangaea Cafe & Pub
(p564)

➡ Etna Brewing Company
(p582)

Best Places to Sleep

➡ McCloud River Mercantile
Hotel (p574)

➡ Holiday Harbor Resort
(p556)

➡ Quincy Courtyard Suites
(p564)

➡ Shasta MountInn (p569)

➡ Feather River Canyon
Campgrounds (p564)

Why Go?

'Hidden California' gets bandied around fairly casually, but here you have an entire corner of the state that does seem forgotten. The coast and foggy redwood groves are far away, so prepare yourself for something completely different: vast expanses of wilderness – some 24,000 protected acres – divided by rivers and streams, dotted with cobalt lakes, horse ranches and alpine peaks; further east is a stretch of shrubby, high desert cut with amber gorges, caves and dramatic light that is a photographer's dream. Much of it doesn't look the way people envision California – the topography more resembles the older mountains of the Rockies than the relatively young granite Yosemite. The towns are tiny but friendly, with few comforts; come to get lost in vast remoteness. Even the two principal attractions, Mt Shasta and Lassen Volcanic National Park, remain uncrowded (and sometimes snow-covered) at the peak of the summer.

When to Go

Lassen Volcanic National Park

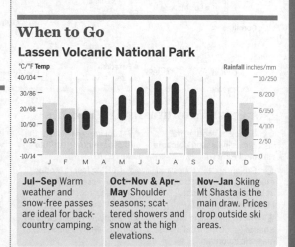

Jul–Sep Warm weather and snow-free passes are ideal for backcountry camping.

Oct–Nov & Apr–May Shoulder seasons; scattered showers and snow at the high elevations.

Nov–Jan Skiing Mt Shasta is the main draw. Prices drop outside ski areas.

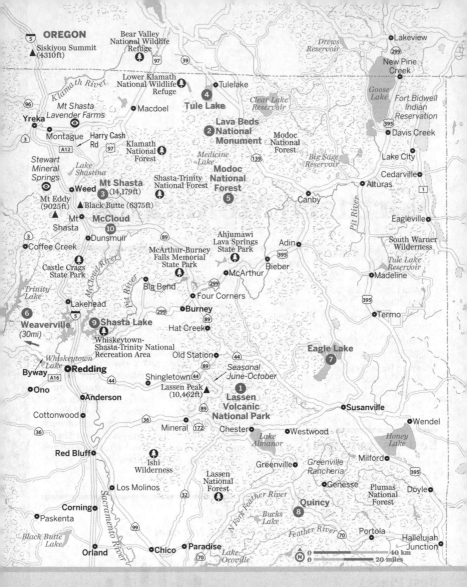

Northern Mountains Highlights

1 Gaping at geothermal spectacles in **Lassen Volcanic National Park** (p556).

2 Exploring deep caves and examining ancient petroglyphs at **Lava Beds National Monument** (p575).

3 Hiking and skiing **Mt Shasta** (p566), NorCal's most majestic mountain.

4 Looking overhead at the bird superhighway at **Tule Lake** (p576).

5 Getting lost in **Modoc National Forest** (p577), California's most remote national forest.

6 Enjoying the small-town charm of **Weaverville** (p578)

and wading in the trout-filled water nearby.

7 Camping along the shores of remote **Eagle Lake** (p563).

8 Chilling out in the mountain town of **Quincy** (p563).

9 Floating with a dozen pals on a **Shasta Lake** (p555) houseboat.

REDDING & AROUND

North of Red Bluff the dusty central corridor along I-5 starts to give way to panoramic mountain ranges on either side. Redding is the last major outpost before the small towns of the far north, and the surrounding lakes make for easy day trips or overnight camps. If you get off the highway – way off – this can be an exceptionally rewarding area of the state to explore.

Redding

Originally called Poverty Flats during the gold rush for its lack of wealth, Redding today has a whole lot of tasteless new money – malls, big-box stores and large housing developments surround its core. A tourist destination it is not, though it is the major gateway city to the northeast corner of the state and a useful spot for restocking before long jaunts into the wilderness. Recent constructions like the Sundial Bridge and Turtle Bay Exploration Park are enticing lures and worth a visit...but not a long one. A surge of good eating and drinking spots makes it an excellent pit stop for a meal if you're taking a long road trip on I-5. Downtown is bordered by the Sacramento River to the north and east. Major thoroughfares are Pine and Market Sts and there's often lots of traffic.

◉ Sights & Activities

★ Sundial Bridge   BRIDGE
(Map p552; http://turtlebay.org/sundialbridge) Resembling a beached cruise ship, the shimmering-white 2004 Sundial Bridge spans the river and is one of Redding's marquee attractions, providing an excellent photo op. The glass-deck pedestrian overpass connects the Turtle Bay Exploration Park to the north bank of the Sacramento River and was designed by renowned Spanish architect Santiago Calatrava.

The bridge/partially working sundial attracts visitors from around the world, who come to marvel at this unique feat of engineering artistry. It is accessed from the park and connects to the Sacramento River Trail system. The surrounding river scenery is beautiful.

Turtle Bay Exploration Park   MUSEUM, GARDENS
(Map p552; ☑800-887-8532; www.turtlebay.org; 844 Sundial Bridge Dr; adult/child $16/12, after 3:30pm $11/7; ⊙9am-5pm Mon-Sat, from 10am Sun, closes 1hr earlier Nov–mid-Mar; ⊞) Situated on 300 meandering acres, this is an artistic, cultural and scientific center for visitors of all ages, with an emphasis on the Sacramento River watershed. The complex houses art and natural-science museums, with fun interactive exhibits. There are also extensive arboretum gardens, a butterfly house and a 22,000-gallon, walk-through river aquarium full of regional aquatic life (yes, including turtles).

The on-site Café at Turtle Bay (p553) serves hot and cold drinks.

Courthouse Museum   MUSEUM
(☑530-243-8194; www.parks.ca.gov; 15312 CA 299; $2; ⊙10am-5pm Thu-Sun; ⊞) This building was the courthouse for over 30 years in the late 1800s and now houses a fun and informative museum and visitor center.

Redding Trails   HIKING, CYCLING
(Map p552; www.reddingtrails.com) Eighty miles of trails loop through parks, along rivers and up hills for strolling, hiking and mountain biking. Check the website for maps or pick up the pamphlet at almost any hotel. The star is the Sacramento River Trail, which meanders along the river all the way to Shasta Dam. There are several access points, including the Sundial Bridge.

Waterworks Park   WATER PARK
(www.waterworkspark.com; 151 N Boulder Dr; day pass adult/child $23/19; ⊙usually late May-Sep) Redding gets really hot, and although most hotels and motels have pools, you'll have more fun splashing around at this water park, including on the four-story-high, cliff-steep Avalanche, a simulated white-water river, giant waterslides, plus a 'Lazy Lagoon' and kiddie pool. Great for kids or kidlike adults.

⌷ Sleeping

Redding's many motels and hotels (most large chains are represented and have swimming pools) huddle around noisy thoroughfares. A couple of rows lie close to the I-5 at the southern end of town: just west of the freeway close to the Cypress Ave exit on Bechelli Lane, and on the east side of the freeway on Hilltop Dr. Aim for the ones on less busy N Market St.

Apples' Riverhouse B&B   B&B $$
(Map p552; ☑530-243-8440; www.applesriver house.com; 201 Mora Ct; r $105-120; ☞) Just steps from the Sacramento River Trail, this

Redding

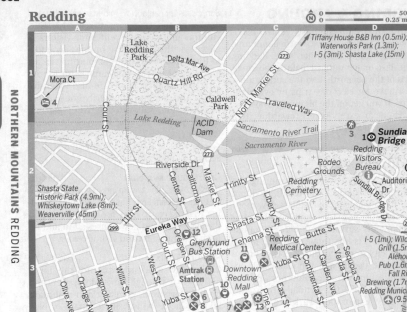

modern, ranch-style home has three comfortable upstairs rooms, two with decks. It's a bit suburban, but it's the best independent stay in Redding. In the evening the sociable hosts invite you for cheese and wine. Bikes are yours to borrow and the proximity to the trail is inviting.

Tiffany House B&B Inn B&B $$
(☎530-244-3225; www.tiffanyhousebb.com; 1510 Barbara Rd; r $125-170; ☎❀) In a quiet cul-de-sac, a mile north of the river, this Victorian cottage has an expansive garden with sweeping views. Cozy rooms are packed with antiques, rosebuds and ruffles. Affable hosts make a big yummy to-do over breakfast.

✖ Eating

While it's certainly not a foodie hub, Redding has some surprisingly good places to eat, including for those on a budget.

Ma Der Ma Der Sap House & Grill LAOTIAN $
(Map p552; ☎530-691-4194; 1718 Placer St; ⊙11am-7pm Mon-Sat) Try the 'Sappritto,' a Laotian-inspired burrito with meat, eggs, veggies, sticky rice and a choice of hot sauce. Or go with pad thai, Lao-sausage tacos, cheesesteak sub or Lao-style wings. Sap means delicious in Lao and we agree. Everything from the hot sauces to the sausage are housemade daily. Call for to-go orders or eat in.

Wilda's Grill HOT DOGS, VEGETARIAN $
(1712 Churn Creek Rd; mains $6-7; ⊙11am-6pm Mon-Fri; ✍) The combo sounds weird but it works: big, excellent hot dogs with toppings from roasted garlic to homemade chili or blue cheese – or go vegetarian with outrageously delicious falafel or the much-lauded Buddha Bowl, made from rice, veggies and yummy, spicy sauces. Expect a line at peak hours. The mini-mall location lacks pizazz but it's very convenient from I-5.

Redding

Vintage Wine Bar & Restaurant
CALIFORNIAN $$

(Map p552; ☑530-229-9449; www.vintageredding.com; 1790 Market St; mains $13-28; ☺5-9pm Tue-Sat) Go here to try the region's best wines (and many more beyond) alongside unpretentious yet classy food and live entertainment most nights. Ask the staff to pair a wine or wine flight with your meal.

Cafe Paradisio
MEDITERRANEAN $$

(Map p552; ☑530-215-3499; www.cafeparadisio.com; 1270 Yuba St; mains lunch $6-12, dinner $10-32; ☺5-9pm Mon, Wed & Thu, to 10pm Fri & Sat; ☑) Take Mediterranean food and give it a bit of Asian flair and you have the comforting fare of this casual and friendly little nook. Start with the baked brie platter then continue with salmon with coconut curry or three-cheese lasagne. The portions are huge and there are lots of vegetarian choices.

Carnegie's
CALIFORNIAN $$

(Map p552; ☑530 246 2926; 1600 Oregon St; mains $12; ☺10am-3pm Mon & Tue, to 11pm Wed-Fri; ☑) This hip and homey, split-level cafe serves up healthy food: big fresh salads, garlicky prawns and pasta, and homemade tomato soup. There's a good selection of beer and wine too. Friday nights get a little rowdy, and there can be a wait.

Moonstone Bistro
CALIFORNIAN $$$

(☑530-241-3663; www.moonstonebistro.com; 3425 Placer St; mains lunch $13-22, dinner $23-44; ☺11am-9pm Tue-Thu, to 10pm Fri & Sat, 10am-2pm Sun; ☑) ✦ Organic, local, free range, line-caught, you name it, if the word is associated with sustainable food, you can use it to describe this place. Try the fish tacos at lunch and the hickory-smoked pork chops with

adobo chilies for dinner, but don't skip dessert – the chocolate soufflé in particular is to die for. Top it off with a microbrew.

Jack's Grill
STEAK $$$

(Map p552; ☑530-241-9705; www.jacksgrillredding.com; 1743 California St; mains $17-42; ☺restaurant 5-11pm, bar 4-11:30pm Mon-Sat) This funky little old-time place doesn't look so inviting – the windows are blacked out and it's dark as a crypt inside – but its popularity with locals starts with its stubborn ain't-broke-don't-fix-it ethos and ends with its steak – a big, thick, charbroiled decadence.

Regulars start lining up for dinner at 4pm, when cocktail hour begins. There are no reservations, so it easily takes an hour to get a seat.

☕ Drinking & Entertainment

Café at Turtle Bay
CAFE

(Map p552; 844 Arboretum Dr; coffee from $1.50; ☺8:30am-5pm Mon-Sat, from 9:30am Sun) Cafe in the Turtle Bay Museum Store serving hot and cold drinks and light snacks.

Alehouse Pub
PUB

(☑530-221-7990; www.reddingalehouse.com; 2181 Hilltop Dr; ☺3pm-midnight Mon-Thu, to 1:30am Fri & Sat, 11am-5pm Sun) Too bad for fans of the cheap stuff, this local pub keeps a selection of highly hopped beers on tap and sells T-shirts emblazoned with 'No Crap on Tap.' It's a fun local place that gets packed after Redding's young professionals get out of work.

Cascade Theatre
LIVE MUSIC

(Map p552; ☑530-243-8877; www.cascadetheatre.org; 1733 Market St) Try to catch some live music downtown at this refurbished 1935 art deco theater. Usually it hosts second-tier

GETTING CRAFTY & DRAFTY IN REDDING

Redding has never gotten much praise for its food-and-beverage scene but that may be changing. Four new craft breweries, all making their own very unique brews, have opened in the last few years, giving folks more of a reason to veer off I-5 to stay a night or more. **Woody's Brewing Co.** (Map p552; ☑530-768-1034; www.woodysbrewing.biz; 1257 Oregon St; bar snacks from $3, meals $12-14; ⊙11am-10pm Tue-Thu, to 11pm Fri & Sat, to 9pm Sun) and **Fall River Brewing** (☑530-605-0230; www.fallriverbrewing.com; 1030 E Cypress Ave D; ⊙3-10pm Mon-Thu, noon-midnight Fri & Sat, to 8pm Sun) were the two earliest, serving the more classic styles of beer, while the new **Final Draft Brewing Company** (Map p552; ☑530-338-1198; www.finaldraftbrewingcompany.com; 1600 California St; ⊙11am-10pm Sun-Thu, to 11pm Fri & Sat) offers barrel-aged, sour beers and more. **Wildcard Brewing Company** (Map p552; ☑530-255-8582; www.wildcardbrewingco.com; 1321 Butte St; ⊙2-9pm Sun-Thu, to 10pm Fri & Sat) is the happy in-betweener with a little of everything and a convivial downtown location.

national acts, but if nothing else, take a peek inside; this is a neon-lit gem.

ℹ Information

California Welcome Center (☑530-365-1180; www.shastacascade.org; 1699 Hwy 273, Anderson; ⊙9am-6pm Mon-Sat, from 10am Sun) About 10 miles south of Redding, in Anderson's Prime Outlets Mall. It's an easy stop for northbound travelers, who are likely to pass it on the I-5 approach. It stocks maps for hiking and guides to outdoor activities, and the website has an excellent trip-planning section for the region.

Redding Visitors Bureau (Map p552; ☑530-225-4100; www.visitredding.com; 777 Auditorium Dr; ⊙9am-6pm Mon-Fri, 10am-5pm Sat) Near Turtle Bay Exploration Park.

Shasta-Trinity National Forest Headquarters (☑530-226-2500; 3644 Avtech Pkwy; ⊙8am-4:30pm Mon-Fri) South of town, in the USDA Service Center near the airport. Has maps and free camping permits for all seven national forests in Northern California.

ℹ Getting There & Away

Redding Municipal Airport (RDD; http://ci.redding.ca.us/transeng/airports/rma.htm; 6751 Woodrum Circle) is 9.5 miles southeast of the city, just off Airport Rd. United Express flies to San Francisco.

The **Amtrak station** (www.amtrak.com; 1620 Yuba St), one block west of the Downtown Redding Mall, is not staffed. For the Coast Starlight service, make advance reservations by phone or via the website, then pay the conductor when you board the train. Amtrak travels once daily to Oakland ($44, six hours), Sacramento ($27, four hours) and Dunsmuir ($23, 1¾ hours).

The **Greyhound bus station** (Map p552; 1321 Butte St), adjacent to the Downtown Redding

Mall, never closes. Destinations include San Francisco ($40, 8½ hours, four daily) and Weed ($16, 1½ hours, three daily). The Redding Area Bus Authority (RABA; www.rabaride.com) has a dozen city routes operating until around 6pm Monday to Saturday. Fares start at $1.50 (exact change only).

Around Redding

Shasta State Historic Park

On Hwy 299, 6 miles west of Redding, this **state historic park** (☑520-243-8194; www.parks.ca.gov; 15312 CA 299; museum entry adult/child $3/2; ⊙10am-5pm Thu-Sun) preserves the ruins of an 1850s gold rush mining town called Shasta – not to be confused with Mt Shasta City. When the gold rush was at its heady height, everything and everyone passed through this Shasta. But when the railroad bypassed it to set up in Poverty Flats (present-day Redding), poor Shasta lost its raison d'être.

An 1861 courthouse contains the excellent museum, the best in this part of the state. With its amazing gun collection, spooky holograms in the basement and gallows out back, it's a thrill ride. Pick up walking-tour pamphlets from the information desk and follow trails to the beautiful Catholic cemetery, brewery ruins and many other historic sites.

Whiskeytown Lake

Sparkling **Whiskeytown Lake** (☑530-242-3400; www.nps.gov/whis; off Hwy 299, Whiskeytown; 7-day pass per car $10; 🅿🚻) takes its name from an old mining camp. When the lake was created in the 1960s by the construction of a 263ft dam, designed for power generation and Central Valley irrigation, the few remaining buildings of old Whiskeytown were moved and the camp was submerged. Today, the lake's serene 36 miles of forested shoreline is a perfect place to camp while enjoying nonmotorized water sports.

The **visitors center** (☑530-246-1225; www.nps.gov/whis; Hwy 299 at JFK Memorial Dr, Whiskeytown; ⊙10am-4pm) has knowledgeable staff that can answer your questions about the area. Look for ranger-led interpretive programs and guided walks. The hike from the visitors center to roaring **Whiskeytown Falls** (3.4 miles round-trip) follows a former logging road and is a good quick trip.

On the western side of the lake, the **Tower House Historic District** contains the El Dorado mine ruins and the pioneer Camden House, open for summer tours. In winter it's an atmospheric place to explore.

On the southern shore of the lake, Brandy Creek is ideal for swimming. Just off Hwy 299, on the northern edge of the lake, Oak Bottom Marina rents boats.

The nice but tightly packed **Oak Bottom Campground** (☑800-365-2267; www.whiskeytownmarinas.com; tent/RV sites $24/21; 🐾) is near the shore of Whiskeytown Lake. There's a parking lot for tent campers and you have to walk in a short distance to the campsites.

Shasta Lake

About 15 minutes north of Redding, Shasta Lake (www.shastalake.com) was created in the 1940s when Shasta Dam flooded towns, railways and 90% of the local Wintu tribal lands to make the largest reservoir in California. Today it's home to the state's biggest population of nesting bald eagles. Surrounded by hiking trails and campgrounds, the lake gets packed in summer. The lake is also home to more than 20 different kinds of fish, including rainbow trout.

◉ Sights & Activities

The lake is known as the 'houseboat capital of the world,' and is very popular with boaters of all kinds. **Packer's Bay** is the best area for leg-stretcher hikes with easy access off the I-5 (follow the Packer's Bay signs), but the prettiest trail (outside of summer months when the lack of shade can make it intensely hot) is the 7.5-mile loop of the **Clikapudi Trail**, which is also popular with

mountain bikers and horse-back riders. To get there, follow Bear Mountain Rd several miles until it dead-ends.

Lake Shasta Caverns   CAVE
(☑530-238-2341, 800-795-2283; www.lakeshastacaverns.com; 20359 Shasta Caverns Rd, Lakehead; 2hr tour adult/child 3-15yr $26/15; ⊙tours every 30min 9am-4pm late May-early Sep, hourly 9am-3pm Apr-late May & early-late Sep, 10am, noon & 2pm Oct-Mar; P🐾) High in the limestone megaliths at the north end of the lake hide these impressive caves. Tours through the many chambers dripping with massive formations operate daily and include a boat ride across Lake Shasta. Bring a sweater as the temperature inside is 58°F (14°C) year-round. With over 600 stairs, a decent level of fitness is required.

To get there, take the Shasta Caverns Rd exit from I-5, about 15 miles north of Redding, and follow the signs for 1.5 miles.

Shasta Dam   DAM
(☑530-275-4463; www.usbr.gov/mp/ncao/shasta-dam.html; 16349 Shasta Dam Blvd; ⊙visitor center 8am-5pm, tours 9am, 11am, 1pm & 3pm; P🐾) FREE On scale with the enormous natural features of the area, this colossal, 15-million-ton concrete dam is second only in size to Grand Coolie Dam in Washington state and second in height only to Hoover Dam in Nevada. The dam is located at the south end of the lake on Shasta Dam Blvd.

Built between 1938 and 1945, its 487ft spillway is nearly three times as high as Niagara Falls. Woody Guthrie wrote 'This Land Is Your Land' while he was here entertaining dam workers. The **Shasta Dam visitors center** offers fascinating free guided tours daily of the structure's rumbling interior – but skip the movie.

🛏 Sleeping & Eating

Hike-in camping and recreational vehicle (RV) parks are sprinkled around the

---

DETOUR AROUND THE I-5 DOLDRUMS

A good alternative for travelers heading north and south on I-5 is to drive along Hwy 3 through the Scott Valley, which rewards with world-class views of the Trinity Alps. Compared to rushing along the dull highway, this scenic detour will add an additional half-day of driving.

lakeshore, and houseboats are wildly popular. Most houseboats require a two-night minimum stay. Reserve as far in advance as possible, especially in summer. Houseboats usually sleep 10 to 16 adults and cost $1600 to $8400 per week. RV parks are often crowded and lack shade, but they have on-site restaurants. For exploring the area on a day trip, stay in Redding.

Holiday Harbor Resort
HOUSEBOATS, CAMPGROUND $

(✆530-238-2383; www.lakeshasta.com; Holiday Harbor Rd; tent & RV sites $42.50, houseboat per 2 nights from $975; ☎☀) Primarily an RV campground, it also rents houseboats (note that off-season rates are almost 50% lower) and the busy marina offers parasailing and fishing-boat rentals. A little cafe (✆530-238-2383; www.lakeshasta.com/service/the-harbor-cafe; 20061 Shasta Caverns Rd; meals around $10; ⊗8am-3pm Memorial Day-Labor Day) sits lakefront. It's off Shasta Caverns Rd, next to the lake.

Antlers RV Park & Campground
CAMPGROUND, CABINS $

(✆530-238-2322; www.shastalakevacations.com; 20679 Antlers Rd; tent & RV sites $32-45, trailer rentals $88-105; ☎☀☎) East of I-5 in Lakehead, at the north end of the lake, this very popular, family-oriented campground has cabins, a country store and a marina renting watercraft and houseboats.

Lakeshore Inn & RV
CAMPGROUND $

(✆530-238-2003; www.shastacamping.com; 20483 Lakeshore Dr; RV sites $25-40, cabins from $100; ☎☀☎) On the western side of I-5, this lakeside vacation park has a restaurant and tavern, horseshoes and basic cabins.

US Forest Service Campgrounds
CAMPGROUND $

(✆info 530-275-1587, reservations 877-444-6777; www.recreation.gov; tent sites free-$35; P☎) About half of the campgrounds around Shasta Lake are open year-round. The lake's

---

KNOW ABOUT THE SNOW

Lassen Volcanic National Park has a very short season from around the beginning of June to the beginning of September. Lower elevations open up earlier but you can expect many services to be shut between October and May. That said, the winter is an incredibly peaceful time to visit as long as the roads are open!

---

many fingers have a huge range of camping, with lake and mountain views, and some of them are very remote. Free boat-in sites are first-come, first-served – sites without boat launches will be far less busy.

Dispersed camping outside organized campgrounds requires a campfire permit, available free from any USFS office.

MT LASSEN REGION

The dramatic crags, volcanic formations and alpine lakes of Lassen Volcanic National Park seem surprisingly untrammeled when you consider they are only a few hours from the Bay Area. Snowed in through most of winter, the park blossoms in late spring. While it is only 50 miles from Redding, and thus close enough to be enjoyed on a day trip, to really do it justice you'll want to invest a few days exploring the area along its scenic, winding roads. From Lassen Volcanic National Park you can take one of two very picturesque routes: Hwy 36, which heads east past Chester, Lake Almanor and historic Susanville; or Hwy 89, which leads southeast to the cozy mountain town of Quincy.

Lassen Volcanic National Park

The dry, smoldering, treeless terrain within this 106,000-acre national park (✆530-595-4480; www.nps.gov/lavo; 38050 Hwy 36 E, Mineral; 7-day entry per car mid-Apr–Nov $20, Dec–mid-Apr $10; P⊕) ✐ stands in stunning contrast to the cool, green conifer forest that surrounds it. That's the summer; in winter tons of snow ensure you won't get too far inside its borders. Still, entering the park from the southwest entrance is to suddenly step into another world. The lavascape offers a fascinating glimpse into the earth's fiery core. In a fuming display the terrain is marked by roiling hot springs, steamy mud pots, noxious sulfur vents, fumaroles, lava flows, cinder cones, craters and crater lakes.

In earlier times the region was a summer encampment and meeting point for Native American tribes, namely the Atsugewi, Yana, Yahi and Maidu. They hunted deer and gathered plants for basketmaking here. Some indigenous people still live nearby and work closely with the park to help educate visitors on their ancient history and contemporary culture.

DRIVING TOUR: THE LASSEN SCENIC BYWAY

Even in the peak of summer, you'll have the Lassen Scenic Byway mostly to yourself. The long loop though Northern California wilderness skirts the edge of Lassen Volcanic National Park and circles Lassen Peak, one of the largest dormant volcanoes on the planet. It mostly covers the big green patches on the map: expansive areas perfect for hiking, fishing, camping or just getting lost. This is a place where few people venture, and those who do come back with stories.

The launching point for this big loop could be either Redding or Sacramento, but there are few comforts for travelers along this course. The only cities in this neck of the woods – little places like Chester and Susanville – aren't all that exciting on their own; they're mostly just places to gas up, buy some beef jerky and enjoy the week's only hot meal. But the banner attractions are visible in every direction – the ominous, dormant volcanic peak of Lassen, the windswept high plains and the seemingly endless wilderness of the Lassen and Plumas National Forests.

This loop is formed by Hwy 36, Hwy 44 and Hwy 89. (You can see the map and some of the highlights at www.byways.org/explore/byways/2195.) It's best to do the drive between late June and mid-October. During other times of the year some of these roads close due to snow.

Sights & Activities

Lassen Peak, the world's largest plug-dome volcano, rises 2000ft over the surrounding landscape to 10,457ft above sea level. Classified as an active volcano, its most recent eruption was in 1917, when it spewed a giant cloud of smoke, steam and ash 7 miles into the atmosphere. The national park (p556) was created the following year to protect the newly formed landscape. Some areas destroyed by the blast, including the aptly named **Devastated Area** northeast of the peak, are recovering impressively.

Hwy 89, the road through the park, wraps around Lassen Peak on three sides and provides access to dramatic geothermal formations, pure lakes, gorgeous picnic areas and remote hiking trails.

In total, the park has 150 miles of **hiking trails**, including a 17-mile section of the **Pacific Crest Trail**. Experienced hikers can attack the **Lassen Peak Trail**; it takes at least 4½ hours to make the 5-mile round-trip but the first 1.3 miles up to the Grandview viewpoint is suitable for families. The 360-degree view from the top is stunning, even if the weather is a bit hazy. Early in the season you'll need snow and ice-climbing equipment to reach the summit. Near the Kom Yah-mah-nee visitor facility, a gentler 2.3-mile trail leads through meadows and forest to **Mill Creek Falls**. Further north on Hwy 89 you'll recognize the roadside **sulfur works** by its bubbling mud pots, hissing steam vent, fountains and fumaroles. At **Bumpass Hell** a moderate 1.5-mile trail and boardwalk leads to an active geothermal area, with bizarrely colored pools and billowing clouds of steam.

The road and trails wind through cinder cones, lava and lush alpine glades, with views of Juniper Lake, Snag Lake and the plains beyond. Most of the lakes at higher elevations remain partially and beautifully frozen in summer. Leave time to fish, swim or boat on **Manzanita Lake**, a slightly lower emerald gem near the northern entrance.

Sleeping & Eating

From the north on Hwy 89, you won't see many gas/food/lodgings signs after Mt Shasta City. Aside from the eight developed **campgrounds** (518-885-3639, reservations 877-444-6777; www.recreation.gov; tent & RV sites $12-24; P) in the park, there are many more in the surrounding Lassen National Forest. The nearest hotels and motels are in Chester, which accesses the south entrance of the park. There are some basic services near the split of Hwy 89 and Hwy 44, in the north.

There are a few basic places to eat in the small towns surrounding the park but for the most part you'll want to pack provisions.

North Entrance of the Park

Manzanita Lake Camping Cabins CABIN $
(May-Oct 530-335-7557, Nov-Apr 530-840-6140; www.lassenrecreation.com; Hwy 89, near Manzanita Lake; cabins $71-95; P) These recently built log cabins enjoy a lovely position on one of

Lassen Volcanic National Park

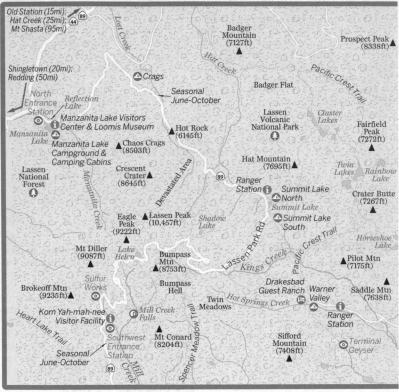

Lassen's lakes, and they come in one- and two-bedroom options and slightly more basic eight-bunk configurations, which are a bargain for groups. They all have bear boxes, propane heaters and fire rings, but no bedding, electricity or running water. Shared bathrooms and coin-op hot showers are nearby.

Those who want to get a small taste of Lassen's more rustic comforts can call ahead to arrange a 'Camper's Amenity Package,' which includes basic supplies for a night under the stars (starting at $100, it includes a s'mores kit).

Manzanita Lake Campground   CAMPGROUND $
(☑ reservations 877-444-6777; www.recreation.gov; tent & RV sites $15-24; ☀) The biggest camping area in these parts has lake access, views of Lassen, and 179 sites with fire rings, picnic tables and bear boxes. There's a store, hot showers and kayak rentals here as well.

Hat Creek Resort & RV Park   CABIN, CAMPGROUND $
(☑ 530-335-7121; www.hatcreekresortrv.com; 12533 Hwy 44/89, Old Station; tent sites from $25, RV sites with/without hookups from $38/17, yurts $69-149, r $69-229, cabins $89-299; ☎☀) Outside the park, Old Station makes a decent stop before entering and is an OK choice. It sits along a fast-moving, trout-stocked creek. Some simple motel rooms and cabins have full kitchens. Stock up at the convenience store and deli, then eat on a picnic table by the river.

🛏 South Entrance of the Park

Mt Lassen/Shingletown KOA   CAMPGROUND $
(☑ 530-474-3133; www.koa.com; 7749 KOA Rd; tent sites $39, RV sites from $69, cabins $71-169; ☺ mid-Mar–Nov; ☎☀☀) Enjoy all the standard Kampgrounds of America (KOA) amenities: a playground, a deli and laundry facilities.

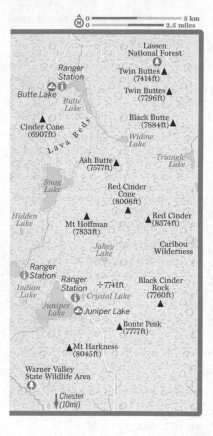

are repeat visitors, use the hot-springs-fed swimming pool or go horseback riding. Except in the main lodge, there's no electricity (the kerosene lamps and campfires give things a lovely glow). Rates include country-style meals (vegetarian options available) and campfire barbecues every Wednesday.

This is one of the few places in the region to book up solidly, so make advance reservations as soon as possible.

ℹ️ Information

Whether you enter at the north or southwest entrance, you'll be given a free map with general information.

Kom Yah-mah-nee Visitor Facility (☏530-595-4480; www.nps.gov/lavo; ⊙9am-5pm, closed Mon & Tue Nov-Mar; ♿) About half a mile north of the park's southwest entrance, this handsome center is certified at the highest standard by the US Green Building Council. Inside there are educational exhibits (including a cool topographical volcano), a bookstore, an auditorium, a gift shop and a restaurant. Visitor information and maps available.

Manzanita Lake Visitors Center & Loomis Museum (☏530-595-4480; ⊙9am-5pm Jun-Sep) Just past the entrance-fee station at the park's northern boundary, you can see exhibits and an orientation video inside this museum. During summer, rangers and volunteers lead programs on geology, wildlife, astronomy and local culture. Visitor information and maps available.

Park Headquarters (☏530-595-4444; www.nps.gov/lavo; 38050 Hwy 36; ⊙8am-4:30pm daily Jun-Sep, 8am-4:30pm Mon-Fri Oct-May) About a mile west of the tiny town of Mineral, it's the nearest stop for refueling and supplies.

ℹ️ Getting There & Away

There's virtually no way to visit this park without a car, though all the two-lane roads around the park and the ample free national-forest camping options make for excellent, if fairly serious, cycle touring.

The park has two entrances. The northern entrance, at Manzanita Lake, is 50 miles east of Redding via Hwy 44. The southwest entrance is on Hwy 89, about 5 miles north of the junction with Hwy 36. From this junction it is 5 miles west on Hwy 36 to Mineral and 44 miles west to Red Bluff. Heading east on Hwy 36, Chester is 25 miles away and Susanville about 60 miles. Quincy is 65 miles southeast from the junction on Hwy 89.

It's off Hwy 44 in Shingletown, about 20 miles west of the park.

Village at Childs Meadow   CABIN **$**
(☏530-595-3383; www.thevillageatchildsmeadow.
com; 41500 E Hwy 36, Mill Creek; tent/RV sites from $25/35, tiny homes $110-185; 🛜) Rustic, run-down 'tiny homes' – some of them more like permanently parked RV trailers – sit at the edge of a spectacularly lush mountain meadow 9 miles outside the park's southwest entrance. Don't expect the Ritz; it's an old-fashioned, fittingly grungy, mountain-resort experience, but it's very close to the park. Expect some changes as it's under new management.

Drakesbad Guest Ranch   RESORT **$$$**
(☏530-529-1512, ext 120; www.drakesbad.com; Warner Valley Rd; r per person $147-199; ⊙Jun-early Oct; ☀) Seventeen miles northwest of Chester, this fabulously secluded place lies inside the park's boundary. Guests, many of whom

WORTH A TRIP

WILD HORSE SANCTUARY

Since 1978 the **Wild Horse Sanctuary** (☑530-335-2241; www.wildhorsesanctuary. com; 5796 Wilson Hill Rd, Shingletown; free; ☉10am-4pm Wed & Sat) **FREE** has been sheltering horses and burros that would otherwise have been destroyed. You can visit its humble visitor center on Wednesdays and Saturdays to see these lovely animals or even volunteer for a day, with advance arrangement. To see them on the open plains, take a two- to three-day weekend pack trip in spring or summer (from $435 per person). Shingletown lies 20 miles to the west of Lassen Volcanic National Park.

Lassen National Forest

The vast Lassen National Forest (www.fs.fed. us/r5/lassen) surrounding Lassen Peak and Lassen Volcanic National Park is so big that it's hard to comprehend: it covers 1.2 million acres (1875 sq miles) of wilderness in an area called the Crossroads, where the granite Sierra, volcanic Cascades, Modoc Plateau and Central Valley meet. It's largely unspoiled land, though if you wander too far off the byways surrounding the park, you'll certainly see evidence of logging and mining operations that still happen within its borders.

The Lassen National Forest supervisor's office is in Susanville. Other ranger offices include **Eagle Lake Ranger District** (☑530-257-4188; 477-050 Eagle Lake Rd, Susanville), **Hat Creek Ranger District** (☑530-336-5521; 43225 E Hwy 299, Fall River Mills; ☉Mon-Fri) and **Almanor Ranger District** (☑530-258-2141; www.fs.usda.gov; 900 CA 36, Chester; ☉8am-4:30pm Mon-Fri), about a mile west of Chester.

Lake Almanor Area

Calm, turquoise Lake Almanor lies south of Lassen Volcanic National Park via Hwys 89 and 36. This man-made lake is a crystalline example of California's sometimes awkward conservation and land-management policy: the lake was created by the now-defunct Great Western Power Company and is now ostensibly owned by the Pacific Gas & Electric Company. The lake is surrounded by lush meadows and tall evergreens and was once little-visited. Now, a 3000-acre ski

resort sits on the hills above, with properties continually being developed near its shore and power boats zipping across its surface. The northeastern section in particular has become particularly ritzy and there are even a few gated communities. On the rugged southern end you'll find miles with nothing but pine trees.

The main town near the lake, Chester (population 2144, elevation 4528ft), isn't a looker. Though you could whiz right by and dismiss it as a few blocks of nondescript roadside storefronts, this little community, while outwardly drab, has a fledgling art scene hidden along the back roads for those willing to explore. It also offers some comfy places to stay but none as exciting or woodsy as you'll find along the lake.

🏃 Activities

You can rent boats and water-sports equipment at many places around the lake.

Bodfish Bicycles & Quiet Mountain Sports   CYCLING, OUTDOORS
(☑530-258-2338; www.bodfishbicycles.com; 149 Main St, Chester; bicycle rental per hour/day $10/33; ☉10am-5pm Tue-Sat, noon-4pm Sun, shorter off-season hours) This outfit rents bicycles, cross-country skis and snowshoes, and sells canoes and kayaks. It's a great source of mountain-biking and bicycle-touring advice. If you want just a taste of the lovely rides possible in this part of the state, make this a priority stop.

Coppervale Ski Hill   SKIING
(www.lassencollege.edu; Westwood; day passes $20-25; ☉1-4:30pm Tue & Thu, 9:30am-4pm Sat & Sun) Run by Lassen Community College, this little place caters to downhill and cross-country skiers as well as snowboarders. There are eight trails and 740ft of vertical drop.

🛏 Sleeping & Eating

The best sleeping options for campers are in the surrounding national forest.

🛏 Chester

Along Chester's main drag you'll find a scattering of 1950s-style inns and a few chain lodgings (the nicest of which is the fairly overpriced Best Western Rose Quartz Inn). Many of these places keep seasonal hours, and when you live in a place where it can snow in mid-June, the season is short.

St Bernard Lodge
B&B $$

(☑530-258-3382; www.stbernardlodge.com; 44801 E Hwy 36, Mill Creek; d without bath from $99; ☎) Located 10 miles west of Chester, this old-world charmer has seven B&B rooms with views to the mountains and forest. All have knotty-pine paneling and quilted bedspreads. There are stables where those traveling with a horse can board them and have access to the nearby network of Lassen's trails. The tavern is good too, serving meaty American-style fare.

Bidwell House B&B
B&B $$

(☑530-258-3338; www.bidwellhouse.com; 1 Main St; r $125-260, without bath $80-115, cottage $185-285; ☎) Set back from the street, this historic summer home of pioneers John and Annie Bidwell is packed with antiques. The classic accommodations come with all the modern amenities (including a spa in some rooms) – no roughing it here. Enjoy goodies like a three-course breakfast, home-baked cookies and afternoon sherry.

🛏 Around the Lake

Book ahead for lakefront lodgings in summer. There are restaurants at the resorts.

PG&E Recreational Area Campgrounds
CAMPGROUND $

(☑916-386-5164; http://recreation.pge.com; tent & RV sites $14-22; ☺May-Sep; P ❀) A favorite for tents and RVs, Rocky Point Campground is right on the lake, with some sites basically on the beach. For something more remote,

try Cool Springs Campground or Ponderosa Flat Campground, both at Butt Reservoir near the lake's south shore, at the end of Prattville Butt Reservoir Rd.

These campgrounds lie within the surrounding Lassen and Plumas National Forests on the lake's southwest shore. Sites tend to be more tranquil than the RV-centric private campgrounds that are right on the water.

Lake Almanor Campgrounds
CAMPGROUND $

(☑877-444-6777; www.recreation.gov; tent sites $15-18, RV sites $29-33) Large wooded campground on the lake. While RVs can camp here, there are no hookups.

North Shore Campground
CABINS, CAMPGROUND $

(☑530-258-3376; www.northshorecampground. com; 541 Catfish Beach Rd; tent sites $36, RV sites $45-56, pop-up trailer $89, cabins $119-269; ☎) Two miles east of Chester on Hwy 36, these expansive, forested grounds stretch for a mile along the water, and get filled up with mostly RVs. Ranch-style cabins have kitchens and are great for families. This place is fine if you want to spend all your time water-skiing on the lake, but those seeking the solitude of nature should look elsewhere.

Knotty Pine Resort & Marina
CABIN $$

(☑530-596-3348; www.knottypine.net; 430 Peninsula Dr; r $165, 2-bedroom cabins with kitchen $180; ☎❀❀) This full-service lakeside alternative, 7 miles east of Chester, has simple cabins and rents boats, kayaks and canoes.

LASSEN NATIONAL FOREST HIKES

The forest has some serious hikes, with 460 miles of trails, ranging from the brutally challenging (120 miles of the **Pacific Crest Trail**) to ambitious day hikes (the 12-mile Spencer Meadows National Recreation Trail), to just-want-to-stretch-the-legs-a-little trails (the 3.5-mile Heart Lake National Recreation Trail). Near the intersection of Hwys 44 and 89, visitors to the area will find one of the most spectacular features of the forest, the pitch-black 600yd **Subway Cave** lava tube. Other points of interest include the 1.5-mile volcanic **Spattercone Crest Trail**, **Willow Lake** and **Crater Lake**, 7684ft **Antelope Peak** and the 900ft-high, 14-mile-long **Hat Creek Rim** escarpment.

For those seeking to get far off the beaten trail, the forest has three wilderness areas. Two high-elevation wilderness areas are the **Caribou Wilderness** and the **Thousand Lakes Wilderness**, best visited from mid-June to mid-October. The **Ishi Wilderness** (named after Ishi, the last surviving member of the Yahi people, who walked out of this wilderness in 1911), at a much lower elevation in the Central Valley foothills east of Red Bluff, is more comfortable in spring and fall, as summer temperatures often climb to over 100°F (37°C). It harbors California's largest migratory deer herd, which can be upwards of 20,000 head.

★ **Cravings** AMERICAN $
(☑530-258-2229; 278 Main St; mains $5-13; ⊙7am-2pm Thu-Tue; 🛜🍴) You will get cravings for this place once you're gone. Think fresh, all homemade classics like crispy waffles or rustic Reuben sandwiches made to big-city-worthy standards. They make their own delectable pastries and pump out quality espresso while keeping small-town smiles. The new historic-building location includes a dedicated cafe, bookstore and creekside dining. Gluten-free and vegetarian friendly.

Tantardino's ITALIAN $$
(☑530-596-3902; www.tantardinos.com; 401 Ponderosa Dr, Lake Almanor Peninsula; mains $16-20, pizzas $12-26; ⊙11:30am-9pm Tue-Sat) This is the locals' favorite place to eat in the region hands down – even folks from Susanville drive the 32 miles to get here, with pleasure, for the excellent Sicillian-style lasagna, yummy pizzas and meatball or caprese sandwiches at lunchtime. It's lively, friendly and you can eat and imbibe outside in summer. Reserve ahead for dinner.

★ **Red Onion Grill** MODERN AMERICAN $$$
(☑530-258-1800; www.redoniongrill.com; 303 Peninsula Dr, Westwood; mains $12-36; ⊙11am-9pm, shorter hours Oct-Apr) Head here for the finest dining on the lake with upscale New American, Italian-influenced cuisine (like the simply prepared shrimp scampi), and bar food that's executed with real panache. The setting is casual and fun, made all the more warm by the wine list.

❶ Information

Get information about lodging and recreation around the lake, in Lassen National Forest and in Lassen Volcanic National Park at **Chester & Lake Almanor Chamber of Commerce** (☑530-258-2426; www.chester-lakealmanor.com; 529 Main St, Chester; ⊙9am-4pm Mon-Fri)

❶ Getting There & Away

Plumas Transit (☑530-283-2538; www.plumastransit.com; fares $1-4) runs buses to Quincy with connections to Redding, while **Lassen Rural bus** (☑530-252-7433; www.lassentransportation.com; fares $1-4) runs to/from Susanville.

Susanville

Though it sits on a lovely high desert plateau, the Lassen County seat isn't much of a charmer; it's a resupply post with a Wal-Mart, a few stop lights and two prisons. Although not a tourist destination in itself, it provides good services for travelers passing through. It lies 35 miles east of Lake Almanor and 85 miles northwest of Reno – and is home to a couple of modest historic sites. The best event in town is the **Lassen County Fair** (☑530-251-8900; www.lassencountyfair.org; $6; ⊙Jul), which swings into gear in July.

The restored **Susanville Railroad Depot**, south of Main St, off Weatherlow St, sits beside the terminus of the Bizz Johnson Trail.

The town's oldest building, **Roop's Fort** (1853), is named after Susanville's founder, Isaac Roop. The fort was a trading post on the Nobles Trail, a California emigrant route. The town itself was named after Roop's daughter, Susan.

Beside Roops Fort is the friendly **Lassen Historical Museum** (☑530-257-3292; 75 N Weatherlow St; admission by donation; ⊙hours vary, closed Sun), which has well-presented displays of clothing and memorabilia from the area, which are worth a 20-minute visit.

The **Railroad Depot Visitors Center** (☑530-257-3252; 601 Richmond Rd; ⊙10am-4pm May-Oct) rents bicycles and has brochures on mountain-biking trails in the area.

Motels along Main St average $65 to $90 per night. **High Country Inn** (☑530-257-3450; www.high-country-inn.com; 3015 Riverside Dr; r $87-159; 🛜🍴) is the best of these. For more character, try **Roseberry House B&B** (☑530-257-5675; www.roseberryhouse.com; 609 North St; r/ste $125/150; 🛜). This sweet 1902 Victorian house is two blocks north of Main St. Striking dark-wood antique headboards and armoires combine with rosebuds and frill. There are nice little touches, like bath salts and candy dishes. In the morning expect homemade muffins and jam as part of the full breakfast.

To eat, head to **Lassen Ale Works** (☑530-257-7666; www.lassenaleworks.com; 724 Main St; mains $9-21; ⊙4-10pm Mon, 11am-10pm Tue-Thu, 11am-11pm Fri & Sat). In the renovated c 1862 Pioneer Saloon, this place looks like nothing from the outside but opens up to a big and bustling space. It's known for it's fish-and-chips but everything from steaks to Reuben sandwiches are fresh and as good as the service. Try one of the seven signature brews like the Pioneer Porter or Almanor Amber.

For local information about the town visit the **Lassen County Chamber of Commerce** (☑530-257-4323; www.lassencountychamber.org; 84 N Lassen St; ⊙9am-4pm Mon-Fri), while the

Lassen National Forest supervisor's office ([☑]530-257-2151; 2550 Riverside Dr; [⊙]8am-4:30pm Mon-Fri) has maps and recreation information for getting into the surrounding wilds.

SageStage([☑]530 203-0410;www.sagestage.com) runs buses to Redding via Alturas ($18) and south to Reno ($22). Susanville City Buses ([☑]530-252-7433) makes a circuit around town (fare $2).

Eagle Lake

Those who have the time to get all the way out to Eagle Lake, California's second-largest natural lake, are rewarded with a stunningly blue jewel on the high plateau. From late spring until fall this lovely lake, about 15 miles northwest of Susanville, attracts a smattering of visitors who come to cool off, swim, fish, boat and camp. On the south shore, you'll find a pristine 5-mile **recreational trail** and several busy **campgrounds** ([☑]information 530-257-4188, reservations 877-444-6777; www.recreation.gov; tent/RV sites from $20/30) administered by Lassen National Forest and the **Bureau of Land Management** (BLM; [☑]530-257-0456; 2550 Riverside Dr, Susanville). **Eagle Lake Marina** ([☑]877-444-6777; www.eaglelakerecreationarea.com), close by, has shower and laundry facilities, and can help you get out onto the lake with a fishing license.

Eagle Lake RV Park ([☑]530-825-3133; www.eaglelakeandrv.com; 687-125 Palmetto Way; tent/RV sites $25/36.50, cabins $37-100; [❄][🐾]), on the western shore, and **Eagle Lake Resort** ([☑]530-251-6770; www.eaglelakerv.com; Stones Landing; RV sites $33; [❄][🐾]), on the quieter northern shore, both rent boats.

Quincy

Idyllic Quincy is one of the northern mountains' three mountain communities, which teeter on the edge of becoming an incorporated town (the other two are Burney, in Shasta County, and Weaverville). Nestled in a high valley in the northern Sierra, southeast of Lassen Volcanic National Park via Hwy 89, it's a lovely little place, endowed with just enough edge by the student population of the local Feather River College. Nearby Feather River, Plumas National Forest, Tahoe National Forest and their oodles of open space make Quincy an excellent base from which to explore.

In town, Hwy 70/89 splits into two one-way streets, with traffic on Main St heading east, and traffic on Lawrence St heading west. Jackson St runs parallel to Main St, one block south, and is another main artery. Just about everything you need is on or close to these three streets, making up Quincy's low-key commercial district.

◉ Sights & Activities

Pick up free hiking-, biking- and driving-tour pamphlets from the Plumas National Forest Headquarters (p565) to guide you through the gorgeous surrounding **American Valley**. The **Feather River Scenic Byway** (Hwy 70) leads into the Sierra. In summer the icy waters of county-namesake **Feather River** (*plumas* is Spanish for 'feathers') are excellent for swimming, kayaking, fishing and floating in old inner tubes. The area is also a wonderland of winter activities, especially at Bucks Lake.

Plumas County Museum　　MUSEUM
([☑]530-283-6320; www.plumasmuseum.org; 500 Jackson St, at Coburn St; adult/child $2/1; [⊙]9am-4:30pm Tue-Sat, 10am-3pm Sun; [P][🐾]) In the block behind the courthouse, this multifloor county museum has flowering gardens, as well as hundreds of historical photos and relics from the county's pioneer and Maidu days, its early mining and timber industries, and construction of the Western Pacific Railroad. For the price, it's definitely worth the stop.

Plumas County Courthouse　HISTORIC BUILDING
(www.plumascourt.ca.gov; 520 Main St) Pop into the 1921 Plumas County Courthouse, at the west end of Main St, to see enormous interior marble posts and staircases, and a 1-ton bronze-and-glass chandelier in the lobby.

Big Daddy's Guide Service　　FISHING
([☑]530-283-4103; www.bigdaddyfishing.com; trips per person from $175) Captain Bryan Roccucci is Big Daddy, the best-known fishing guide in Northeast California. He knows the lakes well and leads trips for all levels.

✪ Festivals & Events

★**High Sierra Music Festival**　　MUSIC
(www.highsierramusic.com; [⊙]Jul) On the first weekend in July, quiet Quincy is host to this blowout festival, renowned statewide. The four-day extravaganza brings a five-stage smorgasbord of art and music from a spectrum of cultural corners (indie rock, classic

blues, folk and jazz). Past acts include Thievery Corporation, Lauryn Hill, Primus, Ben Harper and Neko Case.

Sure, a curmudgeonly local might call it the Hippie Fest, but it's pretty tame in comparison to some of Northern California's true fringe festivals. If you plan to attend, reserve a room or campsite a couple of months in advance. For those who don't want to camp in nearby national-forest land, Susanville, one hour away, will have the largest number of rooms.

🛏 Sleeping

Ranchito Motel
MOTEL $

(📞 530-286-2265; www.ranchitomotel.com; 2020 E Main St; r from $79; 🛜) With antique timber pillars, white-painted brick walls, old barn-style doors and the occasional wagon wheel for decoration, this friendly motel (in the eastern half of town) definitely has a Mexican ranch feel. Inside, rooms are modern, freshly painted and very comfortable for the price. The motel offers plenty more choices on the wooded land that extends back a few acres.

Pine Hill Motel
MOTEL $

(📞 530-283-1670; www.pinehillmotel.com; 42075 Hwy 70; s/d/cabins from $70/75/150; ❄️🛜🐾) A mile west of downtown Quincy, this little hotel is fronted by a manicured, flower-bedecked lawn dotted with white tables and chairs. The units are nothing fancy, but they're clean and in a constant state of renovation. Each is equipped with microwave, coffeemaker and refrigerator; some cabins have full kitchens.

Feather River Canyon Campgrounds
CAMPGROUND $

(📞 reservations 877-444-6777; www.fs.usda.gov; tent & RV sites $25) Area campgrounds are administered through the Mt Hough Ranger District Office (p565). They are in a cluster along the north fork of the Feather River west of Quincy – five are no-fee, but also have no piped water. All are first-come, first-served.

★ Quincy Courtyard Suites
APARTMENT $$

(📞 530-283-1401; www.quincycourtyardsuites.com; 436 Main St; apt $129-169; 🅿️♿🛜) Staying in this beautifully renovated 1908 Clinch building, overlooking the small main drag of Quincy's downtown, feels just right, like renting the village's cutest apartment. The warmly decorated rooms are modern – no

fussy clutter – and apartments have spacious, modern kitchens, claw-foot tubs and gas fireplaces.

Ada's Place
B&B $$

(📞 530-283-1954; www.adasplace.com; 562 Jackson St; cottages $110-145; 🛜) Even though it feels like a B&B, it's a bit of a misnomer. Without breakfast, Ada's is just an excellent B. No problem, as each of the three brightly painted garden units has a full kitchen. Ada's Cottage is worth the slight extra charge, as its skylights offer an open feel. It's very quiet and private, yet right in town.

Greenhorn Guest Ranch
RANCH $$$

(📞 800-334-6939; www.greenhornranch.com; 2116 Greenhorn Ranch Rd; per person per day incl trail rides from $260; 🕙May-Oct; 🛜🏊🐾) Not a 'dude' ranch but rather a 'guest' ranch: instead of shoveling stalls, guests are pampered with mountain-trail rides, riding lessons, even rodeo practice. Or you can just fish, hike, square-dance and attend evening bonfires, cookouts and frog races – think of it as a cowboy version of the getaway resort in *Dirty Dancing*.

Before you raise an eyebrow at the price, note that meals and riding are all included.

🍴 Eating & Drinking

★ Pangaea Cafe & Pub
CAFE $

(📞 530-283-0426; www.pangaeapub.com; 461 W Main St; mains $10-13; 🕙11:30am-8:30pm Mon-Fri; 🛜🍽♿) 🍃 Like a stranger you feel you've met before, this earthy spot feels warmly familiar, all the more lovable when you consider its commitment to serving local produce. Choose from regional beef burgers, salmon sushi, a slew of panini sandwiches (many veggie), burritos and rice bowls. It's hopping with locals drinking craft brews, kids running around and lots of hugging.

Farmers Market
MARKET $

(www.quincyfarmersmarket.org; 530 W Main St; 🕙4:30-7:30pm Thu mid-Jul–mid-Sep) Everything from fruits and veggies to handmade soaps, crafts and more. Enjoy it all to live music.

Patti's Thunder Café
BREAKFAST $

(📞 530-283-3300; 557 Lawrence St; mains $9-16; 🕙7am-2pm; 🍽) Homey and hip, this is the best place in town for breakfast, and the vine-shaded patio is a lovely way to start the day. The menu has plenty of meaty or vegetarian options and portions are huge. Try the 'vegetaters' (roasted veg and potatoes smothered in cheese). The restaurant is a no-cell-phone zone so bring a friend or a book.

Sweet Lorraine's
CALIFORNIAN $$
(384 Main St; mains $18-24; ⊙ 11:30am-2pm Mon-Fri, 5-8pm Tue-Sat) On a warm day – or, better yet, evening – the patio here is especially sweet. The menu features basic Californian cuisine (ribs, pork chops, half a roast chicken, soups and salads) and the ambience is woodsy and local. Finish things off with the delicious whiskey bread pudding.

Moon's
ITALIAN $$
(☑530-283-0765; www.moons-restaurant.com; 497 Lawrence St; mains $13-24; ⊙ daily Jun-Oct, 5-9pm Tue-Sun Nov-May) Follow the aroma of garlic to this welcoming little chalet with a charming ambience. Dig into choice steaks and Italian-American classics, including excellent pizza and rich lasagna.

Drunk Brush
WINE BAR
(www.facebook.com/TheDrunkBrush; 438 Main St; ⊙ 2-7pm Mon-Wed, to 10pm Thu & Fri, to 8pm Sat) A sweet little courtyard wine bar that pours 25 wines and a few beers. Sample delicious appetizer pairings in a welcoming, arty atmosphere and sometimes to live music.

ⓘ Information

Mt Hough Ranger District Office (☑530-283-0555; 39696 Hwy 70; ⊙ 8am-4:30pm Mon-Fri) Five miles northwest of town. Has maps and outdoors information.

Plumas National Forest Headquarters (☑530-283-2050; 159 Lawrence St; ⊙ 8am-4:30pm Mon-Fri) For maps and outdoors information.

Bucks Lake

This clear mountain lake is cherished by locals in the know. Surrounded by pine forests, it's excellent for swimming, fishing and boating. It's about 17 miles southwest of Quincy, via the white-knuckle roads of Bucks Lake Rd (Hwy 119). The region is lined with beautiful hiking trails, including the Pacific Crest Trail, which passes through the adjoining 21,000-acre Bucks Lake Wilderness in the northwestern part of Plumas National Forest. In winter, the last 3 miles of Bucks Lake Rd are closed by snow, making it ideal for cross-country skiers.

Bucks Lake Lodge (☑530-283-2262; www.buckslakelodge.com; 16525 Bucks Lake Rd; d $99-109, cabins $119-195; 🛰🐾) is right on the lakeshore and its restaurant is popular with locals. **Haskins Valley Inn** (☑530-283-9667; www.haskinsvalleyinn.com; 1305 Haskins Circle; r $129-149; 🛰) is actually a B&B just across the street from the lake, with cozily overstuffed furnishings, woodsy paintings, Jacuzzis, fireplaces and a deck.

Five first-come, first-served campgrounds (p563) are open from June to September. Get a map at the Plumas National Forest Headquarters (p565) or Mt Hough Ranger District Office (p565), both in Quincy.

Aside from the lodge and B&B, you'll need to bring your own grub to this rustic area.

MT SHASTA REGION

'Lonely as God, and white as a winter moon,' wrote poet Joaquin Miller about this lovely mountain. The sight of it is so awe-inspiring that the new-age claims about its power as an 'energy vortex' sound plausible even after a first glimpse.

There are a million ways to explore the mountain and surrounding Shasta-Trinity National Forest – take scenic drives or get out and hike, mountain bike, raft, ski or snowshoe. At Mt Shasta's base sit three excellent little towns: Dunsmuir, Mt Shasta City and McCloud. Each has a distinct personality, but all hold a wild-mountain sensibility and first-rate amenities. Find the snaggle-toothed peaks of Castle Crags just 6 miles west of Dunsmuir.

A long drive northeast of Mt Shasta and a world away is eerily beautiful Lava Beds National Monument, a blistered badland of petrified fire. The contrasting wetlands of Klamath Basin National Wildlife Refuges lie just west.

Many services and some roads close in winter so summer is a far easier time to visit. However, winter is a peaceful and beautiful time to come here.

Mt Shasta

'When I first caught sight of it I was 50 miles away and afoot, alone and weary. Yet all my blood turned to wine, and I have not been weary since,' wrote naturalist John Muir of Mt Shasta in 1874. Mt Shasta's beauty is intoxicating, and the closer you get to her the headier you begin to feel. Dominating the landscape, the mountain is visible for more than 100 miles from many parts of Northern

Mt Shasta Area

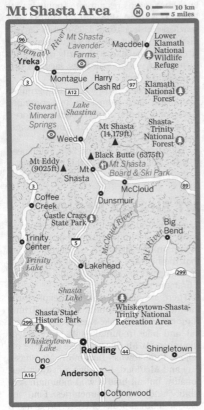

California and southern Oregon. Though not California's highest peak (at 14,162ft it ranks fifth), Mt Shasta is especially magnificent because it rises alone on the horizon, unrivaled by other mountains.

Mt Shasta is part of the vast volcanic Cascade chain that includes Lassen Peak to the south and Mt Rainier to the north in Washington state. Thermal hot springs indicate that Mt Shasta is dormant, not extinct. The last eruption was about 200 years ago.

History

The story of the first settlers here is a sadly familiar one: European fur trappers arrived in the area in the 1820s, encountering several Native American tribes, including the Shasta, Karuk, Klamath, Modoc, Wintu and Pit River people. By 1851, hordes of Gold Rush miners had arrived and steamrolled the place, destroying the tribes' traditional life and nearly causing their extinction.

Later, the newly completed railroad began to import workers and export timber for the booming lumber industry. And since Mt Shasta City (called Sisson at the time) was the only non-dry town around, it became *the* bawdy, good-time hangout for lumberjacks.

The lumberjacks have now been replaced by middle-aged mystics and outdoor-sports enthusiasts. While the slopes have immediate appeal for explorers, spiritual seekers are attracted to the peak's reported cosmic properties. In 1987, about 5000 believers from around the world convened here for the Harmonic Convergence, a communal meditation for peace. Reverence for the mountain is nothing new; for centuries Native Americans have honored the mountain as sacred, considering it to be no less than the Great Spirit's wigwam.

◉ Sights & Activities

◉ The Mountain

You'll come across views of **Mt Shasta** (☑ 530-926-4511; www.fs.fed.us/r5/shastatrinity; Everitt Memorial Hwy; P ♿) ∅ either peaking over a ridge or completely dominating the landscape, from the Oregon border and even into the east toward Tule Lake. The mountain has two cones: the main cone has a crater about 200yd across, and the younger, shorter cone on the western flank, called Shastina, has a crater about half a mile wide.

You can drive almost the whole way up the mountain via the Everitt Memorial Hwy (Hwy A10) and see exquisite views at any time of year. Simply head east on Lake St from downtown Mt Shasta City, then turn left onto Washington Dr and keep going. **Bunny Flat** (6860ft), which has a trailhead for Horse Camp and the Avalanche Gulch summit route, is a busy place with parking spaces, information signboards and a toilet.

The section of highway beyond Bunny Flat is only open from about mid-June to October, depending on snow, but if it's clear, it's worth the trouble. This road leads to **Lower Panther Meadow**, where trails connect the campground to a Wintu sacred spring, in the upper meadows near the **Old Ski Bowl** (7800ft) parking area. Shortly thereafter is the highlight of the drive, **Everitt Vista Point** (7900ft), where a short interpretive walk from the parking lot leads to a stone-walled outcrop affording exceptional views of Lassen Peak to the south, the Mt Eddy and Marble Mountains to the west and the whole Strawberry Valley below.

Climbing the summit is best done between May and September, preferably in spring and early summer, when there's still enough soft snow on the southern flank to make footholds easier on the nontechnical route. Although the elements are occasionally volatile and the winds are incredibly strong, the round-trip could conceivably be done in one day with 12 or more hours of solid hiking. A more enjoyable trip takes at least two days with one night on the mountain. How long it actually takes depends on the route selected, the physical condition of the climbers and weather conditions (for weather information, call the recorded message of the Forest Service Mt Shasta climbing advisory on 530-926-9613).

The hike to the summit from Bunny Flat follows the **Avalanche Gulch Route**. Although it is only about 7 miles, the vertical climb is more than 7000ft, so acclimatizing to the elevation is important – even hearty hikers will be short of breath. Additionally, this route requires crampons, an ice axe and a helmet, all of which can be rented locally. Rock slides, while rare, are also a hazard. If you want to make the climb without gear, the only option is the **Clear Creek Route** to the top, which leaves from the east side of the mountain. In late summer, this route is usually manageable in hiking boots, though there's still loose scree, and it should be done as an overnight hike. Novices should contact the Mt Shasta Ranger Station (p570) for a list of available guides.

There's a charge to climb beyond 10,000ft: a three-day summit pass costs $25; an annual pass is $30. Contact the ranger station for details. You must obtain a free wilderness permit any time you go into the wilderness, whether on the mountain or in the surrounding area.

Mt Shasta Ski Park   SNOW SPORTS
(✍ snow reports 530-926-8686; www.skipark.com; full-day weekend lift tickets adult/child $58/32; ⏰9am-9pm Thu-Sat, to 4pm Sun-Tue) On the south slope of Mt Shasta, off Hwy 89 heading toward McCloud, this winter skiing and snowboarding park opens depending on snowfall. The park has a 1435ft vertical drop, 32 alpine runs and 18 miles of cross-country trails. These are all good for beginner and intermediate skiers, and are a less crowded alternative to the slopes around Lake Tahoe.

Rentals, instruction and weekly specials are available; lift tickets are cheapest on weekdays. It's Northern California's largest night-skiing operation. There are lots of inexpensive options for skiing half a day or just at night, when hitting the slopes and taking in a full moon can be enchanting.

In summer the park occasionally hosts mountain-biking events.

◉ The Lakes

There are a number of pristine mountain lakes near Mt Shasta. Some of them are accessible only by dirt roads or hiking trails and are great for getting away from it all.

The closest lake to Mt Shasta City is lovely **Lake Siskiyou** (also the largest), 2.5 miles southwest on Old Stage Rd, where you can peer into **Box Canyon Dam**, a 200ft-deep chasm. Another 7 miles up in the mountains, southwest of Lake Siskiyou on Castle Lake Rd, lies **Castle Lake**, an unspoiled gem surrounded by granite formations and pine forest. Swimming, fishing, picnicking and free camping are popular in summer; in winter folks ice-skate on the lake. **Lake Shastina**, about 15 miles northwest of town, off Hwy 97, is another beauty.

Mt Shasta City

Comfortable and practical Mt Shasta City glows in the shadow of the white pyramid of Mt Shasta. The downtown is charming; you can spend hours poking around galleries and boutiques. Orienting yourself is easy with the mountain looming over the east side of town and you may get a kink in your neck from admiring it. The downtown area is a few blocks east of I-5. Take the Central Mt Shasta exit, then drive east on Lake St past the visitor center, up to the town's main intersection at Mt Shasta Blvd, the principal drag.

◉ Sights & Activities

To head out hiking on your own, first stop by the ranger station or the visitors center for excellent free trail guides, including several access points along the **Pacific Crest Trail**. Gorgeous **Black Butte**, a striking, treeless, black volcanic cone, rises almost 6436ft. The 2.5-mile trail to the top takes at least 2½ hours for the round-trip. It's steep and rocky in many places, and there is no shade or water, so don't hike on a hot summer day. Wear good, thick-soled shoes or hiking boots and bring plenty of water. If you want an easier amble, try the 10-mile **Sisson-Callahan National Recreation Trail**, a partially paved trail that affords great views of Mt Shasta and the jagged Castle Crags, following a historic route established in the mid-1800s by prospectors, trappers and cattle ranchers to connect the mining town of Callahan with the town of Sisson, now called Mt Shasta City.

Mt Shasta City Park & Sacramento River Headwaters PARK
(http://msrec.org; Nixon Rd) FREE Off Mt Shasta Blvd, about a mile north of downtown, the headwaters of the Sacramento River gurgle up from the ground in a large, cool spring. It's about as pure as water can get – so bring a bottle and have a drink. The park also has walking trails, picnic spots, sports fields and courts, and a children's playground.

Sisson Museum MUSEUM
(http://mtshastamuseum.com; 1 Old Stage Rd; suggested donation $1; ⊙10am-4pm Jun-Sep, 1-4pm Fri-Sun Oct-Dec & Apr-May) A half-mile west of the freeway, this former hatchery headquarters is full of curious mountaineering artifacts and old pictures. The changing exhibitions highlight history – geological and human – but also occasionally showcase local artists. Next door, the oldest operating hatchery in the West maintains outdoor ponds teeming with rainbow trout that will eventually be released into lakes and rivers.

Siskiyou Ice Rink SKATING
(www.siskiyourink.org; cnr Rockfellow & Adams Drs; adult/child $10/7; ⊙9am-7:15pm Mon-Thu, to 9pm Fri & Sat, 8am-5pm Sun Dec-Mar) East of downtown, the immense outdoor skating rink is open to ice-skaters in winter and has lessons available.

River Dancers Rafting & Kayaking RAFTING
(☑530-925-0237; www.riverdancers.com; 705 Kenneth Way; half-day trips from $78) Excellent outfit run by active environmentalists who guide one- to five-day white-water-rafting excursions down the area's rivers: the Klamath, Sacramento, Salmon, Trinity and Scott. Chose from half-day to multiday adventures.

Shasta Mountain Guides OUTDOORS
(☑530-926-3117; http://shastaguides.com; 2-day climbs from $625 per person) Offers two-day guided climbs of Mt Shasta between April and September, with all gear and meals included. The experienced mountaineers have operated in Shasta for 30 years.

🍂 Courses

Mt Shasta Mountaineering School ADVENTURE SPORTS
(www.swsmtns.com; 210a E Lake St; 2-day summit climbs $600) Conducts clinics and courses for serious climbers, or those looking to get serious on Mt Shasta.

☞ Tours

Note that hiking Mt Shasta doesn't require an operator, but those wanting one have plenty of options; ask at the visitor center.

Shasta Vortex Adventures OUTDOORS, MEDITATION
(☑530-926-4326; www.shastavortex.com; 400 Chestnut St) For a uniquely Mt Shasta outdoor experience, Shasta Vortex offers low-impact trips accented with the spiritual quest as much as the physical journey. The focus of the trips includes guided meditation and an exploration of the mountain's metaphysical power. Full-day tours for two people cost $474; larger groups get a slight discount.

🛏 Sleeping

Shasta has it all, from free rustic camping to plush boutique B&Bs. If you're intent on staying at the upper end of the spectrum, make reservations well in advance, especially on weekends and holidays and during ski season.

Many modest motels stretch along S Mt Shasta Blvd (costing $60 to $140 depending on how recently they were remodeled). Most offer discount ski packages in winter and lower midweek rates year-round.

★Historic Lookout & Cabin Rentals CABIN $
(☑information 530-994-2184, reservations 877-444-6777; www.fs.usda.gov/stnf; q $75; ⊙May/Jun–mid-Oct; ⊛) What better way to rough it in style than to bunk down in a fire lookout on forested slopes? Built from the 1920s to '40s, cabins come with cots, tables and chairs, have panoramic views and can accommodate four people. Details about Little Mt Hoffman, Girard Creek and other lookouts can all be found on the national forest website.

Note that these cabins have become *very* popular and you'll need to reserve far in advance.

Panther Meadows
CAMPGROUND $

(www.fs.usda.gov; tent sites free; ☺ usually Jul-Nov) Ten walk-in tent sites (no drinking water) sit at the timberline, right at the base of the mountain. They're a few miles up the mountain from other options, but are still easily accessible from Everitt Memorial Hwy. No reservations; arrive early to secure a site.

Swiss Holiday Lodge
MOTEL $

(☑530-926-3446; www.swissholidaylodge.com; 2400 S Mt Shasta Blvd; r $66-110; P ☻ ✹ 🕾 ☒ ☝) Run by a friendly family and a small, energetic dog; you get a peek of the mountain from the back windows of these clean, well-priced rooms.

McBride Springs
CAMPGROUND $

(tent sites $10; ☺ Memorial Day-late Oct, depending on weather) Easily accessible from Everitt Memorial Hwy, this campground has running water and pit toilets, but no showers. It's near mile marker 4, at an elevation of 5000ft. It's no beauty – a recent root disease killed many of the white fir trees that shaded the sites – but it's convenient. Arrive early in the morning to secure a spot (no reservations).

Lake Siskiyou Beach & Camp
CAMPGROUND $

(☑888-926-2618; www.lakesiskiyouresort.com; 4239 WA Barr Rd; tent/RV sites from $20/29, cabins $107-152; 🕾☝) Tucked away on the shore of Lake Siskiyou, this sprawling place has a summer-camp feel (there's an arcade and an ice-cream stand). Hardly rustic, it has a swimming beach, and kayak, canoe, fishing-boat and paddle-boat rentals. Lots of amenities make it a good option for families on an RV trip.

Horse Camp
HUT $

(www.sierraclubfoundation.org; per person with/without tent $5/3) This 1923 alpine lodge run by the Sierra Club is a 2-mile hike uphill from Bunny Flat, at 8000ft. The stone construction and natural setting are lovely. Caretakers staff the hut from May to September only.

★ Shasta MountInn
B&B $$

(☑530-926-1810; www.shastamountinn.com; 203 Birch St; r $150-175; P ☻🕾) Only antique on the outside, this bright Victorian 1904 farmhouse is all relaxed minimalism, bold colors and graceful decor on the inside. Each airy room has a great bed and exquisite views of the luminous mountain. Enjoy the expansive garden, wraparound deck, outdoor hot tub and sauna. Not relaxed enough yet? Chill on the perfectly placed porch swings.

Mt Shasta Resort
RESORT $$

(☑530-926-3030; www.mountshastaresort.com; 1000 Siskiyou Lake Blvd; r from $119, 1-/2-bedroom chalets from $179/239; 🕾☝) Divinely situated away from town, this upscale golf resort and spa has arts-and-crafts-style chalets nestled in the woods around the shores of Lake Siskiyou. They're a bit soulless, but they're immaculate, and each has a kitchen and gas fireplace. Basic lodge rooms are near the golf course, which boasts some challenging greens and amazing views of the mountain.

The restaurant has excellent views and serves Californian cuisine with a large selection of steaks.

Strawberry Valley Inn
B&B $$

(☑530-926-2052; 1142 S Mt Shasta Blvd; d $109-169; 🕾) The understated rooms surround a garden courtyard, allowing you to enjoy the intimate feel of a B&B without the pressure of having to chat with the darling newlyweds around the breakfast table. A continental breakfast is included and guests can use the kitchen.

Dream Inn
B&B $$

(☑530-926-1536; www.dreaminnmtshastacity. com; 326 Chestnut St; r without bath $80-160, ste $120-160; 🕾☝) Made up of two houses in the center of town: one is a meticulously kept Victorian cottage stuffed with fussy knick-knacks; the other a Spanish-style two-story building with chunky, raw-wood furniture and no clutter. A rose garden with a koi pond joins the two properties. A good-sized breakfast is included. Excellent midtown location.

Finlandia Motel
MOTEL $$

(☑530-926-5596; www.finlandiamotel.com; 1612 S Mt Shasta Blvd; r $65-120, with kitchen $115-200) An excellent deal, the standard rooms are... standard – clean and simple. The suites get a little chalet flair with vaulted pine ceilings and mountain views. There's an outdoor hot tub and the Finnish sauna is available by appointment.

✖ Eating & Drinking

Trendy restaurants and cafes here come and go with the snowmelt, but there are still some tried-and-true places, favored by locals and visitors alike. For more options head 6 miles south to Dunsmuir, an unexpected hot spot for great food. A **farmers market** (p570) sets up on Mt Shasta Blvd during summer.

Poncho & Lefkowitz MEXICAN, INTERNATIONAL $
(401 S Mt Shasta Blvd; meals $4-9; ⊙11am-4pm Tue-Sat; 🖉) Surrounded by a picnic table or three, this classy, wood-sided food cart turns out juicy Polish sausage, bratwurst and hot dogs, and big plates of nachos, tamales and burritos (including vegetarian options). It's a good bet for food on the go.

Berryvale Grocery MARKET, CAFE $
(🖉530-926-1576; www.berryvale.com; 305 S Mt Shasta Blvd; cafe items from $5; ⊙store 8am-8pm, cafe to 7pm; 🖉🖟) 🖋 This market sells groceries and organic produce to health-conscious eaters. The excellent cafe serves good coffee, fresh juices and an array of tasty – mostly veggie – salads, sandwiches and wraps.

Farmers Market MARKET $
(www.mtshastafarmersmarket.com; 400 block of N Mt Shasta Blvd; ⊙3:30-6pm Mon mid-May–mid-Oct) Stock up on farm-fresh produce or graze the stalls of delicious tamales, bakery goods, pastas and more.

Mount Shasta Pastry BAKERY $
(🖉530-926-9944; www.mountshastapastry.com; 610 S Mt Shasta Blvd; mains $5-11; ⊙7am-4pm Mon-Fri, to 1pm Sat & Sun, closed Mon & Tue Oct-May; 🖉🖟) Walk in hungry and you'll be plagued with an existential breakfast crisis: the feta spinach quiche or the Tuscan scramble? The flaky croissants or a divine apricot turnover? It also serves terrific sandwiches, gourmet pizza, Peet's coffee and mimosas.

Lily's CALIFORNIAN $$
(www.lilysrestaurant.com; 1013 S Mt Shasta Blvd; mains breakfast & lunch $10-17, dinner $14-28; ⊙8am-2pm & 5-9pm; 🖉🖟) Enjoy quality Californian cuisine – Asian- and Mediterranean-touched salads, fresh sandwiches and all kinds of veg options – in a cute, white, clapboard house. Outdoor tables overhung by flowering trellises are almost always full, especially for breakfast. A Shasta classic, you can now expect vegan and gluten-free options.

Andaman Healthy Thai Cuisine THAI $$
(🖉530-926-5288; 313 N Mt Shasta Blvd; mains $12-22; ⊙11am-9pm Mon, Tue, Thu & Fri, from 4pm Sat & Sun) The food is pretty good, but the kitchen and the staff can't keep up with the crowds. It also serves burgers if you're traveling with fussy folk.

Seven Suns Coffee & Cafe CAFE
(1011 S Mt Shasta Blvd; ⊙5:30am-7pm; 🖥) This snug little hangout serves organic, locally roasted coffee, light meals (around $10) and is consistently busy. There's live acoustic music some evenings.

🔒 Shopping

Looking for an imported African hand drum, some prayer flags or a nice crystal? You've come to the right place. The downtown shopping district has a handful of cute little boutiques to indulge a little shopping for the spiritual seeker.

Fifth Season Sports SPORTS & OUTDOORS
(🖉530-926-3606; http://thefifthseason.com; 300 N Mt Shasta Blvd; ⊙9am-6pm Mon-Fri, from 8am Sat, 10am-5pm Sun) A favorite outdoor store in Shasta, this place rents camping, mountain-climbing and backpacking gear and has staff familiar with the mountain. It also rents skis, snowshoes and snowboards.

ℹ Information

Mt Shasta Ranger Station (🖉530-926-4511; www.fs.usda.gov/stnf; 204 W Alma St; ⊙8am-4:30pm Mon-Fri) One block west of Mt Shasta Blvd. Issues wilderness and mountain-climbing permits, good advice, weather reports and all you need for exploring the area. It also sells topographic maps.

Mt Shasta Visitors Center (🖉530-926-4865; www.mtshastachamber.com; 300 Pine St; ⊙9am-4:30pm) Detailed information on recreation and lodging across Siskiyou County.

ℹ Getting There & Away

Greyhound (www.greyhound.com) buses heading north and south on I-5 stop at the **depot** (628 W Sweed Blvd) in Weed, 8 miles north on I-5. Services include Redding ($15, one hour and 20 minutes, three daily), Sacramento ($40, 5½ hours, three daily) and San Francisco ($50, 10½ hours, two or three times daily).

The **STAGE bus** (🖉530-842-8295; www. co.siskiyou.ca.us; 914 Pine St; fares $2.50-8) includes Mt Shasta City in its local I-5 corridor route (fares $2.50 to $8, depending on distance), which also serves McCloud, Dunsmuir, Weed and Yreka several times each weekday. Other buses connect at Yreka.

Dunsmuir

In 1886 Canadian coal baron Alexander Dunsmuir came to Pusher (named after the 'pusher' train engines) and was so enchanted that he promised the people a fountain if they would rename the town after him. The fountain stands in the park today. Stop

WEED & STEWART MINERAL SPRINGS

Just outside Weed, **Stewart Mineral Springs** (☑530-938-2222; http://stewartmineral springs.com; 4617 Stewart Springs Rd, Weed; sauna/mineral baths $18/30; ⊙10am-6pm Thu-Sun, from noon Mon) is a popular clothing-optional hangout on the banks of a mountain stream. Henry Stewart founded these springs in 1875 after Native Americans revived him from a near-death experience. He attributed his recovery to the properties of the mineral waters, said to draw toxins from the body.

Today you can soak in a private claw-foot tub or steam in the dry-wood sauna. Other perks include massage, meditation, a Native American sweat lodge and a riverside sun-bathing deck. Call ahead to be sure there's availability. Dining and **accommodations** (tent & RV sites $35, tipis $45, d $80-120; P ☺) are on-site. To reach the springs, go 10 miles north of Mt Shasta City on I-5, past Weed to the Edgewood exit, then turn left at Stewart Springs Rd and follow the signs.

While in the area, tickle your nose at **Mt Shasta Lavender Farms** (☑530-926-2651; www.mtshastalavenderfarms.com; 9706 Harry Cash Rd, Montague; ⊙9am-4pm mid-Jun–early Aug; P), or drink up the tasty porter at the **Mt Shasta Brewing Company Alehouse** (☑530-938-2394; www.weedales.com; 360 College Ave, Weed; mains $11-18; ⊙11am-9pm or 10pm).

there for a drink; it could easily be – as locals claim – 'the best water on earth.'

This town has survived avalanche, fire, flood, even a toxic railroad spill in 1991. Long since cleaned up, the river has been restored to pristine levels and the community has a plucky spirit, though today a number of empty storefronts attest to the community's greatest challenge: the Global Economic Crisis.

Still, it's home to a spirited set of artists, naturalists, urban refugees and native Dunsmuirians, who are rightly proud of the fish-stocked rivers around their little community. Its downtown streets – once a bawdy gold rush district – hold cafes, restaurants and galleries.

◉ Sights & Activities

The Dunsmuir Chamber of Commerce (p573) stocks maps of **cycling trails** and **swimming holes** on the Upper Sacramento River.

Dunsmuir City Park PARK
(www.dunsmuirparks.org; ⊙dawn-dusk) FREE
As you follow winding Dunsmuir Ave north over the freeway, look for this park with its local native **botanical gardens** and a **vintage steam engine** in front. A forest path from the riverside gardens leads to a small waterfall, but **Mossbrae Falls** are the larger and more spectacular of Dunsmuir's waterfalls.

It's actually illegal to walk to the falls since the trail is partially on the railroad tracks and a woman was hit by a train here in 2011. Still, plenty of people go. Be extremely careful of trains as you walk by the tracks – the river's sound can make it impossible to hear them coming and to escape a train you'll have to run for it or jump in the river. Park by the railroad tracks (there's no sign), then walk north along the right-hand side of the tracks for a half-hour until you reach a railroad bridge built in 1901. Backtracking slightly from the bridge, you'll find a little path going down through the trees to the river and the falls. The community is discussing making a safer trail, so ask around.

California Theater HISTORIC BUILDING
(5741 Dunsmuir Ave) At downtown's north end stands what was the town's pride. This once-glamorous venue was being restored to its original glory, then the work stopped. First opened in 1926, the theater hosted stars such as Clark Gable, Carole Lombard and the Marx Brothers. Today the very sporadic lineup includes second-run films, musical performances and yoga classes.

🛏 Sleeping

Dunsmuir Lodge MOTEL $
(☑530-235-2884; www.dunsmuirlodge.net; 6604 Dunsmuir Ave; r $59-153; ☎☒) Toward the south entrance of town, the simple but tastefully renovated rooms have hardwood floors, big chunky blond-wood bed frames and tiled baths. A grassy communal picnic area overlooks the canyon slope. It's a peaceful little place and very good value.

Cave Springs
MOTEL, CABIN $

(☑530-235-2721; www.cavesprings.com; 4727 Dunsmuir Ave; r/cabins from $75/89; ✿🛜❄) These creekside cabins seem unchanged since the 1920s, even though the interiors were recently updated. They are rustic – *very* rustic – but their location, nestled on a piney crag above the Sacramento River, is lovely and ideal for anglers. At night the sound of rushing water mingles with the haunting whistle of trains.

The motel rooms are bland, but they're up to modern standards and have more amenities than the cabins.

Dunsmuir Inn & Suites
MOTEL $

(☑530-235-4395; www.dunsmuirinn.com; 5400 Dunsmuir Ave; r $79-159; ✿🛜) Straightforward, immaculately clean motel rooms make a good, no-fuss option. Great location in the main part of town.

Railroad Park Resort
INN, CAMPGROUND $$

(☑530-235-4440; www.rrpark.com; 100 Railroad Park Rd; tent/RV sites from $29/37, d $135-165; ✿🛜❄🐾) About 2 miles south of town, off I-5, visitors can spend the night inside refitted vintage railroad cars and cabooses. The grounds are fun for kids, who can run around the engines and plunge in a centrally situated pool. The deluxe boxcars are furnished with antiques and claw-foot tubs, although the cabooses are simpler and a bit less expensive.

You get tremendous views of Castle Crags, a peaceful creekside setting and tall pines shading the adjoining campground. In 2017 it came under enthusiastic new ownership.

✗ Eating

★ Dunsmuir Brewery Works
PUB FOOD $

(☑530-235-1900; www.dunsmuirbreweryworks.com; 5701 Dunsmuir Ave; mains $9-13; ⊙11am-10pm May-Sep, to 9pm Tue-Sun Oct-Apr; 🛜) It's hard to describe this little microbrew pub without veering into hyperbole. Start with the beer: the crisp ales and porter are perfectly balanced and the India Pale Ale (IPA) is apparently pretty good too, because patrons are always drinking it dry. Soak it up with awesome bar food: a warm potato salad, bratwurst, or a thick Angus or perfect veggie nut burger.

The atmosphere, with a buzzing patio and aw-shucks staff, completes a perfect picture.

Cornerstone Bakery & Café
CAFE $

(5759 Dunsmuir Ave; mains $6-15; ⊙8am-2pm Thu-Mon; 🖉) Smack in the middle of town, this homey place serves strong coffee, espresso and friendly service. It's more of a diner than a bakery and the offerings – basic to creative omelettes, French toast and some fun specials like chai sweet-potato waffles – are consistently delicious. The baked goods, including gooey cinnamon rolls, are often warm from the oven.

Yaks
AMERICAN $

(www.yaks.com; 4917 Dunsmuir Ave; mains $8-19; ⊙11am-9pm Mon-Sat, to 8pm Sun; 🛜) Hiding under the Hitching Post sign just off I-5, this is the lplace to come to blow your diet. Breakfast means Cuban pepper-steak hash or perhaps home-baked cinnamon-roll French toast with your choice of house syrups like Baileys-and-bourbon. Lunch offers a huge range of burgers (try the one with the house-roasted coffee rub). There's also a take-out counter.

Wheelhouse
CAFE $

(☑530-235-0754; 5841 Sacramento Ave; mains $7-12; ⊙7am-3pm Wed-Sun, to 8pm Fri & Sat; 🛜🖉) This casual, high-ceilinged, brick-walled hangout (formerly the Brown Trout Gallery & Dogwood Diner and originally the town mercantile) serves organic, healthy yet hefty and delicious New American–style breakfasts. If you're not feeling like bacon and eggs, try the Zephyr, ciabatta bread in a custard batter, grilled and topped with pineapple, brown sugar and brandied caramel syrup.

★ Café Maddalena
EUROPEAN, NORTH AFRICAN $$

(☑530-235-2725; www.cafemaddalena.com; 5801 Sacramento Ave; mains $15-26; ⊙5-9pm Thu-Sun Feb-Dec) Simple and elegant, this cafe put Dunsmuir on the foodie map. The menu was designed by chef Bret LaMott (of Trinity Cafe fame) and changes seasonally to feature dishes from southern Europe and northern Africa. Some highlights include pan-roasted king salmon with basil cream, wild mushroom soup or sautéed rabbit with carrots and morel sauce.

The wine bar is stocked with rare Mediterranean labels, including a great selection of Spanish varietals.

Railroad Park Dinner House
CALIFORNIAN $$

(☑530-235-4440; www.rrpark.com; Railroad Park Resort, 100 Railroad Park Rd; mains $15-30; ⊙5-9pm Fri & Sat Apr, 5-9pm Wed-Sun May-Oct) Set inside a vintage railroad car with views of Castle Crags, this popular restaurant-bar offers trainloads of dining-car ambience and Californian cuisine. Prime-rib specials are on Friday and Saturdays. A new chef started in 2017 so expect some surprises.

Sengthongs THAI, VIETNAMESE $$
(☑ 530-235-4770; http://sengthongs.com; 5855 Dunsmuir Ave; mains $17-27; ☺ 4:30-8:30pm Thu-Sun) This funky joint serves up sizzling Thai, Lao and Vietnamese food and books first-rate jazz, reggae, salsa or blues some nights. Many dishes are simply heaping bowls of noodles, though the meat dishes – flavored with ginger, scallions and spices – are more complex and uniformly delicious. It's a Dunsmuir classic.

Information

Dunsmuir Chamber of Commerce (☑ 530-235-2177; www.dunsmuir.com; 5915 Dunsmuir Ave, Suite 100; ☺ 10am-3:30pm Tue-Sat) Free maps, walking-guide pamphlets and excellent information on outdoor activities.

ⓘ Getting There & Away

Amtrak Station (www.amtrak.com; 5750 Sacramento Ave) Dunsmuir's Amtrak station is the railroad hub for the region and bus connections are available to the surrounding towns.

STAGE Bus (☑ 530-842-8295) This local bus service covers the Shasta region, including Shasta City and Weed.

Castle Crags State Park

The stars of this glorious **state park** (☑ 530-235-2684; www.parks.ca.gov; per car $8; ☺ sunrise-sunset) alongside Castle Crags Wilderness Area are its soaring spires of ancient granite formed some 225 million years ago, with elevations ranging from 2000ft along the Sacramento River to more than 6500ft at the peaks. The crags are similar to the granite formations of the eastern Sierra. Castle Dome resembles Yosemite's famous Half Dome.

Rangers at the park entrance station have information and maps covering nearly 28 miles of **hiking trails**. There's also **fishing** in the Sacramento River at the picnic area on the opposite side of I-5.

If you drive past the campground, you'll reach **Vista Point**, near the start of the strenuous 2.7-mile **Crags Trail**, which rises through the forest past the Indian Springs spur trail, then clambers up to the base of

Castle Dome. You're rewarded with unsurpassed views of Mt Shasta, especially if you scramble the last 100yd or so up into the rocky saddle gap. The park also has gentle **nature trails** and 8 miles of the **Pacific Crest Trail**, which passes through the park at the base of the crags.

You can camp anywhere in the Shasta-Trinity National Forest surrounding the park if you get a free campfire permit, issued at park offices. At the time of writing, the future of this state park was uncertain because of budget issues.

The **campground** (☑ reservations 800-444-7275; www.reserveamerica.com; tent & RV sites $15-30) is one of the nicer public campgrounds in this area, and very easily accessible from the highway. It has running water, hot showers and three spots that can accommodate RVs but have no hookups. Sites are shady, but suffer from traffic noise.

McCloud

This tiny, historic mill town sits at the foot of the south slope of Mt Shasta, and is an alternative to staying in Mt Shasta City. Quiet streets retain a simple, easygoing charm. It's the closest settlement to Mt Shasta Board & Ski Park and is surrounded by abundant natural beauty. Hidden in the woods upriver are woodsy getaways for the Western aristocracy, including mansions owned by the Hearst and Levi Strauss estates.

◉ Sights & Activities

The **McCloud River Loop**, a gorgeous, 6-mile, partially paved road along the Upper McCloud River, begins at Fowlers Camp, 5.5 miles east of town on Hwy 89, and re-emerges about 11 miles east of McCloud. Along the loop, turn off at Three Falls for a pretty trail that passes...yep, three lovely falls and a riparian habitat for bird-watching in the Bigelow Meadow. The loop can easily be done by car, bicycle or on foot, and has five first-come, first-served campgrounds.

Other good hiking trails include the **Squaw Valley Creek Trail** (not to be confused with the ski area near Lake Tahoe), an easy 5-mile loop trail south of town, with options for swimming, fishing and picnicking. Also south of town, **Ah-Di-Na** is the remains of a Native American settlement and historic homestead once owned by the William Randolph Hearst family. Sections of the **Pacific Crest Trail** are accessible from

Ah-Di-Na Campground, off Squaw Valley Rd, and also up near Bartle Gap, offering head-spinning views.

Fishing and swimming are popular on remote **Lake McCloud** reservoir, 9 miles south of town on Squaw Valley Rd, which is signposted in town as Southern. You can also go fishing on the Upper McCloud River (stocked with trout) and at the Squaw Valley Creek.

McCloud Mercantile   HISTORIC BUILDING
(www.mccloudmercantile.com; 222-245 Main St) The huge McCloud Mercantile anchors the downtown. There's a hotel (p574) upstairs and it hosts a couple of restaurants that warrant a longer stay, but those just passing through can get a bag of licorice at the old-world candy counter or browse the main floor. The collection of dry goods is very Nor-Cal: Woolrich blankets, handmade soap and interesting gifts for the gardener, outdoors person or chef.

Historical Museum   MUSEUM
(☑530-964-2604; 320 Main St; ⊙11am-3pm Mon-Sat, 1-3pm Sun May-Sep) **FREE** The tiny historical museum sits opposite the McCloud Chamber of Commerce and could use a bit of organization – it has the feel of a cluttered, messy thrift store – but tucked in the nooks and crannies are plenty of worthwhile curiosities from the town's past.

🛏 Sleeping & Eating

Lodging in McCloud is excellent and reservations are recommended. For camping, the McCloud Ranger District Office (p575) has information on the half-dozen campgrounds nearby. Fowlers Camp is the most popular. The campgrounds have a range of facilities, from primitive (no running water and no fee) to developed (hot showers and fees of up to $15 per site). Ask about nearby fire-lookout cabins for rent for amazing, remote views of the area.

McCloud's eating options are few. For more variety, make the 10-mile trip over to Mt Shasta City.

Stoney Brook Inn   B&B $
(☑530-964-2300; www.stoneybrookinn.com; 309 W Colombero Dr; d $94, s/d without bath $53/79, ste with kitchen $99-156; ☎❄) Smack in the middle of town, under a stand of pines, this alternative B&B also sponsors group retreats. Creature comforts include an outdoor hot tub, a sauna, a Native American sweat

lodge and massage by appointment. Downstairs rooms are nicest. Vegetarian breakfast available.

McCloud Dance Country RV Park   CAMPGROUND $
(☑530-964-2252; www.mccloudrvpark.com; 480 Hwy 89, at Southern Ave; tent sites $30, RV sites $39-46, cabins $140-175; ☎❄) Chock-full of RVs, with campsites under the trees and a small creek, this is a good option for families. The view of the mountain is breathtaking and there's a large, grassy picnic ground. Cabins are basic but clean.

★McCloud River Mercantile Hotel   INN $$
(☑530-964-2330; www.mccloudmercantile.com; 241 Main St; r $129-250; P⊝❄) Stroll upstairs to the 2nd floor of McCloud's central Mercantile Hotel and try not to fall in love; it's all high ceilings, exposed brick and a perfect marriage of preservationist class and modern panache. Antique-furnished rooms have open floor plans. Guests are greeted with fresh flowers and can drift to sleep on feather beds after soaking in claw-foot tubs.

One of the best hotels in the northern mountains.

McCloud Hotel   HISTORIC HOTEL $$
(☑530-964-2822; www.mccloudhotel.com; 408 Main St; r $145-255; ❄) Regal, butter-yellow and a whole block long, this grand hotel opened in 1916 and has been a destination for Shasta's visitors ever since. The elegant historic landmark has been restored to a luxurious standard and Sage, the on-site restaurant, serves the most upscale meals in town. Many rooms have Jacuzzis; one room is accessible for travelers with disabilities.

McCloud River Inn   B&B $$
(☑530-964-2130; www.mccloudriverinn.com; 325 Lawndale Ct; r $99-199; ❄) Rooms in this rambling, quaint Victorian are fabulously big – the bathrooms alone could sleep two. In the morning look out for the frittatas; in the evening have a bottle of wine delivered to your room. There's also an on-site day spa. The relaxed and familial atmosphere guarantees that it books up quickly.

White Mountain Cafe   AMERICAN $
(☑530-964-2005; 241 Main St; mains from $8; ⊙8am-4pm Wed-Sun, to 2pm Oct-May) In the window-lined corner of the Mercantile, this old-fashioned yet classy diner serves classic American breakfasts, hot or cold sandwiches, burgers and shakes. The 'Not the Dolly

Varden' is an excellent vegetarian sandwich with roasted zucchini, red peppers and garlic aioli.

🍷 Drinking & Entertainment

Siskiyou Brew Works BREWERY
(☑530-925-5894; 110 Squaw Valley Rd; ☺4-8pm Wed-Sun) In a not-obvious spot in the McCloud Dairy Barn just off Hwy 89, this rustic little spot churns out the town's first craft beers and decent, heavily topped pizzas. Get a beer sampler to find your favorite.

★McCloud Dance Country DANCE
(www.mcclouddancecountry.com; cnr Broadway & Pine Sts; packages from $299 per couple) Dust it up on the 5000-sq-ft maple dance floor in the 1906 Broadway Ballroom. Square dancing, round dancing, ballroom dancing – they do it all. Multiday packages include lessons and evening dances. It's a worthwhile centerpiece to a weekend getaway. Visit the website to see what's on and to sign up.

ℹ️ Information

McCloud Chamber of Commerce (☑530-964-3113; www.mccloudchamber.com; 205 Quincy St; ☺10am-4pm Mon-Fri) Has basic info and friendly staff.

McCloud Ranger District Office (☑530-964-2184; 2019 Forest Rd; ☺8am-4:30pm Mon-Sat summer, 8am-4:30pm Mon-Fri rest of year) A quarter-mile east of town. Detailed information on camping, hiking and recreation.

McArthur-Burney Falls Memorial State Park & Around

This beautiful **state park** (☑530-335-2777; www.parks.ca.gov; Hwy 89, Burney; per car $8; P🐾) ✿ lies southeast of McCloud, near the crossroads of Hwys 89 and 299 to Redding. Fed by a spring, the splashing 129ft-tall waterfalls flow at the same temperature, 42°F (6°C), year-round. Rangers are quick to point out that it might not be California's highest waterfall, but it may be the most beautiful (Teddy Roosevelt considered it the eighth wonder of the world). Clear, lava-filtered water surges over the top and also from springs in the waterfall's face.

Hiking trails include a portion of the **Pacific Crest Trail**, which continues north to Castle Crags State Park. The 1.3-mile **Burney Falls Trail** is the one you shouldn't miss.

Upgraded with guardrails, it's an easy loop for families and allows close-up views of water rushing right out of the rock. You can **camp** (☑information 530-335-2777; summer reservations 800-444-7275; www.reserveamerica.com; off Hwy 89, Burney; tent & RV sites $35, cabins $83-105; P🐾) here.

A visit to nearby **Ahjumawi Lava Springs State Park** (☑530-335-2777; www.parks.ca.gov; ☺sunrise-sunset) ✿ comes with serious bragging rights as the abundant springs, aquamarine bays and islets, and jagged flows of black basalt lava are truly off the beaten path, and can be reached only by boat. After you paddle out, the hikes are glorious: there are basalt outcroppings, lava tubes, cold springs bubbling and all kinds of volcanic features.

Lava Beds National Monument

A wild landscape of charred volcanic rock and rolling hills, this remote **national monument** (☑530-667-8113; www.nps.gov/labe; 1 Indian Well HQ, Tulelake; 7-day entry per car $15; P🐾) ✿ is reason enough to visit the region. Off Hwy 139, immediately south of Tule Lake National Wildlife Refuge, it's a truly remarkable 72-sq-mile landscape of volcanic features – lava flows, craters, cinder cones, spatter cones, shield volcanoes and amazing lava tubes.

Lava tubes are formed when the surface of hot, spreading lava cools and hardens upon exposure to cold air. The lava inside is thus insulated and stays molten, flowing away to leave an empty tube of solidified lava. Nearly 400 such tubular caves have been found in the monument, and many more are expected to be discovered. Approximately two dozen are currently open for exploration by visitors.

On the south side of the park, the **visitors center** (☑530-667-8113; www.nps.gov/labe; Tulelake; ☺8am-6pm late May-early Sep, to 5pm mid-Sep–mid-May) has free maps, activity books for kids, and information about the monument and its volcanic features and history.

From the visitors center rangers loan mediocre flashlights (and rent helmets and kneepads in the summer season only) for cave exploration and lead summer interpretive programs, including campfire talks and guided cave walks. To explore the caves it's essential you use a high-powered flashlight, wear good shoes and long sleeves (lava is sharp), and do not go alone.

Near the visitors center, a short, one-way **Cave Loop** drive provides access to many lava-tube caves. **Mushpot Cave**, the one nearest the visitors center, has lighting and information signs and is beautiful, besides being a good introductory hike. There are a number of caves that are a bit more challenging, including Labyrinth, Hercules Leg, Golden Dome and Blue Grotto. Each one of these caves has an interesting history – visitors used to ice skate by lantern light in the bottom of Merrill Cave, and when Ovls Cave was discovered, it was littered with bighorn sheep skulls. There are good brochures with details about each cave available from the visitors center. We found Sunshine Cave and Symbol Bridge Cave (the latter is reached via an easy 0.8-mile hike) to be particularly interesting. Rangers are stern with their warnings for new cavers, though, so be sure to check in with the visitors center before exploring to avoid harming the fragile geological and biological resources in the park.

The tall black cone of **Schonchin Butte** (5253ft) has a magnificent outlook accessed via a steep 1-mile hiking trail. Once you reach the top, you can visit the fire-lookout staff between June and September. **Mammoth Crater** is the source of most of the area's lava flows.

The weathered Modoc **petroglyphs** at the base of a high cliff at the far northeastern end of the monument, called Petroglyph Point, are thousands of years old, but unfortunately the cliffside is now sheltered behind a cyclone fence because of vandalism. There's also a short trail at the top of the hill that offers amazing views over the plains and Lower Klamath Lake. At the visitors center, be sure to take the leaflet explaining the origin of the petroglyphs and their probable meaning. Look for the hundreds of nests in holes high up in the cliff face, which provide shelter for birds that sojourn at the wildlife refuges nearby.

Also at the north end of the monument, be sure to go to the labyrinthine landscape of **Captain Jack's Stronghold**, the Modoc Indians' very effective ancient wartime defense area. A brochure will guide you through the breathtaking Stronghold Trail.

Forty-three first-come first-served sites are available at **Indian Well Campground** (www.nps.gov/labe/planyourvisit/campgrounds. htm; tent & RV sites $10; ☎) 0.5 miles from the Lava Beds National Monument Visitors Center. Each has a picnic table and a fire ring and there are communal flush toilets and sinks. It's legal to collect dead wood for fires in the nearby Modoc National Forest.

Klamath Basin National Wildlife Refuges

Of the six stunning national wildlife refuges in this group, Tule Lake and Clear Lake refuges are wholly within California, Lower Klamath refuge straddles the California–Oregon border, and the Upper Klamath, Klamath Marsh and Bear Valley refuges are across the border in Oregon. Bear Valley and Clear Lake (not to be confused with the Clear Lake just east of Ukiah) are closed to the public to protect their delicate habitats, but the rest are open during daylight hours.

These refuges provide habitats for a stunning array of birds migrating along the Pacific Flyway. Some stop over only briefly; others stay longer to mate, make nests and raise their young. The refuges are always packed with birds, but during the spring and fall migrations, populations can rise into the hundreds of thousands.

The **Klamath Basin National Wildlife Refuge Complex Visitor Center** (☎530-667-2231; www.klamathbasinrefuges.fws.gov; 4009 Hill Rd, Tulelake; ◷8am-4:30pm Mon-Fri, 9am-4pm Sat & Sun) sits on the west side of the Tule Lake refuge, about 5 miles west of Hwy 139, near the town of Tule Lake. Follow the signs from Hwy 139 or from Lava Beds National Monument. The center has an interesting video program, as well as maps, information on recent bird sightings and updates on road conditions. It rents photo blinds. Be sure to pick up the excellent, free *Klamath Basin Birding* Trail brochure for detailed lookouts, maps, color photos and a species checklist.

The spring migration peaks during March, and in some years more than a million birds fill the skies. In April and May the songbirds, waterfowl and shorebirds arrive, some to stay and nest, others to build up their energy before they continue north. In summer ducks, Canada geese and many other water birds are raised here. The fall migration peaks in early November. In and around February, the area hosts the largest wintering concentration of bald eagles in the lower 48 states, with 1000 in residence. The eagles prey on migrating geese, and yes, seeing an eagle catch and eat a goose is very dramatic. The Tule Lake and Lower Klamath refuges are by far the best places to see eagles and other raptors.

The Lower Klamath and Tule Lake refuges attract the largest numbers of birds year-round, and **auto trails** (driving routes) have been set up; a free pamphlet from the visitor center shows the routes. Self-guided canoe trails have been established in three of the refuges. Those in the Tule Lake and Klamath Marsh refuges are usually open from July 1 to September 30; no canoe rentals are available. Canoe trails in the Upper Klamath refuge are open year-round. Here, canoes can be rented at **Rocky Point Resort** (☑541-356-2287; 28121 Rocky Point Rd, Klamath Falls, OR; canoe & kayak rental per hour/half-day/day $20/45/60; ☻Apr-Oct; ⛱🐾), on the west side of Upper Klamath Lake.

Camp at nearby Lava Beds National Monument. Alternatively, a couple of RV parks and budget motels cluster along Hwy 139 near the tiny town of Tulelake (4035ft), including the friendly **Ellis Motel** (☑530-667-5242; 2238 Hwy 139; d with/without kitchen $95/75; 🐾) and **Fe's B&B** (☑877-478-0184; www.fesbandb.com; 660 Main St; s/d without bath $70/80; 🐾). **Wild Goose Lodge** (☑541-331-2701; www.wildgoosemotel.com; 105 E Court Dr, Merrill, OR; RV sites/r/cabins $30/57/115; ⛱🐾🐾) – a good-value, locally owned motel with country charm – is the best option near Lava Beds National Monument outside of Klamath Falls. Klamath Falls, OR, 29 miles from Tulelake, is the closest real town, and there are lots of lodging options there.

Modoc National Forest

This enormous national forest (www.fs.usda.gov/modoc) covers almost two million spectacular, remote acres of California's northeastern corner. Fourteen miles south of Lava Beds National Monument, on the western edge of the forest, **Medicine Lake** is a stunning crater lake in a caldera (collapsed volcano), surrounded by pine forest, volcanic formations and campgrounds. The enormous volcano that formed the lake is the largest in area in California. When it erupted it ejected pumice followed by flows of obsidian, as can be seen at **Little Glass Mountain**, east of the lake.

Pick up the *Medicine Lake Highlands: Self-Guided Roadside Geology Tour* pamphlet from the McCloud ranger district office to find and learn about the glass flows, pumice deposits, lava tubes and cinder cones throughout the area. Roads are closed by snow from around mid-November to mid-June, but the area is still popular for winter sports, and accessible by cross-country skiing and snowshoeing.

Congratulations are in order for travelers who make it all the way to the **Warner Mountains**. This spur of the Cascade Range in the east of the Modoc National Forest is probably the least visited range in California. With extremely changeable weather, it's also not so hospitable; there have been snowstorms here in every season of the year. The range divides into the North Warners and South Warners at **Cedar Pass** (elevation 6305ft), east of Alturas. Remote **Cedar Pass Snow Park** (☑530-233-3323; www.facebook.com/NCCPSP/; all-day pass $20; ☻10am-4pm Sat, Sun & holidays during ski season) offers downhill and cross-country skiing. The majestic **South Warner Wilderness** contains 77 miles of hiking and riding trails. The best time to use them is from July to mid-October.

Maps, campfire permits and information are all available at the **Modoc National Forest supervisor's headquarters** (☑530-233-5811; 800 W 12th St; ☻8am-5pm Mon-Fri) in Alturas.

If you are heading east into Nevada from the forest, you'll pass through **Alturas**, the pancake-flat, eerily quiet seat of Modoc County. The town was founded by the Dorris family in 1874 as a supply point for travelers, and it serves the same function today, providing basic services, motels and family-style restaurants.

WEST OF I-5

The wilderness west of I-5 is right in the sweet spot: here are some of the most rugged towns and seductive wilderness areas in the entire state of California - just difficult enough to reach to discourage big crowds. The **Trinity Scenic Byway** (Hwy 299) winds spectacularly along the Trinity River and beneath towering cliffs as it makes its way from the plains of Redding to the coastal redwood forests around Arcata. It provides a chance to cut through some of the northern mountains' most pristine wilderness and passes through the vibrant gold rush town of Weaverville.

Heavenly Hwy 3 (a highly recommended – although slower and windier – alternative route to I-5) heads north from Weaverville. This mountain byway transports you through the Trinity Alps – a stunning granite range dotted with azure alpine lakes – past the shores of Lewiston and Trinity Lakes, over the Scott Mountains and finally into emerald, mountain-rimmed Scott Valley. Rough-and-ready Yreka awaits you at the end of the line.

Weaverville

In 1941 a journalist asked James Hilton, the British author of *Lost Horizon:* 'In all your wanderings, what's the closest you've found to a real-life Shangri-La?' Hilton's response? 'A little town in northern California. A little town called Weaverville.'

Cute as a button, Weaverville's streets are lined with flower boxes in the summer and banks of snow in the winter. The seat of Trinity County, it sits amid an endless tract of mountain and forest. At almost 3300 sq miles, the county is roughly the size of Delaware plus Rhode Island, yet has a population of only 13,500 and not one freeway.

This gem of a town is on the National Register of Historic Places and has a laid-back, bohemian feel (thanks in part to the back-to-landers and marijuana-growing subculture). You can spend the day here strolling around the quaint storefronts and visiting art galleries or hit the great outdoors.

◉ Sights & Activities

There are 40 miles of hiking and mountain-biking trails in the Weaverville Basin Trail System, or you can cast a line along the Trinity River, Trinity Lake or Lewiston Lake for steelhead, salmon and trout.

★ **Weaverville Joss House**
State Historic Park   HISTORIC BUILDING
(☑530-623-5284; www.parks.ca.gov; 630 Main St; tour adult/child $4/2; ☺tours hourly 10am-4pm Thu-Sun; ℗) The walls here actually talk – they're papered inside with 150-year-old donation ledgers from the once-thriving Chinese community, the immigrants who built Northern California's infrastructure, a rich culture that has all but disappeared. It's a surprise that the oldest continuously used Chinese temple in California (and an exceptionally beautiful one at that), dating from 1874, is in Weaverville.

The blue-and-gold Taoist shrine contains an ornate altar, more than 3000 years old, which was brought here from China. The adjoining schoolhouse was the first to teach Chinese students in California. It's rare to see a Chinese temple with all of the ancient features so well preserved.

Alpen Cellars   WINERY
(☑530-266-9513; www.alpencellars.com; East Fork Rd, Trinity Center; ☺10am-4pm summer, by appointment Oct-May) Jaunt over to little-known, utterly picturesque Alpen Cellars. Specializing in Riesling, *Gewürztraminer,* Chardonnay and Pinot Noir, the vineyard is open for tours, tastings and picnicking on idyllic riverside grounds.

To get there from Weaverville, take Hwy 3 for about 35 miles to the north end of Trinity Lake (5 miles past Trinity Center), then turn right on East Side Rd; 8 miles further, head left on East Fork Rd and continue for 2 miles.

JJ Jackson Memorial Museum & Trinity
County Historical Park   MUSEUM
(www.trinitymuseum.org; 508 Main St; donation requested; ☺10am-5pm daily May-Oct, noon-4pm daily Apr & Nov-Dec 24, noon-4pm Tue & Sat Dec 26-Mar) Next door to the Joss House you'll find gold-mining and cultural exhibits, plus vintage machinery, memorabilia, an old miner's cabin and a blacksmith shop.

Highland Art Center   GALLERY
(www.highlandartcenter.org; 691 Main St; ☺10am-5pm Mon-Sat, 11am-4pm Sun) Stroll through this large central gallery showcasing local artists.

Coffee Creek Ranch   FISHING, HIKING
(☑530-266-3343; www.coffeecreekranch.com; 4310 Coffee Creek Rd, Coffee Creek; all-inclusive per-person rates per day from $329; 👪) In Trinity Center, these guys run a dude ranch and lead fishing and fully outfitted pack trips into the Trinity Alps Wilderness.

🛏 Sleeping

There are a few basic motels at the edge of town in addition to the inn and hotel. The ranger station (p579) has information on many USFS campgrounds in the area, especially around Trinity Lake. Commercial RV parks, some with tent sites, dot Hwy 299.

Red Hill Motel & Cabins   MOTEL $
(☑530-623-4331; www.redhillresorts.com; 116 Red Hill Rd; d $52, cabins with/without kitchen $68/56;

🖥🖨) This very quiet and rustic motel is tucked under ponderosa pines at the west end of town, just off Main St, next to the library. It's a set of red wooden cabins built in the 1940s and they're equipped with kitchenettes and minifridges. The rooms are simple and good value. It sometimes fills with visiting groups, so book ahead.

Whitmore Inn HISTORIC HOTEL **$$**
(📞530-623-2509; www.whitmoreinn.com; 761 Main St; r $100-165; ✱🖥) Settle into plush, cozy rooms in this downtown Victorian with a wraparound deck and abundant gardens. One room is accessible for travelers with disabilities. Only kids over five years old are welcome.

Weaverville Hotel HISTORIC HOTEL **$$**
(📞800-750-8957, 530-623-2222; www.weaverville hotel.com; 481 Main St; r $110-390; 🅿🖥✱🖥) Play like you're in the Old West at this upscale hotel and historic landmark, refurbished in grand Victorian style. It's luxurious but not stuffy, and the very gracious owners take great care in looking after you. Guests may use the local gym, and a $10 credit at local restaurants is included in the rates. Kids under 12 years are not allowed.

✗ Eating

Downtown Weaverville caters to all, from hungry hikers to foodies. There's also a fantastic **farmers market** (www.weaverville tailgate.org; 691 Main St; ⊙4-7pm Wed May-Oct), which takes over Main St in the warmer months. In winter the tourist season dries up and opening hours can be hit or miss.

Trinideli DELI **$**
(📞530-623-5856; www.trinideli.com; 201 Trinity Lakes Blvd; sandwiches $6-10; ⊙6:30am-4pm Mon-Fri, 10am-3pm Sat; 🍴) Cheerful staff prepare decadent sandwiches stuffed with fresh goodness. The 1.5lb 'Trinideli' with four types of meat and three types of cheese will fill the ravenous, while simple turkey and ham standards explode with fresh veggies and tons of flavor. Breakfast burritos are perfect for a quick prehike fill up.

Mountain Marketplace MARKET **$**
(📞530-623-2656; 222 S Main St; ⊙9am-6pm Mon-Fri, 10am-5pm Sat; 🍴) Stock up on natural foods or hit its juice bar and vegetarian deli.

★ **Cafe at Indian Creek** CALIFORNIAN **$$**
(📞530-623-1951; www.thecafeatindiancreek.com; 59741 Highway 299 W, Douglas City; mains $14-28; ⊙5-9pm Tue-Sun) About 8 miles south of Weaverville, this unlikely spot in a roadside lodge serves up the area's finest meals. Try anything with elk, the gnocchi is superb and there's a wine list to match. It also serves a much-lauded brunch on summer weekends.

La Grange Cafe CALIFORNIAN **$$**
(📞530-623-5325; 520 Main St; mains $15-28; ⊙11am-9pm Tue-Sat) For years this has been Weaverville's more upscale offering, specializing in American favorites from burgers and steaks to ribs and grilled salmon. It's a homey, friendly place that's gone through management changes in the past few years and is still finding its new feet. You may not eat your most memorable meal here but expect it to be plenty tasty.

🍷 Drinking & Entertainment

Mamma Llama CAFE
(www.mammallama.com; 490 Main St; breakfasts & sandwiches $3.50-8; ⊙6am-6pm Mon-Fri, 7am-6pm Sat, 7am-3pm Sun; 🖥) A local institution, this coffeehouse is a roomy and relaxed chill spot. The espresso is well made, there's a selection of comic books and CDs, and there are couches for lounging. The small menu does breakfasts, wraps and sandwiches, and there's microbrew beer available by the bottle. Live folk music (often including a hand drum) takes over occasionally.

Red House CAFE
(📞530-623-1635; 218 S Miner St; ⊙6:30am-5:30pm Mon-Fri, 7:30am-1pm Sat) 🍴 This airy, light and bamboo-bedecked spot serves a wide selection of teas, light snacks (soups from $3) and organic, fair-trade, shade-grown coffee. The daily food specials include a delicious chicken-and-rice soup on Mondays. If you're in a hurry (rare in Weaverville), there's a drive-through window.

Trinity Theatre CINEMA
(www.trinitytheatre.us; 310 Main St; adult/child $8.50/7) This newly renovated and inviting theater plays first-run movies.

ℹ Information

Trinity County Chamber of Commerce (📞530-623-6101; www.trinitycounty.com; 215 Main St; ⊙10am-4pm) Knowledgeable, friendly staff with lots of useful information.

Weaverville Ranger Station (📞530-623-2121; www.fs.usda.gov/stnf; 360 Main St; ⊙8am-4:30pm Mon-Fri) A homey little office with maps, information and permits for all lakes, national forests and wilderness areas in and near Trinity County.

❶ Getting There & Away

A local **Trinity Transit** (📞 530-623-5438; www.trinitytransit.org; fares from $1) bus makes a Weaverville–Lewiston loop via Hwy 299 and Hwy 3 from Monday to Friday. Another one runs between Weaverville and Hayfork, a small town about 30 miles to the southwest on Hwy 3.

Lewiston Lake

Adorable Lewiston is little more than a collection of rickety historic buildings beside a crossroad, 26 miles west of Redding. It's right beside the Trinity River, and the locals here are in tune with the environment – they know fishing spots on the rivers and lakes, where to hike and how to get around.

The lake is about 1.5 miles north of town and is a serene alternative to the other area lakes because of its 10mph boat speed limit. Migrating bird species sojourn here – early in the evening you may see ospreys and bald eagles diving for fish. The **Trinity River Fish Hatchery** (📞 530-778-3931; www.wildlife.ca.gov/Fishing/Hatcheries/Trinity-River; 1000 Hatchery Rd; ⏱ 7am-3pm) **FREE** traps juvenile salmon and steelhead and holds them until they are ready to be released into the river. The only marina on the lake, **Pine Cove Marina** (www.pine-cove-marina.com; 9435 Trinity Dam Blvd), has free information about the lake and its wildlife, boat and canoe rentals, potluck dinners and guided off-road tours.

🛏 Sleeping & Eating

Several commercial campgrounds dot the rim of the lake. For information on USFS campgrounds, contact the ranger station in Weaverville. Two of these campgrounds are on the lake: the wooded **Mary Smith** (📞 877-444-6777; www.fs.usda.gov/recarea/stnf/recarea/?recid=6489; tent sites $11; ⏱ May-Sep), which is more private; and the sunny **Ackerman** (📞 877-444-6777; www.fs.usda.gov; tent sites $13), which has more grassy space for families. If there's no host, both have self-registration options. There are also all kinds of RV parks, cabins for rent and motels in Lewiston.

★ **Lewiston Hotel** HISTORIC HOTEL $
(📞 530-778-3823; www.lewistonhotel.biz; 125 Deadwood Rd; r without bath $65; 🅿 🐾 🛜) This 1862 rambling, ramshackle hotel has small,

rustic rooms with quilts, historic photos and river views – all have tons of character but none have attached bathrooms. Ask (or don't ask) for the room haunted by George. Explore the building to find giant stuffed moose heads, old girly calendars, rusty saws and so much more.

On-site are a friendly locals' bar, a dancehall and a restaurant (with sporadic opening hours, especially in winter) that specializes in prime rib. Call to book a room.

Old Lewiston Bridge RV Resort CAMPGROUND $
(📞 530-778-3894; www.lewistonbridgerv.com; 8460 Rush Creek Rd, at Turnpike Rd; tent/RV sites $15/30, trailers $65; 🐾) A pleasant place to park the RV, with campsites beside the river bridge. It also rents travel trailers that sleep four people (bed linens not included).

Lakeview Terrace Resort CABIN, CAMPGROUND $
(📞 530-778-3803; www.lakeviewterraceresort.com; 9001 Trinity Dam Rd; RV sites $32, cabins $85-165; 🌸🛜🐾🐾) Five miles north of Lewiston, this is a woodsy Club Med, and rents boats.

Old Lewiston Inn B&B B&B $$
(📞 530-778-3385; www.theoldlewistoninn.com; 71 Deadwood Rd; r $125; 🌸🛜🐾) The prettiest place in town and right beside the river, this B&B is in an 1875 house and serves country-style breakfasts. Enjoy the hot tub, or ask about all-inclusive fly-fishing packages. There's one two-bedroom suite, which is great for families.

🔒 Shopping

Country Peddler ANTIQUES
(4 Deadwood Rd; ⏱ hours vary) Impossible to miss, this funky old barn welcomes you with rusty vintage gas pumps (no gas) and beckons you inside for a simply wondrous collections of junk and treasures.

Trinity Lake

Placid Trinity Lake, California's third-largest reservoir, sits beneath dramatic snowcapped alps north of Lewiston Lake. In the off season it is serenely quiet, but it attracts multitudes in the summer, who come for swimming, fishing and other water sports. Most of the campgrounds, RV parks, motels, boat rentals and restaurants line the west side of the lake.

Spreading over 22 acres on the shores of Trinity Lake, **Pinewood Cove Resort**

(📞530-286-2201; www.pinewoodcove.com; 45110 Hwy 3; tent/RV sites $29/46, cabins $98-158; ⊙May 1-Oct 1; ✱) offers quality camping, cabins and marina facilities.

Klamath & Siskiyou Mountains

A dense conglomeration of rugged coastal mountains gives this region the nickname 'the Klamath Knot.' Coastal, temperate rainforest gives way to moist inland forest, creating an immense diversity of habitats for many species, some found nowhere else in the world. Around 3500 native plants live here. Local fauna includes the northern spotted owl, the bald eagle, the tailed frog, several species of Pacific salmon and carnivores like the wolverine and the mountain lion. One theory for the extraordinary biodiversity of this area is that it escaped extensive glaciation during recent ice ages. This may have given species refuge and longer stretches of relatively favorable conditions during which to adapt.

The region also includes the largest concentration of wild and scenic rivers in the US: the Salmon, Smith, Trinity, Eel and Klamath, to name a few. The fall color change is magnificent.

Five main wilderness areas dot the Klamath Knot. The **Marble Mountain Wilderness** in the north is marked by high rugged mountains, valleys and lakes, all sprinkled with colorful geological formations of marble and granite, and a huge array of flora. The **Russian Wilderness** is 8000 acres of high peaks and isolated, beautiful mountain lakes. The **Trinity Alps Wilderness**, west of Hwy 3, is one of the area's most lovely regions for hiking and backcountry camping, and has more than 600 miles of trails that cross passes over its granite peaks and head along its deep alpine lakes. The **Yolla Bolly-Middle Eel Wilderness** in the south is less visited, despite its proximity to the Bay Area, and so affords spectacular, secluded backcountry experiences. The **Siskiyou Wilderness**, closest to the coast, rises to heights of 7300ft, from where you can see the ocean. An extensive trail system crisscrosses the wilderness, but it is difficult to make loops.

The Trinity Scenic Byway (Hwy 299) follows the rushing **Trinity River** to the Pacific coast and is dotted with lodges, RV parks and blink-and-you'll-miss-'em burgs.

There's river rafting at Willow Creek, 55 miles west of Weaverville. **Bigfoot Rafting Company** (📞530-629-2263; www.bigfootrafting.com; 31221 State Hwy 299, Junction City; half-/full-day trips per person $69/89) leads guided trips and also rents rafts and kayaks (from $69 per day).

Scott Valley

North of Trinity Lake, Hwy 3 climbs along the gorgeous eastern flank of the Trinity Alps Wilderness to Scott Mountain Summit (5401ft) and then drops gracefully down into verdant Scott Valley, a bucolic agricultural area nestled between towering mountains. There are good opportunities for hiking, cycling and mountain biking, or taking horse trips to mountain lakes. For a bit of history, pick up the *Trinity Heritage Scenic Byway* brochure from the Weaverville ranger station (p579) before taking this world-class drive.

Etna (population 711), toward the north end of the valley, is known by its residents as 'California's Last Great Place,' and they might be right. Folks are uncommonly friendly, birdsong is more prevalent than road noise and if you're in town in summer and see lots of dirty people with backpacks, these are hard-core hikers taking a break from the nearby **Pacific Crest Trail** – Etna is a favorite pit stop.

Beyond Etna, **Fort Jones** (population 839) is just 18 miles from Yreka. The **visitors center** (📞530-468-5442; 11943 Main St; ⊙10am-5pm Tue-Sat, noon-4pm Sun) sits at the back of the Guild Shop mercantile. Down the street, a small **museum** (📞530-468-2444; www.fortjonesmuseum.com; 11913 Main St; donation requested; ⊙10am-4pm Mon-Fri, 11am-3pm Sat Memorial Day-Labor Day) houses Native American artifacts.

There are a few places to stay in the valley, from family-run motels to bucolic B&Bs. The clean, family-run **Motel Etna** (📞530-467-5338; www.theetnahotel.com; 317 Collier Way; s/d/tw $64/74/84; ✱🤖) on the outskirts of town, is a favorite with Pacific Crest Trail hikers and a good choice for anyone on a budget. The storybook-perfect 1877 mansion **Alderbrook Manor B&B** (📞530-467-3917; www.alderbrookmanor.com; 836 Sawyers Bar Rd; r $135, without bathroom $120, dm $35; 🤖✱) has a handful of pretty and bright antique-decorated rooms and a hikers' hut with dorm beds.

People talk about the **Etna Brewing Company** (www.etnabrew.com; 131 Callahan St; brewery tours free; ⊘noon-8pm Wed-Sat) from Redding to Yreka. Don't miss a stop for a meal and one of its beers on tap if you're in Etna.

Yreka

Inland California's northernmost town, Yreka (wy-*ree*-kah) was once a booming gold rush settlement and has the gorgeous turn-of-the-century architecture to prove it. Most travelers only pass through en route to Oregon, but the new-age-tinged yet authentically Wild West–feeling historic downtown makes a good spot to stretch, eat and refuel before heading out into the hinterlands of the Scott Valley or the northeastern California wilderness.

◉ Sights & Activities

Siskiyou County Museum   MUSEUM
(☑530-572-1099; www.siskiyoucountyhistorical society.org; 910 S Main St; adult/child $3/1; ⊘9am-3pm Tue-Sat) Several blocks south of Yreka's downtown grid, this exceptionally well-curated museum brings together pioneer and Native American history. The native basketry collection is particularly impressive. An outdoor section contains historic buildings brought from around the county.

**Siskiyou County
Courthouse**   HISTORIC BUILDING
(☑530-842-0199; www.siskiyou.courts.ca.gov; 311 4th St; ⊘8am-noon & 1-4pm Mon-Fri) This hulking downtown building was built in 1857 and has a collection of gold nuggets, flakes and dust in the foyer.

Yreka Creek Greenway   WALKING, CYCLING
(www.yrekagreenway.org) Behind the museum, the Yreka Creek Greenway has walking and cycling paths winding through the trees.

🛏 Sleeping & Eating

Motels, motels and more motels: budget travelers can do lots of comparison shopping along Yreka's Main St for mid-century motels galore. Klamath National Forest runs several campgrounds; the supervisor's office (p582) has information. RV parks cluster on the edge of town.

Klamath Motor Lodge   MOTEL $
(☑530-842-2751; www.klamathmotorlodge.net; 1111 S Main St; s/d from $51/60; 🛜🖥) Folks at

this motel are especially friendly, the rooms are clean and – bonus for those headed in from the wilderness – it has an on-site laundry. Of all the motels in Yreka, this is tops. Book by phone for better rates than you'll find online.

Nature's Kitchen   HEALTH FOOD, BAKERY $
(☑530-842-1136; 412 S Main St; dishes $8-14; ⊘8am-5pm Mon-Sat; 🖊) Friendly and quirky natural-foods store and bakery, serving healthy and tasty vegetarian and nonvegetarian dishes, fresh juices and good espresso. The adjoining store has all kinds of fairies, crazy socks, herbal supplements and new-agey trinkets.

Klander's Deli   DELI $
(☑530-842-3806; 211 S Oregon St; sandwiches $6-9; ⊘9am-3pm Mon-Fri) Local to the core, this deli's long list of yummy sandwiches is named after regulars. Bob is a favorite, named for the first owner and stacked with ham, turkey, roast beef and Swiss cheese.

🍸 Drinking & Nightlife

Etna Brewery & Taphouse   BREWERY
(☑530-841-0370; www.etnabrew.com; 231 W Miner St; mains $9-12; ⊘11am-9pm Tue-Sat) Serving delicious Etna brews on tap, come here for the beer more than the ambience or food (mostly burgers).

ⓘ Information

Klamath National Forest Supervisor's Office
(☑530-842-6131; www.fs.usda.gov/klamath; 1711 S Main St; ⊘8am-4:30pm Mon-Fri) Has the lowdown on recreation and camping.
Yreka Chamber of Commerce (☑530-842-1649; www.yrekachamber.com; 117 W Miner St; ⊘9am-5pm, with seasonal variations; 🛜) Has information about Yreka and surrounding areas.

ⓘ Getting There & Away

STAGE buses (☑530-842-8295; www.co.siskiyou.ca.us; fares $1.75-6) run throughout the region from a few different stops in Yreka. There are several daily services on weekdays along the I-5 corridor to Weed, Mt Shasta, McCloud and Dunsmuir. Other buses depart daily for Fort Jones (25 minutes), Greenview (35 minutes) and Etna (45 minutes) in the Scott Valley. On Monday and Friday only, buses go out to Klamath River (40 minutes) and Happy Camp (two hours).

Sacramento & Central Valley

Why Go?

The Central Valley is visible from space – a vast expanse of green between the Sierra Nevada and Pacific Ocean. The area is divided in two parts: the Sacramento Valley in the north and the San Joaquin Valley in the south. For millennia, the rivers cutting through these valleys flooded seasonally, creating extremely fertile soil. Today, those waterways are tamed by mighty public works projects that support massive agricultural endeavors. Half the produce in the US is grown in these valleys – including almost every almond, olive and bulb of garlic.

Like the birds that commute overhead, most travelers are just passing through – zipping along the highway to more popular parts of the state. But those who linger are rewarded with stately Victorian-era mansions, uniquely scenic byways and quirky small towns.

Best Places to Eat

➡ Empress Tavern (p591)

➡ Noriega's (p611)

➡ Towne House Restaurant (p602)

➡ Shubert's Ice Cream & Candy (p598)

Best Places to Sleep

➡ Padre Hotel (p610)

➡ Citizen Hotel (p589)

➡ Greens Hotel (p589)

When to Go

Sacramento

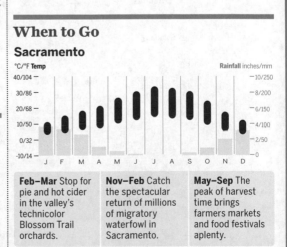

°C/°F **Temp**   Rainfall inches/mm

40/104 —   —10/250
30/86 —   —8/200
20/68 —   —6/150
10/50 —   —4/100
0/32 —   —2/50
-10/14 —   —0

J F M A M J J A S O N D

Feb–Mar Stop for pie and hot cider in the valley's technicolor Blossom Trail orchards.

Nov–Feb Catch the spectacular return of millions of migratory waterfowl in Sacramento.

May–Sep The peak of harvest time brings farmers markets and food festivals aplenty.

Sacramento & Central Valley Highlights

1 Strolling between **breweries in Sacramento** (p591), the self-proclaimed mecca of beer.

2 Driving bumper cars, eating fried Twinkies and checking out blue-ribbon livestock at the **California State Fair** (p588).

3 Uncorking the region's emerging fine-wine scene in **Lodi** (p603).

4 Tasting the valley's bounty in Sacramento's abundant **farmers markets** (p589).

5 Sipping cold beer and listening to country music in **Buck Owens' Crystal Palace** (p611), Bakersfield.

6 Rushing down world-class rapids on the mighty **Kern River** (p612).

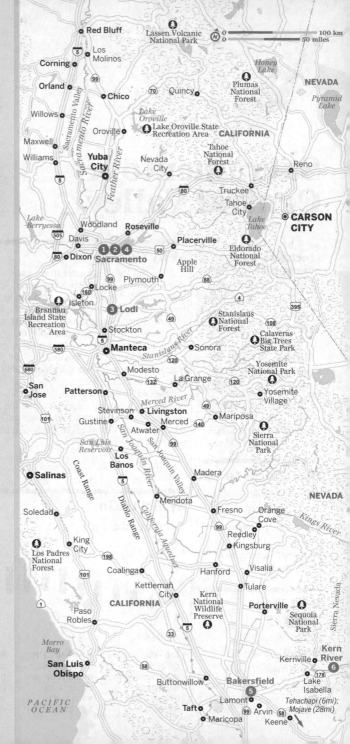

SACRAMENTO VALLEY

The labyrinth of waterways making up the Sacramento–San Joaquin River Delta feeds San Francisco Bay and divides the Central Valley in half, with the Sacramento Valley in the north and the San Joaquin Valley in the south.

The Sacramento River, California's largest, rushes out of the northern mountains from Shasta Lake before hitting the Sacramento Valley basin above Red Bluff. It snakes south across grassy plains and orchards before skirting the state capital, fanning across the Delta and draining into San Francisco Bay. The valley is most beautiful in the bloom of spring. The shaded gardens and stately homes of Sacramento and its progressive neighbor, Davis, offer friendly respites from the blistering summer sun. If you're driving through the region on the way to one of California's marquee attractions, make time for a pit stop in Sacramento, which has a surprisingly vibrant food and beer scene.

Sacramento

Sacramento is a city of contrasts. It's a former cow town where state legislators' SUVs go bumper-to-bumper with farmers' muddy, half-ton pickups at rush hour. It has sprawling suburbs, but also new lofts and upscale boutiques squeezed between aging mid-century storefronts.

The people of 'Sac' are a resourceful lot that have fostered small but thriving food, art and nightlife scenes. They rightfully crow about Second Saturday, the monthly Midtown gallery hop that is the symbol of the city's cultural awakening. Their ubiquitous farmers markets, farm-to-fork fare and craft beers are another point of pride.

History

The history of the state is contained in this city. Paleo-era peoples fished the rivers and thrived before colonists arrived. By the 1800s, the native communities were largely wiped out by colonizers. Control changed from Spanish to Mexican to American hands, when in 1847, a Swiss named John Sutter came seeking fortune. Recognizing the strategic importance of the major rivers, Sutter built an outpost and raised a militia. Soon the outpost became a safe haven for traders, and Sutter expanded his business operations in all directions.

It was at his lumber mill near Coloma that something glittered in the river in 1848. Eureka! Gold rushers stampeded to the trading post, which was eventually christened 'Sacramento.' Though plagued by fires and relentless flooding, the riverfront settlement prospered and became the state capital in 1850.

After the discovery of gold, a quarter of a million Chinese people arrived in California, often traveling through Sacramento. Although many were indentured servants who traded passage to the US in return for years of labor, they developed a thriving Chinatown and left an indelible mark on the region. These communities literally built the infrastructure of the city – as well as the levees and roads in the surrounding valley.

Chinese also built much of the Transcontinental Railroad, though you won't see any among the faces of the 'Big Four' – Leland Stanford, Mark Hopkins, Collis P Huntington and Charles Crocker. These wealthy men founded Central Pacific Railroad, which began construction here in 1863, and connected to the Union Pacific in Promontory, UT, in 1869.

⊙ Sights

Sacramento is roughly halfway between San Francisco and Lake Tahoe. The city is boxed in by four main highways: Hwy 99, which is the best route through the Central Valley; I-5, which runs along its west side; I-80 skirts downtown on the city's northern edge, heading west to the Bay Area and east to Reno; and Hwy 50 runs along downtown's southern edge (where it's also called Business Route 80) before heading east to Tahoe.

In the middle is the Grid, where numbered streets run from north–south and lettered streets run east–west (Capitol Ave replaces M). One-way J St is a main drag east from Downtown to Midtown.

⊙ The Grid

It's easy finding sights along the Grid, but everything is spread out.

★ **California Museum**   MUSEUM
(Map p586; ☏916-653-0650; www.california museum.org; 1020 O St; adult/child $9/6.50; ☺10am-5pm Tue-Sat, from noon Sun; ☞) This modern museum is home to the California Hall of Fame and so the only place to simultaneously encounter César Chávez, Mark Zuckerberg and Amelia Earhart. The *Cali-*

Downtown Sacramento

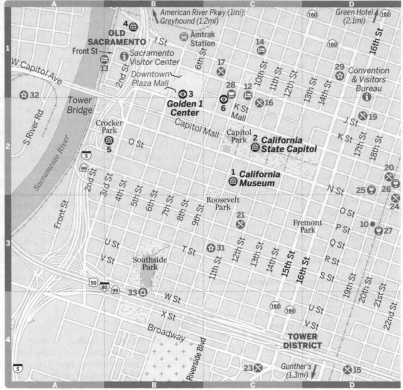

fornia Indians exhibit is a highlight, with artifacts and oral histories of more than 10 tribes.

★**California State Capitol** HISTORIC BUILDING
(Map p586; ☎916-324-0333; http://capitolmuseum.ca.gov; 1315 10th St; ⊗8am-5pm Mon-Fri, from 9am Sat & Sun; ♿) **FREE** The gleaming dome of the California State Capitol is Sacramento's most recognizable structure. A painting of Arnold Schwarzenegger in a suit hangs in the West Wing along with the other governors' portraits. Some will find Capitol Park, the 40 acres of gardens and memorials surrounding the building more interesting than what's inside. Tours run hourly until 4pm.

Sutter's Fort
State Historic Park HISTORIC SITE
(Map p586; www.suttersfort.org; 2701 L St; adult/child $5/3; ⊗10am-5pm) Originally built by John Sutter, this park was once the only trace of white settlement for hundreds of

miles. Reserve a couple hours to stroll within its walls, where furniture, medical equipment and a blacksmith shop are straight out of the 1850s.

State Indian Museum MUSEUM
(Map p586; www.parks.ca.gov; 2618 K St; adult/child $5/3; ⊗10am-5pm) It's with some irony that the Indian Museum sits in the shadow of Sutter's Fort. The excellent exhibits and tribal handicrafts on display – including the intricately woven and feathered baskets of the Pomo – are traces of cultures nearly stamped out by the fervor Sutter ignited.

⊙ Old Sacramento

This historic river port by Downtown remains the city's stalwart tourist draw. The aroma of saltwater taffy and restored buildings give Old Sac the vibe of a second-rate Frontierland, but it's good for a stroll on summer evenings, when boomers on Har-

Downtown Sacramento

leys rumble through the brick streets, and tourists and natty legislative aides stroll the promenade. California's largest concentration of buildings on the National Register of Historic Places is here. Most now peddle Gold Rush trinkets and fudge. There are a few quality attractions, but the restaurant scene is a bust – head to Midtown. Right at the edge of Midtown is the gleaming new Golden 1 Center (p587), home to the Sacramento Kings.

★ **Golden 1 Center** STADIUM
(Map p586; ☎ 916-701-5400; www.golden1center. com; 500 David J Stern Walk; ♿) ⚲ Welcome to the arena of the future. This gleaming home to the Sacramento Kings is one of the most advanced sports facilities in the country. Made with the highest sustainability standard, it's built from local materials, powered by solar and cooled by five-story airplane hangar doors that swing open to capture the pleasant Delta breeze.

The building is also pushing the envelope of interactivity, with a free app that allows fans to monitor bathroom lines, order concessions (which follow a farm-to-fork philosophy, of course) and watch replays of the action on the court.

DON'T MISS

CALIFORNIA STATE FAIR

For two weeks in late July, the **California State Fair** (☎916-263-3247; www.castatefair.org/home; 1600 Exposition Blvd; adult/child $12/8; ☺Jul; 🖝) fills the Cal Expo, east of I-80 on the north side of the American River, with a small city of cows and carnival rides. It's likely the only place on earth where you can plant a redwood tree, watch a pig give birth, ride a roller coaster, catch some barrel racing and taste exquisite Napa vintages within one (exhausting) afternoon. Make time to see some of the auctions ($500 for a dozen eggs!) and the interactive agricultural exhibits run by the University of California Davis. Hotels near Cal Expo run regular shuttles to the event.

Crocker Art Museum MUSEUM
(Map p586; ☎916-808-7000; https://crockerart museum.org; 216 O St; adult/child $10/5; ☺10am-5pm Tue, Wed & Fri-Sun, to 9pm Thu) Housed in the ornate Victorian mansion (and sprawling additions) of a railroad baron, this museum has striking architecture and an excellent collection. Works by California painters and European masters hang beside an enthusiastically curated collection of contemporary art.

California State Railroad Museum MUSEUM
(Map p586; ☎916-323-9280; www.csrmf.org; 125 I St; adult/child museum $10/5, train ride $12/6; ☺10am-5pm; P🖝) Train buffs will delight in this incredible collection of vintage locomotives (even if history buffs will question the candy-coated presentation about the plight of workers who built the rails). You can also hop aboard a restored passenger train from the Sacramento Southern Railroad for a 45-minute jaunt along the river.

Weather permitting, train rides run hourly from 11am to 4pm on weekends from April to September and on select dates in October, November and December.

K Street Mall PLAZA
(Map p586; www.kstreetmall.com) Known by locals as 'The Kay,' this formerly blighted neighborhood is undergoing a major redevelopment effort that has transformed it into a weekend hot spot. The pedestrian mall draws a party on weekends.

Sacramento History Museum MUSEUM
(Map p586; www.historicoldsac.org/museum; 101 I St; adult/child $6/4, Underground Tour Mar-Dec $15/10; ☺10am-5pm; 🖝) Exhibits, stories and artifacts of some of Sacramento's most fascinating citizens, though much of the information is focused on the Gold Rush. Get tickets here for the **Underground Tour**, a 45-minute look at what's under Old Sac's streets.

◉ Tower District

South of Midtown, at the corner of Broadway and 16th St, the Tower District is dominated by Tower Theatre (p592), a beautiful 1938 art-deco movie palace that's easy to spot on the way into town. From the theater, head east on Broadway to a stretch of the city's most eclectic and affordable eateries. The **Tower Records** chain started here in 1960 and closed in 2006, a digital music casualty, but the original neon sign survives.

🏃 Activities

American River Parkway OUTDOORS
(www.arpf.org; north bank of American River) The American River Parkway is a natural treasure. This massive urban park stretches along the north bank of the American River for over 20 miles, skirting one of the most extensive riparian habitats in the continental US.

The park's network of trails and picnic areas is easily accessed from Old Sacramento by taking Front St north until it becomes Jiboom St and crosses the river, or by taking the Jiboom St exit off I-5/Hwy 99.

The parkway includes a nice walking/running/bicycling path called the Jedediah Smith National Recreation Trail that's accessible from Old Sacramento at the end of J St. You can rent bicycles at the waterfront (per day $25).

City Bicycle Works CYCLING
(Map p586; www.citybicycleworks.com; 2419 K St; per hour/day from $5/20; ☺10am-7pm Mon-Fri, to 6pm Sat, 11am-5pm Sun) The perfect spot to get a bike for cruising the amazing American River Parkway (p588) for a couple of hours. Road bikes and cruisers are in good condition and the staff is enthusiastic and helpful.

👉 Tours

Sacramento Beer Tour BREWERY
(☎916-852-5466; www.sacramentobrewtour.com; 1751 Enterprise Blvd, West Sacramento) These

tours offer a fun, safe way to taste breweries around the city. Perfectly suited for larger groups, they offer a pick-up and drop-off service, and have great relationships with local beer makers. A three-brewery tour is led by a certified beer cicerone. It takes five hours and includes private tours, taster flights and local brews.

Sac Brew Bike BREWERY
(Map p586; ☑916-952-7973; www.sacbrewbike. com; tours depart from 1519 19th St; 15-person tour from $350, individual pricing available) You can pedal your way between the city's best breweries on the multi-peddler 'Brew Bike.' You can join a mixed tour with random beer-and-bike loving strangers for about $20 per person, but tours are ideal for groups. The whole bike accommodates 15 people and two-hour tours start at $300. Rates increase on the weekends.

⚝ Festivals & Events

★ **Second Saturday** CULTURAL
(www.2ndsaturdaysacramento.com) Look no further for evidence of Sacramento's cultural revival. Galleries and shops in Midtown draw crowds to the streets on the second Saturday of each month for open-air music, openings and cultural events.

Sacramento Central Farmers Market FOOD & DRINK
(www.california-grown.com; cnr 8th & W St, under Hwy 80 overpass; ⊘8am-noon Sun; 🖷) You're never far from a mind-blowing farmers market in Sacramento. They're hosted all year round and every day of the week in the summer and fall. Most will have food trucks and street performers.

Gold Rush Days CULTURAL
(www.sacramentogoldrushdays.com; ⊘Sep; 🖷) Old Sacramento comes alive in early September with horse races, historic costumes, music and kids' events. You can even pan for gold.

🛏 Sleeping

The capital is a magnet for business travelers, so Sacramento doesn't lack hotels. Many have good deals during legislative recesses. Unless you're in town for something at Cal Expo, stay Downtown or Midtown, where there's plenty to do within walking distance. If you're into kitschy motor lodges from the 1950s, cross the river into West Sac for the last-standing members of Motel Row on Rte 40.

HI Sacramento Hostel HOSTEL $
(Map p586; ☑916-443-1691; http://norcalhostels. org/sac; 925 H St; dm $30-33, r from $86, without bath from $58; ⊘reception 2-10:30pm; 🅿🕸@🛜) In a grand Victorian mansion, this hostel offers impressive trimmings at rock-bottom prices. It's within walking distance of the capitol, Old Sac and the train station, and has a piano in the parlor and large dining room. It attracts an international crowd often open to sharing a ride to San Francisco or Lake Tahoe.

★ **Citizen Hotel** BOUTIQUE HOTEL $$
(Map p586; ☑916-442-2700, 877-829-2429; www.thecitizenhotel.com; 926 J St; r from $180; 🅿🕸🐾@🛜🐾) After an elegant, ultra-hip upgrade, this long-vacant 1927 beaux-arts tower became Downtown's coolest place to stay. The details are spot-on: luxe linens, wide-striped wallpaper and a roof-top patio with a great view of the city. There's an upscale farm-to-fork **restaurant** (Map p586; ☑916-492-4450; www.grangesacramento.com; mains $19-39; ⊘6:30-10:30am, 11:30am-2pm & 5:30-10pm Mon-Thu, to 11pm Fri, 8am-2pm & 5:30-11pm Sat, to 10pm Sun; 🛜) on the ground floor.

Greens Hotel BOUTIQUE HOTEL $$
(www.thegreenshotel.com; 1700 Del Paso Blvd.; r from $127; 🅿🕸🐾@🛜🐾) This stylishly updated mid-century motel is one of Sacramento's hippest places to stay. Even though the neighborhood is a bit rough around the edges, the Greens' secure parking, pool and spacious grounds make it an ideal place for families to stop en route to or from Tahoe. The chic rooms are also classy enough for a romantic getaway.

Delta King B&B $$
(Map p586; ☑800-825-5464, 916-444-5464; www.deltaking.com; 1000 Front St; d from $145; 🅿🐾🕸🛜) It's a kitschy treat to sleep aboard the *Delta King*, a 1927 paddle wheeler docked on the river in Old Sacramento. It lights up like a Christmas tree at night.

Amber House B&B $$
(Map p586; ☑800-755-6526, 916-444-8085; www.amberhouse.com; 1315 22nd St; r $199-279; 🕸@🛜) This Dutch Colonial home in Midtown has been transformed into a B&B, where rooms have Jacuzzis, fireplaces and lots of frill. The Mozart and Vivaldi rooms have private balconies perfect for enjoying breakfast.

DON'T MISS

THE GREAT MIGRATION

The Sacramento Valley serves as a rest stop for countless migrating species that arrive in such great numbers they are a spectacle even without binoculars.

October to February Four million waterbirds winter in the warm tules (marshes) on their way along the Great Pacific Flyway. Tours available at Sacramento National Wildlife Refuge (p596).

October to January Endangered chinook and steelhead fight their way upstream to spawn. Spot them along the American River Parkway (p588) and the **Nimbus Fish Hatchery** (⏱916-358-2884; www.dfg.ca.gov; 2001 Nimbus Rd, Gold River; ⏰9am-3pm) FREE.

March to June Cabbage white, painted lady and Western tiger swallowtail butterflies come to party. Their offspring will gorge and then grow wings to fly north. Sacramento National Wildlife Refuge (p596) has details.

June to August Hundreds of thousands of Mexican free-tailed bats shelter under the Yolo Causeway. Tours (www.yolobasin.org) catch them alighting at twilight.

✗ Eating

Skip the overpriced fare in Old Sacramento or by the capitol and head Midtown or to the Tower District. A cruise up J St or Broadway passes a number of hip, affordable restaurants where tables spill onto the sidewalks in the summer. Many source farm-fresh ingredients.

Shoki II Ramen House   JAPANESE $
(Map p586; ⏱916-441-0011; www.shokiramenhouse. com; 1201 R St; mains $8-16; ⏰11am-10pm Mon-Fri, from noon Sat, 11am-8pm Sun) Like its tiny original location on 24th St, this cozy ramen house under the direction of Yasushi Ueyama makes amazing housemade noodles that live up to the motto of 'a bowl of dreams.' The fresh spinach, grass-fed beef and shiitake are organic and local.

Gunther's   ICE CREAM $
(⏱916-457-6646; www.gunthersicecream.com; 2801 Franklin Blvd; sundaes $4; ⏰10am-10pm; 🚗) Look for 'Jugglin Joe' – a cheerful, ice-cream-slinging neon giant – towering above this 1940s soda fountain. Gunther's makes its own ice cream and frozen novelties.

La Bonne Soupe Cafe   DELI $
(Map p586; ⏱916-492-9506; 920 8th St; items $5-8; ⏰11am-3pm Mon-Sat) Divine soup and sandwiches assembled with such care that the line of Downtown lunchers snakes out the door. If you're in a hurry, skip it. This humble lunch counter is focused on quality that predates drive-through haste.

Andy Nguyen's   VIETNAMESE, VEGETARIAN $
(Map p586; www.andynguyenvegetarian.com; 2007 Broadway; mains $9-15; ⏰11:30am-9pm Sun-Thu, to 9:30pm Fri & Sat; 🚗) 🍃 This tranquil vegetarian Buddhist diner serves steaming clay pots and curries. The Peaceful Existence Clay Pot – which includes a 'chicken' drumstick with a little wooden bone – lives up to its divine name.

Tank House BBQ and Bar   BARBECUE $
(Map p586; www.tankhousebbq.com; 1925 J St; pork butt sando $10; ⏰11:30am-2am Mon-Fri, from 11am Sat & Sun) The classy roadhouse vibe suits this historic railway stop, where you can get passable BBQ and soak in the mix of local characters, families and wayward tourists. Sidle up to the bar to order and start a tab. The smoker goes all day, so if you sit outside, position upwind.

Tower Cafe   BREAKFAST $
(Map p586; ⏱916-441-0222; www.towercafe.com; 1518 Broadway; mains $7-18; ⏰8am-10pm Sun-Thu, to midnight Fri & Sat) Best bet for big ol' breakfasts – custardy French toast, chorizo sausage with eggs – at a 1938 art-deco movie theater.

Localis   BRUNCH $$
(Map p586; ⏱916-737-7699; www.localissacramento. com; 2031 S St.; ⏰5-9pm Tue-Thu, to 10pm Fri & Sat, 10am-2pm Sun) The 'hyper-seasonal' menu includes the city's best fancy brunch (the lamb benedict is a decadent delight) and artfully prepared comfort food, all served in a sunny atrium.

Waterboy   CALIFORNIAN $$
(Map p586; ⏱916-498-9891; www.waterboy restaurant.com; 2000 Capitol Ave; mains $13-29; ⏰11:30am-2:30pm Mon-Fri, 5-9:30pm Sun-Thu, to 10:30pm Fri & Sat) The wicker and palm in the windowed dining room offer a preview

of the chef's style – a French-Italian spin on Central Valley ingredients. The day's catch is always stellar.

Lucca   ITALIAN $$

(Map p586; www.luccarestaurant.com; 1615 J St; ⊙11:30am-10pm Mon-Thu, to 11pm Fri, noon-11pm Sat, 4-9pm Sun) Within a stroll of the convention center is this quality Italian eatery. Parmesan frites with truffle aioli are the way to start.

★ Empress Tavern   NEW AMERICAN $$$

(Map p586; ☑916-662-7694; www.empresstavern. com; 1013 K St; mains $13-40; ⊙11:30am-9pm Mon-Thu, to 10pm Fri, 5-10pm Sat) In the catacombs under the historic Crest Theater, this gorgeous restaurant hosts a menu of creative, meat-focused dishes (including family-style options like the falling-off-the-bone lamb osso buco). The space itself is just as impressive as the food; the arched brick ceilings and glittering bar feel like a speakeasy supper club from a bygone era.

Kitchen Restaurant   CALIFORNIAN $$$

(☑916-568-7171; www.thekitchenrestaurant.com; 2225 Hurley Way; prix-fixe dinner $125; ⊙5-10pm Wed-Sun) Husband-and-wife team Randall Selland and Nancy Zimmer's cozy dining room in the northeast 'burbs is the pinnacle of Sacramento's food experience. Their demonstration dinners focus on — what else? — local, seasonal, organic food, immaculately prepared before your eyes. Reservations are essential.

Mulvaney's B&L   MODERN AMERICAN $$$

(Map p586; ☑916-441-6022; www.mulvaneysbl. com; 1215 19th St; dinner mains $33-45; ⊙11:30am-2:30pm & 5-10pm Tue-Fri, 5-10pm Sat) ✐ With effortless class and obsessive commitment to seasonality, this converted 19th-century firehouse offers delicate pastas (such as a fresh lamb tortellini) and grilled local meats on a menu that changes daily. As one of the area's farm-to-table pioneers, it's also deeply invested in community programs and sustainable food production.

♟ Drinking & Nightlife

Sacramento has a split personality when it comes to drinking – upscale joints where hipster bartenders shake cocktails, and sans-bullshit dive bars with vintage neons and menus that begin and end with a-shot-ana-beer. Both options dot the Grid. If you're looking to party, head to the K Street Mall (p588), which has booming clubs and great restaurants.

Temple Coffee Roasters   COFFEE

(Map p586; www.templecoffee.com; 1010 9th St; ⊙6am-11pm; 🛜) ✐ Hip young patrons nurse organic free-trade coffee and chai morning to night in this steel and concrete space.

Mercantile Saloon   GAY

(Map p586; ☑916-447-0792; 1928 L St; ⊙10am-2am) Down an alley in a yellow Victorian, stiff drinks go for less than $5. Personal space is nil in this rowdy dive. Start here

---

SACTOWN BEER HEAVEN

In the past few years, Sacramento has developed one of California's best craft beer scenes. A number of excellent breweries is clustered on the Grid, and some of the most promising newer spots are just a bit further afield. If you want to taste all that Sacramento has to offer, sign up for one of the fun, safe guided trips from Sacramento Beer Tour (p588) or pedal your way from one brewery to the next on a 15-person human-powered contraption from Sac Brew Bike (p589). If you're going it alone, these are some of our favorites.

Fieldwork Brewing Company (Map p586; ☑916-329-8367; www.fieldworkbrewing.com; 1805 Capitol Ave; ⊙11am-9pm Sun-Thu, to 11pm Fri & Sat)

Big Stump Brew Company (Map p586; ☑916-668-7433; www.bigstumpbrewco.com; 1716 L St; ⊙3-10pm Mon-Wed, to 11pm Thu, noon-midnight Fri & Sat, noon-10pm Sun)

Rubicon Brewing Company (Map p586; www.rubiconbrewing.com; 2004 Capitol Ave; ⊙11am-11:30pm Mon-Thu, to 12:30am Fri & Sat, to 10pm Sun)

Sactown Union Brewery (☑916-917-5555; www.sactownunion.com; 1210 66th St; ⊙4-10pm Mon-Thu, 2-11pm Fri, noon-11pm Sat, to 8pm Sun)

Track 7 Brewing (www.track7brewing.com; 3747 W Pacific Ave, Suite F; ⊙3-9pm Mon-Thu, from noon Fri-Sun)

before touring the four-block radius of gay bars and clubs that locals call 'Lavender Heights.'

58 Degrees and Holding Co WINE BAR
(Map p586; www.58degrees.com; 1217 18th St; ⊙11am-10pm Mon, Wed & Thu, to 11pm Fri & Sat, to 9pm Sun) A wide selection of California and European reds and a refined bistro menu make this a favorite for young professionals on the prowl.

Old Tavern Bar & Grill PUB
(Map p586; 1510 20th St; ⊙6pm-2am) This friendly dive stands out from Sac's many workaday joints with its huge beer selection, tall pours and 1980s-loaded jukebox.

☆ Entertainment

Pick up a copy of the free weekly *Sacramento News & Review* (www.newsandreview.com) for a list of current happenings around town.

Harlow's LIVE MUSIC
(Map p586; www.harlows.com; 2708 J St; ⊙7pm-midnight) Quality jazz, R&B and the occasional salsa or indie act in a classy joint. Just beware of the potent martinis.

California Musical Theatre PERFORMING ARTS
(Map p586; www.californiamusicaltheatre.com; 1419 H St) This top-notch company holds court at the Community Center Theater and the Wells Fargo Pavilion in town.

Crest Theatre CINEMA
(Map p586; www.thecrest.com; 1013 K St) A classic old movie house that's been restored to its 1949 splendor. Hosts indie and foreign films and the annual **Trash Film Orgy** (trashfilmorgy.com) on Saturdays in July and August.

Old Ironsides LIVE MUSIC
(Map p586; www.theoldironsides.com; 1901 10th St; cover $5-10; ⊙8am-2am Tue-Fri & Sun, from 6pm Sat) The tiny back room of this cool dive hosts some of the best indie bands that come through town.

Tower Theatre CINEMA
(Map p586; ☑916-442-4700; www.ReadingCinemasUS.com; 2508 Landpark Dr) Classic, foreign and indie films screen at this historic movie house with a digital upgrade.

Sacramento River Cats BASEBALL
(Map p586; www.milb.com; Raley Field, 400 Ballpark Dr; tickets $8-60; ⊙Apr-Sep) Sacramento's minor-league baseball team plays across the river at Raley Field, with views of the art-deco Tower Bridge.

❶ Information

Convention & Visitors Bureau (Map p586; www.visitsacramento.com; 1608 I St; ⊙8am-5pm Mon-Fri) Local information, including event and bus schedules.

Sacramento Visitor Center (Map p586; ☑916-442-7644; www.visitsacramento.com; 1002 2nd St; ⊙10am-5pm) A great local resource that's well-equipped with information and suggestions for travelers.

❶ Getting There & Away

At the intersection of major highways, you'll likely pass through Sacramento en route to other California destinations. The **Sacramento International Airport** (SMF; www.sacramento.aero/smf; 6900 Airport Blvd) is one of the nearest options for those traveling to Yosemite National Park.

Sacramento–San Joaquin River Delta

The Sacramento Delta is a sprawling web of waterways and one-stoplight towns plucked out of the 1930s. On weekends, locals gun powerboats on glassy waterways and cruise winding levy roads. This wetland area encompasses a huge swath of the state – from the San Francisco Bay to Sacramento, and all the way south to Stockton. Here the Sacramento and San Joaquin Rivers converge to drain into the San Francisco Bay. If you have the time to smell the grassy delta breezes on the slow route between San Francisco and Sacramento, travel the iron bridges of winding Hwy 160. You'll lazily make your way past rice fields, vast orchards, sandy swimming banks and little towns with long histories.

The region's best-known winery, **Bogle** (☑916-744-1092; www.boglewinery.com; 37783 Country Rd 144, Clarksburg; ⊙10am-5pm Mon-Fri, from 11am Sat & Sun; ℗) 🎫 **FREE**, is a few miles southwest of Clarksburg via County Rds 141 and 144. It's set among vineyards on a sixth-generation family farm.

Old Sugar Mill (☑916-744-1615; www.oldsugarmill.com; 35265 Willow Ave, Clarksburg; ⊙11am-5pm; ℗ 🐾) **FREE** is the hub of a thriving community of local winemakers. A jazz combo echoes through the space to complement wines of the Carvalho family, who own

THE DELTA DETOUR

Locke (☎ 916-776-1661; www.locketown.com; 13920 Main St, Walnut Grove; tours adult/student $5/3; ☺ visitors center noon-4pm Tue & Fri, 11am-3pm Sat & Sun) is the most fascinating of the Sacramento Delta towns, founded by Chinese laborers who also built the levees that ended perpetual flooding and allowed agriculture to flourish here. After a malicious fire wiped out the settlement in 1912, a group of community leaders approached land baron George Locke for a leasehold; at the time, California didn't allow people of Chinese descent to own property. Locke became the only freestanding town built and managed by Chinese people in the US, most of whom spoke the Chungsan dialect of Cantonese. Tucked below the levee, Locke's main street feels like a ghost town these days, but the weather-beaten buildings are protected on the National Register of Historic Places.

The colorful **Dai Loy Museum** (☎ 916-776-1661; www.locke-foundation.org; 13951 Main St, Locke; donations appreciated; ☺ noon-4pm Fri-Sun; ♿), housing dusty *pai gow* tables and an antique safe, is the main stop. Nearby is **Al's Place** (☎ 916-776-1800; 13943 Main St, Walnut Grove; mains $7-21; ☺ 11am-9pm), a saloon that's been pouring since 1915 and serves peanut-butter-slathered Texas toast. Below are creaking floorboards; above, the ceiling's covered in crusty dollar bills and more than one pair of erstwhile undies.

Hwy 160 also passes through Isleton, so-called Crawdad Town USA, whose main street has more shops, restaurants, bars and buildings that reflect the region's Chinese heritage. Isleton's Cajun Festival, at the end of June, draws folks from across the state, but you can get very lively crawdads year round at **Bob's Bait Shop** (☎ 916-777-6666; http://themasterbaiter.tripod.com; 302 2nd St, Isleton; ☺ 6am-noon Tue-Wed, to 5pm Thu-Sat, to 3pm Sun).

Further west on Hwy 160 you'll see signs for the Delta Loop, a drive that passes boater bars and marinas where you can rent something to take on the water. At the end is the **Brannan Island State Recreation Area** (☎ 916-777-6671; www.parks.ca.gov; 17645 Hwy 160, Rio Vista; per car $10; ☺ sunrise-sunset; P ♿), which has boat-in, drive-in and walk-in campsites.

In the 1930s the Bureau of Reclamation issued an aggressive water-redirection program – the Central Valley and California State Water Projects – that dammed California's major rivers and directed 75% of their supply through the Central Valley for agriculture and Southern California. The siphoning affected the delta, its wetlands and estuaries, and sparked debate. Learn about the area's unique legacy by bus or on a self-guided tour with **Delta Heartbeat Tours** (☎ 916-776-4010; www.deltaheartbeattours.com; Deckhands Marina, 14090 Hwy 160, Walnut Grove), which also has leads on boat rides. If you have a car, taste the fruits of the delta on the **Delta Grown Farm Trail** (☎ 916-775-1166; www.sacriverdeltagrown.org).

this custom crushing facility. The wines of the Clarksburg region have developed a lot over the last decade, benefiting from the blazing sun and cool delta breezes.

Brannan Island State Park Recreation Area Campgrounds (☎ 800-444-7275; www.reserveamerica.com; 17645 Hwy 160, Rio Vista; tent & RV sites $31-49, cabin $56; P ☺) is a tidy facility in a protected wetland marsh that provides drive-in and walk-in campsites. There's a hike-in log cabin with electricity that sleeps four; bring sleeping bags.

In nearby Isleton, **Rogelio's** (☎ 916-777-5878; www.rogelios.net; 34 Main St, Isleton; mains $8-15; ☺ 4-8pm Wed & Thu, from noon Fri-Sun) makes the most of the delta's multiethnic history, serving a mash-up of Mexican and

Chinese dishes, with a few Italian and American standards mixed in. But nothing beats the carnitas chow mein.

Davis

Bicycles whir through the streets of Davis, a vibrant oasis of culture, food and progressive politics. Much of the energy comes from the students who flock to the University of California, Davis (UCD), which boasts one of the nation's leading viticulture departments. Bikes outnumber cars two-to-one (it has more bikes per capita than any other American city) and students make up half the population. It's a fun and free-spirited place that makes an excellent pit stop when traveling in or out of the Bay Area.

Strolling the downtown grid, you'll pass family-operated businesses (city council has forbidden any store over 50,000 sq ft – sorry, Wal-Mart), public art projects and affordable international restaurants.

I-80 skirts the south edge of town, and you can reach downtown via the Richards Blvd exit. UCD is southwest of downtown, bordered by A St, 1st St and Russell Blvd.

◉ Sights & Activities

UC Davis Arboretum PARK
(http://arboretum.ucdavis.edu; 1 Shields Ave; 🚼)
FREE With well-marked botanical collections, picnic grounds and family tours, the 100-acre 'Arb' is a treasure. Follow the peaceful 3.5-mile loop along one of the state's oldest reservoirs, dug in the 1860s.

Pence Gallery GALLERY
(www.pencegallery.org; 212 D St; ⊙11:30am-5pm Tue-Sun) This community gallery exhibits contemporary art and hosts classes, lectures and films. It offers a free reception 6pm to 9pm on the second Friday of each month.

Davis Transmedia Art Walk WALKING
(http://davisartwalk.com; 🚼) FREE This two-hour walking tour winds through Davis' public art collection, mostly clustered on D and G Sts. There's a free smartphone app with audio and interactive media. If you're low-tech, get a map at the Yolo County Visitors Bureau (p595) or **John Natsoulas Center for the Arts** (www.natsoulas.com; 521 1st St; ⊙11am-5pm Wed & Thu, to 9pm Fri, noon-5pm Sat & Sun) FREE.

🛏 Sleeping

Hotel rates are stable until graduation or special campus events, when they skyrocket and sell out fast. Worse, the trains that roll through the town will infuriate a light sleeper. For a utilitarian (if bland) stay, look for chains along the highway.

University Park Inn & Suites HOTEL $$
(☎844-277-4752; www.universityparkinn.com; 1111 Richards Blvd; r $149-200; 🅿️❄@🛜🚾🐕) Right off the highway, this independent hotel isn't the Ritz but it's clean, serves breakfast and offers free bikes for guests. Rates double in June.

Aggie Inn HOTEL $$
(☎530-756-0352; www.aggieinn.com; 245 1st St; r from $139; ❄🛜) Across from UCD's east entrance, the Aggie is neat, modern and unassuming. Cottages are not much more than regular rooms with kitchenettes and Jacuzzis.

🍴 Eating

College students love to eat and drink cheaply, and downtown has no short supply of lively spots for a quick plate of Pad Thai or slice of pizza. The Davis farmers market (p594) is incredible, and features food vendors, picnic supplies and buskers. More excellent self-catering options can be found at the **Davis Food Co-op** (http://davisfood.coop; 620 G St; ⊙7am-10pm).

★Davis Farmers Market MARKET $
(www.davisfarmersmarket.org; cnr 4th & C Sts; ⊙8am-1pm Sat year-round, 4:30-8:30pm Wed Mar-Oct.) With more than 150 vendors and an awe-inspiring selection of local produce, meat, flowers and baked goods, this is the vibrant heart of Davis. It's justly considered among the best farmers markets in the nation.

On Wednesday evenings in summer, browse for provisions for a dreamy dinner picnic in the park.

Sam's Mediterranean Cuisine MIDDLE EASTERN $
(☎530-758-2855; 301 B St; shawarma $6.99; ⊙11:30am-7:30pm Mon-Fri, from noon Sat) Delicious and cheap shawarma (get the beef with tangy yogurt and chili sauce) makes this little spot a university institution. Cash only.

Burgers and Brew PUB FOOD $
(☎530-750-3603; www.burgersandbrew.com; 403 3rd St; burgers $10; 🚼) It's all in the name; the brilliantly simple formula of this buzzing brewpub makes it a charming local favorite. The 30 craft beers on tap include the best of the region and a delicious house IPA. When you're a few deep, the 'Beast Mode Fries' (caramelized onions, cheese, and spicy sauce) are a fantastic idea.

Woodstock's PIZZA $
(www.woodstocksdavis.com; 219 G St; slice $3.50, pizzas $8-28; ⊙11am-1am Mon-Wed, to 2am Thu-Sat, to midnight Sun; 🚼) The most popular pizza joint in town serves slices at lunch and gets boisterous at happy hour. Besides the usual combos, it has a fun selection of gourmet pizzas. (Sriracha, bacon, pineapple and green onions? Yes, please.)

Woodstock's also hosts some weekly events that are popular when the students are in town, including a trivia night, live rock bands and an open mike.

Davis Noodle City   ASIAN $
(129 E St; mains $7-10; ☉11am-9:30pm Mon-Sat, to 8:30pm Sun) Students and locals tuck into wooden booths at this cozy spot to slurp up thick homemade noodles, fresh dumplings and scallion pancakes.

Delta of Venus Cafe & Pub   CAFE $
(www.deltaofvenus.org; 122b St; mains $7-11; ☉7:30am-10pm, hours vary seasonally; 🖉) This converted Arts and Crafts bungalow has a social, shaded front patio, delicious homemade granola, and tons of vegetarian and vegan options. At dinner, Chef Iwaca turns out fantastic Caribbean dishes while indie and folk songwriters add ambience. In the warm months, the cafe stays open late and sometimes has live music, but in winter it closes earlier.

🍸 Drinking & Nightlife

During the school year, downtown bars lure students with every trick in the book – drink specials, open mike nights, karaoke and trivia. In the summer, things are a bit quieter, but the downtown grid is the place to wander if you're thirsty.

Three Mile Brewing Company   MICROBREWERY
(🖉530-564-4351; www.threemilebrewing.com; 231 G St, Suite 3; ☉3-10pm Thu-Fri, noon-10pm Sat, to 8pm Sun; 🖥) This welcome upstart microbrew has a fantastic flight of crisp, hoppy beer made from local ingredients. Get a taster of four 5oz sips for $7. The list is always changing, but if you're lucky, it will have the smoky Big Deal Scotch on tap, which is made from peated malt.

Davis Beer Shoppe   BEER HALL
(🖉530-756-5212; 211 G St; bottle from $3; ☉11am-11pm Mon-Wed, to 12:30am Thu-Sat, to 9pm Sun) This mellow beer hall and shop stocks 650 varieties of craft beer, bottled and on tap, import and brewed down the block. Pull any bottle from the back, or order one of its daily changing draft flights. BYO food.

☆ Entertainment

The college has fostered a thriving cultural scene – bulletin boards around town will announce readings and performances galore. For tickets and information to UC Davis' arts events, call the Mondavi Center (p595). For athletic events, call the UC Davis Athletic Ticket office (🖉530-752-2471; http://campus recreation.ucdavis.edu; Aggie Stadium, off La Rue Rd).

Mondavi Center for the Performing Arts   CONCERT VENUE
(www.mondaviarts.org; 1 Shields Ave) Major theater, music, dance and other performances take place at this state-of-the-art venue on the UCD campus.

Varsity Theatre   FILM
(www.davisvarsity.net; 616 2nd St) Davis' beloved art house movie theater has discerning programming and occasional Q&As with filmmakers.

ℹ Information

The exhaustive www.daviswiki.org is fascinating.
Yolo County Visitors Bureau (🖉530-297-1900; www.visityolo.com; 132 E St, Suite 200; ☉8:30am-4:30pm Mon-Fri) Free bike maps, travel brochures and transit info.

ℹ Getting There & Away

Amtrak (🖉530-758-4220; 840 2nd St) Davis' station is on the southern edge of downtown. Trains connect with Sacramento ($9, 26 minutes) or San Francisco ($31, two hours) throughout the day.
Yolobus (🖉530-666-2877; ☉5am-11pm) Routes 42A and B ($2.25) loop between Davis and the Sacramento International Airport. The route also connects Davis with Woodland and Downtown Sacramento.

TULE FOG

As thick as the proverbial pea soup, tule (too-lee) fog causes chain collisions each year on area roads. In 2007, more than 100 cars and big rigs collided on a stretch of Hwy 99. At its worst, these dense, immobile clouds can limit visibility up to a foot.

Tule fog, named after a marsh grass common here, is thickest from November to March, when cold mountain air settles on the warm valley floor and condenses. The fog burns off for a few afternoon hours, just long enough for the ground to warm again and perpetuate the cycle.

If you find yourself driving in fog, turn on your low beams, give other cars extra distance and maintain an easy, constant speed. Avoid passing.

❶ Getting Around

Unitrans (☑530-752-2877; http://unitrans.ucdavis.edu; one-way $1) If you're not biking, this student-run outfit shuttles people around town and campus in red double-deckers.

Ken's Bike, Ski, Board (www.kensbikeski.com; 650 G St; ☉9am-8pm Mon-Fri, to 7pm Sat, noon-5pm Sun) Rents basic bikes (from $21 per day), as well as serious road and mountain bikes.

Oroville

North of Sacramento's bustle, the quiet town of Oroville has seen quite a reversal. In the mid-19th century the lust for gold brought a crush of white settlers, who drove out the native community. Today, crowds still seek riches – in the thriving tribal casinos on the outskirts of town. Aside from slots, the local economy relies on tourists headed to the rugged northern reaches of the Sierra Nevada.

Oroville's most enduring attraction, aside from the nearby lake, is an excellent museum established by descendants of a long-dispersed Chinese community. Oroville's other historic attractions revolve around the gold rush.

Hwys 162 and 70 head northeast from Oroville into the mountains and on to Quincy. Hwy 70 snakes along the magnificent **Feather River Canyon**, an especially captivating drive in autumn.

OROVILLE DAM CRISIS

In February 2017, Oroville made national headlines when a dam east of town threatened catastrophe. After heavy rains, several flood control measures failed and the swollen waters of Lake Oroville – California's second-largest reservoir and the water source for farms of the Central Valley and 23 million people – threatened disaster. In a chaotic evacuation, 188,000 people were given just an hour to leave their homes, while news helicopters live streamed the traffic jam. The dam held, but the crisis caused millions in damage and added another hot-button issue to the complex debate about California's water management, climate change and crumbling infrastructure.

◉ Sights & Activities

Lake Oroville State Recreation Area   LAKE
(☑530-538-2219; www.parks.ca.gov; 917 Kelly Ridge Rd; ☉park 8am-8pm, visitor center 9am-5pm; **P**🐾) This artificial lake was formed by the USA's tallest earth-filled dam, rising 770ft above the Feather River. There are boat-in, floating campsites available. The lake's **visitor center** (☑530-538-2219; www.parks.ca.gov; 917 Kelly Ridge Rd; ☉9am-5pm) has exhibits on the California State Water Project and local tribe history, plus a viewing tower and loads of recreational information.

The area surrounding Lake Oroville is also full of hiking trails, and a favorite is the 7-mile round-trip walk to 640ft Feather Falls. The Brad Freeman Bicycle Trail is a 41-mile, off-road loop that takes cyclists to the top of 770ft Oroville Dam, then follows the Feather River back to the Thermalito Forebay and Afterbay storage reservoirs, east of Hwy 70. The ride is mostly flat, but the dam ascent is steep. Get a free map of the ride from the Oroville Area Chamber of Commerce (p597). The Forebay Aquatic Center (p596) rents non-motorized watercraft to get out on the water.

**Chinese Temple
& Museum Complex**   MUSEUM
(☑530-538-2496; 1500 Broderick St; adult/child $3/free; ☉noon-4pm; **P**) This restored temple and museum offers a fascinating glimpse into Oroville's Chinese legacy and is well worth exploring. Built in 1863, it served the Chinese community, which built the area's levees and at its peak numbered 10,000. Inside is an unrivaled collection of 19th-century stage finery, religious **shrines** and a small **garden** with fine Qing-era relics.

**Sacramento National
Wildlife Refuge**   BIRDWATCHING
(www.fws.gov; $6; ☉1hr before sunset-1hr after sunset) Serious bird-watchers sojourn here in winter, when millions of migratory waterfowl are spectacular. The visitor center (p597) is off I-5 near Willows; a splendid 6-mile driving trail and walking trails are open daily. The peak season to see birds is between October and late February, with the largest skein of geese arriving in December and January.

Forebay Aquatic Center   BOATING
(www.forebayaquaticcenter.com; 930 Garden Dr; kayaks per day from $40; ☉10am-6pm Wed-Sun May-Sep) A pair of docks and a beach for easy water access for canoeing, kayaking, rowing,

pedal boats, hydro bikes, paddle boarding or just swimming in a motor-boat free area of the Thermalito Forebay. Rentals and lessons available.

🛏 Sleeping

★Lake Oroville State Recreation Area Campground
CAMPGROUND $

(✏information 530-538-2219, reservations 800-444-7275; www.reserveamerica.com; tent & RV sites $20-45; P) Drive-in campgrounds aren't the most rustic choice, but there are good primitive campsites if you're willing to hike or – perhaps the coolest feature of the park – boat. There's a cove of floating platform sites (per night $175).

🍸 Drinking & Nightlife

Keg Room
BAR

(✏530-534-1394; 3035 Oro Dam Blvd E; ⊙7am-2am) Our favorite of Oroville's no-frills watering holes serves very cold beer and spicy Bloody Marys and has a shuffleboard table.

❶ Information

For road conditions, phone 800-427-7623.

Feather River Ranger District (Plumas National Forest; ✏530-534-6500; www.fs.usda.gov; 875 Mitchell Ave; ⊙8am-4:30pm Mon-Fri) This US Forest Service (USFS) office has maps and brochures.

Oroville Area Chamber of Commerce (www.orovillechamber.net; 1789 Montgomery St) A source for free biking and trail maps and other area activities.

Sacramento National Wildlife Refuge Visitor Center (✏530-934-2801; 752 County Rd, Willows; ⊙9am-4pm, closed Mon Nov-Feb, closed Sat & Sun Mar-Oct) An Audubon Society bookstore and exhibits on all things birds at this well-run visitor center. Pick up maps for self-guided wetland walks here.

❶ Getting There & Away

Although **Greyhound buses** (✏800-231-2222; www.greyhound.com; 420 Richards Blvd) stop near the **Valero gas station** (✏530-533-2328; 555 Oro Dam Blvd E) a few blocks east of Hwy 70, a car is far and away the simplest and most cost effective way to reach the area. There are two buses daily between Oroville and Sacramento ($20, 1½ hours).

Chico

With its huge population of students, Chico has the wild energy of a college kegger during the school year, and a lazy, lethargic

hangover during the summer. An oak-shaded downtown and university makes it one of Sacramento Valley's more attractive hubs, where folks mingle late in the restaurants and bars, which open onto patios when it's warm.

Though Chico wilts in the heat during summer, the swimming holes in Bidwell Park offer an escape, as does floating down the gentle Sacramento River. The brews of the Sierra Nevada Brewing Company, near downtown, are another of Chico's refreshing blessings.

It's ironic a town so widely celebrated for its beer was founded by John Bidwell, a California pioneer who made a bid for US president with the Prohibitionist party. In 1868, Bidwell and his philanthropist wife, Annie Ellicott Kennedy Bidwell, moved to the mansion that is now the Bidwell Mansion State Historic Park.

⊙ Sights

Nearly all the sights are downtown, west of Hwy 99, easily reached via Hwy 32 (8th St). Main St and Broadway are the central downtown streets; from there, Park Ave stretches south and the tree-lined Esplanade heads north.

Sierra Nevada Brewing Company
BREWERY

(✏530-899-4776; www.sierranevada.com; 1075 E 20th St; brewery tour free, Beer Geek tour $45; ⊙tours 11am-4pm Sun-Thu, to 5:30pm Fri & Sat) 🍺 Hordes of beer fans gather at the birthplace of the nationally distributed Sierra Nevada Pale Ale and Schwarber, a Chico-only black ale. You can also stock up on eccentric 'Beer Camp' collaborations, short-run craft beers brewed by über-beer nerds at invitation-only seminars. Free brewhouse tours are given regularly.

Chico Creek Nature Center
SCIENCE CENTER

(www.bidwellpark.org; 1968 E 8th St; suggested donation adult/child $4/2; ⊙11am-4pm Wed-Sun; 🚼) If you plan on spending the afternoon in Bidwell Park, stop here first for displays on local plants and animals and excellent hands-on science programs for families. The exhibit hall is closed on Wednesdays.

Chico State University
UNIVERSITY

Ask for a free map of the Chico State University campus, or about campus events and tours at the **CSU Information Center** (✏530-898-4636; www.csuchico.edu; cnr 2nd & Normal Sts; ⊙7am-11pm Mon-Thu, to 10pm

Fri, 11am-10pm Sat, noon-11pm Sun school year), on the main floor of Bell Memorial Union. The attractive campus is infused with floral sweetness in spring, and there's a rose garden and several stately Romanesque buildings at its center.

Bidwell Mansion State Historic Park HISTORIC BUILDING

(☑530-895-6144; www.parks.ca.gov; 525 Esplanade; adult/child $6/3; ☉noon-5pm Mon, 11am-5pm Sat & Sun) ✦ Chico's most prominent landmark, the opulent Victorian home was built for Chico's founders, John and Annie Bidwell. The 26-room mansion was built between 1865 and 1868. It hosted many US presidents and John Muir, who was a personal friend of Annie. Tours start every hour from 11am to 4pm.

Honey Run Covered Bridge HISTORIC SITE

(www.honeyruncoveredbridge.com; parking $3) The historic 1894 bridge is an unusual style this side of the country and a favorite spot for engagement photos. Take the Skyway exit off Hwy 99 on the southern outskirts of Chico, head east and go left on Honey Run-Humbug Rd. The bridge is in a small park 5 miles up the road.

🏃 Activities

In summer you can cool off by tubing the Sacramento. Inner tubes can be rented at grocery stores and other shops along Nord Ave (Hwy 32) for $7 to $12. Tubers enter at the Irvine Finch Launch Ramp on Hwy 32, a few miles west of Chico, and come out at Washout Beach, off River Rd.

Bidwell Park SWIMMING

(www.bidwellpark.org) Growing out of downtown, the 3670-acre Bidwell Park is the nation's third-largest municipal park. It stretches 10 miles northwest along Chico Creek with lush groves and miles of trails. The upper part of the park is an untamed oasis. Several classic movies have been shot here, including parts of *Gone with the Wind* and *The Adventures of Robin Hood*.

The park is full of swimming spots. You'll find pools at One-Mile and Five-Mile recreation areas and swimming holes (including Bear Hole, Salmon Hole and Brown Hole) in Upper Bidwell Park, north of Manzanita Ave. Don't be surprised if some opt to swim au naturel.

Adventure Outing OUTDOORS

(☑530 898-4011; www.aschico.com/adventure-outings; Bell Memorial Union basement, 2nd & Chestnut Sts; life jackets $4-8; ☉9am-5pm Mon-Fri) The CSU-student-run outfitter rents equipment like life jackets, rafts and even coolers at very reasonable prices by the weekend or week. It also leads popular trips further afield.

🎉 Festivals & Events

With the students out of town, family-friendly outdoor events take over each summer. The Thursday Night Market fills several blocks of Broadway from April to September. At City Plaza (www.downtownchico.com; W 4th & Broadway Sts), you'll find free Friday night concerts starting in May.

🛏 Sleeping

There's plenty of decent independent motels with swimming pools, some of them along the shaded Esplanade north of downtown. Chico State's graduation and homecoming mania (May and October, respectively) send prices skyward.

Hotel Diamond

(☑866-993-3100; www.hoteldiamondchico.com; 220 W 4th St; r $150-399; ❄@🛜) is the most luxurious place to lay your head in Chico, with high thread counts and attentive room service. The Diamond Suite, with its spacious top-floor balcony, is a-*maz*-ing. There's also a swanky piano bar and top-notch restaurant, Two Twenty, downstairs.

🍴 Eating

Downtown Chico is packed with fun places to eat, many of them catering to a student budget. The outdoor farmers market (p598) draws from the plentiful surrounding valley.

Shubert's Ice Cream & Candy ICE CREAM $

(www.shuberts.com; 178 E 7th St; ☉9:30am-10pm Mon-Fri, from 11am Sat & Sun) Five generations of Shuberts have produced delicious homemade ice cream, chocolates and confections for more than 75 years at this beloved pastel-colored Chico landmark. The flavors change with the season; consider yourself lucky to get the boysenberry sundaes in the spring.

Chico Certified Farmers Market MARKET $

(☑530-893-3276; www.chicofarmersmarket.com; Chico Municipal parking lot, 305 Wall St; ☉7:30am-1pm Sat May-Sep) Rain or shine, this excellent open-air market brings in the best from the valley, artisanal baked goods and coffee.

El Paisa Taco Truck
MEXICAN $
(cnr 8th & Pine Sts; mains $1.50-5; ⊙11am-8pm) Debate about which of Chico's taco trucks is best can quickly lead to fisticuffs, but the smoky carnitas tacos served at this mobile kitchen are a dream.

Sin of Cortez
CAFE $
(www.sinofcortez.com; 2290 Esplanade; mains $6-16; ⊙7am-2pm; 🍸) The service won't win awards for speed, but this local favorite draws both vegetarian and omnivorous mobs with its burly breakfast plates. Order anything with the soy chorizo.

Sierra Nevada Taproom & Restaurant
PUB FOOD $$
(www.sierranevada.com; 1075 E 20th St; mains $10-32; ⊙11am-9pm Sun-Thu, to 10pm Fri & Sat; 🍸) What's on tap is the main draw at the on-site restaurant of the Sierra Nevada Brewery Company (p597). This genuine Chico destination is great for downing brews but lacks ambience – the huge, loud dining room is basically a cafeteria. Still, it has better-than-average pub food and superbly fresh ales and lagers, some not available elsewhere.

Red Tavern
AMERICAN $$
(www.redtavern.com; 1250 Esplanade; mains $17-28; ⊙from 5pm Tue-Sat, 10am-2pm Sun) 🍸 The Red Tavern is one of Chico's favorite fine-dining experiences, with a sophisticated menu that uses local, seasonal and organic ingredients. On Sundays, it offers a delicious brunch and family-style dinners.

Celestino's Live from New York Pizza
PIZZA $$
(101 Salem St; pizzas from $14; ⊙10:30am-10pm Sun-Thu, to 11pm Fri & Sat) A convincing imitation of 'real' New York pizza, it serves thin-crust pizzas and playful variations like the meaty Godfather. There's a budget slice-n-a-soda lunch for $4.75.

Leon Bistro
CALIFORNIAN $$$
(www.leonbistro.com; 817 Main St; mains $18-35; ⊙from 5pm Wed-Sat) When the most ordinary thing on the menu is a wagyu beef burger with bacon-onion marmalade, you know you're in for something nice. Chef Ann Leon cooked in several fine kitchens before opening her namesake restaurant, a go-to among Chico tastemakers. She regularly shares her skills in cooking classes.

5th Street Steakhouse
AMERICAN $$$
(www.5thstreetsteakhouse.com; 345 W 5th St; steaks from $26; ⊙11:30am-2:30pm Fri, from 4:30pm daily) This is where college kids take their visiting parents. It features crisp white tablecloths, steaks tender enough to cut with a reproachful look, and occasional live jazz loud enough to drown out any disapproval.

🍷 Drinking & Nightlife

Given Chico's party-school rep, you won't be thirsty. There's a strip of bars on Main St if you want to go hopping.

Naked Lounge
COFFEE
(☑530-895-0676; www.nakedcoffee.net; 118 W 2nd St; ⊙6:30am-8pm; 🍸) With excellent coffee, mellow music and a choice selection of beer on tap, this inviting downtown cafe is perfect for an easygoing morning.

Madison Bear Garden
BAR
(www.madisonbeargarden.com; 316 W 2nd St; ⊙11am-1:45am Mon-Sat, from 10am Sun; 🍸) This spacious brick building with adjoining big beer garden isn't only the most reliable scene in Chico – it's an institution. The walls are loaded with kitsch, and students pack the place for big burgers and cold pints.

Panama Bar & Cafe
BAR
(www.panamabarcafeinchico.com; 177 E 2nd St; iced tea from $3; ⊙11:30am-1:30am Tue-Sat, 11am-9pm Sun) The house specializes in 31 variations of Long Island iced teas (most of which are around $3), so brace yourself. The only way to take in alcohol any faster would be by IV drip. There are several adjoining dance clubs which get packed on the weekends.

☆ Entertainment

For entertainment options, pick up the free weekly *Chico News & Review* (www.newsandreview.com). For theater, films, concerts, art exhibits and other cultural events at the CSU campus, contact the **CSU Box Office** (☑530-898-6333; www.csuchico.edu; Sierra Hall, cnr 3rd & Chestnut; ⊙11am-6pm Mon-Fri) or the CSU Information Center (p597).

Pageant Theatre
CINEMA
(www.pageantchico.com; 351 E 6th St; tickets $8) Screens international and alternative films. Monday is 'cheap skate night,' with all seats just $4.

1078 Gallery
PERFORMING ARTS
(☑530-343-1973; www.1078gallery.org; 820 Broadway; ⊙12:30-5:30pm) Chico's

contemporary gallery exhibits artworks, and hosts boundary-pushing literary readings, music and theater.

ⓘ Information

Chico Chamber of Commerce & Visitor Center (☑800-852-8570, 530-891-5556; www.chicochamber.com; 441 Main St; ☻10am-4pm Mon-Fri) Local information including bike maps.

ⓘ Getting There & Around

Greyhound (www.greyhound.com) buses stop multiple times a day at the **Amtrak station** (www.amtrak.com; 450 Orange St) heading to San Francisco ($48, six hours 40 minutes), Reno ($57, 10 hours), Los Angeles ($65, 11 hours) and points between. The platform is unattended so purchase tickets in advance or from the driver.

Amtrak trains on the *Coast Starlight* line depart Chico in the middle of the night for Redding ($20, one hour) and Sacramento ($26, 2½ hours). Amtrak's connecting buses travel through the region as well, but require booking a connecting train.

B-Line (Butte Regional Transit; ☑530-342-0221; www.blinetransit.com; W 2nd St at Salem; adult/child $1.40/1) handles all buses throughout Butte County, and can get you around Chico and down to Oroville in 50 minutes.

Car is the easiest way to get around, but Chico is one of the best biking towns in the country. Rent from **Campus Bicycles** (www.campusbicycles.com; 330 Main St; rental half/full day $20/35).

Red Bluff

The smoldering streets of Red Bluff – one of California's hottest towns due to the hot-air trap of the Shasta Cascades – aren't much of a draw on their own. But a glimpse toward the mountainous horizon reveals what brings most travelers this way.

Peter Lassen laid out the town site in 1847 and it grew into a key port along the Sacramento River. Now it's a pit stop on the way to the national park that bears his name.

Cowboy culture is alive and well here. Catch it in action the third weekend of April at the **Red Bluff Round-Up** (www.redbluffroundup.com; tickets $10-27), a major rodeo event dating back to 1918, or in any of the dive bars where the jukeboxes are stocked with country and plenty of cowboys belly up to the bar. You can also stock up on your own Western wear from one of several historic storefronts in the business district.

⊙ Sights & Activities

Red Bluff Recreation Area   PARK
(www.fs.usda.gov) On the east bank of the Sacramento River this sprawling park of meadows has interpretive trails, bicycle paths, boat ramps, a wildlife-viewing area with excellent bird-watching, and a salmon and steelhead ladder (most active July to September).

William B Ide Adobe
State Historic Park   HISTORIC SITE
(☑530-529-8599; 21659 Adobe Rd; per car $6; ☻10am-4pm Fri-Sun) Set on a beautiful, shaded piece of land overlooking a languorous section of the Sacramento River, this park preserves the original one-room adobe house, old forge and grounds of pioneer William B Ide, who 'fought' in the 1846 Bear Flag Revolt at Sonoma. He became president of the California Bear Republic, which lasted 25 days.

Head about a mile north on Main St, turn east onto Adobe Rd and go another mile, following the signs.

Sacramento River
Discovery Center   SCIENCE CENTER
(www.sacramentoriverdiscoverycenter.com; 1000 Sale Lane; admission by donation; ☻11am-3pm Tue-Sat; ⌖) This kid-friendly center has exhibits on the river and the Diversion Dam just outside its doors, which has been permanently opened to allow endangered chinook and green and white sturgeon to migrate. Though the fish aren't visible, up to 120 species of birds are. Bird walks along the 4.2 miles of wheelchair-accessible trails start the first Saturday of each month at 8am.

🛏 Sleeping & Eating

Sycamore Grove
Camping Area   CAMPGROUND $
(☑530-824-5196; www.recreation.gov; tent/RV sites $16/30) Beside the river in the Red Bluff Recreation Area is this quiet USFS campground. Campsites for tents and RVs are first-come, first-served, and offer new, shared showers and flush toilets. You can reserve a large group campground, Camp Discovery, which has basic screened-in cabins that must be booked as a block ($175 for all 11 cabins per night).

Los Mariachis   MEXICAN $
(www.redblufflosmariachis.com; 604 S Main St; mains $5-14; ☻9am-9pm Mon-Fri, to 9:30pm Sat & Sun; ⌖) This bright, family-run Mexican

spot overlooks the central junction of Red Bluff. It has great salsa and *molcajetes* (meat or seafood stew, served in a stone bowl) big enough to satisfy hungry campers.

From The Hearth CAFE **$**
(📋 530-727-0616; www.fthcafe.com; 638 Washington St; sandwiches $7-10; ⊘ 7am-9pm Mon-Sat, to 6pm Sun) Pastries and expert coffee drinks in the morning, crispy panini on just-baked bread for lunch and dinner. Everything is very fresh, colorful and made-to-order. This sophisticated, no-fuss cafe is a dream for travelers who want to get a quick bite and get back on the road.

Thai House THAI **$**
(www.newthaihouse.com; 248 S Main St; mains $5-14; ⊘ 11am-3pm & 4-8:30pm Mon-Fri, 11am-8:30pm Sat, from noon Sun; P❄🖉) 🍴 A remarkably solid Thai restaurant with excellent curries and soups.

🍸 Drinking & Nightlife

Cedar Crest Brewing BREWERY
(615 Main St; ⊘ 11am-8pm Mon-Thu, to 10pm Fri & Sat, noon-5pm Sun) Situated inside a local specialty food spot called Enjoy The Store, this young craft brewery (Red Bluff's first!) pours floral IPAs and a delicious Dark Matter Porter. The surrounding store is a great spot to stock up on fancy snacks, such as local cheese, olives and nuts.

E's Locker Room BAR
(📋 530-527-4600; 1075 Lakeside Dr; ⊘ 4-9:30pm Tue-Thu, to 10pm Fri & Sat, 3-9pm Sun) Framed photos of local legends and sports heroes clutter the walls of this friendly, casual Red Bluff watering hole. Take your pint out to the big porch out back, overlooking a lazy bend of the Sacramento River.

ℹ Information

Red Bluff Chamber of Commerce (📋 530-527-6220; www.redbluffchamber.com; 100 Main St; ⊘ 8:30am-4pm Mon, to 5pm Tue-Thu, to 4:30pm Fri) To get your bearings and a stack of brochures, find this white building just south of downtown.

ℹ Getting There & Away

Most visitors pull into Red Bluff to take a break from the busy I-5. By highway, the town is three hours north of San Francisco and 15 minutes north of Sacramento. **Amtrak** (www.amtrak.com; cnr Rio & Walnut Sts) and **Greyhound** (www.greyhound.com; 22700 Antelope Blvd) connect it with other California cities via bus.

SAN JOAQUIN VALLEY

The southern half of California's Central Valley – named for the San Joaquin River – sprawls from Stockton to the turbine-covered Tehachapi Mountains, southeast of Bakersfield. Everything stretches to the horizon in straight lines – railroad tracks, two-lane blacktop and long irrigation channels.

The tiny towns scattering the region retain their Main St Americana appeal while slowly embracing the influence of the Latino labor force.

This is a place of seismic, often contentious, development. Arrivals from the coastal cities have resulted in unchecked sprawl. What were once actual ranches and vineyards are now nostalgically named developments: a big-box shopping complex named Indian Ranch, a tidy row of McMansions named Vineyard Estates. More green lawns appear as the irrigation systems drain dry. Water rights is *the* issue on everyone's minds.

Lodi

Although Lodi was once the 'Watermelon capital of the world,' today, full-bodied wine rules this patch of the valley. Breezes from the Sacramento River Delta soothe the area's hot vineyards, where some of the world's oldest Zinfandel vines grow. Lodi's diverse soil is sometimes rocky, sometimes fine sandy loam, giving its grapes a range of distinctive characteristics that allow for experimentation with some less common varietals.

Lodi also hosts a slew of festivals dedicated to their famous export, including the **Wine & Chocolate Weekend** in February and **ZinFest** in May.

◉ Sights

Jessie's Grove at Olde Ice House Cellars WINERY
(📋 209-368-0880; www.jessiesgrovewinery.com; 27 E Locust St; tasting $5; ⊘ noon-5pm Fri & Sat, from 1pm Sun; P) Several wineries have opened tasting rooms within a few blocks of one another downtown, including Jessie's Grove, which pours Zinfandel, Chardonnay, Merlot and more inside a historical ice house by the railroad tracks, north of the Lodi Arch.

Micke Grove Regional Park & Zoo ZOO
(📋 209-331-2010; www.mgzoo.com; 11793 N Micke Grove Rd; adult/child $5/3, parking $5; ⊘ 10am-

5pm; 🚼) For the seriously underage, Lodi's Micke Grove Regional Park and Zoo is a good stop, with a water play area, hissing cockroaches and some barking sea lions. There are also kiddie rides in a section called Fun Town. The park also houses an exceptional **Japanese Garden** (www.sjparks.com; 11793 N Micke Grove Rd; ⊙9am-2pm Mon-Thu, to 1pm Fri-Sun) FREE.

🛏 Sleeping & Eating

Wine & Roses
HOTEL $$
(☑209-334-6988; http://winerose.com; 2505 W Turner Rd; r $179-240, ste from $335; P🐾❄ @🛜🐾) Surrounded by a vast rose garden, this is the most luxurious offering to spring up amid Lodi's vineyards. Tasteful and romantic, the rooms have slate bathrooms, high-quality toiletries and lots of square footage. There's an acclaimed restaurant (p602) and spa too.

Dancing Fox Winery & Bakery
AMERICAN, BAKERY $
(☑209-366-2634; www.dancingfoxwinery.com; 203 S School St; mains from $11; ⊙7:30am-9pm Tue-Sat, 9am-3pm Sun) Everything here celebrates grapes – from the Lewis Family Estate's own wines to the bread cultures created from the vineyard's petite sirah grapes. The best selections from the overly broad menu involve the wood-burning oven.

Farm Cafe
AMERICAN $
(☑206-368-7384; www.michaeldavidwinery.com; 4580 W Hwy 12; mains $7-14; ⊙7:30am-3pm; 🚼) On the outskirts of town at Michael David Winery, this farmstand cafe slings big breakfast plates of fluffy omelets with country potatoes, cinnamon pancakes and homemade breads with strawberry jam.

Towne House Restaurant
CALIFORNIAN $$$
(☑209-371-6160; www.loditownehouse.com; 2505 W Turner Rd; mains $20-55; ⊙7-10:30am, 11am-2pm & from 5pm Mon-Fri, 8am-2pm & from 5pm Sat & Sun) The bright, crisply designed on-site restaurant of Wine & Roses draws on locally sourced ingredients in an elegant preparation. There's often live jazz in the evening in the adjoining lounge, which pours cocktails and a selection of local wines.

🍷 Drinking & Nightlife

Blend Ultra Lounge
COCKTAIL BAR
(www.blendlodi.com; 115 S School St, Suite 13; ⊙5-9pm Wed, to 2am Thu-Sat, 1-6pm Sun) Patrons sip colorful cocktails while bathed in blue neon at this (almost) swanky lounge. When the Giants are on, it takes on the vibe of a (almost) swanky sports bar. It also serves tapas and good burgers (mains $11 to $22).

🛍 Shopping

Cheese Central
FOOD
(www.cheesecentrallodi.com; 11 N School St; ⊙10am-6pm Mon-Sat, 1- 5pm Sun) Ask Cindy the cheesemonger for thoughtful pairings with Lodi wines. If you want to make a weekend out of Lodi's wine region, try one of the cooking classes.

Stockton

Stockton has had its share of ups and downs – including recent challenges with the housing crisis and large civic debt – but the downtown and waterfront redevelopment is one of the valley's more promising grassroots efforts. In the summer, when festivals take over the Weber Point Events Center (p603), Stockton makes for a fun detour.

The city has an interesting past that is just under the surface of its checkered

---

WATER WARS

Through the elaborate politics and machinery of water management, this once-arid region ranks among the most agriculturally productive places in the world, though the profits often go to agribusiness shareholders, not the increasingly disenfranchised family farmer. The region's water issue became dire in 2015, when a severe drought parched the region, bringing usage restrictions and heated debate. In 2016, things settled down when an extremely rainy winter brought deep snow to the Sierra Nevada and refilled the reservoirs. But the increasingly noticeable impact of climate change and population growth aren't going away, and water will continue to be a divisive issue in these communities. Plenty of roadside signs along Hwy 99 emblazoned with bold-font political slogans about the water crisis will keep the issue on travelers' minds as well.

TOP LODI WINERIES

Lodi's underrated wineries make an fun escape from the Bay Area, and the quality of grapes will delight true oenophiles. This is the source of many master blenders' secret weapons.

The region is easily accessed from I-5 or Hwy 99 and just as easy to navigate, as roads are well marked. For maps, check the **Lodi Wine & Visitor Center** (☑209-367-4727; www.lodiwine.com; 2545 W Turner Rd; ☻10am-5pm).

Jessie's Grove (www.jessiesgrovewinery.com; 1973 W Turner Rd; ☻noon-5pm) With its summer concert series and very long history, this is an anchor of Lodi wine producers. There's a new **tasting room** (p601) downtown on E Locust St.

Harney Lane (www.harneylane.com; 9010 E Harney Lane; tasting $5; ☻11am-5pm Thu-Mon) A sweet family outfit that's been around Lodi forever; their Tempranillo is an overachiever. Tasting fee refunded with purchase.

d'Art (www.dartwines.com; 13299 N Curry Ave; tasting $5; ☻noon-5pm Thu-Mon) Helen and Dave Dart's bold Cabernet Sauvignon is as fun and inviting as the tasting room. Tasting fee refunded with purchase.

LangeTwins (www.langetwins.com; 1525 East Jahant Rd, Acampo; tasting $5-10; ☻11am-4pm Thu-Sun) The Viognier and reserve blends are worth the 7-mile drive north of town to this state-of-the-art steel-and-redwood winery.

Riaza Wines (www.riazawines.com; 20 W Elm St; ☻1-6pm Fri & Sat, to 5pm Sun) The downtown tasting room pours Spanish varietals that only recently were discovered to grow like mad in the Lodi sun.

Jeremy Wine Co (www.jeremywineco.com; 6 W Pine St; ☻1-5pm Wed-Sun) Friendly folk in this brass- and wood-fitted tasting room downtown pour a bright fruit-forward Sangiovese.

Michael David (☑209-368-7384; www.michaeldavidwinery.com; 4580 W Hwy 12; tasting $5-10; ☻10am-5pm; ℗) These brothers have built an enthusiastic following with their oaky, fruity wines. Their renowned Zinfandel, '7 Deadly Zins,' is a standout. The cafe and farmstand make this tasting room a perfect lunch stop. Tasting fee refunded with purchase; last entry is at 4:30pm.

facades. It is a major inland port and was once the main supply hub for gold rushers. During WWII it became a major center of American shipbuilding, and remains home to a few maritime transportation facilities.

A block east of Weber Point, the **Department of Tourism** (☑209-938-1555; www.visitstockton.org; 125 Bridge Pl; ☻9am-5pm Mon-Fri) has complete information about the goings-on in town.

◉ Sights & Activities

★ Wat Dhammararam
Buddhist Temple　　BUDDHIST TEMPLE
(☑209-943-2883; www.watdhammararam buddhist.org; 3732 Carpenter Rd) **FREE** With elaborate grounds, brightly painted statues and a 50ft reclining Buddha, this is a vibrant home to the area's Cambodian population. The celebration of the Cambodian New Year

in mid-April draws thousands of people who celebrate with music, dance and an amazing pot-luck lunch.

Weber Point Events Center　　LANDMARK
(www.stocktongov.com; 221 N Center St) Downtown on the McLeod Lake waterfront, the modern white edifice standing in the middle of a grassy park looking rather like a pile of sailboats is the Weber Point Events Center and marks the center of the action. This is also the site of the huge April San Joaquin Asparagus Festival (p604), a series of open-air concerts, and fountains where squealing kids cool off.

Banner Island Ballpark　　STADIUM
(☑209-644-1900; www.stocktonports.com; 404 W Fremont St) The beautiful Banner Island Ballpark is where the minor-league Stockton Ports play ball April to September.

DON'T MISS

SAN JOAQUIN ASPARAGUS FESTIVAL

Of all the Central Valley food celebrations, perhaps none pay such creative respect to the main ingredient as the **San Joaquin Asparagus Festival** (www.asparagusfest.com; N Center St, btwn Oak St & W Weber Av; adult/child $13/free; ☺Apr), which brings together more than 500 vendors to serve these green stalks – more than 10 tons of them! – every way imaginable. It sprouts along the waterfront at the end of April.

Haggin Museum   MUSEUM
(www.hagginmuseum.org; 1201 N Pershing Ave; adult/child $8/5; ☺1:30-5pm Wed-Fri, noon-5pm Sat & Sun) This city gem houses a 26ft boat by Stockton's own Stephens Bros company, and an excellent collection of American landscape and 'Golden Age' paintings.

Opportunity Cruises   CRUISE
(www.opportunitycruises.com; Stockton Marina, 445 W Weber Ave; cruises with/without meal $55/37) Cruises around the Sacramento Delta in open-sided river boats depart from the Marina.

🛏 Sleeping & Eating

University Plaza Waterfront Hotel   HOTEL $$
(☑209-944-1140; www.universityplazawaterfronthotel.com; 110 W Fremont St; r from $125; 🛜) If you're spending the night here, the best option is University Plaza Waterfront Hotel, where business travelers mingle with University of the Pacific students and the mayor, who all live in the lofts on the upper floors. The very modern building overlooking the harbor and historic park, unlike the highway chains, is walkable from other locations in the city center.

**Open-Air Asian and
Farmers Market**   MARKET $
(200 E Washington St; ☺5:30-11am Sat) You can find fresh fish and a huge variety of Asian vegetables each Saturday, under the elevated freeway.

Papa Urb's Grill   FILIPINO $
(☑209-227-8144; www.papaurbsgrill.com; 331 E Weber Ave; mains $5-10; ☺10am-7:30pm Mon-Fri, from 11am Sat, 11am-4pm Sun) Filipino flavors drive the menu of fusion fast food at this bright cafe: there's adobo and *longanisa* (Filipino pork sausage) in many of the typically Mexican presentations. If you want to expand your horizons, go for the *sisig* fries, a savory mess of pork, cheese and tangy cilantro dipping sauce.

Smitty's Wings & Things   CHICKEN $
(☑209-227-7479; 946 Acacia St; mains $9-15; ☺noon-7pm Tue-Thu, to 8pm Fri & Sat) This checker-tiled neighborhood wing joint is run by a former NFL player and his wife, who turn out perfectly crispy wings (which were recently featured on the Food Network) and pizzas. They have specials every day and a selection of cold beer on tap. The sauces for the wings are all amazing, but we love the tingling spice of the 'damn hot' and garlic chili.

On Lok Sam   CANTONESE $$
(www.newonlocksam.com; 333 S Sutter St; mains $10-25; ☺11am-9pm) Venture south of the Crosstown Freeway (Hwy 4) to (New) On Lok Sam, established in 1895 in the center of Stockton's lively Chinese settlement. The garlic chicken and spicy, deep-fried green beans are delicious.

🍷 Drinking & Nightlife

Abbey Trappist Pub   CRAFT BEER
(www.abbeystockton.com; 2353 Pacific Ave. Suite B; ☺4-10pm Tue-Wed, to 11:30pm Thu, to 1am Fri, 11am-1am Sat) The beer menu is deep at this excellent local favorite, which also boasts a raucous trivia night and quality European pub food, such as the sausage plate, Scotch eggs and frog legs with spicy remoulade.

AVE on the Mile   BAR
(www.aveonthemile.com; 2333 Pacific Ave.; ☺3:30pm-midnight Tue-Thu, to 1am Fri, 4:30pm-1am Sat, 10am-2pm Sun) Exposed brick and a glittering wall of bottles make this the most elegant option on the block. It has a full menu of upscale pub food and Sunday brunch comes with bottomless mimosas.

ⓘ Getting There & Away

By train, boat or car, Stockton is easy to reach; it sits between I-5 and Hwy 99. You can also take Amtrak's San Joaquin line or the regional **Altamont Commuter Express** (☑800-411-7245; www.acerail.com; 949 East Channel St; one-way tickets $6-$14.50) from the **Robert J Cabral Station** (☑800-872-7245; 949 East Channel St), or float from the downtown marina to the Sacramento–San Joaquin River Delta.

Modesto

Cruising was banned in Modesto in 1993, but the town still touts itself as the 'cruising capital of the world.' The pastime's notoriety stems mostly from homegrown George Lucas' 1973 film *American Graffiti*. You'll still see hot rods and flashy wheels around town, but they no longer clog thoroughfares on Friday nights.

This is a good spot for getting off the dusty highway. Old oaks arch over the city's streets and you can eat well and stretch your legs in the compact downtown. The **Ernest & Julio Gallo Winery**, makers of America's best-selling jug wines, is one of the town's biggest businesses.

Classic car shows and rock and roll fill the streets every June for **Graffiti Summer** (www.visitmodesto.com; ☺Jun). Amid all the 1950s charm, the sparkling Gallo Center for the Arts (p605) brings huge acts to the valley. For details, check the **Modesto Convention & Visitors Bureau** (☑888-640-8467; www.visitmodesto.com; 1150 9th St; ☺8am-5pm Mon-Fri).

✖ Eating & Drinking

Thailand Restaurant   THAI **$**
(☑209-544-0505; 950 10th St, Suite 17; mains $9-15; ☺10:30am-9pm Mon-Fri, from 11am Sat; ✐)
Go immediately for the spicy noodles and green papaya salad at this friendly, spotless Thai restaurant.

Brighter Side   SANDWICHES **$**
(www.brighter-side.com; 1125 K St, cnr 13th & K Sts; sandwiches $5-6; ☺11am-3:30pm Mon-Fri; ✐)
An earthy little sandwich shop housed in a wood-shingled, former gas station, serves up sandwiches such as the Larry (Polish sausage, mushrooms, green onions on rye) or the veggie Christine on the sunny patio.

A&W Drive-In   AMERICAN **$**
(www.awrestaurants.com; 1404 G St, cnr 14th & G Sts; cheeseburger $3, float $4; ☺10am-9pm, to 8pm Oct-Mar) A vintage burger stand (part of a chain founded in nearby Lodi), where roller-skating carhops and classic cars on display move a lot of root beer floats. George Lucas supposedly cruised here as a youth.

Commonwealth   AMERICAN **$$**
(☑209-248-7451; www.commonwealthmodesto.com; 1022 11th St; mains $11-30; ☺11am-10pm Mon-Wed, to midnight Thu-Fri, 9am-midnight Sat, 9am-9pm Sun) Elegant without being stuffy, there's a great selection of local wine and indulgent sandwiches at this downtown spot (try the M80, which joins jalapeño fried chicken and thick bacon). In the morning, it serves picture-perfect waffles.

Tiki Cocktail Lounge   GAY & LESBIAN
(☑209-577-9969; 932 McHenry Ave; ☺5pm-2am)
Campy decor, friendly bartenders and an indoor fire pit give this gay hangout lots of cozy atmosphere.

☆ Entertainment

Gallo Center for the Arts   PERFORMING ARTS
(☑209-338-2100; www.galloarts.org; 1000 I St; ☺10am-6pm Mon-Fri, from noon Sat) This huge, state-of-the-art performing arts complex in downtown Modesto brings great musical, dance and theater acts to town.

State Theatre   THEATER
(www.thestate.org; 1307 J St) This historic theater has stood here since 1934 and continues to put on films and live music.

Merced

You can jog over to Yosemite from many of the small towns in this part of the valley, but this is a convenient staging area, right on Hwy 140. The machine of progress has not been kind to Merced, as it suffers more than its share of strip malls. Still, you'll find tree-lined streets, historic Victorian homes and a magnificent 1875 courthouse at the city's core. The downtown business district is a work in progress, with 1930s movie theaters, antique stores and a few casual eateries undergoing constant renovation.

Merced is right in the midst of a population makeover, thanks to the newest University of California campus, opened in 2005. UC Merced's first freshman class numbered just 1000 students, but the school continues to grow with a diverse student body and has begun to dramatically shape the city.

At the **Castle Air Museum** (☑209-723-2178; www.castleairmuseum.org; 5050 Santa Fe Dr, Atwater; adult/child $15/10; ☺10am-4pm), aerospace buffs will enjoy strolling down the rows of vintage military aircraft, ranging from pre-WWII to the present, on former Air Force base grounds. Military mechanics volunteer their time restoring these planes and are often on-site to answer questions.

The museum recently acquired a gigantic Douglas RA-3 Skywarrior, a reconnaissance bomber with a wingspan of 72ft. It is the largest, heaviest jet to ever land on an aircraft carrier. More than 1200 wing bolts had to be unscrewed just to move it to the museum.

🛌 Sleeping

HI Merced Home Hostel
HOSTEL $

(📞 209-725-0407; www.hiusa.org; dm $20-23; ⊙ reception 5:30-10pm) A night in this six-bed homestay in the northeast part of town feels like staying with your long-lost Aunt Jan and Uncle Larry, the kind of folks happy to lend advice about Yosemite at the kitchen table. Beds fill quickly and must be reserved in advance (call between 5:30pm and 10pm). They can shuttle you to/from the bus and train stations.

Hooper House Bear Creek Inn
B&B $$

(📞 209-723-3991; www.hooperhouse.com; 575 W North Bear Creek Dr; r $139-169; ❄ 🛜) In a grand old Colonial-style mansion, Hooper House Bear Creek Inn is a leisurely retreat. Rooms are large and beautifully furnished with hardwood furniture, soft beds and tiled bathrooms. A full breakfast is included, which you can have sent to your room.

🍴 Eating & Drinking

Little Oven Pizza
PIZZA $

(www.littleovenmerced.com; 433 W Main St; slices $3-4; ⊙11:30am-9pm Tue-Thu, to 11pm Fri, 4-11pm Sat; 🛜) Turning out picture-perfect, New York–style thin crust, this tidy downtown spot offers daily specials and makes a quick, cheap option. The Pesto Bango – a pesto, garlic and mushroom combination – is delicious. Like everything else on the menu, the ingredients are sourced from the Central Valley.

New Thai Cuisine
THAI $

(📞 209-726-1048; 909 W 16th St; mains $10-19; ⊙11am-8pm) Hardly the fanciest digs in town – just four bare walls and a few tables – but this downtown Thai restaurant makes an excellent combination pho soup, sweet-and-savory honey sesame wings and a nice duck curry.

Branding Iron
STEAK $$

(www.thebrandingiron-merced.com; 640 W 16th St; mains lunch $9-11, dinner $10-27; ⊙11:30am-2pm Mon-Fri, 5-10pm Sun-Thu, to 9:30pm Fri & Sat) The Branding Iron roadhouse, a favorite of ranchers in the area, has been spruced up

a bit for the tour buses, but locals still dig the hearty steak platters and Western atmosphere. Presiding over the dining room is 'Old Blue,' a massive stuffed bull's head from a local dairy farm.

17th Street Public House
BAR

(📞 209-354-4449; www.17thstpub.com; 315 W Main St; noon-10pm Sun-Wed, to midnight Thu-Fri) This haven for serious beer drinkers has an excellent and often-updated rotation of taps and a huge selection of bottles.

ℹ️ Getting There & Away

YARTS (Yosemite Area Regional Transportation System; 📞 209-388-9589; www.yarts.com) buses depart three (winter) to five (summer) times daily for Yosemite Valley from several Merced locations, including the **Merced Transpo Center** (www.mercedthebus.com; cnr 16th & N Sts) and the **Amtrak station** (www.amtrak.com; 324 W 24th St, cnr 24th & K Sts). The trip takes about 2½ hours and stops include Mariposa, Midpines and the Yosemite Bug Lodge & Hostel. Round-trip adult/child costs $26/20 and includes park entry (quite a bargain!). There's limited space for bicycles, so show up early if you have one.

Greyhound (710 W 16th St) also operates from the Transpo Center (Los Angeles $20, 6½ hours, four times daily).

Fresno

Smack in the arid center of the state, Fresno is the biggest city in the Central Valley. It's hardly scenic, but it is beautifully situated, just an hour's drive from four national parks (Yosemite, Sierra, Kings Canyon and Sequoia), making it the ideal last stop for expeditions.

In recent years, Fresno's agriculture-based economy has suffered from catastrophic droughts and plummeting food prices. A local farm movement in the area seeks to revolutionize food production through organic, sustainable practices and fair wages. Fresno's proximity to these progressive farms has fostered a food renaissance. The produce and meat is the freshest you'll find anywhere. Fresno? Oh, Fresyes.

Like many valley towns, Fresno is home to diverse Hmong, Mexican, Chinese and Basque communities, which arrived in successive waves. The longstanding Armenian community is famously represented by author and playwright William Saroyan, who was born, lived and died in this city he loved.

◉ Sights & Activities

One of the most bustling parts of town is the Tower District, north of downtown, an oasis of gay-friendly bars, book and record stores, music clubs and a handful of stylish restaurants. Many of the historic buildings are along the Santa Fe railroad tracks and downtown, including the 1894 **Fresno Water Tower** and the 1928 **Pantages (Warnors) Theatre**. The crowds gather at the sprawling **Convention Center** and **Chukchansi Park**, home of Fresno's Triple-A baseball team, the Grizzlies.

Downtown lies between Divisadero St, Hwy 41 and Hwy 99. Two miles north, the Tower District sits around the corner of E Olive and N Fulton Aves.

Forestiere Underground Gardens   GARDENS
(☑ 559-271-0734;   www.undergroundgardens. info; 5021 W Shaw Ave; adult/child $17/8; ☺ tours 10am-4pm hourly Wed-Sun May-Sep, reduced hours Oct-Apr) If you see only one thing in Fresno, make it this intriguing historic landmark, two blocks east of Hwy 99. The gardens were built by Sicilian immigrant Baldassare Forestiere, who dug out some 70 acres beneath the hardpan soil to plant citrus trees, starting in 1906. This utterly fantastical accomplishment took 40 years to complete.

Roeding Park   PARK
(www.fresno.gov; 890 W Belmont Ave; per vehicle $5; ☺ 6am-10pm Apr-Oct, to 7pm Nov-Mar) Just east of Hwy 99, this large and shady park is home to the small **Fresno Chaffee Zoo** (☑ 559-498-5910; www.fresnochaffeezoo.org; 894 W Belmont Ave; adult/child $10/5.50; ☺ 9am-6pm; 🖐). Adjacent to it are **Storyland** (☑ 559-264-2235; www.storylandplayland.com; 890 W Belmont Ave; adult/child $5/3.50; ☺ 10am-4pm Sat & Sun; 🖐), a kitschy children's fairy-tale world dating from 1962, and the freshly remodeled **Playland** (www.storylandplayland.com; 890 W Belmont Ave; adult/child $5/3.50; ☺ 10am-4pm Wed-Sun; 🖐), which has kiddie rides and games.

Fresno Art Museum   MUSEUM
(☑ 559 441-4221;   www.fresnoartmuseum.org; 2233 N 1st St; adult/child $10/5; ☺ 11am-5pm Thu-Sun; 🖐) This museum has rotating exhibits of contemporary art – including work by local artists – that are among the most intriguing in the valley.

Woodward Park   PARK
(www.fresno.gov; 7775 Friant Rd; per vehicle $5; ☺ 6am-10pm Apr-Oct, to 7pm Nov-Mar) The city's largest park has 300 acres of barbecue facilities, lakes and ponds, a **Japanese garden** (adult/child $5/1), and a huge amphitheater for Shakespeare and other performances. A 6-mile network of bike trails connects to the **Lewis S Eaton Trail**, which runs 22 miles from the northeast corner along Friant Rd to Friant Dam.

🛏 Sleeping & Eating

Fresno has room to grow when it comes to world-class accommodations, but those using it as a launch pad for visiting Sequoia and Kings Canyon National Parks have plenty of options in the cluster of chains near the airport or a couple of high-rise offerings downtown.

For food, the best stuff is scattered around town – making this, most definitely, a driving town. Trendy eateries and breweries are in the Tower District and hidden among abandoned storefronts downtown. Food trucks circle up every Thursday accompanied by live music in front of Fresno Brewing Company. For fantastic raw ingredients, Fresno's excellent farmers markets are abundant all year round.

Piccadilly Inn Shaw   HOTEL $$
(☑ 559-348-5520; www.picadillyinn.com; 2305 W Shaw Ave; r $89-159; ❄ @ 🛜 ≋) This is Fresno's nicest option, with a lovely pool, big rooms and tons of amenities. Ask for a room with a fireplace to cuddle by in winter.

Rocket Dog Gourmet Brats & Brew   BREW PUB $
(☑ 559-283-8096; www.rocketdogbratsandbrew. com; 88 E Shaw Ave; hot dogs $8; ☺ 11am-9pm Sun-Thu, to 10pm Fri) Sure, something like 'Hansel's Heaven' – a bratwurst served on a pretzel roll and covered in mac 'n' cheese – isn't health food, but this excellent, ultra-efficient brewpub is the perfect highway pit stop if you're on the way in or out of Yosemite and not counting calories. It has a long list of excellent, elaborate hot dogs and local beer on tap.

Sam's Italian Deli & Market   DELI $
(www.samsitaliandeli.com; 2415 N 1st St; mains $5-9; ☺ 9am-6pm Mon-Sat) This Italian market and deli is the real deal, stacking up the 'New Yorker' pastrami and some mean prosciutto and mozzarella.

Fresno Farmers Market   MARKET $
(☑ 559-222-0182;   www.vineyardfarmersmarket. com; ☺ 3-6pm Wed, 7am-noon Sat) Local booths

serve the freshest seasonal food from surrounding farms.

CartHop
FAST FOOD $

(http://carthopfresno.com; Fulton Mall; ⊙10am-2pm Thu) Every Thursday, a fleet of independent food trucks from around the valley park on the Fulton Mall, serving grab-and-go lunch options from every corner of the globe.

☆ Entertainment

Tower Theatre for the Performing Arts
PERFORMING ARTS

(www.towertheatrefresno.com; 815 E Olive Ave) In the center of Fresno's hippest neighborhood, it's hard to miss the neon deco palace that opens its stage to touring rock and jazz acts and seasonal cultural events.

ℹ Information

Fresno/Clovis Convention & Visitors Bureau
(☑800-788-0836, 559-981-5500; www.playfresno.org; 1550 E Shaw Ave, Suite 101; ⊙8am-5pm Mon-Fri) Visitor information in a nondescript office complex. Brochures are also stocked in the Water Tower and airport. Its website is a good place to look for comprehensive listings about local farmers markets and events.

ℹ Getting There & Around

Amtrak (Santa Fe station; ☑559-486-7651; 2650 Tulare St; ⊙5:30am-9:45pm) The most scenic way to travel these parts, the San Joaquin service stops in a white Mission

---

DOWN ON THE FARM

There's no better way to get a taste of this agricultural region than on its farms. Many offer tours and seasonal opportunities to pick your own. Central Valley visitor's bureaus can point you to popular stops. Here are a few family farms paving the way with progressive practices.

➜ **Page River Bottom Farms** (☑559-638-3124; 17780 E Vino Ave, Reedley; ⊙8am-5pm Mon-Sat)

➜ **Organic Pastures** (www.organicpastures.com; 7221 S Jameson Ave; ⊙8am-5pm Mon-Fri)

➜ **T&D Willey Farm** (☑559-673-9058; www.tdwilleyfarms.com; 13886 Road 20, Madera)

---

building smack in downtown Fresno on its way to other tourist destinations, including Yosemite ($40, four hours, twice daily) and San Francisco ($55, four hours).

Fresno Area Express (FAX; ☑559-621-7433; www.fresno.gov; one-way $1.25) The local service that has daily buses to the Tower District (bus 22 or 28) and Forestiere Underground Gardens (bus 20) from the downtown transit center at Van Ness Ave and Fresno St.

Fresno Yosemite International Airport (FAT; www.flyfresno.com; 5175 E Clinton Way) In the Central Valley.

Greyhound (☑559-268-1829; 1033 H St) Stops downtown near the Chukchansi ballpark. Multiple regular/express rides daily to Los Angeles ($24, four hours) and San Francisco ($20, five hours).

Visalia

Its agricultural prosperity and well-maintained downtown make Visalia one of the valley's convenient stops en route to Sequoia and Kings Canyon National Parks or the Sierra Peaks. Bypassed a century ago by the railroad, the city is 5 miles east of Hwy 99, along Hwy 198. Its downtown has old-town charm and makes for a nice stroll.

The original Victorian and Arts-and-Crafts–style homes in Visalia are architectural gems worth viewing on foot. Maps for many self-guided tours are available via the website of the **Visalia Convention & Visitor's Bureau** (☑559-334-0141; www.visitvisalia.org; 303 E Acequia Ave; ⊙8am-5pm Mon-Fri).

The main draw in the area is the **Kaweah Oak Preserve** (www.sequoiariverlands.org; 29979 Rd 182, Exeter; donation adult/child $3/1; ⊙8am-sunset), about 7 miles east of town. With 324 acres of majestic oak trees, it is a gorgeous setting for easy hikes. From Hwy 198, turn north onto Rd 182; the park is about a half mile along on your left.

🛏 Sleeping & Eating

Lamp Liter Motel
MOTEL $

(☑559-732-4511; www.lampliter.net; 3300 W Mineral King Ave; r $75-125; ❄@🛜🐕) It could be a run-of-the-mill two-story courtyard motel, but this family-owned establishment surprises with its spotlessly clean, if dated, rooms and country cottages facing an outdoor pool. The Sequoia Shuttle stops here.

Spalding House B&B $
(☑ 559-739-7877; www.thespaldinghouse.com;
631 N Encina St; s/d $85/95; ✳ 🌐) Built by a
lumber baron, this atmospheric 1901 Colonial Revival–style home offers three cozy
guest suites with private sitting areas and
gorgeous details, such as mosaic-tiled bathrooms, a stained-glass ceiling or a sleigh bed.

Char-Cu-Te-Rie CAFE $
(☑ 559-733-7902; www.char-cu-te-rie.com; 211 W
Main St; mains $6-9; ☺ 8am-3pm) Truffled eggs
on brioche French toast, sourdough sandwiches spread with goat cheese and sweet
figs, maple-bacon popcorn, date and Nutella
ice-cream shakes and artisan coffee are just
a few of the treats at this downtown storefront.

**Visalia Farmers Market –
Downtown** MARKET $
(www.visaliafarmersmarket.com; cnr E Main & N
Church Sts; ☺ 5-8pm Thu mid-Mar–Sep; 🚸) Fresh
fruits and veggies sold downtown.

Brewbakers Brewing Company AMERICAN $
(☑ 559-627-2739; www.brewbakersbrewingco.com;
219 E Main St; mains $8-18; ☺ 11:30am-10pm; 🌐)
Always jam-packed, Brewbakers beckons
thirsty hikers with house-made sodas and
craft beers. A huge menu of burgers, pizzas,
pastas and salads promises more than it delivers, but it's a great place to refuel after a
few days in the mountains.

☆ Entertainment

Visalia Fox Theatre CINEMA, LIVE MUSIC
(☑ 559-625-1369; www.foxvisalia.org; 300 W Main
St) A 1930s 'talkie' movie palace, the Fox has
a stunning East Indian temple–themed interior and occasionally hosts film screenings,
live music concerts, stand-up comedy and
special events.

Cellar Door LIVE MUSIC
(☑ 559-636-9463; www.cellardoor101.com; 101 W
Main St; ☺ from 6pm Tue, Thu-Sat) Serving pizza,
wine and live music in a subterranean club
on Main St. The events are all over the place
– a Metallica cover band one night, salsa
dancing the next – but there's always something going on.

🔒 Shopping

Big 5 Sporting Goods SPORTS & OUTDOORS
(☑ 559-625-5934; www.big5sportinggoods.
com; 1430 S Mooney Blvd; ☺ 10am-9pm Mon-Fri,
9am-9pm Sat, 9:30am-8pm Sun) Stock up on

camping, fishing and outdoor-sports equipment here, less than a mile south of Hwy 198.

ℹ Getting There & Around

Visalia's transit options, including direct access
to **Sequoia National Park** (p486), all funnel
through the **Visalia Transit Center** (www.
ci.visalia.ca.us; 425 E Oak Ave). **Amtrak** (☑ 800-
872-7245; www.amtrak.com) shuttles run
between the Transit Center and Hanford station
a half hour away by reservation only (use local
buses as an alternative). From Hanford, you can
connect to all other Amtrak routes in the state,
including the *San Joaquin*, which travels north to
Sacramento ($32, two direct daily) or south to
Bakersfield ($22.50, 1½ hours, six
daily).

The convenient, bike-rack equipped **Sequoia
Shuttle** (☑ 877-287-4453; www.sequoiashuttle.
com; round-trip incl park entry fee $15; ☺ late
May-late Sep) picks up from major hotels and
takes two hours to reach the **Giant Forest
Museum** (p491) in Sequoia National Park. The
Visalia Towne Trolley (425 East Oak Ave; ticket
25¢; ☺ 7:30am-5:30pm Mon-Wed, to 11pm
Thu-Fri, 9:30am-11pm Sat) hits most downtown
sights over two circuits.

Bakersfield

Nearing Bakersfield, the landscape has evidence of California's *other* gold rush: rusting rigs alongside the route burrow into
Southern California's vast oil fields. Black
gold was discovered here in the late 1800s,
and Kern County, the southernmost along
Hwy 99, still pumps more than some OPEC
countries.

This is the setting of Upton Sinclair's *Oil!*,
which was adapted into the 2007 Academy
Award–winning film, *There Will Be Blood*.
In the 1930s the oil attracted a stream of
'Okies' – farmers who migrated out of the
Great Plains – to work the derricks. The
children of these tough-as-nails roughnecks
put the 'western' in country and western by
creating the 'Bakersfield Sound' in the mid-
1950s, with heroes Buck Owens and Merle
Haggard waving a defiant middle finger at
the silky Nashville establishment.

Downtown Bakersfield is making moves
to fancy-up, evident in the upbeat mix of restored buildings and new restaurants, theaters and clubs.

◉ Sights

The Kern River flows along Bakersfield's
northern edge, separating it from its

blue-collar neighbor, Oildale, and a host of oil fields. Truxtun and Chester Aves are the main downtown thoroughfares. Though currently suffering from some neglect, Old Town Kern, located east of downtown around Baker and Sumner Sts, still has character underneath the decay. **Bakersfield Historic Preservation Commission** (which you can find with a quick search of www.bakersfieldcity.us) has downloadable maps of walking tours covering Old Town Kern and Bakersfield's historic downtown.

Cesar E Chavez National Monument
HISTORIC SITE

(☑ 661-823-6134; www.chavezfoundation.org; 29700 Woodford-Tehachapi Rd, Keene; $3; ☺10am-4pm) This newly designated national monument, Nuestra Señora Reina de la Paz, is the national headquarters of the United Farmworkers of America and was the home of civil rights leader César Chávez from 1971 until his death in 1993. On view are exhibits on Chávez's work, his office and grave. Keene is 27 miles southeast of Bakersfield down Hwy 58.

Chávez was born near Yuma, AZ, in 1927, and was 11 when his family lost their farm and became migrant farm workers in California. At 14, he left school to labor in the fields. Eventually, he became a champion of nonviolent social change, negotiating for better wages and access to water and bathrooms in the fields. His work resulted in numerous precedents, including the first union contracts requiring safe use of pesticides and the abolition of short-handled tools that had crippled generations of farm workers.

Kern County Museum
MUSEUM

(www.kcmuseum.org; 3801 Chester Ave; adult $10, child $7-9; ☺10am-5pm Tue-Sat, from noon Sun; P❋) ⏀ This museum brings local history to life with a pioneer village of more than 50 restored and replicated buildings (including Merle Haggard's childhood home) and courtyard with beautifully restored vintage neon signs. The main structure has a large (and fairly disturbing) display of taxidermy wildlife and pristine memorabilia from Bakersfield's musical heyday.

Five & Dime Antique Mall
LANDMARK

(☑ 661-321-0061; Woolworth Bldg, 1400 19th St; ☺10am-5pm Mon-Sat, from noon Sun) Three stories hold vintage wares that date back to at least the same era as the Woolworth building they're housed in. Try to go when the diner (p610) is open.

🛌 Sleeping & Eating

Chain motels sprout like weeds off the highways near Bakersfield. Old-school budget motels, starting from about $50, line Union Ave south heading south from Hwy 178, but can be a little seedy.

★Padre Hotel
BOUTIQUE HOTEL $$

(☑ 661-427-4900; www.thepadrehotel.com; 1702 18th St; r $119-229, ste from $459) A stylish update revived this exceptional historic hotel, adding an upscale restaurant and two bars that instantly became *the* places for cocktails in Bakersfield. The service is excellent and the rooms have lavish details: thick mattresses, plush sheets and designer furniture. The two themed suites – the 'Oil Baron' and 'Farmer's Daughter' – have playful decor and showers for two.

Cafe Smitten
CAFE $

(www.cafesmitten.com; 909 18th St; mains $9-11; ☺6:30am-7pm Mon-Thu, to 9pm Fri, 8:30am-9pm Sat) This bright cafe in the heart of downtown has a great vibe, serving lighter fare, such as a savory 'avocado smash' sandwich, and buttery pastries. It has excellent coffee drinks and a sunny patio that attracts a fun crowd for after-work drinks.

Luigi's
ITALIAN $

(www.shopluigis.com; 725 E 19th St; mains $7.75-11.95; ☺11am-2:30pm Tue-Sat; ✔) Lined with black-and-white photos of sporting legends, this amazing lunch spot has been around for over 100 years. The stuffed chicken melts in your mouth and the excellent bakery turns out soft, buttery rolls and an exceedingly rich Butterfinger Pie. The adjacent bar and deli stay open until 4pm.

Dewar's Candy Shop
ICE CREAM $

(☑ 661-322-0933; 1120 Eye St; sundaes from $4.50; ☺10am-9pm Mon-Sun; ❋) Perched on the pink stools at the counter, families dig into homemade ice cream with ingredients sourced from surrounding farms since 1930. Dreamy flavors like lemon flake and cotton candy change seasonally.

Woolworth Diner
DINER $

(☑ 661-321-0061; Five & Dime Antique Mall, 1400 19th St; burgers $5.95; ☺11am-4pm Mon-Sat, noon-4pm Sun) The soda jerks flip fantastic cheeseburgers and pour thick shakes at the store's original soda counter, buffed to its former glory.

WORTH A TRIP: WEEDPATCH CAMP

In the Depression era, more than a million poor, white laborers from the Dust Bowl states in the South and the Great Plains arrived in the Central Valley with dreams of opportunity. Branded 'Okies' by the locals (whether from Oklahoma or not), the majority found only more hardship in the Golden State.

Weedpatch Camp (Arvin Farm Labor Center; ☑661-832-1299; 8701 Sunset Blvd, Bakersfield; ☺by appointment) is one of about 16 Farm Security Administration camps built in the US during the 1930s to aid migrant workers, and today it is the only one with original buildings still standing (as of press time, they were undergoing renovation). A reporter named John Steinbeck researched the people in this camp and their lives inspired *The Grapes of Wrath*. Nearby tract housing still shelters migrant workers for the six-month grape harvest.

From Bakersfield, take Hwy 58 east to Weedpatch Hwy; head south for about 7 miles, past Lamont; then turn left on Sunset Blvd, driving another half mile. Look for the 'Arvin Farm Labor Center' sign on your right. The **Dust Bowl Festival** is a free celebration of Okie history held here the third Saturday of October.

SACRAMENTO & CENTRAL VALLEY BAKERSFIELD

★**Noriega's** BASQUE $$
(☑661-322-8419; www.noriegahotel.com; 525 Sumner St; breakfast $10, lunch $17, dinner $22; ☺7am-9am, from noon, from 7pm Tue-Sun) Surly Basque gentlemen pass the communal wine carafes at Bakersfield's family-style Basque institution. The fixed menu includes a procession of dishes leading to silky oxtail stew, ribs and amazing garlic fried chicken (check online for the day's menu). The magical ambience and the food earned a prestigious James Beard award. Reserve in advance, seating hours are strict.

The Mark AMERICAN $$
(☑661-322-7665; www.atthemark.com; 1623 19th St; mains from $17; ☺11am-10pm Mon-Fri, 4pm-11:30pm Sat, 7:30-11:30pm Sun) One of downtown Bakersfield's swanky spots has red banquettes and big-city classics such as cioppino and pistachio-crusted lamb chops.

Wool Growers BASQUE $$
(☑661-327-9584; www.woolgrowers.net; 620 E 19th St; lunch $15, dinner mains $18-32; ☺11:30am-2pm & 6-9pm Mon-Sat) A simple Basque eating hall loaded with character. You can order the nine – yes nine – sides without a main dish, or loosen your belt and get it all.

🍷 Drinking & Nightlife

Dionysus Brewing Company BREWERY
(☑661-833-6000; www.dionysusbrewing.com; 6201 Schirra Ct, Suite 13; ☺4-9pm Mon-Fri, from noon Sat, 11am-5pm Sun) Craft beer nerds should go out of their way for a snifter at this exceptional small brewery. It specializes in adventurous sour beers, but has something for every palette, from the Super Funkadelic sour aged with fresh guava and pomegranate to the crisp, clean Berliner Weisse.

Temblor Brewing Company BREWERY
(☑661-489-4855; www.temblorbrewing.com; 3200 Buck Owens Blvd; 🛜) Housed in a cavernous, sleekly renovated industrial space, this brewpub is a welcome newcomer to Bakersfield's nightlife. It serves quality flatbreads with fresh ingredients and main dishes ($9 to $15), and excellent beer, including a refreshing Belgian with a hint of blood orange. It's particularly fun here when it hosts comedy and live music.

☆ Entertainment

★**Buck Owens' Crystal Palace** LIVE MUSIC
(☑661-328-7560; www.buckowens.com; 2800 Buck Owens Blvd) For fans of the Bakersfield Sound, this is the first stop – just look for the huge neon homage to Buck's famous red, white and blue guitar. Part museum, honky-tonk and steakhouse (dinner from 5pm, brunch 9:30am to 2pm Sunday), it has top-drawer country acts nearly nightly. Locals in snap-button shirts, shiny boots and pressed jeans tear up the dance floor.

Trout's & the Blackboard Stage LIVE MUSIC
(www.therockwellopry.webs.com; 805 N Chester Ave at Decatur St, Oildale; ☺11am-late Mon-Sat) The legendary Trout's, north of town, is the only remaining honky-tonk in these parts, hobbling along after half a century as a testament to hell-raisin' days past. Hundreds of old guitars hang from the ceiling of this ramshackle dive, while Bakersfield legends and their disciples take the stage.

Bakersfield Music Hall of Fame ARTS CENTER
(☑661-864-1701; www.bakersfieldmusichalloffame.
com; 2230 Q St; ⊙10am-6pm Mon-Fri) Housing
a small theater, recording studios and displays on local legends, this space celebrates
past icons and fosters new talent. Check the
schedule for local up-and-comers, who take
the state-of-the-art stage and are quite a bit
more civilized than the rowdy honky-tonks
that made this town famous.

ℹ Information

**Greater Bakersfield Convention & Visitors
Bureau** (☑661-852-7282; www.bakersfieldcvb.
org; 515 Truxtun Ave; ⊙8am-5pm Mon-Fri) A
spacious building with maps and brochures.

ℹ Transport

Airport Valet Express (☑661-363-5000;
www.airportvaletexpress.com; 201 New Stine,
Suite 120; one-way/round-trip $49/89; ⊙to
LAX 3am, 8am, 5pm) Star-spangled buses
travel between Bakersfield (from the north side
of the San Joaquin Valley College campus) and
LAX (2½ hours, three daily). Book in advance
for a sizable discount.

Amtrak Station (☑800-872-7245; 601 Truxtun
Ave at S St) Trains travel north from here to
Sacramento ($45 to $65, five hours, two direct
trains). Buses head to LA, but fares must be
purchased in combination with a train ticket.

Golden Empire Transit (GET; www.getbus.org;
Transit Center, 1830 Golden State Ave; fares
from $1.25) The efficient local bus system's
Route 22 runs north on Chester Ave to the
Kern County Museum (p610) and Oildale (22
minutes).

Greyhound (☑661-327-5617; 1820 18th St at G
St) Cheap rides from downtown Bakersfield to
Los Angeles ($9, two hours).

Kern River Area

A half-century ago, Kern River originated
on the slopes of Mt Whitney and journeyed
close to 170 miles before finally settling into
the Central Valley. Now, after its wild descent from the high country – 60ft per mile
– the Kern is dammed in several places and
almost entirely tapped for agricultural use.

Its pristine upper reaches, declared wild
and scenic by the Secretary of the Interior,
is nicknamed 'Killer Kern' for its occasionally lethal force and makes for world-class
rafting.

There are two USFS Ranger Stations in
the area, one in **Kernville** (☑760-376-3781;

www.fs.usda.gov; ⊙8am-4:30pm Mon-Fri) and
another in **Lake Isabella** (☑760-379-5646;
⊙8am-4:30pm Mon-Fri). Both have hiking and
camping information, maps and wilderness
permits.

🏃 Activities

This part of the state is all about white water, and rafting is the banner attraction. The
town of **Lake Isabella** is a dreary strip of
local businesses on the south end of the lake,
but Hwy 155 runs north to **Kernville**, a cute
little town straddling the Kern River that
is *the* hub for local water sports. While the
lake is popular for cooling off, note that the
river's currents can be extremely dangerous.

The Upper Kern and Forks of the Kern
(both sections of the river north of Kernville)
yield Class IV and V rapids during spring
runoff and offer some of the most awe-inspiring white-water trips in the country.
You'll need experience before tackling these
sections, though there are still opportunities
for novices. Below Lake Isabella, the Kern is
tamer and steadier.

Currently seven rafting companies are licensed to operate out of Kernville; all offer
competitive prices and run trips from May
to August, depending on conditions. Excursions include popular one-hour runs (from
$40) and day-long Lower Kern trips (from
$120) and multiday Wild Forks of the Kern
experiences (from $600). Walk-ins are wel-
come and experience is not necessary. Kids
ages six and up can usually participate.

Kern River Outfitters RAFTING
(☑800-323-4234; www.kernrafting.com; 6602
Wofford Heights Blvd, Wofford Heights; ⊙8:30am-
5:30pm Mon-Fri) Offers the staple menu of
trips plus an adults-only Pub & Grub trip,
which includes beer tastings from the Kern
River Brewery.

Mountain & River Adventures RAFTING
(☑800-861-6553, 760-376-6553; www.mtnriver.
com; 11113 Kernville Rd) Besides rafting, this
outfit offers combo–kayak and rafting,
mountain-biking and winter excursions. It
also has a campground right on the banks
of the Kern.

Sierra South RAFTING
(☑760-376-3745, 800-457-2082; www.sierrasouth.
com; 11300 Kernville Rd) Rafting or for something calmer, paddle boarding, on Lake
Isabella.

WORTH A TRIP

A LITTLE SWEDEN IN THE VALLEY

The quiet hamlet of Kingsburg has a vibrant ethnic heritage. Around 1873, when it was established as a rail stop called 'Kings River Switch,' two Swedes arrived. Their countrymen soon followed, and by 1921, 94% of Kingsburg's residents, as it had become known, were of Swedish heritage. Today, the Swedish past mixes with more recent Mexican immigrants who drive the agricultural economy.

Draper St, the main drag, is decked out in Swedish Dala horses and crests of Swedish regions. Inside the cutesy Tudor buildings are gift shops and little bakeries stocked with buttery pastries. Diane at **Diane's Village Bakery & Cafe** (☑559-897-7460; Kingsburg Village Mall, 1332 Draper St; mains under $8.25; ◉8am-2:30pm Mon-Sat) cooks with her grandmother's recipes. Pick up Nordic decor and insight on the town from June, town icon and proprietor of **Svensk Butik** (☑559-897-5119; 1465 Draper St; ◉9am-5pm Mon-Sat). Sure, the town plays up its heritage for the crowds, but there is genuine pride in every 'Valkommen!'

The town has gone through pains to preserve its oldest structures. Under the coffee-pot water tower, the **city jail** (www.kingsburghistoricalpark.org; 1400 Marion St; ◉24hr) **FREE** is a quick stop. On the east end of town, a general store, schoolhouse and windmill, as well as artifacts and farm equipment, make up **Kingsburg Historical Park** (www.kingsburghistoricalpark.org; 2321 Sierra St; ◉1-4pm Fri).

Good times to visit are during the holiday explosion that is the Santa Lucia Festival (first Saturday of December) and the Swedish Festival (parades, maypole dancing and a real smorgasbord) in May. The Chamber of Commerce keeps a calendar.

Whitewater Voyages RAFTING
(☑660-376-8806, 800-400-7238; www.whitewatervoyages.com; 11006 Kernville Rd) The first outfitter to dare guide clients down the entire Wild and Scenic Forks of the Kern back in 1980.

🛏 Sleeping

USFS Campgrounds CAMPGROUND $
(☑877-444-6777; www.fs.usda.gov; developed/undeveloped tent sites $24/20) These campgrounds line the 10-mile stretch between Lake Isabella and Kernville, and several more lie north of Kernville on Mountain Hwy 99. There are seven in total, mostly undeveloped. Rangers recommend the Fairview and Limestone (marked on the map) for their seclusion. Campgrounds without running water and electricity are free.

Whispering Pines Lodge B&B $$
(☑760-376-3733; www.pineskernville.com; 13745 Sierra Way; r $189-219, house incl breakfast $359; ❄) This secluded B&B, blending rustic character with luxurious comfort, is just north of town. Rooms with kitchens book up quickly in the summer.

🍷 Drinking & Nightlife

Kern River Brewing Company BREWERY
(☑760-376-2337; www.kernriverbrewing.com; 13415 Sierra Hwy, Kernville; ◉11am-10pm Sun-Thu, to 11pm Fri & Sat) An excellent hub for local rafting guides and outdoor types, this brewery has a rotation of excellent seasonal beers. The Isabella Blonde is light and refreshing when the weather is sweltering. It also has a reliably tasty menu with pulled pork tacos, fish and chips, and fancy burgers.

Gold Country

Best Places to Eat

➡ New Moon Cafe (p621)
➡ Argonaut Farm to Fork Cafe (p627)
➡ La Cocina de Oro Taqueria (p624)
➡ Taste (p630)
➡ Ike's Quarter Cafe (p620)

Best Places to Sleep

➡ Outside Inn (p620)
➡ Lure Resort (p624)
➡ Camino Hotel (p628)
➡ Imperial Hotel (p630)
➡ Victoria Inn (p635)

Why Go?

Hollywood draws the dreamers and Silicon Valley lures fortune-hunters, but this isn't the first time droves of aspiring young folk have streamed into the Golden State. After a sparkle in the American River caught James Marshall's eye in 1848, more than 300,000 prospectors from America and abroad started digging for gold in the Sierra foothills. Soon California entered statehood with the official motto 'Eureka' solidifying its place as the land of opportunity.

The miner forty-niners are gone, but a ride along Hwy 49 through sleepy hill towns, past clapboard saloons and oak-lined byways is a journey back to the wild ride that was modern California's founding: umpteen historical markers tell tales of gold rush violence and banditry. Many travelers hardly hit the brakes while rushing between California's coasts and mountains, but those who do are rewarded with a taste of the helter-skelter era that kick-started the heartbeat of this state.

When to Go

Nevada City

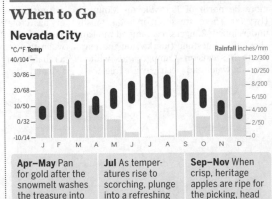

Apr–May Pan for gold after the snowmelt washes the treasure into Jamestown's hills.

Jul As temperatures rise to scorching, plunge into a refreshing South Yuba swimming hole.

Sep–Nov When crisp, heritage apples are ripe for the picking, head to Apple Hill's sprawling ranches.

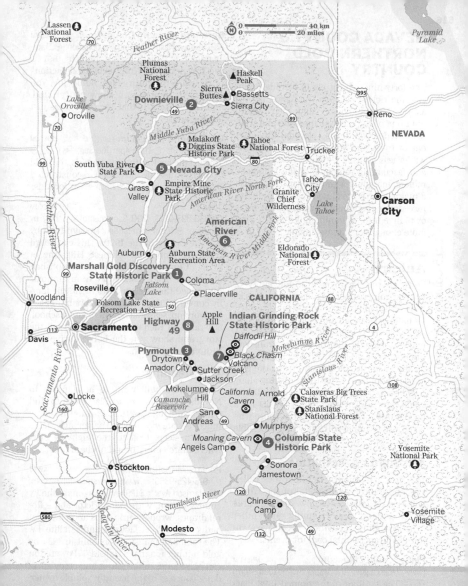

Gold Country Highlights

1 Witnessing the birthplace of modern California at **Marshall Gold Discovery State Historic Park** (p627).

2 Rumbling down the premier single-track bike trails above **Downieville** (p623).

3 Tasting wines made from grapes grown in the **Plymouth** (p630) hills.

4 Stepping back in time in the living history of **Columbia State Historic Park** (p637), the 'Gem of the Southern Mines.'

5 Wandering the historic streets of **Nevada City** (p619), Gold Country's relaxing jewel of a town.

6 Riding the white-water **American River** (p626).

7 Discovering rock art created by the Miwoks who once thrived near **Indian Grinding Rock State Historic Park** (p632).

8 Traveling down **Highway 49** (p625) through El Dorado and Amador counties in pursuit of antiques and ice cream.

NEVADA COUNTY & NORTHERN GOLD COUNTRY

The forty-niners hit it big in Nevada County – the richest score in the region known as the Mother Lode – and their wealth built one of the most picturesque and well-preserved boomtowns, Nevada City. Get out of town and you'll find lovely, remote wilderness areas, a clutch of historic parks and fascinating remnants of the long-gone miners, including a ghost town. This is also a magnet for adrenaline junkies looking to race down singletracks on mountain bikes or plunge into swimming holes that are remote enough for skinny-dipping.

Auburn

Look for the big man: a 45-ton effigy of French gold panner Claude Chana marks your arrival in Placer County's Gold Country. Its hallmarks are all here – ice-cream shops, strollable historic districts and antiques. A major stop on the Central Pacific's transcontinental route, Auburn still welcomes trains on the Union Pacific's main line to the east and is a popular stop for those rushing along I-80 between the Bay Area and Lake Tahoe. You'll have to venture along Hwy 49 for a deeper taste of Gold Country, but those who want just a sample will enjoy this accessible town.

◉ Sights & Activities

The fact that Auburn is sometimes called the 'Endurance Sport Capital of the World' will give you a sense of how good the area is for cycling, trail running and other heart-pounding activities. See www.auburnendurancecapital.com for events.

Placer County Museum   MUSEUM
(www.placer.ca.gov; 101 Maple St; ☉10am-4pm) FREE The 1st floor of the domed 1898 Placer County Courthouse has Native American artifacts and displays of Auburn's transportation heritage, including a classic 1877 stage coach. It's the easiest museum to visit and gives a good overview of area history; there's also the glitter of the museum's gold collection with huge chunks of unrefined gold on display.

Hour-long walking tours of the town leave from the museum at 10am each Saturday.

Bernhard Museum Complex   MUSEUM
(291 Auburn-Folsom Rd; entry by donation; ☉11am-4pm Tue-Sun) This museum, built in 1851 as the Traveler's Rest Hotel, exhibits depictions of typical 19th-century-farm family life. Volunteers in period garb show you around, and the concept is that the family has just left the house.

Gold Country Museum   MUSEUM
(1273 High St; ☉11am-4pm Tue-Sun; ⊕) FREE Toward the back of the fairgrounds, the Gold Country Museum includes a reconstructed mine and gold panning, both great for kids.

Joss House   MUSEUM
(☏530-823-0373; 200 Sacramento St; entry by donation; ☉10am-4pm 1st Sat of month) Built by the Yue family in the 1920s, this clapboard residence stands on 'Chinese Hill,' one of many Chinese communities established during the gold rush. After a 'mysterious' fire ripped through the settlement, the family converted their home into a public space for worship, seasonal boarders and a school.

Grandson Richard is on hand to tell the story, and show you the house shrine and rudimentary kitchen.

⌖ Sleeping

Most visitors will want to head north to Nevada City or south to Placerville to find a more enticing spot to stay: Auburn is very much a gateway town. For an affordable place to sleep, look to the highway exits where there's every brand of chain hotel.

Powers Mansion Inn   B&B $$
(☏916-425-9360; www.powersmansioninn.com; 195 Harrison Ave; r $129; ☎) An unabashedly chintzy option, with much Victoriana – floral drapes, wrought-iron beds and claw-foot baths – as well as Jacuzzis and satellite TV. The rambling mansion was built in 1884 by gold-mining magnate Harold T Power. You can play games in the parlor and enjoy anecdotes courtesy of the friendly, voluble owner.

✖ Eating & Drinking

Lincoln Way toward the Chamber of Commerce (p617) has several restaurants popular with locals, and there's plenty of sunny outdoor eating right off the highway around Sacramento St.

Ikedas   DINER $
(www.ikedas.com; 13500 Lincoln Way; sandwiches $6-9; ☉11am-7pm Mon-Thu, 10am-8pm Fri-Sun; ✍) If you're cruising this part of the state

without time to explore, the best pit stop is this expanded farm stand – now a diner/market – off I-80 a few miles north of downtown. Thick, grass-fed beef or tofu burgers, homemade sweet and savory pies and the seasonal fresh-peach shake are deliriously good.

Katrina's BREAKFAST $
(www.katrinascafe.com; 456 Grass Valley Hwy; mains $10-15; ⊘7am-2:30pm Wed-Sat, to 2pm Sun) Lemon yogurt or banana nut pancakes, great omelets and all manner of hot sandwiches dished up in a homey atmosphere.

Auburn Alehouse BREWERY
(www.auburnalehouse.com; 289 Washington St; mains $8-21; ⊘11am-10pm Mon & Tue, to 11pm Wed & Thu, to midnight Fri, 9am-midnight Sat, 9am-10pm Sun) One of those rare brewpubs with both excellent craft beer *and* food; patrons dig into burgers, sweet-potato fries, 'adult mac 'n' cheese' and sweet-and-savory salads. The beer sampler is a great deal, as Auburn brings home tons of medals for its ales and pilsners, and the setting, with swirly stucco and a pressed-metal ceiling, is impressive.

ℹ Information

Auburn Area Chamber of Commerce (☑530-885-5616; www.auburnchamber.net; 1103 High St; ⊘10am-4pm Tue-Fri) In the Southern Pacific railroad depot at the north end of Lincoln Way, it has lots of useful local info and a monument to the Transcontinental Railroad nearby.
Auburn State Recreation Area Office (☑530-885-4527; 501 El Dorado St; ⊘9am-4pm Mon-Fri) Information on sights and outdoor activities in the area.
California Welcome Center (Placer County Visitors Center; ☑530-887-2111; www.visitplacer.com; 1103 High St; ⊘9am-4:30pm Mon-Sat, 11am-4pm Sun) Great information on Gold Country and eastward.

ℹ Getting There & Away

Amtrak (☑800-872-7245; www.amtrak.com; 277 Nevada St) runs one train a day along the Capital Corridor route (http://capitolcorridor.org) linking Auburn with Sacramento ($16, one hour); other destinations require connecting with Thruway buses. There is also one train daily east to Reno ($62, eight hours; requires a change).

Amtrak's *California Zephyr* stops in Auburn on its daily run between the Bay Area and Chicago via Reno and Denver (to San Francisco takes three hours and costs $39).

SUCTION DREDGING FOR GOLD

Floating down Gold Country's waterways, you may see someone trying to strike it rich with a suction dredge – a vacuum that sucks up the river bed and the gold in it. This method of prospecting was banned in California in 2009 for its destructive side effects, including disturbing riparian habitat and stirring up toxic quicksilver, the mercury that the forty-niners used to extract gold from ore.

The **Gold Country Stage Bus Service** (☑888-660-7433; www.goldcountrystage.com; adult $1.50-3, child free) links Auburn, including its Amtrak station, with Grass Valley and Nevada City five times a day on weekdays (limited service on Saturdays). Kids and bikes ride free. **Placer County Transit** (☑530-885-2877; www.placer.ca.gov/transit; 11460 F Ave; fare $2.50) also runs bus services in the Auburn area.

Auburn State Recreation Area

This is a **park** (☑530-885-4527; www.parks.ca.gov; per car $10; ⊘7am-sunset) of deep gorges cut by the rushing waters of the North and Middle Forks of the American River, which converge below a bridge on Hwy 49, 4 miles south of Auburn. In early spring, when waters are high, this is immensely popular for white-water rafting, as the rivers are Class II to V runs. Late summer, calmer waters allow for sunning and swimming, especially around the confluence. Numerous trails are shared by hikers, mountain bikers and horses.

One of the most popular hikes is the **Western States Trail**, which connects Auburn State Recreation Area to **Folsom Lake State Recreation Area** and Folsom Lake. It's the site of the **Western States 100-Mile Endurance Run** (www.wser.org), and the **Tevis Cup** (www.teviscup.org), an endurance race on horseback. The **Quarry Trail** takes a level path from Hwy 49, just south of the bridge, along the Middle Fork of the American. Several side trails reach the river.

The best tours of the American, Tuolumne and Stanislaus rivers are offered spring through fall by the family-run **All-Outdoors California Whitewater Rafting** (☑925-932-

8993; www.aorafting.com; 1250 Pine St, Walnut Creek; trips from $108). Its single- and multi-day wilderness rafting excursions include breaks for hiking among the boulders and historically significant sights in the canyons. Meals are provided (the burrito lunch might be worth the trip alone). Check online for discounts.

For **camping** (campsites $25-35), there are basic sites on a sweeping bend of the Middle Fork at the blackberry-dotted Ford's Bar that are accessible only by a 2-mile hike from Rucky-A-Chucky Rd, or a half-day raft. Required permits for these sites are available from the Auburn State Recreation Area Office (p617).

Grass Valley

From the margins, Grass Valley is the ugly utilitarian sister to Nevada City, a place to stock up on supplies and get an oil change, not necessarily vacation. But there are treasures if you dig, including a dense cluster of Victorian and art-deco buildings, some great independent boutiques and cafes, and a few surprisingly rowdy bars.

TRIBAL HISTORY IN GOLD COUNTRY

. . . .

A few dedicated museums tell part of the stories of the Miwok, Maidu, Konkow, Monache, Nisenan, Tubatulabal, Washo and Foothill Yokuts – the people who called this region home, way before the rush for gold.

➡ **Maidu Museum & Historical Site** (www.roseville.ca.us; 1970 Johnson Ranch Dr, Roseville; adult/child $4.50/4; ⊘ 9am-4pm Mon-Fri, to 1pm Sat, plus 6:30-8:30pm every 3rd Sat) is built on the site of an ancient Maidu village, occupied for over 3000 years.

➡ The roundhouse museum in **Indian Grinding Rock State Historic Park** (p632) has a variety of artifacts representing different tribes of the area. The limestone outcrop outside is dimpled with mortar holes for grinding acorns.

➡ The **State Indian Museum** (p370) in Sacramento features the most varied collections, with a redwood canoe and extraordinary beaded garments.

Historic Mill and W Main Sts mark the town center. E Main St leads north to modern shopping centers and mini-malls and into Nevada City. On Thursday nights in late June through August, Mill St closes to traffic to serve up farmstead food, arts and crafts and music. On the town's outskirts are some of the state's oldest shaft mines. Being the first to exploit lode-mining (tunneling to find veins of gold in hard rock) rather than placer techniques (sifting debris carried by waterways), these were among the most profitable claims.

◉ Sights

Empire Mine State Historic Park   HISTORIC SITE
(☑ 530-273-8522; www.empiremine.org; 10791 Empire St; adult/child $7/3; ⊘ 10am-5pm; ℗ ⊛) Atop 367 miles of mine shafts tunneling almost a vertical mile beneath the surface, Gold Country's best-preserved gold-quartz-mining operation is worth a solid half-day's exploration. From 1850 to 1956 the miners here, mostly Cornish, produced 5.8 million ounces of gold (worth about $8 billion today). The visitor center has maps and leads guided tours (schedules vary).

It's very well worth paying to enter the mine yard, littered with mining equipment and buildings constructed from waste rock, and to view the main shaft's claustrophobic entry, next to the head frame (a tall structure used to haul ore and people from underground). Nearby is the English-manor-style cottage and rose garden of the Bourn family, who originally owned the mine; though this now appears incongruously idyllic, the noise of the mining activity must have been deafening.

Hiking the trails that meander past abandoned mines and equipment is free. Trailheads are located at the parking lots behind the visitor center and Penn Gate to its west.

North Star Mining Museum   MUSEUM
(Powerhouse & Pelton Wheel Museum; www.nevadacountyhistory.org; 10933 Allison Ranch Rd; entry by donation; ⊘ 11am-5pm Tue-Sat, noon-4pm Sun May-Oct) A museum for those who ache when they see machinery set aside to rust. The engineering-minded docents here have polished and oiled their extensive collection of 19th-century mining equipment to a shine. See stamp mills, dredges, dynamite packing machines, Cornish pumps and the

largest Pelton wheel ever constructed in action.

The grassy banks of the creek that once powered the North Star mine are perfect for a picnic.

🍴 Sleeping & Eating

The menus around here don't vary much but the quality is good. There are several good brunch spots and bars around downtown, and every imaginable chain among the strip malls by the highway.

Holbrooke Hotel   HISTORIC HOTEL **$$**
(🖉 530-273-1353; www.holbrooke.com; 212 W Main St; r $129-179, ste $249; ❈ 🛜) The register in this 1862 hotel boasts the signatures of Mark Twain and President Ulysses S Grant; rooms are aging but neat. The restaurant (mains $11 to $22) serves casual fare in the ornate dining room or on the shaded patio, but the best tables overlook the Main St action. Weekday rates drop by 15% to 30%.

There's live music in the saloon bar every night except Monday, with a regular slot for Celtic bands on a Sunday. Beware the haunted loo downstairs from reception.

Cousin Jack Pasties   BAKERY **$**
(100 S Auburn St; meals $5.25-9; ⊙ 10:30am-6pm Mon-Sat, 11am-5pm Sun; 🖉) Cousin Jack and his kin have been serving flaky pasties – a meat-and-potato-stuffed pastry beloved by Cornish miners – for five generations. The pies – Basque lamb, pot roast and several vegetarian options – are all made from local ingredients. Anyone homesick for other British fare can buy Bramley pies, Bakewell tarts and Marmite here.

Lazy Dog Ice Cream   ICE CREAM **$**
(www.spotlazydog.com; 111 Mill St; ice-cream bars $4; ⊙ 10am-9pm Sun-Thu, to 10pm Fri & Sat) This colorful ice-cream and candy shop explodes with sugar in all its forms. Besides scoops, there are hand-dipped bars, chocolates and old-timey candies from 'juicy wax sticks' to swirly suckers.

Tofanelli's   ITALIAN **$$**
(🖉 530-272-1468; www.tofanellis.com; 302 W Main St; mains $8-23; ⊙ 8am-9pm) Hugely popular with locals in the know, this creative restaurant has everything from salads to hearty steaks and seasonal specials such as summer squash ravioli. Portions are burly and the patio is a treat.

☆ Entertainment

Center for the Arts   ARTS CENTER
(🖉 530-274-8384; http://thecenterforthearts.org; 314 W Main St) Grass Valley punches above its weight with this excellent arts center. The varied program includes local and international music, dance, visual arts, comedy and literary events.

ℹ Information

Greater Grass Valley Visitor Center (🖉 530-273-4667; www.grassvalleychamber.com; 128 Main St; ⊙ 10am-5pm Mon-Fri, to 3pm Sat & Sun; ❈) In the thick of the historical sights stands this brick livery stable, which is stocked with maps and brochures covering the county and more. There's a very comprehensive walking-tour map.

ℹ Getting There & Away

Transit in Grass Valley is by **Gold Country Stage Bus Service** (🖉 888-660-7433; www.goldcountrystage.com; 13083 John Bauer Ave), which links to Nevada City hourly from 7am to 6pm weekdays, 8am to 4pm Saturday. Fares are $1.50 to $3 for adults. Kids and bikes ride free. Check the website for connections to Auburn and schedule changes.

Amtrak (p617) bus connections are in Colfax, 12 miles south.

Nevada City

Nevada City knows it's charming, but it doesn't like to brag. The shops sell prayer flags and chia smoothies, while the drinking holes sling all manner of liquid enlightenment. The person browsing the history museum with you is just as liable to be a crusty old-timer, a road-weary backpacker or a mystical folk artist. In the midst of all that are the requisite Victorian and gold rush tourist attractions – an elegantly restored town center and frilly B&Bs.

This is the gateway to Tahoe National Forest, but linger a few days to experience some inviting NorCal culture. The theater companies, alternative film houses, bookstores and venues put on shows almost every night; tune into radical local radio station kvmr.org at 89.5FM to catch the vibe and hear what's on.

Nevada City's strollable streets are especially lively in summer. In December the snow blanket and twinkling lights are something from a storybook.

◉ Sights

The main attraction is the town itself – its restored buildings, all brick and wrought-iron trimmings, wear their history proudly. There are intriguing (if pricey) boutiques, galleries and places for food and drink everywhere, all with exhaustive posted histories.

Firehouse No 1 Museum　　　MUSEUM
(☑ 530-265-3937;　　　www.nevadacountyhistory. org; 214 Main St; by donation; ⊙ 1-4pm Tue-Sun May-Oct, by appointment Nov-Apr) This small, painstakingly curated museum is run by the Nevada County Historical Society from a unique white wooden building with a tall bell tower. From stunning Nisenan baskets to preserved Victorian bridal wear, its collections tell the story of the local people. The prize exhibits are relics from the Chinese settlers who often built but seldom profited from the mines.

By 1880, miners of Chinese origin constituted more than a fifth of all engaged in the industry and were nearly exclusively subject to a hefty Foreign Miners' License Tax. The Chinese altar was saved by a local merchant who hid the pieces around town to keep it from marauders.

Nevada City Winery　　　WINERY
(☑ 530-265-9463; http://ncwinery.com; 321 Spring St; ⊙ tasting room noon-5pm Sun-Thu, to 6pm Fri & Sat) This popular winery excels with Syrah and Zinfandel varietals, which you can savor while touring the production facility in the old Miners' Foundry Garage. It's a good place to get information on touring all of the surrounding wine region.

🛏 Sleeping

Weekends, Nevada City fills up with urban refugees who inevitably weigh themselves down with real-estate brochures. There are B&Bs everywhere. The cheapest options are the National Forest campgrounds, just outside town in any direction.

★ Outside Inn　　　INN, COTTAGE $$
(☑ 530-265-2233; http://outsideinn.com; 575 E Broad St; d $79-210; 🅿 ❄ ✿ 🤵 🛜 🐾 🐕) The best option for active explorers, this is an unusually friendly and fun inn, with 12 rooms and three cottages maintained by staff who love the outdoors. Some rooms have a patio overlooking a small creek; all have nice quilts and access to BBQ grills. It's a 10-minute walk from downtown and there's a small unheated outdoor pool.

★ Two Room Inn　　　APARTMENT $$
(☑ 415-891-9022; http://tworoominn.com; 431 Broad St; d from $125) Nevada City isn't short on pretty buildings, but this is one of the most enchanting: a two-room cottage with a Hansel and Gretel vibe, latticed stained-glass windows and a redwood interior. The upstairs master bedroom has a pitched wooden roof; an alcove converts into a second bedroom. Located in the heart of town, this little gem has all the mod cons.

★ Broad Street Inn　　　INN $$
(☑ 530-265-2239; www.broadstreetinn.com; 517 W Broad St; r $119-134; ❄ 🛜 🐾) 🍽 This six-room inn in the heart of town is a favorite because it keeps things simple. (No weird old dolls, no yellowing lace doilies.) The good-value rooms are modern, brightly but soothingly furnished and elegant. No breakfast served.

National Hotel　　　HISTORIC HOTEL $$
(☑ 530-265-4551; www.thenationalhotel.com; 211 Broad St; r $80-140; 🅿 ⊜) This historic 1850s hotel in the heart of downtown claims to be the oldest continuously operating hotel west of the Rocky Mountains and its unreconstructed charm supports this. Most of the rooms are en suite, but don't come here if you're looking for home comforts, as it's pretty spartan.

✗ Eating

In a town of holistic thinkers, it's no surprise most menus emphasize organic and seasonal ingredients. The options are mostly clustered in a three-block radius on Commercial and Broad Sts.

★ Ike's Quarter Cafe　　　CREOLE, BREAKFAST $
(☑ 530-265-6138; www.ikesquartercafe.com; 401 Commercial St; mains $11-15; ⊙ 8am-3pm Thu-Mon; 🍴 🐾) 🍽 Right out of New Orleans' Garden District, Ike's serves splendid brunch fare with a sassy charm. Sit outside under the cherry tree or in the cluttered, funky interior. There's eggs Sardou, jambalaya, vegetarian po'boy sandwiches and more. It's an excellent place to get 'Hangtown Fry' – a cornmeal-crusted mess of oysters, bacon, caramelized onions and spinach.

Vegan and gluten-free options are available, including gluten-free cornbread.

Sopa Thai　　　THAI $
(☑ 530-470-0101; www.sopathai.net; 312 Commercial St; mains $10-15; ⊙ 11am-3pm & 5-9:30pm Mon-Fri, noon-9:30pm Sat & Sun) Huge quantities

of delicious mango red curry, steamed mussels and spring rolls in the region's best and most popular Thai restaurant. The rugged red-brick interior is furnished with imported carvings, silks and lanterns, and the patio seating in back makes for a busy scene midday. The $10.95 lunch special is great value.

Three Forks Bakery & Brewing Co CAFE $
(☑ 530-470-8333; www.threeforksnc.com; 211 Commercial St; pizzas $10-15, cakes $4-5 per slice; ⊘ 7am-10pm Mon, Wed & Thu, 7am-11pm Fri, 8am-11pm Sat, 8am-10pm Sun) An open-plan modern place, open all day and serving cakes, pizzas and beer brewed on site. It has a generic feel compared to some of the quirky options in town, but it's functional, fast and friendly.

Treats DESSERTS $
(http://treatsnevadacity.com; 110 York St; items $3.50-5; ⊘ 1-9pm Mon-Sat, 1-8pm Sun; ☒) It's a crowded contest for Gold Country's best ice-cream shop, but this cute little spot – the brilliant second career of avuncular scooper Bob Wright – wins in a walk. Many flavors are sourced from ripe local produce like the River Hill Red sorbet (sweet red peppers and strawberry), mint chip and pear ginger.

★**New Moon Cafe** CALIFORNIAN $$$
(☑ 530-265-6399; www.thenewmooncafe.com; 203 York St; dinner mains $23-38; ⊘ 11:30am-2pm Tue-Fri, 5-8:30pm Tue-Sun) ☒ Pure elegance, Peter Selaya's organic- and local-ingredient menu changes with the seasons. If you visit during spring or summer, go for the line-caught fish or the house-made, moon-shaped fresh ravioli. The wine list is excellent.

🍷 Drinking & Entertainment

This little village has a vibrant arts scene, with two theater-cinemas and an ambitious arts center. The entertainment section of the *Union* newspaper (www.theunion.com) comes out on Thursday, and lists what's going on throughout the county. Bar-hopping in Nevada City is a delight, with friendly bar staff and locals, and delectable local brews to sample.

Crazy Horse Saloon Grill BAR
(☑ 530-265-4000; http://crazyhorsenc.com; 230 Commercial St; ⊘ 11:30am-1:30am) A fantastic town-center saloon with a long convivial bar where you can eat burgers and nachos, shoot the breeze with the friendly staff, then hit the dance floor. The little raised stage, wreathed in lanterns, hosts almost nightly live music, with jazz, funk, indie pop and rock, plus DJ nights.

★**Miners Foundry** ARTS CENTER
(☑ 530-265-5040; http://minersfoundry.org; 325 Spring St; ⊘ 10am-5pm, plus evenings for events) As the name suggests, this was once an industrial building, constructed in 1856 and used to manufacture Pelton wheels. It has been brilliantly converted into an eclectic arts center, hosting music workshops, youth theater, dance classes and gigs.

★**Magic Theatre** CINEMA
(www.themagictheatre.com; 107 Argall Way) This beloved and adorably quirky theater screens a matchless lineup of unusual films and is about a mile south of downtown Nevada City. It serves bowls of fresh popcorn, coffee in real mugs and hot brownies. At the time of writing the owners were about to renovate and add a new screen, with a promise to keep the charm intact.

Nevada Theatre THEATER, CINEMA
(www.nevadatheatre.com; 401 Broad St) This brick fortress is one of California's first theaters (1865) and has welcomed the likes of Jack London, Emma Nevada and Mark Twain to its stage. Now it's home to a number of small, top-notch theater companies and an off-beat indie film series.

ℹ️ Information

Nevada City Chamber of Commerce (☑ 530-265-2692; www.nevadacitychamber.com; 132 Main St; ⊘ 9am-5pm Mon-Fri, 11am-4pm Sat, 11am-3pm Sun) Ideally located at the east end of Commercial St, this has two welcome traveler comforts – expert local advice and public toilets right next door.

Tahoe National Forest Headquarters (☑ 530-265-4531; www.fs.usda.gov/tahoe; 631 Coyote St; ⊘ 8am-4:30pm Mon-Fri) A useful and friendly resource for trail and campground information, covering the area from here to Lake Tahoe. It sells topographical maps.

ℹ️ Getting There & Away

Nevada City is served by the **Gold Country Stage Bus Service** (☑ 530-477-0103; www.goldcountrystage.com; fares $1.50-3), which links it with Grass Valley (adult $1.50, 30 minutes) hourly from 6:30am to 5:30pm weekdays and 7:30am to 4:30pm Saturdays. Kids and bikes ride free. Check the website for connections to Auburn and schedule changes.

Amtrak (p617) bus connections are in Colfax, 15 miles south.

GOLD COUNTRY NEVADA CITY

LOCAL KNOWLEDGE

SWIMMING HOLE 101

Gold Country's rivers carved out precious metals as well as emerald pools perfect for late-summer dips.

On the South Yuba River, 8 miles northeast of Nevada City on Bloomfield Rd, under the **Edwards Crossing** bridge is a lively, popular pool. Just a mile hike downstream you'll find the scenic cascade of waterfalls known as **Mountain Dog**, perfect for a more secluded skinny dip.

For an even more remote spot, head to the Stanislaus River, to Parrots Ferry Rd 7 miles south of Murphys, and then turn north on Camp Nine Rd. Near the end, where the river splits, a half-mile hike up the right fork will lead you to **Camp Nine**, a peaceful, limestone-bordered pool and beach.

Some keys to swimming hole usage: always test rope swings and currents before jumping in. Never dive. Pack in your supplies and pack out your trash. No glass. And always stay at least 100yd from the water when nature calls.

South Yuba River State Park

Cool off with a dip at **South Yuba River State Park** (☑530-432-2546; www.parks. ca.gov; 17660 Pleasant Valley Rd, Penn Valley; ⊙park sunrise-sunset, visitor center 11am-4pm May-Sep, to 3pm Thu-Sun Oct-Apr; P ⊞ ❀) **FREE**, which has popular swimming holes and hiking trails. It's near Bridgeport, which has the USA's longest covered wooden bridge (temporarily closed for restoration at the time of research), a 30-minute drive northwest of Nevada City or Grass Valley.

This area has a growing network of trails, including the wheelchair-accessible Independence Trail, which starts from the south side of the South Yuba River bridge on Hwy 49 and continues for a couple of miles with canyon overlooks. June is the best time, when the rivers are rushing and the wildflowers are out.

The longest, single-span, wood-truss covered bridge in the USA, all 251ft of it, crosses the South Yuba River at Bridgeport (not to be confused with the Eastern Sierra town of the same name). It's easy to spend a whole

day hiking and swimming in this wild area, where crowds can be left behind with little effort. The Buttermilk Bend Trail skirts the South Yuba for 1.4 miles, offering river access and bountiful wildflowers around April.

Maps and park information are available from the state park headquarters in Bridgeport, or from the Tahoe National Forest Headquarters (p621) in Nevada City. The South Yuba River Park Association (www. southyubariverstatepark.org) is another great resource.

Malakoff Diggins State Historic Park

An otherworldly testament to the mechanical determination of the gold hunt, **Malakoff Diggins** (☑530-265-2740; 23579 N Bloomfield Rd; per car $8; ⊙sunrise-sunset) is a place to get lost on fern-lined trails and take in the raw beauty of a landscape recovering from brutal hydraulic mining. There is a mesmerizing ghost town here, with a barber shop, ice-cream parlor and saloon, abandoned and now frozen in time. Join a tour of the town at the **museum** (☑530-265-2740; http:// malakoffdigginsstatepark.org; 23579 North Bloomfield Rd; ⊙9am-5pm, tours 1:30pm Fri-Sun May-Sep) or stay at the **campground** (☑800-444-7275; www.reserveamerica.com; North Bloomfield Rd; tent sites $35, cabins $40; ⊙May-Sep) or in one of three humble miners' cabins.

California's largest hydraulic mine left behind massive gold and crimson cliffs and small mountains of tailings, which were carved from the land by mighty streams of water. The forestland has recovered since the legal battles between mine owners and downstream farmers shut down the mine in 1884, and makes for a pleasant hike.

In 1852, a French miner named Anthony Chabot channeled the Yuba through a canvas hose to blast away at the bedrock. To reach the veins of gold inside, miners eventually carved a canyon 600ft deep. To speed up the sorting process, they mixed the slurry of gravel with quicksilver (mercury) to recover the gold, and then washed all the leftovers into the Yuba River. When a few decades later, 20ft high glaciers of tailings and toxic waste choked the rivers and caused deadly flooding, farmers and miners collided in the courtroom. In 1884, the Sawyer Decision set a critical precedent: a profitable industry can be stopped for the public good. No longer able to reap profits by dumping in the Yuba, most fortune hunters moved on. North Bloomfield, the mining community at the center of Malakoff's operation, is the eerie ghost town that stands within the park's limits.

Tours of the town – which had a population of 1229 back in 1880 – provide the chance to see some impressive gold nuggets. The 1-mile Diggins Loop Trail is the quickest way to get a glimpse of the scarred moonscape.

Access Tyler-Foote Crossing Rd, the turnoff for the park, 10 miles northwest of Nevada City on Hwy 49.

North Yuba River

The northernmost segment of Hwy 49 follows the North Yuba River through some stunning, remote parts of the Sierra Nevada, known for a tough, short season of white water and great fly-fishing. An entire lifetime outdoors could hardly cover the trail network that hikers, mountain bikers and skiers blaze every season. In summer, snow remains at the highest elevations and many places have roaring fireplaces year-round. The best source of trail and camping information is the **Yuba River Ranger Station** (☑530-288-3231; 15924 Hwy 49, Camptonville; ☺8am-4:30pm Mon-Fri).

Downieville

Downieville, the biggest town in remote Sierra County (though that's not saying much), is located at the junction of the North Yuba and Downie Rivers. With a reputation that quietly rivals Moab, UT (before it got big), this is one of the premier places for mountain-bike riding in the US, and a staging area for true wilderness adventures.

As with most gold rush towns, it wasn't always fun and games: the first justice of the peace was the local barkeep, and a placard tells the story of the racist mob that hanged a Chicana named Josefa on the town bridge in 1851, the only recorded lynching of a woman in California. The town retains a grisly affection for frontier justice and its ghosts; a reconstructed gallows is across the river, by the civic building.

🏃 Activities

The mountains and rivers in these parts beg to be explored in summer. Favorite hikes include the **Sierra Buttes Fire Lookout**, a

moderate 6 miler that joins the **Pacific Crest Trail** before a 1500ft elevation gain to epic views from the lookout tower, and **North Yuba Trail**, 12 miles along the canyon ridge, starting behind the courthouse in town. There are many more options. Pick up maps and a shuttle ride from the local outfitters.

Downieville Downhill MOUNTAIN BIKING
(www.downievilleclassic.com) This world-class mountain biking trail shoots riders over the Sierra Buttes and a molar-rattling 4000ft down into Downieville. There are plenty of other scenic biking trails to explore, including **Chimney Rock**, **Empire Creek** and **Rattlesnake Creek**, but this route is the reason why pro-riders arrive in August for the **Downieville Classic**, a mix of cross-country and downhill racing and revelry.

Local outfitters run hourly shuttles to the start.

Yuba Expeditions MOUNTAIN BIKING
(☑530-289-3010; www.yubaexpeditions.com; 208 Main St; bike rentals $80-100, shuttle $20; ☺shuttles 9am-5pm May-Oct, reserve Nov-Apr) Yuba Expeditions is run by Sierra Buttes Trail Stewardship, a nonprofit in the center of the trail-bike scene. Non-bikers will find it helpful with maps and general trail advice.

Downieville Outfitters MOUNTAIN BIKING
(☑530-289-0155; www.downievilleoutfitters.com; 114 Main St; bike rental per day $65, shuttle $20; ☺8:30am-5pm Mon-Thu, 8am-6pm Fri-Sun, shuttles May-Oct) A good option for trail information, bike rental and shuttles in Downieville.

🎉 Festivals & Events

Downieville Mountain Brewfest BEER
(www.downievillebrewfest.com; ☺Aug) This August event is focused around the consumption of craft beer, but it also involves fabulous food vendors, live music and lots of fresh Downieville air.

🛏 Sleeping & Eating

In downtown Downieville, the soft roar of the rapids lull saddle-sore bikers to sleep in several small B&Bs. More secluded options are along Hwy 49 east of town.

Tahoe National Forest
Campgrounds CAMPGROUND $
(☑information 530-994-3401, reservations 877-444-6777; www.recreation.gov; tent & RV sites $24; ☺May-Sep; P🐾) West of town on Hwy 49 are a string of beautiful campsites. Most have vault toilets, running water and

reservable sites along the North Yuba River. Of these, the prettiest is Fiddlecreek, which has tent-only sites right on the river.

★ **Lure Resort** CABIN, CAMPGROUND $$
(📞530-289-3465; www.lureresort.com; 100 Lure Bridge Lane; camping cabins $80, housekeeping cabins $180-290; 📶🐾) A great option if you want to come with biking buddies or a family, this circle of tidy, modernized log cabins is along a sublime stretch of river open to fly fishing with big lawns for the kids to play on. The basic camping cabins, which are BYO sleeping bag and have shared bathrooms, sleep four tightly.

Riverside Inn HOTEL $$
(📞530-289-1000; www.downieville.us; 206 Commercial St; r $95-125, ste $180-190; 🅿🐾📶🐾) There is a secluded, rustic charm to these 11 stove-warmed rooms and a suite overlooking the river near the heart of Downieville. About half have kitchens and all have balconies for enjoying the river. The delightful innkeepers share excellent information about hiking and biking in the area, and in winter lend snowshoes.

Carriage House Inn INN $$
(📞530-289-3573; www.downievillecarriagehouse.com; 110 Commercial St; r $95-195; 📶🐾) This renovated homey inn has country-style charms, which include decks with rockers and river views. Rooms have wing-backed chairs and wrought-iron beds; two rooms share a shower.

★ **La Cocina de Oro Taqueria** MEXICAN $
(📞530-289-9584; 322 Main St; tacos from $2.50, burritos $10; ⊙11am-8pm Thu-Sat, to 5pm Sun Apr-Dec; 🐾) Chef-owner Feather Ortiz uses herbs and peppers from her garden and sources everything else from local growers to make the freshest food around. The burritos are the size of Chihuahuas. No credit cards.

Sierra City & The Lakes Basin

Sierra City is the primary supply station for people headed to the **Sierra Buttes**, a rugged, rocky shock of mountains that are probably the closest thing to the Alps you'll find in California without hoisting a backpack. It's also the last supply point for people headed into the fishing paradise of the Lakes Basin. There's information about lodging and area activities at www.sierracity.com.

There's just one main drag in town, and that's the Golden Chain Hwy (Hwy 49). All commerce happens here. The hotels often

have the best restaurants – when they're open. Winter time is quiet.

◉ Sights & Activities

There's a vast network of trails, including access to the famed **Pacific Crest Trail**. The Sierra Country Store (p625) is about the only consistently open place in town, and it welcomes Pacific Crest Trail refugees with its laundromat and deli.

To reach the Sierra Buttes, and many lakes and streams nearby, take Gold Lake Hwy north from Hwy 49 at Bassetts, 9 miles northeast of Sierra City. An excellent hiking trail leads 1.1 miles to **Haskell Peak** (8107ft), where you can see from the Sierra Buttes right to Mt Shasta and beyond. To reach the trailhead, turn right from Gold Lake Hwy at Haskell Peak Rd (Forest Rd 9) and follow it for 8.5 miles to the marked parking lot.

Sierra City's local museum, the **Kentucky Mine** (📞530-862-1310; www.sierracountyhistory.org; 100 Kentucky Mine Rd; museum $1, tour adult/child $7/3.50; ⊙10am-4pm Wed-Sun late May-early Sep; 🅿🐾), is a worthy stop that introduces the famed 'Golden Chain Hwy' (California's Hwy 49). Its gold mine and stamp mill are just northeast of town.

🛏 Sleeping & Eating

This is very much outdoorsy terrain, and the campsites are excellent. The cheapest sleeps are in the USFS campgrounds east from Sierra City along Hwy 49. Wild Plum, Sierra, Chapman Creek and Yuba Pass all have vault toilets and running water (Sierra has river water only), and first-come, first-served sites. If you're not bringing your tent, Buttes Resort is the best option.

Salmon Creek Campground CAMPGROUND $
(📞information 530-994-3401, reservations 877-444-6777; www.recreation.gov; Gold Lake Hwy, Calpine; tent & RV sites $24; ⊙mid-May–late Sep; 🅿🐾) With dramatic views of the Sierra Buttes, this USFS campground in the Tahoe National Forest is 2 miles north of Bassetts on Gold Lake Hwy, off Hwy 49. It has vault toilets, running water and sites for tents and RVs, but no hookups.

Sites 16 and 20 are separated from the rest by a creek.

Wild Plum Campground CAMPGROUND $
(📞530-993-1410; tent sites $18) Of the handful of camping areas east of Sierra City, this is the most scenic, along a rushing stretch of the river. The facilities – vault toilets and 47

GOING FOR THE GOLD

California's gold rush started in 1848 when James Marshall was inspecting the fatefully sited lumber mill he was building for John Sutter near present-day Coloma. He saw a sparkle in the mill's tailrace water and pulled out a tiny nugget. Marshall hightailed it to Sacramento and consulted Sutter, who tested the gold by methods described in an encyclopedia. Sutter still wanted to finish his mill so he made a deal with his laborers, allowing them to keep gold they found after-hours if they kept working. Before long, word of the find leaked out.

Sam Brannan was among those who went to Coloma to investigate the rumors shortly after Marshall's find. After finding 6oz of gold in one afternoon, he paraded through San Francisco's streets proclaiming, 'Gold on the American River!' Then he snapped up every piece of mining equipment – from handkerchiefs to shovels – in the area. When gold seekers needed equipment for their adventure, Brannan sold them goods at a 100% markup and was a rich man before the gold seekers even reached the foothills.

The mill's construction was finished in the spring of 1848 when the first wave of miners arrived from San Francisco. Only a few months later, the cities were depleted of able-bodied men, while towns near the 'diggins,' as the mines were called, swelled to thousands. News of the gold rush spread around the world, and by 1849 more than 60,000 people (who became widely known as forty-niners) rushed into California. Everyone was looking for the mother lode: the mythical deposit believed to be the source of all the gold washing into the streams and riverbeds.

Most prospectors didn't stick around after the initial diggings petered out; gold-extraction processes became increasingly equipment-dependent and environmentally disastrous, culminating in the practice of hydraulic mining, by which miners drained lakes and rivers to power their water cannons and blast away entire hillsides. The most extreme example was the still-stark moonscape created at the Malakoff Diggins (p622). People downstream were inundated by the muck and floods and finally sued in 1884. The Sawyer court held the environmental cost was too great to justify the miners staying in business.

first-come, first-served sites – are basic but clean.

★ Buttes Resort
CABIN, LODGE $$

(☑530-862-1170; www.buttesresort.com; 230 Main St; d $95-160; 🅿🐾) In the heart of Sierra City, the small Buttes Resort occupies a lovely spot overlooking the river and is a favorite with hikers looking to recharge. Most cabins have a private deck and barbecue, and some have full kitchens. You can borrow games from the wilderness-loving owners and there's a wood-lined communal area with a pool table.

Red Moose
CAFE $

(☑530-862-1024; www.redmoosecafe.com; 224 Main St; ⏱7:30am-2pm, closed Tue) This rugged old-school wooden building on the main street houses a great little cafe, with an unlikely specialty in the British favorite fish and chips. It also serves big breakfast scrambles, burritos and burgers.

🛍 Shopping

Sierra Country Store
MARKET

(☑530-862-1560; www.sierracountrystore.com; 213 Main St; ⏱8am-8pm May-Sep, 10am-6pm Oct-Apr; 🛜) A welcome sight for Pacific Crest Trail (PCT) hikers and anyone else needing a laundromat, deli, groceries, ATM and wi-fi.

EL DORADO & AMADOR COUNTIES

In the heart of the pine- and oak-covered Sierra foothills, this is where gold was first discovered – Spanish-speaking settlers named El Dorado County after a mythical city of riches.

Today, SUVs en route to South Lake Tahoe pull off Hwy 50 to find a rolling hillside dotted with the historic towns, sun-soaked terraces and fertile soil of one of California's burgeoning wine-growing regions. If you make the stop, don't leave without tasting a glass of regional Zinfandel, which, like the locals, is packed with earthy attitude and regional character. It's also worth the detour to pause at the shore where a glint of gold caught James Marshall's eye.

Coloma-Lotus Valley

Coloma-Lotus Valley surrounds Sutter's Mill (the site of California's first gold discovery) and Marshall Gold Discovery State Historic Park (p627). It is also a great launching pad for rafting operations. The South Fork of the American River gets the most traffic, since it features exciting rapids but is still manageable. Adrenaline junkies who have never rafted before should try the Middle Fork.

☆ Activities

Half-day rafting trips usually begin at **Chili Bar** and end close to the Marshall Gold Discovery State Historic Park (p627). Full-day trips put in at the **Coloma Bridge** and take out at **Salmon Falls**, near Folsom Lake. The half-day options start in Class III rapids and are action-packed (full-day trips start out slowly, then build up to Class IV as a climax). Full-day trips include a lavish lunch. The season usually runs from May to mid-October, depending on water levels. Prices are generally lower on weekdays.

Don't want to get wet? Watch people navigate the **Troublemaker Rapids**, upstream from the bridge near Sutter's Mill in the state park.

Monroe Ridge Trail   WALKING
This 3-mile hike follows a steep route from Coloma. Take High St from the town center, then Marshall Park Way, winding through oak woodland to the Marshall Monument, via James Marshall's rugged cabin and an 1865 Catholic church and pioneer cemetery. You then join the Monroe Ridge Trail, which leads along the ridge, looping back down into Coloma.

Whitewater Connection   RAFTING
(📞530-622-6446; www.whitewaterconnection. com; half-day trips $95-115, full-day $129-149; ⊙Apr-Oct) Whitewater Connection is typical of the area's operators, with knowledgeable guides and excellent food.

Bekeart's Gun Shop   OUTDOORS
(329 Hwy 49, Coloma; per person $7; ⊙10am-3pm Sat & Sun; 🅿) Panning for gold is always popular at Bekeart's Gun Shop, across the street from the Gold Discovery Museum & Visitor Center (p627). It's sometimes open on weekdays.

🛏 Sleeping & Eating

Unless you want to camp, for which you're very well served here, it's best to head south to Placerville, or get a cheap motel bed around Auburn.

American River Resort   CAMPGROUND, CABIN $
(📞530-622-6700; www.americanriverresort.com; 6019 New River Rd; tent & RV sites $25-50, cabins $185-280; 🛜🏊) A quarter mile off Hwy 49, just south of the Marshall Gold Discovery State Historic Park (p627), this site is more built-up than other area campgrounds. There's a small convenience store, free wi-fi, a playground, fishing pond and pool. The sites are basic, but some are right on the river. The most spacious and pretty oak-shaded sites are 14 to 29.

Coloma Club Cafe & Saloon   AMERICAN $
(📞530-626-6390; http://colomaclub.com; 7171 Hwy 49, Coloma; mains from $9; ⊙restaurant 6:30am-9pm, bar 10am-2am; 🛜) The patio at this rowdy old saloon comes alive with guides and river rats when the water is high. It hosts bands and DJ nights on summer weekends.

Cafe Mahjaic   AMERICAN, INTERNATIONAL $$
(Lotus Inn; 📞530-622-9587; www.cafemahjaic. com; 1006 Lotus Rd, Lotus; mains $17-23; ⊙from 5pm Wed-Sun; 🛜) House-baked breads and organic meats, with a sophisticated menu and Japanese and Mexican influences in the cooking. The four-course prix fixe for $35 is a great deal. The owners also run the three-room Lotus Inn (rooms $109 to $139), tucked in the brick house behind the restaurant.

❶ Getting There & Away

Hwy 49 runs right through the heart of Coloma. Boaters can use the **Coloma Shuttle** (p627), which serves the South Fork of the American River. **Coloma Shuttle** (📞530-303-2404; https:// colomashuttle.com; River Park Village, 7308 Suite F; daily membership fee $10) A van that connects local campsites to rafting spots on the river, with a trailer rigged up for boats and gear.

Marshall Gold Discovery State Historic Park

This **state park** (📞530-622-3470; www.parks. ca.gov; Hwy 49, Coloma; per car $8; ⊙8am-8pm late May-early Sep, to 5pm early Sep-late May; 🅿🍴🛜) comprises a fascinating collection of buildings in a bucolic riverside setting at the site of James Marshall's riot-inducing discovery. Buy your ticket at the **museum** (📞530-622-6198; http://marshallgold.com; 310

Back St, Coloma; free with park entry, guided tour adult/child $3/2; ⊘10am-4pm, guided tours 11am & 1pm year-round; P⚒) to display on the dashboard, return to the museum for some background, then explore a replica of **Sutter's Mill**, mosey round the blacksmith's and Chinese store and even try panning for gold.

Compared to the stampede of gun-toting, hill-blasting, hell-raising settlers that populate tall tales along Hwy 49, the Marshall Gold Discovery State Historic Park is a place of tranquility, with two tragic protagonists in John Sutter and James Marshall.

Sutter, who had a fort in Sacramento, partnered with Marshall to build a sawmill on this swift stretch of the American River in 1847. It was Marshall who discovered gold here on January 24, 1848, and though the men tried to keep their findings secret, prospectors from around the world stampeded into town. In one of the ironies of the gold rush, the men who made this discovery died nearly penniless. In another, many of the new immigrants who arrived seeking fortune were indentured, taxed and bamboozled out of anything they found. Meanwhile, as the site museum stresses, the world of the local Native American Nisenan tribespeople was collapsing due to disease and displacement.

In the rare moments when there aren't a million schoolkids running around, the pastoral park by the river makes for a solemn stroll. A trail leads, via displays on panning and hydraulic mining and past the 1860 **Wah Hop Chinese Store**, to the spot on the bank of the wide American River where Marshall found gold and started the revolutionary birth of the 'Golden State.'

On a hill overlooking the park is the **James Marshall Monument**, where he was buried in 1885, a ward of the state. You can drive the circuit but it's much better to meander up to the monument on foot, and then continue on the Monroe Ridge Trail for views of the town and the river.

Panning for gold ($7, free if you have your own equipment) is popular. From 10am to 3pm in the summer, or by request, you get a quick training session and 45 minutes to pan.

Coloma Resort (☎530-621-2267; www.colomaresort.com; 6921 Mt Murphy Rd; tent & RV sites $48-65, cabins & on-site RVs $95-375; 🛜🏊) is a long-established riverside campground with the feel of a summer camp and a good choice for RVs. It comes with wi-fi and a full range of activities: scavenger hunts, a rock wall, karaoke and face-painting. There's a

range of accommodations, from camping to cabins and a country cottage.

Truly delicious soups, sandwiches, baked goods and coffee from well-known Sacramento and local purveyors find their way to **Argonaut Farm to Fork Cafe** (☎530-626-7345; www.argonautcafe.com; 331 Hwy 49, Coloma; items $3-10; ⊘8am-4pm; 🛜📶⚒). Crowds of schoolkids waiting for gelato can slow things down.

Placerville

Placerville is a great little place to explore while traveling between Sacramento and Tahoe on Hwy 50. It has a thriving and well-preserved downtown with antique shops and bars, and local wags who cherish the wild reputation of 'Hangtown' – a name earned when a handful of men swung from the gallows in the mid-1800s. Among the many awesome local legends is 'Snowshoe' John A Thompson, a postal carrier who regularly delivered 80lb of mail on skis from Placerville over the Sierras to Carson Valley during the winter.

Placerville has always been a travelers' town: it was originally a destination for fortune hunters who reached California by following the South Fork of the American River. In 1857 the first stagecoach to cross the Sierra Nevada linked Placerville to Nevada's Carson Valley, which eventually became part of the nation's first transcontinental stagecoach route.

◉ Sights

Main St is the heart of downtown Placerville and runs parallel to Hwy 50 between Canal St and Cedar Ravine Rd. Hwy 49 meets Main St at the west edge of downtown. Looking like a movie set, most buildings along Main St are false fronts and sturdy brick structures from the 1850s, dominated by the spindly **Bell Tower**, a relic from 1856 that once rallied volunteer firemen.

★**El Dorado County Historical Museum** MUSEUM
(http://museum.edcgov.us; 104 Placerville Dr; entry by donation; ⊘10am-4pm Wed-Sun) On the El Dorado County Fairgrounds west of downtown (exit north on Placerville Dr from Hwy 50), is this complex of restored buildings, mining equipment and re-created businesses telling the story of old 'Hangtown.' There are displays on the pony express, wanted posters and wagons, a reconstructed old-time grocery and luxurious silk gowns.

WORTH A TRIP

PLACERVILLE WINERIES

The Placerville region's high heat and rocky soil produces excellent wines, which frequently appear on California menus. Oenophiles could spend a long afternoon rambling through the welcoming vineyards of El Dorado County alone (though a full weekend of tasting could be had if it was coupled with adjoining Amador County). Details can be found at the **El Dorado Winery Association** (☑800-306-3956; www.eldorado wines.org) or **Wine Smith** (p629), a local shop with just about everything grown in the area.

Some noteworthy wineries, all north of Hwy 50, include **Lava Cap Winery** (☑530-621-0175; www.lavacap.com; 2221 Fruit Ridge Rd; tasting fee free-$5; ⊙10am-5pm; ℗), which has an on-hand deli for picnic supplies, and **Boeger Winery** (p628) with its 1872 fieldstone building and blacksmith.

Hangtown's Gold Bug Park & Mine
HISTORIC SITE

(☑530-642-5207; www.goldbugpark.org; 2635 Gold Bug Lane; adult/child $7/4; ⊙10am-4pm Apr-Oct, from noon Sat & Sun Nov-Mar; ℗⏍) About 1 mile north of town via Bedford Ave, this historical park stands on the site of four mining claims that yielded gold from 1849 to 1888. You can descend into the Gold Bug Mine with a self-guided audio tour, do some gem panning ($2 per hour) or just explore the grounds and picnic area for free.

Boeger Winery
WINERY

(☑530-622-8094; www.boegerwinery.com; 1709 Carson Rd; tasting $5-15; ⊙10am-5pm; ℗) Amid vineyards that were planted in the gold rush era, relegated to producing sacramental wine for the local church during Prohibition, and then restored in the 1970s, this historic winery pours a mind-boggling number of varietals, but the flagship wine is Barbera. The place was first settled by an Italian in 1872, and the rugged homestead he built looks straight out of Tuscany.

🛏 Sleeping

There are some wonderful historic accommodations here, and chain motels can be found at either end of the center of Placerville along Hwy 50.

★ Camino Hotel
B&B $

(☑530-644-1800; www.caminohotel.com; 4103 Carson Rd, Camino; r $60-125) A former lumberjack bunkhouse that's every bit as creaky as you'd hope but with rooms that have been redone. The rates are a steal, especially on weekdays, and room 4 is perfect for families with two rooms adjoined by a central sitting room. Breakfast is made to order. A great spot to hunker down while touring Apple Hill's (p633) farms.

National 9 Inn
MOTEL $

(☑530-622-3884; www.national9inns.com; 1500 Broadway; r $50-89; ❄🐾) This mid-century motel, recently renovated by a young couple, is the best bargain in Placerville, even if it lies at the lonely north end of town. The building's exterior is ho-hum, but the rooms are sparkling with refrigerators, microwaves and remodeled baths. It's a great option for travelers who want a clean, no-frills stay and want to support independent businesses.

Cary House Hotel
HISTORIC HOTEL $$

(☑530-622-4271; www.caryhouse.com; 300 Main St; r from $121; ❄@🐾) This historic hotel in the middle of downtown Placerville has a large, comfortable lobby with backlit stained glass depicting scenes from the region's history. Once a major staging stop, it has updated rooms (some with kitchenettes) with period decor. Ask for a room overlooking the courtyard to avoid street noise, or try room 212, a rumored supernatural haunt.

Seasons Bed & Breakfast
B&B $$

(☑530-626-4420; www.theseasons.net; 2934 Bedford Ave; r $90-190; 🐾) Stay near the heart of Placerville at this leafy inn, built as a stamp mill in 1859. A creek runs through the lush garden; you stay in little wooden cottages in the grounds or in an art-deco-themed room in the main house. The owner serves excellent homemade continental breakfasts.

🍴 Eating

Z-Pie
AMERICAN $

(3182 Center St; pies $7.25-7.95; ⊙11am-9pm) With its whimsical take on the all-American comfort-food staple, this casual stop stuffs flaky, butter-crusted pot pies with a gourmet flourish (steak Cabernet! Thai chicken! tomatillo stew!). California beers are on tap. The four-beer sampler ($8) is ideal for the indecisive.

Sweetie Pie's
BREAKFAST $

(www.sweetiepies.biz; 577 Main St; mains $5-12; ⊙6:30am-3pm Mon-Fri, 7am-3pm Sat, 7am-1pm

Sun) Ski bunnies and bums fill this diner and bakery counter on the weekends en route to Tahoe, filling up with egg dishes and top-notch homemade baked goods including heavenly cinnamon rolls. Breakfast is the specialty, with an array of omelets, waffles, scrambles and pancakes, but it also does a capable lunch.

Farm Table Restaurant MEDITERRANEAN $$
(☑530-295-8140; https://ourfarmtable.com; 311 Main St; sandwiches from $8, mains from $14; ☺11am-5pm Mon, 11am-8pm Wed, 11am-9pm Thu-Sat, 9am-5pm Sun; ☑) A lovely deli-style place dishing up well-cooked farm-fresh food with a Mediterranean feel, alongside homespun fare such as rabbit pot pie. It specializes in charcuterie and preserving, and has plenty of gluten-free and veggie options on the menu too.

Heyday Café CAFE $$
(www.heydaycafe.com; 325 Main St; mains $9-25; ☺11am-9pm Tue-Thu, to 10pm Fri & Sat, to 8pm Sun) Fresh and well-executed, the menu here leans toward simple Italian comfort food including pizza, made all the more comfortable by the wood-and-brick interior. The wine list is long on area vineyards. Locals rave about lunch.

🍸 Drinking & Entertainment

Liar's Bench BAR
(☑530-622-0494; 255 Main St; ☺8am-1am) The Liar's Bench survives as the town's classic watering hole under a neon martini sign that beckons after dark. Karaoke nights, a pool table and darts provide entertainment.

★Cozmic Café LIVE MUSIC
(☑530-642-8481; http://ourcoz.com; 594 Main St; ☺cafe 7am-8pm Tue-Sun, pub 6pm-midnight Thu-Sun; ☺🕸) Located in the historic Placerville Soda Works building attached to a mine shaft: ask staff if you can have a peek. The upstairs hall is a fantastic venue for high-quality homespun gigs, including a Thursday open mike night, while the feel-good cafe spotlights organic, vegetarian and healthy fare plus fresh-fruit smoothies. There's a good selection of wine and craft beer.

🛍 Shopping

★Hangtown Antiques ANTIQUES
(452 Main St; ☺11:30am-6pm Mon, Thu & Sun, to 10pm Fri & Sat) Specialists in kitsch and highly collectible Americana, with Hawaiian shirts, alternative vinyl, guitars, ukuleles and even pinball machines. In their words: 'no dishes, no dollies.'

Wine Smith WINE
(☑530-622-0516; www.thewinesmith.com; 346 Main St; ☺11am-8pm Mon-Sat, from noon Sun) The Placerville wine shop that specializes in local vintages – and beers too. It pairs wines with beer and chocolate for tasting sessions.

Placerville Hardware HOMEWARES
(☑530-622-1151; 441 Main St; ☺8am-6pm Mon-Sat, 9am-5pm Sun) The 1852 building, an anchor of Placerville's main drag, is the oldest continuously operating hardware store west of the Mississippi and a place to pick up a brochure for a self-guided tour of the town. The store has a smattering of Gold Country bric-a-brac but most of what clutters the place are bona-fide dry goods, like hammers and buckets.

Bookery BOOKS
(326 Main St; ☺10am-5:30pm Mon-Thu, to 7pm Fri & Sat, to 4pm Sun) A great used-book store to stock up on vacation reading, including Americana and travel and music books.

ℹ Information

El Dorado County Visitors Authority (Chamber of Commerce; ☑530-621-5885; http://visit-eldorado.com; 542 Main St; ☺9am-5pm Mon-Fri) Maps and local information on everything from farm trails to films, breweries and Tahoe.

ℹ Getting There & Away

Amtrak (☑877-974-3322; www.capitolcorridor.org; Mosquito Rd) Runs several buses daily to Sacramento ($20, 1½ hours), though some require train connections to points further along the Capital Corridor route.

El Dorado Transit (☑530-642-5383; www.eldoradotransit.com; 6565 Commerce Way, Diamond Springs; adult/child $1.50/75¢) Operates hourly weekday commuter buses between 7am and 4pm to every corner of town out of the Placerville Station Transfer Center (2984 Mosquito Rd), a charming covered bus stop with benches and restrooms. It's about half a mile from downtown, on the north side of Hwy 50.

Plymouth & Amador City

Two small, sunny villages make equally good bases for exploring Amador County's wine region. The first, Plymouth, is where the region's gold rush history is evident in its original name, Pokerville. Few card sharks haunt the slumbering town today; it wakes late when the tiny main street fills with the smell of barbecue, a few strolling tourists and the odd rumble of a motorcycle posse.

DON'T MISS

AMADOR COUNTY WINE REGION

Amador County might be an underdog among California's winemaking regions, but a thriving circuit of family wineries, gold rush history and local characters make for excellent imbibing without a whiff of pretension. The region lays claim to the oldest Zinfandel vines in the United States and the surrounding country has a lot in common with this celebrated variety – bold, richly colored, earthy and constantly surprising.

The region has two tiny towns, Plymouth and Amador City. Start in Amador and follow Hwy 49 north through the blip known as Drytown, continue on Hwy 49 to Plymouth, and then follow Shenandoah Rd northeast, which takes you past rolling hills of neatly pruned vines. Most hosts are exceedingly welcoming and helpful, offering free tastes and information on their operations. In July, 38 wineries throw an annual 10-day tasting extravaganza.

Maps are available at the wineries, and from the Amador Vintners Association (www.amadorwine.com).

Deaver Vineyards (☑ 209-245-4099; www.deavervineyards.com; 12455 Steiner Rd, Plymouth; tasting fee $5; ⊙ 10:30am-5pm; ℗) A true family affair going back 150 years, where nearly everyone pouring has the last name on the bottles.

Drytown Cellars (☑ 209-245-3500; www.drytowncellars.com; 16030 Hwy 49, Drytown; ⊙ 11am-5pm; ℗) This is one of the most fun tasting rooms in Amador County, thanks to vintner Allen Kreutzer, a gregarious host, and his array of big reds. At the time of research, there was no tasting fee.

Sobon Estate (www.sobonwine.com; 14430 Shenandoah Rd, Plymouth; ⊙ 10am-5pm) Founded in 1977, this is an environmentally conscious family-run estate.

Wilderotter Vineyard (☑ 209-245-6016; www.wilderottervineyard.com; 19890 Shenandoah School Rd, Plymouth; tasting fee $10; ⊙ 10:30am-5pm; ℗) As if the fine rosé and award-winning Sauvignon Blanc weren't enough, here tastings are paired with complimentary artisanal cheeses.

Amador 360 Wine Collective (www.amador360.com; 18950 Hwy 49, Plymouth; ⊙ 11am-6pm) Run by the couple that organizes Amador's annual Barbera extravaganza (http://barberafestival.com), this expansive shop reserves special billing to boutique vintners who otherwise would not offer tastings.

Six miles to the south, Amador City was once home to the Keystone Mine – one of the most prolific gold producers in California – but the town lay deserted from 1942 (when the mine closed) until the 1950s, when a family from Sacramento bought the dilapidated buildings and converted them into antique shops.

☉ Sights

Chew Kee Store Museum MUSEUM
(www.fiddletown.info; Fiddletown; entry by donation; ⊙ noon-4pm Sat Apr-Oct) Remnants of the bygone era are just outside of Plymouth. The Chew Kee Store Museum, 6 miles east in Fiddletown, is an old herbal shop that once served railroad workers. The dusty collection of artifacts frozen in time are objets d'art.

Amador Whitney Museum MUSEUM
(☑ 209-267-5250; www.amador-city.com; Main St, Amador City; ⊙ noon-4pm Fri-Sun) FREE This

rugged little 1860s building looks like something straight out of a John Ford movie, and houses a replica schoolhouse scene and the obligatory mine shaft.

🛏 Sleeping & Eating

★ Imperial Hotel B&B $$
(☑ 209-267-9172; www.imperialamador.com; 14202 Hwy 49, Amador City; r $110-155, ste $125-195; ❄🕾) Built in 1879, this is one of the area's most inventive updates to the typical antique-cluttered hotel, with sleek art-deco touches accenting the warm red brick, a genteel bar and a very good, seasonally minded restaurant (dinner mains $14 to $30). On weekends and holidays, expect a two-night minimum.

★ Taste CALIFORNIAN $$$
(☑ 209-245-3463; www.restauranttaste.com; 9402 Main St, Plymouth; small plates $5-16, dinner mains $24-41; ⊙ 11:30am-2pm Fri-Sun, 5-9pm Mon, Tue,

Thu & Fri, from 4:30pm Sat & Sun) Book a table at Taste, where excellent Amador County wines are paired with a fine menu of California-style cooking (big on meat and game). There's open seating in the wine bar.

🍸 Drinking & Nightlife

Drytown Club BAR
(15950 Hwy 49, Drytown; ⊘ noon-midnight Wed-Fri, to 2am Sat, to 9pm Sun) Tired of wine? Hit the Drytown Club, the local rowdy roadhouse with a Wild West vibe. The bands on weekends are bluesy, boozy and sometimes brilliant: the Doghouse Blues Band plays every Sunday at 4:40pm.

Sutter Creek

Perch on the balcony of one of the gracefully restored buildings on this particularly scenic Main St and view Sutter Creek, a gem of a Gold Country town with raised, arcade sidewalks and high-balconied buildings with false fronts that are perfect examples of California's 19th-century architecture. This is a good option for staying the night when visiting Amador and El Dorado County wineries.

Begin the visit at volunteer-operated Sutter Creek Visitors Center (p632) to collect a walking-tour map of historic traces left by Cornish, Yugoslavian and Italian arrivals, or pick up the excellent, free driving-tour guide to local gold mines.

⦿ Sights

Monteverde General Store HISTORIC BUILDING
(📞209-267-0493; www.suttercreek.org; 11 Randolph St; entry by donation; ⊘ by appointment) This building goes back in time to when the general store was the center of the town's social and economic life, represented by the chairs that circle the pot-belly stove and the detailed historic scale. Senior docents lead tours by appointment. If you're lucky, sometimes the building is open on weekends.

Knight Foundry MINE
(www.knightfoundry.org; 81 Eureka St) In its prime, Sutter Creek was Gold Country's main supply center for all things forged. Three foundries operating in 1873 made pans and rock crushers, but only this one operated until 1996 – it was the last water-powered foundry and machine shop in the US. At the time of research, the interior was closed to visitors, with plans in the works to reopen.

🛏 Sleeping

Eureka Street Inn B&B $$
(📞209-267-5500; www.eurekastreetinn.com; 55 Eureka St; r $145; ❋ 🐾 🛜) Each of the four rooms in this 1914 arts-and-crafts-style home has unique decor and gas fireplaces. Once the home of a wealthy stagecoach operator, the inn is on a quiet side street.

Hotel Sutter HOTEL $$
(📞209-267-0242; www.hotelsutter.com; 53 Main St; r $115-175; P ❋ 🛜) There was some controversy when they started gutting the beloved American Exchange, which had stood in repose for more than 150 years. The bricks and facade may be the only things left, but the modern rooms (some with en-suite bathrooms), very fine restaurant (mains $24 to $32) and cool cellar bar seem to have quelled the protest.

Sutter Creek Inn B&B $$
(📞209-267-5606; www.suttercreekinn.com; 75 Main St; r $120-210; ❋) The 17 rooms and cottages here vary in decor and amenities (antiques, fireplaces, sunny patios). All have private bathrooms. Guests can snooze in the hammock by the gardens or curl up with a book on a comfy chair on the sprawling lawn.

Hanford House Inn B&B $$
(📞209-267-0747; www.hanfordhouse.com; 61 Hanford St; d $145-245; P 🐾 ❋ @ 🛜 🐾) Nod off on platform beds in contemporary rooms or fireplace cottage suites. Chef-prepared breakfasts are harvested from the inn's garden, freshly baked goods appear every afternoon and evening brings wine tasting.

🍴 Eating

Sutter Creek Ice Cream Emporium SWEETS $
(📞209-267-0543; 51 Main St; ⊘11am-6pm Thu-Sun) This sweet shop gets downright enchanting when town icon Stevens Price takes to the 1919 Milton piano and plays ragtime. The former proprietor still stops by in between organizing the Sutter Creek Ragtime Festival each August. Order ice-cream sodas, floats, sundaes or splits.

Gold Dust Pizza PIZZA $
(20 Eureka St; pizzas $14; ⊘11am-9pm, closed Mon winter; 🍴) Crisp, crusty pizza and pitchers of beer make this a favorite; it's the perfect place to hang out and chat to the locals. Combinations like the BBQ pizza put it over the top; you can order (huge) whole pizzas, or opt for slices.

Sutter Creek Cheese Shoppe MARKET $
(209-267-5457; www.suttercreekcheese.com; 33b Main St; 10am-5pm) A stop for cheeses from California and beyond. Call ahead for a picnic box of cheese, a baguette and even a little cutting board and knife to enjoy on your winery hop.

☆ Entertainment

Sutter Creek Theatre PERFORMING ARTS
(916-425-0077; www.suttercreektheater.com; 44 Main St; tickets $15-40) One of several excellent Gold Country arts venues, the theater has nearly a 100-year-long history of presenting live drama, but nowadays schedules mostly musical concerts, as well as films and other cultural events.

ⓘ Information

Sutter Creek Visitors Center (209-267-1344; www.suttercreek.org; 71a Main St; 10am-6pm) Volunteers stand by with maps, information and souvenirs. The printed walking tour through historic downtown is also available online.

Volcano

One of the fading plaques in Volcano, 12 miles upstream from Sutter Creek, tellingly calls it a place of 'quiet history.' Even though the little L-shaped village on the bank of Sutter Creek yielded tons of gold and a Civil War battle, today it slumbers away in remote solitude. Only a smattering of patinated bronze monuments and some characterfully battered buildings attest to Volcano's lively past.

Large sandstone rocks line Sutter Creek, which skirts the center of town. The rocks, now flanked by picnic tables, were blasted from surrounding hills by hydraulic mining before being scraped clean of their gold. The process had dire environmental consequences, but generated miners nearly $100 of booty a day.

⊙ Sights & Activities

**★ Indian Grinding Rock
State Historic Park** HISTORIC SITE
(Chaw'se; 209-296-7488; www.parks.ca.gov; 14881 Pine Grove-Volcano Rd; per car $8; museum 11am-4pm) Two miles southwest of Volcano, this sacred area for the local Miwok comprises a museum in a traditional wooden roundhouse, a village site, a limestone outcrop covered with petroglyphs – 363 originals and a few modern additions – and

over 1000 mortar holes called *chaw'se*, used for grinding acorns and seeds into meal.

During the last weekend of September, the time of the acorn harvest, the Big Time festival at the site features crafts, dances and games. Look out for the wonderful feathered dance capes in the museum.

Daffodil Hill FARM
(209-296-7048; 18310 Rams Horn Grade; donations accepted; 10am-4pm mid-Mar–mid-Apr) This hilltop farm, 2 miles northeast of Volcano, is blanketed with more than 300,000 daffodil blooms in the spring. The McLaughlin and Ryan families have operated the farm since 1887 and keep hyacinths, tulips, violets, lilacs and the occasional peacock among the daffodils.

Black Chasm Cavern CAVE
(888-762-2837; www.caverntours.com; 15701 Pioneer Volcano Rd, Pine Grove; adult/child $17.50/9.50; 9am-5pm mid-May–early Sep, 10am-4pm early Sep–mid-May; P) Less than 1 mile east of Volcano, this National Natural Landmark has the whiff of a tourist trap, but one look at the array of helictite crystals – rare clusters that grow horizontally – makes the crowd more sufferable. Guides for the one-hour tours are all experienced cavers.

⌂ Sleeping & Eating

Union Inn HISTORIC HOTEL $$
(209-296-7711; www.volcanounion.com; 21375 Consolation St; r $130-150; P) The more comfortable of the two historic hotels in Volcano: there are four lovingly updated rooms with crooked floors, two with street-facing balconies. Flat-screen TVs and modern touches are a bit incongruous in the old building, but it's a cozy place to stay. The on-site Union Pub (p633) has the best food in town, and a lovely patio garden.

St George Hotel HISTORIC HOTEL $$
(209-296-4458; www.stgeorgevolcano.com; 16104 Main St; r $79-209) Up the crooked stairs of this charming galleried hotel are 20 rooms that vary in size and amenity (most have shared bathrooms) and are free of clutter. The restaurant (open for dinner Thursday to Sunday and brunch Sunday) has a menu anchored by steak. Hang out in the saloon and try to spot the rumored ghosts.

Union Pub PUB FOOD $$
(209-296-7711; www.volcanounion.com; 21375 Consolation St; mains $10-30; 5-8pm Mon & Thu, to 9pm Fri, noon-9pm Sat, noon-8pm Sun) The Un-

ion Inn's (p633) pub has a superb menu of big burgers, salads and steaks, plus an array of local wines and beers.

☆ Entertainment

Volcano Theatre Company PERFORMING ARTS
(☑209-419-0744; www.volcanotheatre.org; 16121 Main St; tickets adult/child $16/11; ⊙Sat & Sun Apr-Nov) On weekends between April and November, this highly regarded company produces live dramas in an outdoor amphitheater and in the tiny 1856 Cobblestone Theater.

🛍 Shopping

Country Store FOOD & DRINKS
(☑209-296-4459; 16146 Main St; ⊙10am-6pm Mon-Sat, 11am-5pm Sun) In continuous use since 1852, this fantastically atmospheric and authentic old store has creaky floorboards, a long wooden counter and inbuilt stools, and shelves groaning with tins and bottles. The shopkeeper whips up canned beef sandwiches and hamburgers in the small cafe.

Jackson

Jackson has some historic buildings and a small downtown, but it ain't much to look at. It stands at the junction of Hwy 49 and Hwy 88, which turns east from Hwy 49 here and heads over the Sierra Nevada near the Kirkwood ski resort.

◉ Sights

Kennedy Gold Mine HISTORIC SITE
(☑209-223-9542; http://kennedygoldmine.com; 12594 Kennedy Mine Rd; adult/child $10/6) You can't miss the ominous steel headframe of the mine from the road, rising to 125ft. Its pulleys lifted ore and miners from the bowels of the earth. Guided tours last about 90 minutes and take you past the stamp, gold recovery mill and massive tailing wheels. The parking lot is off North Main St.

On-site **Kennedy Tailing Wheels Park** has marvelous examples of engineering and craftsmanship – four iron and wood wheels, 58ft in diameter, that transported tailings from neighboring Eureka Mine over two low hills. Once the deepest mine in the area, this is now a peaceful park good for a stroll. Be sure to climb to the top of the hill behind the wheels to see the impounding dam.

Mokelumne Hill HISTORIC SITE
(www.mokehill.org) The somewhat undiscovered settlement of Mokelumne Hill is 7 miles

WORTH A TRIP

APPLE HILL
....
In 1860, a miner planted a Rhode Island Greening apple tree on a hill and with it established the foundation for bountiful Apple Hill, a 20-sq-mile area east of Placerville and north of Hwy 50 where there are more than 60 orchards. Apple growers sell directly to the public, usually from August to December, and some let you pick your own. Other fruits and Christmas trees are available during different seasons.

Maps of Apple Hill are available online through the **Apple Hill Association** (☑530-644-7692; www.applehill.com; 2461 Larsen Dr, Camino), or use the El Dorado **Farm Trails Guide** (http://visit-eldorado.com).

A great place to hunker down while touring the farms is the **Camino Hotel** (p628).

south of Jackson just off Hwy 49. Settled by French trappers in the early 1840s, it's a good place to see historic buildings without the common glut of antique stores and gift shops. Stay at the old-style Hotel Leger (p634) if you want to soak up the peace and quiet.

🛏 Sleeping & Eating

Hotel Leger HERITAGE HOTEL $
(☑209-286-1401; www.hotelleger.com; 8304 Main St, Mokelumne Hill; r $85) A grand and pleasingly old-fashioned place with an impressive galleried frontage and pretty decent food in the restaurant, plus characterful creaky floorboards and a stuck-in-time saloon bar. Get a room on the street side for a view of the picturesque little hillside town of Mokelumne Hill.

National Hotel HISTORIC HOTEL $$
(☑209-223-0500; www.national-hotel.com; 2 Water St; r $140-160) Jackson's historic hotel has had a serious upgrade from the gold rush era. While the restored building retains its historical details, all rooms are newly refurbished with luxurious details like gas fireplaces and heated floors. The top-notch steakhouse and bar downstairs complete the picture.

Mel's & Faye's Diner AMERICAN $
(http://melandfayes.homestead.com; 31 N Hwy 49; meals $7-12; ⊙10am-11pm Sun-Thu, to 2am Fri & Sat) A local institution near Hwy 88 that dates back to 1956: there's a takeout window

but it's not meant for quick stops. Take a seat on the bottle-green leather benches for solid diner fare that includes huge breakfasts, classic burgers (try the chili-soaked 'Miner'), luscious milkshakes and – to balance the grease binge – a decent salad bar.

ℹ Information

Amador County Chamber of Commerce (☎209-223-0350; www.amadorcountychamber.com; 115 Main St; ⊗8am-4pm Mon-Fri, 10am-2pm Sat & Sun) Stop off on Main St to pick up information about sights and stays.

ℹ Getting There & Away

The only way to easily travel through this area is with your own wheels. By car, Jackson is 2½ hours from San Francisco and just over one hour to the ski resorts of South Lake Tahoe.

Placer County runs its bus system out of Jackson, but good luck catching a bus – they're few and far between. **Amador Transit** (☎209-267-9395; http://amadortransit.com; 115 Valley View Way; fares $1-3; ⊗Mon-Fri) is a bit better. It makes a weekday connection through Sutter Creek to Sacramento ($1, one hour) and, if you have enough patience, you can connect to Calaveras County and southern Gold Country.

CALAVERAS COUNTY & SOUTH GOLD COUNTRY

The southern region of Gold Country is hot as blazes in the summer, so cruising through its historic gold rush hubs will demand more than one stop for ice cream. The tall tales of yesteryear come alive here through the region's famous former residents: author Mark Twain, who got his start writing about a jumping frog contest in Calaveras County, and Joaquin Murrieta, a controversial symbol of the lawlessness of the frontier era who somehow seems to have frequented every old bar and hotel in the area.

Angels Camp

On the southern stretch of Hwy 49 one figure looms over all others: literary giant Mark Twain, who got his first big break with the story of *The Celebrated Jumping Frog of Calaveras County*, written and set in Angels Camp. There are differing claims as to when or where Twain heard this tale, but Angels Camp makes the most of it. There are gentlemanly Twain impersonators and statues, and bronze frogs on Main St honoring the champions of the past 80 years, as well as the **Jumping Frog Jubilee** (www.frogtown.org; 2465 Gun Club Rd; from $8; ⊗May; 🅷) on the third weekend in May (in conjunction with the county fair and something of a Harley rally). Look for the plaque of Rosie the Ribeter, who set an impressive 21ft record in 1986. Today the town is an attractive mix of buildings from the gold rush to art-deco periods.

It's perhaps not the greatest natural beauty, but Moaning Cavern, 7 miles east of Angels Camp, does have the most thrills. Visitors can rappel 165ft to the bottom ($72). A pile of bones discovered here are some of the oldest human remains in the US. There's also above-ground zip lines and a self-guided nature walk. Winter events like caroling utilize cave acoustics.

Strung out along Hwy 49 are a number of motels, including the simple **Jumping Frog** (☎209-736-2191; 330 Murphys Grade Rd; d $70; 🅰🅰🅰).

For food, the class act in downtown Angels Camp is **Crusco's** (www.cruscos.com; 1240 S Main St; mains $14-26; ⊗11am-3pm & 5-9pm Thu-Mon), which puts out a serious, authentic northern Italian menu. The owners regularly hit Italy for more recipes, like the Polenta Antonella (creamy cornmeal with chicken and mushroom sauce).

There are a couple of bars in town, but your best bet for a night out here is the wonderful restored art-deco **cinema** (☎209-736-2472; www.cinemawest.com; Angels 6 Theatres, 1228 S Main St; tickets $9.25).

Calaveras Transit (☎209-754-4450; http://transit.calaverasgov.us; 750 Industrial Way, San Andreas; fare $2) operates the most reliable public transportation system in the region from the Government Center in downtown San Andreas. Use it to connect to Angels Camp ($2, 30 minutes, several times daily) and other surrounding towns. You can catch it mid-route – just flag it down. To connect via public transportation to the rest of California, you have to catch Route 1 to San Andreas, switch to Route 3 to Mokelumne Hill and finally transfer to Amador Transit (p634).

Murphys

With its white picket fences and old-world charm, Murphys is one of the more scenic towns along the southern stretch of Gold Country, befitting its nickname as 'Queen of the Sierra.' It lies 8 miles east of Hwy 49 on

Murphys Grade Rd, and is named for Daniel and John Murphy, who founded a trading post and mining operation on Murphy Creek in 1848. They employed the struggling local Miwok and Yokut people as laborers. While some settlers continued to persecute the tribes, John eventually married Pokela, a chieftain's daughter.

The town's Main St is refined, with tons of wine-tasting rooms, boutiques, galleries and good strolling. For information and a town overview, look to www.visitmurphys.com.

◉ Sights & Activities

Ironstone Vineyards   WINERY
(www.ironstonevineyards.com; 1894 Six Mile Rd; tasting fee $5; ⊙11am-5pm; 🐾) 🍴 The unusually family-friendly atmosphere makes the wine feel secondary at Ironstone. There's a natural spring waterfall, a mechanical pipe organ, frequent exhibits by local artists, and blooming grounds. By the deli, the museum displays the world's largest crystalline gold leaf specimen (it weighs 44lb and was found in Jamestown in 1992). The enormous tasting room accommodates crowds.

Murphys Old Timers Museum   MUSEUM
(www.murphysoldtimersmuseum.com; 470 Main St; donation requested; ⊙noon-4pm Fri-Sun) The name is a good hint that this place approaches history with a humorous touch. Housed in an 1856 building, it has an inscrutable tintype of the outlaw Joaquin Murrieta and the entertaining 'Wall of Comparative Ovations.' Guided tours of town leave from the museum every Saturday at 10am.

California Cavern   CAVING
(☎209-736-2708; www.caverntours.com; adult/child $14.95/7.95; ⊙10am-5pm Apr-Oct; 🐾) In Cave City, 12 winding miles north of Murphys (take Main St to Sheep Ranch Rd to Cave City Rd), is a natural cavern, which John Muir described as 'graceful flowing folds deeply placketed like stiff silken drapery.' Regular tours take 60 to 90 minutes.

🛏 Sleeping

Most accommodations in Murphys are top-end B&Bs. For the same price, there are some attractive rental cottages (p636) just off Main St, or check nearby Angels Camp or Arnold for cheaper alternatives.

★ Victoria Inn   B&B $$
(☎209-728-8933; www.victoriainn-murphys.com; 402 Main St; r $135-320, cottages from $295;

CALAVERAS BIG TREES STATE PARK

Calaveras Big Trees State Park (☎209-795-2334; www.parks.ca.gov; 1170 Hwy 4, Arnold; per car $10; ⊙sunrise-sunset; 🅿🐾) Home to giant sequoia trees that reach as high as 250ft with trunk diameters of over 25ft, these leftovers from the Mesozoic era are thought to weigh upwards of 2000 tons, or close to 10 blue whales. The giants are distributed in two large groves, one easily seen on the **North Grove Trail**, a 1.5-mile self-guided loop, near the park entrance. On the more remote **South Grove Trail**, it's a 5-mile round-trip hike to **Agassiz Tree**, the park's largest specimen.

Camping (☑reservations 800-444-7275; www.reserveamerica.com; off Hwy 4; tent & RV sites $25-35, cabins $165-185; 🅿) is popular and reservations essential. North Grove Campground is near the park entrance; less charming is Oak Hollow Campground, 4 miles further on the park's main road. Most atmospheric are the hike-in environmental sites. Store food and toiletries in the provided bear lockers at all times.

🅿🐾🛜) This newly built B&B has glamorous rooms with claw-foot slipper tubs, sleigh beds and balconies. Some rooms have wood-burning stoves and balconies overlooking the courtyard fountain. The common spaces, like the long verandah for enjoying tapas and wine from the **restaurant and bar** (☎209-728-0107; http://vrestaurantandbar-murphys.com; 402 Main St; mains $11-32; ⊙bistro 11:30am-8:30pm, restaurant from 5:30pm Wed-Sun), have chic, modern country appeal.

Murphys Vacation Rentals   COTTAGE $$
(☎209-736-9372; www.murphysvacationrentals.com; 549 S Algiers St; cottages $140-245) For the same price as a frilly B&B, picturesque cottages clustered just off Main St are available for rent. The charming Church St cottage has two bedrooms that sleep four and feels like the set of a 1950s TV show. Cleaning fee extra.

Murphys Historic Hotel   INN $$
(☎209-728-3444; www.murphyshotel.com; 457 Main St; d $130-205, with shared bath $95-215; 🅿🐾) Since 1856, this hotel has been an anchor on Main St. A must-stop on the

Mark-Twain-slept-here tour, the original structure is a little rough around the edges. The adjoining buildings have bland, modern rooms that cost more. Make your way down to the dining room for fried chicken ($21) at dinner.

✗ Eating

Firewood AMERICAN, PIZZA **$**
(📞 209-728-3248; www.firewoodeats.com; 420 Main St; mains $8-15; ⊘ 11am-9pm Sun-Thu, to 9:30pm Fri & Sat; 🖟) A rarity in a town with so much historical frill, Firewood's exposed-concrete walls and corrugated metal offer a minimalist respite. When the weather's nice, the front wall is opened for alfresco dining. There are wines by the glass, half a dozen beers on tap and basic pub fare, but the wood-fired pizzas are the hallmark.

Grounds MODERN AMERICAN **$$**
(📞 209-728-8663; www.groundsrestaurant.com; 402 Main St; dinner mains $17-26; ⊘ 7am-3pm Mon & Tue, to 8:30pm Wed-Sun; 🖟) This casually elegant cafe does everything competently – expert breakfast foods, a roster of light lunch mains and weekend dinners of steak and fresh fish. Iced herbal tea and fresh vegetarian options are key when temperatures outside rise. Opening hours vary.

Alchemy Market & Cafe CALIFORNIAN **$$**
(📞 209-728-0700; www.alchemymarket.com; 191 Main St; mains $13-25; ⊘ 11am-8pm Mon, Tue, Thu & Fri, from 10:30am Sat & Sun) The stellar cafe menu here has a long wine list and many dishes, from parsley truffle fries to iron-skillet mussels, all great for sharing on the patio. Live jazz every Tuesday from 5:30pm to 8pm.

Columbia

More than any other place in Gold Country, Columbia blurs the lines between present and past with a carefully preserved gold rush town – complete with volunteers in period dress – at the center of a modern community. In 1850 Columbia was founded over the 'Gem of the Southern Mines,' and as much as $150 million in gold was found here. The center of the town (run by the state parks system) looks almost exactly as it did in its heyday. On the fringe of these blocks are homes and businesses that blend in so well it's hard to tell what's park and what's not.

Docents lead free hour-long tours weekends at 11am from the Columbia Museum (p637).

◉ Sights

Columbia State Historic Park HISTORIC SITE
(📞 209-588-9128; www.parks.ca.gov; Main St; ⊘ most businesses 10am-5pm; P 🖟) **FREE** The so-called 'Gem of the Southern Mines' is like a miniature Gold Rush Disneyland, but with more authenticity and heart. Four blocks of town have been preserved, where volunteers perambulate in 19th-century dress and demonstrate gold panning. The blacksmith's shop, theater, hotels and saloon are all carefully framed windows into California's past. The yesteryear illusion of Main St is shaken only a bit by fudge shops and the occasional banjo-picker or play-acting forty-niner whose cell phone rings.

Columbia Museum HISTORIC SITE
(📞 209-532-3184; www.parks.ca.gov; cnr Main & State Sts; ⊘ 10am-5pm Apr-Sep, to 4pm Oct-Mar) **FREE** Looking rather like dinosaur bones, limestone and granite boulders are noticeable around town. These were washed out of the surrounding hills by hydraulic mining and scraped clean by prospectors. There's a fascinating explanation of this technique at this renovated museum inside Knapp's Store.

🛏 Sleeping & Eating

Fallon Hotel HISTORIC HOTEL **$**
(📞 information 209-532-1470, reservations 800-444-7275; www.reserveamerica.com; 11175 Washington St; r $50-115; 🕸🛜) The historic Fallon

---

GOLD COUNTY'S BEST CAVES
....

➡ **California Cavern** (p636) in Murphys, marveled at by John Muir, offers a wide variety of tours and lengthy adventure trips.

➡ **Moaning Cavern** (📞 209-736-2708; www.caverntours.com; 5350 Moaning Cave Rd, Vallecito; adult/child $17.50/9.50; ⊘ 10am-5pm) in Angels Camp has the deepest cave rappelling in California and an above-ground zip line.

➡ **Black Chasm** (p633) in Volcano features a quiet self-guided Zen Garden walk above ground and rare helictite crystals below.

Hotel hosts the most professional theater troupe in the region, the Sierra Repertory Theatre (p637). The (apparently haunted) building is done out in period style, with floral wallpaper, glass lanterns and gleaming wooden furnishings.

Cottages COTTAGE $$
(☑information 209-532-1479, reservations 800-444-7275; www.reserveamerica.com; 1-/2-/3-bedroom cottage $127/149/171; P☻) A cozy alternative to staying in a hotel are these cottages, two at the end of Main St, and the largest with three bedrooms on Columbia St.

City Hotel HISTORIC HOTEL $$
(☑information 209-532-1479, reservations 800-444-7275; www.reserveamerica.com; 22768 Main St; r $85-115; P☻✿☎) Among a handful of restored Victorian hotels in the area, City Hotel is the most elegant, with rooms that overlook a shady stretch of Main St. Adjoining the on-site restaurant Christopher's at the City Hotel (mains $10 to $30), What Cheer Saloon is an atmospheric Gold Country joint with oil paintings of lusty ladies and striped wallpaper.

☆ Entertainment

Sierra Repertory Theatre THEATER
(☑209-532-3120; www.sierrarep.org; 11175 Washington St) This theater mixes up Shakespeare, musicals, farce and popular revues.

Sonora & Jamestown

Settled in 1848 by miners from Sonora, Mexico, this area was once a cosmopolitan center of commerce and culture with parks, elaborate saloons and the Southern Mines' largest concentration of gamblers and gold. Racial unrest drove the Mexican settlers out and their European immigrant usurpers got rich on the Big Bonanza Mine, where Sonora High School now stands. That single mine yielded 12 tons of gold in two years (including a 28lb nugget).

Today, people en route to Yosemite National Park use Sonora as a staging post. The historic center is so well preserved that it's a frequent backdrop in films.

Smaller Jamestown is 3 miles south of Sonora, just south of the Hwy 49/108 junction. Founded around the time of Tuolumne County's first gold strike in 1848, today the place limps along on tourism and antiques. It has its charm but is only a few blocks long.

⦿ Sights & Activities

Sonora is a base for **white-water rafting**: the Upper Tuolumne River is known for Class IV and V rapids and its population of golden eagles and red-tailed hawks, while the Stanislaus River is more accessible with Class III rapids. **Sierra Mac River Trips** (☑209-591-8027; www.sierramac.com; 27890 Hwy 120, Groveland; trips from $269) and All-Outdoors (p617) both have good reputations and run trips of one day or more on multiple rivers.

Tuolumne County Museum MUSEUM
(www.tchistory.org; 158 W Bradford St, Sonora; ☺10am-4pm Mon-Fri, to 3:30pm Sat) FREE In the former 1857 Tuolumne County Jail, you'll find this great little museum with a fortune's worth of gold on display in the form of nuggets and gold-bearing quartz. Each of the former jail cells takes on a different theme, one of which is the little-told story of African Americans during the gold rush.

The museum also explores the story of former slave William Suggs, who set up a leather harness business, built a mansion in the town and successfully campaigned to overturn segregation in local schools.

Railtown 1897
State Historic Park STATE PARK
(☑209-984-3953; www.railtown1897.org; 10501 Reservoir Rd, Jamestown; adult/child $5/3, incl train ride $15/10; ☺9:30am-4:30pm Apr-Oct, 10am-3pm Nov-Mar, train rides 10:30am-3pm Sat & Sun Apr-Oct; P♿) Five blocks east of Jamestown's Main St, this 26-acre collection of trains and railroad equipment is the photogenic sister to Sacramento's rail museum. It's served as a backdrop for countless films and TV shows including *Back to the Future III*, *Unforgiven* and *High Noon*. On some weekends and holidays, you can ride the narrow-gauge railroad that once transported ore, lumber and miners.

California Gold Panning Lessons OUTDOORS
(☑209-694-6768; www.gold-panning-california.com; 17712 Harvard Mine Rd, Jamestown; sluicing & panning specials per 2hr from $180; ☺9am-3pm Jun-Oct, or by appointment) Miner John and his crew provide boots and all needed equipment for a genuine experience panning at Woods Creek and beyond. Be warned: real prospecting involves lots of digging. A couple of hours in, you'll have gold fever, a blister or both. Take a right onto Harvard Mine Rd and drive to the parking lot with a 'Gold Panning' sign. Best to call ahead.

🛏 Sleeping & Eating

⭐ Bradford Place Inn
B&B $$

(☑209-536-6075; www.bradfordplaceinn.com; 56 W Bradford St, Sonora; r $145-265; ❄@🖙) Gorgeous gardens and inviting porch seats surround this four-room B&B, which emphasizes green living. With a two-person claw-foot tub, the Bradford Suite is the definitive, romantic B&B experience. Breakfast can be served on the verandah: try the crème brûlée French toast or the filling Mother Lode Skillet.

Gunn House Hotel
HISTORIC HOTEL $$

(☑209-532-3421; www.gunnhousehotel.com; 286 S Washington St, Sonora; r $84-140; P🖙❄🖙) For a lovable alternative to Gold Country's cookie-cut chains, this historic hotel hits the sweet spot. Rooms feature period decor and guests take to rocking chairs on the wide porches in the evening. A nice pool and a breakfast buffet also make it a hit with families.

⭐ Legends Books, Antiques & Old-Fashioned Soda Fountain
CAFE $

(☑209-532-8120; 131 S Washington St, Sonora; ⊙11am-5pm) The place to sip sarsaparilla, snack on a Polish dog or share a scoop of huckleberry ice cream at a 26ft-long mahogany bar here since 1850. Then browse antiques and books downstairs in the old tunnel miners used to secret their stash directly into the former bank; there's even an in-house stream downstairs.

Lighthouse Deli & Ice Cream Shop
DELI $

(www.thelighthousedeli.com; 28 S Washington St, Sonora; sandwiches $8-9; ⊙8am-4pm Mon-Sat) The flavors of N'Awlins make this unassuming deli an unexpected delight. The muffeletta – a toasted piece of Cajun paradise that's stacked high with ham, salami, cheese and olive tapenade – is the best sandwich within 100 miles.

🍷 Drinking & Entertainment

The free and widely available weekend supplement of the *Union Democrat* comes out on Thursday and lists movies, music, performance art and events for Tuolumne County.

Iron Horse Lounge
BAR

(☑209-532-4482; 97 S Washington St, Sonora; beer $3-6; ⊙8:30am-2am) Sonora's classic and fairly rugged hangout in the center of town. Bottles glitter like gold on the backlit bar.

Sierra Repertory Theatre
PERFORMING ARTS

(☑209-532-3120; www.sierrarep.com; 13891 Hwy 108, Sonora; tickets adult $26-32, child $18) Located in a restored tin warehouse in East Sonora, close to the Junction Shopping Center. This critically acclaimed company also performs in the Fallon Hotel (p637) in Columbia.

🛍 Shopping

Sierra Nevada Adventure Company
SPORTS & OUTDOORS

(www.snacattack.com; 173 S Washington St, Sonora; ⊙10am-6pm) This flagship is stocked with maps and has equipment for rent and sale. There's also friendly advice from passionate guides with knowledge of ways to get outdoors in the area.

❶ Information

Mi-Wuk Ranger District Office (☑209-586-3234; 24695 State Hwy 108; ⊙8am-4:30pm Mon-Fri) For information and permits for the Stanislaus National Forest up in the Sierra Nevada on Hwy 108.

Tuolumne County Visitors Bureau (☑209-533-4420; www.yosemitegoldcountry.com; 193 S Washington St, Sonora; ⊙9am-6pm daily Jun-Sep, Mon-Sat Oct-May) More so than other brochure-jammed chamber of commerce joints, the staff here offer helpful trip-planning advice throughout Gold Country as well as Yosemite National Park and Stanislaus National Forest.

❶ Getting There & Away

Hwy 108 is the main access road here, and it links up with I-5, 55 miles west near Stockton. A summer-only entrance to Yosemite National Park lies 60 scenic miles south on Hwy 120.

A limited service is provided weekdays by **Tuolumne County Transit** (☑209-532-0404; www.tuolumnecountytransit.com; 48 Yaney Ave, Sonora; fare $1.50; ⊙Mon-Fri) buses, which make a circuit from Sonora hourly from 7am to 7:46pm; they also stop in Columbia and Jamestown less frequently.

Gleaming green **trolleys** (☑209-532-0404; www.tuolumnecountytransit.com; Washington St, Sonora; adult/child $1.50/free; ⊙11am-9pm Sat, to 4pm Sun mid-May–early Sep) link the sights in Columbia, Sonora and Jamestown.

YARTS (☑209-388-9589; www.yarts.com; adult/child return $25/18, one-way $13/9) For Yosemite visitors staying in the Sonora area, YARTS operates two round-trip buses connecting downtown Sonora, Jamestown's Main St and Yosemite from June 14 to September 1. There is just one round-trip bus in May and September. Ask nicely to be dropped off at unscheduled stops in Yosemite.

Lake Tahoe

Best Places to Eat

➜ Moody's Bistro & Lounge (p666)

➜ Cafe Fiore (p653)

➜ Fire Sign Cafe (p658)

➜ Fat Cat (p660)

➜ Old Granite Street Eatery (p673)

Best Places to Sleep

➜ Cedar House Sport Hotel (p665)

➜ Hostel Tahoe (p668)

➜ PlumpJack Squaw Valley Inn (p662)

➜ Deerfield Lodge at Heavenly (p650)

➜ Sorensen's (p650)

Why Go?

Shimmering in myriad shades of blue and green, Lake Tahoe is the USA's second-deepest lake and, at 6255ft high, it is also one of the highest-elevation lakes in the country. Driving around the spellbinding 72-mile scenic shoreline will give you quite a workout behind the wheel. Generally, the north shore is quiet and upscale; the west shore, rugged and old-timey; the east shore, undeveloped; the south shore, busy and tacky, with aging motels and flashy casinos; and nearby Reno, the biggest little city in the region.

The horned peaks surrounding the lake, which straddles the California–Nevada state line, are year-round destinations. The sun shines on Tahoe three out of every four days. Swimming, boating, kayaking, windsurfing, stand up paddle surfing (SUP) and other water sports take over in summer, as do hiking, camping and wilderness backpacking adventures. Winter brings bundles of snow, perfect for hitting Tahoe's top-tier ski and snowboard resorts.

When to Go

South Lake Tahoe

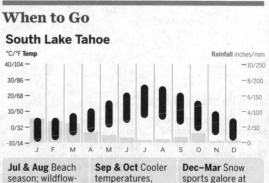

Jul & Aug Beach season; wildflowers bloom, and hiking and mountain-biking trails open.

Sep & Oct Cooler temperatures, colorful foliage and fewer tourists after Labor Day.

Dec–Mar Snow sports galore at resorts; storms bring hazardous roads.

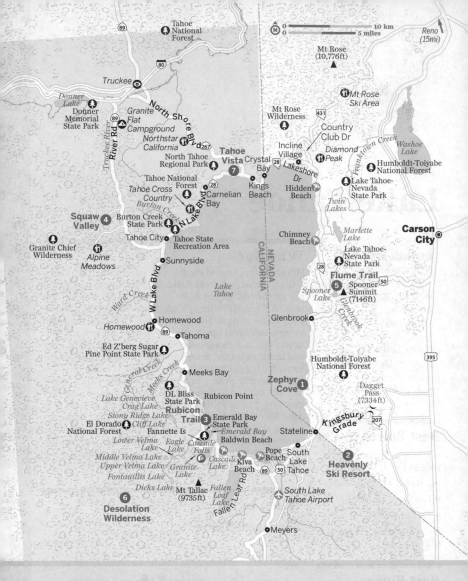

Lake Tahoe Highlights

1 Surveying the shimmering expanse of Lake Tahoe from a kayak or from the sandy beach at **Zephyr Cove** (p646).

2 Swooshing down the vertiginous double-black-diamond runs of **Heavenly** (p645) ski resort.

3 Trekking **Rubicon Trail** (p655) from Vikingsholm

Castle on sparkling Emerald Bay to DL Bliss State Park.

4 Swimming in an outdoor lagoon or ice-skating above 8000ft atop the cable-car line in **Squaw Valley** (p661).

5 Thundering down **Flume Trail** (p670) on a mountain bike to tranquil Spooner Lake.

6 Escaping summer crowds with an overnight backpack to alpine lakes and high-country meadows in the **Desolation Wilderness** (p652).

7 Cozying up with your family around a lakefront beach fire pit or inside a comfortable cabin at **Tahoe Vista** (p667) on the no-fuss northern shore.

SOUTH LAKE TAHOE & STATELINE

Highly congested and arguably overdeveloped, South Lake Tahoe is a chockablock commercial strip bordering the lake and framed by picture-perfect alpine mountains. At the foot of the world-class Heavenly (p642) mountain resort, and buzzing from the gambling tables in the casinos just across the border in Stateline, NV, Lake Tahoe's south shore draws visitors with a cornucopia of activities, lodging and restaurant options, especially for summer beach access and tons of powdery winter snow.

◉ Sights

Heavenly Gondola   CABLE CAR

(Map p644; www.skiheavenly.com; Heavenly Village; adult/child 5-12yr/youth13-18yr from $45/27/37; ☉10am-5pm Jun-Aug, reduced off-season hours; ⊕) Soar to the top of the world as you ride this gondola, which sweeps you from Heavenly Village to some 2.4 miles up the mountain in just 12 minutes. From the observation deck at 9123ft, get gobsmacking panoramic views of the entire Tahoe Basin, the Desolation Wilderness and Carson Valley, then jump back on for the final, short hop to the top.

From here there's a range of activities to enjoy (climbing, zip-lining, tubing) and decent eating (**Tamarack Lodge** restaurant and bar), or jump on the **Tamarack Express** chairlift to get all the way to the mountain summit.

Tallac Historic Site   HISTORIC SITE

(Map p644; www.tahoeheritage.org; Tallac Rd; optional tour adult/child $10/5; ☉10am-4pm daily mid-Jun–Sep, Fri & Sat late May–mid-Jun; ⊕) **FREE** Sheltered by a pine grove and bordering a wide, sandy beach, this national historic site sits on the archaeologically excavated grounds of the former Tallac Resort, a swish vacation retreat for San Francisco's high society around the turn of the 20th century. Feel free to just amble or cycle around the breezy forested grounds, today transformed into a community arts hub, where leashed dogs are allowed.

Inside the 1921 **Baldwin Estate**, the museum has exhibits on the history of the resort and its founder, Elias 'Lucky' Baldwin, who made a bundle off Nevada's Comstock Lode. Nearby is the 1894 **Pope Estate**, now used for art exhibits and open for guided tours (daily except Wednesday). The boathouse of the **Valhalla Estate** functions as a theater venue. The 1923 **Grand Hall** contains an art

---

SKIING IN TAHOE

Lake Tahoe has phenomenal skiing, with thousands of acres of the white stuff beckoning at more than a dozen resorts. Winter-sports complexes range from the giant, jet-set slopes of Squaw Valley (p661), Heavenly (p645) and Northstar (p663), to the no-less-enticing insider playgrounds like Sugar Bowl (p664) and Homewood (p657). Tahoe's simply got a hill for everybody, from kids to kamikazes. Ski season generally runs November to April, although it can start as early as October and last until the last storm whips through in May or even June. All resorts have ski schools, equipment rental and other facilities; check their websites for snow conditions, weather reports and free ski-season shuttle buses from area lodgings.

Downhill Skiing & Snowboarding

Tahoe's downhill resorts are usually open every day from December through April, weather permitting. See Winter Sports listings for Truckee & Donner Lake, Tahoe City and South Lake Tahoe & Stateline. All of these resorts rent equipment and have places to warm up slope side and grab a quick bite or après-ski beer. Most offer group ski and snowboard lessons for adults and children (a surcharge applies,but usually no reservations are required).

Cross-Country Skiing & Snowshoeing

Tahoe's cross-country ski resorts are usually open daily from December through March, and sometimes into April. See Winter Sports listings for Truckee & Donner Lake, Tahoe City and South Lake Tahoe & Stateline. Most rent equipment and offer lessons; reservations typically aren't taken for either, so show up early in the morning for the best availability.

Lake Tahoe

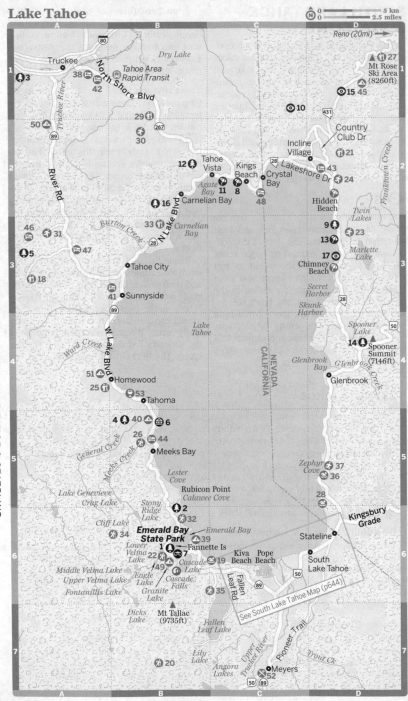

See South Lake Tahoe Map (p644)

Lake Tahoe

LAKE TAHOE SOUTH LAKE TAHOE & STATELINE

gallery and gift shop. In summer concerts, plays and other cultural events happen here, most notably the three-decade-old Valhalla Festival of Arts, Music & Film (p649).

The parking lot is about 3 miles north of the 'Y' junction of Hwys 89 and 50.

Lake Tahoe Historical Society Museum   MUSEUM
(Map p644; ☑530-541-5458; 3058 Lake Tahoe Blvd; ☺ usually 11am-3pm Sat & Sun) FREE This small but interesting museum displays artifacts from Tahoe's pioneer past, including Washoe tribal baskets, vintage black-and-

white films, hoary mining memorabilia and a model of a classic Lake Tahoe steamship. On summer Saturday afternoons, join a volunteer-led tour of the restored 1930s cabin out back.

🏃 Activities

Tahoe Treetop Adventure Park   ADVENTURE SPORTS
(Map p642; ☑530-581-7563; www.tahoetreetop. com; 725 Granlibakken Rd, off Hwy 89; adult/child 5-12yr $55/45; ☺10am-5:30pm Sat & Sun Jan-late

South Lake Tahoe

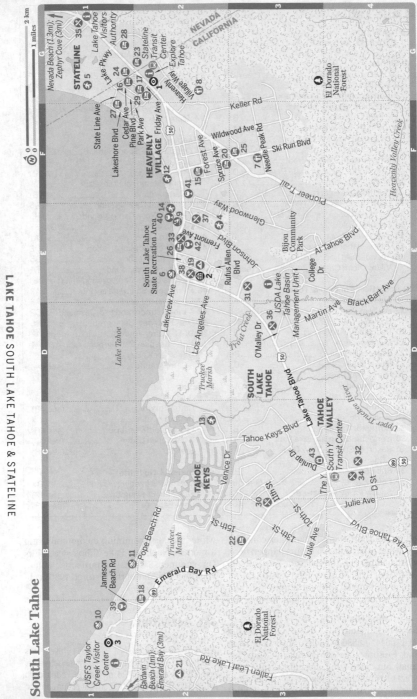

South Lake Tahoe

May, 9am-7:30pm daily late May-Aug, reduced hours Sep-Dec; ⊛) At the Granlibakken (p660) resort, take a 2½-hour monkey-like romp between tree platforms connected by zip lines and swinging bridges. Various courses are geared to everyone from little kids (no more than 10ft off the ground) to daredevils (two 100ft zip lines and one that's 300ft). Reserve ahead.

Winter Sports

★ **Heavenly** SNOW SPORTS
(Map p644; ☎775-586-7000; www.skiheavenly. com; 4080 Lake Tahoe Blvd; adult/child 5-12yr/ youth 13-18yr $135/79/113; ⊙9am-4pm Mon-Fri, from 8:30am Sat, Sun & holidays; ⊛) The 'mother' of all Tahoe mountains boasts the most acreage, the longest run (5.5 miles), great tree-skiing and the biggest vertical drop around. Follow the sun by skiing on the Nevada side in the morning, moving to the California side in the afternoon. Views of the lake and the high desert are heavenly indeed.

Two terrain parks won't strand snowboarders of any skill level, with the High Roller for experts only. Stats: 28 lifts, 3500 vertical feet, 97 runs.

Sierra-at-Tahoe SNOW SPORTS
(☎530-659-7453; www.sierraattahoe.com; 1111 Sierra-at-Tahoe-Rd, off Hwy 50, Twin Bridges; adult/child 5-12yr/youth 13-22yr $90/30/83; ⊙9am-4pm Mon-Fri, 8:30am-4pm Sat, Sun & holidays; ⊛) About 18 miles southwest of South Lake Tahoe, this is snowboarding central, with five raging terrain parks and a 17ft-high superpipe. A great beginners' run meanders gently for 2.5 miles from the summit, but there are also gnarly steeps and chutes for speed demons.

Tahoe Ski Areas

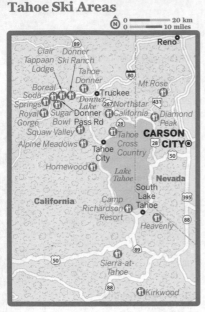

Kirkwood
SNOW SPORTS

(📞 209-258-6000; www.kirkwood.com; 1501 Kirkwood Meadows Dr, off Hwy 88, Kirkwood; adult/child 5-12yr/youth 13-18yr $96/65/80; ⊙9am-4pm) Off-the-beaten-path Kirkwood, set in a high-elevation valley, gets great snow and holds it longer than almost any other Tahoe resort. It has stellar tree-skiing, gullies, chutes and terrain parks, and is the only Tahoe resort with backcountry runs accessible by snowcats. Novice out-of-bounds skiers should sign up in advance for backcountry safety-skills clinics.

It's 35 miles southwest of South Lake Tahoe via Hwy 89; ski-season shuttles are available (from $15). Stats: 15 lifts, 2000 vertical feet, 72 runs.

Hiking

Many miles of summer hiking trails start from the top of the Heavenly Gondola (p641), many with mesmerizing lake views. On the Nevada side of the state line, **Lam Watah Nature Trail** meanders for just over a mile each way across United States Forest Service (USFS) land, winding underneath pine trees and beside meadows and ponds, on its way between Hwy 50 and Nevada Beach, starting from the community park off Kahle Dr.

Several easy kid- and dog-friendly hikes begin near the USFS Taylor Creek Visitor Center (p655) off Hwy 89. The mile-long, mostly flat **Rainbow Trail** loops around a creekside meadow, with educational panels about ecology and wildlife along the way. On the opposite side of Hwy 89, the gentle, rolling 1-mile **Moraine Trail** follows the shoreline of Fallen Leaf Lake; free trailhead parking is available near campsite No 75. Up at cooler elevations, the mile-long round-trip to **Angora Lakes** is another popular trek with kids, especially because it ends by a sandy swimming beach and a summer snack bar selling ice-cream treats. You'll find the trailhead on Angora Ridge Rd, off Tahoe Mountain Rd, accessed from Hwy 89.

For longer and more strenuous day hikes to alpine lakes and meadows, several major trailheads provide easy access to the evocatively named Desolation Wilderness (p651): Echo Lakes (south of town); Glen Alpine (near Lily Lake, south of Fallen Leaf Lake), to visit a historic tourist resort and waterfall; and Tallac (p651) (opposite the entrance to Baldwin Beach). The latter two trailheads also lead to the peak of Mt Tallac (9735ft), a strenuous 10- to 12-mile day hike. Self-serve wilderness permits for day hikers only are freely available at trailheads; overnight backpacking permits are subject to quotas.

Beaches & Swimming
On the California side, the nicest strands are **Pope Beach** (Map p644; per car $7), **Kiva Beach** (Map p644) and **Baldwin Beach** (Map p642; per car $7), each with picnic tables and barbecue grills; Kiva offers free parking and allows leashed dogs too. They're all found along Emerald Bay Rd (Hwy 89), running west and east of Tallac Historic Site (p641). Nearby, **Fallen Leaf Lake**, where scenes from the Hollywood flicks *The Bodyguard* and *City of Angels* were filmed, is also good for summer swims. **El Dorado Beach** (Map p644) is a free public beach in town, just off Lake Tahoe Blvd.

Many folks prefer to head over to Stateline and keep driving north 2 miles to pretty **Nevada Beach** (Map p642; per car $7), where the wind really picks up in the afternoons, or always-busy **Zephyr Cove** (Map p642; 📞775-589-4901; www.zephyrcove.com; 760 Hwy 50; per car $10; 🐾), which has rustic resort and marina facilities along its sandy mile-long shoreline.

Boating & Water Sports

Ski Run Boat Company (Map p644; ☑530-544-0200; www.tahoesports.com; 900 Ski Run Blvd; parasailing $55-80), at the **Ski Run Marina** (Map p644; ☑530-544-9500; 900 Ski Run Blvd), and **Tahoe Keys Boat & Charter Rentals** (Map p644; ☑530-544-8888; www.tahoesports.com; 2435 Venice Dr; per hour $110-235), at the **Tahoe Keys Marina** (Map p644; ☑530-541-2155; www.tahoekeysmarina.net; 2435 Venice Dr E), both rent motorized powerboats, pontoons, sailboats and Jet Skis (rentals $110 to $235 per hour), as well as human-powered kayaks, canoes, hydro bikes, paddleboats and paddleboard sets (per hour $25 to $35). If you want to go parasailing up to 1200ft above Lake Tahoe's waves, the Ski Run Marina branch can hook you up (rides $55 to $80).

Kayak Tahoe KAYAKING, WATER SPORTS
(Map p644; ☑530-544-2011; www.kayaktahoe.com; 3411 Lake Tahoe Blvd; kayak single/double 1hr $25/35, 1 day $65/85, lessons & tours from $40; ⊙9am-5pm Jun-Sep) Rent a kayak or stand up paddleboard, take a lesson or sign up for a guided tour, including sunset cove paddles, trips to Emerald Bay and explorations of the Upper Truckee River estuary and the eastern shore. Five seasonal locations at **Timber Cove Marina** (Map p644; ☑530-544-2942; 3411 Lake Tahoe Blvd), Vikingsholm (Emerald Bay) and Baldwin, Pope and Nevada Beaches.

Zephyr Cove Resort & Marina WATER SPORTS
(Map p642; ☑775-589-4901; www.zephyrcove.com; 760 Hwy 50, NV; ⊙9am-5pm) Rents powerboats, pedal boats, wave runners, Jet Skis, canoes, kayaks and stand up paddleboards; also offers single and tandem parasailing flights.

Camp Richardson Resort Marina WATER SPORTS
(Map p644; ☑530-542-6570; www.camprichardson.com; 1900 Jameson Beach Rd; ⊙kayaks, paddleboats & paddleboards per 1hr $25) Rents powerboats, paddleboats, water skis, kayaks and SUP gear.

Mountain Biking

For expert mountain bikers, the classic **Mr Toad's Wild Ride**, with its steep downhill sections and banked turns reminiscent of a Disneyland theme-park ride, should prove sufficiently challenging. Usually open from June until October, the one-way trail along Saxon Creek starts off Hwy 89 south of town near Grass Lake and Luther Pass.

Intermediate mountain bikers should steer toward the mostly single-track **Powerline Trail**, which traverses ravines and creeks. You can pick up the trail off Ski Run Blvd near the Heavenly (p642) resort, from the western end of Saddle Rd. For a more leisurely outing over mostly level terrain, you can pedal around scenic **Fallen Leaf Lake**. Anyone with good lungs might try the **Angora Lakes Trail**, which is steep but technically easy and rewards you with sweeping views of Mt Tallac and Fallen Leaf Lake. It starts further east, off Angora Ridge and Tahoe Mountain Ridge Rds.

ⓘ TOP WAYS TO SKI TAHOE FOR LESS MONEY

Midweek and half-day afternoon discounts on lift tickets are usually available, but expect higher prices on weekends and holidays. Lift-ticket rates go up incrementally almost every year too. Parents should ask about the interchangeable 'Parent Predicament' lift tickets offered by some resorts, which let one parent ski while the other one hangs with the kids, then switch off later.

The **Bay Area Ski Bus** (☑925-680-4386; www.bayareaskibus.com) allows you to leave the headache of driving I-80 to others. Round-trips start at $109 including lift tickets, with various add-on packages available. Pick-up locations include San Francisco and Sacramento.

In San Francisco, **Sports Basement** (https://shop.sportsbasement.com) sells deeply discounted lift tickets and has the best deals on multiday rental equipment because it doesn't charge for pickup or drop-off days.

Handy money-saving websites:

Ski Lake Tahoe (www.skilaketahoe.com) Portal for the seven biggest Tahoe resorts, with deals covering all.

Sliding on the Cheap (www.slidingonthecheap.com) Homegrown website listing discounts and deals on lift tickets.

For shuttle service and mountain-bike rentals for Mr Toad's Wild Ride, the Tahoe Rim Trail (p656) and other downhill adventures, as well as family friendly tours, talk to **Wanna Ride** (☑ 775-588-5800; www.wannaridetahoe.com; ⊙ 8am-4pm Tue-Sat). For mountain-biking trail conditions, race schedules, volunteer days and other special events, contact the Tahoe Area Mountain Biking Association (www.tamba.org).

Cycling

The **South Lake Tahoe Bike Path** is a level, leisurely ride suitable for anyone. It heads west from El Dorado Beach (p646), eventually connecting with the **Pope-Baldwin Bike Path** past Camp Richardson (p650), Tallac Historic Site (p641) and the USFS Taylor Creek Visitor Center (p655). Visitor centers carry the excellent Lake Tahoe bike route map, available online from the Lake Tahoe Bicycle Coalition (www.tahoebike.org), which has an info-packed website for cycling enthusiasts. **Anderson's Bike Rental** (☑ 530-541-0500; www.laketahoebikerental.com; 645 Emerald Bay Rd/Hwy 89; per hour $10; 🐾) rents hybrid bikes with helmets.

Golf

Edgewood Tahoe Golf Course   GOLF
(Map p644; ☑ 775-588-3566; www.edgewood-tahoe.com/golf; 100 Lake Pkwy, Stateline, NV; green fee $110-260) Stunning lakeside scenery is a major distraction at this challenging championship 18-hole course designed by George Fazio, a favorite for celebrity golf tournaments. Tee-time reservations are required; cart and club rentals available.

Bijou Golf Course   GOLF
(Map p644; ☑ 530-542-6097; www.cityofslt.us; 3464 Fairway Ave; green fee $18, club/cart rental $15/5; ⊙ mid-Apr–Oct) So you don't know your putter from your nine iron? That's OK at this laid-back, no-reservations municipal course with views of Heavenly Mountain. Built in the 1920s, it's got just nine holes, which you can play twice around.

Horseback Riding

Both **Camp Richardson Corral & Pack Station** (Map p644; ☑ 530-541-3113; www.camprichardsoncorral.com; Emerald Bay Rd/Hwy 89; trail rides $50-168; 🐾) and **Zephyr Cove Stables** (Map p642; ☑ 775-588-5664; www.zephyrcovestable.com; Hwy 50, NV; trail rides $40-80; 🐾), about 4 miles north of Stateline casinos,

---

SOUTH LAKE TAHOE FOR CHILDREN

With oodles of outdoor activities, families will never run out of mountains to explore and beaches to dig. If the kids start to get fractious though, try one of these local favorites to mix things up a little.

Major ski resorts such as Heavenly (p642) and Kirkwood (p642) around South Lake Tahoe, and Squaw Valley (p661) and Northstar California (p664) near Truckee, offer sledding hills for the kiddos, some with tubing rentals and thrilling rope tows. Smaller ski mountains including Sierra-at-Tahoe (p642) outside South Lake Tahoe, and Boreal (p664), Soda Springs (p664) and Tahoe Donner (p664), all near Truckee, also offer child-friendly slopes.

To avoid the crowds, bring your own sleds to designated local snow-play areas at North Tahoe Regional Park (p667) in Tahoe Vista on the north shore, or to Nevada's Incline Village (p669), Tahoe Meadows (p669) off the Mt Rose Hwy (Hwy 431) or **Spooner Summit** on Hwy 50, all along the east shore. Back in California, DIY **Sno-Parks** (☑ 916-324-1222; www.parks.ca.gov; pass per day/year $5/25) are found along Hwy 89 at **Blackwood Canyon**, 3 miles south of Tahoe City on the west shore, and **Taylor Creek**, just north of Camp Richardson at South Lake Tahoe. Coming from Sacramento or the San Francisco Bay Area, two Sno-Parks are along I-80 at **Yuba Gap** (exit 161) and **Donner Summit** (exit 176 Castle Peak/Boreal Ridge Rd); their parking lots often fill by 11am on winter weekends. Buy required Sno-Park parking passes online or at local shops.

For private groomed sledding and tubing hills, swing by **Hansen's Resort** (Map p644; ☑ 530-544-3361; www.hansensresort.com; 1360 Ski Run Blvd; per person incl rental per hour $15; ⊙ 9am-5pm) in South Lake Tahoe or **Adventure Mountain** (☑ 530-577-4352; www.adventuremountaintahoe.com; 21200 Hwy 50; per car $20, tube/2-person sled rental per day $20/10; ⊙ 10am-4:30pm Mon-Fri, 9am-4:30pm Sat, Sun & holidays), south of town at Echo Summit.

offer daily horseback rides in summer, varying from one-hour kid-friendly trips through the forest, to extended treks with meadow and lake views (reservations required).

☞ Tours

Lake Tahoe Balloons BALLOONING
(Map p644; ☏ 530-544-1221; www.laketahoe balloons.com; per person $299) From May through October (weather permitting), you can cruise on a catamaran launched from Tahoe Keys Marina (p647), then clamber aboard a hot-air balloon launched right from the boat's upper deck. The lake and Sierra Nevada mountain views may take away what little breath you have left up at 10,000ft. Reservations required.

Woodwind Cruises CRUISE
(Map p642; ☏ 775-588-3000; www.tahoecruises. com; 760 Hwy 50, NV, Zephyr Cove Marina; 1hr cruise adult/child 2-12yr from $49/18) Sunset champagne and happy-hour floats aboard this sailing catamaran are the perfect way to chill after a sunny afternoon lazing on the beach. Five daily departures during summer; reservations recommended.

Lake Tahoe Cruises CRUISE
(Map p644; ☏ 800-238-2463; www.zephyrcove. com; 900 Ski Run Blvd; adult/child from $55/20; ☻) Two paddle wheelers ply Lake Tahoe's 'big blue' year-round with a variety of sightseeing, drinking, dining and dancing cruises, including a narrated two-hour daytime trip to Emerald Bay. The *Tahoe Queen* leaves from Ski Run Marina (p647) – summer parking fee $8 – in town, while the MS *Dixie II* is based at Zephyr Cove Resort & Marina (p647) on the eastern shore in Nevada.

Action Watersports BOATING
(Map p644; ☏ 530-544-5387; www.action-watersports.com; 3411 Lake Tahoe Blvd, Timber Cove Marina; adult/child under 13yr $69/35) In a hurry to get to Emerald Cove? Wanna avoid those near-constant traffic jams on Hwy 89? Jump on board the *Tahoe Thunder* speedboat, which zips across the lake – watch out, though, you'll get wet! Also offers parasailing rides (from $75).

✸ Festivals & Events

Valhalla Festival of Arts, Music & Film CULTURAL
(☏ 530-541-4975; www.valhallatahoe.com; ☻Jun-Aug) A summerlong cultural bonanza of music and theater held at a 1930s Nordic hall.

SNOWSHOEING UNDER THE STARS

A crisp quiet night with a blazing glow across the lake. What could be more magical than a full-moon snowshoe tour? Reserve ahead, as ramblings at these places are very popular:

➡ Ed Z'Berg Sugar Pine Point State Park (p657)

➡ Squaw Valley (p661)

➡ Tahoe Donner (p664)

➡ Northstar California (p664)

➡ Kirkwood (p642)

🛏 Sleeping

🛏 South Lake Tahoe

South Lake Tahoe has a bazillion choices. Lodging options line Lake Tahoe Blvd (Hwy 50) between Stateline and Ski Run Blvd. Further west, closer to the intersection of Hwys 50 and 89, a string of budget motels ranges from adequate to inexcusable. For ski condos and rooms near the slopes, contact Heavenly (p642).

Fallen Leaf Campground CAMPGROUND $
(Map p644; ☏ info 530-544-0426, reservations 877-444-6777; www.recreation.gov; 2165 Fallen Leaf Lake Rd; tent & RV sites $33-35, yurts $84; ☻mid-May–mid-Oct; ☻) Near the north shore of stunning Fallen Leaf Lake, this is one of the biggest and most popular campgrounds on the south shore, with pay showers and approximately 200 wooded sites and six canvas-sided yurts that can sleep a family of five (bring your own sleeping bags).

Big Pines Mountain House MOTEL $
(Map p644; ☏ 530-541-5155; www.thebigpines. com; 4083 Cedar Ave; r $50-129, pet fee $15; ❄@🕾🐾🐕) Choose from over 70 comfortable rooms in various sizes – some with blissful mountain views – and in summertime, stroll to the private beach nearby or take a dip in the heated pool. Gas fireplaces cozy up the king kitchenette rooms.

Camp Richardson Resort CABIN, CAMPGROUND $
(Map p644; ☏ 530-541-1801; www.camprichardson. com; 1900 Jameson Beach Rd; tent sites from $35, RV sites with partial/full hookups from $40/45, r $95-215, cabins $125-263; 🕾) Removed

from downtown's strip-mall aesthetic, this sprawling family camp is a hectic place offering seasonal camping (expect marauding bears all night long!), forested cabins rented by the week in summer, and so-so beachside hotel rooms. Sports-gear and bicycle rentals are available, and there's a popular ice-cream parlor across the road. Wi-fi in lobby only.

Blue Lake Inn   MOTEL $
(Map p644; ☑530-544-6459; www.thebluelakeinn. com; 944 Friday Ave; r $89-104, pet fee $15; ❄️🛜🐾🏊) A good-value choice near the Heavenly Gondola (p641), these ample motel rooms have the core amenities: microwave, refrigerator, coffeemaker and flat-screen TV, plus a hot tub and outdoor pool.

Campground by the Lake   CAMPGROUND $
(Map p644; ☑530-542-6096; www.cityofslt.us; 1150 Rufus Allen Blvd; tent & RV sites with/without hookups from $40/29, cabins $49-80; ☺Apr-Oct; 🛜🐾) Highway noise can be an around-the-clock irritant, though proximity to the city pool and ice rink make this wooded in-town campground with an RV dump station a decent choice. Basic sleeping-platform cabins are available between Memorial Day (late May) and Labor Day (early September).

★ Sorensen's   CHALET $$
(☑800-423-9949; www.sorensensresort.com; 14255 Hwy 88; r $135-195) A truly delightful option in the Hope Valley, with snug pine cottages and cabins, decked out with fairy lights and hammocks. There's a wealth of activities, including skiing, fishing and hiking. Magical in the snow, but just as lovely in summer. Bird-watching and stargazing events are held. The on-site cafe serves seasonal fish, steaks and salads.

Deerfield Lodge at Heavenly   BOUTIQUE HOTEL $$
(Map p644; ☑530-544-3337; www.tahoedeerfield lodge.com; 1200 Ski Run Blvd; r/ste from $179/229, pet fee $25; ❄️🛜) A small boutique hotel close to Heavenly ski resort, Deerfield has a dozen intimate rooms and spacious suites that each have a patio or balcony facing the green courtyard, along with a whirlpool tub, flickering gas fireplace and amusing coat racks crafted from skis and snowboards.

There's complimentary wine in the lobby, s'mores to be made over the fire pit, and barbecue grills appear in summer.

Alder Inn   MOTEL $$
(Map p644; ☑530-544-4485; www.alderinn.com; 1072 Ski Run Blvd; r $89-149; 🅿️♿🛜🏊) Even better than staying at your best friend's house by the lake, this hospitable inn on the Heavenly ski-shuttle route charms with color schemes that really pop, pillow-top mattresses, organic bath goodies, mini-refrigerators, microwaves and flat-screen TVs. Dip your toes in the kidney-shaped pool in summer.

Fireside Lodge   INN $$
(Map p644; ☑530-544-5515; www.tahoefireside lodge.com; 515 Emerald Bay Rd/Hwy 89; d $149-219, pet fee $25; 🛜🐾) This woodsy cabin B&B wholeheartedly welcomes families, with free bikes, kayaks and snowshoes to borrow and evening s'mores and wine and cheese. Kitchenette rooms and suites have river-rock gas fireplaces, cozy patchwork quilts and pioneer-themed touches like wagon wheels or vintage skis.

Heavenly Valley Lodge   B&B $$
(Map p644; ☑530-564-1500; www.heavenlyvalley lodge.com; 1261 Ski Run Blvd; d $145-255, pet fee $25; 🛜🐾) Located along the Heavenly shuttle route, this family-run place perfects the balance of old Tahoe – all-fireplace rooms of knotty pine and river rock – and great amenities, like DVD players and a huge movie library, a fire-pit patio and afternoon happy hour. Some kitchenette units.

Basecamp Hotel   BOUTIQUE HOTEL $$
(Map p644; ☑530-208-0180; www.basecamphotels. com; 4143 Cedar Ave; d $109-229, 8-person bunk room $209-299, pet fee $40; 🛜🐾) ❂ Recycled wood, original nature-themed canvases and artsy artifacts gussy up this stylish former motel. Lucky couples can rough it in the 'Great Indoors' room with a tented bed and faux campfire, and families can overnight in spacious bunk-bed rooms. A rooftop hot tub, beer and wine bar, and communal dinner nights sweeten the deal.

Timber Lodge   HOTEL $$
(Map p644; ☑530-542-6600; www.marriott.com; 4100 Lake Tahoe Blvd; r $150-230, ste from $230; ❄️@🛜🏊) Don't let the Marriott chain-gang brand put you off this modern ski lodge with an enviable position, where you can watch the Heavenly Gondola (p641) whoosh by outside your window. Cookie-cutter hotel rooms have kitchenettes, while apartment-style 'vacation villa' suites come with

full kitchens, gas fireplaces and deep soaking tubs for après-ski warm-ups.

Paradice Inn MOTEL $$
(Map p644; ☑530-544-6800; www.paradicemotel tahoe.com; 953 Park Ave; r $150-220; ❇ 📶) Harried travelers will appreciate the fabulous hospitality (turndown service!) at this small two-story motel. Step outside your minimalist room bordered by flower baskets, then stroll across the street to the Heavenly Gondola (p641). Families should ask about the two-bedroom suites.

Spruce Grove Cabins CABIN $$
(Map p644; ☑530-544-0549; www.sprucegrove tahoe.com; 3599-3605 Spruce Ave; 4-/6-person cabins $169/215, cleaning fee $30, refundable pet deposit $100; 📶🐾) Away from the Heavenly hubbub, these tidy, private cabins are fenced off on a quiet residential street. The vintage look of the kitchen-equipped cabins, from knotty pine walls to the stone-bordered gas fireplaces, will make you feel like you're staying lakeside. Let your dogs cavort in the yard while you swing in the hammock or soak in outdoor hot tubs.

Inn by the Lake HOTEL $$
(Map p644; ☑530-542-0330; www.innbythelake. com; 3300 Lake Tahoe Blvd; r $180-300, pet fee $20; ❇@📶♨🐾) Rooms here are rather nondescript, although a bilevel outdoor hot tub, spa suites with kitchens, and bicycles and snowshoes to borrow are nifty. Rooms out back are cheaper and quieter, but then you'll miss the lake views.

Landing HOTEL $$$
(Map p644; ☑855-700-5263; www.thelandingtahoe. com; 4104 Lakeshore Blvd; d/ste from $319/619, pet fee $100; ❇@📶♨🐾) South Lake's newest and most luxurious lakeside resort dazzles

with an in-house spa, marble bathrooms with toilet night lights and heated seats, Keurig coffeemakers, a private beach and the swank Jimmy's restaurant. Each room has a fireplace seating arrangement, and other perks include a complimentary town shuttle, a year-round outdoor pool and nightly wine tasting.

Stateline, NV

At Nevada's high-rise casinos, prices rise and fall like a gambler's luck. In winter ask about ski-and-stay packages.

Nevada Beach Campground CAMPGROUND $
(Map p642; ☑775-588-5562, reservations 877-444-6777; www.recreation.gov; off Hwy 50; tent & RV sites $32-38; ☉mid-May–mid-Oct; 🐾) Bed down on a carpet of pine needles at this tidy lakeside campground, about 3 miles north of Stateline, where 48 sites are nestled amid pines. Leashed dogs are allowed at campsites, but not the beach.

Harrah's CASINO HOTEL $$
(Map p644; ☑775-588-6611; https://caesars.com/harrahs-tahoe; 15 Hwy 50; r $85-369; ❇@📶♨) Clad in an oddly tasteful forest-green facade, this buzzing casino hotel is Stateline's top contender. Let yourself be swallowed up by even standard 'luxury' rooms, which each have two bathrooms with telephones, or spring for a luxury suite with panoramic lake-vista windows. For more eye-popping views, snag a window table at one of Harrah's upper-floor restaurants.

MontBleu CASINO HOTEL $$
(Map p644; ☑775-588-3515; www.montbleuresort. com; 55 Hwy 50; r $70-210, ste from $240; ❇@📶♨) The public areas may sport ubercool modern boutique decor, but hallways

LAKE TAHOE SOUTH LAKE TAHOE & STATELINE

---

❶ NAVIGATING SOUTH TAHOE TRAFFIC

South Lake Tahoe's main east–west thoroughfare is a 5-mile stretch of Hwy 50 called Lake Tahoe Blvd. Most hotels and businesses hover around the California–Nevada state line and Heavenly Village. Casinos are located in Stateline, which is officially a separate city.

West of town, Hwy 50 runs into Hwy 89 at the 'Y' junction. Heavy snowfall sometimes closes Hwy 89 north of the Tallac Historic Site (p641). The section of Hwy 89 between South Lake Tahoe and Emerald Bay is also known as Emerald Bay Rd.

Traffic all along Hwy 50 between the 'Y' junction and Heavenly Village gets jammed around lunchtime and again by 5pm Monday to Friday in both summer and winter, but Sunday afternoons, when skiers head back down the mountain, are the worst.

An alternate, less crowded route through town is Pioneer Trail, which branches east off the Hwy 89/50 junction (south of the 'Y') and reconnects with Hwy 50 at Stateline.

DON'T MISS

HIKING & BACKPACKING THE DESOLATION WILDERNESS

Sculpted by powerful glaciers aeons ago, this relatively compact **wilderness area** (Map p642; www.fs.usda.gov/detail/eldorado/specialplaces/?cid=fsbdev7_019062) spreads south and west of Lake Tahoe and is the most popular in the Sierra Nevada. It's a 100-sq-mile wonderland of polished granite peaks, deep-blue alpine lakes, glacier-carved valleys and pine forests that thin quickly at the higher elevations. In summer wildflowers nudge out from between the rocks.

All this splendor makes for some exquisite backcountry exploration. Six major trailheads provide access from the Lake Tahoe side: Glen Alpine, **Tallac** (Map p642; Mt Tallac Rd B trailhead), Echo Lakes (near Echo Summit on Hwy 50), **Bayview** (Map p642), **Eagle Falls** (p655) and **Meeks Bay** (Map p642). Tallac and Eagle Falls get the most traffic, but solitude comes quickly once you've scampered past the day hikers.

Wilderness permits are required year-round for both day and overnight explorations. Day hikers can self-register at the trailheads, but overnight permits must be either reserved online (fee $6) at www.recreation.gov and printed at home, or picked up in person at one of the three USFS offices in South Lake Tahoe and Pollack Pines. Permits cost $5 per person for one night, $10 per person for two or more nights.

Quotas are in effect from late May through the end of September. Over half of the permits for the season may be reserved online, usually starting in late March or April; the other permits are available on a first-arrival basis on the day of entry only.

Bear-proof canisters are strongly advised in all wilderness areas (hanging your food in trees will not work – these bears are too smart!). Borrow canisters for free from the USFS offices. Bring bug repellent as the mosquitoes can be merciless. Wood fires are a no-no, but portable stoves are OK. Dogs must be leashed at *all* times.

are seriously dim. Remodeled rooms have fluffy duvets and art-deco-esque accents, and some of the marble-accented bathrooms sport hedonistic circular tubs. Rooms above the 5th floor are best, and those in the premiere category have lake views. Unwind in the lavish indoor-pool lagoon, accented by a rockscape and mini waterfalls.

Harvey's CASINO HOTEL **$$**
(Map p644; ☑ 775-588-2411; www.harveystahoe.com; 18 Hwy 50; r $80-229, pet fee $75; ❋@♠❋❋) Harvey's was South Lake Tahoe's first casino, and with 740 rooms, is also its biggest. Mountain Tower rooms have fancy marble bathrooms and oodles of space, but renovated Lake Tower rooms are more chic and design-savvy. The heated outdoor pool is open year-round, for beach and snow bunnies alike. Wi-fi costs $11 daily.

✗ Eating

For late-night cravings, each of the big casinos in Stateline has a 24-hour coffee shop for hangover-helper and night-owl breakfasts. If you're just looking for filling pub grub or après-ski appetizers and cocktails, most bars and cafes also serve just-OK food, some with waterfront views and live music too.

Sprouts VEGETARIAN **$**
(Map p644; www.sproutscafetahoe.com; 3123 Harrison Ave; mains $7-10; ⊘8am-9pm; ✔♠) Cheerful chatter greets you at this energetic, mostly organic cafe that gets extra kudos for its smoothies. A healthy menu will have you noshing happily on satisfying soups, rice bowls, sandwiches, burrito wraps, tempeh burgers and fresh salads.

Sugar Pine Bakery BAKERY **$**
(Map p644; http://sugarpinecakery.com; 3564 Lake Tahoe Blvd; pastries $1-5; ⊘8am-5pm Tue-Sat, to 4pm Sun) Organic crunchy baguettes, ooey-gooey cinnamon rolls, fruit tarts and choco-chunk cookies.

Cork & More DELI **$**
(Map p644; www.thecorkandmore.com; 1032 Al Tahoe Blvd; sandwiches $5-10; ⊘10am-7pm) Specialty foods, gourmet deli (sandwiches, soups, salads) and picnic baskets to go.

Ernie's Coffee Shop DINER **$**
(Map p644; ☑ 530-541-2161; http://erniescoffeeshop.com; 1207 Hwy 50; mains $8-14; ⊘6am-2pm; ♠) A sun-filled local institution, Ernie's dishes out filling three-egg omelets, hearty biscuits with gravy, fruity and nutty waffles and bottomless cups of locally roasted coffee. Breakfast is served all day.

Burger Lounge
FAST FOOD $

(Map p644; ☑530-542-2010; 717 Emerald Bay Rd; dishes $4-10; ⊙10am-8pm Jun-Sep, 11am-7pm Thu-Mon Oct-May; ☻) You can't miss that giant beer mug standing outside a shingled cabin. Step inside for the south shore's tastiest burgers, including the crazy 'Jiffy burger' (with peanut butter and cheddar cheese), the zingy pesto fries or the knockout ice-cream shakes.

★Cafe Fiore
ITALIAN $$

(Map p644; ☑530-541-2908; www.cafefiore. com; 1169 Ski Run Blvd; mains $18-34; ⊙5:30-9pm) Serving upscale Italian without pretension, this tiny romantic eatery pairs succulent pasta, seafood and meats with an award-winning 300-vintage wine list. Swoon over the veal scaloppine, homemade white-chocolate ice cream and near-perfect garlic bread. With only seven tables (a baker's dozen in summer when the candle-lit outdoor patio opens), reservations are essential.

Freshie's
FUSION $$

(Map p644; ☑530-542-3630; www.freshiestahoe. com; 3330 Lake Tahoe Blvd; mains $14-28; ⊙11:30am-9pm; ☑) From vegans to seafood-lovers, everybody should be able to find a favorite on the extensive menu at this Hawaiian fusion joint with sunset upper-deck views. Most of the produce is local and organic, and the blackened fish tacos are South Lake Tahoe's best. Check the webcam to see if there's a wait.

Off the Hook
SUSHI $$

(Map p644; www.offthehooksushi.com; 2660 Lake Tahoe Blvd; mains $14-23; ⊙5-10pm) Sushi, so far from the ocean? Yup. Locals keep on coming back to this dynamite little sushi shack, where you can feast on bento boxes and *nigiri* (oblong-shaped sushi) combos, or big steaming bowls of floury udon noodles and pan-fried halibut steaks off the Japanese, Hawaiian and Californian menu.

Latin Soul
LATIN AMERICAN $$

(Map p644; ☑775-588-7777; www.lakesideinn. com; 168 Hwy 50, Stateline, NV; mains $9-28; ⊙8am-11pm) For something completely different, steal away to this little casino kitchen with a big, bold menu of spicy south-of-the-border flavors: Argentinean churrasco-grilled steak, Veracruz shrimp ceviche, goat *bírria* (stew) and outrageously mixed mojitos.

Blue Angel Cafe
CALIFORNIAN $$

(Map p644; ☑530-544-6544; www.theblueangel cafe.com; 1132 Ski Run Blvd; lunch $11-16, dinner $12-25; ⊙11am-9pm; ☎☑☻☺) Inside a cute wooden house on the way uphill to ski at Heavenly (p642), this modern international-inspired kitchen churns out seafood, club sandwiches, elaborate salads, pastas and flank steaks to stuff your belly. Turn up for happy hour or the rotating lunch and dinner specials.

Getaway Cafe
AMERICAN $$

(Map p642; www.getawaycafe.com; 3140 Hwy 50, Meyers; mains breakfast & lunch $8-13, dinner $10-19; ⊙11am-10pm Mon-Thu, to 11pm Fri & Sat, 8:30am-10pm Sun; ☻) On the outskirts of town, just south of the agriculture inspection checkpoint, this place really lives up to its name; avoid the weekend crowds here. Friendly waitstaff sling heaped-up buffalo chicken salads, barbecue burgers, chiles rellenos, coconut-encrusted French toast and more.

Lake Tahoe Pizza Co
PIZZA $$

(Map p644; ☑530-544-1919; www.laketahoepizzaco. com; 1168 Emerald Bay Rd/Hwy 89; pizzas $11-23; ⊙4-9:30pm; ☻) Since the '70s, this classic pizza parlor has been hand rolling its house-made dough (cornmeal or whole wheat, anyone?), then piling the pizzas with crafty combos such as the meaty 'Barnyard Massacre' or vegan 'Green Giant.'

✕ Self-Catering

Grass Roots Natural Foods
FOOD & DRINKS

(Map p644; http://grassrootstahoe.com; 2030 Dunlap Dr; ⊙9am-8pm) 🖉 This store sells a wealth of organic produce, lifestyle products and grocery goods, as well as sandwiches and fresh pizzas.

Safeway
SUPERMARKET $

(Map p644; www.safeway.com; 1020 Johnson Blvd; ⊙24hr) Standard supermarket fare, with an in-house deli and bakery.

🍷 Drinking & Entertainment

The siren song of blackjack and slot machines calls the masses over to Stateline, NV. Published on Thursdays, the free alt-weekly newspaper *Reno News & Review* (www.newsreview.com/reno) has comprehensive Stateline entertainment and events listings. For what's going on around South Lake Tahoe, pick up a copy of the free weekly *Lake Tahoe Action,* published by the *Tahoe Daily Tribune* (www.tahoedaily tribune.com).

Beacon Bar & Grill BAR
(Map p644; www.camprichardson.com; 1900 Jameson Beach Rd, Camp Richardson Resort; ☺11am-10pm) Imagine all of Lake Tahoe is your very own front yard when you and your buddies sprawl across this big wraparound wooden deck. If you want to get schnock- ered, order the signature Rum Runner cock- tail. Bands rock here in summer.

Boathouse on the Pier BAR
(Map p644; 3411 Lake Tahoe Blvd; ☺11am-9pm, extended hours Jun-Sep) On the lake behind the Beach Retreat complex, this upstairs and upscale restaurant at the Timber Cove marina is the perfect spot for sunset cock- tails, with outdoor tables to feel the summer breeze.

MacDuffs Pub PUB
(Map p644; www.macduffspub.com; 1041 Fremont Ave; ☺11:30am-9:30pm) With excellent beers rotating on tap, a dartboard on the wall, and fish-and-chips and shepherd's pie (as well as gourmet burgers and wood-fired pizzas) on the menu, this dark and bustling gastropub wouldn't look out of place in Edinburgh. Sports fans and beer drinkers, step right up.

Brewery at Lake Tahoe BREWERY
(Map p644; www.brewerylaketahoe.com; 3542 Lake Tahoe Blvd; ☺11am-10:30pm) This crazy-pop- ular brewpub pumps its signature Bad Ass Ale into grateful local patrons, who may sniff at bright-eyed out-of-towners. The barbecue is dynamite and a roadside patio opens in summer. Don't leave without a bumper sticker!

Opal Ultra Lounge CLUB
(Map p644; ☎775-586-2000; www.montbleuresort. com; 55 Hwy 50, MontBleu, Stateline, NV; cover free- $10; ☺10pm-4am Wed-Sat) With DJ booths and go-go dancers, this Top 40 and electro dance club draws a young party crowd that enjoys getting their bodies painted in-house. Ladies may get in free before midnight. On summer Sunday nights, hit up the casino's poolside DJ parties. Dress to impress.

Stateline Brewery BREWERY
(Map p644; www.statelinebrewery.com; 4118 Lake Tahoe Blvd; ☺11am-9pm Sun-Thu, to 10:30pm Fri & Sat) Seat yourself by the shiny industrial brewing vats at this subterranean eating and drinking spot. German- and American-style ales taste mighty good after a day of sunning

yourself on the lakeshore or skiing Heavenly (p642) (the gondola swings nearby).

Improv COMEDY
(Map p644; www.caesars.com/harveys-tahoe; 18 Hwy 50, Stateline, NV; tickets $25-30; ☺usually 9pm Wed, Fri & Sun, 8:30pm & 10:30pm Sat) Catch up-and-coming stand-up comedians doing their funny shtick at the intimate cabaret theater inside Harvey's (p652) old-school casino.

ℹ Information

Barton Memorial Hospital (☎530-541-3420; www.bartonhealth.org; 2170 South Ave; ☺24hr) Around-the-clock emergency room. Barton's urgent-care clinic is inside the Stateline Medical Center at 155 Hwy 50, Stateline, NV.

Explore Tahoe (Map p644; ☎530-542-4637; www.cityofslt.us; 4114 Lake Tahoe Blvd, Heav- enly Village Transit Center; ☺9am-5pm) Find information on transport and recreation at **Heavenly** (p642).

Lake Tahoe Visitors Authority (Map p644; ☎800-288-2463; www.tahoesouth.com; 169 Hwy 50, Stateline, NV; ☺9am-5pm Mon-Fri) A full range of tourist information.

South Lake Tahoe Library (☎530-573-3185; www.eldoradolibrary.org/tahoe.htm; 1000 Rufus Allen Blvd; ☺10am-8pm Tue & Wed, to 5pm Thu-Sat; ☎) First-come, first-served free internet terminals.

Tahoe Urgent Care (☎530-553-4319; www. tahoeurgentcare.com; 2130 Lake Tahoe Blvd; ☺8am-6pm) Walk-in medical clinic for nonemergencies.

USDA Lake Tahoe Basin Management Unit (Map p644; ☎530-543-2600; www.fs.usda. gov/ltbmu; 35 College Dr; ☺8am-4:30pm Mon- Fri) Find out about camping and outdoor op- tions, plus acquire permits for wilderness trips.

USFS Taylor Creek Visitor Center (Map p644; ☎530-543-2674; www.fs.usda.gov/ltbmu; Visitor Center Rd, off Hwy 89; ☺8am-5pm late May-Sep, to 4pm Oct) Outdoor information, wilderness permits and daily ranger-led walks and talks during July and August.

ℹ Getting There & Away

From Reno-Tahoe International Airport, **South Tahoe Airporter** (☎775-325-8944; www.south tahoeexpress.com; adult/child 4-12yr $30/17) operates several daily shuttle buses to Stateline casinos; the journey takes from 75 minutes up to two hours.

Amtrak (☎800-872-7245; www.amtrak.com) has a daily Thruway bus service between Sacramento and South Lake Tahoe ($34, 2½ hours), stopping at the **South Y Transit Center** (p655).

ℹ️ Getting Around

South Lake Tahoe's main transportation hubs are the **South Y Transit Center** (Map p644; 1000 Emerald Bay Rd/Hwy 89), just south of the 'Y' intersection of Hwys 50 and 89; and the more central **Stateline Transit Center** (Map p644; 4114 Lake Tahoe Blvd).

BlueGO (☑530-541-7149; www.tahoe transportation.org/transit; single/day pass $2/5) local buses operate year-round from 6am to 11pm daily, stopping all along Hwy 50 between the two transit centers.

On summer weekends, BlueGO's **Emerald Bay Trolley** (☑531-541-7149; www.tahoe transportation.org; fare $2; 🚐) heads north from the South Y Transit Center to the Vikingsholm and Eagle Falls parking lot at Emerald Bay, but confirm the schedule as it changes from year to year. During winter ski season, BlueGO provides free and frequent shuttle service from Stateline and South Lake Tahoe to all **Heavenly** (p642) base operations every 30 minutes from stops along Hwy 50, Ski Run Blvd and Pioneer Trail.

LAKE TAHOE WESTERN SHORE

Lake Tahoe's densely forested western shore, between Emerald Bay and Tahoe City, is idyllic. Hwy 89 sinuously wends past gorgeous state parks with swimming beaches, hiking trails, pine-shaded campgrounds and historic mansions. Several trailheads also access the rugged splendor of the Desolation Wilderness (p651).

All campgrounds and many businesses shut down between November and May. Hwy 89 often closes after snowfall for plowing or due to imminent avalanche danger. Once you drive its tortuous slopeside curves, you'll understand why. The further south you are, the more of a roller coaster it is, no matter the season – so grip that steering wheel!

Emerald Bay State Park

Sheer granite cliffs and a jagged shoreline hem in glacier-carved **Emerald Bay** (Map p642; ☑530-541-6498; www.parks.ca.gov), a teardrop cove that will have you digging for your camera. Its most captivating aspect is the water, which changes from cloverleaf green to light jade depending on the angle of the sun.

DON'T MISS

TAHOE RIM TRAIL

The 165-mile **Tahoe Rim Trail** (Map p642; www.tahoerimtrail.org) **FREE** treks the lofty ridges of the Lake Tahoe Basin. Day hikers, equestrians and – in some sections – mountain bikers are rewarded by high-altitude views of the lake and Sierra Nevada peaks while tracing the footsteps of early pioneers, Basque shepherds and Washoe tribespeople.

◎ Sights

You'll spy panoramic pullouts all along Hwy 89, including at **Inspiration Point** (Map p642), opposite USFS Bayview Campground. Just south, the road shoulder evaporates on both sides of a steep drop-off, revealing a postcard-perfect view of Emerald Bay to the north and Cascade Lake to the south.

Fannette Island, an uninhabited granite speck, is Lake Tahoe's only island. It holds the vandalized remains of a tiny 1920s teahouse belonging to heiress Lora Knight, who would occasionally motorboat guests to the island from **Vikingsholm Castle** (Map p642; http://vikingsholm.com; tour adult/child 7-17yr $10/8; ⊙10:30am-3:30pm or 4pm late May–Sep; 🅿🚐), her Scandinavian-style mansion on the bay. The focal point of the state park, Vikingsholm Castle is a rare example of ancient Scandinavian-style architecture. Completed in 1929, it has trippy design elements aplenty, including sod-covered roofs that sprout wildflowers in late spring. The mansion is reached by a steep 1-mile trail, which also leads to a visitor center.

🏃 Activities

Hiking

Vikingsholm Castle is the southern terminus of the famous **Rubicon Trail** (Map p642).

Two popular trailheads lead into the Desolation Wilderness. From the Eagle Falls parking lot ($5), the **Eagle Falls Trail** (Map p642) travels one steep mile to Eagle Lake, crossing by Eagle Falls along the way. This scenic short hike often gets choked with visitors, but crowds disappear quickly as the trail continues up to the Tahoe Rim Trail and Velma, Dicks and Fontanillis Lakes (up to 10 miles round-trip). From the back of USFS Bayview Campground, it's a steep 1-mile climb to glacial Granite Lake or a moderate

1.5-mile round-trip to Cascade Falls, which rushes with snowmelt in early summer.

Boating
Fannette Island is accessible by boat, except during Canada goose nesting season (typically February to mid-June). Rent boats at Meeks Bay (p656) or South Lake Tahoe; from the latter, you can also catch narrated bay cruises or speedboat tours.

Scuba Diving
Divers prepared for chilly high-altitude plunges can explore sunken barges, a submerged rockslide and artifacts at a historic dumping ground at the unique Underwater State Parks of Emerald Bay and DL Bliss State Park. Reno-based Sierra Diving Center (www.sierradive.com) and Adventure Scuba Center (www.renoscuba.com) offer classes and trips.

🛏 Sleeping

Eagle Point Campground CAMPGROUND $
(Map p642; ☑ 530-525-7277, reservations 800-444-7275; www.reserveamerica.com; Hwy 89; tent & RV sites $38; ⊗ mid-Jun–early Sep) With over 90 sites perched on the tip of Eagle Point, this state-park campground provides flush toilets, hot pay showers, beach access and bay views. Another 20 scattered sites are reserved for boat-in campers.

USFS Bayview Campground CAMPGROUND $
(Map p642; Hwy 89; tent & RV sites $15; ⊗ Jun-Sep; 🐾) This rustic, nay, primitive forest-service campground has 13 no-reservation sites and vault toilets, but its potable water supplies are often exhausted sometime in July. It's opposite Inspiration Point (p655).

DL Bliss State Park

DL Bliss State Park (Map p642; ☑ 530-525-7277; www.parks.ca.gov; per car $10; ⊗ late May–Sep; P 🐾) 🏊 has the western shore's nicest beaches at Lester Beach and Calawee Cove. A short nature trail leads to the Balancing Rock, a giant chunk of granite perched on a rocky pedestal. Pick up information from the visitor center by the park entrance.

Near Calawee Cove is the northern terminus of the scenic one-way Rubicon Trail. The park's campground (Map p642; ☑ 800-444-7275; www.reserveamerica.com; tent & RV sites $35-45, hike-and-bike sites $7; ⊗ mid-May–Sep; 🐾) has 145 sites, including some coveted spots near the beach, along with flush toilets, hot pay showers, picnic tables, fire rings and an RV dump station.

The small visitor parking lot at Calawee Cove usually fills up by 10am, in which case it's a 2-mile walk from the park entrance to the beach. Alternatively, ask park staff at the entrance station about closer access points to Rubicon Trail.

Meeks Bay

With a wide sweep of shoreline, sleek and shallow Meeks Bay has warm water by Tahoe standards and is fringed by a beautiful, but busy, sandy beach. West of the highway, north of the fire station, is a trailhead for the Desolation Wilderness.

A mostly level, shaded path parallels Meeks Creek before heading steeply uphill through the forest to Lake Genevieve (9 miles round-trip), Crag Lake (10 miles round-trip) and other backcountry ponds, all surrounded by scenic Sierra peaks.

🛏 Sleeping & Eating

USFS Meeks Bay Campground CAMPGROUND $
(Map p642; ☑ 530-525-4733, reservations 877-444-6777; www.recreation.gov; tent & RV sites $27-29; ⊗ mid-May–mid-Oct) This developed campground offers 36 reservable sites along the beach, along with flush toilets, picnic tables and fire rings. For pay showers, head to Meeks Bay Resort (p656) next door.

Meeks Bay Resort CABIN, CAMPGROUND $$
(Map p642; ☑ 530-525-6946; www.meeksbayresort.com; 7941 Emerald Bay Rd/Hwy 89; tent/RV sites with full hookups $30/50, cabins $125-400; ⊗ May-Oct) The Washoe tribe offers various lodging options (cabins require minimum stays) plus kayak, canoe and paddleboat rentals. If you're hungry, swing by the waterfront grill or small market, which stocks limited groceries and camping, fishing and beach gear, as well as Native American crafts and cultural books.

Ed Z'berg Sugar Pine Point State Park

Ed Z'berg Sugar Pine Point State Park (Map p642; ☑ 530-525-7982; www.parks.ca.gov; per car $10) occupies a promontory blanketed by a fragrant mix of pine, juniper, aspen and fir. It has a swimming beach, hiking trails and abundant fishing in General Creek. A paved bike path travels north to Tahoe City and Squaw Valley. In winter, 12 miles of groomed cross-country trails await inside the park; book ahead for ranger-guided full-moon snowshoe tours. In summer the park offers kayak and hiking tours through the Sierra State Parks Foundation (www. sierrastateparks.org).

Historic sights include the modest 1872 cabin of William 'General' Phipps, an early Tahoe settler, and the considerably grander 1903 Queen Anne–style **Hellman-Ehrman Mansion** (Map p642; tours adult/youth 7-17yr $10/8; ⊙10:30am-3:30pm mid-Jun–Sep).

The park's secluded **General Creek Campground** (Map p642; ✆800-444-7275; www.reserveamerica.com; tent & RV sites $25-35; ⊙late May–mid-Sep) has 120 fairly spacious, pine-shaded sites, plus flush toilets and hot pay showers; a dozen sites stay open year-round (but without showers).

Tahoma

A blink-and-you'll-miss-it lakeside outpost, Tahoma has a post office and a handful of places to stay and eat. Within striking distance of Tahoe City, Tahoma offers a more secluded base for outdoor enthusiasts.

If you don't want to camp, the best option is **Tahoma Meadows B&B Cottages** (✆530-525-1553; www.tahomameadows.com; 6821 W Lake Blvd; cottages $119-239, pet fee $20; P ❀ 🐾 🛜 🐕), set in a pine grove.

You can booze all day long at **Chamber's Landing** (Map p642; ✆530-525-9190; 6400 W Lake Blvd; ⊙noon-8pm Jun-Sep) if you so desire.

Homewood

This quiet and very alpine-looking **resort hamlet** (Map p642; ✆530-525-2992; www. skihomewood.com; 5145 Westlake Blvd, off Hwy 89; adult/child 5-12yr/youth 13-19yr $83/35/65; ⊙9am-4pm; 🚡) is popular with summertime boaters and, in winter, skiers and snowboarders. **West Shore Sports** (✆530-525-9920; www.westshoresports.com; 5395 W Lake Blvd; ⊙8am-5pm) rents out all the winter and summer gear you'll need.

🛏 Sleeping & Eating

USFS Kaspian Campground   CAMPGROUND $ (Map p642; ✆877-444-6677; www.recreation.gov; tent sites $20; ⊙mid-May–mid-Oct) The closest campground is this nine-site, tent-only spot set among ponderosa and fir trees; amenities include flush toilets, picnic tables and fire rings.

West Shore Inn   INN $$$ (✆530-525-5200; www.westshorecafe.com; 5160 W Lake Blvd; r/ste from $199/349; ❀ 🛜) Oriental rugs and arts-and-crafts decor give this luxurious six-room inn a classic, aged ambience, and the lake's so close you feel like you could dive in. It's an upscale mountain lodge where crisp, modern suites feel decadent, and each has a fireplace and lake-view balcony. Rates include complimentary use of bicycles, kayaks and stand up paddleboards.

West Shore Café   CALIFORNIAN $$ (✆530-525-5200; www.westshorecafe.com; 5160 W Lake Blvd; mains $12-33; ⊙11am-9:30pm mid-Jun–Sep, 5-9:30pm Oct–mid-Jun) At the West Shore Inn's (p657) cozy destination restaurant, chef Mike Davis whips up worthy meals using fresh produce and ranched meats, from juicy burgers to Arctic char with spaghetti squash and hedgehog mushrooms. Dinner reservations recommended.

Sunnyside

Sunnyside is a lakeshore hamlet that may be just a dot on the map, but it has a couple of detour-worthy restaurants. To work off all that dang-good eating, rent a bicycle from an outpost of **West Shore Sports** (✆530-583-9920; www.westshoresports.com; 1785 W Lake Blvd), where you can get the scoop on all sorts of local outdoor information. You can pedal all the way north to Tahoe City along the paved bike path, or rent a stand up paddling set and hit the popular local beaches.

🛏 Sleeping & Eating

Sunnyside Lodge   INN $$ (✆530-583-7200; www.sunnysidetahoe.com; 1850 W Lake Blvd; d $150-380, pet fee $35; 🛜 🐕) This recently upgraded lodge features modern rooms with new bathrooms, pillow-top mattresses and flat-screen TVs, afternoon tea and cookies, and a guests-only sitting room overlooking the lake. The less expensive 'garden view' rooms lack good lake views. Note that there's lots of activity from the restaurant, and boat dock and marina next door.

★ **Fire Sign Cafe**   AMERICAN $ (www.firesigncafe.com; 1785 W Lake Blvd; mains $7-13; ⊙7am-3pm; 🍴 🐕) For breakfast, everyone heads to the friendly Fire Sign for down-home omelets, blueberry pancakes, eggs Benedict with smoked salmon, fresh made-from-scratch pastries and other carbo-loading bombs, plus organic coffee. In summer, hit the outdoor patio. Lines are usually very long, so get here early.

Spoon   AMERICAN $
(☑530-581-5400; www.spoontakeout.com; 1785 W Lake Blvd; mains $9.50-15; ⊙3-9pm, closed Tue & Wed Oct-May; ⊕) Call ahead for takeout, or squeeze yourselves into the cozy upstairs dining room at this little slat-sided cabin by the side of the highway. Barbecue tri-tip beef sandwiches, roasted veggies, soups, baked pastas and chicken enchiladas are the comfort-food staples, with brownies and ice cream for dessert.

Sunnyside Restaurant   CALIFORNIAN $$
(☑530-583-7200; www.sunnysidetahoe.com; 1850 W Lake Blvd; mains lunch $10-13, dinner $16-35) Classic and innovative contemporary takes on steak and seafood – think porterhouse pork with cherry chutney or roasted chicken with braised fennel – pervade this lakeside dining room. In summer you'll probably have more fun doing lunch – or drinks with the signature zucchini sticks and a piece of hula pie – on the huge lakefront deck.

❶ Getting There & Around

Tahoe Area Rapid Transit (TART; Map p642; ☑530-550-1212; www.laketahoetransit. com; 10183 Truckee Airport Rd; single/day pass $2/4) buses can take you to and from Sunnyside.

TAHOE CITY

The western shore's commercial hub, Tahoe City straddles the junction of Hwys 89 and 28, making it almost inevitable that you'll find yourself breezing through here at least once during your round-the-lake sojourn. The town is handy for grabbing food and supplies and renting sports gear. It's also the closest lake town to Squaw Valley. The main drag, N Lake Blvd, is chockablock with outdoor outfitters, touristy shops and cafes.

◎ Sights

Gatekeeper's Museum & Marion Steinbach Indian Basket Museum   MUSEUM
(☑530-583-1762; www.northtahoemuseums.org; 130 W Lake Blvd/Hwy 89; adult/child under 13yr $5/ free; ⊙10am-5pm daily late May-Sep, 11am-4pm Fri & Sat Oct-Apr) In a reconstructed log cabin close to town, this museum has a small but fascinating collection of Tahoe memorabilia, including Olympics history and relics from the early steamboat era and tourism explosion around the lake. In the museum's rear wing, uncover an exquisite array of Native American baskets collected from over 85 indigenous California tribes.

Fanny Bridge   BRIDGE
Just south of the always-jammed Hwy 89/28 traffic stoplight junction, the Truckee River flows through dam floodgates and passes beneath this bridge, cutely named for the most prominent feature of people leaning over the railings to look at fish (in American slang, 'fanny' means your rear end). The side facing the lake displays historical photos and hydrological facts.

Watson Cabin   MUSEUM
(☑530-583-8717; www.northtahoemuseums.org; 560 N Lake Tahoe Blvd; adult/child under 13yr $2/ free; ⊙noon-4pm Thu-Sun mid-Jun–early Sep) A few blocks east of Fanny Bridge (p658) over the Truckee River, this well-preserved 1908 settlers' cabin made from hand-hewn logs is one of the town's oldest buildings, built overlooking the beach.

Commons Beach   PARK
(400 N Lake Blvd) Commons Beach is a small, attractive park with sandy and grassy areas, picnic tables, barbecue grills, a climbing rock and playground, as well as free summer concerts (www.concertsatcommonsbeach. com) and outdoor movie nights. Leashed dogs welcome.

🏃 Activities

Winter Sports

Alpine Meadows   SNOW SPORTS
(Map p642; ☑530-452-4356; www.skialpine.com; 2600 Alpine Meadows Rd, off Hwy 89; adult/child under 13yr/youth 13-22yr $124/75/109; ⊙9am-4pm) Though now owned by neighboring Squaw (tickets are good at both resorts and a free shuttle connects them), Alpine remains a no-nonsense resort with challenging terrain and without the fancy village, attitude or crowds. It gets more snow than Squaw and it's the most backcountry-friendly resort around. Boarders jib down the mountain in a terrain park designed by Eric Rosenwald.

Also look for the supersmart and adorable ski-patrol dogs. The turnoff is 4 miles northwest of Tahoe City. Stats: 13 lifts, 1800 vertical feet, over 100 runs.

Tahoe Cross Country
SKIING

(Map p642; ☑530-583-5475; www.tahoexc.org; 925 Country Club Dr, off N Lake Blvd/Hwy 28; adult/child under 12yr/youth 13-17yr $24/free/20; ⊙8:30am-5pm; 🅰🅰) Run by the nonprofit Tahoe Cross Country Ski Education Association, this center, about 3 miles north of Tahoe City, has 40 miles of groomed tracks (23 trails) that wind through lovely forest, suitable for all skill levels. Group lessons come with good-value equipment-rental packages; half-day and twilight trail-pass discounts are also available.

Ask about free skate clinics and beginners' cross-country midweek lessons.

Dogs are allowed on three trails.

Tahoe City is within easy reach of a half dozen downhill and cross-country skiing and snowboarding resorts.

Tahoe Dave's
OUTDOORS

(☑530-583-0400,530-583-6415; www.tahoedaves. com; 590 N Lake Tahoe Blvd; ski & snowboard rentals per day from $32) The main regional outfitter, with additional branches at Squaw Valley, Kings Beach and Truckee (rentals can be returned to any shop); reservations accepted.

River Rafting

Truckee River Raft Rentals
RAFTING

(☑530-583-0123; www.truckeeriverraft.com; 185 River Rd; adult/child 6-12yr $30/25; ⊙8:30am-3:30pm Jun-Sep; 🅰) The Truckee River here is gentle and wide as it flows northwest from the lake – perfect for novice paddlers. This outfit rents rafts for the 5-mile float from Tahoe City to the River Ranch Lodge (p660), including transportation back to town. Reservations strongly advised.

Hiking

Explore the fabulous trails of the **Granite Chief Wilderness** (Map p642) north and west of Tahoe City. For maps and trailhead directions, stop by the visitor center. Recommended day hikes include the moderately strenuous **Five Lakes Trail** (over 4 miles round-trip), which starts from Alpine Meadows Rd off Hwy 89 heading toward Squaw Valley, and the easy trek to **Paige Meadows**, leading onto the Tahoe Rim Trail (p656). Paige Meadows is also good terrain for novice mountain bikers and snowshoeing. Wilderness permits are not required, even for overnight trips, but free campfire permits are needed, even for gas stoves. Leashed dogs are allowed on these trails.

Cycling

The paved 4-mile **Truckee River Bike Trail** runs from Tahoe City toward Squaw Valley, while the multi-use **West Shore Bike Path** heads 9 miles south to Ed Z'berg Sugar Pine Point State Park (p657), including highway-shoulder and residential-street sections. Both are fairly easy rides, but expect crowds on summer weekends. The whole family can rent bicycles from any of several shops along N Lake Blvd. Park and head out from the **64 Acres Park** trailhead behind the Tahoe City Transit Center (p661). The excellent bike-trail map of Lake Tahoe Bicycle Coalition (www.tahoebike.org) is available on its website.

🛏 Sleeping

If you show up without reservations, dingy, last-resort budget motels are along N Lake Blvd. For camping, head north to USFS campgrounds off Hwy 89 or south along Hwy 89 to state parks and small towns along the lake's western shore.

USFS William Kent
Campground
CAMPGROUND $

(☑877-444-6777; www.recreation.gov; Hwy 89; tent & RV sites $27-29; ⊙mid-May–mid-Oct) About 2 miles south of Tahoe City, this roadside campground offers over 85 nicely shaded but cramped sites that often fill up. Amenities include flush toilets, picnic tables and fire rings, along with swimming-beach access.

Mother Nature's Inn
INN $$

(☑530-581-4278; www.mothernaturesinn.com; 551 N Lake Blvd; r $65-155, pet fee $15; 🅰🅰) Right in town behind the Cabin Fever knickknack boutique, this good-value option offers quiet motel-style rooms with a tidy country look, fridges and coffeemaker, eclectic furniture and comfy pillow-top mattresses. It's within walking distance of Commons Beach.

Granlibakken
LODGE $$

(Map p642; ☑530-583-4242; www.granlibakken. com; 725 Granlibakken Rd, off Hwy 89; r/ste from $150/242, 1-/2-/3-bedroom town house from $330/409/516; 🅰🅰) Sleep old-school at this cross-country ski area and kitschy wedding and conference venue. Basic lodge rooms are spacious, but time-share town houses with kitchens, fireplaces and lofts can be a decent deal for families and groups. Amenities include tennis courts, a full spa, year-round outdoor pool and hot tub, and winter shuttle service to Homewood (p657).

Pepper Tree Inn MOTEL $$
(☑530-583-3711; www.peppertreetahoe.com; 645 N Lake Blvd; r $96-199; 🌐🛏) The tallest building in town, this somberly painted establishment redeems itself with some bird's-eye lake views. Fairly comfortable modern rooms with that familiar log-cabin decor each have a microwave and mini-refrigerator. Top-floor rooms with hot tubs are most in demand.

✕ Eating

★Fat Cat CALIFORNIAN $
(www.tahoefatcat.com; 599 N Lake Blvd; mains $9-17; ⊙11am-9pm, bar to 2am; 🛏) This casual, family run restaurant with local art splashed on the walls does it all: from-scratch soups, heaped salads, sandwiches, incredible burgers, pasta bowls and plenty of fried munchies for friends to share. Look for live indie music on Friday and Saturday nights.

Tahoe House Bakery BAKERY $
(www.tahoe-house.com; 625 W Lake Blvd; items $2-10; ⊙6am-6pm; 🌐) Before you take off down the western shore for a bike ride or hike, drop by this mom-and-pop shop that opened in the 1970s. Their motto: 'While you sleep, we loaf.' Sweet cookies, European pastries, fresh-baked deli sandwiches and homemade salads and soups will keep you going all afternoon on the trail.

New Moon Natural Foods DELI, HEALTH FOOD $
(505 W Lake Blvd; mains $6-12; ⊙9am-8pm Mon-Sat, 10am-7pm Sun; 🍴) 🌿 A tiny but well-stocked natural-foods store, its gem of a deli concocts scrumptious ethnic food to go, all packaged in biodegradable and compostable containers. Try the fish tacos or Thai salad with organic greens and spicy peanut sauce.

Dam Cafe CAFE $
(55 W Lake Blvd; mains $6-11; ⊙6am-3pm) This cute cottage is right by the Truckee River dam and Fanny Bridge (p658); stash your bikes in the racks outside and walk inside for a breakfast burrito, ice-cream fruit smoothie or pick-me-up espresso.

Syd's Bagelry & Espresso CAFE $
(550 N Lake Blvd; items $2-8.50; ⊙7am-5pm; 🌐) A handy spot on the main drag that serves bagels and locally roasted coffee, plus smoothies and breakfast burritos made with organic produce.

★Dockside 700
Wine Bar & Grill AMERICAN $$
(☑530-581-0303; www.dockside700.com; 700 N Lake Blvd; lunch $10-17, dinner $14-32; ⊙11:30am-8pm Mon-Thu, to 9pm Fri-Sun; 🛏🍴) On a lazy summer afternoon, grab a table on the back deck that overlooks the boats bobbing at Tahoe City Marina. Barbecue chicken, ribs and steak light a fire under dinner (reservations advised), alongside seafood pastas and pizzas.

Rosie's Cafe DINER $$
(www.rosiescafe.com; 571 N Lake Blvd; breakfast & lunch $7-14, dinner $14-20; ⊙7:30am-9:30pm; 🍴) With antique skis, shiny bikes and lots of pointy antlers belonging to stuffed wildlife mounted on the walls, this quirky place serves breakfast until 2:30pm. The all-American hodgepodge menu with items such as Yankee pot roast is all right, but the convivial atmosphere is a winner.

River Ranch Lodge MODERN AMERICAN $$
(Map p642; ☑530-583-4264; http://riverranchlodge.com; Hwy 89 at Alpine Meadows Rd; mains patio & cafe $8-13, restaurant $22-30; ⊙lunch Jun-Sep, dinner year-round, call for seasonal hours) This stone-built riverside dining room is a popular stop, drawing rafters and bikers to its patio for summer barbecue lunches.

♟ Drinking & Nightlife

There's an unpretentious and enjoyable nightlife scene here, with several restaurants joining in the fun by staging live music.

Tahoe Mountain Brewing Co BREWERY
(www.tahoebrewing.com; 475 N Lake Blvd; ⊙11:30am-10pm) Brewed in nearby Truckee, the Sugar Pine Porter, barrel-aged sours and award-winning Paddleboard Pale Ale here pair splendidly with sweet-potato fries, burgers and other pub grub on the outdoor lake-facing patio.

Bridgetender Tavern & Grill PUB
(www.tahoebridgetender.com; 65 W Lake Blvd; ⊙11am-11pm, to midnight Fri & Sat) Après-ski crowds gather for beer, burgers and chili-cheese or garlic waffle fries at this woodsy bar (mains $8 to $14). In summer, grab a seat on the open-air patio.

❶ Information

Tahoe City Downtown Association (www.visittahoecity.org; 425 N Lake Blvd; ⊙9am-

5pm Mon-Thu) Tourist information and online events calendar.

Tahoe City Library (☑530-583-3382; 740 N Lake Blvd, Boatworks Mall; ⊙10am-5pm Tue & Thu, 11am-6pm Wed & Fri, 10am-2pm Sat; 🔊) Free wi-fi and walk-in internet terminals.

Tahoe City Visitors Information Center (☑530-581-6900; www.gotahoenorth.com; 100 N Lake Blvd; ⊙9am-5pm) At the Hwy 89/28 split.

Truckee Tahoe Medical Group (☑530-581-8864, ext 3; www.ttmg.net; 925 N Lake Blvd, Trading Post Center; ⊙9am-6pm Mon-Sat year-round, also 10am-5pm Sun Jul-early Sep) Walk-in clinic for nonemergencies.

❶ Getting There & Away

Just south of the Hwy 28/89 split, the modern new **Tahoe City Transit Center** (www.nextbus.com/tahoe; 870 Cabin Creek Rd, off Hwy 89) is the main bus terminal, with a comfy waiting room. Behind it you'll find trailhead parking for the **Tahoe Rim Trail** (p656) and various bike-path routes. Regular buses connect the town with other spots on the lake.

SQUAW VALLEY

The nirvana of the north shore, Squaw Valley played host to the 1960 Olympic Winter Games and still ranks among the world's top ski resorts. The stunning setting amid granite peaks, though, makes it a superb destination in any season, and this deluxe family-friendly resort stays almost as busy in summer as in winter.

◎ Sights & Activities

Much summertime action centers on 8200ft **High Camp** (☑800-403-0206; http://squawalpine.com; cable car adult/child 5-12yr/youth 13-22yr $39/15/25, all-access pass $46/19/38; ⊙11am-4:30pm; 🌊), reached by a cable car, and offering swimming, disc golf, tennis and ice/roller-skating. Other activities down below include a ropes course with zip lines, a climbing wall, mini-golf and a bungee trampoline, all operated by **Squaw Valley Adventure Center** (Map p642; ☑530-583-7673; www.squawadventure.com). Golfers tee off at the **Resort at Squaw Creek Golf Course** (Map p642; ☑530-583-6300; www.squawcreek.com; green fee incl cart $59-99).

Several hiking trails radiate out from High Camp, or try the lovely, moderate **Shirley Lake Trail** (round-trip 5 miles), which follows a sprightly creek to water-falls, granite boulders and abundant wildflowers. It starts at the mountain base, near the end of Squaw Peak Rd, behind the cable-car building. Leashed dogs are allowed.

★**Squaw Valley**   SNOW SPORTS
(Map p642; ☑530-452-4331; www.squaw.com; 1960 Squaw Valley Rd, off Hwy 89, Olympic Valley; adult/child 5-12yr/youth 13-22yr $124/75/109; ⊙9am-4pm Mon-Fri, from 8:30am Sat, Sun & holidays; 🐕) Few ski hounds can resist the siren call of this megasized, world-class, see-and-be-seen resort that hosted the 1960 Winter Olympic Games. Hard-core skiers thrill to white-knuckle cornices, chutes and bowls, while beginners practice their turns in a separate area on the upper mountain. There's also a great après-ski scene, and relatively short chairlift waits.

The valley turnoff is 5 miles northwest of Tahoe City. Stats: 29 lifts, 2850 vertical feet, over 170 runs.

Olympic Museum   MUSEUM
(☑800-403-0206; http://squawalpine.com; High Camp; entry incl with cable car adult/child 5-12yr/youth 13-22yr $39/15/25; ⊙11am-4pm Sat & Sun) A fun retro exploration of the 1960 Olympics, featuring a film and much memorabilia. Located at High Camp (p661).

🎊 Festivals & Events

WinterWonderGrass Tahoe   MUSIC
(www.winterwondergrasstahoe.com; ⊙Mar) Book early for this great little outdoor festival of bluegrass and acoustic roots music, the stage encircled by the snow and pines of Squaw Valley. It's a family-oriented event, with an ethos of sustainability.

🛏 Sleeping & Eating

There are some premier accommodations here, with boutique options as well as more rugged places.

River Ranch Lodge   INN $$
(Map p642; ☑530-583-4264; www.riverranchlodge.com; Hwy 89 at Alpine Meadows Rd; r $115-190; 🔊🌊) Though there's some noise from traffic outside and the bar downstairs, request a river-facing room so you can drift off to dreamland as the Truckee River tumbles below your window. Rooms bulge with lodgepole-pine furniture; those upstairs have wistful balconies. Pet-friendly rooms available in summer only.

★**PlumpJack**
Squaw Valley Inn BOUTIQUE HOTEL **$$$**
(Map p642; ☑530-583-1576; www.plumpjack
squawvalleyinn.com; 1920 Squaw Valley Rd, Olym-
pic Valley; r summer $205-385, winter $340-645;
❄@🕸✉🐾) Bed down at this artsy bou-
tique hotel in the village, where every room
has mountain views and extracomfort fac-
tors like plush terry-cloth robes and slippers.
Ski-in, ski-out access doesn't hurt either, but
a $150 pet fee will. The chic **PlumpJack
Cafe**, with its crisp linens and plush ban-
quettes, serves seasonally inspired Califor-
nia cuisine with ace wines.

Le Chamois & Loft Bar PIZZA, PUB FOOD **$**
(Map p642; www.squawchamois.com; 1970 Squaw
Valley Rd; mains $7-17; ⊙11am-6pm Mon-Fri, to
8pm Sat & Sun, bar open to 9pm or 10pm; 🐾🐾)
For a social bite after shedding your bind-
ings, this slopeside favorite is handily posi-
tioned between the cable-car building and
the rental shop. Slide on over to devour a hot
sammy or pizza and a beer with eye-pleasing
mountain views.

ℹ️ **Getting There & Away**
The village at Squaw Valley, at the base of the
mountain cable car, is about a 20-minute drive
from Tahoe City or Truckee via Hwy 89 (turn off
at Squaw Valley Rd).
Tahoe Area Rapid Transit (p658) buses be-
tween Truckee and Tahoe City, Kings Beach and
Crystal Bay stop at Squaw Valley every hour
or so between 6am and 5pm daily, with a free
morning ski shuttle from December to April.

TRUCKEE & DONNER LAKE

Cradled by mountains and the Tahoe Na-
tional Forest, Truckee is a thriving town
steeped in Old West history. It was put on
the map by the railroad, grew rich on log-
ging and ice harvesting, and even had its
brush with Hollywood during the 1924 film-
ing of Charlie Chaplin's *The Gold Rush*. To-
day tourism fills much of the city's coffers,
thanks to a well-preserved historical down-
town and its proximity to Lake Tahoe and
no fewer than six downhill and four cross-
country ski resorts.

🔘 **Sights**
The aura of the Old West still lingers over
Truckee's teensy one-horse downtown,

where railroad workers and lumberjacks
once milled about in raucous saloons, bawdy
brothels and shady gambling halls. Most of
the late 19th-century buildings now contain
restaurants and upscale boutiques. Donner
Memorial State Park (p662) and **Donner
Lake** (www.donnerlakemarina.com; P🐾), a busy
recreational hub, are 3 miles further west.

Donner Memorial State Park STATE PARK
(Map p642; ☑530-582-7892; www.parks.ca.gov;
Donner Pass Rd; per car $8; ⊙10am-5pm; P🐾)
At the eastern end of Donner Lake (p662),
this state-run park occupies one of the sites
where the doomed Donner Party (p663)
got trapped during the fateful winter of
1846. Though its history is gruesome, the
park is gorgeous and has a sandy beach,
picnic tables, hiking trails and wintertime
cross-country skiing and snowshoeing. The
entry fee includes admission to the **visitor
center**, which has fascinating, if macabre,
historical exhibits and a 25-minute film
reenacting the Donner Party's horrific plight.
There are also displays about the Chi-
nese workers who turned from gold mining
to building California's railways. Outside,
the **Pioneer Monument** has a 22ft pedes-
tal – the exact depth of the snow piles that
horrendous winter. A short trail leads to a
memorial at one family's cabin site.

Old Jail HISTORIC BUILDING
(www.truckeehistory.org; 10142 Jiboom St, cnr
Spring St; suggested donation $2; ⊙11am-4pm Sat
& Sun late May & mid-Jun–mid-Sep) Continuous-
ly in use until the 1960s, this 1875 redbrick
building is filled with relics from the wild
days of yore. George 'Machine Gun' Kelly was
reportedly once held here for shoplifting at
a local variety store, and 'Baby Face' Nelson
and 'Ma' Spinelli and her gang did time too.

🏃 **Activities**
**Northstar Mountain
Bike Park** MOUNTAIN BIKING
(Map p642; www.northstarcalifornia.com; 5001
Northstar Dr, off Hwy 267; lift ticket adult/child
9-12yr $55/35; ⊙Jun-Sep) Sure, there's great
cross-country skiing, but the downhill at this
lift-serviced ski resort brings on the adren-
aline with lots of intermediate and expert
singletrack and fire roads. Over 100 miles of
trails; bikes and body-armor rental available.

Back Country OUTDOORS
(☑530-582-0909; www.thebackcountry.net; 11400
Donner Pass Rd; ⊙8am-6pm, call ahead in winter

& spring) Rents bicycles and snowshoes, and rents and sells new and used climbing gear, as well as backcountry ski gear.

Winter Sports

★ **Royal Gorge** SKIING
(☑530-426-3871; www.royalgorge.com; 9411 Pahatsi Rd, off I-80 exit Soda Springs/Norden, Soda Springs; adult/youth 13-22yr $32/25; ☺9am-5pm during snow season; ⊕⛇) Nordic-skiing aficionados won't want to pass up a spin around North America's largest cross-country resort (now operated by Sugar Bowl), with its mind-boggling 125 miles of groomed track crisscrossing 6000 acres of terrain. It has great skating lanes and diagonal stride tracks and also welcomes telemark skiers and snowshoers.

Group lessons are offered a few times daily, with ski camps for kids aged five to 12 (reservations recommended). For a twist, catch some air at the on-site Sierra Snowkite Center (www.sierrasnowkite.com).

Northstar California SNOW SPORTS
(Map p642; ☑530-562-1010; www.northstar california.com; 5001 Northstar Dr, off Hwy 267; adult/child 5-12yr/youth 13-18yr $130/77/107; ☺8am-4pm; ⊕) An easy 7 miles south of I-80, this hugely popular resort has great intermediate terrain as well as long black runs. Northstar's relatively sheltered location makes it the second-best choice after Homewood (p657) when it's snowing, and the eight terrain parks and pipes are top-ranked. Advanced and expert skiers can look for tree-skiing challenges on the back of the mountain.

Sugar Bowl SNOW SPORTS
(☑530-426-9000; www.sugarbowl.com; 629 Sugar Bowl Rd, off Donner Pass Rd, Norden; adult/

THE DOOMED DONNER PARTY

In the 19th century, tens of thousands of people migrated west along the Overland Trail with dreams of a better life in California. Among them was the ill-fated Donner Party.

When the families of George and Jacob Donner and their friend James Reed departed Springfield, IL, in April 1846 with six wagons and a herd of livestock, they intended to make the arduous journey as comfortable as possible. But the going was slow and, when other pioneers told them about a shortcut that would save 200 miles, they jumped at the chance.

However, there was no road for the wagons in the Wasatch Mountains, and most of the livestock succumbed under the merciless heat of the Great Salt Lake Desert. Arguments and fights broke out. James Reed killed a man, was kicked out of the group and left to trundle off to California alone. By the time the party reached the eastern foot of the Sierra Nevada, near present-day Reno, morale and food supplies were running dangerously low.

To restore their livestock's energy and stock up on provisions, the emigrants decided to rest here for a few days. But an exceptionally fierce winter came early, quickly rendering what later came to be called Donner Pass impassable and forcing the pioneers to build basic shelter near today's Donner Lake. They had food to last a month and the fervent hope that the weather would clear by then. It didn't.

Snow fell for weeks, reaching a depth of 22ft. Hunting and fishing became impossible. In mid-December a small group of 15 made a desperate attempt to cross the pass. They quickly became disoriented and had to ride out a three-day storm that killed a number of them. One month later, less than half of the original group staggered into Sutter's Fort near Sacramento, having survived on one deer and their dead friends.

By the time the first rescue party arrived at Donner Lake in late February, the trapped pioneers were still surviving – barely – on boiled ox hides. The rescuers themselves fell into difficulty, and when the second rescue party, led by the banished James Reed, made it through in March, evidence of cannibalism was everywhere. Journals and reports tell of 'half-crazed people living in absolute filth, with naked, half-eaten bodies strewn about the cabins.' Many were too weak to travel.

When the last rescue party arrived in mid-April, only a sole survivor, Lewis Keseberg, was there to greet them. The rescuers found George Donner's body cleansed and wrapped in a sheet, but no sign of Tasmen Donner, George's wife. Keseberg admitted to surviving on the flesh of the dead, but denied charges that he had killed Tasmen for fresh meat. He spent the rest of his life trying to clear his name.

In the end, only 47 of the 89 members of the Donner Party survived. They settled in California, their lives forever changed by the harrowing winter at Donner Lake.

child 6-12yr/youth 13-22yr $85/35/76; ☻9am-4pm; ⊛) Cofounded by Walt Disney in 1939, this is one of the Sierra's oldest ski resorts and a miniature Squaw Valley in terms of variety of terrain, including plenty of exhilarating gullies and chutes. Views are stellar on sunny days, but conditions go downhill pretty quickly, so to speak, during stormy weather.

The resort is 4 miles southeast of I-80 (exit Soda Springs/Norden). Stats: 13 lifts, 1500 vertical feet, 103 runs.

Boreal   SNOW SPORTS
(☑530-426-3666; www.rideboreal.com; 19659 Boreal Ridge Rd, off I-80 exit Castle Peak/Boreal Ridge Rd; adult/child 5-12yr/youth 13-17yr $64/34/54, night skiing adult/child $30/25, tubing $35; ☻9am-9pm; ⊛) Fun for newbies and intermediate skiers, Boreal is traditionally the first resort to open each year in the Tahoe area. For boarders, there are five terrain parks including a competition-level 450ft superpipe. Boreal is the only North Tahoe downhill resort besides Squaw that offers night skiing. Stats: seven lifts, 500 vertical feet, 33 runs.

Soda Springs   SNOW SPORTS
(☑530-426-3901; www.skisodasprings.com; 10244 Soda Springs Rd, off I-80 exit Soda Springs/Norden, Soda Springs; adult/child under 18yr $43/35, snowmobiling $16, tubing $35; ☻10am-4pm Thu-Mon, daily during holidays; ⊛) This cute little resort is a winner with kids, who can snow-tube, ride around in pint-sized snowmobiles, or learn to ski and snowboard. Stats: two lifts, 650 vertical feet, 15 runs.

Donner Ski Ranch   SNOW SPORTS
(☑530-426-3635; www.donnerskiranch.com; 19320 Donner Pass Rd, Norden; adult/child 7-12yr/youth 13-17yr $69/29/59; ☻9am-4pm; ⊛) Generations of skiers have enjoyed this itty-bitty family-owned resort. It's a great place to teach your kids how to ski, or for beginners to build skills. Prices drop after 12:30pm. It's 3.5 miles southeast of I-80 exit Soda Springs/Norden. Stats: six lifts, 750 vertical feet, 52 runs.

Tahoe Donner   SNOW SPORTS
(☑530-587-9444; www.tahoedonner.com; 11603 Snowpeak Way, off I-80 exit Donner Pass Rd; adult/child 7-12yr/youth 13-17yr $48/25/45; ☻9am-4pm; ⊛) Small, low-key and low-tech, Tahoe Donner is a darling resort with family-friendly beginner and intermediate runs only. Stats: five lifts, 600 vertical feet, 14 runs.

Clair Tappaan Lodge   SKIING
(☑530-426-3632; http://clairtappaanlodge.com; adult/child under 12yr $9/5; ☻9am-5pm; ⊛) You can ski right out the door if you're staying at this rustic mountain lodge near Donner Summit. Its 7 miles of groomed and tracked trails are great for beginner and intermediate skiers, and connect to miles of backcountry skiing. Stop by the lodge for ski and snowshoe rentals, and value-priced ski lessons at all skill levels (sign-up 9am daily).

Beaches & Water Sports

Warmer than Lake Tahoe, tree-lined Donner Lake (p662) is great for swimming, boating, fishing (license required), water-skiing and windsurfing.

West End Beach   SWIMMING, WATER SPORTS
(☑530-582-7720; www.tdrpd.com; off Donner Pass Rd; adult/child 2-17yr $4/3; ⊛) This Donner Lake (p662) beach is popular with families for its roped-off swimming area, snack stand, volleyball nets, and kayak, paddleboat and SUP rentals.

Tributary Whitewater Tours   RAFTING
(☑530-346-6812; www.whitewatertours.com; half-day trip per adult/child 7-17yr $69/62; ⊛) From roughly mid-May through September, this long-running outfitter operates a 7-mile, half-day rafting run on the Truckee River over Class III-plus rapids that will thrill kids and their nervous parents alike.

Hiking & Climbing

Truckee is a great base for treks in the **Tahoe National Forest** (Map p642), especially around **Donner Summit**. One popular 5-mile hike reaches the summit of 8243ft **Mt Judah** for awesome views of Donner Lake (p662) and the surrounding peaks. A longer, more strenuous ridge-crest hike (part of the **Pacific Crest Trail**) links **Donner Pass** to Squaw Valley (15 miles each way), skirting the base of prominent peaks, but you'll need two cars for this shuttle hike.

Donner Summit is also a major rock-climbing mecca, with over 300 traditional and sport-climbing routes. To learn the ropes, so to speak, take a class with **Alpine Skills International** (☑530-582-9170; www.alpineskills.com; 11400 Donner Pass Rd).

☞ Tours

Tahoe Adventure Company   ADVENTURE
(☑530-913-9212; www.tahoeadventurecompany.com; 7010 N Lake Blvd; tours per person from $55) A great option for guided Sierra adventures.

Staff know the backcountry inside out and can customize any outing to your interest and skill level, from kayaking, hiking, mountain biking and rock climbing to any combination thereof. They also offer full-moon snowshoe tours, SUP lessons and guided lake paddles.

🛏 Sleeping

A few dependable midrange chain motels and hotels are found off I-80 exits, plus there's a great hostel (p665) behind the train station.

★ Redlight   HOSTEL $
(⟋ 530-536-0005; www.redlighttruckee.com; 10101 West River St; dm $30, d from $70; 🛜) The name pays tribute to this hostel's 19th-century incarnation as a brothel. With a mix of dorms beds, doubles and even a suite with kitchenette, this is a great option for travelers on a budget. Communal areas are decked out in brocade and red drapes, and there's a good shared kitchen, board games and even a dry sauna.

Donner Memorial
State Park Campground   CAMPGROUND $
(Map p642; ⟋ 530-582-7894, reservations 800-444-7275; www.reserveamerica.com; tent & RV sites $35; ⊘ late May-late Sep) Brace yourself to camp near Donner Lake (p662): this family-oriented campground has 138 campsites with flush toilets and hot pay showers.

USFS Campgrounds   CAMPGROUND $
(Map p642; ⟋ 518-885-3639; www.recreation.gov; campsites $17-48; 🐾) Conveniently located along Hwy 89 (though with street noise) are three minimally developed riverside camping areas within a few minutes' drive of each other: Granite Flat, Goose Meadow and Silver Creek. All have potable water and vault toilets.

★ Cedar House
Sport Hotel   BOUTIQUE HOTEL $$
(Map p642; ⟋ 530-582-5655; www.cedarhouse sporthotel.com; 10918 Brockway Rd; r $170-295, pet fee $50; P♿@🛜🐾) ⏀ This chic, environmentally conscious contemporary lodge aims at getting folks out into nature. It boasts countertops made from recycled paper, 'rain chains' that redistribute water from the green roof garden, low-flow plumbing and in-room recycling. However, it doesn't skimp on plush robes, sexy platform beds with pillow-top mattresses, flat-screen TVs or the outdoor hot tub. It also houses Stella (p666) dining room.

Guided tours and multisport outdoor adventures can be arranged in house.

Truckee Hotel   HISTORIC HOTEL $$
(⟋ 530-587-4444; www.truckeehotel.com; 10007 Bridge St; r $79-229; 🛜) Tucked behind an atmospheric four-story redbrick streetfront arcade, Truckee's most historic abode has welcomed weary travelers since 1873. A recent remodel has updated the carpets and furniture to genteel Victorian-infused modern luxury, and there's regular live music in its restaurant Moody's Bistro & Lounge (p666). Parking available across the street. Expect some train noise and no elevator.

Truckee Donner Lodge   HOTEL $$
(⟋ 530-582-9999; www.truckeedonnerlodge.com; 10527 Cold Stream Rd, off I-80 exit Donner Pass Rd; r $84-204; ✳🛜🐾) Just west of Hwy 89, this ex–Holiday Inn property gives you easy driving access to area ski resorts, shaving time off your morning commute to the slopes. No-nonsense, spacious hotel rooms come with microwaves and mini-refrigerators, and some have gas fireplaces. The hot-and-cold continental breakfast bar is complimentary.

River Street Inn   B&B $$
(⟋ 530-550-9290; www.riverstreetinntruckee.com; 10009 E River St; r $145-220; 🛜) On the far side of the tracks, this sweet 1885 Victorian inn in Truckee's historic downtown has 11 rooms that blend nostalgic touches like claw-foot tubs with down comforters, but have few amenities other than TVs. Mingle with other guests over breakfast in the lounge. Bring earplugs to dull the occasional train noise.

Hotel Truckee-Tahoe   HOTEL $$
(Map p642; ⟋ 530-587-4525; www.hoteltruckee tahoe.com; 11331 Brockway Rd; r $189-229, pet fee $50; ✳@🛜🐾) Forget about retro ski-lodge kitsch as you cozy up inside these crisp, earth-toned and down-to-earth hotel rooms that abound in sunny, natural woods. Sink back onto the feather-topped mattresses, refresh yourself with spa-quality bath amenities or hit the seasonal outdoor heated pool by the hot tub.

🍴 Eating & Drinking

Coffeebar   CAFE $
(⟋ 530-587-2000; www.coffeebartruckee.com; 10120 Jiboom St; items $3-9; ⊘ 6am-6pm Sun-Thu, to 7pm Fri & Sat; 🛜) ⏀ This beatnik, barebones industrial coffee shop serves Italian gelato, delectable pastries and home-brewed

kombucha. Go for tantalizing breakfast crepes and overstuffed panini on herbed focaccia bread, or for a jolt of organic espresso or flavored tea lattes.

Squeeze In
DINER $

(www.squeezein.com; 10060 Donner Pass Rd; mains $8-15; ☺7am-2pm; 🖼) Across from the Amtrak station, this snug locals' favorite dishes up breakfasts big enough to feed a lumberjack. Over 60 varieties of humongous omelets – along with burgers, burritos and big salads – are served in the funky space crammed with silly tchotchkes and colorful handwritten notes on the walls.

★ Moody's Bistro & Lounge
CALIFORNIAN $$

(📿530-587-8688; www.moodysbistro.com; 10007 Bridge St; mains lunch $12-18, dinner $13-32; ☺11:30am-9:30pm) 🍴 With its sophisticated supper-club looks and live jazz (Thursday to Saturday evenings), this gourmet restaurant in the Truckee Hotel (p665) oozes urbane flair. Only fresh, organic and locally grown ingredients make it into the chef's perfectly pitched concoctions like pork loin with peach barbecue sauce, roasted beets with shaved fennel or pan-roasted Arctic char.

★ Stella
CALIFORNIAN $$$

(Map p642; 📿530-582-5665; www.cedarhouse sporthotel.com; 10918 Brockway Rd; mains $28-59; ☺5:30-8:30pm Wed-Sun) 🍴 Housed at the trendy Cedar House Sport Hotel (p665), this modern mountain-lodge dining room elevates Truckee's eating scene with Californian flair, harmonizing Asian and Mediterranean influences on its seasonal menu of housemade pastas, grilled meats and pan-roasted seafood. Bonuses: veggies grown on-site, housemade artisan bread and a killer wine list.

Fifty Fifty Brewing Co
BREWERY

(Map p642; www.fiftyfiftybrewing.com; 11197 Brockway Rd; ☺11:30am-9pm Sun-Thu, to 9:30pm Fri & Sat) Inhale the aroma of toasting grains at this brewpub south of downtown, near the Hwy 267 intersection. Sip the popular Donner Party Porter or Eclipse barrel-aged imperial stout while noshing a huge plate of nachos or other pub grub.

ⓘ Information

Truckee Donner Chamber of Commerce
(📿530-587-2757; www.truckee.com; 10065 Donner Pass Rd; computer access per 15min $3; ☺9am-6pm; 🛜) Inside the Amtrak train depot; free walking-tour maps and wi-fi.

USFS Truckee District Ranger Station
(📿530-587-3558; www.fs.usda.gov/tahoe; 10811 Stockrest Springs Rd, off I-80 exit 188; ☺8am-5pm Mon-Sat, Mon-Fri winter) Tahoe National Forest information.

ⓘ Getting There & Around

Truckee straddles the I-80 and is connected to the lakeshore via Hwy 89 to Tahoe City or Hwy 267 to Kings Beach. The main drag through downtown Truckee is Donner Pass Rd, where you'll find the **Amtrak Depot** (📿800-872-7245; www.amtrak.com; 10065 Donner Pass Rd) and metered on-street parking. Brockway Rd begins south of the river, connecting over to Hwy 267.

Though the Truckee Tahoe Airport has no commercial air service, **North Lake Tahoe Express** (📿866-216-5222; www.northlaketahoeexpress. com; per person to Truckee $49) shuttles to the closest airport at Reno. Buses make several runs daily from 3:30am to midnight, serving multiple northern and western shore towns and **Northstar** (p664) and **Squaw Valley** (p661) ski resorts. Make reservations in advance.

Greyhound (📿800-231-2222; www.greyhound. com) has twice-daily buses to Reno ($22, one hour), Sacramento ($51, 2½ hours) and San Francisco ($45, six hours). Greyhound buses stop at the train depot, as do Amtrak Thruway buses and the daily *California Zephyr* train to Reno ($16, 1½ hours), Sacramento ($41, 4½ hours) and Emeryville/San Francisco ($47, 6½ hours).

Truckee Transit (📿530-587-7451; www. laketahoetransit.com; single/day pass $2.50/5) links the Amtrak depot with Donner Lake hourly from 9am to 5pm Monday through Saturday. For Tahoe City and other towns on the lake's north, west or east shores, hop on the **Tahoe Area Rapid Transit** (p658) bus at the train depot. During ski season, additional buses run to many area ski resorts.

LAKE TAHOE NORTHERN SHORE

Northeast of Tahoe City, Hwy 28 cruises through a string of cute, low-key towns, many fronting superb sandy beaches, with reasonably priced roadside motels and hotels all crowded together along the lakeshore. Oozing old-fashioned charm, the north shore is a blissful escape from the teeming crowds of South Lake Tahoe, Tahoe City and Truckee, but still puts you within easy reach of winter ski resorts and snow parks, and summertime swimming, kayaking, hiking trails and more.

The **North Lake Tahoe Visitors' Bureaus** (📞800-468-2463; www.gotahoenorth.com) can help get you oriented, although the closest walk-in office is at Incline Village, NV.

Tahoe Vista

Pretty little Tahoe Vista has more **public beaches** (www.northtahoeparks.com) than any other lakeshore town. Sandy strands along Hwy 28 include small but popular **Moon Dunes Beach**, with picnic tables and fire pits opposite the Rustic Cottages (p667); **North Tahoe Beach** (Map p642; 7860 N Lake Blvd), near the Hwy 267 intersection, with picnic facilities, barbecue grills and beach-volleyball courts; and **Tahoe Vista Recreation Area** (7010 N Lake Blvd; parking $10), a locals' favorite with a small grassy area and marina and the **Tahoe Adventure Company** (📞530-913-9212; www.tahoeadventure company.com; 7010 N Lake Blvd; activities $15-80) renting kayaks and SUP gear.

Away from all the maddening crowds, **North Tahoe Regional Park** (Map p642; 📞530-546-4212; www.northtahoeparks.com; 6600 Donner Rd, off National Ave; per car $5; ☉7am-9pm Jun-Aug, to 7pm Sep & Oct, to 5pm Nov-May; P 🏕) offers forested hiking and mountain-biking trails, an 18-hole disc-golf course, a children's playground and tennis courts lit up for night play. In winter a sledding hill (rentals available) and ungroomed cross-country ski and snowshoe tracks beckon.

🛏 Sleeping

★**Cedar Glen Lodge**   CABIN **$$**
(📞530-546-4281; www.tahoecedarglen.com; 6589 N Lake Blvd; r, ste & cottages $139-350, pet fee $30; @ 🏕 🛏 🐾) Completely renovated and upgraded, these gorgeous cabins and rustic-themed lodge rooms across from the beach have pine paneling, new mattresses and kitchenettes or full kitchens. Kids go nuts over all the freebies, from Ping-Pong tables, a horseshoe pit and volleyball to an outdoor swimming pool, putting green and toasty fire pit.

Franciscan Lakeside Lodge   CABIN **$$**
(📞530-546-6300; www.franciscanlodge.com; 6944 N Lake Blvd; cabins $109-399; P 🐾 🏕 🛏) Spend the day on a private sandy beach or in the outdoor pool, then light the barbecue grill after sunset – ah, now that's relaxation. All of the simple cabins, cottages and suites have kitchenettes. Lakeside lodgings have

better beach access and views, but roomier cabins near the back of the complex tend to be quieter and will appeal to families.

Firelite Lodge   MOTEL **$$**
(📞530-546-7222; www.tahoelodge.com; 7035 N Lake Blvd; r $79-154; 🏕🛏) Upgraded with thick walls, soundproofed windows, and kitchenettes and gas fireplaces in every room, the family-run Firelite is a good-value stay in a prime walkable location, with the Tahoe Vista Recreation Area (p667) right across the street. The upstairs king-bed rooms have perfect lake-view balconies. Outside amenities include bikes to rent and a hot tub.

Rustic Cottages   CABIN **$$**
(📞530-546-3523; www.rusticcottages.com; 7449 N Lake Blvd; cottages $109-244; 🏕🛏) These cottages consist of a cluster of about 20 little storybook houses in the pines, with name tags fashioned from hand saws. They sport beautiful wrought-iron beds and a bevy of amenities. Most cabins have full kitchens, and some have gas or real wood-burning fireplaces.

Other perks: waffles and homemade muffins at breakfast, and free sleds and snowshoes to borrow in winter.

🍴 Eating & Drinking

★**Old Post Office Cafe**   AMERICAN **$**
(📞530-546-3205; 5245 N Lake Blvd; mains $8-12; ☉6:30am-2pm; 🏕) Head west of town toward Carnelian Bay, where this always-packed, cheery wooden shack (never, in fact, a post office) serves scrumptious breakfasts: buttery potatoes, eggs Benedict, biscuits with gravy, fluffy omelets with lotsa fillings and fresh-fruit smoothies. Waits for a table get long on summer and winter weekends, so roll up early.

Gar Woods Grill & Pier   BAR
(📞530-546-3366; www.garwoods.com; 5000 N Lake Blvd; ☉11:30am-11:30pm) A shoreline hot spot, Gar Woods pays tribute to the era of classic wooden boats. Don't show up for the lackadaisical grill fare, but instead to slurp a Wet Woody cocktail while watching the sun set over the lake. Be prepared to duke it out for a table on the no-reservations side of the beachfront deck out back.

Kings Beach

The utilitarian character of fetchingly picturesque Kings Beach lies in its smattering of back-to-basics retro motels all lined up along the highway (and belies the fact that the town has some of the area's best restaurants). This is one of the more ethnically diverse lakeshore communities, with a large Latino population, many of whom work in the tourism industry around Lake Tahoe.

Activities

Adrift Tahoe
OUTDOORS

(530-546-1112; www.standuppaddletahoe.com; 8338 N Lake Blvd; rentals per hour $25-50, per day from $80;) At **Kings Beach State Recreation Area** (Map p642; 530-583-3074; www.parks.ca.gov; off Hwy 28; per car $10; 6am-10pm;), Adrift Tahoe handles kayak, outrigger canoe and SUP rentals, and offers private lessons and tours.

North Tahoe Event Center
HEALTH & FITNESS

(http://northtahoeevents.com; 8318 N Lake Blvd) Hosts jazzercise, yoga and other classes.

Old Brockway Golf Course
GOLF

(530-546-9909; www.oldbrockwaygolf.com; 400 Brassie Ave, cnr Hwys 267 & 28; green fees $35-60, club/cart rental from $25/20) Just inland from the lake, the 1920s Old Brockway Golf Course runs along pine-bordered fairways where Hollywood celebs once swung their clubs.

Sleeping

Hostel Tahoe
HOSTEL $

(530-546-3266; www.hosteltahoe.com; 8931 N Lake Blvd; dm/d/q $33/60/80;) Minutes from Northstar (p664) and the beach, this former motel has private rooms and single-sex dorms with hand-painted murals and gauzy hanging textiles. A separate common building is the pièce de résistance, sunlight bathes the fireplace living room and a well-equipped honor kitchen stocks coffee, tea and food staples. Free loaner bikes, and breakfast included on Saturday and Sunday.

Eating & Drinking

Log Cabin Caffe
DINER $

(530-546-7109; www.logcabinbreakfast.com; 8692 N Lake Blvd; mains $8-16; 7am-2pm) Come early (especially on weekends) to join the queue for the North Shore's best breakfast. Eggs Benedict, whole-wheat pancakes with hot fresh fruit and cranberry-orange waffles are just a few highlights from the huge menu. Tip: call ahead to put your name on the waiting list. It sells ice cream out back in summer.

Char-Pit
FAST FOOD $

(www.charpit.com; 8732 N Lake Blvd; items $3-12; 11am-9pm;) No gimmicks at this 1960s fast-food stand, which grills juicy burgers and St Louis–style baby back ribs, and also fries up crispy onion rings and breaded mozzarella sticks. Somebody call an ambulance!

Lanza's
ITALIAN $$

(530-546-2434; www.lanzastahoe.com; 7739 N Lake Blvd; mains $12-23; 5-10pm, bar from 4:30pm) Next to the Safeway supermarket stands this beloved Italian trattoria where a tantalizing aroma of garlic, rosemary and 'secret' spices perfumes the air. Dinners, though undoubtedly not the tastiest you've ever had, are hugely filling and include salad and bread. Look for the owner's sepia-colored family photos in the entranceway.

Jason's Beachside Grille
BAR

(www.jasonsbeachsidegrille.com; 8338 N Lake Blvd; 11am-10pm) Looking for the party around sundown? Hit this waterfront deck with a schooner of microbrew. Never mind the unexciting American fare (dinner mains $13 to $25), like smoked chicken pasta, alongside an overflowing salad bar. On colder days, red-velvet sofas orbiting a sunken fireplace are the coziest, but in summer it's all about sunset views.

Grid Bar & Grill
PUB

(www.thegridbarandgrill.com; 8545 N Lake Blvd; 11am-2am) This locals' dive bar looks rough around the edges, but happy hours are supercheap and you can catch live music, from bluegrass to punk, DJs, dancing or karaoke, or trivia nights.

Getting There & Around

Tahoe Area Rapid Transit (p658) buses between Tahoe City and Incline Village make stops in Tahoe Vista, Kings Beach and Crystal Bay hourly from approximately 6am until 6pm daily. Another TART route connects Crystal Bay and Kings Beach with the **Northstar** (p664) resort every hour or so from 8am until 5pm daily; in winter this bus continues to Truckee (between May and November, you'll have to detour via Tahoe City first).

Crystal Bay (Nevada)

Crossing into Nevada, the neon starts to flash and old-school gambling palaces pant after your hard-earned cash. Though currently closed, historic Cal-Neva Resort literally straddles the California–Nevada border and has a colorful history involving ghosts, mobsters and Frank Sinatra, who once owned the joint. Ask about the guided secret tunnel tours if it ever reopens. **Crystal Bay Casino** (Map p642; ☑775-833-6333; www.crystal baycasino.com; 14 Hwy 28; ℗) is open though, and there you can try your luck at the gambling tables or catch a live-music show.

For a breath of pine-scented air, flee the smoky casinos for the steep 1-mile hike up paved Forest Service Rd 1601 to Stateline Lookout. Sunset views over Lake Tahoe and the mountains are all around. A nature trail loops around the site of the former fire lookout tower – nowadays there's a stone observation platform. To find the trailhead, drive up Reservoir Rd, just east of the Tahoe Biltmore parking lot, then take a right onto Lakeview Ave and follow it uphill just over a half-mile to the (usually locked) iron gate on your left.

🍴 Sleeping & Eating

**Tahoe Biltmore Lodge
& Casino**   CASINO HOTEL $
(Map p642; ☑800-245-8667; www.tahoebiltmore. com; 5 Hwy 28; r $84-129; 🖥�ﬆ) An old-school lodge and casino that has definitely seen better days.

Cafe Biltmore   AMERICAN $
(Map p642; 5 Hwy 28; mains $8-15; ☉7am-9pm) With floral carpet and a mirrored ceiling, this meat-heavy joint is visually bizarre enough to merit a peek.

LAKE TAHOE EASTERN SHORE (NEVADA)

Lake Tahoe's eastern shore lies entirely within Nevada. Much of it is relatively undeveloped thanks to George Whittell Jr, an eccentric San Franciscan playboy who once owned a lot of this land, including 27 miles of shoreline. Upon his death in 1969, it was sold off to a private investor, who later wheeled and dealed most of it to the USFS and Nevada State Parks. And lucky it was, because today the eastern shore offers some of Tahoe's best scenery and outdoor diversion.

Incline Village

One of Lake Tahoe's ritziest communities, Incline Village is the gateway to **Diamond**

Peak (Map p642; ☑775-832-1177; www.diamond peak.com; 1210 Ski Way, off Tahoe Blvd/Hwy 28; adult/child 7-12yr/youth 13-23yr $74/29/54; ☉9am-4pm; ﬆ) and **Mt Rose** (Map p642; ☑775-849-0704; http://skirose.com; 22222 Mt Rose Hwy/Hwy 431, Reno; adult/child 0-5yr/youth 6-15yr $60/20/30; ☉9am-4pm) ski resorts. The latter is a 12-mile drive northeast via Hwy 431 (Mt Rose Hwy). During summer, the nearby **Mt Rose Wilderness** (Map p642; www.fs.usda.gov/ltbmu) offers miles of unspoiled terrain, including a strenuous 10-mile round-trip to the summit of majestic **Mt Rose** (10,776ft). The trail starts from the deceptively named Mt Rose Summit parking lot, 9 miles uphill from Incline Village. For a more mellow meadow stroll that even young kids can handle, pull over a mile or so earlier at wildflower-strewn **Tahoe Meadows** (Map p642; Mt Rose Hwy; ﬆ). Stay on the nature loop trails to avoid trampling the fragile meadows; leashed dogs are allowed.

In summer, you can also visit George Whittell's mansion, **Thunderbird Lodge** (Map p642; ☑800-468-2463; http://thunderbird tahoe.org; adult/child 6-12yr from $39/19; ☉Tue-Sat mid-May–mid-Oct; ﬆ), where he spent summers with his pet lion, Bill.

🛏 Sleeping

Hyatt Regency Lake Tahoe   RESORT $$$
(Map p642; ☑775-832-1234; https://laketahoe. regency.hyatt.com; 111 Country Club Dr; r Sun-Thu/Fri & Sat from $199/379, ste & cottages Sun-Thu/Fri & Sat from $319/629; 🖥@�'�)
Decorated like an arts-and-crafts-style mountain lodge, every room and lakeside cottage here looks lavish, and the spa is even bigger than the casino. In summer you can sprawl on a private lakefront beach or in winter let the heated outdoor swimming lagoon warm you up after a day on the slopes.

🍴 Eating & Drinking

Austin's   AMERICAN $
(Map p642; www.austinstahoe.com; 120 Country Club Dr; mains $9-17; ☉11am-9pm; ☑ﬆ) A hearty welcome for the whole family is what you'll find at this wood-cabin diner with an outdoor deck. Buttermilk fries with jalapeño dipping sauce, chicken-fried steak, classic meatloaf, burgers, huge salad bowls and sandwiches will fill you up – and so will mountain-sized martinis.

Bite
CALIFORNIAN $$

(☑775-831-1000; www.bitetahoe.com; 907 Tahoe Blvd; shared plates $8-19; ◎5-10pm, closed Wed Oct-May; ☑) Don't let the strip-mall location stop you from rocking this creative, eclectic tapas and wine bar. Mix light, seasonal, veggie-friendly dishes with modern takes on rib-sticking comfort food like honeyed baby back ribs or green-chili mac 'n' cheese. An après-ski crowd turns up for happy hour.

Lone Eagle Grille
COCKTAIL BAR

(Map p642; https://laketahoe.regency.hyatt.com; 111 Country Club Dr; ◎11:30am-10pm Sun-Thu, to 11pm Fri & Sat) At the Hyatt Regency's (p669) many-hearthed cocktail lounge, sip a divine orange-flavored margarita, then head outside for sunset and to hang out by the beach fire pit.

Lake Tahoe-Nevada State Park

Back on the lake, heading south, is **Lake Tahoe-Nevada State Park** (Map p642; ☑775-831-0494; www.parks.nv.gov; per car $7-12; P 🚻), which has beaches, lakes and miles of trails. Just 3 miles south of Incline Village is beautiful **Sand Harbor** (Map p642; ☑775-831-0494; www.parks.nv.gov/parks/sand-harbor; 2005 Hwy 28; per car $7-12), where two sand spits have formed a shallow bay with brilliant, warm turquoise water and white, boulder-strewn beaches. It gets very busy here, especially during July and August, when the **Lake Tahoe Shakespeare Festival** (☑800-747-4697; www.laketahoeshakespeare.com; ◎Jul & Aug) is underway.

At the park's southern end, just north of the Hwy 50/Hwy 28 junction, **Spooner Lake** (Map p642; ☑775-749-5980; www.parks.nv.gov; per car $7-10) is popular for catch-and-release fishing, picnicking, nature walks, backcountry camping and cross-country skiing. Spooner Lake is also the start of the famous 13-mile **Flume Trail** (Map p642), a holy grail for experienced mountain bikers. From the trail's end near Incline Village you can either backtrack 10 miles along the narrow, twisting shoulder of Hwy 28 or board a shuttle bus. Arrange shuttles and rent bikes by the trailhead inside the park at **Flume Trail Bikes** (Map p642; ☑775-298-2501; http://flumetrailtahoe.com; 1115 Tunnel Creek Rd; mountain-bike rental per day $39-100, shuttle $15, state park entrance $2).

RENO (NEVADA)

Reno has a compact clutch of big casinos in the shadow of the Sierra Nevada. It has a reputation for being a 'poor man's Vegas,' but while in some ways that cap fits, we're here to set the record straight: Reno is oh, so much more. Beyond the garish downtown, with its photoworthy mid-century modern architecture, neon signs and alpine-fed Truckee River, sprawls a city of parks and pretty houses inhabited by a friendly bunch eager to welcome you.

Stealing a piece of California's tech-pie, the gargantuan Tesla Gigafactory will open its doors here in 2020, bringing plenty of cashed-up youngsters to town, and Reno is ready: the transformation of the formerly gritty Midtown District continues, injecting a dose of funky new bars, top-notch restaurants and vibrant arts spaces into Reno's already unique and eclectic mix.

If you like pleasant surprises or just go for the underdog, chances are you'll love Reno.

⊙ Sights

★**National Automobile Museum**
MUSEUM

(☑775-333-9300; www.automuseum.org; 10 S Lake St; adult/child 6-18yr $10/4; ◎9:30am-5:30pm Mon-Sat, 10am-4pm Sun) Stylized street scenes illustrate a century's worth of automobile history at this engaging car museum. The collection is enormous and impressive, with one-of-a-kind vehicles – including James Dean's 1949 Mercury from *Rebel Without a Cause,* a 1938 Phantom Corsair and a 24-karat gold-plated DeLorean – and rotating exhibits with all kinds of souped-up and fabulously retro rides.

Nevada Museum of Art
MUSEUM

(☑775-329-3333; www.nevadaart.org; 160 W Liberty St; adult/child 6-12yr $10/1; ◎10am-5pm Wed & Fri-Sun, to 8pm Thu) In a sparkling building inspired by the geological formations of the Black Rock Desert north of town, a floating staircase leads to galleries showcasing temporary exhibits and eclectic collections on the American West, labor and contemporary landscape photography. In 2016 the museum opened its $6.2-million Sky Room function area. Visitors are free to explore and enjoy the space – essentially a fabulous rooftop penthouse and patio with killer views – providing it's not in use.

Fleischmann Planetarium & Science Center
MUSEUM

(☑775-784-4811; http://planetarium.unr.nevada.edu; 1664 N Virginia St; planetarium adult/child under 12yr $8/6; ☺noon-8pm Mon-Thu, to 9pm Fri, 10am-9pm Sat, to 6pm Sun; ⊞) Pop into this flying-saucer-shaped building at the University of Nevada for a window on the universe during star shows and feature presentations.

Nevada Historical Society Museum
MUSEUM

(☑775-688-1190; www.nvdtca.org/historical society; 1650 N Virginia St; adult/child under 17yr $5/free; ☺10am-4:30pm Tue-Sat) Within the main campus of the University of Nevada, the state's oldest museum includes permanent exhibits on neon signs, local American Indian culture and the presence of the federal government.

Circus Circus
CASINO

(☑775-329-0711; www.circusreno.com; 500 N Sierra St; ☺24hr; ⊞) The most family-friendly of Reno's casinos, Circus Circus has free circus acts to entertain kids beneath a giant, candy-striped big top, which also harbors a gazillion carnival and video games that look awfully similar to slot machines.

Silver Legacy
CASINO

(☑775-329-4777; www.silverlegacyreno.com; 407 N Virginia St; ☺24hr) A Victorian-themed place, the Silver Legacy is easily recognized by its white landmark dome, where a giant mock mining rig periodically erupts into a fairly tame sound-and-light spectacle. The casino's hotel tower is usually lit emerald green at night and looks like something out of *The Wizard of Oz*.

Eldorado
CASINO

(☑775-786-5700; www.eldoradoreno.com; 345 N Virginia St; ☺24hr) Right downtown, near the Reno Arch, the Eldorado has a kitschy Fountain of Fortune that probably has Italian sculptor Bernini spinning in his grave.

Harrah's
CASINO

(☑775-786-3232; www.harrahsreno.com; 219 N Center St; ☺24hr) Founded by Nevada gambling pioneer William Harrah in 1946, Harrah's is still one of the biggest and most popular casinos in town.

★Atlantis
CASINO

(☑775-825-4700; www.atlantiscasino.com; 3800 S Virginia St; ☺24hr) Looking like it's straight out of a 1970s B-grade flick on the outside,

THE RENO ARCH

Be sure to check out the iconic **Reno Arch** (cnr Virginia St & Commercial Row), a fabulously retro neon sign spanning Virginia St at the intersection of Commercial Row, denoting the epicenter of 'casino central' and proclaiming Reno to be 'The Biggest Little City in the World.' First built in 1926, the arch has had a number of incarnations in different locations downtown. Its slogan was chosen by competition in 1929, and has held tight, despite attempts to change it: proud locals love that Reno remains the 'biggest little city' to this day.

Atlantis is all fun on the inside, modeled on the legendary underwater city, with a mirrored ceiling and tropical flourishes like indoor waterfalls and palm trees. It's one of Reno's most popular offerings, though not downtown.

🏃 Activities

While gamblers feed their addictions indoors, countless others relish Reno's outdoor activities, from river floats and kayaking to mountain biking, climbing and skiing.

Reno is under an hour's drive from Lake Tahoe ski resorts – most hotels and casinos offer stay-and-ski packages.

For information on regional hiking and mountain-biking trails, including the Mt Rose summit trail and Tahoe-Pyramid Bikeway, download the *Truckee Meadows Trails Guide* (www.washoecounty.us/parks/trails/trail_challenge.php).

Truckee River Whitewater Park
OUTDOORS

(www.reno.gov; Wingfield Park) Mere steps from the casinos, the park's class II and III rapids are gentle enough for kids riding inner tubes, yet sufficiently challenging for professional freestyle kayakers. Two courses wrap around Wingfield Park, a small river island that hosts free concerts in summertime. Tahoe Whitewater Tours (p672) and Sierra Adventures (p672) offer kayak trips and lessons.

Tahoe Whitewater Tours
OUTDOORS

(☑775-787-5000; www.gowhitewater.com; 400 Island Ave; 2hr kayak rental/tour from $48/68) Tahoe Whitewater Tours rents tubes and kayaks and leads guided tours.

LAKE TAHOE RENO (NEVADA)

Sierra Adventures OUTDOORS
(☑866-323-8928, 775-323-8928; www.wildsierra.
com; Truckee River Lane; kayak rental from $22)
This affable outfitter offers tons of adventure: kayaking, tubing, mountain biking, skiing, horseback riding and snowmobiling.

☞ Tours

Historic Reno
Preservation Society WALKING
(☑775-747-4478; www.historicreno.org; suggested
donation $10) Dig deeper with a walking or biking tour of Reno that highlights subjects including architecture, politics and literary history. Check the website for the exhaustive list of tours available.

⚘ Festivals & Events

Hot August Nights CULTURAL
(www.hotaugustnights.net; ☺Aug) Catch the
American Graffiti vibe during this celebration of hot rods and rock and roll in early August held over separate dates and various locations around Reno and Virginia City. Hotel rates skyrocket.

Tour de Nez SPORTS
(www.tourdenez.com; ☺Jul) Called the 'coolest
bike race in America,' the Tour de Nez brings together pro and amateur cyclists for five days of races and partying in July.

Reno River Festival SPORTS
(www.renoriverfestival.com; ☺May) The world's
top freestyle kayakers compete in a mad paddling dash through Whitewater Park in mid-May. Free music concerts as well.

⌂ Sleeping

Reno has a wide range of accommodations, from budget motels to boutique hotels and decadent casino suites. Room rates in smoky casino towers can sometimes seem

GREAT BALLS OF FIRE!

For a week in August during the **Burning Man** (www.burningman.com; entry $425; ☺Aug) festival, 'Burners' from around the world descend on the Black Rock Desert to build the temporary Black Rock City, only to tear it all down again and set fire to an effigy of man. In between, there's peace, love, music, art, nakedness, drugs, sex and frivolity in a safe space where attendees uphold the principles of the festival.

ridiculously inexpensive – this is to get as many people through the doors as possible. Many casinos also whack on a resort fee to your bill. Reno's prices are generally higher than in other parts of the state, especially on weekends.

Mt Rose Campground CAMPGROUND $
(Map p642; ☑877-444-6777; www.recreation.
gov; Mt Rose Hwy/Hwy 431; RV & tent sites $20-50; ☺mid-Jun–Sep; ℗⚘) Reserve your spot a minimum of four days in advance for this gorgeous and popular high-altitude (9300ft!) campsite overlooking Lake Tahoe. It's located within the Humboldt-Toiyabe National Forest, 28 miles from downtown Reno. Reservations can be made via the website.

Sands Regency HOTEL $
(☑775-348-2200; www.sandsregency.com; 345
N Arlington Ave; r from $49 Sun-Thu, from $89 Fri & Sat; ℗⚘⚘⚘⚘⚘) The Sands Regency has some of the largest standard digs in town. Its rooms are decked out in a cheerful tropical palette of upbeat blues, reds and greens – a visual relief from typical motel decor. Empress Tower rooms are best. The 17th-floor gym and Jacuzzi are perfectly positioned to capture the drop-dead panoramic mountain views, and an outdoor pool opens in summer.

Peppermill CASINO HOTEL $$
(☑775-826-2121; www.peppermillreno.com; 2707 S
Virginia St; r from $69 Sun-Thu, from $149 Fri & Sat; ℗⚘@⚘⚘) ✈ With a dash of Vegas-style opulence, the ever-popular Peppermill boasts Tuscan-themed suites in its newest 600-room tower, and plush remodeled rooms throughout the rest of the property. The two sparkling pools (one indoors) are dreamy, with a full spa on hand. Geothermal energy powers the resort's hot water and heat. The nightly resort fee is $20.

Renaissance Reno Downtown HOTEL $$
(☑775-682-3900;www.marriott.com/hotels/travel/
rnobr-renaissance-reno-downtown-hotel; 1 Lake St; r from $149; ℗⚘⚘) Formerly the boutique Siena hotel, this property joined the Renaissance group in 2017 and at the time of writing was undergoing an extensive transformation. Renovated, oversized guest rooms will follow a contemporary theme using tones and textures that complement its fabulous riverside position, moments from downtown. With the best rooftop pool in town, this is a smart alternative to casino hotels.

✖ Eating

Reno's dining scene is coming of age, finally going beyond the cheap casino buffets and ubiquitous old-school diners. Many downtown restaurants are open around the clock, or at least until the wee hours. The Midtown District has an impressive selection of new restaurants across a wide genre of cuisine.

★ **Gold 'n Silver Inn**   DINER $
(☑ 775-323-2696; www.goldnsilverreno.com; 790 W 4th St; mains $6-20; ☺ 24hr) A Reno institution for over 50 years, this slightly divey but superfriendly 24-hour diner has a huge menu of homestyle American favorites such as meatloaf, plated dinners, all-day breakfasts and burgers, not to mention seriously incredible caramel milkshakes.

Pho 777   VIETNAMESE $
(☑ 775-323-7777; 102 E 2nd St; mains $6-8; ☺ 10am-9pm) A no-frills Vietnamese noodle shop just off the casino strip that serves up bowls and bowls of steamy soup.

Peg's Glorified Ham & Eggs   DINER $
(www.eatatpegs.com; 420 S Sierra St; mains $7-16; ☺ 6:30am-2pm; ⊞) Locally regarded as having the best breakfast in town, Peg's offers tasty grill food that's not too greasy.

★ **Old Granite Street Eatery**   AMERICAN $$
(☑ 775-622-3222; www.oldgranitestreeteatery. com; 243 S Sierra St; dinner mains $12-29; ☺ 11am-10pm Mon-Thu, to 11pm Fri, 10am-11pm Sat, to 3pm Sun; ☑) A lovely well-lit place for organic and local comfort food, old-school artisanal cocktails and craft beers, this antique-strewn hot spot enchants diners with its stately wooden bar, water served in old liquor bottles and lengthy seasonal menu. Forgot to make a reservation? Check out the iconic rooster and pig murals and wait at a communal table fashioned from a barn door.

Silver Peak Restaurant & Brewery   PUB FOOD $$
(☑ 775-324-1864; www.silverpeakbrewery.com; 124 Wonder St; dinner mains $15-26; ☺ restaurant 11am-10pm Sun-Thu, to 11pm Fri & Sat, pub open 1hr later; ⊞) Casual and pretense-free, this place hums with the chatter of happy locals settling in for a night of microbrews and great eats, from pizza with barbecue chicken to filet mignon.

★ **Wild River Grille**   GRILL $$
(☑ 775-847-455; www.wildrivergrille.com; 17 S Virginia St; mains lunch $11-16, dinner $21-37; ☺ 11am-9pm; ☑) At the Wild River Grille you'll love the smart-casual dining and the varied menu of creative cuisine, from the Gruyère croquettes to the lobster ravioli, but most of all the wonderful patio overlooking the lovely Truckee River: it's also the best spot in town for a drink on a balmy summer's evening and a great place to take a date.

WORTH A TRIP

PYRAMID LAKE

Pyramid Lake is a stunning stand-alone sight, with shores lined with beaches and eye-catching tufa formations. This piercingly blue expanse in an otherwise-barren landscape is 25 miles north of Reno on the Paiute Indian Reservation. Iconic pyramid-like Anaho Island, nearer its east side, is a bird sanctuary for American white pelicans.

Permits for camping on the beach on the west side of the lake and fishing are available online, at outdoor suppliers and CVS drugstore locations in Reno, and at the **ranger station** (☑ 775-476-1155; http://plpt.nsn.us/rangers; 2500 Lakeview Dr, Sutcliffe; ☺ 9am-1pm & 2-6pm Thu-Mon) east of SR445 in Sutcliffe.

🍸 Drinking & Nightlife

Reno is a fun place with plenty going on, including regular monthly pub crawls, the only gay bars in Nevada outside Las Vegas and an emerging arts scene.

★ **Imperial Bar & Lounge**   BAR
(☑ 775-324-6399; www.imperialbarandlounge. com; 150 N Arlington Ave; ☺ 11am-2am Fri & Sat, to 10pm Sun-Thu) A classy bar inhabiting a relic of the past – this building was once an old bank, and in the middle of the wood floor you can see cement where the vault once stood. Sandwiches and pizzas go with 16 beers on tap and a buzzing weekend scene.

Chapel Tavern   COCKTAIL BAR
(☑ 775-324-2244; www.chapeltavern.com; 1099 S Virginia St; ☺ 2pm-2am Mon-Wed, to 4am Thu-Sun) Midtown's cocktail mecca makes its own infusions – try the bourbon with fig – and a seasonal drinks menu attracts year-round interest to its antler-adorned bar and outdoor patio. DJs keep it jamming on Friday and Saturday, and patrons comprise a diverse age mix.

Jungle
CAFE, WINE BAR

(☑775-329-4484; www.thejunglereno.com; 246 W 1st St; ☺coffee 6am-midnight, wine 3pm-midnight Mon-Thu, 3pm-2am Fri, noon-2am Sat, noon-midnight Sun; 🛜) A side-by-side coffee shop and wine bar with a cool mosaic floor and riverside patio all rolled into one. The wine bar has weekly tastings, while the cafe serves breakfast bagels and lunchtime sandwiches ($6 to $8) and puts on diverse music shows.

☆ Entertainment

The free weekly *Reno News & Review* (www.newsreview.com/reno/home) is your best source for listings.

Knitting Factory
LIVE MUSIC

(☑775-323-5648; http://re.knittingfactory.com; 211 N Virginia St) This midsized music venue books mainstream and indie favorites.

ℹ Information

Galena Creek Visitor Center (☑775-849-4948; www.galenacreekvisitorcenter.org; 18250 Mt Rose Hwy; ☺9am-6pm Tue-Sun) Check in with this center when you arrive at the Galena Creek Recreation Area for the latest conditions and friendly advice.

Reno-Sparks Convention & Visitors Authority Visitor Center (☑775-682-3800; www.visitrenotahoe.com; 135 N Sierra St; ☺9am-6pm) Stop by this conveniently located center when you get to town for the latest on what's on, where and when.

ℹ Getting There & Away

About 5 miles southeast of downtown, the **Reno-Tahoe International Airport** (RNO; www.renoairport.com; 🛜) is served by most major airlines, with connections throughout the US to international routes.

The **North Lake Tahoe Express** (☑866-216-5222; www.northlaketahoeexpress.com; 1 way $49) operates a shuttle (six to eight daily, 3:30am to midnight) to and from the airport to multiple North Shore Lake Tahoe locations including Truckee, Squaw Valley and Incline Village. Reserve in advance.

The **South Tahoe Airporter** (☑866-898-2463; www.southtahoeairporter.com; adult/child 1 way $29.75/16.75, round-trip $53/30.25) operates several daily shuttle buses from the airport to Stateline casinos; the journey takes from 75 minutes to two hours.

RTC Washoe (☑775-348-0400; www.rtcwashoe.com) operates six wi-fi-equipped RTC Intercity buses per day from Monday to Friday to Carson City ($5, one hour), which loosely connect to BlueGo buses – operated by **Tahoe Transportation District** (☑775-589-5500; www.tahoetransportation.org) – to the Stateline Transit Center in South Lake Tahoe (adult/child $4/2 with RTC Intercity transfer, one hour).

Greyhound (☑800-231-2222; www.greyhound.com) offers up to five direct buses a day to Reno from San Francisco (from $8, from five hours): book in advance for these lowest fares.

Discount bus company **Megabus** (www.megabus.com) has two daily departures to San Francisco (from $15, 4½ hours) via Sacramento.

The **Amtrak** (☑800-872-7245; www.amtrak.com) *California Zephyr* train makes one daily departure from Emeryville/San Francisco ($52, 6¾ hours) to Reno, onwards to Chicago (from $122, 44¾ hours): a shared sleeper berth will set you back $467. Up to three other daily services depart Emeryville/San Francisco for Sacramento, connecting with a bus service to Reno ($60, from 6½ hours).

ℹ Getting Around

It's easy to get around Reno on foot, but parts of downtown beyond the 24-hour casino area can be sketchy after dark. Exercise caution when walking along Ralston St, between W 4th and 5th Sts, especially at night.

Casino hotels usually offer frequent free airport shuttles for their guests (and generally don't ask to see reservations – just saying...).

The local **RTC Washoe** (p674) RTC Ride buses blanket the city, and most routes converge at the RTC 4th St station downtown (between Lake St and Evans Ave). Useful routes include the RTC Rapid line for S Virginia St, 11 for Sparks and 19 for the airport.

The Sierra Spirit bus (50¢) loops around all major downtown landmarks – including the casinos and the university – every 15 minutes from 7am to 7pm.

Yosemite & the Sierra Nevada

Why Go?

An outdoor-adventurer's wonderland, the Sierra Nevada is a year-round pageant of snow sports, white-water rafting, hiking, cycling and rock climbing. Skiers and snowboarders blaze through hushed pine-tree slopes, and wilderness seekers come to escape the stresses of modern civilization.

With fierce granite mountains standing watch over high-altitude lakes, the eastern spine of California is a formidable but exquisite topographical barrier enclosing magnificent natural landscapes. And interspersed between its river canyons and 14,000ft peaks are the decomposing ghost towns left behind by California's early white settlers, bubbling natural hot springs and Native American tribes that still call it home.

In the majestic national parks of Yosemite and Sequoia & Kings Canyon, visitors will be humbled by the groves of solemn giant sequoias, ancient rock formations and valleys, and the ever-present opportunity to see bears and other wildlife.

Best Places to Eat

➡ Evergreen Lodge (p692)

➡ Lakefront Restaurant (p721)

➡ Majestic Yosemite Dining Room (p693)

➡ Erick Schat's Bakkerÿ (p728)

➡ Mono Inn (p716)

➡ Fork & Love (p698)

Best Places to Sleep

➡ Sequoia High Sierra Camp (p703)

➡ Majestic Yosemite Hotel (p690)

➡ Rush Creek Lodge (p693)

➡ Yosemite Bug Rustic Mountain Resort (p697)

➡ Inn at Benton Hot Springs (p730)

➡ Hotel Charlotte (p698)

When to Go

Yosemite National Park

May & Jun The Yosemite waterfalls are gushing and spectacular in spring.

Jul & Aug Head for the mountains for wilderness adventures and glorious sunshine.

Dec–Mar Take a wintertime romp through snowy forests.

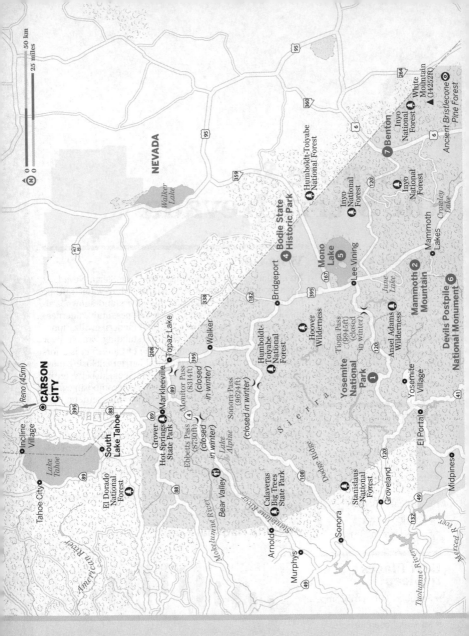

Yosemite & the Sierra Nevada Highlights

1 **Yosemite National Park**
(p678) Marveling at the waterfall gush in spring.

2 **Mammoth Mountain** (p718)
Whooshing down the wintertime heights of this snow-draped mountain.

3 **Sequoia & Kings Canyon National Parks** (p698) Gazing heavenward through the celestial sequoia canopies.

4 **Bodie State Historic Park** (p713)
Ambling around this evocative ghost town.

5 **Mono Lake**
(p716) Canoeing or kayaking amid the lake's haunting tufa.

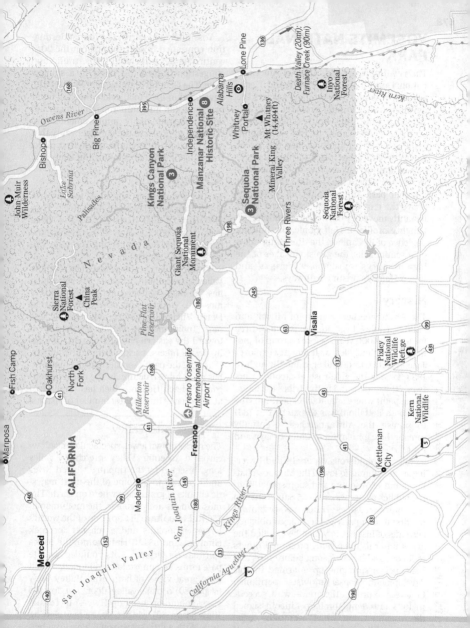

CALIFORNIA

Nevada

San Joaquin Valley

Merced

Fresno

Mariposa
Fish Camp
Oakhurst
North Fork
Madera

Lone Pine
Big Pine
Bishop

Owens River
Lake Sabrina
Palisades

John Muir Wilderness
Sierra National Forest
China Peak

Kings Canyon National Park ③
Manzanar National Historic Site ⑧
Independence
Alabama Hills
Whitney Portal
Mt Whitney (14,494ft)
Sequoia National Park ③
Mineral King Valley

Giant Sequoia National Monument

Pine Flat Reservoir
Millerton Reservoir

Yosemite International Airport

San Joaquin River
Kings River
California Aqueduct

Three Rivers
Sequoia National Forest

Visalia
Pixley National Wildlife Refuge
Kern National Wildlife

Kettleman City

Death Valley (20mi): Furnace Creek (90mi)
Inyo National Forest
Kern River

⑥ **Devils Postpile National Monument** (p728) Viewing this bizarre volcanic formation.

⑦ **Benton Hot Springs** (p730) Soaking your troubles away at these hot springs.

⑧ **Manzanar National Historic Site** (p729) Visiting the museum and site of one of the darkest events in US history.

YOSEMITE NATIONAL PARK

The jaw-dropping head-turner of America's national parks, and a Unesco World Heritage site, Yosemite (yo-*sem*-it-ee) garners the devotion of all who enter. From the waterfall-striped granite walls buttressing emerald-green Yosemite Valley to the skyscraping giant sequoias catapulting into the air at Mariposa Grove, the place inspires a sense of awe and reverence – four million visitors wend their way to the country's third-oldest national park annually. But lift your eyes above the crowds and you'll feel your heart instantly moved by unrivalled splendors: the haughty profile of Half Dome, the hulking presence of El Capitan, the drenching mists of Yosemite Falls, the gemstone lakes of the high country's subalpine wilderness and Hetch Hetchy's pristine pathways.

History

The Ahwahneechee, a group of Miwok and Paiute peoples, lived in the Yosemite area for around 4000 years before a group of pioneers, most likely led by legendary explorer Joseph Rutherford Walker, came through in 1833. During the gold-rush era, conflict between the miners and native tribes escalated to the point where a military expedition (the Mariposa Battalion) was dispatched in 1851 to punish the Ahwahneechee, eventually forcing the capitulation of Chief Tenaya and his tribe.

Tales of thunderous waterfalls and towering stone columns followed the Mariposa Battalion out of Yosemite and soon spread into the public's awareness. In 1855 San Francisco entrepreneur James Hutchings organized the first tourist party to the valley. Published accounts of his trip, in which he extolled the area's untarnished beauty, prompted others to follow, and it wasn't long before inns and roads began springing up. Alarmed by this development, conservationists petitioned Congress to protect the area – with success. In 1864 President Abraham Lincoln signed the Yosemite Grant, which eventually ceded Yosemite Valley and the Mariposa Grove of Giant Sequoias to California as a state park. This landmark decision, along with the pioneering efforts of conservationist John Muir, led to a congressional act in 1890 creating Yosemite National Park; this, in turn, helped pave the way for the national-park system that was established in 1916.

Yosemite's popularity as a tourist destination continued to soar throughout the 20th century and, by the mid-1970s, traffic and congestion draped the valley in a smoggy haze. The General Management Plan (GMP), developed in 1980 to alleviate this and other problems, ran into numerous challenges and delays. Despite many improvements, and the need to preserve the natural beauty that draws visitors to Yosemite in the first place, the plan still hasn't been fully implemented.

◉ Sights

There are four main entrances to the park: South Entrance (Hwy 41), Arch Rock (Hwy 140), Big Oak Flat (Hwy 120 W) and Tioga Pass (Hwy 120 E). Hwy 120 traverses the park as Tioga Rd, connecting Yosemite Valley with the Eastern Sierra.

Visitor activity is concentrated in Yosemite Valley, especially in Yosemite Village, which has the main visitor center, a post office, a museum, eateries and other services. Half Dome Village is another hub. Notably less busy, Tuolumne (too-*ahl*-uh-*mee*) Meadows, toward the eastern end of Tioga Rd, primarily draws hikers, backpackers and climbers. Wawona, the park's southern focal point, also has good infrastructure. In the northwestern corner, Hetch Hetchy, which has no services at all, receives the smallest number of visitors.

◉ Yosemite Valley

The park's crown jewel, spectacular meadow-carpeted Yosemite Valley stretches 7 miles long, bisected by the rippling Merced River and hemmed in by some of the most majestic chunks of granite anywhere on earth. The most famous are, of course, the monumental 7569ft **El Capitan** (El Cap), one of the world's largest monoliths and a magnet for rock climbers, and 8842ft **Half Dome**, the park's spiritual centerpiece – its rounded granite pate forms an unmistakable silhouette. You'll have great views of both from **Valley View** (Map p680) on the valley floor, but for the classic photo op, head up Hwy 41 to **Tunnel View** (Map p680), which boasts a new viewing area. With a little sweat you'll have even better postcard panoramas – sans the crowds – from **Inspiration Point** (Map p680). The trail (2.6-mile round-trip) starts at the tunnel.

Yosemite's waterfalls mesmerize even the most jaded traveler, especially when the spring runoff turns them into thunderous cataracts. **Yosemite Falls** (Map p680) is considered the tallest in North America, dropping

2425ft in three tiers. A slick wheelchair-accessible trail leads to the bottom of this cascade or, if you prefer solitude and different perspectives, you can also clamber up the **Yosemite Falls Trail**, which puts you atop the falls after a grueling 3.4 miles. No less impressive is nearby **Bridalveil Fall** (Map p680) and others scattered throughout the valley.

Any aspiring Ansel Adams should lug their camera gear along the 1-mile paved trail to **Mirror Lake** (Yosemite Valley) early or late in the day to catch the ever-shifting reflection of Half Dome in the still waters. The lake all but dries up by late summer.

South of here, where the Merced River courses around two small islands, lies **Happy Isles** (Map p682), a popular area for picnics, swimming and strolls. It also marks the start of the **John Muir Trail** and **Mist Trail** to several waterfalls and Half Dome.

Yosemite Museum   MUSEUM
(Map p682; www.nps.gov/yose; 9037 Village Dr, Yosemite Village; ☺9am-5pm summer, 10am-4pm rest of year, often closed noon-1pm) 🏃 **FREE** The Yosemite Museum has Miwok and Paiute artifacts, including woven baskets, beaded buckskin dresses and dance capes made from feathers. Native American cultural demonstrators engage visitors with traditional basket weaving, tool making and crafts. There's also an **art gallery** with paintings and photographs from the museum's permanent collection. Behind the museum, a self-guided **interpretive trail** winds past the reconstructed 1870s **Indian Village of Ahwahnee**, with pounding stones, an acorn granary, a ceremonial roundhouse and a conical bark house.

Majestic Yosemite Hotel   HISTORIC BUILDING
(Map p682) About a quarter-mile east of Yosemite Village, the former Ahwahnee Hotel is a graceful blend of rustic mountain retreat and elegant mansion dating back to 1927. You don't need to be a guest to have a gawk and a wander. Built from local granite, pine and cedar, the building is splendidly decorated with leaded glass, sculpted tiles, Native American rugs and Turkish kilims. You can enjoy a meal in the baronial dining room or a casual drink in the piano bar.

Around Christmas, the hotel hosts the **Bracebridge Dinner** (☑888-413-8869; www.bracebridgedinners.com), a combination of banquet and Renaissance fair. Book early.

Nature Center at Happy Isles   MUSEUM
(Map p682; www.nps.gov/yose; ☺9am-5pm late May-Sep; 👶) 🏃 An aging but still fun hands-on nature museum, the Nature Center has displays explaining the differences between the park's various pinecones, rocks, animal tracks and (everyone's favorite subject) scat. Out back, don't miss an exhibit on the 1996 rockfall, when an 80,000-ton slab plunged 2000ft to the nearby valley floor, killing a man and felling about 1000 trees. The center is off Southside Dr in Yosemite Valley.

👁 Glacier Point

If you drove, the views from 7214ft **Glacier Point** (Map p682) might make you feel like you cheated – superstar sights present themselves to you with you making hardly any physical effort. A quick mosey up from the parking lot and you'll find the entire eastern Yosemite Valley spread out before you, from **Yosemite Falls** to **Half Dome**, as well as the distant peaks that ring Tuolumne Meadows. Half Dome looms practically at eye level, and if you look closely you can spot hikers on its summit.

To the left of Half Dome lies the glacially carved **Tenaya Canyon**, and to its right are the wavy white ribbons of **Nevada and Vernal Falls**. On the valley floor, the Merced River snakes through green meadows and groves of trees. Sidle up to the railing, hold on tight and peer 3200ft straight down at Half Dome Village. **Basket Dome** and **North Dome** rise to the north of the valley, and **Liberty Cap** and the **Clark Range** can be seen to the right of Half Dome.

Almost from the park's inception, Glacier Point has been a popular destination. It used to be that getting up here was a major undertaking. That changed once the Four Mile Trail opened in 1872. A wagon road to the point was completed in 1882, and the current Glacier Point Rd was built in 1936.

At the tip of the point is **Overhanging Rock**, a huge granite slab protruding from the cliff edge like an outstretched tongue, defying gravity and once providing a scenic stage for daredevil extroverts. Through the years, many famous photos have been taken of folks performing handstands, high kicks and other wacky stunts on the rock. The precipice is now off-limits.

👁 Tioga Road & Tuolumne Meadows

Tioga Rd (or Hwy 120 E), the only road through the park, travels through 56 miles of superb high country at elevations ranging from 6200ft at Crane Flat to 9945ft at

Yosemite National Park

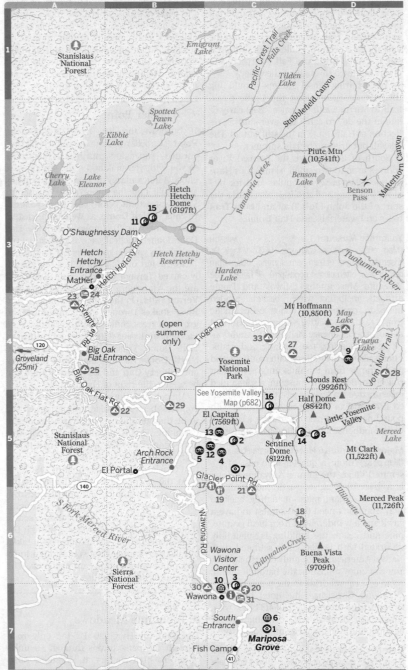

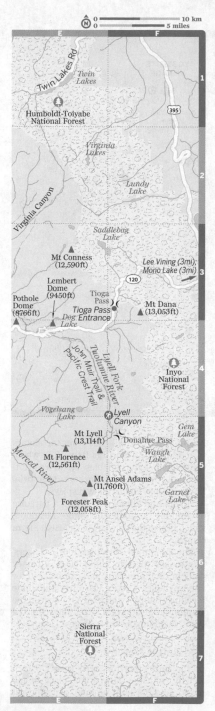

Tioga Pass. Heavy snowfall keeps it closed from about November until May. Beautiful views await after many a bend in the road, the most impressive being **Olmsted Point** (Map p680; ⓘ), where you can gawp all the way down Tenaya Canyon to Half Dome. Above the canyon's eastern side looms the aptly named 9926ft **Clouds Rest**. Continuing east on Tioga Rd soon drops you at **Tenaya Lake**, a placid blue basin framed by pines and granite cliffs.

Beyond here, about 55 miles from Yosemite Valley, 8600ft **Tuolumne Meadows** is

Yosemite Valley

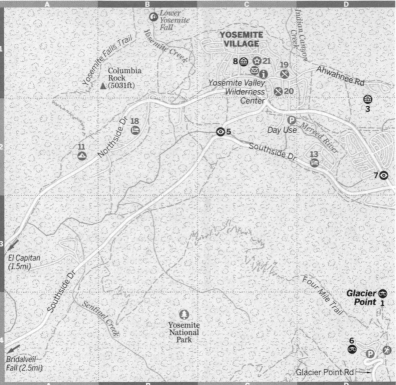

the largest subalpine meadow in the Sierra. It provides a dazzling contrast to the valley, with its lush open fields, clear blue lakes, ragged granite peaks and domes, and cooler temperatures. If you come during July or August, you'll find a painter's palette of wildflowers decorating the shaggy meadows.

Tuolumne is far less crowded than the valley, though the area around the campground, lodge store and visitor center does get busy, especially on weekends. Some hiking trails, such as the one to **Dog Lake**, are also well traveled. Remember that the altitude makes breathing a lot harder than in the valley, and nights can get nippy, so pack warm clothes.

The main meadow is about 2.5 miles long and lies on the northern side of Tioga Rd between **Lembert Dome** (Map p713) and **Pothole Dome** (Map p713). The 200ft scramble to the top of the latter – preferably at sunset – gives you great views of the meadow.

An interpretive trail leads from the stables to muddy **Soda Springs** (Map p713), where carbonated water bubbles up in red-tinted pools. The nearby **Parsons Memorial Lodge** (Map p713) has a few displays.

Hikers and climbers will find a paradise of options around Tuolumne Meadows, which is also the gateway to the High Sierra camps.

The Tuolumne Meadows Tour & Hikers' Bus makes the trip along Tioga Rd once daily in each direction, and can be used for one-way hikes. There's also a free Tuolumne Meadows Shuttle, which travels between the Tuolumne Meadows Lodge and Olmsted Point, including a stop at Tenaya Lake.

Hetch Hetchy

In the park's northwestern corner, Hetch Hetchy, which is Miwok for 'place of tall grass,' gets the least amount of traffic yet

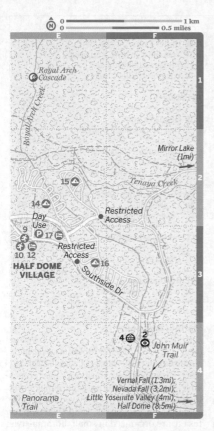

sports waterfalls and granite cliffs that rival its famous counterparts in Yosemite Valley. The main difference is that Hetch Hetchy Valley is now filled with water, following a long political and environmental battle in the early 20th century. It's a lovely, quiet spot and well worth the 40-mile drive from Yosemite Valley, especially if you're tired of the avalanche of humanity rolling through that area. The 2013 Rim Fire charred a huge section of the forest in this region, but its beauty has not been significantly diminished.

The 8-mile-long Hetch Hetchy Reservoir, its placid surface reflecting clouds and cliffs, stretches behind O'Shaughnessy Dam, site of a parking lot and trailheads. An easy 5.4-mile (round-trip) trail leads to the spectacular Tueeulala (Map p680) (*twee*-lala) and Wapama Falls (Map p680), which each plummet more than 1000ft over fractured granite walls on the north shore of the reservoir. Hetch Hetchy Dome rises up in the distance. This hike is best in spring, when temperatures are moderate and wildflowers poke out everywhere. Keep an eye out for rattlesnakes and the occasional bear, especially in summer.

There are bathrooms but no other visitor services at Hetch Hetchy. The road is open only during daylight hours; specifics are posted at the Evergreen Rd turnoff.

◉ Wawona

Wawona, about 27 miles south of Yosemite Valley, is the park's historical center, home to its first headquarters (supervised by Captain AE Wood on the site of the Wawona Campground) and its first tourist facilities.

★ Mariposa Grove   FOREST

(Map p680) With their massive stature and multi-millennium maturity, the chunky high-rise sequoias of Mariposa Grove will make you feel rather insignificant. The largest grove of giant sequoias in the park, Mariposa is home to approximately 500 mature trees spread over 250 acres. Walking trails wind through this very popular grove; you can usually have a more solitary experience if you come during the early evening in summer or anytime outside of summer.

Closed to visitors since the start of a major restoration project in July 2015, at the time of writing the grove was scheduled to reopen in fall 2017. Visitors will benefit from new trails, including accessible boardwalks, and the removal of most of the parking lot, gift shop, tram tours and grove roads should translate to less traffic congestion and a more natural visitor experience. Another multimillion-dollar grant from the Yosemite Conservancy is funding the building of a new trail, scheduled to open in 2018, from the South Entrance to Mariposa Grove.

On your right as you enter the lower grove, the Fallen Monarch may be familiar to you from an iconic 1899 photo of the US 6th Cavalry – and their horses – posed on the tree's length. Its exposed roots illustrate the sequoias' shallow but diffuse life-support system.

Walk a half-mile up to the 1800-year-old Grizzly Giant, a bloated beast of a tree with branches that are bigger in circumference than most of the pine trees in this forest. The walk-through California Tunnel Tree is close by, and the favored spot for 'I visited the tall forest' photos. Incredibly, this tree

Yosemite Valley

continues to survive, even though its heart was hacked out back in 1895.

In the upper grove, the more famous **Fallen Wawona Tunnel Tree**, however, fell over in a heap in 1969 – its 10ft-high hole was gouged from a fire scar in 1881. Other notable specimens include the **Telescope Tree** and the **Clothespin Tree**. It's about a mile round-trip from the Fallen Wawona Tunnel Tree to the wide-open overlook at **Wawona Point** (6810ft), which takes in the entire area.

Depending on your energy level, you could spend half an hour or a few hours exploring the forest. Between the new shuttle stop and the Wawona Tunnel Tree in the upper grove, the elevation gain is about 1000ft, but the trail is gentle.

In summer, and during weekends and holidays, parking at the grove is limited to visitors with accessible placards; others must take the free shuttle bus from the South Entrance unless they arrive outside of the to-be-determined shuttle hours. It takes at least an hour to drive from Yosemite Valley to the grove shuttle at the South Entrance. Snowfall closes Mariposa Grove Rd to cars from about November to April, but you can always hike, ski or snowshoe in (2 miles, 500ft of elevation gain) and experience it during its quiet hibernation.

Mariposa Museum & History Center MUSEUM

(Map p680; ☎209-966-2924; www.mariposa museum.com; 5119 Jessie St; adult/child $5/ free; ⊙10am-4pm; 🐾) Mariposa's past comes alive, well, as much as possible, considering the fairly fusty objects displayed in this museum. Menus, logbooks, train tickets, photos etc are organized in small diorama-style rooms to tell the stories of specific historical epochs or people. Some gems, like actual gold-miners' letters, can be found if you have the time.

Several period buildings and a Yosemite Miwok bark house can be visited on the museum grounds.

Pioneer Yosemite History Center HISTORIC BUILDING

(Map p680;☎209-372-0200; www.nps.gov/yose; Wawona; rides adult/child $5/4; ⊙24hr, rides Wed-Sun Jun-Sep; 🅿🐾) **FREE** Off Wawona Rd, about 6 miles north of Mariposa Grove, you can take in the manicured grounds of the elegant Big Trees Lodge and cross a covered bridge to this rustic center, where some of the park's oldest buildings were relocated. It also features stagecoaches that brought early tourists to Yosemite, and offers short horse-drawn **stagecoach rides** in summer.

✗ Activities

Hiking

Over 800 miles of hiking trails cater to hikers of all abilities. Take an easy half-mile stroll on the valley floor; venture out all day on a quest for viewpoints, waterfalls and lakes; or go camping in the remote outer reaches of the backcountry.

Some of the park's most popular hikes start right in Yosemite Valley, including to the top of Half Dome (17 miles round-trip), the most famous of all. It follows a section of the John Muir Trail and is strenuous, difficult and best tackled in two days with an overnight in Little Yosemite Valley. Reaching the top can only be done after rangers have installed fixed cables. Depending on snow conditions, this may occur as early as late May or as late as July, and the cables usually come down in mid-October. To whittle down the cables' notorious human logjams, the park now requires permits for day hikers, but the route is still nerve-racking as hikers must 'share the road.' The less ambitious or physically fit will still have a ball following the same trail as far as **Vernal Falls** (Map p680) (2.6 miles round-trip), the top of **Nevada Fall** (Map p680) (6.5 miles round-trip) or idyllic Little Yosemite Valley (8 miles round-trip). The Four Mile Trail (9.2 miles round-trip) to Glacier Point is a strenuous but satisfying climb to a glorious viewpoint.

Along Glacier Point Rd, **Sentinel Dome** (Map p682) (2.2 miles round-trip) is an easy hike to the crown of a commanding granite dome. And one of the most scenic hikes in the park, the **Panorama Trail** (8.5 miles one way), descends to the valley (joining the John Muir and Mist Trails) with nonstop views, including Half Dome and Illilouette Fall.

If you've got kids in tow, easy destinations include Mirror Lake (p679) (2 miles round-trip, or 4.5 miles via the **Tenaya Canyon Loop**) in the valley, the **McGurk Meadow** (Map p680) (1.6 miles round-trip) trail on Glacier Point Rd, which has a historic log cabin to romp around in, and the trails meandering beneath the big trees of Mariposa Grove (p683) in Wawona.

The Wawona area also has one of the park's prettiest (and often overlooked) hikes to **Chilnualna Falls** (Map p680) (8.6 miles round-trip). Best done between April and June, it follows a cascading creek to the top of the dramatic overlook falls, starting gently, then hitting you with some grinding switchbacks before sort of leveling out again.

The highest concentration of hikes lies in the high country of **Tuolumne Meadows**, which is only accessible in summer. A popular choice here is the hike to **Dog Lake** (2.8 miles round-trip), but it gets busy. You can also hike along a relatively flat part of the John Muir Trail into lovely **Lyell Canyon** (17.6 miles round-trip), following the Lyell Fork of the Tuolumne River.

Backpacks, tents and other equipment can be rented from the Yosemite Mountaineering School. The school also offers two-day Learn to Backpack trips for novices, and all-inclusive three- and four-day guided backpacking trips ($375 to $500 per person), which are great for inexperienced and solo travelers. In summer the school operates a branch from Tuolumne Meadows.

Rock Climbing

With its sheer spires, polished domes and soaring monoliths, Yosemite is rock-climbing nirvana. The main climbing season runs from April to October. Most climbers, including some legendary stars, stay at Camp 4 (p690) near El Capitan, especially in spring and fall. In summer another base camp springs up at Tuolumne Meadows Campground (p690). Climbers looking for partners post notices on bulletin boards at either campground.

Yosemite Mountaineering School (Map p682; ☏ 209-372-8344; www.travelyosemite.com;

IMPOSSIBLE TIOGA PASS

Hwy 120, the main route into Yosemite National Park from the Eastern Sierra, climbs through Tioga Pass, the highest pass in the Sierra at 9945ft. On most maps of California, you'll find a parenthetical remark – 'closed in winter' – printed next to the pass. While true, this statement is also misleading. Tioga Rd is usually closed from the first heavy snowfall in October until May, June or even July! If you're planning a trip through Tioga Pass in spring, you're likely to be out of luck. According to official park policy, the earliest date the road will be plowed is 15 April, yet the pass has been open in April only once since 1980. Other mountain roads further north, such as Hwys 108, 4 and 88/89, may also be closed due to heavy snow, albeit only temporarily. Call ☏ 800-427-7623 for road and weather conditions.

YOSEMITE THROUGHOUT THE YEAR

January

Short days and freezing temperatures mostly empty out the parks, and ice-quiet solitude has never looked so stunning. Skiing and other snow sports reign supreme.

A TASTE OF YOSEMITE

At the Majestic Yosemite Hotel (p690), meet top chefs from around the country as they lead cooking demonstrations and offer behind-the-scenes kitchen tours in January and February. It's all topped off by a sumptuous gala dinner.

February

Daytime temperatures gradually begin to inch up the thermometer as the days get longer. The ski and snowboarding season hits its stride and the long Presidents' Day weekend brings out the snow hounds.

HORSETAIL FALL

For two weeks at the end of the month, this thin, seasonal cascade becomes Yosemite's most photographed attraction. When the sun sets on clear evenings, the flow lights up like a river of fire.

March

When it's sunny, Yosemite Valley can top out at almost 60°F (15°C), though ice forms in the evenings. Spring feels like it's creeping closer at lower elevations.

YOSEMITE SPRINGFEST

Yosemite Ski & Snowboard Area (www.travelyosemite.com) hosts this winter carnival on the last weekend of each ski season, usually in late March or early April. Events include slalom racing, costume contests, obstacle courses, a barbecue and snow sculpting.

April

Don't forgo the tire chains – there's still the possibility of snowstorms during winter's last gasp. But by the end of the month, the dogwoods start to bloom and the waterfalls begin awakening.

FISHING SEASON BEGINS

Anglers froth at the mouth counting the days until the last Saturday of the month. Why? It's the kickoff date of the fishing season, and the trout are just waiting to bite (www.wildlife. ca.gov).

May

Things really start stirring on Memorial Day weekend, when flocks of vacationers flood the area and the spring snowmelt courses through park waterfalls. Chilly nights punctuate the occasional 70°F (21°C) day.

WATERFALL SEASON

For falls fanatics, the warmer weather means one thing: cascades gushing off the hook. Yosemite's most famous attractions demonstrate their vigor, and seasonal flows like Hetch Hetchy's Tueeulala Falls (p683), and Silver Strand Falls and Sentinel Falls in Yosemite Valley briefly come to life.

June

The high country has begun to thaw, and the summer visitor influx begins. It's the best time to explore trails below 8000ft, though you'll want snow gear to hike much higher.

TIOGA ROAD OPENS

Though it varies year to year, by now this crucial trans-Sierra highway is usually plowed and open. The Eastern Sierra suddenly feels a little closer, and hikers feel that itch to strike the trail.

July

Snow has usually receded from the higher elevations, though mosquitoes often wait to greet you there. At exposed lower ground, summer heat may leave you wilting at midday.

BADWATER ULTRAMARATHON

About 30 years ago someone came up with a preposterous idea: why not run a race (www. badwater.com) between the highest and lowest points in the continental US? Over 60 hours, runners attempt a nonstop course from Death Valley (35 miles southeast of Lone Pine) to Whitney Portal.

August

Temperatures in Yosemite Valley and the lower areas of Sequoia and Kings Canyon keep rising, making an escape to the higher altitudes a refreshing relief.

TUOLUMNE MEADOWS POETRY FESTIVAL

A poetry festival on the grass in Tuolumne Meadows – how can you beat that? Wildflowers and words take center stage during a weekend of workshops and readings.

September

The summer heat begins to fizzle as the month progresses, giving way to brisk days and frigid evenings. The crowds recede and waterfalls are at a trickle.

YOSEMITE FACELIFT

The biggest volunteer event of the year – in Yosemite or any other national park – sees climbers and other grateful souls arrive for a major cleanup (www.yosemiteclimbing.org) at the end of the season. The result? Over 100,000lb of garbage removed.

October

The weather's hit and miss, with either Sierra Nevada sunshine or bucketfuls of chilling rain. Mountain businesses wind up their season and diehards take one last hike before the first snowflakes appear.

AUTUMN FOLIAGE

Fall colors light up the Sierra Nevada and leaf-peeping photographers joyride looking for the best shot. Black oaks blaze dramatically in the undulating foothills, but it's the stands of aspen that steal the show as they flame gold under blue high-elevation sky.

November

Deep snow shuts Tioga Rd and – ta-da! – it's the unofficial start of winter. The Thanksgiving holiday reels in families, and backcountry campers tune up their cross-country skis.

December

Vacationers inundate the resorts during the week between Christmas and New Year's Day, though otherwise the parks remain frosted and solitary. Think snowshoe hikes and hot chocolate.

BRACEBRIDGE DINNER

Held at the Majestic Yosemite Hotel, this traditional Christmas pageant (p679) is part feast and part Renaissance fair. Guests indulge in a multicourse meal while being entertained by more than 100 actors in 17th-century costume.

MANDATORY HALF DOME PERMITS

To stem lengthy lines (and increasingly dangerous conditions) on the vertiginous cables of Half Dome, the park now requires that all day hikers obtain an advance permit to climb the cables. There are currently three ways to do this, though check www.nps.gov/yose/planyourvisit/hdpermits.htm for the latest information. Rangers check permits at the base of the cables.

Preseason permit lottery (www.recreation.gov) Lottery applications ($10) for the 300 daily spots must be completed in March, with confirmation notification sent in mid-April; an additional fee of $10 per person confirms the permit. Applications can include up to six people and seven alternate dates.

Daily lottery Approximately 50 additional permits are distributed by lottery two days before each hiking date. Apply online or by phone (☑877-444-6777) between midnight and 1pm Pacific Time; notification is available late that same evening. It's easier to score weekday permits.

Backpackers Those with Yosemite-issued wilderness permits that *reasonably include* Half Dome can request Half Dome permits (from $12.50 per person) without going through the lottery process. Backpackers with wilderness permits from a National Forest or another park can use that permit to climb the cables.

Half Dome Village; ⊘Apr-Oct) offers top-flight instruction for novice to advanced rock hounds, plus guided climbs and equipment rental. All-day group classes for beginners are $148 per person.

The meadow across from El Capitan and the northeastern end of Tenaya Lake (off Tioga Rd) are good for watching climbers dangle from granite (you need binoculars for a really good view). Look for the haul bags first – they're bigger, more colorful and move around more than the climbers, making them easier to spot. As part of the excellent **'Ask a Climber' program**, climbing rangers set up telescopes at El Capitan Bridge from 11am to 3pm (mid-May through mid-October) and answer visitors' questions.

Cycling

Mountain biking isn't permitted within the park, but cycling along the 12 miles of paved trails is a popular and environmentally friendly way of exploring the valley. It's also the fastest way to get around when valley traffic is at a standstill. Many families bring bicycles, and you'll often find kids doing laps through the campgrounds. Hard-core cyclists brave the skinny shoulders and serious altitude changes of the trans-Sierra Tioga Rd. Bike rentals are available at **Yosemite Valley Lodge** and **Half Dome Village** (per hour/day $12.50/30.50; ⊘9am-6pm Mar-Oct).

Swimming

On a hot summer day, nothing beats a dip in the gentle Merced River, though if chilly water doesn't float your boat, you can always pay to play in the scenic outdoor swimming pools at **Half Dome Village** (adult/child $5/4; ⊘end May-Sep) and **Yosemite Valley Lodge** (adult/child $5/4; ⊕). With a sandy beach, Tenaya Lake is a frigid but interesting option, though White Wolf's Harden Lake warms up to a balmy temperature by midsummer.

Horseback Riding

The park's concessionaire runs guided trips to such scenic locales as Mirror Lake and Chilnualna Falls from Wawona's **Big Trees Lodge Stable** (☑209-375-6502; www.travelyosemite.com; ⊘7am-5pm Jun-Sep) and **Yosemite Valley Stable** (☑209-372-8348; www.travelyosemite.com). The season runs from May to October, although this varies slightly by location. No experience is needed, but reservations are advised, especially at Yosemite Valley Stable. Some mounts are horses, but most likely you'll be riding a sure-footed mule.

Rafting

From around late May to July, floating along the Merced River from Stoneman Meadow, near Half Dome Village, to **Sentinel Bridge** (Map p682) is a leisurely way to soak up Yosemite Valley views. Four-person **raft rentals** (Map p682; ☑209-372-4386; per person $30; ⊘late May-late Jul) for the 3-mile trip are available from the concessionaire in Half Dome Village and include equipment and a shuttle ride back to the rental kiosk. Children must be over 50lb. Or bring your own raft and pay $5 to shuttle back.

River rats are also attracted to the fierce **Tuolumne River**, a classic class IV run that plunges and thunders through boulder gardens and cascades. Outfitters **OARS** (☑20 9-736-4677, 800-346-6277; www.oars.com) and Groveland-based **Sierra Mac** (☑20 9-591-8027, 800-457-2580; www.sierramac.com; 27890 Hwy 120) offer guided trips.

Winter Sports

The white coat of winter opens up a different set of things to do, as the valley becomes a quiet, frosty world of snow-draped evergreens, ice-coated lakes and vivid vistas of gleaming white mountains sparkling against blue skies. Winter tends to arrive in full force by mid-November and peter out in early April.

Cross-country skiers can explore 350 miles of skiable trails and roads, including 90 miles of marked trails and 25 miles of machine-groomed track near the Yosemite Ski & Snowboard Area. The scenic but grueling trail to Glacier Point (21 miles roundtrip) also starts from here. More trails are at Crane Flat and Mariposa Grove. The ungroomed trails can also be explored with snowshoes.

A free shuttle bus connects the valley and the Yosemite Ski & Snowboard Area. Roads in the valley are plowed, and Hwys 41, 120 and 140 are usually kept open, conditions permitting. Tioga Rd (Hwy 120 E), however, closes with the first snowfall. Be sure to bring snow chains with you, as prices for them double once you hit the foothills.

Yosemite Ski & Snowboard Area   SNOW SPORTS

(☑209-372-8430; www.travelyosemite.com; lift ticket adult/child $47/29; ☺9am-4pm mid-Dec–Mar) Most of the action converges on one of California's oldest ski resorts, about 22 miles from the valley on Glacier Point Rd. The gentle slopes are perfect for families and beginner skiers and snowboarders. There are five chairlifts, 800 vertical feet and 10 runs, a full-service lodge and equipment rental ($27 to $37 for a full set of gear).

The excellent **Yosemite Ski & Snowboard Area School** (Map p680; www.travel yosemite.com), where generations of novices have learned how to get down a hill safely, offers group lessons (from $47).

Ostrander Ski Hut   SKIING

(Map p680; ☑209-379-5161; www.yosemitecon-servancy.org) More experienced skiers can trek 10 miles out to this popular hut on Ostrander Lake, operated by Yosemite Conservancy. The hut is staffed all winter and open to backcountry skiers and snowshoers for $35 to $55 per person, per night, on a lottery basis. See the website for details.

Half Dome Village Ice Skating Rink   SKATING

(Map p682; 2½hr session adult/child $10/9.50, skate rental $4; ☺noon-2:30pm, 3:30-6pm & 7-9:30pm Mon-Fri, 8:30-11am, noon-2:30pm, 3:30-6pm & 7-9:30pm Sat & Sun Nov-Mar; 👶) A delightful winter activity is taking a spin on the outdoor rink, where you'll be skating under the watchful eye of Half Dome.

☞ Tours

The nonprofit **Yosemite Conservancy** (☑209-379-2317; www.yosemiteconservancy.org) has scheduled tours of all kinds, plus custom trips.

First-timers often appreciate the year-round, two-hour **Valley Floor Tour** (☑20 9-372-1240; www.travelyosemite.com; adult/child $35/25; ☺year-round; 👶), which covers the valley's highlights.

For other options, stop at the tour and activity desks at **Yosemite Valley Lodge** (☑209-372-1240; ☺7:30am-7pm), Half Dome Village or Yosemite Village, call ☑209-372-4386 or check www.travelyosemite.com.

🛏 Sleeping

Competition for campsites is fierce from May to September, when arriving without a reservation and hoping for the best is tantamount to getting someone to lug your Barcalounger up Half Dome. Even first-come, first-served campgrounds tend to fill by noon, especially on weekends and around holidays. Campsites can be reserved up to five months in advance. Reservations become available from 7am PST on the 15th of every month in one-month blocks, and often sell out within minutes.

Without a booking, your only chance is to hightail it to an open first-come, first-served campground or proceed to one of four campground-reservation offices in Yosemite Valley, Wawona, Big Oak Flat and Tuolumne Meadows (the latter three are only open seasonally). Try to get there before they open at 8am (the Yosemite Valley office may open at 7:30am in summer), put your name on a waiting list and then hope for a cancellation or early departure. Return when the ranger tells you to (usually 3pm) and if you hear your name, consider yourself very lucky indeed.

All campgrounds have flush toilets, except for Tamarack Flat, Yosemite Creek and Porcupine Flat, which have vault toilets and no potable water. Those at higher elevations get chilly at night, even in summer, so pack accordingly. The Yosemite Mountaineering School (p685) rents camping gear.

If you hold a wilderness permit, you may spend the nights before and after your trip in the backpacker campgrounds at Tuolumne Meadows, Hetch Hetchy, White Wolf and behind North Pines in Yosemite Valley. The cost is $5 per person, per night, and reservations aren't necessary.

Opening dates for seasonal campgrounds vary according to the weather.

🛏 Yosemite Valley

Camp 4 CAMPGROUND $
(Map p682; www.nps.gov/yose; shared tent sites per person $6; ⊙year-round) Walk-in campground at 4000ft, popular with climbers and entwined in climbing history; sites are shared.

North Pines Campground CAMPGROUND $
(Map p682; tent & RV sites $26; ⊙Apr-Oct; 🐾) Within walking distance of some of the valley's most popular trailheads, North Pines (4000ft) has 81 sites near Mirror Lake; reservations required. Can feel crowded and cramped with recreational vehicles (RVs).

Upper Pines Campground CAMPGROUND $
(Map p682; www.nps.gov/yose; tent & RV sites $26; ⊙year-round; 🐾) Busy, busy, busy – and big (238 sites, 4000ft); reservations required mid-March through November. Sites are fairly small and close to one another.

Lower Pines Campground CAMPGROUND $
(Map p682; www.nps.gov/yose; tent & RV sites $26; ⊙Apr-Oct; 🐾) Jam-packed and noisy, with 60 sites at 4000ft; reservations required.

Housekeeping Camp CABIN $$
(Map p682; www.travelyosemite.com; Southside Dr; q $112; ⊙Apr-Oct) This cluster of 266 cabins, each walled by concrete on three sides and lidded by a canvas roof, is crammed and noisy, but the setting along the Merced River has its merits. Each unit sleeps six and has electricity, light, a table and chairs, and a covered patio with picnic tables. Laundry and shower facilities are open to guests and non-guests.

Half Dome Village CABIN $$
(Map p682; 📞 reservations 888-413-8869; www. travelyosemite.com; tent cabins from $143, r

from $260, cabins with shared/private bath from $170/225; ⊙daily mid-Mar–late Nov, Sat & Sun early Jan–mid-Mar; P🐾♿🐕🛖) Founded in 1899 as summertime Camp Curry, Half Dome Village has hundreds of units squished together beneath towering evergreens. The canvas cabins (heated or unheated) are basically glorified tents, so for more comfort, quiet and privacy get one of the cozy wood cabins, which have vintage posters. There are 18 motel-style rooms in Stoneman House, including a loft suite that sleeps six.

Cabin 819, with its fireplace, sofa bed and king-sized bed, is probably the most luxurious of the bunch. The village is off Southside Dr.

★ Majestic Yosemite Hotel HISTORIC HOTEL $$$
(📞 reservations 888-413-8869; www.travelyosemite. com; 1 Ahwahnee Dr; r/ste from $480/590; P🐾♿@🐕🛖) The crème de la crème of Yosemite's lodging, this sumptuous historic property (formerly called the Ahwahnee) dazzles with soaring ceilings and atmospheric lounges with mammoth stone fireplaces. Classic rooms have inspiring views of Glacier Point and (partial) Half Dome. Cottages are scattered on the immaculately trimmed lawn next to the hotel. For high season and holidays, book a year in advance.

Suite 332 has a fireplace, a chandelier and incredible panoramic views.

The Majestic is the gold standard for upscale lodges, but even if you're not staying here you can still soak up the ambience during afternoon tea, a drink in the bar or a gourmet meal.

Yosemite Valley Lodge MOTEL $$$
(Map p682; 📞 reservations 888-413-8869; www. travelyosemite.com; 9006 Yosemite Lodge Dr; r from $260; P🐾♿@🐕🛖) ✈ Situated a short walk from Yosemite Falls, this large complex contains a wide range of eateries, a lively bar, a big pool and other handy amenities. The rooms, spread out over 15 buildings, feel somewhat lodge like, with rustic wooden furniture and striking nature photography. All have cable TV, telephone, fridge and coffeemaker, and great patio or balcony panoramas.

🛏 Tioga Road & Tuolumne Meadows

Tuolumne Meadows Campground CAMPGROUND $
(Map p713; www.nps.gov/yose; Tioga Rd; tent & RV sites $26; ⊙Jul-Sep; 🐾) Biggest campground

in the park (8600ft), with 304 fairly well-spaced sites; half of these can be reserved.

Porcupine Flat Campground   CAMPGROUND $
(Map p680; www.nps.gov/yose; tent & RV sites $12; ☺Jul–mid-Oct; 🐾) Primitive 52-site area at 8100ft; some sites near the road.

Tamarack Flat Campground   CAMPGROUND $
(Map p680; Old Big Oak Flat Rd; tent sites $12; ☺late Jun-Sep; 🐾) Quiet and primitive (pit toilets only) at 6315ft; the 52 tent sites are a rough 3-mile drive off Tioga Rd. Despite its relatively secluded location, you'll need to show up early to snag a spot, especially on weekends. Bring plenty of water.

White Wolf Campground   CAMPGROUND $
(Map p680; www.nps.gov/yose; tent & RV sites $18; ☺Jul–early Sep; 🐾) Attractive setting at 8000ft, but the 74 sites are fairly boxed in.

Yosemite Creek Campground   CAMPGROUND $
(Map p680; www.nps.gov/yose; tent sites $12; ☺Jul–early Sep; 🐾) The most secluded and quiet campground (7659ft) in the park, reached via a rough 4.5-mile road. There are 75 first come, first-served primitive sites (no potable water).

Tuolumne Meadows Lodge   CABIN $$
(Map p713; ☑reservations 888-413-8869; www.travelyosemite.com; tent cabins $137; ☺mid-Jun–mid-Sep) Set amid the magnificent high country, about 50 miles from Yosemite Valley off Tioga Rd, this option attracts hikers to its 69 canvas tent cabins with two or four beds each, a wood-burning stove and candles (no electricity). Breakfast and dinner are available (surcharge applies; dinner reservations required). A fork of the Tuolumne River runs through the property.

White Wolf Lodge   CABIN $$
(Map p680; www.travelyosemite.com; White Wolf Rd; tent cabins without bath $140, cabins $170; ☺Jun–mid-Sep) This complex enjoys its own little world a mile up a spur road, away from the hubbub and traffic of Hwy 120 and Yosemite Valley. There are 24 spartan four-bedded tent cabins without electricity and four very-in-demand hard-walled cabins that feel like rustic motel rooms. The generator cuts out at 11pm, so you'll need a flashlight until early morning.

There's also a dining room with somewhat-overpriced fare and a tiny counter-service store.

🛏 Hetch Hetchy & Big Oak Flat Road

Crane Flat Campground   CAMPGROUND $
(Map p680; www.nps.gov/yose; Big Oak Flat Rd; tent & RV sites $26; ☺Jun–mid-Oct; 🐾) Large family campground at 6192ft, with 166 sites; reservations required. The **Clark Range**

WILDERNESS PERMITS FOR OVERNIGHT CAMPING

Shedding the high-season crowds is easiest in Yosemite's backcountry wilderness. Start by identifying a route that matches your schedule, skill and fitness level. Then secure a wilderness permit (www.nps.gov/yose/planyourvisit/wpres.htm), which is mandatory for overnight trips. The advance-reservation fee is $5, plus there's a fee of $5 per person; walk-ins are free. To prevent tent cities sprouting in the woods, a quota system limits the number of people leaving from each trailhead each day. For trips between mid-May and September, 60% of the quota may be reserved by fax (209-372-0739), phone (☑20 9-372-0740) or mail (PO Box 545, Yosemite National Park, CA 95389) from 26 weeks to two days before your trip. Faxes received between noon (the previous day) and 7:30am (the first morning you can reserve) get first priority.

The remainder are distributed by the office closest to the trailhead on a first-come, first-served basis (beginning at 11am one day before your planned hike) at Yosemite Valley Wilderness Center, Tuolumne Meadows Wilderness Center, the information stations at Wawona and Big Oak Flat, and the Hetch Hetchy Entrance Station. Hikers who turn up at the wilderness center nearest the trailhead get priority over those at another wilderness center. For example, if a person who's been waiting for hours in the valley wants the last permit left for Lyell Canyon, the Yosemite Valley Wilderness Center calls the Tuolumne Meadows Wilderness Center to see if any hikers in Tuolumne want it. If a hiker waltzing into the Tuolumne office says 'yes!', they get priority over the person in the valley.

Reservations are not available from October to April, but you'll still need to get a permit by self-registering at the park.

overlook hike, 4 miles out and back, begins from here.

Hodgdon Meadow Campground
CAMPGROUND $

(Map p680; Tuolumne Grove Rd; tent & RV sites $18-26; ☺ year-round; 🐾) Utilitarian and crowded 105-site campground at 4875ft; reservations required mid-April to mid-October.

Dimond O Campground
CAMPGROUND $

(Map p680; ☎ 877-444-6777; www.recreation.gov; Evergreen Rd; tent & RV sites $24; ☺ May-Sep) Away from the valley bustle and 4 miles off Hwy 120 in the Stanislaus National Forest, this reservable United States Forest Service (USFS) campground has 35 forested sites adjacent to the Tuolumne River. Arriving from the west, it's the last campground before the Big Oak Flat Entrance, and a good fallback if you can't get a campsite inside the park.

★ Evergreen Lodge
CABIN $$$

(Map p680; ☎ 209-379-2606; www.evergreenlodge. com; 33160 Evergreen Rd, Groveland; tents $90-125, cabins $180-415; ☺ usually closed Jan–mid-Feb; 🅿☺🐾@🛜🐕) 🏊 Outside Yosemite National Park near the entrance to Hetch Hetchy, this classic, nearly century-old resort consists of lovingly decorated and comfy cabins (each with its own cache of board games) spread among the trees. Accommodations run from rustic to deluxe, and all cabins have private porches without distracting phone or TV. Roughing-it guests can cheat with comfy, prefurnished tents.

🍴 Wawona & Glacier Point Road

Bridalveil Creek Campground CAMPGROUND $

(Map p680; www.nps.gov/yose; tent & RV sites $18; ☺ Jul-early Sep; 🐾) Quieter than the Yosemite Valley campgrounds, with 110 sites at 7200ft.

Wawona Campground
CAMPGROUND $

(Map p680; www.nps.gov/yose; Wawona; tent & RV sites $26; ☺ year-round; 🐾) Idyllic riverside setting at 4000ft with 93 well-spaced sites; reservations required May to September.

🍴 Eating

You can find food options for all budgets and palates within the park, from greasy slabs of fast food to swanky cuts of top-notch steak. All carry good vegetarian options. The **Village Store** (Yosemite Village; ☺ 8am-8pm, to 10pm summer) has the best selection (including health-food items and some or-

ganic produce), while stores at Half Dome Village, Wawona, Tuolumne Meadows and the Yosemite Valley Lodge are more limited.

Yosemite Valley Food Court
CAFETERIA $

(Map p682; Yosemite Valley Lodge, 9006 Yosemite Lodge Dr, Yosemite Valley; mains $5.50-13.50; ☺ 6:30am-10pm, to 8pm winter; 🖋🍴) This self-service restaurant has several tummy-filling stations serving a large choice of pasta, burgers, pizza and sandwiches, either made to order or served from beneath heat lamps. Proceed to the cashier (lines can be long) and find a table inside or on the patio. At the time of writing it was scheduled to be fully remodeled after the 2017 summer season.

Degnan's Loft
PIZZA $$

(Map p682; www.travelyosemite.com; Yosemite Village) Above the new Degnan's Kitchen, off Village Dr, the Loft retains its old name but has also received a top-to-bottom remodeling. Kick back and enjoy artisan pizzas, specialty appetizers and desserts, and beer and wine in this space with high-beamed ceilings and a many-sided fireplace.

Meadow Grill
FAST FOOD $

(Map p682; Half Dome Village; mains $8; ☺ 11am-5pm Sep-Apr, to 7pm summer) Hot dogs, burgers and a few salads are available on a deck near the parking area. Even when lines are long, the food's served up fairly quickly.

Tuolumne Meadows Grill
FAST FOOD $

(Map p713; Tioga Rd; mains $7-12; ☺ 8am-5pm mid-Jun–mid-Sep) You can hardly say you've visited Tuolumne without scoffing down a chili burger and a basket of crispy fries in the parking lot in front of the Tuolumne Meadows Grill. The soft-serve ice-cream cones and hearty breakfasts – not to mention the people-watching at the picnic tables – are equally mandatory.

Village Grill
FAST FOOD $

(Map p682; Yosemite Village; mains $6-13; ☺ 11am-6pm mid-Mar–Oct; 🖋) Fight the chipmunks for burgers, hot sandwiches, salads and fries alfresco. Expect crowds and lines.

★ Evergreen Lodge
AMERICAN $$

(☎ 209-379-2606; www.evergreenlodge.com; 33160 Evergreen Rd; breakfast & lunch $12-18, dinner $20-34; ☺ 7-10:30am, noon-3pm & 5-9pm; 🖋🍴) Creative and satisfying, the Evergreen's restaurant serves some of the best meals around, with big and delicious breakfasts, three types of burger (Black Angus beef, buffalo and veggie) and dinner choices including rib-eye steak, grilled venison and vegan tamales.

The homey wooden tavern is a perennial favorite for evening cocktails, beers on tap over a game of pool and live music on select weekends. A general store fills the gaps with to-go sandwiches, snacks and dreamy gelato.

Majestic Yosemite Dining Room
CALIFORNIAN $$$

(Map p682; ☑209-372-1489; Majestic Yosemite Hotel, 1 Ahwahnee Dr, Yosemite Valley; breakfast $7-22.50, lunch $15-22, dinner $28-46; ⊙7-10am, 11:30am-3pm & 5:30-9pm; ☑) ☑ The formal ambience (mind your manners!) may not be for everybody, but few would not be awed by the sumptuous decor, soaring beamed ceiling and palatial chandeliers here. The menu is constantly in flux, but most dishes have perfect pitch and are beautifully presented. There's a dress code at dinner, but otherwise shorts and sneakers are OK.

Sunday brunch (adult/child $45/15; 7am to 3pm) is amazing. Reservations highly recommended for brunch and dinner.

☷ Drinking & Nightlife

No one will mistake Yosemite for nightlife central, but there are some nice spots to relax with a cabernet, cocktail or cold beer. Outside the park, the Yosemite Bug Rustic Mountain Resort (p697), **Rush Creek Lodge** (☑209-379-2373; www.rushcreeklodge.com; 34001 Hwy 120; @ ⧖ ☑) ☑ and Evergreen Lodge (p692) have lively lounges.

Mountain Room Lounge
BAR

(Map p682; www.travelyosemite.com; Yosemite Valley Lodge, 9006 Yosemite Lodge Dr, Yosemite Valley; ⊙4:30-11pm Mon-Fri, noon-11pm Sat & Sun) Catch up on the latest sports news while knocking back draft brews at this large bar that buzzes in wintertime. The small food menu (mains $9 to $16) features tacos, salads and chili. Order a s'mores kit (graham crackers, chocolate squares and marshmallows) to roast in the open-pit fireplace. Kids welcome until 10pm.

Majestic Bar
BAR

(Map p682; www.travelyosemite.com; Majestic Yosemite Hotel, 1 Ahwahnee Dr, Yosemite Valley; ⊙11am-10pm) The perfect way to experience the Majestic Yosemite Hotel without dipping too deep into your pockets; settle in for a drink at this cozy bar completely remodeled in 2016. Appetizers and light meals ($10.50 to $25) provide sustenance.

☆ Entertainment

In addition to events at the Yosemite Theater, other activities scheduled year-round include campfire programs, children's photo walks, twilight strolls, night-sky watching, ranger talks and slide shows, and the tavern at the Evergreen Lodge (p692) has live bands some weekends. Scan the *Yosemite Guide* for full details.

Yosemite Theater
THEATER

(Map p682; www.yosemiteconservancy.org/yosemite-theater; 7pm film screenings adult/child $8/4; ⊙9:30am-4:30pm; ☑) Behind the Yosemite Valley Visitor Center (p694), this theater screens two films: Ken Burns' *Yosemite: A Gathering of Spirit*, a celebration of the Yosemite Grant's 150th anniversary, and the painfully dramatic but beautifully photographed *Spirit of Yosemite*. The movies alternate, starting every half-hour between 9:30am and 4:30pm (from noon on Sunday), and offer a free, air-conditioned respite from the summer heat.

In the evening, take your pick from a rotating selection of films. Actor Lee Stetson portrays the fascinating life and philosophy of John Muir, and park ranger Shelton Johnson re-creates the experiences of a buffalo soldier. Other films explore search-and-rescue missions and rock climbing in the park. There are also special children's shows.

☷ Information

Yosemite's entrance fee is $30 per vehicle or $15 for those on a bicycle or on foot and is valid for seven consecutive days. Passes are sold (you can use cash, checks, traveler's checks or credit/debit cards) at the various entrance stations, as well as at visitor centers in Oakhurst, Groveland, Mariposa and Lee Vining. Upon entering the park, you'll receive a National Park Service (NPS) map and a copy of the seasonal *Yosemite Guide* newspaper, which includes an activity schedule and current opening hours of all facilities. The official NPS website (www.nps.gov/yose) has the most comprehensive and current information.

For recorded park information, campground availability, and road and weather conditions, call ☑209-372-0200.

The park has a bare-bones **dog kennel** (☑209-372-8326; www.travelyosemite.com; Yosemite Valley Stable; per dog per day $9.50; ⊙late May-early Sep), at which dogs are kept in outdoor cages (no food is allowed, due to wildlife concerns) and stay unattended. No overnight stays are allowed. You must provide a written copy of vet immunization records. Reservations are strongly recommended.

A-frame Building (☑209-372-0409; Yosemite Ski & Snowboard Area; ⊙9am-4pm winter) In winter, wilderness permits are available by self-registration at the A-frame Building, where the first-aid station and ski patrol are also situated. Rangers usually staff the office from 8am to 5pm.

Big Oak Flat Information Station (☑209-372-0200; ⊙8am-5pm late May-Oct) Has a wilderness permit desk.

Tuolumne Meadows Visitor Center (Map p713; ☑209-372-0263; ⊙9am-6pm Jun-Sep) Information desk, bookstore and small exhibits on the area's wildlife and history.

Tuolumne Meadows Wilderness Center (Map p713; ☑209-372-0309; ⊙8am-5pm Jun-Sep) Issues wilderness permits.

Wawona Visitor Center (☑209-375-9531; Wawona; ⊙8:30am-5pm May-Oct) Located off Wawona Rd in the historic studio of artist Thomas Hills; has information and issues wilderness permits.

Yosemite Valley Visitor Center (☑209-372-0200; 9035 Village Dr, Yosemite Village; ⊙9am-5pm; ♿) Park's busiest information desk. Shares space with bookstore run by Yosemite Conservancy and part of the museum complex in the center of Yosemite Village.

Yosemite Valley Wilderness Center (☑209-372-0745; Yosemite Village; ⊙8am-5pm May-Oct) Wilderness permits, maps and back-country advice.

DANGERS & ANNOYANCES

Yosemite is prime black-bear habitat. Follow park rules on proper food storage and utilize bear-proof food lockers when parked overnight. Mosquitoes can be pesky in summer, so bug spray's not a bad idea. And please don't feed those squirrels. They may look cute but they've got a nasty bite.

INTERNET ACCESS

Yosemite Valley Lodge (p690), **Majestic Yosemite Hotel** (p690) and **Half Dome Village** (p690) offer free wi-fi to guests.

Half Dome Village Lounge (Half Dome Village) Next to the food pavilion; free wi-fi.

Mariposa County Public Library (☑209-372-4552; 58 Cedar Ct, Girls Club Bldg, Yosemite Valley; ⊙9am-noon Mon & Tue, to 1pm Wed & Thu; ☏) Free internet terminals and wi-fi.

MEDICAL SERVICES

Yosemite Medical Clinic (☑209-372-4637; 9000 Ahwahnee Dr, Yosemite Village; ⊙9am-7pm daily late-May–late Sep, to 5pm Mon-Fri late Sep-late May) A 24-hour emergency service is available.

MONEY

Stores in Yosemite Village, Half Dome Village and Wawona all have ATMs, as do the **Yosemite Valley Lodge** (p690) and the **Majestic Yosemite Hotel** (p690).

POST

The main **post office** (9017 Village Dr; ⊙8:30am-5pm Mon-Fri, 10am-noon Sat) is in Yosemite Village, but **Wawona** (☑209-375-6574; 1 Forest Dr; ⊙9am-5pm Mon-Fri) and the **Yosemite Valley Lodge** (9006 Yosemite Lodge Dr; ⊙12:30-2:45pm Mon-Fri) also have year-round services. A seasonal branch operates in **Tuolumne Meadows** (☑209-372-8236; ⊙9am-5pm Mon-Fri, to noon Sat, closed mid-Sep–mid-Jun).

TELEPHONE

There are payphones at every developed location throughout the park. Cell-phone reception is sketchy, depending on your location; AT&T and Verizon have the only coverage and both are best in the Yosemite Village area near the visitor center.

❶ Getting There & Away

CAR & MOTORCYCLE

Yosemite is accessible year-round from the west (via Hwys 120 W and 140) and south (Hwy 41), and in summer also from the east (via Hwy 120 E). Roads are plowed in winter, but snow chains may be required at any time. In 2006 a mammoth rockslide buried part of Hwy 140, 6 miles west of the park; traffic there is restricted to vehicles under 45ft. Big Oak Flat Rd was closed for several months after a 'slide', really of an entire hillside, in February 2017.

Gas up year-round at Wawona inside the park (you'll pay dearly), at El Portal on Hwy 140 just outside its western boundary or Lee Vining at the junction of Hwys 120 and 395 outside the park in the east. In summer, gas is also sold at Crane Flat; the gas station in Tuolumne Meadows is now closed.

PUBLIC TRANSPORTATION

Yosemite is one of the few national parks that can easily be reached by public transportation. **Greyhound** buses and **Amtrak** trains serve Merced, west of the park, where they are met by buses operated by the **Yosemite Area Regional Transportation System** (YARTS; ☑877-989-2787; www.yarts.com), and you can buy Amtrak tickets that include the YARTS segment all the way into the park. Buses travel to Yosemite Valley along Hwy 140 several times daily year-round, stopping along the way.

In summer (roughly June through September), another YARTS route runs from Mammoth Lakes along Hwy 395 to Yosemite Valley via Hwy 120.

One-way tickets to Yosemite Valley are $13 ($9 child and senior, three hours) from Merced and $18 ($15 child and senior, 3½ hours) from Mammoth Lakes, less if boarding in between.

YARTS fares include the park-entrance fee, making them a super bargain, and drivers accept credit cards.

ⓘ Getting Around

BICYCLE

Bicycling is an ideal way to take in Yosemite Valley. You can rent a wide-handled cruiser (per hour/day $11.50/32) or a bike with an attached child trailer (per hour/day $19/59) at the **Yosemite Valley Lodge** (p690) or **Half Dome Village** (p690). Strollers and wheelchairs are also rented here.

CAR

Roadside signs with red bears mark the many spots where bears have been hit by motorists, so think before you hit the accelerator, and follow the pokey posted speed limits. Valley visitors are advised to park and take advantage of the Yosemite Valley Shuttle Bus. Even so, traffic in the valley can feel like rush hour in LA.

Glacier Point and Tioga Rds are closed in winter.

Village Garage (☑ 209-372-8320; Tecoya Rd; ⊙ 8am-5pm) provides emergency repairs and even gasoline when you're in an absolute fix.

PUBLIC TRANSPORTATION

The free, air-conditioned **Yosemite Valley Shuttle Bus** (www.nps.gov/yose) is a comfortable and efficient way of traveling around the park. Buses operate year-round at frequent intervals and stop at 21 numbered locations, including parking lots, campgrounds, trailheads and lodges. For a route map, see the *Yosemite Guide*.

Free buses also operate between Yosemite Valley and the Yosemite Ski & Snowboard Area (winter only). The **Tuolumne Meadows Shuttle** (1 way adult/child 5-12yr $9/4.50; ⊙ 7am-7pm Jun-mid Sep) runs between Tuolumne Lodge and Olmsted Point in Tuolumne Meadows (usually mid-June to early September), and the **El Capitan Shuttle** runs a summertime valley loop from Yosemite Village to El Capitan.

Two fee-based hikers' buses also travel from Yosemite Valley. For trailheads along Tioga Rd, catch the **Tuolumne Meadows Hikers' Bus** (☑ 209-372-1240; www.travelyosemite.com), which runs once daily in each direction. Fares depend on distance traveled; the trip to Tuolumne Meadows costs $14.50/23 one way/round-trip. The **Glacier Point Hikers' Bus** (☑ 888-413-8869; 1 way/return $25/49; ⊙ mid-May–Oct) is good for hikers as well as for people reluctant to drive up the long, windy road themselves. Reservations are required.

YOSEMITE GATEWAYS

Fish Camp

Fish Camp, just south of Yosemite on Hwy 41, is more of a bend in the road, but it does have some good lodging options as well as the ever-popular **Sugar Pine Railroad** (☑ 559-683-7273; www.ymsprr.com; 56001 Hwy 41; rides adult/child $24/12; ⊙ approximately Mar-Oct; 🖤).

🛏 Sleeping & Eating

Summerdale Campground   CAMPGROUND $
(www.fs.usda.gov; tent & RV sites $30; ⊙ May-Sep; 🐾) The closest campground to Yosemite, Summerdale is a pleasant spot along Big Creek, with 28 well-dispersed sites in a grassy meadow with shade trees.

White Chief Mountain Lodge   MOTEL $$
(☑ 209-742-7777; www.whitechiefmountainlodge.com; 7776 White Chief Mountain Rd; r $159-179; ⊙ Apr-Oct; 🐾) The cheapest and most basic option in Fish Camp, this 1950s-era motel has simple kitchenette rooms with uninspiring furnishings. It's located a few hundred yards east of Hwy 41; watch for the sign and go up the wooded country road. An on-site restaurant with dreary decor usually serves breakfast and dinner in summer.

Big Creek Inn B&B   B&B $$$
(☑ 559-641-2828; www.bigcreekinn.com; 1221 Hwy 41; r $259-299; 🐾) Each of the three white-palette rooms has peaceful creek views and a private balcony, and two have gas fireplaces. From the comfortable rooms or the back patio you can often spot deer and beavers, or hummingbirds lining up at the patio feeder. Amenities include in-room DVD/Blu-ray players and a large movie library, kitchenette use and big soaking tubs with bath salts.

★ Narrow Gauge Inn   AMERICAN $$$
(☑ 559-683-7720; 48571 Hwy 41; mains $18-35; ⊙ 5-9pm late Apr-Oct) Excellent food and knockout views make the dining experience at the Narrow Gauge Inn one of the finest in the Yosemite region. The dinners are creatively prepared, the lodge-like atmosphere is casual but elegant, and the windows look out on lush mountain vistas.

Cozy up to the fireplace on colder evenings or warm yourself up at the small Buffalo Bar, perfect for a cocktail or a glass of wine. Reservations recommended.

SIERRA VISTA SCENIC BYWAY

Set entirely within Sierra National Forest, this scenic route follows USFS roads in a 100-mile loop that takes you from 3000ft to nearly 7000ft. Along the way are dramatic vistas, excellent fishing, and camping almost anywhere you like (dispersed camping is allowed in most areas). It's a great way for car campers – and curious day trippers – to lose themselves within the mountains.

From its start in **North Fork**, the route takes a half-day to complete, emerging on Hwy 41 a few miles north of **Oakhurst**. Open from June to November, the road is paved most of the way, but it's narrow and laced with curves. See www.fs.usda.gov for a map and information on sights and the best overlooks.

Oakhurst

Although only about 16 miles south of Yosemite's southern entrance (and the Mariposa Grove), at the junction of Hwys 41 and 49, Oakhurst feels worlds away from the park's natural majesty. It's the most quotidian of Yosemite's gateway towns: think strip malls and fast-food joints. For park-goers it functions primarily as a service town and is your last chance to stock up on reasonably priced groceries, gasoline and camping supplies.

Sleeping & Eating

★Sierra Sky Ranch LODGE $$
(☎559-683-8040; www.sierraskyranch.com; 50552 Road 632; r $199-279;) This 1875 former ranch encompasses 14 attractive acres. The homespun rooms are phone-free and pet friendly, with double doors that open onto shady verandas. The rambling and beautiful old lodge features a **restaurant** (☎559-658-2644; dinner mains $28-35; ⊙5-9pm Wed-Sun), a rustic saloon and loads of comfortable lounging areas. A major renovation following new ownership in 2015 upgraded the room furnishings and public spaces.

With a storied history including previous uses as a tuberculosis hospital and a bordello, the ranch counts such past guests as Marilyn Monroe and John Wayne. Many swear that it's cheerfully haunted by former residents.

Hounds Tooth Inn B&B $$
(☎559-642-6600; www.houndstoothinn.com; 42071 Hwy 41; r $180-230;) A few miles north of Oakhurst, this gorgeous garden B&B is swimming in rosebushes and Victorianesque charm. Its 12 airy rooms and two cottages, some with spas and fireplaces, have a slight English-manor-house feel. Complimentary wine and hot drinks are available in the afternoon.

Château du Sureau BOUTIQUE HOTEL $$$
(☎559-683-6860; www.chateaudusureau.com; 48688 Victoria Lane; r $420-645, 2-bedroom villas $2950; @) Never in a billion years would you expect to find a place like this in Oakhurst. A luxe and discreet full-service European-style hotel and world-class spa, this serene destination property boasts an exceptional level of service.

★Erna's Elderberry House CALIFORNIAN, FRENCH $$$
(☎559-683-6860; www.chateausureau.com/ernas-elderberry-house-restaurant; Château du Sureau, 48688 Victoria Lane; prix-fixe dinner $75-112, Sun brunch mains $18-24, tasting menu $68; ⊙dinner daily, plus 11am-1pm Sun;) With wall tapestries, oil paintings and ornate chandeliers, the Californian-French restaurant at Château du Sureau (p696) could be a castle. But you don't have to be royalty to eat here (and the service is notably unstuffy), only willing to shell out for dishes like fois-gras parfait, truffle gnocchi and Pacific halibut, wonderfully presented and enhanced with locally sourced herbs and vegetables.

Merced River Canyon

The approach to Yosemite via Hwy 140 is one of the most scenic routes to the park, especially the section that meanders through Merced River Canyon. Right outside the Arch Rock entrance, and primarily inhabited by park employees, **El Portal** makes a convenient Yosemite base.

The canyon is a top spot for **river rafting**, with many miles of class III and IV rapids. (Age minimums vary with water levels.) Outfitters include OARS (p689), a worldwide rafting operator with a solid reputation.

🛏 Sleeping & Eating

★**Yosemite Bug**
Rustic Mountain Resort   HOSTEL, CABIN **$**
(☑209-966-6666; www.yosemitebug.com; 6979 Hwy 140, Midpines; dm $30, tent cabins from $65, r with/without bath from $165/95; 🅿🐾@🤙) 🍴 This folksy oasis is tucked away on a forested hillside about 25 miles west of Yosemite. A wide range of accommodations types lines the narrow ridges; some require more walking from parking areas and bathrooms than others. The June Bug Cafe (p697) is highly recommended. Also available are yoga lessons, massages and a spa with hot tub.

★**June Bug Cafe**   CALIFORNIAN **$$**
(☑206-966-6666; www.yosemitebug.com/cafe.html; Yosemite Bug Rustic Mountain Resort, 6979 Hwy 140, Midpines; mains $8-22; ⊗7-10am, 11am-2pm & 6-9pm; 🍴🚴) Guests of all ages and backgrounds at the Yosemite Bug resort convene at this friendly cafe to share stories and delicious, freshly prepared meals, beer and wine in the evenings, and live music some nights. More than a half-dozen healthy and hearty dishes are on the whiteboard menu and served cafeteria-style.

Mariposa

About halfway between Merced and Yosemite Valley, Mariposa (Spanish for 'butterfly') is the largest and most interesting town near Yosemite National Park. Established as a mining and railroad town during the gold rush, it has the oldest courthouse in continuous use (since 1854) west of the Mississippi, loads of Old West pioneer character and a couple of good museums dedicated to the area's history.

Rock hounds should drive to the Mariposa County Fairgrounds, 2 miles south of town on Hwy 49, to see the 13lb 'Fricot Nugget' – the largest crystallized gold specimen from the California gold-rush era – and other gems and machinery at the **California State Mining & Mineral Museum** (☑209-742-7625; www.parks.ca.gov/?page_id=588; 5005 Fairgrounds Rd; adult/under 13yr $4/free; ⊗10am-5pm Thu-Sun May-Sep, to 4pm Oct-Apr). An exhibit on glow-in-the-dark minerals is also very cool.

🛏 Sleeping & Eating

River Rock Inn   MOTEL **$$**
(☑209-966-5793; 4993 7th St; r $135-179; ❄🤙🐾) Updated kitchenette rooms are done up in artsy earth tones at this inn that claims to be the oldest motel in town. It features a courtyard deck and a small cafe serving breakfast to guests. It's a block removed from Hwy 140 on a quiet side street.

Mariposa Hotel Inn   HISTORIC HOTEL **$$**
(☑209-966-7500; www.mariposahotelinn.com; 5029 Hwy 140; r $149-169; ❄🤙) This creaky 1901 building has six king or queen rooms with quilts and period-style furniture, and a corridor crammed with old town photos and newspaper clippings. Room 6 has an original claw-foot tub. Hummingbirds love the flowery back patio where breakfast is served.

★**Happy Burger**   DINER **$**
(☑209-966-2719; www.happyburgerdiner.com; Hwy 140, cnr 12th St; mains $8-14; ⊗5:30am-9pm; 🤙🐾🚴🐕) Burgers, fries and shakes served with a heavy dose of nostalgic Americana. Happy Burger, decorated with old LP album covers, and boasting the largest menu in the Sierra, offers one of the cheaper meals in town. Besides burgers, there are sandwiches, Mexican food, salads and a ton of sinful ice-cream desserts. Free computer terminal inside and a 'doggy dining area' outdoors.

You can call and order in advance and pick up your food at the restaurant's to-go window.

Sugar Pine Cafe   AMERICAN **$**
(☑209-742-7793; www.sugarpinecafe.com; 5038 Hwy 140; mains breakfast $6-9, dinner $7-21; ⊗7am-8:30pm Tue-Sat, to 3pm Sun & Mon) Gussied up with chrome soda-counter stools and red circular booths, this 1940s-era diner serves yummy breakfast items, hot or cold sandwiches, and burgers on whole-wheat buns. Dinner fare is pure comfort food like spaghetti and meatballs, and pork chops.

Savoury's   AMERICAN **$$**
(☑209-966-7677; 5034 Hwy 140; mains $17-35; ⊗5-9:30pm, closed Wed winter; 🍴) Upscale yet casual Savoury's is the best restaurant in town. Black lacquered tables and contemporary art create tranquil window dressing for dishes like wild-mushroom ravioli, Cajun-spiced New York steak with pan-seared onions, and crab cakes with cilantro-lime aioli.

ℹ Information

Mariposa County Visitor Center (☑209-966-7081; cnr Hwys 140 & 49; ⊗8:30am-5:30pm; 🤙) Helpful staff and racks of brochures; public restrooms.

❶ Getting There & Away

YARTS (☎209-388-9589, 877-989-2787; www.yarts.com) buses run year-round along Hwy 140 into Yosemite Valley ($6 one way, 1¾ hours), stopping at the Mariposa visitor center. Tickets include admission to Yosemite.

Groveland

From the Big Oak Flat entrance to Yosemite, it's 22 miles to Groveland, an adorable town with restored gold-rush-era buildings and lots of visitor services.

About 15 miles east of Groveland, in the Stanislaus National Forest, **Rainbow Pool** (www.fs.usda.gov/stanislaus) is a popular swimming hole with a small cascade; it's signed on the south side of Hwy 120.

⌖ Sleeping & Eating

★**Hotel Charlotte** BOUTIQUE HOTEL **$$**
(☎209-962-6455; www.hotelcharlotte.com; 18736 Main St; r $149-249; ✱@☎❄) Casually sophisticated and designed with a mix of vintage flair and contemporary conveniences, the Charlotte is the nicest spot in Groveland. Some of the rooms have beautifully restored claw-footed bathtubs, and the owners, a husband-and-wife team, work diligently to help guests with their Yosemite stay. A sophisticated bistro and bar serves a creative small-plates menu.

The owners also have six three-bedroom vacation rentals in the nearby gated community of Pine Mountain Lake.

★**Blackberry Inn Bed & Breakfast** B&B **$$$**
(☎209-962-4663; www.blackberry-inn.com; 7567 Hamilton Station Loop; r $205-295; ☉mid-Mar–Oct; ✱@☎) On a rural road right off Hwy 120, this stunningly converted house and newer wing offer 10 sumptuous rooms showcasing stained-glass scenes of Yosemite, soaking tubs and electric fireplaces that give off real heat or just cozy ambience. Its *big* breakfasts can be delivered to your room or patio so you can spy on the hummingbirds. Two-night minimum stay.

Cocina Michoacana MEXICAN **$**
(☎209-962-6651; 18730 Main St; mains $9-14; ☉10am-10pm) Quick and friendly service and large servings of tasty Mexican fare make this the most popular restaurant with Groveland locals. The chicken mole is especially recommended and there's a good selection of Mexican beers.

★**Fork & Love**
Restaurant MODERN AMERICAN **$$**
(www.forkandlove.com; 18736 Main St; mains $17-28; ☉6-9pm Thu-Sat, 9am-1pm Sun Mar-Nov) Scarce in these parts, 'local, organic and sustainable' is done right at this rustically refined restaurant in a historic saloon space in the Hotel Charlotte. The small plates, as well as the mains, like pork spatzle, carne masala (black Angus beef with homemade masala sauce) and artichoke fried rice, are innovative and best enjoyed by sharing.

❼ Drinking & Nightlife

★**Iron Door Grill & Saloon** BAR
(☎209-962-6244; www.iron-door-saloon.com; 18761 Main St; ☉restaurant 7am-10pm, bar 11am-2am, shorter hours winter) Claiming to be the oldest bar in the state, the Iron Door is a dusty, atmospheric place, with swinging doors, a giant bar, high ceilings, mounted animal heads and hundreds of dollar bills tacked to the ceiling. There's live music summer-weekend nights, and the adjacent, more contemporary dining room serves good steaks, ribs and pasta dishes (mains $9.50 to $25).

Also hosts open-mike and karaoke nights.

SEQUOIA & KINGS CANYON NATIONAL PARKS

The twin parks of Sequoia and Kings Canyon dazzle with superlatives, though they're often overshadowed by Yosemite, their smaller neighbor to the north (a three-hour drive away). With towering forests of giant sequoias containing some of the largest trees in the world, and the mighty Kings River careening through the depths of Kings Canyon, one of the deepest chasms in the country, the parks are lesser-visited jewels where it's easier to find quiet and solitude. Throw in opportunities for caving, rock climbing and backcountry hiking through granite-carved Sierra landscapes, and backdoor access to 14,494ft Mt Whitney – the tallest peak in the lower 48 states – and you have all the ingredients for two of the best parks in the country.

The two **parks** (Map p700; ☎559-565-3341; www.nps.gov/seki; 7-day entry per car $30; ⓟ♿) ✍, though distinct, are operated as one unit with a single admission fee; for 24-hour recorded information, including road conditions, call the number listed or visit the parks' comprehensive website. At either entrance station (Big Stump or Ash Mountain), you'll receive an NPS map and a copy of the parks' the *Guide* newspaper, with information on seasonal activities, camping and special programs, including those in the surrounding national forests and the Giant Sequoia National Monument (Map p700; www.fs.usda.gov). It's easy enough to explore sections of both parks in a single day.

History

In 1890 Sequoia became the second national park in the USA (after Yellowstone). A few days later, the 4 sq miles around Grant Grove were declared General Grant National Park and, in 1940, absorbed into the newly created Kings Canyon National Park. In 2000, to protect additional sequoia groves, vast tracts of land in the surrounding national forest became the Giant Sequoia National Monument.

ⓘ Dangers & Annoyances

➡ Air pollution wafting up from the Sequoia Central Valley and Kings Canyon often thwarts long-range visibility, and people with respiratory problems should check with a visitor center about current pollution levels.

➡ Black bears are common and proper food storage is always required.

➡ Heed park instructions on wildlife procedures.

Kings Canyon National Park

With a dramatic cleft deeper than the Grand Canyon, Kings Canyon offers true adventure to those who crave seemingly endless trails, rushing streams and gargantuan rock formations. The camping, backcountry exploring and climbing here are all superb. Big

Stump Entrance (Map p700; Hwy 180), not far from Grant Grove Village, is Kings Canyon National Park's only entrance station.

◉ Sights & Activities

Kings Canyon National Park has two developed areas with markets, lodging, showers and visitor information. Grant Grove Village is only 4 miles past Big Stump Entrance (in the park's west), while Cedar Grove Village, with a simple lodge and snack bar, is 31 miles east at the bottom of the canyon. The two are separated by the Giant Sequoia National Monument and are linked by Kings Canyon Scenic Byway (Hwy 180).

General Grant Grove   FOREST
(Map p700; P 🚻) This sequoia grove off Generals Hwy is nothing short of astounding. The paved half-mile General Grant Tree Trail is an interpretive walk that visits a number of mature sequoias, including the 27-story General Grant Tree. This giant holds triple honors as the world's second-largest living tree, a memorial to US soldiers killed in war, and the nation's official Christmas tree since 1926. The nearby Fallen Monarch, a massive, fire-hollowed trunk you can walk through, has been cabin, hotel, saloon and stables.

To escape the bustling crowds, follow the more secluded 1.5-mile North Grove Loop, which passes wildflower patches and bubbling creeks as it gently winds underneath a canopy of stately sequoias, evergreen pines and aromatic incense cedars.

The magnificence of this ancient sequoia grove was nationally recognized in 1890 when Congress first designated it General Grant National Park. It took another half-century for this tiny parcel to be absorbed into the much larger Kings Canyon National Park, established in 1940 to prevent damming of the Kings River.

OVERNIGHT BACKPACKING

For overnight backcountry trips you'll need a wilderness permit (per group $15), which is subject to a quota system in summer; outside the quota season, permits are free and available by self-registration. About 75% of spaces can be reserved, while the rest are available in person on a first-come, first-served basis. Reservations can be made from March 1 until two weeks before your trip. For details, see www.nps.gov/seki/planyourvisit/wilderness_permits.htm. There's also a dedicated wilderness desk at the Lodgepole Visitor Center (p710).

All ranger stations and visitor centers carry topo maps and hiking guides. Note that you need to store your food in park-approved bear-proof canisters, which can be rented at markets and visitor centers (from $5 per trip).

Sequoia & Kings Canyon National Parks

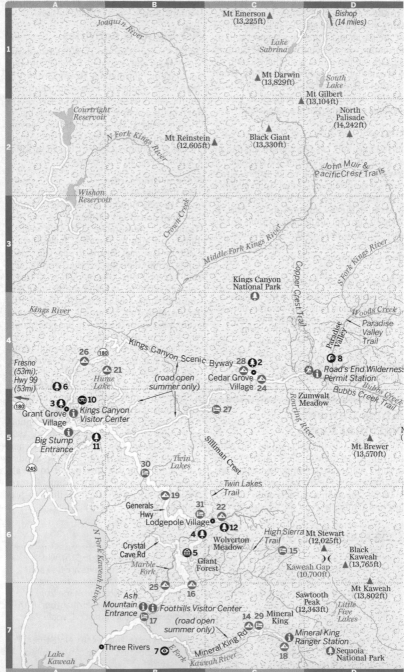

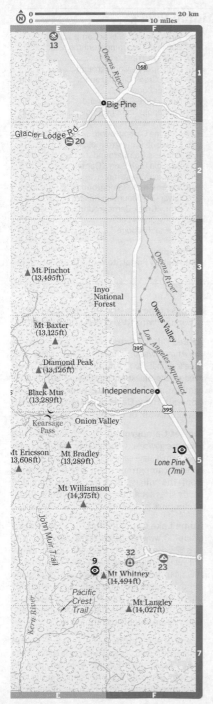

Panoramic Point
VIEWPOINT

(Map p700) For a breathtaking view of Kings Canyon, head 2.3 miles up narrow, steep and winding Panoramic Point Rd (trailers and RVs aren't recommended), which branches off Hwy 180. Follow a short paved trail uphill from the parking lot to the viewpoint, where precipitous canyons and the snowcapped peaks of the Great Western Divide unfold below you. Snow closes the road to vehicles during winter, when it becomes a cross-country ski and snowshoe route.

From Grant Grove's visitor center, follow the paved side road east, turning left after 0.1 miles, then right at the John Muir Lodge.

Redwood Canyon
FOREST

(Map p700) Over 15,000 sequoias cluster in Redwood Canyon, making it one of the world's largest groves of these giant trees. In an almost-forgotten corner of the park, this secluded forest lets you revel in the grandeur of the trees away from the crowds while you hike mostly moderate trails. What you won't find here, however, are any of California's coast-redwood trees – that's what early pioneers mistook these giant sequoias for, hence the erroneous name.

The trailheads are at the end of a 2-mile bumpy dirt road (closed in winter) that starts across from the Hume Lake/Quail Flat signed intersection on the Generals Hwy, just over 5 miles southeast of Grant Grove Village. It's a good spot for a picnic before heading out on a hike.

Cedar Grove
FOREST

(Map p700) Cedar Grove is the last outpost of civilization before you reach the rugged grandeur of the Sierra Nevada backcountry. A popular day hike climbs 4 miles one way to roaring Mist Falls from Road's End; continue uphill alongside the river 2.5 more miles to **Paradise Valley**. A favorite of birders, an easy 1.5-mile nature trail loops around **Zumwalt Meadow**, just west of Road's End. Watch for rattlesnakes, black bears and mule deer.

Mist Falls
WATERFALL

(Map p700) One of the most popular destinations for a day hike from the Cedar Grove area of Kings Canyon, Mist Falls is a fairly Edenic spot, with massive boulders and interesting rock formations. It's ideal for a picnic and a rest before you turn back or venture higher into the backcountry.

Sequoia & Kings Canyon National Parks

🛏 Sleeping & Eating

Accommodations (and pay showers) are offered in Grant Grove and Cedar Grove Villages. Unless otherwise stated, all campsites are first-come, first-served. Apart from the campsites, facilities in Cedar Grove Village don't start operating until mid-May.

Potential campers should keep in mind that there are great free, uncrowded and undeveloped campgrounds off Big Meadows Rd in the Sequoia National Forest. They're some of the only empty campsites in the Sierra Nevada during peak summer season. Free roadside camping is also allowed in the forest, but no campfires are allowed without a permit (available from the Grant Grove Visitor Center).

🛏 Grant Grove

Crystal Springs Campground CAMPGROUND $
(www.nps.gov/seki; tent & RV sites $18; ☺ mid-May–Sep; 🐾) At the smallest campground in the Grant Grove area, off Generals Hwy, a few dozen wooded, well-spaced sites are generally very quiet.

Princess Campground CAMPGROUND $
(Map p700; www.fs.usda.gov; Hwy 180; tent & RV sites $25-27; ☺ late May-late Sep; 🐾) Just off the scenic byway and only a few miles from Hume Lake, here almost 90 reservable sites border a pretty meadow, with sequoia

stumps at the registration area. It's especially popular with RVs. Reservations essential.

Azalea Campground CAMPGROUND $
(www.nps.gov/seki; tent & RV sites $18; ☺ year-round; 🐾) Among stands of evergreens, the nicest of the 110 sites at this busy campground border a green meadow. It's off Generals Hwy; General Grant Grove (p701) is a short walk downhill.

Sunset Campground CAMPGROUND $
(www.nps.gov/seki; Generals Hwy; tent & RV sites $22; ☺ mid-May–early Sep; 🐾) Grant Grove's biggest campground is a five-minute walk from the village and has more than 150 shady sites set among evergreen trees. Ranger campfire programs in summer.

Hume Lake Campground CAMPGROUND $
(Map p700; www.fs.usda.gov; Hume Lake Rd; tent & RV sites $22; ☺ mid-May–mid-Sep; 🐾) Almost always full yet still managing a laid-back atmosphere, this campground operated by California Land Management offers almost 75 relatively uncrowded, shady campsites, a handful with lake views. It's on the lake's northern shore. Reservations highly recommended.

Grant Grove Cabins CABIN $$
(📞 866-807-3598; www.visitsequoia.com; Grant Grove Village; cabins $78-148; ☺ some cabins Apr-Oct only) Set amid towering sugar pines, the accommodations here include aging tent-

top shacks, rustic camp cabins with electricity and outdoor wood-burning stoves, and heated duplexes (a few wheelchair accessible) with private bathrooms and double beds. Number 9 is the lone hard-sided, free-standing 'Honeymoon Cabin' with a queen bed, and it books up fast.

John Muir Lodge LODGE $$
(☑866-807-3598; www.visitsequoia.com; Grant Grove Village; r from $225; P👚😊🤶) An atmospheric building hung with historical black-and-white photographs, this is a place to lay your head and still feel like you're in the forest. Wide porches have rocking chairs, and homespun rooms, completely renovated a couple of years ago, contain rough-hewn wooden furniture and patchwork bedspreads. On chilly nights, cozy up to the big stone fireplace with a board game.

Grant Grove Market MARKET $
(Grant Grove Village; ⊘8am-9pm late May-early Sep, shorter hours Apr-late May & early Sep-Oct) This small grocery store has firewood, camping supplies and packaged food, with a small selection of fruit and veggies, as well as pizza by the slice (plus an ATM).

▣ Cedar Grove

Cedar Grove's **Sentinel** (www.nps.gov/seki; Hwy 180, Cedar Grove Village; tent & RV sites $18; ⊘late Apr–mid-Nov; P🈲) campground, next to the village area, is open whenever Hwy 180 is open; **Sheep Creek** (Map p700; www.nps.gov/seki; Hwy 180, Cedar Grove Village; tent & RV sites $18; ⊘late May–mid-Sep), **Canyon View** (www.nps.gov/seki; Hwy 180; tent sites $40; ⊘late May–Sep) (tent only) and **Moraine** (Map p700; www.nps.gov/seki; Hwy 180; tent & RV sites $18; ⊘late May & early Jul-early Sep) are opened as overflow when needed. These campgrounds are usually the last to fill up on busy summer weekends and are also good bets early and late in the season thanks to their comparatively low elevation (4600ft). All have flush toilets. Other facilities in the village don't start operating until mid-May.

★ **Sequoia High Sierra Camp** CABIN $$
(Map p700; ☑866-654-2877; www.sequoiahigh sierracamp.com; tent cabins without bath incl all meals adult/child $250/150; ⊘mid-Jun–mid-Sep) A mile's hike deep into the Sequoia National Forest, this off-the-grid, all-inclusive resort is nirvana for those who don't think luxury camping is an oxymoron. Canvas bungalows are spiffed up with pillow-top mattresses,

feather pillows and cozy wool rugs. Restrooms and a shower house are shared. Reservations are required, and there's usually a two-night minimum stay.

Cedar Grove Lodge LODGE $$
(☑559-565-3096; www.visitsequoia.com; 86724 Hwy 180, Cedar Grove Village; r from $130; ⊘mid-May–mid-Oct; P👚❄🤶) The only indoor sleeping option in the canyon, this riverside lodge offers 21 unexciting motel-style rooms. A recent remodel has updated some of the frumpy decor. Three ground-floor rooms with shady furnished patios have spiffy river views and kitchenettes. All rooms have phone and TV.

Cedar Grove Snack Bar AMERICAN $
(Hwy 180, Cedar Grove Village; mains $6-15; ⊘7:30-10:30am, 11:30am-2:30pm & 5-8pm mid-May–mid-Oct; 🤶🏃) This basic counter-service grill dishes up hot meals and cold deli sandwiches. Dine outside on the riverside deck. In summer barbecue gets smoked all afternoon long through dinnertime.

ⓘ Information

Cedar Grove Visitor Center (☑559-565-3793; Hwy 180, Cedar Grove Village; ⊘9am-5pm late May-late Sep) Small, seasonal visitor center in Cedar Grove Village selling books and maps.

Kings Canyon Visitor Center (Map p700; ☑559-565-4307; Hwy 180, Grant Grove Village; ⊘9am-5pm) The park's main facility in Grant Grove Village; open year-round with a bookstore and gift shop inside.

Road's End Wilderness Permit Station (Map p700; ⊘ usually 7am-3:45pm late May-late Sep) Dispenses wilderness permits, rents bear canisters and sells a few trail guides and maps.

BUFFALO SOLDIERS

Beginning in 1899, US Army infantry and cavalry troops drawn from well-respected, though segregated, African American regiments of 'Buffalo Soldiers' were sent to patrol the Sierra Nevada's new national parks. In Sequoia National Park and what was then General Grant National Park, the troops impressively built roads, created a trail system and set a high precedent as stewards of the land. These first park rangers were commanded by Captain (later Colonel) Charles Young, who at the time was the army's only African American captain. In 1903 he became the first African American acting superintendent of a US national park.

It's 6 miles east of Cedar Grove Village, at the end of Hwy 180.

ℹ️ Getting There & Away

BUS

An option in summer only is to use **Big Trees Transit** (📞800-325-7433; www.bigtreestransit.com; round-trip incl park entry fee $15; ☺late May–early Sep) to travel between Fresno and Grant Grove ($15 round-trip, 2½ hours) in Kings Canyon.

CAR & MOTORCYCLE

From the west, Kings Canyon Scenic Byway (Hwy 180) travels 53 miles east from Fresno to the Big Stump Entrance. Coming from the south, you're in for a long 46-mile drive through Sequoia National Park along sinuous Generals Hwy. Budget about two hours' driving time from the Ash Mountain Entrance to Grant Grove Village. The road to Cedar Grove Village is only open from around April or May until the first snowfall.

Sequoia National Park

Picture unzipping your tent flap and crawling out into a 'front yard' of trees as high as a 20-story building and as old as the Bible. Brew some coffee as you plan your day in this extraordinary park with its soul-sustaining forests and gigantic peaks soaring above 12,000ft.

◉ Sights

Nearly all of the park's star attractions are conveniently lined up along the Generals Hwy, which starts at the Ash Mountain Entrance and continues north into Kings Canyon. Tourist activity concentrates in the Giant Forest area and in Lodgepole Village, which has the most facilities, including a visitor center and market. The road to remote Mineral King veers off Hwy 198 in the town of Three Rivers, just south of the park's Ash Mountain Entrance.

Giant Forest   FOREST
(Map p700) Hugging the trees is a daunting prospect in this 3-sq-mile grove protecting the park's most gargantuan specimens. Among them is the world's biggest tree, the **General Sherman** (Map p700; 🚶), rocketing

HIKING IN SEQUOIA & KINGS CANYON NATIONAL PARKS

NAME	REGION	DESCRIPTION	DIFFICULTY
Mist Falls	Cedar Grove	partly shaded forest & granite hike to a gushing waterfall	moderate
Rae Lakes Loop	Cedar Grove	passes a chain of jewel-like lakes in the heart of the Sierra Nevada high country	difficult
Zumwalt Meadow Loop	Cedar Grove	flat, meadow boardwalk loop traces the Kings River beside canyon walls	easy
Marble Falls	Foothills	lower-elevation hike parallels a river canyon to a thundering cascade	moderate
Big Trees Trail	Giant Forest	paved, kid-friendly interpretive trail circling a sequoia-bordered forest meadow	easy
Crescent Meadow Loop	Giant Forest	beautiful subalpine meadow ringed by giant sequoias & summer wildflowers	easy
General Sherman Tree to Moro Rock	Giant Forest	huge sequoias, peaceful meadows & the pinnacle of Moro Rock	moderate
High Sierra Trail to Bearpaw Meadow	Giant Forest	gorgeous sequoia-grove & canyon-view hike crossing mountain streams	difficult
Moro Rock	Giant Forest	steep granite dome ascent for panoramic peak & canyon views	easy
General Grant Tree Trail	Grant Grove	paved interpretive loop through a giant-sequoia grove	easy
Tokopah Falls	Lodgepole	one of Sequoia's largest, most easily accessed scenic waterfalls	easy
Monarch Lakes	Mineral King	high-country hike to two alpine lakes at base of Sawtooth Peak	difficult

275ft into the sky. Pay your respects via a short descent from the Wolverton Rd parking lot, or join the Congress Trail, a paved 2-mile pathway that takes in General Sherman, the Washington Tree (the world's second-biggest sequoia) and the see-through Telescope Tree. The 5-mile Trail of the Sequoias helps you lose the crowds.

The top destination in the park, Giant Forest was named by John Muir in 1875. At one point over 300 buildings, including campgrounds and a lodge, encroached upon the sequoias' delicate root systems. In 1997, recognizing this adverse impact, the park began to remove structures and resite parking lots. It also introduced a convenient, free seasonal visitor shuttle, significantly cutting traffic congestion and reducing the potential harm to these majestic trees.

Giant Forest Museum   MUSEUM

(Map p700; ☑ 559-565-4480; www.nps.gov/seki; cnr Generals Hwy & Crescent Meadow Rd; ⊙ 9am-4:30pm; P ⊕) ✐ FREE For a primer on the intriguing ecology and history of giant sequoias, this pint-sized modern museum will entertain both kids and adults. Hands-on exhibits teach about the life stages of these big trees, which can live for over 3000 years, and the fire cycle that releases their seeds and allows them to sprout on bare soil. The museum is housed in a historic 1920s building designed by Gilbert Stanley Underwood, famed architect of the Majestic Yosemite (formerly Ahwahnee) Hotel.

The museum is crushed with visitors in summer. To avoid parking headaches, take the free in-park shuttle bus. You can also try the information desk here when the Lodgepole Visitor Center is closed in winter.

Mineral King   HISTORIC SITE

(Map p700; Mineral King Rd) A scenic subalpine valley at 7500ft, Mineral King is Sequoia's backpacking mecca and a good place to find solitude. Gorgeous and gigantic, its glacially sculpted valley is ringed by massive mountains, including the jagged 12,343ft Sawtooth Peak. The area is reached via Mineral King Rd – a slinky, steep and narrow 25-mile road not suitable for RVs or speed demons; it's usually open from late May through

DURATION	ROUND-TRIP DISTANCE	ELEVATION CHANGE	FEATURES	FACILITIES
3-5hr	8 miles	+800ft	view; waterfall	restrooms; drinking water; ranger station
5 days	40 miles	+7000ft	wildlife-watching; view; waterfall	restrooms; drinking water; ranger station; backcountry campsite
1hr	1.5 miles	+100ft	wildlife-watching; view; great for families	
3-4hr	7 miles	+2000ft	view; waterfall	restrooms; drinking water
45min	1.2 miles	+100ft	wildlife-watching; great for families	restrooms; drinking water; transportation to trailhead
1hr	1.6 miles	+200ft	wildlife-watching; great for families	restrooms; drinking water; transportation to trailhead
2½-4hr	6 miles	+1600ft	wildlife-watching; view; rock climbing	restrooms; drinking water; transportation to trailhead
2 days	22 miles	+2200ft	wildlife-watching; view	restrooms; drinking water; ranger station; backcountry campsite
40min	0.5 miles	+300ft	view; great for families; rock climbing	transportation to trailhead
30min	0.5 miles	+100ft	view; great for families	restrooms; drinking water
2hr	3.5 miles	+500ft	wildlife-watching; view; great for families; waterfall	restrooms; drinking water; transportation to trailhead
4-6hr	8.5 miles	+2700ft	wildlife-watching; view	restrooms; drinking water; backcountry campsite; swimming

DON'T MISS

CRYSTAL CAVE

Discovered in 1918 by two parks employees who were going fishing, this unique cave (www.explorecrystalcave. com; Crystal Cave Rd; tours adult/child/youth from $16/5/8; ☺May-Sep; ℗ ♿) 🪨 was carved by an underground river and has marble formations estimated to be 10,000 years old. Stalactites hang like daggers from the cave ceiling, and milky-white marble formations take the shape of ethereal curtains, domes, columns and shields. The cave is also a unique biodiverse habitat for spiders, bats and tiny aquatic insects that are found nowhere else on earth.

Tickets for the 50-minute introductory tour are only sold online in advance or, during October and November, at the Giant Forest Museum and Foothills Visitor Center, not at the cave. Bring a jacket.

YOSEMITE & THE SIERRA NEVADA SEQUOIA NATIONAL PARK

October. Plan on spending the night unless you don't mind driving three hours round-trip.

Hiking anywhere from here involves a steep climb out of the valley along strenuous trails, so be aware of the altitude, even on short hikes. Enjoyable day hikes go to Crystal, Monarch, Mosquito and Eagle Lakes. For long trips, locals recommend the Little Five Lakes and, further along the High Sierra Trail, Kaweah Gap, surrounded by Black Kaweah, Mt Stewart and Eagle Scout Peak – all above 12,000ft.

In spring and early summer, hordes of hungry marmots terrorize parked cars at Mineral King, chewing on radiator hoses, belts and wiring to get the salt they crave after their winter hibernation. If you're thinking of going hiking during that time, you'd be well advised to protect your car by wrapping the underside with a diaper-like tarp – apparently, the marmots have learned to get around the previously recommended chicken wire.

From the 1860s to the 1890s, Mineral King witnessed heavy silver mining and lumber activity. There are remnants of shafts and stamp mills, though it takes some exploring to find them. A proposal by the Walt Disney Corporation to develop the area into a massive ski resort was thwarted when Congress annexed it to make it part of the national park in 1978. The website of the Mineral King Preservation Society (www.mineralking.org) has all kinds of info on the area, including its rustic and still-occupied historic mining cabins.

🏃 Activities

With an average elevation of about 2000ft, the foothills in the park's south are much drier and warmer than the rest of the park. Hiking here is best in spring, when the air is still cool and wildflowers put on a colorful show. Summers are buggy and muggy, but fall again brings moderate temperatures and lush foliage.

Swimming holes abound along the Marble Fork of the Kaweah River, especially near Potwisha Campground. Be careful, though – the currents can be deadly, especially when the river is swollen from the spring runoff.

🛏 Sleeping & Eating

Wuksachi Lodge (p707) is the only accommodation in the main section of the park proper. Two other lodges are in the adjoining Sequoia National Forest, and Grant Grove Village in Kings Canyon has a couple of options. Three Rivers, just outside the Ash Mountain Entrance, has the widest choice of accommodations. Otherwise, camping is the highly recommended way to go.

Generals Highway

A handful of campgrounds line the highway and rarely fill up, although space may get tight on holiday weekends. Those in the foothills area in the south of the park are best in spring and fall when the higher elevations are still chilly, but they get hot and buggy in summer. Unless noted, sites are available on a first-come, first-served basis. Free dispersed camping is possible in the Giant Sequoia National Monument (p699). Stop by a visitor center or ranger station for details or a fire permit. Lodgepole Village (p710) and Stony Creek Lodge (p709) have pay showers.

Stony Creek Campground CAMPGROUND $
(Map p700; www.fs.usda.gov; Generals Hwy; tent & RV sites $24; ☺mid-May–late Sep; 🐶) A mile north of the national-park boundary near Stony Creek Lodge, this forest campground operated by California Land Management fills with families in summer. Its nearly 50 sites are spacious and shady.

Lodgepole Campground CAMPGROUND $
(Map p700; www.nps.gov/seki; Lodgepole Rd; tent & RV sites $22; ☺late Apr–Nov; 🐶) Closest to the Giant Forest area, with over 200 closely

packed sites, this place fills quickly because of its proximity to Kaweah River swimming holes and Lodgepole Village amenities. The 16 walk-in sites are more private. Reservations available (and strongly recommended) from late May through late September.

Potwisha Campground   CAMPGROUND $
(Map p700; www.nps.gov/seki; Generals Hwy; tent & RV sites $22; ☺year-round; 🐾) Popular campground with decent shade near swimming spots on the Kaweah River. It's 3 miles northeast of the Ash Mountain Entrance, with 42 sites. Reservations (highly recommended) taken May through September.

Dorst Creek Campground   CAMPGROUND $
(Map p700; www.nps.gov/seki; Generals Hwy; tent & RV sites $22; ☺mid-Jun–early Sep; 🐾) Big and busy campground with more than 200 sites. The quieter back sites are for tents only, while the front loops can fill with RVs. It's about 7 miles northwest of Wuksachi Village. No reservations accepted.

Buckeye Flat Campground   CAMPGROUND $
(Map p700; www.nps.gov/seki; tent sites $22; ☺late Mar-late Sep; 🐾) This tent-only campground is off Generals Hwy in an open stand of oaks, about 6 miles northeast of the Ash Mountain Entrance, down a winding road that's off-limits to RVs and trailers. Reservations accepted (and strongly advised) between late May and late September.

Stony Creek Lodge   LODGE $$
(Map p700; ☑reservations 559-565-3388, reservations 877-828-1440; www.sequoia-kingscanyon.com; 65569 Generals Hwy; r $179-199; ☺mid-May–early Oct; 🐾) About halfway between Grant Grove Village and Giant Forest, this wood-and-stone lodge has a big river-rock fireplace in its lobby and a dozen aging motel rooms with telephones and TVs. Laundry facilities and coin-operated showers are available for nonguests.

Wuksachi Lodge   LODGE $$
(Map p700; ☑information 866-807-3598, reservations 317-324-0753; www.visitsequoia.com; 64740 Wuksachi Way; r $215-290; Ⓟ🐾🐾🐾) Built in 1999, Wuksachi Lodge is the park's most upscale option. But don't get too excited: the wood-paneled atrium lobby has an inviting stone fireplace and forest views, but the motel-style rooms are fairly generic, with coffeemakers, minifridges, oak furniture and thin walls. The location near Lodgepole Vil-

lage, however, can't be beat, and staff members are friendly and accommodating.

Rooms, many of which were renovated in the winter and spring of 2017, are spread out over three three-story buildings a short walk from the lobby and restaurant and from each building's respective parking lot. If you have a lot of gear, it's best to ask for help lugging things to your room.

🛏 Backcountry

Bearpaw High Sierra Camp   CABIN $$
(Map p700; ☑reservations 317-324-0753; www.visitsequoia.com; per person incl breakfast & dinner $175; ☺usually mid-Jun–mid-Sep) An 11.3-mile hike east of Crescent Meadow on the High Sierra Trail, this canvas-tent village at 7800ft is ideal for exploring the backcountry without lugging your own gear. Rates include showers, dinner and breakfast, as well as bedding and towels. Bookings start at 7am PST every January 2 and places sell out almost immediately, though you can always check for last-minute cancellations.

🛏 Mineral King

Mineral King's two pretty campgrounds, **Atwell Mill** (Map p700; www.nps.gov/seki; Mineral King Rd; tent sites $12; ☺late May-late Oct; 🐾) and **Cold Springs** (Map p700; www.nps.gov/seki; Mineral King Rd; tent sites $12; ☺late May-late Oct; 🐾), often fill up on summer weekends. Pay showers are available at the rustic **Silver City Mountain Resort** (Map p700; ☑559-561-3223; www.silvercityresort.com; Mineral King Rd; cabins with/without bath from $175/110, chalets from $250; ☺late May-late Oct; 🐾), the only food-and-lodging option anywhere near these parts.

🛏 Three Rivers

Named for the nearby convergence of three Kaweah River forks, Three Rivers is a friendly small town populated mostly by retirees and artsy newcomers. The town's main drag, Sierra Dr (Hwy 198), is sparsely lined with motels, eateries and shops.

Sequoia Village Inn   CABIN, COTTAGE $$
(Map p700; ☑559-561-3652; www.sequoiavillageinn.com; 45971 Sierra Dr; d $155-319; ❄🐾🐾🐾) These 10 cottages, cabins and chalets (most with kitchens and the rest with kitchenettes) border the park and are great for families or groups. Most have outdoor woodsy decks and BBQs; the largest can sleep 12 people.

California Wildlife

Unique creatures great and small inhabit the land, sky and waters of California's diverse ecosystems. Visit them at the ocean or in the forest, or just scan the skies.

1. Elephant seal
Equipped with a trunk-like nose, the enormous males noisily battle for dominance on the beach.

2. Black bear
The name is misleading, as bear fur can be shades of brown, black, cinnamon or tawny blonde.

3. California condor
A 10ft wingspan is the hallmark of these endangered carrion scavengers. Captive breeding has increased the population, though lead bullet poisoning remains its biggest threat.

4. Gray whale
Dramatic breaches and the puffs of water spouts mark the passage of these school-bus-sized mammals. Pods of whales migrate yearly between Mexico and Alaska, with peak viewing between December and April.

5. California sea lion
With dog-like faces and oversized flippers, vocal sea lions typically haul out in large social groups. The crowd-pleasing colony at San Francisco's Pier 39 mysteriously appeared soon after the 1989 Loma Prieta earthquake.

6. Mule deer
Ubiquitous throughout the state, mule deer are recognizable by their ample ears and black foreheads. Bucks wear forked antler racks.

7. Desert tortoise
Able to live for over half a century, these high desert reptiles burrow underground to survive extreme heat and cold.

8. Hawk
Frequently seen riding the thermal currents on windy ridges, a dozen types of hawks can be found in California. These speedy birds of prey are known for their keen eyesight and strong talons.

9. Mountain lion
Also known as cougars, panthers or pumas, these territorial big cats primarily stalk and feed on deer. They hunt from dusk to dawn, and can sprint at up to 50 miles per hour.

10. Banana slug
Tread carefully along the forest floor so you don't slip on these large and squishy bright yellow specimens.

11. Monarch butterfly
These orange and black beauties flutter thousands of miles to complete their annual migration.

12. Elk
Three subspecies of elk roam the state, with majestic males parading chandeliers of velvety antlers, and bugling dramatically during the fall rutting season.

709

Buckeye Tree Lodge
MOTEL $$

(Map p700; ☑559-561-5900; www.buckeyetree
lodge.com; 46000 Sierra Dr; d $159; ❄🅿🛜❄🐾)
🍳 Sit out on your grassy back patio or
perch on the balcony and watch the river
ease through a maze of boulders. Fairly ge-
neric motel rooms, one with a kitchenette,
feel airy. The outdoor picnic area has BBQ
grills.

❶ Information

Foothills Visitor Center (Map p700; ☑559-
565-4212; 47050 Generals Hwy; ⊙8am-
4:30pm) Just past the Ash Mountain Entrance;
a good place to stop, get your bearings and
check out campground availability further up
the road.

Lodgepole Village This complex includes
grocery store, gift shop, snack bar, visitor
center, and coin-operated showers and laundry
facilities.

Lodgepole Visitor Center (☑559-565-4436;
Lodgepole Village; ⊙7am-5pm late Apr-early
Oct, to 7pm peak season) Often less than help-
ful or informative; non-NPS staff members sell
books and maps, and rangers issue wilderness
permits. Off the Generals Hwy.

Mineral King Ranger Station (Map p700;
☑559-565-3768; Mineral King Rd; ⊙8am-
4pm late May-late Sep) Almost 24 miles east
of Three Rivers; small, seasonal ranger station
issuing wilderness permits, renting bear canis-
ters and selling a few books and maps.

❶ Getting There & Around

BUS
Sequoia Shuttle (☑877-287-4453; www.
sequoiashuttle.com; ⊙late May-late Sep)
buses run five times daily between Visalia
and the Giant Forest Museum ($15, 2½ hours)
via Three Rivers; reservations required. Cost
includes park admission fee.

CAR & MOTORCYCLE
Hwy 198 runs north from Visalia through Three
Rivers past Mineral King Rd to the Ash Mountain
Entrance. Beyond here the road continues as the
Generals Hwy, a narrow and windy road snaking
all the way into Kings Canyon National Park,
where it joins the Kings Canyon Scenic Byway
(Hwy 180) near the western Big Stump Entrance.
Vehicles over 22ft long may have trouble ne-
gotiating the steep road with its many hairpin
curves. Budget about one hour to drive from the
entrance to the Giant Forest/Lodgepole area
and another hour from there to Grant Grove
Village in Kings Canyon.

There are no gas stations in the park.

EASTERN SIERRA

Cloud-dappled hills and sun-streaked moun-
taintops dabbed with snow typify the land-
scape of the Eastern Sierra, where slashing
peaks – many over 14,000ft – rush abruptly
upward from the arid expanses of the Great
Basin and Mojave Deserts. It's a dramatic
juxtaposition that makes for a potent cock-
tail of scenery. Pine forests, lush meadows,
ice-blue lakes, simmering hot springs and
glacier-gouged canyons are only some of the
beautiful sights you'll find in this region.

The Eastern Sierra Scenic Byway, official-
ly known as Hwy 395, runs the entire length
of the range. Turnoffs dead-ending at the
foot of the mountains deliver you to pristine
wilderness and countless trails, including
the famous Pacific Crest Trail, John Muir
Trail and main Mt Whitney Trail. The most
important portals are the towns of Bridge-
port, Mammoth Lakes, Bishop and Lone
Pine. Note that in winter, when traffic thins,
many facilities are closed.

❶ Information
Check out www.thesierraweb.com for area events
and links to local visitor information, and *Sierra
Wave* (www.sierrawave.net) for regional news.

❶ Getting There & Around
The Eastern Sierra is easiest to explore under
your own steam. Keep in mind that mountain
roads close in winter, as do most of the passes
that take you over the Sierras from east to west.

BUS
Eastern Sierra Transit Authority (☑800-922-
1930, 760-872-1901; www.estransit.com) buses
make a round-trip between Lone Pine and Reno
($59, six hours) on Monday, Tuesday, Thursday
and Friday, stopping at all Hwy 395 towns
in between. Fares depend on distance, and
reservations are recommended. There's also
an express bus between Mammoth and Bishop
($7, one hour, three times daily) that operates
Monday to Friday.

In summer, connect to Yosemite via **YARTS
bus** (p694) in Mammoth Lakes or Lee Vining.

Mono Lake Region

Bridgeport

Barely three blocks long, set amid an open
high valley and in view of the peaks of Saw-
tooth Ridge, Bridgeport flaunts classic West-
ern flair with charming old storefronts and

a homey ambience. Most everything shuts down or cuts back its hours for the brutal winters, but the rest of the year the town is a magnet for anglers, hikers, climbers and hot-spring devotees.

◉ Sights & Activities

Mono County Courthouse HISTORIC BUILDING
(cnr Main & School Sts; ⊙9am-5pm Mon-Fri) The gavel has been dropped since 1880 at this courthouse, an all-white italianate dreamboat surrounded by a gracious lawn and a wrought-iron fence. On the street behind it, look for the Old County Jail, a spartan facility fashioned with iron latticework doors and stone walls 2ft thick. Unlucky inmates overnighted in its six cells from 1883 until 1964.

Mono County Museum MUSEUM
(⌨760-932-5281; www.monocomuseum.org; Emigrant St; adult/child $2/1; ⊙9am-4pm Tue-Sat Jun-Sep) In an 1880 schoolhouse, this museum has mining artifacts on display from all the local ghost towns, plus a room of fine Paiute baskets.

★**Travertine Hot Spring** HOT SPRINGS
(Map p713) **FREE** A bit south of town, head here to watch a panoramic Sierra sunset from three hot pools set amid impressive rock formations. To get here, turn east on Jack Sawyer Rd just before the ranger station, then follow the dirt road uphill for about 1 mile.

Ken's Sporting Goods FISHING
(⌨760-932-7707; www.kenssport.com; 258 Main St; ⊙7am-7pm Mon-Thu, to 8pm Fri & Sat mid-Apr–Oct, 9am-4pm rest of year) Stop by Ken's for information and fishing gear. If you're trolling for trout, try the Bridgeport Reservoir and the East Walker River.

🛏 Sleeping & Eating

Redwood Motel MOTEL $
(⌨760-932-7060; www.redwoodmotel.net; 425 Main St; d $89-99; ⊙Apr-Nov; ❋🐾🛜) A bucking bronco, an ox in a Hawaiian shirt and other wacky farm-animal sculptures provide a cheerful welcome at this little kitchenette motel. Rooms are homey and simply furnished, and your dog-friendly host is super helpful in dispensing local-area tips.

Bodie Victorian Hotel HISTORIC HOTEL $
(⌨760-616-1977; www.bodievictorianhotel.com; 85 Main St; r $60-125; ⊙May-Oct; ❋🛜) To experience an 1800s boarding house in all its rickety glory, try a room in this building transplanted from the abandoned mining town of Bodie (p712). It can feel rundown despite the great-great-grandmother-style antiques, bold Victorian wallpaper and striking bordello accoutrements. If no one's here, poke your head into the Sportsmens Bar & Grill next door to rustle up an employee.

WILDERNESS PERMITS FOR THE EASTERN SIERRA

➡ Free wilderness permits for overnight camping are required year-round in the Ansel Adams, John Muir, Golden Trout and Hoover Wilderness areas.

➡ For the first three areas, trailhead quotas are in effect from May to October; about 60% of the quota may be reserved online at www.recreation.gov for a $5 fee (per person).

➡ From November to April, you can pick up permits at most ranger stations. If you find a station closed, look for self-issue permits outside the office.

➡ Wilderness permits for the Inyo National Forest can be picked up in Lone Pine, Bishop, Mammoth Lakes or its Mono Basin ranger stations.

➡ For information, call the Inyo National Forest Wilderness Permit Office (p728) in Bishop.

➡ Yosemite's Tuolumne Meadows Wilderness Center can also issue permits for trips from Saddlebag Lake.

➡ Permits for the Hoover Wilderness that depart from the Humboldt-Toiyabe National Forest (seasonal quotas on some trails) are issued at the Bridgeport Ranger Station & Visitor Center (p712).

➡ The forums on High Sierra Topix (www.highsierratopix.com) are an excellent resource for planning trips.

Mono Lake Area

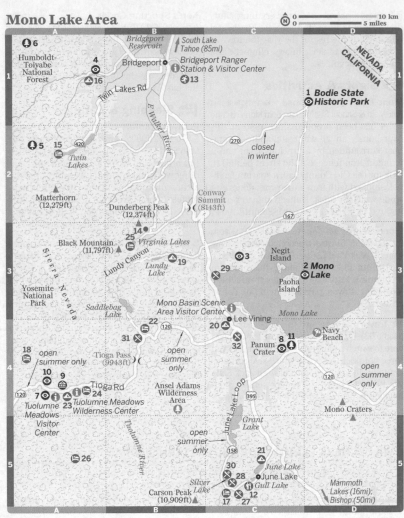

ℹ Information

Bridgeport Ranger Station & Visitor Center
(Map p713; ☎760-932-7070; www.fs.usda.
gov/htnf; Hwy 395; ⊙8am-4:30pm daily
Jun–mid-Sep, 8am-12:30pm & 1-4:30pm Mon-
Fri mid-Sep–May) The local office for maps,
information on the Humboldt-Toiyabe Forest
(Map p713; www.fs.usda.gov) (in both California
and Nevada) and Hoover Wilderness (Map p713;
www.fs.usda.gov) permits.

Twin Lakes

Eager anglers line the shoreline of Twin
Lakes, a gorgeous duo of basins cradled by

the fittingly named Sawtooth Ridge. The area's famous for its fishing – especially since
some lucky guy bagged the state's largest
ever brown trout here in 1987 (it weighed in
at a hefty 26lb). Lower Twin is quieter, while
Upper Twin allows boating and waterskiing.
Other activities include mountain biking
and, of course, hiking in the Hoover Wilderness Area and on into the eastern, lake-
riddled reaches of Yosemite National Park.

The main trailhead is at the end of Twin
Lakes Rd just past Annett's Mono Village;
weekly overnight parking is $10 per vehicle.
From here, hikers can set off along Robinson

Mono Lake Area

Creek for adventures in the stunning **Hoover Wilderness** and overnight backpacking trips (wilderness permit required from the Bridgeport Ranger Station & Visitor Center (p711)) into northeastern Yosemite. The day hike to lovely **Barney Lake** (8 miles round-trip) takes in magnificent views of jagged granite spires in **Little Slide Canyon** – where rock climbers detour to scale a fierce wall called the Incredible Hulk – and steep boulder rockslides on the ridge to the north.

For a hike with great views of Twin Lakes, go south from Annett's on the **Horse Creek trail**, which soon leads to the cascades of **Horsetail Falls**. It continues up to skirt the wilderness boundary and then descends back to Twin Lakes on the **Cattle Creek trail**. Loop back along the lake for 7.5 miles in total. In *Dharma Bums*, Beat author Jack Kerouac describes an ascent he made from Horse Creek Canyon to nearby Matterhorn Peak (12,300ft) with poet Gary Snyder.

A stroll down a hillside brings you to the out-of-the-way (though it can still get crowded) **Buckeye Hot Spring** (Map p713). Water emerges piping hot and cools as it trickles down into several rock pools right by the side of lively Buckeye Creek, which is handy for taking a cooling dip. One pool is partially tucked into a small cave made from a rock overhang. Clothing is optional.

USFS campgrounds (☏ 800-444-7275; www.recreation.gov; tent & RV sites $17-22; ☉ late Apr–Sep) in the Humboldt-Toiyabe National Forest are generally open from late April to early October. You can also set up tents for free in undeveloped spots along both sides of nearby Buckeye Creek.

Buckeye Campground (Map p713; tent & RV sites $18; ☉ May–mid-Oct), west of Bridgeport and north of Twin Lakes in the Humboldt-Toiyabe National Forest, has tables, fire grates and toilets, but you'll need to bring or treat water. Take Twin Lakes Rd from Bridgeport for 7 miles before turning right onto Buckeye Rd. It's another 3 miles and then left at a fork to reach the campground.

Bodie State Historic Park

At **Bodie State Historic Park** (Map p713; ☏ 760-647-6445; www.parks.ca.gov/bodie; Hwy 270; adult/child $8/4; ☉ 9am-6pm mid-Mar–Oct, to 4pm Nov–mid-Mar; 🅿🚻), a gold-rush ghost town is preserved in a state of 'arrested decay.' Weathered buildings sit frozen in time on a dusty, windswept plain. To get there, head east for 13 miles (the last three unpaved) on Hwy 270, about 7 miles south of Bridgeport. The access road is often closed by snow in winter.

Gold was first discovered here in 1859, and within 20 years the place grew from a rough mining camp to an even rougher boomtown with a population of 10,000 and a reputation for unbridled lawlessness. Fights and murders took place almost daily, the violence no doubt fueled by liquor dispensed in the town's 65 saloons, some of which did double duty as brothels, gambling halls or opium dens. The hills disgorged some $35 million worth of gold and silver in the 1870s and '80s, but when production plummeted, so did the population, and eventually the town was abandoned to the elements.

Peering through the windows of the 200 weather-beaten buildings, you'll see stocked stores, furnished homes, a schoolhouse with desks and books, and workshops filled with tools. The jail is still there, as are the fire station, churches, a bank vault and many other buildings.

The former Miners' Union Hall now houses a museum and visitor center. Rangers conduct free general tours. In summer, they also offer tours of the landscape and the cemetery; call for details. The second Saturday of August is **Friends of Bodie Day** (www.bodiefoundation.org), with stagecoach rides, history presentations and lots of devotees in period costumes.

Lee Vining

Hwy 395 skirts the western bank of Mono Lake, rolling into the gateway town of Lee Vining, where you can eat, sleep, gas up (for a pretty penny) and catch Hwy 120 to Yosemite National Park when the road's open. A superb base for exploring Mono Lake, Lee Vining is only 12 miles (about a 30-minute drive) from Yosemite's Tioga Pass entrance. **Lee Vining Canyon** is a popular location for **ice climbing.**

The **Upside-Down House** (Map p713; www.monobasinhistory.org; 129 Mattly Ave; donation $2; ☺10am-4pm Thu-Mon late May–early Oct), a kooky tourist attraction created by silent-film actress Nellie Bly O'Bryan, is worth a quick look. Originally situated along Tioga Rd, it now resides in a park in front of the tiny **Mono Basin Historical Society Museum.** To find it, turn east on 1st St and go one block to Mattley Ave.

EBBETTS PASS SCENIC BYWAY

For outdoor fanatics, a scenic 61-mile section of Hwys 4 and 89 called the Ebbetts Pass Scenic Byway (www.scenic4.org) is a road trip through paradise. Heading northeast from **Arnold**, gaze up at the giant sequoias of **Calaveras Big Trees State Park** (p635) and in winter stop at the family-friendly ski resort of **Bear Valley** (✆209-753-2301; www.bearvalley.com; 2280 Hwy 207, Bear Valley; ski-lift ticket adult/6-12yr/13-19yr $79/32/68; ☺hours vary end Nov-May; ⚐). Nearby is the **Bear Valley Adventure Company** (✆209-753-2834; www.bearvalleyxc.com; 1 Bear Valley Rd, Bear Valley; ☺hours vary; ⚐), a one-stop shop for other outdoor adventures in the area. Continuing east, the stunningly beautiful **Lake Alpine** is skirted by slabs of granite, has several great beaches, and boasts excellent water sports, fishing and hiking. A handful of campgrounds line the lakefront, as well as the rustic **Lake Alpine Resort** (✆209-753-6350; www.lakealpineresort.com; 4000 Hwy 4, Bear Valley; tent cabins $70-80, cabins with kitchenette or kitchen $170-280; ☺May-Oct; P☻☷).

The next stretch is the most dramatic, when the narrow highway continues past picturesque **Mosquito Lake** and the **Pacific Grade Summit** (8060ft) before slaloming through historic Hermit Valley and finally winding up and over the 8730ft summit of **Ebbetts Pass**. North on Hwy 89 and just west of **Markleeville**, you can visit the two developed pools and seasonal campground at **Grover Hot Springs State Park** (✆530-694-2249, 530-694-2248; www.parks.ca.gov; 3415 Hot Springs Rd, Markleeville; pool adult/child $10/5; ☺hours vary; ⚐). It's worth returning to Markleeville for dinner at the **Stone Fly** (✆530-694-9999; www.stoneflyrestaurant.com; 14821 Hwy 89, Markleeville; mains $15-24; ☺5-9pm Fri-Sun) restaurant.

The relatively little-known **Hope Valley Wildlife Area** (✆916-358-2900; www.wildlife.ca.gov; P) ⚐FREE, a gorgeous reserve of meadows, streams and forests ringed by high Sierra peaks, is not far northwest of Markleeville. **Sorensen's Resort** (✆800-423-9949, 530-694-2203; www.sorensensresort.com; 14255 Hwy 88, Hope Valley; r $145-210, cabins $145-325; P☻☷), with a variable collection of cabins and rooms, makes an excellent base camp.

From San Francisco, it's a three-hour drive east to Arnold, via Hwy 108 and Hwy 49. Ebbetts Pass closes after the first major snowfall and doesn't reopen until June, but Hwy 4 is usually plowed from the west as far as Bear Valley.

VIRGINIA LAKES

South of Bridgeport, Hwy 395 gradually arrives at its highest point, Conway Summit (8143ft), where you'll be whipping out your camera to capture the awe-inspiring panorama of Mono Lake, backed by the Mono Craters, and June and Mammoth Mountains.

Also at the top is the turnout for **Virginia Lakes Road**, which parallels Virginia Creek for about 6 miles to a cluster of lakes flanked by Dunderberg Peak (12,374ft) and Black Mountain (11,797ft). A trailhead at the end of the road gives access to the Hoover Wilderness Area and the **Pacific Crest Trail**. The trail continues down Cold Canyon through to Yosemite National Park. With a car shuttle, the excellent 10.5-mile hike to **Green Creek** visits a bevy of perfect lakes; an extra mile (each way) takes you to windswept – check out the mammoth tree blowdown! – **Summit Lake** at the Yosemite border. Check with the folks at the Virginia Lakes Resort, opened in 1923, for maps and tips about specific trails.

Nearby, **Virginia Lakes Pack Outfit** (Map p713; ☑760-937-0326; www.virginialakes. com; half-/full-day rides $90/150) offers horseback-riding trips.

🛏 Sleeping

Lodging rates drop when Tioga Pass is closed. Psst, campers: **Mono Vista RV Park** (Map p713; ☑760-647-6401; www.monovistarv park.net; 57 Beaver Lane; tent/RV sites $27/35; ⊙9am-6pm Apr-Oct) has the closest pay showers to Tuolumne Meadows. Most of the options in town are fairly ordinary, but the Tioga Pass Resort (p714) is in an extraordinary setting, way up Hwy 120 near Yosemite. Mammoth Lakes, with an abundance of accommodations, is only 31 miles south.

El Mono Motel　　　　　　　　　　MOTEL **$**
(☑760-647-6310; www.elmonomotel.com; cnr Hwy 395 & 3rd St; r $75-99; ⊙mid-May–Oct; 🐾) Grab a board game or soak up some mountain sunshine in this friendly, flower-ringed place attached to an excellent cafe. In operation since 1927, it's often booked solid, and each of its 11 simple rooms (a few share bathrooms) is unique, decorated with vibrant and colorful art and fabrics.

★ Tioga Pass Resort　　　　　　　CABIN **$$**
(Map p713; www.tiogapassresort.com; Hwy 120; d $145, cabins $180-280; ⊙Jun-Sep) Situated at a whopping 9550ft and only 2 miles east of Tioga Pass, this is as close to a Yosemite experience as you can get without staying in the park. Founded in 1914, this high-country resort attracts a fiercely loyal clientele to its quiet, comfortable, woodsy cabins (most with full kitchen) beside Lee Vining Creek. Walk-ins can sometimes snag a cancellation.

The thimble-sized **cafe** (mains lunch $10-11.50, dinner $22; ⊙7am-9pm Jun-Sep; 🐾) serves excellent fare all day at a few tables and a broken horseshoe counter, with a house pastry chef concocting dozens of freshly made desserts.

At the time of writing, record winter snowfall had caused the resort to close temporarily. Check the website for updates.

Yosemite Gateway Motel　　　　MOTEL **$$**
(☑760-647-6467; www.yosemitegatewaymotel. com; 51340 Hwy 395; r $159-229; ⊛🐾) Think vistas. This is the only motel on the eastern side of the highway, and the views of Mono Lake and surroundings from some of the rooms are phenomenal. The somewhat-tired rooms have comfortable beds with thick duvets and big bathrooms.

Murphey's Motel　　　　　　　　MOTEL **$$**
(☑760-647-6316; www.murpheysyosemite.com; 51493 Hwy 395; r $80-150; ⊛🐾🐾) At the northern end of town, this large, two-story, log-cabin-style place offers comfy rooms with all mod cons. It's one of the few hotels in Lee Vining open year-round. A little cafe serving pastries and espresso drinks is attached.

🍴 Eating

Latte Da Coffee Cafe　　　　　　CAFE **$**
(cnr Hwy 395 & 3rd St; sandwiches $6; ⊙7am-8pm; 🐾) Located at the El Mono Motel, this cafe is a charming spot for sandwiches, scones and excellent espresso drinks. The cozy wood floored interior is bested by the front porch and tiny backyard garden.

★ Whoa Nellie Deli　　　　　AMERICAN **$$**
(Map p713; ☑760-647-1088; www.whoanelliedeli. com; Tioga Gas Mart, 22 Vista Point Rd; mains $9-19; ⊙6:30am-8:30pm late Apr-Oct; 🐾) Years after its famed chef moved on to Toomey's (p721) at Mammoth Lakes, this Mobil-gas-station restaurant off Hwy 120 is still, surprisingly,

LUNDY LAKE

After Conway Summit, Hwy 395 twists down steeply into the Mono Basin. Before reaching Mono Lake, Lundy Lake Rd meanders west of the highway for about 5 miles to Lundy Lake. This is a gorgeous spot, especially in spring, when wildflowers carpet the canyon along Mill Creek, or in fall when the landscape is brightened by colorful foliage. Before reaching the lake, the road skirts first-come, first-served **Lundy Canyon Campground** (Map p713; tent & RV sites $16; ☺late Apr-Oct; 🐾), with vault toilets; there's water available, but it must be boiled or treated. At the end of the lake, there's a ramshackle resort on the site of an 1880s mining town, plus a small store and boat rentals.

Past the resort, a dirt road leads into Lundy Canyon; after 2 miles, it dead-ends at the trailhead for the Hoover Wilderness Area. A fantastic 1.5-mile hike follows Mill Creek to the 200ft-high **Lundy Falls**. Industrious beavers define the landscape along the trail, with gnawed aspens scattered on the ground and a number of huge dams barricading the creek. Ambitious types can continue on via Lundy Pass to **Saddlebag Lake** and the **Twenty Lakes Basin**, though the final climb out of the canyon uses a very steep talus chute.

a damn good place to eat. Stop in for delicious burgers, fish tacos, wild-buffalo meatloaf and other tasty morsels, and live bands some nights.

★**Mono Inn**   AMERICAN $$$
(Map p713; ☎760-647-6581; www.themonoinn.com; 55620 Hwy 395; mains $20-38; ☺5-9pm Tue-Sat, to 8pm Sun Apr–mid-Nov) A restored 1922 lodge owned by the family of photographer Ansel Adams, this elegant yet casual lakefront restaurant makes everything from scratch and has correspondingly delectable views. Stop in for the occasional live band on the creekside terrace. It's located about 5 miles north of Lee Vining.

Mono Lake

North America's second-oldest lake is a quiet and mysterious expanse of deep blue water whose glassy surface reflects jagged Sierra peaks, young volcanic cones and the unearthly tufa (too-fah) towers that make the lake so distinctive. Jutting from the water like drip sand castles, tufas form when calcium bubbles up from subterranean springs and combines with carbonate in the alkaline lake waters.

In *Roughing It,* Mark Twain described **Mono Lake** (Map p713; www.monolake.org) as California's 'dead sea.' Hardly. The brackish water teems with buzzing alkali flies and brine shrimp, both considered delicacies by dozens of migratory bird species that return here year after year. So do about 85% of the state's nesting population of California gulls, which take over the lake's volcanic islands from April to August. Mono Lake has also

been at the heart of an environmental controversy, lasting decades, that involves the diversion of the lake's freshwater feeder streams to Los Angeles' drinking-water supply.

◉ Sights & Activities

South Tufa   NATURE RESERVE
(Map p713; adult/child $3/free) Tufa spires ring Mono Lake, but the biggest grove is on the southern rim, with a mile-long interpretive trail. Ask about ranger-led tours at the Mono Basin Scenic Area Visitor Center (p717). To get to the reserve, head south from Lee Vining on Hwy 395 for 6 miles, then east on Hwy 120 for 5 miles to the dirt road leading to a parking lot.

Navy Beach   BEACH
The best place for swimming in Mono Lake is at Navy Beach. It's also the best place to put in canoes or kayaks.

Panum Crater   NATURAL FEATURE
(Map p713) Rising above southern shore of Mono Lake, Panum Crater is the youngest (about 640 years old), smallest and most accessible of the craters that string south toward Mammoth Mountain. A panoramic trail circles the crater rim (about 30 to 45 minutes), and a short but steep 'plug trail' puts you at the crater's core. A dirt road leads to the trailhead from Hwy 120, about 3 miles east of the junction with Hwy 395.

Black Point Fissures   NATURAL FEATURE
(Map p713) On the north shore of Mono Lake are the Black Point Fissures, narrow crags that opened when a lava mass cooled and contracted about 13,000 years ago. Access is from three places: east of Mono Lake County

Park, from the western shore off Hwy 395, or south off Hwy 167. Check at the Mono Basin Scenic Area Visitor Center for specific directions.

ℹ️ Information

Mono Basin Scenic Area Visitor Center (Map p713; ☑760-647-3044; www.fs.usda.gov/inyo; 1 Visitor Center Dr; ⊘ generally 8am-5pm Apr-Nov; 🖟) Half a mile north of Lee Vining, this center has maps, interpretive displays, Inyo National Forest wilderness permits, bear canister rentals, a bookstore and a 20-minute movie about Mono Lake.

June Lake Loop

Under the shadow of massive Carson Peak (10,909ft), the stunning 16-mile June Lake Loop (Hwy 158) meanders through a picture-perfect horseshoe canyon, past the relaxed resort town of **June Lake** and four sparkling, fish-rich lakes: Grant, Silver, Gull and June. It's especially scenic in fall, when the basin is ablaze with golden aspens. Catch the loop a few miles south of Lee Vining.

🏃 Activities

June Lake is backed by the Ansel Adams Wilderness area, which runs into Yosemite National Park. Hiking and horse-riding trips into the backcountry are the equal of any in the Sierra Nevada.

June Mountain Ski Area　　　SKIING
(Map p713; ☑888-586-3686, 24hr snow info 760-934-2224; www.junemountain.com; lift tickets adult/13-18yr & senior/under 13yr $72/48/free; ⊘8:30am-4pm; 🖟) Winter fun concentrates in this area, which is smaller and less crowded than nearby Mammoth Mountain (p718) – Mammoth lift passes can be used here – and perfect for beginner and intermediate skiers. Some 35 trails crisscross 500 acres of terrain served by seven lifts, including two high-speed quads. Boarders can get their adrenaline flowing at three terrain parks with a kick-ass super pipe.

Ernie's Tackle & Ski Shop　SPORTS & OUTDOORS
(☑760-648-7756, 2604 Hwy 158; ⊘6am-7pm) One of the most established outfitters in June Lake village.

🛏️ Sleeping & Eating

June Lake Campground　　　CAMPGROUND $
(☑800-444-7275; www.recreation.gov; tent & RV sites $22; ⊘mid-Apr–Oct; 🖟) On the June

Lake shoreline and a short walk from town. Accepts reservations.

Oh! Ridge Campground　　　CAMPGROUND $
(Map p713; ☑800-444-7275; www.recreation.gov; tent & RV sites $27; ⊘mid-Apr–Oct; 🖟) Large open-air campground popular with families because of its access to a swimming beach on June Lake. Accepts reservations.

June Lake Motel　　　　　　MOTEL $$
(☑760-648-7547; www.junelakemotel.com; 2716 Hwy 158; r with kitchenette/kitchen $115/165; ❋@🛜🖟) Enormous rooms – most with full kitchens – catch delicious mountain breezes and sport attractive light-wood furniture. There's a fish-cleaning sink and barbecues.

Silver Lake Resort　　　　　CABIN $$
(Map p713; ☑760-648-7525; www.silverlakeresort.net; 6957 Hwy 158; cabins $131-212; ⊘late Apr–mid-Oct) Across the road from Silver Lake and astride Alger Creek, this sweet cabin compound opened in 1916 and has a duck pond and boat rentals in addition to almost 20 rustic cabins with full kitchens. Its tiny old-time **cafe** (mains $8-11; ⊘7am-2pm; 🅿) displays the requisite antique winter-sports equipment and serves diner fare like burgers, sandwiches and grilled chicken; it's most popular for excellent big breakfasts.

Double Eagle Resort & Spa　　RESORT $$$
(Map p713; ☑760-648-7004; www.doubleeagle.com; 5587 Hwy 158; r $249, cabins $369; 🛜♨🖟) A swanky spot for these parts, Double Eagle has sleek two-bedroom log cabins and balconied hotel rooms that lack no comfort. Worries disappear at the elegant spa, and there's a heated indoor pool and a fully equipped gym. The **restaurant** (mains $15-35; ⊘7:30am-9pm) exudes rustic elegance, with cozy booths, a high ceiling and a huge fireplace.

★Ohanas 395　　　　　　FOOD TRUCK $
(www.ohanas395.com; 131 S Crawford Ave; mains $8-14; ⊘11:30am-6:30pm Mon & Wed-Sat, noon-5pm Sun) Check out this food truck parked at **June Lake Brewing** (www.junelakebrewing.com; 131 S Crawford Ave; ⊘11am-8pm Wed-Mon, to 9pm Fri & Sat; 🖟), serving wait-worthy 'Hawaiian soul food' with a dash of Mexican fusion. Try the kalua pig or naan tacos (the Korean beef brisket and the portobello mushroom are favorites), a classic plate lunch or an ahi *poke* (raw-fish salad) bowl.

Tiger Bar　　　　　　　AMERICAN $$
(☑760-648-7551; www.tigerbarcafe.com; 2620 Hwy 158; mains $9-20; ⊘8am-10pm) After a

day on the slopes or trails, people gather at the long bar or around the pool table of this no-nonsense, no-attitude place, around in some form or another since 1932. The kitchen feeds all appetites, with burgers, salads, tacos and other tasty grub, including homemade fries; there are fresh-baked pies for dessert.

Carson Peak Inn AMERICAN $$$
(Map p713; ☑760-648-7575; Hwy 158, btwn Gull & Silver Lakes; meals $24-40; ☺5-10pm, shorter hours winter) Inside a cozy house with a fireplace, this restaurant is much beloved for its tasty old-time indulgences, such as fried chicken, pan-fried trout and chopped sirloin steak. Portion sizes can be ordered for regular or 'hearty' appetites.

Mammoth Lakes

Mammoth Lakes is a small mountain-resort town endowed with larger-than-life scenery – active outdoorsy folks worship at the base of its dizzying 11,053ft Mammoth Mountain. Long-lasting powder clings to these slopes, and when the snow finally fades, the area's an outdoor wonderland of mountain-bike trails, excellent fishing, endless alpine hiking and blissful hidden spots for hot-spring soaking. The Eastern Sierra's commercial hub and a four-season resort, outdoorsy Mammoth is backed by a ridgeline of jutting peaks, ringed by clusters of crystalline alpine lakes and enshrouded by the dense Inyo National Forest.

◉ Sights

★**Earthquake Fault** NATURAL FEATURE
(Map p724) On Minaret Rd, about 1 mile west of the Mammoth Scenic Loop, detour to gape at Earthquake Fault, a sinuous fissure half a mile long gouging a crevice up to 20ft deep into the earth. Ice and snow often linger at the bottom until late summer, and Native Americans and early settlers used it to store perishable food.

Mammoth Museum MUSEUM
(Map p719; ☑760-934-6918; www.mammoth museum.org; 5489 Sherwin Creek Rd; suggested donation $5; ☺10am-6pm mid-May–Sep; 🐾) For a walk down memory lane, stop by this little museum inside the historic Hayden log cabin, with photographs and artifacts from its heyday as a hunting and fishing lodge.

🏃 Activities

The excellent website of the **Mammoth Lakes Trail System** (www.mammothtrails. org) contains a comprehensive guide to local hiking, biking and cross-country ski trails, with maps and information on services available.

McGee Creek Pack Station HORSEBACK RIDING
(☑800-854-7407, 760-935-4324; www.mcgeecreek packstation.com; McGee Creek Rd; half-/full-day rides $80/140; 🐾) Whether it's backcountry multiday packing trips or hour-long rides on nearby trails, the owners of this company offer decades of experience and knowledge.

Rock Creek Pack Station HORSEBACK RIDING
(☑760-872-8331; www.rockcreekpackstation.com; Rock Creek Rd; half/full-day ride $90/140; 🐾) Old, experienced hands run this backcountry packing company high up in the Rock Creek wilderness. Short of dressage, nearly every equine activity, as well as hiking and fishing trips, is on offer.

Caldera Kayaks KAYAKING
(☑760-935-1691; www.calderakayak.com) Caldera Kayaks has single ($30 for a half-day) and double kayaks ($50) for use on Crowley Lake.

Skiing & Snowboarding

Mammoth Mountain (Map p724; ☑800-626-6684, 760-934-2571, 24hr snow report 888-766-9778; www.mammothmountain.com; adult/13-18yr/7-12yr $125/98/35; 🐾) is one of California's premier ski resorts. There's free cross-country skiing along the more than 300 miles of ungroomed trails in town and in the Inyo National Forest. Pick up a free map at the Mammoth Lakes Welcome Center (p722) or head to **Tamarack Cross-Country Ski Center** (☑760-934-2442; www.tamaracklodge.com/xc-ski-center; 163 Twin Lakes Rd; all-day trail pass incl equipment adult/child/senior $58/52/29; ☺8:30am-5pm).

Hiking

Mammoth Lakes rubs up against the **Ansel Adams Wilderness** (Map p724; www.fs.usda. gov) and **John Muir Wilderness** (Map p724; www.fs.usda.gov) areas, both laced with fabulous trails leading to shimmering lakes, rugged peaks and hidden canyons. Major trailheads leave from the Mammoth Lakes Basin, Reds Meadow and Agnew Meadows; the latter two are accessible only by shuttle. **Shadow Lake** is a stunning 7-mile day hike from Agnew Meadows, and **Crystal Lake**

Mammoth Lakes

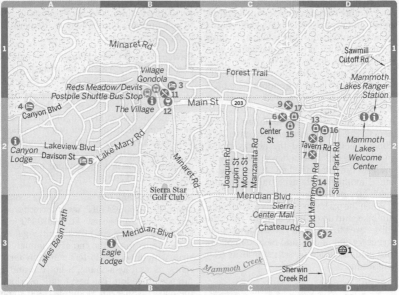

Mammoth Lakes

◎ Sights
1 Mammoth Museum.................................D3

✪ Activities, Courses & Tours
2 Mammoth Rock 'n' Bowl......................D3

🛏 Sleeping
3 Alpenhof Lodge.......................................B1
4 Austria Hof Lodge..................................A2
5 Davison Street Guest House................A2
   Mammoth Creek Inn ....(see 2)

✕ Eating
6 Base Camp Café C2
7 Good Life Café.......................................D2
   Mammoth Rock Brasserie.............(see 2)
   Petra's Bistro & Wine Bar..............(see 3)

Schat's Bakery.................................(see 6)
8 Sierra Sundance Whole Foods.............D2
9 Stellar Brew...C2
10 Stove..D3
11 Toomey's..B1

🍷 Drinking & Nightlife
   Clocktower Cellar...........................(see 3)
12 Mammoth Brewing Company B2

🛍 Shopping
13 Footloose..D2
14 Mammoth Mountaineering Supply.......D2
15 Rick's Sports Center.............................C2
16 Troutfitter...D2
17 Wave Rave...C2

makes a worthy 2.5-mile round-trip trek from Lake George in the Lakes Basin.

From various spots along the Reds Meadow area, long-distance backpackers with wilderness permits and bear canisters can easily jump onto the **John Muir Trail** (to Yosemite to the north and Mt Whitney to the south) and the **Pacific Crest Trail** (fancy walking to Mexico or Canada?).

Cycling & Mountain Biking
Stop at the Mammoth Lakes Welcome Center (p722) for a free biking map with area route descriptions.

Mammoth Mountain
Bike Park
MOUNTAIN BIKING
(Map p724; ☎ 800-626-6684; www.mammoth mountain.com; day pass adult/7-12yr $45/24; ☉ 9am-4:30pm Jun-Sep) Come summer, Mammoth Mountain morphs into the massive

Mammoth Mountain Bike Park, with more than 80 miles of well-kept single-track trails. Several other trails traverse the surrounding forest. In general, Mammoth-style riding translates into plenty of hills and soft, sandy shoulders, which are best navigated with big, knobby tires.

But you don't need wheels (or a medic) to ride the vertiginous **gondola** (Map p724; ☑800-626-6684; www.mammothmountain.com; adult/13-18yr/5-12yr $29/24/12; ⊗hours vary; P⚿) to the apex of the mountain, where there's a cafe and an interpretive center with scopes pointing toward the nearby peaks. And for kids 12 and under, a $40 Adventure Pass buys unlimited day access to a zip line, climbing wall, bungee trampoline and child's bike-park area.

When the park's open, it runs a free mountain-bike **shuttle** (9am to 5:30pm) from the Village area to the Main Lodge. Shuttles depart every 30 minutes, and mountain bikers with paid mountain passes get priority over pedestrians.

Lakes Basin Path
CYCLING

One of Mammoth's fantastic multi-use paths, the 5.3-mile Lakes Basin Path begins at the southwestern corner of Lake Mary and Minaret Rds and heads uphill (1000ft, at a 5% to 10% grade) to Horseshoe Lake, skirting lovely lakes and accessing open views of the Sherwin Range. For a one-way ride, use the free Lakes Basin Trolley, which tows a 12-bicycle trailer.

Fishing & Boating

From the last Saturday in April, the dozens of lakes that give the town its name lure in fly- and trout fishers from near and far. California fishing licenses ($15/47 for a one-day license for California residents/nonresidents) are available at sporting-goods stores throughout town. For equipment and advice, head to **Troutfitter** (Map p719; ☑760-924-3676; www.thetroutfitter.com; 2987 Main St; ⊗8am-4pm) or **Rick's Sports Center** (Map p719; ☑760-934-3416; 3241 Main St; ⊗6am-8pm).

🛏 Sleeping

Mammoth B&Bs and inns rarely sell out midweek, when rates tend to be lower. During ski season, reservations are recommended at weekends and essential during holidays. Many properties offer ski-and-stay packages. Condo rentals often work out cheaper for groups.

The Mammoth Lakes Welcome Center (p722) has a full list of campgrounds, dispersed free camping locations (don't forget to pick up a free but mandatory fire permit) and public showers.

Davison Street Guest House
HOSTEL $

(Map p719; ☑760-924-2188; www.mammoth-guest.com; 19 Davison St; dm $35-45, d $75-125; 🛜) A charming and interesting five-room A-frame chalet hostel on a quiet residential street, this place has a stocked kitchen, plus mountain views from the living room (with fireplace) or sundeck. There's a nifty electronic self-registration system when the manager isn't around. Fills with long-distance backpackers in June and July.

Mammoth Creek Inn
INN $$

(Map p719; ☑760-934-6162; www.mammothcreekinn.com; 663 Old Mammoth Rd; r $139-149, with kitchen $199-209; @🛜🏊) It's amenities galore at this pretty inn at the end of a commercial strip, with down comforters and fluffy terry robes, as well as a sauna, a hot tub and a fun pool-table loft. The best rooms overlook the majestic Sherwin Mountains, and some have full kitchens and can sleep up to six.

Austria Hof Lodge
LODGE $$

(Map p719; ☑760-934-2764; www.austriahof.com; 924 Canyon Blvd; r $109-215; 🛜) Close to Canyon Lodge, rooms here have modern knotty-pine furniture, thick down duvets and DVD players. Ski lockers and a sundeck hot tub make winter stays here even sweeter. The lodge restaurant (dinner mains $25 to $40) serves meaty gourmet German fare in a muraled cellar dining room.

Alpenhof Lodge
HOTEL $$

(Map p719; ☑760-934-6330; www.alpenhof-lodge.com; 6080 Minaret Rd; r $99-199; @🛜🏊) A snowball's toss from the Village, this Euro-flavored inn has updated lodge rooms with tasteful accent walls and ski racks, plus more luxurious accommodations with gas fireplaces or kitchens. The basement houses the Clocktower Cellar (p721).

🍴 Eating

Good Life Café
CALIFORNIAN, MEXICAN $

(Map p719; ☑760-934-1734; www.mammothgoodlifecafe.com; 126 Old Mammoth Rd; mains $8-17; ⊗6:30am-8:30pm; 🍴) Healthy food, generously filled veggie wraps and big bowls of salad make this a perennially popular place. It's been around for over 20 years and the diner-style decor is showing its age. A few tables on the front patio facing the parking lot are great for a long brunch on a warm day.

Stellar Brew
CAFE $

(Map p719; www.stellarbrewnaturalcafe.com; 3280 Main St; salads & sandwiches $5.50-10; ⊙5:30am-5pm; 🛜🍴🐾) 🍃 Proudly locavore and mostly organic, Stellar entices you to settle into a comfy sofa for your daily dose of locally roasted coffee, homemade granola, breakfast burritos and scrumptious vegan (and some gluten-free) pastries.

Base Camp Café
AMERICAN $

(Map p719; www.basecampcafe.com; 3325 Main St; mains $7-15; ⊙7:30am-3pm Sun-Fri, to 9pm Sat; 🛜🍴) Fuel up with a bracing dose of organic tea or coffee and a filling breakfast, or comfort food like Tex-Mex jalapeño-onion straws, turkey chili in a bread bowl and pesto-chicken fajitas. Decorated with various backpacking gear and beer mats, the bathroom has a comical photo display of backcountry outhouses.

Sierra Sundance Whole Foods
HEALTH FOOD $

(Map p719; 26 Old Mammoth Rd; ⊙9am-7pm Mon-Sat, to 5pm Sun; 🍴) Stock up on organic produce, free-range meats and healthy bulk foods at this large store and deli.

Toomey's
AMERICAN $$

(Map p719; 760-924-4408; www.toomey scatering.com; 6085 Minaret Rd; mains $12-33; ⊙7am-9pm; 🍴) Since 2012, Toomey's chef, once of legendary Whoa Nellie Deli (p715) in Lee Vining, has been preparing his eclectic menu of wild-buffalo meatloaf, seafood jambalaya and lobster *taquitos* (filled, rolled and fried tortillas) with mango salsa. The central location's perfect for grabbing a to-go breakfast or a sit-down dinner near the Village Gondola.

Stove
AMERICAN $

(Map p719; www.thestoverestaurantmammoth.com; 644 Old Mammoth Rd; breakfast items $6-13, lunch mains $10-13; ⊙6:30am-2pm) Great coffee and carbs; try the cinnamon-bread French toast and fresh-baked fruit pies. Excellent soups, salads and sandwiches for lunch.

Lakefront Restaurant
AMERICAN $$$

(760-934-2442; www.lakefrontmammoth.com; 163 Twin Lakes Rd; mains $30-70; ⊙5-9:30pm, plus 11am-2pm summer, closed Tue & Wed fall & spring) The most atmospheric and romantic (and pricey) restaurant in Mammoth, this intimate dining room at Tamarack Lodge overlooks the lovely Twin Lakes. The chef crafts

delights like halibut and pan-seared duck accompanied by creative seasonal vegetable sides, and the staff is superbly friendly. Reservations recommended.

Petra's Bistro & Wine Bar
CALIFORNIAN $$$

(Map p719; 760-934-3500; www.petrasbistro. com; 6080 Minaret Rd; mains $23-36; ⊙5-9:30pm Tue-Sun) Settle in for seasonal cuisine and wines recommended by the staff sommeliers. In wintertime the best seats in the house are the cozy fireside couches. Start the evening with a cheese course, and choose from 36 wines available by the glass (250 by the bottle) or from the excellent cocktail menu. Reservations recommended.

Mammoth Rock Brasserie
AMERICAN $$$

(Map p719; 760-934-4200; 3029 Chateau Rd; mains $19-34; ⊙5:30-9pm Mon-Thu, to 10pm Fri-Sun) The classically trained French chef at this swanky brasserie at Mammoth Rock 'n' Bowl serves tasty small plates and meaty main courses like elk medallions and pork mignon. Breathtaking views of the Sherwin Range are available from the 2nd-floor dining room.

🍷 Drinking & Nightlife

Clocktower Cellar
PUB

(Map p719; www.clocktowercellar.com; 6080 Minaret Rd; ⊙4-11pm) In winter especially, locals throng this dive bar–pub in the basement of the Alpenhof Lodge (p720). The ceiling is tiled with a swirl of bottle caps, and the bar has 150 whiskies, about 30 beers on tap and about 50 bottled varieties.

Mammoth Brewing Company
BREWERY

(Map p719; 760-934-7141; www.mammoth brewingco.com; 18 Lake Mary Rd; ⊙10am-9:30pm Sun-Thu, to 10:30pm Fri & Sat) You be the judge whether beer is brewed best at high altitude. Boasting the highest West Coast brewery, at 8000ft, Mammoth Brewing Company offers more than a dozen brews on tap (flights $5 to $7) – including special seasonal varieties not found elsewhere. Tasty bar food's available, and you can pick up some IPA 395 or Double Nut Brown to go.

🛍 Shopping

Gear heads will find no shortage of shops staffed by passionate young enthusiasts indulging their own outdoor adventures on days off. Most sell ski and snowboard equipment, with great sales in low season. In-town shops, especially for equipment rentals, are usually cheaper than those at Mammoth Mountain.

Footloose
SPORTS & OUTDOORS

(Map p719; ☑760-934-2400; www.footloose sports.com; 3043 Main St; ◷8am-8pm) Full range of footwear and seasonal equipment; local biking info and rentals.

Mammoth Mountaineering Supply
SPORTS & OUTDOORS

(Map p719; ☑760-934-4191; www.mammothgear. com; 361 Old Mammoth Rd; ◷8am-8pm) Offers friendly advice, topo maps and all-season equipment rentals.

Wave Rave
SPORTS & OUTDOORS

(Map p719; ☑760-934-2471; www.waverave snowboardshop.com; 3203 Main St; ◷7:30am-9pm Sun-Thu, to 10pm Fri & Sat, shorter hours low season) Snowboarders worship here. In summer it rents stand-up paddleboards and electric bikes.

ℹ Information

The **Mammoth Lakes Welcome Center** (Map p719; ☑760-924-5500, 888-466-2666; www. visitmammoth.com; 2510 Hwy 203; ◷9am-5pm) and the **Mammoth Lakes Ranger Station** (Map p719; ☑760-924-5500; www.fs.usda.gov/ inyo; ◷9am-5pm) share a building on the northern side of Hwy 203. This one-stop information center issues wilderness permits and rents bear canisters, helps find accommodations and campgrounds, and provides road- and trail-condition updates. From May to October, when trail quotas are in effect, walk-in wilderness permits are released at 11am the day before, though numbers are given to those lined up at 8am; permits are self-issue the rest of the year.

The following are locations where you can purchase lift tickets to Mammoth Mountain:
➜ **Canyon Lodge** (Map p719; 1000 Canyon Blvd)
➜ **Eagle Lodge** (Map p719; 4000 Majestic Pines Dr)
➜ **Main Lodge** (Map p724; 1001 Minaret Rd)
➜ **Mill Cafe** (Map p724; 1 Minaret Rd)
➜ **The Village** (Map p719; 72 Canyon Blvd)

ℹ Getting There & Away

AIR

Mammoth Yosemite Airport (MMH; www. visitmammoth.com/fly-mammoth-lakes; 1300 Airport Rd) has nonstop flights to San Francisco and Denver, operating winter through to spring on **United** (www.united.com). **Alaska Airlines** (www.alaskaair.com) runs year-round service to Los Angeles and ski-season service to San Diego. All flights are about an hour.

Taxis meet incoming flights, some lodgings provide free transfers and Mammoth Express buses (run by Eastern Sierra Transit; one way $3.50) ply the route to Mammoth Lakes. **Mammoth Taxi** (☑760-934-8294; www.mammoth-taxi.com) does airport runs as well as hiker shuttles throughout the Sierra.

BUS

Mammoth is a snap to navigate by public transportation year-round. In summer, **YARTS** (☑877-989-2787; www.yarts.com) runs buses to and from Yosemite Valley, and the **Eastern Sierra Transit Authority** (p710) has year-round service along Hwy 395, north to Reno, NV, and south to Lone Pine.

ℹ Getting Around

Within Mammoth Lakes, a year-round system of free and frequent **bus shuttles** – operated by the **Eastern Sierra Transit Authority** (p710) – connects the whole town with the Mammoth Mountain lodges; in summer, routes with bicycle trailers service the **Lakes Basin Path** (p720) and **Mammoth Mountain Bike Park** (p719). Check the website for details on routes and schedules.

The **Reds Meadow/Devils Postpile shuttle** (Map p719) (adult/child $7/4, season pass $35) provides public transportation to Reds Meadow and the **Devils Postpile National Monument** (p728). From 9am to 5pm it runs nearly every 20 minutes, departing from just under the base of the gondola in the Village.

Around Mammoth Lakes

Reds Meadow

One of the beautiful and varied landscapes near Mammoth Lakes is the Reds Meadow Valley, west of Mammoth Mountain. Drive on Hwy 203 as far as Minaret Vista for eye-popping views (best at sunset) of the Ritter Range, the serrated Minarets and the remote reaches of Yosemite National Park.

The road to Reds Meadow is only accessible from about June until September, weather permitting. To minimize impact when it's open, the road is closed to private vehicles beyond Minaret Vista unless you are camping, have lodge reservations or are disabled, in which case you must pay a $10 fee per car. Otherwise you must use a mandatory shuttle bus ($7/4 adult/child). The bus leaves from a lot in front of the Adventure Center (next to the mammoth statue) approximately every 30 minutes between 7:15am and 7pm (last bus out leaves Reds Meadow at 7:45pm), and you must buy tickets inside before joining the queue. There are also three direct departures from the Village (on Canyon Blvd, under the gondola) before 9am, plus the option of using the free mountain-bike shuttle between the Village and the Adventure Center. The bus stops at trailheads, viewpoints and campgrounds before completing the one-way trip to Reds Meadow (45 minutes to an hour).

The valley road provides access to six campgrounds along the San Joaquin River. Tranquil, willow-shaded **Minaret Falls Campground** (www.fs.usda.gov; tent & RV sites $22; 🐾) is a popular fishing spot where the best riverside sites have views of the namesake cascade.

Hot Creek Geological Site

For a graphic view of the area's geothermal power, journey just south of Mammoth Lakes to where chilly Mammoth Creek blends with hot springs and continues its journey as **Hot Creek** (www.fs.usda.gov/inyo; Hot Creek Hatchery Rd; ⊙sunrise-sunset) FREE. It eventually enters a small gorge and forms a series of steaming, bubbling cauldrons, with water shimmering in shades of blue and green reminiscent of the tropics. In 2006 a significant increase in geothermal activity began sending violent geysers of boiling water into the air, so swimming is strictly prohibited.

To reach the site, turn off Hwy 395 about 5 miles south of Mammoth Lakes and follow signs to the Hot Creek Fish Hatchery. From here it's another 2 miles on gravel road to the parking area, and a short hike down to the canyon and creek.

Convict Lake

One of the area's prettiest lakes, **Convict Lake** has emerald water embraced by massive peaks. A hike along the gentle trail skirting the lake, through aspen and cottonwood trees, is great if you're still adjusting to the altitude. A trailhead on the southeastern shore gives access to Genevieve, Edith, Dorothy and Mildred Lakes in the John Muir Wilderness. To reach the lake, turn south from Hwy 395 on Convict Lake Rd (across from the Mammoth airport) and go 2 miles.

In 1871 Convict Lake was the site of a bloody shoot-out between a band of escaped convicts and a posse that had given chase. The posse leader, Sheriff Robert Morrison, was killed during the gunfight and the tallest peak, Mt Morrison (12,268ft), was later

named in his honor. The bad guys got away, only to be apprehended later near Bishop.

McGee Creek

Eight miles south of Mammoth Lakes, off Hwy 395, McGee Creek Rd rises into the mountains and dead-ends in a dramatic aspen-lined canyon, a particularly beautiful spot for autumn foliage. From here, the **McGee Pass Trail** enters the John Muir Wilderness, with day hikes to **Steelhead Lake** (10 miles round-trip) via an easy walk to subtle **Horsetail Falls** (4 miles round-trip).

On the drive up, the McGee Creek Pack Station (p718) offers trail rides. Spacious **McGee Creek Campground** (www.fs.usda. gov; McGee Creek Rd; tent & RV sites $23; ⊙late Apr-Oct; 🐾) has 28 reservable sites at 7600ft, with sun-shaded picnic tables along the creek and stunning mountain vistas.

Don't miss the coffee and home-baked goodies at the cute **East Side Bake Shop** (📞760-914-2696; www.facebook.com/EastSide BakeShop; 1561 Crowley Lake Dr; mains $8-15; ⊙6:30am-3pm Wed, Thu & Sun, to 9pm Fri & Sat, shorter hours winter); check its calendar for fun local music at weekends.

Rock Creek

South off Hwy 395 and roughly equidistant between Mammoth Lakes and Bishop, Rock Creek Rd travels 11 miles into some of the dreamiest landscapes in the Sierra. At road's end, the Mosquito Flat trailhead into the **Little Lakes Valley** (part of the John Muir Wilderness) clocks in at a whopping 10,300ft of elevation. Mountaintops seem to be everywhere, with the 13,000ft peaks of Bear Creek Spire, Mt Dade, Mt Abbot and Mt Mills bursting out along the southwestern horizon and lush canyon meadows popping with scores of clear blue lakes. Ecstatic hikers and climbers fan out to explore – an excellent day-hike destination is the second of the **Gem Lakes** (7 miles round-trip), a lovely aquamarine bowl and five-star lunch spot.

A dozen popular **USFS campgrounds** (📞877-444-6777; www.recreation.gov; tent & RV sites $22; ⊙late May-Sep; 🐾) line Rock Creek Rd; most are along Rock Creek and a few are reservable. In wintertime there's a Sno-park 7 miles in, and during summer the Rock Creek Pack Station (p718) offers trail rides from its location just before the trailhead.

The area is deservedly popular, and trailhead parking can be challenging; be

Mammoth Lakes Area

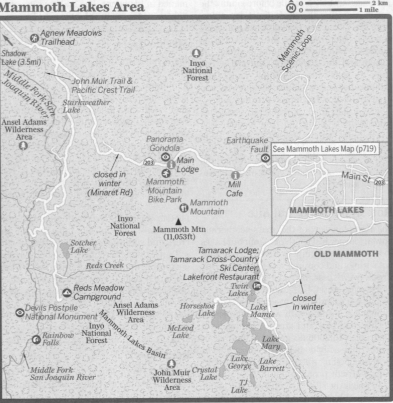

N
0 — 2 km
0 — 1 mile

Agnew Meadows Trailhead

Shadow Lake (3.5mi)

Middle Fork San Joaquin River

John Muir Trail & Pacific Crest Trail

Starkweather Lake

Ansel Adams Wilderness Area

Inyo National Forest

Mammoth Scenic Loop

Panorama Gondola

203

Main Lodge

closed in winter (Minaret Rd)

Mammoth Mountain Bike Park

Mammoth Mountain

Inyo National Forest

Mammoth Mtn (11,053ft)

Earthquake Fault

See Mammoth Lakes Map (p719)

Main St 203

MAMMOTH LAKES

Mill Cafe

OLD MAMMOTH

Sotcher Lake

Reds Creek

Tamarack Lodge; Tamarack Cross-Country Ski Center; Lakefront Restaurant

Twin Lakes

closed in winter

Reds Meadow Campground

Devils Postpile National Monument

Ansel Adams Wilderness Area

Inyo National Forest

Mammoth Lakes Basin

Horseshoe Lake

McLeod Lake

Lake Mamie

Lake Mary

Rainbow Falls

Middle Fork San Joaquin River

John Muir Wilderness Area

Crystal Lake

Lake George

Lake Barrett

TJ Lake

prepared to trek an extra half-mile from the overflow lot.

Bishop

The second-largest town in the Eastern Sierra, Bishop is about two hours from Yosemite's Tioga Pass entrance. A major recreation hub, Bishop offers access to excellent fishing in nearby lakes, climbing in the Buttermilks just west of town, and hiking in the John Muir Wilderness via Bishop Creek Canyon and the Rock Creek drainage. The area is especially lovely in fall, when dropping temperatures cloak aspen, willow and cottonwood in myriad glowing shades.

The earliest inhabitants of the Owens Valley were Paiute and Shoshone Native Americans, who today live on four reservations. White settlers came on the scene in the 1860s and began raising cattle to sell to nearby mining settlements.

◉ Sights

★ Laws Railroad Museum & Historic Site   MUSEUM

(🖉760-873-5950; www.lawsmuseum.org; Silver Canyon Rd; donation $5; ⊙10am-4pm; 🖶) Railroad and Old West aficionados should make a detour off Hwy 6 to this museum. It recreates the village of Laws, an important stop on the route of the *Slim Princess*, a narrow-gauge train that hauled freight and passengers across the Owens Valley for nearly 80 years. You'll see the original 1883 train depot, a post office, a schoolhouse and other rickety old buildings. Many contain funky and eclectic displays (dolls, fire equipment, antique stoves etc) from the pioneer days.

Mountain Light Gallery   GALLERY

(🖉760-873-7700; www.mountainlight.com; 106 S Main St; ⊙10am-5pm Mon-Sat, 11am-4pm Sun) **FREE** To see the Sierra on display in all its majesty, pop into this gallery, housed in the historic Monument Bank building, which features the stunning outdoor images of the late Galen Rowell. An accomplished mountaineer and a *National Geographic* photographer, Rowell produced work that bursts with color, and his High Sierra photographs are some of the best in existence.

Besides the stunning fine-art prints that are for sale, the gallery sells a good selection of books on the Sierras and mountaineering in general.

Owens Valley Paiute Shoshone Cultural Center
CULTURAL CENTER

(☏760-873-8844; www.bishoppaiutetribe.com/cultural-center.html; 2300 W Line St; ⊙10am-5pm Tue-Sat) FREE A mile west of Hwy 395, this underutilized tribal cultural center and museum, run by the local Paiute Shoshone tribe, includes exhibits on local basketry, tools and the use of medical herbs; behind the building is an interpretive native-plant walk.

🏃 Activities

In the summer, fishing is good in the high-altitude lakes of **Bishop Creek Canyon** (west of town along Hwy 168). Other fine spots include the scenic, twisty and downright magical **Owens River** (northeast) and the **Pleasant Valley Reservoir** (Pleasant Valley Rd, north of town).

Climbing

Bishop is prime bouldering and rock-climbing territory, with terrain to match any level of experience and any climbing style. The main areas are the granite **Buttermilk Country**, nearly 8 miles west of town on Buttermilk Rd, and the stark **Volcanic Tablelands** and **Owens River Valley** (Happy and Sad Boulders) to the north. The tablelands are also a wellspring of Native American petroglyphs – tread lightly.

Hiking

Hikers will want to head to the high country by following Line St (Hwy 168) west along Bishop Creek Canyon, past Buttermilk Country and on to several lakes. Trailheads lead into the John Muir Wilderness and on into Kings Canyon National Park. Check with the White Mountain information station (p728) for suggestions, maps and wilderness permits for overnight stays.

Swimming

Keough's Hot Springs
SWIMMING

(Map p700; ☏760-872-4670; www.keoughshotsprings.com; 800 Keough Hot Springs Rd; adult/

child 3-12yr/child under 2yr $12/7/4; ⊙11am-7pm Wed-Fri & Mon, 9am-8pm Sat & Sun, longer hours Jun-Aug; 🏊) About 8 miles south of Bishop, this historic institutional-green outdoor pool (dating from 1919) is filled with bath-warm water from local mineral springs and doused with spray at one end. A smaller and sheltered 104°F (40°C) soaking pool sits beside it. Camping and tent cabins are also available.

🛏 Sleeping

Bishop is loaded with economically priced motels, mostly chains. The majority are located on or just off Main St. A couple of campgrounds at the foot of the Volcanic Tablelands just to the north of town are open year-round.

USFS Campgrounds
CAMPGROUND $

(www.recreation.gov; tent & RV sites $23; ⊙May-Sep; 🏊) For a scenic night, stretch out your sleeping bag beneath the stars. The closest USFS campgrounds, all but one first-come, first-served, are between 9 miles and 15 miles west of town on Bishop Creek along Hwy 168, at elevations between 7500ft and 9000ft.

Hostel California
HOSTEL $

(☏760-399-6316; www.hostelbishop.com; 213 Academy Ave; dm $28-39, d $70, 6-person r $170; ❋🐾🛜) A rambling, historic Victorian house located in the center of town, this hostel packs in dusty long-distance backpackers during June and July, with a more varied mix of hikers, anglers, climbers and international travelers the rest of the year. Visitors love the full kitchen, laundry-time loaner clothes, and bicycles, as well as the communal outdoors-loving atmosphere. Adults only.

Owner Matt Meyers, an avid climber, is an excellent source of information. Showers for nonguests are available for $5.

★ Bishop Creekside Inn
MOTEL $$

(☏760-872-3044; www.bishopcreeksideinn.com; 725 N Main St; r $130-209, ste $140-230; ❋@🛜🐾) Bishop's most upscale lodging, with an enviable location alongside Bishop Creek, underwent a full-scale renovation completed in summer 2017. Woodsy art and Western-style leather armchairs outfit rooms that come with marble bathrooms (with walk-in glass showers), roomy armchairs, Keurig coffeemakers and thick duvet bedding. Whistling Trout, the hotel's new restaurant, was set to open in fall 2017 at the time of writing.

Joseph House Inn Bed & Breakfast
B&B $$

(☏760-872-3389; www.josephhouseinn.com; 376 W Yaney St; r $153-188; ❋🛜🐾) This beautifully

DAVID TOUSSAINT/GETTY IMAGES ©

1. Lundy Lake (p716) **2.** John Muir Trail (p719) **3.** Little Lakes Valley (p723)

Best Hikes of the Sierra Nevada

Packed with ancient granite peaks, icy-blue lakes and serpentine stream meadows, the Sierra Nevada beckons mountain worshippers. Though the sights may look lovely from the car, you need to stop, smell and touch to really experience the landscape. And once you witness its burning alpenglow, you'll understand why Sierra Club cofounder John Muir called it the 'Range of Light.'

Lundy Canyon

In the Hoover Wilderness west of Mono Lake, ambitious beavers gnaw and stack stands of leafy aspens, and frothy waterfalls draw you deeper and deeper into this stunning and solitary canyon.

John Muir Trail

Load up that pack and connect the dots from the heart of Yosemite to the pinnacle of Mt Whitney, the highest peak in the contiguous USA. This 200-plus-mile trek goes step by step up and over six passes topping 11,000ft. Cross chilly rivers and streams between bumper-to-bumper Yosemite Valley, the roadless backcountry of Sequoia and Kings Canyon and the oxygen-scarce summit of Mt Whitney.

Little Lakes Valley

Marvel at this perfect chain of alpine lakes nestled between snow-tipped summits. With the Sierra's highest trailhead, there's no need to earn your elevation here.

Yosemite High Sierra Camps

Tour Yosemite's high country without a bulging backpack and share the sights with pudgy whistling marmots. Highlights include overnights at pristine May Lake, the waterfalls of Glen Auli and lake-studded Vogelsang.

DEVIL'S POSTPILE
....

The most fascinating attraction in Reds Meadow is the surreal volcanic formation of **Devils Postpile National Monument** (Map p724; ☎760-934-2289; www.nps.gov/depo; shuttle day pass adult/child $7/4; ☺late May-Oct). The 60ft curtains of near-vertical, six-sided basalt columns formed when rivers of molten lava slowed, cooled and cracked with perplexing symmetry. This honeycomb design is best appreciated from atop the columns, reached by a short trail. The columns are an easy half-mile hike from the Devils Postpile Ranger Station.

From the monument, a 2.5-mile hike passing through fire-scarred forest leads to the spectacular **Rainbow Falls** (Map p724), where the San Joaquin River gushes over a 101ft basalt cliff. Chances of actually seeing a rainbow forming in the billowing mist are greatest at midday. The falls can also be reached via an easy 1.5-mile walk from the Reds Meadow area, which has a cafe, a store, the **Reds Meadow campground** (Map p724; tent & RV sites $22; ☻) and a pack station. Shuttle services run to the Reds Meadow area in season.

restored ranch-style home with a patio overlooking a tranquil 3-acre garden has six nicely furnished rooms, some with fireplaces, all with TV. Guests enjoy a complimentary gourmet breakfast and afternoon wine.

✖ Eating

★ Erick Schat's Bakkerÿ   BAKERY $

(☎760-873-7156; www.erickschatsbakery.com; 763 N Main St; sandwiches $6-9; ☺6am-6pm Sun-Thu, to 7pm Fri; ☻) A deservedly hyped tourist mecca filled to the rafters with racks of fresh bread, Schat's has been making its signature sheepherder bread and other baked goodies since 1938. Some of the desserts, including the crispy cookies and bear claws, are addictive, and call for repeated trips while in town. Also has a popular sandwich bar and outdoor tables.

Great Basin Bakery   BAKERY, CAFE $

(☎760-873-9828; www.greatbasinbakerybishop. com; 275d S Main St; salads & sandwiches $5-8; ☺6am-4pm Mon-Sat, from 6:30am Sun; ☻🖉) 🖉 In the southern part of town, this excellent mom-and-pop bakery serves locally roasted coffee, breakfast sandwiches on freshly baked bagels with local eggs, homemade soups and lots of delectable baked goods (with vegan and gluten-free options). Enter from Lagoon St.

Back Alley   AMERICAN $$

(www.thebackalleybowlandgrill.com; 649 N Main St; mains $15-24; ☺11:30am-10pm, to 9pm Sun) Tucked off the main drag, behind Yamatani's Restaurant, this busy bowling-alley bar and grill (with bowling-pin carpeting!) earns the locals' affection with huge portions of fresh fish, rib-eye steak and burgers. Specials come with loads of sides and the homemade

desserts are surprisingly good amid the tattered Tiki-meets-televisions surf decor.

ℹ Information

Bishop Area Visitors Bureau (☎760-873-8405; www.bishopvisitor.com; 690 N Main St; ☺10am-5pm Mon-Fri, to 4pm Sat & Sun; ☻) Helpful staff with information on accommodations and activities in Bishop and the surrounding region.

Inyo National Forest Wilderness Permit Office (☎760-873-2483; www.fs.usda.gov/inyo; 351 Pacau Lane, suite 200) Offices for Inyo National Forest staff and wilderness-permit office.

White Mountain Public Lands Information Station (☎760-873-2500; www.fs.usda.gov/inyo; 798 N Main St; ☺8am-5pm daily May-Oct, Mon-Fri Nov-Apr) Wilderness permits, trail and campground information for the entire area.

Public showers are available in town at **Wash Tub** (☎760-873-6627; 236 N Warren St; ☺9am-6pm Mon-Fri, 8am-10pm Sat & Sun; ☻).

Big Pine

This blink-and-you-missed-it town has a few motels and basic eateries. It mainly functions as a launchpad for the **Ancient Bristlecone Pine Forest** (☎760-873-2500; www. fs.usda.gov/inyo; ☺usually mid-May–Nov; P☻) 🖉 and to the granite **Palisades** in the John Muir Wilderness, a rugged cluster of peaks including six above 14,000ft. Stretching beneath the pinnacles is **Palisades Glacier**, the southernmost in the USA and the largest in the Sierra Nevada.

To get to the trailhead, turn onto Glacier Lodge Rd (Crocker Ave in town), which follows trout-rich Big Pine Creek up Big Pine Canyon, 10 miles west into a bowl-shaped valley. The strenuous 9-mile hike to Palisades Glacier via the North Fork Trail skirts several lakes – turned a milky turquoise color by glacial runoff – and a stone cabin built by horror-film actor Lon Chaney in 1925.

Glacier Lodge (Map p700; ☑ 760-938-2837; www.glacierlodge395.com; tent sites $25, RV sites $35, cabins $160-190; ☺ mid-Apr–mid-Nov; 🐾) is a bunch of rustic cabins with kitchens, as well as a campground. Though the original building no longer exists, it was one of the earliest Sierra getaways when built in 1917. Two-night minimum stay.

Independence

This sleepy highway town has been a county seat since 1866, but it's on the map because of its proximity to the Manzanar National Historic Site south of town and to wilderness trails in the Sierra Nevada. West of town via Onion Valley Rd (Market St in town), pretty **Onion Valley** harbors the trailhead for the **Kearsage Pass** (9.4 miles round-trip), an old Paiute trade route. This is also the quickest east-side access to the **Pacific Crest Trail** and Kings Canyon National Park.

Fans of **Mary Austin** (1868–1934), renowned author of *The Land of Little Rain* and vocal foe of the desertification of the Owens Valley, can follow signs leading to her former house at 253 Market St.

◉ Sights

★Manzanar National Historic Site   HISTORIC SITE
(Map p700; ☑ 760-878-2194; www.nps.gov/manz; 5001 Hwy 395; ☺ 9am-5:30pm Apr–mid-Oct, 10am-4:30pm mid-Oct–Mar; 🅿️📶) 🎫 FREE A stark wooden guard tower alerts drivers to one of US history's darkest chapters, which unfolded on a barren, windy sweep of land some 5 miles south of Independence. Little remains of the infamous war concentration camp, a dusty square mile where more than 10,000 people of Japanese ancestry were corralled during WWII. The camp's lone remaining building, the former high-school auditorium, houses a superb interpretive center. A visit is one of California's historical highlights and should not be missed.

Watch the 20-minute documentary, then explore the thought-provoking exhibits chronicling the stories of the families that languished here yet built a vibrant community. Afterward, take a self-guided 3.2-mile driving tour around the grounds, which includes a recreated mess hall and barracks, vestiges of buildings and gardens, and the haunting camp cemetery.

Eastern California Museum   MUSEUM
(☑ 760-878-0364; www.inyocounty.us/ecmsite; 155 N Grant St; donation requested; ☺ 10am-5pm; 🅿️📶) This museum contains one of the most complete collections of Paiute and Shoshone baskets in the country, as well as artifacts from the Manzanar National Historic Site and historic photographs of primitively equipped local rock climbers scaling Sierra peaks, including Mt Whitney.

🛌 Sleeping

USFS Campgrounds   CAMPGROUND $
(www.fs.usda.gov; tent & RV sites $18; ☺ approx May-Sep; 🐾) There are three USFS campgrounds alongside Independence Creek, including one at the Kearsage Pass trailhead. Reservations available at www.recreation.gov.

Mt Williamson Motel & Base Camp   CABIN $
(☑ 760-878-2121; www.mtwilliamsonmotel.com; 515 S Edwards St; r $85-95, ste $125; 🏧📶🐾) A low-key hiker favorite, Mt Williamson has cute cabins with flat-screen TVs, calico bedspreads, tea kettles and arresting prints of the local bighorn sheep, all nestled among fruit trees. Ask about the hiker packages that include trailhead transportation. Full breakfast included mid-June to October.

🍴 Eating

Owens Valley Growers Co-op   SUPERMARKET, CAFE $
(☑ 760-915-0091; 149 S Edwards St; mains $8; ☺ cafe 5-7pm Fri, supermarket hours vary; 📶🐾) The cafe, serving locally grown produce and other products, is open for Friday-night dinners; an outdoor farmers market is held at the same time from late May to September. Lunch and dinner other days of the week are a possibility.

Still Life Cafe   FRENCH $$
(☑ 760-878-2555; 135 S Edward St; lunch $9-16, dinner $16-24; ☺ 11am-3pm & 6-9:30pm Wed-Mon) Fairly upscale and unexpected in such a flyspeck town, the Still Life Cafe prepares escargot, steak au poivre and other French bistro faves and serves them with Gallic charm in this dimly lit, eclectically decorated dining room.

Lone Pine

A tiny town, Lone Pine is the gateway to big things, most notably Mt Whitney, the loftiest

BENTON HOT SPRINGS

Soak in your own hot-springs tub and snooze beneath the moonlight at **The Inn at Benton Hot Springs** (☏866-466-2824, 760-933-2287; www.historicbentonhotsprings.com; Hwy 120, Benton; tent & RV sites for 2 people $40-50, d with/without bath $129/109; ✲❖✲), a small, historic resort in a 150-year-old former silver-mining town nestled in the White Mountains. Choose from nine well-spaced campsites with private tubs or themed, antique-filled B&B rooms with semiprivate tubs. Daytime dips ($10 per person per hour) are available. Reservations essential.

The inn is reachable from Mono Lake via Hwy 120 (in summer), Mammoth Lakes by way of Benton Crossing Rd, or Bishop via Hwy 6; the first two options are undulating drives with sweeping red-rock vistas that glow at sunset, and all take approximately one hour. An Eastern Sierra Transit Authority bus connects Bishop and Benton ($6, one hour) on Tuesday and Friday, stopping right at the resort.

If you have time, ask for directions to the Volcanic Tablelands petroglyphs off Hwy 6, where ancient drawings decorate scenic rock walls.

---

peak in the contiguous USA, and Hollywood. In the 1920s cinematographers discovered that the nearby Alabama Hills were a picture-perfect movie set for Westerns, and stars from Gary Cooper to Gregory Peck could often be spotted swaggering about town.

◉ Sights

★Alabama Hills   NATURAL FEATURE

The warm colors and rounded contours of the Alabama Hills, located on Whitney Portal Rd, stand in contrast to the jagged, snowy Sierras just behind. The setting for countless ride-'em-out movies, the popular *Lone Ranger* TV series and, more recently, parts of *Iron Man* (Jon Favreau, 2008) and Quentin Tarantino's *Django Unchained* (2012), the stunning orange rock formations are a beautiful place to experience sunrise or sunset.

You can drive, walk or mountain bike along dirt roads rambling through the boulders, and along Tuttle and Lone Pine Creeks. A number of graceful rock arches are within easy hiking distance of the roads. Head west on Whitney Portal Rd and either turn left at Tuttle Creek Rd, after a half-mile, or north on Movie Flat Rd, after about 3 miles. Following the latter route, the road eventually turns into Moffat Ranch Rd and brings you back to Hwy 395, only 3½ miles south of Manzanar National Historic Site (p729). The websites of the Lone Pine Chamber of Commerce (p732) and the Museum of Western Film History have excellent movie-location maps.

Mt Whitney   MOUNTAIN

(Map p700; www.fs.usda.gov/inyo) West of Lone Pine, the jagged incisors of the Sierra surge skyward in all their raw and fierce glory. Cradled by scores of smaller pinnacles, Mt Whitney is a bit hard to pick out from Hwy 395, so, for the best views, take a drive along Whitney Portal Rd through the Alabama Hills.

As you get a fix on this majestic megalith, remember that the country's lowest point is only 80 miles (as the crow flies) east of here: Badwater in Death Valley. Climbing to Mt Whitney's summit (p731) is among the most popular hikes in the entire country.

Museum of Western Film History   MUSEUM

(☏760-876-9909; www.museumofwesternfilmhistory.org; 701 S Main St; adult/under 12yr $5/free; ◷10am-6pm Mon-Wed, to 7pm Thu-Sat, to 4pm Sun Apr-Oct, 10am-5pm Mon-Sat, to 4pm Sun Nov-Mar; Ⓟ♿) More than 400 movies, not to mention numerous commercials (mostly for rugged SUVs and Jeeps), have been shot in the area, and this museum contains exhibits of paraphernalia from locally set films. One of the most fascinating pieces in the collection is the 1928 Lincoln camera car, acquired in 2016 – the mounted cameras caught the action while cars drove alongside galloping horses. The museum's theater screens a well-made film about the history of Westerns shot in the Alabama Hills.

The museum hosts a film festival – geared to Westerns, of course – on the first weekend in October.

🛏 Sleeping

⭐ Alabama Hills Bureau
of Land Management   CAMPGROUND
(Alabama Hills) **FREE** You can't go wrong with free camping amid some of the most striking scenery in the Sierras. Pull off onto any of the dirt roads to find a private spot behind a rock formation with snowcapped mountains towering above. Of course, services are nonexistent, but for those you can head into Lone Pine, a short drive away.

⭐ Whitney Portal
Hostel & Hotel   HOSTEL, MOTEL $
(☎760-876-0030; www.whitneyportalstore.com; 238 S Main St; dm/d $25/85; ❄🛜🐾) A popular launchpad for Mt Whitney trips and a locus of posthike washups (public showers are available), the Whitney has the cheapest beds in town – reserve dorms months ahead for July and August. There's no common space, just well-maintained single-sex bunk-bed rooms,

though amenities include towels, TVs, in-room kitchenettes and stocked coffeemakers.

The majority of the establishment consists of plush, modern motel rooms, and many look towards Whitney and its neighbors. The ground-floor general store (p732) is an excellent place to stock up on basic gear and food supplies.

Tuttle Creek   CAMPGROUND $
(Horseshoe Meadows Rd; tent & RV sites $5; 🐾) Off Whitney Portal Rd, this first-come, first-served Bureau of Land Management campground has 83 primitive sites with panoramic 'pinch-me!' views of the Sierras, the White Mountains and the rosy Alabama Hills (p730). There's not much shade, though.

Lone Pine Campground   CAMPGROUND $
(Map p700; www.fs.usda.gov; Whitney Portal Rd; tent & RV sites $22; ⏱mid-Apr–Oct; 🐾) About midway between Lone Pine and Whitney Portal, this popular creekside USFS

HIKING MT WHITNEY

The mystique of 14,505ft **Mt Whitney** (p731) captures the imagination, and conquering its hulking bulk becomes a sort of obsession for many. The main **Mt Whitney Trail** (the easiest and busiest one) leaves from Whitney Portal, about 13 miles west of Lone Pine via Whitney Portal Rd (closed in winter), and climbs about 6000ft over 11 miles. It's a super-strenuous, really, really long walk that'll wear out even experienced mountaineers, but it doesn't require technical skills if attempted in summer or early fall. Earlier or later in the season, you'll likely need an ice axe and crampons, and to overnight.

Many people in good physical condition make it to the top, although only superbly conditioned, previously acclimatized hikers should attempt this as a day hike. Breathing becomes difficult at these elevations and altitude sickness is a common problem. Rangers recommend spending a night camping at the trailhead and another at one of the two camps along the route: **Outpost Camp** at 3.5 miles or **Trail Camp** at 6 miles up the trail.

When you pick up your permit and pack-out kits (hikers must pack out their poop) at the Eastern Sierra Interagency Visitor Center (p733) in Lone Pine, get the latest info on weather and trail conditions. Near the trailhead, the **Whitney Portal Store** (p732) sells groceries and snacks. It also has public showers ($5) and a cafe with enormous burgers and pancakes. The message board on its website is a good starting point for Whitney research.

The biggest obstacle in getting to the peak may be to obtain a **wilderness permit**, which is required for all overnight trips and for day hikes past Lone Pine Lake (about 2.8 miles from the trailhead). A quota system limits daily access to 60 overnight and 100 day hikers from May to October. Because of the huge demand, permits are distributed via the online **Mt Whitney lottery** (www.fs.usda.gov/inyo; per group $6, plus per person $15), with applications accepted from February to mid-March.

Want to avoid the hassle of getting a permit for the main Mt Whitney Trail? Consider ascending this popular pinnacle from the west, using the **backdoor route** from Sequoia & Kings Canyon National Parks. It takes about six days from Crescent Meadow via the High Sierra Trail to the John Muir Trail – with no Whitney Zone permit required – and wilderness permits are much easier to secure.

NAMING THE ALABAMA HILLS

Wouldn't the Alabama Hills to the west of Lone Pine have more suitably been named the 'California Hills'? So why Alabama? It turns out that a group of miners digging in these hills during the Civil War years were supporters of the Confederacy and chose the moniker in honor of the CSS *Alabama*, which was wreaking havoc on Union ships.

campground (elevation 6000ft) offers vault toilets and potable water.

Dow Hotel & Dow Villa Motel HOTEL, MOTEL **$$**
(☏760-876-5521; www.dowvillamotel.com; 310 S Main St; hotel r with/without bath from $89/70, motel r $117-158; P❀❋@⚡⚡⚡) John Wayne and Errol Flynn are among the stars who have stayed at this venerable hotel. Built in 1922, the place has been restored but retains much of its rustic charm. The rooms in the newer motel section have air-con and are more comfortable and bright, but also more generic.

✖ Eating

Alabama Hills Cafe DINER **$**
(☏760-876-4675; 111 W Post St; mains $8-14; ⏱7am-2pm; ⚡⚡⚡) At everyone's favorite breakfast joint, the portions are big, the bread is fresh baked, and the hearty soups, sandwiches and fruit pies make lunch an attractive option too. You can also plan your drive through the Alabama Hills (p730) with the help of the map on the menu.

Lone Pine Smokehouse BARBECUE **$**
(☏760-876-4433; www.lonepinesmokehouse.com; 325 S Main St; sandwiches $9; ⏱noon-8pm Mon, to 9pm Thu-Sun; ❀) The quality seems to be hit or miss – the beef brisket and pulled pork are most consistent – at this friendly Texas-style-barbecue place. And, despite the Western-themed facade, the dining room is utterly unadorned. It's best to grab an outdoor table on a sunny day (dogs allowed).

Lone Star Bistro SANDWICHES **$**
(107 N Main St; sandwiches $5-8; ⏱6am-7pm Tue-Sun, to noon Mon; ⚡) You can satisfy most of your needs at this mash-up of a gift shop, deli, ice-cream parlor and cafe. Soups, pastries and hiking fare to go are also offered.

Seasons AMERICAN **$$**
(☏760-876-8927; 206 N Main St; mains $17-30; ⏱5-9pm daily Apr-Oct, Tue-Sun Nov-Mar) Seasons has everything you fantasized about the last time you choked down freeze-dried rations. Sautéed trout, roasted duck, filet mignon and plates of carb-replenishing pasta will revitalize your appetite, and nice and naughty desserts will leave you purring. Reservations recommended.

🛍 Shopping

★ **Whitney Portal Store** FOOD & DRINKS
(Map p700; ☏760-876-0030; www.whitneyportal store.com; ⏱hours vary May-Oct; ⚡) Food, beer, souvenirs and excellent advice from the friendly staff make this *the* (only) place to visit before and/or after your hike up Mt Whitney. It sits just a few yards from the trailhead and is only open during the peak hiking season.

Elevation SPORTS & OUTDOORS
(☏760-876-4560; www.sierraelevation.com; 150 S Main St, cnr Whitney Portal Rd; ⏱call for hours) Rents bear canisters and crampons, and sells hiking, backpacking and climbing gear.

Lone Pine Sporting Goods SPORTS & OUTDOORS
(☏760-876-5365; 220 S Main St; ⏱call for hours) Sells camping gear, clothing, fishing licenses (cash only) and maps.

ℹ Information

Eastern Sierra Interagency Visitor Center
(☏760-876-6222; www.fs.fed.us/r5/inyo; cnr Hwys 395 & 136; ⏱8am-5pm) USFS information center for the Sierra Nevada, Death Valley and Mt Whitney; about 1.5 miles south of town.

Lone Pine Chamber of Commerce (☏760-876-4444; www.lonepinechamber.org; 120 S Main St; ⏱8:30am-4:30pm Mon-Fri) Housed in a historic building with loads of brochures and friendly and helpful staff.

Understand California

California Today

California is a crazy dream that has survived more than 150 years of reality. The Golden State has surged ahead of France to become the world's sixth-largest economy. But like a kid that's grown too fast, California still hasn't figured out how to handle the hassles that come along with such rapid growth, including housing shortages, traffic gridlock and rising costs of living. Escapism is always an option here, thanks to Hollywood blockbusters and legalized marijuana dispensaries. But California is coming to grips with its international status and taking leading roles in such global issues as environmental standards, online privacy, marriage equality and immigrant rights.

Best on Film

The Maltese Falcon (1941) Humphrey Bogart as a San Francisco private eye.
Sunset Boulevard (1950) The classic bonfire of Hollywood vanities.
Vertigo (1958) Alfred Hitchcock's noir thriller, set in SF.
The Graduate (1967) Surviving life in 1960s California suburbia.
Blade Runner (1982) Ridley Scott's futuristic cyberpunk vision of LA.
Pulp Fiction (1994) Quentin Tarantino's outrageous interlocking LA stories.
LA Confidential (1997) Neo-noir tale of corruption and murder in 1950s LA.
The Big Lebowski (1998) Through myriad misadventures in the Coen brothers' zany LA farce, 'The Dude' abides.

Best in Print

On the Road (Jack Kerouac; 1957) The epic road trip that inspired free spirits everywhere to come to California.
My California: Journeys by Great Writers (Angel City Press; 2004) Insightful stories by talented California chroniclers.
Where I Was From (Joan Didion; 2003) California-born essayist shatters palm-fringed fantasies.
Hollywood Babylon (Kenneth Anger; 1959) The tell-all book that exposed the scandals behind Hollywood's silver screen.

California Dreams vs Reality

Even after you've seen it 1000 times on movies and TV, California still comes as a shock to the system. Venice Beach skateboarders, Santa Cruz hippies, Rodeo Dr poseurs and Silicon Valley billionaires aren't on different channels here – this is their natural habitat. California is all over the map politically: by turns liberal and conservative, Californians have also cultivated a certain wackiness that blurs party lines. California's long track record of conspiracy theories and fringe movements can only partly be explained by the state's legendary fondness for marijuana, legalized here in 2017.

Californians may not seem to have much in common, but they're not afraid to take controversial stances on issues affecting their communities. California's trailblazing support for LGBT rights was instrumental in securing marriage equality in 2013. With first- and second-generation immigrants making up more than half the state's population, Californians vocally opposed federal immigration bans by nationality and religion in 2017. Even under threat of federal defunding, Californians continue to march, file lawsuits and support passing a statewide sanctuary law to ensure that all are welcome here.

Environmental Roots

California's culture of conspicuous consumption is world famous, thanks to soda-shilling Hollywood movies and reality TV stars who have spawned entire butt-padding industries. But ever since John Muir established the Sierra Club in the 19th century, many Californians have deliberately sought out a more sustainable way of life. In the midst of lumber and oil booms, Californians helped kick-start the world's conservation movement. They passed trailblazing laws curbing industrial dumping, set aside swaths of prime real estate as urban green space, and protected California wilderness as national, state and county parks.

Fast Companies, Slow Food

Perhaps you've heard of PCs, iPhones, Google and the internet? Then California's technological innovations need no introduction. Between Silicon Valley and biotech, Northern California is rapidly overtaking Southern California's gargantuan entertainment industry as California's main economic engine. While building the infrastructure for the AI-enabled Internet of Things, multitasking Silicon Valley pioneers are also busy laying the the groundwork for online ethics, including net neutrality, data privacy and online civil liberties through the Electronic Frontier Foundation.

Less than 10% of Californians live in rural areas, but they sustain California's other powerhouse industry: agriculture. Each year, 80,000 Californian farms raise $42 billion worth of food, including specialty produce that has changed American diets and created new food cravings worldwide. Climate change and drought are top of mind for many Californians, but especially farmers and foodies.

You may notice that Californians seem downright religious about their food. They proselytize about their diets, worship star chefs and ritually photograph dishes before they take a single bite. Sounds ludicrous – but after a few bites, you may begin to understand the obsession. Local menus reflect values close to many Californians' hearts: organic and non-GMO farming, protections against animal cruelty, sustainable natural-process winemaking, fair-trade coffee and support for small local businesses. Californians coined the term 'locavore' – people who eat food grown locally – and once you've tasted the difference for yourself, you may become California's newest convert.

New World Religions

Though they may not have many followers outside their yurt villages, California's alternative religions and utopian communities have long captivated the popular imagination. Since its inception California has been a magnet for spiritual seekers, from modern-day pagans to new-age healers. Many Californians have pursued quiet contemplation, forming the largest Zen communities outside Japan and establishing Quaker silent-retreat centers in the redwoods.

But California is better known for making sensational headlines in the 1960s and '70s with hippie spiritualism, primal scream therapy, Jim Jones' ill-fated People's Temple, and Erhard Seminars Training (EST) hype-heavy self-help movement. Founded in 1954, the controversial Church of Scientology has attracted converts with celebrity endorsements from the likes of Tom Cruise and John Travolta. Californian doomsday cults caused commotions in the 1990s with the Heaven's Gate UFO cult in San Diego, and again when Oakland radio minister Harold Camping proselytized that the Rapture was imminent. That was back in 2011 – perhaps it's a miracle we survived. So there's still time to find religion, or invent your own in California.

POPULATION: **39.5 MILLION**

AREA: **155,780 SQ MILES**

GDP: **$2.46 TRILLION**

MEDIAN HOUSEHOLD INCOME: **$64,500**

UNEMPLOYMENT: **5.2%**

if California were 100 people

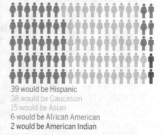

39 would be Hispanic
38 would be Caucasian
15 would be Asian
6 would be African American
2 would be American Indian

belief systems
(% of population)

32 Protestant
3 Jewish
2 Buddhist
28 Roman Catholic
27 None
8 Other

population per sq mile

California   San Francisco   Los Angeles

≈ 250 people

History

Five hundred Native American nations called this land home for some 150 centuries before 16th-century European arrivals gave it a new name: California. Spanish conquistadors and priests came here for gold and god, but soon relinquished their flea-plagued missions and ill-equipped presidios (forts) to Mexico. The unruly territory was handed off to the US in the Treaty of Hidalgo mere months before gold was discovered here in 1848. Generations of California dreamers continue to make the trek to these Pacific shores for gold, glory and self-determination, making homes and history on America's most fabled frontier.

Native Californians

Native Californian Sites

Indian Canyons & Tahquitz Canyon (Palm Springs)

Autry National Center (Griffith Park, LA)

Indian Grinding Rock State Historic Park (Gold Country)

California State Indian Museum (Sacramento)

Maidu Museum & Historical Site (Roseville)

Patrick's Point State Park (North Coast)

Immigration is hardly a new phenomenon in California, where settlers have been arriving for millennia. Humans were settling California as early as 19,000 years ago, leaving behind traces of early California cuisine in large middens of seashells along the beaches and campfire sites on the Channel Islands.

From the beginning, the Californian menu was abundant and varied. Seafood and small game such as rabbits and deer were sopped up with acorn-meal bread. Native Californians were highly skilled at preparing foods, and did not need to stray far from their small communities to secure their staple foods with fishing nets, bows, arrows, and spears with chipped stone points. Food and water were carried in finely woven baskets decorated with elegant geometric patterns.

Native Californians spoke at least 100 distinct languages, and passed knowledge of hunting grounds and turf boundaries from generation to generation in song. Northern coastal fishing communities such as the Ohlone, Miwok and Pomo built subterranean roundhouses and sweat lodges, where they held ceremonies, told stories and gambled for fun. Northern hunting communities, including the Hupa, Karok and Wiyot, constructed big houses and redwood dugout canoes, while the Modoc lived in summer tipis and winter dugouts – but all their paths converged during California's seasonal salmon runs. Kumeyaay and Chumash villages dotted the central coast, where they fished and paddled canoes as far out into the Pacific as the Chan-

TIMELINE	13,000 BC	AD 1542–43	1769
	Native American communities settle this land, from Yurok redwood plank houses in the north to Kumeyaay thatch-domed dwellings in the south.	Portuguese navigator Juan Rodríguez Cabrillo and his Spanish crew are among the first Europeans to sail California's coast. His journey ends in the Channel Islands with untimely death from a gangrenous wound.	Franciscan friar Junípero Serra and Captain Gaspar de Portolá lead a Spanish expedition to establish missions, rounding up Native Californians as converts and conscripted labor.

nel Islands. Southern Mojave, Yuma and Cahuilla nations made sophisticated pottery and developed irrigation systems for farming in the desert.

When English sea captain Sir Francis Drake harbored briefly on Miwok land north of San Francisco in 1579, the English were taken to be the dead returned from the afterworld, and shamans saw the arrival as a warning of apocalypse. The omens weren't far wrong: within a century of the arrival of Spanish colonists in 1769, California's indigenous population would be decimated by 80% to 90%, falling to just 20,000 due to foreign diseases, conscripted labor, violence, marginalization and hunger in their own fertile lands.

The Spanish Mission Period

In the 18th century, when Russian and English trappers began trading valuable pelts from Alta California, Spain concocted a plan for colonization. For the glory of God and the tax coffers of Spain, missions would be built across California. According to plan, these missions would be going concerns run by local converts within 10 years. This venture was approved by quixotic Spanish colonial official José de Gálvez of Mexico, who was full of grand schemes, including controlling Baja California with a trained army of apes.

Almost immediately after Spain's missionizing plan was approved in 1769, it began to fail. When Franciscan friar Junípero Serra and Captain Gaspar de Portolá made the overland journey to establish Mission San Diego de Alcalá in 1769, only half the sailors on their supply ships survived. Portolá had heard of a fabled cove to the north, but failing to recognize Monterey Bay in the fog, he gave up and turned back.

Portolá reported to Gálvez that if the Russians or English wanted California, they were welcome to it. But Serra wouldn't give up, and secured support to set up presidios (forts) alongside missions. When soldiers weren't paid regularly, they looted and pillaged local communities. Clergy objected to this treatment of potential converts, but still relied on soldiers to round up conscripts to build missions. In exchange for their forced labor, Native Californians were promised one scant meal a day and a place in God's kingdom – which came much sooner than expected, due to diseases such as smallpox and syphilis that the Spanish introduced.

California's indigenous tribes often rebelled against the Spanish colonists, and the missions barely managed to become self-sufficient. Although they did plant California's first vineyards, the Spanish failed to colonize California. Spanish colonists gave up, other foreigners moved in, and more Native Californians died than were converted.

California Under Mexican Rule

Spain wasn't sorry to lose California to Mexico in the 1810–21 Mexican War of Independence – and Californian settlers known as *rancheros*

Find out more about the traditions and lifestyles of indigenous tribes with *California Indians and Their Environment*, an engaging and accessible natural history guide by Kent Lightfoot and Otis Parrish.

The distance between each of California's Spanish colonial missions equaled a day's journey by horseback. Learn more about the missions' historical significance and cultural influence at www.missions california.com.

1781	1821	1835	1846
Spanish governor Felipe de Neve sets out from Mission San Gabriel with a tiny band of settlers, trekking west all of 9 miles before putting down stakes and establishing the future Los Angeles.	Mexican independence ends Spanish colonization of California. Mexico inherits 21 missions, along with unruly cowboys and a radically reduced Native Californian population.	An emissary of US President Andrew Jackson makes a formal offer to buy Alta California, but Mexico unsuccessfully tries to sell it off to Britain instead.	Sierra Nevada blizzards strand the Donner Party of settlers, some of whom avoid starvation by eating their dead companions. Five women and two men survive, snowshoeing 100 miles for help.

(ranchers) saw an opportunity. The Spanish, Mexican and American ranchers who had intermarried with Native Californians had become a sizable constituency known as 'Californios', but the best grazing land was still reserved for the missions. So in 1834 Californios convinced Mexico to secularize the missions.

Californios quickly snapped up deeds to privatized mission property, and capitalized on the growing market for cowhides and tallow (a key ingredient in soap). Only a few dozen Californios were literate in the entire state, so boundary disputes that arose were settled with muscle, not paper. By law, half the lands were supposed to go to Native Californians who worked at the missions, but few actually received their entitlements.

Through marriage and other mergers, most of the land and wealth in California was held by just 46 *ranchero* families by 1846. The average *rancho* (ranch) was now 16,000 acres, having grown from cramped shanties to elegant haciendas where women were ordered to stay confined to quarters at night. But *rancheras* (ranch women) weren't so easily bossed around: women owned some Californian ranches, rode horses as hard as men and caused romantic scandals worthy of modern *telenovelas* (soap operas).

Meanwhile, Americans were arriving at the trading post of Los Angeles via the Old Spanish Trail. Northern passes through the Sierra Nevada were trickier, as the Donner Party tragically discovered in 1846 – stranded by snow near Lake Tahoe, some survivors resorted to cannibalism.

Still, the US saw potential in California. When US president Andrew Jackson offered the financially strapped Mexican government $500,000 for the territory in 1835, the offer was tersely rejected. After the US annexed the Mexican territory of Texas in 1845, Mexico broke off diplomatic relations and ordered all foreigners without proper papers deported from California. The Mexican–American War was declared in 1846, lasting two years with very little fighting in California. Hostilities ended with the Treaty of Guadalupe Hidalgo, in which Mexico ceded much of its northern territory (including Alta California) to the US. The timing was lucky for the US, and most unfortunate for Mexico: just a few weeks after the US took possession of California, gold was discovered.

Stranded in Sierra Nevada blizzards in 1846, some pioneers took extreme survival measures, including eating their dead companions. Their harrowing tale is captured in *Desperate Passage: The Donner Party's Perilous Journey West* (2008) by, Ethan Rarick.

THE BEAR FLAG REPUBLIC

In June 1846, American settlers tanked up on liquid courage declared independence in the northern town of Sonoma. Not a shot was fired – instead, they captured the nearest Mexican official and hoisted a hastily made flag. Locals awoke to discover they were living in the independent 'Bear Republic,' under a flag painted with a grizzly that looked like a drunken dog. The Bear Flag Republic lasted only a month before US orders telling settlers to stand down arrived.

1848	1850	1851	1869
Gold is discovered near present-day Placerville by mill employees. San Francisco tabloid publisher, speculator and bigmouth Sam Brannan lets the secret out, and the gold rush is on.	With hopes of solid-gold tax revenues, the US declares California the 31st state. When miners find tax loopholes, SoCal ranchers are left carrying the tax burden, creating early north–south rivalries.	The discovery of gold in Australia means cheering in the streets of Melbourne and panic in the streets of San Francisco, as the price for California gold plummets.	On May 10 the 'golden spike' is nailed in place at Promontory, Utah, completing the first transcontinental railroad and connecting California with the East Coast.

California's Gold Rush

The gold rush era in California began with a bluff. Real-estate speculator, lapsed Mormon and wily tabloid publisher Sam Brannan was looking to unload some California swampland in 1848 when he heard rumors of gold flakes found near Sutter's Mill in the Sierra Nevada foothills. Figuring this news should sell some newspapers and raise real-estate values, Brannan published the rumor as fact.

At first Brannan's story didn't generate much excitement – gold flake had surfaced in southern California as far back as 1775. So he ran another story, this time verified by Mormon employees at Sutter's Mill who had sworn him to secrecy. Brannan kept his word until he reached San Francisco, where he legendarily ran through Portsmouth Sq brandishing gold entrusted to him as tithes for the Mormon church, shouting, 'Gold on the American River!'

Other newspapers around the world weren't scrupulous about the facts either, hastily publishing stories of gold near San Francisco. By 1850 – the year California was fast-tracked for admission as the 31st US state – California's non-native population had ballooned from 15,000 to 93,000. Early arrivals from across the country and around the world panned for gold side by side, slept in close quarters, guzzled locally made wine and slurped Chinese noodles. When they struck it rich, miners ordered the 'Hangtown Fry,' an omelette made with salt-cured bacon and local oysters – ingredients worth up to $200 in today's terms.

With each wave of new arrivals, profits dropped and gold became harder to find. In 1848 each prospector earned an average of about $300,000 in today's terms. By 1849 earnings were less than half that, and by 1865 they had dipped to $35,000. When surface gold became scarce, miners picked, shoveled and dynamited through mountains. The work was grueling and dangerous and, with few doctors around, injuries often proved lethal. The cost of living in cold, filthy mining camps was sky-high – and with only one woman for every 400 men in some camps, many turned to paid company, booze and opium for consolation.

Vigilantes, Robber Barons & Railroads

Gold prospectors who did best arrived early and got out quick, while those who stayed too long either lost fortunes searching for the next nugget or became targets of resentment. Native Californian laborers who helped miners strike it rich were denied the right to hold claims. Successful Peruvians and Chileans were harassed and denied renewals to their mining claims, and most left California by 1855. The 'Chilecito' neighborhood they established in San Francisco is now called Jackson Sq, but you can still order the drink these early settlers brought to San Francisco circa 1848: Pisco punch.

Top California History Books

Slouching Towards Bethlehem (Joan Didion)

Strangers from a Different Shore (Ronald Takaki)

Alice: Memoirs of a Barbary Coast Prostitute (Ivy Anderson and Devon Angus)

California: A History (Kevin Starr)

City of Quartz (Mike Davis)

HISTORY CALIFORNIA'S GOLD RUSH

1882	1906	1928	1934
The US Chinese Exclusion Act suspends new immigration from China, denies citizenship to those already in the country and sanctions racially discriminatory laws that remain on the books until 1943.	An earthquake levels entire blocks of San Francisco in 42 seconds, setting off fires that rage for three days. Survivors start rebuilding immediately.	*The Jazz Singer* premieres – as the first feature-length 'talkie' movie, it kicks off Hollywood's Golden Age.	A longshoremen's strike ends with two strikers dead, 34 sympathizers shot and 40 gassed or beaten by police in San Francisco. After mass funeral processions and citywide strikes, shipping magnates meet union demands.

As mining became industrialized, fewer miners were needed, and jobless prospectors turned anger toward a convenient target: Chinese workers. Frozen out of mining claims, many Chinese opened service-based businesses that survived when mining ventures went bust. By 1860 enough Chinese pioneers had endured to become the second-most populous group in California after Mexicans, but this hard-won resilience met with irrational resentment. Discriminatory Californian laws restricting housing, employment and citizenship for anyone born in China were passed and extended with the 1882 US Chinese Exclusion Act, which remained law until 1943.

Inter-ethnic rivalries obscured the real competitive threat posed not by fellow workers, but by those who controlled the means of production: California's 'robber barons.' These Californian speculators hoarded the capital and industrial machinery necessary for deep-mining operations. Laws limiting work options for Chinese arrivals served the needs of robber barons, who needed cheap labor to build railroads to their mining claims and reach East Coast markets.

To blast tunnels through the Sierra Nevada, workers were lowered down sheer mountain faces in wicker baskets, planted lit dynamite sticks in rock crevices then urgently tugged the rope to be hoisted out of harm's way. Those who survived the day's work were confined to bunkhouses under armed guard in cold, remote mountain regions. With little other choice of legitimate employment, an estimated 12,000 Chinese laborers blasted through the Sierra Nevada, meeting the westbound end of the transcontinental railroad in 1869.

Immigrants denied entry under the Asian Exclusion Act carved heartbreaking poems into cell-block walls at Angel Island detention center. Poet Genny Lim championed the effort to preserve and translate their poignant words in *Island: Poetry and History of Chinese Immigrants on Angel Island, 1910-1940* (2014).

Oil & Water

During the US Civil War (1861–65), California couldn't count on food shipments from the East Coast, and started growing its own. California recruited Midwestern homesteaders to farm the Central Valley with shameless propaganda. 'Acres of Untaken Government Land...for a Million Farmers...Health & Wealth without Cyclones or Blizzards,' trumpeted one California-boosting poster, neglecting to mention earthquakes or ongoing land disputes with *rancheros* and Native Californians. The hype worked: more than 120,000 homesteaders came to California in the 1870s and '80s.

These homesteaders soon discovered that California's gold rush had left the state badly tarnished. Hills were stripped bare, vegetation wiped out, streams silted up and mercury washed into water supplies. Cholera spread through open sewers of poorly drained camps, claiming many lives. Because mining claims leased by the US government were granted significant tax exemptions, there were insufficient public funds for cleanup programs or public water works. Smaller mineral finds in Southern

1942	1955	1965	1966
Nearly 120,000 Japanese Americans are sent to internment camps. Legal defenses raised by the Japanese American Citizens League help lead to the 1964 Civil Rights Act and, 47 years later, a presidential apology.	Disneyland opens in Anaheim on July 17. As crowds swarm the park, plumbing breaks and Fantasyland springs a gas leak. Walt Disney calls a do-over, relaunching successfully the next day.	20,000 National Guards are ordered to suppress the Watts Riots in LA. Six days of violent clashes result in death, devastation and more than $40 million in property damage. That same year, Rodney King is born.	Ronald Reagan is elected governor of California, setting a career precedent for fading entertainment figures. He served until 1975 then in 1981 became the 40th US President.

California mountains diverted streams, turning the green valleys below into deserts. Recognizing at last that water, not gold, was the state's most precious resource, Californians passed a pioneering law preventing dumping into rivers in 1884.

Amid California's first water crisis, frustrated farmers south of Big Sur voted to secede from California in 1859. These calls for secession were set aside during the Civil War, but were soon back on the table. With the support of budding agribusiness and real-estate concerns, Southern Californians passed bond measures to build aqueducts and dams that made large-scale farming and real-estate development possible. By the 20th century, the lower one-third of the state claimed two-thirds of available water supplies, inspiring Northern California's own calls for secession.

Meanwhile, flat-broke mining prospector and failed real-estate speculator Edward Doheny made an unexpected discovery in Los Angeles: oil. In 1892 Doheny drilled his first oil well near where Dodger Stadium now stands, and within a year it was yielding 40 barrels daily. Five years later, 500 wells were operational in Southern California. By 1900 the state was producing four million barrels of 'black gold' annually, Downtown LA had boomed to 100,000 inhabitants, and California oil kickbacks greased the palms of politicians all the way to DC. Doheny's own back-door dealings were exposed in the 1920s Teapot Dome bribery scandal, inspiring Upton Sinclair's darkly satirical 1926 novel *Oil!* and the 2007 Oscar-winning oil drama *There Will Be Blood*.

While pastoral Southern California was urbanizing, Northern Californians who had witnessed mining and logging devastation firsthand were jump-starting the nation's first conservation movement. Scottish immigrant John Muir moved to San Francisco to make his living, but found his true calling as a naturalist on a week-long trip to the Yosemite Valley. Muir founded the Sierra Club in 1892 and devoted his life to defending Yosemite and vast tracts of California's wilderness against the encroachments of dams and pipelines to urban centers. After backpacking with Muir in Yosemite in 1903, President Theodore Roosevelt was convinced to preserve Yosemite as a national park. Muir's passionate objections, however, couldn't prevent Woodrow Wilson from signing the 1913 bill to build Hetch Hetchy Reservoir, which supplies Bay Area water today. In drought-prone California, tensions between land developers and conservationists still run high.

Roman Polanski's classic neo-noir thriller *Chinatown* (1974) is a fictionalized yet surprisingly accurate account of the brutal early 20th century water wars waged to build Los Angeles.

Hollywood & California Counterculture

By the 1920s California's greatest export was the sunny, wholesome image it projected to the world through its homegrown film and TV industry. With consistent sunlight and versatile locations, Southern California proved to be an ideal movie location. Early in its career, SoCal was a

1967	1968	1969	1969
The Summer of Love kicks off on January 14 in Golden Gate Park, where the Human Be-In blows minds and conch shells, and draft cards are used as rolling papers.	Presidential candidate, former US attorney-general and civil-rights ally Robert Kennedy is fatally shot in Los Angeles after winning the critical California presidential primary.	A UCLA computer connects to another at Stanford University, just long enough to read two characters before the system crashes. The internet is born.	Native American activists symbolically reclaim Alcatraz until ousted by the FBI in 1971. Public support for protesters strengthens self-rule concessions for Native American nations.

stand-in for more exotic locales, and got dressed up for period-piece productions such as Charlie Chaplin's *Gold Rush* (1925). But with its beach sunsets and palm-lined drives, California soon stole the scene in Technicolor movies and iconic TV shows. California shed its bad-boy Wild West reputation to become a movie star, dominating the screen behind squeaky-clean beach boys and bikini-clad blondes.

But Northern Californians didn't picture themselves as extras in *Beach Blanket Bingo* (1965). The Navy discharged WWII sailors for insubordination and homosexuality in San Francisco, as though that would teach them a lesson. Instead they found themselves at home in North Beach's bebop jazz clubs, bohemian coffeehouses and City Lights Bookstore. San Francisco was an outpost of free speech and free spirits, and soon everyone who was anyone was getting arrested here, including dancer Carol Doda for going topless, comedian Lenny Bruce for dropping F-bombs onstage, and City Lights founder Lawrence Ferlinghetti for publishing Allen Ginsberg's epic poem *Howl*. Doda won and kept dancing for 45 years. Writers including Woody Allen, James Baldwin and Bob Dylan vocally defended Bruce, who was posthumously pardoned. City Lights continues to celebrate its landmark 1957 victory for free speech, publishing thousands of volumes of fresh verse and provocative prose annually.

The final button of convention was popped not by San Francisco artists, but by the CIA. To test psychoactive drugs intended to create the ultimate soldier, the CIA gave LSD to writer Ken Kesey. He saw the potential not for war but for a wild party, and spiked the punch at the 1966 Trips Festival organized by Stewart Brand. The psychedelic era hit an all-time high at the January 14, 1967 Human Be-In in Golden Gate Park, where trip-master Timothy Leary urged a crowd of 20,000 hippies to dream a new American dream and 'turn on, tune in, drop out.' As the high wore off and hippy 'flower power' faded, other Bay Area rebellions, including Black Power and gay pride, grew in its place.

Northern California had the more attention-grabbing counterculture in the 1940s to '60s, but nonconformity in sunny SoCal shook the country to the core. In 1947, when Senator Joseph McCarthy attempted to root out suspected communists in the film industry, 10 writers and directors refused to admit to communist alliances or to name names. The 'Hollywood Ten' were charged with contempt of Congress and barred from working in Hollywood, but their impassioned defenses of the US Constitution were heard nationwide. Major Hollywood players boldly voiced dissent and hired blacklisted talent until lawsuits finally curbed McCarthyism in the late 1950s.

California's beach-paradise image – and its oil-industry dealings – would be permanently changed not by Hollywood directors, but Santa Barbara beachgoers. On January 28, 1969, an oil rig dumped 100,000

Marc Reisner's *Cadillac Desert: The American West and Its Disappearing Water* examines the contentious, sometimes violent water wars that gave rise to modern California.

1977	1989	1992	1994
San Francisco Supervisor Harvey Milk becomes the first openly gay man elected to public office in California. Milk sponsors a gay-rights bill before being murdered by political opponent Dan White.	On October 17, the Loma Prieta Earthquake hits 6.9 on the Richter scale near Santa Cruz, collapsing a two-level section of Interstate 880 and resulting in 63 deaths and almost 4000 injuries.	Four white police officers charged with assaulting African American Rodney King are acquitted by a predominantly white jury. Following the acquittal, Los Angeles endures six days of riots.	Orange County, one of the wealthiest municipalities in the US, declares bankruptcy after the county treasurer loses $1.7 billion in risky derivatives investments and pleads guilty to felony charges.

CALIFORNIA'S CIVIL RIGHTS MOVEMENT

Before the 1963 march on Washington, DC, the civil rights movement was well under way in California. When almost 120,000 Japanese Americans living along the West Coast were ordered into internment camps by President Roosevelt in 1942, the Japanese American Citizens League immediately filed suits that advanced all the way to the US Supreme Court. These lawsuits established groundbreaking civil rights legal precedents, and in 1992 internees received reparations and an official letter of apology signed by President George HW Bush.

Adopting the nonviolent resistance practices of Mahatma Gandhi and Martin Luther King Jr, labor leaders César Chávez and Dolores Huerta formed United Farm Workers in 1962 to champion the rights of immigrant laborers. Four years later Chávez and Californian grape pickers marched on Sacramento, bringing the issue of fair wages and the health risks of pesticides to the nation's attention. When Bobby Kennedy was sent to investigate, he sided with Chávez, bringing Latinos into the US political fold.

California was again on the front lines during the fight for marriage equality. In open defiance of the 1996 US Defense of Marriage Act (DOMA) that defined marriage as between opposite-sex partners, San Francisco mayor Gavin Newsom began issuing marriage certificates to same-sex couples in 2004. The issue went to the courts, which found DOMA in conflict with California's constitution. Opponents of marriage equality rallied around Proposition 8, a ballot measure that proposed to change California's constitution to invalidate same-sex marriage. Proposition 8 passed by a narrow margin, but was found unconstitutional in 2008 and on appeal in 2013. With this key legal precedent established, the US Supreme Court declared DOMA unconstitutional the same day, and marriage equality was established nationwide.

Today civil rights remains top of mind in California, where new Americans represent over half the population, including 26.9% foreign-born immigrants, and 30.7% naturalized citizens or US-born children of immigrants. A dozen California cities have passed sanctuary statutes, including Berkeley's pioneering 1971 sanctuary resolution and San Francisco's 1989 citywide sanctuary law. These laws protect local police stations, schools and hospitals from having to detain undocumented people not charged with any crime for deportation by federal authorities. Under threat of the removal of federal funds by the Trump administration in 2017, San Francisco and Berkeley reaffirmed their sanctuary policies, and California legislators are considering measures that would extend sanctuary statewide.

barrels of crude oil into the Santa Barbara Channel, killing dolphins, seals and thousands of birds. Playing against type, the laid-back SoCal beach community organized a highly effective protest, spurring the establishment of the US Environmental Protection Agency, the California Coastal Commission and pioneering legislation against environmental pollution.

1994	2000	2003	2005
The 6.7-magnitude Northridge earthquake strikes LA on January 17, killing 72 and causing $20 billion in property damage – one of the costliest natural disasters in US history.	The Nasdaq crashes, ending the dot-com boom. Traditional industries gloat over the bubble burst, until knock-on effects lead to a devalued dollar and NYSE slide starting in 2002.	Republican Arnold Schwarzenegger (aka 'The Governator') is elected governor of California. Schwarzenegger breaks party ranks on environmental issues and wins re-election in 2007.	Antonio Villaraigosa is elected mayor of LA, becoming the first Latino to hold that office since 1872. Born poor in East LA, he says in his victory speech, 'I will never forget where I came from.'

Geeking out in California

When Silicon Valley introduced the first personal computer in 1968, advertisements breathlessly gushed that Hewlett-Packard's new 'light' (40lb) machine could 'take on roots of a fifth-degree polynomial, Bessel functions, elliptic integrals and regression analysis' – all for just $4900 (over $33,000 today). Consumers didn't know quite what to do with such computers, but Trips Festival organizer Stewart Brand had a totally psychedelic idea: what if all that technology could fit into the palm of your hand? Maybe then, the technology governments used to run countries could empower ordinary people.

When Brand shared this radical notion of 'personal computing' in his 1969 *Whole Earth Catalog*, it inspired a generation of technologists. At the 1977 West Coast Computer Faire, 21-year-old Steve Jobs and Steve Wozniak introduced the Apple II, a personal computer with unfathomable memory (4KB of RAM!) and microprocessor speed (1MHz!). But the question remained: what would ordinary people do with all that computing power?

By the mid-1990s an entire dot-com start-up industry boomed in Silicon Valley, and suddenly people were getting everything – mail, news, pet food and, yes, sex – online. But when dot-com profits weren't forthcoming, venture-capital funding evaporated. Fortunes in stock options disappeared when the Nasdaq plummeted on March 10, 2000, popping the dot-com bubble. Overnight, 26-year-old vice-presidents and Bay Area service-sector employees alike found themselves jobless.

But online users continued to look for useful information and human connection in those billions of web pages, and search engines and social media boomed. Technology became ever more personal, and Steve Jobs was finally able to call Stewart Brand in 2007 with some news: he'd finally shrunk computers to fit into the palm of a hand. Smartphones took off, and more than two million apps have been launched since.

Meanwhile, California's biotech industry has been quietly booming. An upstart company called Genentech was founded in a San Francisco bar in 1976, and quickly got to work cloning human insulin and introducing the Hepatitis B vaccine. In 2004 California voters approved a $3-billion bond measure for stem-cell research, and by 2008 California had become the USA's biggest funder of stem-cell research, as well as the focus of Nasdaq's new Biotechnology Index. With cloud computing to store and access data, machine learning is now able to make rapid advancements in medical imaging and diagnostics.

So will machines save us all, or surpass us? Dude, that sounds like a good subject for a Hollywood movie – or at least a far-out conversation in a California marijuana dispensary (legal as of 2017, in case you're wondering). No matter what happens next, you can say you saw it coming in California.

In his 2017 bestseller *The Upstarts*, tech reporter Brad Stone captures the giddy rise and dubious ethics of Uber, Airbnb and other Silicon Valley titans behind the fast-growing 'sharing economy.'

Werner Herzog's documentary *Lo and Behold* (2016) explores the California origins of the internet and its impact on society.

2007	2008	2013	2017
Wildfires sweep drought-stricken Southern California, forcing one million people to evacuate their homes. Migrant workers, state prisoners and Tijuana firefighters help curb the blazes.	California voters pass Proposition 8, defining legal marriage as between a man and a woman. Courts eventually rule the law, and others like it, unconstitutional, establishing marriage equality nationwide in 2013.	After years of construction delays and engineering controversies, the eastern span of the Bay Bridge opens. At more than $6 billion, it is the costliest public-works project in California history – so far.	Threatened with defunding from the federal government, San Francisco and a dozen other California cities reinforce their sanctuary statutes, and California legislators consider expanding the law statewide.

The Way of Life

In a California dreamworld, you'd wake up with an espresso and a side of wheatgrass and roll down to the beach while the surf's up. Lifeguards wave hello as they go jogging past in sleek bathing suits and sweatproof smartwatches. You skateboard down the boardwalk to your yoga class, where everyone admires your downward dog. A food truck pulls up with your favorite low-carb, sustainable fish tacos with organic mango chipotle salsa...and then you wake up.

Living the Dream

What's that you say? You're not ready for this dream to end? OK, let's hit the snooze button and see how far this California dream takes you.

Snoozing on the beach after yoga class, you awake to find a casting agent hovering over you, blocking your sunlight, imploring you to star in a movie based on a best-selling graphic novel. You say you'll have your lawyer look over the papers, and by your lawyer you mean your roommate who plays one on TV. The conversation is cut short when you get a text to meet up with some friends at a bar.

That casting agent was a stress case – she was, like, all business, dude – so you swing by your medical marijuana dispensary and a tattoo parlor to get 'Peace' inscribed on your bicep in Tibetan script as a reminder to yourself to stay chill. At the bar you're called onstage to guest DJ, and afterwards you tell the bartender how the casting agent harshed your mellow. She recommends a wine country getaway, but you're already doing that Big Sur primal scream chakra-cleansing retreat this weekend. Maybe next time.

You head back to your beach house to update your status on your social-networking profile, alerting your one million online friends to the major events of the day: 'Killer taco, solid downward dog, major tattoo, random movie offer thingy, sick beats.' Then you repeat your nightly self-affirmations: 'I am a child of the universe...I am blessed, or at least not a New Yorker...tomorrow will bring sunshine and possibility...om.'

Riptionary (www.riptionary.com) is the definitive online lexicon of surfer slang, so that you'll know what Californians mean when they say: 'The big mama is fully mackin' some gnarly grinders!'

Regional Identity

Now for the reality check. Any Northern Californian hearing your California dream is bound to get huffy. What, political protests and Silicon Valley start-ups don't factor in your dreams? But Southern Californians will also roll their eyes at these stereotypes: they didn't create NASA's Jet Propulsion Lab and almost half of the world's movies by slacking off.

But there is some truth to your California dreamscape. Some 80% of Californians live near the coast rather than inland, even though California beaches aren't always sunny or swimmable. Self-help, fitness and body modification are major industries throughout California, successfully marketed since the 1970s as 'lite' versions of religious experience – all the agony and ecstasy of the major religions, without all those heavy commandments. Exercise and healthy food help keep Californians among the fittest in the nation. Yet millions of Californians are apparently ill enough to merit medical prescriptions for marijuana. Ahem.

Not everything is invented in Silicon Valley: SoCal innovations include the space shuttle, Mickey Mouse, whitening toothpaste, the Hula-Hoop, Barbie, skateboard and surfboard technology and the Cobb salad.

At least Northern and Southern Californians do have one thing in common: they're all baffled by New Yorkers' delusion that the world revolves around them. Whatever, dudes. We'll just be over here on the Best Coast, building your technology, growing your food and providing your entertainment. No need to thank us, really. (Californians don't resort to sarcasm all that often, but we've totally mastered the eye roll. Insert one here.)

Thousands of Southern Californians practice Santeria, a fusion of Catholicism and Yoruba beliefs brought by West African slaves to the Caribbean, South America and sunny SoCal. Drop by a *botànica* (herbal folk-medicine shop) for charms and candles.

Lifestyle

The charmed existence you dreamed about is a stretch, even in California. Few Californians can afford to spend entire days tanning and networking, what with all the aging UVA rays and sky-high rents out here. Eight of the 10 most expensive US housing markets are in California, and in the two most expensive areas, Newport Beach and Palo Alto, the average house price is over $2.5 million. Only multi millionaires can afford a beach dream-home here. With a modest median household income of $64,500 per year, most Californians rent rather than own.

As for those roommates you dreamed about: if you're a Californian aged 18 to 24, there's a 50/50 possibility that your roomies are your parents. Among adult Californians, one in four live alone, and about half are unmarried. If you're not impressed with your dating options in Californian, stick around: of those who are currently married, about a third won't be in 10 years. Increasingly Californians are shacking up: the number of unmarried cohabiting couples has increased 40% since 1990.

If you're like most Californians, you effectively live in your car. Californians commute an average of 29 minutes each way to work and spend at least $1 out of every $5 earned on car-related expenses. Small wonder that six of the US cities with the highest air-pollution levels are in California. But Californians are zooming ahead of the national energy-use curve in their smog-checked cars, buying more hybrid and fuel-efficient cars than any other state. With all these statewide efforts to spare the air, two of the 25 US cities with the cleanest air are now in California (kudos, Redding and Salinas!).

Almost half of all Californians reside in cities, but most of the other half live in the suburbs, where the cost of living is just as high – only without all the cultural perks of city living. The Silicon Valley hub of San Jose has been ranked the most overpriced city in America, yet other Californian cities (especially San Francisco and San Diego) consistently top national quality-of-life indexes, with a sunny outlook dubbed the 'Golden State of Mind.' According to a recent Cambridge University study, creativity, imagination, intellectualism and mellowness are all defining characteristics of Californians, compared with inhabitants of other US states.

Homelessness is not part of the California dream, but it's a reality for at least 115,000 Californians, representing more than 20% of the total US homeless population. Some are teens who have run away or been kicked out by their families, but the largest contingent of homeless are US military veterans – 25% of the nation's homeless vets are in California. What's more, in the 1970s mental-health programs were cut, and state-funded drug treatment programs were dropped in the 1980s, leaving many Californians with mental illnesses and substance-abuse problems no place to go.

Also standing in line at homeless shelters are the working poor, unable to afford to rent even a small apartment on minimum-wage salaries. Recent California minimum-wage increases still don't cover the cost of living here – you'd need to earn $33 an hour to pay the average rent in Los Angeles. Rather than addressing the underlying causes of homelessness, some California cities have criminalized loitering, panhandling and even sitting on sidewalks. More than three out of every 1000 Californians already sit in the state's notoriously overcrowded jails, mostly for minor drug-related offenses.

Population & Multiculturalism

With more than 39 million residents, California has more people than any other state. One in every eight Americans lives here. It's also one of the fastest-growing states, with three of America's 10 biggest cities (Los Angeles, San Diego and San Jose) and more than 300,000 newcomers each year. Although the high Sierras and southern deserts are sparsely populated, California's overall population density is 251 people per square mile – almost triple the national average.

If you were the average Californian, you'd be statistically likely to be Latina, aged about 36 and living in densely populated LA, Orange or San Diego Counties. You'd speak more than one language, and there's a one in four chance you were born outside the US. If you were born in the US, the odds are 50/50 you moved here recently from another state.

Far from being a new development, immigration has been key to California's growth since its inception. California was a territory of Mexico and Spain before it became a US state, and has sustained one of the world's most diverse populations ever since. One of every four immigrants to the US lands in California, with twice as many coming from Asia as from Latin America. Most arrivals in recent years come from Mexico, followed by China, the Philippines, Vietnam and India. But most immigrants don't arrive as strangers – they move to California to join family members already settled here. An estimated three million undocumented immigrants currently live in California, often with documented or naturalized family members.

Most Californians see their state as a laid-back, open-minded multicultural society that gives everyone a chance to live the American dream. Sanctuary laws reinforce social acceptance of all who become Californian, no matter whether they arrive here seeking safety, family, opportunity, or fellow dreamers. No one is expected to give up their cultural or personal identity to become Californian: Chicano pride, Black Power and gay pride all built political bases here.

Hard-won civil rights are a source of pride in California, but equal opportunity remains elusive. Historically California's Chinatowns, Japantowns and other ethnic enclaves were often the result of segregationist sentiment, not created by choice. Today Californian cities are among the nation's most racially integrated, yet some neighborhoods remain quite segregated by income, language, education and – even here in the birthplace of the web – internet access.

California is one of the most religiously diverse US states, but also one of the least religious. Less than half of Californians consider religion very important, and a quarter of all Californians profess no religion at all. Of those Californians who do practice a religion, a third identify as Protestant and about a quarter are Catholic. California is home to most of the nation's practicing Hindus, the biggest Jewish community outside New York, a sizable Muslim community and the largest number of Buddhists anywhere outside Asia. Californians have also established their own spiritual practices, including the Church of Satan, EST self-help movement and UFO cults.

Californian culture reflects the composite identity of the state. Over one third of the nation's Asian American population lives in California, and Latinos became the state's majority ethnic group in 2014. As relatively late arrivals during the WWII shipping boom, California's African Americans have historically represented just 7% of the population, but they have been a driving force in California popular culture and politics. The bond holding the Golden State together isn't a shared ethnic background, religion, or common language: it's choosing to be Californian.

In his column 'iAsk a Mexican!', *OC Weekly* comic columnist Gustavo Arellano tackles such burning Californian questions as whether sour cream belongs on burritos, alongside weighty issues such as gentrification and immigrant rights. Read it at www.ocweekly.com.

THE WAY OF LIFE POPULATION & MULTICULTURALISM

LOVE IS IN THE AIR IN CALIFORNIA

California believes in love, and isn't afraid to show it. In 2004 San Francisco Mayor Gavin Newsom issued marriage licenses to same-sex couples in defiance of the federal Defense of Marriage Act, and 4000 same-sex couples promptly got hitched. Four years later California courts found banning same-sex marriage in conflict with California's constitutional protections against discrimination. Opponents rallied around Proposition 8, amending the state's constitution to limit marriage to between one man and one woman, and it narrowly passed.

But California civil-rights activists took their case against Prop 8 all the way to the US Supreme Court, which decided to uphold a lower court's ruling that the measure was unconstitutional. The 2013 decision was a definitive blow against laws blocking marriage equality, and promptly sparked a $2.6-billion wedding boom nationwide. Meanwhile in California, star-crossed same-sex couples were finally able to celebrate their legal marriages, including some getting hitched for the third time to the same person. Massive LGBT Pride parades across the state doubled as wedding receptions, with free cake, veils and garters galore, and an eternally romantic hashtag: #LoveWins.

Sports

Californians seem laid-back by nature, until you see them at a game. California has more professional sports teams than any other state, and loyalties to NBA basketball, NFL football and major-league baseball teams run deep. To catch them in action, get your wallet ready. Tickets aren't cheap but sell out fast, especially for Golden State Warriors or LA Lakers basketball, Oakland Raiders or San Diego Chargers football, San Francisco Giants or LA Dodgers baseball, or LA Kings or San Jose Sharks hockey. Except for championship playoffs, the regular season for major-league baseball runs from April to September, NFL football from September to January, NBA basketball from October to April, WNBA basketball from May to August, NHL ice hockey from October to April and major-league soccer from April to October.

Over 200 different languages are spoken in California, with Spanish, Chinese, Tagalog, Russian, Hindi and Arabic in the top 10. Around 44% of state residents speak a language other than English at home.

According to a recent study, Californians are less likely to be couch potatoes than other Americans. But when Californian teams play against one another, the streets empty and all eyes are on the game. The ultimate grudge matches are between the San Diego Chargers and Oakland Raiders, the San Francisco Giants and LA Dodgers, and the LA Lakers and LA Clippers. California college-sports rivalries are equally fierce, especially UC Berkeley's Cal Bears versus the Stanford University Cardinals and the USC Trojans versus UCLA Bruins.

To see small but dedicated crowds of hometown fans – and score cheaper tickets – watch women's pro basketball in LA, men's pro basketball in Sacramento, pro hockey in Anaheim or pro soccer in San Jose and LA. You may luck onto tickets for San Diego Padres and Anaheim Angels major-league baseball games, and you can catch minor-league baseball teams up and down the state, especially the Sacramento River Cats.

Californians have a reputation as daredevils, and if you can't join them, you can always watch them from the comfort of a beach chair. Surfing first hit California in 1914, when Irish-Hawaiian surfer George Freeth gave demonstrations at Huntington Beach in Orange County. But it was the Santa Cruz TV legend Gidget the surfer girl who turned this Hawaiian pastime into a California obsession, and she is duly honored alongside California surf legends in the city's Surfing Museum (p289). Today the annual Titans of Mavericks big-wave riding competition in Half Moon Bay is the world's premier surfing challenge, with pro surfers risking life and limb to take on waves 10 stories high.

On Location: Film & TV

Picture Orson Welles whispering 'Rosebud,' Judy Garland clicking her ruby-red heels three times, or the Terminator threatening 'I'll be back': California is where these iconic film images came to life. Shakespeare claimed 'all the world's a stage,' but in California, it's actually more of a movie set. With over 40 TV shows and scores of movies shot here annually, every palm-lined boulevard or beach seems to come with its own IMDb resume.

The Industry

You might know it as the TV and movie business, but to Southern Californians it's simply 'the Industry.' It all began in the humble orchards of Hollywoodland, a residential suburb of Los Angeles where entrepreneurial moviemakers established studios in the early 20th century. Within a few years, immigrants turned a humble orchard into Hollywood. In 1915 Polish immigrant Samuel Goldwyn joined with Cecil B DeMille to form Paramount Studios, while German-born Carl Laemmle opened nearby Universal Studios, selling lunch to curious guests to help underwrite his moving pictures. A few years later, a family of Polish immigrants arrived from Canada, and Jack Warner and his brothers soon set up a movie studio of their own.

With perpetually balmy weather and more than 315 days of sunshine a year, SoCal proved an ideal shooting location, and moviemaking flourished. In those early Wild West movie-making days, patent holders such as Thomas Edison sent agents to collect payments, or repossess movie equipment. Fledgling filmmakers saw them coming, and made runs for the Mexican border with their equipment. Palm Springs became a favorite weekend hideaway for Hollywood stars, partly because its distance from LA (just under 100 miles) was as far as they could travel under restrictive studio contracts.

Seemingly overnight, Hollywood studios made movie magic. Fans lined up for premieres in LA movie palaces for red-carpet glimpses of early silent-film stars such as Charlie Chaplin and Harold Lloyd. Moviegoers nationwide celebrated the first big Hollywood wedding in 1920, when swashbuckler Douglas Fairbanks married 'America's sweetheart' Mary Pickford. Years later, their divorce would be one of Hollywood's biggest scandals,

1913
Cecil B DeMille directs the first full-length Hollywood feature movie: a silent Western drama called *The Squaw Man*.

1927
The silent film era ends with the first talkie, *The Jazz Singer*. Sid Grauman opens his Chinese Theatre in Hollywood, where stars have been leaving their handprints ever since.

1939
The Wizard of Oz is the first wide-release movie shown in glorious Technicolor. It's a hit, but loses the Oscar for Best Picture to *Gone with the Wind*. Both were filmed in Culver City.

1950s
On a witch hunt for communists, the federal House Un-American Activities Committee investigates and blacklists many Hollywood actors, directors and screenwriters.

1975
The age of the modern blockbuster begins with the thriller *Jaws,* by a young filmmaker named Steven Spielberg, whose later blockbusters include *ET* and *Jurassic Park*.

2001
In the Hollywood & Highland Complex on Hollywood Blvd, the new Kodak (now Dolby) Theatre becomes the permanent home of the Academy Awards ceremony.

but the United Artists studio they founded with Charlie Chaplin endures today. When the silent-movie era gave way to 'talkies' with the 1927 musical *The Jazz Singer*, the world hummed along.

Hollywood & Beyond

By the 1920s Hollywood had become the industry's social and financial hub, but it's a myth that most movie production took place there. Of the major studios, only Paramount Pictures is in Hollywood proper, surrounded by block after block of production-related businesses, such as lighting and post-production. Most movies have long been shot elsewhere around LA, in Culver City (at MGM, now Sony Pictures), Studio City (at Universal Studios) and Burbank (at Warner Bros and later Disney).

Moviemaking hasn't been limited to LA, either. Founded in 1910, the American Film Manufacturing Company (aka Flying 'A' Studios) churned out box-office hits in San Diego and then Santa Barbara. Balboa Studios in Long Beach was another major silent-era dream factory. Contemporary movie-production companies based in the San Francisco Bay Area include Francis Ford Coppola's American Zoetrope, Pixar Animation Studios and George Lucas' Industrial Light & Magic. Both San Francisco and LA remain major hubs for independent filmmakers and documentarians.

But not every Californian you meet is in the Industry, even in Tinseltown. The Los Angeles Economic Development Council reports that only 1.6% of people living in LA County today are employed directly in film, TV and radio production. The high cost of filming has sent location scouts far beyond LA's San Fernando Valley (where most of California's movie and TV studios are found) to Vancouver, Toronto and Montreal, where film production crews are welcomed with open arms (and sweet deals) to 'Hollywood North.' California recently passed a $330 million tax

From the 1930s to the 1950s, many famous US writers, including F Scott Fitzgerald, Dorothy Parker, Truman Capote, William Faulkner and Tennessee Williams, did stints as Hollywood screenwriters.

CALIFORNIA ON CELLULOID

California is a sneaky scene-stealer in many Hollywood films, stepping out of the background to become a main topic and character in its own right. From sunny capers to moody film-noir mysteries, California has proved its versatility in these movie classics:

The Maltese Falcon (1941) John Huston directs Humphrey Bogart as Sam Spade, the classic San Francisco private eye.

Sunset Boulevard (1950) Billy Wilder's classic stars Gloria Swanson and William Holden in a bonfire of Hollywood vanities.

Vertigo (1958) The Golden Gate Bridge dazzles and dizzies in Alfred Hitchcock's noir thriller.

The Graduate (1967) Dustin Hoffman flees status-obsessed California suburbia to search for meaning, heading across the Bay Bridge to Berkeley (in the wrong direction).

Chinatown (1974) Roman Polanski's gripping version of the early-20th-century water wars that made and nearly broke LA.

Blade Runner (1982) Ridley Scott's sci-fi cyberpunk thriller projects a future LA of high-rise corporate fortresses and chaotic streets.

The Player (1992) Directed by Robert Altman and starring Tim Robbins, this satire on 'the Industry' features dozens of cameos by actors spoofing themselves.

The Big Lebowski (1998) Through myriad misadventures in the Coen brothers' zany LA farce, The Dude abides.

Milk (2008) Gus Van Sant directs Sean Penn in an Oscar-winning performance as Harvey Milk, the first openly gay man to hold a major US political office.

credit to lure filmmakers back to Cali, and it seems to be working – more 2016 TV pilots were shot here than in any other location.

Still, for Hollywood dreamers and movie buffs, LA remains *the* place for a pilgrimage. You can tour major movie studios, be part of a live TV studio audience, line up alongside the red carpet for an awards ceremony, catch movie premieres at film festivals, wander the Hollywood Walk of Fame and discover what it's like to live, dine and party with the stars.

The Art of Animation

In 1923 a young cartoonist named Walt Disney arrived in LA, and within five years he had a hit called *Steamboat Willie* and a breakout star called Mickey Mouse. That film spawned the entire Disney empire, and dozens of other California animation studios have followed with films, TV programs and special effects. Among the most beloved are Warner Bros (Bugs Bunny et al in *Looney Tunes*), Hanna-Barbera (*The Flintstones, The Jetsons, Yogi Bear* and *Scooby-Doo*), DreamWorks (*Shrek, Madagascar, Kung-Fu Panda*) and Film Roman (*The Simpsons*). Even if much of the hands-on work takes place overseas (in places such as South Korea), concept and supervision still takes place in LA and the San Francisco Bay Area.

In San Francisco, George Lucas' Industrial Light & Magic is made up of a team of high-tech wizards who produce computer-generated special effects for blockbuster series such as *Star Wars, Jurassic Park, Indiana Jones* and *Harry Potter*. Just across the San Francisco Bay, Pixar Animation Studios has produced an unbroken string of animated hits, including *Toy Story, Finding Dory, Inside Out, WALL-E, Cars* and *Brave*.

The Small Screen

After a year of tinkering, San Francisco inventor Philo Farnsworth transmitted the first television broadcast in 1927 of...a straight line. Giving viewers something actually interesting to watch would take a few more years. The first TV station began broadcasting in Los Angeles in 1931, beaming iconic images of California into living rooms across America and around the world with *Dragnet* (1950s), *The Beverly Hillbillies* (1960s), *The Brady Bunch* and *Charlie's Angels* (1970s), *LA Law* (1980s), and *Baywatch, Buffy the Vampire Slayer* and *The Fresh Prince of Bel-Air* (1990s). *Beverly Hills 90210* (1990s) made that LA zip code into a status symbol, while *The OC* (2000s) glamorized Orange County and *Silicon Valley* (2014–now) satirizes NorCal start-ups. Reality-TV fans will recognize Southern California locations from *Top Chef, Real Housewives of Orange County* and *Keeping Up with the Kardashians*.

A suburban San Francisco start-up changed the TV game in 2005, launching a streaming video on a platform called YouTube. With on-demand streaming services competing with cable channels to launch original series, we are entering a new golden age of California television. Netflix Studios (in Silicon Valley and LA), Amazon Studios (Santa Monica) and Hulu Studios (Santa Monica) are churning out original series, feeding binge-watching cravings with futuristic dystopias such as *Stranger Things, Man in the High Castle* and *The Handmaid's Tale*. Only time will tell if streaming services will also yield breakthrough Californian comedies to compare with Showtime's sharp-witted suburban pot-growing dramedy *Weeds*, Showtime's *Californication* adventures of a successful New York novelist gone Hollywood, or HBO's *Curb Your Enthusiasm*, an insider satire of the industry featuring *Seinfeld* co-creator Larry David and Hollywood celebrities playing themselves.

Top California Film Festivals

AFI Fest (www.afi.com/atifest)

LA Film Fest (www.lafilmfest.com)

Frameline LGBT Film Fest (www.frameline.org)

Palm Springs International Film Festival (www.psfilmfest.org)

San Francisco International Film Festival (www.sffs.org)

Sonoma International Film Festival (www.sonomafilmfest.org)

Music & the Arts

Go ahead and mock, but when Californians thank their lucky stars – or good karma, or the goddess – that they don't live in New York, they're not just talking about beach weather. This place has long supported thriving music and arts scenes that aren't afraid to be completely independent, even outlandish. In the US's most racially and ethnically diverse state, expect eclectic playlists, involving performances and vivid shows of pride and individuality.

Music

In your California dream, you're a DJ – so what kind of music do you play? Beach Boys covers, West Coast rap, bluegrass, original punk, classic soul, hard bop, heavy-metal riffs or opera? To please Californian crowds, try all of the above. To hear the world's most eclectic playlist, just walk down a city street in California.

Much of the traditional recording industry is based in LA, and SoCal's film and TV industries have produced many pop princesses and airbrushed boy bands. But the NorCal DIY tech approach is launching YouTube artists daily, and encouraging Californians to make strange sounds in their garages with Moog synthesizers and keytars. None of this would be possible without California's decades of innovation, musical oddities and wild dance parties.

An Eclectic Early Soundtrack

Chronologically speaking, Mexican folk music arrived in California first, during the rancho era. The gold rush brought an influx of new arrivals, and rancheros had to belt to be heard over competing sounds of bluegrass, Chinese classical music and bawdy dancehall ragtime. But Italian opera arias became the breakout hits of early California, with divas paid fortunes in gold dust for encores.

By the turn of the 20th century, the city of San Francisco alone had 20 concert and opera halls before the 1906 earthquake literally brought down the houses. Performers converged on the shattered city for marathon free public performances that turned arias into anthems for the city's rebirth. San Francisco's War Memorial Opera House today is home to North America's second-largest opera company, after NYC's Metropolitan Opera.

Swing Jazz, Blues & Soul

Swing was the next big thing to hit California. In the 1930s and '40s, big bands sparked a Lindy-Hopping craze in LA, and sailors on shore leave hit San Francisco's integrated underground jazz clubs.

California's African American community grew with the 'Great Migration' during the WWII shipping and manufacturing boom, and from this thriving scene emerged the West Coast blues sound. Texas-born bluesman T-Bone Walker worked in LA's Central Ave clubs before making hit records of his electric-guitar stylings for Capitol Records. Throughout the 1940s and '50s, West Coast blues was nurtured in San Francisco and

In the 1950s, the hard-edged, honky-tonk Bakersfield Sound emerged inland in California's Central Valley, where Buck Owens and the Buckaroos and Merle Haggard performed their own twists on Nashville country hits for hard-drinkin' audiences of Dust Bowl migrants and cowboy ranchers.

Oakland by guitarists such as Pee Wee Crayton and Oklahoma-born Lowell Fulson.

With Beat poets riffing over improvised bass lines and audiences finger-snapping their approval, the cool West Coast jazz of Chet Baker and Bay Area–born Dave Brubeck emerged from San Francisco's North Beach neighborhood in the 1950s. Meanwhile, in the African American cultural hub along LA's Central Ave, the hard bop of Charlie Parker and Charles Mingus kept SoCal's jazz scene alive and swinging.

In the 1950s and '60s, doo-wop, rhythm and blues, and soul music were all in steady rotation at nightclubs in South Central LA, considered the 'Harlem of the West.' Soulful singer Sam Cooke ran his own hit-making record label, attracting soul and gospel talent to LA.

Waiting for the Sun: A Rock 'n' Roll History of Los Angeles (1996) by Barney Hoskyns follows the twists and turns of the SoCal music scene from the Beach Boys to Black Flag.

MUSIC & THE ARTS MUSIC

Rockin' Out

The first homegrown rock-and-roll talent to make it big in the 1950s was Richie Valens, born in the San Fernando Valley, whose 'La Bamba' was a rockified version of a Mexican folk song. Dick Dale experimented with reverb effects in Orange County in the 1950s, becoming known as 'the King of the Surf Guitar.' He topped the charts with his band the Del-Tones in the early '60s, influencing everyone from the Beach Boys to Jimi Hendrix – you might recognize his recording of 'Miserlou' from the movie *Pulp Fiction.*

Guitar got psychedelic in 1960s California. When Joan Baez and Bob Dylan had their Northern California fling in the early 1960s, Dylan plugged in his guitar and pioneered folk rock. Janis Joplin and Big Brother & the Holding Company developed their own shambling musical stylings in San Francisco, splintering folk rock into psychedelia. Emerging from the same San Francisco Fillmore scene, Jefferson Airplane turned Lewis Carroll's children's classic *Alice's Adventures in Wonderland* into the psychedelic hit 'White Rabbit.' For many 1960s Fillmore headliners, the show ended too soon with drug overdoses – though for the original jam band, the Grateful Dead, the song remained the same until guitarist Jerry Garcia died in rehab in 1995.

On LA's famous Sunset Strip, LA bands were also blowing minds at the legendary Whisky a Go Go nightclub – especially the Byrds and

PUNK'S NOT DEAD IN CALIFORNIA

In the 1970s American airwaves were jammed with commercial arena rock that record companies paid DJs to shill like laundry soap, inspiring the articulate ire of California rock critics Lester Bangs and Greil Marcus. California teens bored with prepackaged anthems started making their own with secondhand guitars, three chords and crappy amps that added a loud buzz to unleashed fury.

LA punk paralleled the scrappy local skate scene with the hardcore grind of Black Flag from Hermosa Beach and LA's the Germs. LA band X bridged punk and new wave from 1977 to 1987 with John Doe's rockabilly guitar, Exene Cervenka's angsty wail, and disappointed-romantic lyrics inspired by Charles Bukowski and Raymond Chandler. Local LA radio station KROQ rebelled against the tyranny of playlists, putting local punk on the airwaves and launching punk-funk sensations the Red Hot Chili Peppers and Jane's Addiction.

San Francisco's punk scene was arty and absurdist, in rare form with Dead Kennedys singer (and future San Francisco mayoral candidate) Jello Biafra mocking Golden State complacency in 'California Uber Alles.' In one legendary 1978 San Francisco punk show, the Sex Pistols broke up and the all-women Avengers took the punk scene by storm. Green Day and Blink 182 put pop-punk on the radio, but there's nothing like hearing next-gen punk kids rip through all three chords they know in a grimy California club.

the Doors, fronted by the legendary Jim Morrison. But the California sound also got down with iconic funk bands War from Long Beach, Tower of Power from Oakland, and San Francisco's Sly and the Family Stone.

The '70s music scene in LA was divided by zip codes and production values. High in the hills above the Sunset Strip was Laurel Canyon, where Joni Mitchell, David Crosby and Graham Nash held legendary jam sessions. Meanwhile down at Sunset Strip's seedy Tropicana Motel, local characters found their way into the bluesy storytelling of singer-songwriters Tom Waits and Rickie Lee Jones. Record labels produced arena bands to a high polish, creating the slick country-pop of the Eagles and Jackson Browne and finessing Mexican–American fusion with Linda Ronstadt and Santana. But in tiny clubs with battered guitars, a bunch of kids (Black Flag, The Germs, X) were making up songs and the LA punk scene as they went along.

Post-Punk to Pop

The 1980s saw the rise of such influential LA crossover bands as Bad Religion (punk) and Suicidal Tendencies (hardcore/thrash), while more mainstream all-female bands the Bangles and the Go-Gos, new wavers Oingo Boingo, and California rockers Jane's Addiction and Red Hot Chili Peppers took the world by storm. Hollywood's Guns N' Roses set the '80s standard for arena rock, while San Francisco's Metallica showed the world how to headbang with a vengeance. Avant-garde rocker Frank Zappa earned a cult following and a rare hit with the 1982 single *Valley Girl*, in which his 14-year-old daughter Moon Unit taught the rest of America to say 'Omig*o*-o-o-od!' like an LA teenager.

By the 1990s California's alternative rock acts took the national stage, including songwriter Beck, political rockers Rage Against the Machine and Orange County's ska-rockers No Doubt, fronted by Gwen Stefani. Hailing from East LA, Los Lobos was king of the Chicano (Mexican–American) bands, an honor that has since passed to Ozomatli.

Berkeley's 924 Gilman Street club revived punk in the '90s, launching the career of Grammy Award–winning Green Day. Riding the wave were Berkeley ska-punk band Rancid, surf-punk Sublime from Long Beach, San Diego–based pop-punksters Blink 182, and Orange County's resident loudmouths, the Offspring.

Rap & Hip-Hop

Since the 1980s, West Coast rap and hip-hop have spoken truth and hit the beat. When the N.W.A. album *Straight Outta Compton* was released in 1988, it launched the careers of Eazy E, Ice Cube and Dr Dre, and established gangsta rap. Dre co-founded Death Row Records, which helped launch megawatt talents such as Long Beach bad boys Snoop Dogg, Warren G and the late Tupac Shakur. The son of a Black Panther leader who'd fallen on hard times, Tupac combined party songs and hard truths learned on Oakland streets until his untimely shooting in 1996 in a suspected East Coast/West Coast rap feud. Feuds also checkered the musical career of LA rapper Game, whose 2011 *The R.E.D. Album* brought together an all-star lineup of Diddy, Dr Dre, Snoop Dogg and more.

Throughout the 1980s and '90s, California maintained a grassroots hip-hop scene in Oakland and LA. Reacting against the increasing commercialization of hip-hop in the late 1990s, the Bay Area scene produced underground 'hyphy' (short for hyperactive) artists such as E-40. Political commentary and funk hooks have become signatures of East Bay groups Blackalicious, The Coup and Michael Franti & Spearhead.

Tune into the 'Morning Becomes Eclectic' show on Southern California's KCRW radio station (www.kcrw.com) for live in-studio performances and musician interviews.

Architecture

There's more to California than beach houses and boardwalks. Californians have adapted imported styles to the climate and available materials, building cool, adobe-inspired houses in San Diego and fog-resistant redwood-shingle houses in Mendocino. After a century and a half of Californians grafting on inspired influences and eccentric details as the mood strikes them, the element of the unexpected is everywhere: tiled Maya deco facades in Oakland, Shinto-inspired archways in LA, English thatched roofs in Carmel and chinoiserie streetlights in San Francisco. California's architecture was postmodern before the word even existed.

Spanish Missions & Victorian Queens

The first Spanish missions were built around courtyards, using materials that Native Californians and Spaniards found on hand: adobe, limestone and grass. Many missions crumbled into disrepair as the church's influence waned, but the style remained practical for the climate. Early California settlers later adapted it into the rancho adobe style, as seen in Downtown LA's El Pueblo de Los Angeles and San Diego's Old Town.

Once the mid-19th-century gold rush was on, California's nouveau riche imported materials to construct grand mansions matching European fashions. Many millionaires favored the gilded Queen Anne style, raising the stakes with ornamental excess. Outrageous examples of colorful, gingerbread-swagged Victorian 'Painted Ladies' can be found in San Francisco, Ferndale and Eureka.

But Californian architecture has always had its contrarian streak. Many turn-of-the-20th-century architects rejected frilly Victorian styles in favor of the simpler, classical lines of Spanish designs. Spanish Colonial Revival architecture (also known as Mission Revival style) recalls early California missions with their restrained functional details: arched doors and windows, long covered porches, fountain courtyards, solid walls and red-tile roofs. Downtown Santa Barbara showcases this revival style, as do stately buildings in San Diego's Balboa Park, Scotty's Castle in Death Valley and several SoCal train depots, including in Downtown LA, San Diego, San Juan Capistrano and Santa Barbara, as well as Kelso Depot in the Mojave National Preserve.

Arts & Crafts & Art Deco

Simplicity and harmony were hallmarks of California's early 20th-century Arts and Crafts style. Influenced by both Japanese design principles and England's Arts and Crafts movement, its woodwork and handmade touches marked a deliberate departure from the industrial revolution's mechanization. Bernard Maybeck and Julia Morgan in Northern California, and SoCal architects Charles and Henry Greene, popularized the versatile one-story bungalow. Today you'll spot them in Berkeley and Pasadena with their overhanging eaves, airy terraces and sleeping porches harmonizing warm, livable interiors with the natural environment outdoors.

California was cosmopolitan from the start, and couldn't be limited to any one set of international influences. In the 1920s, the international art-deco style took elements from the ancient world – Mayan glyphs, Egyptian pillars, Babylonian ziggurats – and flattened them into modern motifs to cap stark facades and outline streamlined skyscrapers in Oakland, San Francisco and LA. Streamline moderne kept decoration to a minimum, and mimicked the aerodynamic look of ocean liners and airplanes.

Post-Modern Evolutions

True to its mythic nature, California couldn't help wanting to embellish the facts a little, veering away from strict high modernism to add unlikely postmodern shapes to the local landscape. Hearst Castle is an early

Oddball California Architecture

Hearst Castle

Winchester Mystery House

Tor House

Theme Building, LAX Airport

Wigwam Motel

Integratron

MUSIC & THE ARTS ARCHITECTURE

CALIFORNIA'S NAKED ARCHITECTURE

Clothing-optional California has never been shy about showcasing its assets. Starting in the 1960s, California embraced the stripped-down, glass-wall aesthetics of the International Style championed by Bauhaus architects Walter Gropius, Ludwig Mies van der Rohe and Le Corbusier. Open floor plans and floor-to-ceiling windows were ideally suited to the see-and-be-seen culture of Southern California.

Austrian-born Rudolph Schindler and Richard Neutra brought early modernism to LA and Palm Springs, where the signature desert modern style is still celebrated every February during Modernism Week. Neutra and Schindler were also influenced by Frank Lloyd Wright, who designed LA's Hollyhock House in a style he dubbed 'California Romanza.'

With LA-based designers Charles and Ray Eames, Neutra contributed to the experimental open-plan Case Study Houses, several of which jut out of the LA landscape. You may also recognize Neutra houses from the movies – they've served as filming locations for *Boogie Nights* and *LA Confidential*.

example, built over decades by a patient Julia Morgan to suit William Randolph Hearst's every whim with Greco-Roman columns, Spanish Mission arches and Persian tiles.

In 1997 Richard Meier made his mark on West LA with the Getty Center, a cresting white wave of a building on a sunburned hilltop. Canadian-born Frank Gehry relocated to Santa Monica, and his billowing, sculptural style for LA's Walt Disney Concert Hall winks cheekily at shipshape streamline moderne. Also in Downtown LA, the Cathedral of Our Lady of the Angels, designed by Spanish architect Rafael Moneo, echoes the grand churches of Mexico and Europe from a controversial deconstructivist angle. Renzo Piano's signature inside-out industrial style can be glimpsed in the sawtooth roof and red-steel veins of the Broad in Los Angeles.

The Bay Area's iconic postmodern building is the San Francisco Museum of Modern Art, which Swiss architect Mario Botta capped with a black-and-white striped, marble-clad atrium in 1995 and Snøhetta architects expanded with wings shaped like ship sails in 2016. Lately SF has championed a brand of postmodernism by Pritzker Prize–winning architects that magnify and mimic the great outdoors, especially in Golden Gate Park. Swiss architects Herzog & de Meuron clad the MH de Young Memorial Museum in copper, which promises to oxidize green to match its park setting. Nearby, Renzo Piano literally raised the roof on sustainable design at the LEED platinum-certified California Academy of Sciences, capped by a living-roof garden.

To find museums, art galleries, fine-art exhibition spaces and calendars of upcoming shows throughout SoCal, check out *ArtScene* (www.artscenecal.com) and *Artweek LA* (www.artweek.la) magazines.

Visual Arts

Although the earliest European artists were trained cartographers accompanying Western explorers, their images of California as an island show more imagination than scientific rigor. This mythologizing tendency continued throughout the gold-rush era, as Western artists alternated between caricatures of Wild West debauchery and manifest-destiny propaganda urging pioneers to settle the golden West. The completion of the Transcontinental Railroad in 1869 brought an influx of romantic painters, who produced epic California wilderness landscapes. After the 20th century arrived, homegrown colonies of California impressionist plein-air painters emerged at Laguna Beach and Carmel-by-the-Sea.

With the invention of photography, the improbable truth of California's landscape and its inhabitants was revealed. Pirkle Jones saw expressive potential in California landscape photography after WWII, while San Francisco–born Ansel Adams's sublime photographs had already started doing justice to Yosemite. Adams founded Group f/64 with Edward Weston and

Imogen Cunningham in San Francisco. Berkeley-based Dorothea Lange turned her unflinching lens on the plight of Californian migrant workers in the Great Depression and Japanese Americans forced to enter internment camps during WWII, producing poignant documentary photos.

As the postwar American West became crisscrossed with freeways and divided into planned communities, Californian painters captured the abstract forms of manufactured landscapes on canvas. In San Francisco, Richard Diebenkorn and David Park became leading proponents of Bay Area Figurative Art, while San Francisco–born sculptor Richard Serra captured urban aesthetics in massive, rusting monoliths resembling ship prows and industrial Stonehenges. Meanwhile pop artists captured the ethos of conspicuous consumerism, through Wayne Thiebaud's gumball machines, British émigré David Hockney's LA pools and, above all, Ed Ruscha's studies of SoCal pop culture. In the Bay Area, artists showed their love for rough-and-ready-made 1950s Beat collage, '60s psychedelic rock posters from Fillmore concerts, earthy '70s funk and beautiful-mess punk, and '80s graffiti art.

Today's California contemporary-art scene brings all these influences together with muralist-led social commentary, an obsessive dedication to craft and a new-media milieu pierced by cutting-edge technology. LA's Museum of Contemporary Art puts on provocative and avant-garde shows, as does LACMA's Broad, San Francisco's Museum of Modern Art and the Museum of Contemporary Art San Diego, which specializes in post-1950s pop and conceptual art. To see California-made art at its most experimental, browse the SoCal gallery scenes in Downtown LA and Culver City then check out independent NorCal art spaces in San Francisco's Mission District and the laboratory-like galleries around SoMa's Yerba Buena Center for the Arts.

In 1919 newspaper magnate William Randolph Hearst commissioned California's first licensed female architect, Julia Morgan, to build Hearst Castle. It would take her decades to finish.

Theater

In your California dream you're discovered by a movie talent scout, but most Californian actors actually get their start in theater. Home to about 25% of the nation's professional actors, LA is the USA's second-most influential city for theater, after NYC. Meanwhile San Francisco has been a national hub for experimental theater since the 1960s.

Spaces to watch around LA include the Geffen Playhouse close to UCLA, the Ahmanson Theatre and Mark Taper Forum in Downtown LA, and the Actors' Gang theater, co-founded by actor Tim Robbins. Small theaters flourish in West Hollywood (WeHo) and North Hollywood (NoHo), the West Coast's versions of off- and off-off-Broadway. Influential multicultural theaters include Little Tokyo's East West Players, while critically acclaimed outlying companies include the innovative Long Beach Opera and Orange County's South Coast Repertory in Costa Mesa.

San Francisco's priorities have been obvious since the great earthquake of 1906, when survivors were entertained in tents set up amid the smoldering ruins, and its famous theaters were rebuilt well before City Hall. Today SF is undergoing a performing-arts renaissance. Tickets are affordable and programs sensational at historic theaters, and new venues are opening mid-Market, in the Tenderloin and in North Beach. Major productions destined for the lights of Broadway and London premiere at the American Conservatory Theater, and its new experimental venue, The Strand. The Magic Theatre gained a national reputation in the 1970s, when Sam Shepard was the theater's resident playwright, and it still premieres innovative California playwrights today. An audience-interactive troupe, We Players, stages classic plays, including Shakespearean dramas, at unusual locations such as Alcatraz. Across the Bay the Berkeley Repertory Theatre has launched acclaimed productions based on such unlikely subjects as the rise and fall of Jim Jones' Peoples Temple.

Timeless, rare Ansel Adams photographs are paired with excerpts from canonical Californian writers such as John Steinbeck and Joan Didion in *California: With Classic California Writings* (1997), edited by Andrea Gray Stillman.

By the Book

Californians make up the largest market for books in the US, and read much more than the national average. Skewing the curve is bookish San Francisco, with more writers, playwrights and book purchases per capita than any other US city. The West Coast is a magnet for novelists, poets and storytellers, and California's multicultural literary community today is stronger than ever.

Early Voices of Social Realism

Arguably the most influential author to emerge from California was John Steinbeck, born in Salinas in 1902 in the heart of Central Valley farm country. He explored the lives and struggles of diverse California communities: Mexican American WWI vets adjusting to civilian life in *Tortilla Flat*, flat-broke wharf characters attempting to throw a party on *Cannery Row,* and migrant farm workers just trying to survive the Great Depression in his Pulitzer Prize–winning book *The Grapes of Wrath.* Acclaimed social realist Eugene O'Neill took his 1936 Nobel Prize money and transplanted himself near San Francisco, where he wrote the autobiographical play *Long Day's Journey into Night.*

Novelists took on the myth of California's self-made millionaires, exposing the tarnish on the Gold State. Classics in this vein include Upton Sinclair's *Oil!,* exposing the schemes of real-life LA oil-tycoon Edward Mahoney that resulted in the Teapot Dome bribery scandal. Aldous Huxley's *After Many a Summer* is based on the life of publisher William Randolph Hearst, the reclusive and vengeful media mogul who also inspired the Orson Welles' film *Citizen Kane.* When F Scott Fitzgerald moved to Hollywood to write scripts, he found the inspiration for his final novel, *The Last Tycoon,* the story of a 1930s movie producer slowly working himself to death.

California became synonymous with adventure through the talents of early chroniclers such as Mark Twain and Bret Harte. Professional hell-raiser Jack London was a wild child from the Oakland docks who traveled the world with little more than his wits and a canoe. He became the world's most successful adventurer and travel writer, sailing the seven seas, getting swept up in the Klondike gold rush, and dictating his adventures with an early recording device on his pioneering permaculture ranch in Sonoma.

Feel the pulse of California's heartland in *Highway 99: A Literary Journey Through California's Central Valley* (1996), edited by Oakland-based writer Stan Yogi. It's full of multicultural perspectives, from early European settlers to 20th-century Mexican and Asian immigrant farmers.

Pulp Noir & Science Fiction

With mysterious fog and neon signs to set the mood, San Francisco and Los Angeles became crime-drama pulp-fiction capitals and the setting of choice for noir mystery movies. Dashiell Hammett *(The Maltese Falcon)* made a cynical San Francisco private eye into a modern antihero, while hard-boiled crime writer Raymond Chandler set the scene for murder and double-crossing dames in Santa Monica. The masterminds behind California's 1990s neo-noir crime fiction renaissance were James Ellroy *(LA Confidential),* the late Elmore Leonard *(Get Shorty)* and Walter Mosley *(Devil in a Blue Dress),* whose Easy Rawlins detective novels are set in South Central LA.

California technology has long inspired science fiction. Raised in Berkeley, Philip K Dick imagined dystopian futures, including a Los Angeles ruled by artificial intelligence in *Do Androids Dream of Electric Sheep?* It was adapted into the 1982 sci-fi movie classic *Blade Runner.* Dick's novel *The Man in the High Castle* presents the ultimate what-if scenario: imagine San Francisco circa 1962 if Japan, fascist Italy and Nazi Germany had won WWII. Berkeley-born Ursula K Le Guin *(The Left Hand of Darkness, A Wizard of Earthsea)* brings feminism to the genre of fantasy, imagining parallel realities where heroines confront forces of darkness.

Social Movers & Shakers

After surviving WWII, the Beat Generation refused to fall in line with 1950s conformity, defying McCarthyism with poignant, poetic truths. San Francisco Beat scene luminaries included Jack Kerouac *(On the Road)*, Allen Ginsberg *(Howl)* and Lawrence Ferlinghetti, the Beats' patron publisher who co-founded City Lights Bookstore. Censors called *Howl* obscene, and Ferlinghetti was arrested for publishing it – but he won his trial in a landmark decision for free speech. Beat poets broke style rules and crossed genres, including poet–painter–playwright Kenneth Rexroth and Buddhist philosopher–poet Gary Snyder.

But no author has captured California culture with such unflinching clarity as Joan Didion, whose prose burns through the page like sun on a misty California morning. Her collection of literary nonfiction essays *Slouching Towards Bethlehem* captures 1960s flower power at the exact moment it blooms and wilts. Didion pioneered immersive first-person New Journalism with fellow '60s California chroniclers Hunter S Thompson *(Hells Angels: A Strange and Terrible Saga)* and Tom Wolfe *(The Electric Kool-Aid Acid Test)*.

In the 1970s, Charles Bukowski's semiautobiographical novel *Post Office* captured down-and-out Downtown LA, while Richard Vasquez' *Chicano* took a dramatic look at LA's Latino barrio. Armistead Maupin captured the rise of disco, cults, medical marijuana, feminism and gay pride in 1970s San Francisco as it happened in his serialized *Tales of the City*. Bret Easton Ellis followed the short lives and fast times of coked-up Beverly Hills teenagers in *Less Than Zero*, the definitive chronicle of '80s excess. Amy Tan's *The Joy Luck Club* weaves together the stories of four Chinese immigrants and their American-born daughters in a textured tale of aspiration and survival in San Francisco's Chinatown.

Ever since the rise of California's underground comics in the '60s, no California bookshelf can be considered complete without graphic novels and 'zines. As you travel through California, you'll recognize characters straight out of local comics – arty, angsty teens from Daniel Clowes' *Ghostworld* and *Art School Confidential*, street-corner prophets from Wendy McNaughton's *Meanwhile in San Francisco*, and soul-searching techies from Paul Madonna's *Everything Is Its Own Reward*. To see what's on California's mind lately, pick up the latest copies of literary magazines *The Believer* and *McSweeney's*, founded by author Dave Eggers. You'll find them at his youth literary nonprofit 826 Valencia and its LA offshoot, the Time Travel Mart.

Road-trip through California with local storytellers as your copilots in *My California: Journeys by Great Writers*. Proceeds from purchases via Angel City Press (www.angelcitypress.com) support the California Arts Council.

Each word Berkeley-based US Poet Laureate Robert Hass commits to the page in his Pulitzer Prize–winning *Time and Materials* is as essential and uplifting as a rivet in the Golden Gate Bridge.

BY THE BOOK SOCIAL MOVERS & SHAKERS

READING CALIFORNIA

Crack open these classics from some of California's less-likely literary locations:

Central Coast *Selected Poetry of Robinson Jeffers* – In the looming, windswept pines surrounding his Tor House, Jeffers found inspiration for hauntingly beautiful poems.

Central Valley *Woman Warrior: Memoirs of a Girlhood Among Ghosts* (Maxine Hong Kingston) – A gripping tale of growing up Chinese American, and finding Californian identity.

Gold Country *Roughing It* (Mark Twain) – The master of sardonic wit tells of earthquakes, silver booms and busts, and getting by for a month on a dime in the Wild West.

Sierra Nevada *Riprap and Cold Mountain Poems* (Gary Snyder) – Influenced by Japanese and Chinese spirituality and classical literature, the Beat poet captures the meditative nature of open wilderness.

The Land & Wildlife

You'll never have to leave California for a change of scenery. From snowy peaks to scorching deserts, golden-sand beaches and sun-dappled redwood forests, California is the most biodiverse place in North America. Species that are rare elsewhere thrive in this balmy Mediterranean climate, with its dry summers and mild wet winters. California has more people than any other US state, which puts a tremendous strain on precious natural resources, but for more than 150 years, conservation-minded Californians have worked hard to protect the state's iconic wildlife and natural wonders.

Lay of the Land

California is the third-biggest US state after Alaska and Texas, covering more than 155,000 sq miles – that's larger than 85 of the world's smallest nations. It shares borders with Oregon to the north, Mexico to the south, Nevada and Arizona to the east, and has 840 miles of glorious Pacific shoreline to the west.

Geology & Earthquakes

According to the US Geological Survey, the odds of a magnitude 6.7 or greater earthquake hitting California in the next 30 years are 99.7%... but the odds of getting hit by a car in that time are far higher. Might as well take that California vacation now.

California is a complex geologic landscape formed from fragments of rock and earth crust squeezed together as the North American continent drifted westward over hundreds of millions of years. Crumpled coastal ranges, fault lines rippling through the Central Valley and jagged, still-rising Sierra Nevada mountains all reveal gigantic forces at work, as the continental and ocean plates crush together.

Everything changed about 25 million years ago, when the ocean plates stopped colliding and instead started sliding against each other, creating the massive San Andreas Fault. This contact zone catches and slips, rattling California with an ongoing succession of tremors and earthquakes.

In 1906 the state's most famous earthquake measured 7.8 on the Richter scale and demolished San Francisco, leaving more than 3000 people dead. The Bay Area was again badly shaken in 1989, when the Loma Prieta earthquake (6.9) caused a section of the Bay Bridge to collapse. In Los Angeles the last 'big one' was in 1994, when the Northridge quake (6.7) caused parts of the Santa Monica Fwy to fall down, resulting in damage that made it the most costly quake in US history.

The Coast to the Central Valley

Rugged mountains take the brunt of winter storms along California's coast, leaving inland areas more protected. San Francisco marks the midpoint of the Coast Ranges, with fog swirling along the sparsely populated North Coast. To the south, beach communities enjoy balmier climates along the Central and Southern California coasts.

The northernmost reaches of the Coast Ranges get 120in of rain in a typical year, and persistent summer fog contributes another 12in of precipitation in some spots. This may not sound like the best climate for beach-going, but California's northern coastal lowlands are sublime for coastal wine tasting. Nutrient-rich soils and abundant moisture foster stands of towering coast redwoods, growing as far south as Big Sur and all the way north to Oregon.

On their eastern flanks, the Coast Ranges taper into gently rolling hills that slide into the sprawling Central Valley. Once an inland sea, this flat basin is now an agricultural powerhouse producing about half of America's fruits, nuts and vegetables. Stretching about 450 miles long and 50 miles wide, the valley sees about as much rainfall as a desert, but gets huge volumes of water runoff from the Sierra Nevada.

Before the arrival of Europeans, the Central Valley was a natural wonderland – vast marshes with flocks of geese that blackened the sky, grasslands carpeted with flowers sniffed by millions of antelopes, elk and grizzly bears. Virtually this entire landscape has been plowed under and replaced with non-native plants (including agricultural crops and vineyards) and livestock ranches. So when you savor your next great California meal, raise a glass to the flora and fauna that came before you.

Browse through more than 1200 aerial photos covering almost every mile of California's gorgeously rugged coastline, stretching from Oregon to Mexico, at www.california coastline.org.

Mountain Ranges

On the eastern side of the Central Valley looms California's most prominent topographic feature: the Sierra Nevada, nicknamed the 'Range of Light' by conservationist John Muir. At 400 miles long and 70 miles wide, this is one of the world's largest mountain ranges, punctuated with 13 peaks over 14,000ft high. The vast wilderness of the High Sierra (mostly above 9000ft) is an astounding landscape of shrinking glaciers, sculpted granite peaks and remote canyons. This landscape is beautiful to look at but difficult to access, and it was one of the greatest challenges for 19th-century settlers attempting to reach California.

The soaring Sierra Nevada captures storm systems and drains them of their water, with most of the precipitation above 3000ft turning to snow, creating a premier winter-sports destination. Melting snow flows down into a half-dozen major river systems on the range's western and eastern slopes, providing the vast majority of water needed for agriculture in the Central Valley and for the metro areas of San Francisco and LA.

At its northern end, the Sierra Nevada merges imperceptibly into the volcanic Cascade Mountains, which continue north into Oregon and Washington. At its southern end, the Sierra Nevada makes a funny westward hook and connects via the Transverse Ranges (one of the USA's few east–west mountain ranges) to the southern Coast Ranges.

California claims both the highest point in contiguous US (Mt Whitney, 14,505ft) and the lowest elevation in North America (Badwater, Death Valley, 282ft below sea level) – and they're only 90 miles apart, as the condor flies.

The Deserts & Beyond

With the west slope of the Sierra Nevada capturing most of the precipitation, lands east of the Sierra crest are dry and desertlike, receiving less than 10in of rain a year. Some valleys at the eastern foot of the Sierra Nevada, however, are well watered by creeks, so that they're able to support livestock and agriculture.

At the western edge of the Great Basin, the elevated Modoc Plateau in far northeastern California is a cold desert blanketed by hardy sagebrush shrubs and juniper trees. Temperatures increase as you head south, with a prominent transition on the descent from Mono Lake into the Owens Valley east of the Sierra Nevada. This southern hot desert (part of the

CALIFORNIA: ALMOST AN ISLAND

Cut off from the rest of North America by the soaring peaks of the Sierra Nevada, California is as biologically distinct as an island. Under these biologically isolated conditions, evolution and local adaptation have yielded unique plants and animals ranging from bristlecone pines in the north, to Joshua trees in the south. California ranks first in the nation for its number of endemic plants, amphibians, reptiles, freshwater fish and mammals. In fact, 30% of all plant species, 50% of all bird species and 50% of all mammal species in the USA can be found here.

Mojave Desert) includes Death Valley, one of the hottest places on the planet. Further south the Mojave Desert morphs into the Colorado Desert (part of Mexico's greater Sonoran Desert) around the Salton Sea.

California's Flora & Fauna

Although the staggering numbers of animals that greeted the first foreign settlers are now distant memories, you can still easily spot wildlife thriving in California. Some are only shadow populations, and some are actually endangered – all the more reason to take the opportunity to stop by California's designated wildlife areas to appreciate their presence and support their conservation.

Peak mating season for northern elephant seals along California's coast just happens to coincide with Valentine's Day (February 14).

Marine Mammals

Spend even one day along California's coast and you may spot pods of bottle-nosed dolphins and porpoises swimming, canoodling and cavorting in the ocean. Playful sea otters and harbor seals typically stick closer to shore, especially around public piers and protected bays. Since the 1989 earthquake, sea lions have taken to sunbathing on San Francisco's Pier 39, where delighted tourists watch the city's resident beach bums nap, goof off and recover from their seafood dinners. To see more wild pinnipeds, visit Point Lobos State Natural Reserve near Monterey, or Channel Islands National Park in Southern California.

Once threatened by extinction, gray whales now migrate in growing numbers along California's coast between December and April. Adult whales live up to 60 years, grow longer than a city bus and can weigh up to 40 tons, making quite a splash when they leap out of the water. Every year they travel from summertime feeding grounds in the arctic Bering Sea, down to southern breeding grounds off Baja California then all the way back up again, making a 6000-mile round trip.

Also almost hunted to extinction by the late 19th century for their oil-rich blubber, northern elephant seals have made a remarkable comeback along California's coast. North of Santa Cruz, Año Nuevo State Reserve is a major breeding ground for northern elephant seals. California's biggest elephant seal colony is found at Piedras Blancas, south of Big Sur. There's a smaller rookery at Point Reyes National Seashore in Marin County. When marine mammals are hurt or stranded, they're cared for at Marin's Marine Mammal Center, where you can meet rescued seals and learn how you can help protect their habitats.

The Audubon Society's California chapter website (www.ca.audubon.org) offers helpful birding checklists, photos and descriptions of key species, conservation news and a Pacific Flyway blog (www.audublog.org).

Land Mammals

Lumbering across California's flag is the state mascot: the grizzly bear. Grizzlies once roamed California's beaches and grasslands in large numbers, eating everything from acorns to whale carcasses. Grizzlies were particularly abundant in the Central Valley, but retreated upslope into the Sierra Nevada as they were hunted to extinction in the 1920s.

California's mountain forests are still home to an estimated 25,000 to 30,000 black bears, the grizzlies' smaller cousins. Despite their name, their fur ranges in color from black to dark brown, auburn or even blond. These burly omnivores feed on berries, nuts, roots, grasses, insects, eggs, small mammals and fish, but can become a nuisance around campgrounds and cabins where food and trash are not secured.

As settlers moved into California in the 19th century, many other large mammals fared almost as poorly as grizzlies. Immense herds of tule elk and antelope in the Central Valley were particularly hard hit, with antelope retreating in small numbers to the northeastern corner of the state, and tule elk hunted into near-extinction. A small remnant herd was moved to Point Reyes, where it has since rebounded.

Geography Map

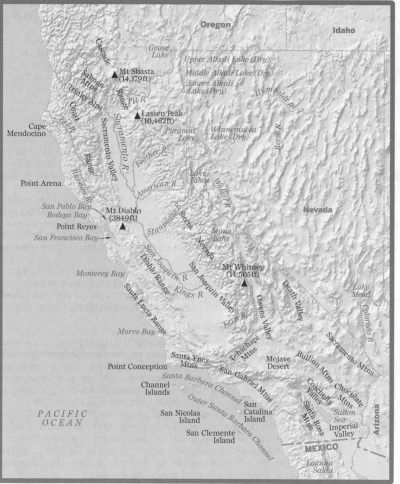

Mountain lions (also called cougars) hunt throughout California's mountains and forests, especially in areas teeming with deer. Solitary lions can grow 8ft in length and weigh 175lb, and are formidable predators. Few attacks on humans have occurred, happening mostly where suburbs have encroached on the lions' wilderness hunting grounds.

Birds & Butterflies

You might think this picture-postcard state is made for tourists, but California is totally for the birds. California is an essential stop on the migratory Pacific Flyway between Alaska and Mexico. Almost half the bird species in North America use the state's wildlife refuges and nature preserves for rest and refueling. Migration peaks during the wetter winter season starting in October/November, when two million fowl gather at the Klamath Basin National Wildlife Refuges for the world's biggest game of duck, duck, goose.

CALIFORNIA'S DESERT CRITTERS

California's deserts are far from deserted, but most animals are too smart to hang out in the daytime heat. Most come out only in the cool of the night, as bats do. Roadrunners (black-and-white mottled ground cuckoos) can often be spotted on roadsides – you'll recognize them from their long tails and punk-style Mohawks. Other desert inhabitants include burrowing kit foxes, tree-climbing gray foxes, hopping jackrabbits, kangaroo rats, slow-moving (and endangered) desert tortoises and a variety of snakes, lizards and spiders. Desert bighorn sheep and migrating birds flock to watering holes, often around seasonal springs and native fan-palm oases – look for them in Joshua Tree National Park and Anza-Borrego Desert State Park.

Year-round you can see birds dotting California's beaches, estuaries and bays, where herons, cormorants, shorebirds and gulls gather. Point Reyes National Seashore and the Channel Islands are prime year-round bird-watching spots.

As you drive along the Big Sur coastline, look skyward to spot endangered California condors. You may also spot condors inland, soaring over Pinnacles National Park and the Los Padres National Forest. Keep an eye out for regal bald eagles around their winter home at Big Bear Lake in the mountains near LA, and on the Channel Islands, where they've started to make a comeback.

Monarch butterflies are glorious orange creatures that take epic long-distance journeys in search of milkweed, their only source of food. They winter in California by the tens of thousands, clustering along the Central Coast at Santa Cruz, Pacific Grove, Pismo Beach and Santa Barbara County.

The California condor is the largest flying bird in North America. In 1987 there were only two dozen or so birds left in the wild. Thanks to captive breeding and release programs, there are about 240 flying free today.

Wildflowers & Trees

Like human Californians, California's 6000 kinds of plants are by turns shy and flamboyant. Many species are so obscure and similar that only a dedicated botanist could tell them apart, but in the spring they merge into shimmering carpets of wildflowers that will take your breath away. The state flower is the native California poppy, which shyly closes at night and unfolds by day in a shocking display of golden orange.

California is also a region of superlative trees: the oldest (bristlecone pines of the White Mountains live to nearly 5000 years old), the tallest (coast redwoods reach 380ft) and the largest (giant sequoias of the Sierra Nevada exceed 36ft across). Sequoias are unique to California, adapted to survive in isolated groves on the Sierra Nevada's western slopes in Yosemite, Sequoia and Kings Canyon National Parks.

An astounding 20 native species of oak grow in California, including live (evergreen) oaks with holly-like leaves and scaly acorns. Other common trees include the aromatic California bay laurel, whose long slender leaves turn purple. Rare native trees include Monterey pines and Torrey pines, gnarly species that have adapted to harsh coastal conditions such as high winds, sparse rainfall and sandy, stony soils. Torrey pines only grow at Torrey Pines State Reserve near San Diego and in the Channel Islands, California's hot spot for endemic plant species.

Heading inland, the Sierra Nevada has three distinct eco-zones: the dry western foothills covered with oak and chaparral; conifer forests starting from an elevation of 2000ft; and an alpine zone above 8000ft. Almost two dozen species of conifer grow in the Sierra Nevada, with mid-elevation forests home to massive Douglas firs, ponderosa pines and, biggest of all, the giant sequoia. Deciduous trees include the quaking aspen, a white-trunked tree with shimmering leaves that turn pale yellow in the fall, helping the Golden State live up to its name in the Eastern Sierra.

Cacti & Other Desert Flora

In Southern California's deserts, cacti and other plants have adapted to the arid climate with thin, spiny leaves that resist moisture loss (and deter grazing animals). Their seed and flowering mechanisms kick into high gear during brief winter rains. Desert flora can bloom spectacularly in spring, carpeting valleys and drawing thousands of onlookers and shutterbugs.

One of the most common species is cholla, which looks so furry that it's nicknamed 'teddy-bear cactus,' but don't be fooled by its cuddly appearance. Cholla will bury extremely sharp, barbed spines in your skin at the slightest touch. Also watch out for the aptly named catclaw acacia, nicknamed 'wait-a-minute bush' because its small, sharp, hooked thorny spikes will try to grab your clothing or skin as you brush past.

You may also recognize prickly pear, a flat, fleshy-padded cacti whose juice is traditionally used as medicine by Native Americans. You can hardly miss spiky ocotillo, which grows up to 20ft tall and has canelike branches that sprout blood-red flowers in spring. Creosote may look like a cactus, but it's actually a small evergreen bush with a distinctive smell.

With gangly arms and puffy green sleeves, Joshua trees look like Dr Seuss characters from afar, but up close you can see they're actually a type of yucca. In spring they burst into blossom with greenish-white flowers. Joshua trees grow throughout the Mojave Desert, although their habitat and long-term survival is severely threatened by climate change. According to local legend, they were named by Mormons who thought their crooked branches resembled the outstretched arms of a biblical prophet.

California's National & State Parks

Most Californians rate outdoor recreation as vital to their quality of life, and the amount of preserved public lands has steadily grown since the 1960s with support from key legislation. The landmark 1976 California Coastal Act saved the coastline from further development, while the controversial 1994 California Desert Protection Act passed over the objections of ranchers, miners and off-highway vehicle (OHV) enthusiasts.

Today, California State Parks (www.parks.ca.gov) protect nearly a third of the state's coastline, along with redwood forests, mountain lakes, desert canyons, waterfalls, wildlife preserves and historical sites. In recent decades, state budget shortfalls and chronic underfunding of California's parks have contributed to closures, limited visitor services and increased park entry and outdoor-recreation fees. But with state revenues from recreational tourism consistently outpacing resource-extraction industries such as mining, California has a considerable vested interest in protecting its wilderness tracts.

While you could be disappointed to find a park closed or full, bear in mind that some limits to public access are necessary to prevent California's parklands from being loved to death. Too many visitors can stress the natural environment. To avoid the crowds and glimpse wilderness at its most untrammeled, plan to visit popular parks such as Yosemite outside of peak season. Alternatively, less-famous natural areas managed by the National Park Service (www.nps.gov/state/CA) often receive fewer visitors, which means you won't have to reserve permits, campsites or lodging many months in advance.

There are 18 national forests in California managed by the US Forest Service (USFS; www.fs.usda.gov/r5), comprising lands around Mt Whitney, Mt Shasta, Lake Tahoe, Big Bear Lake and Big Sur. Beloved by birders, national wildlife refuges (NWR), including the Salton Sea and Klamath Basin, are managed by the US Fish & Wildlife Service (USFWS; www.fws.gov/refuges). More wilderness tracts in California, including the Lost Coast and Carrizo Plain, are overseen by the Bureau of Land Management (BLM; www.blm.gov/ca/st/en.html).

In 2006 the world's tallest-known living tree was discovered in a remote area of Redwood National Park – its location is kept secret to protect it. It's named Hyperion and stands a whopping 379ft tall.

THE LAND & WILDLIFE CALIFORNIA'S NATIONAL & STATE PARKS

California's Top Parks

Yosemite National Park

Sequoia & Kings Canyon National Parks

Death Valley National Park

Joshua Tree National Park

Lassen Volcanic National Park

Redwood National & State Parks

GO WILD FOR WILDFLOWERS

The famous 'golden hills' of California are actually native plants and grasses that have adapted to local conditions over millennia, and learned to dry up in preparation for the long hot summer. Many local plants have adjusted their growing cycles to long periods of almost no rain, growing prolifically during California's mild wet winters, blooming as early as February, drying out in early summer and springing to life again with the first rains of fall.

In Southern California's desert areas, wildflower blooms usually peak in March, with carpets of wildflowers covering lowland areas of the state into April. Visit Anza-Borrego Desert State Park, Death Valley National Park, the Antelope Valley California Poppy Preserve and Carrizo Plain National Monument for some of the most spectacular annual wildflower displays.

As snows melt later at higher elevations in the Sierra Nevada, Yosemite National Park's Tuolumne Meadows is another prime spot for wildflower walks and photography, with blooms usually peaking in late June or early July.

Conserving California

As you take in California's stunning natural landscapes, pause to appreciate the human effort it has taken to preserve and reclaim these natural wonders. In California rapid development and unchecked growth have often come at great environmental cost. Starting in 1849, gold-rush miners hacked and blasted through the California countryside in search of a lucky strike. More than 1.5 billion tons of debris and uncalculated amounts of poisonous mercury were carried downstream into the Central Valley, where rivers and streams became clogged and polluted. When you see forests in high Sierra gold country and salmon runs in the Sacramento Delta, you are admiring the resilience of nature and the work of many determined conservationists.

Water, or the lack thereof, has led to epic environmental struggles and catastrophes in California. Despite campaigning by John Muir, California's greatest environmental champion, the Tuolumne River was dammed at Hetch Hetchy in Yosemite National Park to supply Bay Area drinking water. Pipelines diverting water supplies for arid Los Angeles have contributed to the destruction of Owens Lake and its fertile wetlands, and the degradation of Mono Lake in the Eastern Sierra. Statewide, the damming of rivers and capture of water for houses and farms has ended inland salmon runs and dried up marshlands. The Central Valley's underground aquifer is subsiding, with some land sinking as much as 1ft each year.

Although air quality in California has improved markedly in past decades, it's still among the worst in the country. Along with industrial emissions, the main pollutants are auto exhaust and fine particulates generated by the wearing down of vehicle tires. An even greater health hazard is ozone, the principal ingredient in smog, which makes sunny days around LA, Sacramento, the Central Valley and the western Sierra Nevada look hazy. California road trips are fantastic adventures, but if you rent a hybrid, take a train, carpool or hop public transit for short distances, you can breathe easier knowing you're helping to spare the air.

All these efforts add up to a more sustainable future for California and its wildlife. Low-emission vehicles are becoming one of the most sought-after types of car in the state – California's own Tesla electric cars may yet replace gas-guzzling SUVs as the Hollywood celebrity car of choice. While environmental controls, emissions standards and renewable energy support have been eroding at the federal level, Californians have voted to raise standards for pollution control and construct solar-power plants. By law, California's utilities must get 33% of their energy from renewable resources by 2020 – the most ambitious target yet set by any US state. When you bask in the California sun, you may be seeing the future.

Co-founded by naturalist John Muir in 1892, the Sierra Club (www.sierraclub.org) was the USA's first conservation group. It remains the nation's most active, offering educational programs, group hikes, organized trips and volunteer vacations.

Survival
Guide

Directory A–Z

Accommodations

Amenities

➡ Budget accommodations include campgrounds, hostels and motels. Because midrange properties generally offer better value for money, most of our accommodations fall into this category.

➡ At midrange motels and hotels, expect clean, comfortable and decent-sized rooms with at least a private bathroom, and standard amenities such as cable TV, direct-dial telephone, a coffee maker, and perhaps a microwave and mini-fridge.

➡ Top-end lodgings offer top-notch amenities and perhaps a scenic location, high design or historical ambience. Pools, fitness rooms, business centers, full-service restaurants and bars and other convenient facilities are often included.

➡ In Southern California, nearly all lodgings have air-conditioning, but in perpetually cool Northern California, most don't. In coastal areas as far south as Santa Barbara, only fans may be provided.

➡ Accommodations offering online computer terminals for guests are designated with the internet icon. A fee may apply, including at full-service hotel business centers.

➡ There may be a fee for wireless internet, especially for in-room access. Look for free wi-fi hot spots in hotel public areas such as the lobby or poolside.

➡ Many lodgings are now exclusively nonsmoking. Where they still exist, smoking rooms are often left unrenovated and in less desirable locations. Expect a hefty 'cleaning fee' ($100 or more) if you light up in designated nonsmoking rooms.

Rates & Reservations

➡ Generally midweek rates are lower, except at urban hotels geared toward business travelers. Hotels in Silicon Valley, downtown San Francisco, LA and San Diego may lure leisure travelers with weekend deals.

➡ Discount membership cards (such as AAA and AARP) may get you about 10% off standard rates at participating hotels and motels.

➡ Look for freebie-ad magazines packed with hotel and motel discount coupons at gas stations, highway rest areas, tourist offices and online at HotelCoupons (www.hotelcoupons.com).

➡ High season is from June to August everywhere, except the deserts and mountain ski areas, where December through April are the busiest months.

➡ Demand and prices spike around major holidays and for festivals, when some properties may impose multiday minimum stays.

➡ Reservations are recommended for weekend and holiday travel year-round, and every day of the week during high season.

➡ Bargaining may be possible for walk-in guests without reservations, especially at off-peak times.

B&Bs & Vacation Rentals

If you want an atmospheric or romantic alternative to impersonal motels and hotels, try bed-and-breakfast inns. Many are converted Victorian mansions or other heritage buildings, bedecked with floral wallpaper and antique furnishings. Travelers who prefer privacy may find B&Bs too intimate.

Rates often include breakfast, but occasionally don't – never mind what the name 'B&B' suggests. Amenities

---

BOOK YOUR STAY ONLINE

For more accommodations reviews by Lonely Planet authors, check out http://lonelyplanet.com/hotels/. You'll find independent reviews, as well as recommendations on the best places to stay. Best of all, you can book online.

vary widely, but rooms with TV and telephone are the exception; the cheapest units may share bathrooms. Standards are high at places certified by the California Association of Boutique & Breakfast Inns (www.cabbi.com). Quality and price vary at home shares and vacation rentals listed with Airbnb (www.airbnb.com) and Vacation Rentals By Owner (www.vrbo.com).

Most B&Bs require advance reservations; only a few will accommodate drop-in guests. Smoking is generally prohibited and children are usually not welcome in B&Bs – vacation rentals are generally more flexible. Multiple-night minimum stays may be required, especially on weekends and during high season.

Camping

In California, camping is much more than just a cheap way to spend the night. The best campgrounds offer moonlit ocean views by the beach, cushioned spots under pine trees next to an alpine lake, or stargazing in desert sand dunes. The state park system has a variety of campgrounds. To reserve, check out www.reservecalifornia.com.

Hostels

California has 18 hostels affiliated with **Hostelling International USA** (✆240-650-2100; www.hiusa.org).

Dorms in HI hostels are typically gender-segregated and alcohol and smoking are prohibited. HI membership cards (adult/senior $28/18 per year, free for under 18s) get you $3 off per night.

California also has dozens of independent hostels, particularly in coastal cities. They generally have more relaxed rules, with frequent guest parties and activities. Some hostels include a light breakfast in their rates, arrange local tours or offer pickups at transportation hubs. No two hostels are alike, but facilities typically include mixed dorms, semi-private rooms with shared bathrooms, communal kitchens, lockers, internet access, coin-op laundry and TV lounges.

Some hostels say they accept only international visitors (basically to keep out homeless locals), but Americans who seem to be traveling (eg you're in possession of an international plane ticket) may be admitted, especially during slow periods.

Dorm-bed rates range from $30 to $55 per night, including tax. Reservations are always a good idea, especially in high season. Most hostels take reservations online or by phone. Booking services such as www.hostels.com, www.hostelz.com and www.hostelworld.com sometimes offer lower rates than the hostels directly.

Hotels & Motels

Rooms are often priced by the size and number of beds, rather than the number of occupants. A room with one double or queen-size bed usually costs the same for one or two people, while a room with a king-size bed or two double beds costs more.

There is often a small surcharge for the third and fourth person, but children under a certain age (this varies) may stay free. Cribs or rollaway cots usually incur an additional fee. Be aware that suites or 'junior suites' may simply be oversized rooms; ask about the layout when booking.

Recently renovated or larger rooms, or those with a view, are likely to cost more. Descriptors like 'oceanfront' and 'ocean view' are often too liberally used, and you may require a telescope to spot the surf.

You can make reservations at chains by calling their central reservation lines, but to learn about specific amenities and local promotions, call the property directly. If you arrive without reservations, ask to see a room before paying for it, especially at motels.

Rates may include breakfast, which could be just a stale donut and wimpy coffee, an all-you-can-eat hot and cold buffet, or anything in between.

Customs Regulations

Currently, non-US citizens and permanent residents may import:

➡ 1L of alcohol (if you're over 21 years of age)

➡ 200 cigarettes (one carton) or 100 cigars (if you're over 18 years)

➡ $100 worth of gifts Amounts higher than $10,000 in cash, traveler's checks, money orders and other cash equivalents must be declared. Don't even think about bringing in illegal drugs.

For more complete, up-to-date information, check the US Customs and Border Protection website (www.cbp.gov).

Discount Cards

'America the Beautiful' Annual Pass (http://store.usgs. gov/pass; 12-month pass $80) Admits four adults and all children under 16 years for free to all national parks and federal recreational lands (eg USFS, BLM) for 12 months from the date of purchase. US citizens and permanent residents aged 62 years and older are eligible for a lifetime Senior Pass ($10), which grants free entry and 50% off some recreational-use fees such as camping.

American Association of Retired Persons (AARP; ☑888-687-2277; www.aarp.og) This advocacy group for Americans 50 years and older offers member discounts (usually 10%) on hotels, car rentals and more. Annual membership costs $16.

American Automobile Association (AAA; ☑800-922-8228; www.aaa.com) Members of AAA and its foreign affiliates (eg CAA, AA) enjoy small discounts (usually 10%) on Amtrak trains, car rentals, motels and hotels, chain restaurants and shops, tours and theme parks. Annual membership from $56.

Go Los Angeles, San Diego & San Francisco and San Francisco Explorer Cards (www. smartdestinations.com; 1-day pass adult/child from $65/49) The Go LA Card and pricier Go San Diego Card include admission to major SoCal theme parks (but not Disneyland). The cheaper Go San Francisco Card covers museums, bicycle rental and a bay cruise. You've got to do a lot of sightseeing over multiple days to make passes come close to paying off. Alternatively, the San Francisco Explorer pass gives you 30 days to visit three to five attractions (excluding Alcatraz cruises and tours). For discounts, buy online.

International Student Identity, Youth Travel & Teacher Identity Cards (www.isic.org; 12-month card $25) Offers savings on airline fares, travel insurance and local attractions for full-time students (ISIC), for nonstudents 30 years of age or younger (IYTC) and for employed teachers (ITIC). Cards are issued online and by student unions, hosteling organizations and youth-oriented budget travel agencies.

Senior Discounts People over the age of 65 (sometimes 50, 55, 60 or 62) often qualify for the same discounts as students; any ID showing your birth date should suffice as proof.

Southern California CityPass (www.citypass.com/south-ern-california; adult/child from $346/314) If you're visiting SoCal theme parks, CityPass covers three-day admission to Disneyland and Disney California Adventure and one-day admission each to Legoland California and SeaWorld San Diego, with add-ons available for the San Diego Zoo or Safari Park. Passes are valid for 14 days from the first day of use. It's cheapest to buy them online in advance.

Student Advantage Card (☑877-256-4672; www.studen-tadvantage.com) For international and US students, this card offers 15% savings on Amtrak trains and 10% on Greyhound buses, plus discounts of 10% to 25% on some motels and hotels, rental cars, ride-sharing services and shopping. A 12-month card costs $22.50.

Electricity

Type A
120V/60Hz

Food

➡ Lunch is generally served between 11:30am and 2:30pm, and dinner between 5pm and 9pm daily, though some restaurants stay open later, especially on Friday and Saturday nights.

➡ If breakfast is served, it's usually between 7:30am and 11am. Some diners and cafes keep serving breakfast into the afternoon, or all day. Weekend brunch is a laid-back meal, usually available from 11am until 3pm on Saturdays and Sundays.

➡ Californian restaurant etiquette tends to be informal. Only a handful of restaurants require more than a dressy shirt, slacks and shoes that aren't flip-flops. At other places, T-shirts, shorts and sandals are fine.

➡ Tipping 18% to 20% is expected anywhere you receive table service.

➡ Smoking is illegal indoors. Some restaurants have patios or sidewalk tables where smoking is tolerated (ask first, or look around for ashtrays), but don't expect your neighbors to be happy about secondhand smoke.

➡ You can bring your own wine to most restaurants; a 'corkage' fee of $15 to $30 usually applies. Lunches rarely include booze, though a glass of wine or beer is socially acceptable.

➡ If you ask the kitchen to divide a plate between two (or more) people, there may be a small split-plate surcharge.

➡ Vegetarians, vegans and travelers with food allergies or dietary restrictions are in luck – many restaurants are used to catering to specific dietary needs.

Health

Before You Go
HEALTH INSURANCE

➡ Keep all medical receipts and documentation for billing and insurance claims and reimbursement later.

➡ Some health-insurance policies require you to get pre-authorization over the phone for medical treatment before seeking help.

➡ Overseas visitors with travel-health-insurance policies may need to contact a call center for an assessment by phone before getting medical treatment.

RECOMMENDED VACCINATIONS

Currently there are no vaccination requirements for visiting the USA. California has recently had outbreaks of measles and whooping cough, since fewer parents have been choosing to vaccinate their children. Before visiting California, make sure you've had all of the standard immunizations, including but not limited to MMR (measles, mumps and rubella), Hepatitis A and B, varicella (chickenpox) and Tdap (tetanus-diphtheria-acelluar pertussis) within the last 10 years, and the annual seasonal influenza vaccine.

Availability & Cost of Health Care

➡ Medical treatment in the USA is of the highest caliber, but the expense could kill you. Many health-care professionals demand payment at the time of service, especially from out-of-towners or international visitors.

➡ Except for medical emergencies (in which case call 911 or go to the nearest 24-hour hospital emergency room, or ER), phone around to find a doctor who will accept your insurance.

Environmental Hazards

DEHYDRATION, HEAT EXHAUSTION & HEATSTROKE

➡ Take it easy as you acclimatize, especially on hot summer days and in Southern California's deserts. Drink plenty of water. A minimum of 3L per person per day is recommended when you're active outdoors. Be sure to eat a salty snack too, as sodium is necessary for rehydration.

➡ Dehydration (lack of water) or salt deficiency can cause heat exhaustion, often characterized by heavy sweating, fatigue, lethargy, headaches, nausea, vomiting, dizziness and muscle cramps.

➡ Long, continuous exposure to high temperatures can lead to possibly fatal heatstroke, when body temperatures rise to dangerous levels. Warning signs include altered mental status, hyperventilation and flushed, hot and dry skin (ie sweating stops).

➡ For heatstroke, immediate hospitalization is essential. Meanwhile get out of the sun, remove clothing that retains heat (cotton is OK), douse the body with cool water and fan continuously. Ice packs can be applied to the neck, armpits and groin.

HYPOTHERMIA

➡ Skiers and hikers will find that temperatures in the mountains and desert can quickly drop below freezing, especially during winter. Even a sudden spring shower or high winds can lower your body temperature dangerously fast.

➡ Instead of cotton, wear synthetic or woolen clothing that retains warmth even when wet. Carry waterproof layers (eg Gore-Tex jacket, plastic poncho, rain pants) and high-energy, easily digestible snacks such as chocolate, nuts and dried fruit.

➡ Symptoms of hypothermia include exhaustion, numbness, shivering, stumbling, slurred speech, dizzy spells, muscle cramps and irrational or even violent behavior.

➡ To treat mild hypothermia, get out of bad weather and change into dry, warm clothing. Drink hot liquids (no caffeine or alcohol) and snack on high-calorie food.

➡ For more advanced hypothermia, seek immediate medical attention. Do not rub victims, who must be handled gently.

PRACTICALITIES

DVDs Coded for region 1 (USA and Canada only)

Electricity 110/120V AC, 50/60Hz

Newspapers *Los Angeles Times* (www.latimes.com), *San Francisco Chronicle* (www.sfchronicle.com), *Mercury News* (www.mercurynews.com), *Sacramento Bee* (www.sacbee.com)

Radio National Public Radio (NPR), lower end of FM dial

TV PBS (public broadcasting); cable: CNN (news), ESPN (sports), HBO (movies), Weather Channel

Weights & Measures Imperial (except 1 US gallon equals 0.83 imperial gallons)

TAP WATER

It's fine to drink water from the tap anywhere in California, except at some wilderness campgrounds where the water may not be potable (look for signs or ask the campground host).

Insurance

Getting travel insurance to cover theft, loss and medical problems is highly recommended. Some policies do not cover 'risky' activities such as scuba diving, motorcycling and skiing, so read the fine print. Make sure the policy at least covers hospital stays and an emergency flight home.

Paying for your airline ticket or rental car with a credit card may provide limited travel accident insurance. If you already have private health insurance or a homeowners or renters policy, find out what those policies cover and only get supplemental insurance. If you have prepaid a large portion of your vacation, trip-cancellation insurance may be a worthwhile expense.

Worldwide travel insurance is available at www.lonely planet.com/travel-insurance. You can buy, extend and claim online anytime – even if you're already on the road.

Internet Access

➡ Cybercafes typically charge $6 to $18 per hour for online access.

➡ With branches in major cities and towns, **FedEx** (☑800-463-3339; www.fedex.com/us/office) offers internet access at self-service computer workstations (30¢ to 40¢ per minute) and sometimes free wi-fi, plus digital-photo printing and CD-burning stations.

➡ Free or fee-based wi-fi hot spots can be found at major airports, many hotels, motels and coffee shops (eg Starbucks) and some tourist information centers, campgrounds (eg KOA), stores (eg Apple), bars and restaurants (including fast-food chains such as McDonald's).

➡ Free public wi-fi is proliferating and even some of California's state parks are now wi-fi–enabled (get details at www.parks.ca.gov).

➡ Public libraries have internet terminals (online time may be limited, advance sign-up required and a nominal fee charged for out-of-network visitors) and, increasingly, free wi-fi.

Legal Matters

Drugs & Alcohol

➡ Possession of up to 1oz of marijuana (if you are 21 years or older) for recreational use is no longer a crime in California, but it is still illegal to use marijuana in public (subject to fines of up to $250, as well as mandatory community-service hours and drug-education classes).

➡ Possession of any other drug or more than 1oz of marijuana is a felony punishable by lengthy jail time. For foreigners, conviction of any drug offense is grounds for deportation.

➡ Police can give roadside sobriety checks to assess if you've been drinking or using drugs. If you fail they'll require you to take a breath, urine or blood test to determine if your blood alcohol is over the legal limit (0.08%). Refusing to be tested is treated the same as if you had taken and failed the test.

➡ Penalties for driving under the influence (DUI) of drugs or alcohol range from license suspension and fines to jail time. It's illegal to carry open containers of alcohol inside a vehicle, even if they're empty. Unless they're full and still sealed, store them in the trunk.

➡ Consuming alcohol anywhere other than at a private residence or licensed premises is a no-no, which puts most parks and beaches off limits (although many campgrounds legally allow it).

➡ Bars, clubs and liquor stores often ask for photo ID to prove you are of legal drinking age (21 years). Being 'carded' is standard practice, so don't take it personally.

Police & Security

➡ For police, fire and ambulance emergencies, dial 911. For nonemergency police assistance, contact the nearest local police station (dial 411 for directory assistance).

➡ If you are stopped by the police, be courteous. Don't get out of the car unless asked. Keep your hands where the officer can see them (eg on the steering wheel) at all times.

➡ There is no system of paying fines on the spot. Attempting to pay the fine to the officer may lead to a charge of attempted bribery.

➡ For traffic violations the ticketing officer will explain your options. There is usually a 30-day period to pay a fine; most matters can be handled by mail or online.

➡ If you are arrested you have the right to remain silent and are presumed innocent until proven guilty. Everyone has the right to make one phone call. If you don't have a lawyer, one will be appointed to you free of charge. Foreign travelers who don't have a lawyer, friends or family to help should call their embassy or consulate; the police can provide the number upon request.

➡ Due to security concerns about terrorism, never leave your bags unattended, especially at airports or bus and train stations.

LGBT Travelers

California is a magnet for LGBTQ travelers. Hot spots include the Castro in San Francisco, West Hollywood (WeHo), Silver Lake and Long Beach in LA, San Diego's Hillcrest neighborhood, the desert resort of Palm Springs, Guerneville in the Russian River Valley and Calistoga in Napa Valley.

Same-sex marriage is legal in California. Despite widespread tolerance, homophobic bigotry still exists. In small towns, especially away from the coast, tolerance often comes down to a 'don't ask, don't tell' policy.

Helpful Resources

Advocate (www.advocate.com/travel) Online news, gay travel features and destination guides.

Damron (www.damron.com) Classic, advertiser-driven gay travel guides and 'Gay Scout' mobile app.

LGBT National Hotline (888-843-4564; www.glbthotline.org) For counseling and referrals of any kind.

Out Traveler (www.outtraveler.com) Free online magazine articles with travel tips, destination guides and hotel reviews.

Purple Roofs (www.purpleroofs.com) Online directory of LGBTQ-friendly accommodations.

Maps

➡ GPS navigation is handy, but cannot be relied upon 100% of the time, especially in remote wilderness and rural areas.

➡ Visitor centers distribute free (but often very basic) maps. If you're doing a lot of driving around California, you'll need a more detailed road map or map atlas.

➡ Members of the **American Automobile Association** (AAA; ☏800-922-8228; www.aaa.com) or its international affiliates (bring your membership card from home) can get free driving maps from local AAA offices.

➡ DeLorme's comprehensive *California Atlas & Gazetteer* ($25) shows campgrounds, hiking trails, recreational areas and topographical land features; it's less useful for navigating urban areas.

Money

ATMs

➡ ATMs are available 24/7 at most banks, shopping malls, airports and grocery and convenience stores.

➡ Expect a minimum surcharge of around $3 per transaction, in addition to any fees charged by your home bank.

➡ Most ATMs are connected to international networks and offer decent foreign-exchange rates.

➡ Withdrawing cash from an ATM using a credit card usually incurs a hefty fee and high interest rates; contact your credit-card company for details and a PIN number.

Cash

Most people don't carry large amounts of cash for everyday use, relying instead on credit and debit cards. Some businesses refuse to accept bills over $20.

Credit Cards

➡ Major credit cards are almost universally accepted. In fact, it's almost impossible to rent a car, book a hotel room or buy tickets over the phone without one. A credit card may also be vital in emergencies.

➡ Visa, MasterCard and American Express are the most widely accepted credit cards.

Moneychangers

➡ You can exchange money at major airports, bigger banks and currency-exchange offices such as American Express (www.americanexpress.com) or Travelex (www.travelex.com). Always enquire about rates and fees.

➡ Outside big cities, exchanging money may be a problem, so make sure you have a credit card and sufficient cash on hand.

Taxes & Refunds

➡ California state sales tax (7.5%) is added to the retail price of most goods and services (gasoline and groceries are exceptions). Local and city sales taxes may tack on up to 2.5%.

➡ Tourist lodging taxes vary statewide, but average 10.5% to 15.5% in major cities.

➡ No refunds of sales or lodging taxes are available for visitors.

Traveler's Checks

➡ Traveler's checks have pretty much fallen out of use.

➡ Big-city restaurants, hotels and department stores will often accept traveler's checks (in US dollars only), but small businesses, markets and fast-food chains may refuse them.

➔ Visa and American Express are the most widely accepted issuers of traveler's checks.

Opening Hours

Businesses, restaurants and shops may close earlier and on additional days during the winter off-season (November to March). Otherwise, standard opening hours are as follows:

Banks 9am–6pm Monday to Friday, some 9am–1pm or later Saturday

Bars 5pm–2am daily

Business hours (general) 9am–5pm Monday to Friday

Nightclubs 10pm–4am Thursday to Saturday

Post offices 8:30am–5pm Monday to Friday, some 8:30am–noon or later Saturday

Restaurants 7:30am–10am, 11:30am–2pm and 5pm–9pm daily, some open later Friday and Saturday

Shops 10am–6pm Monday to Saturday, noon–5pm Sunday (malls open later)

Supermarkets 8am–9pm or 10pm daily, some 24 hours

Post

➔ The **US Postal Service** (USPS; ☎800-275-8777; www.usps.com) is inexpensive and reliable.

➔ For sending important documents or packages internationally, try **Federal Express** (FedEx; ☎800-463-3339; www.fedex.com/us) or **United Parcel Service** (UPS; ☎800-742-5877; www.ups.com).

Public Holidays

On the following national holidays, banks, schools and government offices (including post offices) are closed, and transportation, museums and other services operate on a Sunday schedule. Holidays falling on a weekend are usually observed the following Monday.

New Year's Day January 1

Martin Luther King Jr Day Third Monday in January

Presidents' Day Third Monday in February

Good Friday Friday before Easter in March/April

Memorial Day Last Monday in May

Independence Day July 4

Labor Day First Monday in September

Columbus Day Second Monday in October

Veterans Day November 11

Thanksgiving Day Fourth Thursday in November

Christmas Day December 25

School Holidays

➔ Schools take a one- or two-week 'spring break' around Easter, sometime in March or April. Some hotels and resorts, especially at beaches and near SoCal's theme parks, raise their rates during this time.

➔ School summer vacations run from mid-June until mid-August, making July and August the busiest travel months.

Safe Travel

Despite its seemingly apocalyptic list of dangers – guns, violent crime, riots, earthquakes – California is a reasonably safe place to visit. The greatest danger is posed by car accidents (buckle up – it's the law), while the biggest annoyances are metro-area traffic and crowds. Wildlife poses some small threats, and of course there is the dramatic, albeit unlikely, possibility of a natural disaster.

Earthquakes

Earthquakes happen all the time, but most are so tiny they are detectable only by sensitive seismological instruments. If you're caught in a serious shaker:

➔ If indoors, get under a desk or table or stand in a doorway.

➔ Protect your head and stay clear of windows, mirrors or anything that might fall.

➔ Don't head for elevators or go running into the street.

➔ If you're in a shopping mall or large public building,

TIPPING

Tipping is *not* optional. Only withhold tips in cases of outrageously bad service.

Airport skycaps & hotel bellhops $2 or $3 per bag, minimum $5 per cart

Bartenders 15% to 20% per round, minimum $1 per drink

Concierges Nothing for simple information, up to $20 for securing last-minute restaurant reservations, sold-out show tickets, etc

Housekeeping staff $2 to $4 daily, left under the card provided; more if you're messy

Parking valets At least $2 when your car keys are handed back

Restaurant servers & room service 18% to 20%, unless a gratuity is already charged (common for groups of six or more)

Taxi drivers 10% to 15% of metered fare, rounded up to the next dollar

expect the alarm and/or sprinkler systems to come on.

➡ If outdoors, get away from buildings, trees and power lines.

➡ If you're driving, pull over to the side of the road away from bridges, overpasses and power lines. Stay inside the car until the shaking stops.

➡ If you're on a sidewalk near buildings, duck into a doorway to protect yourself from falling bricks, glass and debris.

➡ Prepare for aftershocks.

➡ Turn on the radio and listen for bulletins.

➡ Use the telephone only if absolutely necessary.

Wildlife

➡ Never feed or approach any wild animal, not even harmless-looking critters – it causes them to lose their innate fear of humans, which in turn makes them dangerously aggressive. Many birds and mammals, including deer and rodents such as squirrels, carry serious diseases that can be transmitted to humans through a bite.

➡ Disturbing or harassing specially protected species, including many marine mammals such as whales, dolphins and seals, is a crime, subject to enormous fines.

➡ Black bears are often attracted to campgrounds, where they may find food, trash and any other scented items left out on picnic tables or stashed in tents and cars. Always use bear-proof containers where they are provided. For more bear-country travel tips, visit the **SierraWild website** (http://sierrawild.gov/bears).

➡ If you encounter a black bear in the wild, don't run. Stay together, keeping small children next to you and picking up little ones. Keep back at least 100yd. If the bear starts moving toward you, back away slowly off-trail and let it pass by, being careful not to block any of the

bear's escape routes or to get caught between a mother and her cubs. Sometimes a black bear will 'bluff charge' to test your dominance. Stand your ground by making yourself look as big as possible (eg waving your arms above your head) and shouting menacingly.

➡ Mountain lion attacks on humans are rare, but can be deadly. If you encounter a mountain lion stay calm, pick up small children, face the animal and retreat slowly. Make yourself appear larger by raising your arms or grabbing a stick. If the lion becomes menacing, shout or throw rocks at it. If attacked, fight back aggressively.

➡ Snakes and spiders are common throughout California, not just in wilderness areas. Always look inside your shoes before putting them back on outdoors, especially when camping. Snake bites are rare, but occur most often when a snake is stepped on or provoked (eg picked up or poked with a stick). Antivenom is available at most hospitals.

Telephone

Cell Phones

➡ You'll need a multiband GSM phone to make calls in the USA. Popping in a US prepaid rechargeable SIM card is usually cheaper than using your network.

SMOKING

➡ Smoking is generally prohibited inside all public buildings, including airports, shopping malls and train and bus stations.

➡ There is no smoking allowed inside restaurants, although lighting up may be tolerated at outdoor patio or sidewalk tables (ask first).

➡ At hotels you must specifically request a smoking room, but note some properties are entirely nonsmoking by law.

➡ In some cities and towns, smoking outdoors within a certain distance of any public business is illegal.

➡ SIM cards are sold at telecommunications and electronics stores. These stores also sell inexpensive prepaid phones, including some airtime.

➡ You can rent a cell phone at San Francisco (SFO) International Airport from TripTel (www.triptel.com); pricing plans vary, but typically are expensive.

Dialing Codes

➡ US phone numbers consist of a three-digit area code followed by a seven-digit local number.

➡ When dialing a number within the same area code, use the seven-digit number (if that doesn't work, try all 10 digits).

➡ For long-distance calls, dial 1 plus the area code plus the local number.

➡ Toll-free numbers (eg beginning with 800, 855, 866, 877 or 888) must be preceded by 1.

➡ For direct international calls, dial 011 plus the country code plus the area code (usually without the initial '0') plus the local phone number.

➡ If you're calling from abroad, the country code for the US is 1 (the same as Canada, but international rates apply between the two countries).

Payphones & Phonecards

➡ Where payphones still exist, they're usually coin-operated, though some may only accept credit cards (eg in state or national parks). Local calls cost 50¢ minimum.

➡ For long-distance and international calls, prepaid phonecards are sold at convenience stores, supermarkets, newsstands and electronics and convenience stores.

Time

Pacific Standard Time (UTC minus eight hours). Clocks are set one hour ahead during Daylight Saving Time (DST), from the second Sunday in March until the first Sunday in November.

Toilets

Free public restrooms are easy to find inside shopping malls, public buildings and some transportation hubs, as well as outdoors at parks and beaches. It's more challenging to find them in urban areas – try the nearest public library, grocery store, pharmacy, gas station, bar or coffee shop (where you might have to buy something to eat or drink before borrowing the bathroom key).

Tourist Information

➡ For pretrip planning, peruse the information-packed website of the **California Travel & Tourism Commission** (Visit California; ☏877-225-4367, 916-444-4429; www.visitcalifornia.com).

➡ The same government agency operates more than a dozen statewide California Welcome Centers (www.visitcwc.com), where staff dispense maps and brochures and may be able to help find accommodations.

➡ Almost every city and town has a local visitor center or a chamber of commerce where you can pick up maps, brochures and information.

Travelers with Disabilities

More-populated areas of coastal California are reasonably well equipped for travelers with disabilities, but facilities in smaller towns and rural areas may be limited.

Download Lonely Planet's free Accessible Travel guide from http://lptravel.to/AccessibleTravel.

Accessibility

➡ Most traffic intersections have dropped curbs and some have audible crossing signals.

➡ The Americans with Disabilities Act (ADA) requires public buildings built after 1993 to be wheelchair-accessible, including restrooms.

➡ Motels and hotels built after 1993 must have at least one ADA–compliant accessible room; state your specific needs when making reservations.

➡ For nonpublic buildings built prior to 1993, including hotels, restaurants, museums and theaters, there are no accessibility guarantees; call ahead to find out what to expect.

➡ Most national and many state parks and some other outdoor recreation areas offer paved or boardwalk nature trails that are graded and accessible by wheelchair.

➡ Many theme parks go out of their way to be accessible to wheelchairs and guests with mobility limitations and other disabilities.

➡ US citizens and permanent residents with a permanent disability quality for a free lifetime **'America the Beautiful' Access Pass** (http://store.usgs.gov/pass/access.html), which waives entry fees to all national parks and federal recreational lands and offers 50% discounts on some recreation fees (eg camping).

➡ California State Parks' disabled discount pass ($3.50) entitles people with permanent disabilities to 50% off day-use parking and camping fees; for an application, click to www.parks.ca.gov.

Communications

➡ Telephone companies provide relay operators (dial 711) for the hearing impaired.

➡ Many banks provide ATM instructions in braille.

Transportation

➡ All major airlines, Greyhound buses and Amtrak trains can accommodate people with disabilities, usually with 48 hours of advance notice required.

➡ Major car-rental agencies offer hand-controlled vehicles and vans with wheelchair lifts at no extra charge, but you must reserve these well in advance.

➡ For wheelchair-accessible van rentals, also try **Wheelchair Getaways** (☏800-642-2042; www.wheelchairgetaways.com) in LA and San Francisco, or **Mobility Works** (☏877-275-4915; www.mobilityworks.com) in LA, San Diego, San Francisco, Oakland and San Jose.

➡ Local buses, trains and subway lines usually have wheelchair lifts.

➡ Seeing-eye dogs are permitted to accompany passengers on public transportation.

➡ Taxi companies have at least one wheelchair-accessible van, but you'll usually need to call and then wait for one.

Helpful Resources

A Wheelchair Rider's Guide to the California Coast (www.wheelingcalscoast.org) Free accessibility information covering beaches, parks and trails, plus downloadable PDF guides to the San Francisco Bay Area and

Los Angeles and Orange County coasts.

Access Northern California (www.accessnca.org) Extensive links to accessible-travel resources, including outdoor recreation opportunities, lodgings, tours and transportation.

Access San Francisco Guide (www.sftravel.com) Search the city's official tourism site for this free, downloadable PDF guide – dated, but useful.

Access Santa Cruz County (www.scaccessguide.com) Free online accessible-travel guide for visiting Santa Cruz and around, including restaurants, lodging, beaches, parks and outdoor recreation.

California State Parks (http://access.parks.ca.gov) Searchable online map and database of accessible features at state parks.

Disabled Sports Eastern Sierra (http://disabledsportseastern-sierra.org) Offers summer and winter outdoor-activity programs around Mammoth Lakes.

Achieve Tahoe (http://achieve tahoe.org) Organizes summer and winter sports, 4WD adventures and adaptive-ski rental around Lake Tahoe in the Sierra Nevada (annual membership $50).

Flying Wheels Travel (📞507-451-5005; www.flyingwheels travel.com) Full-service travel agency for travelers with disabilities, mobility issues and chronic illnesses.

Los Angeles for Disabled Visitors (www.discoverlos angeles.com/search/site/disabled) Tips for accessible sightseeing, entertainment, museums and transportation.

Yosemite National Park Accessibility (www.nps.gov/yose/planyourvisit/accessibility.htm) Detailed, downloadable accessibility information for Yosemite National Park, including services for deaf visitors.

Wheelchair Traveling (www. wheelchairtraveling.com) Travel articles, lodging and helpful California destination info.

Visas

➡ Visa information is highly subject to change. Depending on your country of origin, the rules for entering the USA keep changing. Double-check current visa requirements *before* coming to the USA.

➡ Currently, under the US Visa Waiver Program (VWP), visas are not required for citizens of 38 countries for stays up to 90 days (no extensions) as long as you have a machine-readable passport that meets current US standards and is valid for six months beyond your intended stay.

➡ Citizens of VWP countries must still register with the **Electronic System for Travel Authorization** (ESTA; https://esta.cbp.dhs.gov) at least 72 hours before travel. Once approved, ESTA registration ($14) is valid for up to two years or until your passport expires, whichever comes first.

➡ For most Canadian citizens traveling with Canadian passports that meet current US standards, a visa for short-term visits (usually up to six months) and ESTA registration aren't required.

➡ Citizens from all other countries, or whose passports don't meet US standards, need to apply for a visa in their home country. The process has a nonrefundable fee (minimum $160), involves a personal interview and can take several weeks, so apply as early as possible.

➡ For up-to-date information about entry requirements and eligibility, check the visa section of the US Department of State website (http://travel.state.gov), or contact the nearest USA embassy or consulate in your home country (for a complete list, visit www. usembassy.gov).

Volunteering

Casual drop-in volunteer opportunities, where you can socialize with locals while helping out nonprofit organizations, are most common in cities. Browse upcoming projects and activities and sign up online with local organizations such as **One Brick** (www. onebrick.org) in San Francisco and Silicon Valley, **HandsOn Bay Area** (www.handsonba-yarea.org), **LA Works** (www. laworks.com) and Orange County's **OneOC** (www.oneoc. org). For more opportunities, check local alternative weekly tabloids and **Craigslist** (www. craigslist.org) online.

Helpful Resources

California Volunteers (www. californiavolunteers.org) State-run volunteer directory and matching service, with links to national service days and long-term programs.

Habitat for Humanity (www. habitat.org) Nonprofit organization that helps build homes for impoverished families across California; has day, weekend and week-long projects.

Idealist (www.idealist.org) Free searchable database that includes both short- and long-term volunteer opportunities.

Sierra Club (www.sierraclub. org) Day or weekend projects and longer volunteer vacations (including for families) that focus on environmental conservation (annual membership from $15).

TreePeople (www.treepeople. org) Organizes half-day group tree planting, invasive-weed pulling and habitat-restoration projects around LA, from urban parks to mountain forests.

Wilderness Volunteers (www. wildernessvolunteers.org) Week-long trips that help maintain national parks, preserves, forests, seashores and other wilderness conservation and outdoor recreation areas.

Worldwide Opportunities on Organic Farms (www.wwoofusa. org) Long-term volunteering opportunities on local organic farms (annual membership from $40).

Transportation

GETTING THERE & AWAY

Getting to California by air or overland by car, train or bus is easy, although it's not always cheap. Flights, cars and tours can be booked online at www.lonelyplanet.com/bookings.

Entering the Region

Under the US Department of Homeland Security's Orwellian-sounding Office of Biometric Identity Management, almost all visitors to the USA (excluding, for now, many Canadians, some Mexican citizens, children under the age of 14 and seniors over the age of 79) will be digitally photographed and have their electronic (inkless) fingerprints scanned upon arrival.

Regardless of your visa status, immigration officers have absolute authority to refuse entry to the USA. They may ask about your plans and whether you have sufficient funds; it's a good idea to list an itinerary, produce

DEPARTURE TAX

There is no separate departure tax for domestic or international flights leaving California.

an onward or round-trip ticket and have at least one major credit card. Don't make too much of having friends, relatives or business contacts in the US, because officers may think this makes you more likely to overstay. For more information, visit the US Customs and Border Protection website (www.cbp.gov).

California is an important agricultural state. To prevent the spread of pests and diseases, certain food items (including meats, fresh fruit and vegetables) may not be brought into the state. Bakery items, chocolates and hard-cured cheeses are admissible. If you drive into California from Mexico, or from the neighboring states of Oregon, Nevada or Arizona, you may have to stop for a quick questioning and inspection by California Department of Food and Agriculture (www.cdfa.ca.gov) agents.

Passport

➡ Under the Western Hemisphere Travel Initiative (WHTI), all travelers must have a valid machine-readable passport (MRP) when entering the USA by air, land or sea.

➡ The only exceptions are for some US, Canadian and Mexican citizens traveling by land who can present other WHTI-compliant documents (eg pre-approved 'trusted traveler' cards). A

regular driver's license is *not* sufficient.

➡ All foreign passports must meet current US standards and be valid for at least six months beyond your intended stay.

➡ MRPs issued or renewed after October 26, 2006, must be e-passports (ie have a digital photo and integrated chip with biometric data).

➡ For more information, consult www.cbp.gov/travel.

Air

➡ To get through airport security checkpoints (30- to 45-minute wait times are standard), you'll need a boarding pass and photo ID.

➡ Some travelers may be required to undergo a secondary screening, involving hand pat downs and carry-on-bag searches.

➡ Airport security measures restrict many common items (eg pocket knives, scissors) from being carried on planes. Check current restrictions with the Transportation Security Administration (TSA; www.tsa.gov).

➡ Currently TSA requires that all carry-on liquids and gels be stored in 3oz or smaller bottles placed inside a quart-sized clear plastic zip-top bag.

Exceptions, which must be declared to checkpoint security officers, include medications.

➡ All checked luggage is screened for explosives. TSA may open your suitcase for visual confirmation, breaking the lock if necessary. Leave your bags unlocked or use a TSA-approved lock.

Airports & Airlines

California's major international airports are **Los Angeles International Airport** (LAX; www.lawa.org/welcomeLAX.aspx; 1 World Way) in Southern California and **San Francisco International Airport** (SFO; www.flysfo.com; S McDonnell Rd) in Northern California. Smaller regional airports throughout the state are mainly served by domestic US airlines. Many domestic and international air carriers offer direct flights to and from California.

Land
Border Crossings

It's relatively easy crossing from the USA into Mexico; it's crossing back into the USA that can pose problems if you haven't brought all of the required documents. Check the ever-changing passport and visa requirements with the US Department of State (http://travel.state.gov) beforehand.

The US Customs & Border Protection (http://bwt.cbp.

gov) tracks current wait times at every US border crossing. On the US–Mexico border between San Diego and Tijuana, San Ysidro is the world's busiest border crossing, with average wait times of an hour or more.

US citizens do not require a visa for stays of 72 hours or less within the Mexican border zone (ie as far south as Ensenada). But to reenter the USA, US citizens need to present a US passport or other WHTI-compliant travel document (see www.cbp.gov/travel); a regular US driver's license is no longer enough.

CAR & MOTORCYCLE

➡ If you're driving into the USA from Canada or Mexico, bring your vehicle's registration papers, liability insurance and driver's license; an International Driving Permit (IDP) is a good supplement but is not required.

➡ If you're renting a car or a motorcycle, ask if the agency allows its vehicles to be taken across the Mexican or Canadian border – chances are it doesn't.

TO & FROM MEXICO

➡ Unless you're planning an extended stay in Mexico, taking a car across the Mexican border is more trouble than it's worth. Instead take the trolley from San Diego or park your car on the US side and walk across instead.

➡ If you do decide to drive across, you must buy Mexican car insurance either beforehand or at the border crossing.

➡ Expect long border-crossing waits, especially on weekends and holidays and during weekday commuter rush hours.

TO & FROM CANADA

➡ Canadian auto insurance is typically valid in the USA and vice versa.

➡ If your papers are in order, taking your own car across the US–Canada border is usually quick and easy.

➡ On weekends and holidays, especially in summer, border-crossing traffic can be heavy and waits long.

➡ Occasionally the authorities of either country decide to search a car *thoroughly*. Remain calm and be polite.

Bus
Greyhound (☏800-231-2222; www.greyhound.com) is the major long-distance bus company, with routes throughout the USA, including to/from California. Routes trace major highways and may stop only at larger population centers, with services to many small towns having been cut.

Train
Amtrak (☏800-872-7245; www.amtrak.com) operates a fairly extensive rail system throughout the USA. Trains are comfortable, if a bit slow, and

CLIMATE CHANGE & TRAVEL

Every form of transport that relies on carbon-based fuel generates CO_2, the main cause of human-induced climate change. Modern travel is dependent on airplanes, which might use less fuel per kilometer per person than most cars but travel much greater distances. The altitude at which aircraft emit gases (including CO_2) and particles also contributes to their climate change impact. Many websites offer 'carbon calculators' that allow people to estimate the carbon emissions generated by their journey and, for those who wish to do so, to offset the impact of the greenhouse gases emitted with contributions to portfolios of climate-friendly initiatives throughout the world. Lonely Planet offsets the carbon footprint of all staff and author travel.

WARNING!

As of April 2016, the US State Department (http://travel.state.gov) has reissued a travel warning about drug-trafficking violence and crime along the US–Mexico border. Travelers should exercise extreme caution in Tijuana, avoid large-scale gatherings and demonstrations and refrain from venturing out after dark. Cars with US license plates can be targets for carjackings, especially at night and on isolated roads.

are equipped with dining and lounge cars and sometimes wi-fi on long-distance routes. Fares vary according to the type of train and seating (eg coach or business class, sleeping compartments).

Amtrak's major long-distance services to/from California:

California Zephyr Daily service between Chicago and Emeryville (from $136, 52 hours), near San Francisco, via Denver, Salt Lake City, Reno, Truckee and Sacramento.

Coast Starlight Travels the West Coast daily from Seattle to LA (from $97, 35½ hours) via Portland, Sacramento, Oakland, San Jose, San Luis Obispo and Santa Barbara.

Southwest Chief Daily departures from Chicago and LA (from $141, 43 hours) via Kansas City, Albuquerque, Flagstaff and Barstow.

Sunset Limited Thrice-weekly service between New Orleans and LA (from $136, 46½ hours) via Houston, San Antonio, El Paso, Tucson and Palm Springs.

TRAIN PASSES

Amtrak's USA Rail Pass is valid for coach-class train travel only (and not Thruway buses) for 15 ($459), 30 ($689) or 45 ($899) days; children aged two to 12 pay half price. Travel is limited to eight, 12 or 18 one-way 'segments,' respectively. A segment is not the same as a one-way trip; if reaching your destination requires riding more than one train, you'll use multiple pass segments. Purchase passes online, then make advance reservations for each trip segment.

Sea

Several international cruise lines dock along California's coast at piers and cruise-ship terminals in San Diego, Long Beach and San Francisco.

GETTING AROUND

Air

Several major US carriers fly within California. Flights are often operated by their regional subsidiaries, such as American Eagle, Delta Connection and United Express. Alaska Airlines/Virgin America, Frontier Airlines, Horizon Air and JetBlue serve many regional airports, as do low-cost airlines Southwest and Spirit.

Bicycle

Although cycling around California is a nonpolluting 'green' way to travel, the distances involved demand a high level of fitness and make it hard to cover much ground. Forget about the deserts in summer and the mountains in winter.

Helpful Resources

Adventure Cycling Association (☎800-755-2453; www.adventurecycling.org) Online resource for purchasing bicycle-friendly maps and long-distance route guides; also organizes van-supported cycling tours for members (annual membership from $45).

Better World Club (☎866-238-1137; www.betterworldclub.com) Annual membership in the bicycle club (from $40) gets you two 24-hour emergency roadside-assistance calls and transport within a 30-mile radius.

California Bicycle Coalition (http://calbike.org) Links to cycling route maps, events, safety tips, laws, bike-sharing programs and community nonprofit bicycle shops.

Rental & Purchase

➡ You can rent bikes by the hour, day or week in most cities and tourist towns.

➡ Rentals start around $10 per day for beach cruisers, and up to $45 or more for mountain bikes; ask about multiday and weekly discounts.

➡ Most rental companies require a large security deposit using a credit card.

➡ Buy new models from specialty bike shops and sporting-goods stores, or used bicycles from noticeboards at hostels, cafes etc.

➡ To buy or sell used bikes online, check Craigslist (www.craigslist.org).

Road Rules

➡ Cycling is allowed on all roads and highways – even along freeways if there's no suitable alternative, such as a smaller parallel frontage road; all mandatory exits are marked.

➡ Some cities have designated bicycle lanes, but make sure you have your wits about you in traffic.

➡ Cyclists must follow the same rules of the road as vehicles. Don't expect drivers to always respect your right of way.

➡ Wearing a bicycle helmet is mandatory for riders under 18 years of age.

➡ Ensure you have proper lights and reflective gear, especially if you're pedaling at night or in fog.

Transporting Bicycles

➡ Greyhound transports bicycles as luggage (surcharge $35 to $45), provided the bicycle is disassembled and placed in a rigid container ($10 box may be available for purchase at some terminals).

➡ Amtrak's *Cascades, Capitol Corridor, Pacific Surfliner* and *San Joaquins* trains have onboard racks where you can secure your bike unboxed; try to reserve a spot when making your ticket reservation ($5 to $10 surcharge may apply).

➡ On Amtrak trains without racks, bikes must be put in a box ($15 at most staffed terminals) and checked as luggage (fee $10 to $20). Not all stations or trains offer checked-baggage service, however.

➡ Before flying, you'll need to disassemble your bike and box it as checked baggage. Contact airlines directly for details, including surcharges ($75 to $150 or more).

Boat

Boats won't get you around California, although there are a few offshore routes, notably to Catalina Island off the coast of Los Angeles and Orange County, and to Channel Islands National Park from Ventura or Oxnard, northwest of LA heading toward Santa Barbara. On San Francisco Bay, regular ferries operate between San Francisco and Sausalito, Larkspur, Tiburon, Angel Island, Oakland, Alameda and Vallejo.

Bus

Greyhound (📞800-231-2222; www.greyhound.com) buses are an economical way to travel between major cities and to points along the coast, but won't get you off the beaten path or to national parks or small towns. Frequency of service varies from rarely to constantly, but the main routes have service several times daily.

Greyhound buses are usually clean, comfortable and reliable. The best seats are typically near the front, away from the bathroom. Limited on-board amenities include freezing air-con (bring a sweater) and slightly reclining seats, and select buses have electrical outlets and wi-fi. Smoking on board is prohibited. Long-distance buses stop for meal breaks and driver changes.

Bus stations are typically dreary, and often in dodgy areas – if you arrive at night, take a taxi into town or to your lodgings. In small towns where there is no bus station, know exactly where and when the bus arrives, be obvious as you flag it down and pay the driver with exact change.

Costs

You may save money by purchasing tickets in advance and by traveling between Monday and Thursday.

Discounts (on unrestricted fares only) are offered to seniors over 62 (5% off), students with a Student Advantage card (10%) and children under 16 years (20%). Tots under two years of age ride for free only if they don't require a seat.

Special promotional discounts, such as 50% off companion fares, are often available, though they may come with restrictions or blackout periods. Check Greyhound's website for current fare specials or ask when buying tickets.

Tickets & Reservations

It's easy to buy tickets online with a credit card then pick them up (bring photo ID) at the terminal. You can also buy tickets over the phone, or in person from a ticket agent. Greyhound terminal ticket agents also accept debit cards, traveler's checks (in US dollars) and cash.

General boarding is first-come, first-served. Buying tickets in advance doesn't guarantee a seat on any particular bus unless you also purchase priority boarding, available only on some routes. Otherwise, arrive at least one hour prior to the scheduled departure to get a seat; allow extra time on weekends and holidays.

Travelers with disabilities who need special assistance should call (📞800-752-4841 (TDD/TTY 📞800-345-3109) at least 48 hours before traveling. Wheelchairs and mobility scooters are accepted as checked baggage (or carry-on, if space allows) and service animals are allowed on board.

Car & Motorcycle

California's love affair with cars runs deep for at least one practical reason: the state is so big, public transportation can't cover it. For flexibility and convenience, you'll probably want a car, but rental rates and gas prices can eat up a good chunk of your trip budget.

Automobile Associations

For 24-hour emergency roadside assistance, free maps and discounts on lodging, attractions, entertainment, car rentals and more, consider joining an auto club.

American Automobile Association (AAA; 📞800-922-8228; www.aaa.com) Walk-in offices throughout California, add-on coverage for RVs and motorcycles, and reciprocal agreements with some international auto clubs (eg CAA in Canada, AA in the UK) – bring your membership card from home.

Better World Club (☎866-238-1137; www.betterworldclub.com) Ecofriendly auto club supports environmental causes and offers add-on or stand-alone emergency roadside assistance for cyclists as well.

Driver's Licenses

➡ Visitors may legally drive a car in California for up to 12 months with their home driver's license.

➡ If you're from overseas, an International Driving Permit (IDP) will have more credibility with traffic police and simplify the car-rental process, especially if your license doesn't have a photo or isn't written in English.

➡ To ride a motorcycle, you'll need a valid US state motorcycle license, or a specially endorsed IDP.

➡ International automobile associations can issue IDPs, valid for one year, for a fee. Always carry your home license together with the IDP.

Fuel

➡ Gas stations in California, nearly all of which are self-service, are ubiquitous, except in national and state parks and some sparsely populated desert and mountain areas.

➡ Gas is sold in gallons (one US gallon equals 3.78L). At time of writing, the average cost for mid-grade fuel was around $3 a gallon.

Insurance

California law requires liability insurance for all vehicles. When renting a car, check your auto-insurance policy from home or your travel insurance policy to see if you're already covered. If not, expect to pay about $20 per day.

Insurance against damage to the car itself, called Collision Damage Waiver (CDW) or Loss Damage Waiver (LDW), costs another $10 to $20 or more per day. The deductible may require you

to pay the first $100 to $500 for any repairs.

Some credit cards cover CDW/LDW, provided you charge the entire cost of the car rental to the card. Check with your credit-card issuer first to determine the extent of coverage and policy exclusions. If there's an accident you may have to pay the rental-car company first, then seek reimbursement from the credit-card company.

Parking

➡ Parking is usually plentiful and free in small towns and rural areas, but often scarce and/or expensive in cities.

➡ When parking on the street, read all posted regulations and restrictions (eg street-cleaning hours, permit-only residential areas) and pay attention to colored curbs, or you may be ticketed and towed.

➡ You can pay municipal parking meters and sidewalk pay stations with coins (eg quarters) and sometimes credit or debit cards.

➡ Expect to pay $30 to $50 for overnight parking in a city lot or garage.

➡ Flat-fee valet parking at hotels, restaurants, nightclubs etc is common in major cities, especially Los Angeles and Las Vegas, NV.

Rental

CARS

To rent your own wheels, you'll typically need to be at least 25 years old, hold a valid driver's license and have a major credit card, not a check or debit card. A few companies may rent to drivers under 25 but over 21 for a hefty surcharge. If you don't have a credit card, large cash deposits are infrequently accepted.

With advance reservations, you can often get an economy-size vehicle with unlimited mileage from around $30 per day, plus insurance, taxes and fees.

Weekend and weekly rates are usually the most economical. Airport locations may have cheaper rates but higher add-on fees; if you get a fly-drive package, local taxes may be extra when you pick up the car. City-center branches sometimes offer free pickups and drop offs.

Rates generally include unlimited mileage, but expect surcharges for additional drivers and one-way rentals. Child or infant safety seats are legally required; reserve them when booking for $10 to $15 per day.

If you'd like to minimize your carbon footprint, some major car-rental companies offer 'green' fleets of hybrid or biofueled rental cars, but these fuel-efficient models are in short supply. Reserve them well in advance and expect to pay significantly higher rates.

To find and compare independent car-rental companies, try Car Rental Express (www.carrentalexpress.com).

Avis (☎800-633-3469; www.avis.com)

Budget (☎800-218-7992; www.budget.com)

Dollar (☎800-800-5252; www.dollar.com)

Enterprise (☎855-266-9289; www.enterprise.com)

Fox (☎855-571-8410; www.foxrentacar.com)

Hertz (☎800-654-3131; www.hertz.com)

National (☎877-222-9058; www.nationalcar.com)

Payless (☎800-729-5377; www.paylesscar.com)

Rent-a-Wreck (☎877-877-0700; www.rentawreck.com) Minimum rental age and under-25 driver surcharges vary at six locations, including in LA and the San Francisco Bay Area.

Simply Rent-a-Car (☎323-653-0022; www.simplyrac.com) ✐ Rents hybrid, electric and flex-fuel vehicles in LA; ask about free delivery and pickup.

Super Cheap! Car Rental (☎310-645-3993; www.super

cheapcar.com) No surcharge for drivers ages 21 to 24; nominal daily fee applies for drivers ages 18 to 21 (full-coverage insurance required). Locations in the San Francisco Bay Area, LA and Orange County.

Sixt (☏888-749-8227; www.sixt.com)

Thrifty (☏800-847-4389; www.thrifty.com)

Zipcar (☏866-494-7227; www.zipcar.com) 🖋 Currently available in the San Francisco Bay Area, LA, San Diego and Sacramento, this car-sharing club charges usage fees (per hour or day), including free gas, insurance (a damage fee of up to $1000 may apply) and limited mileage. Apply online (foreign drivers accepted); application fee $25, annual membership from $70.

MOTORCYCLES

Motorcycle rentals and insurance are not cheap, especially if you've got your eye on a Harley. Depending on the model, renting a motorcycle costs $100 to $250 per day plus taxes and fees, including helmets, unlimited miles and liability insurance; one-way rentals and collision insurance (CDW) cost extra. Discounts may be available for multiday and weekly rentals. Security deposits can be up to $2000 (credit card required).

California Motorcycle Adventures (☏800-601-5370, 650-969-6198; www.californiamotorcycleadventures.com; 2554 W Middlefield Rd, Mountain View) Harley-Davidson and BMW rentals in Silicon Valley.

Dubbelju (☏415-495-2774, 866-495-2774; www.dubbelju.com; 274 Shotwell St; per day from $99; ⊙9am-6pm Mon-Sat) Rents Harley-Davidson, Japanese and European imported motorcycles, as well as scooters.

Eagle Rider (☏888-900-9901, 310-321-3180; www.eaglerider.com) Nationwide company with 11 locations in California, as well as Las Vegas, NV.

RECREATIONAL VEHICLES

Gas-guzzling recreational vehicles (RVs) remain popular despite fuel prices and being cumbersome to drive. That said, they do solve transportation, accommodation and cooking needs in one fell swoop. It's easy to find RV campgrounds with electricity and water hookups, yet there are many places in national and state parks and in the mountains they can't go. In cities RVs are a nuisance, because there are few places to park or plug them in.

Book RVs as far in advance as possible. Rental costs vary by size and model, but you can expect to pay more than $100 per day. Rates often don't include mileage, bedding or kitchen kits, vehicle-prep fees or taxes. If pets are allowed, a surcharge may apply.

Camper USA (☏310-929-5666; www.camperusa.com) Campervan rentals in the San Francisco Bay Area, LA and Las Vegas, NV.

Cruise America (☏480-464-7300, 800-671-8042; www.cruiseamerica.com) Nationwide RV-rental company with 20 locations statewide.

El Monte (☏562-483-4985, 888-337-2214; www.elmonterv.com) Over a dozen locations in California. This national RV-rental agency offers AAA discounts.

Escape Campervans (☏877-270-8267, 310-672-9909; www.escapecampervans.com) Awesomely painted campervans at economical rates in the San Francisco Bay Area, LA and Las Vegas, NV.

Jucy Rentals (☏800-650-4180; www.jucyrentals.com) Campervan rentals in the San Francisco Bay Area, LA and Las Vegas, NV.

Road Bear (☏866-491-9853, 818-865-2925; www.roadbearrv.com) RV rentals in the San Francisco Bay Area and LA.

Vintage Surfari Wagons (☏714-585-7565; www.vwsurfari.com) VW campervan rentals in Orange County.

Road Conditions & Hazards

For up-to-date highway conditions, including road closures and construction updates, check with the **California Department of Transportation** (CalTrans; ☏800-427-7623; www.dot.ca.gov). For Nevada highways, call 877-687-6237 or check www.nvroads.com.

In places where winter driving is an issue, snow tires and tire chains may be required in mountain areas. Ideally carry your own chains and learn how to use them before you hit the road. Otherwise, chains can usually be bought or rented (but not cheaply) on the highway, at gas stations or in the nearest town. Most car-rental companies don't permit the use of chains and also prohibit driving off-road or on dirt roads.

In rural areas, livestock sometimes graze next to unfenced roads. These areas are typically signed as 'Open Range,' with the silhouette of a steer. Where deer and other wild animals frequently appear roadside, you'll see signs with the silhouette of a leaping deer. Take these signs seriously, particularly at night.

In coastal areas thick fog may impede driving – slow down and if it's too soupy, get off the road. Along coastal cliffs and in the mountains, watch out for falling rocks, mudslides and avalanches that could damage or disable your car if struck.

Road Rules

➡ Drive on the right-hand side of the road.

➡ Talking, texting or otherwise using a cell (mobile) phone or other mobile electronic device without hands-free technology while driving is illegal.

➡ The driver and all passengers must use seat belts in a private vehicle.

In a taxi or limo, back-seat passengers are not required to buckle up.

➜ Infant and child safety seats are required for children under eight years of age, or who are less than 4ft 9in tall.

➜ All motorcyclists must wear a helmet. Scooters are not allowed on freeways.

➜ High-occupancy (HOV) lanes marked with a diamond symbol are reserved for cars with multiple occupants, sometimes only during signposted hours.

➜ Unless otherwise posted, the speed limit is 65mph on freeways, 55mph on two-lane undivided highways, 35mph on major city streets and 25mph in business and residential districts and near schools.

➜ Except where indicated, turning right at a red stoplight after coming to a full stop is permitted, although intersecting traffic still has the right of way.

➜ At four-way stop signs, cars proceed in the order in which they arrived. If two cars arrive simultaneously, the one on the right has the right of way. When in doubt, politely wave the other driver ahead.

➜ When emergency vehicles (ie police, fire or ambulance) approach from either direction, carefully pull over to the side of the road.

➜ California has strict anti-littering laws; throwing trash from a vehicle may incur a $1000 fine.

➜ Driving under the influence of alcohol or drugs is illegal. It's also illegal to carry open containers of alcohol, even empty ones, inside a vehicle. Store them in the trunk.

Local Transportation

Except in cities, public transit is rarely the most convenient option, and coverage to out-lying towns and suburbs can be sparse. However, it's usually cheap, safe and reliable.

Bicycle

➜ Cycling is a feasible way of getting around smaller cities and towns, but it's not much fun in traffic-dense areas such as LA.

➜ San Francisco, Napa, Arcata, South Lake Tahoe, West Sacramento, Chico and Santa Monica are among California's most bike-friendly communities, as rated by the League of American Bicyclists (www.bikeleague.org).

➜ Bicycles may be transported on many local buses and trains, sometimes during off-peak, non-commuter hours only.

Bus, Cable Car, Streetcar & Trolley

➜ Almost all cities and larger towns have reliable local bus systems (average $1 to $3 per ride). Outside of major metro areas, they may provide only limited evening and weekend service.

➜ San Francisco's extensive Municipal Railway (MUNI) network includes not only buses and trains, but also historic streetcars and those famous cable cars.

➜ San Diego runs trolleys around some neighborhoods and to the Mexican border.

Taxi

➜ Taxis are metered, with flag-fall fees of $2.50 to $3.50 to start, plus around $2 to $3 per mile. Credit cards may be accepted, but bring cash just in case.

➜ Taxis may charge extra for baggage and airport pickups.

➜ Drivers expect a 10% to 15% tip, rounded up to the next dollar.

➜ Taxis cruise the streets of the busiest areas in large cities, but elsewhere you may need to call for one.

Train

➜ LA Metro is a combined, ever-expanding network of subway and light-rail trains around Los Angeles. Metrolink commuter trains connect LA with surrounding counties.

➜ San Diego's Coaster commuter trains run from downtown and Old Town to Carlsbad, Encinitas, Solana Beach and Oceanside in the North County.

➜ To get around the San Francisco Bay Area, hop aboard Bay Area Rapid Transit (BART) or Caltrain.

Tours

Green Tortoise (✆800-867-8647, 415-956-7500; www.greentortoise.com) Youthful budget-backpacker trips utilize converted sleeping-bunk buses for adventure tours of California's national parks, northern redwood forests, southern deserts and Pacific Coast.

Train

Amtrak (✆800-872-7245; www.amtrak.com) runs comfortable, if occasionally tardy, trains to major California cities and some towns. Amtrak's Thruway buses provide onward connections from many train stations. Smoking is prohibited aboard trains and buses.

Amtrak routes within California:

California Zephyr Daily service from Emeryville (near San Francisco) via Davis and Sacramento to Truckee (near Lake Tahoe) and Reno, NV.

Capitol Corridor Links San Francisco's East Bay (including Oakland, Emeryville and Berkeley) and San Jose with Davis and Sacramento several times daily; on-board wi-fi available. Thruway buses connect to San Francisco, Auburn (in Gold Country), Truckee (near Lake Tahoe) and Reno, NV.

Coast Starlight Chugs roughly north–south almost the entire length of the state. Daily stops include LA, Burbank, Santa Barbara, San Luis Obispo, Paso Robles, Salinas, San Jose, Oakland, Emeryville, Davis, Sacramento, Chico, Redding and Dunsmuir.

Pacific Surfliner Eight daily trains ply the San Diego–LA route, stopping at San Diego's North County beach towns and Orange County's San Juan Capistrano and Anaheim, home of Disneyland. Three trains continue north to Santa Barbara via Burbank, Ventura and Carpinteria, with one going all the way to San Luis Obispo. Trains hug the scenic coastline for much of the route. On-board wi-fi may be available.

San Joaquins Several daily trains with on-board wi-fi run between Bakersfield and Oakland or Sacramento. Thruway bus connections include San Francisco, LA, Palm Springs and Yosemite National Park.

Costs

Purchase tickets at train stations, by phone or online (in advance for the cheapest prices). Fares depend on the day of travel, the route, the type of seating etc. Fares may be slightly higher during peak travel times (eg summer). Round-trip tickets typically cost the same as two one-way tickets.

Usually seniors over 62 and students aged 13 to 25 with a valid student ID card receive a 15% discount, while up to two children aged two

---

---

to 12 who are accompanied by an adult get 50% off. AAA members save 10%. Special promotions can become available anytime, so check Amtrak's website or ask when making reservations.

Reservations

Amtrak reservations can be made up to 11 months prior to departure. In summer and around holidays, trains sell out quickly, so book tickets as early as possible. The cheapest coach fares are usually for unreserved seats; business-class fares come with guaranteed seats.

Travelers with disabilities who need special assis-

tance, wheelchair space, transfer seats or accessible accommodations should call 800-872-7245 (TDD/TTY 800 523 6590). Also inquire about discounted fares when booking.

Train Passes

Amtrak's California Rail Pass costs $159 ($80 for children ages two to 12) and is valid on all trains (except certain long-distance routes) and most connecting Thruway buses for seven days of travel within a 21-day period. Pass holders must reserve each leg of travel in advance and obtain hard-copy tickets prior to boarding.

Behind the Scenes

SEND US YOUR FEEDBACK

We love to hear from travelers – your comments keep us on our toes and help make our books better. Our well-traveled team reads every word on what you loved or loathed about this book. Although we cannot reply individually to your submissions, we always guarantee that your feedback goes straight to the appropriate authors, in time for the next edition. Each person who sends us information is thanked in the next edition – the most useful submissions are rewarded with a selection of digital PDF chapters.

Visit **lonelyplanet.com/contact** to submit your updates and suggestions or to ask for help. Our award-winning website also features inspirational travel stories, news and discussions.

Note: We may edit, reproduce and incorporate your comments in Lonely Planet products such as guidebooks, websites and digital products, so let us know if you don't want your comments reproduced or your name acknowledged. For a copy of our privacy policy visit lonelyplanet.com/privacy.

OUR READERS

Many thanks to the travelers who used the last edition and wrote to us with helpful hints, useful advice and interesting anecdotes:

Samuel Akologo, Richard Ault, Jonas Elliott Gerson, Matt Knipe, Susanna Seppala, Maaike van de Pijpekamp, Wes Wallace

AUTHOR THANKS
Andrea Schulte-Peevers

Big heartfelt thank-yous go to the following people for their invaluable tips, insights and hospitality (in no particular order): Valerie Summers, Kristin Schmidt, Joyce Kiehl, Andrew Bender, Abigail Wines, Bruce Moore, Susan Witty, Brandy Marino and Mona Spicer.

Brett Atkinson

Thanks to everyone who made my exploration of California's Central Coast so enjoyable, especially Christina Glynn in Santa Cruz. In Santa Cruz thanks also to Margaret Leonard for travel inspiration beyond the borders of Monterey Bay. The staff at the region's visitor centers were all uniformly helpful, and at Lonely Planet, huge thanks to Cliff Wilkinson for the opportunity to return to Big Sur.

Andrew Bender

Thanks to Denise Lengyeltoti, Christie Bacock, Melissa Perez, Jackie Alvarez, Jennifer Tong, Erin Ramsauer, Michael Ramirez, Jenny Wedge, Ashley Johnson and the many information center, hotel and restaurant staffers who gave me way more of their time than I deserved. In house, thanks especially to Clifton Wilkinson, Sarah Stocking, Anita Isalska, Judith Bamber and Kathryn Rowan.

Alison Bing

Thanks to Cliff Wilkinson, Sarah Sung, Lisa Park, DeeAnn Budney, PT Tenenbaum, and above all, Marco Flavio Marinucci, for making a Muni bus ride into the adventure of a lifetime.

Cristian Bonetto

A heartfelt thank you to the many Angelenos (and New Yorkers) who shared their LA secrets and insights with me, especially John-Mark Horton, Michael Amato, Andy Bender, Norge Yip, Calvin Yeung, Douglas Levine, Daphne Barahona, Nicholas Maricich, David Singleman, William J Brockschmidt, Richard Dragisic and Andy Walker. Thanks also to fellow Aussies in SoCal, Mary-ann Gardner and Natalie Yanoulis. At Lonely Planet, much gratitude to Cliff Wilkinson.

Celeste Brash

Thanks to my Aunt Kem and Uncle Ken for Susanville roots, Gerad in Mt Shasta City for great beer and info, countless friends and family for tips and suggestions, and my husband and kids for being the best people to come home to. Last but not least, big love to the glorious state of California, where my heart will always live.

Jade Bremner

Thanks to Destination Editor Clifton Wilkinson for his support and endless knowledge about LP. Plus, everyone working their socks off behind the scenes – Cheree Broughton, Dianne, Jane, Neill Coen, Evan Godt and Helen Elfer. Last but not least, thanks to the friendly staff at Fig Tree Cafe for making those marvelous egg Bennies, which often set me up for the day.

Nate Cavalieri

Many thanks to my partner Florence, who is always game for a last-minute road trip to Bakersfield. Thanks to Cliff, Daniel, Jane, Diane and the staff at Lonely Planet for all the support, and to my colleague Alison Bing, who inspired me to get back in the travel-writing game after a long and ill-advised hiatus.

Michael Grosberg

Thanks especially to Carly, Rosie and Booney for keeping the home fires burning, and Carly especially for sharing her experiences as a forest ranger in Mammoth Lakes and Mono Lake all those years ago. Thanks also to Peter Bartelme of Yosemite Conservancy, Lisa Cesaro from Aramark, Joe Juszkiewicz at Rush Creek Lodge, Lauren Burke in Mammoth, Tawni Thompson in Bishop and Julie Wright for help in Sequoia.

Ashley Harrell

Thanks to my coauthors and editors for their diligence and support, the kind people all over Wine Country for their time and recommendations, David Roth and Andy Wright (dumb people) for the endless amusement, Amy Benziger for letting me trash her apartment, Shane Henegan for his glorious Airstream, Paul Stockamore for David Applebaum, Adele Fox for being the best Gumpy, Anne Murphy for sharing her ranch and wise/hilarious opinions, and Andy Lavender for his innumerable contributions and unrelenting care.

Josephine Quintero

Thanks to Cliff Wilkinson for the opportunity of researching this fabulous region of California. Also to my road trip buddy Robin Chapman and my good local resident pals who invaluably assisted me: Janice Crowe and Linda Sinclair. Also thanks to the helpful folk in the various visitor centers and, last but not least, those at the SPP help desk for helping me when I had a serious technical glitch!

Helena Smith

Many thanks to everyone who offered warm hospitality in the Gold Country and Lake Tahoe, most especially Naomi Terry for keeping us company, and Anna and her family for hospitality and local expertise. King was a great road-trip buddy, and so was Art Terry, who drove and DJ'd me round California, and made every exploration a joy.

John A Vlahides

Thanks to destination editor Clifton Wilkinson and my coauthor Alison Bing, with whom it's always lovely to work. And most of all, thanks to you, dear reader – you make my life so joyful and I'm grateful for the honor of being your guide through the cool grey city of love.

Clifton Wilkinson

Thanks to the Santa Barbara County tourism people (Karna, Danielle, Chrisie) who provided excellent recommendations, including my favorite meal of the whole update. Thanks too to all the in-house LP team, especially colleagues who listened patiently to all my pre-trip plans. And final thanks to the weather, which mostly played along with my research – except for all the mud on Santa Cruz Channel Island (if anyone finds some sunglasses, they might be the ones I lost falling over).

ACKNOWLEDGEMENTS

Climate map data adapted from Peel MC, Finlayson BL & McMahon TA (2007) 'Updated World Map of the Köppen-Geiger Climate Classification', Hydrology and Earth System Sciences, 11, 163344.

Illustration pp84-85 by Michael Weldon.

Cover photograph: McWay Falls, Big Sur, Supreecha Samansukumal/Shutterstock.

THIS BOOK

This 8th edition of *California* was researched and written by Andrea Schulte-Peevers, Brett Atkinson, Andrew Bender, Sara Benson, Alison Bing, Cristian Bonetto, Celeste Brash, Jade Bremner, Nate Cavalieri, Michael Grosberg, Ashley Harrell, Josephine Quintero, Helena Smith, John A Vlahides, Benedict Walker and Clifton Wilkinson. The previous edition was researched and written by John A Vlahides, Sara Benson, Alison Bing, Celeste Brash, Tienlon Ho and Beth Kohn. This guidebook was produced by the following:

Destination Editors Clifton Wilkinson, Sarah Stocking

Product Editors Will Allen, Kate Mathews

Senior Cartographer Alison Lyall

Assisting Editors Sarah Bailey, Andrew Bain, Judith Bamber, Michelle Coxall, Andrea Dobbin, Carly Hall, Kellie Langdon, Jodie Martire, Gabrielle Stefanos, Amanda Williamson

Book Designer Katherine Marsh

Assisting Book Designer Meri Blazevski

Cover Image Researcher Brendan Dempsey-Spencer

Thanks to Sasha Drew, Shona Gray, Kate Kiely, Anne Mason, Rachel Rawling, Tony Wheeler

Index

INDEX M

Map Legend

Sights

- Beach
- Bird Sanctuary
- Buddhist
- Castle/Palace
- Christian
- Confucian
- Hindu
- Islamic
- Jain
- Jewish
- Monument
- Museum/Gallery/Historic Building
- Ruin
- Shinto
- Sikh
- Taoist
- Winery/Vineyard
- Zoo/Wildlife Sanctuary
- Other Sight

Activities, Courses & Tours

- Bodysurfing
- Diving
- Canoeing/Kayaking
- Course/Tour
- Sento Hot Baths/Onsen
- Skiing
- Snorkeling
- Surfing
- Swimming/Pool
- Walking
- Windsurfing
- Other Activity

Sleeping

- Sleeping
- Camping

Eating

- Eating

Drinking & Nightlife

- Drinking & Nightlife
- Cafe

Entertainment

- Entertainment

Shopping

- Shopping

Information

- Bank
- Embassy/Consulate
- Hospital/Medical
- Internet
- Police
- Post Office
- Telephone
- Toilet
- Tourist Information
- Other Information

Geographic

- Beach
- Gate
- Hut/Shelter
- Lighthouse
- Lookout
- Mountain/Volcano
- Oasis
- Park
- Pass
- Picnic Area
- Waterfall

Population

- Capital (National)
- Capital (State/Province)
- City/Large Town
- Town/Village

Transport

- Airport
- BART station
- Border crossing
- Boston T station
- Bus
- Cable car/Funicular
- Cycling
- Ferry
- Metro/Muni station
- Monorail
- Parking
- Petrol station
- Subway/SkyTrain station
- Taxi
- Train station/Railway
- Tram
- Underground station
- Other Transport

Note: Not all symbols displayed above appear on the maps in this book

Routes

- Tollway
- Freeway
- Primary
- Secondary
- Tertiary
- Lane
- Unsealed road
- Road under construction
- Plaza/Mall
- Steps
- Tunnel
- Pedestrian overpass
- Walking Tour
- Walking Tour detour
- Path/Walking Trail

Boundaries

- International
- State/Province
- Disputed
- Regional/Suburb
- Marine Park
- Cliff
- Wall

Hydrography

- River, Creek
- Intermittent River
- Canal
- Water
- Dry/Salt/Intermittent Lake
- Reef

Areas

- Airport/Runway
- Beach/Desert
- Cemetery (Christian)
- Cemetery (Other)
- Glacier
- Mudflat
- Park/Forest
- Sight (Building)
- Sportsground
- Swamp/Mangrove

Celeste Brash

Northern Mountains Like many California natives, Celeste now lives in Portland, Oregon. She arrived, however, after 15 years in French Polynesia, a year and a half in Southeast Asia and a stint teaching English as a second language in Brighton, England – among other things. She's been writing guidebooks for Lonely Planet since 2005 and her travel articles have appeared in *BBC Travel* and *National Geographic*.

Jade Bremner

San Diego Jade has been a journalist for more than a decade. Wherever she goes she finds action sports to try – the weirder the better – and it's no coincidence many of her favorite places have some of the best waves in the world. Jade has edited travel magazines and sections for *Time Out* and *Radio Times* and has been a correspondent for the *Times*, CNN and the *Independent*.

Nate Cavalieri

Sacramento & the Central Valley Nate is a writer and musician based in Oakland, California, and has authored over a dozen titles for Lonely Planet including guides to California, the Caribbean and Latin America, and *Epic Bike Rides of the World*. He's cycled across China and Southern Africa as a guide with Tour d'Afrique, played third chair percussion in an Orlando theme park and accompanied modern dance classes.

Michael Grosberg

Yosemite & the Sierra Nevada Michael has worked on over 45 Lonely Planet guidebooks, from Myanmar to New Jersey. Other work has included development on the island of Rota in the western Pacific, writing about political violence in South Africa, and teaching in Ecuador. He has a Masters in Comparative Literature, and taught literature and writing as an adjunct professor at several New York colleges.

Ashley Harrell

Napa & Sonoma Wine Country After a brief stint selling day-spa coupons door-to-door in South Florida, Ashley decided she'd rather be a writer. She has traveled widely and moved often, from a tiny NYC apartment to a vast California ranch to a jungle cabin in Costa Rica, where she started writing for Lonely Planet. Her travels since became more exotic and farther-flung, and she still laughs when paychecks arrive.

Josephine Quintero

North Coast & Redwoods Josephine began her journalism career with a wine-and-lifestyle magazine in the Napa Valley. This was followed, ironically, with a move to 'dry' Kuwait, where she was editor of the *Kuwaiti Digest* for six years until August 1, 1990 – the day Iraq invaded. After six weeks as a hostage and escape to Turkey, Josephine moved to Andalucia, where she mainly earned a crust as a ghostwriter.

Helena Smith

Lake Tahoe; Gold Country Helena is an award-winning writer and photographer, and has written guidebooks on destinations from Fiji to Norway. Helena is from Scotland but was partly brought up in Malawi, so Africa always feels like home. She also enjoys her multicultural home area of Hackney and wrote, photographed and published *Inside Hackney*, the first guide to the borough (https://insidehackney.com).

John A Vlahides

San Francisco John has been a cook in a Parisian bordello, a luxury-hotel concierge, a television host, a safety monitor in a sex club and a French–English interpreter, and he is one of Lonely Planet's most experienced and prolific guidebook authors. A native New Yorker living in San Francisco, John has contributed to 18 Lonely Planet guidebooks since 2003.

Benedict Walker

The Deserts Berlin-based Ben grew up in the 'burbs of Australia, spending weekends and long summers by the beach, and while he's magnetically drawn to big mountains, beach life is in his blood. Ben thinks that the best thing about travel isn't as much about where you go as who you meet: living vicariously through the stories of kind strangers really adds to one's own experience.

Clifton Wilkinson

Santa Barbara County Christmases spent near Sacramento, bike rides across the Golden Gate Bridge and hiking in Yosemite National Park have all reinforced Clifton's opinion that the Golden State is the best state in the whole US, and Santa Barbara is one of its most beautiful corners. Having worked for Lonely Planet for more than 11 years, he's now based in the London office.

OUR STORY

A beat-up old car, a few dollars in the pocket and a sense of adventure. In 1972 that's all Tony and Maureen Wheeler needed for the trip of a lifetime – across Europe and Asia overland to Australia. It took several months, and at the end – broke but inspired – they sat at their kitchen table writing and stapling together their first travel guide, *Across Asia on the Cheap*. Within a week they'd sold 1500 copies. Lonely Planet was born.

Today, Lonely Planet has offices in Franklin, London, Melbourne, Oakland, Dublin, Beijing and Delhi, with more than 600 staff and writers. We share Tony's belief that 'a great guidebook should do three things: inform, educate and amuse'.

OUR WRITERS

Andrea Schulte-Peevers

Curator; The Deserts Born and raised in Germany and educated in London and at UCLA, Andrea has earned her living as a professional travel writer for over two decades and authored or contributed to nearly 100 Lonely Planet titles, as well as to newspapers, magazines and websites around the world. She also works as a travel consultant, translator and editor.

Brett Atkinson

Central Coast Brett is based in Auckland, New Zealand, but is frequently on the road for Lonely Planet. He's a full-time travel and food writer. Since becoming a Lonely Planet author in 2005, Brett has covered areas as diverse as Vietnam, Sri Lanka, the Czech Republic, New Zealand, Morocco, California and the South Pacific.

Andrew Bender

Los Angeles; Disneyland & Orange County An award-winning travel and food writer, Andrew Bender has written three dozen Lonely Planet guidebooks, plus numerous articles for lonelyplanet.com. Outside of Lonely Planet, he writes the Seat 1A travel site for Forbes.com and is a frequent contributor to the *Los Angeles Times*, in-flight magazines and more.

Sara Benson

Marin County & the Bay Area After graduating from college in Chicago, Sara jumped on a plane to California with one suitcase and just $100 in her pocket. Today she makes her home in Oakland. The author of more than 70 travel and non-fiction books, she has written for Lonely Planet guides covering Peru, Japan, Malaysia, Las Vegas, California, Southwest USA, Canada, Australia and Hawaii.

Alison Bing

San Francisco Over 10 guidebooks and 20 years in San Francisco, author Alison Bing has spent more time on Alcatraz than some inmates, become an aficionado of drag and burritos, and willfully ignored Muni signs warning that safety requires avoiding unnecessary conversation.

Cristian Bonetto

Los Angeles Cristian has contributed to over 30 Lonely Planet guides to date, covering New York City, Italy, Venice & the Veneto, Naples & the Amalfi Coast, Denmark, Copenhagen, Sweden and Singapore. His writing has appeared in numerous publications around the world, including the *Telegraph* (UK) and *Corriere del Mezzogiorno* (Italy). He lives in Melbourne, Australia.

OVER PAGE | MORE WRITERS

Published by Lonely Planet Global Limited
CRN 554153
8th edition – February 2018
ISBN 978 1 78657 348 3
© Lonely Planet 2018 Photographs © as indicated 2018
10 9 8 7 6 5 4 3 2 1
Printed in China